THE TECHNIQUE OF PSYCHOTHERAPY

PART TWO

OTHER BOOKS BY DR. WOLBERG

THE PSYCHOLOGY OF EATING
HYPNOANALYSIS
MEDICAL HYPNOSIS
    Volume I: Principles of Hypnotherapy
    Volume II: Practice of Hypnotherapy
SHORT-TERM PSYCHOTHERAPY (Editor)
PSYCHOTHERAPY AND THE BEHAVIORAL SCIENCES
THE DYNAMICS OF PERSONALITY (with John P. Kildahl)
HYPNOSIS: IS IT FOR YOU?
MICROART
GROUP THERAPY (Editor)
    1973
    1974
    1975
    1976
    1977

THE TECHNIQUE OF PSYCHOTHERAPY

THIRD EDITION

LEWIS R. WOLBERG, M.D.

Clinical Professor of Psychiatry
New York University Medical School
and Emeritus Dean
Postgraduate Center for Mental Health
New York, New York

PART TWO

GRUNE & STRATTON
A Subsidiary of Harcourt Brace Jovanovich, Publishers
New York · San Francisco · London

Library of Congress Cataloging in Publication Data
Wolberg, Lewis Robert, 1905–
    The technique of psychotherapy.

    Bibliography
    Includes indexes.
    1. Psychotherapy. I. Title. [DNLM: 1. Psy-
chotherapy. WM420 W848t]
RC480.W6 1977   616.8'914   77-7017
ISBN 0-8089-1009-4

Grune & Stratton, Inc.
111 Fifth Avenue
New York, New York 10003

Distributed in the United Kingdom by
Academic Press, Inc. (London) Ltd.
24/48 Oval Road, London NW 1

Library of Congress Catalog Number 77-7017
International Standard Book Number 0-8089-1009-4
Printed in the United States of America

CONTENTS

PART TWO

IV.   The Terminal Phase of Treatment

V.   Special Aspects

Contents   vii

VII.   Appendices and References

III

The Middle Phase of Treatment (continued)

44
The Handling of Resistances to Cure

Despite our best intentions and the most heroic efforts, even where the patient expresses hope and determination to conquer his problems, he may sometimes be unwilling to relinquish them. Personality change is painful as progress takes hold. Anachronistic patterns regressively pull the individual back to the dreams and demands of his past. Temporary secondary gains from exploiting symptoms and the desire to avoid anxiety at all costs inherent in facing difficulties and revising routines hold the patient in a grip from which he may be unable to release himself.

Interpretations of these defensive operations help the patient gradually to an understanding of his unhealthy patterns and to a discovery of what if any vicarious satisfactions he gains from them. In this way the patient learns to master some of the anxiety that made the defenses necessary. However, because certain drives serve a protective function and yield intense gratifications, the individual is apt to fight treatment desperately. Under these circumstances he interprets therapy as an attack on his philosophy of existence and as an assault on his secret wishes and expectations.

FORMS OF RESISTANCE

In his book, *Inhibitions, Symptoms and Anxiety,* Freud emphasizes five types of resistance: (1) "repression resistance," which is motivated to protect the ego from anxiety; (2) "transference resistance," inspired by a refusal to give up hopes for regressive gratifications from the analyst, along with a desire to frustrate him; (3) "epinosic gain resistance," which follows upon a need to indulge secondary gains and the advantages of symptoms; (4) "repetition compulsion resistance," motivated by a drive to repeat neurotic impulses under the lash of a self-destructive principle; and (5) the need for punishment to appease guilt. Psychoanalysis is a "never ending duel between the analyst and the patient's resistance" (Menninger, K, 1961).

Resistance operates not only in psychoanalysis but in all forms of psychotherapy. This is not remarkable because therapy threatens to upset the delicate balance between various elements of the personality. To give up defenses, however, maladaptive as they may be, exposes the patient to dangers that he considers far greater than

609

the inconveniences already suffered as a result of the symptoms.

Resistance may take myriad forms, limited only by the repertory of the individual's defenses. The patient may spend time on evasive and aggressive tactics: fighting the therapist; or proving he is wrong; or winning him over with gestures of helplessness, praise, or devotion; or seeking vicarious means of escaping or evading treatment. Fatigue, listlessness, inhibitions in thinking, lapses in memory, prolonged silences, intensification of complaints, pervasive self-devaluation, resentment, suspiciousness, aggression, forced flight into health, spurious insight, indulgence in superficial talk, engagement in irrational acts and behavior (acting-out), and expressed contempt for normality may occupy the patient to the detriment of his progress.

Resistances may consume the total energy of the patient, leaving little zeal for positive therapeutic work. Sometimes a skilled therapist may bypass resistance by prodding reality into the face of the patient. Sometimes it may be handled by interpretations. Often it operates in spite of attempts to dissipate it, bringing the best efforts of the therapist to a halt. Because resistance is so often concealed and rationalized, it may be difficult to expose. Even an experienced therapist may be deceived by its subtleties.

In supportive therapy resistance may be manifested in a refusal to acknowledge environmental disturbance or in a defensiveness about one's life situation. There may be a greater desire to cope with present known vexations than to chance unknown and perhaps grievous perils. There may be a reluctance to yield inimical conditions that gratify needs for self-punishment and justify one's recriminations against the world. In reeducative therapy resistance to the changing of modes of relating to people cannot be avoided. New interpersonal relations are, in the mind of the patient, fraught with danger. They can be approached only tentatively and with great hesitation. The patient may accordingly remain oblivious to his interpersonal distortions, no matter how frequently they are brought to his attention and how thoroughly they are interpreted.

He will repeat the same patterns, with continuous bouts of suffering, and seemingly little insight into what is going on. In reconstructive therapy impediments are even more manifest. A most complex array of resistances may materialize. This is especially the case where a weak ego creates an inability to face and to master anxiety related to unconscious conflicts.

Suppression and Repression

Any material that is emotionally disturbing will be suppressed or repressed by the patient until enough strength is gained to handle the anxieties evoked by its verbalization. This material may seem, and actually may be, insignificant or innocuous. It is essential to remember, however, that it is not so much the events or ideas that are disturbing, but rather the emotions that are related to them. Thus, a patient suffering from feelings of hopelessness and depression, relieved through excessive alcoholic indulgence, could talk about her present homosexual and heterosexual exploits and her bouts of antisocial behavior that bordered on the criminal, with little disturbance; yet she required one year of therapy before she could relate an experience of removing the clothing of her younger brother and observing and handling his penis. The excitement of this experience and the guilt engendered by it were so intense that she had isolated the memory in her mind. Only when I had proved myself to be a noncondemning person, who would not punish or reject her for the desires that produced this incident, was she able to bring it up and to reevaluate it in the light of her present-day understanding.

Intensification of Symptoms

One of the earliest symptoms of resistance to cure is a reenforcement of those neurotic devices that had previously kept the individual free from anxiety. Something to anticipate, consequently, is an acute exacerbation of neurotic symptoms. An explanation that the patient may possibly get worse before getting better is often a safeguard against interruption of therapy.

Self-devaluation

An insidious type of resistance is that of self-devaluation. Here the patient refuses to concede that there is anything about him of an estimable nature or that he has any chance whatsoever of standing on his own feet. To every interpretation, he responds with the allegation that he is lost, that there is no need for him to continue, that he is hopeless, that it is too late in life to expect a change for the better. The inner image of himself is often that of a hideous, contemptible person, and any attempt to show him that this is a distorted picture usually serves to throw him into a panic; his self-contempt is used as a bulwark to progress in therapy. There may be, in addition, a deep wish to be cared for like a child by rendering himself helpless. The desire to depreciate himself may be in the nature of escaping criticism by anticipatory self-punishment. A masochistic indulgence is also a cover for a fear that if one acknowledges himself to be an able person, active and independent efforts will be expected of him. Patients with this misconception will hang on to their self-contempt with a determination that is astonishing, and only painstaking analysis of this resistance can lead them out of their morass.

Forced Flight into Health

Another form of resistance is "forced flight into health." Here the individual tries to convince himself and the therapist that he is well and that he no longer needs treatment. Any implication that he is not making a good adjustment is resisted with vigor. Actually, the patient may conduct his affairs with a semblance of normality in that he appears to be confident, self-reliant, and normally assertive. Yet the trained observer may detect a false note and often can perceive the tremendous effort that is needed to maintain the illusion of health. This form of resistance is usually associated with the need to maintain a rigid watch over everything one says for fear one will lose control. From a pragmatic point of view, it makes little difference if a patient flies, swims, walks, or crawls to health, as long as he gets there. However, assumed health, fashioned by resistance, is generally short-lived.

Intellectual Inhibitions

The urge to ward off the therapist may result in an inability to think, to talk, or to feel. The patient, if he yields to this urge, will insist that there is absolutely nothing on his mind, and he will exhibit a singular sterility in his associations and in his ability to think constructively about his problems.

The patient may break appointments, come late, forget to mention significant aspects of his day, block off memory of his dreams and fantasies, manifest inattention, show an inability to concentrate or to remember what has gone on before, relapse into silence during the interview, or display a mental fogging that persists both inside and outside of therapy.

The following excerpt from a session illustrates this phenomenon. The patient, a divorcee of 32 years of age, with an hysterical, infantile personality, involved sexually with two men who were supporting her, came to therapy after making a suicidal attempt. After one year of treatment, her recognition of her dependency caused her to decide to get rid of her lovers and to get a productive job. The patient came a half hour late for the session that follows:

Pt. (apologetically) I've been forgetting things lately. Absent-mindedness for about 6 months. Last week I forgot to go to an important meeting. I will make appointments and completely forget them. I forget things to do.

Th. Let's explore that and see if we can learn something about it.

Pt. I keep forgetting names and telephone numbers. I don't know why. Maybe I'm so preoccupied with what's to become of me.

Th. Are you preoccupied?

Pt. I am. I can't remember anything.

Th. What *is* on your mind?

Pt. I have the constant worry that I better hurry and do what I have to do. I am concerned with dying. I keep thinking I may not be here long. I noticed yesterday that my shoes on the floor were empty. I then said, "What will people do with my shoes when I die? I wonder who'll go over my papers."

Th. What's this all about? Do you feel the life you are now living is not worth living?

Pt. I feel threatened by giving up these people who are supporting me. I wonder if I can live and get along. What will become of me?

Th. Maybe you resent giving up these dependent patterns?

Pt. I must resent it; yet even though I do, I can't tolerate them any longer. I've gotten to the point where I can be casual with my supporters and tell them exactly what I feel. I told Max that I can't go to bed with him; he's too old for me. This is terribly threatening for me because the instant I do that my income is cut off.

Th. Mm hmm.

Pt. And Max told me he would give me money without strings tied to it.

Th. This must be a great temptation.

Pt. It is, and I see myself not wanting to give it up. I've accepted it in my mind to try it out.

Th. You may be in a great conflict between being dependent and being active and independent.

Pt. Yes, I don't know which to do.

Th. That's something that you yourself will have to work through.

Pt. I suppose my mind is in a fog because I don't know what to do, but somehow I feel I'm getting stronger. [*The mental fog and her coming late for the session are apparently signs of resistance.*]

Very frequently, negativistic resistant states develop several weeks or several months after the patient appears to have entered into the spirit of treatment, spontaneously analyzing difficulties and making what appears to be good progress. Suddenly, without warning, he will go into a blocked, inhibited pattern.

Acting-out

Along with unwillingness to verbalize ideas and impulses, the patient may indulge in irrational acts and behavior in everyday life. This "acting-out" appears to be a way of supporting the inability to talk during treatment. The acts serve to drain off anxiety and leave little energy available for ideational processes during the treatment hour.

Superficial Talk

Another form of resistance is a veering around one's problems in superficial talk. Here verbal comments are used as a defense to ward off basic issues. The patient may spend the entire time of treatment in talk that embraces topics of the day, current events, or past experiences portraying personal tragedy and martyrdom. There is little of deep significance in the conversation, and, if allowed to, the patient may continue for years to discuss material that is interesting enough but that actually has little to do with deeper problems. Often he will want to monopolize the interview, and he will resent the therapist getting a comment or an interpretation in edgewise. Rarely will he talk about his attitudes toward the therapist, who may begin to feel merely like a sounding board for the patient's boasts and diatribes. It is almost as if in superfluous conversation the patient defies the world to make him talk about his innermost self. Associated with this, there may be an attempt to intellectualize his problems, to figure out connections, and to present a rigid and logical system of what must have happened to him.

Insight as Resistance

A device that is apt to be confusing to the therapist is the use of insight as a form of resistance. Here the patient will routinely go through a detailed accounting of how well he understands himself, using the best accepted terminology, presenting the dynamics and mechanisms of his disorder in approved textbook style. To all appearances he has gained complete insight into the origin of his problems, into his compulsive trends and distorted relationships, and into the consequences and destructive influences of his neurosis. Yet in his daily experiences he goes right on with his usual neurotic modes of adjustment, manifesting the same symptoms that originally brought him to treatment. It is probable in such cases that the patient's insight is a highly intellectualized affair that he employs to confuse himself and the therapist.

There are many reasons why a person

utilizes insight as a smoke screen behind which to indulge customary neurotic trends. One of the most common reasons is the desire to escape criticism and detection. Here, a dissociation exists between how the patient thinks and feels. It is often easy for the therapist to minimize the seriousness of the patient's disorder when confronted during treatment with a beautiful recitation of psychopathology. Behind the camouflage of insight it is apparent that the patient uses knowledge of mechanisms as an instrument to allay guilt and to forestall criticism in regard to daily actions.

This mechanism is often found in the extremely dependent patient who has magical expectations of what therapy will do for him. The chief motivation for entering treatment is the feeling that the therapist will bring about those neurotic objectives that he, himself, has failed to obtain through his own efforts. Compliance here is the keynote, and the patient, by reciting his spurious insights, will feel that the therapist must reward his aptitudes in learning with anticipated bounties. The facade is at least partially unconscious, and the patient may really believe that he understands himself thoroughly. The clue to what is going on is usually furnished by the tremendous hostility and aggression that eventually is exhibited toward the therapist when, after months of precise and punctilious performance, the patient does not magically get what he originally set out to achieve.

Dissociating the Treatment Hour from Life

Sometimes resistance takes the form of the patient's utilizing the treatment hour as a special event dissociated from life. Regarding it as such, he will go into the mechanisms of his interpersonal relationships with complete freedom, but it is obvious that with the therapist he is operating under a set of standards entirely different from those that he uses with people in general. There seems to be something recondite about the treatment hour, for it is set apart from all other experiences. The special resistance here is that of not seeing how the material that is uncovered in the treatment

hour relates to the everyday situation. This isolation of treatment from life is often rationalized by the patient on the basis that the therapist is a scientist who does not condemn him for acts for which he would be punished by others. In this way he will lead a dual existence and seemingly be unable to fill the chasm between what happens in treatment and experiences outside of treatment.

Contempt for Normality

An insidious kind of resistance expresses itself in a fear of, or a contempt for, normality. Associated is a refusal to assume responsibility or to make an effort on one's own. By substituting new patterns for old, the patient believes that he is yielding up something valuable, something he may never be able to replace, that he will become a prosaic bore, or that he may be exposing himself to dangers with which he will be unable to cope. This type of resistance appears most intensely after the patient has gained insight and is ready to execute it into action.

A patient with a phobic reaction extended to subway travel made a trip to my office by subway for the first time since treatment had started. She entered the room sullenly and remarked fretfully that she was furious with me. Her anger had started when she discovered that she had no great anxiety riding on the train. A fragment of the session follows:

Pt. I am so angry and resentful toward you. *(pause)*

Th. I wonder why.

Pt. I feel you are gloating over my taking a subway. I feel mother is gloating too. I resent her too. I felt she was pushing me, trying to force me to break away from her. She gloats if I do something that makes me independent. I feel that when I go ahead you gloat too. [*The patient had become so pathologically dependent on her mother that she was scarcely able to let her out of her sight. Mastering some dependency and walking alone was achieved previously in therapy, although the patient was very reluctant to give up this aspect of her dependent relationship.*]

Th. It sounds as if you are angry about being able to travel on the subway.

Pt. Mother seems to be anxious to give up

her responsibility for me. I resent that. But I also don't like the idea of my being so close to mother too.

Th. I see, as if you want to continue being dependent and yet resenting it.

Pt. When I get sick at night, I ask her to make me some tea; and then I resent her patrician attitude when she does this.

Th. But what about your feeling about me?

Pt. It's like giving in to you. But yesterday I felt liberated by the idea that I'm in the middle of a conflict and that coming here offers me hope. I realize that my neurosis is threatened by my getting well. *(laughs)*

Th. What part of your neurosis do you want to hold onto?

Pt. (laughs) None. But I have a feeling that I don't want to be normal, that in giving in to you I'll be like anybody else. Also that you'll expect more things of me. And *(laughs)* that if I get too well you'll kick me out. [*Here the patient verbalizes a variety of resistances: namely, a desire for uniqueness, a contempt for normality, a fear she will be expected to face more anxiety-provoking situations, a reluctance to give up her dependence on me, a punishing of her mother and of me by refusing to acknowledge improvement, and an unwillingness to yield her masochism and the various secondary gain elements accruing to her neurosis.*]

Occasionally a psychosomatic complaint may be a manifestation of resistance, as illustrated in the following fragment from a session with a male patient:

Pt. Everything was going well until this morning when I got stomach cramps. They have been with me all day.

Th. Mm hmm.

Pt. I find it hard to concentrate because my stomach bothers me so much. Mondays I always have a hard time for some reason. It's happened the last few Mondays.

Th. Seems like an unlucky day for you. *(pause)*

Pt. I was thinking about how long it takes to get well, and I was wondering if others did any better than I do. Of course, things are a lot better now, and I was thinking of taking a course in journalism up at the New School. The only thing is that it comes on Mondays, and that's hard. I . . . uh . . . uh . . . *(Patient brings hand to his abdomen.)* I had something I wanted to say . . . but I can't think of anything but these cramps. *(He takes a cigarette from a pack, reaches into his pocket for matches but cannot find them.)* Do you have a match?

Th. I believe so. Here's one. *(pause)*

Pt. Well . . . *(coughs)*

Th. You were saying that Mondays are pretty tough on you? Perhaps something happens to you on Mondays that upsets you.

Pt. I . . . I . . . I don't know.

Th. You do come *here* on Mondays.

Pt. Why . . . yes . . . yes . . . I mean I do.

Th. Maybe something is upsetting you in coming here?

Pt. I don't know what it might be. *(pause)* Maybe I'm upset that you feel I'm not doing well. [*We discuss his feelings that he is not living up to expectations. This is what has been giving him anxiety. His cramps are manifestations of internalized resentment and act in the service of resistance.*]

Reluctance to Yield the Pleasure Values of the Treatment Hour

A form of resistance that is frequently overlooked is one that involves reluctance to yield the positive pleasures that the patient gets out of the treatment itself. He may derive such comfort from the therapeutic hour that other gratifications seem dubious, and he may refuse to give up his neurosis because of a desire to continue to see the therapist. This is frequently the case in a very dependent patient who looks forward to the hour to get a "lift," who perhaps pays lip homage to all the dynamic principles uncovered during treatment, but whose chief motive for therapy is to get suggestions and courage to carry on with his daily routines. Unless one watches oneself carefully, the therapist will fall into a trap laid out by the patient and may, by the patient's helplessness and apparent inability to do things voluntarily, feel forced to load the patient with advice and admonishments, which the patient absorbs as if these were pronouncements from the Deity.

Transference Resistances

Perhaps the most common and disturbing of resistances are those that are produced in response to the relationship with the therapist or that take the form of transference. Contact with the therapist is understandably disturbing when it mobilizes attitudes, impulses, and feelings that threaten the repressive forces. The patient will, in the attempt to escape from the associated anxiety, exhibit his usual characterologic defenses to detach himself, to control and overwhelm the therapist, or to render himself invincible. In supportive and some types of reeducative psychotherapy the patient will manage to restore his equilibrium through the medium of such defenses, and he will, more or less successfully, repress disturbing irrational, unconscious drives. In reconstructive therapy, on the other hand, the therapist constantly interprets the nature and purpose of the various defenses as they arise. This constitutes an assault on the integrity of the repressive system and will precipitate much tension. Eventually the patient cannot help coming to grips with the emotions and drives that hitherto have been successfully avoided. The patient will then mobilize further protective devices to reinforce the shattered repressions.

One of the earliest manifestations of this struggle is an intensification of symptoms, which seems to serve the desperate function of restoring psychic equilibrium. Soon the struggle becomes more personalized as the patient realizes that relationship with the therapist is the womb of the distress. Resistance may be exerted against the original unconscious material or to its projected and animated representations in the transference.

The patient may exhibit a clinging dependent attitude toward the therapist, who is regarded as a godlike individual, the embodiment of all that is good and strong and noble in the universe. This kind of resistance is often found in individuals who are characterologically submissive, subordinate, and ingratiating and who strive to adjust to life by clinging parasitically to a more powerful person. It is as if the individual had an amputated self that could be restored only by symbiosis with a stronger individual. There is an associated tendency to overvalue the characteristics and qualities of the therapist. This type of relationship is extremely shaky because the patient regards therapy as a magical means to secu-

rity and power. Consequently, the therapist must always live up to the inordinate expectations of the patient, which are so sheerly in the realm of fantasy that they are beyond possibility of fulfillment. The patient will demand more and more of the therapist, and, failing to get what he secretly wants, he will be filled with hostility and contempt. It is essential that the therapist recognize a dependency trend in order to point out to the patient the need for activity and the necessity of avoiding acceptance of interpretations on the premise of faith.

Another form of relationship that may develop is based on an intense fear of the therapist as one who is potentially capable of injuring or enslaving the patient. This attitude stems from a hostile image of the parent and is usually applied to all authoritative individuals. Treatment in such cases proceeds only when the patient realizes that the therapist does not desire to punish or condemn him for his ambitions or fantasies but instead is benevolently neutral toward them. Little progress is possible until the patient accepts the therapist as a friend. Until then resistance will be intense.

Sometimes the patient displays a need to be victimized and unfairly treated. He will maneuver himself into a situation with the therapist in which he feels that the latter is taking advantage of him. He may exhibit various symptoms that he attributes to the harmful effects of therapy. In order to reinforce his waning repressive system, he may seek to transform the therapist into a stern authority who commands and punishes him. Where this happens, he will experience severe anxiety if the therapist is tolerant and condones his inner impulses.

Resistance is frequently displayed in the form of hostility. The resulting reaction patterns depend on the extent to which the patient is able to express aggression. Where the character structure makes it mandatory to inhibit rage, the patient may respond with depression and discouragement. He may then want to terminate therapy on the grounds that he has no chance of getting well. He may mask his aggression with slavish conformity and perhaps evince an interest in the therapist's personal life, assuming an attitude of comradery and good fellowship. There is in such efforts a desire to ally himself with the therapist in order to lessen the danger to himself.

On the other hand, where the patient is able to express hostility, he may exhibit it in many ways. He may become critical, then defiant, challenging the therapist to make him well. Irritability is often transmuted into contempt, and the patient may accuse the therapist of having exploitative or evil designs on him. Feeling misunderstood and humiliated, he will manufacture, out of insignificant happenings in his contact with the therapist, sufficient grounds to justify his notion of being mistreated. He will become suspicious about the therapist's training, experience, political convictions, and social and marital adjustment. He may enter actively into competition with the therapist by analyzing the latter, by reading books on psychoanalysis to enable him to point out the therapist's shortcomings. He may become uncooperative and negativistic to the point of mutism.

Sometimes hostility is handled by attempts at detachment. The need to keep the therapist from getting too close may burn up a great deal of the patient's energy. He may refuse to listen to what the therapist says. He may ridicule in his mind proffered interpretations. He may forget his appointments or seek to discontinue therapy, inventing many rationalizations for this. He may strive to ward the therapist off by discussing irrelevant subjects or by presenting a detailed inventory of his symptoms. In his effort to keep aloof he may attempt to take over therapy, interpreting in advance his unconscious conflicts, the existence of which he suspects. An insidious type of defense is a preoccupation with childhood experiences. Here the patient will overwhelm the therapist with the most minute details of what must have happened to him when he was little, presenting a fairly consistent and logical survey of how previous inimical experiences must have produced all of his present difficulties.

Occasionally the impulse toward detachment is bolstered by contempt for the therapist's values; the patient will feel that his own values are what really count. Because of this he will be convinced that the therapist cannot like him and will "let him down." He will rationalize these feelings and say to himself that the therapist is no good, or incompetent, or of no importance, or that psychotherapy is nothing but nonsense.

The desire to control the situation may reflect itself in many ways. The patient may seek to shower the therapist with gifts and favors, or he may develop a sentimental attachment that assumes a sexual form. Therapy may be regarded as a seduction, the patient experiencing in it intense erotic feelings. One of the motives involved in falling in love with the therapist is to put him in a position where he will not pry too closely into the patient's deepest secrets. There are often hostile components associated. The incentive may be to devaluate the therapist, to enslave him, to test his convictions, or to fuse with him; in this way taking a shortcut to cure. Progress may suddenly stop as the patient blocks himself in his love experience. The real purpose of this type of attachment is resistance, although the patient will seek other gains, such as the living out of fantasied neurotic gratifications.

Many patients come to treatment not because they desire to function more adequately in their interpersonal relationships, but rather because they seek to obtain from treatment the fulfillment of neurotic demands that they have been unable to gratify through their own efforts. In such cases resentment and resistance develop when the patient does not receive from the therapist the specific type of help that he has expected.

Upon analyzing the evidence as to what the patient seeks from the therapist, it turns out that what is sought is not a cure for the neurosis, but an infallible method of making it work. Many patients particularly desire to achieve their neurotic expectations without having to pay the penalty of suffering. The individual with a power drive may thus insist on a formula whereby she can function in an invincible manner in all activities in which she participates. The perfectionist will want to find a way to do things flawlessly, with as little effort as possible. The dependent individual will expect to amalgamate himself with the therapist and to have all of his whims gratified without activity on his own part. The detached soul will seek the fruits of social intercourse, though she wants at the same time to keep her distance from people. When these drives are not gratified in therapy, when patients sense that these are instead being challenged, they will become tremendously resistive.

Frequently resistance is exerted against accepting the idea that it is possible to function adequately without repairing a fantasied injury to the genital organs. In the female the resistance may be to continuing life without the possibility of ever procuring for herself a penis, which she regards as the bridge to activity and self-fulfillment. In males the assumption of a passive role is often interpreted as equivalent to being castrated, and resistance may be directed against assuming any role that does not involve aggressive fighting. Even accepting help from the therapist may symbolize passivity.

Psychotherapy may produce other unfavorable resistance reactions in patients with immature ego structures. The transference becomes so dramatic and disturbing to these patients that they respond to it in an essentially psychotic manner. They will accuse the therapist of being hostile, destructive, and rejecting, and they will refuse to acknowledge that their attitudes may be the product of their own feelings. The reasonable ego here is very diminutive and cannot tolerate the implications of unconscious drives and conflicts. The patient acts out inner problems and constantly avoids subjecting them to reason. The acting-out tendency permits the neurosis to remain intact. Where the therapist is seen as a cruel or lecherous or destructive being who threatens the patient with injury or abandonment, any action or interpretation is twisted in the light of this delusional system. Fear and anxiety issuing from the functioning of the patient's irrational strivings lie like boulders in his path, barring the way to a more congenial therapeutic relationship. In such cases therapy will be prolonged, and the relationship must be worked on actively so as to constitute for the patient a gratifying human experience.

METHODS OF HANDLING RESISTANCE

As soon as the therapist realizes that resistance is interfering with therapy, it is necessary to concentrate on the resistance to the exclusion of all other tasks. This may be done in a number of ways.

Identifying the Resistance and Exploring Its Manifestations

Calling the patient's attention to the resistance itself and exploring its manifestations are essential procedures for the therapist. For example, a patient has for the past few sessions arrived 5 to 10 minutes late. The sessions are spent in a discursive account of family events, including the impending marriage of his son, the forthcoming graduation of his daughter, and the attacks of "gall-bladder trouble" suffered by his wife for which she may need an operation. The responsibilities imposed on him by his business and social position also occupy his attention. He mentions having suggested a 2-week vacation in Florida, but his wife promptly vetoed the idea. He pauses in his conversation and then remarks that there is nothing on his mind. Sensing resistance, I direct the interview along the following lines:

Th. I wonder if there is something on your mind that bothers you that you are not talking about.

Pt. Why, no, not that I'm aware of.

Th. The reason I bring this up is that you have been coming late to your sessions, and during your sessions you have kind of rambled along, not talking about things that bothered you too much. At least I have that impression. [*pointing out possible resistances*]

Pt. Why no, I mean you want me to talk about anything on my mind. I'm supposed to do that, am I not?

Th. Yes.

Pt. Well, I haven't had anything else bothering me.

Th. Perhaps not, but have you had any symptoms that upset you?

Pt. No. I've noticed though that my jaws tighten up sometimes. And my wife tells me I'm grinding my teeth in my sleep.

Th. Mm hmm. That sounds like tension of some kind.

Pt. I know I feel a little tense.

Th. A little tense?

Pt. I've been upset that I have to do, do, do for other people, give, give, give, and get little in return.

Th. As if people expect things from you and do not want to give anything?

Pt. Yes, I'm getting fed up with my life, the way it's been going.

Th. I see. This could be upsetting.

Pt. I suppose you'd say I feel frustrated.

Th. Well, what do *you* say?

Pt. (laughs) It's hard to admit it, but I am. Sometimes I'd like to chuck up the whole thing, and be single again, without responsibilities, to do what I want to do.

Th. I should think you would feel frustrated that you can't.

Pt. Lately I've been getting this way. [*The patient discusses his secret ambition of wanting to be a writer and admits that he was embarrassed to talk about this. He was also, he remarks, afraid to admit that he resents being tied down to a routine family life. His resistance to talk about these things along with his internalized rage at his life situation seemed responsible for his muscular symptoms.*]

Pointing Out Possible Reasons for the Resistance

Where the patient is cognizant of his resistance but does not recognize its purpose, the therapist should point out various reasons possible for the resistance. The defensive objects of the resistance may be interpreted along with the various facades that the patient elaborates to block himself. The patient may be shown that his resistance protects him against the threat of change. Thus, a patient blocks repeatedly during a session; the periods of silence are not broken by the usual interview techniques.

Th. I wonder what the long silences mean.

Pt. Nothing comes to my mind, that's all. I kind of wish the time was up.

Th. Perhaps you are afraid to bring up certain things today. [*suggesting that her silence is a resistance to prevent her from bringing up painful material*]

Pt. Like what?

Th. Well, is there any event that happened since I saw you that you have not mentioned to me?

Pt. (silence) Yes, there was. I met a man last Wednesday who sent me. I made a big play for him and am going to see him Sunday. [*The patient's infidelity to her husband is one of her symptoms, of which she is ashamed.*]

Th. I see.

Pt. I have wondered why I did this. I realized you wouldn't tell me not to, but I feel guilty about it.

Th. Was that the reason why you were silent?

Pt. (laughing) Honestly, I thought there wasn't much to talk about. I minimized the importance of this thing. But I realize now that I didn't want to tell you about it.

Th. What did you think my reaction would be?

Pt. (laughs) I guess I thought you'd think I was hopeless or that you'd scold me.

Reassuring Tactics

Reassuring the patient in a tangential way about that which is being resisted necessitates an understanding by the therapist of the warded-off aspects. For instance, a woman with an obsessional neurosis comes into a session with symptoms of exacerbated anxiety. She has no desire to talk about anything but her suffering. This seems to me a sign of resistance. When I inquired about dreams that she may have had, the patient reveals one that, in a disguised way, indicates murderous attitudes toward her offspring. The idea occurs to me that she is attempting to suppress and repress thoughts about her children. A significant portion of the session follows:

Th. I wonder if you haven't been overly concerned about thoughts of your children.

Pt. I'm frightened about them, the thoughts.

Th. You know, every mother kind of resents being forced into playing the role of housewife. This is a cramped life to many persons. Most women may resent their children and from time to time wish they weren't around. It's natural for them to feel that. [*reassuring the patient about possible hostility*]

Pt. (rapidly) That's how I feel.

Th. They may even get a feeling sometime that if the children pass away, that will liberate them. Not that they really want that, but they look at it as an escape. [*more reassurance*]

Pt. That's what I didn't want to say. I've felt that it was horrible to be like that.

Focusing on Material Being Resisted

Bringing the patient's attention to the material against which the resistance is being directed must be done in a very diplomatic way, preferably by helping the patient to make his own interpretation or by a tentative interpretation. A patient with a problem of dependency complained of an intense headache and a general feeling of disinterest in life. The interview was rather barren, but enough material was available to bring the patient to an understanding of what he was trying to repudiate.

Pt. My wife has been telling me that I just am not like the other husbands. I come home and read the newspaper and don't go grubbing around in the garden.

Th. What does that make you feel like?

Pt. I guess she's right. But as hard as I try, I know I'm being a hypocrite. I just gave that up.

Th. But your wife keeps pounding away at you.

Pt. Well, what are you going to do. I don't help her around the place. She resents my being as I am.

Th. But what do you feel your reaction is to her pounding away at you?

Pt. (*fists clench*) It drives me nuts. I'd like to tell her to stop, but I know she's right.

Th. Is it possible that you resent her attitude, nevertheless, and would prefer her laying off you when you don't do the chores? [*a tentative interpretation of the material against which there is resistance*]

Pt. God damn it. I think she is being unreasonable when she sails into me. [*The patient takes courage from my interpretation and expresses resentment.*]

Th. Mm hmm.

Pt. After all, I come home tired and I find no interest in planting cucumbers. Besides, it's crazy. My neighbors plant dollar tomatoes. Each tomato costs them a dollar. It's no economy. The whole thing is silly. [*The patient continues in a diatribe, venting his resentment about his wife's attitude. At the end of the session his headache has disappeared.*]

Handling Acting-out

Acting-out is a common manifestation that has been given various interpretations (Abt, 1965). Fenichel (1945) defines acting-out as "an acting which unconsciously re-lieves inner tension and brings a partial discharge to warded-off impulses (no matter whether these impulses express directly instinctual demands, or are reactions to original instinctual demands, i.e., guilt feelings); the present situation, somehow associatively connected with the repressed content, is used as the occasion for the discharge of repressed energies, the cathexis is displaced from the repressed memories to the present, 'derivative,' and this displacement makes the discharge possible." Aronson (1964) considers the essential features of any acting-out sequence to be a reenactment of a childish ("pregenital") memory or fantasy, of which there is no conscious recollection, precipitated by transference or resistance during psychotherapy, displacing itself to some organized "ego-syntonic" action, thus permitting a partial discharge of inner tension. At the same time there is no awareness of any relationship of the old memory or fantasy with the current action.

Prior to coming to therapy the patient, having indulged in acting-out tendencies as a way of expressing unconscious impulses and feelings, may have gotten into certain scrapes. During psychotherapy acting-out may occur even in patients who have, before treatment, shown no evidence of it in their behavior.

There are some psychotherapists who take the view that acting-out can serve a useful purpose in some patients, that it may be growth inducing and, particularly where basic problems originated in the preverbal state, constitute a preliminary step toward gaining insight. Consequently, they tend to encourage and even to stimulate acting-out. Other therapists, however, regard acting-out as always detrimental to therapeutic progress since it drains off the tension that should be employed for a requisite understanding and working through of conflicts. Between these two extremes an intermediate viewpoint may be taken, acting-out being managed in accordance with whether it serves as an obstruction to or as an intermediate stage toward learning.

Some patients who were overindulged and poorly disciplined as children will engage in untoward acting-out behavior to goad the therapist into a setting of limits such as they had never experienced with their own parents. On the other hand, where parents have been to authoritarian and have cowed the patient to a point where the slightest emergence of defiant or antisocial conduct inspires fear of a counterattack, acting-out may constitute a breaking out of restraints. The handling of acting-out in these two instances will be different.

Where acting-out occurs as a resistance to therapy, it is usually inspired by the transference situation. Because the patient refuses to verbalize prior to acting-out and because he may conceal and rationalize his behavior, it may be difficult to deal with it therapeutically. For instance, a prudish female patient, shortly after starting therapy, confessed having involved herself in extramarital love affairs with several men. It was only through a dream that I was able to get a glimpse of her guilt feelings at sexual actions that were totally foreign to her personality. Confronting her with the existence of sexual guilt brought forth divulgence of the information that she had, during the past month, become so sexually aroused that she felt forced to seek satisfaction in outside "affairs." Focusing on her feelings about me, the patient was soon brought to an awareness of how closely she had identified me with her father, and of how her incestuous impulses were being displaced. The establishment of the connections of her current behavior with its infantile roots enabled her to control her acting-out and to work through her fantasies within the therapeutic situation.

The therapist should consequently be alert to extraordinary behavior patterns that occur in the patient. Thus, a man who is ordinarily restrained may engage in random, multiple sexual affairs to the point of satyriasis, or involve himself in dangerous but exciting aggression-releasing situations that are potentially disastrous to him. One patient, for instance, whenever provoked by hostility toward her therapist, would get into her car and drive speedily and recklessly. Only when she narrowly escaped an accident would she slow down.

Whenever the therapist recognizes acting-out, it is necessary to bring this to the attention of the patient. The therapist may suggest that there are reasons why the patient feels forced to engage in certain deeds. Talking about his feelings *prior* to putting them into action will help the therapeutic process. Acting compulsively the way that the patient does tends to interfere with therapy. Should the patient accept these statements and verbalize, he will usually drain off enough energy in the interview to forestall acting-out. Interpretation may also help to dissipate the need for unrestrained behavior. Interpretive activities will require a repeated pointing out to the patient of manifestations of acting-out conduct. At the same time attempts are made to link actions to fantasies or impulses that are preconsciously perceived. Material from free associations and dreams may be valuable here. What helps in most instances is bringing the patient to an awareness of evidences of transference. Should any of the acting-out manifestations contain healthy elements, the therapist should attempt to reinforce these. The strategic timing of interpretations is important. Where acting-out occurs during a session as a manifestation of transference and resistance, interpretations will be particularly effective; nevertheless, a prolonged period of working through may still be required.

Should acting-out persist and should this be potentially dangerous to the patient, the therapist may direct the patient to desist from the acts on the basis of their destructive nature, while enjoining him to talk about his impulses. Of course, in some instances, it may be impossible for the patient voluntarily to stop acting-out. Exhibitionism, voyeurism, and other sexual perversions are examples. However, with persistence it may be possible to get the patient to talk freely about his "temptations" and to help him, to an extent at least, to gain some voluntary control over them. Increasing the frequency of sessions to five times weekly and giving the patient the privilege to telephone the therapist whenever the impulse to act-out occurs are often helpful. As a last resort, if the patient continues dangerous acting-out, the therapist may threaten to withdraw from the therapeutic situation unless the patient exercises control over his impulses. Aversive conditioning techniques are sometimes employed as a means toward checking acting-out that cannot be controlled in any other way. Cooperation of the patient will, of course, be necessary. The patient may also be told, "If you want to continue in this self-destructive behavior, you can do it by yourself; you don't need me. If you want to change, I can help you."

It goes without saying that acting-out within the therapeutic session, like physical attacks on the therapist and lovemaking gestures, are to be prohibited. Patients may be told that they can talk about anything they please but that unrestrained actions are not permitted by rule in therapy. Experience has shown that these interfere with the therapeutic process.

Handling Transference Resistances

Where transference has developed to the point where it constitutes resistance to treatment, it will have to be resolved. If it is not dissipated, it will seriously interfere with the working relationship. Treatment may become interminable, the patient utilizing the therapeutic relationship solely as a means of gratifying neurotic impulses at the expense of getting well. Frustrated by the absence of what he considers to be the proper response to his reasonable demands, the patient may terminate treatment with feelings of contempt for or antagonism toward the therapist.

Superficial manifestations of transference may often be adequately handled by maintaining a steadfast attitude and manner, constantly bringing the patient back to reality. Sometimes a studied avoidance of the role that the patient wants the therapist to play, or acting in an opposite role, minimizes transference. For instance, if the patient expects the therapist to be directive and controlling, on the basis of a conviction that all authority is this way, the therapist deliberately acts permissive, tolerant, and encouraging of those activities toward assertiveness and freedom that the patient himself cherishes but which he believes his parents wanted him to repress.

A patient, conditioned to expect punishment for infractions by a punitive parent, appears for a session depressed and guilt-ridden. She seems to demand that the therapist scold and punish her for having drunk to excess the evening before and for having acted sexually promiscuous. Not being able to stimulate this reaction in the therapist, the patient launches into an attack, upbraiding the therapist for passivity. The therapist continues to react in a tolerant and nonjudgmental manner but interprets the responses of the patient in terms of her desires for punishment and forgiveness to propitiate aroused guilt feelings.

Severe manifestations of transference being rooted in infantile conditionings will usually require prolonged "working through." Strategically timed interpretations of the sources of transference in childhood experiences and fantasies, and of its present functions, will be required.

Among the most disturbing of transference resistances is that of the sexual transference, which takes the form of insistence that one can be cured only in a sexual relationship. While therapy may set off a temporary sexual attraction toward the therapist, this fascination usually disappears as therapy progresses or upon the simple structuring of the therapeutic situation. However, in some patients the sexual preoccupation becomes intense and persistent. A male patient, for example, will pick out from the behavior of a female therapist minor evidences that he will enlarge to justify his belief that the therapist must love him. The protestations of the patient may greatly flatter the therapist, and the urgency of the expressed demands may tempt her to respond partially by touching or holding the patient. These advances are most provoking to the patient and incite greater sexual feeling. Should the therapist engage in any kind of sex play with the patient, this can have only the most destructive effect on both participants. Once the patient has even partially seduced the therapist, he may develop contempt for her weakness and for her abandonment of ethical principles. The therapeutic situation will obviously terminate with any expressed intimacy.

It is important in handling sexual transference not to make the patient feel guilty about sexual feeling. Rather, the feeling should be accepted and an attempt made to find out what it means in terms of the patient's past sexual attitudes and behavior. For instance, sex may indicate being accepted or preferred by someone. It may perhaps have the connotation of vanquishing or humiliating others. Sometimes reassuring comments are helpful in abating the patient's reactions. Thus the patient may be told, "It is usual for persons to develop such feelings for their therapist," or "It is good that you have these feelings because they will enable you to work out important attitudes and relationships," or "The feeling you have toward me is a step in your ability to feel and to relate to other people," or "This will serve as a means toward better relations with others." Where the patient brings in dreams and fantasies, it may be possible to interpret, with all the precautions already mentioned, the sources of the patient's transference reactions.

Another disturbing resistance is that of the hostile transference. Here the patient will react to the therapist as if he is convinced of the reality of the therapist's unfriendliness, destructiveness, ineptness, seductiveness, and maliciousness. He will be importunate, irrascible, and insistent that it is the therapist who misinterprets and not he. He may become retaliatory or destructive in response to the therapist's fancied hostility, or he may experience panic, depression, or psychosomatic symptoms. A resolution of hostility by the introduction of reality and by interpretation is indicated, following some of the suggestions given for the management of the sexual transference.

Where transference cannot be handled in any other way, active steps will have to be taken to minimize it. Such measures include a focusing in the interview on the current life situation rather than on early childhood experiences, avoidance of dreams and fantasies, discouraging discussion of the patient's relationship to the therapist, abandonment of the couch position and free association if these have been employed, decreasing the frequency of the interviews, presenting interpretations in terms of the character structure and current life situation rather than in terms of genetic determinants, and greater activity in the interview.

THE NEED FOR WORKING THROUGH RESISTANCE

Resistance may burn up the entire energy of the patient, and he may concentrate solely on fighting the therapist, or defending himself, or proving the therapist to be wrong, or winning him over with gestures of helplessness, praise, or love, or seeking various means to escape or to evade treatment. The struggle is an intense one and usually goes on below the level of awareness.

When one appreciates the purpose of resistance, one realizes that patience is a great virtue. The therapist must bear with the neurotic individual as he progresses and as he takes refuge over and over again in his customary defenses. Resistance is yielded only after a great struggle, for change is a painful affair.

Since resistance has a dynamic function, an effort is made to help the patient to relinquish it slowly. Too sudden removal may produce severe anxiety and may provoke a reinforcement of the neurotic defenses intended to protect the individual. Relinquishment of resistance will thus be blocked by a threat of repetition of the anxiety experience.

Resistance is best managed by demonstrating its presence, its purpose, its ramifications, its historical origin, and the manner of its operation in the patient's present relationships with the therapist and with people in general. As resistances are gradually analyzed and resolved, repressed material appears in consciousness in a less and less disguised form. Resistances require a constant working through. A single interpretation of a resistance is hardly effective.

The therapist should allow resistance to evolve fully before taking it back to its origins. If a second resistance develops, the therapist must handle it by returning to the first one and demonstrating to the patient the interrelationship of the two. Tackling the patient's defensive reactions inevitably causes him to feel threatened and to resist interpretations of his resistance. This reaction is opposed by a contrary motive, that of retaining the good will of the therapist. Often the patient will attempt to satisfy both of these motivations at the same time by abandoning his defense in the forms recognized by the therapist and changing it to a less obvious type. The understanding of these elaborations and their continued exposure forces the patient to take a real stand against them and, finally, to abandon them entirely.

It is always essential to remember that resistance has a strong protective value. The patient will usually reject any insight that is too traumatic, or he will toy with it for a while, then forget it. However, through careful handling, he may gain insight as to how and why the resistance is operating. First, he must be made aware of the resistance. Merely calling his attention to it makes him concentrate on a specific task. It prevents him from burning up all of his energy in maintaining the resistance; it enables him to use some of his energy in tracing down its meaning.

Once a resistance develops, it is essential to abandon other tasks until it is analyzed because the patient will not be productive while battling the therapist. It is best at first not to probe too deeply for unconscious material, but rather to work intensively upon the immediate interpersonal relationship. To aid in the process, the patient must be impressed with the fact that there is nothing morally bad about showing certain defensive attitudes in the form of resistance.

The dealing with transference resistances may be a prolonged affair in the personality disorders. Here the ego seems blocked in absorbing the full meaning of the unconscious material as it becomes apparent. The patient may acknowledge the presence of certain drives. He may even understand their irrational nature and historical origin, but this pseudoinsight provokes little change in the customary life adjustment. The entire therapeutic process is intellectualized, the patient using insight to fortify himself against pain. His relationship with the therapist never proceeds to a level of positive feeling, shorn of hostility and inordinate expectations.

In infantile, narcissistic character structures particularly, intellectuality serves as a defense against unconscious impulses. Habitually there is a repression of the feeling aspects of the patient's personality, and mastery is sought through intellectual control. Any experience of feeling is regarded as catastrophic. By a curious transformation the defense itself may become a vicarious means of gratifying nonpermissible drives as represented in hostile and sexual impulses. Another secondary gain hoped for from this facade is that of acceptance by the therapist.

Patients who have a tendency to isolate emotional components from emerging unconscious material may make the latter acceptable to themselves by repressing the affective content. Frequently they strive to neutralize their panic by means of foresight and reason. During therapy they give the impression of being very active and at first seem to work extraordinarily well. Even though they make a brilliant feat of minutely analyzing their inner mental processes, little change occurs. Such patients may involve the therapist in long dialectic arguments that take on the nature of debates. Words replace experiences and constitute a defense against feelings.

Interpretation of this type of defense is bound to create great turmoil in the patient. The patient is prone to feel attacked and criticized by the therapist. "Negative therapeutic reactions" are common, the patient responding to important interpretations not with insight or relief, but with depression and discouragement. Hostility may be directed at the therapist in an effort to annihilate the therapeutic work.

It is essential to remind every patient not to get too distressed if cure is not immediate. Some patients are confounded and depressed when they find, in spite of their own wishes, that they go on reacting to their various trends. It may be necessary to explain that reaction patterns that have become established over a long period cannot be removed in a few sessions. They are habits that call for extended working through and reeducation.

In the event the patient insists he cannot get well because he is hopeless, the therapist may say, "You can express your hopelessness, but I will not go along with it. You can spend your energies feeling hopeless, and you don't need me for this; or you can spend them doing something about getting well, and I can help you in this case."

ILLUSTRATIVE CASE MATERIAL

Example 1:

In this session a female patient with a homosexual problem introduces a number of different resistances that block her progress.

Pt. I keep losing my keys constantly. My mind can't seem to concentrate lately. I notice that the only time I want to think about my problem is when I come here. The minute I get out I feel relieved. When I leave here I notice my hands as very cold. [*This sounds like resistance in the form of intellectual inhibition.*]

Th. I see. Can you tell me more about this?

Pt. When I get out of the office, in waiting for the elevator, I push myself up against the wall pretending the wall to be Helen (*the patient's homosexual love object*). I actually kiss that wall and I say, "Who does he think *he* is, trying to pull me away from my darling Helen. I won't have it, I just won't have it." [*This device seems to be a magical way of neutralizing therapy, which she interprets as a threat to her homosexuality.*]

Th. What does it remind you of when you do that?

Pt. Like being united with my mother. Everything seems to be O.K. again, and I can go on living. [*Having lost her mother in childhood, the patient's homosexuality, in part, is a neurotic attempt to reunite herself with her mother.*]

Th. Mm hmm.

Pt. You see. I do that.

Th. But why do you think I want to take you away from your mother?

Pt. I see that. You see, the information I get here, I feel, is going to get rid of the old regime and bring on a new regime.

Th. And the old regime is what?

Pt. Homosexuality. That's strong. It's easier to live in than the new regime.

Th. And the new regime?

Pt. Is getting rid of the mother fantasy and working it out.

Th. So that you would consider any insights that you get here in a certain way.

Pt. As dangerous to my ability to function (*pause*) for the moment.

Th. So when you come here, I upset the balance and you may want to go to the opposite extreme.

Pt. I shift to the opposite extreme so I can function.

Th. You must perhaps think of me as a terrible person to do this to you. [*probing our relationship*]

Pt. You are a horror. (*said facetiously*) I adore you, you know.

Th. You do? Why?

Pt. You know I do. [*Our relationship, though ambivalent, seems good.*]

Th. In spite of what I do?

Pt. In spite of it. (*coughs*)

Th. Maybe I better stop doing this to you. [*challenging her desire for health*]

Pt. Hell, no. I don't go wild. There is a certain amount of control.

Th. The fact that you know all the reasons that exist for your problem . . .

Pt. (*interrupting defiantly*) Doesn't do me any good.

Th. You are still the arbiter of whether you'll do anything about the situation or not. But at least you have the right to know all the facts. There is no magic about this. The whole thing is your choice. Nobody is going to take anything away from you, you don't want to let go of.

Pt. But I don't have the ability to make a choice rationally. (*yawns*)

Th. Right now your choice would be irrational.

Pt. Yes, I'd choose homosexuality. But, not really. You know, my mind is wandering. I'm trying not to listen to you. You know what I'm doing now? I'm trying to figure out my school homework. [*Patient is aware of her resistance.*]

Th. Not paying attention to what I'm saying.

Pt. Isn't that awful. First I yawn and then my mind wanders. And I wasn't even aware of what I was doing. [*Again she recognizes her resistance.*]

Th. But now you've caught yourself.

Pt. I caught myself.

Th. There must be a reason why it's dangerous for you to integrate what we talk about. [*pointing out possible reasons for her resistance*]

Pt. I just won't listen to you. (*coughs*) I'll bet this throat business has something to do with it. Obviously.

Th. You sense your own resistance. Do you want me to leave you alone?

Pt. No, no. But I do want to get well.

Th. It may take time for you to overcome this problem. It started far back in your childhood. And you have been reacting automatically since.

Pt. You know, I didn't hear a word you said. My mind keeps wandering. [*more resistance*]

Th. Do you remember anything we talked about the last session?

Pt. Nothing. My mind's a complete blank. I can't pull myself together at all. *(coughs)* And you know why I can't do this?

Th. Why?

Pt. Because you are sitting back and judging me on my little speeches.

Th. I'm judging you?

Pt. It's not true, but that's how I feel. I sort of feel I'm on trial and that I'm likely to do things wrong. The same thing happens when I get up and speak in class. It's funny that I don't remember a damn word of what you said today.

Th. How about what I said to you last time?

Pt. Oh, I remember that, but I can't put it together.

Th. Suppose you try.

Pt. It's like the only thing that can give me pleasure is my homosexuality and my torture fantasies with masturbation. I feel that you will take these from me. I say to myself that if I let you take these things away, the time will come when I'll need them and I'll be without them. Take life's last spark away.

Th. No wonder you can't concentrate here, if you think this is what really is going to happen. As if there can't be a good substitute for your present pleasures.

Pt. But it's not entirely what I feel because I do want to get well. But I can't seem to do it today. When I leave here, I suppose I'll kiss that wall to get my equilibrium back. Or I will get a hopeless desire and sexual attraction for you. I don't want to listen to what you have to say. I just want to be close to you. [*transference resistance*]

Th. In a way that's the same thing as clinging to and kissing the wall?

Pt. It is exactly the same thing. It's the same thing I have about Helen. Intellectually I'm not interested. I want to get into bed with her. So stop talking and let's have sex. That's how I feel about you. Same kind of feeling.

Th. Sex appeases your tension? Is that what you really want exclusively?

Pt. Obviously not, but I can see how this operates. And another crazy thing I do. When I leave here and get onto the street, I imagine you are watching me from the window. I get into my car and roar off.

Th. What does that mean to you?

Pt. It's like I get my masculinity back again.

Th. Which means you feel you lose it when you come here?

Pt. *(laughs)* Yes, I really do. I know that's silly. I say, "I'll show him. I'll roar off. I'll show him he can't make me into a woman." I try to get my feeling of power. *(laughs)* How silly can you get?

Example 2:

A patient comes in with a hoarseness so severe that she can hardly talk. This symptom came on her several hours prior to her session and was not accompanied by any other signs of a head cold. Exploration reveals the symptom to be a manifestation of various resistances.

Th. I wonder if you have been at all emotionally upset prior to this hoarseness. [*focusing on possible emotional sources of the symptom*]

Pt. I don't know what you mean.

Th. Are you aware of anything emotional that is happening right now? *(long pause)* What about your feeling about therapy?

Pt. The only thing I can say now, which is nuts, is that I'm scared to death of you. *(pause)*

Th. The way you look at me is suggestive that you are afraid of me. *(The patient has a frightened expression on her face.)*

Pt. I was always aware that I had a tenseness before, but it never was like this. *(The patient is so hoarse it is difficult to make out what she is saying.)*

Th. What do you think this is all about?

Pt. I don't know. *(pause)*

Th. Have you had any dreams?

Pt. Yes, I had one dream I can hardly remember. It's scrambled. *(pause)* I dreamed I was in some sort of clinic. It was your clinic. *(pause)* And there was a young chap there who was very attracted to me. He was there for treatment too. I liked him, and he liked me. But I was a patient at the clinic and I was working there, both. I talked to a group of people on the stairs. You were there as an onlooker in a benevolent way. And I was kidding. I said I want to go to Paris and live a couple of years. But this guy I liked and I decided we would have to take you with us. We have to take Dr. Wolberg with us because we have to finish this treatment. I looked at you and said, "That's involved for you, isn't it?" You laughed. It was all said in fun. Then this young chap and I decided to go home, and we walked and walked. And all of a sudden it occurred to me that I was walking without any trouble at all. *(Among the patient's problems are muscular pains and arthritis complaints in both legs which make it hard for her to walk.)*

Th. Mm hmm.

Pt. (pause) And then I was back in the clinic, and this young chap said he wanted me to do his analysis. I said that's impossible. And he sort of grinned at me and disappeared out of the door. That's all I can remember. *[The thoughts that come to my mind are that the patient may represent herself in the dream as her feminine component and the young man as her masculine component. She wants to return to narcissism (loving the man) and feels she can function this way (being able to walk). However, she is unwilling to give up her dependency on me (returns to the clinic) and she relinquishes her masculine component (the man disappears out of the door). Another possibility is that the young man is a disguised symbol for me toward whom the patient feels she can express an erotic feeling. In this way she can dissociate her sexual feeling for me from her therapy.]*

Th. When did this dream occur?

Pt. Last night.

Th. What are your associations to it?

Pt. (pause) I'm blocked off on associations, *(pause)* I'm blocked off on thinking. I'm in a complete state of suspension. *[intellectual resistance]*

Th. What in the dream might give you clues about your fear of me? What might you be planning or thinking of that would make you afraid of me?

Pt. Well, when I said I want to go to Paris, I might want to run away.

Th. What does Paris mean?

Pt. If I could do what I want to do, I'd go to Paris for a couple of years. I love it, just adore it. I love the French people, their relaxation and acceptance. It was wonderful.

Th. What does Paris symbolize to you?

Pt. Fun and sex. It's a sexy place.

Th. And here you wanted to go with this young man.

Pt. Yes, he was cute. *(laughs)*

Th. Was there a sexual feeling about that dream?

Pt. Oh, yes, sure. I was all for this guy. I'll tell you who he was. I never thought of it until now. He was a guy I met at Bob's party last Wednesday night. He turned out to be a young psychiatrist, and he knew you. Which is connected with you. So there you are.

Th. So you really felt attracted to him.

Pt. Yes, but had to take you along.

Th. Why do you think you had to?

Pt. Obviously you two are the same.

Th. So that you may have sexual feelings for me and project them onto another person, or you have a fear of sex and also fear disappointment. *[tentative interpretation]*

Pt. (sighs) Couldn't that be the same thing?

Th. It might. There may also be a desire to leave your therapy and run off and have fun, and wonder about my disapproval of that. There may be many things. What do you think? *[tentative interpretations]*

Pt. Consciously I'm not aware of wanting to run away from therapy. It's very painful to me as you can see. I wouldn't be happy getting out of it; I'd only be happy getting through with it. But the sexual thing troubles me.

Th. What about any sexual feelings toward me?

Pt. I think I've always had that. I block off though and can't talk about it. It's almost impossible. *[She recognizes her resistance.]*

Th. What does talking about the feelings do?

Pt. Make me scared of you. I don't want to talk about it. I'm sure that's what's happening to me now, *(pause)* I'm just preventing talking, that's all. *(pause)* And I feel silly. *[This indicates an awareness that her hoarseness may be a form of resistance against verbalizing sexual feelings toward me.]*

Th. Silly about your feelings?

Pt. Mm hmm. *I* think it does. All my life I've covered up important things, so to let it out is an almost impossible thing. I talk about sex often in a pseudosophisticated way. I can make smart cracks faster than anybody I know, but it has nothing to do with me. To talk about my sexual feelings—no, no. The minute it touches me, I clam up.

Th. Yet you haven't been too inhibited in your sex life.

Pt. I think I was a great deal, even though I didn't act it. *(pause)* I just thought of a dream I had in which you kissed me. I told you about it two months ago. From that time on I haven't been able to talk about my sexual feelings for you.

Th. Mm hmm.

Pt. When I'm lonesome I say you are very attractive to me sexually. *(pause)* I feel sexual contact with you is forbidden, like it would be with a father. *(The patient's voice is much clearer now, as if her hoarseness is vanishing.)*

Th. If it's true that you feel extremely guilty about having sexual thoughts about me, that would cause you not to want to tell me your thoughts. *[interpreting her resistance]*

Pt. That comes close to it, I think. It's silly.

(laughs) I'm beginning to see through you. *(The patient's voice is very clear at this point, her hoarseness having subsided considerably.)*

Th. What do you mean?

Pt. You're trying to make me talk about you. All right. *(laughs)* I have varying emotions about you. First, I say, "To hell with that bastard, I won't go back to see him." Then I say, "That's what he expects me to do, so I shall go back to see him." And then I say you are trying to be my friend, trying to do something decent. Then I get contrite about having had bad thoughts. All of which is a bunch of crap. I know it as well as you know it.

Th. So you must feel resentful toward me sometime.

Pt. I feel, *(long pause)* I feel now, and I have for the last few times I've seen you, that all of the threads that have bothered me have all come together in one knot, which knot has become *you.* If I can get that knot untied, then I'll be free. All the other things that bothered me are minor. I'm pulling out everything I have to resist you.

Th. Resist me in what reference?

Pt. Horribly enough I'm afraid it's a resistance to getting cured. [*recognition of resistance of normality*]

Th. You sound disgusted with yourself.

Pt. I am.

Th. What might cure do to you?

Pt. Well, it could put me back to work. It could eliminate all my excuses for not doing things. It could make me take an aggressive and active role. It could make me stop drinking and take that fun away from me. It could make me take a decisive action about George *(her husband).* I've come through the labyrinth and I'm up to the door, and I'm just resisting like hell. [*The patient elaborates her many resistances against normality.*]

Th. You must be frightened. Because that door is the door people want to reach.

Pt. That's what I've been coming here to reach.

Th. And now that you're approaching it, you are a little afraid of it.

Pt. I'm scared as hell, but I'm beginning a little to understand it.

The following is an excerpt of the very next session that brings out some interesting points:

Pt. I had a very peculiar reaction. Of course, it is almost impossible for me to say it, a very peculiar reaction last time. And I don't know what it was that was said, whether it was something I said or something you said, I don't know. But it was something in connection with our conversation, our relationship. Then all of a sudden I got a "cat-and-canary" deal, which you knew perfectly well, because you couldn't help but see it on my face. I don't see how you couldn't, and then just as I left, I said, "I feel like you're laughing at me." I knew that you weren't laughing at me in the sense of being nasty, but you knew damned well I wouldn't tell you what was on my mind. And, of course, that's the hell of the "cat-and-mouse" thing, because I'm perfectly aware that you know what's on my mind. Or at least you know very well whether I'm holding something back and won't say it or not. And I know that you know; so, therefore, I get into one of these, as I say, "cat-and-mouse" deals.

Th. What makes you feel that I can read your mind, that I know what you're holding back?

Pt. I'll bet 99 times out of 100 you do. It's very difficult, and I feel very silly. Whatever it was, whether that was a part of it or something else, I got a reaction of being very silly and ingenue, and very ridiculous, and I couldn't get over that feeling. Now what tossed me into that?

Th. When did you get this feeling?

Pt. Sometime during the last part of our conversation last time. I don't remember very much what we said, only that I think you asked me how I feel about you.

Th. How *do* you feel?

Pt. Giddy.

Th. Giddy?

Pt. Yeah. I think when I use the word "silly" I probably mean that. *(pause)*

Th. How did you feel *I* must have viewed you? Was it that you thought *I* thought you were silly?

Pt. Yeah. I imagine that's it.

Th. Well, why?

Pt. *(pause)* My reaction when I left was that I wanted to put my arms around you and kiss you. Now whether that is a little-girl reaction or not, I don't know. But that was the feeling I had.

Th. You felt affectionate.

Pt. Yeah. And then I think that's probably why I felt embarrassed. I felt I *(laughs)* wanted to go over and sit on your lap, like a little girl, and I'm probably older than you are.

Th. You think I think you're silly if you want to do that?

Pt. Probably because I had the idea that you've been trying to make me grow up. And goddamn it, I don't want to grow up.

Th. If this is what you feel, this is what you feel. Let's try to understand it. Suppose you do feel like putting your arms around me or sitting on my lap. Do you think there is something wrong with that?

Pt. Apparently I do. I don't think so, but I *feel* there is. I must or I wouldn't react that way. And when I get the "cat-and-canary," as they say, the "cat-that's-robbed-the-canary-look" on my face, I usually have something in my head, which I entertain, which I think is not in order. *(pause)*

Th. You know it is rather interesting that you find it so hard to mention to me what had happened. *[focusing on resistance]*

Pt. Sometimes I'll go for months and won't mention some things to you. And it isn't because I want to hide something. That's the goddamned mechanism of this thing. I blurted out and told you the last time, but, of course, by the time I get to talking about things, it's just when I'm putting on my coat. Like last time I kicked myself around the block when I got outside. I thought, why that's perfectly silly, why shouldn't I have said that; I've said every other goddamned thing. It's a wonder I came back today and said it. Because sometimes I might go for months and I might talk about every subject in the world. But some little thing like that which apparently has significance for me, I can't talk about.

Th. Perhaps it had such deep significance to you for a special reason?

Pt. Well, I find you attractive. *(laughs)* It's silly, but I have a thought it would be nice . . . last time what I failed to say was that I thought it would be nice to go to bed with you. But it kills me to tell you that. *[sexual transference]*

Th. Perhaps you wonder what my reaction would be.

Pt. I can remember one instance now. I don't suppose it was the type of person. It was probably the way I was feeling at the time. But usually men have approached me and I pretty much took what I wanted and left what I didn't want alone. That's always the case. A few times I thought someone was awfully cute, and I have deliberately gone after it, trying to look undelib-

erate. The exception was this once, and I can't remember who this man was. I think I'd read it in a novel, and I decided to try to ask a man to sleep with me, and did. And the result was disastrous. He ran like he was hit by a poisoned arrow.

Th. I see.

Pt. This guy ran. I don't think I ever did see him again. I remember now. Yeah. To show you that I'm embarrassed about it, I can't remember his name. Anyway, he was a guy that I went to Virginia with. I was going on my business. He was going on his business. He was trying to make a business deal with me. He was very good looking, and he was my type. He was dark and not too damned tall and big, and I thought he was very attractive. I had lunch with him several times. And so I was going to Richmond. And I said at lunch one day that I was going to go to Richmond on such and such a day. And he said, "What are you taking?" And I told him the train number. And I got on the train, and he had the compartment right next to me. That I've never figured out. Maybe it was just luck. So anyway, he started making love to me. He came in to my compartment, and we were having a couple of drinks, and we were talking. And he started making love to me and all in a roundabout way, an inch at a time, an inch at a time. He put his arms around me first, and all the pow-wow they go through. So I thought this is going to be silly. I'd been thinking about it for weeks. That looks good. I'd like to have that when I can get a hold of it. So I just turned and looked at him. I said, "You don't have to go through all this, because I *want* to sleep with you." And it scared the hell out of him.

Th. Do you feel that maybe you're afraid of being outspoken with me too?

Pt. Goddamn it, yes. *(laughs)* I see it now. I must be afraid. You will run off and leave me if I'm too outspoken. My parents never let me speak my mind. Everything I learned I got out of being on the go with the other kids on the street. *[We continue to explore her sexual feelings toward me.]*

45

The Management of Untoward Attitudes in the Therapist, Including Countertransference

Two people locked up in the same room are, sooner or later, bound to find their difficulties rubbing off on each other, each personality influencing the other. The patient will regard the therapist in many ways, such as (1) an idealized parental figure, (2) a symbol of his own parents and of authority, and (3) a model after whom he seeks to pattern himself. A therapist too responds to a patient in various ways. There is a tendency to project onto the patient one's own prejudices and values as well as to identify the patient with individuals from one's own past. The therapist's reactions are bound to influence those of the patient. In recognition of the fact that a therapist cannot truly act as a blank screen, no matter how thoroughly adjusted one is, many therapists have devoted themselves to a delineation of the clinical effects of what they have called "countertransference" (Balint & Balint, 1939; Berman, L, 1949; Bonime, 1957; Cohen, M, 1952; Gitelson, 1952; Heiman, 1950; Little, M, 1951; Orr, 1954; Rioch, 1943; Salzman, 1962; Tauber, 1964; Winnicott, 1949; Wolstein, 1959). The importance of countertransference is that it influences all forms of psychotherapy—supportive, reeducative, or reconstructive—usually to their detriment.

Conceptions about countertransference are multifaceted. These range from the traditional idea that it is exclusively confined to feelings derived from repressed unresolved parental attachments (Winnicott, 1949) to strivings provoked by anxiety (Cohen, M, 1952) to the total range of attitudes of the therapist toward the patient (Alexander, F, 1948). The tendency to dilute countertransference with reactions emerging from the habitual character structure has created some confusion. Befuddlement also comes from the tendency to identify all positive or negative feelings toward the patient as forms of countertransference. The therapist as a functioning human being will have a warmth toward, a liking for, and empathy with patients—more with some than with others for realistic reasons. The therapist will also be candidly angry with certain actions of patients, the display of which toward the patient may not at all be destructive. Indeed, the patient may be traumatized by the therapist's failure to respond to his provocations with justified indignation or rage. However, the reactions we are concerned with most in psychotherapy are responses of the therapist not justified by reality but which issue either out of the therapist's transference or that emerge as expressions of neurotic character structure. Therapeutic manipulations fostered by the therapist's needs, rather than by those of the patient, are bound to create rather than to solve problems (Lorand, 1963).

Where disciplined in self-observation, the therapist may become cognizant of troublesome attitudes and feelings toward patients before expressing them in behavior. The more insight one has into one's interpersonal operations, the more capable one is of exercising any necessary control. Where there is little understanding of one's unconscious dynamisms, the therapist is most apt to respond with unmanageable countertransference.

An illustration of how countertransference may act to the detriment of therapeutic competence may be cited by the case of the therapist who, well trained and endowed with more than the usual warmth toward people, was able to achieve good results in psychotherapy with most patients. Notably defective, however, were his results with male patients who had serious difficulties with women. The therapist himself was involved in conflict with his wife, the details of which he was not at all loath to verbalize. This was undoubtedly a manifestation of his unresolved problems with women. Whenever his male patients divulged their difficulties with their wives, the therapist would immediately respond with rancor and vehemently denounce the chicanery of scheming females. This attitude, while temporarily comforting to some patients, ultimately resulted in their distrust of the therapist, engendered by a realization that they could never work through with him some of their basic life problems.

It is rare indeed that a therapist, irrespective of how free from personality blemish that he is, can respond with completely therapeutic attitudes toward all patients. With some patients one may display an adequate degree of sensitivity, flexibility, objectivity, and empathy, so helpful to good psychotherapy. With other patients one may manifest a lack of these qualities and an inability to perceive what is happening in the treatment process. there will be a failure to recognize neurotic projections in the relationship, and to remain tolerant in the face of the patient's irrational and provocative behavior. Thus, infantile requests by the patient for exclusive preference or sexual responsiveness, or expressions of resentment and hostility, or unfounded complaints of being exploited, may bring out in the therapist attitudes that interfere with a working relationship.

If the analyst cannot identify with the patient, he will encounter difficulties, but identification in turn leads to other difficulties . . . the analyst then experiences the patients' intense anxieties fears, rages, lusts and conflicts as his own, and unless he faces these problems and deals with them directly, he may resort to controlling devices to allay the patient's anxiety and his own—such as excessive tenderness or other devices similar to those employed by the patient's parents, or he may resort to primitive defenses similar to those used by the patient, especially paranoid defenses. (Savage, 1961)

Character distortions in the therapist will inevitably have an effect on the patient. Thus, a need in the therapist to be directive and authoritarian, while advantageous in supportive approaches, tends, in insight therapy, to interfere with the individual's growing sense of self, with his expanding assertiveness, and with his independence. Authoritarian attitudes also pander to dependency strivings in the patient and coordinately nurture rebellious tendencies in him. Some therapists are driven by pompousness to make too early and too deep interpretations, which they hope will impress the patient with their erudition and perceptiveness. They may also attempt to force the patient into actions before the latter is ready for them. However, this playing of a directive role with the patient to satisfy certain emotional needs in the therapist must not be confused with a deliberate extension to the patient of emotional support when this is therapeutically indicated. The former is usually based on the motivation to parade one's power and omniscience; the latter is a studied, measured giving of help that is inspired by the needs of the patient.

Tendencies toward passivity and submissiveness in the therapist may also have a detrimental effect on treatment since it is sometimes necessary to be firm with the patient, as in helping him to avoid retreat, in enjoining him to execute insight into action, and in offering him essential guidance and reassurance. Submissive traits in the therapist, furthermore, operate to bring out sadistic, hostile attitudes in the patient.

Impulses toward detachment may develop in the therapist as a defense against entering into close contact with some patients. This trait is particularly destructive to the therapeutic relationship. The patient may be able to establish some sort of relatedness with a domineering or a passive therapist, but he is totally unable to relate to one who is detached.

A therapist who, because of personal anxiety or a depriving life situation, is thwarted in the expression of certain basic drives may attempt to live them through vicariously in the experiences of the patient. The therapist may, therefore, tend to overemphasize certain aspects of the patient's behavior. Thus, if the patient is in a position of fame, or is financially successful, or is expressing sexual or hostile impulses, the therapist, if there is the unconscious need to satisfy such strivings, will focus unduly on these perhaps to the exclusion of other vital psychic aspects. This loss of perspective is particularly pronounced where there is any overidentification with the patient.

Neurotic ambitiousness may cause the therapist to glory in the patient's accomplishments and to push him inexorably into areas that are calculated to lead to success and renown. Overambitiousness may also be extended toward seeking rapid results in treatment. Here the therapist will be unable to wait for the gradual resolution of resistance. Accordingly, the exploratory process will be promoted too hurriedly at the beginning of therapy. Perturbed by the slowness with which the patient acquires insight, the therapist may interpret prematurely, and then respond with resentment at the oppositional tendencies of the patient. The therapist may also propel the patient too vigorously toward normal objectives and then become frustrated at the patient's refusal to utilize insight in the direction of change.

Due to anxiety or guilt, it may be difficult for the therapist to countenance certain needs within himself or herself. When such needs appear in the patient, the therapist may exercise attempts to inhibit their expression. Difficulties here especially relate to impulses toward sexuality, hostility, and assertiveness. Should the patient introduce these topics, the therapist may act disinterested or may deliberately focus on another area. The therapist may be unaware of these personal psychic blind spots that prevent exploring anxiety-inspiring conflicts in the patient. Thus, if the therapist has problems in dealing with hostility, he or she may, upon encountering hostile expressions, reassure the patient compulsively or channelize verbalizations toward a less threatening topic. Fear of hostility may also cause the therapist to tarry, to lose initiative, and to evidence paralysis on occasions when the patient attempts to act in an aggressive or assertive way. Fear of other aspects of the patient's unconscious may cause the therapist to circumvent the discussion of pertinent material to the detriment of reconstructive therapeutic goals.

Other limiting personality manifestations may reflect themselves in neurotic attitudes toward money with an overemphasis of fees and payments, in an inability to tolerate acting-out tendencies in the patient, and in a tremendous desire for admiration and homage. Perfectionistic impulses may cause the therapist to drive the patient compulsively toward goals in treatment that are beyond the patient's capacities. At times some therapists, under pressure of their own neurotic drives, may set up a situation in treatment that parallels closely the traumatizing environment of the patient's childhood. When this happens, transference may become extreme and perhaps insoluble. Certain patients may mobilize in the therapist strong feelings of rejection and intolerance, which will destroy the emotional climate that is so important for personality development. Other therapists, burdened with narcissism, and needing to impress the patient constantly with their brilliance, may utilize interpretation too freely and water down the therapeutic process with intellectualizations.

It must not be assumed that all neurotic displays on the part of the therapist will have a bad effect. If they play into the patient's immediate needs, they may bring him to a rapid homeostasis. Thus, a sadistic therapist may be eagerly responded to by a masochistic patient. An authoritarian, domineering therapist may satisfy the dependent impulses of a depressed person. Restoration of equilibrium will not, of course, alter the basic personality structure. Important to consider also is that growth in a psychotherapeutic relationship with a neurotic therapist may occur in patients with essentially good resources. Such patients will select out of positive aspects of the therapeutic situation elements that they can constructively utilize. They may rationalize the therapist's neurotic weaknesses, or not pay attention to them, or simply blot them out of their cognitive field. It is to be expected that every perceptive patient will eventually discover some neurotic patterns or traits in his therapist. This may at first result in disillusionment, anxiety, resentment, or insecurity. If the relationship is a good one, however, there need be no interference with the therapeutic process, the patient ultimately adjusting himself to the reality of a less-than-ideal therapist image. It may actually be helpful to discard the mantle of perfection with which the therapist has been draped in the early part of therapy. The degree and kind of neurotic disturbance in the therapist is what is important.

At certain phases in therapy therapist improprieties may become much more pronounced than at others. For instance, during periods of resistance the therapist may respond with aggressive or rejecting behavior. Some actions of the patient may also stimulate countertransference. A patient who is frankly seductive may stimulate sexual feelings in the therapist; one who is openly antagonistic may precipitate counterhostile attitudes. The patient may be sensitive to the moods of the therapist and work on these for his own specific gains, the most insidious effect of which is a sabotaging of the treatment effort.

Because countertransference may result in therapeutic failure, it must be handled as soon as possible. Where recognized, the therapist may be able to exercise some control over it. There are therapists, who, though unanalyzed themselves, have an excellent capacity for self-analysis and an ability to restrain annoying expressions of countertransference. This permits the therapeutic process to advance unimpeded. A therapist who has undergone successful personal psychotherapy or psychoanalysis will still be subject to countertransference from time to time. Nevertheless, one should, by virtue of one's training, be capable of detecting and of managing troublesome reactions as soon as they develop.

Instead of denying a neurotic response to the patient, which is the traditional method, some therapists, detecting their own untoward responses, admit them openly and even analyze them with the help of the patient. Alger (1964) suggests that the therapist should "deal with these feelings in no way different than he deals with any other of his reactions. By this is meant that he be willing to include all the reactions he has while he is with his patient as part of the analytic data of that particular situation. . . . In this view, the analysis then becomes a joint activity in which two participants attempt by mutual effort to assemble and openly share with each other their perceptions, their concepts, and most importantly their own feelings." Such therapeutic license will call for great skill on the part of the therapist.

One way of acquiring this skill is to examine oneself honestly rather than defensively when attacked or criticized by a patient. To be sure, it is impossible for a therapist to maintain a consistent attitude toward or interest in patients at all times. Names and events may be forgotten, indicating to the patient lack of rapport; appointments may be broken or confused, connoting unconcern; irrelevant comments may be made, pointing to "noncaringness"; tension and anxiety may be expressed, suggesting instability. Irrespective of the reasons for the therapist's reactions, awareness of what one is doing and willingness to admit one's failings when they are discerned by the patient is of paramount importance. There is nothing so undermining to a patient as to have an observation, predicated on fact, dismissed as fanciful, or to have an obvious error on the part of the therapist converted into a gesture for which the patient is held responsible. Where the therapist is capable of admitting a blunder and of conveying to the patient that this does not vitiate his respect and interest, the liability may actually be converted into an asset.

Certain therapists have taken this as license to articulate every aberrant thought and impulse to the patient, and even to act out with the patient. While this may be accepted by some patients as indications of the therapist's "genuineness," it is destructive for other patients who expect the therapist to function as a rational authority. Therapists who are basically detached, and who are obsessively preoccupied with neurotic impulses, may, nevertheless, come through to the patient more sincerely as people when they engage in such random and undisciplined behavior than when they assume the straitjacket of a "therapeutic" attitude. From this experience of unrestraint, however, they may devise a theory and formulate methodologies, predicated on being free and abandoned in the therapeutic relationship, a stance that for most professionals will prove to be antitherapeutic.

Detection of countertransference and character distortions may not be possible where deep unconscious needs are pressing. It is this unawareness of their inner drives that so frequently causes therapists to rationalize them. Indeed, the very selection of certain methodologies and kinds of therapeutic practice may be determined by unconscious motivations. Thus, a therapist, basically passive, who fears human contacts and has evolved a detached manner as a defense, may be attuned to schools in which extreme passivity and nondirectiveness are the accepted modes. Or, if by personality domineering and aggressive, a therapist may be inclined toward endorsing the doctrines of those schools that advocate directive or coercive techniques.

MANAGEMENT OF COUNTERTRANSFERENCE

Since some countertransferential reactions are unavoidable, most likely breaking through when the therapist's emotional reserve is taxed or when the therapist is distraught and upset, the question arises as to what he can do to neutralize their antitherapeutic effect. Signs of countertransference include impatience with the length of a session or resentment at having to terminate it, doing special out-of-the-ordinary things for select patients, dreaming about a patient, making opportunities to socialize with the patient, sexual fantasies about the patient, unexplained anger at the patient, boredom with the patient, impulses to act out with the patient, and refusal to terminate when planned goals have been achieved.

In order to become sensitized to one's own neurotic manifestations when they appear, all therapists should subject themselves to self-examination throughout the course of therapy. Such questions as the following are appropriate:

1. How do I feel about the patient?
2. Do I anticipate seeing the patient?
3. Do I overidentify with, or feel sorry for the patient?
4. Do I feel any resentment or jealousy toward the patient?
5. Do I get extreme pleasure out of seeing the patient?
6. Do I feel bored with the patient?
7. Am I fearful of the patient?
8. Do I want to protect, reject, or punish the patient?
9. Am I impressed by the patient?

Should answers to any of the above point to problems, the therapist may ask why such attitudes and feelings exist. Is the patient doing anything to stir up such feelings? Does the patient resemble anybody the therapist knows or has known, and, if so, are any attitudes being transferred to the patient that are related to another person? What other impulses are being mobilized in the therapist that account for these feelings? What role does the therapist want to play with the patient?

Mere verbalization to oneself of answers to these queries, permits of a better control of unreasonable feelings. Cognizance of the fact that one feels angry, displeased, disgusted, irritated, provoked, uninterested, unduly attentive, upset, or overly attracted may suffice to bring these emotions under control. In the event untoward attitudes continue, more self-searching is indicated. Of course, it may be difficult to act accepting, noncritical, and nonjudgmental toward a patient who is provocatively hostile and destructive in his attitudes toward people and who possesses disagreeable traits that the therapist in everyday life would criticize.

The ability to maintain an objective attitude toward the patient does not mean that the therapist will not, on occasion, temporarily dislike many of the things the patient does or says. Indeed, one may become somewhat irritated with any patient on certain occasions, especially when being subjected to a barrage of unjust accusations, criticisms, and demands. The stubborn resistances of the patient to acquiring insight and to translating insight into action, and the clinging of the patient to attitudes and action patterns that are maladaptive and destructive, will tax the endurance of any therapist, no matter how well integrated one's personality may be. But the capacity to understand one's own feelings will help the therapist better to tolerate the neurotic strivings of the patient and to maintain a working relationship.

To illustrate how a therapist may control countertransference, we may consider the case of a patient who is having an affair with the wife of his best friend and feels exultant about this situation. The therapist is repulsed by the enthusiasm and sexual abandon displayed by the patient. She may, therefore, have a temptation to interpret the situation as a disgraceful one, with the object of putting pressure on the patient to give up his paramour. With this in mind, she may enjoin, order, or suggest that the patient stop seeing the woman in question or desist from having sexual relations with her. Should the therapist step in boldly in this way, her interference will probably be resented by the patient. Indeed, transference

may be mobilized, the patient regarding the therapist as a cruel, depriving, dangerous mother who prohibits him from having sex or freedom. An artificial note will thus be injected into the relationship, the patient utilizing his affair as a means of defying the therapist. Not only will the patient continue in his infatuation, but the therapeutic situation may deteriorate. Or the patient may yield to the therapist's suggestion and give up the relationship with the woman and then become depressed and detached, as if he has been forced to relinquish something precious. He will feel that his independence has been violated.

In attempting to control her responses, the therapist may indulge in self-searching. Realizing that she feels moralistic, the therapist is better capable of keeping in the forefront the general principle that, right or wrong, the patient is the one who must make the decision about continuing in the affair or giving it up. Accordingly, instead of suggesting to the patient that he stop the illicit relationship, the therapist may say:

"Now here is a situation that seems to have a good deal of value for you. You get fun out of seeing your friend's wife, but you also see that there are difficulties in the situation. Now suppose we discuss the good and bad sides of your predicament." The patient then will verbalize his feelings about the virtues as opposed to the liabilities of his intrigue. Thereupon, the therapist may remark: "Here, you see, there are values as well as liabilities in the situation. It is important for you to consider all the facts and then decide the course of action you want to take." In this way the therapist strives to keep her own feelings from influencing the patient. The patient is then better equipped to evaluate what is happening and to plan his own course of action.

It is unnecessary for therapists to feel that they must strap themselves into an emotional straitjacket to avoid upsetting the patient. Nor is it essential that they be paragons of personality virtues to do good psychotherapy. As long as one is reasonably flexible, objective, and empathic, and provided that a working relationship exists, one may indulge a variety of spontaneous emotional responses, even some that are neurotically nurtured, without hurting the patient or the therapeutic situation. Actually, the patient will adjust to the therapist's specific personality, if he senses that the therapist is a capable, honest, nonhostile person who is interested in helping him get well.

For example, a therapist may be inclined to be active and somewhat domineering. The patient may then exhibit toward the therapist his usual attitudes toward domineering and authoritative people: he may become fearful, or hostile, or submissive, or detached. As the therapist interprets these reactions without rancor, the patient may challenge the therapist's overbearing manner. The therapist, if not threatened by this stand, will acknowledge the operation of some domineering tendencies. The very fact that the therapist admits responsibility, may give the patient a feeling that he is not dealing with the same kind of imperious authority with whom he has always involved himself. He may then question the facades and defenses that he automatically employs with authority, and he may countenance a new kind of relationship. In working out this aspect of his problem, the patient will undoubtedly see connections with other personality facets and begin working on these also.

If, on the other hand, the therapist acts in a passive, retiring way, basic attitudes toward passive people may emerge. Thus, the same patient may become disappointed, sadistic, or depressed. The therapist, observing such reactions, will be able to bring the patient to an awareness of why he is manifesting these tendencies. The patient will learn by this that the therapist is really not an inconsequential person, in spite of a quiet manner. Indeed, the patient may discover that he seeks a godlike authority and that he has contempt for any lesser kind of human being. The patient will learn then that he can respect the therapist, and the therapist's personality, even though this happens to be passive. He will then have resolved one important part of his problem. With this resolution other aspects will come in for consideration, such as his attitudes toward domineering people. Thus, even though the patient deals with two entirely different reactions, he will have been able to work out basic difficulties with each.

What is important, therefore, is not whether the therapist has an impeccable personality that admits no countertransference, but rather that his or her distortions can be sufficiently reduced, controlled, or explicated to provide the patient with a suitable medium in which to work through his neurotic patterns.

46

Translating Insight into Action

A basic assumption in insight approaches is one made originally by Freud that was to the effect that once the individual becomes aware of his unconscious motivations, he can then alter his behavior and get well. That this fortunate consequence does not always follow (a circumstance also recognized by Freud) is the disillusioning experience of many young therapists who have predicated their futures on the premise that analysis of resistances will inevitably bring forth insight and cure like a sunbeam breaking through a cloud.

The fact that a patient acquires a basic understanding of his problems, and delves into their origins as far back as childhood, does not in the least guarantee that he either will or can do anything about them. Even if an incentive to change is present, there are some patterns that cling to a person obstinately as if they derive from a world beyond the reach of reason and common sense. The patient is somewhat in the position of the obese hypertensive who pursues his gluttony with avidity while reviling his weakness and lamenting his inevitable doom. Chided by his physician to reduce his weight to avert the threat of a coronary attack, he is unable to avoid stuffing himself with the foods marked taboo on his reduc-

ing chart, irrespective of how thoroughly he appreciates the folly of his intemperence. In the same way repetitive compulsive patterns lead an existence of their own seemingly impervious to entreaty or logic.

Complicating this enigma further is the fact that the acquisition of even inaccurate insights may register themselves with beneficial effect, particularly if the therapist interprets with conviction and the patient accepts those pronouncements on faith. Marmor (1962) has implied that "insight" usually means the confirmation by the patient of the hypotheses of the therapist that have been communicated by various verbal and nonverbal cues. Having arrived at a presumably crucial understanding as indicated by approving responses from the therapist, the patient experiences what is essentially a placebo effect. The restoration of his sense of mastery reinforces further his belief in the validity of his supposition and encourages him to search for further validations, which he most certainly is bound to find.

One of my patients reported to me what he considered a significant flashback that almost immediately resolved his anxiety: "This," he avowed, "was a cocksucking experience I reconstructed from what must have happened to me in child-hood. It involved an affair with a China-man. My father gave me shirts to take to the Chinaman who had a laundry nearby. I got the slip, but when I brought my father along to collect the laundry, I took him by mis-take to another Chinese laundry. My father had a fight with the Chinaman over the slip. Then I remembered and brought my father to the right laundry. We lived in Cleveland at the time. That's why I know it happened before I was 6. Seems young to be running errands, but I had a dream that convinced me that the Chinaman sucked my cock. I remember he gave me leechie nuts.'' This "memory" served to convince the patient that he now had the key to his fear of wan-dering away from home and his sexual prob-lems. It required no extensive work to re-veal this bit of ''insight'' as false, although it had a most astonishing effect on the patient.

This does not mean that some of the insights patients arrive at may not be cor-rect. But not too much wisdom is needed to recognize that, with all of the doctrines of psychodynamics current among contempo-rary schools of psychotherapy, each one of which finds its theories confirmed in work with patients, factors other than their pre-cepts, reflected as ''insights,'' must be re-sponsible for at least some of the cure. The nonspecific windfalls of insight do not in-validate the specific profits that can accrue from a true understanding of the forces that are undermining security, vitiating self-esteem, and provoking actions inimical to the interests of the individual.

In opening up areas for exploration, a therapist should, in the effort to minimize false insight, confine oneself as closely as possible to observable facts, avoiding speculations as to theory so as to reduce the suggestive component. The more experi-enced one is, the more capable one will be of collating pertinent material from the pa-tient's verbal content and associations, ges-tures, facial expressions, hesitations, si-lences, emotional outbursts, dreams, and interpersonal reactions toward assumptions that, interpreted to the patient, permit the latter to acknowledge, deny, or resist these offerings. Dealing with the patient's resis-

tances, the therapist studies the patient's behavior and continues to reexamine origi-nal assumptions and to revise them in terms of any new data that come forth.

The collaborative effort between pa-tient and therapist made in quest of insight is in itself a learning experience that has an emotional impact on the patient that is at least as strong as any sudden cognitive illumination (Bonime, 1961). Malvina Kramer (1959) has pointed out that ''what appears from the patient-analyst viewpoint to be a matter of insight and intrapsychic rearrangement turns out to be a far more complex process which depends on fields of multiple interaction on many levels.''

Improvement or cure in psychotherapy may be posited on the following proposi-tions:

1. The patient successfully acquires an understanding of the nature of his prob-lem by developing the capacity to con-ceive of it in terms that are meaningful to him.
2. On the basis of his understanding, he begins to organize a campaign of posi-tive action. He acquires symbolic con-trols, replaces destructive with adap-tive goals, and pursues these in a pro-ductive way.

True insight is helpful in this process. It acts as a liberating and an enabling force; it upsets the balance between the repressed and repressing psychic elements; it creates motivations to test the reality of one's at-titudes and values; it gives the person an opportunity to challenge the very philos-ophies with which he governs his life. But insight is not equivalent to cure; by it-self it is insufficient to arrest the neurotic process and to promote new and construc-tive patterns.

Indeed, the development of insight may surprisingly produce not relief from distress, but an accentuation of anxiety. The ensuing challenge to change one's modus operandi, and the sloughing off of neurotic protective devices make the possi-bility of exposure to hurt all the more real. No longer is one capable of hiding behind one's defense mechanisms. One must tear down one's facades and proceed to tackle life on assertive terms. Prior to acquiring insight, one may have envisaged "normality" in fantasy as a desirable quality, but the approaching new way of life fills the individual with a sense of impending doom.

Thus a man with an impotency problem may learn in therapy that his impotence is a defense against a fear of being mutilated by destructive, castrating women. Realizing that his defense is realistically unfounded, he must still expose himself to intercourse. This will continue to be extremely frightening to him until he convinces himself through action that the imagined dangers will not come to pass. A woman, working in an advertising agency, may discover that a fear of competition with men is due to her repudiation, on the basis of anxiety, of a desire for masculinity. Her knowledge then opens up the possibility of her being able to stand up to men. Specifically, she may practice her new insight on a man in her office who has advanced himself professionally over her because she had assumed a retiring and passive attitude. The understanding that she is playing a role with men akin to the subordinate role she had assumed as a child with her brother does not ameliorate the anxiety that she feels at having to compete with her office associate.

To protect himself from facing the threatened perils of action, a patient may throw up a smokescreen of resistance. He may reinforce old and employ new defensive mechanisms. He may devaluate strivings for health even though these had constituted strong incentives for starting therapy. The original motivations may be submerged under the anxiety of impending fulfillment and the patient may then interrupt treatment.

It is an unfortunate fact that only too often does therapy grind to a halt at a point where insight must be converted into action. The impediment encountered by the patient is complicated by resistance against releasing intolerable unconscious fantasies associated with action. In psychoanalysis action inhibition may symbolically be repeated in transference, and analysis of the resistance may liberate the patient. The therapist, while permitting the verbal ex-

pression of the unconscious fantasy in the relationship, does not participate in it; nor does he encourage its sexual or hostile acting-out. Any interventions are predicated on the patient's need, not the countertransferential demands of the therapist. But even under those circumstances translation of insight into action may fail.

MODERN LEARNING THEORY AND PSYCHOTHERAPY

The difficulties that invest the resolution of old patterns and the elaboration of new ones make it necessary for therapists to use every stratagem at their disposal. Since psychotherapy involves a learning process in which the patient acquires abilities to abandon his neurotic adjustment in favor of an adaptation consonant with reality, it may be interesting to consider the therapeutic situation in the light of the theory of learning. A number of attempts have been made to coordinate psychotherapy with the principles of modern learning theory. None of these has proven successful, since the various propounded theories—including the stimulus-response and cognitive theories—are unable to account for the complexities of ego functioning, both normal and pathological. The ego seems to operate under laws of its own that have scarcely been embraced by any of the learning theories. Furthermore, there are various kinds of learning to which different postulates may be applied. The unsolved problems of learning would seem too diffuse to permit of any real application of learning theory to the phenomena of psychotherapy.

It may be helpful, nevertheless, to consider a number of well-known learning principles and to attempt to apply them to psychotherapeutic situations:

Learning is most effective where the individual participates directly in the learning experience. For this reason, the greatest impact on a patient is registered by patterns that come out during his encounter with the therapist—patterns that are a product of the collaborative relationship. Such a learning experience gives the patient a basis on which to reconstitute his ideas of reality. It permits him to experiment with the therapist as a new kind of authority in association with whom he can evolve a more wholesome image of himself.

This eventuality, however, does not always develop in therapy, and when it happens, it does not guarantee an integration of understanding toward productive behavioral change. First, the patient may have an investment in his maladaptive patterns which subserve spurious security needs. To give them up exposes the individual to fantasied dangers or to deprivations. For example, a homosexual may learn that he seeks in the homosexual relationship an image to repair his own damaged genitality. He learns also that avoidance of women is both a safety measure to withdraw him from competition with other men and a way of preventing his being overwhelmed and infantilized by a mother figure. These insights do not subdue his intense sexual interest in males nor stop him from seeking men as a source of gratification. They do not lessen his disgust toward women, with whom he continues to maintain a casual, detached, or hostile relationship.

A second factor that may hinder the occurrence of a meaningful learning experience in therapy is the fact that a patient's reactions may have become so automatic and conditioned that knowledge of their unreasonableness does not suffice to inhibit them; they continue in an almost reflex way. One patient as a boy was constantly being taken to physicians by a hypochondriacal mother. Threats of operations were used as measures to exact cooperation of the boy for various injections and diagnostic procedures. In later life the patient developed a profound fear of doctors to a point where he refused to expose himself to essential medical contacts. An understanding of the sources of these fears, and an attempt to control them, did not inhibit explosive physiological reactions at the sight of a physician.

A third instance in which the learning experience in therapy may not be effective occurs when the attitudes and behavior of the therapist do not provide the conditions most conducive to change; his patterns, perhaps inspired by countertransference, may reinforce the patient's neurotic expectations. A woman patient, burdened in her work by damaging competitiveness with other women and constantly involved in winning the attentions of her male associates through her seductive manner, realizes during therapy the origin of these drives in her competitiveness with her mother for her father's favors. Yet she may cleverly maneuver the therapist into acting overprotective and reassuring toward her by playing on the therapist's personal interests in attractive women.

Repeated attempts to execute healthy responses may lead to their reinforcement. Nevertheless, repeated practice of rational reactions does not necessarily inhibit neurotic responses. The power of the repetition compulsion often neutralizes effective learning through doing. Thus, a man who compulsively fails as soon as success becomes imminent may, on the basis of insight into this distortion, force himself diligently to take advantage of any emoluments his life situation yields. Yet the impulse to fail will become so overbearing that he may yield to it even while trying to succeed. Learning, nevertheless, goes on in the medium of this neurotic relapse, provided that the individual is aware of what is happening and has ideas of why he needs to foster his failure. This "working through" is helped by the therapist who is in a position to be objective. It may be achieved by the person alone if he has the motivation to examine and to correct his behavior.

Learning is facilitated through satisfaction of important needs, such as a gaining of rewards and an avoidance of punishment. However, in the light of our experiences in psychotherapy, we have to recast our ideas about rewards and punishments due to the disordered values of the patient. Rewards to a neurotic person may most keenly be the profits of surviving infantile needs, such as dependency or defiance, which are more or less unconscious. They may be organized around maintenance of various neurotic mechanisms of defense that reduce anxiety. In the latter case the individual will develop not health-oriented behavior but more sophisticated methods of supporting defenses. Thus, a married man, pursuing at the sacrifice of his safety and economic security, a disturbed young woman, who constitutes for him a maternal symbol, is suffused with pleasure whenever the woman favors him with her attention. Due to her narcissism, immaturity, and fears of men, she rejects his advances, yet she demands that he protect and support her. Fearful that he will lose her affection, the man yields to the unsatisfactory arrangement of financing the irresponsible expenditures of the young woman in the hope that she will eventually bestow her favors on him. His hostility and anxiety mount as he becomes more and more trapped by his dependence. In therapy what the man seeks is freedom from his symptoms and, covertly, expert stratagems of breaking down the young woman's resistance. After a period in treatment, he learns the meaning of his involvement. The rewards that he obtains in integrating this learning is the immediate approval of the therapist and the promised reward that his symptoms will be relieved if he extricates himself from his untenable situation. These satisfactions threaten the rewards he really seeks in terms of overcoming the young woman's rejection of him and of establishing himself as her favorite "son" and lover. What he does then is to utilize his psychological insights to understand the reactions of his desired mistress in order to outmaneuver her. Her momentary sexual yieldings are followed by violent scenes and threats of separation, which, precipitating anxiety in the man, binds him more firmly in his enslavement. The punishment that he receives is really no deterrent to his continued acting-out of this drama. Indeed, it fulfills an insidious need to appease his guilt feeling. Thus, as in many psychological problems, punishment becomes a kind of masochistic reward.

We cannot, therefore, apply the same criteria of rewards and punishments to the complex problems of learning in psychotherapy as we do to some other forms of learning. This is why conditioning techniques that are utilized in behavior therapy fail to influence certain kinds of neurotic disturbance. As the working-through process continues in treatment, the patient may, however, eventually rearrange his value systems. He may then approximate healthy goals as rewards and conventional pain and suffering as punishments. Conditioning under these circumstances may then prove successful.

Rational understanding is a sine qua non of learning. Rational understanding in itself, as has repeatedly been emphasized, does not seem to help many emotional problems. This is because behavioral change is predicated on complex rearrangements of thinking, feeling, and acting that are bound together in tangled disorder. We attempt a disentwining of this yarn by plucking away at the surface strands. There may be no other way of getting at the disorganized psychophysiological structure inside. Hopefully, our efforts will be rewarded. Even from superficial intellectual unravelings behavioral, and even physiological, readjustments may ensue. As Freud (1928) once said, "The voice of the intellect is a soft one, but it does not rest until it has gained a hearing." Ultimately our therapeutic operations may overcome the tumultuous emotions of the psychologically ill individual. Unfortunately, patterns and values acquired early in life may obstruct meaningful adult learning. The most obstructive interferences are systems that have been repressed and yet obtrude themselves in devious ways. For example, sexual education as it is now being taught in high schools and colleges may have little impact on a young woman who has developed, as a result of childhood anxieties, the practice of shunting sexual material out of her mind. Defiance of authority, developed to preserve autonomy and to neutralize overprotective and interfering parental figures, may subtly block the incorporation of factual data. Perfectionistic tendencies and fear of failure, residues of a damaged self-image, may interfere with effective recall in situations where performance is a measure of self-worth. The powerful imprint of early impressions and experiences on the total behavior of the individual cannot be overemphasized, and learning may be blocked until some resolution of inner conflict has been instituted.

Is it completely hopeless, then, to try

to take advantage of any basic learning propositions in order to expedite psychotherapy? Let us attempt to answer this question by considering some of the positive learning factors that Hilgard (1956) has described so well:

Motivation is important in learning. The individual who is motivated to learn will apply himself to the learning task and more readily overcome his resistances. Rewards are much more effective learning stimulants than are punishments. In psychotherapy rewards may be offered to the patient in the form of encouragement and approval when he has come to important understandings or has engaged in constructive actions. The benefits of his activities may be pointed out in terms of what progress will do for him.

When learning failures occur, the person may be helped to tolerate them by pointing out his previous successes. In psychotherapy failures are inevitable, partly due to resistance and partly to the repetitive nature of neurotic drives. Reassurance of the patient when he becomes discouraged by failure and helping him to see why the failure occurred may encourage him to try again. The therapist may accent the patient's constructive activities that he has initiated in the past.

Setting realistic goals during learning is an important step. The individual may be unable to achieve success where his objectives are beyond his capacities or opportunities. Where his goals are too modest, also, he will not make the effort that would be most rewarding. In psychotherapy, where the therapist senses that the patient is overly ambitious and that his plans are unrealistic, it is essential that the therapist bring the patient back to earth. There are some memories he may be unable to recover, some patterns so imbedded in his past that he cannot overcome them. Pointing some of these facts out to him may prevent the individual from engaging in frustrating efforts that discourage productive learning. On the other hand, when his targets are too limited, for instance, where he insists that he is so seriously and irretrievably ill that he cannot achieve certain gains or execute essential actions, the therapist has a responsibility in stimulating the patient toward more ambitious aims.

Learning is most effective where there is a good relationship with the teaching authority and where mutual respect prevails. This is, of course, the essence of good psychotherapy. Where the patient's habitual contacts with authority are predicated on fear, hostility, or excessive dependence, the patient will probably display these patterns, which will then inhibit learning. He may be diverted from the task of learning toward fulfillment of regressive needs in his association with the therapist. The therapist must be alert to these maneuvers and must constantly keep the working relationship at the proper pitch, devoting efforts to this above all other tasks.

Active participation by the individual in the learning process is more effective than a passive feeding of materials to him. If the learner is able to figure out facts for himself and to apply these to a variety of situations through his own efforts, he will learn most readily. In therapy problem-solving tasks are given to the patient; questions are directed at him; a thinking through of solutions is encouraged. The motto is "Let's figure this thing out together" rather than "Here are the answers." The patient is constantly encouraged to enter into new situations and to observe his reactions to these challenges.

Where learning materials and tasks are understood by the individual, he will integrate knowledge better than where they are meaningless. Knowledge of how to perform well in the learning task, recognition of his errors in operation, and the understanding of what constitutes effective performance are most helpful. In therapy the treatment situation is structured for the patient; the purpose of different techniques is presented to him in terms that he can understand. There are a number of routines that may seem mysterious to the patient, for instance, the use of the couch and the employment of dreams. A careful explanation of their rationale is conducive to greater cooperation.

Repetition makes for the greatest success in learning. Where recall can be spaced over an expanded span, material will be better retained. In psychotherapy the patient is continuously engaged in examining his neurotic behavior; he acquires an increasing understanding of why he acts in certain ways. Repetition of successful behavioral responses is encouraged. The working-through process constitutes a continuous learning experience.

BUILDING MOTIVATION FOR ACTIVITY

If empirically we are to pay credence to these concepts of learning, we have to abide by the rule that the first step in helping a patient to translate insight into action is to build adequate incentives toward the abandoning of old patterns of living. A constant analysis of the individual's habitual drives—their purpose, their origin, their contradictions, and the conflicts that they inevitably inspire—enables the patient to doubt their values. Gradually he realizes that his strivings do him more harm than they do him good, that they are responsible for much of his maladjustment, and that they promote many of his symptoms. Eventually he understands that the pleasures that he derives from the fulfillment of his patterns are minute, indeed, compared to the devastation that they produce in his life. He then becomes willing to challenge the validity of his customary modes of adjustment.

For example, a woman with a strong dependency drive discovers that her need for dependence dominates every aspect of her thinking and feeling. Finding an omnipotent person on whom to lean fills her with a sense of "goodness" and security. Life then becomes a bountiful place; she is suffused with vitality, imagination, and creativeness. But not long after this metamorphosis a curious change takes place in the way that she feels. Fear and panic begin to overwhelm her; she becomes sleepless and she feels depressed; headaches, dyspepsia, and muscle tension develop. To her consternation she seems to invite suffering, masochistically assuming the manner of a martyr, and then undermining the person who acts as her host. She appears also to want to capitalize on her plight, by holding forth physical weakness

and infirmity as reasons for her avoidance of responsibility.

These patterns become apparent to her during psychotherapy. She learns that while she is driven to submit herself to a powerful parental agency, this crushes her assertiveness and fosters feelings of helplessness. Exploration of the genesis of her patterns may show her how her dependency resulted from subjugation by an overprotecting mother who stifled her independent emotional growth. This knowledge gives impetus to her desires for freedom. She sees how continued pursuit of dependency since childhood causes reflex helplessness and crushing of independence. Such insights are fostered in a nonjudgmental and tolerant treatment atmosphere, the therapist never holding himself out as an authority who orders the patient to change her way of life.

On the basis of her new understanding much dissatisfaction may be created in the patient with her present life situation. She will also be motivated to experiment with different modes of adjustment. The desire to give up dependency as a primary adaptive technique may, however, be blocked by a fear of, and a contempt for, normal life goals. Anxiety here may mask itself as anhedonia—an indifference to or boredom with pleasures and impulses accepted as valuable by the average person—for, compared with the ecstatic, albeit spurious, joys of neurotic fulfillment, customary routines seem uninspiring indeed. The therapist accordingly engages in a constant analysis of misconceptions about normality in terms of their anxiety-avoidance components.

When our patient, for instance, manifests disinterest in certain people, it may be possible to show her that she harbors contempt for any individual who does not possess a glamorous omniscience. She may actually classify people into two categories: those who are "superior" and who potentially can serve as parental substitutes and those who are "inferior" and, therefore, are "utter bores." The immense narcissism and grandiosity inherent in her attitudes about herself may become apparent to the patient as she realizes how she strives to gain omnipotence through passive identification with a godlike figure. At this point the patient may become aware of why she refuses to have children. She realizes that she does not want to be replaced as the favorite child of her husband. She does not want to "give" and be a parent to a child, since she herself wants to be that child. She conceives it her right to take from others.

This analysis of anxieties and expectations, and the continued verbalization by the patient of fears and anticipated pleasures, provides increased motivation to attempt a different life expression. But no new patterns can be learned unless the motivation to acquire them is greater than the motivation that promotes the survival of the existing neurotic habits. Therapist activities, therefore, must embrace encouragement of any desires that the patient voices for mental health, emotional growth, and freedom from suffering. The therapist must attempt to undermine the pleasure and security values that the patient seeks from the prosecution of her neurosis. Thus, the therapist may show the patient that the rationale of her dependency need is inescapable if one accepts the premise that she is incorrigibly helpless. While it is true that conditions in her childhood made dependency and related patterns necessary, she now continues to operate under assumptions that are no longer true. Her expectations of injury approximate those of a child. If she analyzes her situation today, she will see that conditions no longer necessitate anachronistic reactions that are so destructive to her adjustment. She is challenged to revise her assumption of life as a repetitive phenomenon that is blackened by shadows of her past.

PROVIDING A FAVORABLE ENVIRONMENT FOR ACTION

With expanding insights the patient tends to relate neurotic strivings with suffering and maladjustment. Their operation and even their appearance begin to evoke discomfort. This provides motivation for their inhibition. Involved in the inhibitory response are incidental stimuli or cues that are associated with the neurotic patterns and that once could initiate them. More and more the patient becomes capable of controlling reactions and of engaging in productive responses.

It may be necessary for the therapist to prepare the patient in advance for any foreseen disappointments that may occur in the course of executing a new response. Thus, if our dependent patient decides that she must assert herself with her husband, she may resolve to do this by asking him for a regular allowance weekly, from which she can budget her household expenses, purchase her clothing, and provide for certain luxuries. Hitherto her husband has doled out funds whenever she needed to make a purchase, requesting an itemized accounting in order to check on her spending. He has considered his wife irresponsible—an attitude the patient has sponsored, partly out of ignorance and partly out of hostility—because she has made many unnecessary purchases. He has for this reason restricted her spending. We may, therefore, anticipate that he will react negatively to her suggestion that he provide her with a weekly sum and that she be entrusted with the family purchasing. Because she has chosen this area as a test for her assertiveness, a negative or violent reception of her assertive gesture will probably mobilize anxiety and result in defeat. She may then suffer a decisive setback in her therapy and perhaps never again dare to approach her husband assertively.

To forestall this contingency, the therapist may, when the patient presents her plan, ask her to anticipate her husband's reaction. In her reply the patient may be fully expectant that her husband's response will be negative. She may then be asked to anticipate her own reaction should he refuse to cooperate. The therapist may even predict for the patient a violent response on the part of her husband and get her to verbalize how she would feel if he became recalcitrant and punitive. Once the patient accepts the possibility that her request may bring forth hostility and once she recognizes that her husband may, on the basis of her past performance, perhaps be justified in his refusal to trust her management, the therapist may encourage her to approach her husband on a different basis. Discussing with him the need for practice in making herself more independent, she may suggest that he allow her to assume greater responsibility in the handling of finances. However, since even this prudent method of presentation may be rejected, the patient should be prepared for a disappointment. What is accomplished by this tactic is that the patient is desensitized to failure and musters the strength to cope with an absence of rewards for her new responses.

In many patients insight is translated into action without too great activity on the part of the therapist. In some patients, however, considerable activity may be required before therapeutic movement becomes perceptible.

PSYCHODRAMATIC TECHNIQUES

In occasional instances role playing may be efficacious, the therapist taking the role of the individual with whom the patient seeks to relate on different terms. Or the therapist may suggest that the patient assume the role of the person, while the therapist takes the part of the patient. The patient, in addition to building up immunity to rebuffs, enjoys in this technique an opportunity for emotional catharsis. The therapist is, in turn, possessed of a means of bringing the patient's undercurrent feelings and responses to his awareness. If the therapist does group psychodrama, the patient may be introduced into the group while continuing to be seen on an individual basis too.

Conferences with Family Members

An element often overlooked in the resistance to getting well is the impact of the reactions on the patient of significant other persons. The patient's interpersonal relationships are bound to change as he begins to break out of the shackles of his neurosis. The threat to the existing balance will mobilize defensive attack and withdrawal maneuvers on the part of those with whom the patient is in close bond who are

threatened by change, often creating such turmoil that the patient will block off progress and perhaps retreat to former patterns of interaction, only to be rewarded by a return of symptoms. The therapist may imagine that it is the therapy that is ineffective, an unhappy thought that the patient may well instigate and sustain. By being constantly on the lookout for possibilities of retrenchment into former behavioral patterns, the therapist will best be able to explain failure of progress as a form of resistance. This phenomenon is most clearly apparent in children, adolescents, and young people who live closely with their families, particularly those who are withdrawn and schizoid. Therapy in releasing independent or rebellious activities may create a crisis in the family homeostasis.

It is also present, though less apparent, in older adults. If interpretation fails to resolve this form of resistance, family therapy with the significant others present is often very successful where the related persons are not too emotionally disturbed. Where an adult lives in a close relationship with another person, like a mate, and his security is bound up with this person, his ability to respond with different patterns toward this person will be circumscribed by the permissiveness extended to the patient by the person. In the event that the person has problems that interlock with those of the patient, and if the person utilizes the patient as a means of insuring a neurotic adjustment, the person is bound to react with anxiety when the patient threatens to upset present routines. Thus, the mate of our patient with the dependency problem will probably regard any change in the patient in her striving for freedom as an assault on his own rights. He may then attempt to undermine the patient's treatment.

Surmising such a contingency, we might find it expedient to arrange for a talk with the person in question. The consultation will have to be arranged with the knowledge and even cooperation of the patient. One or several conferences with the person can often make the difference between success or failure in the patient's initial effort at a new response. Once the person sees the rationale of the new plan of action (and senses that he is not being blamed by the therapist), once he realizes that his own problems and needs are being taken into account, he may voluntarily cooperate. Even hostile reactions of the patient may be tolerated by him, if the person is alerted to the possibilities of such reactions. In our dependent patient, for example, an interview may be geared around the discussion with the husband of what he has noticed about his wife. Any troublesome attitudes and behavior mentioned may then be pointed out as manifestations of her problem of lack of assertiveness. In order for her to overcome this problem, which is so crippling to her adjustment, including her marital adjustment, it will be necessary to give her an opportunity to grow. Even though she may make mistakes, the husband is enjoined to exercise tolerance, since this is how people learn and grow. It would be better for her to make a few mistakes, for instance, in the way that she budgets her allowance, and to help her to learn through her mistakes, than to let her continue in her present state of turmoil.

Obviously, in order for the husband to adjust to the patient's assertiveness, it will be necessary for him to master some of his own needs that are being satisfied by the patient's passivity and dependence. A fear for his own masculinity, and/or a compulsive striving for superiority and power may demand that his wife relate to him as a subordinate. Consequently, the husband may have to experience a therapeutic change himself in order to allow his wife to exercise assertiveness in the relationship. He may go through an emotional crisis before this happens, even though he appreciates the purpose behind the plan as explained to him by the therapist.

The following excerpt from a session with a woman whose dependency problem resembled that of the hypothetic patient we are considering as an example illustrates this point:

Pt. And Sunday morning I was in church and I got a little nervous. Then when I came home, my husband started acting funny, wanting to go here, wanting to go there. I told him I thought he didn't really want to go anywhere. He brought up a lot of things. All of a sudden I looked at him and saw hatred on his face, and my mind stopped working. He said, "You care more about the doctor than you do me." He acted very jealous, and I got upset.

Th. I see.

Pt. And in the last few months we had been getting along so well. You know I just am never going to go back again to what I was. I got upset at his attitude and wanted to throw something at him, but instead I turned it on me. I cried and tore my hair. He got me so angry, I lost control. I don't want to live with a man I have to appease. I told him he is a mean man and that I would leave him.

Th. And then what happened?

Pt. He got upset and cried. He told me it was his fault. He said he always was this way and that he could see he was wrong. Then I started feeling sorry for him. Then I got mad at him. I don't think I can stand him. He's brutal and mean. He isn't happy until he sees me groveling on my knees. Then he's happy. Maybe I'm not the woman for him. *(pause)*

Th. But you *could* assert your rights. You *could* define what you feel your rights to be.

Pt. But I have. I don't see what I did to aggravate him. I know he has a problem in wanting to treat me like a slave. Maybe someone else could stand it, but I can't. And I told him and threatened to walk out. *(pause)*

Th. So what happened then?

Pt. Surprising. He broke down and cried. Then he said it was all his fault. He said he could see how he treated me, that it was all his fault. He said he didn't know how I could stand it so long. He said he would try to treat me more like an equal.

There are many instances in which improvement in therapy of one marital partner results in increasing emotional disturbance of the mate. Indeed, a disturbed adaption of the patient may be a condition necessary for the equilibrium of the mate. Thus, a man, domineered by a power-driven wife, may satisfy masochistic needs under a domain of tyranny. He may be unable to adjust to an atmosphere of cooperative equality brought about by the wife's improvement through psychotherapy. Or a frigid woman, receiving treatment, may make sexual demands on her impotent husband who will then develop strong anxiety. Where the mate of a patient has good ego strength, he may possibly be able to progress spontaneously on the basis of new demands made on him by the patient toward a healthier adjustment. The outcome of psychotherapy in one partner then will be emotional improvement in both members. However, it may be necessary for the mate of the patient to receive psychotherapy also where spontaneous improvement does not occur. Conjoint marital therapy and even family therapy, including as many involved members of the family as possible, may be in order.

Adjusting the Patient's Environment

Where the patient's environment is disturbed, it may have to be altered before insight can adequately be translated into action. Thus, if there is undernourishment, shabby physical attire, bad housing, and other consequences of a subminimal budget standard, which are outside of the patient's control, a community or private agency may have to render assistance. An individual who is living with a brutal or neurotic parent or marital partner may be unable to achieve mental health until an actual separation from the home is brought about. Domineering parents who resent their offspring's self-sufficiency may cause a patient to feel hopeless since compliance seems to be a condition for his security.

The majority of patients are capable of modifying their environment through their own actions, once the disturbance is clearly identified and the proper resources are made available to them. Occasionally the adjunctive services of a trained social worker may be required, especially with children and patients with weak ego structures. The therapist, with the help of a social worker, may materially alleviate certain problems by simple environmental manipulation. This is particularly the case where the people with whom the patient lives are capable of gaining insight into existing defects in the family relationship. Such factors as favoritism displayed toward another sibling, lack of appropriate disciplines and proper habit routines, the competitive pitting of the child against older siblings, overprotective and domineering influences of the patient's parents or mate may sometimes be eliminated by inculcating proper

insights. The correction of sources of discord and tension frequently is rewarded by disappearance of anxiety.

Such situational treatment, while admittedly superficial, can have a definite therapeutic value and may permit an individual to proceed to a more favorable development. Often family members become so subjectively involved with the problems of the patient, so defensive and indignant about them that they are unable to see many destructive influences that exist in the household. An honest and frank presentation of the facts may permit intelligent people to alter the situation sufficiently to take the strain off the patient.

It must not be assumed, however, that all situational therapy will be successful, even when gross disturbances exist in the household. Frequently the family is unable or unwilling to alter inimical conditions because of severe neurotic problems in other members or because of physical factors in the home over which they have no control. Here the social worker, through repeated home visits, may start interpersonal therapy that may bring the family around toward accepting the recommendations of the therapist. The worker may, in specific instances, render material aid to the family, or may assist in the planning of a budget or a home routine. Direct contact of the social worker with the family may reveal that others need attention or therapy.

Another function that the social worker can fulfill is to make available to the individual the various church, school, and neighborhood recreational facilities. Persons with emotional problems frequently become so rooted to their homes, out of a sense of insecurity, that they fear outside contacts. Establishing a relationship with the patient and introducing him to groups outside the home may start a social experience that becomes increasingly meaningful for him, helping to release forces that make for self development.

In cases where the destructive elements within the family are irremediable or where the individual is rejected with little chance of his eventual acceptance, it may be necessary to encourage him to take up residence elsewhere. Temporary or permanent placement in a foster family or rest home may be essential. Although there is evidence that such change of environment rarely has an effect on deeper problems, residence in a home with kindly and sympathetic adults may serve to stabilize the individual and to give him an opportunity to execute in action the insight that he has learned. The most significant factor in changes of residence is the meaning that it has to the patient himself. If he regards it as another evidence of rejection, it can have an undermining rather than a constructive influence. Instead of getting better, he may regress to more immature patterns of behavior. Above all, the patient must be adequately prepared for residence change or placement and should look forward to it as a therapeutic experience rather than as a form of punishment.

Caution must, however, be exercised in effecting drastic and permanent changes in the work or home situation, and thorough study of the patient is essential before one is justified in advising anything that may recast his entire life. This applies particularly to problems of divorce and separation.

Many patients seek therapeutic help while on the crest of a wave of resentment which compels them to desire separation or divorce. Mere encouragement on the part of the therapist serves to translate these desires into action. The therapist should, therefore, always be chary of giving advice that will break up a marriage unless completely convinced that there is nothing in the marital situation that is worthy of saving or until certain that the relationship is dangerously destructive to the patient and that there is no hope of abatement. This precaution is essential because the patient may completely bury, under the tide of anger, positive qualities of his mate to win sympathy from the therapist or to justify his own resentment.

When the therapist is swept away by the patient's emotion and encourages a breakup of the home, many patients will be plunged into despair and anxiety. They will blame the therapist for having taken them so seriously as to destroy their hopes for a reconciliation. It is advisable in all cases, even when the home situation appears hopeless,

to enjoin the patient to attempt the working through of his problems in his present setting, pointing out that his mate may also suffer from emotional difficulties for which treatment will be required. The patient will, in this way, not only help himself but also his mate, and constructive features of the relationship will be preserved. It is wise to get the patient to talk about positive qualities possessed by his spouse instead of completely absorbing himself with the latter's negative characteristics.

On the other hand, it is undesirable, indeed manifestly impossible, to restrict every patient from making fundamental changes in his life during therapy. Conversion of understanding into action presupposes that the life situation must be altered. The rule that no changes be made during the period of therapy is more honored in its breach than its observance. The important thing is that the patient discuss with the therapist his plans to effectuate change *before* making them in order to explore the possibilities of a neurotic decision, for instance one that may be in service of masochistic self-defeating impulses.

Learning New Patterns within the Therapeutic Relationship

The reexperiencing by the patient, within the therapeutic situation, of early unresolved fears, attitudes, and needs and the proper management by the therapist of these strivings are important means of learning. The patient has an opportunity to work out, in a more favorable setting, problems that could not be resolved in relationships with early authorities. The new patterns resulting are gradually absorbed into the ego and become a part of the patient's personality.

For this to happen, the therapeutic situation must serve as a corrective experience and must not repeat early disappointments and mishandlings. While the patient is motivated to grow and to develop within the relationship, he is hampered by anxiety, residual in expectations of hurt from domineering, rejecting, overprotecting, and punitive authorities, which he may project toward the therapist. The therapist may be tempted by the patient's unprovoked attitudes and behavior to repeat the prohibitions, penalties, and retribution of authoritative figures in the patient's past. Should the therapist respond in this way, the patient's convictions that authority is not to be trusted will be reinforced. No modifications of attitudes can occur under these circumstances.

Realizing that the patient must verbalize or act out unreasonable strivings in order to get well, the therapist will have an opportunity to react to these in an entirely different way from that anticipated by the patient. The therapist acts in a warm, accepting, and nonjudgmental manner. These attitudes inspire the patient to retest the original traumatic situation. He does this anticipating hurt. If the therapist, by virtue of understanding and the ability to remain objective, can avoid repeating the punitive and rejecting threats, the patient may be permitted to live through in a new setting crucial experiences that he should have resolved as a child. The therapist will constantly have to interpret to the patient the latter's expectation of hurt, and to help him to realize that the circumstances under which he failed to develop security and self-esteem were peculiar to his disturbed childhood.

This will call for a high degree of mental health on the part of the therapist, whose own value system is bound to incorporate many of the judgments and arbitrary attitudes residual in the culture, which, incorporated in the parent's attitudes, have crushed the patient's growth.

Within the therapeutic relationship itself, therefore, the patient is helped to find a new and healthier means of adjustment. A virtue of the working relationship is that it acts as a prototype of better interpersonal relationships. It fosters the patient's faith in other people and ultimately in himself.

One way that the working relationship is utilized is to resolve resistances to action. It is sometimes necessary to encourage the patient to face certain situations that have paralyzed him with fear. Utilizing the relationship as a fulcrum, the patient may be urged to experiment with new patterns while observing his responses. A program sometimes may be planned cooperatively with the patient, the therapist occasionally making positive suggestions. While advice giving is best eschewed, the advantages and disadvantages of alternative courses of action may be presented, the patient being encouraged to make a final choice for himself. Thus, if the patient wants the therapist to decide something for him, the therapist may ask, "What do *you* feel about this?" Possibilities of failure, as well as anticipated reactions to entering into new situations may be explored. The patient may be cautioned by such statements as, "It isn't easy to do this" or "This may be hard for you." A method of stimulating action is to confront the patient with the question, "What are you doing about this situation?" whenever he expresses dissatisfaction with his progress.

Even with these promptings the patient may shy away from executing actions that threaten to promote old anxieties. If the initiative is put in the patient's hands, a stalemate may result. Although an analysis of resistances may encourage a cautious step into dangerous territory, the patient may need a gently firm push by the therapist before boldly approaching a new activity. In phobias, for instance, the patient may have to be strongly urged to face the phobic situation, on the basis that it is necessary to learn to master a certain amount of anxiety before one can get well. Where the relationship with the therapist is good, the patient will be motivated to approach the danger situation with greater courage.

Success and pleasure in constructive action constitute the greatest possible rewards for the patient. Occasionally the therapist may indicate approval in nonverbal or in cautiously phrased verbal terms. Conversely, whenever the patient fails in an attempted action, sympathy, reassurance, encouragement, and active analysis of the reasons for the failure are indicated. The patient may be reminded that the difficulty has been present a long time and that he need not be discouraged if he does not conquer his trouble abruptly. The patient may be given an explanation such as the following: "You know, an emotional problem is often like a hard rock. You can pound on it with a hammer one hundred times without making any visible impression. The hundred-and-first time, however, it may crumble to pieces. The same thing happens in therapy. For months no visible change is present, but the neurotic structure is constantly being altered under the surface. Eventually in therapy, and even after therapy, signs of crumbling of the neurosis occur.''

Eventually the rewards of positive achievement and enjoyment issue out of the new and healthy patterns themselves. Surcease from suffering, reinforced by joys of productive interpersonal relationships, enable the patient to consolidate gains.

Adjunctive devices are often helpful during the action phase of therapy. These include the prescription of tranquilizing drugs, to help master anxiety associated with attempting new tasks, as well as hypnosis, self-hypnosis, and behavior therapy. (See Chapters 49 and 53.)

ILLUSTRATIVE CASE MATERIAL

The following is a portion of a session in which a man with a personality problem of dependency, submissiveness, passivity, and detachment indicates how he has put his insight into action and asserted himself.

Pt. There has been a great change in me. I haven't felt this way in my whole life. And it has been going on for weeks.

Th. Is that so?

Pt. Yes. Of course, I used to have spurts of good feeling for different reasons. Once I felt as happy as a lark when I was about 13. I had had eczema for years and x-ray treatments took it away. I felt grand for a short time. And then I felt wonderful when I met my wife, but it lasted only a short while. But all these things came from external causes. The way I feel now seems to be coming from inside of me. All my life I seem to have been a zombie, really dead, because I carried inside of me all sorts of standards of other people. I was like an automaton. If you would press a button, I would react in a certain way. I never had a sense of myself.

Th. Mm hmm.

Pt. Things have happened these weeks, which I think I handled well, and my reactions

were good too. I have never had a prolonged period like this. Several times I'd say to myself, "I wonder if I can keep this up?" People mean different things to me now, you know. They are not powerful and threatening. My daughter was operated on at the hospital, for example. I regarded it in a sensible way. I said, "It's a minor operation. I'm concerned about her, but it's a simple thing and nothing to be upset about." I used to have a whole string of emotional responses that go along with illness. Now my wife has this worrying bug that was instilled in her by her mother. So I had to go along handling various things with her feelings which used to suck me into a trap before and arouse guilt feelings in me.

Th. I see.

Pt. So she started to hammer at me a few days before the operation to see to it that the room in the hospital was a good one, that there was a television set there, and so on. Now this is a good hospital, I know, but their policy is annoying. I know they have a program, and you could stand on your ear and get nowhere by ordering them around. So I said to my wife, "I'm not going to follow out your directions and do this and do that because I don't think it's right. Everything will go smoothly." So I did it my way, and everything went smoothly.

Th. Previously how would you have done it?

Pt. To tell you this is a revolution is an understatement. I'd always appease my wife like I did my mother. I'd do what she said without questioning it. This time I did what *I* wanted, and I felt no guilt. I had a sense of power. Everything went smoothly. When I got to the hospital, my wife was frantic because they gave my daughter a rectal sedative and she expelled it. The nurse was all confused and didn't know what to do. Then they called for her to go to the operation. I said, "I won't let her out of the room until she is properly sedated. I don't care if they get the whole hospital on my head; I'm just not going to do it." And I did this with ease. There was nothing to it. Before this I would say, "Look, I'm making these people wait, and so forth, and so forth." So the interne came up and gave her a sedative. They called the surgeon who agreed that the child shouldn't come down until she was sedated. *(laughs)* Everyone was chewing their nails, but I stuck to my guns. Not that I was unreasonable, but I did stick to what I felt was right.

Th. And things came out well?

Pt. Better than well. It's like a miracle. To think how fearful I was, before therapy, to take a stand with anybody. Especially, I wasn't able to be firm with my wife. When I got home, though, my wife started on me and said that I should have acted more cooperative. That burned me up because that questioned my stand. I told her calmly *(laughs)* that I had sized up the situation and felt this is what had to be done, and the proof was that things turned out well. Even if they didn't, I was sure I was doing the right thing.

Th. I see.

Pt. I then realized that my wife was under a strain, and I told her I was sorry if I talked rough to her. And then she said, "Yes, you're sorry," sarcastically. I said to her, "Look, I said I was sorry. I'm not going to crawl; I'm not going to stand on my head or any goddamn thing." And I didn't feel any anxiety or any guilt or anything. This morning my wife was as happy as a lark, as if nothing had happened.

Th. That made you feel you could take a stand and nothing bad would happen.

Pt. I just brought that up to show that I wasn't drawn in; I felt I was right and I wasn't going to try to dope out my wife's neurotic reactions to things and turn myself inside out trying to please her. I felt wonderful about this. So that was that.

Th. Yes.

Pt. I get a lot of resentment now at certain women mostly, and say, "Why did I have to knock myself out for years? What's so great about them? They are just people, and there are plenty of them around. Why were women so important to me?" I know what it springs from, and it seems so crazy to me now. *(laughs)*

Th. What *did* it spring from actually? [*testing his insight*]

Pt. Well, I would say that there were many factors involved and the picture becomes clearer; my whole life becomes clearer all the time. I would say it all started out, leaving psychologic terms out, with getting a terrible deal with my mother—she killed me. She must have acted in such a way that I was terribly uncertain of her love, and I must have gotten the feeling that if I didn't do exactly as she wanted me to do, she wouldn't love me any more. And there was no approbation given to me as a person. I became a thing. I became something that was used as a ground for other people's neurotic problems. My mother, on the one hand, being defeated in her life, used me to a point of smothering me with affection, which, I have a feeling now, covered a lot of repressed hostility and a lot of rebellion against being a mother. My father, on the other hand, showered on me his own lack of confidence as a man. He impressed me with what a man should be, that when he was with people, he wouldn't let them get away with anything. If a cab driver said anything to him, he'd beat him up. He had a tremendous temper.

He'd say, "You got to fight; don't take anything from anybody." He never gave me any affection. He couldn't. I think he has a lot more qualities than my mother, but he is very compulsive in the matter, as shown by the fact that he couldn't be warm. He was compulsive about his own work and emphasized to me not to procrastinate or put off to tomorrow what could be done today. The approbation came from getting good marks in school. That was the big thing.

Th. Yes.

Pt. So, I grew up with two big areas that were involved—the love area with my mother and the work area with my father. And then, in addition to that, my mother presenting the picture of what a bastard an aggressive man is. My father was a bastard, she said. "I love you," she said, "so don't be a bastard to me. If you do certain things that I don't like, then you are a bastard to me." So I grew up that way with no confidence in myself, no feeling about myself as having worth. The only worth I had was getting good marks to please my father and giving in to please my mother. So with one thing and another I started to crack up.

Th. What happened with your wife?

Pt. She became a mother, and the same thing would have happened with every woman. No matter what the woman was, she was irreplaceable because I had no confidence I could get another woman.

Th. How would you say your attitudes are now in that respect?

Pt. Well, I would say, number one, I know they are not irreplaceable. I think I use sex in an abnormal way. First, it was to prove being a man and to get this feeling of being approved and accepted by a woman like my wife, which after a while stopped working because it proved nothing. So I feel now they are not irreplaceable. I know they have problems, and I don't have to get involved in their problems. I don't have to be sucked in again into being an automaton who is prey to their whims. Pleasing a woman, no matter what her problems, is good as long as it is a reciprocal thing; but doing it just to please her becomes detrimental to the relationship. I suppose in our culture women are more insecure than men and have problems; but I don't have to get involved in their problems. I also have learned that making a woman insecure by making her feel uncertain about you is not the answer. Because, while it works temporarily to incite her interest, it breaks up the relationship after a while.

Th. So that you feel your attitudes are altogether more wholesome.

Pt. My, yes. I realize that my feelings and

my needs are just as important as the woman's. All this time I've been making an intellectual exercise about resolving conflict. Instead, the drives I feel now are healthy and good. After all, if it's a fifty-fifty proposition; you can't be too submissive and you can't be too aggressive. I feel a lot more strength within myself. I feel more alive and more vital. The reactions of other people don't matter as much as my own, or I'd say better that my reactions are equally important as the opinions of other people.

47

The "Working-through" Process

Mental health is won only after a long and painful fight. Even in supportive therapy, where goals are minimal, the person clings to symptoms with a surprising tenacity. In reeducative therapy the patient returns repetitively to old modes of living while making tentative thrusts in a new and more adaptive direction. In reconstructive therapy the struggle is even more intense, the patient shuttling back and forth, for what seems to be an interminable period, between sick and healthy strivings.

The initial chink in the patient's neurotic armor is made by penetrations of insight. The patient tries stubbornly to resist these onslaughts. The implementation of any acquired insight in the direction of change is resisted even more vigorously. Only gradually, as anxieties are mastered, does the patient begin to divest neurotic encumbrances.

Change is never in a consistently forward direction. Progress takes hold, and the patient improves. This improvement is momentary, and the patient goes backward with an intensified resistance, retrenching with all previous defenses as the problem is investigated more deeply. Anxiety forces a reverse swing toward familiar modes of coping with fear and danger. This is not a setback in the true sense because the individual integrates what has happened to him into the framework of his rational understanding. Usually he will gain from this experience and take another step forward. Again, however, as he experiences anxiety, he will return to his old methods of dealing with stress or will resort to disguised adaptations of his defenses. In association with this there may be discouragement and a feeling of helplessness. But this time, the reintrenchment is more easily overcome. With the development of greater mastery there is further progress; and there may again be a regression to old defenses. The curve of improvement is jerky, but with each relapse the patient learns an important lesson. The neurotic way of adaptation is used less and less, and as the patient gains strength through what is happening to him, he is rewarded with greater and greater progress.

It is discouraging to some therapists to encounter such curious reluctances in their patients toward moving ahead in treatment. The therapist is bound to respond with discouragement or resentment when, after having made an estimable gain, the patient experiences a recrudescence of his symptoms. Should the therapist communicate dismay to the patient, the latter is apt to regard this as a sign that he is hopeless or that he has somehow failed the therapist. Actually, there is no need for despondency or pessimism should the patient fumble along, repeat the same mistakes, or backslide when logic dictates that he forge ahead.

One way the therapist may maintain control of personal feelings is to anticipate setbacks in all patients. He must decide that no patient will be able to acquire new patterns overnight and must also recognize that each patient has his own rate of learning, which may not be accelerated by any technical tricks.

Before structural psychic change can take place, it is necessary for the patient to amalgamate changes that he has achieved in one area with other areas of his personality. Analogically, it is as if in a business institution that is failing specific enlightenment comes to one department of the organization. After a new policy is accepted and incorporated by this department, it is presented to the other organizational divisions for consideration. Resistance against changing the status quo will inevitably be encountered, with eventual painful yielding by department heads, executives, and other administrative personnel. Many months may go by before the recommended reforms are generally accepted and put into practice. Not until then will the influence on the business be felt. In emotional illness, too, enlightenment produced by understanding of one facet of the individual's behavior will have little effect on the total behavior until it is reconciled with the various aspects of the patient's personality.

This process of "working through" is usually extremely slow, particularly where basic character patterns are being challenged. One may painstakingly work at a problem with little surface change. Then, after a number of months something seems to "give," and the patient begins responding in a different way to his environment. Gaining satisfaction from the new response, he integrates it within his personality. The old patterns continue to appear from time to time, but he becomes increasingly capable of controlling them and of replacing them with new reactions. Having achieved a par-

tial goal, he is motivated to tackle more ambitious aims. The investigative operation is extended toward these new objectives, and the working-through exercise then goes on with retreats and advances until constructive and established action eventuates.

Thus, a patient with a disturbing personality problem came to therapy because of the symptom of impotence. Understanding of his sexual misconception, with a working through of his fear of performance, opened up the possibility of more advanced objectives. A portion of an important session with this patient follows:

Pt. I saw Jane after I spoke to you. Sexually we got along better than we ever had. She had a good orgasm, and it was really the first time. We've been seeing each other for about 5 months, so it was sort of a milestone as far as I was concerned. And yet, I wasn't, I didn't feel as though I'd done a great thing, as though I'd "arrived" or anything like that.

Th. Previously you had felt—I can even recapture your own words—that if an occasion ever occurred with a person like Jane where you could really function to your own satisfaction and to hers, it would really mean you had achieved your goal. Now that it's come about, it hasn't proved to be anything like you anticipated.

Pt. I said to myself that something seems to be stopping me almost from thinking about it. I said, "Now, let's think about this thing because this is supposedly very important." And I just didn't grasp it, as though there's something you want so much, and you get it, and it doesn't mean anything. I said this ought to give you a wonderful feeling; this should be good for you, that this happened. It was good, but it didn't solve all my problems like I imagined it would. And I don't know whether it's because it's become less important to me. It continually demonstrates this business of I could do such-and-such, if only this were the case. How foolish that is because I thought to myself, "Well, really it's just once. Maybe it should be another time. Maybe I should prove myself again. Once really isn't enough." But I feel I could do it three or four times, or a hundred, and it still wouldn't be enough. [*The patient is apparently aware of the fact that sexual success will not solve all of his problems.*]

Th. As a matter of fact, it is possible that the reason you weren't functioning well sexually with her is that you weren't permitting yourself to enjoy sex for the pleasure value but rather for its value in building you up. [*interpreting his neurotic use of sex*]

Pt. I would guess that I have certainly changed in that respect. It bothered me though that it didn't mean more to me than it did. I thought, "Well maybe that's why it happened," because it didn't mean so much to me. So that we're still really on the same basis, as far as this business is concerned.

Th. Mm hmm.

Pt. I say to myself, "Well, there's three women, Barbara, Martha, and Jane, that I'm sleeping with. I have now reached a point where I, they've all been able to have orgasms. It made me feel comfortable, but not . . . maybe I could be better off if I could think, 'Jesus, I'm terrific, or what a great man I am now'." But I don't feel that way.

Th. It would be a very neurotic thing to build up your self-esteem solely and completely, or largely, on the basis of how you function sexually. That's a facade that will cross you up.

Pt. It would be like evaluating a man on the basis of his appetite. If I would be with a woman and I could only have one orgasm, I would think to myself, "Well, you're not as much of a man as if you had two or three orgasms." And yet, it would be like saying, "If a man eats a plate of oysters, if he eats only one plate, he's not as much a man as if he'd eaten two or three plates." I realize my attitude is ridiculous.

Th. But still you seem to think one way and feel the other way.

Pt. It really is a tough situation. This sort of thing seems to be pretty much the kernel of my difficulty. It radiates in all actions and all spheres. I mean the sexual element now seems to, right now, this week anyhow, seems to be receding somewhat into the background and other aspects becoming important. I see where it's necessary to do more, to alter your personality and your attitudes. A whole new set of values have to be evolved, what's good and what's bad, what's right and what's wrong, the sort of life you want to live and what you want to do about it, which, I presume most people never really figure out. I have toyed with the idea before, but now I want to get into myself more.

Another patient with sexual fears and problems in his marital life was, with continued working through, able to make good progress. His relationship with his wife improved. Sexuality became less compulsive a function; he began to achieve greater assertiveness and a feeling of increased self-esteem. These changes are illustrated in the following fragment of the session that follows:

Pt. Tuesday night I decided to bring some flowers home. It was like a miracle, a tremendous response. In fact my wife's face was so overjoyed that I really felt a little sorry that—well, she'd been so miserable—it just required little things like that, not much to make her happy. I talked to her last night about my work, and she interpreted my actions as rejection. But it wasn't so, I told her. I said the things you really want are the important ones. She said that it's true. I explained to her about my work and eventually I thought I'd be able to spend more time with the children, and I was working toward that end. I feel much more comfortable in the situation. I was afraid that I'd have a compulsion to want to do as many things as possible along these lines, so that she'd know I was thinking of her. And the result would be that I'd have a conflict between wanting to do those things and other things like my work. But I find it's not so. I feel very comfortable, much more comfortable in the situation. I feel that I can do those things if I want to. If I think of something to make her know that I'm thinking of her, it's not an effort really on my part. I don't feel a compulsion to want to do them. In fact, when I got the flowers, I really enjoyed getting them. I would say right now that my situation, therefore, on the whole is a little better. These other things aren't important to me. My wife is enjoyable. I'm more in control of the situation.

Th. You'll be able to make even further progress if you can think objectively about your situation and not act impulsively as you once did.

Pt. Yes, I guess so. I guess being tied up in a situation makes you lose your perspective, but I was so interested in the things that she was actually finding fault with me for, I felt that I concentrated on those, taking them as a personal affront, instead of realizing what they were. I suppose that the situation will change again in some way, but right now I guess things are fairly peaceful, considering everything. I have a great deal of work to do, but I think I'm less neurotic about it; for the first time, I would say, since I've been in business, I am willing and eager to strip myself of as much detail work as possible. Before I was just holding on to it. I made up my mind that this work has to be done and that until I do it, I won't be able to take it easy. The work has to be done before I can take it easy. So I said to myself, "Well, it's really awful because if I had three days like Saturday, where no one bothered me, in a row, I could do it all." So I told my wife that I'm going to have to work a few nights and she said O.K. In fact, last night, I did one of the things that she complained about, I came home late again. But it was wonderful; she didn't complain about it. She greeted me with a smile and said nothing about it. So I could see that that wasn't the important thing. I would say that I feel on the whole that I sort of climbed a little and reached a little plateau, if such a thing is possible.

Th. Well, let us examine that plateau, and see what incentives there are to move ahead. Because virtually, in terms of your goals that you came to see me for originally, you've pretty much achieved those, haven't you?

Pt. I suppose so. The physical symptoms that I had, I don't have them any more. I assume they'll just fade away, because I never think of them. Sexually, I'm functioning much better than I ever did before. So I guess on those two counts I've come a long way. That's true.

Th. In your assertiveness, in your capacity to stand up for your own rights, what about that?

Pt. Well, I'd say there is probably less progress made on that score. We haven't been working on it as much as the other thing.

Th. Well, do you feel that it's been a problem? Do you feel that that constitutes a problem for you?

Pt. Yes, definitely, but now I feel more like a person with rights and things like that, more of an individual than I felt before. But I think I still have a long way to go to feel really an assertive person, I would say. And this may be just a temporary peace that I've achieved. All the elements that caused me anxiety for the past few months have reached the point of equilibrium.

Therapeutic progress is gauged by the ability of the patient to apply what has been learned toward a more constructive life adaptation. The recognition of disturbing drives and the realization that they are operating compulsively do not guarantee that any modification will occur. Nor do they mean that the patient has the capacity for change. The ability to progress depends upon many factors. Foremost is the desire for change. Among the motivating influences here are a sense of frustration induced by an inability to fulfill normal needs and growing awareness that neurotic strivings are associated with suffering far in excess of compensatory gratifications.

The detection of contradictions in the personality structure also acts as a powerful incentive to change. It is, however merely the first step in the reintegrative process. Thus, if a patient exhibits a pattern of compulsive dependency, the mere recognition of dependency and its consequences will not alter the need to cling tenaciously to others. While it may point the way to the more basic problem of inner helplessness and devaluated self-esteem, there is still a need to examine the meaning of the patient's impaired self-esteem as well as to determine its source. Furthermore, there is required an appreciation of the motivating factors in the individual's present life that perpetuate feelings of helplessness. Understanding the origins of one's dependency trend and tracing it to determining experiences with early authorities are important steps, but these too are usually insufficient for cure. As long as basic helplessness continues, dependency has subjective values the individual cannot and will not relinquish. While he may recognize the irrationality of his drive or its unfortunate consequences, he will desperately cling to it, at the same time rationalizing his motives. He may even have partial insight regarding his dependency, but deep down he feels that he must become reconciled to it the remainder of his life.

Working through, as has been previously indicated, is especially difficult in reconstructive therapy. The releasing of the self from the restraint and tyranny of an archaic conscience, freeing it from paralyzing threats of inner fears and conflicts, is an extremely slow process. Ego growth gradually emerges, with the development of self-respect, assertiveness, self-esteem, and self-confidence. It is associated with liberation of the individual from a sense of helplessness and from fears of imminent rejection and hurt from a hostile world.

The process of ego growth during reconstructive therapy is complex and merits a more elaborate description. Fundamentally to encourage such growth it is necessary to cajole the ego into yielding some of its defenses. Within himself the individual feels too weak to do this and too terrified to face inner conflicts. Unconscious material is invested with such anxiety that its very acknowledgment is more than the patient can bear. Rooted in past conditionings, this anxiety possesses a fantastic quality, since it is usually unmodified by later experiences. It is as if the anxiety had been split off and were functioning outside the domain of the ego. In therapy it is essential to reunite the conscious ego with the repressed material and its attendant anxiety, but resistance constantly hampers this process. Promoting resistance is the hypertrophied set of standards and prohibitions that developed out of the individual's relationships with early authorities. These standards oppose not only the uncovering of unconscious material, but also the expression of the most legitimate biologic and social needs.

Working through in reconstructive therapy must be accompanied by a strengthening of the ego to a point where it can recognize the disparity between what is felt and what is actually true, where it can divest the present of unconscious fears and injuries related to the past, where it can dissociate present relationships with people from attitudes rooted in early interpersonal experiences and conditionings. Ego growth is nurtured chiefly through a gratifying relationship with the therapist. The exact mechanism that produces change is not entirely clear. However, the therapist–patient relationship acts to upset the balance of power between the patient's ego, his conscience, and his repressed inner drives. The ultimate result is an expansion of the ego and a replacement of the tyrannical conscience by a more tolerant superego patterned around an identification with the therapist.

The relationship with the therapist may, however, light up the individual's fears of injury, his inordinate demands and expectations, and his forbidden erotic and hostile desires. Despite the lenity of the therapist, the patient will keep subjecting him to tests in order to justify a returning to his old way of life. If the therapist is too expressive in tolerance of the patient's deepest impulses, the patient will look upon treatment as a seduction for which he will pay penalties later on. On the other hand, a repressive attitude expressed by the therapist will play in with the patient's residual concept of authority as restrictive and, therefore, deserving of customary eva-

sions and chicaneries. At all times the patient will exploit his usual characterologic defenses to prevent relating himself too intimately to the therapist. He has been hurt so frequently in his previous interpersonal relationships that he is convinced that danger lurks in the present one. Under the latter circumstance the working-through experiences may take place within the transference relationship itself particularly when the patient is in long-term therapy and the therapist encourages the development of a transference neurosis, which is the focus in classical analysis. Obviously the therapist must have had psychoanalytic training to lead the patient through the rigors of the neurotic transference experience.

Many months may be spent in dealing with resistances that ward off the threat of a close relationship with, and the acknowledgment of certain irrational feelings toward, the therapist. The therapist acts to dissolve these facades by direct attack. Perhaps for the first time the patient permits himself to feel, to talk, and to act without restraint. This freedom is encouraged by the therapist's attitude, which neither condones nor condemns destructive impulses. The patient senses that the therapist is benevolently neutral toward his impulses and will not retaliate with counterhostility in response to aggression. Gradually the patient develops reactions to the therapist that are of a unique quality, drawing upon emotions and strivings that have hitherto been repressed. The release of these submerged drives may be extremely distressing to the patient. Because they conflict so strongly with his standards, he is bound to reject them as wholly fantastic or to justify them with rationalizations. There is an almost psychotic quality in projected inner feelings and attitudes, and the patient may fight desperately to vindicate himself by presenting imagined or actual happenings that put the therapist in a bad light.

As the patient experiences hostility toward the therapist and as he finds that the dreaded counterhostility does not arise, he feels more and more capable of tolerating the anxiety inevitable to the release of his unconscious drives. He finds that he can bear frustration and discomfort and that such tolerance is rewarded by many positive gains. Finally, he becomes sufficiently strong to unleash his deepest unconscious drives and feelings, which previously he had never dared to express. Projecting these onto the person of the therapist, the patient may live through infantile traumatic emotional events with the therapist that duplicate the experiences initially responsible for his disorder. The latter phase occurs when the patient has developed sufficient trust and confidence in the therapist to feel that he is protected against the consequences of his inner destructive impulses.

Sexual wishes, perverse strivings, and other drives may also suddenly overwhelm the patient and cause him to react compulsively, against his better judgment. The patient almost always will exhibit behavior patterns, both inside and outside the therapeutic situation, that serve either to drain off his aroused emotions or to inhibit them. He may, for instance, in response to feelings of rage, have a desire to frustrate and hurt the therapist. Accordingly, he will heap imprecations and derisive remarks upon the therapist, minimizing the latter's intelligence, or emphasizing any shortcomings. He may become sullen, or mute, or negativistic.

These reactions do not always appear openly and may be manifested only in dreams and fantasies. Sometimes hostility is expressed more surreptitiously in the form of a sexual impulse toward the therapist, which often has its basis in the desire to undermine or to depreciate. At the same time the patient realizes that he needs the love and help of the therapist, and he may feel that expression of hostility will eventuate in rejection. He may then try to solve his conflict by maintaining a detached attitude toward the therapist, by refusing to talk, by forgetting his appointments, or by terminating treatment.

A danger during this working-through process is that the patient may act out inner impulses and feelings and fail to verbalize them. This is particularly the case where the patient is given no chance to express everything that comes to mind. Such acting-out has a temporary cathartic effect, but it is not conducive to change. If the patient does not

know what he is reliving, he will think that his reactions are completely justified by reality. If acting-out goes on unchecked, it may halt the therapeutic process. The most important task of the therapist here is to demonstrate to the patient what in the therapeutic relationship is being avoided by acting-out.

As the patient realizes that his emotions and impulses are directly a product of his relationship with the therapist, he will attempt to justify himself by searching for factors in the therapist's manner or approach that may explain his reactions. Inwardly he is in terror lest the therapist call a halt to therapy and thus bring to an end the possibility of ever establishing an unambivalent relationship with another human being. Yet he continues to respond with contradictory attitudes. On the one hand, he seeks praise and love from the therapist, and, on the other, he tries to injure and destroy the therapist. He resents the tender emotions that keep cropping up within himself. The battle with the therapist rages back and forth, to the dismay of both participants.

One of the effects of this phase of the therapy is to mobilize ideas and fantasies related to past experiences and conditionings. The transference relationship is the most potent catalyst the therapist can employ to liberate repressed memories and experiences. As the patient expresses irrational impulses toward the therapist, he becomes tremendously productive, verbalizing fantasies and ideas of which he was only partially aware.

Sooner or later the patient discovers that his attitudes and feelings toward the therapist are rooted in experiences and conditionings that have gone before; he realizes that they have little to do with the therapist as a real person. This has a twofold effect: first, it shows him why exaggerated expectations and resentments develop automatically in his relationships with others; second, it permits him to see that he is able to approach people from a different point of view.

The transference is a dynamic, living experience that can be intensely meaningful to the patient. Recovery of repressed material is in itself insufficient. The material has to be understood, integrated, and accepted. During therapy much material of an unconscious nature may come to the surface, but the patient will, at first, be unable to assimilate this material because it lies outside the scope of his understanding. In the transference relationship the patient is able to feel his unconscious impulses in actual operation. He realizes them not as cold intellectual facts but as real experiences. The learning process is accelerated under such circumstances.

The transference not only mobilizes the deepest trends and impulses, but also it teaches the patient that he can express these without incurring hurt. This is unlike the ordinary authority-subject relationship, in which the person feels obligated to hold back irrational feelings. Because of the therapist's tolerance, the patient becomes capable of countenancing certain attitudes consciously for the first time. He appreciates that when he expresses destructive attitudes toward the therapist, these do not call forth retaliatory rejection, condemnation or punishment. He gradually develops a more tolerant attitude toward his inner drives, and he learns to reevaluate them in the light of existing reality rather than in terms of unconscious fantasies and traumatic events in the past. As he undergoes the unique experience of expressing his deepest strivings without retaliation, he also begins to permit healthy, congenial social attitudes to filter through his defenses. The therapist becomes an individual who fits into a special category. He or she is less the authority and more the friend.

The tolerant and understanding attitude of the therapist provides a peculiar attribute of protectiveness; for the patient alone is unable to accept inner conflicts and impulses and uses the therapist as a refuge from danger. The conviction that he has a protector enables him to divulge his most repulsive impulses, emotions, memories, and fantasies, with an associated release of affect. Along with growing awareness of his unconscious drives and the recalling of their existence in earliest childhood, the patient sooner or later discovers that there is a dif-

ference between what he feels and what is actually going on in reality; he finds that his guilt feeling and anxiety actually have no basis in fact.

The patient may bring up more and more painful material. Encouraged to express himself, he begins to regard the therapist as one who bears only good will toward his repressed drives. He will continue to exhibit all of his customary interpersonal attitudes and defenses in his relationship with the therapist, but he can clarify them to himself under a unique set of conditions—conditions in which he feels accepted and in which there is no condemnation or retaliatory resentment.

The reorientation in his feeling toward the therapist makes it possible for him to regard the therapist as a person toward whom he need nurture no ambivalent attitude. His acceptance of the therapist as a real friend has an important effect on his resistances. These are genetically related to the hurt that he experienced in his relationships with early authorities. The removal of resistances is dynamically associated with an alteration in his internalized system of restraints, for, if he is to yield his defenses, he must be assured that the old punishments and retributions will not overtake him. It is here that his experience with the therapist plays so vital a role because in it he has gained an entirely new attitude toward authority. His own conscience is modified by adoption of a more lenient set of credos.

One of the chief aims of reconstructive therapy is to render the conscience less tyrannical and to modify it so as to permit the expression of impulses essential for mental health. Perhaps the most important means toward this alteration is through acceptance of the therapist as a new authority whose standards subdue and ultimately replace the old and intolerable ones. In the course of the therapeutic relationship the patient tends to identify himself with the therapist and to incorporate the therapist's more temperate values. The ultimate result is a rearrangement of the dynamic forces of the personality and a reduction in the harshness of the superego.

The identification with the therapist

also has a remarkable effect on the patient's ego. Progress in reconstructive therapy is registered by the increasing capacity of the reasonable ego to discern the irrationality of its actions, feelings, and defenses. The rebuilding of ego strength promotes a review of old repressions, some of which are lifted, while others are accepted but reconstructed with more solid material, so that they will not give way so easily to unconscious fears. Growth in the rational power and judgment of the ego makes it possible to identify these destructive strivings, which, rooted in past experiences, are automatically operative in the present.

Ego strength, consequently, results both from liberation of the self from the repressive and intolerant standards of the tyrannical conscience, and from identification with the accepting, nonhostile figure of the therapist. Ultimately, ego growth involves an identification with a healthy group. This is, of course, the final aim in therapy, and a good relation with the group eventually must supplement and partly replace the personal identification.

The undermining of the superego and the strengthening of the ego give the patient courage to face his fearsome impulses, such as hate. He becomes increasingly more capable of expressing rage openly. The possibility of his being physically attacked by the therapist becomes less and less real to him. As he resolves his hate and fear, he is likely to experience an onrush of loving emotions. Particularly where a transference neurosis has been allowed to develop, they may burst forth in a violent form, as in a compulsive desire for sexual contact. In this guise they may be so loathsome and terrifying that they are promptly repressed. Sexuality, to the mind of the patient, may mean unconditional love or surrender or a desire to attack or to merge with another person. Inextricably bound up with such destructive feelings are healthful ones, but because the patient has been hurt so frequently in expressing tender impulses, he has customarily been forced to keep them under control. In his relationship with the therapist he learns that normal demands for understanding and affection will not be frustrated and that they have nothing to do with hateful and sexual attitudes.

As the therapist comes to be accepted as an understanding person, the unconscious impulses come out in greater force, and the patient discovers that he is better able to tolerate the anxiety that is created by their expression. In contrast to what occurs in real life, resistance to their divulgence is not reinforced by actual or implied threats of retaliation or loss of love. The patient then becomes conscious of the fact that his terror has its source within himself rather than in an implied threat of hurt from the therapist. This insight does not help much at first, but gradually it permits the patient to experiment in tolerating increased doses of anxiety.

The development of the capacity to withstand pain makes it possible for the patient to work out more mature solutions for his problems, instead of taking refuge in repression, a defense hitherto necessitated by his inability to tolerate anxiety. The discovery that he has not been destroyed by his impulses and the realization that he has not destroyed the therapist, whom he both loves and hates, are tremendous revelations to him, lessening the inclination to feel guilty and to need punishment and contributing to his security and self-respect.

At this stage in therapy the patient becomes more critical of the therapist and more capable of injecting reality into the relationship. He attempts to test out his new insights in real life. He does this with considerable trepidation, always anticipating the same kind of hurt that initially fostered his repression. As he discovers that he can express himself and take a stand with people, a new era of trust in the therapist is ushered in with a definite growth of self-confidence. Over and over he works through with the therapist his own characterologic strivings, reexperiencing his unconscious impulses and his reactions of defense against them. Gradually he becomes aware of the meaning of his emotional turmoil, as well as of the futility of his various defenses. The continuous analysis of the transference enables him to understand how his neurotic drives have isolated him from people and have prevented expression of his healthy needs.

A new phase in his relationship with the therapist ensues. Realizing that the therapist means more to him than does anyone else, he seeks to claim his new ally for himself. He may wish to continue the relationship indefinitely, and he may look upon the completion of therapy as a threat. Clinging to his illness may then have positive values. However, he soon begins to understand that there are reality limitations in his present relationship, and he begins to realize that he does not get out of it the things that he is beginning to demand of life, that the outside world is the only milieu in which he can gratify his needs. He finds the relationship with the therapist gratifying, but not gratifying enough; his reality sense becomes stronger, and his ability to cope with frustration is enhanced. Finally, he sets out in the world to gain those satisfactions that he has never before felt were available to him.

The working-through process is not always accompanied by the intensive transference manifestations such as have been described. Indeed, the relationship with the therapist may be maintained on a more or less equable level, the working through of attitudes, feelings, and conflicts being accomplished exclusively in relation to persons and situations outside of therapy. This is particularly the case in supportive, reeducative, and psychoanalytically oriented psychotherapies in which a transference neurosis is more or less discouraged. But even in the latter therapies it may not be possible to keep transference from erupting; if this occurs, some of the working through will have to be focused on the patient–therapist relationship.

Again it must be emphasized that circumvention and avoidance of a transference neurosis do not necessarily limit the extent of reconstructive change that may be achieved by skilled therapists with less intensive therapies than classical analysis. Nevertheless there are some patients in whom repression is so extreme that only a transference neurosis will serve in its resolution.

EXPEDITING WORKING-THROUGH

It is salutory to avoid reinforcing the patient's concept that he is a laboratory of pathological traits. Our focus on symptoms, conflicts, defenses, and personality distortions may divert us from accenting the sound, constructive, and healthy elements that coexist. The patient is sufficiently alarmed by his difficulties not to need constant reminders of the various ways that they obtrude themselves in his life. In a subtle way he perceives that the therapist is more interested in his pathological traits than in other aspects, and he may respond to this reinforcement by concentrating on them at the same time that he builds a shell of hopelessness around himself. As he repetitively indulges his neurosis, and the therapist keeps pointing this out to him, he may begin to feel out of control. Ultimately, he may give up and assume the attitude that if he is unavoidably neurotic, he might as well act like a hero in a Greek legend, marching with head up to his inevitable doom.

Neurotic trends are tenacious things and do not yield by constant exposure of their existence or source. They must gradually be neutralized through replacement with more effective and adaptive substitutes. This process will require that the therapist mobilize all positive resources at the disposal of the patient. While one should not avoid acquainting the patient with what he is doing to sabotage his adjustment, and perhaps the reason why, one should at the same time point out what constructive elements are present simultaneously. For example, a salesperson in therapy who is burdened by a need to fail, destroys again the opportunity of advancement by insulting the vice president of the company, who is in charge of her operations and who is considering her and a colleague for a post that is more interesting, better paying, and more prestigious. The patient eager to have this new job, to her own consternation finds herself engaging angrily in complaints and recriminations about the company's policies and operations charging that the vice president must in some way be involved. The patient reports to her therapist:

Pt. I did it again. I was so furious with myself. I even realized what I was doing while I was letting off steam. I'm just a mess.

Improper Response

Th. You aren't, but what you're doing to your life is. You shouldn't have allowed yourself to criticize your superior directly.

Proper Response

Th. It's obvious to me that you care enough about yourself to be disturbed by what happened. When a similar situation presents itself that invites you to fail, you will most likely be able to anticipate your response in advance and alert yourself to any sabotage talk.

The patient should be apprised of her active need for cooperation. She must be told that one cannot change without experimenting with certain new actions. Like any experiments she must take some risks, and she must be prepared to face some failure and disappointments, even a few hurts. Successes cannot occur without some failures. The therapist should extend as much help and encouragement as is necessary— but no more. It is important that the patient assume as much responsibility as possible. Role playing here can be helpful.

To summarize, the following principles may be found helpful:

1. The patient must proceed at a pace unique for himself and contingent on his readiness for change and on his learning abilities.
2. Reinforcement for progress is needed in the form of therapist verbal approval whenever the patient takes a reasonable step forward.
3. If resistances to movement develop, the focus on therapy must be concentrated on understanding and interpreting the patient's resistances.
4. Adjuncts, like assigning homework practice sessions, for the gradual mastery of certain problems may help deal with obdurate resistances.
5. Encouraging the patient to generalize

from the immediate situation one aspect of his experience, or the control of a symptom, to other experiences may be important. This eventually enables him to view his immediate disturbance in the light of his total personality structure.
6. Adjuncts like role playing may be indispensable.

ILLUSTRATIVE CASE MATERIAL

Illustrative of the working through of transference is the case of a young divorcée with a personality problem of detachment, whose marriage had disintegrated because of her general apathy. Sexually frigid and with little affectionate feeling for people, she had never been able to establish a relationship in which she could feel deep emotion. After a prolonged period of working on her resistances, she began to evince positive transference feelings toward me, as manifested in the following fragment of a session:

Pt. I had a dream yesterday. We were dancing together, and then you make love to me. Then the scene changes, and there is a fellow sitting on a bench, and you kiss me and in jest ask him to leave. And then you sit down, and I lie down with my head against you. You put your arms around me. And then the scene shifts again, and you and I are in the kitchen. And my daughter, Georgia, is climbing over the sink toward the window, and I pull her in. Then I'm standing there with my son, John, in the hallway and you very professionally ask if there is anyone else I am waiting for. You came to find out about John. You forget the fact that you asked me for dinner, and I'm very let down and wake up with that let-down feeling.
Th. What are your associations to this dream?
Pt. I awoke with the feeling that I'm very much in love with you. I want you to love me very much. It's a desperate feeling that I can't control.
Th. How long has this feeling been with you?
Pt. It's been accumulating over a time, but it suddenly hit me last night, and when I awoke

this morning, I knew. *(pause)* This is a funny thing to ask you, but I feel sexually attracted to you. Is it ever permissible to . . . to . . . I mean *(blushes)*

Th. You mean to have an affair?

Pt. Yes.

Th. Well, I appreciate your feeling very much. It often happens that in therapy the patient falls in love with the therapist. This is understandable because the patient takes the therapist into her confidence and tells him things she wouldn't dare tell herself. But in therapy for the therapist to respond to the patient by making love would destroy therapy completely.

Pt. I can understand perfectly. But I felt that you responded to me, *(laughs)* that *you* were in love with me. I think you are the most wonderful man in the world.

Th. You may possibly feel I reject you. It is important though to explore your feelings for me, no matter what these may be.

Pt. I agree, agree with you, of course. I can't see how this happened to me though. It never happened before. It's a hell of a note, but as you say, it must inevitably happen.

There ensued a prolonged period of strife in which the patient veered from sexual to hostile and destructive feelings toward me. The following session, for example, reflects negative impulses.

Pt. I'm furious at you. I don't, didn't want to come today.

Th. Can you tell me why?

Pt. Because you've gotten, gotten me to feel like a human being again instead of a piece of wood, and there's nothing to do about it. You know very well there's nothing to do about it.

Th. You mean, now you're able to feel about people and there's nothing you can do about expressing yourself?

Pt. *(angrily)* Oh, please be quiet will you. *(pause)* Here you went and got me all stirred up for absolutely nothing. It's like you want to torture and hurt me.

Th. What makes you think that I want to torture you and hurt you?

Pt. I didn't say you wanted to. I don't believe I've reproached you at all. I never reproach anybody for anything, I never have.

Th. But . . .

Pt. Have I ever implied or said one word of reproach to you? I don't believe I have.

Th. No.

Pt. No. I don't think so. I don't reproach anybody for anything. I don't want you to do anything at all, except just let me walk out of that door.

Th. Do you really want to walk out of that door?

Pt. I'm going to walk out of that door. You see, what you don't know about me yet is that I've a very, very strong will. *(pause)* You sit there in that chair, and I sit here opposite you, and you've got that lovely warm darn way of speaking, and before I reach that door, you'll freeze like an icicle. And I can do exactly the same thing, exactly the same thing.

Th. You mean just to get even with me?

Pt. Have you ever seen me try to get even with anybody? I don't think you have. I'm not a very vindictive person.

Th. Do you think I really act icy to you?

Pt. But you do.

Th. When?

Pt. I went out of here the last time ashamed of myself. I went down that street crying. I was crying. I felt you rejected me, cold to me.

Th. You felt that I rejected you? You felt that I acted cold toward you? When did I act cold toward you?

Pt. Let's drop that rejection business, shall we? It isn't a question of being rejected. It has nothing to do with it at all. And if we get right down to it, what difference does it make whether you do or you don't?

Th. It makes this difference, that I am very much interested in helping you.

Pt. If I walked out of this room, you'd never think of me again.

Th. You feel that if you walk out of this room, I'll never even think of you again.

Pt. That's exactly how I feel! Exactly what I feel. Yes. Suppose you had to do the same thing for every patient. You couldn't last, any more than any other doctor could last, any more than any trained nurse could last. They can't. *(pause)* Well, I'm feeling a lot better getting that off my chest.

Th. I'm glad you're feeling better.

Pt. Yes. I'm sure. I think you owe me quite a little time. I don't believe I've ever stayed here 45 minutes, have I? I don't think so. I've always looked at that clock and I've gone. I've gone to the second at 40 minutes after I got here. [*This is not exactly correct, but I decide not to challenge it.*]

Th. Why?

Pt. Because I don't want anything from anybody. Because I don't want one minute of anybody's time.

Th. You just want to be completely independent?

Pt. Yes, I do.

Th. I wonder if you trust me?

Pt. I've always trusted you. What do you

think I'm coming here for? There isn't anybody that is forcing me to come. Who is it that drags me any place on a chain? If I didn't want to come, there isn't anybody that could make me come.

Th. Indeed. You know, too, that it's good that there's nobody that forces you to be here. It has to be completely a free thing with you, a voluntary thing with you, a thing that you really believe in.

Pt. I don't know what I'm going to do when I have to leave you, when I'm through with this.

Th. Why?

Pt. I can't depend on anybody, see?

Th. You're afraid to get dependent on me?

Pt. I'm afraid to get dependent on any human being, because there isn't a living human being that I can trust. Not even you. I can't trust anybody on earth. And that's the truth.

Th. I can't force you to trust me, but I hope you will. I'll do everything in my power to be worthy of that trust. But I can appreciate the suffering and torment that you must go through as you begin to feel feelings for me.

Pt. But you do torment me.

Th. How do I torment you?

Pt. I think you resent me, even despise me.

Th. Did I ever do anything to give you that impression?

Pt. No, but . . . I guess I must *think* you reject me. But you really don't.

The working through of her feelings toward a more constructive solution is shown in this portion of an interview that occurred several months after the initial onset of transference:

Pt. When I came to you, you were exactly what I needed at that moment, and you comforted me when I came, and for the first few weeks—it was no more than that—then I began to like you. I liked you more and more, and it was interesting to me that I could feel that way about a person because I had not up to that point. You were the first person that I felt anything for since many, many years ago. So I reasoned it out, and I felt that you were probably . . . I didn't know what you were like as a man. I knew you only from a professional standpoint, what you were like. Maybe I would not feel that way if I did know you, I don't know. I was trying to tell myself I didn't know enough about you to feel that way. It wasn't anything sound. And another thing I felt was that you were probably a symbol of what I would like to have or feel for someone, that you just were a symbol. Actually,

I didn't know enough about you to feel that way, and I kept telling myself that, and, during your vacation when I left I thought I didn't know how I was going to get along without seeing you. It was really the high point of my week when I came to see you. I looked forward to it, and I really enjoyed that more than anything else that I did. So, during the summer, I thought, "Well, I am going to miss him. How will I get along?" I sort of leaned on you, and I had gotten so much comfort. Then, something began to happen to me, and I felt that even if I felt that way, maybe you did like me very much, maybe you didn't. I don't know whether what you say is all professional. I felt that as far as you were concerned, even if you did like me, and I liked you as you said, which was what I had figured out for myself, that any sort of very close friendship was not possible and isn't practical. I felt that I needed you much more as a doctor than a man at that point and that I should forget about it. So it was something that I was putting on. I probably needed something, maybe it wasn't necessarily you. So I sort of started to look around at men. I was aware more of the attention they paid me. I responded more, which I had never done. I found that I was giving them a little more encouragement because I never radiated any encouragement. I felt that if I were to find someone, I was very happy that I could feel that way about someone. I really was because I didn't think I could any more, I just didn't. I missed seeing you, which was very unusual for me, because I hadn't felt that way about anyone in many years. So I started to look around; as I say I have responded, but I haven't found anyone that I do feel that way about. Of course, I haven't had the opportunity.

Th. At least you are not running away and are not guilt-ridden. You may feel that if the right sort of person came along, there may be a possibility for a relationship. But what about me right now?

Pt. Well, I'll tell you how I feel about that. When I first came here, not the first few weeks, but a little later, I felt that you did like me personally. I don't know how justified I was, but I did feel that.

Th. You mean that I was in love with you?

Pt. Not that you were in love with me, but that you were attracted to me, that you did like me. But, of course, again I said that maybe I was so keyed up; I thought maybe I had sort of colored it, which was unusual for me, because I have never in all my life responded to any man or made the first steps without his feeling a great interest in me. I have never, so that if it was so, it was different than it had ever been because that was never so before. I have never made the first move or picked someone and said I liked him and want to know him, and I'd like to be in love with him. I never felt that way.

Th. It was always as a result of somebody's else's actions first.

Pt. Of somebody radiating more than the usual amount of interest. So that I felt that it was different and I was rarely wrong, I mean, I was always right, but, of course, as I say, I was in a different state of mind than I am today. I am much calmer, probably see things a little clearer. So that I felt that you didn't love me, and I hoped that you didn't. In a way I wanted it, and yet I realized that I hoped you didn't because I might respond. I just felt it was wrong because you were the wrong person, because you are my doctor. "So, find somebody else," I said to myself. *(laughs)* As a matter of fact a very funny thing happened. I ran into my uncle who referred me to you shortly after first starting with you. I was beginning to feel that way about you, and I was curious about you. I met him in a restaurant. We talked for a few minutes. He asked me how I was getting along. I said I was making progress. He asked me how I liked you, and I said very much indeed, you were grand. He said he thought so too. You were practical, and he

recommended you because he thought you would be what I needed. So I said, "Is he married?" And I was blushing. So he said, "He has an awfully nice wife and some lovely children." I realized then that probably I had radiated something that I hadn't intended to. I must have radiated some interest.

Th. Your reaction to me was one that occurs commonly in psychotherapy.

Pt. I realize this.

Th. Sometimes it's necessary to have such a reaction to get well.

Pt. That's the thing, that's the reason I bring it up.

Th. You might never get well if you didn't have a positive attitude toward me. That attitude we can use as a bridge to better relationships with men. There is a possibility that you may not find a man right away. There is a possibility of that, but at least you will know that it's not because of any block in you; it's not because you have no capacity to love.

Pt. Well, it's been, and I'll tell you it's been an amazing thing. I used to wonder at it myself because I certainly am not cold. I used to wonder at myself because it didn't seem to concern me. I mean sex. That's the truth of it. But I'm getting myself interested now.

48

Supportive and Reeducative Techniques during Middle Treatment Phase

Supportive approaches are employed during the middle phases of treatment under the following conditions:

As a Principal Form of Therapy

1. Where the patient possesses a fairly well-integrated personality but has temporarily collapsed under severe stress, a short period of palliative psychotherapy may suffice to restore the habitual stability. Supportive techniques may also be efficacious where the problem has not yet been structuralized, as in behavior disorders in children. Actually, supportive therapy may be the treatment of choice in a sizable number of patients who consult a psychotherapist.

2. Patients who require more intensive psychotherapy, but are temporarily too ill to utilize reconstructive therapy, may benefit from supportive approaches as an emergency measure.

3. Supportive therapy is often mandatory in patients whose symptoms interfere drastically with proper functioning or constitute sources of danger to themselves and to others. Among such symptoms are severe depression, suicidal impulses, homicidal or destructive tendencies, panic reactions, compulsive acting-out of perverse sexual strivings, severe alcoholism, drug addiction, and disabling physical symptoms of psychologic origin.

4. Where motivation for extensive therapeutic goals is lacking, supportive treatment may prove sufficient or may constitute a preparatory period for reconstructive or reeducative therapy.

5. Where the personality has been severely damaged during the formative years so that there is little on which to build, the objective may be to stabilize the individual through supportive measures. Some patients with severe infantile, dependent personality disorders, and with borderline and psychotic reactions, may be unable to tolerate the anxieties of exploration and challenge.

6. Supportive treatment may be indicated where the patient lacks adequate intelligence, or where the available time and finances are limited, or where there is extreme character rigidity, or where the personality is so constituted that the patient can respond only to commanding authoritative injunctions. Even though manifest neurotic difficulties continue in force following therapy, life may become more tolerable and the individual may adopt a more constructive attitude toward reality.

As an Adjunctive Form of Treatment during Reeducative and Reconstructive Therapy

1.   Where the coping resources of the ego are failing, as evidenced in feelings of extreme helplessness, severe depression, intense anxiety, and disabling psychosomatic symptoms, extension of support is usually necessary.

2.   In cases where the environment is grossly disturbed so as to impede progress, supportive techniques like environmental manipulation may be required.

MODE OF ACTION OF SUPPORTIVE THERAPY

Supportive therapy owes its efficacy to a number of factors:

1.   A correction or modification of a disturbed environment or other stress source may serve to strengthen coping resources.

2.   The improved situation that results may permit the individual to exact gratifications essential to his well-being.

3.   The patient may fulfill, in the supportive relationship with the therapist, important interpersonal needs, the deprivation of which has created tension. The supplying of emotional needs in the relationship constitutes what is sometimes known as "transference cure." For instance, the patient, feeling helpless, may desire the protection and security of a stronger individual on whom he may become dependent. Finding this with the therapist, he feels the comfort akin to a child who is being cared for by a loving and powerful parental agency. This relieves him of responsibility and fills him with a sense of comfort and security. Reinforcing these effects are the influences of the placebo element and of suggestion.

4.   In the medium of the therapeutic situation the patient may verbalize freely and gain a cathartic release for his fears, guilt feelings, damaging memories, and misconceptions that he has suppressed or repressed, having no opportunity for such discharge in his customary life setting. The draining off of tension, which has been converted into symptoms, brings about relief and usually a temporary abatement of symptomatic complaints.

5.   The patient may rebuild shattered old defenses or erect new ones that serve to repress more effectively his offending conflicts. Supportive therapy is suppressive in nature, helping to keep conflicts from awareness or modifying attitudes toward the elements of conflict.

6.   Under the protective aegis of the therapist the patient is enabled to face and to master life problems that have hitherto baffled him. Greater capacity to deal with these problems not only helps to rectify current sources of stress, but also gives the patient confidence in his ability to adjust to other aspects of his environment. The resultant expansion of security may eliminate the patient's need to exploit inadequate defense mechanisms.

7.   There may be an alleviation of guilt and fear through reassurance or through prohibitions and restrictions, which, imposed by the therapist, are interpreted as necessary disciplines by the patient.

8.   Certain measures, like drugs and relaxing exercises, may remove tension or moderate its effects.

9.   An outlet for excessive energy and tension may be supplied through prescribed physical exercises, hobbies, recreations, and occupational therapy.

THE THERAPIST–PATIENT RELATIONSHIP IN SUPPORTIVE THERAPY

The different techniques employed in supportive therapy presuppose a relationship of therapist to patient that varies from strong directiveness to a more passive permissiveness. In most cases the therapist is essentially authoritarian.

Success in treatment is usually contingent on acceptance of the therapist as a wise or benevolent authority. A consistent effort is made to establish and maintain a congenial atmosphere. Because hostile attitudes oppose the incorporation of therapeutic suggestions, it is essential to try to avoid a negative transference. Hostilities, therefore, are dissipated as soon as they arise, and an attempt is made to win the patient over to a conviction that the therapist is a helpful friend. Whenever the patient manifests attitudes that interfere with the relationship, therapy is focused on discussion and clarification in the attempt to restore the original rapport. Much skill may be required to halt negative feelings as soon as they start developing; but unless this is done, the therapist may encounter resistance that cannot be controlled.

Forcefulness of personality, and an ability to inspire confidence are important qualities in the therapist. The ideal attitude toward the patient is sympathetic, kindly, but firm. The therapist must be constituted so as neither to derive sadistic pleasure from the patient's submission nor to resent the latter's display of aggression or hostility. One must not succumb to blandishments of praise or admiration. A noncondemning, accepting attitude, shorn of blame or contempt, secures best results. The neurotic patient may, of course, display provocative impulses and attitudes; but if the therapist is incapable of controlling his or her resentment, this practitioner will probably be unable to do productive work with the patient. The irritation cannot usually be concealed by a judicious choice of words.

The attitudes of the therapist are important because some of the patient's responses have been conditioned by antagonistic reactions of other people. At the start of therapy the patient will expect similar displays from the therapist, especially rejection or condemnation. When such responses do not appear even under badgering, the patient's attitude toward the therapist will hopefully change. Different from how he acts in other relationships, he may begin to feel accepted as he is, and genuine warmth toward the therapist may begin to trickle through. The patient may then recognize the therapist as an ally with whom he can identify and whose values he may respect.

There are therapists who attempt, in a supportive framework, to deal boldly with pathogenic conflicts by manipulating the therapeutic relationship. Here the therapist deliberately plays a role with the patient in order to reinforce or subdue the parental image or to introduce himself or herself as an idealized parental substitute. Transference responses are deliberately cultivated by employing permissiveness or by enforcing prohibitions graded to a desired effect. Thus, acting as a "good" parental figure is considered helpful with patients who need an accepting "giving" situation. Deprived in childhood of an understanding maternal relationship, certain patients are presumed to require a "living through" with another human being of an experience in which they are protected and loved without stint. Another role assumed by the therapist is that of a commanding, stern authoritarian figure. This is believed to be helpful in patients whose superegos are relatively undeveloped, who still demand controls and disciplines from the outside.

Sometimes role playing is combined with support on the theory that it is essential for the patient to live through with the therapist emotional incidents identical in type with the traumatizing experiences of his childhood. Only by dramatizing his problems, it is alleged, can the patient be prodded out of the rigid and circumscribed patterns through which he avoids coming to grips with life. In order to mobilize activity and to release inner drives, the therapist attempts to create a relationship that is charged with tension. The ensuing struggle between patient and therapist is said to catalyze the breaking down of the neurosis.

One may rightfully criticize this technique on the grounds that the patient actually experiences frustration as a direct result of the therapeutic situation. The hostility may thus be justified. The tension and hostility that are mobilized may eventually become sufficiently intense to break through repression, with an acting-out of impulses; however, this may be destructive to the patient and to the therapeutic relationship.

A misdirected positive use of role playing is also to be impugned. Even though open demonstrations of affection may seem logical in making the patient feel loved and lovable, such gestures are usually ineffective because of the patient's ambivalence.

Love is so fused with hate that the patient may completely misinterpret affectionate tokens. This does not mean that the therapist must be cold and withdrawn, for a refrigerated attitude will even more drastically reinforce the patient's feelings of rejection.

Manipulations of the relationship call for a great deal of skill and stamina on the part of the therapist. They are responded to best by relatively healthy persons. Borderline patients, schizophrenics, paranoiacs, and profoundly dependent individuals may react badly to such active gestures.

GUIDANCE

In the supportive technique of guidance the therapist acts as a guide or mentor, helping the patient to evolve better ways of adjusting to the reality situation. Therapeutic interviews are focused around immediate situational problems. While the therapist may formulate an hypothesis of the operative dynamics, this is not interpreted to the patient unless the dynamics are clearly manifest and the interpretation stands a chance of being accepted by the patient without too great resistance. The employment of guidance requires that the therapist encourage the patient toward a better understanding and evaluation of his situation, toward a recognition of measures that will correct his difficulty, and toward the taking of active steps in effectuating a proposed plan. The patient is usually required to make the choices, although the therapist may clarify issues, outline the problem more succinctly, present operational possibilities, suggest available resources, and prompt the patient to action. Reassurance is utilized in proportion to the existing need, while as much responsibility is put on the patient as he can take.

Guidance suggestions must always be made in such a manner that the patient accepts them as the most expedient and logical course of action. It may be essential to spend some time explaining the rationale of a tendered plan until the patient develops a conviction that he really wishes to execute it. In this choice the patient should always be led to feel that his wishes and resistances will be respected by the therapist.

There are, however, a few patients whose personalities are so constituted that they resent a kindly and understanding authority. Rather they are inclined to demand a scolding and commanding attitude without which they seem lost. Such patients appear to need a punitive reinforcement of their conscience out of fear of yielding to inner impulses over which they have little control. At the start of therapy it may sometimes be tempting to respect the needs and demands of such personalities, but an effort must always be made later on to transfer the disciplinary restraints to the individual himself. Unless such an incorporation of prohibitions is achieved and becomes an integral part of the individual's conscience, he will demand a greater and greater display of punitive efforts on the part of the therapist. To complicate this, when he has responded to dictatorial demands, he will burn inwardly with resentment and hate for the therapist, and he will feel a tremendous contempt for himself for being so weak as to need authoritative pressure.

One way of conducting the guidance interview is to try to avoid, as much as possible, the giving of direct advice. Rather, the therapist may couch ideas and suggestions in a way that the patient participates in the making of decisions. Furthermore, advice should be proffered in a nondictatorial manner so that the patient feels he may accept or reject it in accordance with his own judgment.

The sicker the individual, the more he will need active guidance and direction. How long the supportive relationship will have to be maintained will depend on the strength of the patient's ego. Usually, as the patient gains security and freedom from symptoms, he will want to take more and more responsibility for his own destiny. Even those persons who offer resistance to assertiveness and independence may be aided in developing incentive toward greater independence. This may require considerable time and patience, but in most instances such constructive motivation can be achieved.

ENVIRONMENTAL MANIPULATION

The special environment in which the individual lives may sponsor conditions inimical to mental health. This does not mean that mental health will be guaranteed by a genial atmosphere because personal conflicts may continue to upset the individual even under the most propitious circumstances. One may be burdened with blocks that obstruct available opportunities. Indeed one may initiate and foster a disturbance of the environment even where none has existed in order to satisfy inner needs. Be this as it may, the therapist has a responsibility to help rectify discordant living conditions so as to give the patient the best opportunities for growth. Even though the effort may be palliative, the relief that the patient experiences, even temporarily, will provide the most optimal conditions for psychotherapy. It is obviously best for the patient to execute necessary changes in the environment for himself. The therapist, however, may have to interfere directly or through an assistant by doing for the patient what he cannot do for himself.

Conditions for which environmental manipulation may be required are the following:

1. *Economic situation.*
   a. Location of resources for financial aid.
   b. Budgeting and managing of income.
   c. Home planning and home economics.
2. *Work situation.*
   a. Testing for vocational interests and aptitudes. (Referral to a clinical psychologist may be required.)
   b. Vocational guidance and vocational rehabilitation. (Referral to a clinical psychologist or rehabilitation resource may be required.)
3. *Housing situation.*
   a. Locating new quarters.
   b. Adjusting to present housing situation.
4. *Neighborhood situation.*
   a. Moving to a new neighborhood.
   b. Locating and utilizing neighborhood social, recreational, or educational resources.
   c. Adjusting to present neighborhood.
5. *Cultural standards.*
   a. Interpreting meaning of current cultural patterns.
   b. Clarifying personal standards that do not conform with community standards.
   c. Clarifying legality of actions.
6. *Family and other interpersonal relations.*
   a. Consulting with parents, siblings, relatives, mate, child, or friend of patient.
   b. Promoting education in such matters as sexual relations, child rearing, and parenthood.
   c. Helping in the selection of a nursery school, grade school, camp, or recreational facilities for the patient's children.
   d. Referring patient to legal resources in critical family or interpersonal situations.
7. *Daily habits, recreations, and routines.*
   a. Referring patient to resources for correction of defects in dress, personal hygiene, and grooming.
   b. Referring patient to appropriate recreational, social, and hobby resources.
8. *Health.*
   a. Clarifying health problems to patient or relative.
   b. Referring patient to hospital or institution.
   c. Referring patient to resources for correction of remediable physical disabilities.

The therapist may have to interfere actively where the environmental situation is grossly inimical to the best interests of the patient. This usually implies work with the patient's family, since it is rare that a patient's difficulties are limited to himself.

Various family members may require psychotherapy before the patient shows a maximal response to treatment. Indeed, the cooperation of the family is not only desirable, but in many instances unavoidable. A psychiatric social worker can render invaluable service to the therapist here. In some cases family therapy may be required.

Where the immediate environment does not offer good opportunities for rehabilitation, the patient may be referred to resources that will reinforce the therapist's efforts, such as day-and-night hospitals, halfway houses, sheltered workshops, rehabilitation centers, and social therapy clubs. For instance, day-and-night hospitals keep even moderately disturbed patients in the community and help support their work capacities. Halfway houses may serve as a sheltered social environment in which the patient's deviant behavior is better tolerated than elsewhere. The patient is capable of experimenting there with new roles while being subject to the modifying pressures of group norms. Discarding of disapproved patterns and adoption of new attitudes may become generalized to the social environment (Wechsler, H, 1960, 1961). Sheltered work programs have been shown to help patients make a slow adjustment to conditions and conflicts at work (Olshansky, 1960). Tolerating an individual's reactions allows him to restructure his defenses at his own pace without countenancing violent or rejecting responses on the part of supervisors and employers. A reconditioning process that prepares the patient for a regular occupation in the community may in this way be initiated. Rehabilitation centers, such as Altro Health and Rehabilitation Services, provide a variety of benefits that are made available to the patient and that permit him to achieve the best adjustment within the limitations of his handicap. At such centers the following may be accomplished:

1. Handling the patient's lack of motivation and resistance to work.
2. Helping him in his efforts at reality testing.
3. Educating him in methods of coping with daily problems as well as in developing working skills.
4. Aiding him in recognizing early signs of emotional upset and suggesting means of removing himself from sources that upset him before he goes to extremes.
5. Working with the patient's family to secure their cooperation and manage problems within the family structure.
6. Providing aftercare services to prevent relapses (Benney et al, 1962; Fisher & Beard, 1962).

Social therapy clubs provide an extraordinary medium for a variety of experiences, either in themselves or as part of a therapeutic community (Bierer, 1948, 1958; Fleischl, 1962, 1964; Lerner, 1960; Ropschitz, 1959; Waxenberg & Fleischl, 1965).

EXTERNALIZATION OF INTERESTS

The turning of the patient's interests away from himself may be considered important as part of a supportive program. Hobbies, occupational therapy, and recreational activities may be exploited here.

A most effective hobby is one that provides an acceptable outlet for impulses that the person cannot express directly. The need to experience companionship, to give and to receive affection, to be part of a group, to gain recognition, to live up to certain creative abilities, and to develop latent talents may be satisfied by an absorbing hobby interest.

External activities can provide compensations that help the individual to allay some inferiority feelings. Instead of concentrating on failings, the patient is encouraged to develop whatever talents and abilities he possesses. For instance, if he is proficient as a tennis player or has a good singing voice, these aptitudes are encouraged so that the patient feels that he excels in one particular field. Whatever assets the individual has may thus be promoted. Calisthenics and gymnastics, even setting-up exercises, act as excellent outlets for inner resentments that have no other way of being drained off. Some patients harbor within themselves strong hostilities of a disturbing nature, with needs to vanquish, defeat and to overwhelm others. Hostility may have to be repressed as a result of fear of retaliatory rejection or punishment. Sometimes even ordinary forms of self-assertiveness may be regarded as aggression. As a consequence, such a person may have to lead a life of detachment in order to avoid giving expression to what are considered forbidden impulses. For these patients hobbies that do not involve competition will be most acceptable, at first. The ultimate object is to interest the patient in a hobby that has some competitive element. The patient may come around to this himself. For example, one patient chose photography as an outlet principally because it involved no contact with other people. Gradually, as she became more expert, she exhibited her work to friends, and, finally, she entered pictures in various photographic contests. Later on, with encouragement, she learned to play bridge, which acted as a spur to an interest in active competitive games and sports.

The ability to express hostility through activities that involve the larger muscle groups permits of a most effective expression of disquieting aggression. Boxing, wrestling, hunting, archery, marksmanship, fencing, and such work as carpentry and stone building can burn up a tremendous amount of energy. In some individuals the mere attendance at games and competitive sports, such as baseball, football, and boxing, has an aggression-releasing effect. It must be remembered, however, that this release is merely palliative; it does not touch upon the dynamic difficulties in the life adjustment of the person that are responsible for the generation of hostility.

Many other impulses may be satisfied through occupational or diversional activities. Hobbies may foster a sense of achievement and can help the individual to satisfy a need for approval. Energy resulting from inhibited sexual strivings may gain expression sometimes in an interest in pets or naturalistic studies. Frustrated parental yearnings may be appeased by work with children at children's clubs or camps.

One must expect that the patient will try to employ hobbies as a means of reinforcing the neurotic patterns by which he adjusts to life. If he has a character structure of perfectionism, he will pursue his hobby with the goal of mastering intricate details. If he is compulsively ambitious, he will strive to use his interest as a way to fame or fortune. The same holds true for any of the other character traits that he may possess.

Most patients gain temporary surcease from neurotic difficulties during the period when they are working at a new interest; however, their illness will become exacerbated when the hobby has failed to come up to their expectations. In spite of this, the diversion may open up avenues for contact with others that will neutralize this tendency.

Neurotic difficulties are often associated with disturbances that cause the individual to isolate himself from the group. The pleasures derived from social activities do not compensate for the tensions and anxieties incurred in mingling with people. Occupational therapy, hobbies, and recreations give the person an opportunity to participate with others in a project of mutual enjoyment. Pleasure feelings radiate to those with whom the patient is related and help lessen his defenses against people. They may even lead him to find values in a group.

Once the patient has established a group contact, there may be sufficient pleasures to sustain interest. It is to be expected, nevertheless, that the patient will manifest customary withdrawal defenses. But the benefits derived from the group may more than make up for the discomfiture.

In some instances it may be possible to convince the patient to engage in activities or work that contribute to the general welfare of the community. This can create a feeling of active participation with others and a conviction that something is being done that is socially useful.

REASSURANCE

Some reassurance may be necessary at certain phases of psychotherapy. This is sometimes given in verbal form; more commonly it is indicated through nonverbal behavior, as by maintenance of a calm and objective attitude.

Verbal reassurance, when used, should not be started too early, since the patient at first may not have sufficient faith in the therapist to be convinced of his sincerity. He may imagine that the therapist is secretly ridiculing him, or does not know how serious the situation really is, or is merely delivering therapeutic doses of solace without deep conviction.

In practicing reassurance, the therapist must listen to the patient with sincerity and respect, pointing out that his difficulties may perhaps seem overwhelming because they represent much more than appears on the surface. Under no circumstances should the patient be disparaged for illogical fears. He usually appreciates that his worries are senseless, but he is unable to control them.

One of the most common fears expressed by the neurotic person is that of going insane. Panicky feelings, bizarre impulses, and a sense of unreality lead him to this assumption. He becomes convinced that he will lose control and perhaps inflict injury on himself or others. He may attempt to justify his fear of insanity by revealing that he has a relative who was insane, from whom he believes he has inherited a taint. It is essential to show him that fear of insanity is a common neurotic symptom and to acquaint him with the fact that there is scarcely a family in which one cannot find cases of mental illness. A presentation may be made of the facts of heredity, with an explanation that insanity is not inevitable even in families that have a history of mental illness. He may be furthermore reassured that his examination fails to reveal evidence of insanity.

Another ubiquitous fear relates to the possession of a grave physical disease or abnormality. The patient may believe that through masturbation, physical excesses, or faulty hygiene he has procured some irremediable illness. A physical examination with x-ray and laboratory tests should be prescribed, even though negative findings may not convince the patient that his fear is founded on emotional factors. Assurance may be given the patient that anxiety and worry can produce physical symptoms of a reversible nature. Where his fears are not too integral a part of the patient's neurosis, these explanations may suffice. Even where fears are deep, as in obsessional patients, and where the patient does not accept the results of the physical examination, his more rational self will toy with the idea that he may be wrong. At any rate, the absence of manifest physical illness will give the therapist the opportunity to demonstrate to the patient that his problem is not really just a physical one and that feelings of being ill or damaged may serve an important psychologic function.

Masturbatory fears are often deep-seated and operate outside the awareness of the person. The patient may, through reading and discussions with enlightened people, rationalize his fears, or he may conceal them under an intellectual coating. Either because of actual threats on the part of early authorities, or through his own faulty deductions, he may believe that his past indulgences have injured him irreparably. He may shy away from masturbatory practices in the present or else engage in them with conscious or unconscious foreboding. Assurance that he has misinterpreted the supposedly evil effects of masturbation, coupled with assigned reading of books that present scientific facts on the subject, have remarkably little effect on the patient's qualms. He is unable to rid himself of childish misapprehensions that seem invulnerable to reason. Nevertheless, the therapist's point of view should be presented in a sincere and forthright manner, with the statement that the patient, for emotional reasons, may not now be able to accept the explanation. Eventually, as he realizes the depth of his fears, he may be able to understand how victimized he has been all his life by faulty ideas about masturbation absorbed during his childhood.

Reassurance may also be needed in regard to other aspects of the individual's sexual life. Frigidity, for instance, is the concern of many women who often expect that it will disappear automatically with marriage. Projecting their disappointment, some women tend to blame their mates for their sexual incompetence. In therapy this misconception will have to be clarified carefully with a focusing on guilt and other provocative conflicts.

In men reassurance may be required in conditions of temporary impotence. Many males are excessively concerned with their sexual powers and have exorbitant expectations of themselves insofar as sexual performance is concerned. Discussions may be organized around the theme that episodes of impotence are quite natural in the lives of most men. Temporary feelings of resentment toward a marital partner or attempts at intercourse during a state of exhaustion, or without any real desire, will normally inhibit the erective ability. On the basis of several such failures in performance, the individual may become panicky, and his sense of tension may then interfere with proper sexual performance thereafter. The patient may be shown the necessity for a different attitude toward sex, treating it less as a means of performance and more as a pleasure pursuit. Reassurance that his impotence is temporary and will rectify itself with the proper attitude may suffice to restore adequate functioning.

Another concern shown by patients is that of homosexuality. Fears of homosexuality may be overwhelming. It is helpful sometimes to reassure the patient regarding homosexual fears or impulses with which he happens to be concerned. Elucidation that a liking for people of the same sex may occasionally be associated with sexual inclinations toward them, that this impulse is not a sign that one is evil or depraved, and that it need not be yielded to may be extremely reassuring. An effort may be made to explain how, in the development of a child, sexual curiosities and sex play are universal and may lead to homosexual explorations. Usually this interest is later transferred to members of the opposite sex, but in some persons, for certain reasons, an arrest in development occurs. The patient may be informed that when homosexuality represents a basic attitude toward people as part of a neurotic problem, it need not be considered any more significant than any other problem that requires psychological treatment.

Reassurance is often necessary in the event of infidelity of one's marital partner.

Where a man or woman is extremely upset because their spouse has been unfaithful, they may feel not only a threat to their security, but, more importantly, they may experience a shattering of self-esteem. The therapist may affirm that infidelity on the part of one's marital partner is indeed hard to bear, but that it is far from a unique experience in our culture. The patient must be urged not to be stampeded into a rash divorce simply because he or she feels outraged. It is natural that knowledge of a spouse's infidelity should have filled them with indignation, but in their own interest, they must not act precipitously. They may find themselves encouraged by friends, family, and public opinion to hate their spouses and to cut themselves off from them. There is good logic in resisting a dramatic act and not precipitating a divorce over an affair that is in all probability quite insignificant. Such reassurance may convince the patient that he or she really does not desire a divorce but that they can work out a better relationship with their spouses and perhaps discover why they had drifted apart.

One use of reassurance that is practiced by some therapists is helping the process of ego building. Patients become so preoccupied with their troubles and pain that they are apt to lose sight of the constructive aspects of their personality. They may, consequently, minimize their good points or be unaware of them. The therapist here selects aspects of the individual's life adjustment and personality that the patient may underestimate. Positive qualities of the patient may be indicated with emphasis on how these have been sabotaged by the patient's neurosis.

Direct reassurance in response to inferiority feelings, however, is generally futile. One of the most common symptoms of neurosis is devaluated self-esteem, which fosters inhibitions in action, perfectionistic strivings, and feelings of worthlessness, inadequacy, and self-condemnation. Any attempt here to inflate the patient's ego by reassurance accomplishes little.

Self-devaluation may be a symptom that serves a useful purpose for the patient, protecting him from having to live up to the expectations of other people or of his own ego ideal. Rebuilding his self-esteem by reassurance, therefore, threatens to remove an important coping mechanism. Many persons who devaluate themselves insidiously do penance for forbidden strivings and desires. Reassurance here may actually plunge the person into anxiety.

Apart from the instances mentioned, reassurance is not too commonly employed even in supportive therapy. It can, however, serve a useful purpose where indicated. Where the patient has sufficient ego resources, reassurance even though necessary should be tempered, the patient being apprised that responsibility for investigating his patterns has to be borne by himself. If this precaution is not taken, the patient will lose initiative in getting at the source of his difficulties, and he will tend to seek more and more reassurance from the therapist.

PERSUASION

Persuasive techniques are sometimes helpful as supportive measures, particularly in obsessive-compulsive personalities. The object is to master conflict by forces of will power, self-control, and powers of reasoning.

Persuasive suggestions have arbitrarily been subdivided into several categories. They represent a point of view and a slant on life that may not always be accurate but that, if accepted by the patient, may help alleviate his distress. In general, suggestions tend toward a redirection of goals, an overcoming of physical suffering and disease, a dissipation of the "worry habit," "thought control," and "emotion control," a correcting of tension and fear, and a facing of adversity. These suggestions are superficial, but their pursuit is considered justified by some therapists as a means of helping the patient control symptoms. The following suggestions are a summary of a number of different "systems" of persuasion. Superficial as they sound they are sometimes eagerly accepted by some patients who are not amenable to other approaches and seem to need a wise authority to structure their lives.

Redirection of Goals

If the patient's goals in life are obviously distorted, the patient is instructed that the most important aim in living is inner peace rather than fame, fortune, or any other expedient that might be confused with real happiness. In order to gain serenity, he may have to abandon hopes of becoming rich, famous, or successful. He may be causing himself much harm by being overambitious. If he is content to give up certain ambitions, and to make his objective in life that of mental serenity and enjoyment, he should try living on a more simple scale. He should give up struggling for success. Health and freedom from suffering are well worth this sacrifice.

One can attain happiness and health by learning to live life as it should be lived, by taking the good with the bad, the moments of joy with the episodes of pain. One must expect hard knocks from life and learn to steel oneself against them. It is always best to avoid fearsome anticipations of what might happen in the future. Rather one should strive for a freer, more spontaneous existence in the present. One should take advantage of the experiences of the moment and live for every bit of pleasure that one can get out of each day. The place to enjoy life is here. The time is now. By being happy oneself, one can also make others happy.

It is profitable to concern oneself with the problems of other people. Many persons who have suffered pain, disappointment, and frustration have helped themselves by throwing their personal interests aside and living to make others happy. We are social creatures and need to give to others, even if we must force ourselves to do so. Thus, we can take a little time out each day to talk to our neighbors, to do little things for them. We can seek out a person who is in misery and encourage him to face life. In giving we will feel a unity with people.

A person may be enjoined to avoid the acting-out of a sense of despair. A pitfall into which most "nervous" people fall is a hopeless feeling that paralyzes any constructive efforts. One must not permit oneself to yield to feelings of hopelessness, for life is always forward moving. Hopelessness and despair are a negation of life. If we stop holding ourselves back, we will automatically go forward, since development and growth are essential parts of the life process.

Overcoming Physical Suffering and Disease

The patient, if he is suffering from ailments of a physical nature, may be told that physical symptoms are very frequently caused by emotional distress. Studies have shown that painful thoughts can affect the entire body through the autonomic nervous system. For instance, if we observe an individual's intestines by means of a fluoroscope, we can see that when the person thinks fearful or painful thoughts, the stomach and intestines contract, interfering with digestion. On the other hand, peaceful, happy thoughts produce a relaxation of the intestines and a restoration of peristaltic movements, thus facilitating digestion. The same holds true for other organs.

Understanding the powerful effect that the mind has over the body lucidly demonstrates that physical suffering can be mastered by a change in attitudes. By directing one's thoughts along constructive lines, by keeping before the mind's eye visions of peace and health, a great many persons who have been handicapped by physical ailments, and by even incurable diseases, have conquered their suffering and even have outlived healthy people. This is because a healthy mind fosters a healthy body and can neutralize many effects of a disabling malady.

Physical aches and pains, and even physical disease, may be produced by misguided thoughts and emotions. The body organs and the mind are a unity; they mutually interact. Physical illness can influence the mind, producing depression, confusion, and disturbed thought process. On the other hand, the psyche can also influence the body, causing an assortment of ailments. In the latter instance the institution of proper thought habits can dispel physical distress.

It is natural for a person who is suffering from physical symptoms to imagine that there is something organically wrong with him. He cannot be blamed if he seeks the traditional kinds of relief. But palliation is not found in medicines or operations. Relief is found in determining the cause of his trouble and correcting the cause. Worry, tension, and dissatisfaction are causes for many physical complaints; the treatment here lies in abolishing destructive thoughts.

The first step in getting relief from physical suffering is to convince oneself that one's troubles are not necessarily organic. The difficulties may lie in one's environment, but usually they are due to improper thinking habits. If there is a remediable environmental factor, this must, of course, be remedied. Where it cannot be altered, the person must learn to change himself so that he can live comfortably in his difficult environment. In the latter case he has to reorganize his patterns of thinking.

Where a patient actually has an organic ailment that is not amenable to medical or surgical correction, an attempt may be made to get the patient not only to accept the illness, but also to change his attitude toward it. It is essential to help the patient reorganize his philosophy so that he can find satisfactions in life consistent with his limited capacities.

In physical conditions of a progressive nature, such as coronary disease, cancer, or malignant hypertension, the patient may be in a constant state of anxiety, anticipating death at any moment. Here it is wise to emphasize the fact that death is as much a part of living as is life and that the horrors attached to it are those that come from a misinterpretation of nature. Life must go on. Babies are born, and people pass on to a peaceful sleep that is death. The chances are that the patient still has a long useful life ahead that can be prolonged by adopting a proper attitude toward one's condition. If suffering and pain do not exist, this should be pointed out as a fortunate occurrence. The person should think about the present and avoid dwelling too much on the future. No one can anticipate what the future may bring. Accidents can happen to anyone, and even a young person in the best of health does not know when an illness or accident will strike. The only rational philosophy is to glean whatever pleasure one can from the moment and to leave the future to take care of itself. Hypnosis and self-hypnosis may be employed as aids for the alleviation of pain and physical distress.

The patient is encouraged to develop hobbies and to engage in activities that will divert his thinking from himself. A list of diversions that the patient can pursue may be prepared and the patient guided into adopting new interests.

Dissipating the "Worry Habit"

Patients who are obsessed with worrying about themselves may be urged to remember that much energy is expended ruminating about one's problems and fears instead of doing something positive about a solution. Worry tends to magnify the importance of petty difficulties; it usually paralyzes initiative. The worrier is constantly preoccupied with ideas of fear, dread, and morbid unpleasantness. These thoughts have a disastrous effect on the motor system, the glands, and the organs.

In order to overcome the "worry habit," it is first necessary to formulate in one's mind the chief problem with which one is concerned. To do this it will be necessary to push apprehensions boldly aside. In a seemingly insurmountable problem, one should attempt to reformulate the situation to bring clearly to mind the existing difficulty. If one is honest with oneself, one will realize that most of one's energy has been spent in hopeless despair, in anxiety, or in resentful frustration rather than in logical and unemotional thinking that can bring about tranquility.

First, it is necessary to review all possible answers to the problem at hand. Next, the best solution is chosen, even though this may seem inadequate in coping with all aspects of the problem. A plan of action must then be decided on. It is necessary to proceed with this design immediately and to abandon all worry until the plan is carried out as completely as possible. Above all the person must stick to the project, even if it is distasteful.

If the person cannot formulate a scheme, the therapist may help to do so. The patient should be told that it is better to be concerned about a constructive plan than to get tangled up in the hopelessness of an apparently insoluble problem. Until the patient can work out something better, it is best to adjust to the present situation, striving always to externalize energy in a constructive way.

The patient may be urged to stop thinking painful thoughts. He may be told that forgetting is a process that goes on of its own accord if one does not interfere with it. Worry is a process that has been learned. One can, therefore, help oneself by controlling one's thoughts and avoiding painful ideas. If action is impossible for the moment, one can try to crowd out apprehensions by simply resolving to stop worrying.

Discussing painful topics with other people should also be avoided. If the patient must ventilate disturbing feelings, this should be done with the therapist. "Blowing off steam" and relating troubles to friends often does more harm than good because the suggestions offered are usually unsound. It is better for the patient to underestimate his difficulties than to become too emotional about them. It is also necessary for him to ask his friends and relatives to stop talking about his personal problems, if such discussions are aggravating. It is understandable that people close to him will be much concerned with his illness, but they must be reminded that their solicitude may aggravate his condition. Often a person can forestall trouble by insisting that he feels "fine" when questioned by others about his health.

"Thought Control" and "Emotion Control"

Patients who seem to be at the mercy of painful thoughts and emotions may be enjoined never to permit their minds to wander like flotsam, yielding to every passing thought and emotion. It is necessary to try to choose deliberately the kinds of thoughts to think and the kinds of emotions to feel. It is essential to eschew ruminating about re-sentiments, hatreds, and disappointments, about "aches and pains," and about misery in general.

One must think thoughts that nourish the ego and permit it to expand to a better growth. A woman with multiple complaints unresponsive to various types of psychotherapy was told by her therapist that if she wants to be without pain, she must fill her mind with painless ideas. If she wants to be happy, she must smile. If she wants to be well, she must act as if she *were* well. She must straighten her shoulders, walk more resolutely, talk with energy and verve. She must face the world with confidence. She must look life in the face and never falter. She must stand up to adversity and glory in the struggle. She must never permit herself to sink into the quagmire of helplessness or give herself up to random worries, thus feeling sorry for herself. She must replace thoughts of doubt and fear with those of courage and confidence. She must think firmly of how she can accomplish the most in life, with whatever resources she has. She must feel those emotions that lead to inner harmony.

She must picture herself as above petty recriminations, avoiding the centering of her interest around herself. Even if she suffers from pain and unhappiness, she must stop thinking about her daily discomforts. She must give to others and learn to find comfort in the joys of giving. She must become self-reliant and creative. Emancipation from tension and fear can come by training one's mind to think joyous and peaceful thoughts. But new thought habits do not come immediately. One must show persistence and be steadfast in one's application. One must never permit oneself to be discouraged. One must practice, more and more. Only through persistent practice can perfection be obtained so that the mind shuts out painful thoughts automatically.

It is not necessary to force oneself impetuously to stop worrying or feeling pain. Will power used this way will not crowd out the painful emotions. One must instead substitute different thoughts or more appropriate actions. If one starts feeling unhappy or depressed, one should determine to rise above this emotion. One should talk cheerfully to others, try to do someone a good turn; or one may lie down for a short while, relax the body and then practice thinking about something peaceful and pleasant. As soon as this occurs, unhappy thoughts will be eradicated. A good practice is to think of a period in one's life when one was happiest. This may have been in the immediate past or during childhood. One may think of people one knew, the pleasant times one had with them. This substitution of pleasant for unpleasant thoughts may take several weeks before new thinking habits eventuate.

These injunctions had an almost immediate effect on the patient. Instead of preoccupying herself with her symptoms she concentrated on putting into practice the suggestions of her therapist, with a resultant dramatic cessation of complaints.

Correcting Tension and Fear

Where undifferentiated tension and fear exist, the patient may be told that difficulties may come from without, but that one's reactions to these difficulties are purely personal and come from within. By changing these reactions, one can avoid many of the consequences of stress. If one is confronted with tension, anxiety, or feelings of inner restlessness, it is best to start analyzing the causes. Are these emotions due to disappointment or failure? Or are they the product of a sense of hopelessness? Once the cause is found, it is necessary to face the facts squarely and take corrective steps. It is urgent to plan a course to follow and to execute this immediately. If facts cannot be altered, one must change attitudes toward them. It is essential to stop thinking about the painful side of things and to find instead something constructive on which to concentrate.

One may be unable to prevent anxious thoughts from coming into one's mind, but they can be prevented from staying there. The person must stop saying, "I can't," and think in terms of "I can." As long as one says, "I can't," one is defeated. Being resolute and persistent in saying "I can" will eventually bring results.

The first step in overcoming tension is to stop indulging oneself in self-pity. Tension will drag one's life down if not interrupted. It is necessary to learn to love life for the living. One must learn not to exaggerate troubles. One must let other people live *their* lives, and one should live one's own.

Many people suffering from tension and fear have helped themselves by saying, "Go ahead and hurt all you want; you will not get me down." Fears are best faced by courageously admitting them. They can be conquered by stopping to fight them or by refraining from trying to master them by sheer will power. Acknowledging that one is afraid is the first step. Thereafter one must determine to rid oneself of fear by developing the conviction that one will overcome it. A sense of humor is of unparalleled help here. If one laughs at one's fears instead of cringing before them, one will not be helpless and at the mercy of forces one cannot control.

Practicing relaxation sometimes is useful. Each day a person may lie on his back, on the floor or on a hard surface, for 20 minutes, consciously loosening up every muscle from forehead to feet, even fingers and toes. He may then start breathing deeply, with slow, deep exhalations through pursed lips. At the same time he may think of a peaceful scene at the mountains or seashore. Mental and muscular relaxation are of tremendous aid in overcoming states of tension.

Facing Adversity

In the event a patient has an irremediable environmental difficulty, he may be reminded that there are many dire conditions in one's environment that cannot be changed no matter how diligently one tries. Poor financial circumstances, an unstable mate, overactive youngsters who make noise and tax one's patience, a physical handicap, or an incurable physical illness can create a great deal of worry, tension, and anxiety. It is not so much these difficult conditions that are important as it is the reaction of the person to them. Life is usually full of struggle; but the individual need not permit himself to get embroiled in the turmoil and misery of the world. There are many persons who are deformed, or deprived of sight, hearing, and of vital parts of their body, who live happily and courageously because they have learned to accept their limitations and to follow the rule to live life as it is right now. There are many persons who, forced to exist under the most miserable conditions of poverty, with no resources or education, are not distressed by worry or nervousness because they have not yielded themselves to their emotions.

It is a human tendency to exaggerate one's plight. If one compares oneself with many other people, however, one will discover that one is not so badly off. An individual may not be able to achieve all of the ambitions that he has in life. He may not be as intellectual as he wants to be, or as strong, or successful, or rich, or famous. He may have to earn a living at work he detests. As bad as he imagines his state to be, if he were to be faced with the possibility of changing places with some other persons, he would probably refuse to do so. He might be dissatisfied with his appearance, and he may long for features that would make him look more handsome and distinguished. If this were possible, he might instead find that his health had become impaired or his intellect was not up to its present level.

It is necessary to make the most out of the little one has. Every person possesses weaknesses and must learn to live with them. Each of us must pattern our life so as to make our weaknesses as little manifest as possible. We must expand all of our good qualities to the limit. One's facial appearance may not be handsome, but one may have nicer hair and teeth than many other people. These may be emphasized in hair style or proper facial expression. One can appear well groomed with well-tailored clothing. If one's voice is good, one should cultivate it. In this way one may take advantage of every good feature one possesses.

Instead of resigning oneself to a sense of hopelessness, it is wise to turn one's mind toward creative activities and outlets. It will take much perseverance to conquer feelings of helplessness and frustration, but this can be done, particularly by living honestly and courageously. The wealthiest person is he who has not riches but strength of spirit. If an individual is dissatisfied with himself, he may try to imagine himself as the kind of person who he would like to be. He may then find that he can do those things that he has hitherto felt were impossible. He must never yield to despair or discouragement. Crippled persons have learned to walk by sheer perseverance of will. On the other hand, one should not set goals for oneself that are impossible of fulfillment. Thwarted ambition can give rise to bitterness and greed.

A sign of character is to change those conditions that can be remedied and to accept those that cannot be changed. To accomplish this one must face the problem squarely. What is to be done about a difficult situation? What can be done? How will one go about accomplishing the change? This calls for a plan of action that, once made, must be pursued diligently without discouragement.

There are always, of course, situations one must accept. Unalterable facts must be faced. If one cannot change things as they are, he can change his own attitude so that he will not overreact to his difficulties. As soon as a person has decided to make the best of things, his condition will improve immediately. If one is unable to possess the whole loaf, he must learn to content himself with part of a loaf. He must disregard minor discomforts, and pay less and less attention to them. His symptoms may be annoying, but they are not fatal. Keeping two written lists, outlining on one side the things that have troubled him, on the other side the things that have gone in his favor, will often convince the person, after a while, that the balance is on the positive side.

It is particularly important to train oneself to overcome the effects of frustration and disappointment. These may be expressed in the form of quarreling, or holding grudges against others, or by depression or physical symptoms. There are many dangers associated with permitting oneself to become too discouraged. It is best here to forestall despair before it develops, by adopting the attitude that one will not allow himself to get too upset if things go wrong. One must force himself to regard all adversity dispassionately, with the idea of modifying the cause if possible, or changing his point of view, if the cause cannot be removed.

The above persuasive suggestions do not represent a scientific point of view. However, their use is believed, especially by nondynamically oriented therapists, to be consonant with a pragmatic approach to therapy in certain patients who do not respond well to insight approaches.

EMOTIONAL CATHARSIS AND DESENSITIZATION

Release of painful feelings and desensitization to their effects constitutes an important supportive technique. The patient is encouraged to talk about those things in his past life or in his present-day relationships that bother him most. His responsiveness will depend on the confidence and trust he has in the therapist.

The patient may be told that most people have bottled up within themselves memories and experiences that, though seemingly under control, continue to have a disturbing effect on them. The attempt to obliterate emotional experiences by banishing them from the mind is not ordinarily successful. Disturbing ideas keep obtruding themselves into the stream of thought. Even when will power triumphs and suppression succeeds, casual everyday happenings may remind the person of his conflict. In addition to memories, there are also impulses and desires of which the person is thoroughly ashamed and which he dares not permit himself to think about. Among these are desires for extramarital sexual gratification, homosexual interests, hostile strivings, and impulses of a fantastic and infantile nature.

Emotional catharsis must never be foisted on the patient. To force him to reveal inner fears of a traumatic nature prematurely may cause him such panic that his resistance to further revelations will be increased. Actually, the patient has built up so hard a crust of repression that it keeps him from admitting his deepest fears even to himself. It is essential to let him feel his own way and choose his own pace with casual encouragement.

In continued discussions with the patient it may be emphasized that every individual has difficulties and problems of which he is ashamed, that the patient probably is no exception and may have had experiences that make him feel that he is wicked. Discussing the patient's problem in this roundabout way makes it possible for him to talk about his worries more openly. For instance, where it is obvious that the patient has a suppressed homosexual wish, the therapist may weave into the discussions the fact that every person, at certain times in life, develops friendships with and crushes on people of the same sex. This is by no means abnormal; it is merely a developmental phase in the life of the individual. Some persons, for certain reasons, continue to have ideas that were normal at an earlier phase of growth. As a matter of fact, most people have fears of homosexuality. The patient may be told that it would be unusual if he did not have such ideas at one time. He may then casually be asked whether or not this is so. In opening up discussions of this kind there are certain risks that must be countenanced. Sometimes patients prevent themselves from acting-out their desires by not thinking about or exposing them. Such persons may interpret the therapist's interest as condonation of their suppressed impulses, particularly where the therapist relieves them too freely of their guilt. Guilt, of course, is, not too trustworthy an opposing force, but it may be the only deterrent to rebellious tendencies that the patient has. An effort to supply the patient with rational deterrents should be made where his cravings may involve the patient in unforeseen dangers.

The ability of the patient to discuss his impulses, fears, and experiences openly, without encountering condemnation, enables him to tolerate the implications of the suppressed material.

In the event the patient confesses to a truly reprehensible incident in his life, the ventilation of these facts may have to be followed by active reassurance. He may be reminded that the incidents he has revealed do not necessarily pollute him, that many persons are compelled, for neurotic reasons, to do things that they regret later, and that their subsequent actions can fully neutralize what they have done. The patient may be urged to spend his energy doing something positive in the present rather than to wear himself out regretting the past. He may, if he desires, make some restitution to any person who has been injured by his act, or to society in general.

In cases where the individual has irrational feelings that issue out of his relationships with people or where he has phobias, he may be repeatedly urged, for purposes of desensitization, to expose himself to those situations that incite painful emotions. His experiences are then subjected to discussion, and the patient is trained to face those situations gradually, without quaking. For instance, if the patient has a fear of closed spaces, he may be instructed to lock the door of his room for a brief instance for the first day, to increase the interval to the count of 10 the next day, then to one-half minute, extending the time period daily, until he discovers through actual experience that he can tolerate the phobic situation. Other phobias may be treated in a similar way by varying the offered suggestions. The therapist must appreciate, of course, that the patient's fears may be rooted in deep unconscious conflicts and may not yield to such desensitization techniques until the sources of fear are uprooted through insight approaches. These tactics actually are reeducative and therefore will be discussed in the next chapter on Behavior Therapy.

MISCELLANEOUS
SUPPORTIVE MEASURES*

Relaxation exercises and massage may be prescribed for muscle tension, spasms, contractures, and tremors, the patient being

* See also Chapter 53, Adjunctive Aids in Psychotherapy.

referred to a physiotherapist when this is necessary. Enforced rest is sometimes advised for fatigue and exhaustion in the form of a prolonged vacation or a sojourn in a spa or country place. Subcoma insulin therapy is sometimes prescribed for unyielding anxiety states, delirium tremens, and confusional syndromes. Electrical (convulsive) therapy is helpful in manic-depressive psychosis, involutional depression, severe psychoneurotic depression, and senile depression. Drug therapy is employed where indicated; for example, sedatives and tranquilizers in excitement or insomnia, amphetamine and anti-depressants in depression or listlessness, antabuse in alcoholism, and glandular products in endocrine disorders. Brain surgery, such as transorbital lobotomy and leucotomy, is used as a last resort in severe, intractable schizophrenia, chronic disabling obsessive-compulsive neurosis, and hypochondriasis. These somatic therapies will be discussed later. Inspirational group therapy is a helpful procedure in certain problems, for instance, for dependent, characterologically immature, alcoholic, drug addictive, and mentally ill patients.

Supportive measures during reconstructive treatment must be employed cautiously because the patient may invest the therapist with directive, authoritarian qualities that interfere with a good working relationship. Moreover, alleviation of symptoms and suffering may remove a most important motivation for continued treatment in some patients.

There are, nevertheless, certain circumstances under which support is necessary. The challenging of one's defenses exposes basic conflicts and may revive the early anxieties that inspired them. A period of some instability and turmoil is to be expected with reconstructive procedures, and the therapist may, where the reactions are severe, temporarily have to assume the role of a helping authority.

The specific kinds of supportive measures implemented will vary according to the patient's needs. Where severe environmental disturbance exists, the therapist may suggest available resources that hold forth promise of mediation. The therapist may

also aid the patient in resolving resistances toward utilizing the prescribed resources effectively. Active reassurance may be dispensed where the patient harbors gross misconceptions or where there is a threat of a dangerous shattering of the ego. There may be a cautious extension of advice when the patient is thoughtlessly embarking on a potentially destructive course of action. Encouragement certainly may be voiced when the patient does a significant job in thinking through a problem or in effectuating insight into action.

The degree of emotional support employed will depend upon the strength of the patient's ego. A withholding of support by the therapist, when the patient actually needs it, may be harmful. On the other hand, excessive support may interfere with assertiveness and activity. The person's reactions to support will depend on its symbolic meaning to him. The most common response is an abatement of symptoms and a cessation of anxiety. Occasionally, however, anxiety breaks out due to fears of being overwhelmed and mutilated in a protective relationship. The emotion will have to be handled promptly, should it emerge.

REEDUCATIVE APPROACHES*

Reeducative measures are employed both as a complete goal-limited form of treatment and as interventions that are strategically incorporated into a reconstructive therapeutic program.

Current interest in cognitive therapy (Beck A, 1971, 1976) accents the value of certain reeducational techniques during psychotherapy. The individual's cognitive set often determines what he feels and how he interprets reality. Utilizing this paradigm, patients are enjoined to examine how their *interpretation* of an event determines their feelings and whether the interpretation is based on facts or insubstantialities. Sometimes patients are asked to keep a diary and

* See also Chapters 9, 49, and 53, Reeducative Therapy, Techniques in Behavior (Conditioning) Therapy, and Adjunctive Aids in Psychotherapy, respectively.

jot down the thoughts that immediately precede certain feelings. In this way they learn first to identify provocative thinking patterns that inspire upsetting feelings and then to challenge the validity of their ideas.

The value of examining the connection of events with succeeding disturbing emotions is shown by the pilot study of A. Beck and Kovacs (1977), in which depressed patients who were treated with cognitive therapy did better than those who were given antidepressant drugs. Some forms of cognitive therapy focus on the various ego states of the individual during his daily operations. There is exploration of the interfaces of these states, elaboration of the dissimilar roles assumed during these states, explication of the multiform self-representation and differentiations between self and object, and identification of the different values and needs emerging with each ego state. In this way the individual becomes aware of habitual shifts in his orientations, some of the forces producing the shifts, and perhaps tactics through which control may be achieved before his emotions take over. During therapy, an integration of dissociated self- and object representations is attempted, with the aim of bringing the patient's self-concepts to a more mature level. Sicker patients, such as those who are borderline cases and those who have narcissistic character disorders, are apt to show splitting and confusion of self–object identities. Here the patient may utilize the therapist as an aspect of himself during transference. This will call for therapeutic interventions, such as interpretations, that are more attuned to reconstructive than reeducative premises.

In some forms of reeducative therapy efforts are made to rehabilitate the individual as rapidly as possible by discovering and modifying factors that provoked the emotional illness and by surveying the available assets and liabilities in order to mobilize positive forces of the personality. In the medium of a warm relationship with the therapist, the patient is brought to an awareness of interpersonal conflicts that have contaminated his adjustment. Maladaptive attitudes are explored to point out to the patient the difficulties that they

create for him. The individual learns the reasons for their development in his past life and for their persistence in the present. Finally, he is helped to adjust with new, healthful, more adaptive patterns. In other forms of reeducative therapy, namely, behavior and conditioning therapies, there is a minimization of insight and a concentration on learning and reconditioning.

In reeducative therapy less weight is placed on exploring the origins of patterns, while more emphasis is put on reorganization of habits, regardless of their sources in constitution or in specific inimical experiences. During the process of retraining early difficulties that originally produced disturbing character traits may spontaneously be remembered by the patient. As part of his schooling, the patient must be taught to face early childhood experiences and, if necessary, to change attitudes toward them.

The patient is encouraged to rectify remediable environmental difficulties, to adjust to irremediable handicaps while finding adequate compensations and sublimations, to enhance personality resources through education and activity, to abandon unrealistic goals, and to coordinate ambitions with capacities. The therapist concentrates on all of the healthy personality elements, actual and potential, that can neutralize, control, or rectify pathologic adjustment.

In dealing with abnormal traits and patterns, the therapist may strive to bring the patient to where he can reason unemotionally, facing facts bravely, adjusting to painful memories and impulses without panic, meeting stresses of life with courage, and forsaking fantasy in thinking. Each trait that the patient exhibits may be taken up in detail, discussing its origin, purpose, value, and the ways it interferes with his happiness and adjustment. More adaptive substitive patterns may then be explored, and the patient may be urged to take positive courses of action.

A discussion of the patient's life history may reveal to the therapist that the patient has insight into his inordinate attachment to a domineering parent who continues to infantalize him. Evidences of how dependency undermines him are brought to his attention, and the patient may be shown how some of his symptoms are produced by his conflict over his dependent need. If the patient evidences a desire to overcome his dependency on his family, the wisdom of visiting his family at increasingly infrequent intervals, of making his own decisions, and of finding outlets for his energy and interests may be indicated. It is to be expected, because neurotic reaction patterns are so deeply imbedded, that this advice will not be heeded at first; but as the patient constantly experiences untoward emotions associated with the giving up of his independence, he may agree with the therapist's observations and gradually experiment with new modes of adjustment.

Where a patient is too compliant and recognizes his compliance, it may be pointed out that he has probably always felt the need to be overrespectful to authority. His security is perhaps bound up with this reaction. However, he has a right, as a human being, to his own opinions, and he need not accept the wishes or orders of other people unless he wants to do so. He can review in his mind the pros and cons of any advice given him, and he may then accept or reject it as he sees fit. If he does not wish to abide by the orders or judgments of other people, he can try to explain to them why his own plans seem best. Should he decide to conform with the wishes of others, he must be sure that this is what he really wants, and that it is not what he feels forced to want. Above all, he must be logical rather than emotional in his choices of action. Specific ideas on how to function independently may be advanced. The help of other people with whom the patient lives may be enlisted in this training process.

An individual who is aware of a power drive may be shown how this is a dominating force in his life, preoccupying his thoughts and actions. He may be partly aware of how he strives for power and strength in all of his interpersonal relationships. What he may not realize is how mercilessly his drive rules him and how it results in his forfeiting normal goals. The person may be alerted to how his power trend brings him into conflict with others and evokes retaliatory hostilities. It is necessary

to get the patient to see the need of adopting a more mature attitude and of readjusting his standards in line with the reality situation. Other outlets than power may then be suggested to satisfy the patient's drive for self-assertiveness and self-esteem.

The same technique may be used in dealing with other compulsive neurotic patterns, such as detachment, aggression, and perfectionism. Their manifestations are repeatedly brought to the patient's attention, and he is shown why they stir up difficulties for him. He is challenged in his assumption that they are the only ways of adjusting to life, and substitutive responses are suggested.

The patient may be acquainted with the ways in which his character drives operate insidiously. He may be shown that, unknown to himself, he lashes out at others, or vanquishes them in actual deeds or in fantasy, or renders himself invulnerable and strong, or retreats from competition, or engages in any number of facades that become for him basic goals in life, making average pursuits meaningless.

Such unhealthy attitudes perhaps might be understandable were we to insist on what is probably not true—that the patient really is an inferior person who has to eliminate adult and realistic methods of dealing with his problems. The patient must be shown the need to stop taking refuge in childhood defenses, and he must be apprised of the wisdom of facing his difficulties with decision and courage. However, because he has utilized his defenses for so many years, he must understand that they will not vanish immediately. Indeed, they will keep cropping up from time to time. If they do, there is no need for discouragement. When he becomes sufficiently strong, his defenses will no longer be required. Yet, he must not abandon his patterns out of a sole conviction that they are wrong or out of a desire to please the therapist. Rather, as he realizes the implications of his neurotic drives, he will want to substitute creative goals and patterns for those that have resulted in his present unhappiness.

The therapist should, in this way, actively encourage a conscious analysis by the patient of his customary trends as well as stimulate him to substitute new ways of thinking and acting. If the old patterns reappear, it may be necessary for the patient to try to bring them to as complete a halt as possible by deliberate effort. The patient should be encouraged to feel that he has the capacity to change, that others sicker than himself have done so successfully.

Usually the patient will be dismayed to find that his character patterns are regarded as problems because he has accepted them as natural and normal. As he realizes that they constantly bring him into difficulties with people and are responsible for much of his turmoil, he is supplied with a valid motivation to alter his scheme of life. He is confronted with a choice for which he, himself, will have to assume a measure of responsibility.

Many persons faced with this choice are unwilling or unable to give up their destructive drives. The knowledge that frustration or pain will follow observance of their patterns is not enough to make them give up the gratifications that accrue from the propitiation of neurotic goals. An extreme example of this is the alcoholic who appreciates the physical, social, and moral hardships that inevitably follow his bouts of drinking but seems unable to do anything about it. In cases where the patient refuses to abandon his immature objectives, the knowledge that he is responsible for his own plight is healthier, from a therapeutic viewpoint, than the conviction that may have existed previously, to the effect that the sources of his misery lay outside of himself.

Where the person is convinced that his adjustment is eminently unsatisfactory, where he realizes that his gratification does not compensate for the suffering that comes from indulgence of his immature drives, where he is aware of how his patterns interfere with biologic and social goals, he will be motivated toward experimenting with new reactions toward people.

Once patterns that are inimical to adjustment are clearly defined and more adaptive substitutive reactions are suggested, a long period of experiment and training is necessary before unhealthy attitudes are replaced by those of a more mature nature. Even where the patient has the motiva-

tion to change, a struggle will be necessary to achieve reeducative effects. In spite of all good resolutions, the patient, at first, will find himself responding automatically, in line with his customary habits. He will, however, become more and more conscious of his reactions, and, as they occur, he will better be able to subject them to analysis and control. Even though this may fail to stop him from following his usual patterns, he will become more and more aware of their irrational nature, and he will have a greater determination to substitute for them constructive behavior tendencies.

For instance, a perfectionistic person may become conscious of the fact that his impulse to do everything meticulously extends itself into every aspect of his life and poisons his relationships with people. He will see, as the therapist brings it to his attention, that the slightest failure to perform flawlessly suffices to create tension and panic. He may learn that the reason for his disturbance lies in the fact that when he is not perfect, his image of himself is shattered and he feels unloved and unlovable. Life then becomes a constant series of frustrations, since it is obviously impossible to do things perfectly every minute of the day and still be human. The patient will, as he becomes aware of his inordinate expectations, find himself toying with the philosophy of self-tolerance, which he will not wish to accept at first, probably because being mediocre is equivalent to being no good at all, and because he is unconvinced that perfectionism is not really the keynote of life. As he tests the truth of the therapist's exhortations and as he realizes the extent to which his perfectionistic strivings dominate him, he may attempt to restrain himself before yielding to perfectionistic impulses. He will review in his mind the reasons why he must be perfect on every occasion. He may eventually even try to substitute for this impulse the attitude that he can do things without needing to be perfect.

In these ways the individual eventually undergoes reeducation of his attitudes, values, and customary modes of dealing with people, which encourage the various neurotic symptoms for which he seeks relief.

49
Techniques in Behavior (Conditioning) Therapy

The Freudian economic concept of the personality as a closed energy system sponsored the idea that libido removed from one area must be relocated and that energy released by symptom removal must inevitably wreak its mischief elsewhere. The removal of symptoms, therefore, was considered irrational and the rewards dubious since energy soon displaced itself in other and perhaps more serious symptoms. No myth has survived as tenaciously as has this concept, which continues to be promulgated as dogma despite the fact that in practice symptoms are constantly being lifted with beneficial rather than destructive results.

In its early days behavior therapy was viewed by some clinicians as a viable and powerful means of bringing about symptom relief and removal. The assumption was that, even when effective, the net outcome would be primarily of an adjunctive or patching-up nature that had to be supplemented by more depth-directed, non-behavioral approaches geared toward the total personality. Contemporary behavior therapy, however, is multidimensional and aims, in systematic fashion, at the modification of every relevant facet of the personality. This will include both maladaptive be-

havioral excesses (e.g., tics) and/or deficits (e.g., lack of assertion). It will embrace affective and cognitive modes of functioning; it will stress control from within (self control) rather than control from without. It will take the form of a collaborative project with the patient rather than a laissez faire, "leave it to the patient to decide or not to decide," direction, on the one hand, or authoritarian direction, on the other.

Behavior therapy is rooted in concepts derived from conditioning and learning theory (Hilgard, 1956; Kimble, 1961) particularly from formulations of Pavlov, Skinner, and Hull. It is based on the hypothesis that since neurosis is a product of learning, "its elimination will be a matter of unlearning" (Wolpe, 1958). It embraces a wide and seemingly disparate array of procedures, all of which share certain common attributes: an unswerving allegiance to data and the methodology of the behavioral scientist, a rejection of metaphysical concepts and mentalistic processes, and predilection for what is now known as social learning theory (Wolpe & Lazarus, 1966; Bandura, 1969; Wolpe, 1971; Birk et al, 1973; O'Leary & Wilson, 1975). These techniques may be directly physiological or narrowly S-R (stimulus-response) in nature (e.g., aversive conditioning), highly imaginal (e.g., real-life–graded desensitization of an elevator phobia), stimulus specific (e.g., thought stoppage), stimulus situation complex (e.g., assertion training, behavioral rehearsal), of a contractual nature (e.g., contingency contracting), directly cognitive (e.g., cognitive behavior therapy, rational emotive therapy) conducted with the individual or in groups, or utilizing complex interpersonal interactions as in group behavior therapy (not to be confused with behavior therapy in groups), etc., etc. Affects, cognitions, and behavior will all come within the purview of the behavior therapist of the seventies (as contrasted with the behavior therapist of a decade ago) as indicated by the outcome of his or her carefully engineered behavioral analysis of the total situation. As more therapists apply themselves to this area of treatment, they introduce their own original procedures and unique interpretations regarding operative learning mechanisms. The rapid growth of behavior therapy and the introduction into its orbit of a profusion of techniques has led to some confusion, although attempts are being made to establish a methodical way of looking at the different approaches (Kanfer & Phillips, 1966).

The practice of behavior modification is most expediently executed where the therapist and patient both agree on the behaviors to be altered or required, on immediate and ultimate goals, and on the methods to be employed to achieve these objectives. Where the patient is unable to make adequate decisions, these determinations are sometimes made with a relative or other representative, who is kept informed about progress and changes in goals or methods. An assessment of the problem initially includes the history of the behavioral difficulty, the circumstances under which it now appears, its frequency, and the consequences following its occurrence. A careful record of the frequency of the distortion is generally kept during therapy by the patient or a member of his family. A search for overt or hidden reinforcements that maintain the noxious behavior is also pursued. The formulation of the treatment plan will depend on many factors, including the type of symptom, the forces that bring it about

and maintain it, and the kind of environment in which the patient functions, including the influence of individuals with whom he is living.

The two chief avenues to behavioral therapy are through classical (respondent) and operant (instrumental) conditioning.*

SYSTEMATIC DESENSITIZATION

Techniques organized around classical conditioning are tailored for anxiety situations such as phobias, the product of unfortunate associations that continue to burden the individual without too much secondary gain or other subversive benefits. Therapy consists of a progressive desensitization to the anxiety situation, either by a slow exposure to gradually increasing increments of the anxiety stimulus, under as pleasurable or otherwise rewarding circumstances as possible, or by a mastery of fantasies of such stimuli in ever increasing intensity in the presence of an induced state of inner relaxation. Even where the anxiety situation is highly symbolized—for instance, phobic projection, which nonbehavioral therapists view as a product of deep inner conflict—it may be possible to overcome the symptom without the formality of insight. However, an understanding of the sources of the problem may be helpful in avoiding a relapse by dealing correctively with some of the core problems that initiate the anxiety. This, too, would be taken into account by modern behavior therapists in their treatment strategy without recourse to concepts such as the unconscious or the achievement of "insight." On the other hand, insight alone, without reconditioning, may leave the symptom unrelieved. An understanding and use of behavioral approaches can be helpful even to the practitioner who aims at personality reconstruction. These techniques may be especially valuable during phases of treatment where the patient offers severe resistances to the execution of insight into action.

While increasingly deemphasized in the armamentarium of the behavior therapist, perhaps the best known ap-

* See also pages 102–117.

proach, and the easiest one to learn, is that of desensitization. In desensitization methods anxiety-provoking cues are presented in a positive or pleasurable climate. These cues must be graduated so that the responses that they evoke are always of lesser intensity than the positive feelings that coexist. In this way the aversive stimuli are gradually mastered in progressively stronger form. The method is most readily applicable to anxiety that is set loose by environmental cues. In the arrangement of stimulus hierarchies both environmental and response-produced cues are listed to encompass as many complex aversive social stimuli as possible. The most common positive anxiety-reversing stimulus, jointly presented with and calculated to neutralize and eventually extinguish the aversive stimuli, is muscular relaxation, often induced by hypnosis.

To his use of this technique Wolpe (1958) has given the name "reciprocal inhibition." Treatment is initiated by the construction of an "anxiety hierarchy." The patient is given the task to prepare a list of stimuli to which he reacts with unadaptive anxiety. The items are ranked in accordance with the intensity of anxiety that they induce. The least anxiety-provoking stimulus is placed at the bottom. The most disturbing stimulus is put at the top. The remainder are placed in accordance with their anxiety-arousing potential. The patient is then hypnotized and relaxed as deeply as is possible. In the trance it is suggested that he will imagine the weakest item in the anxiety hierarchy. If he is capable of doing this without disturbing his relaxation, the next item on the list is presented at the following session. With each successive session the succeeding intense anxiety stimulus is employed during relaxation until "at last the phobic stimulus can be presented at maximum intensity without impairing the calm relaxed state." At this point the patient will presumably have ceased to react with his previous anxiety, to be able to face in real life "even the strongest of the once phobic stimuli."

Wolpe denies that his therapy is useful only in simple phobias. He believes that even difficult "character neurosis" can be treated, since they consist of intricate systems of phobias that have been organized in complex units. "This," he says, "is not remarkable, if as will be contended, most neuroses are basically unadaptive conditioned anxiety reactions." Wolpe insists that in contrast to measures of success by all methods of therapy, ranging from traditional counseling to psychoanalysis, of a recorded 50 percent, his special method brings about an "apparently cured" and "much improved" rate of over 90 percent. It is important, however, to stress, as do sophisticated behavior therapists, that the presenting complaint is not necessarily either the one that requires desensitization or, if it is, that it may not be the one that should be given sole, or even primary, attention. For example, to desensitize an attorney to a fear of public speaking (the presenting complaint) may be of far less significance than desensitization to the fear of losing face should the attorney not win the case. Which desensitization strategy to employ, or whether to employ desensitization at all, or what other necessary behavioral techniques to employ in the restructuring of this particular individual's life can only be determined by a detailed and comprehensive behavioral analysis of the total life style of that individual and the relevant contingencies operating in his life and the lives of meaningful others.

Attempts to standardize Wolpe's procedure have been made by Lazovik and Lang (1960). The pretraining procedure of five sessions includes the construction of an anxiety hierarchy (a series including the phobic object, graded from most to least frightening). Training in deep muscle relaxation after the method of Jacobson (1938) is followed by training in hypnosis, efforts being made to get the patient to learn to visualize hypnotic scenes vividly. Eleven sessions of systematic desensitization follow the pretraining period. During these the patient is instructed to relax deeply, and items on the anxiety hierarchy are presented as scenes that are to be visualized clearly. The least frightening scene is presented first. When this is experienced for about 3 to 10 seconds without anxiety, the next item in the hierarchy is introduced. All scenes are presented at least twice. If any of the scenes make the patient anxious or apprehensive, he is instructed to raise his left hand a few inches. Should this happen, the scene is immediately discontinued and not repeated until the next session; rather, the last successfully completed item of the hierarchy is presented. From two to four scenes are attempted during each session of 45 minutes. The authors confirm Wolpe's method as remarkably effective for treating cases of phobia and insist that there is no substitution of other fears. This has also been my personal experience.

Edward Dengrove has prepared a leaflet for "fearful" patients that introduces them to the technique of systematic desensitization:*

The type of treatment that is being offered to you is known as systematic desensitization. It is based upon scientific studies of conditioned reflexes and is particularly helpful to persons who are fearful. It makes little difference what these fears are: whether of closed places, or being alone, walking alone, driving or flying; or whether one fears loss of self-control, criticism by others, and the like.

Kindly list *all* of the fears that disturb you. Make the list as complete as possible. We will go over the list together and reduce it to its basic units. Treatment will be directed to each individual fear.

The next step will be to teach you how to relax. There are several methods by which this may be accomplished. The particular method that suits your needs will be chosen. This is very important, for the more relaxed you are, the more rapid your progress to health. You cannot be relaxed and remain anxious or fearful at the same time.

When you are completely relaxed— not partially, but completely—I shall present to your visual imagination a series of situations. These will be based upon your presenting fears. They will be

organized in series, graded from the most mild to the most intense. Each forms a hierarchy.

As you visualize each scene in the relaxed state, you may find yourself unmoved by what you see. Or you may experience an uneasiness or restlessness (anxiety). This is a critical point in treatment, and must be signalled to me. No matter how slight, I must be made aware of it.

I may ask, "Do you feel relaxed? Do you feel at ease?" If you do, then move your head up and down ever so slightly. If you do not, move it from side to side.

This is a critical point, for we can only proceed as fast as you are able to accept these visualized situations with ease. I shall not push or prod you. It is only by the ability to maintain your relaxed state that you are able to overcome these fears.

The desensitization takes place gradually by getting you to cope with small doses of anxiety at first, then gradually increasing the dosage a small amount at a time.

With children, desensitization is done in a less subtle manner. Consider a child who is afraid of dogs. The child is held by a trusted person who allows him to suck on a lollipop and point to a dog on a leash in the distance. A little later, the child, still held, is encouraged to view a dog through a pet-shop window. Still later, he is brought closer to a dog; and later, closer still. With the pleasure of the food and security of being held by a trusted person, the child gradually overcomes his fear. At first there are pictures of dogs, then toy dogs, small, friendly dogs, medium-sized dogs, and so forth. At last, he will be able to reach out and touch a dog.

This gives you a clue to a second part of treatment. You are to do the very things that you fear. One cannot overcome a fear by avoiding it, as you have done in the past, nor by trying to drown it out with continued medication. Medicine is helpful, but only a crutch, to be reduced and gradually thrown away.

The same principles of gradual desen-

* Reprinted with the permission of Dr. Dengrove.

sitization must be employed. You are not to attempt any activity that produces overwhelming anxiety. However, you can and should try those tasks that are only mildly upsetting, at the same time attempting to quiet yourself. If the anxiety persists, stop what you are doing, for this will only set you back. Instead, return to doing those things that you can do without getting upset.

With this approach you will find yourself gradually doing more of these tasks that you avoided in the past. One can get used to almost any new situation that is approached gradually.

Interestingly, as the milder fears are overcome, the more strong ones lose their intensity and lessen, much as the contents of a gum machine diminish with the discharge of each piece of gum. The more one attempts with relaxation, the more rapid the improvement. But one must keep in mind that these attempts deal only with those productive of mild anxiety.

A warning: everyone must proceed at his or her own pace. Some slowly, others more rapidly. There is no reason to feel guilt or shame if one's progress is slow. The process of desensitization cannot be hurried by rushing into highly anxious situations. You will not be thrown into the water and made to swim or sink on your own. At times, under the pressure of need or anger, a few of you will make large strides but this is the exception to the rule.

Consider the woman who is afraid to leave her home. Her first move is to step outside her front door and back again into the house. From there she gradually makes it to the street in front of her home, then around the house—by herself or with someone or while someone trusted is in the house. Each day this is extended until she is able to walk a house away, then two houses, then half-a-block; with someone, without someone, with someone at home, with no one there. Again, no new step is made until the previous step is mastered, and until it can be accomplished without any anxiety whatsoever. Each

fear is attacked individually, daily or as frequently as this can be done.

Gradually you find yourself doing things without thinking about them. Sometimes it will be only after you have done something that you realize you have done it without forethought or anxiety. It may be that someone else will point out to you that you have done something you would not have attempted in the past.

A cooperative spouse is not only helpful and understanding but an essential part of this approach. He or she can be tremendously important to this undertaking. Marital problems tend to hold back progress and should be resolved.

It is by doing what we do in the office, and what you do for yourself away from the office, that will lead you to health. One or other of these techniques may be used alone, but when both are employed, progress is so much faster.

Systematic desensitization is sometimes expedited by the use of drugs, like Brevital, 1 percent solution, in small doses (Brady, 1966; Friedman & Silverstone, 1967). Slow intravenous injections to produce relaxation without drowsiness are particularly valuable for patients who are unable to relax or who are extraordinary anxious. Pentothal (2 percent solution) is preferred by some therapists to Brevital.

OPERANT CONDITIONING

Techniques of operant (instrumental) conditioning, in which the subject is active in bringing about a situation toward achieving reward or avoiding punishment, supplement classical Pavlovian conditioning procedures (Krasner, L, 1971). Essentially, these techniques consist of reinforcements in the form of rewards or the withdrawal of an aversive (punishing) stimulus or event when the subject executes a desired act. The subject is free to respond or not to respond instead of, as in classical conditioning, being passively subjected to events over which he has no control. The techniques are designed to strengthen existing constructive responses and to initiate new ones.

Operant approaches depend on the fact that human beings like other animals are influenced toward specific kinds of behavior by the reinforcers they receive for this behavior. Where a desired behavior is sought, the patient must first be helped to accept the desirability of this behavior in terms of the rewards that will accrue from it. Many patients are confused regarding appropriate courses of action. The therapist's positive attention and approval following a remark that indicates a willingness to try a tactic, or the execution of the desired behavior itself, or approximations of this behavior may be reinforced through nodding, utterances of approval, or paying rapt attention to these desirable responses. On the other hand, when the patient repeats a pathological pattern or verbally indicates nonproductive choices, the therapist may act disinterested and fail to respond to this behavior.

Operant conditioning works best in an environment that can be controlled. It is indicated in nonmotivated patients in institutions whose behavior must be modified to enable them to adjust more appropriately. The "token economy" of Ayllon and Azrin (1968), established in a state institution, illustrates an imaginative use of substitutive reinforcers. Since the desired reinforcers (ground passes, TV, cigarettes, canteen purchases, trips to town, and ordering items from a mail order catalogue) would not in all cases be immediately produced, tokens to exchange for these when available were found to be effective. Tokens were earned for better self-care and for work on and off the ward. The results in terms of morale and behavioral improvement, which in some cases led to recovery, were astonishing.

Bachrach provides an example of anorexia nervosa treated by operant-conditioning techniques. Considering etiology, explained by such concepts as "fear of oral impregnation" as unfounded, and without regard for the initiating source, he simply increased the response of frequency of food intake; consequently, the amount of food consumed was increased. Since food obviously did not have its expected rein-

forcing characteristics, a study was made of the stimuli that could act as reinforcers. Because the subject enjoyed visits from people, music, reading and television, she was at first deprived of these by being put in a barren room. Being visited by people, listening to records, seeing television, or reading books were made contingent upon eating and weight gain. In a little over a year of such operant conditioning, she doubled her weight.

Ayllon and Michael (1959) describe an experiment in operant-conditioning therapy done on the ward of a mental hospital by the nursing staff working under the supervision of a clinical psychologist. The patient load consisted of 14 schizophrenics and 5 mentally defective patients. The kind of disturbing behavior (psychotic talk, acts, etc.) in each patient was recorded along with the nature and frequency of the naturally occurring reinforcements (giving the patient attention, social approval, candy, cigarettes). Then the nurses were instructed to observe the patients for about 1 to 3 minutes at regular intervals, to give them reinforcements only during desirable behavior, and to ignore undesirable behavior. Nonsocial behavior was to be reinforced temporarily if it replaced violent behavior. For instance, two patients who refused to eat unless spoon fed had a penchant for neat and meticulous appearance of their clothing. The nurses were instructed to spill food on their clothing during periods when they resisted feeding and to present social reinforcements when the patients fed themselves. The patients soon spontaneously began to reach for their spoons and eventually were feeding themselves. In a group of mentally defective patients who were collecting papers, rubbish, and magazines in their clothing next to their skin, the nurses were instructed not to pay attention (i.e., not to reinforce) this behavior, while flooding the ward with magazines to overcome the shortage. The hoarding tendency was overcome.

In the experimental control of behavior the specification of the response may be simple to describe, but the identification of the stimulus that brings on the response may be obscure. Hence, one must work toward the desired response employing appropriate scheduled reinforcements in terms of what the subject considers to be significant rewards. At first, the most that can be expected are approximations of the final response. Reinforcement is restricted progressively to responses that are closer and closer to the end response. In this way behavior is "shaped." Complex behavior patterns may be evolved by developing a series of coordinated responses, linking them together like a chain. Thus, employing food as the reinforcing stimulus, Ayllon and Michael (1959, 1964), as described above, brought chronic schizophrenics out of their disturbed behavior and psychotic isolation. Lindsley (1960) has also written about the operant conditioning of severely sick patients, and N. Ellis and his colleagues (1960) have had some interesting experience in retraining disturbed mental defectives.

Operant conditioning is suited for the removal of habits and patterns that serve a neurotic function from which the person derives some immediate benefit (such as delinquent behavior, temper tantrums, etc.) at the expense of his total adjustment. It is also helpful in developing new constructive patterns that are not in the individual's current repertoire. In the main, the treatment procedure consists of an identification of the untoward patterns and a careful delineation of the stimuli that bring them about. Next, the nature of the reinforcements to be employed are determined (attention, food, bribes, etc.) as well as the nature of any aversive stimuli that may help to interrupt the pattern to be corrected. In general, reinforcements are withheld (or aversive stimuli applied) when the behavior to be corrected is manifested, but reinforcements are given (or aversive stimuli removed) when substitutive and more adaptive behavior is displayed. In this way the individual is helped to develop more frustration tolerance and to control his untoward behavior in favor of acts for which rewards are forthcoming.

Ferster (1964), in an article that details the tactics of operant conditioning, describes the treatment of autistic children. As is known, tantrums and destructive behavior in the autistic child are usually reinforced by the persons with whom the child is in contact by their yielding to the child and satisfying his whims. Thus, a child may have learned that he can get candy if he screams loud enough or bangs his head on the floor. Much of the child's behavior is operant, being contingent on reactions from the social environment. Ferster found that food was the most effective reinforcing agent. The sound of the candy dispenser prior to the release of candy acted as a secondary reinforcer. With some training, coins became the conditioned reinforcer, the coins operating devices within the room that could deliver the candy reward. Later, the coins were to be held for a period prior to their use before the reward was allotted. Then five coins were to be accumulated. Delays were increased by introducing a towel or life jacket that later could be used in swimming or water play (another reinforcer) following the experimental session. While the repertory of the autistic child was limited, it was possible for the child to develop some frustration tolerance and controls.

Next, Ferster examined the circumstances in the early life of the child that originally had brought about, and still could bring about, behavioral disorders. The parental environment was also put under surveillance to see what factors weakened the child's performance, the resultant behavior, and the effect of this behavior on the people surrounding the child. This was done to determine what reinforcements were operating and the possible ways of discouraging such reinforcements. It is likely that the atavistic and uncontrollable behavior of the autistic child starts with the reinforcement of small magnitudes of behavior such as whining. A shaping into violent responses occurs by differential reinforcement. By refusing to provide reinforcements of his behavior, we may expect the child gradually to abandon the behavior (extinction). Changing the environment gradually may be helpful in this respect, since the habitual reinforcing agencies on whom and which the child depends are no longer present. By withholding positive reinforcements and rewarding conduct that slowly approximates adaptive behavior, it may be possible to effectuate behavioral change not only in psychotic children but also in psychotic adults without using aversive stimuli.

The techniques of operant conditioning are particularly suited for patients who are not accessible for traditional interviewing techniques, for example, delinquents, psychopaths, drug addicts, psychotics, and mental defectives. The results may be rewarding where the reinforcements stem from remediable environmental sources, such as reasonable and relatively nonneurotic individuals with whom the patient is in contact. The results are not so good where the agencies, such as parents, participate in the family neurosis and support the patient's acting-out as a way of satisfying their own needs. It is indeed difficult to prevent reinforcement of the patient's untoward behavior in many families since the reinforcing drives are usually in the unconscious of the parents and are subject to their conscious denial. Such parents become frustrated when the patient begins to get better. Subtly the patient may be maneuvered back to his old way of behavior with restoration of the defensive protesting of the parent.

Where the reinforcements are of an inner, perhaps unconscious nature, such as sexual excitation and a masochistic desire for punishment, operant conditioning may be of little use. For example, where shoplifting in a well-to-do matron occurs against all reason, it is difficult to find external reinforcements to put this compulsive behavior to a halt.

In intelligent patients, however, a recognition of some of their unconscious motivations may enable them to execute the principles of operant conditioning for themselves. An executive in a large business firm, presumably happily married and adjusted, periodically would involve himself with prostitutes, whom he enjoined to strap him down to a bed and beat him unmercifully. Struggling to escape from this humiliation, he responded with a strong orgasm. After this experience his shame and guilt feelings, as well as his fears of being discovered, overwhelmed him to the point of depression and suicidal impulses. Although he pursued every device at his command, including exercise, prayer, and involvement in charitable activities to counteract his de-

sire, his intervals of abstinence from flagellant impulses would, without reason, be interrupted and he would go forth again toward another beating orgy.

In studying this case it was determined that what particularly delighted this man was sailing in Long Island Sound, where he had a boat. This, it was felt, could be employed as a reinforcement for the ability to control his masochism. It was first necessary, however, to add to the leverage of his will power some understanding of the meaning of his peculiar deviation. This, it was determined from dreams and free associations, related particularly to spankings from his mother during his childhood when he masturbated or was otherwise "bad." A fusion of orgiastic feelings with punishment apparently was the conditioning underlying his symptom. The origins of this affiliation were repressed and could only be restored through analytic techniques. This provided him with a new motivation to decondition himself. A plan was organized so that sailing was to be indulged only in the intervals of control. If a relapse occurred and he acted out his masochism, sailing was to be avoided for a month thereafter. If the impulse appeared and he could control it, he was rewarded by taking a short sea voyage (which he enjoyed as much as sailing) to Bermuda. During the winter, if he had been able to vanquish his symptom, he was to take a sailing vacation in southern waters. Within a year of this regime the patient's symptom was arrested, and whenever the desire returned minimally, he was able to overcome it by reviewing the history of the original development of the symptom. Coordinate with symptom improvement was a better personal and sexual relationship with his wife.

The problem in utilizing operant conditioning as an adjunctive technique consists in finding external reinforcements that are sufficiently interesting and important for the patient to induce him to challenge patterns that have open and subversive values for him. However, if the therapist reviews areas of interest with a patient who is willing to cooperate, a sufficiently provocative reward or diversion that will help incite the patient to change may be uncovered.

The schedules of reinforcement may preferably be arranged at varying intervals and at unpredictable times. This is to produce an anticipatory set and to help prevent the extinguishing of a response that may come about if the patient expected reinforcement uniformly as a consequence of a new behavior. It may so happen that circumstances make it impossible to reward new behaviors each time. If the patient does not envision fulfillment without fail, he will not be too disappointed and angry when reinforcements do not appear. Rather, he will anticipate their arrival at some point.

Other conditioning techniques have been employed. For instance, Efron (1964) helped a patient stop uncinate seizures by inhaling from a vial odors of various aromatic chemicals (these had been proven effective in controlling the seizures) that were conditioned to a nonspecific visual stimulus, namely an inexpensive silvered bracelet. This was done by presenting simultaneously every 15 minutes, for a period of 8 days, the concentrated odor of essence of jasmine and the bracelet. The instructions were to stare intently for 15 to 30 seconds at the bracelet while sniffing a vial of jasmine. Except for 7 hours of sleep at night, the conditioning continued during the rest of the 17-hour period. At the end of 8 days of conditioning, the bracelet alone presented to the patient produced the experience of odor of jasmine, which receded in a few seconds when the bracelet was removed from the patient's sight. The patient was exposed to reinforcements twice a day for the next week. A spontaneous seizure developing during the second week was stopped by the patient's merely staring at the bracelet for a few seconds. Thereafter the bracelet continued without fail to arrest seizures.

An excellent account of conditioning techniques toward painless childbirth is given by Bonstein (1958). Contained in the article are general suggestions for pain control.

Conditioning techniques have been utilized as diagnostic aids. Gantt (1964), employing the methods of Krasnogorsky and of Ivanov-Smolensky, has described a method for the study of motor conditional reflexes that can be applied to psychiatric diagnosis. Through the use of his technique he claims to be able to distinguish psychogenic from organic psychoses. This is because in psychogenic problems the patient inhibits the expression of the elaborated conditional reflex, while in organic psychoses he fails absolutely in the function of forming new adaptive responses. L. Alexander (1964), employing a conditional psychogalvanic reflex technique, has developed a test for the differentiation of physical from psychogenic pain. Ban and Levy (1964) describe a diagnostic test based on conditioned-reflex therapy that measures evidence of change in patients exposed to any treatment regime. Conditioned-reflex techniques can also be employed to investigate the effectiveness of drugs in psychiatry (Alexander, 1964). How conditioning may enter into the genesis of attacks of asthma is discussed by Dekker, Pelser, and Groen (1965).

PUNISHMENT AND DEPRIVATION

Punishment rarely works as a means of halting undesirable behavior. It is usually temporary in its effect and likely to exaggerate rather than solve problems. Getting the individual to stop hurtful activities because he gets adequate rewards in exchange is much more effective. The patient may not be able to anticipate the rewards that accrue from constructive behavior until he has yielded his destructive activities, and it will be necessary for the therapist to provide interim reinforcements.

A child who consistently misbehaves, who refuses to eat, sleep, or give up childish habits like thumb-sucking and bedwetting will frustrate the parents and provoke angry responses. The parent will be tempted to punish the child for his refusal to cooperate. This may do little other than to mobilize the child's guilt feelings and lead to self-punitive activities (masochism) or to stimulate retaliating anger and defiance. Logic has little to do with these reactions. Or the parent may be tempted to remove certain privileges, such as taking away something that the child enjoys (e.g., allowance, desserts, or TV viewing). The consequences of such deprivation are usually the same as punishment. Yet punishment and deprivation may rarely be an expedient in temporarily stopping destructive behavior that the child refuses to halt. For instance, of his own accord, an older child who is mercilessly beating a younger sibling may be forcefully required to retire to his room until he feels he can control himself. But the expedient of punishment or deprivation must be used only in emergencies to put a stop to immediate destructive outbursts that do not yield to reason, verbal reprimand, or the ignoring of the behavior. In any event, the punishment or deprivation should be reasonable and never so drastic as to leave an enduring residue of anger and desire for revenge.

Far more effective are actions that tend to *extinguish* improper behavior. This may require little more than refusal to reinforce the behavior by paying too much attention to it or being ostensibly provoked by it. Thus, a parent may interrupt an undesirable activity by diverting a child's attention and substituting another activity for the disturbing one. Reinforcing the substitute activity by providing a proper reward for its indulgence will help extinguish the unwanted activity.

AVERSIVE CONTROL

There are times when all methods employed to halt disturbing behavior, particularly those that are life threatening or destructive, may fail, and the therapist may, with the consent and cooperation of the patient, have to resort to measures of blocking the behavior by associating it with unpleasant stimuli (Rachman & Teasdale, 1969; Lovibond, 1970).

Aversive conditioning is sometimes employed to overcome certain undesirable behavioral components. Emetic drugs (apomorphine or emetine hydrochloride) were used for years in the treatment of alcoholism by conditioning methods. E. C. Miller, Dvorak, and Turner (1964) have described a technique of establishing aversion to alcohol through the employment of emetics in a group setting. A unique form of aversive stimulus—paralysis and suppression of respiration through intravenous injection of succinylcholine-chloride dihydrate—has been reported by Sanderson et al. (1964). In addition to drugs, electric shock has been employed as an aversive stimulus for a variety of syndromes (McGuire & Vallance, 1964). Needless to say, unless one has an excellent working relationship with a patient, aversive conditioning poses some risk and may play into a patient's masochistic need. And, as noted in the preceding section, punitive conditioning is never employed in isolation by the modern behavior therapist; nowhere is this more evident than in the behavioral treatment of the alcoholic (Franks & Wilson, 1975).

In certain cases self-induced aversive conditioning may be helpful in controlling violently upsetting thoughts or impulses, such as occur in compulsive-obsessive reactions. The patient is supplied with a toy "shocking machine." This may be purchased in a store that sells "tricks" for the practical joker. It consists of a simulated book with a spicy title or a pack of cards, which, when opened, delivers a shock from a battery within. The shock (buzz) is harmless, yet annoying and even frightening. The patient, with the contraption in his hands, is requested to shut his eyes and then bring his offensive thoughts to his mind. As soon as they appear, he is to open the book or cards and keep it open until the thoughts completely disappear. After six to ten trials patients are usually surprised to find themselves unable to bring obsessive ideas to their minds, even when they try to force themselves to do so. The patient may be asked to practice this "exercise in thought control" two times daily, with as many trials as are necessary to eliminate the obsessions or impulses, even when the patient tries to bring them on. Aversive conditioning may give the patient confidence in his ability to occupy himself with useful rather than self-destructive concerns. Carrying the device in his pocket may become a conditioned reassuring stimulus even though it is not used. Should the patient complain that the shock is too strong, he may reduce its intensity by interposing a piece of facial tissue between his fingers and the box.

Hypnosis may be induced, if desired, and the aversive conditioning employed in the trance state.

HUMAN AVOIDANCE OR AVERSIVE CONDITIONING (HOMEWORK)*

You can help yourself to get rid of undesirable, torturesome thoughts and habits after you and the doctor or his associates have agreed that these thoughts or habits are damaging to you. Repeated practice is necessary for most people at least one or more times per day in the beginning and then at gradually decreasing intervals until the thought or habit is gone. The doctor or his associates may help prescribe the intervals and amount of time most helpful to you as well as other helpful ideas.

I. Repetitive, self-damaging thoughts (thought-stopping)**
a. Close your eyes, hypnotize, or relax yourself and force the repetitive thought or the picture of the undesirable habit to be visualized in your mind for at least 2–3 seconds.
b. Almost immediately, shout STOP or if this is not possible, think STOP or if this is not possible, think STOP emphatically and promptly give yourself an unpleasant buzz with the buzzer at the same moment. Holding your breath can be used with the buzzer, or something unobtrusive for you, e.g., a clenched fist can be used at the same time in place of "STOP." (It is important that during the pleasant and restful time after you have stopped the shock, visualize a successful, positive, helpful image or valuable substitute activity.) As soon as these secondary

A typewritten form such as the following may be given to the patient so that he may practice at home:

things (breath holding, fist, etc.) work, use buzzer less and less frequently.

Repeat this entire procedure at the same sitting until you can no longer get the thought at that time or until at least 20 satisfactory repetitions have occurred. The entire procedure is to be repeated up to six times per day for 1 to 15 weeks. This will be prescribed in accordance with the severity of your problem and the length of time you have had it. Make a note each day on the back of an appointment card or some other record such as a homework sheet of how frequently and for what number of repetitions you have been using the buzzer, or the word STOP, breath holding, fist, etc. A list of possible pleasant thoughts, activities, assets should be available.

II. Modification

In addition, you can carry the buzzer, or special pen if you prefer, with you and use it whenever you find yourself thinking repetitively or continuing your undesirable habit. If circumstances are such that it is impossible for you to use the buzzer during the larger part of the day, think the word STOP, etc. and imagine the uncomfortable buzz when you find yourself going back to the thought or habit. This will gradually become more successful after actual practice when practice is possible. Unless good success is being maintained with the STOP, breath holding, or other simultaneous gesture, and the pleasant thought or activity substitution, report to doctor.

---

* Reprinted by permission of the author, Dr. Irwin Rothman.

** Modified by Rothman after J. Wolpe.

Note: The buzzer should be held firmly with two fingers and the buzz should not be pleasant.

If it seems too much to endure, however, even though it contains only a single pen-light type of battery, a single thickness of Kleenex placed under the fingers will modify the buzz sufficiently.

Another form of aversive control is the withholding of positive reinforcements, such as the loss of certain privileges or the levying of fines, as a consequence of certain behaviors. Even though the effects of aversive control may be limited, it may have to be resorted to where self-injurious behavior cannot be stopped by any other method. For example, I have had referrals of patients with hair plucking that had failed to

respond to years of insight therapy. They stopped their self-denuding habit after several sessions with a small shocking machine, which they carried with them thereafter. Obviously, desirable behavior that opposes the noxious habit should be rewarded. A variation of aversive control is "overcorrection," whereby an individual is obliged not only to restore the original situation disrupted by his behavior, but also to engage in other corrective tasks that can prove tedious (Foxx & Azrin, 1972; Webster & Azrin, 1973).

IMPLOSIVE THERAPY

Implosive therapy is a modality utilized to help extinguish avoidance responses (e.g., phobias) as an alternative to relaxation-desensitization treatment (Kirchner & Hogan, 1966; Hogan & Kirchner, 1967; Stampfl, 1967). Here the patient is flooded with the very stimuli that he fears under conditions where avoidance responses are blocked or prevented. Forced exposure to the feared stimulus has been shown in certain cases to facilitate extinction (Boulougouris & Marks, 1969), although this is not always a consistent finding (Hodgson & Rachman, 1970; Willis & Edwards, 1969). There are so many variables in therapy that one cannot credit results exclusively to the methods employed, since the skill of the therapist, his personality, case selection, etc. crucibly influence results. Be this as it may, implosive therapy in the hands of a skilled operator may dramatically cure some phobias, particularly if the phobia is combined with intravenous infusions of a short-acting barbiturate. The patient at the start of therapy may be given a slow intravenous injection of Pentothal (thiopental sodium) in dilution of 2 percent, sufficient to produce relaxation without drowsiness. Pentothal is available in 500 mg vials in combination packages with diluent (20 ml vial of sterile water). Some therapists utilize a 1.25 percent concentration (Hussain, MZ, 1971), but the diluent here should be sterile sodium chloride to prevent hemolysis. A very slow injection of the drug is essential to avoid sleepiness. Once relaxation is obtained, the patient is shown pictures related to the phobic object or phobic situation and asked to picture himself touching or holding the object or being involved in the situation. This continues throughout the session, the patient being asked to continue to imagine himself immersed in the scene. Where artificial objects similar to the phobic object can be obtained (snakes, worms, mice, roaches, etc.), he is enjoined

to handle these. The session is brought to an end with the patient in a drug-relaxed state. As mastery occurs, sessions are conducted with lesser and lesser amounts of the drug and finally without it. Some therapists prefer a 1 percent solution of Brevital (methohexital sodium) to Pentothal.

Home practice sessions may be valuable for some patients. These can cover a wide range of themes. A technique that I have found valuable for some phobias is illustrated by the following directions given to patients:

Running away from fearful situations or trying to crowd out of your mind a fearsome thought only reinforces your fear. If you practice producing the fearful situation deliberately in your mind as completely as possible, while studying your bodily reactions, you will begin extinguishing the fear. If when you are not practicing the fear comes upon you, do not push it aside; try to exaggerate it, experiencing the fear as fully as possible. Practice bringing on the fear at least three times daily. If you have a sympathetic friend whom you can talk to about your reactions while practicing, this can help.

SELF-IMAGERY

Practicing self-imagery sometimes serves the interests of ego building. The patient can be given varied instructions that can be easily followed at home. A mimeographed or typed sheet, such as the one that follows, will enable the patient to select that which is best for him. A small shocking machine as described in "Aversive Control" is used to deliver a "buzz" in indicated sections.

A number of useful images are detailed in the book by Kroger and Fezier (1976).

ASSERTIVE TRAINING

Assertive training strives to equip the individual to stand up for his own rights, to express anger when justified and to make demands when these are reasonable. Fear of one's own anger and aggression and terror at fancied retaliation tend to support attitudes of passivity, obsequiousness, and retreat. These defenses are counter to self-

IMPROVING HUMAN SELF-IMAGES RAPIDLY*
(some newer and some experimental methods)

INTRODUCTION: You and the doctor or his associates have agreed that a less self-critical self-image of yourself is desirable; or a self-concept in which you feel less inferior and more self-confident, or less childlike, more active at finding a new job—remedying a situation—doing more housework—getting more exercise—or more comfortable physical and social activity—or some other changes in your innermost self-concept are necessary or desirable.

Method I: Ego Building. Under self-hypnosis or relaxation leave yourself with the self-image of pleasant feelings and times in your life you, and possibly others, thought you were at least somewhat successful. Tell yourself, "I promise to act in accordance with this image."

Method II: A gradual stepladder of improved self-images can be used under self-hypnosis or relaxation, and you can move up this imaginary ladder of improved self-images until you feel a tinge of anxiety. Step down to the last comfortable self-image you could get. As soon as possible, act in daily life according to this improved image—as if it is now you.

Method III: Visualize your "lazy" or passive self-image as perhaps you have looked after avoiding some important work—a picture that we have agreed should be changed. After imagining this picture for 2–3 seconds, give yourself a buzz, usually until the image stops. Repeat as prescribed, usually for about 20 pictures at a sitting, with at least daily repetition. Substitute an image of a time when you were slightly more pleased with yourself each time you relax from the buzz.

Method IV: This can be used if you have been taught self-hypnosis with body imagery changes. (a) Hypnotize yourself to picture how some of your character (expressed as face and body) looks to you. Usually the doctor or his associates will have agreed with you on a given signal or word for this unconscious image to appear clearly. If you find difficulty in separating "bad mother or bad father" (or other image previously discussed with the therapist) from your image, i.e., they stick, then try using the buzzer to break up the fusion and leave you with an independent self-image, or with "good" mother and father's love. (b) Then you may attempt to modify by fusing your image with someone who has, as you and your therapist have agreed, some desirable traits you'd gradually like to work toward in a realistic fashion. (c) If the old image is stubborn in leaving, or fusing with the image you and your therapist have agreed upon, use the buzzer as described in Method III and #1 under AVERSIVE CONDITIONING to modify the old image by buzzing it and thereby speeding up the desired fused image. Report changes to your therapist, and keep your goals practical and within easy steps forward.

NOTE: It is most important that you keep careful records of frequency of use, and just what happens with the images, and discuss this with the therapist. These methods are not the same as daydreaming. Homework time is limited to approved and improved images as prescribed and should be tried out in reality.

---

* Reprinted by permission of the author, Dr. Irwin Rothman.

---

fulfillment and mobilize self-hatred and subversive aggression. A variety of programs to enhance assertiveness may be set up, such as those of Eisler et al. (1973 , b; 1974) and Hersen et al. (1973a, b). Role-playing sessions are valuable where the therapist plays the part of the challenging adversary, then alternates roles with the patient to indicate appropriate assertive responses, and finally reassumes the pose of the adversary to observe how well the patient has benefitted by the modeling exercises. Assignments may be given the patient deliberately to put himself into situations that call for challenging and affirmative behavior. It need hardly be mentioned that constant vigilence by the therapist will be required to prevent the patient from forgetting or bypassing assignments due to anxiety and resistance.

The following outline, modified after J. Wolpe and prepared by I. Rothman and M. L. Carroll, provide examples of practice exercises in assertiveness.

SELF-DESENSITIZATION OR ANXIETY REDUCTION TECHNIQUES IN MAN*

A. Frequently you will be given a choice of self-relaxation or self-hypnotic techniques described in a booklet or in instructions given to you by the doctor. Practice the method you choose. Other types of training for self-help may also be shown you.

B. Make a written stepladder of situations which disturb you or are problems to you. Arrange these in order from the most disturbing to the least, or from least to most if you prefer. Please provide a clear copy of your stepladder for the doctor.

C. During your 70% successful relaxation periods, visualize dramatically (get a vivid mental picture of) yourself successfully handling the situations (going up your stepladder) from the least to slightly disturbing until you feel slightly tense, then stop. Relax until you are again at ease. This procedure should be done daily, usually for not more than 10 minutes at bedtime, or some other convenient time. This visualization should be about things you actually want and intend to do and not just daydreaming. Make it a practice to try the things you have successfully pictured yourself doing whenever possible. After a few days, longer or more frequent practice periods or several separate stepladders may be prescribed.

D. Try to record where you are on the list daily. The faithfulness with which you practice daily visualization is an indication of how much your healthy self is willing to cooperate in the treatment against your self-destructive side. If your mind wanders from successful picturing, repeat the last successful picture. Remember that the mind can only concentrate on one thing at a time, although it may skip quickly. Bring back the thought you wish to work with for at least 2–3 seconds at a time. Your visualization will improve with practice. Stop when you feel anxiety at the same step on the stepladder more than three times, go back to a comfortable relaxation, and later add extra smaller steps between the worrisome ones.

E. The situations listed below are merely suggestions of areas which may be problems to you and how to handle them with this method. If any of the examples do apply to you, include them in your own stepladder (s), along with any other problem areas not listed here. Each area can be divided into as many as 20 or more gradual steps to visualize and to conquer in actuality. If you do not experience any anxiety while first visualizing situations which you find much too difficult to accomplish in real daily life, consult the doctor or his associates concerning this.

EXAMPLES:

(The first example is broken down to give you an idea of how to place situations on your own list.)

I. ASSERTION EXAMPLES:

Asserting yourself with other people without guilt, listing different types of people in order of decreasing difficulty from the boss (possible #1) to the office boy (possible #9) to the janitor (possible #15). This is a most important category for people with depression, strong self-damaging tendencies, and anxieties in dealing with other people.

Picture yourself:

(a)   expressing affection openly for (1) pets, (2) children, (3) immediate family, (4) more distant relatives, (5) friends, (6) acquaintances—possibly in that order of difficulty for you.

(b)   being assertive with your family, clerks, waitresses, policemen, and authority figures in the degree and order of difficulty fitting you.

(c)   Discussing topics which are of interest to you with your family, other relatives, and close friends.

(d)   Making an effort and succeeding in discussing their interests.

(e)   Stating your wishes without guilt to family, relatives, and close friends.

(f)   Expressing disagreement without guilt to family, friends, other relatives.

(g)   Following the same steps with casual friends and acquaintances.

(h)   Requesting firmly that clerks, janitors, or any subordinates do their jobs promptly and properly.

(i)   Expressing disagreement or your feeling of annoyance with those who do not fulfill their duties correctly.

(j)   Talking about your job with fellow workers or firmly requesting that they do their share of any mutual job.

(k) Giving a report and expressing disagreement if necessary with your immediate superior in a tactful way.

(l) Giving a report and expressing disagreement if necessary to the highest superior with whom you must deal in a tactful way.

Other problem areas which can be broken down may include:

II. FEAR OF CRITICISM, REJECTION, DISAPPROVAL, OR HEALTHY DISAGREEMENT:

(1) Successfully facing sarcasm from family, friends, or associates.

(2) Successfully facing direct disapproval or criticism from family, friends, or associates.

(3) Successfully arguing and being unafraid of arguments.

(4) Successfully facing feelings of being excluded by others.

(5) Successfully facing being ignored or reprimanded.

(6) Successfully dealing with persons you feel dislike you, etc.

III. MEDICAL SYMPTOMS: Symptoms you have been told have no medical importance: getting busy with activities and ignoring symptoms such as rapid heartbeat, buzzing in ears, constant or intermittent pain from rheumatism, or similar symptoms if you know that they are not medically important. Arrange a stepladder of increasing time for enduring them and carrying on despite them.

IV. STAGE FRIGHT: successfully speaking to a group. Perhaps start with an empty room and gradually increase the number of people present to 100.

V. SOCIAL FRIGHT: enjoying entertaining and parties of increasing size from one friendly couple to any number of relative strangers.

VI. CROWDS: At ease in crowds of increasing size. (elevators, trains, cramped quarters, open spaces, etc.)

VII. JOB SEEKING: Being at ease in applying for a job, starting with one you do not really want. Actually having several interviews before taking a job.

VIII. OPPOSITE SEX: Being at ease with members of the opposite sex, starting with someone unimportant to you and increasing periods of time and difficulty.

IX. DECISION MAKING: Being at ease in making your own decisions, without regrets and afterthought. Start with small decisions and increase importance.

* Reprinted by permission of the authors, Dr. I. Rothman and M. L. Carroll.

ROLE OF COGNITIVE PROCESSES

Some forms of behavior therapy, such as "rational emotive imagery" (REI) recognize the role of cognitive processes in maintaining neurotic problems and thus attempt to deal with behavioral difficulties by a restructuring of the thinking process (Ellis, A, 1963). Instead of attempting to win the patient over toward adopting a new philosophy toward life, or different attitudes toward himself and others, as in persuasion (q.v.) the patient is given daily relearning exercises to change his thinking habits toward rational goals that he is trying to achieve. First the patient is trained for several sessions in rational self-analysis to get at the basis of his problem. Next he is enjoined to practice rational emotive imagery for a minimum of three 10-minute periods each day during which the patient sees himself acting in constructive ways in relation to the upsetting or challenging situations in his life (Maultsby, 1970).

A GENERAL OUTLINE OF BEHAVIOR THERAPY PRACTICE

There are many designs for the practice of behavioral modification. One that I have found useful follows:

1. Ask the patient which behaviors he wishes to strengthen and which he wishes to diminish or extinguish.

2. Find out the situations under which undesirable traits or symptoms lessen or increase. Do not be concerned with explaining why the problem developed except insofar as the positive and aver-

sive reinforcements that maintain it can be detected.

3. Select jointly with the patient (on the basis of the patient's priorities) which behaviors or reactions are to be altered first, leaning toward those that, in your opinion, are most modifiable.

4. Explore the degree of motivation of the patient for therapy, the consequences of his present demeanor and the rewards anticipated from newly developed behavior. Challenge and work on the patient's motivation until it is certain that he unequivocally wishes to change for himself and not to please others.

5. Examine in depth the behavioral constellation to be altered or strengthened, going into past history to determine the reinforcements that have maintained the problem. Can the patient clearly define what it is that he desires to change? Does he accept your formulation of the problem? If not, you, the therapist, assume an educational role to teach the patient the full implications and complete description of the behaviors that are appropriate for the desired change. Does the patient clearly understand what is expected of him?

6. Identify the rewards (reinforcers) if any that are to be employed making sure that they have value for the patient. These reinforcers are made contingent on the desired behavior. A contract— verbal or, better, written—is drawn stating what is expected of the patient and the rewards for maintenance of the contract. The contract time should be made short, say a few days, with the idea of renewing the contract at the end of the contract time.

Sometimes "contingency contracting" is utilized, the patient and therapist deciding mutually not only on the kind of reinforcements that the patient is to receive on controlling problem behaviors or substituting constructive alternatives, but also the penalties to be imposed, if any, for perpetuation of disturbed behaviors. We, the therapists, may also impose penalties on ourselves should we not live up to our contract (appearing late for appointments, missing appointments, etc.), for example, reducing or cancelling fees. Token reinforcement systems may be set up, the patient receiving tokens for constructive behavior that he can exchange for luxuries, privileges etc. (Ayllon & Azrin, 1968; O'Leary & Drabman, 1971). Token economies have been found to work well in some institutions and classrooms.

7. Work out a planned schedule with the patient to begin to approach his new behaviors under the least traumatic circumstances possible. If interpersonal relations are involved in the plan, the least challenging individuals are selected so that the patient may be minimally uncomfortable. In the shaping of a difficult behavior the start should strive for minimal gains and immediate reinforcements, with the object of approximating the desired change, more and more reinforcements being given step by step as changes progress.

8. Ask the patient to keep a diary that lists each day the frequencies of new behaviors practiced. Praise is proferred for each success, but no criticism is given for failure. If no progress occurs, explore with the patient the reasons for failure. Encourage the patient to try again and make suggestions as to new assignments that the patient is prepared to execute.

Behavior modeling by the therapist and role playing are introduced when necessary. If anxiety prevents the patient from following through on his behavioral assignments, systematic desensitization may be tried and/or a mild tranquilizer suggested. At each session the patient is given "homework" to expand his skills.

9. Where it is obvious that the patient is confused in acting in a constructive way, try behavior rehearsal (Casey, GA, 1973).

Here the therapist rehearses the patient in what to say and how to say it, covering a broad zone of interpersonal behavior, with both real and fantasied authorities and peer figures. The gestures to make, the words to say, the facial expressions to exhibit are all acted out. The rehearsal will bring out feelings in the patient that will need discussion. Sometime it is helpful to make a recording (audio and video if available) to play responses back for the patient after each rehearsal. The therapist advantageously can play dual roles: first, that of the individual with whom the patient cannot seem to deal with in real life, and then, by changing chairs with the patient (role reversal), that of the patient with appropriate comments and gestures to indicate preferred reactions (modeling) while the patient is asked to put himself in the position of the adversary. The patient may need constant or periodic coaching while this role playing goes on.

10. Individual sessions may later be complimented with family and group sessions where these are deemed helpful.

In family therapy sessions the attendant members are apprised of the circumstances that create and maintain behavioral difficulties. Appropriate ways of reacting with each other are suggested. Group sessions are usually conducted with the object of allowing each member about 10 minutes of time to describe what each has accomplished since the last session and his reactions. The members then make suggestions to each other as to how difficulties may be overcome or progress increased.

11. Should a relapse occur, the best way to manage it is not to reward it with too much attention. Ignoring the relapse must be followed by adequate reinforcement when improvement resumes. Punishment should assiduously be avoided.

12. In the event resistance is obdurate and no progress occurs, explore frankly and openly the relationship with the patient. You as the therapist may very well look into your own feelings about the patient (countertransference) to see if you can perceive deleterious effects on the relationship.

There is, in my opinion, no reason why behavioral therapy cannot be practiced in a dynamic framework, although this may horrify some behavioral purists. Often dreams will reveal the nature of the resistance more readily than any other communication. Once the resistance is detected and explored, clarification or interpretation may turn the tide toward success in the behavioral effort.

A great deal of ingenuity is required to set up the design that will govern behavior therapy in a particular case. The treatment undergoes continued modifications in line with the observed behavioral change. Wide differences exist in the susceptibility of subjects to conditioning. However, the greater the quantum of anxiety, the more easily are conditioned responses established and the more difficult are these to extinguish. Generalized anxiety does not respond too well to behavior therapy unless it is possible to differentiate the conditioned stimuli that sponsor anxiety. It may be possible to break down anxiety or disturbed behavior into a number of phobic hierarchies and to deal with each hierarchy as a separate unit.

50

Techniques in Group, Marital, and Family Therapy

Group psychotherapy is a valuable and, in some cases, indispensible treatment method. Its historical development and uses in supportive (see page 99), reeducative (see page 136), and reconstructive (see page 238) approaches have been amply delineated and some of the important bibliography listed in the respective chapters. Group therapy may be employed both as an adjunctive aid to individual psychotherapy and as a treatment modality in its own right. There are some therapists who claim that not only are the results they obtain with groups equivalent to those of individual treatment, but in many cases even superior to it. Consequently, they dispense with individual therapy, except as an adjunct to a group approach. Other therapists, not so skilled in its use, tend to depreciate the effect and "depth" of group treatment.

Evolving in a group are a number of processes that are intimately bound up with the outcome. Among the most important are the developing group cohesiveness and mutual assistance. What one finds evolving in the group are manifestations of empathy, support, challenge, confrontation, and interpretation; availability of identification models; opportunities for introducing one's projective identifications; investigative explorations; and a joint sharing of problems.

Needless to say, the specific way that the group is employed, its composition, the degree of activity or passivity of the therapist, the extent of the therapist's authoritarianism, maneuvers, and kinds of participation, the pursuits sanctioned within and outside the group, and the interpretations will vary with the skill, experience, theoretical bias, and personality of the therapist. For example, some therapists assume an almost completely detached attitude, on the assumption that this will dredge up the dependent resentments of the group members, in the wake of which basic inner conflicts will be exposed. Other therapists cast anonymity to the winds and virtually become participating patients in the group, acting-out as enthusiastically as any other member. Both methods in the opinion of their sponsors are promoted as the "best" and even "only way" to do group therapy. Actually, there is no "best" group method; this will vary with the predilections of the therapist. After blundering through a number of sessions, each therapist will settle down to a procedure that works best for him or her.

Group therapy may be utilized (1) independently, during which both intrapsychic and interpersonal operations are considered; (2) in combination with individual therapy conducted by the same therapist ("combined therapy")—individual sessions deal with the patient's resistances, his transferential responses to the therapist, and his primary separation anxiety, while group sessions focus chiefly on interpersonal phenomena; (3) in conjunction with individual therapy conducted by another therapist ("conjoint therapy"); and (4) as leaderless groups particularly after formal group therapy has ended (Kline, 1975).

Meetings in independent, combined, and conjoint therapy may take place from one to three times weekly and, in institutional settings, even daily. They may be supplemented with regularly scheduled meetings that are not attended by the therapist ("coordinated meetings")—the members may congregate before a regular session ("pre-meetings"), after a regular session ("postmeetings"), or at other times at specially designated places ("alternate meetings"). Coordinated meetings enable patients to discuss their feelings about the therapist more freely. They are generally less formal and more spontaneous than regular meetings. Acting-out is more than a casual possiblity here, which may or may not prove to be beneficial to the patient. ("Closed groups" maintain a constant membership although new members may rarely be added for special reasons. "Open groups" operate continuously with new members being added as regular members complete therapy and leave the group.)

Treatment in group therapy may be "therapist-centered," in which the therapist takes a directive and more authoritarian role, moderating member-to-member communication, presenting interpretations, and limiting the patient's intragroup and extragroup activities ("triangular communication"). It may be "group-centered," in which the group operates as the primary authority, the therapist functioning in a kind of consultative role. Here peer (sibling) and authority (parental) relationships are considered equally important; rotating leadership is encouarged; there is no interference with the relationships between patients ("circular communication"), which are constantly being broken, restored, and new ones formed, the therapist controlling his

anxiety about neurotic alliances; or there is "authority-denying" ("horizontal communication") in which the therapist is on an equal plane with the patient, a structured relationship between therapist and patient being considered limiting to growth. In the latter case emotional interactions are considered more important than rational ones; direct experience in the group is encouraged; the therapist presents his own problems to the group ("The group can grow if I grow with them").

How a therapist conducts a group will be determined

1. By the goals that the therapist sets—supportive, reeducative or reconstructive.
2. By the constituent members—alcoholics, drug addicts, psychotics, stutterers, delinquents, psychoneurotics, character disorders, patients with heterogeneous problems.
3. By the therapist's training—group dynamics, rehabilitation, behavior therapy, existential therapy, psychodrama, psychoanalytically oriented psychotherapy, psychoanalysis.
4. By the therapist's personal ambitions and needs—characterologic and countertransferential.

INFLUENCES OF THE GROUP ON THE INDIVIDUAL

When people gather together in a group, phenomena are mobilized that may have an influence on each individual. One of the effects is an immediate impression of strangeness and embarrassment. This soon gives way to a realization that others present are not too different from oneself in problems, weaknesses, and ways of relating. This encourages the person to express himself openly. He soon discovers that the group fosters free expression of feelings or attitudes on any subject. There are no social taboos on content usually avoided in everyday interactions. The ability to open up varied forbidden topics, and the recognition that fellow members harbor the same fears and doubts, can be reassuring. Apart from the emotional catharsis experienced, the individual finds that he can share his problems with others without being rejected or ridiculed. His self-esteem and self-confidence are thereby enhanced. He begins to realize in his expression that he is not a reprehensible person deserving of blame or repudiation. The usual drives through which an individual achieves status and prestige receive no sanction in the group. Indeed, they are analyzed in terms of their neurotic components.

Every human being is a group creature and is constantly looking to others for validation of his or her own ideas. One of the most powerful molding influences in group therapy is the impact of group standards and values. These can have a markedly transforming influence on the personal persuasions by which individuals customarily govern themselves. A gradual incorporation of group convictions and judgments in a cohesive and developed group neutralizes self-oriented neurotic needs. The presence of the therapist is a safeguard that the prevailing group values are not along improper lines. There is some validity in the belief that patients in a group reinforce each other's normal reactions. This is because they collectively make up the norm from which they individually deviate. This is particularly true in a therapeutic group presided over by a therapist who has healthy values himself; it is not so true in a group left to its own destiny, which so often will be diverted and taken over by a power-driven member with qualities of leadership.

Group patterns evolve related to the roles members assume and the ways they perceive themselves; how and when they take over leadership; the specific motives assigned to them by other members; and the existing defensive maneuvers, such as competitiveness, struggles for control, dominance, submissiveness, ingratiation, masochistic devices, aggressiveness, and violence. The fluctuating group interaction is influenced by levels of tension that affect participation, the sharing of ideas, and decision making. Arguments, the taking over of a session by a monopolizer, coming late, absenteeism, and the formation of subgroup clusters manifesting special likings and dis-

likings raise tensions that stimulate action; however, if tension is too high, it will paralyze action. Extremes of harmony and congeniality will also tend to subdue activity.

A successful solution to a problem enables the person better to extend his success to relationships with people outside of the group. It is to be expected that the person will react to different members selectively with his full range of prejudices. Awe, infatuation, disgust, anger, hate, and sexual interest will be expressed toward members who are identified with archaic or idealized models. Whereas in the usual group setting these feelings are controlled and verbalizations related to them suppressed or repressed, in the therapeutic group they are encouraged and even rewarded by approval from the therapist. The reactions of the person with whom one is immediately entangled presents opportunities to examine the reasonableness or unreasonableness of one's responses. The individual gradually learns that he can accept criticism and aggression. This is a most crucial lesson; indeed soon recognized is the fact that aggression and criticism can be either proper or unjustified and that the individual can differentiate the two and manage responses accordingly.

The effect of interpretations from other group members may be pronounced. The individual begins to distinguish prejudiced opinions from factual ones; he learns to tolerate projections with clemency which he may then generalize to the world at large. He may master his fear of becoming violent and in turn being subject to physical attack and humiliation. The group judgment is a moving force that he cannot resist. Where a number of members share an opinion about him or his behavior, the effect on him may be more intense than an interpretation by the therapist. The group strengthens the individual's ability to express his feelings toward the therapist—rational or irrational; he may be unable to do this during individual therapy.

One of the most important consequences of being in a group geared toward reconstructive goals is learning how emotional processes operate by observing how other members react and how problem solving takes place. Dynamic thinking soon becomes a dominant mode in the group. Immediate symptoms are related to basic adaptational patterns. As these are traced to destructive past conditionings, resistance and transference are mobilized and explored. In this way the patient begins to think more dynamically about himself— about the genetic origins of his patterns, their manifestations in his present life, and his defensive maneuvers. Awareness of his inner psychological operations is also sharpened through emotional involvements with the group members around him, through his own spontaneous discoveries, and through interpretations from fellow members and the therapist. Instead of withdrawing, as in a usual life situation, the patient is encouraged to hold his ground and to express and analyze his feelings and defenses. It is here that a psychotherapist trained in reconstructive therapy can make the greatest impact on the patient.

ADVANTAGES OF GROUP VERSUS INDIVIDUAL THERAPY

Group therapy has certain advantages over individual treatment. It is capable of registering deep impressions by virtue of the fact that the patient is exposed to the judgments of not one person, but a host of people. In individual therapy the patient soon learns how to cope with and to neutralize the influence of the therapist. It is much more difficult to do this in a group setting. Change is scored on different levels of the intrapsychic organization. This includes his system of values, which is altered through percussion of disparate ideologies in the group. It is much simpler for the individual to recast his standards in a setting that is a reflection in miniature of the world than in the isolated confines of the dyadic therapeutic relationship.

Diversified intrapsychic defenses come out toward members of the group with whom the patient plays varying roles. Multiple transferences are readily established. The opportunity to relate in different ways to fellow members enables the individual to work through his insights in the direction of change. Thus, if the patient finds it difficult to express himself aggressively or assertively, he will first be able to practice this with the least threatening member, and then, as he grows stronger, he may progressively challenge others who are more threatening to him. In individual treatment the therapist may continue to be too powerful a figure to vanquish. Moreover, even though the patient masters his fear and guilt, he may find it difficult to transfer what he has learned during individual therapy to the envirionment outside of the therapeutic setting.

Within the group the patient feels more protected, both by the therapist and by members with whom he has formed alliances, and he may be able to practice his new attitudes more propitiously. For example, if Mary Smith has a problem in accepting any aggression and hostility that are being directed toward her, the group will offer her the opportunity of exposure to these emotions in graduated doses. She will become more and more tolerant of the resentment extended toward her. She will learn to accept criticism—to reflect on it and to see whether it is justified or not—instead of reacting automatically with indignant or violent responses. Rigid character defenses often yield in group therapy as patients observe their ego-syntonic traits operating in others.

On the other hand, one advantage of individual therapy is that the focus is on the patient's personal problems, which often become diluted in a group setting. With so many other members of the group expressing themselves, it is not always possible for the patient to clarify significant feelings at the time he is experiencing them. Individual therapy enables the patient to look into his private world of fantasy and conflict and to explore intrapsychic mechanisms in greater depth.

Outlining some of the benefits a patient may derive from group therapy, we may include the following: (1) the opportunity to see that he is not alone in his suffering and that problems he felt were unique are shared by others; (2) the opportunity to break down his detachment and tendencies to isolate himself; (3) the opportunity to correct misconceptions in his ideas about human behavior by listening to others and by exposing himself to the group judgment; (4) the opportunity to observe dynamic processes in other people and to study his own defenses in clear perspective in relation to a variety of critical situations that develop in the group; (5) the opportunity to modify his personal destructive values and deviancies by conforming with the group norm; (6) the opportunity to relieve himself of tension by expressing his feelings and ideas to others openly; (7) the opportunity to gain insight into intrapsychic mechanisms and interpersonal processes, (particularly as multiple and split transferences develop), the group acting as a unit that replicates the family setting and sponsors reenactment of parental and sibling relationships; (8) the opportunity to observe his reactions to competition and rivalry that are mobilized in the group; (9) the opportunity to learn and to accept constructive criticism; (10) the opportunity to express hostility and to absorb the reactions of others to his hostility; (11) the opportunity to consume hostility from others and to gauge the reasonableness of his reactions; (12) the opportunity to translate understanding into direct action and to receive help in resolving resistances to action; (13) the opportunity to gain support and reassurance from the other members when his adaptive resources are at a breaking point; (14) the opportunity to help others which can be a rewarding experience in itself; (15) the opportunity to work through problems as they precipitate in relationship with others; (16) the opportunity to share his difficulties with his fellow members; (17) the opportunity to break down social fears and barriers; (18) the opportunity to learn to respect the rights and feelings of others, as well as to stand up to others when necessary; (19) the opportunity to develop new interests and make new friends; (20) the opportunity to perceive his self-image by seeing a reflection of himself in other people; (21) the opportunity to develop an affinity with others, the group supplying identification-models; (22) the opportunity to relate unambivalently and to give as well as to receive; (23) the opportunity to enter into productive social relationships, the group acting as a bridge to the world.

ORGANIZING A GROUP

In organizing a group the therapist will be limited by the patients available. Nevertheless, one should choose patients who are sufficiently advanced in their understanding of themselves to be able to perceive their patterns as they will appear in the group setting. While the clinical diagnosis is not too important, experience shows that the following conditions and patients do poorly in a group; except perhaps when implemented by an experienced group therapist in a homogenous group within an inpatient setup through supportive or reeducative group methods.

1. Psychopathic personalities and those with poor impulse control
2. Acute depressions and suicidal risks
3. Stutterers
4. True alcoholics
5. Hallucinating patients and those out of contact with reality
6. Patients with marked paranoidal tendencies
7. Hypomanics
8. Patients with a low intelligence

The age difference should preferably not exceed 20 years. Homogeneity in educational background and intelligence is desirable but not imperative. A well-balanced group often contains an "oral-dependent," a "schizoid-withdrawn," a "rigid-compulsive," and perhaps a "provocative" patient, such as one who is in a chronic anxiety state. This variety permits the members to observe a wide assortment of defense mechanisms and to experience tensions they might otherwise evade.

The number of group members may range optimally from 6 to 10. If a therapist feels uncomfortable with a large group, then the size of the group should be reduced. Marital status is relatively unimportant. A balance of males and females in the group allows for an opportunity to project and to experience feelings in relation to both sexes, although acting-out is more likely in a mixed group.

A heterogeneous group in terms of age, sex, and syndrome is most effective for reconstructive goals. A homogeneous group, composed of patients with the same problem, is best for alcoholics, drug addicts, stutterers, and psychopathic personalities, the goals being both supportive and reeducative. Severely handicapped persons, such as paraplegics and laryngectomized patients, feel unrelated to the norm and do better in homogeneous groups. Adolescents seem to be more responsive in same-sex groups.

In introducing the matter of group therapy to a prospective member, the therapist may explain that he or she is organizing a group of patients for purposes of treatment. Talking over problems or ideas in a group tends to expedite getting well. The patient may then be invited to join with the statement that perhaps a group may facilitate his progress. This, if the patient is in individual treatment, may be presented as a "promotion."

One of the problems that plagues the neurotic individual is the loss of a sense of group belongingness. To an extent, it is because he devalues himself and feels rejected by others; partly it is because he anticipates that his own hostility will be reciprocated. As a consequence of his isolation, he loses his identity with people and thus is robbed of a vital source of security. When a suggestion is made that he enter a group, he may imagine that his worst fears will come to pass. He will then pose a number of questions, which usually reflect his resistance, and the therapist will be obliged to answer them.

The following are common questions and suggested replies:

Q. How can other mixed-up people like myself help me?

A. People in a group actually do help each other. They become extremely sensitive and perceptive about problems, and they often may be of considerable service to other members. In the group the person has an opportunity to observe how he interacts and to witness the nature of reactions to him. The therapist is present during the sessions to see that it goes along well.

Q. I would be ashamed to bring up my problems to a group of people I don't know.

A. This is understandable. It is not necessary for you to divulge anything you do not wish to talk about. [*Actually this reassurance does not retard the patient from divulging his most intimate problems readily as soon as he begins to articulate.*] Without your permission I shall not bring up anything about you or your problems. This is up to you. Most people fear not being able to talk in a group. In reality, being with a group with whom you can be yourself is consoling, not frightening.

Q. What am I supposed to do in the group?

A. There is no need for you to do anything special. You may talk or you may remain silent as you wish. Generally one is not as embarrassed as he would imagine.

Q. Won't these people reveal things about each other outside the group?

A. One of the rules is that no mutual confidences are to be revealed to outsiders. Should this happen (and it rarely does), the person is dropped from the group.

Q. Supposing I meet someone in the group I know?

A. When it happens, it may actually prove to be an advantage. Any problems between two people who know each other can be worked out.

Q. Won't the problems of the other people rub off on me?

A. Without any reservation I can say, "no." On the contrary, you may gain a great deal from observing how other people face and resolve their troubles. It can be a great educational experience for you.

Q. Do I continue seeing you individually?

A. Generally yes, but we will decide how frequently. Sometimes I may want you to try the group alone, but if that comes up, we can talk about it.

Q. Can I raise any issues I want in the group, even about you?

A. Unless you do, you will not get as much benefit out of the group as you might. It is important to talk about your feelings and ideas in relation to yourself, to outside people, to the group members and to me. That is, if you wish to do so.

Q. Supposing my feelings are unreasonable?

A. This is why the group is of such value. In life there is very little opportunity to examine the reasonableness or unreasonableness of one's attitudes and responses. The group offers you an opportunity to test your assumptions. In the protected setting of the group a person can express his ideas and emotions.

The length of a group therapy session is approximately 1½ to 2 hours. The frequency of meetings is one to two sessions weekly, with alternate sessions once weekly if desired. The best seating arrangement is in a circle.

There are many advantages in employing cotherapists in a group, provided that problems between them do not prevent their working together. The literature on the subject of cotherapy and the difficulties that can occur between cotherapists that can sabotage their usefulness and destroy the group process are pointed out by J. B. Strauss (1975). Her own study deals with the results of a questionnaire that explores the ways therapists conceptualize their problems and how they try to cope with them. A most interesting finding was the difference of role perceptions of male and female therapists.

THE OPENING SESSIONS

At the first session the members are introduced by their first names, and the purpose of group discussions is clarified. This will vary with different therapists and different groups. Advanced patients will already have worked through some of their individual resistances in their sessions alone with the therapist. Newer patients may need more explanations in the group setting. The more passive-dependent the patient, the more leadership he will demand of the therapist. The technique employed during the opening session will be determined by the therapist's orientation and level of anxiety. Many therapists who use the group as an adjunct may assume a very passive role so as to elicit spontaneous reactions from different members for use in later individuals sessions.

Some therapists begin by simply stating that the group offers members an opportunity to talk about their feelings and eventually to understand their individual patterns. It is not necessary for the members to feel compelled to reveal something that they want to keep to themselves. However, communicating freely will help them to get a better grip on their problems. For instance, each member must have had certain definite feelings about entering the group;

he may have been embarrassed, upset, or fearful. The therapist may attempt to elicit these emotions, and, as one member expresses himself, others will join in, leading to a general airing of difficulties shared by all.

Before the close of the first session, some therapists find it advisable to stress the confidential nature of the meetings and to caution that each member is expected not to reveal to others the identity of the members and the subject matter discussed in the group. While no member will have to divulge his secrets before he is ready, he will be encouraged to relate any incidents involving accidental or planned contacts with other members of the group outside of the sessions. Therapists who strongly believe that acting-out it deleterious will, in all probability, discourage any contact outside of the group. Sexual involvements may be forestalled by fostering verbalization of the patients' feelings and impulses toward each other. Usually the anxiety level drops markedly at the end of the first session.

During the early stages of treatment some therapists who are anxious to prevent acting-out at any cost will, at first, assume a despotic role that contrasts sharply with their role in individual sessions. Parenthetically, this may lead to more acting-out. They may try to keep patients from exposing painful revelations before the group is ready to support them. On the other hand, free verbal interaction may be encouraged in the group in order to bring out each member's customary facades and defenses.

Later in the course of therapy authority is shared by various members, who are, from time to time, "elevated" and "dethroned" by the group according to its needs. Often individual members in their temporary authority posts may initiate ways of eliciting meaningful material. This may take the form of giving each person an opportunity to express himself at each session, or there may be a much more informal arrangement with the members spontaneously expressing what is on their minds at the moment. Actually, by the time emotions are beginning to flow freely within the group, there is no further need for procedural structuring; indeed, this should not be rigidly controlled at any time. The content of discussions will vary greatly, covering current incidents of importance in the lives of each member, dreams, attitudes toward others in the group or toward the therapist, and general areas, such as family relations and sex.

LATER SESSIONS

Ezriel (1973) believes principles of classical individual psychoanalysis can be advantageously adapted to group therapy. Essentially mechanisms of the unconscious are uncovered and their meaning explicated through interpretation. The core of the neurotic process are unconscious need structures that constantly strive for satisfaction through transference reactions and that are dynamically related to resistances. "Here-and-now interpretations" of transference maneuvers with group members does not preclude examination of extra-transference projections toward persons outside of the group. However, the therapist must be constantly on the alert to covert transference manifestations that relate directly to the therapist that are being diluted by references away from him or her. Interpretation of transference with the therapist ("the required relationship") brings the patient closer to behavior patterns that the patient has been repudiating ("the avoided relationship") and permits reality testing that can demonstrate that anticipated calamities will not come to pass. Often such experiences enable the patient to make a connection between his contemporary life and his unresolved infantile conflicts. Unconscious common group tensions lead to the development of a group structure within which each member seeks to express his transference needs. The therapist can advantageously analyze the structure of the group as it displays itself in a particular session and designate the roles played by the different members, thus delineating the defense mechanisms displayed by the individual members. Interpretation can thus be both individual-centered and group-centered; ideally the focus is on the two during each session. All activity in the group, as in classical individual analysis, other than interpretation must be assiduously avoided to prevent gratification of transference needs, which, while momentarily tension relieving, keep basic conflicts alive.

Other authorities insist that the classical model is too limiting and introduce many modifications and active maneuvers. A dynamic viewpoint, nevertheless, is desirable even if nonanalytic methods are employed.

As the group becomes integrated and develops an "ego" of its own, members feel free to air intimate vexations. The patient gains more insight into his own difficulties when he finds that many troubles he believed were unique to himself have a common base. The therapist should, therefore, direct energies toward stimulating thinking around universally shared problems, getting responses from other group members even though the subject under consideration is out-of-the-ordinary. The therapist may ask a patient to talk about what role he believes the therapist is playing in the group; then the therapist may suggest that the group discuss the verity of the patient's assumptions.

As Grotjahn (1973) has pointed out transference is a most important element of the group experience. He describes three trends in transference: (1) transference to the therapist and central figure (e.g., paternal figure), (2) transference to peers (e.g., sibling), and (3) transference to the group itself (e.g., pregenital mother symbol). These different transference relationships are always present simultaneously, patients treating the group as if it were their own family. In working through transference and defenses dreams are advantageously utilized; but they are utilized in a somewhat different manner than in individual therapy, the group members and the therapist associating directly to the dream, without waiting for the associations of the dreamer. In this way the dream becomes a part of group experience. Sometimes the therapist's reactions to a group member may be perceived correctly by a third member and interpreted.

Many therapists practicing individual psychoanalysis contend that group therapy waters down transference reactions, minimizes regressive reactions, and neutralizes emergence of a genuine transference neurosis. Character changes in depth are, therefore, circumvented. Durkin and Glatzer (1973) have elaborated on how a constant focus on process rather than content and how selective exploration of origins of defensive behavior during group therapy can effectively bring forth pre-Oedipal as well as Oedipal conflicts. Systematic analysis of intragroup transferences may act as a vehicle for successful transference interpretations and can lead to reconstructive personality changes of a deep and enduring nature.

Of vital importance is the opportunity for the development of multiple transferences during which varying members of the group function as vehicles for the projection of feelings, attitudes, and relationships with important persons in the individual's past existence. Of significance, too, is the fact that the group situation allows for "split transferences"—for example, projection of a "good" mother image on one member (or the therapist or the group as a whole) and of a "bad" image on another.

The basic rule in a group setting is for members individually to express themselves as freely and without restraint as possible. This encourages the disclosure of forbidden or fearsome ideas and impulses without threat of rejection or punishment. The patterns of some individual members usually irritate and upset others in the group, mobilizing tension and stimulating appropriate and inappropriate responses. The monopolizing of most of the session's time and competitiveness for the therapist's attention bring about rapid responses from the other members. Many patients will react to a trait in a member that they despise in themselves, even though they may not be immediately aware of possessing that trait.

Some therapists work even at the start on group resistance. For example, they may believe that mobilization and release of hostility is essential toward the development of positive and cooperative attitudes. The activity they engage in, therefore, is designed to stir up hostility and to facilitate hostile verbalizations. Other therapists try to facilitate the activity of the members as "adjunct therapists." The interactional processes virtually do put the various group members in the role of cotherapists. Under the guidance of the therapist this role can be enhanced. The specific effect of member "cotherapists" may be analytic or it may be more supportive, encouraging, accepting, and empathic, thus providing an important dimension to supplement the analytic work of the therapist. One way to enhance cotherapeutic participation is, even at the start, to analyze motivations of one or more members to stimulate curiosity and communication. The members are invited to put themselves into the place of a member chosen for analysis, e.g., to imagine dreaming the same dream as the member and to interpret the meaning.

Sensing that the group and the therapist are supporting him, a patient finds it easier to examine the inner feelings that he has been repudiating. If his expressed feelings seem to elicit a sympathetic response from other members, the ensuing discussion often leads to a lifting of tension and a sharpening awareness of his neurotic patterns. In the kaleidoscopic illuminations of the group each person's vision is broadened by taking advantage of the opportunity to observe and study his own and other members' reactions within the group—e.g., manifestations of hostility, fear, suspicion, or sexual feeling—and to relate them to his basic character structure. In this context the difficulties and antagonisms among members may, through analysis of the operative projections, lead to a constructive solution.

Among the therapist's activities are comments, interventions, structuring, focusing, timing, interpreting individual and group resistance, encouraging group interaction, and clarifying group interrelations. The therapist's ability to accept hostility and criticism from one member paves the way for other members to engage in further examination—and a working through—of their own hostile emotions. Reactions of the patient occur in complex clusters as a release of feeling within the group is accelerated. Lack of restraint in one group member results in a similar lack of restraint in the others. A climate that tends to remove repression enables the patient to work toward a better understanding of his inner conflicts, particularly in an analytic group.

The matter of alternate sessions calls for special attention. Although it is regarded by some as a sanctioned vehicle for acting-out, experience shows that it can provide opportunities for free interaction, testing, and exploring. It enables patients to speak more freely about their feelings about the therapist and thereby to consolidate their separation from parental authority. It is essential, however, that activities at alternate sessions or elsewhere involving group members with each other be reported at the regular group sessions. Acting-out members should be seen also in individual therapy.

TECHNICAL OPERATIONS OF THE GROUP THERAPIST

The role of the group leader is to catalyze participation of the various members, to maintain an adequate level of tension, to promote decision making and problem solving, to encourage identifications, to foster an interest in the goals to be achieved, and to resolve competitiveness, resentments, and other defenses that block activity. Groups have a tendency to develop many resistances; for instance, the members form cliques, they come late, they socialize too much, they get frozen into interlocking roles. The therapist has a responsibility to deal with these overt obstructions, as well as with those that are more concealed and come through in acts like passivity, detachment, and ingratiation. The group interactions will permit the therapist to witness how individuals function with others, their enmities, and their alliances.

How the leader communicates himself or herself to the group will vary with the orientation and personal idiosyncrasies of the leader. Some leaders are mercilessly authoritarian, and they take over firm control, directing the various activities with despotic regulation. Others are so passive that they scarcely make their presence known. There are therapists who conceive of their role as a benevolent authority who graces his subjects with kindly guidance. There are those who insist that the function of the leader is to liberate the affects of his patients that cause their paralysis as people. This, they believe, is accomplished best not by interpretation, but by establishing meaningful, deep relationships. To do this, a therapist must avoid setting oneself up as a paradigm of health or virtue, one who is falsely objective, which may be merely a cover for the therapist's omnipotence. They contend that there is no reason why the therapist cannot reveal his weaknesses and grow with patients, relating himself to their strengths. Experience convinces, however, that most therapists will do best in group therapy if they function with some discipline and if they sensitize themselves for countertransference manifestations, which are more easy to elicit and more difficult to control in a group than in an individual setting since they may unconsciously experience the group as their personal family. This does not mean that one must keep oneself in a straitjacket and not react to provocations. Expression of anger toward the group when this is justified, without threatening incriminations, may be exactly what the group needs.

There is always a temptation in group therapy to allow the group to indulge in social chatter, in mutual analysis, and in the recounting of dreams and personal experiences at length. This interferes with proper interaction in the group. The therapist must constantly remind the members that they are not there to act as professional psychoanalysts, attempting to figure out dynamics and to expound on theory. The best use of their time is in exploring their own immediate reactions. The principle activity of the therapist will be to resolve resistances to talking about feelings regarding one another and to try to break up fixed role behavior patterns.

The specific communicative media will also vary with the training of the therapist and the goals in treatment. A recounting of dreams, and particularly recurrent dreams and nightmares, may be encouraged by the analytically oriented therapist, as may the reporting of fantasies and daydreams. Interpersonal interaction may be facilitated by encouraging the free association of each patient about the others in what Alexander Wolf has called "going around." Patients are enjoined to recite whatever comes to their minds about their fellow members, whether logical or not. Free association about the therapist is also invited. Interpretation is an instrumentality considered essential for the proper working-through of pathogenic conflicts.

Other therapist activities include:

1. Focusing the conversational theme around pertinent subjects when topics become irrelevant.
2. Creating tension by asking questions and pointing out interactions when there is a slackening of activity in the group.
3. Posing pointed questions to facilitate participation.
4. Dealing with individual and group resistances.
5. Supporting upset members.
6. Encouraging withdrawn members to talk.
7. Interfering with hostile pairings who upset the group with their quarreling.
8. Reminding the group that communication about and understanding of mutual relationships is more important than interpreting dynamics.
9. Managing silence, which tends to mobilize tension in the group.

Role playing and psychodrama may be introduced periodically. They have advantages and liabilities, as may touching (Spotnitz, 1972).

An important aspect of the therapist's function in the group is that of gauging and regulating group tension and anxiety. It is well known that some degree of anxiety is one of the moving forces in therapy making possible growth and change. But anxiety can also be disorganizing—if too much of it is aroused, the group cannot function, there is low cohesiveness, and dropouts occur. It is up to the therapist to step in and deal with excessive tension and maintain not a minimal level of tension, but an optimal one. If too little tension exists, a "dead" session may be resuscitated by requesting that the members "go around" associating freely

about each other. A group that has settled into pallid social interchanges may also be revived by introducing a new active, disturbed member.

Perhaps the main task of the therapist is to detect resistances of the group as a whole as well as of the individual members. The dealing with resistance will depend on its manifestations and functions. The question is sometimes asked, "Should one share one's feelings with one's patients and act as a 'real' person rather than as a detached observer?" This depends on how it is done and the kind of relationship that the therapist has with the patients. To bring out one's *serious neurotic problems* may destroy the confidence of some group members in the therapist's capacity for objectivity, as well as his ability to help them, and the general effectiveness of the therapeutic process. On the other hand, to share *feelings and reactions* will reveal the therapist as more human and less omniscient and give the patients confidence to talk more openly about their own anxieties.

As has been mentioned, a huge variety of resistances precipitate out in group therapy. Their dissolution has resulted in many innovative techniques. In a humanistic contribution Livingston (1975) describes two major forms of resistance that block progress in group therapy: contempt and masochism (sadomasochism). These defenses may, through the assumption of a special role on the part of the leader, be broken through in what the author calls the "vulnerable moment." During such intervals a patient allows himself to be open and honest, and through a constructive sharing of his experience with the group and therapist, he may score substantial reconstructive gains. Describing how awareness of such readiness for change came about in his own group therapy as a patient, Livingston suggests techniques, some derived from Gestalt therapy, that may facilitate the working-through process.

A particularly insidious and masked form of resistance is acting-out. The initial reaction to a therapeutic group experience is generally a profoundly inspiring one. A good deal of the reaction is marshalled by hope, the patient projecting his wishes to be accepted, understood, and loved without qualification. While his defenses continue to operate, they are softened by the emotional catharsis that he experiences in verbalizing to strangers and by an idealization that he projects onto them. Sooner or later he plummets back to his original defensive baseline as he discovers flaws in the idealized images of the group; as criticisms, challenges, and attacks justifiably and unjustifiably are leveled at him; and as his multiple transference reactions come forth that, unfoundedly, make the group a facsimile of his original family, with some members even sicker than those of his own family. Frustration, disappointment, and even despair are apt to dominate his responses, and acting-out may then occur verbally and behaviorally.

In groups conducted by unsophisticated therapists the acting-out dimension may be openly encouraged, the patient being helped or goaded into unrestrained speech and behavior without relating his responses to underlying motivations. The temporary relief of tension and the pseudo-assertive expostulations are confused with cure. Follow-up almost invariably demonstrates how futile are the results. Many of the members become welded into reciprocal sadomasochistic alliances, and therapy becomes interminable. Others find excuses to leave the group.

The ability of the therapist to establish and to maintain proper communication is the principal means of averting this therapeutic impasse. A. Wolf (1975) illustrates how a therapist may utilize his own personality characteristics, for example, solicitude, capacity for healthy engagement, self-discipline, and sheer human decency, to resolve resistances and to enhance interaction. He refers to methods employed by Asya Kadis, which tend to encourage working through rather than acting-out and help foster character restructuring.

The control of acting-out requires a differentiation of acting-out behavior from impulsive and compulsive acts (Spotnitz, 1973). It is generally agreed that there is a greater tendency toward acting-out in group therapy than in individual treatment. A primary function of acting-out, according to Spotnitz, is to avoid experiencing unpleasant emotions, often of preverbal origin, that cannot be tolerated. Action becomes tension alleviating. It often conveys information in a dramatic form to the effect that the individual is unable to express himself verbally. More constructively, it may serve as a means of attempting to master traumatic events, and it may actually help prevent the outbreak of psychosomatic illness or psychosis by discharging tension. However, the validity of acting-out is always justifiably challenged unless it results in reality testing or enables a patient to master a tendency toward resistive emotional action. Under these circumstances his actions may be considered constructive and in some instances even maturational. If, on the other hand, investigation reveals that emotional action serves as a resistance to communication, it must be therapeutically handled as a form of resistance. Particularly damaging are actions that are destructive to the continuity of the group or to any of its members. Inadequate communication of understanding on the part of the therapist and failure to meet the patient's emotional needs may be responsible for acting-out, which may then take the form of the patient dropping out of the group. Awareness of this contingency may help the therapist deal with such behavior at its inception. Methods for minimizing destructive acting-out are outlined by Spotnitz.

Another type of resistance is encountered particularly in family therapy on the part of members who refuse to participate in the treatment process. Innovative therapeutic approaches here may cut through the defensive system by constructively involving family members through the use of videotape recording and playback. R. L. Beck et al. (1975) describe such a program in which dance movement therapy is employed to demonstrate how incongruence between verbal and behavioral communication as a form of resistance may be resolved. Success may be scored through this approach (whereas traditional therapeutic modes are ineffective) and can lead to a more constructive use of verbal psychotherapy.

Special patients and syndromes may also require innovative methods. The unique personality needs and defenses of adolescents (for example, their lability of affect, their struggle for identity) require an atypical format in the conduct of group psychotherapy. There are differences in respect to activity, depth and content of discussion, and roles taken within the group. Adolescents bring into the group (which influences its Gestalt) the rapidly shifting values of the contemporary social scene and their distinctive reactions to delights and horrors of our modern technological era. Their reactions vary from those of their parents, who were subjected to a different type of social conditioning. Moreover, the ease with which runaways may survive away from home in a commune and participation in the drug culture that surrounds them must be taken into account in any group psychotherapeutic plan. Kraft and Vick (1973) present an approach that acknowledges the pressing need in adolescents for expressions of their identity and creativeness by introducing into the group psychodramatic techniques and artistic activities, such as dance or movement, music, poetry, and various visual stimuli (e.g., psychedeliclike light box) and by employing where indicated auxiliary therapists. Major conflicts of adolescents worked through in the group included individual excessive competitive behavior versus withdrawal tendencies, inadequate outlets for emotional expression versus emotional blocking, growing up toward individual responsibility versus dependency, self-identification versus expected role assumption and various breakdowns in defensive operations. This type of group, according to the authors, provides a growth experience for the members, results being reflected in enhanced school performance, better peer relationships, and a general strengthening of ego functioning.

Riess (1973) describes in the conduct of a group of adolescents, or family of the adolescent, a structured "consensus technique" that he believes is ideally suited for diagnostic and therapeutic purposes. In this technique a problem situation in written or oral form is presented to each member who writes out what he believes would be the appropriate outcome or way of action. The members then discuss the "solutions" and are given a limited time to come to a unanimous decision. In the course of the ensuing interactions, individual styles, reactions, and defenses become apparent and relationship problems emerge. The results may be utilized diagnostically. By mobilizing conflict and anxiety defensive operations precipitate out rapidly, and where the therapist is trained dynamically to deal with defenses, therapy may become catalyzed.

One of the poignant problems of the group therapist is how to deal with "difficult" borderline patients, that is, those who do not respond to the usual tactics or maneuvers during the group session, who are extraordinarily self-involved, sensitive, dissatisfied, and angry. Their impact on the group may be intense and not always constructive, since they attempt to destroy, to monopolize, and to provoke counteraggression from other members. Moreover, they engage in struggles with the group leader that can be disturbing to the latter, to say the least. Pines (1975) has described the dynamics of the "difficult" patient, employing some of the ideas of Foulkes, Kohut, and Kernberg. He makes some useful suggestions on how to manage their reactions and resistances.

Efforts to expedite group therapy and catalyze movement have resulted in therapists' evolving their own unique techniques. Thus, Vassiliou and Vassiliou (1974) employ a transactional method "synallactic collective image technique," which actualizes psychodynamic concepts within the framework of general systems theory. Utilizing artistic creations made by group members (free paintings, doodlings, or scribblings), the participants choose, through majority vote, one creation around which discussion is organized. In this way the members "talk" to each other through a common stimulus. Gradually, as different projections evolve, communalities are compared and a "collective image" of the group emerges that revolves around a central theme with individual variations. Throughout, the therapist operates actively in a key "catalytic regulatory" role, participating continuously in the group transaction.

Encounter and marathon techniques are capable, through the intense emotional atmosphere that they create, of cutting through defenses and rapidly reaching repressed feelings and impulses rarely accessible through the use of conventional techniques. However, such active procedures are unfortunately utilized by therapists as a means of dealing with their own countertransference. Thus, the sessions may be employed as an outlet for the therapist's hostility, boredom, need for social and physical contact, desire for dramatic "instant insights," and solution of professional and personal identity conflicts. The avoidance by encounter therapists of traditional concepts and practices, such as the analysis of countertransference, is a great liability and accounts for the bulk of negative therapeutic reactions and treatment failures. A. W. Rachman (1975) points out the importance of countertransference analysis and suggests methods of examining countertransference.

Corsini (1973) describes a "behind-the-back" (BTB) technique that may serve a useful purpose for groups of people. The problem in ordinary group therapy is that people find it hard to be honest with one another to their faces. The BTB technique is a stylized and formalized procedure that requires a minimum amount of time on the part of the therapist and is one that a suitable group may utilize without a professional therapist in attendance. Members of the group are prepared by informing them that the method is designed to help a person express himself to others and to learn what others really think of him. They are then asked to volunteer their participation as both patients and therapists. Each member in the present and following sessions is given a half hour to tell all about himself without interruption. At the end of this time the involved patient is requested to sit with his back to the group while each member talks about the "absent" member. This requires 20 to 40 minutes. The "absent" member is asked to face the group again while the therapist briefly summarizes what has been said. The patient is given about 5 minutes to make his rebuttal, his responses being studied by the therapist in terms of denials, agreements, evasions and other defenses. Then the patient sits in the center of the group exposed to the interrogation of the group. The therapist may interrupt these questions and terminate the session by sending the patient out of the room should emotions become too violent. It is to be expected that the patient will be upset by his inquisition, but this very turmoil causes him to unfreeze, better to face up to himself, realizing how he impresses others. At the very next session the patient is asked to summarize the meaning of the past session for himself. The BTB technique is planned to facilitate the release of emotions and to expedite change through altered behavior.

It is sometimes propitious, in the opinion of some therapists, once a dynamic understanding of a patient's emotional problems becomes clear to expedite change through arranging an appropriate scenario that encourages the patient to act out his conflicts in a controlled way. E. E. Mintz (1974) presents a number of such episodes from her experience with marathon groups. The procedures employed, some of which draw from psychodramatic and Gestalt therapeutic techniques, are bounded only by the imagination and dramatic proclivities of the group leader and participant members. Patients who are vulnerable or resistant to "interpretations" in individual sessions are often, with this technique, better capable of cutting into core problems and facing their difficulties. Moreover, the process stimulates the other group members to open up many personal painful areas for discussion.

Bach (1974) utilizes and describes a technique of aggressive therapeutic group leadership through participating actively in fights that occur between members of marathon groups. He considers neutrality and passive objectivity, the preferred stance of psychoanalysis, a form of alienation and not caring, which violates the intimate participative spirit of the marathon experience. The therapist "attacks" by frank verbal explosions and expressions of frustration, irritation, and indignation justified by what is happening in the group.

Such actions may be leveled at a passive cotherapist who refuses to participate actively in the group work, at a whole group of "ground-rule" violators (e.g., people who avoid confronting each other with their feelings), at subgroups (e.g., those who hide in a cozy, pairing maneuver), and at individual members who manifest patterns that interfere with the group experience (e.g., monopolizing, controlling, etc.). Bach provides amusing examples of his "attack therapy," which, though seemingly countertransferentially inspired at times, appear, according to his accounts, to result in a more intimate, experience-sharing communion among the members. He expresses his philosophy of therapy in this way: "We must all relearn how to fight to regain our genuineness. Only after this are we ready to share love."

C. Goldberg (1975), on the other hand, stresses an existential stance and believes that patients can be actively taught skills in interpersonal relationships which can mediate their own and others' loneliness and despair, and which can probe ubiquitous alienation and existential exhaustion. Toward this end, the group leader actively participates in the group by his openness, self-disclosures, display of congruence of feeling, and modeling of behavior. There is a minimization of verbal and nonactive interaction. Interpersonal skills are actively taught through such methods as a deciphering of nonverbal "body language," a listing and checking of one's irrational attitudes and an exposure of one's manipulations and defenses in order to influence situations outside of the group and to revise strategies and core attitudes.

SPECIAL PROBLEMS

It can be seen from the previous discussion that some group therapists develop their unique techniques and ways of looking at group phenomena that, while valid for them, may not be sound, plausible, or found useful by all of their patients. Experimenting with these procedures and ideas, however, will reveal their value.

The management by the therapist of special problems among patients will be essential where they obstruct group interaction. Among these are the following:

The Silent Patient

Behind silence may lurk a variety of dynamisms. Sometimes detached, withdrawn persons may be drawn out by the therapist's asking them a pointed question in relation to what is currently going on in the group: "How do *you* feel about this?" Since the response will be hesitant and unsure, more aggressive patients may attempt to interrupt to take the floor over for themselves. The therapist may block this subterfuge and continue to encourage the reluctant patient to articulate. The patient may also be asked directly to report on any dreams. What sometimes helps is to allot a certain amount of time to each member, say, 5 minutes.

The Monopolizer

The person who attempts to monopolize the session may be manifesting a power struggle with the therapist or a masochistic maneuver to bring on his wrath. The aggressive, narcissistic patient who insists on consuming the session for himself will usually be interrupted by one or more members who resent his self-seeking. Where this does not occur, the therapist may halt the patient by asking another member what he is thinking about or by directing a question at the group as to whether they want the monopolizing patient to carry on all the discussion. The same tactics may apply to an interacting pair who interminably carry on a discussion between themselves.

The Quarreling Dyad

A manifestation of unresolved sibling or parental rivalry are two patients who constantly engage in verbal dogfights. This eventually becomes boring for the rest of the group and may sponsor a withdrawal into fantasy. The best way to deal with this phenomenon is by working toward each participant's tracing the transferential roots of the enmity. This should not be too difficult from their dreams and free associations. An interruption by the therapist of uncontrollable outbreaks of bickering is, of course, in order.

Acting-out Patients

Because groups are action-oriented, because multiple transferences are set loose, because individuals other than the therapist are available for the discharge of erotic or hostile impulses, because not enough opportunity is given each patient to verbalize, and because upsetting revelations on the part of the group members may set off identical problems in the patient, acting-out is a frequent phenomenon in groups. The therapist may caution the members to talk out rather than to act out. The group members may be required to report at a regular session the activities engaged in between members outside the group. The therapist may try to reduce the anxiety level of the group. It is possible that the therapist's own countertransference is encouraging the acting-out. One should be constantly on guard for this. It may be necessary to reorganize the group when too many acting-out members are present. The therapist may insist on acting-out members being simultaneously in individual therapy.

The Private Session in the Group

Some patients will attempt to utilize the group time to get a private session with the therapist. They will look at and direct their conversation to the therapist, ignoring the presence of the group. This reaction is especially common in a patient who wants to be the preferred sibling. When this happens, the therapist may ask the patient to focus his remarks on the group, may question the group as to how they feel about the patient's carrying on an intimate discussion with him, may ask other members to associate to the patient's verbalizations, and

finally, he may suggest that the patient come in for a private session.

The Habitual Latecomer

Drifting into the session after it is under way will mobilize resentment among the members, particularly where it is constantly indulged. This resistance should be handled as a special problem, requesting the patient to try to understand what is behind his neglectful conduct. He ultimately may be threatened with removal from the group if he does not come on time. This may bring to the surface the resentment toward the group that he is expressing in his symptom.

The Patient Who Insists that He Is Getting Worse not Better

There are patients who display a negative therapeutic reaction that they are only too eager to communicate to the group. Dependent patients who have been in the group for years, and who cling to it for emotional sustenance, usually join in to complain regarding the ineffectuality of therapy. This can influence the group morale and may be disturbing, especially to new members. The therapist may handle such a reaction by citing examples from the progress made by various members of the group to disprove the thesis that therapy does not help and, where applicable, may point out the aim of the complainant to drive certain members (especially new members) out of the group.

The Accessory Therapist

A variety of mechanisms operate in the patient who is trying to replace the therapist. It may be a protest on the part of a dependent patient to the therapist's passivity. It may be an attempt to undermine authority. It may be a way of seeking favor with the therapist. It may be a gesture to compete with and replace the therapist. Irrespective of its basis, the patient may soon gather about him a group of followers as well as adversaries. The best way to handle this maneuver is to ask the other members what they think is happening, until the therapeutic pretender quiets down. The therapist may also ask the competing patient why he feels obliged to "play psychoanalyst."

Mobilizing Activity

Where progress has bogged down and members seem to be in a stalemate, one may stir up activity by (1) asking the group why this is so, (2) introducing psychodrama or role playing, (3) asking a member to talk about what role he feels that he has been assuming in the group, then "going around," the other members commenting on what role they feel that he is playing, (4) asking each member to talk about his feelings concerning the two people on each side of him, (5) utilizing one or more techniques of encounter therapy, (6) extending the length of a session up to a marathon session, (7) introducing several new members into the group, (8) determining the nature of the resistance and interpreting it.

When a Therapist Becomes Bored with a Session

In this situation the therapist may ask, "Is anybody else besides myself bored with this conversation?" Then the group could explore the basis for such a reaction.

MISCELLANEOUS GROUP APPROACHES

Preintake and Postintake Groups

Preintake groups, which act as a forum for discussion and orientation, are a valuable aspect of clinic functioning where a delay is unavoidable before formal intake. Up to 20 people may attend, and sessions may be given at weekly, bimonthly and even monthly intervals. Parents of children awaiting intake may be organized into a group of this type, which may go on for three to six monthly sessions. Postintake

groups may take place before assignment, and meetings may be spaced up to one month apart. Here some therapeutic changes are possible as disturbing problems are introduced and elaborated. These pretherapy groups serve as useful means of selecting patients for ongoing group therapy. They are worthy orientation devices and help prepare and motivate patients for therapy.

Special Age Groups

Group therapy with children is usually of an activity nature. The size of children's groups must be kept below that of adult groups (Geller, 1962). For instance, in the age group up to 6 years, two or three children constitute the total. Both boys and girls can be included. Single-sex groups are (1) from 6 to 8 years, which optimally consist of three to five members; (2) from 8 to 12 years, which may have four to six members; (3) from 12 to 14 years, which may contain six to eight youngsters; and (4) from 14 to 16 years, which have the same number. Mixed-sex groups at the oldest age level are sometimes possible.

Play therapy is the communicative medium up to 12 years of age, the focus being on feelings and conflicts. It is obvious that the ability to communicate is a prerequisite here. Beyond 12 years discussions rather than play constitute the best activity medium. Techniques include analysis of behavior in the group, confrontation, and dream and transference interpretation. Both activity (during which acting-out may be observed) and discussion take place at various intervals. Interventions of the therapist should be such so as not to hamper spontaneity. Discussion is stimulated by the therapist, and silences are always interrupted. Ideally, individual therapy is carried on conjointly with group therapy, particularly at the beginning of treatment.

Group psychotherapy with older people has met with considerable success in maintaining interest and alertness, in promoting social integration, and in enhancing the concept of self in both affective and organic disorders (Goldfarb, AI, & Wolk, 1966). Where the goal is reconstructive, oldsters may be mixed with younger people.

Behavior Therapy in Groups

Behavioral techniques (Lazarus 1968; Meacham & Wiesen, 1969; Wolpe, 1969; Liberman, 1970; Fensterheim, 1971) lend themselves admirably to group usage, and results, as well as controlled studies, indicate that behavioral change may be achieved by the employment of methods such as behavioral rehearsal, modeling, discrimination learning, and social reinforcement. The group process itself tends to accelerate behavioral strategies. Homogeneous groups seem to do best, the selection of members being restricted to those who may benefit from the retraining of specific target behaviors. Thus, the control of obesity, shyness, speaking anxiety, insomnia, and phobias (flying, insects, mice, closed spaces, etc.) can best be achieved in a group where the participants are focused on the abolition of similar undesireable behaviors. In institutional settings, particularly with psychotic patients, group decision-making strategies may be practiced, reinforcement being offered through token economies. Short-term hospitalization for severe obsessive-compulsives, and perhaps alcoholics and drug addicts, treated in special groups of populations with similar maladaptive behaviors can often be a rewarding enterprise (Rachman, S., et al, 1971).

Individually oriented behavioral interventions [see Chapter 49, Techniques in Behavior (Conditioning) Therapy] may be employed alone in a group setting, or in combination with psychodrama, role playing, Gestalt tactics, encounter maneuvers, or formal group therapy procedures (inspirational, educational, or analytic) depending on the training and flexibility of the therapist.

A routine practiced commonly is to see the patient initially in individual therapy to take a history, to explore the problem area in depth as to origin, circumstances under which it is exaggerated, reinforcements it receives as well as secondary gains, and goals to be approached, employing the traditional processes of behavioral analysis. If group therapy is decided on, it is best to introduce the patient into a newly formed group with persons suffering from the same difficulties and who have approximately the same level of intelligence and knowledge of psychological processes. The size of the group varies from 5 to 10 individuals. A cotherapist is valuable and sometimes indispensable as in the treatment of sexual problems. The initial few sessions may be relatively unstructured to help facilitate the group process. The time of sessions varies from 1½ to 3 or 4 hours. During the starting sessions members are encouraged to voice their problems and to define what they would like to achieve in the sessions, the therapist helping to clarify the goals.

A. P. Goldstein and Wolpe (1971) have outlined the following operations important in group behavioral treatment: feedback, modeling, behavior rehearsal, desensitization, motivational stimulation, and social reinforcement. *Feedback* is provided by the patient being confronted with the reactions of the other members to his own verbalizations and responses. This gives him an opportunity to alter these if he so desires. *Modeling* oneself after how others approach and master the desired behavior is an important learning modality. The therapists may engage in role playing or psychodrama to facilitate modeling. *Behavior rehearsal* similarly employs role playing involving the patient directly. Repetition of the process with different members helps solidify appropriate reactions, the patient engaging in role reversal when necessary. Here video playbacks may be important so that patients may see how they come across. Counter-conditioning and extinction methods (systematic desensitization, role playing with the introduction of the anxiety-provoking stimulus, encouraging expression of forbidden emotions in the group like anger) eventually lead to *desensitization*. The therapist provides direction and guidelines for appropriate behavior which with the pressure of the group helps create *motivation* and *social reinforcement*. Support is provided the patient when necessary. Specific assignments outside the group may be given the patient.

Relaxation methods may be employed in a group for the relief of tension and such symptoms as insomnia. Any of the hypnotic or meditational methods outlined in this volume (q.v.) may be utilized; their impact is catalyzed by implementation in a group atmosphere.

Behavioral tactics are ideally suited for habit disorders related to eating, such as obesity, smoking, gambling, alcoholic overindulgence, and drug addiction. Members for each group must be chosen who suffer from the same problem and possess adequate motivation to cooperate with the interventions.

Where problems are centered around lack of assertiveness, assertiveness training can be highly effective. Fensterheim (1971) describes his method of dealing with this problem. Groups of 9 or 10 consisting of men and women in approximately the same number, roughly homogeneous as to age, marital status, achievement, education, and socioeconomic status (to enhance modeling) meet 2¼ hours once weekly. Seats are arranged in a horseshoe configuration, the opening serving as a stage for role playing and behavior rehearsal. Sessions are begun by each member reporting on the assignment given him the previous week. Successes are rewarded with approval by therapist and members. Failures are discussed. On the basis of the report the assignment for the following week may be formulated. Special problems will evoke discussion by the group. Members are asked to keep their own records of assertive incidents that they indulged in during the past week. Special exercises are employed with role playing depending on problems of individual members, such as talking in a loud voice, behaving unpleasantly, telling an interesting story, expressing a warm feeling toward other group members, practicing progressive expressions of anger (reading a dialogue and portraying an angry role, improvising one's own dialogue, role playing angry scenes and incidents reported by other members, role playing scenes from one's own life and experience). About 5 to 10 minutes of each session is spent doing these exercises over a 4-month period. Roughly 10 to 15 minutes may be used for systematic group desensitization from a common hierarchy prepared by the group. At the end of each session members formulate their own next assignment or if they are blocked, this is suggested.

Phobias respond remarkably well to group behavioral methods. Here the patient selection must also be homogeneous as in assertive training. Aronson (1974) describes a program that has been successful in 90 percent of his patients completing it. The program is designed for fear of flying (but the ideas can be adapted to other phobias, such as fear of cars, ships, elevators, tunnels, bridges, high places, etc.). Initial individual consultations are geared toward establishing a working relationship with the applicant, and essentially to do a behavioral analysis, although Aronson stresses a dynamic accent. A high degree of motivation is desirable. "How much do you want to get over this fear?" may be asked. At the first session the therapist structures the program (the first five sessions devoted to a discussion of fear of flying; one or two educational briefings with safety experts, pilots, and other air personnel to answer questions; seven to eight sessions on discussion and methods of overcoming the fears). The optional size of the group is 8 to 12 persons. Meetings are for 1½ hours once weekly. Presession and postsession meetings of ½ hour each without the therapist may be recommended. Pertinent reading materials on air travel and development should be available.

The following rules are delineated: (a) Each member will within the time limitations, be permitted to talk freely about his fears. (b) At the second session each member is to bring in a drawing depicting the most pleasurable aspect that he can imagine about a commercial air flight and a second drawing depicting the most unpleasant consequences. He is also invited to talk about any dreams that he has had about travel. (In recounting such dreams no associations are encouraged nor interpretations made regarding defenses.) (c) The following exercises (Aronson, 1974) aimed at anxiety control are introduced:

1. While lying down or seated comfortably on a chair, visualize all the sensations and anxieties you experience while on a plane. Simply visualizing yourself on a plane may make you anxious at first. You may find yourself wanting to avoid thinking about it. If so, let your mind dwell on pleasant thoughts for a while. As soon as you feel somewhat more relaxed, reenter the fantasy of being anxious on a plane. Focus initially on the least frightening aspects of flight. Gradually allow yourself to visualize more frightening fears. Each time you practice this exercise you will be able to get closer to the dangerous situation and stay with it longer. Do this exercise twice a day for a week (based on Wolpe, 1969).

2. Picture yourself in the *most pleasant* situation you can imagine. Let your mind dwell on this situation as long as possible. Then imagine yourself on a plane. Some of the positive feelings you experienced in your fantasy will come back with you and help allay your anxiety when you next imagine yourself on a plane or actually fly (based on Perls, 1969).

3. Visualize the most unpleasant situation you can possibly think of— a situation even *more unpleasant* to you than being on a plane. You will find that when you leave this fantasy and imagine yourself flying or actually on a flight, you will experience less anxiety (based on Perls, 1969).

Should any of these exercises stir up anxiety, the members must indicate this to prevent it from getting too deep. (d) Should members start feeling strongly hostile to each other, the therapist encourages verbalization and explains that strong, positive feelings among all group members will be necessary for success. (e) Talking about personal matters other than those related to fears of flying is to be discouraged. (f) After the fourth or fifth session one or two educational sessions are held with local airline representatives to answer technical questions about flying and safety measures. (g)

After the eighth session the entire group visits an airport and, if possible, meets in a stationary airliner for about 1 hour. Members talk about their fears every step of the way. Around the tenth and twelfth session the group leader suggests a target date for a short flight. If too much anxiety prevails, this date can be temporarily postponed until the anxiety recedes. The leader must set the time with the airline representatives and accompany the group. After the flight the group reconvenes to discuss the reactions. (h) Members are encouraged to arrange their own flights and to continue in group therapy for a few sessions thereafter.

Following this format, other phobias may be treated in a group setting, introducing whatever modifications are essential considering the nature of the target symptom. Videotaping and playback may be employed, should the therapist possess the apparatus, particularly for role-playing exercises.

Experiential (Encounter and Marathon) Therapy

The group therapy movement has mushroomed out to include a variety of forms. The traditional model, which focused on inspiration, education, and insight acquisition, has been supplemented by groups whose objective is experiential with a wide variety of techniques. Many names have been given to these new arrangements including Gestalt, human relations training, human awareness, leadership training, T-groups, sensitivity therapy, and encounter therapy. The time element (traditionally 90 minutes) has been stretched sometimes to several hours, 12 hours, 24 hours, or several days with time off for sleep (marathon groups). Encounter therapy may be an ongoing process like any other form of group therapy, or it may be brief, from one to a dozen sessions.

A constructive group experience with a small group of people who are educationally on a relatively equal level and who permit themselves to disclose their self-doubts and personal weaknesses can be most liberating to the participants. The fact that one can expose himself to others and reveal his fears and his desires of which he is ashamed, without being rejected or ridiculed, can be reassuring and strengthening. The person feels accepted for himself, with all his flaws, rather than for the pose that he presents to the world. Whereas previously he may have regarded interpersonal relationships as threatening, he finds that they can embrace a sustaining richness. As communication between the members broadens, they share more and more their hidden secrets and anxieties. They begin to trust and accept themselves as they learn to trust and accept the other participants. Interpersonal confrontations, while temporarily upsetting, may even ultimately bring the individual into contact with repudiated aspects of himself.

By communicating without restraint the members are enabled to learn that other individuals have problems similar to and even more severe than their own. The realization enables them to relax their guards and to open up more with one another. The "encounters" in the group will probably sooner or later release underlying patterns of conflict, such as hostility toward certain members, excessive tendencies to defy and obstruct, inferiority feelings, unrealistic expectations, grandoise boastings, and other maneuvers that have little to do with the immediate group situation but rather are manifestations of fundamental characterologic flaws. Under the guidance of a skilled group leader the encounter group becomes a means through which the members become aware of how they are creating many of their own troubles. By talking things out they are able to correct some of their misperceptions.

Some observers would call this process psychotherapy. We are dealing here with semantics. The effects of the encounter group can be psychotherapeutic, particularly in persons who are ready for change and who already have, perhaps in previous psychotherapeutic experiences, worked through their resistances to change. But psychotherapy, in most cases, is not the achieved objective. What is accomplished is an educational realignment that challenges certain attitudes and teaches the person how to function better in certain situa-

tions. If one happens in the course of this education to change a neurotic pattern of behavior, so much the better, but it must be emphasized that psychotherapeutic groups are run differently from encounter groups. They are organized on a long-term basis and focused on neurotic symptoms and intrapsychic processes.

Even though there is some evidence that encounter group experiences may have a therapeutic effect on neurotic personality structure, our observations at the Postgraduate Center for Mental Health indicate that personality changes, when they do occur, are temporary, rapidly disappearing once the participant leaves the encounter group and returns to his habitual life setting. We have worked with the staffs of various institutional units, including psychiatric clinics, correctional institutions, schools, and a host of professional and nonprofessional organizations. Our delight at "depth" changes brought about by encounter techniques has been generally short-lived when we do follow-up studies after a reasonable time has elapsed. This fact does not depreciate what the encounter group can do for a participant, because in many instances it does alert the individual to his neurotic shortcomings and motivates him to seek psychotherapy on a more intensive level. Many of our "cured" encounter clients later ask for more thorough psychotherapeutic help, once they have an inkling of their problems.

The usual marathon group exposes group members to constant association of approximately 30 hours, generally in the course of which a 5-hour break is taken. During the first 15 hours of interaction there is a gradual sloughing off of defenses, and, in the last hours, a "feedback" is encouraged in which the therapist enjoins the patients to utilize the understanding of themselves to verbalize or execute certain constructive attitudes or patterns. Highly emotional outbursts are encountered with this intensity of exposure, and corrective emotional experiences may occur. The therapist participates actively with the group, expressing his or her own reactions to the members but avoiding interjecting personal needs and problems. A variety of techniques may be employed. For example, at Esalen a combination of theories and methods are used, including Perls' Gestalt therapy, Freud's unconscious motivational ideas, Rolf's structural integration and body balance, Lowen's bioenergetic theory, Moreno's psychodrama, Shutz's encounter tactics, and other sensitivity training methods (Quaytman, 1969).

These experiential therapies are sometimes resorted to by psychotherapists when their patients have reached a stalemate in individual or group therapy. In many cases the specific working on the resistance resolves such blockage of progress without the need for dramatic interventions. However, in spite of this, there are some patients who seem unable to move ahead. Productions dry up, boredom develops, motivation to continue therapy dwindles away. Under these circumstances some therapists have found that referring their patients for encounter therapy or a weekend marathon suddenly opens them up, producing a flood of fresh material to work on, and sponsoring more enthusiasm for continued treatment.

Not too many therapists are qualified to do experiential therapy. Apart from experience which may be gained by participation as a patient in encounter groups or in several marathons, it requires a special personality structure of great extraversiveness, spontaneous enthusiasm, and histrionic inventiveness. Sufficient flexibility must exist to permit a rapid switching of tactics and changing of formats to meet individual and group needs. The role of the leader will vary, of course, with the individual. Most therapists view themselves as participant observers who, while admitting and sharing some of their own problems, hold themselves up as models of expected behavior. Emotional stability of the therapist and control of countertransference are under these circumstances vital. The presence of a trained cotherapist is often of value in the service of objectivity. Both therapists who do marathon therapy and patients who receive it are usually enthusiastic. Follow-up studies have been more conservative as to the actual benefits. The immediate experience may be an intensely moving one, and participants usually believe that they have benefited and are reluctant to end their relationship. They feel that they have acquired a new understanding of themselves. Often they do. But we may anticipate that benefits will not persist unless the environment to which the member returns reinforces the new behaviors and attitudes that have been learned. This is usually not the case, however. One would anticipate that unless some intrapsychic change has occurred, the old defensive balances will usually be restored. It is for this reason that results will be best if the individual continues in individual or group therapy to work on the significance to him of the encounter or marathon experience.

It has been the practice, unfortunately, to offer encounters or marathons for unscreened applicants willing to pay the price of admission on the theory that even a bit of confrontation, challenge, and encounter can provide fruitful bounties. Undoubtedly there are persons who may get a good deal out of an intensive interpersonal experience without formally entering into structured psychotherapy. This does not compensate for the unstable souls, balanced precariously on the razor edge of rationality, who can be damaged by exposure to such groups. There are some patients (usually borderline cases) who cannot tolerate the intense emotional relationships of the marathon experience (Stone, WN, & Tieger, 1971; Yalom & Lieberman, 1971). Such individuals may develop frank psychoses as a result of breakdown of their defenses. Unless the therapist is well trained and does diagnostic interviews on all applicants (which is not often the case), he or she is risking trouble, however infrequent this is reported.

Even where an initial diagnostic study qualifies a person for this type of therapy, difficulties can occur in those with fragile defenses. The task of the leader is to pick out of the group those members who in their speech and behavior are beginning to lose control. Removing such vulnerable persons from the group, temporarily by assigning to them isolated tasks and perhaps giving them supportive reassurance in a brief interview, may permit them to reenter the group when their reality sense is restored. The therapist will have to interrupt any challenges or attacks that are levied at such persons, refocusing attention elsewhere.

Generally, the individual entering an experiential or marathon group is instructed in the responsibility that he has in the group, the need for physical restraint and abstinence from drugs and alcohol, and the fact that while his behavior in the group is related to his life style, that there may be new and better ways of relating that he can learn. Sometimes a contract is drawn up as to what changes a person desires to achieve. Accordingly, the individual may gauge for himself how far ahead he moves. Emphasis is on the "here-and-now" rather than on the past.

As to encounter techniques, these vary with the inventiveness of the leader. In a small group the members may be asked to "go around" and give their impressions of all the other members, positive and negative. The leader may then say, "Reach out and put your hands on the shoulders of the person next to you. He (or she) will do likewise. Look into each other's eyes and say whatever comes into your mind." Or, "Hold the hands of the person next to you, and describe what you feel these hands are saying."

Utilizing art materials (crayons, chalk, pastels, etc.), the members may be asked to draw anything that represents how they feel and also how they would like to feel. The group later associates to or discusses these productions. The same may be done with clay or plasticene materials.

Two members may be asked to approach each other in front of the group and to communicate in nonverbal terms, i.e., by touching, gestures, facial expressions, etc. The group then discusses the nature of the communication.

Schutz (1967a) has described a number of "warm-up" and other techniques that may be used. One technique in helping a person give up rigid controls and distrust of others is to encourage him to stand with his back to the therapist and to shut his eyes and fall straight back with trust that the therapist will not let him hurt himself. Patients show many defenses to this maneuver, and the discussion of their fears and

other feelings provides a stimulus for elaboration in the group. Later members may try this maneuver with each other when they develop confidence in permitting themselves to fall back.

Many touching maneuvers are employed for the same purpose. One is to invite patients to stretch out on a couch and to have them lifted by many hands and passed along, their bodies being stroked in the process. Associations to this are, as may be imagined, often interesting.

Negative outcomes with experiential groups are to be expected in view of the superficial screening of the participants and the large number of untrained leaders who contact these groups with few or no limits on the selection of techniques. It would seem propititious to set up certification and licensure requirements for potential leaders of encounter groups to minimize hazards (Hartley, Roback, & Abramowitz, 1975).

It is to be expected that when people come together for an extended therapeutic experience that hopes are high and that there may be unreasonable expectations of benefit. Despite efforts to control postures and defenses and to substitute for them conventional modes of relating, the facades soon break down, particularly when the individual is criticized and challenged. The close contact, the extended time period of interaction, the developing fatigue, the actual and implied pressures for change all add to the uniqueness of the experience. Intimacies develop that the participant needs to control since subgroups and pairing are strongly discouraged. As the individual realizes the consequence of his own acts for the reactions of others, his motivation for change may be increased. This is further augmented by reinforcements that he receives in the form of group approval for any changes that he exhibits. Where patients are not in ongoing groups or individual therapy, it is advisable to schedule a follow-up meeting 3 or 4 weeks later to discuss postmarathon impressions and experiences.

The literature on encounter (experiential groups) has proliferated since the mid-1960s. The following are recommended: Back (1972), Burton (1969), M. Goodman

(1972), Kuehn and Crinella (1969), E. E. Mintz (1967), Perls (1969), Rabin (1971), C. R. Rogers (1970), M. Rosenbaum (1969), Strean (1971–1972). The list continues to grow. There is also ample material being published on marathon therapy. A sampling follows: Bach (1966, 1967a–d), Casriel and Deitch (1968), Dies and Hess (1971), A. Ellis (1970), Gendzel (1970, 1972), J. Mann (1970), Rachman (1969, 1975), Sklar et al. (1970), Spotnitz (1968), Stoller (1967, 1968), Teicher et al. (1974), and Yalom and Lieberman (1971).

Transactional Analytic Groups

Transactional analysis is a highly structured group of procedures, developed by Eric Berne in 1950 (see page 233), that are designed to help people achieve an expanded awareness of their interpersonal operations. It is predicated on the idea that human beings carry within themselves a threefold set of directives that influence their behavior in positive and negative ways. The first group of prescripts are residues of parental conditionings, the individual functioning as if driven by the values and attitudes of the parents. When this happens the "parent" (P) within is said to take over. The second group of regulations are the survival remnants of the "child" (C) and consist of immature promptings and habitudes, parcels of his past. The third group, the "adult" (A), is the logical, grown-up self that mediates a reasonable disposition. These divisions roughly correspond to Freud's superego, id, and ego; indeed, there is much in transactional analysis that parodies traditional dynamic formulations. What is unique and original about the method is the crisp, humorous, provocative language tabs assigned to different patterns that people display in their relationship with each other. This enables some persons, confused by the complex concepts and vernacular of psychoanalysis, to acquire insight into their drives and defenses rapidly, to accept more readily responsibility for them, and to work toward a primacy of the "adult" within themselves. It is little wonder that the volumes *Games People Play* by

Berne (1964) and *I'm OK—You're OK* by T. Harris (1967) have stirred the popular imagination, plummeting the books to the top of the best-seller list.

Not all therapists, however, are able to do transactional analysis. What is required is a combination of special traits that include an extremely keen sense of humor, a facility for dramatics, a quick ability to perceive patterns as they come through in the patient's speech and behavior, and a unique capacity to label their use with relevant salty titles.

Treatment in transactional analysis begins with several individual interviews. Patients are instructed in the dynamics of the transactional approach and may be given assigned readings (Berne, 1964; Harris, 1967). A treatment "contract" is drawn up describing the goal of therapy in a specific and clear-cut way, and the patient is introduced to his group. Four overlapping phases of therapy are generally described (Karpman, SB, 1972).

The first phase is structural analysis concerned with understanding and recognizing "ego states," which objectively demonstrate themselves in body attitudes, tone of voice, vocabulary, and effect on others. Only one ego state manifests itself within the person at a time. Thus the individual's "parent" (P) may come through in vocabulary and behavior expressing what is right and wrong and what people should or should not do. The parent can be prejudiced, critical, pompous, and domineering, or nurturing, sympathetic, forgiving, reassuring, smothering, oversolicitous, infantilizing. The "adult" (A) is the "sensible, rational, logical, accurate, factual, objective, neutral, and straight-talking side of the personality." The "child" (C) can be "free," i.e., happy, intuitive, spontaneous, adventurous, and creative; or the child can be "adapted," i.e., showing reactions akin to those of parents like being sulky, frightened, guilty, sad, etc. The patient in the group during the first several weeks is encouraged to identify his ego states within himself and as they come through in his behavior toward the others in the group. He learns also his "skull transactions" (i.e., the internal dialogue that goes on between the ego states) as well as ways of "getting the trash out of your head" (i.e., the adult decision to start new internal dialogues— "A 'go away' or 'That's my Parent talking' often quickly helps a patient 'divorce his parent'"). Catchy slogans are used to identify and describe attitudes of P, A, and C. Decision making, views of the world, modes of cataloging external information, and even examining resistance to therapy are referred to the separate outlooks of parent, adult, and child.

The second phase of therapy is "transactional analysis" (TA), which deals with the clarifying and diagraming of conversations with others, as by drawing arrows from one of the ego states of the person to one of the ego states of the other person. One's child may talk to another's child ("fun talk"), or adult to adult ("straight talk"), or parent to child ("helpful talk"). Various combinations can thus exist. In a group a patient's transactions can be drawn on a blackboard. In this way the patient learns the typical "games" that he plays with people. Transference is handled as a "typical transaction" and the precedents traced to early family transactions.

The third phase is "game analysis." "Games" are involved transactions of a number of people that lead to a "payoff" unless interrupted. They have social and psychological dimensions. Repetitive patterns and defenses are defined by provocative or humorous titles enabling the individual to accept them as part of himself without too great anxiety. This is one of the virtues of transactional analysis. It is less apt than other dynamic therapies to set up resistance to the acknowledgment of destructive drives. The individual is more likely to accept the fact that he is driven by neurotic drives if these are presented humorously as universal foibles. He becomes less defensive and more willing to relinquish them.

One of the four basic positions is taken toward the world: (1) "I'm OK, you're OK," (2) "I'm OK, you're not OK," (3) "I'm not OK, you're OK," (4) "I'm not OK, you're not OK." Games are played for figurative "trading stamps" for the purpose of collecting important prizes. "For instance, a man needing only two more books of mad stamps comes home from work, starts a fight with his wife, collects the two books of mad stamps, and cashes them in at the bar for a justifiable drink." In this way the individual develops rapidly an awareness of both social and psychological levels of behavior—not in abstract terms but by recognizing how he utilizes people to perpetuate his own aims ("payoffs"). Sooner or later, the individual is able to interrupt the games (avoid being "hooked," achieve a "quit point") before they sweep him into his habitual acting-out patterns. He develops a cynical attitude toward his games that gives him motivation to stop them.

The fourth phase is "script analysis." A script is the individual's life plan evolved in early childhood. A "script matrix" charts the relationship with the parents and the crucial injunctions that have circumscribed the individual's life. The "script story" delineates the patient's life pattern and outlines the predicted end of the script. In the course of exploring the script early memories may be revived. The object of working with scripts is to give up old unwanted ones and "get a new show on the road." "'Permission' in therapy is given to break the 'witch mother' injunctions. This is followed by a necessary period of up to 6 weeks of protection for the new ego, and this is dependent on the therapist having more potency than the witch parents. Patients gain a final autonomy in therapy and choose their own style of life or even live script free.'" Countertransference is recognized. "The therapist should be alert to detect witch messages in his own script and should not pass these on to his patients."

Transactional analysis for groups has attracted a sizable number of therapists, some of whom have joined the International Transactional Analysis Association, which holds seminars and study groups in many cities. Clinical membership is acquired after 2 years of supervised therapy and a written and oral examination. Publication on the subject has been ample. A *Transactional Analysis Journal* contains some of the writings.

Psychodrama and Role Playing

Moreno (1934, 1946, 1966b) created a useful group therapy method, "psychodrama," which he first introduced in 1925 and which has evolved into a number of clinical methods, including sociodrama, the axiodrama, role playing, and the analytic psychodrama. Many of these have been incorporated into modern Gestalt, encounter, and marathon therapy.

In the hands of a skilled therapist psychodrama is a valuable adjunct in helping patients work through resistances toward translating their insights into action. The initial tactic in the group is the "warm-up" process to facilitate movement. This may take the form of the director (the therapist) insisting that the group remain silent ("cluster warm-up") for a period. As tension mounts, it will finally be broken by some member expostulating about a problem, his verbalizations drawing a "cluster" of persons around him. Other members may similarly come forth with feelings and stimulate "clusters" interested in what they are saying. Soon the whole group is brought together around a common theme. The "star" chosen is the person whose personality reflects the problem area most clearly. Another warm-up method is the "chain of association." Here the group spontaneously brings up fears and associations until an engrossing theme evolves. The star chosen is the person who is most concerned with the theme. A third warm-up is initiated by the director ("directed warm-up") who, knowing the problems of the constituent members, announces the theme. A "patient-directed warm-up" is one in which a patient announces to the group the subject with which he would like to deal.

The star is groomed for the roles that he is to play with representatives of important people in his past and current life, selected from other group members ("auxiliaries") whose needs for insight preferably fit in with the parts they assume. The director facilitates the working together of the group on their problems, while focusing on one person (the "protagonist"). Among the techniques are (1) "role reversal," during which a protagonist and auxiliary reverse positions; (2) "the double," another member seconding for and supporting the protagonist; (3) "the soliloquy," characterized by a recitation by the protagonist of his insights and projections; and (4) "the mirror," auxiliary egos portraying what the protagonist must feel.

By forcing themselves to verbalize and act parts, the members are helped to break through blocks in perceiving, feeling, and acting. Sometimes the therapist (the director) decides which life situations from the patient's history are to be reenacted in order to work at important conflictual foci. A technique often followed is that assumed by "auxiliary egos," who are trained workers or former patients "standing in" for the patient and spontaneously uttering ideas and thoughts that they believe the patient may not yet be able to verbalize, thus helping "to bring his personal and collective drama to life and to correct it" (Moreno, 1966a). As he reenacts situations, the patient may play not only the role of himself, but also roles of other significant persons in his life, such as his parents or siblings. The therapist, in the role as "director," may remain silent or inject questions and suggestions. Material elicited during psychodrama is immediately utilized in the presence of the "actor" patient and the group "audience." This technique usually has an emotionally cathartic value, and it may also help the patient understand problems revealed by his own actions and thoughts as well as those reflected by other members of the group. By venting his feelings and fantasies in the role of actor, the patient often desensitizes himself to inner terrors, achieves hidden wishes, prepares himself for future contingencies, and otherwise helps to resolve many of his deeper problems and conflicts. Psychodrama may, instead of being protagonist-centered, i.e., focused on private problems of the patient, be group-centered, concerning itself with problems facing all members of the group.

An important function of the auxiliary egos is to represent absentee persons important in the life of the protagonist. Auxiliary egos, thus, are best recruited from those persons present in the group who come from a sociocultural environment similar to that of the patient. The auxiliary egos portray the patient's own internal figures, forcing him to face them in reality. In this way the symbolic representatives of his inner life are experienced as real objects with whom the patient has an opportunity to cope. The director enters into the drama being portrayed with various instructions and interpretations. Choice or rejection of the auxiliary egos is vested in the protagonist or the director. Since auxiliary egos are representations, they may play any role, any age, either sex, even the part of a dead person whose memory is still alive in the protagonist. If necessary, and where the protagonist can tolerate it, bodily contact is made between him and the auxiliary ego to supply reassurances and to restore aspects of closeness that the protagonist has lacked. Thus, a person who never experienced real "fathering" may get this from the actions of an auxiliary ego.

Props are sometimes employed, such as an "auxiliary chair" which may represent an absentee personage. Living or dead family members may be portrayed by several empty chairs around a table, each chair in fantasy being occupied by a different relative. In the dramatic interactions the protagonist may play the role of the relative with whom he is momentarily concerned by sitting in the special chair and speaking for him. Sometimes a tall chair is employed to give a protagonist sitting in it a means of assuming a position of superiority. A fantasy prop sometimes used is the "magic shop," in which the shopkeeper dispenses to all the members of the group imaginary items cherished by each in exchange for values and attitudes that are to be identified and surrendered by each member.

Role reversal is a useful technique in psychodrama, two related individuals, for example, taking the role of one another expostulating how they imagine the other feels or portraying the behavior of the other. Where a protagonist is involved emotionally with an absent person, the latter may be portrayed by an auxiliary ego.

Rehearsal of future behavior is an aspect of psychodrama. The protagonist here will play out a situation that necessitates the execution of skills or the conquest of anxiety that he presently feels he cannot master. Verbalizing his inner doubts and fears, and applying himself to the task of overcoming these, may be helpful in easing him through actions in real life.

The controlled acting-out of fearsome strivings and attitudes helps to expose them to clarification. Thus, obsessive gentleness may be revealed as a defense against the desire to lash out at real or imagined adversaries. A protagonist so burdened may be encouraged to swing away at imagined persons who obstruct him. A woman whose spontaneity is crushed may be enabled to dance around the room, liberating herself from inhibitions that block expressive movement. A suicidal person may portray going through the notions of destroying himself in fantasy, thus helping the therapist to discuss with him an impulse that otherwise may be translated into tragic action.

Moreno (1966a) explains the value of psychodrama in these words:

> Because we cannot reach into the mind and see what the individual perceives and feels, psychodrama tries, with the cooperation of the patient, to transfer the mind 'outside' the individual and objectify it within a tangible, controllable universe . . . . Its aim is to make total behavior directly visible, observable, and measurable.

In this way, patients are presented "with an opportunity for psychodynamic and sociocultural reintegration."

The psychodramatic technique has given rise to a number of *role-playing methods* that are being applied to education, industry, and other fields. Recognizing that the mere imparting of information does not guarantee its emotional acceptance or its execution into action, role playing is employed as a way of facilitating learning (Peters & Phelan, 1957a, b). As an example, a group of four participants and a group leader may be observed by four observers who sit apart from and in the rear of the participants. Initial interviews of 1 hour with each participant and observer are advantageous to determine motivations, expectations, and important psychopathological manifestations. Preliminary mapping of the procedure considers group combinations, problems to be considered, objectives and desired modes of interaction. A short warm-up period is employed at the beginning of each session to establish rapport. Then the participants are assigned roles in a selected conflict situation. A discussion by the group of the issues involved, with delineation of possible alternative courses of action, is followed by the leader's interpretation of why various participants reacted the way that they did. Repetition of the conflict situation with the same participants gives them an opportunity to try out new adaptive methods and tests their capacities for change. It also fosters reinforcement of a new mental set. At the end of the session the group leader renders ego support in the form of praise for individual contributions and reassurance to lower any mobilized tension or anxiety. Approximately six 1-hour group sessions are followed by individual consultation with each member to determine his reactions. Another series of six group sessions, or more, may be indicated. These procedures, while effectively altering attitudes and promoting skills, cannot effectuate significant changes in the basic personality structure. More extensive role-playing tactics have been described by Corsini (1966) that are designed to deal with extensive inner conflicts.

Family Therapy

Family therapy (see page 142) is an involved treatment process. It necessitates an understanding of individual and group therapy, sociology, and group dynamics. During treatment the therapist must skillfully weave back and forth among the various members as resistance, transference, and defensive manifestations break loose. Countertransference is a fluid phenomenon in the process; identification with one or more of the patients in the group commonly occurs.

Many models for family therapy exist—and are still developing as psychotherapists of different professions, with varying theoretical viewpoints, evolve modes of working in relation to the needs of families, and the structure and function of the agencies through which treatment is being implemented (Sager & Kaplan, 1972). Sometimes family therapy is undertaken in clinics and family organizations, particularly those dealing with children for the purpose of reducing waiting lists. Under these circumstances therapy may be started even at the first interview as part of the intake and diagnostic process. Sometimes a group of workers visit the family in the home after an intake interview with the family and a diagnostic interview with the child (Hammer & Shapiro, 1965). Visiting the home has certain advantages since the members will demonstrate less defensiveness at home than at the clinic or office, displaying habitual reactions more easily.

Multiple therapists are often employed, circumventing to an extent the countertransference that develops in a one-to-one relationship. Individual therapy may be done concurrently by the different members of the team with selected members of the family (Hammer, 1967). Resistance is also more easily managed when more than one team member approaches a patient from a different perspective. The family facade is then more easily dissolved, and family members are more readily motivated to relate with their inner and latent feelings.

Problems that therapists experience in dealing with another therapist within a family group are sundry. Disagreements will occur in observation, in emphasis of what is important, in diagnosis, and in the type of intervention best suited for specific situations. Competitiveness among therapists may interfere with their capacity to be objective. They may be offended by disagreements with or criticisms of their operations. There is finally the matter of expense and the finding of qualified professionals who can make their time coincide with that of the therapist. Opportunities are obviously better in a clinic than in a private setting since fixed staff is available. There is an advantage in doing multiple therapy in a training center since a trainee may gain a great deal working with a more advanced therapist. Constructive collaboration between therapists tends to reinforce the impact of interpretations. It helps the resolution of resistance.

Working with a family group may serve purely as a diagnostic procedure to spot psychopathology and to aid in the assignment of therapists to individual family members who most need help. Often family therapy is undertaken as a short-term procedure particularly in family crisis situations (Barten, 1971). The focus may be on the relationships between parents, parents and children, and parents and grandparents. If a tangible problem exists, this may constitute the area around which explorations are organized. Long-term goals are fluid and have to be adapted to the needs of the family. The objective, for example, may be to hold the members together in a fragmented family. It may be to help adolescents separate and find their own individuality. Sometimes asking each member of the family ''What would you like to see changed in the family?'' helps. Each member may have a different idea about what should be changed. This will give the therapist clues that will be helpful. At the end of the first session a statement may be made to the family by the therapist as to what the problem seems to be.

It is vital in family therapy to understand and to respect the cultural background. The therapist must attempt to align himself or herself with the cultural system. Sometimes it is helpful to introduce an individual into the family group as a cotherapist who is part of the same subcultural setting, and who is capable of better translating the family code. This individual must, of course, have had some training as a paraprofessional.

Desirable goals of family therapy include resolution of conflicts, improved understanding and communication among family members, enhanced family solidarity, and greater tolerance for and appreciation of individuality (Zuk, 1974). All of these goals may not be achievable. In crisis resolution, for example, the total of one to six sessions, *which are the maximum number* acceptable to lower-class families may achieve little other than an overcoming of the immediate emergency. Somewhat more extensive are the objectives of short-term family therapy, which, though of longer duration, still may produce little other than symptom reduction, largely because of the reluctance of the family members to involve themselves in extensive verbal interchange. Middle-class families are more willing to regard therapy as a learning experience and, accordingly, do not set strict time limits on treatment, usually exposing themselves to 25 to 30 sessions. They are often rewarded for this middle-range treatment with more enduring changes. Sophisticated middle-class and upper middle-class families are generally better disposed to the more extensive goals of long-term therapy, e.g., alteration of values. Engaging a family in a treatment program and terminating therapy are crucial issues.

It is surprising how much can be done in from 3 to 15 sessions. Should follow-up individual or group therapy be required with both children or adults, this may be arranged. Parents soon begin to realize that problems that have exploded into crises have a long history, the roots of which extend into their own early upbringing. Guilt feelings, defensiveness, indignation, and attacking maneuvers may give way to more rational forms of reaction when even a partial picture of the dynamics unfolds itself.

Individual therapy may be done conjunctively with family therapy or at phases when work on a more intensive level is required. For instance, a husband whose authority is being challenged may require help in mastering his anxiety and in giving him some understanding of what is happening. Or a mother and father may need education regarding the processes that go on during adolescence, which can help them understand and deal with their own rebellious child. The family therapist, accordingly, will need the combined skills of the individual therapist, group therapist, sociologist, educator, and social worker.

Doing family therapy is not without its risks, since the neurotic disturbance of one or more members may be the penalty the family is paying for holding itself together. Complementary symbiotic patterns may interlock the members, which, when examined and resolved, may tend to leave the members without defenses and worse off than before. A child's rebellion may be the only way that the child can preserve his integrity in the face of a neurotic or psychotic parent. To interfere with this may prevent the child from achieving any kind of self-actualization and may result in crippling inhibitions. Disorganization of the family structure may be a consequence of recognition of the neurotic basis for the existing relationships. Divorce, for example, may enable a woman with colitis to live her life without abdominal pain. But she may find herself, as a result, in empty waters, isolated and burdened with children she may not be able to rear by herself. Her need for her husband may then become painfully apparent. Mindful of these contingencies, it is important to work against the too rapid precipitation of drastic changes in the family structure. It is here that experience will stand the therapist in good stead. Intensive individual psychotherapy may have to be employed at points where drastic changes in the life situation are imminent.

Insofar as actual techniques are concerned (supportive, reeducative, and reconstructive), the existing styles are legion. An example of a structured diagnostic technique with families is described by Satir (1964). The total interview consists of seven tasks:

The first task ("Main Problem") involves interviewing each family member separately, starting with the father, then the mother and the children in order of their age. Each is asked to discuss briefly: "What do you think is the main problem in your family?" They are each requested not to discuss their answers with other family members until later. Then the same question is asked of the group as a whole, gathered together in the interviewer's office. They are requested to arrive at some kind of consensus. This will expose the interactions and defenses of the members.

The second task ("Plan Something") is composed of a number of parts: (1) The family as a whole is requested to "plan something to do as a family." This enables the therapist to see how the family approaches joint decisions. (2) Next each par-

ent is requested to plan something with all of the children and then the children to plan something that they can all do together. (3) The father and mother are asked to plan something that they can do as a couple. This reveals data of the operation of family subunits.

The third task ("The Meeting") includes the husband and wife only. The question asked them is, "How, out of all the people in the world, did you two get together?" The role each spouse plays in answering this is noted.

The fourth task ("The Proverb") consists of giving the husband and wife a copy of the proverb, "A rolling stone gathers no moss." Five minutes are devoted to getting the meaning from the couple and coming to a conclusion. They then are asked to call the children in and teach them the meaning of the proverb. This enables the therapist to perceive how the parents operate as peers and then as parents, how they teach things to their children, and how the children react.

The fifth task ("Main Fault and Main Asset") requires that the family sit around a table; then each person is given a blank card on which to write the main fault of the person on his left. The therapist, after stating that this will be done, writes two cards and adds them to the others. These contain the words "too good" and "too weak." The therapist then shuffles the cards and reads out the fault written on the top card. Each person is asked in turn to identify which family member has this fault. This exposes the negative value system of the family and prepares the family for the phase of treatment when the task is assigned to avoid open and direct criticism. Following this, each person is requested to identify his own main fault. This is succeeded by the assignment for each person to write on a card what he admires most about the person on his left. The therapist also fills out two cards: (1) "always speaks clearly" and (2) "always lets you know where you stand with him." Experience shows that this part of the task, which is most difficult, exposes the positive value system of the family.

The sixth task ("Who is in charge") consists of asking the family, "Who do you think is in charge of the family?'' This yields clues regarding how members perceive the leadership structure and their feelings about it.

The seventh task (''Recognition of Resemblance and Difference'') requests the husband and wife to identify which of the children is like him or her and which like the other spouse. Then each child is asked which parent he believes he resembles most and the ways he is like and unlike both parents. The parents are also asked how each is like and unlike the other spouse. This points to the family identification processes.

These structured interviews last from 1 to 1½ hours and are employed as research, diagnostic, and therapeutic tools. The network of communication patterns forms the basis for therapeutic intervention.

Further active procedures include (1) preparation of a list by each member of what they would like to see changed (this may act as a focus for negotiating a joint decision), (2) asking the family to discuss a recent argument, (3) asking each member to discuss what he likes and dislikes about other members, (4) changing the seating order periodically, (5) using puppets, members talking through them. Zuk (1971a), Minuchin (1965), and Minuchin and Montalvo (1967) have outlined a number of other strategies.

The management of socially aggressive children especially constitutes a challenge to parents in our contemporary society. Belligerent and hostile, such children can stir up trouble for the entire family. A number of approaches have developed dealing with this specific problem, one of the best known being the methods developed by G. R. Patterson and his associates (Patterson & Gullion, 1968; Patterson, 1971; Patterson et al, 1975). The social learning approach to family therapy as practiced at the Oregon Research Institute appears to be promising. The social learning approach teaches families to discover the ways in which they reinforce the disturbed child's behavior and how unwittingly they are taught to respond destructively to the child's provocations, thus adding fuel to the fire. Some techniques include immediate *isolation* of the child for 3 to 5 minutes (no

more) when he misbehaves, writing a contract with the child defining his desirable and undesirable behaviors and prescribing rewards and punishments, giving points for good behavior that may be swapped for privileges.

The most difficult problem that the therapist will encounter in family therapy is the need and the determined effort (despite protests avowing a desire for change) to maintain the status quo. Yet there are healthy elements that exist in each family that the therapist can draw on. It is important to emphasize these in therapy rather than the prevailing psychopathology.

Reconstructive family therapy may require sessions for several months or several years, depending on the family pathology and goals. It is often articulated with individual reconstructive psychotherapy for family members who need special help. The focus here is on intrapsychic experience. The methodology will vary with the relationship designs and the communication systems. The focus is on transferential reverberations and resistances. During the group session it may become apparent that the ''primary patient'' is not the one who needs most intensive help. Since he may be responding to neurotic provocations from another family member, the latter may be the one who should be seen individually. The following case-history brings this out:

The primary patient is a 22-year-old man whose chief symptom is undiluted anxiety that interferes with his functioning. His relationships are highly competitive with males, the patient assuming a submissive self-castigating role. With females the patient detaches, fantasies of sexual engagement inspiring anxiety. At home the family is involved in constant quarreling, the patient engaging principally with his father, complaining that his father is excessively passive, manipulated by his mother, and extraordinarily demanding of and ambitious for him. The two younger sisters display rebellious and withdrawal tendencies that have not yet become too pathological. In individual sessions the father presents himself as a misunderstood martyr. During the first few family sessions, however, it becomes obvious that he dominates and criticizes the family, especially the mother. The patient and sisters constantly take pot shots at him for acting too strong and dictatorial. The father responds with the expression that any weakness is inadmissible; it is important to deny illness or fear. This, it soon follows, is a pattern that prevailed in the father's own family. The father's father forced himself to work almost constantly as a duty. He died from a cardiac attack at an early age after refusing to see doctors for what seems to have been anginal pains. The father expresses admiration for his own father's "guts." During this recital the patient slumps in his chair interrupting with deprecatory comments. On questioning, he admits feeling defeated and under attack. Recognizing the father's role in stirring up the family, the father was referred for interviews with a therapist. This resulted in a rapid abatement of the patient's symptoms and a more congenial atmosphere at home.

A multiple family group of several families from the same background and socioeconomic level permits mutual exploration of common problems, the ability to observe difficulties in a more objective light, and the availability of a peer group to whom a family can relate who can help educate and be educated (Laquer, 1968, 1972). The family code is more likely to become translated by a peer family than by a therapist who may come from a different background.

Marital (Couple) Therapy

There is a common adage to the effect that when a man and woman marry they become one. If this be so, then trouble starts when they try to decide which one. Considering the current casualty figures on marriage, one is almost inevitably led to the conclusion that the blessed vessel of marital bliss floats on a risky sea. As awesome as are the divorce and separation rates, the number of unhappy couples miserably chained to each other by bonds they cannot break is even greater.

Marriage calls for intricate adjustments. It involves not only dealing with one's personal difficulties but also the normal problems and the irrationalities of one's partner. Because marital adjustment is one of the most difficult and stressful human challenges, it is little wonder that so many people get disturbed under its impact. Problems in marriage and difficulties with a spouse account for almost 50 percent of the

reasons why people seek professional help (Martin & Lief, 1973; Sager et al, 1968).

The task of marital therapy is primarily to help keep a shaky marriage together where there is even a small chance of its success, to strengthen the couple's psychological defenses in the process, or, if the marriage cannot be saved, to help the partners separate with a minimum of conflict and bad feeling, particularly where children are involved.

Marital relationships are commonly sabotaged by the emotional defects of one or both partners. Where a marriage has deteriorated and the couple is motivated to work toward its betterment, there is a good chance that with proper treatment the relationship will improve. This does not mean that all marriages can be saved. In some cases the "chemical" combination of the union is irreconcilably explosive. Husband and wife are too much at loggerheads in their ideas, values, and goals to achieve even a reasonable meeting of the minds; or there is a barrenness of love and unabating cruelty toward each other; or sexual incompatibilities exist of too great severity; or there is uncontrollable and continued violence toward the children. Many couples are already virtually separated but still living together interlocked in a marital death grip from which they cannot loosen themselves before coming to therapy. Here the marriage may not be worthy of saving. The goal, as has been mentioned, may be to help the couple master their guilt and achieve the strength to separate. Generally, however, where couples are not too contentious and are willing to face their feelings and examine their behavior, marital therapy can help a marriage survive.

It is rare that marital difficulties are totally onesided. It is rare, too, that the mate will not come in to see the therapist if the latter handles the situation correctly. The presenting patient may be asked if he or she can convince the mate to come in to see the therapist. The following is from a recording of an interview:

Pt. She's impossible. She won't listen. She says I'm nuts and it's all my doing—the mess we're in. I can't talk to her.

Th. Do you think she would come into see me if you asked her?

Pt. I already asked her to come here with me, and she refused. Frankly, I think it would be a waste of time.

Th. You must have had some hope that coming here would help the situation.

Pt. I suppose I'm looking for magic. I know she won't change.

Th. Would you mind if I telephoned her to come to see me about your problem? I would tell her it will be of help to me in helping you if she could give me an idea of what you're like. (*smiles*) Sometimes this defuses things. She won't feel I'm getting her here to accuse her.

Pt. By all means, maybe she'll come in if you convince her it's all my fault.

Th. I'm sure it isn't, but I'll do my best to ease her into talking things out.

The entire object of getting the mate into the therapist's office is to start a relationship with her or him. By listening with an empathic ear, emphasizing how difficult things must be, the therapist usually can gain confidence. In the case cited the following telephone conversation took place:

Th. Is this Mrs. B?

Mrs. B. Yes.

Th. This is Dr. Wolberg. I hope you will forgive me for calling you. I know it's an imposition. But your husband came in to see me, as you know.

Mrs. B. Yes, I do.

Th. I know it's been extremely difficult for you. But it would help me to help your husband if you could come in and tell me a little bit about him, and about what's happening.

Mrs. B. If I came in, I wouldn't stop talking. (*laughs*)

Th. So much the better, you could give me an idea of him and what has been going on. It must have been very rough.

Mrs. B. I'll be glad to come in.

The initial interview with Mrs. B went along smoothly, and little difficulty was experienced in starting therapy with the couple.

Unless one of the marital partners is paranoidal or completely unwilling to alter the marriage relationship, it should not be too difficult to convince both members to work with the therapist. The design of therapy will vary with the presenting problems and the preferred style of the therapist.

Some therapists begin joint sessions immediately after the initial interview. Others prefer seeing the mate alone to assess the problem before beginning joint sessions. I find one or more individual sessions useful at the start. It is helpful to ask each partner about the relationship their parents have had with one another. Sometimes just talking about this, patients discover that they are acting out roles patterned after parental models.

Marital therapy techniques draw from multiple fields, including psychoanalysis, behavior therapy, family therapy, group therapy, marriage counseling, child therapy, and family casework. Although the goal is an alteration of the relationship between the couple, a hoped-for, and usually serendipitous, objective is intrapsychic change, which surprisingly may come about in those with a readiness for such change and relief from the distracting cross-fire between the two spouses. Conceptual schemes for the actual conduct of marital therapy are not unified, but the most successful approaches stress the importance of communication (Watzlawick et al, 1967; Minuchin, 1974) toward effecting changes in the transactional system. A system behavioral approach is particularly helpful, concentrating "on observable behavior and rules of current communication (Bolte, 1970; Hurvitz, 1970; Kotler, 1967; Mangus, 1957) without immediate recourse to a historical 'Why'" (Berman & Lief, 1975).

Greene (1972) has pointed out that the great variations in marital patterns require flexibility in therapeutic techniques. He proposes a "six-C" classification of therapeutic modalities:

I. Supportive Therapy
    A. Crisis counseling
II. Intensive Therapy
    A. Classic psychoanalytic psychotherapy
    B. Collaborative therapy
    C. Concurrent therapy
    D. Conjoint marital therapy
    E. Combined therapies
        1. Simple therapy
        2. Conjoint family therapy

3. Combined-collaborative therapy
4. Marital group psychotherapy

"Crisis counseling" stresses sociocultural forces in the "here-and-now" situation. The "classic approach" is the usual dyadic one-to-one relationship with both partners seeing separate therapists who do not communicate. The focus here is on the individual's psychodynamics with the marriage as the backdrop. It is used where one partner has severe acting-out problems of which the other partner is unaware (e.g., continuous infidelity or homosexuality), where there is preference for this approach, where one partner refuses to share the therapist, and where spouses have widely divergent goals in terms of the marriage problem. The "collaborative approach" is similarly dyadic, but it sanctions communication between the two therapists by regularly scheduled meetings (Martin & Bird, 1963). The same therapist treats both partners individually in the "concurrent approach," which is aimed at bringing about insight into behavior patterns as they affect each member (Solomon & Greene, 1963). Where strong sibling rivalry attitudes exist, or where there are severe character disorders, psychoses, or paranoid reactions, this approach cannot be used.

These dyadic approaches may be educationally oriented, focused on the marital relationship and on strategies of straightening it out by utilizing a variety of counseling and behavioral techniques. Should it become apparent that the patient has a severe personality or emotional problem being projected into the marital situation, individual dynamic psychotherapy may be indicated. In considerable cases the marital equilibrium will be restored, and the spouse will change with the stabilization and better adaptation of the patient. However, where the spouse is incapable of change and the patient is unable to adapt to this impasse, the marriage will continue as a traumatic source for both.

The "conjoint marital approach," which is the most common form (Satir, 1965; Fitzgerald, 1969), is used both for counseling and intensive therapy. Here the partners meet jointly with the therapist at the same session. This approach fosters communication between the partners and brings out more clearly the marital dynamics. With the "combined therapies" (1) the "simple" form combines individual, concurrent, and conjoint sessions in various arrangements; (2) "conjoint family therapy" includes one or more of the children; (3) the "combined-collaborative" form permits regular meetings of the partners together with the two therapists at the same session; and (4) "marital group therapy" consists of group therapy with four couples and one or two therapists (Blinder & Kirschenbaum, 1967; Framo, 1973).

Thus, there are many ways of working with couples. The two principal orientations are outlined in Table 50-1. The outline should not be taken too literally since many marital therapists, while employing educational therapy, work within a dynamic framework. A number of short-term intensive "courses" in marriage adjustment are being given that draw from cognitive learning methods, for example, the courses at Seattle given by the Bakkers. At the University Salve Mater in Leuven, Belgium, there is a Couples Communication Center that offers an intensive, short-term (3 weeks) approach to marital problems. Two different kinds of activities are offered: (1) a daily session of 1½ hours of marital therapy by a dual-sex team of therapists and (2) a daily meeting of 3 to 4 hours with the total group of clients (usually 8 to 10 persons). The emphasis is on training and cognitive learning (see p. 117). The stress of the "courses" at the University Salve Mater is on proper communication. Verhulst (1974) writes, "We tend to look upon marriage as a project, as something that can be planned and that involves the learning and training of a number of specific skills . . . towards a relationship of equivalence . . . from conformation to a set of 'external' rules, to sober analysis and confrontation." Many of the techniques are employed that have been outlined in the section on cognitive learning, particularly those stressing "territoriality and marriage" (Bakker & Bakker-Rabdau,

Table 50–1
The Leading Orientations in Marital Therapy

	Dynamically Oriented Marital Therapy	Educationally Oriented Marital Therapy
Goals	Reconstructive with character change	Reeducative with adaptive betterment
Process	Long-term, patterned after a modified psychoanalytic model	Short-term, system-oriented, patterned after an eclectic model (cognitive learning, behavior therapy, etc.)
Interview Focus	Relatively undirected, content being determined by current concerns of one or both members	Directed on topics selected by therapist derived from early diagnostic interviews as to what is needed
Extent of Exploration of Topics	Unlimited, the patient taking the lead in probing into genetic and current problems	Selective and time-limited, pointed at informational distortions and problems in relationships
Self-revelations by the Therapist	Utilized often	Utilized occasionally
Handling of Resistance	Analytic probing for resistance with object of its dissolution	Circumvented when it presents itself
Dreams	Encouraged and analyzed	Not encouraged nor analyzed
Transference	Actively searched for and analyzed	Positive transference encouraged and not analyzed
Formulation of Dynamics	Delayed until patient has at least preconscious awareness of underlying problem	Presented at early stage by therapist to provide a working hypothesis
Activity	Moderate to great, focused on interpersonal interactions rather than on acquisition of skills	Great, focused more on adaptive skills than on interpersonal interactions
Cotherapists	Sometimes employed	Usually employed
Adjunctive Therapies	Utilized occasionally, such as role playing and confrontation	Wide range of adjunctive techniques employed, educational materials utilized, homework assignments given
Follow-up	When essential	Usually routine at set intervals

1973); effective communication techniques; techniques for changing rigid concepts of one's self, partner, and the relationship; parent effectiveness training; techniques of achieving changes and working out the relationship contract; and the fight-training sessions of Bach. There is no active selection of patients and no psychiatric examination, although there is history taking. In follow-up the aftercare is restricted to five sessions of conjoint couples therapy (after 1 week, 1 month, 3, 6, and 12 months).

Again flexibility of approach must be stressed in marital therapy. Some therapists begin by seeing both partners (assuming they are both willing to start) from the initial interview on. In many such instances these therapists, particularly if they are wedded to an educational approach, do not believe that diagnosis is necessary or useful. Other therapists work better, as mentioned previously, by doing individual diagnostic evaluations on each spouse first, taking two or three sessions for this. After these diagnostic sessions the couple is seen together to observe the transaction that takes place between the two. Personally, I prefer the latter method because it enables me to obtain a clearer picture of the defensive attack, placating and retreating maneuvers, and the effects on each other, particularly if I know a little about each partner in advance. Often the behavioral pattern shown individually is in sharp contrast to what one observes when the couple is interacting. Thus, a spontaneous, related individual in the initial sessions may react to the couple's interview with disdainful, biting sarcasm, initiating a counterattack from the mate. There are therapists like Greene (1970, 1972) who at the end of the first individual interview give to the patient two biographical marital questionaires to fill out, one for each partner, asking for specific complaints about the marriage, why help is being sought, description of the courtship and honeymoon, family data, relationship with children, medical history, etc. Other therapists depend solely on the information that they obtain from the interviews.

The structured interview, organized by Satir for the entire family (see pages 731–732), may prove helpful applied to a couple alone, and may serve as a basis for further therapeutic interventions. The intensified transference and countertransference reactions that emerge during conjoint therapy will prove challenging to the psychotherapist who attempts to deal with marital problems on a reconstructive level. The reduction of tensions, the enhancement of communication, and awareness of initiating conflicts and distortions, many of which are

residues of the past—all by-products of conjoint therapy—make the procedure very much worthwhile.

It is important from the outset not to express any condemnatory attitude toward either partner for behavior or characteristics that they are exhibiting either in the interview or outside. There will be ample opportunity later to interpret what is happening, and this is aimed toward insightful rather than punitive objectives. A woman may resent the role that she believes her husband expects of her as a dutiful wife, and she may respond by being defiant and neglectful. Her husband may counterattack by detaching himself from her and the family and by impotence. The chasm of misunderstanding grows deeper and deeper until each has accumulated an enormous bag of justifiable grievances. A therapist who takes sides will probably lose both patients. Once the dynamics become clear, the therapist may point out the inevitability of misunderstanding on the basis of the background, upbringing, value systems, and pressures that are being exerted by the partners on each other without laying down strict rules about male and female roles. If the therapist has the confidence of the couple, they will turn to him or her for some constructive guidance, which may be offered without being dictatorial about what should be done. It may be pointed out that difficulties exist in all relationships and that some compromise is always necessary, the ground rules to be negotiated through constructive communication.

The matter of confidentiality is especially important. The patient is told that information given in private sessions will not be revealed to the other member of the couple. The members may be encouraged to talk freely and not hold anything back, but that is up to them. The therapist will not bring up topics that are taboo unless asked to. This encourages the disclosure of secrets so one can work with what comes out. A great deal of relief occurs—and interpretation then can take place.

When there are cotherapists involved in the therapy, one technique is that the same-sexed member of the team (i.e., if the therapists are male and female) labels a

738   The Technique of Psychotherapy

sneaky maneuver of the mate by a less noxious term. For example, a woman complains that her husband is constantly aggressive and puts her down. When during
therapy the male patient says or does something that the patient says is aggressive, the
female therapist says, "I believe your husband is being assertive here rather than
aggressive."

Willy-nilly, the therapist will be used
by both members as an arbiter, guide, and
potential ally to justify mutual opinions,
disgruntlements, and claims. It takes a good
deal of fancy footwork to avoid being maneuvered into a judgmental role. Countertransference is to be expected, and one's
ability to detect one's own prejudices and
predilections borne out of one's background and experience will help keep the
therapeutic situation afloat. There are instances where one mate is manifestly unfair
in expectations of the other, or in liberties
assumed, and the therapist may find it difficult to remain neutral. It will take ingenuity to get one mate to alter his or her
behavior or to help the other member accept
the situation with whatever compromises
can be negotiated.

For example, one of my male patients
who had married late in life, insisted on
staying out late "with the boys" two nights
weekly. His wife objected on the basis that
she felt neglected and lonesome. At interview it was apparent that she suspected infidelity, which she tried to substantiate on
the basis of decreasing frequency of intercourse. I was able to convince her, from my
interview with her husband, that staying out
late constituted a means for her husband to
maintain his independence, which was being
threatened by feelings of increasing devotion to his wife. He had avoided close involvements with women until he met his
wife. Thwarting his need for independence
would, I hazarded, result in increasing detachment from her as a defense and perhaps
in impotency. The patient's depression, related to hostility at being challenged and
"browbeaten," lifted as his wife recognized
the dynamics and accepted her husband's
need for greater freedom. Joint sessions
during which each partner unburdened
themselves and traced their attitudes to past

experiential circumstances resulted in a
cementing of the relationship.

Whether or not the therapist deals with
factors of transference or projective identification and utilizes dreams will depend on
the training of the therapist, the goals desired, and the level of understanding of both
patients. Dramatic results are sometimes
obtained where marital partners associated
to each other's dreams. This helps them become less defensive with each other. By the
same token, transference phenomena
brought out into the open as they relate to
the therapist and to each other, aired without restraint, will bring forth emotions that
with proper interpretation can prove helpful. Sager (1967) points out that it is important for anyone doing marital therapy "to be
aware and work through her reactions to,
and general philosophy regarding, maleness
and femaleness, maturity, marriage roles,
career, money, relationship to children, and
a host of other cathected concepts." Flexibility and tolerance for values other than
their own are important assets for marital
therapists.

It is to be expected that where couples
have been living in neurotic symbiosis that
an alteration in the accustomed response of
one member to the other's provocations will
arouse anxieties in one or both members.
Resistance will generally take the form of a
desire to halt joint sessions. Interpretations
of the resistance and the reasons behind it
are necessary to keep the couple in therapy.

During sessions one may observe
phsyical movements between husbands and
wives that serve as forms of nonverbal
communication to convey emotional meanings. These are in the form of approach and
separation movements and, at different
stages of treatment, seating rearrangements
among couples, which may be explored with
the object of analyzing the underlying
dynamics. In the process one may observe
one's own countertransference responses,
which one should attempt to understand
and to resolve.

While the therapist may make suggestions from time to time, it is vital that patients be made aware of the fact that they
must work out their own solutions utilizing
their own free will.

There are several impasses that may occur in marital therapy. One of the most difficult is the spouse who has a fixed position about divorce. This usually means that he or she does not want therapy except to try to convince the mate to accept the position. Often the lawyer of one mate may be responsible for this impasse. Another problem is when one member of the couple is in individual therapy with another therapist who differs in philosophy and goals from the marital therapist. Then a conference with the other therapist may be in order. Once contact has been established, coordinated therapy may be essential to break up an impasse.

Important adjuncts to marital therapy are behavioral techniques, including role playing and sexual therapy methods (Masters & Johnson, 1970; Kaplan, 1974). Alger (1967a) illustrates the use of the paradigmatic approach in marital therapy, the goal of which is to imitate a pattern one of the partners displays by acting out a part. Alger (1967b) also employs videotape recordings and playback in couple's sessions. His technique consists of a video recording of the first 15 minutes of a joint marital session, which is immediately played back over a television monitor. The participants may ask to stop the recording at any point to comment on the effect of their behavior on others. Viewing themselves as they talk and interact stimulates a great deal of feeling and expedites communcation. Video viewing is now being employed with increasing frequency (Alger & Hogan, 1969; Berger, MM, 1969).

Brief sexual therapy for couples is designed for pairs who essentially like each other but who have blundered into bad sexual habits. Where partners have open or repressed mutual hostility, progress is less likely. Not that training in the proper attitudes toward sex is useless even in couples seriously in conflict, or in individuals harboring neurotic personality drives registered in disturbances in sexual behavior. But the therapist should not be dismayed by failures in the latter cases. He should regard his presumably unsuccessful efforts as a helpful conduit toward more extensive psychotherapy as a gesture that, if

no more successful than having helped to establish a relationship with his patients, has been useful in its own right. A considerable number of couples who apply for help for sexual dysfunctions, nevertheless, will need no more than exposure to a short span of guidance, reassurance, and behavioral training. These cases are highly motivated for change and eager to grapple with new learnings (see section on Sexual Therapy, pages 809–817.)

The presence of two therapists (cotherapists) lessens the possibility of exclusive alliances and of a dyadic impasse (Alger, 1967a; Markowitz, 1967). Each of the therapists may function as an alternate ego for one of the patients aereating ideas and sentiments the patient does not himself or herself dare express. In this way the patient may gain the strength to face impulses and attitudes on the periphery of his awareness. Substantiating the value of cotherapy are four truisms: (1) Two heads are better than one. (A second therapist may be able to illuminate areas missed by the first. Each may be able to correct bias and detect countertransference in the other.) (2) One therapist may support a patient under attack by mate when he or she needs a helping hand. (3) One therapist may engage in confrontation and challenging maneuvers while the other therapist interprets reactions of the patient or supports the latter if necessary. (4) Two therapists lessen the danger of the therapist being utilized as a judge or as a guru who knows and gives all the answers.

A mixed male–female team has advantages in providing opportunities for identification. The disadvantages of cotherapy are competitiveness and friction between the therapists and alliances of one therapist with one patient against the other therapist and other patient. These may be modified by conferences together. There are advantages and disadvantages in conjoint marriage therapy with a husband-and-wife team (Bellville et al, 1969). The inevitable differences arising between the therapist couple are more volatile and unrepressed than in an unrelated couple and can threaten the therapeutic process. In their resolution, however, they offer the patient couple an opportunity to observe how a well-related couple negotiate differences, make compromises, and adapt themselves to each other's individual way of looking at things. It stands to reason that the therapist couple both must be reasonably adjusted, have an understanding about the therapeutic process, and preferably have been in personal therapy or couples therapy themselves.

Follow-up sessions with the marital partners after therapy are wise to prevent a falling back into the old destructive patterns, the intervals between follow-up visits gradually being increased in the event the better adjustment continues.

QUALITY OF CHANGE IN GROUP PSYCHOTHERAPY

One must not be deceived regarding the quality and depth of changes observed among members of a group as a consequence of continued interaction. Changes are dramatic: the attacking and aggressive person becomes quiet and considerate; the dominant individual shows abilities to be submissive; the withdrawn person comes out of his shell and relates himself flexibly to the other members; the dependent, clinging soul is encouraged to express assertiveness. These effects will become apparent, sooner or later, as products of both group dynamics and the interpretive activities of the therapist and group members. But whether there will be a transfer of learning to the outside world sufficient to influence a better life adaptation is another matter. Often what we find in group therapy (as we witness it also in individual therapy) is that the individual fits his group reactions into a special slot. He plays a role in the group

that is disparate from his role in other situations. The group expects him to behave in certain ways, and he obliges. It offers him a shelter from the harsh realities of the external world. He can "be himself" in the group; but his defenses may be checked at the therapist's door, and when he leaves the therapist's office or the group at postsessions and alternate sessions, he may reclaim them. Only in his haven of safety can he trust himself to act differently.

This confounding resistance is testimony to the fact that interpersonal change is not the equivalent of intrapsychic change. The former change may merely reflect the acquisition of a new set of social roles that the individual fastens onto himself and that enhance his repertoire of patterns. It is like acquiring a new wardrobe to be worn on special occasions. The individual underneath remains the same. From this one must not assume that group therapy is of no real consequence. Intrapsychic changes are possible if the person has the courage appreciably to test his changed assumptions and to apply his learning in the group to the other roles that he plays in life. The therapist has a responsibility here in seeing that the patient does not lock himself into a comfortable stalemate in the group. The patient may be asked why there are differences in his feelings and behavior inside as compared to those outside the group, and if there has been no change, why not. Sometimes the patient's resistance is a persistence of the desire to recreate his original family in the group, with all the ambivalences that this entails from which he refuses to break loose. Supplementary individual sessions may be specifically applied to these questions.

IV

The Terminal Phase of Treatment

51

Goals in Terminating Treatment

Theoretically, psychotherapy is never ending, since emotional growth can go on as long as one lives. Consequently, it is necessary to employ some sort of yardstick in order to determine when to discontinue treatment.

The problem of goals in psychotherapy is one about which there are differences of opinion. On the one hand, there are those who believe that a definition of goals is vital in any psychotherapeutic program. On the other hand, there are many professionals who consider goals to be an extremely arbitrary matter—a manifestation of the authoritarianism of the therapist who seeks to impose on the patient artificial values and standards. "Goallessness" has been mentioned as the procedural stance essential to technical analytic work (Wallerstein, 1965). Nevertheless, therapists of different orientations aim at outcome targets that reflect their special conceptions of dynamics.

Psychological processes may be conceived of in many ways:

1. As energy exchanges within various divisions of the psychic apparatus (the Freudian hypothesis).
2. As interpersonal events mediated by characterologic distortions (the neo-Freudian hypothesis).
3. As forms of faulty learning and conditioning (the Pavlovian hypothesis).

Goals in psychotherapy are fashioned by theoretical conceptions of personality. Thus, in Freudian theory the goal in therapy is genital maturity in which fixations of libido on pregenital levels that foster regression have been resolved. In neo-Freudian theory the objective is self-actualization that frees the individual in interpersonal relationships, enhances self-image, and expands creativity and productiveness. In conditioning theory it is the extinction of destructive old patterns and the learning-through-reinforcement of new and adaptive ones.

Irrespective of how one feels about the uses made of them, goals are understandably of concern to the psychotherapist, for success or failure in the treatment effort can be gauged only in the context of set objectives. Before describing goals, however, we must admit that judgments of "success" in psychotherapy are really a matter of definition and may be viewed differently from the standpoints of the patient, society, and the therapist.

743

SUCCESS JUDGMENTS

From the Standpoint of the Patient

There is a story about a man who confided to a friend that he had just successfully completed an extensive course of psychotherapy. "Why did you need psychotherapy?" asked the friend. "Because," revealed the man, "I thought I was a dog." "Was the treatment successful?" queried the friend. "Decidedly," replied the man, "feel my nose."

Estimates by the patient as to what has been accomplished for him in therapy are in themselves not a reliable index of therapeutic success. Most patients regard symptomatic relief as the best measurement of positive gain. This index, however, is not a completely valid one in assaying the effectiveness of treatment.

Symptomatic improvement may be achieved in several ways. First, it may be associated with the giving up of vital aspects of personality functioning. For example, where anxiety and guilt are aroused by sexual impulses, the abandonment of all forms of sexual expression may relieve symptoms. Or where close interpersonal relations are conceived of as dangerous, the patient may, in the course of therapy, detach himself from people. The bargain that the patient makes with anxiety here cannot be regarded as successful therapy, even though his suffering is relieved. Second, the patient may, during treatment, propitiate certain neurotic drives, gaining thereby a spurious kind of security. Thus, he may make himself dependent on the therapist, acquiring a regressive fulfillment of security needs. His symptoms will abate as long as he conceives of the therapist as a bountiful, loving, and protecting parent. This happy situation may, nevertheless, be placed in jeopardy whenever the therapist fails to live up to the patient's expectations. Under these circumstances we cannot consider the surcease of symptoms a sign of cure. Third, symptom relief may be produced by the repression of damaging conflicts. Many annoying but relatively innocuous symptoms may be blotted out of awareness in the course of supportive therapy, only to be replaced by substitutive symptoms of a more serious nature. Thus, the symptom of anxiety may be relieved during therapy by repressive techniques of one sort or another. Anxiety equivalents may, however, appear in the form of psychosomatic complaints. Damage to viscera may later eventuate, of which the patient is not conscious until an irreversible somatic ailment develops, perhaps years after the presumed "success" in therapy had occurred.

The patient's estimates of failure in therapy must also not be accepted at their face value, since he may base his concepts of failure on a false premise. Thus, he may consider his treatment unsuccessful where he has failed to develop traits that identify him with an ideal. For example, one patient may have secret notions of being a genius, and he may believe that therapy can release potentialities in him that will put him in the genius class. Another patient may regard therapy as unsuccessful unless she has developed complete equanimity and the ability to remain tranquil, to endure tension, and to vanquish discomfort, even in the face of the most devastating environmental conditions. The failure to develop these and other traits, which are, in the patient's mind, considered indices of health, security, and self-esteem, may cast a shadow on even estimable therapeutic results.

From the Standpoint of Society

Judgments as to success in therapy from the standpoint of social standards must also be held suspect. The patient's family, mate, or friends may have ideas about the kind of individual that they want the patient to become that may not correspond with standards of mental health. For instance, parents may expect and even demand that the therapist mold the patient into a creature who is cooperative and pleasant at all times and who never challenges parental authority. A mate may insist that the patient develop a personality that tolerates his or her own shortcomings and never gives vent to resentment. Friends may have stringent standards of character that might apply to themselves but not necessarily to the patient.

The culture or subculture may also impose arbitrary norms that differ from those of the patient or of the therapist. Political and economic forces in one group may make for a value system that is not accepted by, or acceptable to, another group. Thus, a "normal" individual in a totalitarian framework would be expected to submit willingly to the yoke of dictatorship and to subordinate personal freedom for the welfare of the state. In another cultural framework the individual's personal rights and the ability to make one's own choices would be paramount; one would not be expected to yield completely to authoritative demands. It is accordingly, important not to regard as goals of normality traits and drives that, thought culturally condoned, may prove to be at variance with mental health.

From the Standpoint of the Therapist

The therapist may fashion therapeutic goals around certain set standards and values. These may relate to personal concepts of normality or to a general ideal of mental health.

One may, reflecting cultural concepts, pronounce certain traits as normal believing that the patient must acquire these before being considered emotionally balanced. Another therapist may herself operate under a cherished set of attitudes that constitute for her the highest goal. Thus, if she puts value in ambitiousness, perfectionism, detachment, dependency, narcissism, or power devices, she is apt to consider these real assets toward which she must aim her therapeutic sights. A word of caution must especially be voiced in regard to that group of attitudes collectively embraced under the term of compliance. A reasonable compliance to authority is a necessary thing, but compliance is too often utilized by neurotic persons as a form of security. This is most often the case in those cultures in which the child is considered a relative nonentity who is expected to submit without question and to yield without complaint to the dictates

and commands of the stronger, more authoritative individuals with whom the child lives. Where the therapist, himself, has been reared in an atmosphere that makes compliance tantamount with good breeding, he may expect the patient to adopt a submissive attitude. The patient may sense this trend in the therapist and try hard to please, even at the price of crushing self-strivings and needs for independent thought and action. The therapist may also, because of his own character structure, consider any aggression a sign of recalcitrance and ill will. Therapists must be careful not to try to pattern the patient after their own image, for they, themselves, may be the victims of values that are basically faulty.

From the Standpoint of Mental Health Objectives

"Ideal" objectives of mental health are many. They require that the person be capable of deriving pleasure from creature comforts in life—from food, rest, relaxation, sex, work, and play. The individual is capable of satisfying these impulses in conformity with the mores of the group. Mobilizing whatever intellectual and experiential resources are required, one is able to plan creatively and realistically and to execute one's plans in accordance with existent opportunities. This involves an appraisal of one's aptitudes and limitations, and a scaling down of one's ambitions to the level of one's true potentialities. It includes the laying down of realistic life goals, an acceptance of one's abilities and a tolerance of one's shortcomings. Presupposed is a harmonious balance between personal and group standards, and those cultural and individual ideals that contribute both to the welfare of the self and of the group. The individual must be able to function effectively as part of the group, to give and to receive love, and otherwise to relate oneself congenially to other humans. One must be capable of engaging in human relations without indulging neurotic character strivings of detachment, needs to dominate or to be enslaved, or desires to render oneself invincible or perfect. One must be able to assume a subordinate relationship to authority without succumbing to fear or rage and yet, in certain situations, be capable of assuming leadership without designs of control or power. One must be able to withstand a certain amount of disappointment, deprivation, and frustration without undue tension or anxiety when these are considered to be reasonable, shared, or necessary to the group welfare or when the consequences of impulse indulgence entail more than their worth in compensatory pain. One's capacities for adjustment must be sufficiently plastic to adapt to the exigencies of life without taking refuge in childish forms of defense or in fantasy. To achieve a healthy self-regard an individual must have a good measure of self-respect, the capacity to be comfortable within oneself, a willingness to face the past and to isolate from the present anxieties relating to childhood experiences. The individual must possess self-confidence, assertiveness, a sense of freedom, spontaneity, and self-tolerance.

Unfortunately, limitations are imposed by a variety of factors on the achievement through therapy of such ideal goals. Chief among these are obstacles within the patient, such as lack of incentives for change, diminished ego strength, and practical considerations of insufficient time and money. Additionally, society itself imposes insuperable embargoes on certain aspects of functioning. It supports many neurotic values that necessitate the maintenance of sundry defenses for survival reasons. A personality structure that is ideally integrated might actually serve as a source of conflict where the individual has to operate in the framework of a severely neurotic culture.

TOWARD A PRACTICAL GOAL IN THERAPY

Modern philosophers contend that achievement of enduring happiness, while worthy of pursuit, is undoubtedly a dream. Total adaptation must be measured against the backdrop of humanity's continuing involvement with violence, exploitation, and devastation of the earth's resources. These and other inescapable calamities are bound to disturb our equilibrium. Achievement of the most ambitious goal in therapy—reconstruction of the personality structure—would theoretically be most helpful in adapting to society's ills while sponsoring constructive efforts to rectify them. However, goals in therapy are more or less patient regulated. No matter how well trained and skilled the therapist may be, nor how extensively he or she may desire to reconstruct the patient's personality, the latter is always in a position to veto the therapist's intentions. The patient is particularly strategically placed to thwart the ideal goal of personality maturation—the most difficult of all objectives. Irrespective of how thoroughly conversant we, the therapists, may be with the technique of reconstructive psychotherapy, our efforts may prove unsuccessful.

Even where conditions are most favorable, reconstructive efforts may fail. The patient may be able to afford extensive psychotherapy and to make the necessary time arrangements; he may earnestly desire to achieve deep change. Yet he may gain little or no benefit from therapy. This fact has confounded many therapists as well as their patients who are wont, as a result, to regard reconstructive psychotherapy as ineffectual.

When we investigate failures in reconstructive therapy in patients who are adequately motivated, we find a number of operative factors. The patient may have sustained such personality damage during the formative years of life that the chances for complete growth are remote. The secondary gain factors may be so powerful as to make health a handicap rather than an asset. Environmental conditions may be irremediably destructive, and the patient may need some neurotic defenses in order to survive them. Disintegrative forces within the personality may be so strong as to threaten to break loose with the employment of uncovering procedures. Finally, neurotic symptoms or character distortions may constitute the only means of adjusting the patient to his conflicts, even though he possesses insight into their nature.

There are some patients who can make an adaptation solely by employing such neurotic facades. While partially debilitating, they help prevent regression and the upsurge of disintegrative tendencies. Thus, a psychosomatic ailment may serve to drain off hostile and masochistic impulses which, deprived of a somatic expression, may shatter the ego and produce a psychosis.

While the ideal goal of absolute resolution of blocks in personality maturation, with achievement of complete functioning in all areas of living, is a cherished aim in every patient, in practice very few people can reach this objective. Lorand (1946) recognized this when he said that in doing psychoanalysis it is sometimes essential to satisfy oneself with "practical" though superficial results that permit the patient to get along more satisfactorily than he did before therapy.

Clara Thompson (1950), in an excellent discussion of what constitutes a "cure" in therapy, describes the need for goal modification. She contends that, first of all, the patient must be relieved of neurotic suffering. He must also be able to relate to others with a minimum of unrealistically perpetuated attitudes that have their origins in early significant relationships. He must be capable of achieving as complete a development of his powers as his education and life circumstances will permit. If his life situation and the culture in which he functions are favorable, he will be most capable of relating to the group constructively; if not favorable, he may have to learn to endure relative isolation. As long as the person does not deceive himself through neurotic escape mechanisms, he may remain healthy even under inimical conditions. However, since we live in a sick society, some neurotic compromises are necessary in order to function. An absolute cure is thus not possible. As long as the person is relieved of anxiety, inferiority feelings, and other destructive elements and is capable of coping effectively with life difficulties as they arise, this may constitute as much as can be done for him in treatment.

While classical analysts in theory contend that theirs is the only therapy that can regularly and deliberately bring about deep and permanent changes (Strachey, 1937; Menninger, KA, 1958; Wallerstein, 1965),

they are not so confident that they can in practice always achieve these all-embracing results. Annie Reich (1950) considers that the bringing about through analysis of an absolute state of health "would appeal to the narcissistic omnipotence fantasies of the analyst." She adds that an analyst cannot hope to produce perfect human beings, that one should be content if one frees a patient from symptoms, and enables him to work, to adjust to reality, to engage in "adult object relations," and to accept his own limitations. Oberndorf (1942) speaks of a "practical success" of symptomatic relief, and admits that in many psychoanalytic cases "the structure of the disorder with recovery of infantile memories has not been worked out, to say nothing of being worked through." Wallerstein (1965) remarks, "Suffice it to say, that though the most ambitious of therapies in its overall outcome goals, in practice analysis often achieves no more than other less ambitious therapeutic approaches."

These formulations actually repeat what Freud himself conceded were limitations in man's capacities for change. In "Analysis Terminable and Interminable" (1937) he stated that what analysis accomplishes "for neurotics is only what normal people accomplish for themselves without its help," namely, a "taming" of their instincts to bring them into harmony with the ego. Where the ego for any reason becomes enfeebled, as in illness or exhaustion, the "tamed" instincts "may renew their demands and strive in abnormal ways after substitution satisfaction." Proof of this statement is inherent in what takes place in sleep when in reaction to the lessening of the ego's forces there is an awakening of instinctual demands. In altering the character structure, Freud was pessimistic of the outcome. It was not possible, he said, to predict a natural end to the process. "Our object will be not to rub off all the corners of the human character so as to produce 'normality' according to schedule, nor yet to demand that the person who has been 'thoroughly analyzed' shall never again feel the stirrings of passion in himself or become involved in any internal conflict. The business of analysis is to secure the best possible psychological conditions for the functioning of the ego; when this has been done, analysis has accomplished its task.''

R. P. Knight (1941) has condensed the aims of psychoanalytic therapy as follows:

1. *Symptom disappearance.*
2. *Improvement in mental functioning* with (a) understanding of the childhood sources of conflict, the part played by precipitating reality factors, the modes of defense against anxiety, and the specific character of the morbid process, (b) tolerance of the instinctual drives, (c) realistic self-appraisal with the ability to accept oneself objectively, (d) relative freedom from enervating tensions and crippling inhibitions, (e) liberation of aggressive energies required for ''self-preservation, achievement, competition and protection of one's rights.''
3. *Improved adjustment to reality* with (a) better interpersonal relationships, (b) more productive work capacity, (c) ability to sublimate more freely in recreation and avocations, and full heterosexual functioning.

A realistic approach to all forms of psychotherapy, including psychoanalysis, recognizes these principles of goal modification. It acknowledges that we may have to content ourselves with the modest objective of freedom from disturbing symptoms, the capacity to function reasonably well, and to experience a modicum of happiness in living. The patient may continue to be burdened by outbursts of his neurosis, which escapes control from time to time. He may have to circumscribe his activities and employ certain protective devices that hamper him in certain areas. Yet he will be as well adjusted as most persons with whom he is in contact, which means that he may continue to be neurotic, although better able to live with his neurosis and to approach average life objectives.

In the process of modifying goals, cognizance is paid to the fact that while each person is capable of change, there are various levels of change—from the altering of relatively superficial attitudes to the modification of the deepest strata of personality.

The strength of the ego in itself may bear no relationship to the extensiveness of goals approached during therapy. Thus, in many patients with strong egos, who have successfully dealt with infantile conflicts through repression, compensation, and sublimation and whose present illness consists of a breakdown of these defenses, the goals may advantageously be oriented around mediating the stress situation that has provoked collapse, restoring to the person his habitual defenses.

In patients with a weak ego who have dealt with infantile conflicts unsuccessfully, with a serious thwarting of maturation, one may also have to be content with the goal of restoring repression and of strengthening defenses to bring the person back to his customary equilibrium.

There are, in general, three types of patterns that exist in all persons that influence potentialities for personality modification even with depth therapy.

1. *Conditionings acquired during the preverbal period of life that have become so integral a part of the individual that they continue to operate in a reflex way.* Reorganization of these paradigms may be unsuccessful even after prolonged reconstructive or conditioning therapy, especially where they fulfill important needs, promote gratifications or serve as defenses. Surviving in almost pristine form, they defy logic and resist corrective influences.
2. *Systems developed in early life that have been symbolized, then repressed and repudiated because they mobilize anxiety or foster such intense guilt that they cannot be acknowledged.* These patterns, often related to sexual, aggressive and assertive needs, may be expressed on occasion in direct or modified form, rationalizations for them being elaborated. Alteration of these configurations may be possible once insight into their nature is gained, their pleasure or adaptive values harnessed, and motivation for their obliteration developed with substitution of more adaptive trends. Where pleasure gains are high and sacrifice of such gains is resented, or where

substitution of more mature ways of behaving is resisted, insight will not remove or control their expression. Here selective reinforcements may be successful.

3. *Patterns developed in later childhood and in adult life of which the individual is aware.* He may be able to modify or to control these patterns through his will power once he understands their nature and consequences. Yet he may also be motivated to retain these destructive modes because of their pleasure and anxiety-reducing values.

Amendment in all of these categories is possible. Some changes come about "spontaneously" in the medium of a rewarding, bountiful environment that does not repeat the frustrating upsetting experiences of the past. They may be the consequence of a constructive human relationship that acts as a corrective experience, rectifying distortions in past relationships. They occur most frequently, however, through a good psychotherapeutic experience with a skilled empathic therapist, the patient gaining some cognitive understanding of his conflicts, drives, and defenses, and being helped to develop new ways of reacting and relating. In all persons some residues of the disturbed past will remain irrespective of how bountiful one's environment may be, how exhaustively one knows oneself, or how thoroughly one has relearned new patterns.

Were we, in summary, to attempt the definition of a practical goal in therapy, we might say that it is *the achievement by the patient of optimal functioning within the limitations of his financial circumstances, his existing motivations, his ego resources, and the reality situation.* Such a goal would put upon the therapist the responsibility of resolving the patient's resistance in working toward the ideal objective of personality reconstruction. It would, however, admit of the expediency of adopting modified goals, such as dealing with only those aspects of the patient's problem that can be practically handled during the present therapeutic effort.

52

Technical Problems in Termination

The conditions under which termination of therapy is indicated are:

1. Achievement by the patient of planned treatment goals.
2. Decision by the patient or therapist to terminate on the basis of incomplete goals.
3. The reaching of an impasse in therapy or the development of stubborn resistances that cannot be resolved.
4. Countertransference that the therapist is unable to control.
5. Occurrence of physical reasons, such as moving of the residence of patient or therapist.

TERMINATING THERAPY UPON REACHING SET GOALS

Therapy may be terminated after the patient has achieved planned goals, such as the disappearance of symptoms, the mediation of environmental stress sources, the acquisition of greater happiness, productivity and self-fulfillment, the resolution of difficulties in interpersonal relationships, or the establishment of creative and productive patterns in living, with the evolution of greater emotional maturity. Hopefully some intrapsychic structural changes will have occurred in which, through a reworking of infantile conflicts, new defenses crystallize and adaptive solutions for old conflicts take place.

With the accomplishment of the purposes of therapy, termination is best effectuated by discussing the possibility of ending treatment with the patient, handling any resistance he displays, warning of the possibility of relapses, and inviting the patient to return after therapy has ended whenever he believes this to be necessary.

Discussing Termination with the Patient

In advance of the termination date it is wise to discuss with the patient the matter of ending therapy. A tapering-off period may be suggested, and a termination date set, which ideally should be from 6 to 8 weeks. The frequency of sessions may be reduced, and the intervals between visits steadily increased. The following is an excerpt from a session with a patient with a phobic disorder who has achieved adequate improvement in therapy:

Th. It sounds as if you are reaching the end of treatment. How do you feel about stopping?

Pt. Oh, of course I am glad that I am feeling so well, and I am very thankful to you, doctor.

Th. Actually, you did the bulk of the work. Of course, we could go on with treatment indefinitely, reaching more extensive goals in your personality development, but frankly I don't see the need for that, unless you do.

Pt. Well, I suppose I can benefit, but as you say, I am comfortable and happy now with Jim [*the patient's husband*] being so much better now to live with, and all these fears and things are gone now.

Th. If you agree with me that we should begin to terminate, we can cut down our visits to once weekly for the next month, and then a session every 2 weeks.

Pt. All right, doctor.

During the tapering-off period, any relapses or resistances are handled, sessions being again increased, but only if the patient's condition demands this. In occasional cases it may be decided to terminate therapy abruptly without tapering off, in order to expose the patient to a complete break with the therapist. Forced to function on his own, the patient may marshal inner strength more rapidly.

Handling Resistances to Termination

If the therapist has conducted the treatment sessions with the full participation of the patient, and if the therapist has avoided playing too directive a role, termination will not pose too great a problem in the average patient. In supportive therapy, however, where the patient has accepted the therapist as a guiding authority with whom he has conformed or in insight therapy where the patient has, on the basis of a residual dependency drive, made the therapist a necessary factor in his adjustment, termination may present difficulties.

In some patients in whom no manifest dependency operates in the relationship with the therapist, termination may still be troublesome. The patient may be fearful of giving up the protective situation in the therapeutic relationship. Memories of past suffering and anxiety may cause a patient to want to hold on to the security achieved, even at the cost of continuing in therapy indefinitely. M. Hollander (1965) has pointed out "that the role of being a patient in psychotherapy, like being a student in school or a patient on a medical service, may become a way of life instead of a means to an end."

The therapeutic tasks in termination with all patients involve analysis of the dependency elements in the relationship, a search for needs in the patient to perpetuate dependency, and a helping of the patient to achieve as much independence and assertiveness as possible. A shift in the character of the relationship may be necessary where the therapist has operated in a directive manner. Here the therapist behaves nondirectively with the patient, aiding him in establishing his own values and goals in relation to both minor and major aspects of his life.

Resistances in the average dependent patient are multiform. Some patients bluntly refuse to yield dependency, adopting all kinds of guiles, even to relapse in their illness, in order to demonstrate their helplessness. Other patients exhibit a profound fear of assertiveness, perhaps promoted by a neurotic equation of assertiveness with aggression. Resolution of such resistances may consume a great deal of time.

It may be necessary to interpret to the patient the reasons for his self-paralysis and to emphasize the need to make his own choices no matter how inappropriate these may seem. The patient may be told that because of the fact that he never has developed full confidence in himself as an individual, he has doubted his right to experience himself as a constructive human being. The insidious operation of his dependency may be demonstrated, and the patient may be shown how dependency has crippled his efforts toward self-growth. In his relationship with the therapist it is natural for him to expect the therapist to give him the answers and to make his decisions for him. Should the therapist do this, however, the patient will never develop strength within himself. The therapist wants to give the patient the opportunity to grow by encouraging him to take complete responsibility for his own decisions. The patient may be apprised of the fact that he will feel some of his decisions to be wrong; but even though he makes mistakes, the very fact that they are his own mistakes will teach him more than being told what to do at all times. The therapist does not want to withhold support from the patient, but it is necessary to do so now out of consideration for the patient's right to develop.

When the patient accuses the therapist of being cold and distant, the therapist may say:

The reason I'm not more demonstrative is that if I were to act like the traditional authority, it would eventually infantilize you; you would have to keep me around as a leaning post the rest of your life. You'd have to come to me for every decision with such queries as, ''Am I doing something wrong?'' or ''Am I doing the right thing?'' Rather, it's better for you to make mistakes, bad as they may be, and to feel that these are your own decisions than for me to tell you what to do.

A definition of the nondirective nature of the treatment situation in this way will give the patient an incentive to take responsibility. It will not serve to liberate the patient completely from his dependency demands. His neurotic attitudes and behavior patterns will continue in force. He may still exhibit toward the therapist the same insecurity, submissiveness, fear, and aggression that he always has manifested toward authority. He will claim the same ineptitudes in dealing with life and people. He will ingratiate himself, or act destructive, or detach himself in his customary manner. But he will do these with a slight difference, with doubts that they are really necessary.

The following excerpt of a treatment session with a patient resisting termination illustrates some of these points:

Th. You want me to tell you exactly what to do, how to do it, and when. If you really feel that you just don't have strength to do things for yourself, I will do them for you, provided you understand it isn't going to be of help to you if I make your decisions. I'll leave it up to you to decide. If you really feel as bad as you say you do, and you haven't got the confidence to make your own decisions, I'll let you depend upon me, if you *really* want that. [*This statement is offered as a challenge to the patient. She actually has*

become quite assertive through therapy but is evincing a regressive dependency reaction to prevent termination.]

Pt. I do feel just as badly as I told you, but at the same time I can hang on to various little things, one of which is that I long ago accepted the idea that you know what you're doing and I don't want to go against it. [*She seems to doubt the wisdom of her desire to have me function as a parental image.*]

Th. You don't want to go against what I have outlined as the best for you? What do you feel about making your own choices and your own decisions completely, with absolutely no help from me?

Pt. Oh, I think it's great, except that there doesn't seem to be much I can do about it.

Th. Well, what do you think would happen if I told you what to do, if I took you over and acted like a parent?

Pt. I feel two ways about it. I feel, first of all, that it might be an excellent idea because I'm certainly amenable to letting you take me over. But the other way I feel about it is that all this time I've been trying to, more or less, cooperate with you. I trust your judgment and I can see very well that keeping throwing decisions at me is what will in the end make me self-sufficient. Yes, I can see it, but right now I just can't imagine it ever happening or my being able to stand on my own feet. I feel very much as if I have slipped constantly downward during the last few weeks. [*This is since termination was suggested.*] That's all. I mean it's not as if I don't have lucid moments every now and then, but they're very few and far between.

Th. All right, then would you want me to play the role of telling you what to do on the basis that you can't come to decisions for yourself?

Pt. If it was making decisions, I might be able to do it; but I just can't see any decisions to make. There's nothing clear-cut. I don't know where I am at all.

Th. So that you'd like to just let yourself be taken care of by somebody?

Pt. It sounds nice, but I know perfectly well that it wouldn't be so good for me.

Th. You mean my making the decisions for you wouldn't be so good?

Pt. Well, certainly not.

Th. But some people seem to want that.

Pt. Grown people?

Th. Yes, grown people. Their feeling about themselves is so diminutive, their capacity to function so low that they want a parent watching over them all the time. If you'd like to adjust on this level all your life, you'd need to have me around to make your decisions for you indefinitely.

Pt. And then if I wasn't living here, I'd try to find someone else to do it, if I let you go ahead with this plan. [*This is a healthy reluctance to accepting dependency.*]

Th. If you don't develop strengths within yourself so you can figure things out and plan your life and follow it through, right or wrong, then you're going to need somebody around all the time.

Pt. I'd rather not depend on you then.

Because the therapist operates in a more passive role, the patient will be encouraged to act with greater assertiveness, to initiate actions, and to follow them through. Increasingly he will make his own plans and express his own choices. He will experience failures, of course, but he will have successes too. And his inner strength will grow on the bedrock of his successes. He will develop new feelings of integrity and a more complete sense of self.

Ego growth will thus be catalyzed during the terminal phase, eventuating in the patient's desire to manage his own life. Such growth is contingent to a large extent on the continued permissiveness of the therapist and the persistent encouragement of the patient's activity and self-expressiveness. The fact that the patient successfully figures things out for himself during the session eventually shows him that he is not at all at the mercy of forces on the outside. Ultimately he comes to the conclusion that he can live his own life, not because he is given permission, but because he has the right to do so. He feels equality with the therapist and a growing sense of self-respect. The self-confidence he develops in therapy promotes an extension of assertive feeling toward the extratherapeutic environment.

The proper conduct of therapeutic sessions during the terminal phase of reconstructive therapy requires that the therapist be so constituted that he or she can permit the patient to feel equality and to allow separation from treatment. The personalities of some therapists are essentially so authoritarian that they will not be able to function on equal terms with their patients. Automatically they will set themselves up as leaders, making judgments, giving directives, and setting goals for the patient that they insist must be followed. They may respond with hostility if challenged or abused by the patient. This is least apt to occur where the therapist has had personal psychotherapy and can analyze and control his countertransference before it acts to interfere with the treatment situation.

Even the therapist who has undergone personal therapy may manifest attitudes that support the resistances of the patient to termination. There may be a compulsion to overprotect or domineer the patient and thus an inability to assume a nondirective role. Economics may play a part when new referrals are scarce, and the therapist anticipates hard times ahead. This may lead to interminable therapy, until the patient forcefully asserts himself through the marshalling of aggression, and in this way violently breaks his ties with the therapist.

In some instances a complete resolution of the patient's dependence may not be possible, or may not even be attempted, as in supportive and some forms of reeducative therapy. Here the dependency is reduced to as innocuous a level as possible, by encouraging contact with an outside group or, in sick patients who require prolonged treatment, by maintaining a casual therapeutic relationship at extended intervals over an indefinite period.

Warning of the Possibility of Relapses

No matter how thoroughly the patient's neurotic patterns seem to have been eradicated, particularly in reconstructive therapy, shadows of old reactions persist. One may be incapable of eliminating them completely, as one cannot obliterate entirely other aspects of the patient's past. Under conditions of great insecurity, when the patient's sense of mastery is threatened, or during periods of disappointment, frustration, and deprivation, old defenses and strivings characteristic of past neurotic modes of adaptation are apt to be awakened.

Symptoms may return insidiously without the patient even being aware of having entered into the old conflictual situations that propagated them. Thus, migrainous attacks may recur in a man who, having learned to channelize hostility constructively and to avoid competitive relationships that create damaging resentment, changes his job to one where he is judged soley on the basis of comparison of his productivity to that of other employees. A woman with a propensity for dependent involvements may experience a return of her helplessness and her symptoms when she falls in love with, and acts submissive toward, a power-driven individual who constitutes for her an omnipotent father figure. Unconsciously she has yielded to a childish yearning for complete protection, and she is again paying the price in shattered self-esteem and its attendant symptomatic penalties.

It is essential for the patient to realize that getting well is no guarantee that one will experience no further return of symptoms. Indeed, at the point where therapy is being discontinued, the patient may be informed that he will probably undergo several relapses. However, if he investigates himself and analyzes the causes of each relapse, he will realize that the old conflicts that he has explored during therapy have been revived. His ability to understand the circumstances that had restored his trouble will not only help him to overcome the relapse, but also will consolidate his understanding and solidify new, healthy patterns. Some therapists find it profitable to tell patients at termination that they do not consider a person cured until he has suffered at least one relapse and has been able to work it out for himself. This practice forestalls the situation of the patient classifying his therapy as a failure, should a return of symptoms ensue. It alerts him to the insidious operation of his inner conflicts and promotes a continuing self-analysis. His ability to recognize the truth of the lessons he has learned in therapy strengthens his newly acquired traits and expands his personality growth. The therapist may tell the patient:

You are apt to get a flurry of anxiety and a return of symptoms from time to time. Don't be upset or intimidated by this. The best way to handle yourself is first to realize that your relapse is self-limited. It will eventually come to a halt. Nothing terrible will happen to you. Second, ask yourself what has been going on. Try to figure out what created your upset, what aroused your tension. Relate this to the general patterns that you have been pursuing since your childhood. Old habits hold on, but they will eventually get less and less provoking.

Inviting the Patient to Return for Further Sessions

The therapist may advantageously invite the patient to return for additional interviews in the event that this is a relapse and the problem cannot be worked through alone. Should the patient take advantage of this invitation, it will be possible for the therapist rapidly to help the patient gain insight into the conflicts and patterns that have been revived, to connect this understanding with what the patient already has learned in therapy, and to analyze why the patient was unable to get along through his own efforts. This process will occasion much relief in the patient and send him forth into life with a greater sense of mastery. Relatively few sessions will be required to effectuate this objective.

The patient may also desire to return to therapy in order to achieve more extensive personality development. Growth is a never ending process, and the patient may be so dissatisfied with his present status that he insists on inquiring more exhaustively into himself.

For example, a patient in an anxiety state, mobilized by involvement in a love affair that she has been unable to control with her habitual character defense of detachment, may utilize the therapeutic situation to break the relationship with the young man of whom she has become so hopelessly enamored. Restoring her detached defenses and again functioning satisfactorily without anxiety, she may decide that she has accomplished her treatment objective. However, because she has become aware of a conflict that makes close relationships dangerous for her, necessitating withdrawal, she may develop, after she has stopped treatment, an incentive to return to therapy for more extensive work. She will do this with a new goal in mind; namely to be able to relate closely to a person without needing to invoke her defense of detachment. With this expanded motivation, a reconstructive approach may be possible.

Encouraging the Patient to Continue Therapeutic Self-Help

A consistent application of what has been learned in psychotherapy is essential. The patient may be encouraged to engage in self-observation and to challenge neurotic patterns directly should they return, both by trying to understand what brought them back and by actively resisting and reversing them. In some cases the patient may be taught the process of self-relaxation or self-hypnosis to help reduce tension when upset and also to enable the patient, through self-reflection, to arrive at an understanding of elusive precipitating factors that have revived conflicts.

Even where there has been only supportive or a more superficial type of reeducative therapy, the patient may be inspired, as much as he can, (1) to utilize will power for the purpose of facing reality situations, (2) to push his mind away from ruminative obsessional thinking and preoccupations, (3) to cultivate, if possible, a sense of humor about himself and his situation, (4) to develop the philosophy of living in the present rather than regretting the past and dreading the future, (5) to practice expressing controlled resentment in justifiable situations, and (6) to examine any tensions, anxieties, or irrational impulses in terms of possible meanings, connecting them with what he knows of his basic neurotic patterns.

TERMINATING ON THE BASIS OF INCOMPLETE GOALS

Therapy may have to be terminated prior to the achievement of planned goals. There are a number of reasons for this, most important of which is insoluble resistance. Thus, a patient may, with psychotherapy, lose certain symptoms, but other symptoms

may cling to him obstinately. He may relinquish many neurotic patterns but continue to exploit a few without which he feels himself incapable of functioning. He may develop a number of new potentialities, yet be unable to progress to as complete emotional maturity as either he or the therapist may desire. Working on his resistance accomplishes little, and the therapist may then deem it advisable to interrupt treatment. A countertransference resistance that may require resolution is a too strong ambition in the therapist who expects more from a patient than he can produce.

Therapeutic objectives may have to be scaled down considerably in certain individuals. Thus, we may be dealing with a sick borderline patient who is on the verge of a schizophrenic break and who is insistent that he be brought in therapy to a point where he can be more normal than normal. This wish, while admirable, is not realistic, for the patient does not possess the fortitude to endure the rigours of a reconstructive approach. Because he does not have sufficient ego strength to work out a better adaptation, one may have to make a compromise with projected goals.

Sometimes therapy is started with a patient whose motivations are unalterably defective. For instance, she may have a tremendously arrogant notion of her capacities, and she may seek treatment solely because she has read somewhere that psychotherapy can bring out an individual's buried potentialities. The bloated self-image that the patient supports may be the only way she has of counteracting feelings of inner devastation or of rectifying a contemptuous self-image. Therapy with such a patient may be extremely difficult and may have to be terminated due to impenetrable resistance.

The therapist may be confronted with a patient whose life situation obstructs his progress. His environmental difficulty is so irremediable that possibilities of correction are remote, and hence the patient must be persuaded to live with it or be desensitized to its effect. Or the patient's symptoms may possess for him so strong a defensive value that their removal will produce a dangerous reaction. Therapy may have to be terminated on the basis of only partial symptomatic relief.

It may be impossible, due to other obstructions, to get some patients to progress beyond a certain point in therapy. To continue treatment may prove discouraging to the therapist and undermining to the patient. It is better here for the patient to retain some neurotic drives than to be exposed to interminable and frustrating therapy to which, in all probability, the patient will be unable to respond.

As soon as the therapist decides that maximum improvement has been obtained or that a stalemate has been reached, the therapy may be brought to a halt by utilizing the techniques described for termination after the achievement of planned goals. The therapist will, however, have to explain the reason for termination in such a way that the patient does not arrive at the conclusion that he is hopeless. Thus, the patient may be told that therapy has alleviated some of his symptoms, has brought him to an awareness of his basic problems, and has pointed the way to a more adaptive life. Because his difficulties have been with him a long time, his resistances to a complete cure may persist for a period. Putting his insight into practice in real life will give him the best opportunity to achieve a more complete development.

The mere mention of termination, and the discussion of resistances that seem to have blocked progress, may stimulate incentives to break through these hindrances. If a termination date has been set, the patient may work through resistances prior to the expiration date. On the other hand, the termination techniques may not resolve the many impediments to further change. Yet, after the patient has left treatment, spectacular progress may be experienced. The fact that no headway was made while in therapy may have been due to the operation of a subtle transference situation that acted as resistance. For example, hostility toward the therapist may have expressed itself in a refusal to go forward in personality advance; or dependence on the therapist may have taken the initiative away from the patient. Once the patient is functioning away from therapy under his own power, such

resistances no longer operate and a spurt in development is possible.

Planned Interruption of Therapy

Instead of outright termination, a vacation from therapy may be suggested. During this period the patient may experiment with the learning he has gained by attempting productive actions. The interruption may also enable him to experience his neurotic tendencies as they operate in his life situation and to cope with disturbances as they arise without help. He may also become aware of his dependency on the therapist. Discussing his reactions later with the therapist may prove to be invaluable to the patient. The proposed interruption may be presented to the patient as in the following excerpt:

Th. It seems to me that we have reached a plateau in your therapy and that a vacation from treatment may be indicated. How do you feel about that?

Pt. I just can't seem to get any further. I've been thinking of that. How long would you suggest?

Th. Suppose we plan on a month's vacation. After a month call me, and we'll arrange an appointment.

Pt. Do you believe that will be of help?

Th. I do. You might observe yourself during this period and see if you can determine what is happening, what stirs up your symptoms and what alleviates them. We might learn something important, and the interlude may help pull you out of the plateau.

Transferring the Patient

Sending the patient to another therapist may sometimes be preferable to outright termination. Where one believes one is unable to deal with the patient's resistances, where one cannot control destructive countertransference, or where, for any other reason, one feels incapable of helping the patient any more, the decision may then be that the patient will do better with a different therapist. Sometimes a transfer is arranged when it is presumed the patient will benefit by a kind of therapeutic experience other than that provided by the present therapist. For instance, a therapist trained mainly in reconstructive approaches may feel that the patient needs somatic, reeducative, or supportive therapy and may consequently want to refer the patient to a professional person who is highly skilled in these techniques. Or a change to a therapist of the opposite sex may be considered advisable. Should a tranfer be indicated, the therapist may discuss the matter with the patient as illustrated in this fragment of a session:

Th. For some time I have felt that we haven't been making very much progress.

Pt. Yes, I was worried about this. I wondered if you were getting impatient.

Th. Of course not, except that sometimes a snag like this does happen, and a person may be able to work it out better with another therapist.

Pt. You mean you want me to see somebody else?

Th. My desire is for you to get well. What would you feel about seeing someone I would recommend and who I believe can help you? I have a feeling you may do better with another type of technique, and Dr. _____ is very excellent at this.

Pt. Well, I don't know.

Th. Why don't you talk to Dr. _____ after I determine that he has the time for you? Then, after a couple of sessions you can see how you feel.

Pt. If you think this is best, I'll do it.

Th. I do, and I'll make all the arrangements and call you.

TERMINATION NOTE

At the time of termination a note should be entered in the patient's case record indicating the reasons for termination, the patient's condition on discharge, the areas of improvement, the patient's attitude toward the therapist, the recommendations made to the patient, and the final diagnosis. A form, such as in Appendix H may be found useful.

FOLLOW-UP

Prior to discharging the patient it is advisable to ask him whether he would object to receiving an occasional letter from the therapist regarding his progress. Most patients are delighted to cooperate and consider the therapist's gesture a mark of interest in their development. Follow-up letters, briefly inquiring into how things have been progressing, may be sent to the patient yearly, preferably for at least 5 years. This enables the therapist to maintain a good check on what has been happening over a considerable period of time. The patient's replies to the follow-up inquiry may be entered in his case record, and, if necessary, a brief notation may be made of the contents.

PATIENTS' REACTIONS TO THE END OF THERAPY

What follows are some reactions voiced by patients when they finished therapy:

1. All people have problems, and I know now that mine are no worse than anybody else's.

2. I realize I considered my symptoms a sign of weakness. I realize they aren't. I don't pay attention to them and they pass. They aren't such a big deal now.

3. One of the big problems I had was considering myself the center of the universe. It now isn't so important for me to feel so important.

4. I was so full of guilt, I felt I would bust. When I talked things out, I realized my standards were a lot more strict than those of other people. As a matter of fact, I would purposefully do things to prove I was bad; now I don't have to.

5. The price I would pay for my indulgences were just too high. So I don't burn the world up! So I don't get as much of a bang out of doing ridiculous things! The quietness I feel more than compensates for the high life I was leading.

6. Why knock yourself out climbing on top of the heap? You're nowhere when you get there. You kill yourself trying. I was so ambitious and perfectionistic that I had no time for living. Now I try to find pleasure in little things, and it works.

7. I don't have to blame my parents anymore for my troubles; whatever happened, happened. Why should I let the past poison my present life? I feel I can live now for what life has to offer me right now.

8. I used to torture myself about the future. Worry about it so much I couldn't enjoy anything. I knew I was silly, but I couldn't stop

it. Now I just don't care. I do the best I can now and I know the future will happen as it will happen no matter how much I worry about it. I take things as they come.

These ideas are not capricious whims. They are formulations developed after a working through of important conflicts. They indicate an attempt at solution of basic problems, which permit of a style of living more in keeping with reality.

Interestingly, the essence of such precepts may be found in proposals and rules of living laid down by poets and philosophers from the earliest times that humans recorded their hopes and fears and formulated ways of resolving them. Sometimes individuals arrive at such philosophies spontaneously without therapy, usually during emotional crises that force upon them adaptive ways of thinking and behaving. Sometimes the philosophies are evolved as a result of authoritative pressures or out of respect for leaders whom the individual elevates to a protective or powerful position. A good psychotherapeutic experience, however, will give the individual the best opportunity to remold values and to arrive at a more constructive way of living.

V

Special Aspects

53

Adjunctive Aids in Psychotherapy

The principal adjuncts in psychotherapy are relaxation exercises, biofeedback, somatic therapy, hypnosis, narcotherapy, videotape recording, and bibliotherapy.

RELAXATION EXERCISES AND MEDITATION

A certain amount of tension is a normal phenomenon, and every human being experiences it as a concomitant of daily living. It is probably helpful to problem solving and creative adaptation. In psychotherapy it acts as a stimulant to experimentation with new modes of defense and behavior. In excess, however, like too much anxiety, it paralyzes productive work and provokes a variety of physiological and psychological symptoms that divert the victim from concentrating on his therapeutic tasks. Its control, consequently, becomes an expedient objective. While the therapeutic relationship serves to solace the patient, it may not be sufficient to subdue pathological tension. Minor tranquilizing drugs are effective, but they have side effects and may, in susceptible persons, lead to habituation. Fortunately, there are other available modes of tension control that can serve as an adjunct to psychotherapy.

As explained in a previous chapter, there are a number of ways that relaxation may be achieved, including meditation, Yoga practices, self-hypnosis, Zen, autogenic training, biofeedback, and simple breathing exercises. In all of the foregoing similar general principles prevail (Benson et al, 1974).

First, there is a *minimization of external stimuli*. This is achieved by a quiet environment devoid of distractions. An isolated room, a secluded seashore, or quiet woods can suffice. Other people may be present provided that they too participate in the relaxation experience, maintaining strict silence. Experienced meditators are able to "turn off" in almost any environment, withdrawing into themselves, but this will not apply to the great majority of people. Second, *attention is focused* on a simple sound, the repetition of a word or monotonous phrase, or gazing at an object. Some subjects utilize a metronome or listen to their own quiet deep breathing; some stare at a spot in the ceiling; still others recite to themselves a syllable or meaningless expression ("mantra"). Whenever the attention wanders and thoughts and ideas invade one's mind, the subject is enjoined to return to the fixation stimulus. Third, a free-floating, unpressured, languid, unresisting attitude must prevail; the *individual surrenders to passivity*. As images, reflections, ruminations, sentiments, and varied thoughts emerge from inner mental recesses, the subject lets them drift by without concentrating on being concerned with them. This is probably the most difficult task for the subject to learn, but with practice there is less and less focus on performance and greater ability to let things take their own course. Fourth, *a comfortable position* is essential, such as sitting in a chair or, if one is nimble, kneeling. Lying down is conducive to sleep and may defeat some of the aims of the experience.

The specific technique that one employs to achieve the relaxation experience is largely dependent on what is most meaningful for the individual. Some persons are so impressed with the mysteries of the esoteric Eastern philosophies that they are especially attracted to these.

In the practice of Zen Buddhism the meditation experience (Zazen) plays an important part. This, performed in a quiet atmosphere, with eyes open, the mind drifting while focused on breathing, produces a unique kind of physical-mental experience. Strived for are episodes of deep clarity (samadhi), of enlightened unity (satori), and a buildup of energy (joriki). To learn this type of meditation, one practices in a group (sangha), preferably under the guidance of a Zen master.

Transcendential meditation is perhaps the most widely employed form of relaxation utilized in the United States. Introduced by a guru, Maharishi Mahesh Yogi, it has resulted in a movement that has been gaining momentum over the years with development of a large number of societies distributed throughout the land.* It is taught by a trained instructor who designs a word, sound, or phrase (mantra) presumably uniquely fitting to the subject, which is supposed to remain secret. This constitutes the fixation object.

Other forms of meditation include

* See the Maharishi International University Catalogue, obtained from Maharishi International University, 1015 Gayley Avenue, Los Angeles, California 90024.

Yoga, Sufism, Taoism, Krishna Consciousness, and a wide variety of nonreligious practices focused on achieving a higher reality and greater knowledge than can be gathered through the senses. This is done by finding a "unity of being" in the quietness of inner tranquility. Each brand of relaxation has its devotees who attest to its singular usefulness. An excellent review of meditation is found in the book by Carrington (1977).

As practiced in the Social Rehabilitation Clinic of the Postgraduate Center for Mental Health (New York City) with groups, under the direction of Dr. Maria Fleischl and Joan Suval, basically two aspects of meditation therapy are utilized. Their description follows:

One involves effort and concentration, focusing attention upon a particular object or sensation, and the other, a simple watchfulness and observation, allowing a free flow of perceptions. The aims of this approach to meditation are twofold; to give a "total rest to the mind," relieving tension and anxiety, and to clear the mind, so that it is more aware and better able to cope with everyday problems.

The meditation therapist begins the group session by suggesting that the meditators close their eyes, take a deep breath, release it slowly, and allow their shoulders, chest, arms, legs, etc., to relax—to "let go completely." For a few moments focus will be on different parts of the body so that tension can be released in those areas. The therapist may then suggest that the meditators direct their attention for a while to the natural movement of their breathing, or to see if they can be aware of the various pulsations and sensations going on within the body. Other areas of focus could include listening to the sounds coming from the outdoors, or the footsteps in the halls, or the steady vibration of an air conditioner. The meditators are reminded throughout this part of the session that if certain thoughts distract their attention, they should simply observe that this is happening, refocusing their attention each time this occurs.

After 10 or 15 minutes of this aspect of the meditation involving effort and concentration, the therapist then suggests that the meditators now allow their attention to move wherever it is attracted—to a sound, a sensation, a thought—permitting a free flow of perceptions, an "effortless awareness." The therapist reminds the group, from time to time, that it is fine if thoughts are coming and going easily without causing any disturbance, but if the meditator finds that he is becoming anxious because he is *thinking* about his thoughts, he should then focus his attention for a few moments on an area such as his breathing, sensations within the body, sounds outside, etc., until his thoughts have subsided and he feels that he is calmer. Then he can return to watching a free flow of perceptions. Sometimes the therapist will ask the meditators to open their eyes "halfway" so that their gaze is directed downward for a few moments. This allows the meditator to discover that the watchfulness and effortless awareness can be going on even when the eyes are open. The therapist ends the meditation by once again suggesting that the meditators take a deep breath, exhale slowly, and gradually open their eyes.

Meditators at the clinic are encouraged to schedule a 15- to 20-minute formal meditation period for themselves at home, either in the morning or the evening, or both, following the same procedure as outlined above. In addition, the therapist points out that this watchfulness and effortless awareness can go on while the person is involved in his everyday activities—traveling on a bus, in a train, walking, listening to a conversation, observing the thoughts one has following an argument, etc. This allows an individual to be in closer "touch" with his thoughts, his feelings, what he actually IS at each particular moment of observation. Often when a meditator is simply watching a free flow of perceptions in this way, repressed thoughts can come to the surface. The meditation therapist stresses the importance of moving away from thought that creates tension and anxiety, calming the mind by focusing attention on an area that is not one of conflict, and then, when the mind is clear and quiet, allowing him to look once again at the thoughts or the situation that had caused the disturbance. When the mind is quiet and free from anxiety, it can see more easily which thoughts are negative and destructive and which are positive and constructive.

It should be pointed out that this approach to meditation is different from that of transcendental meditation, which limits itself to a formal meditation period, with the meditator concentrating his attention on the silent or verbal repetition of an assigned "mantra" or Sanskrit word or phrase, so that he can enter into a state of relaxation. As indicated earlier, relaxation and concentration are important aspects of the meditation being presented at the Social Rehabilitation Clinic, but even more vital and beneficial is that this practical approach involves an effortless and choiceless awareness that the meditator can incorporate into his daily life, enabling him to be in closer contact with himself and to function more effectively in his relationships.

In addition to the formal meditation period, the therapist answers questions that are asked and stimulates group discussion whenever possible. A strong supportive personality is an important requirement for the meditation therapist, who must also be watchful that there not be overdependency on the part of the meditators. The therapist can avoid this by encouraging individuals to meditate at home and throughout the day, modifying their approach according to their own needs and convenience.*

An outline such as that in Table 53–1 may also be given to the patient as an alternative method.

Biofeedback is another way of achieving relaxation through the use of instrumentation. This allows an individual to recognize and influence certain internal bodily states, like muscle tension, that interfere with relaxation. Among the most useful instruments are the electromyograph and temperature machines. Except where certain pathological physiological states exist, like very marked hypertension, dangerous tachycardia, and arrhythmias and severe migraine, I have found little advantage over the simple relaxation exercises outlined above for tension control.

Schultz's autogenic training (Schultz & Luthe, 1959; Luthe, 1969) is another way of achieving tension control. An outline of modified autogenic training exercises is included at the end of the following section on biofeedback.

What all forms of relaxation correctly done achieve is a decrease in activity of the sympathetic nervous system with lowering of the heart rate, respiration, oxygen consumption, blood lactate level, blood pressure, muscle tension, and probably an increase in alpha brain waves. Where highly charged emotions and conflicts lay dormant, their upsurge into awareness may reverse these physiologic changes, but the proper technique will suppress such interferences. Hypnosis can be useful for the relaxation response, but where the object is to release repressed components through suggestion, cathartic liberation of emotions can occur. However, should strict tension control be the objective, there is no attempt made in hypnosis to probe the unconscious.

For many years I have utilized hypnosis for pure tension control and have taught my patients self-hypnosis (which can easily be learned), shying away from ego-building or exploratory suggestions so as to limit the objective to relaxation. The tech-

* Reprinted with permission of Dr. Maria Fleischl and Joan Suval.

nique is simple. The patient is enjoined to practice for 20 minutes, twice daily, sitting in a comfortable chair in a quiet room, shutting his eyes and breathing gently but deeply, concentrating on the sound of his breathing. He is then asked to relax his muscles progressively starting with his forehead and working down to his finger tips and then shoulders to toes. The reverse can also be done, that is, starting with the toes and slowly relaxing muscle groups to the forehead. Finally, the patient counts very slowly from 1 to 20 listening to his breathing. After the count the patient is enjoined to let his mind become passively languid, avoiding concentrating on thoughts and ideas. Should these obtrude themselves, he is to revert back to listening to his breathing. In a short period these exercises may be learned achieving what the more complex meditation practices accomplish without unnecessary adornments. In some instances I have made a cassette recording for the patient utilizing the format outlined in the section on hypnosis later in this chapter, but eliminating the ego-building suggestions and summation of suggestions. Such relaxation practices have been extremely helpful to patients under excessive tension, without interfering with the psychotherapeutic process.

A letter written by a physician who personally tried meditation to reduce pressures and tensions explains some of the benefits to be derived from it:

> I'm getting back to meditating twice a day instead of just once (after four months of down to once a day). It really makes a big difference for me to have regular meditation. It certainly helps me see things in the larger perspective and less egotistically and egocentrically. Also it's a recharging of my mental battery, clearing the static of constant mental chatter out by tuning in to a clearer, more positive channel. You know, I actually feel much more "free-floating" after meditating—like the contrast between having all that subconscious mental chatter and no mental chatter brings the chatter back into acute focus. It seems like I then

Table 53–1
Self-help Relaxation Methods

I. *Letting Go:* For most, it is a mistake to "try to relax." Just tense the muscle group and then visualize and verbalize to the muscle group "let go and keep on letting go."

II. *Breathing:* A Yogic style of deep slow breathing (6000 years old). Fill up with air from the lower belly (abdomen and diaphragm) toward the chest, like filling a glass of water, and *exhale slowly* thru the nostrils. You can first tense, or suck in the belly and feel tension in these muscles, and then say, "I will allow these muscles to let go," visualizing letting go on exhalation. Place hand below "belly button" and feel area move up on inhalation and down on exhalation. Relaxed breathing should continue throughout remaining exercises of tensing and relaxing.

III. *Forearm:* Many people can most quickly be aware of tensing the forearm and relaxing it on exhalation. Making a fist is one way of tensing and visualizing.

IV. *Face and Forehead:* Wrinkle forehead as tightly as possible, and then say to muscles, "Let go and keep on letting go." Practice this often. Furrow between the brows often and say, "Let go and continue to let go." Clench teeth, feel jaw muscles tighten, and let go with lips and teeth slightly parted. Show teeth and relax these muscles. *Push* tongue against upper palate (top of mouth) and let it relax between lower teeth (just almost touching bottom teeth). Close eyelids tightly and let go slowly.
IMPORTANT: Look as far to left as possible with eyes closed, lids relaxed, and then let go and let eyes go and drift. Same to right and up and down. (Rolling eyeballs up with Yogic breathing and keeping them up is one way to be helpful for inducing self-hypnotism and later

sleep in insomniacs.) Visualize and let the entire face smooth out as though you are smoothing it with both hands and let it stay smooth. *(Relaxation of eyes and tongue often controls unwanted thoughts and helps with insomnia.)*

V. If mind wanders, get it back to thinking of breathing and muscle group pictures as best you can. Tighten on inhalation and let go on exhalation.

VI. *Repetition:* Do not become discouraged since tension patterns have existed all of your life. Practice whenever possible. Soon shortcuts such as deep breathing and words "calm," or "let go," or "relax" or words or pictures of your choosing may help form relaxing a habit. You may find for yourself certain muscle groups, such as face, shoulders, or breathing muscles, that allow you to relax most adequately.

VII. *Neck Practice:* The same procedures of breathing and tensing muscle groups apply to all parts of body. You can, expecially in the beginning, bend head back, relax. Head to the left and right.

VIII. *Shoulders:* Hunch up as far as possible and let go. Backward and forward also.

IX. *Lower Extremities:* Pinch buttocks together; feel tension and let go. Tighten and let go toes.
General: Practice at every available moment to do things in a relaxed fashion; then let yourself consciously breath deeply and relax in situations ordinarily causing tension. If possible, condition or habituate the relaxation of the entire musculature or letting go to deep breathing and the same key words or words that seem to suit you.
Time: Persistence and review are worthwhile since everyone agrees on the desirability and harmlessness of relaxation.

Reprinted by permission of Dr. Irwin Rothman, modified from E. Jacobsen and J. Wolpe.

have greater access to my subconscious. I feel more creative, more in control, and less driven somehow.

BIOFEEDBACK

Through the use of electronic instruments it has been shown that an individual may become aware of changes in bodily functions of which he is usually ignorant, including skin temperature, blood pressure, muscle tension, and brain wave patterns. Changes in these functions activate the instruments designed to measure them and deliver signals (sounds or lights) to the subject permitting him to become aware of certain feelings or states of mind that influence alterations in the studied parameters. The subject gradually learns how to reproduce such feelings or states to secure desired physiological effects. Body and mind become affiliated through this feedback process so that eventually the individual can reproduce reactions without the use of instruments. The full value of biofeedback must still be evaluated. It has certain substantiated uses, for example, the control of tension and headaches, but whether it is superior to other techniques (psychotherapy, drug treatment) has not yet been determined. It is being employed in Raynaud's disease, migraine, cardiac arrhythmias, hypertension, and phobias with promising results, but biofeedback cannot be recommended for everyone. It requires time for learning, studied application, and practice, which not all patients are willing to indulge. It requires also instruments that may be an expensive investment. In spite of these drawbacks, biofeedback is an area of great promise whose full possibilities and applications have opened up a fertile field of research (Segal, J., 1975). A number of volumes of collected research on feedback have already appeared as well as critical reviews of the literature (Shapiro, D., & Schwartz, 1972; Blanchard & Young, 1974), and a journal, *Biofeedback and Self-Regulation* has made its debut.

In the technique of biofeedback "a meditative state of deep relaxation is conducive to the establishment of voluntary control by allowing the individual to become aware of subliminal imagery, fantasies, and sensations" (Pelletier, 1975). This facilitates a link between physiological and psychological processes. The combination of relaxation exercises and biofeedback instrumentation facilitates identification of subjective imagery and physiological sensations that are quieting to the bodily organs.

Where a patient with a serious gastrointestinal, cardiovascular, migrainous, or psychosomatic illness is unable to achieve relief through psychotherapy with the adjunctive use of relaxation exercises, biofeedback training should be considered. Which instruments to employ will depend on the illness and the learning capacities of the patient. In my own practice I have found the galvanic skin reflex (GSR) electromyograph (EMG) and temperature machines most useful.

In muscle tension retraining through the use of an electromyograph (EMG) information may be obtained regarding muscular activity below the threshold of sensory awareness. One may measure the average intensity of neuron firing in microvolts on a meter. An audible feedback delivers sounds registering increases in muscular activity, and by utilizing a threshold control one may provide conditions for optimal training. Where muscle relaxation is the goal, the threshold is set at a high level to produce sound; and as the patient learns to relax, the sound lessens then disappears. The electrodes are in a band that fits around the muscle to be utilized for training purposes. The most useful location is the forehead, the electrodes being placed about 1 inch above the eyebrows.

Signals are picked up not only from the frontalis muscle, but also from other muscles in the head, face, and neck. Thinking activates anxiety thoughts, which can cause a rise in muscular activity. "Turning off thinking" causes a fall.

Relaxation of the frontalis muscle tends to generalize to the entire body. When the level reaches below 4 microvolts, the subject may report a feeling of weightlessness or floating and alterations in the body image. This may create temporary anxiety and increase muscle tension. Should this happen, the patient is reassured that these sensations are normal and to enjoy them. As tension decreases, those patients who are repressing anxiety strongly may experience a sudden burst of anxious thoughts and feelings. Should this happen, the patient is encouraged to verbalize them.

When the subject has been able to maintain EMG activity below 4 microvolts for about 15 minutes, one should instruct the subject to examine internal sensations and feelings associated with deep relaxation in order to recreate the state without the feedback unit. In this way muscle relaxation may be obtained rapidly without the use of instruments.

To control migraine, it is necessary to learn control of blood circulation in the brain to minimize engorgement of the blood vessels. Utilizing the thermal machine, one may learn to send the blood flow from the head to the hand. The machine has two probes that record the surface temperature (a measure of the blood flow). To monitor blood flow between the head and hand, one probe is placed on the forehead, the other probe on the middle finger of the right hand. The thermal unit (machine) detects minute changes in temperature differential. As a difference in temperature occurs between forehead and finger, a slowly pulsed audible tone will be heard in the earphones. The sound means the blood is flowing in the right direction. Training sessions after the relaxation exercises should last no longer than 5 to 10 minutes.

There is no reason why biofeedback cannot be utilized in combination with behavior therapy (e.g., systematic desensitization) and dynamic psychotherapy. In this way the patient monitors his own anxiety level by EMG feedback and becomes more insightful of his fantasy material in an atmosphere of objective detachment (Budzynski et al, 1970).

Further information on available biofeedback machines may be obtained from Autogenic Systems Incorporated, 809 Allston Way, Berkeley, Calif., 94710, and from Cyberg Corporation, 342 Western Ave., Boston, Massachusetts 02135.

A useful means of achieving relaxation prior to biofeedback instrumentation is Schultz's autogenic training or a modification of this as in Table 53–2.

SOMATIC THERAPY

In a previous chapter the rationale and indications for the somatic therapies have been detailed (see page 89). In this section we shall consider some practical applications helpful for the psychotherapist in deciding which patients require medicaments adjunctively and which drugs to prescribe. If the therapist is a nonphysician, it will be necessary to work collaboratively with the prescribing medical person, supplying the proper data in order that the most suitable drug be selected.

Somatic therapy has proven itself to be a great boon to patients suffering from schizophrenia, endogenous depressions, manic phases of manic-depressive psychosis, acute puerperal psychosis, and severe toxic confusional states. Moreover, somatic treatments have had a positive effect on the morale of patients and their families and have helped to increase discharge rates from mental hospitals (Freyhan, 1961). The prevailing attitude of the public regarding the hopelessness and incurability of severe mental illness has given way to optimism that dread psychiatric diseases may now be interrupted and perhaps even cured. Employed in outpatient departments of hospitals and clinics, somatic therapy has brought early psychoses to a halt before they have progressed to a point where patients have had to be institutionalized. It has also helped in the rehabilitation of chronic psychotic patients.

Somatic therapy, particularly drug administration, has also exerted a beneficial effect in psychotherapy (Linn, 1964; Kalinowsky, 1965; Kalinowsky & Hippus, 1969; Hollister, 1973). While some therapists continue to shy away from the use of medications, situations do arise during psychotherapy when drugs may prove helpful, even in psychoanalysis (Ostow, 1962). An important factor is to prescribe drugs in sufficient dosage and over a sufficiently long period to test their efficacy.

Table 53–2
Relaxation Training Procedure

Part I	
Sit quietly in a comfortable position.	Take another deep, slow breath.
	Hold the breath while tightening your stomach
Take a deep, slow breath.	and neck muscles.
Hold the breath for several seconds.	Feel the tension.
Slowly exhale.	
	Breathe out and let your muscles go limp.
Take another deep, slow breath.	
Hold the breath and pull your toes toward your	Take another deep, slow breath.
head, tightening your leg and calf muscles.	Hold the breath and tighten every muscle in your
Feel the tension.	body until you feel your whole body start to
	tremble with tension.
Breathe out and let go completely.	
	Now breathe out and let go completely.
Take another deep, slow breath.	
Hold the breath and make a fist with both hands,	Take another deep, slow breath.
tightening your arm and shoulder muscles.	Hold the breath and tighten every muscle in your
Feel the tension.	body.
	Hold on to the tension.
Breathe out and let go completely.	
	Now breathe out and let go completely.
Take another deep, slow breath.	
Hold the breath and bite down as hard as you can,	Take another deep, slow breath.
tightening your jaw muscles.	Hold the breath and tighten every muscle in your
Feel the tension.	body.
	Hold the tension.
Breathe out and let go completely.	
	Now breathe out and let go, relaxing completely.

Part II	
Concentrate on slow, deep breathing throughout	My stomach and the whole center portion of my
this entire section.	body feel heavy and relaxed.
	My stomach and the whole center portion of my
Slowly repeat each of these phrases to yourself	body feel heavy and relaxed.
as you hear them.	My hands feel heavy and relaxed.
	My hands feel heavy and relaxed.
I feel very calm and quiet.	My arms feel heavy and relaxed.
I feel very comfortable and quiet.	My arms feel heavy and relaxed.
I am beginning to feel quite relaxed.	My shoulders feel heavy and relaxed.
I am beginning to feel quite relaxed.	My shoulders feel heavy and relaxed.
My feet feel heavy and relaxed.	My hands, my arms and my shoulders all feel
My feet feel heavy and relaxed.	heavy and relaxed.
My ankles feel heavy and relaxed.	My hands, my arms and my shoulders all feel
My ankles feel heavy and relaxed.	heavy and relaxed.
My knees feel heavy and relaxed.	My neck feels heavy and relaxed.
My knees feel heavy and relaxed.	My neck feels heavy and relaxed.
My hips feel heavy and relaxed.	My jaws feel heavy and relaxed.
My hips feel heavy and relaxed.	My jaws feel heavy and relaxed.
My feet, my ankles, my knees and my hips all	My forehead feels heavy and relaxed.
feel heavy and relaxed.	My forehead feels heavy and relaxed.
My feet, my ankles, my knees and my hips all	My neck, my jaws and my forehead all feel
feel heavy and relaxed.	heavy and relaxed.

Table 53–2 *(Continued)*

My neck, my jaws and my forehead all feel heavy and relaxed.
My whole body feels heavy and relaxed.
My whole body feels heavy and relaxed.
My breathing is getting deeper and deeper.
My breathing is getting deeper and deeper.
I can feel the sun shining down on me warming the top of my head.
The top of my head feels warm and heavy.
The top of my head feels warm and heavy.
The relaxing warmth flows into my right shoulder.
My right shoulder feels warm and heavy.
My right shoulder feels warm and heavy.
My breathing is getting deeper and deeper.
The relaxing warmth flows down to my right hand.
My right hand feels warm and heavy.
My right hand feels warm and heavy.
The relaxing warmth flows back up to my right arm.
My right arm feels warm and heavy.
My right arm feels warm and heavy.
The relaxing warmth spreads up through my right elbow into my right shoulder.
My right elbow, my right shoulder feel warm and heavy.
My right elbow, my right shoulder feel warm and heavy.
The relaxing warmth flows slowly throughout my whole back.
I feel the warmth relaxing my back.
My back feels warm and heavy.
My back feels warm and heavy.
The relaxing warmth flows up my back and into my neck.
My neck feels warm and heavy.
My neck feels warm and heavy.
The relaxing warmth flows into my left shoulder.
My left shoulder feels warm and heavy.
My left shoulder feels warm and heavy.
My breathing is getting deeper and deeper.
The relaxing warmth flows down to my left hand.
My left hand feels warm and heavy.
My left hand feels warm and heavy.
The relaxing warmth flows back up to my left arm.
My left arm feels warm and heavy.
My left arm feels warm and heavy.
The relaxing warmth spreads up through my left elbow into my left shoulder.

My left elbow, my left shoulder feel warm and heavy.
My left elbow, my left shoulder feel warm and heavy.
The relaxing warmth flows to my heart.
My heart feels warm and easy.
My heart feels warm and easy.
My heartbeat is slow and regular.
My heartbeat is slow and regular.
The relaxing warmth flows down into my stomach.
My stomach feels warm and quiet.
My stomach feels warm and quiet.
My breathing is deeper and deeper.
My breathing is deeper and deeper.
The relaxing warmth flows down into my right thigh.
My right thigh feels warm and heavy.
My right thigh feels warm and heavy.
The relaxing warmth flows down into my right foot.
My right foot feels warm and heavy.
My right foot feels warm and heavy.
The relaxing warmth flows slowly up through my right calf, to my right knee, to my right thigh.
My right leg feels warm and heavy.
My right leg feels warm and heavy.
My breathing is deeper and deeper.
My breathing is deeper and deeper.
The relaxing warmth flows down into my left thigh.
My left thigh feels warm and heavy.
My left thigh feels warm and heavy.
The relaxing warmth flows down into my left foot.
My left foot feels warm and heavy.
My left foot feels warm and heavy.
The relaxing warmth flows slowly up through my left calf, to my left knee, to my left thigh.
My left leg feels warm and heavy.
My left leg feels warm and heavy.
My breathing is deeper and deeper.
My breathing is deeper and deeper.
The relaxing warmth flows up through my abdomen, through my stomach and into my heart.
My heart feels warm and easy.
My heart feels warm and easy.
My heart pumps relaxing warmth throughout my entire body.
My whole body is heavy, warm, relaxed.
My whole body is heavy, warm, relaxed.

Table 53–2 *(Continued)*

My whole body is heavy, warm, relaxed.	I feel serene, secure, still.
I am breathing deeper and deeper.	My thoughts are all turned inward.
I am breathing deeper and deeper.	I am at ease, completely at ease.
My whole body feels very quiet and very serene.	Deep within my mind I can visualize and experience myself as relaxed.
My whole body feels very comfortable and very relaxed.	I am comfortable and still.
My mind is still.	My mind is calm and quiet.
My mind is quiet.	I feel an inward peace.
My mind is easy.	I feel a new sense of well being.
I withdraw my thoughts from my surroundings.	I am breathing more and more deeply.
Nothing exists around me.	

Part III

Now lift your arms slowly, high over your head.	You are breathing deeper and deeper.
Take a deep, deep breath.	Slowly say the following phrases to yourself.
Hold the breath and slowly lower your arms and hands.	My whole body feels quiet, comfortable and relaxed.
When your arms and hands touch your chair breathe out and go completely limp.	My hands and arms feel heavy, warm and relaxed.
Hold your hands in front of you as if you were praying.	My legs feel heavy, warm and relaxed.
	My mind is quiet.
Take a deep, deep breath.	I withdraw my thoughts from my surroundings.
Press your hands together until you feel your arm muscles tremble.	I feel serene and still.
	My thoughts are turned inward.
Breathe out and go completely limp.	I am at ease.
Take a deep, deep breath.	Deep within my mind I can visualize and experience myself as relaxed.
Hold the breath and slowly draw your hands toward your face.	Deep within my mind I can visualize and experience myself as comfortable and still.
	My mind is calm and quiet.
When your hands touch your face, breathe out and let go.	I feel an inward peace and quiet.
Go completely limp.	I am now relaxed and alert. [*If biofeedback training is to be utilized, simply say:* I am now ready to begin my training session.]
You are breathing deeper and deeper.	

Reprinted by permission of the Cyborg Corporation.

Pharmacotherapy

Drugs may influence, beyond the placebo effect, a variety of unwholesome behavioral symptoms, such as hyperactivity, agitation, excitement, violent rage, listlessness, social withdrawal, thinking disturbances including hallucinations and delusions, depression, tension, and anxiety. Initial improvements have been sustained, and patients on a drug regimen for over 10 years have not been deprived of any of their vital functions (Redlich & Freedman, 1966). Drug therapy helps to keep psychotic patients out of hospitals and enables them to assume some productive role in the community. During psychotherapy it permits of a modulation of anxiety, particularly where the individual is so immersed in dealing with its effects that he is unable to apply himself to the tasks of psychological exploration and working through. It may make disturbed patients more accessible to psychotherapy. It also reverses some depressive reactions that drain energy and block initiative.

The exact action of drugs is not entirely known; however, they appear to act both on the underlying disorder and on the secondary reactions (e.g., withdrawal, undermined self-esteem, etc.) of a patient to his illness. They may dissociate symptoms from their attached emotional components; for example, the psycho-inhibiting medicaments, namely phenothiazines, can isolate delusional systems in schizophrenia. They may make available more psychic energy, thus enabling the patient to deal more readily with his conflicts. For instance, the energizing drugs vitalize the individual and increase his general feelings of well-being. They may disrupt the psychic organization, giving symptoms a new meaning, as during psychedelic experiences with LSD. Tranquilizing and energizing drugs are sometimes employed singly or in combination (e.g., Trilafon and Elavil from two to four times daily), and with this alone (with no uncovering of dynamics and no insight) the patient may achieve a psychological balance. Lowinger et al. (1964), in a follow-up study on drug treatments as the exclusive therapeutic agency, found that the favorable outcome rates were comparable to other treatment approaches in similar patients. After a short period of time on medication some patients will reconstitute themselves; others may require prolonged drug administration.

Among the impediments in utilizing psychotropic drugs are:

1. Their side effects, such as allergic responses—hepatocanalicular jaundice with the phenothiazines and tricyclic antidepressants, and agranulocytosis with the phenothiazines and occasionally imipramine (Tofranil) and amitriptyline (Elavil); pigmentary reactions in the skin, lens and cornea with phenothiazines; cardiac changes with certain phenothiazines and tricyclic compounds (especially Mellaril and Tofranil).

2. Their tendency to produce adverse physical and behavioral reactions—for example, hypotension with the phenothiazines and MAO inhibitors; adrenergic crisis in the sympathetic amines (amphetamine, dextroamphetamine); hypertensive crises with MAO inhibitors when tyramine foods are eaten; dyskinesia and Parkinsonism with the neuroleptics.

3. Properties that lead to habituation—for instance, the sympathetic amines (Benzedrine, Dexedrine), the barbiturates, meprobamate (Miltown), chlordiazepoxide (Librium), and diazepam (Valium).

Side effects and allergic responses do not justify discontinuing drug treatments. They usually occur during the early stages of administration and may be controlled by antagonistic substances (like Cogentin or Artane in Parkinsonism). A disturbing and lasting effect of phenothiazines on chronic psychiatric patients in long-term therapy is tardive dyskinesia, which may not respond to any treatment. Habituating drugs may be regulated and should be at least temporarily discontinued after their effects have registered themselves to the benefit of the patient.

Some psychiatrists avoid personal prescription of tranquilizers in reconstructive therapy when they are needed on the basis that this introduces a guidance-supportive element in the relationship. If tranquilizers are indicated, they recommend that the patient consult his regular family physician. Actually, the giving of tranquilizers need not interfere with the management of reconstructive therapy, for the patient's reaction to the therapist as a guiding authority may be handled as part of the treatment process. Prescribing tranquilizers, giving interpretations, sending monthly bills, cancelling appointments, and any other active transactions will be utilized by the patient as vehicles around which he organizes his ideas about authority, providing rich material for study. The nonmedical therapist will certainly need the cooperation of a physician, preferably a psychiatrist, in the event that prescription of a drug is necessary.

In review, then, drugs are no substitute for psychotherapy. But, as has been indicated, drugs can provide adjunctive help during certain phases of psychotherapeutic management. Caution is essential in prescribing drugs, not only because of their potential side effects, and the existence of allergies and sensitivities in the patient, but also because the temporary relief from symptoms that they inspire may induce the patient to utilize them as his first line of defense whenever conflict and tension arise, to the neglect of a reasoned resolution of a developing problem. In certain personality types minor tranquilizing and energizing drugs may come to fashion the individual's way of life, dependence on them producing a habituation whose effects are more serious than the complaints that they initially were intended to subdue. These disadvantages should not act as a deterrent to the proper employment of such medicaments, which, in their judicious use, will tend to help, not hinder, a psychotherapeutic program. Side effects and tendencies to habituation may be managed if the therapist alerts himself or herself to developing contingencies. A great deal of prudence must be exercised in evaluating the worth of any drug, since, as more and more medicaments are introduced into the market, their virtues are flaunted with spectacular and often unjustified claims.

In the main, tranquilizing drugs are employed in psychotherapy during extreme anxiety states when the patient's defenses crumble or when he is so completely involved in protecting himself from anxiety that he is unable to explore its sources. In neurotic patients the principal medicaments employed for anxiety are meprobamate (Miltown, Equanil), chlordiazepoxide (Librium), diazepam (Valium) and oxazepam (Serax). In borderline patients who are decompensating (depersonalization, extreme anxiety, etc.) the best drugs are the neuroleptics, e.g., Stelazine and Haldol. In schizophrenia associated with apathetic and depressive symptoms, Stelazine and Trilafon may be employed. In schizophrenic excitement Thorazine is an excellent drug, although, in office practice, Mellaril is commonly used. Manic phases of manic-depressive psychosis may be helped by lithium and by Haldol. For mood elevation in mild depressions Dexamyl and Ritalin may be employed. For moderate and neurotic depressions the MAO inhibitors, Nardil, and Parnate are sometimes utilized, recognizing the side effects and dangers that may accompany their use. Tofranil, Desipramine, Norpramine, and Aventyl apply themselves well to retarded depressions, while Elavil is often helpful in agitated depressions. For suicidal depressions electroconvulsive therapy or Indokolon are preferred. In drug addiction and alcoholism certain drugs may be valuable—for instance, methadone in the former and antabuse in the latter.

People react uniquely to drugs, not only because of their constitutional physiological makeup, but also because of their mental set, their attitudes toward the medication, and the specific lines of their expectation influencing both beneficial and side effects. Experimentation will be required in dosage and type of drug. Drug administration must be under the direction and control of a qualified psychiatrist who first examines the patient and then prescribes the best chemical adjunct. The psychiatrist should see the patient periodically thereafter to ascertain the results of drug treatment, to manage side effects, and to alter the dosage when necessary.

ANTIPSYCHOTIC DRUGS (NEUROLEPTICS)

Phenothiazines, since the 1960s, have brought about recovery and social remission in more cases of schizophrenia than any previously applied method (Goldman, D, 1966). Halperidol (Haldol), chlorpromazine (Thorazine), and thioridazine (Mellaril), among others, are of great value for all types of schizophrenia as well as manic-depressive manic states and paranoid involutional psychoses. They are generally avoided in neurotic patients. Navane and Moban are excellent alternative antipsychotic drugs and in some cases may be the medications of choice.

A useful method of prescribing is to

begin with 50 mg four times daily for Thorazine or 25 mg four times daily for Mellaril. After 3 days the patient may telephone (or may be seen for a few minutes) to discuss the influence on him of the medication. Side effects, such as drowsiness and dry mouth, will usually disappear after a few more days. Unless the patient is showing an untoward reaction, the drug may be doubled to 400 mg daily (200 mg for Mellaril). The patient is again seen 4 days later to observe what has happened. The dose is then, if symptoms are still present, raised to 600 mg daily (300 mg for Mellaril), and the patient is thereafter seen at weekly intervals (or more frequently if necessary), the dose being increased by 200 mg each week (100 mg for Mellaril) until symptoms abate. Usually 600 to 1600 mg of Thorazine or 300 to 800 mg of Mellaril suffice to control symptoms. The patient may be kept on this optimal dosage for from 3 to 4 weeks. Thereafter the dose is reduced 200 mg weekly (100 mg for Mellaril) to 400 mg (150–200 mg for Mellaril) and kept at this level for 6 months or more. If symptoms reappear, the dose should be increased. Should the patient complain of drowsiness, the dose preceding the time drowsiness develops may be eliminated and instead added to the dose at night.

In the event that an alternative to phenothiazines is necessary, as in a case where the latter have proved ineffective, one may try haloperidol (Haldol) and titrate the dosage individually according to symptomatic progress and side effects. The starting dosage may be 2 mg or 5 mg, three times daily. If there is no improvement in 2 or 3 days, the dosage may be increased in daily increments of 9–15 mg until symptoms recede or extrapyramidal signs develop. The range of effective dosages will vary greatly among individuals. Once symptom control is obtained, long-term maintenance may be kept with dosage of 2–6 mg. Should extrapyramidal signs develop, antiparkinson medication may be given and the dosage reduced.

Where rapid tranquilization is essential, the patient may be given parenteral forms of Thorazine (25–100 mg) or Haldol (3–5 mg) intramuscularly every 4 hours until sedated. Following this, oral medications are given. Rapid tranquilization may also be accomplished in a few hours with adequate initial oral medication (Polak and Laycob, 1971), preferably in a hospital setting. A test dose of 25–50 mg of Thorazine is given orally, and the patient is observed for 1 hour for side effects. If there are none, 50–200 mg of Thorazine are given orally every hour for 6–8 hours, depending on the patient's weight and degree of disturbance. If the patient objects to the tablet form, he may be given chlorpromazine elixir. Should the patient refuse the drug orally, intramuscular administration of about one-third the oral dose is given. The dosage is adjusted upward or downward according to the patient's reaction.

Control is generally established within the first 6 hours of treatment. Variations exist as to the amount of drug required. Once in control, the patient is given a daily dose of approximately 2.5 times what he consumed in the first 6 hours to bring him under control. If he required 800 mg of Thorazine to reach an initial tranquilized state, for example, he is then started on 2000 mg of Thorazine daily. Adjustment of this amount is made up or down several times during the day according to the patient's response. An error is to reduce the medication during the first 3 days because the patient seems drowsy. After the third day, with symptom relief and better ego functioning, the dosage may be reduced to two-thirds on the fourth day, again to one-half the original dosage on the sixth day, and to one-third the original dosage by the seventh day. Discharge from the hospital is usually possible after the seventh day on a dosage of one-fourth the original medication.

Generally, the more anxious the patient, the better the response to antipsychotics. Hallucinations may disappear, and one may not respond too much to delusions.

Side effects are to be expected. Should the patient continue to be drowsy, the bulk of the dose may be administered at night which will help sleep. Dryness of the mouth usually abates. Constipation may appear in older people. Rarely, some female patients develop a secretion from the breasts; they may manifest a weight gain and amenorrhea. Because skin sensitivity is increased, patients should be warned not to expose themselves deliberately to the sun during summer months. If skin sensitivity to sun lasts, Trilafon or Haldol is the best drug. Should dizziness occur due to postural hypotension, the patient may be instructed to stand up slowly from a lying or sitting position. Parkinsonism is considered by some authorities to be a welcome sign, a guide post to maximum dosage. If it occurs, the patient should receive Artane (1–6 mg daily) or Cogentin (1–2 mg two or three times daily) or Kemadrin (2.5–5 mg three times daily). A rare side effect is agranulocytosis, and if the patient complains of a sore throat, a white blood cell and differential count should be obtained. In the event agranulocytosis is present, the drug should be immediately discontinued, and a medical consultation obtained to forestall complications. Jaundice is not too important, occurring mainly in 0.5 or 1 percent of older people. Reactions of skin, retinal, and corneal pigmentation are very rare. The most disturbing effect of long-term neuroleptics is tardive dyskinesia, especially in older patients. Efforts to prevent and manage this disorder can be made (Crane, 1972), but they may be unsuccessful. Drug holidays and lowering dosage to a point where symptoms are controlled are helpful here.

Trifluoperazin (Stelazine) and perphenazine (Trilafon), powerful analogues of chlorpromazine, are commonly employed in apathetic and withdrawn patients who need no further sedation. Other low-dose neuroleptics (Haldol, Navane, Stelazine, Prolixin) may be used. Once the dose is regulated so that a therapeutic effect occurs, it should be maintained for 6 months, then gradually decreased. Akathesia and Parkinsonism are common with high dosage and will require control with Artane, Cogentin, or Kemedrin.

Combinations of various antipsychotic medications are sometimes used with the claim that refractory ''hard-core'' psychiatric patients, drug resistant to individual substances, respond to combined therapy (Talbott, 1964). Such combinations, however, are frowned on by most authorities who claim that advantages compared to the increase of side effects does not justify their use.

In referring to Table 53-3, it is seen that the choice of antipsychotic drugs constitutes a problem in view of the varieties available. In general, only three of the seven classes of drugs need be considered for practical reasons: phenothiazines, butyrophenones, and thioxanthenes. The symptom complexes offer some clues as to choice. Where one desires a highly sedative effect with strong adrenergic blocking actions for an overactive patient, there are chlorpromazine (Thorazine) or thioridazine (Mellaril), the latter having less of a tendency to produce extrapyramidal effects. Among the low-dosage phenothiazines (the piperazine group), trifluoperazine (Stelazine), fluphenazine (Prolixin), and perphenazine (Trilafon) are the most popular. The chief characteristics of the latter drugs is that they are low in sedative value while exerting an antipsychotic effect. Of the thioxanthenes, thiothixene (Navane), and of the butyrophenes, haloperidal (Haldol), are useful additions, the latter drug not uncommonly producing extrapyramidal effects and akathisia as side effects. The responses of people to drugs are unique; their reactions are different to the various drugs in efficacy and complications.

Maintenance drug therapy may be required to keep the patient in some kind of functional equilibrium. In all cases the rule should obtain to reduce the quantity of drug slowly once optimal symptom control has been obtained. This may be accompanied by total abstinence once, then twice weekly to allow the patient to try to make a drug-free adjustment. Psychotherapy and environmental adjustment to relieve the patient from undue stresses should be coordinately instituted. Should symptoms return, the dose levels can be adjusted upward. There are some patients who will need periodic drug therapy for the rest of their lives. Yet it is at least theoretically possible to secure adjustment in most cases

Table 53–3

Uses, Characteristics, and Doses of Psychotropic Drugs (see page 779 for key)

Drug (How Dispensed)	Uses	Dosage	Miscellaneous (Action and Side Effects)
Psychostimulants			
1. Sympathetic amines	1. Very mild depression; appetite control; oversedation and fatigue; alcoholism; enuresis and hyperkinetic reactions in children; narcolepsy.		1. Rapid action. Do not use in schizophrenia, agitation, and hypertension. Can cause irritability and insomnia. Habituation danger serious; use for no more than 3 months. (The amobarbital content in Dexamyl overcomes jitteriness.) Monitor blood pressure, especially in hypertension.
a. amphetamine (Benzedrine: T 5, 10 mg; S 15 mg)		a. 5–10 mg at 9 am & 2 pm; 15 mg. (S.) at 9 am.	
b. dextroamphetamine (Dexedrine: S 5, 10, 15 mg) T5 (Dexamyl: T 5 mg; S 10, 15 mg.) elixir 5 cc = 5 mg		b. 5–15 mg at 9 am & 2 pm; (S.) 10–15 mg at 9 am.	
c. methamphetamine (Desoxyn: 2.5, 10, 15 mg)	c. Analeptic in barbiturate poisoning: minimal brain dysfunction in children.	c. 2.5–5 mg tid.	
2. methylphenidate (Ritalin: T 5, 10, 20 mos.)	2. As in (1), but effects are weaker. For minimal brain dysfunction in children.	2. 10–20–30 mg (T) at 9 am & 2 pm.	2. As in (1).

Drug	Uses	Dosage	Miscellaneous
Antidepressants			
1. Tricyclics	1. a. For retarded depression.	a. 25 mg qid increased to 50 mg qid. Use the 10-mg size in older patients. P-IM- to 100 mg in divided doses.	a. Action in 7–21 days. Do not give with MAO inhibitors. Do not use in schizophrenia, epilepsy, glaucoma, urinary retention. Use cautiously in cardiovascular illness. Dryness of mouth and perspiration are side effects. Insomnia and hypotension seen occasionally. Desipramine is more rapid but less intense; it has an initial stimulant action.
a. imipramine (Tofranil: T 10, 25, 50 mg; P 25 mg in 2 cc; Tofranil: PM, C 75, 100, 125, 150 sustained action.)			
desipramine (Norpramine, Pertofrane: T & caps 25, 50 mg)		100–200 mg daily.	
b. amitriptyline (Elavil: T 10, 25, 50, 75, 100, 150 mg; P 100 mg in 10 cc)	b. For agitated depression.	b. 25 mg tid increased to 50 mg tid; max. 250 mg. Use the 10-mg. size in older patients. Maintenance 50–100 mg.	b. As in (a) but with more sedative features. Action in 10–30 days. Potentiates alcohol and barbiturates.
nortriptyline (Aventyl: T 10, 25 mg; liquid 10 mg per 5 cc)		10 mg bid increased to 10 mg qid; in 1 week 25 mg bid increased to 25 mg qid.	Aventyl is more rapid, but less intense. Avoid in cardiovascular disease.
c. doxepin (Sinequan: caps 10, 25, 50, 75 mg: oral concentrate 10 mg per cc)	c. For neurotic, alcoholic, and psychotic depression.	c. 25 mg tid increased to 50 mg tid (for mild or moderate depression; 50 mg tid increased to 100 mg tid for severe depression.	c. Side effects less than other tricyclics. Can be given with guanethidine unlike other tricyclics. A preferred drug for cardiac patients. Action in 10–21 days.
2. MAO inhibitors	2. For neurotic and hysterical depression		2. Action in 1–4 weeks.
a. phenelzine (Nardil: T 15 mg)		a. 15 mg tid (max d 75 mg.); reduce slowly; maintenance d 15 mg.	a. Potentiates amphetamines, alcohol and barbiturates. May intensify schizoprenia. Produces hypotension, dry mouth, blurred vision, dizziness. Do not use in liver, kidney, or heart diseases. Hypertensive crises can occur. Avoid cheese and other medicaments. Avoid in hypertension.

Table 53–3 *(Continued)*

Drug	Uses	Dosage	Miscellaneous
b. tranylcypromine (Parnate: T 10 mg)		b. 10 mg at 9 am & 2 pm; in 2 weeks, 20 mg at 9 am. & 10 mg at 2 pm.	b. Action in 2–21 days. As in (a).
3. Combination drugs a. perphenazine (2 mg) & amitriptyline (10 mg) (Triavil: 2–10 mg; Etrafon: 2–10 mg) b. perphenazine (2 mg) & amitriptyline (25 mg) (Triavil: 2–25 mg; Etrafon: 2–25 mg) c. perphenazine (4 mg) & amytriptyline (10 mg) (Triavil: 4–10 mg; Etrafon: 4–10 mg) d. perphenazine (4 mg) & amitriptyline (25 mg) (Triavil: 4–25 mg; Etrafon-forte)	3. For anxious and agitated depressions as well as depression in schizophrenia.	3. One T tid or qid., (max. 2 T tid); maintenance 1 T bid, tid, or qid.	3. Contraindicated in glaucoma, urinary retention. Action in a few days or a few weeks. See amitriptyline and perphenazine. Some authorities feel combination drugs are unnecessary and even contraindicated.

Drug	Uses	Dosage	Miscellaneous

Neuroleptics

Drug	Uses	Dosage	Miscellaneous
1. Phenothiazines a. chlorpromazine (Thorazine: T 10, 25, 50, 100, 200 mg; S 30, 75, 150, 200, 300 mg; P 25 mg in 1 cc, 50 mg in 2 cc, 250 mg in 10 cc.; syrup 10 mg in each tsp—5 cc; suppositories 25 mg; concentrate 30 mg in 1 cc and 100 mg in 1 cc)	a. The best phenothiazine for agitated, confused, and hyperactive reactions in schizophrenia, manic-depressive reactions, agitated senile dementia.	a. Min 25 mg tid.; av 300–800 mg d; max 1600 mg d; P for excitements, 25–50 mg (repeated in 1 hour if necessary). Higher doses may be necessary.	a. Action in a few days. Potentiates barbituates. Drowsiness, dryness of mouth, stuffiness of nose, tachycardia, hypotension, photosensitivity, allergic skin reactions, jaundice may occur. Use cautiously in atherosclerosis, cardiovascular diseases. Rarely skin pigmentation, ocular changes, blood dyscrasias. Parkinsonism requires Cogentin, Artane or Kemadrin (qv below).
b. thioridazine (Mellaril: T 10, 15, 25, 50, 100, 150, 200 mg; concentrate 30 mg. per cc and 100 mg per cc)	b. Excellent for ambulatory outpatient treatment of hyperkinetic and agitated psychoses. Helps some depressive reactions.	b. Nonpsychotic patients: 10–25 mg tid or qid. Psychotics: 100 mg tid or qid (Max. 800 mg d).	b. Minimum of side reactions. Action is rapid. High doses may cause pigmentary retinopathy.
c. trifluoperazine (Stelazine: T 1, 2, 5, 10 mg; P 2 mg per cc; concentrate 10 mg per cc)	c. For apathetic, depressed, withdrawn schizophrenics. Low dosage relieves tension and agitation. High dose for manic states, agitated depression, schizophrenia.	c. Office patients: 1–2 mg bid or tid. Hospital patients: 5 mg tid or qid (max. 40–50 mg d.	c. Side effects in high dosage are common, namely extrapyramidal reactions—dystonia and Parkinsonism require Cogentin, Artane, or Kemadrin (qv below).
d. perphenazine (Trilafon: T 2, 4, 8, 16 mg; repetabs 8 mg; concentrate 16 mg per 5 cc: P 5 mg in 1 cc.)	d. For psychotic disorders and control of nausea and vomiting in adults.	d. 2–4 mg tid; increased to 4 mg qid.	d. Photosensitive low. Good for those exposed to sun.
e. fluphenazine (Permitil: T 0.25, 2.5, 5, 10, mg; chronotabs 1 mg; oral concentrate 5 mg per cc)	e. For psychotic agitation, hostility, aggression, behavior problems in children, and senile agitation.	e. Office patients: 0.5–3 mg d to 10 mg. Hospital patients: 2–5 mg bid (max 20 mg). (Children: 0.25–0.5 mg d; (max. 1 mg).	e. Sustained action can be prescribed in single dose. Does not potentiate barbiturates much. Extrapyramidal reactions frequent.
(Prolixin: T 1, 2.5, 5, 10 mg; elixir: 0.5 mg per cc; P 2.5 mg per 5 cc)	As above.	As above. Divided doses at 6–8 hour intervals. Maintenance 1–5 mg d; P 1.25 mg. increased 6–8 hr intervals to 10 mg.	As above. After IM injections for emergencies continue on 2–3 times P dose with oral T.

Table 53-3 *(Continued)*

Drug	Uses	Dosage	Miscellaneous
f. fluphenazine enanthate (Prolixin Enanthate: P 25 mg in 1 cc preassembled syringes; vials of 5 cc)	Potent long-acting injectable. Phenothiazine derivative for psychotic disorders.	25 mg. (1 cc.) IM or subcutaneous every 2 weeks. Adjust dose according to response from 12.5–100 mg. every 2 weeks.	Action in 24–48 hours, lasting about 2 weeks. Useful where oral medication cannot be depended on. Extrapyramidal reactions frequent, which can be controlled with antiparkinsonian drugs. Contraindicated in subcortical brain damage.
g. fluphenazine decanoate (Prolixin Decanoate: P 25 mg in 1 cc preassembled syringes; vials of 5 cc)	Potent, long-lasting injectable phenothiazine derivative for schizophrenia.	12.5–25 IM or subcutaneous every 4 weeks. Adjust dose in small increments to 50 or 100 mg.	Action in 24–72 hours, lasting about 4 weeks. Useful where oral medication cannot be depended on. Extrapyramidal reactions frequent and will require antiparkinsonian drugs.
2. Dibenzoxazepines a. loxapine succinate (Loxitane: C 10, 25, 50 mg; elixir 25 mg per cc)	a. Tranquilizes and suppresses aggressive activities in schizophrenia.	a. 10–25 mg bid, usual maintenance dose 60–100 mg d.	a. Action in ½–2 hours for 12 hours. Contraindicated in drug-induced depressive states (alcohol, barbituates). Lowers convulsive threshold. Use cautiously in cardiovascular disease. Extrapyramidal reactions frequent.
3. Butyrophenones a. haloperidol (Haldol: T ½, 1, 2, 5, 10, mg; concentrate 2 mg per cc; P 5 mg per cc)	a. For psychotic disorders and severe tics.	a. Moderate symptoms and older patients: ½–2 mg bid or tid. Severe symptoms: 3–5 mg bid or tid (max 100 mg); P 2–5 mg, repeated if necessary.	a. May be tolerated in some patients better than phenothiazines. Extrapyramidal reactions common. Excellent in manic excitement.
4. Thioxanthenes a. thiothixene (Navane: C 1, 2, 5, 10, 20 mg: concentrate 5 mg per cc: P 2 mg per cc)	a. For psychotic disorders.	a. Mild symptoms: 2 mg tid (max d 15 mg). More severe symptoms: 5 mg bid to 30 mg (max. d 60 mg).	a. May be tolerated in some cases better than phenothiazines.
b. chlorprothixene Taractan: T 10, 25, 50, 100 mg: P 25 mg in 2 cc)	b. Agitated, anxious schizophrenics.	b. 25–50 mg tid or qid. Max 600 mg d. P 25–50 mg up to tid or qid.	b. Avoid in cardiac and respiratory disease.
5. Dihydroindolones a. molindone (Moban: T 5, 10, 25 mg)	a. For symptoms of schizophrenia.	a. Mild symptoms: 5–15 mg tid or qid; moderate 10–25 mg tid or qid. Severe symptoms: up to 225 mg total.	a. Side reactions less than phenothiazines.
6. Antimanic drugs a. Lithium carbonate (C 300 mg) Also see Haldol, Thorazine, and Mellaril above.	a. For control and prophylaxis of manic episodes in manic-depressive psychosis.	a. Usual dose, 300–600 mg tid. Adjust dosage to maintain serum levels between 1–1.5 mEq/1.	a. Action in 1–3 weeks. Contraindicated in colitis and severe renal and cardiovascular disease, or where diuretics are taken. Test serum levels twice weekly during acute phase; in maintenance therapy at least every 2 months.
7. Anti-Parkinson Drugs (1) Cogentin (T 0.5, 1, 2 mg; P 1 mg in 1 cc) (2) Artane (T 2, 5 mg.; elixir 2 mg each 5 cc) (3) Kemadrin (T 2, 5 mg)		(1) Usual dose, 1–2 mg bid or tid. (2) 1 mg 1st day; 2 mg 2nd day, increased if necessary to 6–10 mg d. (3) 2.5 mg tid increased to 5 mg tid.	After symptoms disappear for 1–2 weeks, withdraw to determine need for drug.

Table 53–3 *(Continued)*

Drug	Uses	Dosage	Miscellaneous
Anxiolytics			
a. meprobamate (Miltown, Equanil: T 200, 400, 600 mg)	a. Anxiety, tension headache, muscle spasms, insomnia.	a. Adults: 400 mg d to tid (max 2400 mg d). Children: 100–200 mg bid.	a. Potentiates alcohol and sedatives. Hypotension possible, especially in older persons. Habituation with prolonged use. Avoid driving until drug dose is stabilized. Avoid rapid withdrawal of drug. Drowsiness, allergic reactions possible. Tolerated by older persons.
b. chlordiazepoxide (Librium: caps 5, 10, 25 mg; P 100 mg in 5 cc)	b. Excellent tranquilizer with palliating qualities for anxiety, alcoholism, muscle spasms. IV in delirium tremors and as an anticonvulsive.	b. 10 mg bid, tid, or qid. Severe anxiety: 20–25 mg tid or qid; P 50–100 mg IM or IV, repeated if necessary in 2–6 hours.	b. Ataxia, especially in older persons.
c. diazepam (Valium: T 2, 5, 10 mg: P 5 mg per cc)	c. Anxiety, muscle spasms, alcoholic withdrawal, insomnia due to anxiety, status epilepticus.	c. 5 mg d to tid. Severe anxiety: 10 mg. tid, or qid; P, IM, or IV 2–20 mg, repeated if necessary in 3–4 hours.	c. Avoid in glaucoma and epilepsy. Drowsiness possible. Reduce dose in elderly patients.
d. oxazepam (Serax: caps 10, 15, 30 mg; T 15 mg)	d. Anxiety, alcoholic withdrawal, senile agitation.	d. Mild anxiety: 15 mg qid. Severe anxiety: 30 mg tid or qid. Older patients: 10 mg tid.	d. Initial drowsiness, usually passes.
e. hydroxyzine (Vistaril: caps 25, 50, 100 mg; P 25–50 mg in 1 cc; oral suspension 25 mg per tsp)	e. Mild anxiety, psychophysiological reactions. IM or IV for extreme anxiety and alcoholic withdrawal.	e. 25–100 mg tid or qid, P, IM: 50–100 mg repeated as necessary, 4–6 hours.	e. Side effects mild. May be used with psychotherapy. Potentiates barbiturates and narcotics.
f. clorazepate dipotassium (Tranxene: (3.75, 7.5, 15 mg; Tranxene SD: 11.25, and 22.5 mg)	f. Anxiety	f. 15–60 mg d. Elderly or debilitated patients: 7.5–15 mg d.	f. Avoid in depression or psychosis.

Drug	Uses	Dosage	Miscellaneous
Sedatives and Hypnotics			
1. Barbituates	1. Helpful in allaying tension, anxiety, and insomnia. P, IV, or IM, for convulsions.		1. Use with caution in liver disease. Habituation possibilities great; not for prolonged use.
a. phenobarbital sodium (T ¼, ½, 1½ gr) (Luminal sodium: P, IM, IV 2 gr per 1 cc; Eskabarb: S. 1, 1½ gr)	a. May be utilized as a tranquilizer for anxiety where sedative effect is not objectionable.	a. Sedation: ¼ gr ½ gr tid. Hypnotic: 1½ gr.	a. Slow acting; long duration.
b. amobarbital sodium (Amytal sodium: P 2, 4, 7½ gr; T ¼, ½, ¾, 1½ gr; caps 1, 3 gr)	b. (IV) amytal sodium useful in narcosynthesis.	b. Hypnotic: 1–3 gr; P (IV or IM) 1–7½ gr (max. 15 gr).	b. Moderately rapid acting; medium duration.
c. butabarbital sodium (Butisol sodium: T ¼, ½, ¾, 1½ gr; elixir, ½ gr per 5 cc; caps ¼, ½ gr)		c. Sedation: ¼–½ gr tid or qid. Hypnotic: 1½ gr.	c. Rapid acting; short duration.
d. pentobarbital sodium (Nembutal: caps ½, ¾, 1½ gr; P 1½ gr in 2 cc, 4 gr in 5 cc. Gradumet: caps 1½ gr; Elixir ⅓ gr in 1 tsp; suppositories ½, 1, 3 gr)		d. Hypnotic: ½–1½ gr; P (IV) up to 3 gr (IM) ¾–1½ gr. Daytime sedation: 1 gradumet cap in am.	d. Moderately rapid acting; short duration.
e. secobarbital sodium (Seconal: pulvules ½, ¾, 1½ gr; P 15 gr in 20 cc, ¾ per 1 cc, 1½ gr per 2 cc in disposable syringe)		e. Hypnotic: 1½ gr; P (IV or IM) ¾–1½ gr.	e. Moderately rapid acting; short duration.

Table 53–3 *(Continued)*

Drug	Uses	Dose	Miscellaneous
f. amobarbital and secobarbital sodium (Tuinal: caps ¾, 1½, 3 gr)		f. Sedation: ¾ gr. Hypnotic: 1½–3 gr.	f. Moderately rapid acting, medium duration.
2. Nonbarbiturates			
a. flurazepam hydrochloride (Dalmane: caps 15–30 mg)	a. Effective hypnotic for all types of insomnia.	a. 15–30 mg before retiring.	a. Low incidence of dependence, but avoid too prolonged administration.
b. glutethimide (Doriden: T 250, 500 mg; caps 500 mg.)	b. Useful in elderly and chronically ill patients.	b. Sedation: 250 mg. Hypnotic: 500 mg.	b. Onset in 15–30 minutes; duration 6 hours. Occasional skin rash.
c. methylprylon (Noludar: T 50, 200 mg; caps 300 mg)	c. Well tolerated and effective.	c. Sedation: 50–100 mg. Hypnotic: 300 mg.	c. Onset in 15–45 minutes; duration 5–8 hours.
d. chloral hydrate (Noctec: caps 3¾, 7½ gr; syrup 7½ gr per tsp)	d. Low toxitity; well tolerated in chronic illness.	d. Hypnotic: 7½ gr.	d. Onset in 20 minutes. Avoid in cardiac incompetence.
e. ethchlorvynol (Placidyl: caps 100, 200, 500, 750 mg)	e. Insomnia due to anxiety or excitement.	e. Sedation: 100 mg bid. Hypnotic: 500 mg.	e. Do not give to patients with suicidal tendency.
f. paraldehyde	f. A safe hypnotic and anticonvulsant in psychotic patients.	f. 2–8 cc in iced fruit juice or milk; 10 cc in agitation. P 1–2 cc IM.	f. Onset in 20 minutes. Avoid in gastrointestinal and liver disease.
Psychodysleptic Drugs			
1. Lysergic acid diethylamide (LSD, LSD–25)	1. Hallucinogen; psycholytic, abreactive to produce model psychoses and hypermnesia.	1. Oral: 0.025–2 mg. d; av 0.05–0.4 mg. Same dose IM in sterile solution of 0.1 mg per cc.	1. Potentially dangerous.
2. Psilocybin	2. As in (1)	2. Oral: 6 mg d.	2. Less powerful than LSD.
3. Mescaline	3. As in (1)	3. 300–400 mg d.	3. Less powerful than LSD.

d = daily; bid = 2 times daily; tid = 3 times daily; qid = 4 times daily.	T = tablets; P = parenteral; S = spansules; caps = capsules; IM = intramuscularly; IV = intravenously.		max = maximum; av = average; gr = grain; mg = milligrams; cc = cubic centimeters.

without medication, provided adequate educational, rehabilitative, and psychotherapeutic facilities are available and utilized. Even hardcore institutional mental patients on long-term maintenance drug therapy have been withdrawn from medications with benefit where social–environmental treatment programs were organized (Paul et al., 1972).

Because some patients who require maintenance therapy are loath to use oral medications or forget to take them, parenteral long-acting phenothiazines (Prolixin Enanthate, 25 mg every 2 weeks or Prolixin Decanoate (12.5–25 mg every 4 weeks) may be given. Such maintenance antipsychotic drugs have been found to play a crucial role in the prophylactic treatment of chronic schizophrenia. Nonmotivated patients may be brought in to the doctor's office by a rela-

tive. As a last resort, some reward, by arrangement with the relative, may be given the patient by the doctor (e.g., his allowance) each time he appears for an injection.

A review of 24 controlled studies on the use of maintenance drugs demonstrated that the percentage of relapse was less than half of that in the groups not taking drugs (Davis, JM, 1975). Against this optimistic note is the dire development of long-term side effects, namely, tardive dyskinesia, which occurs particularly in elderly hospitalized patients who have received medication for many years. It bears mentioning again that to prevent tardive dyskinesia, patients receiving medication over a prolonged stretch should periodically have the dosage lowered and the drugs even withdrawn to test the consequence. In a sizable number of patients the schizophrenia may have "burned out," particularly where the environment poses few stresses and the adaptive level has improved. Should relapse follow on withdrawal, medications may be reinstated.

Lithium carbonate (300–600 mg taken three times daily) is an effective therapeutic and prophylactic agent (with no undue sedative effect) for manic-depressive psychosis where manic attacks are part of the recurrent illness. Since lithium acts slowly, an excited, manic reaction may require initial antipsychotics, like Haldol or Thorazine orally or parenterally. The patient may be started on 300 mg of lithium three times daily, serum levels being tested twice during the first week. The usual dose is 600 mg three times daily, but this must be individualized and regulated by the blood level response. Regular determination of lithium serum levels by a good laboratory at least every 2 months to maintain concentration between 1 and 1.5 mEq/1 is essential. In some cases stabilization of other psychiatric conditions with lithium has been achieved, although this cannot be depended on. Use of lithium to control violent behavior, alcohol abuse, or drug abuse is still in the experimental stage.

Antipsychotic drugs are considered nonhabituating, and withdrawal symptoms are rare. However long-term administration should be accompanied by periodic blood and liver studies (Bloom et al, 1955). Some therapists make it a rule to have their patients who are on substantial medication examined every three months neurologically, in order to forestall development of unfortunate complications.

ANTIDEPRESSANT DRUGS

On the whole, antidepressant drugs are inferior to electroconvulsive therapy in the treatment of severe and suicidal depressions. They do have some utility, however, provided that the selection of the drug is one that will fit in with the prevailing profile of symptoms. A caution to be exercised relates to the fact that antidepressants tend to intensify schizophrenic reactions and to precipitate or exaggerate manic symptomatology.

Helpful in overcoming fatigue and oversedation are the sympathomimetic amines: amphetamine (Benzedrine), dextroamphetamine (Dexedrine), and methamphetamine (Methedrine). Methylphenidate (Ritalin) and pipradol hydrochloride (Meratran) are similar in their effects to the sympathomimetic amines, but relatively weaker. Hyperkinetic children (ages 6 to 14) with both organic brain syndromes and functional disorders respond well to d-amphetamine, which has a calming rather than stimulating affect on them (Zrull et al, 1966). Amphetamine dependency may have serious consequences in the form of restlessness, irritability, insomnia, weight loss, aggressiveness, and general emotional instability (Lemere, 1966). Personality changes may progress to outright psychosis, the form of disorder being patterned by existing inner psychological needs and mechanisms (Commission on Alcoholism & Addiction, 1966). Prolonged addition may result in permanent organic damage to the brain. It is essential, then, that administration of amphetamines be very carefully supervised.

Imipramine (Tofranil) is particularly valuable in inhibited endogenous depressions, approximately one-third being arrested and one-third improved. It is probably not as effective as ECT (minimum of eight treatments), but it may be a substitute where for any reason ECT cannot be easily administered. Imipramine has also been found useful in enuresis (Munster et al, 1961).

Since in some cases it may produce insomnia, Kuhn (1960) recommends that the first does of imipramine be given at bedtime. If the drug helps the patient sleep, it may be taken throughout the day. If insomnia occurs, it should not be given after 3 PM. Starting with one 25 mg tablet three times daily, the dose is increased by one tablet each day until eight tablets daily are taken. When the symptoms remit, the dose is reduced by one tablet daily until a maintenance level is reached. Older people respond more intensely to imipramine and may do well on the smaller 10 mg tablets. Because agranulocytosis has been reported, occasional blood checks are recommended. Imipramine is contraindicated in glaucoma. Should side effects of a disturbing nature occur (skin itching, confusion, loss of appetite, etc.) the drug should be stopped and a phenothiazine substance administered. If an MAO inhibitor (Parnate, Nardil, Marplan) is being taken, this should be discontinued for at least 2 weeks prior to introducing imipramine, since the combination is dangerous. Kline claims that small doses of one can be used in combination with the other (Kline, NS, 1966b). Agitated depressions may require a neuroleptic like Thorazine or Trilafon in addition to imipramine or a sedative antidepressant like Elavil. Following ECT, imipramine may be prescribed for a period to reinforce the antidepressive influence. Side effects include dryness of the mouth, tachycardia, sweating, dizziness, and, occasionally, agitation, which may be controlled by regulating the dosage. In many cases the total dose can be given at night. Imipramine can produce orthostatic hypotension, tachycardia, and arrhythmias and prolong atrioventricular conduction time. It must be used with great caution in patients with bundle-branch disease of the heart.

The newer, more rapidly acting imipramine and amitriptyline substances—desipramine (Norpramine, Pertofrane) and nortriptyline (Aventyl)—appear to be no more effective than the parent compounds. They do have more stimulating properties and hence appear best suited for retarded depressions. Since they aggravate preexisting anxiety and tension, they should not be used where these symptoms are present, except perhaps in combinations with a sedative- tranquilizer.

Amitriptyline (Elavil) is a useful antidepressant with more sedative features than imipramine. Benefits are usually felt within a few weeks (Feldman, PE, 1961; Dorfman, 1961). Depression, tension, loss of appetite, disinterest in the environment and insomnia may be reduced or eliminated in somewhat more than half of the patients to whom the drug is given. It is administered in 25 mg dosage three times daily, increasing the dose by 25 mg daily until a 150 mg

daily intake has been reached. In some cases a dose of 200, 250, and even 300 mg will be required. Older patients do well with a smaller dose, 10 mg tablets being substituted for the 25 mg tablets. The side effects, the contraindications, and the incompatability with the MAO inhibitors are similar to those of imipramine. Elavil potentiates alcohol, anaesthetics, and the barbiturates, and the quantities of the latter substances, if taken, should accordingly be reduced.

Monoamine oxidase (MAO) inhibitors, such as tranylcypromine (Parnate) and phenelzine (Nardil), while less successful than ECT, Tofranil, and Elavil, have some use, especially in the neurotic or hysterical depressions or where a tricyclic cannot be used as in glaucoma, cardiovascular disease, or prostatic enlargement with urinary retention. If a patient has not responded to a tricyclic in 3 to 6 weeks, one can go from a tricyclic to a MAO inhibitor immediately, but not the reverse, a waiting period, as previously explained, being necessary. Especially where anxiety and agitation are disturbing, this may be given with Valium or Librium. Beneficial effects may not occur for about 3 weeks. Parnate, which is often prescribed with Stelazine where anxiety is present, must not be given with other medicaments. Cheeses, pickled herring, chicken livers, beer, Chianti wine, coffee and tea in quantity, and over-the-counter cold remedies must also be eliminated from the diet. Side effects with the MAO inhibitors are potentiation of other drugs (such as barbiturates and amphetamine), hypotension, constipation, dysuria, reduced sexual activity, edema, and occasional liver toxicity (Ayd, 1961 a & b). Such side effects may require an adjusting of the dose. N. S. Kline (1966), differing from other authorities in this country, contends that oral amphetamines and monoamine oxidase inhibitors are not incompatible and that the combination often eliminates the abrupt letdown which is a drawback in using MAO inhibitors alone.

Doxepin (Sinequan) is a useful antidepressant that has fewer side effects than Tofranil or Elavil. It may be given for neurotic depression, depression associated with alcoholism, depression or anxiety related to organic disease, and psychotic depressions with associated anxiety including involutional depression and manic-depressive disorders. It is relatively safe for and well tolerated by elderly patients. The dose for mild or moderate depression is 25 to 50 mg three times daily and for severe depression 50 to 100 mg three times daily. It may be used when the patient is taking guanethidine for hypertension in contradistinction to other tricyclics.

In the event the tricyclics (Tofranil, Elavil, Sinequan) produce too great sedation, Ritalin (10–20 mg) after breakfast may be prescribed. A nonbarbiturate hypnotic, like Doriden or Noludar, may be used for insomnia. Birth control pills should not be taken since they depress the plasma level of tricyclics. Patients over 60 should not be given the total dose at nighttime. Rather one-half the dose after the evening meal and one-half at bedtime. After recovery the total dose should be continued for 3 months, then gradually lowered over several months, and finally discontinued. If the patient fails to respond to tricyclics, a MAO inhibitor (Nardil, Parnate), as mentioned, may be tried with the usual precautions.

Combinations of drugs have been developed for treatment of agitated and anxious depressions (Smith, 1963). For example, Triavil and Etrafon are mixtures of perphenazine (Trilafon) and amitriptyline (Elavil). This combination is supplied in several strengths, as outlined in Table 53-3. Other combinations are Parnate and Stelazine, Nardil and Trilafon, and Thorazine and Dexedrine, the doses being adjusted in accordance with which target symptom (depression, anxiety, agitation) is most in need of control. Such combinations are considered unnecessary by some authorities who advise giving single drugs in adequate dosage and adding accessory drugs only when it is necessary to control certain symptoms not influenced by the original drug.

It is advisable in prescribing antidepressants to instruct and reassure patients regarding possible side effects. The patient should be given a typewritten sheet, such as in Appendix T, including dosages and times to take pills. This is especially necessary for geriatric patients who have a tendency to forget. The patient should be instructed that no alcohol is to be taken for the first 2 weeks of using antidepressant medications. However, after this one can, if desired, drink moderately provided that the medication is not taken at the same time.

If a patient is coordinately using other medications for a physical condition, these medications may dictate the preferred antidepressant to use. For instance, in hypertension where guanethidine (Ismelin, Esimil) is being taken, doxepin (Sinequan) is the best antidepressant to use.

ANTIANXIETY DRUGS (ANXIOLYTICS)

It is unsound to assume that a high level of anxiety is needed to motivate a patient for therapy or to make greater efforts to explore his problems. While tolerable anxiety and tension may require no medication, there is no reason to withhold psychotropic drugs where the patient is in real discomfort. A double-blind study by Whittington et al. (1969) with an unrelated outpatient population experiencing anxiety showed a greater perseverance in and acceptance of treatment of those receiving psychotropic drugs as compared with those receiving placebos. The fact that the patient gets relief from medicaments prescribed by the therapists seemed to help the relationship and to give the patient greater confidence in continuing therapy.

In prescribing anxiolytics, symptoms can sometimes be used as a guide for determining which tranquilizers to use. Thus, inhibited, motor-retarded, and anxious patients may do best on diazepam (Valium); the overactive, anxious patients on chloridazepoxide (Librium); and the hostile, anxious patients on oxazepam (Serax). Where anxiolytics fail to control anxiety, as in borderline patients, one may try neuroleptic drugs, like Stelazine. Occasionally, barbiturates like phenobarbital work better in anxiety than any other drugs. There are some anxieties that do not respond to any psychotropic drugs. These are often found in obsessive individuals who cannot stand the emotional straightjacket that tranquilization imposes on them.

Of all the minor tranquilizers, diazepam (Valium) and chlordiazepoxide

(Librium) are probably best known. Most neurotic anxieties can be treated psychotherapeutically without drugs. It is only where the anxiety is so intense that the patient cannot function or because the anxiety interferes with psychotherapy that drugs should be used. In some cases where the patient as a result of psychotherapy is ready to face a fearful situation but avoids this, a drug can help to break through. There is, however, a tendency to overdose. One way of regulating the dosage of tranquilizers is suggested by Hollister (1974) with Valium. Two hours before bedtime the patient is enjoined to take 2.5 mg Valium and to make a note whether he falls asleep earlier than usual, sleeps longer, and has a slight hangover next morning. If these do not occur, 5 mg are taken the second night. Should the patient still not respond, 10 mg are taken the third night. The hangover effect may be sufficiently great to last the patient throughout the day. If not, one-fourth of the evening dose may be taken during day.

The indications for Valium and Librium besides anxiety are depressions that may respond to its mildly euphoriant effect. They are also valuable in treating the agitation of chronic alcoholics for alcoholic withdrawal, including delirium tremens. In *severe* problems relatively large doses of Valium may be necessary. The starting oral dose is 5 mg three or four times daily. The patient is asked to telephone in 3 days to report how he feels. If there is no effect, the dose is raised to 10 mg four times daily so that the patient takes a total of 40 mg. The patient should be seen 4 days later, and if the symptoms continue, the dosage may be raised to 20 mg three or four times daily. The evening dose may be the largest one in the case of insomnia. When the patient feels better (tranquilization, mild mood elevation, increased appetite), one dose may be removed; 2 weeks later, a second dose is removed; 4 weeks later, all but the evening dose is taken away. Such regulation of the dosage will tend to prevent addiction. With higher doses patients may become ataxic and drowsy. Should this happen, the dose is lowered (it requires about 4 days to eliminate the drug from the system; consequently side effects may last during this

period). Rapid symptomatic relief in alcoholic agitation, acute delirium tremens, hallucinosis, acute anxiety, and acute phobic and panic reactions may sometimes be obtained with 50 to 100 mg. Librium injected intramuscularly or intravenously, repeating in 4 to 6 hours if necessary. Caution in the use of Librium is to be heeded in older people who may become ataxic with even moderate doses.

Meprobamate (Miltown, Equanil) is another drug that has anxiety-alleviating properties when given over a sufficiently extended period. Rickels (1966) reports a study of patients in psychotherapy that showed no significant drug-placebo differences after 2 weeks of drug therapy, but demonstrated differences in favor of meprobamate in all measures at the 4- and 6-week evaluation levels. The study also supported the hypothesis that the addition of meprobamate to psychotherapy may enhance the implementation of psychotherapy. Indications for meprobamate are similar to those of chlordiazepoxide, except that it should not be employed in depressed patients. It is particularly useful where skeletal muscle spasm is present. The symptom profile of anxiety and tension may be helped with 400 mg three or four times daily, which may slowly be increased to as much as 3200 mg daily, this high dose being maintained for only a short time. Allergic reactions (fever, urticaria, bronchial spasm, angioneurotic edema) should be treated by discontinuing the drug and administering antihistamines, epinephrine, and possibly cortisone. Dependence and habituation are possible, consequently meprobamates should not be used for more than 3 months. Withdrawal from high doses should be gradual over a 1- to 2-week period.

Other minor tranquilizers include oxazepam (Serax). This drug (15–30 mg three or four times daily) has been utilized to control anxiety, neurotic depression, alcoholic tremulousness and withdrawal. The agitated reactions of older people (dose 10 mg three times daily) also may respond to Serax.

These minor tranquilizers have a disadvantage of leading to addiction over a long-term period. Where a person has an addictive personality (alcoholic, barbituarte user, etc.), it is best not to prescribe Valium, Librium, or Serax. Rather small doses of a major tranquilizer like Stelazine (1–2 mg), Trilafon (2–4 mg), or Prolixin (0.5–2.5 mg) twice daily may be quite effective, particularly where there are some psychosomatic symptoms.

In obsessional individuals who cannot tolerate losing control or not functioning with top efficiency, lowering performance may prove so upsetting as to obliterate any benefit from these drugs. Such persons may be taught to monitor their own minimal doses while being given reassurance to quiet them down.

Propranolol (Inderal) in doses of 10–40 mg three or four times daily may be of value in anxieties associated with beta-adrenergic overstimulation, as in psycho-cardiac disorders. Sometimes higher doses are required, in which case careful monitoring of the heart is necessary to prevent excessive depression of cardiac function.

SEDATIVES AND HYPNOTICS

Since the advent of tranquilizers, barbiturates have suffered a setback in popularity. Yet, in selected cased, they may still be the best drugs to use as daytime sedatives. Butabarbital (Butisol), phenobarbital sodium (Luminol) and Tuinal in small dosage may be utilized here. Nonbarbiturates like flurazepam (Dalmane), glutethimide (Doriden), methylprylon (Noludar), and ethchlorvynol (Placidyl) are the most common substances employed. Proper dosage is indicated in Table 53–3. Some persons find Valium (5–10 mg) a preferred hypnotic while others do well with a mild antihistamine drug. Sedative-hypnotics, while valuable for occasional use, are habituating with prolonged use. Since they are favorite suicidal agents, these drugs should not be made available in large quantities to depressed patients.

PSYCHODYSLEPTIC
(PSYCHOTOMIMETIC) DRUGS

Employed for the setting up of model psychoses (see page 95) LSD-25, mescaline, and psilocybin have been advocated to induce perceptual and cognitive crises in patients, release emotions, promote abreaction, revive memories, and open up channels to the unconscious. The effect on the individual is influenced by the environmental setting, the existing relationship to the therapist and the activity of the therapist. There are some patients who, frozen in their affects, suddenly are transported into a psychedelic experience which enables them to restructure their value systems somewhat after the manner of a mystical experience (see page 149).

The extraordinary perceptual and hallucinatory irregularities induced by these drugs unfortunately appeal to adolescents in rebellion, thrill seekers, and psychopaths who subject themselves to a wondrous "widening of consciousness" in quest of new insights and powers. "It permits you to see, more clearly than our perishing mortal eye can see, vistas beyond the horizons of this life, to travel backwards and forwards in time, to enter other planes of existence, even—to know God" (Wasson, 1963). Psychiatric patients, disappointed in psychoanalysis, hypnosis, drug therapy, and ECT, often express a demand for the drug on the basis of its vaunted effects on the psyche. Unfortunately, on the debit side of the ledger is the capacity of psychodysleptics, particularly in vulnerable borderline patients, of sweeping away defenses that keep the individual in some kind of functional relationship to reality. "Our accumulating day-to-day experience with patients suffering the consequences of the hallucinogens demonstrates beyond question that these drugs have the power to damage the individual psyche, indeed to cripple it for life" (*JAMA*, 1963). These warnings, timely as they are, have put a damper on responsible research that may appraise the types of persons and syndromes who and which may be helped by psychotomimetic drugs.

Favorable reports on LSD therapy with almost every syndrome have been published by Abramson (1956a & b), Bender et al. (1962), Chandler and Hartman (1960), S. Cohen and Eisner (1959), Cutner (1959), Dahlberg (1963a & b), Eisner and S. Cohen (1958), Feld et al. (1958), Heyder (1964), D. J. Lewis and Sloane (1958), Martin (1957),

Sandison and Whitelaw (1957), Savage et al. (1964), Schmiege (1963), Simmons et al. (1966), and Whitelaw (1959). The book, *Uses of LSD in Psychotherapy* (Abramson, 1960), published by the Josiah Macy, Jr., Foundation, has a wealth of experimental and clinical data. The paper by Spencer (1964) also contains material helpful in evolving a technique. A conference held at South Oaks, Long Island (N.Y.), devoted to LSD therapy expounded its potentialities (Abramson, 1966). LSD has been particularly recommended in the treatment of alcoholism (Hoffer, 1965; Jensen, 1962; Kurland et al, 1966, 1971; McCabe et al, 1972; MacLean et al, 1961; Pahnke et al, 1970; Savage et al, 1969, 1973; Smith, CM, 1958).

Its beneficial uses in group psychotherapy have been described by Bierer (1963) who claims good results for LSD (in combination with methedrine) in "acute neuroses and for some sex difficulties. In addition, our experience with LSD as one aspect of an individual and group psychotherapeutic program for psychotic patients has been sufficiently encouraging to merit its continued use on an experimental basis." Bierer insists that it is not dangerous to treat psychotic, psychopathic, and emotionally immature patients with LSD. Eisner (1964) has also described the facilitating use of LSD in group therapy.

The problem of evaluating the effect of LSD in psychotherapy is as great as, if not greater than, that of assessing any other kind of psychotherapy. Of basic importance is how the therapist (who must be with the patient for 5 hours or more) works with and relates to the patient while he is under the influence of the drug. Where the patient becomes too upset, the psychosis may rapidly be abolished by intravenous administration of 50 mg of chlorpromazine. Motor activity is reduced by chlorpromazine, verbal objectivity lessened, anxiety resolved, feelings of unreality and depersonalization abolished, and though hallucinations or somatic delusions continue, the patient may not react to them adversely

Low doses of dipropyltrytamene (DPT), i.e., 15–20 mg intramuscularly as an initial dose raised in 5-mg increments in later interviews until an optimal reaction is achieved, have been productively employed with alcoholic patients as an adjunct to psychotherapy (Soskin et al., 1973).

What is essential in utilizing hallucinogens therapeutically is familiarity with the effects of the particular drugs employed, obtained by observing other therapists work who are expert in the method. Sufficient time must be spent with a patient prior to the administration of the drug to establish a working relationship and a feeling of trust. The therapeutic surroundings must be quiet, and the therapist and preferably a psychiatric nurse should be with the patient during the period the drug is in effect (which may be as long as 10–12 hours), rendering him support if necessary.

ORTHOMOLECULAR
PSYCHIATRY AND
MEGAVITAMIN THERAPY

There is a theory that schizophrenia is the product of an endogenous hallucinogen that accumulates in susceptible individuals as a result of faulty metabolism. Implicated frequently, it is avowed, is adrenochrome, formed from oxidation of adrenalin and released in large quantities by the excessive methylation of noradrenalin. On the basis of this theory, Hoffer (1966, 1971) administered large quantities of nicotinic acid (3 or more g daily), which he and his associates believed could restore metabolic balances. The theory, as well as the cure, have been rejected by a number of scientific investigators who have been unable to confirm the chemical changes postulated. Nevertheless, a sizable group of psychiatrists (who call themselves "orthomolecular" psychiatrists, a term originated by Linus Pauling) have endorsed the value of large quantities of vitamins (nicotinic acid, nicotinamide, vitamin B6, vitamin C, vitamin B12, and pyridoxine) for schizophrenia in combination with other accepted therapies, such as phenothiazines, ECT, and psychotherapy.

A task force of the American Psychiatric Association was appointed to examine the claims and appraise the results of megavitamin therapy. The report rejected both the theory and practice of orthomolecular treatments (Lipton et al., 1973).

The extravagent claims of the orthomolecular psychiatrists in the public media were considered unfortunate. According to the task force, it has been impossible to replicate the results of the advocates of this form of therapy. Other studies, such as a five year multihospital project sponsored by the Canadian Mental Health Association, have concluded that large doses of nicotinic acid (3000 mg per day or more), the cornerstone of megavitamin therapy, have no therapeutic value other than as a placebo.

Against these reports, the orthomolecular psychiatric group have claimed unfairness and bias. Members of the group cite their own research, including double-blind studies, that substantiates the value of megovitamin treatments in acute cases, often in conjunction with ECT and other therapies (Hawkins & Pauling, 1973). They repudiate the results of attempts to replicate their findings on the basis that the research designs have been faulty. Hoffer claims that where the megavitamin program outlined by him has been followed exactly, all reports published have duplicated his original claims. Pauling (1974) insists that "There is evidence that an increased intake of some vitamins, including ascorbic acid, niacin, pyridoxine, and cyanocobalamin, is useful in treating schizophrenia and this treatment has a sound theoretical base."

The controversy illustrates the difficulty of validating outcome research findings where faith or lack of faith in the modality, along with nonspecific therapeutic elements, are unavoidable contaminents.

Electroconvulsive Therapy

Employed with a muscle relaxant, such as succinylcholine (Anectine), and an anestheticlike methohexital (Brevital), administered by a trained anesthetist, electroconvulsive therapy (ECT) (see page 97) has become a simple and relatively safe procedure. Not only is ECT useful in depression, but in some cases of early schizophrenia its careful employment may bring about a remission. It is also valuable in psychotic disorders that accompany organic mental ailments and in psychoneuroses characterized by intense depression or panic that resists or does not respond to psychotherapy—such as some types of obsessional illness and severe hysteria (e.g., anorexia nervosa). An alternative method to ECT is provided by flurothyl (Indokolon), which induces seizures through chemical means.

Unfortunately, ECT has been overused, and for this reason it has acquired a bad reputation. Refinements in drug therapy have largely displaced the need for ECT, and it is now generally used where drug therapy has not helped, and particularly in suicidal patients.

Electroconvulsive therapy in the hands of an expert is a relatively safe procedure. It has a low mortality rate (one death per 10,000 treatments) and low incidence of adverse side reactions. There are, however, dangers in using ECT in patients with ischemic heart disease, the presence of which increases the risk considerably. An appropriate cardiovascular assessment with an electrocardiogram is indicated especially in middle-aged or elderly persons. An absolute contraindication is brain tumor. Compensated myocardial disease, aortic aneurism, and arteriosclerosis are only relative contraindications.

Conditions under which ECT has been found useful are the following:

1. Inhibited depression and melancholia
2. Agitated depression and melancholia
3. Postpartum depression
4. Manic excitements
5. Involutional psychoses
6. Catatonia

Agitated and excited reactions and intense chronic anxiety will require concentrated sessions (two daily for the first day or two followed by daily sessions) until the symptoms are under control. Too few ECTs may aggravate agitated, anxiety, paranoidal, and hebephrenic reactions. ECT has been employed as a preventive measure in manic-depressive psychosis, being administered bimonthly or monthly following full recovery. In schizophrenia, sufficient numbers of ECT (20) may, in cases treated within 6 months of onset, bring about a satisfactory remission.

Adjunctive drugs have been employed with ECT, although caution prescribes that drugs like neuroleptics be employed only after the course of ECT is ended or in severely resistant patients (with the caution that the morning dose should not be given prior to ECT).

It is essential in using ECT to make sure that an adequate number of treatments are given. In general, depressions and manic excitements require the smallest number of sessions (approximately 6 or 8 ECTs), while schizophrenia will need the largest number (20 ECTs). Excited and agitated reactions may need two treatments daily for 1 or 2 days, followed by a conventional twice weekly schedule.

For the most part, the therapist will refer patients for ECT who are severely depressed. An adequate number of treatments (generally three) are needed during the first week where the patient is a suicidal risk. Following this, one treatment at weekly intervals may suffice. A total of 6 to 10 ECTs are usually required. Intervals should be so spaced that the patient is prevented from developing confusion and excessive memory loss. Excited and panicky schizophrenic or borderline patients may also require referral. Here treatments on the basis of three times weekly may be needed, reduced only to control confusion or regression. The last few treatments are given once weekly. In a few cases "maintenance ECT" may be required on a prolonged basis to keep the vulnerable patient from dissociating. Usually, however, borderline patients with a depressive or panicky overlay which interferes with psychotherapy may be made more accessible and kept from memory impairment by one, two, or three or more ECTs spaced sufficiently apart (Kalinowsky, 1965). Memory loss for recent events, a disturbing by-product of ECT, generally reverses itself within a few weeks.

Unilateral ECT reduces the post-treatment confusion and memory loss of conventional bilateral ECT by placing the treatment electrodes over one side of the head only: the nondominant hemisphere (usually the right side in a right-handed individual). Generalized seizures are obtained with this method, which is otherwise given with anesthesia and muscle relaxation exactly as bilateral ECT. The striking absence of memory loss with unilateral ECT permits treatment to be given on a daily basis (Abrams, 1967). The depression-relieving effects of unilateral ECT are less than for bilateral ECT (Abrams, 1972), however, and this observation has stimulated attempts to increase the therapeutic effects of unilateral ECT by giving more than one treatment in a single session (Abrams & Fink, 1972). If there is no pressure of time and no clinical urgency (e.g., suicidal risk, progressive weight loss, reckless overactivity), unilateral ECT should be given initially, changing to bilateral ECT only if improvement has not occurred after four to six ECTs. Unilateral ECT is also useful for ambulatory patients or those whose work requires unaltered memory function during the treatment course. Unilateral ECT may also be used to avoid cumulative memory loss (retrograde amnesia) in patients who have improved after receiving their first few treatments with bilateral ECT.

Basic Suggestions for Proper Drug Usage (Summary)

When psychotherapy alone does not control disturbing symptoms, the proper medicaments may be of great and often indispensible help. Antipsychotic and antidepressant drugs are of particular importance in reducing morbidity and releasing the individual who is suited for them toward a more productive life. The psychotherapist will need special knowledge in choosing proper medications. The following suggestions may be found helpful:

1. Take a history on each patient regarding previous and present psychotropic drug usage. Which drugs were not and which were effective? Dosage? What side effects if any? Ask about the use of dosage and effect of psychotropic medications by other blood relatives. Due to the operation of genetic factors, we may predict similar

reactions to the same drugs by the patient. Inquire into existing physical illness. This may be dangerously aggravated by some drugs. If the patient is taking certain medications for the illness, these may be incompatible with some psychotropic drugs, for example, guanethidine (for hypertension) and tricyclics (given for depression) do not mix.

2. A diagnosis is important in some disorders in order to prescribe the proper drug, for example, in differentiating between schizophrenia and mania (phenothiazines would be used in the former and lithium in the latter) and schizophrenia and psychotic depression (phenothiazines would be used in the former and antidepressants in the latter.) On the other hand, sometimes symptom profiles may be the basis for drug choice, particularly where a diagnosis is impossible. Agitation, thus, will require drugs like Thorazine or Haldol, and apathy may need a stimulant or a drug like Stelazine where a coordinate calming effect is desired.

3. Try to avoid some drug combinations like hypnotics and antidepressants. They can reduce the desired effect of a drug. Where combinations are necessary, one should be aware that the total antipsychotic effect may be reduced. Thus, Cogentin to eliminate Parkinsonian symptoms may lower the plasma level of a neuroleptic drug so that psychotic symptomatology can reappear necessitating greater dosage.

4. In order to reduce side effects many authorities advise using the more powerful psychotropic drugs that secure therapeutic benefits with smaller dosages. Thus, Prolixin, Stelazine, and Haldol will operate with minimal drowsiness, lesser tendency to jaundice and agranulocytosis, and lower anticholinergic effects (delayed urination, aggravation of glaucoma) than Thorazine and Mellaril. They will also produce lesser hypotension and changes in cardiac rhythm and thus are better in cardiovascular illness. On the other hand, they can cause more extrapyramidal symptoms than the weaker compounds, such as muscle stiffness, and, where given over considerable periods (especially to older people),

the dreaded tardive dyskinesia. Among the antidepressants, Sinequan will produce lesser anticholinergic and cardiovascular symptoms than Tofranil or Elavil. Sometimes, however, we may wish to take advantage of the side effects, for instance, by prescribing Thorazine or Mellaril in restless or agitated schizophrenics.

5. Adequate dosage is essential over a sufficiently long period to test the efficacy of a drug. Build up dosage as rapidly as possible. If a patient fails to respond to one class of drugs over a sufficiently long time, switch to one of the other classes, e.g., from Prolixin to Haldol, to Navane, to Moban. If the patient still fails to respond after 2 months of drug therapy, the chances are the individual is not a good candidate for pharmacotherapy.

6. Since these drugs are retained in the body for relatively long periods, a single total dose at nighttime is preferable, once a therapeutic effect has been obtained, to multiple doses during the day. Sleep is enhanced, and there is a lesser tendency to forget to take the medications.

7. "Drug holidays," such as abstinence over weekends, are advisable in chronic patients on maintenance therapy to reduce side effects. Where a patient is in remission, lower the dosage of drugs or administer them with progressively longer drug-free intervals. If symptoms reappear, dosages may be increased.

8. Where a patient has had a good premorbid personality, has related well to people, and has broken down only under the impact of extremely severe stress, psychogenic rather than biological factors are likely. Psychological treatments here are the approaches of choice, the use of drugs being restricted to extraordinarily severe or recalcitrant symptoms. An acute psychotic break, particularly in a young person, may really be an identity crises or a consequence of drug abuse (marijuana, mescaline, LSD, etc.) It is better, therefore, not to prescribe psychotropic medications routinely. In many cases mere hospitalization suffices to stabilize a patient. One may wait a few days and then institute psychotherapy and reassurance to see if the patient's inner strengths will suffice to bring

about a remission. Obviously, psychotherapy should continue after recovery occurs.

9. In some psychosomatic illnesses the associated or provocative tension may not yield to measures other than drugs. Here long-term drug intake may be resorted to by the patient. It is best under these circumstances to prescribe or, if the patient is already on minor tranquilizers like Valium, to change to low doses of the less addicting drugs, like Stelazine or Prolixin.

10. Where possible, coordinate psychotherapy should be employed in a psychotropic drug regime to help reduce destructive patterns of interpersonal relatedness, to lower self-imposed standards impossible of attainment, to teach social skills, and to facilitate environmental adjustment. So doing will enable the patient more rapidly to make an adaption without the need, or with a reduced need, for medications.

CONFRONTATION

Psychodynamic theory and psychoanalytic methods are often accused of helping the patient to avoid responsibility for his own behavior, blaming inner conflicts foisted on him by past experience over which he has no control. In confrontation techniques it is assumed that the patient must accept responsibility for his own actions and take the consequences for behavior that is counterproductive. The patient is exposed to a surprise or shock stimulus from which there is no escape and to which he must respond. Retreats into unreality and evasive defense are cut off. He is invited to explore his reactions with the aid of the therapist. He must justify aspects of his verbalizations and behavior that the therapist believes are significant. The selection of what to question or impugn is obviously of crucial importance, and here the perceptiveness and diagnostic skill of the therapist is important. Most therapists who utilize confrontation employ it in the medium of a wide assortment of eclectic methods like role playing, Gestalt therapy, psychodrama, transactional therapy, en-

counter therapy, existential therapy, and psychoanalytically oriented psychotherapy.

Utilizing a transactional model, Garner (1970) has developed a confrontation technique that "focuses on the patient's conflict between the unconscious or conscious desire to approach a certain goal and the avoidance tendencies." The technique is characterized by interventions in the form of frequent directive statements made to the patient, with the question, "What do you think or feel about what I told you?" The patient's response is studied, whether it be complete compliance, compliance with critical appraisal, or critical appraisal. In this way an attempt is made to probe *reactions* to statements and to avoid the parroting of insight. The challenging question of the therapist requires that the patient explore the role of the therapist and the interactional dynamics of the relationship. It forces the patient also to examine the stereotyped nature of his thoughts and behavior. The patient is invited to work out a mutually satisfactory solution to conflicts. The statements by the therapist chosen for confrontation may be prohibitive—"You must never, under any circumstances, masturbate''—or expressive or permissive —"it would be better if your husband dies" —or adaptive—"I want you to continue to work at your job.

The focus may be limited or may involve the resolution of a core conflict that existed in the early life of the patient. For example, patients with dependency problems or separation anxiety may be confronted with, "Stop believing you are incapable of taking care of yourself," or "You are acting like the most helpless, inept person in the world," or "I want you to go places and do things as you always have." After each of these statements there is added, "What do you think or feel about what I have told you?" Other statements are made depending on the specific difficulty of the patient, such as "Stop believing you are the most sinful (or destructive) person in the world," or "Stop believing that everything you do will be incorrect," or "Stop believing you have to be the most perfect person in the world''—adding on to any of these, "What do you think or feel about what I have told you?'' The latter question acts like a lever to explore compliance or noncompliance tendencies and to engage in problem-solving activities.

The confrontation formulations may be employed adjunctively in any form or insight therapy when a clearly defined conflict is exposed. They may be employed to reinforce a constructive defense or to challenge a neurotic defense, as in peer groups with addicts (Adler, G, & Buie, 1974). Among their uses is testing how thoroughly the patient has understood a point stressed by the therapist. In this way misinterpretations may be immediately corrected. Confrontation may also be used as an adjunct to behavioral and other educational methods as a wedge into cognitive areas. Obviously, sicker patients, such as borderline cases and schizophrenics, do not respond well to the technique.

GESTALT THERAPY

Establishing its position in the Human Potential Movement, Gestalt therapy (see page 227) gets its inspiration from Gestalt psychology, existentialism, psychodrama, and psychoanalysis (particularly character analysis). It stresses the immediacy of experience in the here and now and nonverbal expressiveness (Fagan & Shepherd, 1970). It describes itself as a philosophy of living in the present rather than the past or future, of experiencing rather than imagining, of expressing rather than explaining or justifying, of avoiding the ''shoulds'' or ''oughts,'' of taking full responsibility for one's actions, feelings, and thoughts, and of surrendering to ''being as one is'' (Naranjo, 1971).

By observing the patient's positive gestures and bodily movements, Gestalt therapists attempt to discern aspects that reflect unconscious feelings. The therapist points out these tendencies and asks the patient to exaggerate them, to express any feelings associated with them. The object is to expand the patient's awareness of himself, his bodily sensations, and the world around him. Gestalt techniques are sometimes employed to catalyze other therapies.

As to the actual techniques, the patient may be asked to observe things about the therapist's waiting room and to comment on them, particularly to speculate on the kind of a person that he believes the therapist to be from this data. If the patient becomes aware of certain bodily sensations like his heart beating, deep breathing, his neck stiffening, etc., he may be asked to talk to his heart, his lungs, his neck, etc. The projective elements of anything that he says are inquired into by asking the patient to relate his comments about others to himself. The patient is encouraged to do, and to even exaggerate doing things, that he avoids or is ashamed of, at first in fantasy and then slowly in realilty. All aspects of the patient's dreams are considered part of himself, and the patient is asked to play these parts, dramatizing them while verbalizing feelings freely. Many of the Gestalt techniques lend themselves to groups as well as individual therapy. The techniques used for the most usual situations encountered in therapy are summarized here:

1. *Dealing with conflict:* When elements of a conflict are perceived (e.g., dominant desires versus passive impulses; masculine versus feminine, etc.), the patient is asked to play both roles in turn, utilizing the empty chair in which an imagined significant person is seated or the counterpart aspect of the self is seated.

2. *Unresolved feelings:* When detected, the therapist may insist that these be expressed.

3. *Difficulties in self-expression:* A game is often played wherein the patient makes a statement and ends it by saying, ''And I take responsibility for it.''

4. *Fear of offending others:* In a group the patient goes around expressing his attitudes and feelings frankly to each member.

5. *Testing projections:* When a patient believes another patient has a problem or characteristic, he is asked to play a role as if he himself has the problem or characteristic.

6. *Challenging reaction formations* (e.g., excessive prudishness): Here the therapist may ask the patient to play

the opposite role deliberately (e.g., verbalizing sexual freedom).

7. *Managing anxiety:* The therapist says, "Why not let it build as far as it likes. Don't try to stop it. Emphasize your shaking. Try to bring it on."

8. *Tendencies to detachment and withdrawal:* The patient is asked to focus on the situations or inner feelings that cause him to withdraw.

9. *Exploring the meaning of gestures or unusual verbal statements:* When these are noticeable, the patient is asked to exaggerate them and detail his associations.

10. *Difficulties in making assertive statements:* The patient is encouraged to say before each statement, "Of course" and "It is certain that."

11. *Use of dreams:* Each aspect of the dream is believed to represent a part of the individual. The patient is asked to identify with each aspect of the dream and act out a role talking to various aspects of himself.

12. *Dealing with distorted values:* The therapist often tries to act as a model by verbalizing and sharing with the patient his or her personal values and feelings.

HYPNOSIS

Trance phenomena have been utilized as part of religious and healing rituals in all ages and cultures since the earliest of recorded history. The loss of control by the subject in the trance, the bizarre muscular movements, and the vivid imagery that is released have suggested "possession" by spirits and extramundane forces that have led observers to link hypnosis with mysticism and the paranormal. It is only relatively recently that attempts have been made at scientific investigation of hypnosis in the effort to understand how it influences behavior and particularly its therapeutic potentials.

Such studies have shown that employed by reasonably trained professionals within the context of a structured therapeutic program, with awareness of limits of its application, hypnosis can make a contribution as an adjunct to any of the manifold branches of psychotherapy, whether these be supportive, reeducative, or psychoanalytic.

Most professionals who are fearful of hypnosis as a therapeutic tool, or exaggerate its virtues, either have never experimented with it for a time sufficient to test the method or else are victims of superstition, prejudices, or naive magical expectancy. A number of spokesmen for hypnosis, some writing extensively, help to discredit it by overdramatizing the process, by exaggerating its powers, by participating in and publishing results of poorly conceived experiments, by engaging in naively organized therapeutic schemes, by offering therapeutic formulations that violate the most elementary precepts of dynamic psychology, or by promulgating its presumed dangers for which there is little basis in fact (Wolberg, LR, 1956).

How hypnosis aids in securing therapeutic effects is not entirely clear, but we may postulate two important influences. First, hypnosis rapidly produces a remarkable rapport with the therapist. Irrespective of the fact that this is probably linked to some anachonistic regressive dependency need, a strong impact is registered on the therapeutic working relationship. The placebo influence, a component of all therapies, is strongly enhanced. Suggestion, another universal component of all treatment processes, is so expanded in hypnosis that the patient responds sensitively and with dramatic readiness to both indirect, subtle persuasions by the therapist and to direct commands and injunctions that are not too anxiety provoking. The relationship with the therapist, in a surprisingly short time, becomes one in which the therapist becomes endowed with noble, protective, and even magical qualities. The ultimate result of these combined forces can be substantive relief from tension, a restoration of homeostasis, and a recapturing of a sense of mastery, which in themselves may restore adaptive defenses and produce a symptomatic cure.

The second influence of hypnosis is upon the intrapsychic processes. Hypnosis promotes an altered state of consciousness. As such, repression may temporarily be lifted with exposure of emotionally charged impulses that have been denied direct expression and that have hitherto partly drained themselves off through substitutive symptomatic channels. This can lead to a release of vivid imagery and emotionally cathartic verbalizations. Such spontaneous outbursts usually occur only in persons who are strongly repressed while nurturing explosive inner conflicts. On the other hand, a therapist utilizing exploratory techniques to probe unconscious ideation may, by direct suggestion or regression and revivification, expose less highly charged but significant fantasies, verbal associations, and memories, thus opening roads to greater self-understanding.

Hypnosis as a relaxing agency has been employed in physical and psychological disturbances that are characterized by stress and tension. Since stress may have a damaging effect on all bodily functions, its amelioration can be important for healing (Wolberg, LR, 1957). Tension relief may, on the basis of suggestion during the trance state, be supplemented perhaps by self-hypnosis (Wolberg, LR, 1965) or by such techniques as autogenic training (Luthe, 1963; Schultz & Luthe, 1959; Luthe et al, 1963).

Where the symptom does not bind too much anxiety or where its pleasure and masochistic values are not too intense, it may be possible to alleviate it by hypnotic suggestion without symptom substitution. Not only may the ensuing relief initiate a better adjustment, but also it may set off a chain reaction that, reverberating through the entire personality structure, influences its other dimensions. Suggestive hypnosis may also be of value in controlling the ruminations of chronic obsessive-compulsive patients whose preoccupations immerse them in interminable misery. By helping such victims to divert their thinking into more constructive channels, it may initiate relief of anxiety and a better adaptation. With caution hypnosis may be adopted as a suggestive instrument in controlling certain habits, such as overeating, excessive smoking, and insomnia. The phrasing of suggestions is important.

The use of hypnosis in exploratory psychotherapy, such as in the insight approaches, is contingent upon the influence of hypnosis on unconscious resistance that in resolution helps the individual establish closer contact with repressed needs and conflicts. It may thus be possible to bring to the surface significant memories and repressed impulses that expedite the analytic process.

Hypnosis is particularly useful in freeing verbalizations, in liberating transference, and in helping the patient to recall dreams. Where anxiety blocks speech, the mere induction of a trance may serve to release a verbal discharge. Moreover, the provocation of transference feelings may bring to the surface painful emotions as well as fantasies that sometimes burst through with intense violence. Where free associations have been blocked for one reason or another, hypnosis may suffice to restore this form of communication. Hypnosis may serve also as a means of stimulating dreams in patients who are unable to remember them or who have "dried up" in their analytic productiveness.

In behavior therapy hypnosis is useful in various ways. First, it establishes in the mind of the patient the authority of the therapist, who will act as the reinforcing agency. Under these circumstances positive counterconditioning, aversive conditioning, extinction, and other tactics will be catalyzed. Second, by promoting relaxation through hypnosis a positive stimulus is supplied that becomes affiliated with the conditioned stimulus and helps to extinguish it. Third, on the basis of suggestion, the objectives of the therapist, once explicitly defined, may be more easily accepted. The patient is encouraged to behave in emotionally constructive ways, in quest of reversing established patterns or correcting behavioral deficits. Thus, in the method of desensitization through reciprocal inhibition anxiety-provoking cues are presented in a climate of relaxation in progressively stronger form.

There is no way of predicating in advance the exact influence hypnosis may have on the patient or his problems since each individual will respond uniquely to the phenomenon of hypnosis in line with the special meanings it has for him. The mental set with which he approaches hypnosis, his motivations to be helped, the depth and quality of his resistances, his preparation for induction, his conception of the therapist and particularly the image he conjures up of him, the skill of the therapist as a hypnotist, the quality of the suggestions administered, the management of the patient's doubts and oppositional tendencies, and the nature of the transference and countertransference will all enter into the responsive Gestalt.

Potentially, hypnosis may catalyze every aspect of the therapeutic process. Whether or not a therapist will want to employ it will depend largely on how much confidence one has in hypnosis and how well one works with hypnotic techniques.

Hypnosis is an intense emotional experience that may affect both patient and therapist. In the trance a dynamic configuration of many kinds of phenomena are constantly interacting in response to functional psychophysiological changes within the individual and the specific significance to him of the hypnotic interpersonal relationship. As attention is shifted from the external world toward the inner self, there is an expansion of self-awareness and a lifting of repressions, with exposure of certain repudiated aspects of the psyche. A regressive kind of relationship develops between the subject and operator, the latter being promoted into the post of a kind of magical authoritative figures.

Hypnosis may also release powerful feelings in the therapist, aspects of which, in the form of countertransference, may be inimical to the therapeutic objective. Particularly offensive are omnipotent, sadistic, and sexual strivings. Only by experimenting with hypnosis can a therapist determine whether he or she is personally capable of employing it as a therapeutic adjunct. While one may be able to do good psychotherapy with the usual psychotherapeutic techniques, attempts at hypnosis may alter one's manner toward one's patient in ways that will prove antitherapeutic. Thus, a therapist may act aggressively toward patients perceived to be in a helpless state. Coordinately, one may become suffused with

feelings of grandiosity. Or one may, as a projected Svengali figure, find oneself sexually attracted to a patient whom one regards as passively seductive. Should these feelings arise in spite of measures to control them, it is best to pursue a pattern of caution and refrain from employing hypnosis in practice.

Hypnosis, then, is merely a device to facilitate the psychotherapeutic process rather than to substitute for it. No problems need be anticipated in the induction of hypnosis, and in the application of hypnotic and hypnoanalytic procedures, if the therapist masters at least one of the standard techniques, applies it confidently, while constantly observing the reactions of the patient and of oneself. Protracted dependency reactions are no more common than in psychotherapy without hypnosis. It goes without saying that hypnosis is no substitute for careful training, extensive experience, and technical competence. It will not make up for lacks in judgment or skill. However, a sophisticated psychotherapist who has learned how to utilize hypnosis has available a most important adjunctive tool.

Induction of Hypnosis

Hypnosis is extremely easy to induce. The object is to bring the patient to a hypersuggestible state. Toward this end the operator executes a number of maneuvers, the most common one being a state of muscular relaxation and the fixation of attention. Important rules to follow are these:

1. Engage the attention of the patient by assigning a task, (muscle relaxation, hand clasp, hand levitation), descriptions of which will follow.
2. Approach the induction with a confident manner. Any faltering or unsureness in vocal expression will influence the patient negatively. Adopt a persuasive, calm, reassuring tone of voice, droning suggestions rhythmically and monotonously.
3. Employ repetition in suggestions to focus the patient's attention.
4. Excite the imagination of the patient by building word pictures so that he practically lives and feels what is suggested.

(In children one can engage their attention by asking them to imagine watching a television screen and observing their favorite programs.)

5. Use positive rather than negative suggestions. For example, where pain is to be deadened, do not say, "You will have no pain." Say, "The sensation will change so that instead of feeling what you have been feeling, it will feel dull, numb, and tolerable." If a hypodermic injection is to be given, do not say, "This will not hurt," but rather, "This will be like a tiny mosquito bite."

6. Should the patient at any time open his eyes and insist he is not hypnotized, put your fingers on his eyelids to shut them and say, "That doesn't matter, I just want you to relax." Then continue with suggestions.

7. Almost universally, patients, after the first induction, even those who have been deeply hypnotized, will insist they were not in a trance. Reply with, "Of course you weren't asleep or anaesthesized. You were in a state of relaxation, and, for the time being, this is all that is necessary. You may go deeper next time." Give the patient a typewritten copy of material describing some phenomena of hypnosis (see Appendix U).

8. Some operators find it important to tell the patient that all that will be achieved in the first session is not hypnosis but a state of relaxation that will help the patient quiet his symptoms: "If you fall asleep, that is fine; if you feel completely awake, that too is fine. The effect will still be there." To some people the word "hypnosis" has many unfortunate connotations. It often embraces expectations of an immediate miracle cure. When the patient fails to go into the depth of trance that he imagines he should achieve with the "hypnotic" indication, he will become upset, feel hopeless, and lose confidence in the therapist.

A simple technique that I have found valuable, particularly for suggestive-persuasive-reeducative therapy, involves muscle relaxation. This method lends itself to teaching the patient self-hypnosis in order that he may carry on suggestions by himself. Helpful in this direction is supplying the patient with a tape recording (he may bring his machine with him and a recording may be made directly on it; or if the therapist's recorder is compatible with that of the patient, he may be given the recorded tape at the end of the session). The patient may be requested to lean back in his chair and shut his eyes (if preferred he can be supine on a couch) and the material below may be dictated, *slowly,* in a persuasive tone (the therapist may have to practice reading the material so that it does not come through in a stereotyped mechanical way). As a preliminary, I tell the patient, "I would like to teach you a simple relaxing technique that should help you." If the patient agrees, I continue:

All that will happen is that you will be pleasantly relaxed, no sleep, no deep trances, just comfortable. Now just settle back and shut your eyes. [*At this point the therapist may read the following material. If a recording is to be made, start the recording.*] Breathe in deeply through your nostrils or mouth, right down into the pit of your stomach. D-e-e-p-l-y, d-e-e-p-l-y, d-e-e-p-l-y; but not so deeply that you are uncomfortable. Just deeply enough so that you feel the air soaking in. In . . . and out. D-e-e-p-l-y, d-e-e-p-l-y. In . . . and out. And as you feel the air soaking in, you begin to feel yourself getting t-i-r-e-d and r-e-l-a-x-e-d. Very r-e-l-a-x-e-d. Even d-r-o-w-s-y, d-r-o-w-s-y and relaxed. Drowsy and relaxed.

Now I want you to concentrate on the muscle groups that I point out to you. Loosen them, relax them while visualizing them. You will notice that you may be tense in certain areas and the idea is to relax yourself completely. Concentrate on your forehead. Loosen the muscles around your eyes. Your eyelids relax. Now your face, your face relaxes. And your mouth . . . relax the muscles around your mouth, and even the inside of your mouth. Your chin; let it sag and feel heavy. And as you relax your muscles, your breathing continues r-e-g-u-l-a-r-l-y and d-e-e-p-l-y, deeply within yourself. Now your neck, your neck relaxes. Every muscle, every fiber in your neck relaxes. Your shoulders relax . . . your arms . . . your elbows . . . your forearms . . . your wrists . . . your hands . . . and your fingers relax. Your arms feel loose and limp; heavy and loose and limp. Your whole body begins to feel loose and limp. Your neck muscles relax; the front of your neck, the back muscles. If you wish, wiggle your head if necessary to get all the kinks out. Keep breathing deeply and relax. Now your chest. The front part of your chest relaxes . . . and the back part of your chest relaxes. Your abdomen . . . the pit of your stomach, that relaxes. The small of your back, loosen the muscles. Your hips . . . your thighs . . . your knees relax . . . even the muscles in your legs. Your ankles . . . your feet . . . and your toes. Your whole body feels loose and limp. [*Pause.*] And now, as you feel the muscles relaxing, your will notice that you begin to feel relaxed and tired all over. Your body begins to feel v-e-r-y, v-e-r-y tired . . . and you are going to feel d-r-o-w-s-i-e-r, and d-r-o-w-s-i-e-r, from the top of your head right down to your toes. Every breath you take is going to soak in deeper and deeper and deeper, and you feel your body getting drowsier and drowsier.

And now, I want you to imagine, to visualize the most relaxed and quiet and pleasant scene imaginable. Visualize a relaxed and pleasant quiet scene. Any scene that is comfortable. ([*The following may be introduced the first, and perhaps the second induction to give the patient an idea of the kind of imagery that is suitable. Once he selects a scene, these suggestions need not be repeated:*] It can be some scene in your past, or a scene you project in the future. It can be nothing more than being at the beach watching the water breaking on the shore. Or a lake with a sailboat floating lazily by. Or merely looking at the blue sky with one or two billowy clouds moving slowly. Any scene that is quiet and pleasant and makes you feel drowsy. Or a sound like Beethoven's sonata, or any other selection that is soothing.) Drowsier and drowsier and drowsier. You are v-e-r-y weary, and every breath will send you in deeper and deeper and deeper.

As you visualize this quiet scene, I shall count from one to twenty, and when I reach the count of twenty, you will feel yourself in deep. [*The count should be made very slowly.*] One, deeper, deeper, Two, deeper and deeper and deeper. Three . . . drowsier and drowsier. Four, deeper and deeper. Five . . . drowsier and drowsier and drowsier. Six . . . seven, very tired, very relaxed. Eight, deeper and deeper. Nine . . . ten, drowsier and drowsier. Eleven, twelve, thirteen; deeper and deeper. D-r-o-w-s-i-e-r and d-r-o-w-s-i-e-r. Fourteen, drowsier and drowsier. Fifteen . . . sixteen . . .

seventeen, deeper and deeper. Eighteen . . . nineteen . . . and finally twenty.

The following "ego-building" suggestions of Hartland (1965)* may be employed in supportive and some reeducative approaches. They are introduced at this point. Should the recorder have been turned off for the deepening suggestions, it should be turned on at this point.

As I talk to you, you will absorb what I say d-e-e-p-l-y into yourself. "Every day . . . you will become physically *STRONGER* and *FITTER*. You will become *MORE ALERT . . . MORE WIDE AWAKE . . . MORE ENERGETIC.* You will become *MUCH LESS EASILY TIRED . . . MUCH LESS EASILY FATIGUED . . . MUCH LESS EASILY DEPRESSED . . . MUCH LESS EASILY DISCOURAGED.* Every day . . . you will become *SO DEEPLY INTERESTED IN WHATEVER YOU ARE DOING . . . SO DEEPLY INTERESTED IN WHATEVER IS GOING ON . . . THAT YOUR MIND WILL BECOME MUCH LESS PREOCCUPIED WITH YOURSELF . . . AND YOU WILL BECOME MUCH LESS CONSCIOUS OF YOURSELF . . . AND YOUR OWN FEELINGS.*

"Every day . . . *YOUR NERVES WILL BECOME STRONGER AND STEADIER . . . YOUR MIND WILL BECOME CALMER AND CLEARER . . . MORE COMPOSED . . . MORE PLACID . . . MORE TRANQUIL.* You will become *MUCH LESS EASILY WORRIED . . . MUCH LESS EASILY AGITATED . . . MUCH LESS FEARFUL AND APPREHENSIVE . . . MUCH LESS EASILY UPSET.* You will be able to *THINK MORE CLEARLY . . .* you will be able to *CONCENTRATE MORE EASILY . . . YOUR MEMORY WILL IMPROVE . . .* and you will be able to *SEE THINGS IN THEIR TRUE PERSPECTIVE . . . WITHOUT MAGNIFYING THEM . . . WITHOUT ALLOWING THEM TO GET OUT OF PROPORTION.*

"Every day . . . you will become *EMOTIONALLY MUCH CALMER . . . MUCH MORE SETTLED . . . MUCH LESS EASILY DISTURBED.*

"Every day . . . you will feel a *GREATER FEELING OF PERSONAL WELL-BEING . . . A GREATER FEELING OF PERSONAL SAFETY . . . AND SECURITY . . .* than you have felt for a long, long time.

* Reprinted with permission of Dr. John Hartland and the editor of the *American Journal of Clinical Hypnosis*, 3:89–93, 1965.

"Every day . . . *YOU* will become . . . and *YOU* will remain . . . *MORE AND MORE COMPLETELY RELAXED . . . AND LESS TENSE EACH DAY . . . BOTH MENTALLY AND PHYSICALLY.*

"And, *AS* you become . . . and, *AS* you remain . . . *MORE RELAXED . . . AND LESS TENSE EACH DAY . . . SO,* you will develop *MUCH MORE CONFIDENCE IN YOURSELF.*

"*MUCH* more confidence in your ability to *DO . . . NOT* only what you *HAVE* to do each day, . . . but *MUCH* more confidence in your ability to do whatever you *OUGHT* to be able to do . . . *WITHOUT FEAR OF CONSEQUENCES . . . WITHOUT UNNECESSARY ANXIETY . . . WITHOUT UNEASINESS.* Because of this . . . every day . . . you will feel *MORE AND MORE INDEPENDENT . . . MORE ABLE TO 'STICK UP FOR YOURSELF' . . . TO STAND UPON YOUR OWN FEET . . . TO 'HOLD YOUR OWN'* . . . no matter how difficult or trying things may be. And, because all these things *WILL* begin to happen . . . *EXACTLY* as I tell you they will happen, you will begin to feel *MUCH HAPPIER . . . MUCH MORE CONTENTED . . . MUCH MORE CHEERFUL . . . MUCH MORE OPTIMISTIC . . . MUCH LESS EASILY DISCOURAGED . . . MUCH LESS EASILY DEPRESSED.*"

These are broad suggestions that cover most problems. The therapist may interpolate specific suggestions in accord with the special needs of the patient.

Now relax and rest for a minute or so, going deeper, d-e-e-p-e-r, d-e-e-p-e-r, and in a minute or so I shall talk to you, and you will be more deeply relaxed. [*Pause for one minute.*]

In summary, there are four things we are going to accomplish as a result of these exercises, the 4S's: symptom relief, self-confidence, situational control and self-understanding. First, your various symptoms [*enumerate*] are going to be less and less upsetting to you. You will pay less and less attention to them, because they will bother you less and less. You will find that you have a desire to overcome them more and more. As we work at your problem, you will feel that your self-confidence grows and expands. You will feel more assertive and stronger. You will be able to handle yourself better in any situations that come along particularly those that tend to upset you [*enumerate*]. Finally, and most importantly, your understanding of yourself will improve. You will understand better and better what is behind your trouble, how it started and why your symptoms developed. Whenever you

feel your symptoms coming on you will be able to understand what is bringing them about, and you will be able to do something constructive about this, more and more easily. You will continue working on what is behind your problem. [*Pause.*]

You should play the recording at least twice daily. The time is up to you. Remember it makes no difference if you are just pleasantly relaxed, or in a deep state, or asleep, the suggestions will still be effective. [*Pause.*]

Relax and rest and, if you wish, give yourself all the necessary suggestions to *yourself* to feel better. Using the word "you." Take as long as you want. Then you can go to sleep or arouse yourself. When you are ready, you will arouse *yourself* no matter when that is, by counting slowly to yourself from one to five. You will be completely out of it then—awake and alert. Remember, the more you practice, the more intense will be your response, the more easily will your resistances give way. Keep on practicing. And now go ahead—relax—and *when* you are ready—wake *yourself* up.

If a recording is being made, the machine may now be turned off. The patient may be permitted to arouse himself as he pleases, or, if too long a period transpires, he may be aroused by saying:

Now, when *I* count to five, you will be awake. Your eyes will open, you will feel alert and well. One . . . [*pause*] . . . two [*pause*] . . . three . . . [*pause*] . . . four . . . [*pause*] . . . five . . . Lift your eyes.

Other induction techniques may be employed although the foregoing induction method may be all that the therapist needs to use. Elsewhere, detailed accounts of trance induction have been elaborated (Wolberg, LR, 1948, pp. 98–185; 1964, pp. 31–67). In brief, the required steps are these:

1. Promoting motivations that will lead to hypnosis by associating the desire to get well with cooperation in the hypnotic process.
2. Removing misconceptions and fears about hypnosis by explanation and clarification.
3. Introducing a suggestibility test, like the hand clasp test, to demonstrate that the patient can follow directions.
4. Giving the patient a short preparatory talk to the effect that he will not really

go to sleep, even though sleep suggestions will help him relax, and that he will not be asked embarrassing questions or forced to do anything he does not want to do.

5. Inducing a trance by any chosen method.
6. Deepening the trance by suggesting more and more complex hypnotic phenomena.
7. Making therapeutic suggestions.
8. Awakening the patient.
9. Discussing with him his trance experiences.

One of the easiest ways of inducing hypnosis is by means of the suggestibility test of the hand clasp. To do this, the patient is made comfortable in an armchair and asked to relax his body progressively, starting with the muscles in his forehead, then his face, neck, shoulders, arms, back, thighs, and legs. Following this, the patient is enjoined to clasp his hands in front of him, a foot or so away from his eyes. With his eyes fixed on his hands, he is asked to clasp his hands together more and more firmly as the therapist counts from one to five. At the count of five, he is told his hands will be so firmly clamped together that it will be difficult or impossible to separate them. After the patient has cooperated with this suggestion, he is told that his hands will relax a little, but his eyes will begin to feel tired and his eyelids heavy as he stares at his hands. They will get heavier and heavier, and he will get drowsier and drowsier until his eyelids feel like lead. He will then let his eyelids close, and he will feel a pleasant sense of tiredness and relaxation sweeping over him. These suggestions are repeated over and over in a monotonous cadence and in a firm, reassuring tone until the eyes close.

An effective way of inducing a deep trance by means of hand levitation. This method is more difficult to master than the other techniques and calls for greater effort and persistence on the part of the therapist. With the patient's hands resting lightly on his thighs, he is asked to concentrate his attention on everything his hands do. As he notices sensations, such as the warmth of the palms of his hands against his thighs, the texture of his clothing, and perhaps the weight of his hands, he will observe one of the fingers wiggle a little. As soon as he notices this, he is to raise the finger that moved first. Thereafter, he will gaze at his right hand and will notice that the fingers will fan out, the spaces between the fingers getting wider and wider. When this happens, suggestions are made that the fingers will slowly lift from the thigh; then the hand will rise as the arm becomes lighter and lighter; the eyes will become tired and the lids heavy. However, much as he wants to, the patient is not to fall asleep until his arm rises and his hand touches his face. As he gets more and more tired, and his lids get heavier and heavier, his arm and hand will get lighter and rise higher until it touches his face. When it touches his face, he will be relaxed and drowsy and his eyes will be firmly shut. Suggestions are repeated constantly until they are acted on by the patient.

The traditional method of hypnosis through staring at a fixation object continues to be useful. Here a coin, pencil, or shiny object is held above the head, the patient being asked to stare at it while suggestions are made to the effect that he is tired, that his eyes begin to water, and his lids blink until he no longer can keep his eyes open.

As soon as the eyelids close by the use of any of the above methods, the trance may be deepened by suggesting, progressively, heaviness and stiffness of the left arm (limb catalepsy), heaviness of the lids until the patient cannot open them (lid catalepsy), inability to move his extremities or to get out of the chair (inhibition of voluntary movements), hyperesthesia of the hand, anesthesia of the hand, and, perhaps, auditory and visual hallucinations. Some therapists do not go through the formality of deepening hypnosis (the first method of trance induction through muscle relaxation described above illustrates this). However, if probing techniques are to be employed, it is wise to induce as deep hypnosis as possible.

As to the actual syndromes potentially

helped by hypnosis, many therapists find that is valuable in the following ways:

1. As a means of removing certain conversion symptoms, like paralysis, aphonia, and some psychophysiologic reactions.
2. As a way of controlling the drinking urge in some alcoholic patients.
3. As a vehicle of establishing the authority of the therapist, which the patient does not dare to defy, thus inhibiting acting-out, especially in psychopathic personalities.
4. As a means of bolstering persuasive therapy in obsessive-compulsive reactions.
5. As treatment for certain habit disorders, like smoking, sexual difficulties, insomnia, overeating, and nail biting.
6. As a mode of reinforcing desensitization and counterconditioning in behavior therapy, as in phobias.

In insight therapy hypnosis may result in the following:

1. Removal of amnesia in stress reactions with release of repressed memories and emotions.
2. Lifting of repression in conversion and dissociative reactions.
3. Resolution of repression in the treatment of other conditions, like anxiety reactions and phobic reactions.
4. Dissipation of certain tranference and content resistances.
5. Facilitation of dreams and free associations.

In certain problems and syndromes, where the objective is resolution of deep characterologic distortions and removal of blocks toward emotional maturation, hypnosis does not seem to contribute too much. In other cases, however, hypnosis may be useful where psychotherapy alone fails. For instance, where repression is so intense that it defies all attempts at resolution, free association, dream interpretation, and other traditional routes to the unconscious are of little avail. Hypnosis here may be singularly effective. In supportive therapy, where an authoritarian relationship cannot be set up with facililty, hypnosis may put the therapist

in a sufficiently omnipotent position to produce better results.

There is another use of hypnosis that has not received the attention it deserves, that is, as an experience in relationship. All therapy requires the establishing of a working relationship between therapist and patient. It is impossible, without good rapport, to help the patient to an understanding of his problem and to the resolution of the manifold resistances in utilizing insight in the direction of change. The mere induction of a trance produces a feeling of closeness and trust in a remarkably short time resolving certain transference resistances and enabling the patient to proceed toward the exploration of anxiety-provoking inner conflicts. In some patients one may employ hypnosis at the start of therapy, and once a relationship has crystallized, one may go on to implement the traditional psychotherapies without hypnosis. This may cut down on the tme required for the establishing of a working relationship.

Another technique utilized occasionally during the exploratory phase of therapy is the training of the patient in self-hypnosis, suggesting to him that he will investigate spontaneously, through dreams and fantasies in the self-induced trance state, puzzling aspects of his problem and also that he will work out various resistances that may arise. In this way the patient actively participates in the investigative process and time may be saved. The first induction method above may easily be adapted to self-hypnosis. More details may be found elsewhere (Wolberg, LR, 1965, pp. 277–280). Self-hypnosis may be employed on a maintenance basis where necessary. Qualms about its use need not be felt; addiction to and dependency on self-hypnosis has not occurred in my experience. Appendix V contains an outline for self-hypnosis that may be given to the patient.

Symptom removal through hypnosis should not pose undue risks. The consequences will depend on the way the removal took place and the attitude of the hypnotist. One does not rush into a complex psychiatric picture like a bull in a china shop. Unfortunate aftermaths are usually the product of a disturbed relationship rather than the result of hypnosis. Unsettling reactions to hypnosis do not seem to be greater than untoward responses to any other therapeutic relationship. A study by Litton (1966) of 19 cases of hysterical aphonias was undertaken to test the hypothesis that rapid removal of a symptom will eventuate in substitutive symptoms or in the precipitation of a breakdown in homeostatis. Removal of the symptom through hypnosis was successful in 14 cases and resisted in 5. Follow-up showed no unpleasant sequelae. In 2 cases there was a return of the symptom after 7 months, and in 1 case after 12 months. Re-administration of hypnosis rapidly removed the symptom.

Hypnosis provides a dynamic interpersonal situation that evokes processes in the patient that may be productively examined as a biopsy of how the patient responds to an intensive interpersonal relationship. The patient will project into the hypnotic situation his basic defenses and demands. His responses to hypnotic induction, and to the trance experience itself, may constitute the material around which the therapeutic work is organized. The specific meaning to him of being put into a trance can bring forth various irrational defenses and fears. For instance, a patient with frigidity was referred to me by her psychoanalyst for some hypnotic work. After the third induction, the patient revealed to me that she was aware of her need to keep her legs crossed during the entire trance state. So tightly did she squeeze her thighs together that they ached when she emerged from the trance. Prior to the next induction, I instructed her to keep her legs separated. As I proceeded with suggestions, she became flushed, opened her eyes, and exlaimed that she knew what upset her. I reminded her of her grandfather who, on several occasions, when she was a small child, tossed her into bed and held her close to his body. She had felt his erect penis against her body, which both excited and frightened her. It became apparent that the hypnotic experience constituted for her an episode during which she hoped for and feared a repetition of this sexual seduction, and her leg crossing constituted a defense against these fantasies. Continued trance inductions desensitized her to her fears and

were followed by an improved sexual functioning with her husband.

The hypnotic situation may also enable the patient to recall important past experiences. A man of 45 with a claustrophobic condition of 10 years duration was referred by an analyst who had treated the patient for several years. While his analysis (four times weekly for 2½ years) had enabled the patient to mature considerably in his relationship with people, the phobic problem remained as an obstinate block to the financial success he potentially could achieve in his business. The phobia made it impossible for him to dine with people, and, whenever he was forced in a situation in which he had to eat with others, he excused himself several times during the meal so that he could go to the bathroom to disgorge his food.

The patient was inducted into a hypnotic state, and the suggestion was made that he would go back to the period in his life when he had first experienced a feeling similar to that in his phobia. After several minutes had gone by, it became apparent from his sweating, bodily movements, and moaning that the patient was undergoing a profound emotional reaction. Asked to talk, he murmured, in a voice scarcely audible:

I have a peculiar feeling; the chair is narrow and you are closer. I get a good feeling, a secure feeling [*breaks out into crying*]; my father, I hated him. He rejected me. He was very critical. He never praised me for anything. There was something in him that wouldn't permit him to like me. I hate him. I hate him. [*The patient beats the side of the chair.*] I feel all choked up. I think of my mother. I am little. I see her [*compulsive crying*].

[*On being brought back to the waking state, the patient exclaimed*] This is one of the most remarkable experiences I ever had. This peculiar feeling. I felt the chair was much narrower than it is and that you were getting closer. I felt a good feeling, a secure feeling, like I sometimes felt when I went to see my analyst. But then something happened. I see myself in a restaurant with my parents, a child. I am that child. I am downstairs eating lobster. I felt as if I was going to throw up, and I didn't want to throw up at the table. I kept it in and went into a panic. I thought of my father. I hated him. He rejected me. He was extremely critical. He never praised me for anything. Something in him that wouldn't permit him to compliment me. When I was 3 or 4 years old, mother used to push food into me and I used to vomit it. When I was 10, I had polio and I was afraid to be alone. I was afraid to let mother go out. I was afraid that something would happen to her. If an accident occurred, what would happen to me? I was afraid to stay alone. I had great anxiety until she came home. Before I was 13 I wasn't allowed to go myself. My mother was a terrific worry-wart about my physical condition and about where I was at nighttime.

The patient's recall of his early traumatic incident enabled us to get into other intimacies. An important one was his relationship with his analyst. It became apparent that he had become bogged down in transference resistance. Discussing this appeared to change his feeling toward his analyst, from one of resentment to that of gratitude that he had been helped significantly in many dimensions. Soon he desensitized himself to the phobic situation.

In working with resistances to the revelation of inner content, the way suggestions are made may help avoid precipitating too much anxiety. The therapist, if he feels the patient is unable to tolerate exposure for the moment, may say: (1) "Perhaps there is some information you do not wish to tell me at this time. It is all right to hold this back until the next time you see me or whenever you are ready." Or (2) "I wonder how long it will be before you will want to let yourself give up these uncomfortable symptoms. I do not want you to give them up all at once. Try hard to hold on to one bit of your symptom and not to let it disappear for at least a week or so after you feel comfortable."

In reconstructive therapy hypnosis may be employed to expedite free association in patients who are blocked. It may also foster dream recall. A patient came to me for hypnosis to help her recover a dream that kept eluding her, but which she felt was significant. It had first appeared, she claimed, a long time ago during her psychoanalysis, but she had forgotten it. Try as hard as she could, she was not able to bring it back. Years had gone by and she had stopped her analysis, but periodically she had the impression that the dream returned, only to vanish with daylight. The situation intrigued me enough to consent to

utilize hypnosis, during which I told her that if she had a spontaneous dream, she would remember it. On awakening she revealed that a most interesting thing had happened to her while she was relaxing. The meaning of the forgotten dream had flashed through her mind.

"All of a sudden I realized that the dream was that I was all alone and I don't want to be alone. I don't want to be alone. I shed copious tears." This experience brought about a "heavy sadness" which haunted the patient for several days. A spontaneous dream followed: "I go over the rooms that we lived in as a child. The rooms are empty. I'm all alone. Where is everybody? My mother, father, sister, brothers, where are they? There is nobody there. Ours was a busy house. Copious tears." Burdened by an even deeper depressive feeling to which she could not associate in the waking state, the patient was rehypnotized and requested to say what was on her mind. She replied: "Please everybody, please everybody, come back, come back. Don't leave me alone again. What did I do, what did I do that this should happen." In bitter tears she revealed a memory of having as a tiny child been sent to a hospital after burning herself. Separation from her mother for a protracted period had initiated fear that she would be punished and sent away if she did "anything bad." The traumatic incident (which was validated) was followed by separation of her father from her mother when she was 3 years of age, for which the patient blamed herself unfairly. Therapy including teaching the patient self-hypnosis, during which she was enjoined to revive these images, to master the emotions related to them, and to revalue them in her mind. It was through this means that she desensitized herself. Ultimately her depression was resolved. Hypnotically induced dreams may, in this way, where insight is fragmented, serve to weave unrelated mental segments into a meaningful fabric.

A case illustration of how hypnosis may aid in the uncovering process, with a recording of hypnosis through the handclasp method, may be found on pages 583–587.

NARCOTHERAPY

The difficulty of inducing hypnosis in certain subjects, the relatively long time required to produce a trance even in susceptible persons, and the inability on the part of some therapists to acquire skill in trance induction, have brought into prominence a simple technique of promoting hypnosis by the intravenous injection of a hypnotic drug, such as, Sodium Amytal (sometimes called the "Amytal interview") or Sodium Pentothal (Horsley, 1936, 1943; Grinker & Spiegel, 1945; Sargant & Shorvon, 1945; Hoch & Polatin, 1952).

These substances produce a cortical depression with relaxation and heightened susceptibility to suggestion, reassurance, and persuasion. The name given to this combined use of narcosis and supportive therapy is "narcosuggestion." The psychologic regression in narcosis, as in hypnosis, incites archaic dependency feelings toward the therapist and expedites authoritative supportive procedures. Acute anxiety reactions, some manic and catatonic reactions which constitute emergencies, or assaultive or self-destructive tendencies may sometimes be effectively treated by narcosuggestion as may other conditions that call for supportive measures. In phobias the patient, in a light state of narcosis, may be exposed to counterconditioning techniques of behavioral therapy, for instance to Wolpe's "reciprocal inhibition" technique (see Chapter 49). As a diagnostic aid narcotherapy is sometimes employed to unmask a schizophrenic tendency that is concealed by defensive reactions in the waking state. This can help in treatment planning.

In some instances narcosis, by releasing cortical inhibition, liberates charges of pent-up emotion that have been kept from awareness by repression. The result is an emotional catharsis. This effect may also be facilitated in narcosis by suggestion, by persistent questioning and probing, and by encouraging the patient to explore painful areas of his life. Recollection of repudiated traumatic memories and experiences may remove mental blocks, flurries of anxiety,

depression, and psychosomatic symptoms associated with the repression of such harassing foci. These effects have been found helpful in the treatment of certain emotional problems, particularly acute stress reactions (traumatic neuroses, transportation and industrial accidents, catastrophes like floods and fire, and war neuroses), and some anxiety and hysterical reactions. In the war neuroses, particularly, beneficial results are possible especially in cases of recent origin treated before rigid defenses have organized themselves. The working through of the repressed or suppressed material in both narcotic and waking states helps to insure the permanency of the "cure." In chronic war and civilian neuroses, however, the patient does not seem to benefit so readily, since the illness has structuralized itself and stubborn resistances block progress. The "cathartic" or "analytic" use of narcosis has been referred to by various observers as "narcoanalysis," "narcosynthesis," and "narcocatharsis." Another effect of drug interviews is to release pleasant positive feelings, which I. Stevenson et al. (1974) have found is conducive to symptomatic improvement.

While narcotherapy is principally employed for purposes of short-term therapy, it is sometimes introduced during the course of long-term insight psychotherapy where little material is forthcoming or obdurate resistance blocks the exploratory effort. Here one may frequently save a treatment situation that has come to a stalemate by inducing narcosis and liberating repressive forces through concerted probing. Transference phenomena that have evaded both patient and therapist sometimes become dramatically operative as emotionally charged material is released. An emergency use of narcotherapy is in the dealing with acute anxiety and panic states that occur during the course of long-term therapy. These symptoms may be so severe that they threaten the therapeutic relationship. In obsessional neurosis, for instance, occasional sessions devoted to narcosis may prevent alarming reactions at phases when defensive forces subside too rapidly. The secret of narcosynthesis in chronic neurosis lies in the facilitated communcation that it induces in severely repressed patients.

Where repressed incidents are of relatively recent origin, cathartic release may provide a dramatic improvement or cure. However in most cases a structuralization of traumatic events has occurred, barricaded by many defenses, including protective character traits, so that the exposure during narcosis (no matter how dramatic the results) seems to do little for the patient. It is essential, therefore, as soon as the patient is capable of remembering the events to subject this material to repeated examination in the waking state, particularly probing for associated emotions. During this process periodic sessions with narcosis may be helpful. Should anxiety be strong or repression too interfering, the anxieties and defensive reactions may yield, and the need for narcosis will them be unnecessary.

Another use of narcosis is to expedite the induction of hypnosis in resistant subjects. During narcosis it may be possible to give the patient suggestions to the effect that he will be susceptible to hypnosis. Suggestions must be detailed and specific, covering every aspect of the induction process. For example, the patient may be told that when she is shown a fixation object, she will gaze at it, and as she does, she will notice that her eyes will water, her lids will get heavy, her breathing will deepen, and she will fall asleep. She will sleep deeper and deeper until she is as deeply asleep as at present. These suggestions should be repeated and the patient may be asked if she understands thoroughly what she is to do. If she seems confused, the suggestions should be repeated when the drug effect is not so pounounced. As soon as the patient understands what is expected of her, she is asked to repeat what will happen at the next session. After the narcotic session, and before the patient is fully awake, she may be shown the fixation object and sleep suggestions given to her with the added suggestion, when she closes her eyes, that the next time she is shown the object, she will go to sleep faster and more deeply. Again, before leaving the room, this suggestion is repeated. The technique works best when positive transference phenomena are operative in the narcotic state. It may not succeed in the event the patient does not understand what to do, or if the patient is in a state of hostile resistance.

Induction of Narcosis

The actual technique of inducing narcosis is simple. Most therapists consider amobarbital sodium (Amytal) the drug of choice. There are various techniques of administration. Sodium Amytal is supplied in sterile powder form in ampules containing 125 mg (2 gr), 250 mg (4 gr) and 500 mg (7½ gr). Ampules of sterile water are also available. The 500 mg size is generally utilized, sterile water being added while rotating (not shaking) the ampule to dissolve the drug. It is important to employ fresh solutions (no older than 30 minutes) and to see to it that they are clear (not cloudy). Some patients require large amounts of the drug, and a second ampule of 7½ gr may be necessary. A small gauge intravenous needle attached to a large syringe is used for administration. The injection should be slow, about 1 cc per minute, to avoid depressing the respiration. While the injection takes place, the patient is asked to count backward from 100 to 1. When the patient becomes confused, mumbles, or stops counting, the injection should stop and treatment begun, such as questioning the patient about feelings, attitudes, and memories. Should too great anxiety intervene, more drug is slowly injected. However, in many cases reassurance that he will feel better after talking will alone suffice without the need for further sedation. The patient may be given interpretations and suggestions that he can if he wishes remember any of the material that he has talked about after he awakens or forget it until he is ready to talk about it. He may be requested to remember his dreams. After the narcotic session he may be allowed to rest or sleep. An ampule of methamphetamine or similar stimulant is held in readiness in the event of respiratory embarrassment, and at the termination of the interview it may be introduced to facilitate awakening. Some therapists inject the 20 mg of methamphetamine intravenously at first.

Slowly then, through the same needle, Sodium Amytal (500 mg in 20 cc sterile water) is injected until drowsiness and dysarthia appear. Or, 500 mg of Sodium Amytal in 9 cc sterilized distilled water are combined with a 20 mg ampule of amphetamine sulfate (Benzedrine) and introduced intravenously at the rate of 1 cc per minute.

Various drugs have been employed instead of amobarbital. Pentothal Sodium (supplied in sterile vials of 500 mg and 1 gm, dissolved in 20 or 50 cc of sterile water, respectively, and injected at the rate of 2 cc a minute) is a common substitute, the dosage (approximately the same as Amytal) varying with individual patients. Methohexital sodium (Brevital), a short-acting barbiturate, is another substitute being supplied in sterile powder in ampules of 500 mg, 2.5 gm, and 5 gm. It may be utilized as a continuous drip, 500 mg of Brevital being added to 250 cc of sterile isotonic sodium chloride solution. This provides a 0.2 percent solution. For slow intermittent injection a 1 percent solution is used titrating the amount injected against the reaction of the patient. Sometimes methamphetamine is given intravenously following a intravenous drip of Brevital (Green, DO, & Reimer, 1974). Scarborough and Denson (1958) described a Pentothal-Desoxyn combination similar to that of Rothman and Sward (1956). The patient lies supine on a couch and Sodium Pentothal (a 10-gm ampule of Sodium Pentothal powder is dissolved in 400 cc of normal sterile saline solution) and Desoxyn (in multiple-dose 30 cc bottles that contains 20 mg of drug per cc) are made available. The equipment consists of a small sterile tray containing two alcohol sponges, a soft rubber tourniquet, a small Band-Aid, a syringe containing the Pentothal, and a second syringe containing the Desoxyn. The dosage of Pentothal and Desoxyn vary with different patients. At the start 5 cc (125 mg) of the Pentothal solution may be injected in the vein *as rapidly as possible*. This results in a dazed state and an abrupt stoppage of respiration from 5 to 20 seconds. The syringe is removed from the needle and ¼ cc (5 mg) of Desoxyn is injected through the same needle. The second session usually requires 8 cc (200 mg) of Pentothal and ½ cc

(10 mg) of Desoxyn; the third session, about 10 cc (250 mg) of Pentothal and 1 cc (20 mg) of Desoxyn. The secret of such small doses lies in the fact that the patient is flooded with the drug rapidly; at the end of the hour he is usually quite alert and able to carry on his regular activities. Under the drug influence even ordinarily uncommunicative patients engage fluently in the psychotherapeutic interview. Where narcosynthesis is done only occasionally, it is simpler to utilize the 500-mg ampules of Pentothal that come in a combination package with a 20-ml (cc) ampule of sterile water. Because of the abuse potential, injectable Desoxyn is no longer available. If a substitute amphetamine can be found, this may be employed in proper dosage.

Methylphenidate hydrochloride (Ritalin) has been found helpful in breaking through blocks in the exploration of the problems of alcoholics (Hartert & Browne-Mayers, 1958). Exploratory interviews are carried out after intravenous injection of 20 to 40 mg of the drug. The patients respond by verbalizing freely with greater introspection and critical self-evaluation as well as more intensive involvement in the therapeutic situation. Since Ritalin in injectable form is not now available, oral administration prior to interviews may be considered with caution since Ritalin may be substituted by the alcoholic for alcohol.

In the course of narcotherapy, as has been mentioned previously, drug injections should be halted temporarily if the patient gets excessively incoherent. Should the patient become too alert, more drug is introduced. It goes without saying that adequate preparations must be made for the patient so that he can sleep off the effects of the medication.

In the event psychotic material is brought up during narcosis, giving evidence of a potential disintegrative tendency, therapeutic goals and methods should be reappraised. Where the patient becomes too upset through release of traumatic material, it is best not to let the excitement mount to the point of overtaxing the ego. More drug is injected to put the patient to sleep, which will enable him to overcome the cathartic effects of the narcosis.

VIDEOTAPE RECORDING

Videotape technology has been advancing at a rapid rate and it is being adapted to increasing areas of health and science. Among its many possibilities are self-observation and self-confrontation (Berger, MM, 1971; Melnick & Tims, 1974), which have been applied to the teaching and learning situation (Torkelson & Romano, 1967). The evolvement of video psychiatry has followed in the wake of this. Videotapes are being produced to teach psychopathology, child development, and psychiatric treatment. A cassette entitled "Electronic Textbook of Psychiatry" has been prepared by the New York State Psychiatric Institute's Department of Educational Research, a typical cassette being "Depression: Retarded and Agitated Forms." (Roche Report, 1974) Written linear-programmed texts are being arranged with interdigitating videotaped clinical illustrations to enliven the teaching of psychiatry.

The recording of psychotherapy sessions with opportunity for repeated playback offers patients an unparalleled learning experience that can catalyze the entire therapeutic process. As recorders and cameras have become less and less expensive, the video adjunct has been employed with increasing frequency in clinics and private practice, particularly in group, family, and marital therapy (Alger & Hogan, 1969; Czajkoski, 1968; Danet, 1969; Stoller, 1967, 1969;). In behavior therapy (Bernal, 1969; Melnick & Tims, 1974), and in role playing and psychodrama, its employment is proving valuable. In selected cases persons in individual therapy may find self-observation of substantial value (Geertsma & Reivich, 1965; Paredes et al., 1969). An additional dividend is the fact that a therapist may observe one's own therapeutic performance and interpersonal conduct including countertransference, which can enhance one's own development and sharpen one's skills. The objective data issuing from even fragments of a single session can provide material for study and discussion over weeks and months. Progress or regress may also be scrutinized by comparing the productions of successful sessions. The videotape recording may also be utilized for the purpose of supervising a therapist's work, providing more authentic data than can be conveyed orally by the therapist.

The technique is simple. There is no need to conceal the equipment because after going through the preliminary brief anxiety and self-consciousness phases, patients readily make an adaptation to videotaping. For use of the tape in therapy, 10 minutes of the beginning of the session may be recorded and then played back through the monitor, or recording may be started when a significant period of the session is being approached. The patients are instructed to interrupt the playback if they wish to comment on discrepancies of behavior or if they desire to describe the feelings that they had at the time or have now.

Replay of small segments over and over may be rewarding either for the purposes of clarification and discussion or for desensitization where patients manifest a "shock" reaction at their images. Most patients are surprised at how often their appearance and behavior fails to reveal their shyness, anger, fear, distress, and other emotions. They become sensitive to the pervasive contradictory and paradoxical communications from verbal and nonverbal sources. For example, some patients are not aware of how angry, argumentative, and unpleasant they are in an interpersonal situation until they objectively see and listen to themselves. Opportunities for clarification, heightened awareness, and more constructive reactions are many. Where, as in group, family, or marital therapy, a patient's responses have been maladaptive and the patient realizes this, he may benefit from repeatedly playing back sessions to grasp incongruities of messages. Should resistance develop in therapy or a stalemate have been reached, videotaping may open up dimensions that succeed in breaking through the block. The availability of split-screen and special-effects generators through which one may obtain video multiimage distortions to elicit repressed material is an interesting new use for this adjunct (Roche Report, 1973). Original and unique ways of employing tapes are being elaborated by researchers and clinicians, and innovations will undoubtedly continue to emerge. These eventually will provide material for scientifically controlled studies to test their utility and validity.

Melnick and Tims (1974) make some excellent suggestions regarding the physical surroundings and equipment for videotaping. The room should be of ample size to accommodate comfortably the patients while providing enough space to operate the camera. It should be well ventilated. Generally a 15 feet by 18 feet size is good for a group of 8 to 10 people. If a group is the subject, the patients are seated in a semicircle with the open end accommodating the camera. Sound-absorbing materials and furniture in the room, such as accoustic tile on the ceiling, carpeting on the floor, draperies on the windows, and cloth covered chairs help the accoustics. As to selection of equipment, various machines are readily available. One-half inch decks are available at moderate price and are usually ample for the average psychotherapist. A 1-inch recorder is excellent for educational institutions. Cassette recorders are now being introduced, such as the Sony Betamax Videocassette Console Recorder (LV 1901), which utilizes low cost one-half inch cassette tapes. Cameras for black and white recording range in price, depending primarily on the type of lens, e.g., a fixed-lens AVC 1420 being considerably cheaper than a zoom lens. The camera should be equipped with a viewfinder for ready focusing. A camera with a zoom lens will require an operator to focus on the entire group and on individuals. The operator can be the therapist, cotherapist, or a group member. Where taping is on the entire group and not on individuals, selecting a camera with a wide-angle lens (12.5 mm) is convenient since once set up it does not need an operator. The best microphone is an omnidirectional dynamic table microphone placed on a table or microphone stand. A monitor for the video and sound signals is the final piece of equipment, and for this purpose an ordinary television set is usually ample. Additional optional equipment is also available, such as the use of two cameras with a camera switcher, split-screen apparatus, a special-

effects generator, and a second recorder with an electronic editor, where tapes are to be used for educational purposes. The original choice of equipment should allow for expansion with optional items should the latter be contemplated. If one cannot afford or utilize the most sophisticated apparatus, the simple portable one-half-inch deck and an inexpensive camera and microphone are sufficient, and they may well merit an investment.

THE TELEPHONE

Discrete use of the telephone as an adjunctive device is valuable in emergencies that arise in the course of psychotherapy. These fortunately are rare. Therapists may, for their patients' own good and for their own peace of mind, discourage patients calling for anything other than severe problems that cannot await solution until the next treatment session. Should it become apparent that the patient is taking advantage of the privilege of discrete telephoning, the therapist may focus during interviewing on the patient's need for telephone contact. The patient may be reminded that making his own decisions during therapy is both strengthening and helpful even where such decisions do not turn out well since this provides material for exploration. If the patient is told that he may telephone whenever he desires to talk, the flood of inconsequential calls that can result will very likely annoy the therapist and create resentments in him; this annoyance will adversely affect relations with the patient. In addition, if allowed at all, the therapist may be unable to stop the calls without hurting the working relationship.

There are several exceptions, however, to the rule of encouraging only the most urgent calls. First, patients with a suicidal tendency do need the assurance of immediate contact when necessary. Here the therapist may have to insist that the patient telephone when he gets too depressed. The lives of many patients have been saved by their ability to communicate with the therapist in crisis situations, and prior to the effective working of prescribed antipsychotic drugs. Moreover, should the patient have taken an overdose of drugs, unintentially or with suicidal design, reporting this will enable the therapist to call an ambulance or the police to bring the patient to an emergency unit of a hospital for therapy. Second, patients for whom drug therapy has been prescribed should routinely be requested to telephone if they have peculiar or upsetting reactions to the medication. Hypotension, symptoms of blood dyscrasias, and severe dystonic reactions may need immediate medical intervention.

It goes without saying that the telephone is a vital therapeutic instrument for crisis intervention (Lester & Brockopp, 1973; Williams, T, 1971). "Hotlines" exist in larger cities where young polydrug abusers, suicidally inclined persons, rape victims, and others seeking help for some misfortune or for general information can make contact with knowledgeable persons for guidance and counseling. There are for some clients advantages in retaining anonymity over the telephone and also in talking to an anonymous person onto whom the client can project his fantasies of an adequate helping person he can use for his own needs (Lester, D, 1974). It is vital where nonprofessional persons staff such services that they be adequately supervised by professional persons. The telephone is an important resource, functioning to provide people with a reassuring human contact and a conduit for referral to available agencies in the community.

Telephone therapy also has a place where patients, for one reason or another, are unable for physical reasons to come to treatment in person (Miller, WB, 1972; Robertiello, 1972). There are times where ill health, or absence of transportation, or travel away from home makes it impossible for a patient in psychotherapy to keep appointments, and yet a continuity of treatment is vital. Interestingly, a telephone may make it easier for a patient to reveal certain kinds of information than a face-to-face interview, particularly where a transference reaction exists. This may initiate a breakthrough when the patient returns for regular sessions.

PLAY THERAPY

Play therapy provides children with a means of giving vent to conflicts, ideas, and fantasies that they cannot ordinarily verbalize. One may look upon it as a special nonverbal language through which a child communicates. It is, in a certain sense, an acting-out, permitting through varied activities overt, nonverbal expressions to innermost feelings. "Play therapy does not belong to any specific school of therapy. Each therapist must first learn to understand and to master this particular language of the child, and then integrate the mastery of the therapeutic tool with the particular tenet of his own therapeutic orientation. The child's play, in and by itself, is no more therapeutic than the patient's free associations and relating of dreams. It is the therapist's skill and sensitivity which helps the adult patient to understand the often meaningless stringing together of seemingly unrelated thoughts in free association. In a similar way the child therapist helps the child to understand the real meaning behind his spontaneous play activities" (Woltman, 1959).

Children, in line with their developmental growth, play act and think differently at different age levels. A 3-year-old may be playing with only a single toy, while an 8- or 10-year-old child may build a complicated structure. It must further be recognized that a child will select that kind of play activity which he feels is best suited for the expression of his particular problem. Burning paper, throwing paper airplanes, or playing out elaborate automobile crashes can be properly used in therapy as long as one understands that all three activities constitute an acting-out of aggressive impulses. The specific meanings that play materials and activities have for the child are described by R. E. Hartley et al. (1952 a & b), who also has summarized play activities of children in terms of year levels (1957). A comprehensive study of children's play activites with miniature life toys has been presented by Lois Murphy (1956). The contributions of schools of therapy to play therapy are found in the writings of Melanie Klein

(1935, 1955), Anna Freud (1928), and Virginia Axline (1947), who is a follower of Carl Rogers. Specific play media and activities have been applied in the therapeutic treatment of children (Bender & Woltman, 1936, 1937; Erikson, EH, 1944, 1951; Gondor, 1954; Lowenfeld, 1939; Lyle & Holly, 1941; Trail, 1945; Whiles, 1941; Woltman, 1940, 1950, 1951, 1952, 1955, 1956). Play group therapy has been described by Ginott (1961). The free play technique of Gitelson (1939) may be useful in some cases. Where it is difficult to create in the child an attitude that is conducive to spontaneous play, or where specific problems or time limitations play a decisive role, the methods described by Conn (1938), D. Levy (1937, 1939), J. C. Solomon (1938, 1940, 1951), Muro (1968), Nelson (1967), and Nickerson (1973) are helpful.

The methods of play therapy appear to be particularly suited to the expression of unconscious aggression and to the acting-out of jealousies in relation to a parent or sibling. They are also an excellent media for exploration of sexual and excretory fantasies. The beneficial effects of play therapy in part accrue from the insight patients gain into their unconscious problems. More immediately, a child acts out in play, hostile, sexual, excretory, and other fantasies as well as in anxiety-provoking life situations. The cathartic effect of play therapy temporarily alleviates tension. This is not as important as the gradual understanding that develops into the nature and effects of unconscious conflict. The noncondemning attitude of the therapist, who neither criticizes nor restricts the patient, but accords the child freedom in expressing overtly impulses and fantasies of a dread nature, alleviates guilt feelings, and eventually makes it possible for the patient to acknowledge and to tolerate repressed drives. As these are repeatedly acted out in play, the patient becomes desensitized to their influence. Understanding and control are developed by the therapist's carefully timed interpretations.

Controversy exists regarding the preferred approach in play therapy. A research study of play therapy in 298 outpatient child clinics in the United States indicated that 75 percent of the reporting clinics regard their theoretical orientation as psychoanalytic, 17 percent as nondirective, 5 percent as directive, and 3 percent as between directive and nondirective (Filmer & Hillson, 1959). At the same time, the majority of clinics considered Frederick Allen (1942) as the authority most representative of their orientation. Allen, whose concepts, reflecting those of Rank, stresses the relationship fostered through play therapy as the very core of the therapeutic process. This is in contrast with the approach of Melanie Klein (1955), which bypasses ego defenses and actively and immediately interprets the deep unconscious meanings of the child's play. The less radical approach of Anna Freud (1946) advocates interpretation of unconscious motivation only after a relationship has been established with the child.

ART THERAPY

The use of artistic media, such as drawing, painting, and finger painting, as ways of exploring and working through unconscious conflict has been advocated by many therapists (Arlow & Kadis, 1946; Bender, 1937; Brick, 1944; Fink et al, 1967; Hartley, RE, & Gondor, 1956; Levick, 1973; Mosse, 1940; Napoli, 1946, 1947; Naumburg, 1947, 1952, 1953, 1966; Schopbach, 1964; Stern, MM, 1952a & b). These productions, whatever their nature, serve as means of emotional catharsis and as vehicles for revealing inner problems, wishes and fears. Art therapy is particularly valuable in patients who find it difficult to talk freely. It is predicated on the principle that fundamental thoughts and feelings, derived from the unconscous, often find expression in images rather than in words (Naumburg, 1966). Through art a method of symbolic communication develops between patient and therapist. Though untrained in art, individuals can often project their conflicts into visual forms, to which they may then expeditiously associate freely. Dreams, fantasies, and childhood memories may also more readily be represented in a pictorial way rather than in speech. Patients who are blocked in verbalizing may find that drawing or painting their dreams and fantasies expedites translation of their thoughts and feelings into words. The function of the art therapist is not to interpret, but to encourage the patient to discover for himself the meaning of his productions that provide symbolic ways of representing unconscious phenomena (Lewis, NDC, 1928; Griffiths, 1935; Fairbairn, 1938a & b; Pickford, 1938; McIntosh & Pickford, 1943). The patient projects into his creations significant emotional meanings. This is very much similar to what happens in the Rorschach test (Vernonon, 1935). Furthermore, the symbolized content permits of an expression of inner impulses without too many guilt feelings. The art therapist accepts the patient's projections without punitive or judgmental responses. Interpretations are offered to the patient at strategic times. Interpretive approaches to art symbols have been described by Appel (1931), Jung (1934), Pfister (1934), Liss (1938), Baynes (1939), Harms (1939, 1941), Reitman (1939), Mira (1940), Naumburg (1944, 1950), and E. Kris (1952). Other informative articles are those of Levy (1934), F. J. Curran (1939), Despert (1937), Mosse (1940), and Bychowski (1947).

In the actual technique, the patient may draw or paint during the treatment hour as he sees fit, or he may work at home and bring his productions to the therapist. Drawing and painting may be employed not only individually, but also in groups (Naumburg & Caldwell, 1959), being especially valuable in therapy with children (Kramer, 1972). Simple, easily manipulable art materials must be made available to patients, particularly if they have never drawn or painted. Semihard pastels and casein or poster paints are to be preferred to oil paints. The therapist may have to instruct and encourage beginners by what is known as the "scribble technique." In this the patient is instructed to draw without a conscious plan by making a continuous line which may assume an irregular pattern as it meanders over the paper in various directions. The patient is then encouraged to search for a design, object, animal or person while holding the paper in different directions. Once the patient has learned that he may draw

and associate freely, he is enjoined to work in art as spontaneously as possible.

Where a patient appears emotionally blocked or does not express appropriate feeling toward a special person or situation, asking him to construct an image or make a drawing representing the person or situation may release productive emotions and associations. The fact that the patient can control his drawings gives him a feeling of greater leverage over his affective life. This is especially important in individuals with weak defenses who in being encouraged to draw have an option of how far they wish to go.

An attempt may be made to influence mood by asking the patient to draw something that depicts a special emotion. Thus, a depressed person may be asked to draw a happy scene, an anxiety-ridden soul to depict a relaxed and peaceful sketch. In a more cathartic vein, a patient may be requested to delineate on paper exactly how he feels or what he would like to express if he could. The patient may also be encouraged, and perhaps helped, to depict the completion of an action essential for his well-being on the theory that he may through this means symbolize a breakthrough of his paralysis and then respond behaviorally. Sometimes the psychotherapist may utilize as an adjunctive helper an art therapist. When such a person is used, regular conferences of the two must be held.

In group therapy some therapists find it useful to suggest that patients draw pictures on a common theme. Comparing the drawings and getting the group members' associations can provide much stimulation and enhance group activity. This technique has also been employed with smaller groups, as in family therapy (Kwiatowska, 1967).

The activity of the therapist in relation to the patient's drawings will vary. One may sit quietly and observe what is being drawn, waiting for the patient's explanations, or may comment on or ask questions about the images, or may interpret what he or she believes the patient is trying to say. The patient may be encouraged to draw certain items, (i.e., dreams, memories, fantasies, members of his family, etc.). The therapist may even sketch on the patient's picture or suggest additions or alterations. Questions about the symbols may be asked, and the patient may be encouraged to make associations.

Where a patient responds to images that he has drawn with fear, anger, or detachment, it is likely that he has not been able cognitively to integrate what he has produced. This may provide valuable leads for the interview focus. Encouraging him to repeat the same theme in drawing may result in therapeutic desensitization and conflict resolution.

Criticism of art therapy relates to the tendency among some art therapists to overvalue the medium of communication—the art production—and to confuse the latter with the therapeutic process itself. While therapy may thus be regarded as a constant uncovering phenomenon that brings up interesting material, there may be a denial or minimization of the true therapeutic vehicle—the relationship between patient and therapist. The use of art as an adjunct in therapy is, nevertheless, considered by some analysts as helpful to patients who express themselves better in drawing and in other artistic ways than in free association or dreams. While the content of therapy may be focused on the art expression, the therapeutic process goes through the usual phases of transference and resistance as in any reconstructive form of psychotherapy.

SEX THERAPY

People with sexual problems as their presenting complaint generally are not motivated to seek intensive treatment. What they desire is to function sexually as rapidly and normally as possible. Catering to this wish is a group of new sex therapies (Kaplan, HS, 1974) originated by the research team of Masters and Johnson (1966, 1970), which are short term, behaviorally oriented, and symptomatically effective for most patients. What these authors advocate is a short intensive course of instruction and guidance in proper sexual attitudes and techniques administered to the patient and his or her sexual partner by a dual-sex team.

This format is undoubtedly an excellent one. Some therapists combine behavioral methods with exploratory techniques. They encourage their patients to verbalize their fears, guilt feelings, and misgivings and deal with resistances in traditional psychotherapeutic ways. Ideally, therapy following the intensive initial course continues on a weekly basis for a period until the newly acquired patterns are solidly integrated and the patients are able to manage relapses by themselves.

There are obviously advantages to the couples working with the dual-sex therapeutic team since cooperation of both patient members is more easily obtained, resistances can be dealt with directly, misconceptions about sexuality can be effectively brought out in the open, questions about technique are less likely to be distorted, and desensitization of embarrassment and alleviation of guilt feelings are enhanced. In many cases the core problem is that of communication, particularly in relation to mutual sexual feelings. Breaking into the facade that sex is dirty, not to be talked about, practiced in the dark, etc. can release both partners and lead to a more natural and spontaneous functioning.

Practical considerations, however, may make it impossible to utilize a dual-sex team, and the therapist may have to operate without a cotherapist. In some cases it will be impossible to get the patient's spouse or sexual partner to come for interviewing. Then the therapist will have to work with the patient alone, briefing him or her on how to instruct and work with the partner. A 2-week vacation period to initiate treatment is best since there will be less distractions. Here, too, modifications may be necessary, thus when the couple is ready for sexual exercises, a 3- or 4-day holiday may be all that is necessary.

Several sessions of history taking and interviewing to clarify misconceptions are customary before starting behavioral conditioning. These preliminary sessions, and particularly history taking, are best done individually with the partners since many personal sensitive areas may be exposed. Where a dual-sex team is used, the male therapist interviews the man and the female therapist the woman. Patients will often ask the therapist not to reveal secrets to their mates. Such secrets range from masturbation to past and present sexual affairs. Some of these secrets are not as dreadful as the patient imagines, and their revelation could clear the air between the couple. However, the therapist must promise (and hold to the promise) not to expose the patient. If it turns out that therapy cannot continue without bringing up the secret, the therapist must ask the patient's permission. But in all likelihood the revelation may not be necessary.

The sexual history should cover the following:

1. The earliest memory of sexual feeling.
2. The kinds of sexual information expounded to the individual as a child.
3. Preparation for and reactions to mensturation in the female and the first ejaculation in the male.
4. The first sexual experience (masturbating or in relation to another person, animal, or object).
5. Sexual feelings toward parents or siblings.
6. Early homosexual or heterosexual activities. (The first sexual experiences are very important and the patient may never have gotten over them.)
7. Present sexual behavior and accompanying feelings and fantasies.
8. Sexual dreams.
9. Attitudes toward masturbation.
10. Conditions under which orgasm occurs.
11. If married the kind of relationship with mate.
12. Tendencies toward promiscuity.

Attitudes toward sexuality should be explored, for example, how the patient feels about kissing of the mouth, breast, body, and genitals, about manual manipulation of the genitals, about mouth-genital contact, and about different sexual positions. What does the patient feel (like, dislike) about the partner? What makes him or her angry? What makes him or her feel sexy? The therapist should look for what positive and pleasurable things are present in the relationship since these can be reinforced.

Often the *way* the patient responds to these questions, the hesitancies, embarrassment, etc., will yield as much information about attitudes as the content of the answers.

The bulk of patients who come for sexual therapy are well motivated. This is very much in their favor and permits the use of short-term approaches. The great majority of these patients can be helped without too great delving into dynamics. The empathic liberated attitude of the therapist coupled with correcting misinformation about sex may in itself suddenly liberate the patient.

Some of the more common questions plaguing patients are the following, suggested answers being indicated.

Q. What is the normal frequency of intercourse?

A. There is no such thing as "normal" frequency. Sexual needs vary with each person and the desire for pleasuring oneself can range from daily to bimonthly.

Q. Doesn't masturbation take away desire for intercourse?

A. If people learn better ways of pleasuring themselves, they engage in self-manipulation less frequently, although they can still derive pleasure from it.

Q. Isn't genital intercourse the most desirable form?

A. Sex has several forms and genital intercourse is certainly desirable, but at times other variations of pleasuring, like oral–genital contact, are indulged by many.

Q. I feel my penis is too small. Isn't this objectionable to women?

A. This is a common foolish concern of many men. The vagina is a flexible organ, accommodating itself and capable of being pleasured by all sizes. If you stop worrying about size and concentrate on pleasure in lovemaking, your partner will undoubtedly be more than satisfied.

Perhaps the most important element in the treatment is the manner and attitude of the therapist (or therapeutic team). In working with patients who are seeking to liberate themselves from their sexual fears and inhibitions, the therapist presents himself or herself as a model of a permissive authority. Therapists have tremendous leverage in working with sexual therapy because they fit into the role of idealized parental figures who can make new rules. An easygoing, noncondemning, matter-of-fact approach is quite therapeutic in its own right. The ideal therapeutic philosophy is that the patient has been temporarily diverted from attaining the true joys of sex and that if there is the desire to do so, it is possible to move toward reaching this goal of enjoyable pleasure without guilt and fear. This posture is difficult to simulate if the therapist has "hang-ups" about sex or harbors Victorian sentiments that harmonize with the patient's unhealthy disposition. Many therapists falsely regard their own sexual attitudes and behavior as a norm. If these are not constructive, they will prevent a full release of the patient's potentialities.

In brief sexual therapy, countertransference phenomena can fleetingly occur. One must expect that a patient of the opposite sex will sometimes openly or covertly express sexual transference. This is usually handled by a casual matter-of-fact attitude of nonresponse. Problems occur when the therapist is deliberately or unconsciously seductive with patients.

The following concepts will have to be integrated by the patient, hence they should be accepted by the therapist:

1. Sex is a normal and natural function.
2. The prime purpose of sex is pleasure not performance.
3. People have many different ways of pleasuring themselves. They can derive satisfaction through manual manipulation, oral-genital contacts, and genital-genital contacts. Unfortunately, the way we are brought up teaches many of us wrong attitudes about sexuality.
4. A person has a right to liberate himself from these crippling attitudes.
5. All people have the potential of enjoying sexuality.

If the therapist has scruples about these concepts, these inhibitions may be passed on to the patient. Therefore, it may be preferable to refer patients with sexual difficulties to another therapist or team skilled in sexual therapy.

It is important to avoid the words "abnormal" or "pathological" since these may have frightening connotations. It is best to shy away from the word "masturbation" but rather refer to it as "deriving pleasure manually or through fondling the genitals oneself." The term "mutual masturbation" should also be avoided. Instead one may say "pleasuring each other manually." It is advisable to ask the patient, "Are there thoughts or fantasies or objects that turn you on?" Patients often have wild fantasies and even covet harmless fetishes, symbolic residues of past conditionings, which help them to release sexual feelings. To ridicule or condemn these when they are revealed will serve merely to discourage the patient. The proper therapeutic stance is casually to emphasize that people have different ways of pleasuring themselves. The therapist may say, "For every lock there is a key, and each person has his own key for the release of sexual feeling. If there is something harmless that turns you on, there is nothing to be afraid of or ashamed of." The reason why it is important not to interfere with sexually releasing fantasies is that to remove them too soon, before other more satisfactory sexually releasing stimuli are developed, may result in paralyzing inhibitions or in resentments that will drive the patient away from therapy.

The patient should be asked to have a complete physical examination if one has not been recently obtained. There are some conditions, like diabetes, that result in impairment of functioning. Such medications as strong tranquilizers and antihypertensive substances also are inhibiting to libido. It may be necessary to reduce or change such medications. Where a depression exists, antidepressant medications may be necessary. In the case of excessive tension mild tranquilization may help.

Following history taking, if a dual-sex team is being used, each therapist interviews the other partner to get to know him or her better and to focus on problem areas. Thereafter a joint conference of partners and therapist (or dual-sex team) is held with the object of outlining the problem or problems and of discussing effective ways that the partners can participate in helping each other toward a better adjustment. An idea is given the couple about the roles of each played in the past that have produced the difficulty. The therapist also comments on the behavior of the couple to each other. Transferential data especially should be looked for: "The way you treat your wife [husband] it seems to me is how you described your mother [father] treated your father [mother]." Empathy must be displayed, and it is urgent to set up as good a working relationship as is possible. Reassurance is important. Sometimes women who have had hysterectomies believe that they will not be able to function sexually again. This mistaken notion should be clarified by the therapist, who may point out that the sexual response has nothing to do with the uterus. People with hysterectomies can function normally sexually. In males who have had suprapublic or transurethral prostatectomies any impotence that follows the operation usually disappears. This information can be reassuring to the prostectomized patient.

It may be advisable to use charts or illustrations to clarify the sex anatomy of male and female, even where no ostensible problems appear to exist. It is astonishing how ignorant some people are of their genital makeup. No matter how sophisticated they may imagine themselves to be, a great gap can exist in their education about how they are built.

Misconceptions will also have to be covered such as (1) that erections and orgasm can be brought on by will power, (2) that all sexual play must lead to intercourse, (3) that orgasms must be simultaneous, (4) that a clitoral orgasm is not an orgasm, (5) that orgasm is always essential during sexual contact, (6) that as one gets older desire for sex disappears.

The couple is then enjoined to start a new mode of sexual communication with each other. The therapist may interject these comments:

1. "Don't ask your spouse what he [she] wants in sex. Start every sentence with 'I want' or 'I would like.'"
2. "Express your feelings rather than act on them. If you are angry, say so. The minute you *act* angry with each other something has gone wrong."
3. "There is no reason not to reveal your performance fears to each other." The

couple (or patient) should also be told: "Until I [we] have given you the permission, to do otherwise, you are to limit your sex activities to getting turned on with each other. There is to be no real intercourse in the meantime." Pressure removed from the male to penetrate with his penis and the female to have an orgasm may almost immediately lead to penile erections and vaginal lubrication. This can form the basis for fruitful reconditioning of responses.

4. "You will make mistakes, but that is the best way to learn."
5. "You are not to analyze your performance, just let things happen as they will. The goal is pleasure, not how well you are doing."
6. "You don't have to have intercourse to give your partner sexual satisfactions."

The basic first step to be practiced* by the couple is what Masters and Johnson have called "sensate focus." The couple is instructed to begin in privacy the following assignment:

Th. You are, in a comfortably warm room, to get into bed completely undressed. Turn on a soft light.

Some couples have actually never closely looked at each other nude. The partner with the problem, or with the most severe problem, is instructed thusly:

Th. You are to do with him [or her] whatever you always wanted to do, like touching the face, body, thighs, etc. But *not* the breasts or genitals. There is absolutely to be no intercourse. If you do anything that causes discomfort, your partner must tell you. Your partner is to get what he [or she] can get out of it. But the important thing is for you to experience pleasure in what you are doing. Do this for 5 to 15 minutes, no more. Then your partner is to do the same thing with you.

Very often this exercise will mobilize strong sexual feelings. Impotent men will have erections; nonorgasmic women will lubri-

---

* Suggestions as to technique, found useful by the author, were adopted from the course given by Alexander Levay at the 1974 Continuing Education Course of the Postgraduate Center for Mental Health.

cate; premature ejaculators will maintain an erection.

The couple may also be told that if they get aroused too much, they may pleasure themselves (masturbate) in the presence of each other, but not to the point of orgasm. Couples often lose their guilt and feel released by the therapist giving them "permission" for them to manipulate themselves in the presence of each other.

If the couple is seen only once weekly rather than the intensive 2-week course at the beginning, they may be told to practice "sensate focus" only twice during the week or at the most three times. They may also utilize a warm body lotion if they desire.

After such practice, the couple, seen together, is asked individually what has happened. The therapist may ask: "Describe how you felt when *you* did it; how did you feel when it was done to you." A good deal of benefit that comes from sexual therapy derives from the emotional catharsis that relieves patients of guilt, fear, and shame as they talk about their preoccupations and feelings. The fact that the therapist is empathic toward and noncondemning of past experiences and current fantasies and compulsions helps them to approach their problems from a less defiant and more objective perspective. They get the impression that there is nothing really "bad" or "evil" about what they are thinking, feeling, or doing; rather they feel that they can move ahead toward areas of greater sexual and emotional freedom and fulfillment. The therapist should search for factors that create anxiety and mutual hostilities. If not corrected, these may neutralize the effects of therapy. Where necessary, the therapist supplies data about physiology, prescribes books, and discusses techniques of symptom control. Useful suggestions may be found in the illustrated book by Helen Kaplan (1974). What went right and what went wrong? The accounts will usually vary. If things did not go well, this should be discussed and the couple sent out to repeat the exercises with the addendum: "Each person is to tell the other what he [or she] likes to have done." A common complaint is being ticklish. If this is the case, the ticklish partner should put his (or her) hands over that of the partner who does the stroking. They may be enjoined, "When you are more relaxed, the tickling will cease." Should the couple complain that there was no sexual feeling, they may be told: "This is not a sexual performance. It is a practice session." Successes should be praised but not analyzed.

As soon as this phase has gone well, the couple may be encouraged to practice genital pleasuring. "You may now gently stroke each others' genitals, directing each other as you go along. It is not necessary to have an orgasm unless you want to and are sufficiently stimulated. But spend not more than 15 minutes from the start." The man may be told: "It is enjoyable for a woman to be touched gently on the clitoris. You can put your forearm on her tummy and let your hand fall over the pubis." The woman is to direct the man's hand on her own pubis, the lips, and the clitoris, and tell him when to stop. If the woman does not lubricate, lubrication should be employed especially on the clitoris.

Where an intensive 2-week program is utilized, it may be arranged as follows, varying it according to the reported reactions:

First day: History taking.
Second day: Joint session. Educational explanations. Correcting misconceptions about sex. Directions about "sensate focus."
Third day: Round table (therapists and couple) to discuss reactions. Directions to examine each other avoiding genitals and breast.
Fourth day: More sensate focus. If no anxiety, genitals may be included.
Fifth day: Sensate focus with stimulation of genitals, but not to orgasm. Orgasm may be reached by pleasuring self if desired.
Sixth day: If no anxiety is reported, a mutually pleasurable thing is to be done.
Seventh day: No sexual practice.
Eighth day: As desired with or without practice.
Ninth day: Insertion of penis into vagina for pleasure, but no orgasm is essential. The goal is pleasure not orgasm even if the penis goes inside. If there is no erection, the soft

penis can still be introduced. It should contact the clitoris if not inserted. "Even the soft penis gives pleasure."
Tenth day: Repetition of ninth day.

If after 4 or 5 sensate focus sessions the couple is not responding and moving ahead, they should not be made to feel that they are failures. Some other form of treatment (like psychoanalytically oriented psychotherapy) may be necessary. The failure is not with the couple. It is due to the limitations of this particular kind of therapy.

Some special techniques may be necessary for different problems. In *premature ejaculation* the "squeeze" technique may be helpful. Here the man lies on his back. The woman with legs spread faces his pelvis. She strokes his body and then the penis until there is erection. She continues stroking the penis and randomly places thumbs on the raphe under the glans on the underside of the penis and the forefinger on the other side. She squeezes four times in 15 seconds, but not to the point of pain. Then he lies on his back, and she squats over him. She slowly inserts the penis and stops all movement for a moment. Then she moves slowly at a 45° angle, and he announces when he is getting too much pleasure. He then withdraws the penis, and the squeeze technique is utilized. Modifications of this technique may be used (Tanner, BA, 1973). Where the sexual partner becomes upset and *insists* on a "better performance," the problem of rapid ejaculation is augmented by guilt and conviction of failure. Tension builds up, which exaggerates the symptom. Here dynamic psychotherapy along with sexual therapy along behavioral lines involving also the partner is the preferred approach.

A problem that disturbs many women is that of being *nonorgasmic.* Where the patient has sensuous feelings and can achieve orgasm with masturbation, the difficulty is generally not a serious one. Should a block to sensuous feelings exist, it is expedient to explore with the patient further the history of her sexual development from childhood and the store of information that she has retained about sexuality.

The first step is helping the patient to develop greater sensuous feeling by exercises in relaxing, stroking her body, and self-pleasuring (masturbating). A book like *The Sensuous Woman,* by Lyle Huart, may be helpful. The sensate focus technique described above is then taught the couple with the object of pleasuring each other while avoiding intercourse. Pleasure in giving pleasure to the partner is the object while providing feedback of how they both feel during the exercises.

McCarthy (1973) describes a technique that may be found helpful.

First day: Stroking and kissing various parts of the partner's body with eyes shut and no genital touching.
Second day: Sensate focus, eyes shut and couple guiding each other with no genital touch.
Third day: Sensate focus, guiding each other and eyes open.
Fourth day: Abstinence.
Fifth day: Sensate focus with lotion, no genital touch.
Sixth day: Sensate focus and genital touch with eyes closed.
Seventh day: Guided sensate focus with genital touch, eyes open.

After this greater spontaneity and experiment are encouraged. Some couples may take several days to execute the directions assigned for one day. When the exercises have been completed, once-a-week visits are possible. Teaching the couple sexual positions may be part of the instructions starting with the "no-demand" position. Oral-genital stimulation techniques may also be introduced and feelings aired about this. Should anxiety develop during any of the stages, a return to sensate focus techniques is advocated. Finally, after orgasms are reached by manual and oral-genital techniques, actual intercourse is encouraged. As much as 2 or 3 months of preliminary stimulation may be required before full intercourse is "permitted."

Some therapists skilled in hypnosis have been able to bring their female patients to orgasm by training them in fantasy formation while the patients are in a trance. They are told they will have feelings of gentle warmth in the vaginal area and will be able to accept these feelings and feel excited and passionate deeply inside the vagina. Thereafter scenes are suggested of the patient meeting her secret lover and making exciting love with him. Because repressive barriers are down and the imagination is so vivid in the trance, some patients are able to experience their first orgasm through such training. Posthypnotic suggestions are made to the effect that orgasms will come with intercourse without guilt or fear. The therapist must be a bit of a romantic poet to make such suggestions sound realistic. Should the therapist decide to utilize this technique, it is wise to have a female helper quietly present during and after trance induction for medico-legal reasons.

The use of vibrators should be avoided in nonorgasmic women, since they will probably respond to the intense stimulation and then find the actual sex experience nonstimulating. Moreover, if vibrators are used too much, they may cause vaginal ulceration.

Where the complaint is *impotence,* we must differentiate between primary and secondary varieties. In *primary impotence,* the patient has never been able to sustain an erection with a partner sufficient for the sexual act. Some individuals here realize their failing, but they ascribe it to moral scruples, which they imagine will be resolved when they get married. Marriage fails to correct the condition and, recognizing that an annulment is imminent, husband and wife usually seek help from a minister or physician who, in turn, may refer the couple to a psychotherapist. Generally primary impotence is an aspect of a severe personality problem characterized by strong feelings of inadequacy, inferiority, and doubts about one's masculinity. The principal approach here is dynamic psychotherapy with sex therapy as a supplementary, albeit useful, accessory that should involve the patient and his partner.

Secondary impotence is where, following a period of more or less successful intercourse, the male experiences a loss of erection. This may occur when he is fatigued, or physically ill, or excessively tense and anxious about some situational problem, or most frequently when he is feeling hostile toward his partner. Ever since women have come to regard sex as a right rather than a burden, the incidence of secondary impotence has risen. Especially effected are men who regard their partner's expectations as a challenge to their masculinity. Their reaction to "failure" is usually related to their self-image. If they have a low feeling about themselves, they will overrespond and look forward to the next attempt with a sense of dread. The need to perform becomes more important to them than the desire to achieve pleasure in the sex act.

Let us assume that we have eliminated physical causes (for example, diabetes, which is sometimes the source of secondary impotence) for the impotence. Therapy will involve restoration of confidence in the ability to function. No more may be required than clarification that impotence can occur temporarily in all males and that it will rectify itself if the person has no stake in maintaining it. The therapist should emphasize and reemphasize, "The best advice to follow is to forget the need for performance and to attempt satisfying yourself to the limit of your capacity without or with an erection." Treatment with sensate focus is generally successful, but cooperation of the partner is mandatory.

We sometimes encounter a situation where a middle-aged man is secondarily impotent with his wife and has become involved in an erotic stimulating situation with a younger woman. He is sexually disinterested in his wife, who he complains is getting obese, is losing her body firmness, developing wrinkles, neglects her grooming, and exposes him to a boring, stereotyped sexual experience. Often the relationship with the wife has deteriorated into one where the man regards her as a maternal substitute. He may come to therapy spontaneously out of guilt and with the hope the therapist will work some miracle and produce an erection even though he may not be interested so much in pleasing himself as in pleasing his wife. Generally, if the man is emotionally involved with the other woman, sex therapy will not work too well and the restoration of adequate sexual functioning will be unsuccessful. At some point it will be necessary to break up the triad. The therapist may under some circumstances, at the start, where the man's motivation to correct the situation is strong, have to tell him that he will need to break up his relationship with the young woman before therapy can be successful. In other cases where the man is deeply entangled in the affair, immediate rupture can be traumatic and may be strongly resisted. Here gradually the effort may be made to help the man see the inadequacy of the relationship with his mistress, an effort that may or may not prove successful. Marital therapy is sometimes useful where the relationship between husband and wife has not deteriorated too badly.

Brief periods of *frigidity* in women are normal, the product resulting from temporary physical disability or fleeting anxieties, tensions, and depressions. Frigidity can also occur when there is anger or irritation with a sexual partner. Short-term therapy with reassurance given that there is nothing seriously wrong, while permitting free verbalization of hostility toward the partner, may be all that is required.

Persistent frigidity may be divided into primary and secondary varieties. In *primary frigidity* the woman has never had an orgasm even during sleep or with masturbation, although she may have experienced some sexual arousal. Usually arousal reaches a pitch and then loss of feeling ensues without orgasm. Responsible for this may be fears of loss of control, of rejection, or of acting foolishly. In *secondary frigidity* the person was once orgasmic and then ceased to respond. Here untoward emotions and attitudes are often implicated, like hostility, distrust, disgust, and fear. Sometimes orgasm may be possible with certain fantasies, like being raped or punished, or with some practices, like being treated roughly, tied down, abused, etc. Sometimes masturbation succeeds while intercourse remains distasteful. Sex therapy may enable some women with secondary frigidity to respond satisfactorily. Should a patient require fantasies, the therapist should not disparage these. The patient may be encouraged to substitute thoughts about her present sexual partner at the start of orgasm in an effort to recondition a new way of thinking.

Long-standing primary frigidity, however, does not usually yield to sex therapy, particularly where it is a product of severe personality problems stemming from disturbed family relationships. There may be a fear of functioning like a woman, a repudiation of femininity, a disgust with and desire to renounce the female sexual organs, consciously or unconsciously conceived of as dirty or repulsive. There may be marked competitiveness and hostility toward men. Long-term psychoanalysis or dynamic psychotherapy offers chances for improvement or cure after reconstructive changes have been brought about.

In *dyspareunia* and *vaginismus* intercourse is so painful that it becomes aversive rather than pleasurably rewarding. Here the patient should be sent to a gynecologist to rule out organic causes. Trauma during the birth of a child, episiotomy, a painful past abortion, a hysterectomy, endometriasis, allergic reactions to birth control sprays and jellies, and other physical factors may be at the root of the problem. In most cases, however, the cause is psychogenic. During vaginismus the muscles go into spasm, a kind of defensive splinting. Penetration is difficult or impossible even for the little finger. Reaction to erotic approaches then sponsors a panicky withdrawal. Sometimes vaginismus is a secondary response to premature ejaculation or impotence in a husband or lover. The woman's reaction frightens and discourages the man and aggravates his problem, which, in turn, creates further symptoms in the woman. The triad of dyspareunia, vaginismus, and impotence are often at the basis of an unconsummated marriage. Couples sometimes shamefacedly seek help for this situation, and sex therapy may be tried.

A useful method of dealing with these reactions is to recondition the pain response through the use of graduated dilators. These may be obtained in a surgical supply house, one form being known as Young's Dilators. The smallest size, well lubricated, is slowly inserted by the woman, at first in the presence of her husband. She is encouraged to retain it for a while. Then gradually each day a larger size, well lubricated, is introduced. Next the husband slowly inserts the dilators in graduated size. The time dilators are retained in the vagina is increased from 15 minutes to 2 hours. The patient must be reassured that the dilators will not disappear in her body, a fearful misconception some patients conceive. Success rates are close to 100 percent, assuming no serious psychiatric problem coexists.

BIBLIOTHERAPY

Attempts are sometimes made by therapists to change faulty attitudes and to influence poor motivation in certain patients through the assigned reading of articles, pamphlets, and books. By these measures the patient is helped to understand how personality is evolved, why adaptation breaks down, the manifestations of collapse in adaptation, and how psychotherapy may help repair the damage. Advice on the handling of specific problems in adjustment, marriage, and child rearing may also be obtained from some reading materials. This therapeutic use of reading has been designated as "bibliotherapy."

Bibliotherapy is of value chiefly to persons who are not yet motivated for psychotherapy and who require more information about emotional illness before they can admit of its existence in themselves or can recognize that beneficial results may be obtained from treatment. It may correct misconceptions about mental health, psychiatry, and psychotherapy. It is sometimes effective in bolstering repression through acceptance of written authoritative statements and directives that help the person to suppress inner fears, to gain reassurance, and to adopt socially acceptable attitudes and values. The latter influence makes bibliotherapy a useful adjunctive device in certain patients receiving psychotherapy. Patients may gain from readings a number of methods by means of which they may regulate their life, inspirational formulas that help in the achievement of happiness and success, and devices that permit of a regulation of those conflicts and strivings that are more or less under volitional control.

Bibliotherapeutic approaches to mental health, while praiseworthy, have definite limitations. People often refuse to accept facts due to a complete or partial unawareness of ego-syntonic personality distortions. To tell a parent that he must accept and love his children in order for them to grow into healthy adults, does not mean that he will appreciate the significance of these precepts. Indeed, even though he rejects his children, despises his wife, and detaches himself from family life, he may not consider his behavior in any way unusual. He may even hold himself up as a parental ideal.

In other instances the person may acknowledge his difficulties but be totally unable to do anything about them. Educational media that warn people of the disasters to children or to society of their reactions may mobilize counterreactions and actually exaggerate the existing problems.

The manner in which reading materials are prepared and presented is important. If they apprise of the fact that all parents commit errors, that children are resilient and can stand many mistakes if they feel loved and respected, and that youngsters with even severe difficulties can change, readings may create a corrective atmosphere.

On the whole, reading adjuncts will not prove themselves to be too valuable for the patient who is receiving insight therapy. This is because no intellectual approach is of great service in modifying deeply repressed conflicts or in ameliorating symptoms that have strong defensive virtues for the individual. Indeed, the educational materials may be utilized by the patient as resistance, items being extracted out of context to justify neurotic patterns. The relative ineffectuality of reading materials in severe neurotic difficulties is attested to by the fact that scores of patients come to psychotherapy after having read more extensively from the psychiatric literature than has the therapist.

Nevertheless, bibliotherapy may help certain individuals to break through specific resistances and to gain limited insight, as, for instance, those patients who, unconvinced of the value of psychotherapy, require examples from the experiences of others of how therapy helps. Resistance to working with dreams may sometimes be handled by asking the patient to read books in which the rationale of dream interpretation is explained. A patient who has in therapy resolved crippling sexual inhibitions may be aided in achieving a more complete sexual life by reading appropriate materials dealing with marriage. Or a patient having problems with her children may benefit greatly from books on child psychology. Personal involvement in short stories and case histories is also possible, and McKinney (1975) lists a bibliography that can be useful.

As a therapeutic medium, bibliotherapy is utilized in child therapy. Children readily get "caught up" in a story. A child identifies with one or more of the characters and releases emotional energy vicariously. This may result in greater awareness by the child of his own needs, feelings, and motivations (Ciancilo, 1965; Nickerson, 1975). Some of the ways that bibliotherapy is employed are described by Bell and Moore (1972), Chambers (1970), Dinkmeyer (1970), Gardner (1974), Heimlich (1972), Mulac (1971), Myrick and Moni (1972), and J. A. Wagner (1970).

The following is a list of recommended books and pamphlets, should the therapist decide that bibliotherapy is indicated. (The source abbreviations are spelled out at the end of these references (see page 829).

Books on General Psychology, Psychiatry, and Psychoanalysis

Brill AA: Basic Principles of Psychoanalysis. New York, Washington Square Press, 1968 (paperback)

Brussel JA: The Layman's Guide to Psychiatry (2d ed) New York, Barnes & Noble, 1967 (paperback)

CRM Books Staff: Psychology Today: An Introduction (3d ed). Del Mar, Calif, CRM Books, 1975

Freud S: A General Introduction to Psychoanalysis: The Authorized English Translation of Sigmund Freud (rev ed). New York, Simon & Schuster, 1969

Mezer RE: Dynamic Psychiatry in Simple Terms (4th ed). New York, Springer, 1970

Wittenberg R: Common Sense About Psychoanalysis. New York, Funk & Wagnalls, 1968 (paperback)

Books Explaining How Personality Problems Operate

English OS, Pearson GH: Emotional Problems of Living (3d ed). New York, Norton, 1963

Fromm E: The Sane Society. New York, Rinehart, 1955 (also paperback—New York, Fawcett World, 1973)

Horney K: The Neurotic Personality of Our Time. New York, Norton, 1937 (also paperback)

Menninger K: The Vital Balance: The Life Process in Mental Health and Illness. New York, Viking, 1967 (paperback)

Wolberg LR, Kildahl JP: The Dynamics of Personality. New York, Grune & Stratton, 1970

Books Explaining How Psychiatry and Psychotherapy Help

Berne E: A Layman's Guide to Psychiatry and Psychoanalysis. New York, Grove, 1975 (original title: The Mind in Action)

Brussel J: The Layman's Guide to Psychiatry (2d ed). New York, Barnes & Noble, 1967 (paperback)

Harris T: I'm OK, You're OK: A Practical Guide to Transactional Analysis. New York, Harper & Row, 1969

Horney K: Are You Considering Psychoanalysis? New York, Norton, 1962 (paperback)

Jones E: What Is Psychoanalysis?
Westport, Conn, Greenwood, 1973 (re-
print of 1948 edition)
Kovel J: A Complete Guide to Therapy:
From Psychoanalysis to Behavior
Modification. New York, Pantheon,
1976
Menninger WC, Leaf M: You and Psychia-
try. New York, Scribner, 1948 (also
paperback)
Saul LJ: Emotional Maturity (3d ed).
Philadelphia, Lippincott, 1971
Whitehead T, Kenny B: Insight: A Guide to
Psychiatry and the Psychiatric Ser-
vices. Mystic, Conn, Verry Press, 1973

PAMPHLETS

A Consumer's Guide to Mental Health Ser-
vices. Alcohol, Drug Abuse, and Men-
tal Health Administration. USGPO
(#017-024-00435-9). 30¢
Facts About Group Therapy. NIMH.
USGPO (#1724–0256). 25¢
Mental Illness and Its Treatment. NIMH.
USGPO (#HSM 73–9056). 25¢
Some Things You Should Know About
Mental and Emotional Illness. NAMH.
10¢ (also available in Spanish)
When Things Go Wrong—What Can You
Do? NAMH. 10¢

Books on Marriage

Bernard J: The Future of Marriage. New
York, Bantam, 1973 (paperback)
Clinebell HJ, Clinebell CH: The Intimate
Marriage. New York, Harper & Row,
1970
Landis M, Landis J: Building a Successful
Marriage (6th ed). Englewood Cliffs,
NJ, Prentice-Hall, 1973
Laswell ME, Laswell TE (eds): Love, Mar-
riage, Family: A Developmental Ap-
proach. Glenview, Ill, Scott, Fores-
man, 1973
Lederer WJ, Jackson DD: The Mirages of
Marriage. New York, Norton, 1968
Rogers CR: Becoming Partners: Marriage
and Its Alternatives. New York, De-
lacorte, 1972 (also paperback—New
York, Dell)
Udry RJ: The Social Context of Marriage

(3d ed). Philadelphia, Lippincott, 1974
(paperback)

PAMPHLETS

Mates and Roommates: New Styles in
Young Marriages (LeShan EJ). PAP
(#468), 1971. 50¢
Marriage and Love in the Middle Years
(Peterson J). PAP (#456), 1970. 50¢
Sexual Adjustment in Marriage (Klemer R,
Klemer M). PAP (#397), 1966. 50¢
What Makes a Marriage Happy? (Mace D).
PAP (#290), 1970. 50¢

**Books on Human
Sexuality**

Barbach LG: For Yourself: The Fulfillment
of Female Sexuality. Garden City, NY,
Anchor/Doubleday, 1976 (paperback)
Brecher R, Brecher E (eds): An Analysis of
Human Sexual Response. New York,
New American Library, 1966
Comfort A: The Joy of Sex. New York,
Simon & Schuster, 1974 (paperback)
Hobson L: Consenting Adult. New York,
Doubleday, 1975
Kempton W, Bass MS, Gordon S: Love,
Sex and Birth Control for the Mentally
Retarded. New York, Planned Par-
enthood Association, 1971 (paperback)
Kirkendall LA, Whitehurst RN (eds): The
New Sexual Revolution. Buffalo,
Prometheus, 1974
McCary JL: Human Sexuality: A Contem-
porary Marriage Manual (2d ed). New
York, Van Nostrand, 1973 (brief edi-
tion in paperback)
McCary JL: Sexual Myths and Fallacies.
New York, Van Nostrand, 1971 (also
paperback)
Masters W: The Pleasure Bond: A New
Look at Sexuality and Commitment.
Boston, Little, Brown, 1975 (also
paperback, 1976)
Money J, Tucker P: Sexual Signatures: On
Being a Man or a Woman. Boston, Lit-
tle, Brown, 1975
Peterson JA: Love in the Later Years: The
Emotional, Physical, Sexual and Social
Potential of the Elderly. New York,
Association Press, 1975
Robbins J, Robbins J: An Analysis of

Human Sexual Inadequacy. New York, Norton, 1970 (also paperback—New York, New American Library)

Schur EM (ed): Family and the Sexual Revolution. Bloomington, Indiana University Press, 1964 (paperback)

Weinberg G: Society and the Healthy Homosexual. New York, St. Martin's, 1972

PAMPHLETS

Characteristics of Male and Female Sexual Responses (Pomeroy WB, Christenson, CV). SIECUS Study Guide No. 4

Homosexuality (rev ed) (Bell AP). SIECUS Study Guide No. 2

Homosexuality in Our Society (Ogg E). PAP (#484), 6th printing 1976. 50¢

Masturbation (Johnson WR). SIECUS Study Guide No. 3

Premarital Sexual Standards (rev ed) (Reiss IL). SIECUS Study Guide No. 5

Sex After Sixty-five (Lobsenz H). PAP (#519), 1975. 50¢

Sex Education (Kirkendall LA). SIECUS Study Guide No. 1

Sex Education for Disabled Persons. PAP (#531), 1975. 50¢

Sex, Science and Values (Christenson HT). SIECUS Study Guide No. 9

Sexual Life in the Later Years (Rubin, I). SIECUS Study Guide No. 12

Sexuality and the Life Cycle: A Broad Concept of Sexuality, (Kirkendall LA, Rubin I). SIECUS Study Guide No. 8

Books on Family Planning

Publications dealing with the subjects of contraception, fertility, or menopausal hormone therapy may not reflect the results of current research. Readers are urged to consult their physicians.

Guttmacher AF: Pregnancy, Birth and Family Planning: A Guide for Expectant Parents in the 1970s. New York, Viking, 1973 (also paperback—New York, Signet)

Kamirsky G: Vasectomy, Manhood, and Sex. New York, Springer, 1972 (paperback)

Nyhan W: The Heredity Factor. New York, Grosset & Dunlap, 1976

Planned Parenthood of New York City: Abortion: A Woman's Guide. New York, Pocket Books/Simon & Schuster, 1975 (paperback)

Pohlman EH, Pohlman JM: The Psychology of Birth Planning. Cambridge, Mass, Schenkman, 1969

Warner MP: Modern Fertility Guide: Practical Advice for the Childless Couple (rev ed). New York, Funk & Wagnalls, 1969

Wheelan EM: A Baby ? . . . Maybe. New York, Bobbs-Merrill, 1975

Wylie EM: The New Birth Control: The Case for Voluntary Sterilization. New York, Grosset & Dunlap, 1972

PAMPHLETS

Abortion: Public Issues, Private Decision (Pilpel H, Zuckerman RJ, Ogg E). PAP (#527), 1975. 50¢

Family Planning—Today's Choices (Millstone D). PAP (#513), 1974. 50¢

Modern Methods of Birth Control (rev ed). PPFA, 1976. 25¢

Voluntary Sterilization (Ogg E). PAP (#507), 1974. 50¢

Books on Pregnancy and Childbirth

Apgar V, Beck J: Is My Baby All Right? A Guide to Birth Defects (rev ed). New York, Trident, 1973 (also paperback)

Bean CA: Methods of Childbirth: A Complete Guide to Childbirth Classes and the New Maternity Care. Garden City, NY, Doubleday, 1974

Boston Children's Medical Center. Pregnancy, Birth and the Newborn Baby: A Publication for Parents. New York: Delacorte/Seymour Lawrence, 1972

Colman AD, Libby L: Pregnancy: The Psychological Experience. New York, Seabury, 1972

Eastman NJ: Expectant Motherhood (5th rev ed). Boston, Little, Brown, 1970

Leboyer F: Birth Without Violence. New York, Knopf, 1975

Schaefer G, Zisowitz ML: The Expectant

Father. New York, Simon & Schuster, 1964

PAMPHLETS

Pregnancy and You (Auerbach AB, Arnstein HS). PAP (#482), 1972. 50¢

Prenatal Care (rev ed). OCD, 1973. $1.05

Sexual Relations During Pregnancy and the Post-Delivery Period (Israel SL, Rubin I). SIECUS Study Guide No. 6

When Your Baby Is on the Way. OCD, 1961. 45¢ (also available in Spanish: Mientras Su Bebe Esta en Camino)

Books on the Woman's Role

Bardwick J: The Psychology of Women: A Study of Biocultural Conflicts. New York, Harper & Row, 1971 (also paperback)

Bernard J: Women, Wives, Mothers: Values and Options. Chicago, Aldine, 1975

de Beauvoir S: The Second Sex. New York, Random House, 1974 (paperback)

Group For the Advancement of Psychiatry: The Educated Woman: Prospects and Problems. New York, GAP, 1975

Huber, J: Changing Women in a Changing Society. Chicago, University of Chicago Press, 1973

Ladner JA: Tomorrow's Tomorrow: The Black Woman. Garden City, NY, Doubleday, 1971

Mead M: Male and Female. New York, Dell, 1968 (paperback)

Weideger P: Menstruation and Menopause: The Physiology and Psychology, the Myth and the Reality. New York, Knopf, 1976

PAMPHLETS

Woman's Changing Place: A Look at Sexism (Doyle N). PAP (#509), 1974. 50¢

Books on Family Problems and Crises

Ambrosino L: Runaways. Boston, Beacon, 1971

Atkin E, Rubin E: Part-Time Father: A Guide for the Divorced Father. New York, Vanguard, 1976

Caine L: Widow. New York, Morrow, 1974

Despert LJ: Children of Divorce. Garden City, NY, Doubleday, 1953

Fisher EO: Divorce—The New Freedom. New York, Harper & Row, 1974

Gardner RA: The Boys and Girls Book About Divorce. New York, Science House, 1970

Klein C: The Single Parent Experience. New York, Walker, 1973 (also paperback—New York, Avon)

Kubler-Ross E: On Death and Dying. New York, Macmillan, 1969

Ludwig S: Out of Work. Syracuse, NY, New Readers Press, 1975

Milt M: Basic Handbook on Alcoholism. Maplewood, NJ, Scientific Aids Publications, 1973

Milt H: Basic Handbook on Mental Illness (rev ed). New York, Scribner, 1974 (paperback)

Pincus L: Death and the Family: The Importance of Mourning. New York, Pantheon, 1974

Rosenthal MS, Mothner I: Drugs, Parents and Children. Boston, Houghton Mifflin, 1972

Ruina E: Moving: A Common-Sense Guide to Relocating Your Family. New York, Funk & Wagnalls, 1970

Stuart IR, Abt LE: (eds): Children of Separation And Divorce. New York, Grossman, 1972

Wolf AW: Helping Your Child to Understand Death (rev ed). New York, Child Study Press, 1973 (paperback)

PAMPHLETS

Alcohol: Some Questions and Answers. NIAAA, 1971. (single copy free from NIAAA; additional copies available from USGPO at 15¢ each)

Crisis in the Family (Cadden V). NRB, 1974. 10¢

Dealing with the Crisis of Suicide (Frederick CJ, Lague L). PAP (#406A), 1972. 50¢

Divorce (Ogg E). PAP (#528), 1975. 50¢

Drugs—Use, Misuse, Abuse (Hill M). PAP (#515), 1974. 35¢

The Dying Person and the Family (Doyle N): PAP (#485), 1972. 50¢

Family Money Problems (Margolius S). PAP (#412), 1976. 50¢

Grief and Mourning (Kentucky Department of Mental Health). MHMC, 1973. 50¢

A Guide for the Family of the Alcoholic (Kellerman JL). Center City, Minn, Hazeldon Literature Department (Box 176), nd. 40¢

The Illness Called Alcoholism. AMA, 1973. 25¢

Living with a Heart Ailment (Irwin T). PAP (#521), 1975. 50¢

Male "Menopause" (Irwin T). PAP (#526), 1975. 50¢

Nursing Home Care. Office for Consumer Services, USDHEW. USGPO, 1973. 45¢

Questions and Answers about Drug Abuse. Special Action Office for Drug Abuse Prevention, National Institute on Drug Abuse. USGPO, 1975. $1.45

Sexual Encounters Between Adults and Children (Gagnon JH, Simon W). SIECUS Study Guide No. 11

Teenage Pregnancy: Prevention and Treatment (Sarrel PM). SIECUS Study Guide No. 14

Treating Alcoholism: The Illness, the Symptoms, the Treatment. NIAA. USGPO (#ADM 74–128), 1974. 50¢

Understand Your Heart (Irwin T). PAP (#514), 1974. 50¢

Watch Your Blood Pressure! (Irwin T). PAP (#483A), 1976. 50¢

The Woman Alcoholic (Lindbeck V). PAP (#529), 1975. 50¢

Books on Family Living and Adjustment

Albrecht M: The Complete Guide for the Working Mother. New York, Award/Universal Publishing, 1970 (paperback)

Arnstein HS, Arnstein B: Getting Along with Your Grown Up Children. New York, Evans, 1970

Denton W: Family Problems and What to Do About Them. Philadelphia, Westminster, 1971

Duvall EM: Faith in Families. Chicago, Rand McNally, 1970

Edwards M, Hoover E: The Challenge of Being Single. Los Angeles, Tarcher, 1974

Glidewell JC: Choice Points: Essays on the Emotional Problems of Living with People. Cambridge, M.I.T. Press, 1970

Levy J, Munroe R: The Happy Family. New York, Knopf, 1938

Satir V: Peoplemaking. Palo Alto, Calif, Science & Behavior Books, 1972

Spock B: Raising Children in a Difficult Time. New York, Norton, 1974

PAMPHLETS

A Guide for Family Living (Jenkins G). SRA. $1.50

The Mother Who Works Outside the Home (Olds SW). New York, Child Study Press, 1975. $1.50

One-Parent Families. CB. USGPO (#1791–00192). 30¢

Familias Con Solo Uno de los Padres. CB. USGPO (#1791–00201). 45¢

Books on General Child Care and Guidance

Biller H, Meredith D: Father Power. New York, McKay, 1974

Boston Children's Medical Center and Richard I. Feinbloom MD: Child Health Encyclopedia. New York, Delacorte/Dial, 1974

Braga J, Braga L: Growing with Children. Englewood Cliffs, NJ, Prentice-Hall, 1974

Brofenbrenner U (ed): Influences on Human Development. New York, Holt, 1972

Comer P, Poussaint AF (eds): Black Child Care. New York, Simon & Schuster, 1975

Erikson EH: Childhood and Society (rev ed). New York, Norton, 1964 (also in paperback)

Gardner GE and others: The Emerging Personality: Infancy Through Adolescence. New York, Delacorte, 1970

Ginott HG: Between Parent and Child: New

Solutions for Old Problems. New York, Macmillan, 1965

Group for the Advancement of Psychiatry. The Joys and Sorrows of Parenthood. New York, Scribner, 1973

Hoover MB: The Responsive Parent: Meeting the Realities of Parenthood Today. New York, Parents' Magazine Press, 1972

Josselyn IM: Happy Child: A Psychoanalytic Guide to Emotional and Social Growth. New York, Random House, 1955

Montessori M: From Childhood to Adolescence. New York, Schocken, 1973

Morris NS: Television's Child. Boston, Little, Brown, 1971

Princeton Center for Infancy: The Parenting Advisor (Caplan F, ed). Garden City, NY, Anchor Press/Doubleday, 1977

Stone LJ, Church J: Childhood and Adolescence: A Psychology of the Growing Person (rev ed). New York, Random House, 1973

Weinstein G: Children and Money: A Guide for Puzzled Parents. New York, McKay, 1975

PAMPHLETS

Behavior: The Unspoken Language of Children (rev ed). CSAA. 75¢

Facts about the Mental Health of Children. NIMH. USGPO (#ADM 75–70). 25¢

Fears of Children (Ross H). SRA. $1.50

A Guide to Successful Fatherhood (English OS, Foster CJ). SRA. $1.50

How to Know Your Child (3d ed). MHMC. 25¢

Play: Children's Business and a Guide to Play Materials. ACEI. $2.95

Preparing Tomorrow's Parents (Ogg E). PAP (#520), 1975. 50¢

The Roots of Self-Confidence (Neisser E). SRA. $1.50

Self-Understanding: A First Step to Understanding Children (Menninger WC). SRA. $1.50

Understanding Hostility in Children, by S. Escalona. SRA. $1.50

What Every Child Needs for Good Mental Health. NAMH. 5¢ (also available in Spanish: $4.50 per 100)

When a Child Goes to the Hospital. Medford, Mass, Tufts University, 1971. $1.00

The Why and How of Discipline (rev ed) (Auerbach AB). New York, Child Study Press, 1974. $1.25

Why Children Misbehave (Leonard CW, Flander MS). SRA. $1.50

Books on Infants and Young Children

Arnstein HS: The Roots of Love: Helping Your Children Learn to Love in the First Three Years of Life. New York, Bobbs-Merrill, 1975

Beadle M: A Child's Mind: How Children Learn During the Critical Years from Birth to Age Five (rev ed). New York, Aronson, 1975

Brazelton TB: Infants and Mothers: Individual Differences in Development. New York, Delacorte/Seymour Lawrence, 1969

Brazelton TB: Toddlers and Parents: A Declaration of Independence. New York, Delacorte/Seymour Lawrence, 1974

Chess S, et al: Your Child Is a Person: A Psychological Approach to Parenthood Without Guilt. New York, Viking, 1972 (paperback)

Fraiberg S: The Magic Years: Understanding and Handling the Problems of Early Childhood. New York, Scribner, 1968

Neisser EG: Primer for Parents of Preschoolers. New York, Parents' Magazine Press, 1972

Pomeranz VE, Schultz D: The First Five Years: A Relaxed Approach to Child Care. Garden City, NY, Doubleday, 1973

Princeton Center for Infancy and Early Childhood: The First Twelve Months of Life (Caplan F, ed). New York, Grosset & Dunlap, 1973

Rozdilsky ML, Banet B: What Now? A Handbook for New Parents. New York, Scribner, 1975

Sime M: A Child's Eye View: Piaget for Young Parents and Teachers. New York, Harper & Row, 1974

Spock, B: Baby and Child Care (4th ed). New York, Pocket Books, Simon & Schuster, 1976 (paperback)

PAMPHLETS

As Your Child Grows: The First Eighteen Months (Wolf K with Auerbach AB). CSAA, 1955. $1.50

Child Development in the Home. CB. USGPO (#017–091–00193–6), 1976. 45¢

Child Training Leaflets (21 in series). MHMC. 8¢ each

Concerns of Parents about Sex Education (Brown TE). SIECUS Study Guide No. 13

How to Give Your Child a Good Start. CSAA. 75¢

Infant Care (rev ed). CB. USGPO, 1973. $1.00 (also available in Spanish)

Some Special Problems of Children: Aged 2 to 5 Years (rev ed) (Ridenour N, Johnson I). CSAA, 1966. $1.25

Some Ways of Distinguishing a Good Early Childhood Program. NAEYC. 25¢

Tips on Drug Abuse Prevention for the Parents of a Young Child. NIMH. USGPO, 1972. 10¢ (single copies free from National Clearinghouse for Drug Abuse Information on request)

When Your Child First Goes Off to School (Brown BS). NIMH. USGPO, 1973

Your Baby's First Year. CB. USGPO, 1963. 50¢

El Primer Año de Vida Su Bebe. Children's USGPO, 1963 (single Spanish copies free on request)

Your Child from 1 to 6. OCD, 1962. $1.05

Your Child from 1 to 3. CB. USGPO (#1791–00019). 35¢ (also available in Spanish—USPGO, #1791–00088, 50¢)

Your Child From 3 to 4. CB. USGPO (#1791–00097). 45¢

Your First Months with Your First Baby (Barman A). PAP (#478), 1972. 50¢

Books on Adoption and Foster Care

Anderson DC: Children of Special Value: Interracial Adoption in America. New York, St. Martin's, 1971

Dywasuk C: Adoption—Is It for You? New York, Harper & Row, 1973

Felker E: Foster Parenting Young Children: Guidelines from a Foster Parent. New York, Child Welfare League of America, 1974

Klibanoff S, Klibanoff E: Let's Talk About Adoption. Boston, Little, Brown, 1973

Lifton BJ: Twice Born: Memoirs of an Adopted Daughter. New York, McGraw-Hill, 1975

Meredith J: And Now We Are a Family. Boston, Beacon, 1972 (a "read to" with children book)

Raymond L: Adoption and After (rev ed) (Dywasuk C). New York, Harper & Row, 1974

Thomson H: The Successful Step-Parent. New York, Funk & Wagnalls, 1968 (paperback)

PAMPHLETS

You and Your Adopted Child (LeShan Ed). PAP (#274), 1958. 50¢

Books on the Child's Middle Years

Chess S, Whitbread J: How to Help Your Child Get the Most Out of School. Garden City, NY, Doubleday, 1974

Elkind D: A Sympathetic Understanding of the Child Six to Sixteen. Boston, Allyn & Bacon, 1974 (also paperback)

Kagan J: Understanding Children: Behavior, Motives and Thought. New York, Harcourt, 1971

LeShan E: What Makes Me Feel This Way? Growing Up with Human Emotions. New York, Macmillan, 1972

Mogal DP: Character in the Making: The Many Ways Parents Can Help the School-Age Child. New York, Parents' Magazine Press, 1972

PAMPHLETS

Moving into Adolescence: Your Child in His Preteens. OCD, 1966. 60¢

Pre-Adolescents—What Makes Them Tick? (rev ed) (Redl F). CSAA. 75¢

Your Child from 6 to 12. CB. USGPO (#1791–0070). $1.15

Books on How to Understand and Relate to the Adolescent

Albrecht M: Parents and Teen-Agers: Getting Through to Each Other. New York, Parents' Magazine Press, 1972

Child Study Association of America: You, Your Child and Drugs. New York, Child Study Press, 1971

Conger JJ: Adolescence and Youth: Psychological Development in a Changing World. New York, Harper & Row, 1973

Esman AH (ed): The Psychology of Adolescence: Essential Readings. New York, International Universities Press, 1975

Erikson EH (ed): Youth: Change and Challenge. New York, Basic Books, 1963

Ginott H: Between Parent and Teenager. New York, Avon, 1973 (paperback)

Group for the Advancement of Psychiatry Committee on Adolescence: Normal Adolescence: Its Dynamics and Impact. New York, The Group, 1968

Josselyn IM: The Adolescent and His World. New York, Family Service Association, 1952 (paperback)

Mead M: Culture and Commitment. Garden City, NY, Doubleday, 1970

Student Association for the Study of Hallucinogens (STASH): Our Chemical Culture: Drug Use and Misuse. Madison, Wis, STASH, 1975

Yankelovich D: The New Morality: A Profile of American Youth in the 70's. New York, McGraw-Hill, 1974

PAMPHLETS

An Adolescent in Your Home. CB. USGPO (#1791–00202), 1975. 50¢ (single copy free on request from CB)

Drug Abuse and Your Child (Hill M). PAP (#448), 1970. 50¢

Drugs—Use, Misuse, Abuse: Guidance for Families (Hill M). PAP (#515), 1974. 50¢

Facts About Adolescence. NIMH. USGPO, 1972. 15¢

Health Care for the Adolescent (Schwartz J). PAP (#463), 1971. 50¢

Parent-Teenager Communication: Bridging the Generation Gap (Bienvenu M). PAP (#438), 1969. 50¢

Parents and Teenagers (Hill M). PAP (#490), 1973. 50¢

Books on How to Explain Sexuality to Children

del Solar C: Parents' Answer Book: What Your Child Ought to Know About Sex. New York, Grosset & Dunlap, 1971 (paperback)

Gordon S: The Sexual Adolescent: Communicating with Teenagers About Sex. North Scituate, Mass, Duxbury, 1973 (paperback)

Kay E: Sex and the Young Teenager. New York, Watts, 1973

PAMPHLETS

The Gift of Life (rev ed). HES. 30¢ (flip chart)

Helping Boys and Girls Understand Their Sex Roles (Levine M, Levine JS). SRA. $1.50

Helping Children Understand Sex (Kirkendall, LA). SRA. $1.50

The Sex Educator and Moral Values (Rubin I). SIECUS Study Guide No. 10

Talking to Preteenagers about Sex (Hofstein S). PAP (#349), 1972. 50¢

What to Tell Your Child About Sex (rev ed). CSAA, 1974. $1.50 (paperback), $4.95 (hard cover)

When Children Ask About Sex (rev ed) (Daniels A, Hoover M). CSAA, 1974. $1.25

Books about Sexuality to Read to or Be Read by Children

Barnes KC: He and She. New York, Penguin, 1962. for ages 12–20 (paperback)

de Schweinitz K: Growing Up: How We Become Alive, Are Born and Grow (4th ed). New York, Collier/Macmillan, 1974 (paperback)

Gordon S, Gordon J: Did the Sun Shine Before You Were Born? New York, Third Press, 1974

Gruenberg, S. M.: The Wonderful Story of How You Were Born, rev ed. New York, Doubleday, 1970. For ages 5–10 (also paperback)

Johnson EW: Love and Sex in Plain Language (rev ed). New York, Bantam, 1973 (paperback)

Lerrigo MO: What's Happening to Me (rev ed). New York, Dutton, 1969

Strain FB: Being Born (rev ed). New York, Hawthorn, 1970

Books for Adolescents

Ayars AL: The Teen-ager and Alcohol. New York, Rosen, 1970

Boston Women's Health Book Collective: Our Bodies, Ourselves (rev ed). New York, Simon & Schuster, 1976

Chesser E: Young Adults' Guide to Sex. New York, Popular Library, 1972 (paperback)

Fedder R: You, the Person You Want to Be. New York, McGraw-Hill, 1957

Gordon S: Facts About Sex for Today's Youth (rev ed). New York, Day, 1973 (also paperback)

Greenberg HR: What You Must Know About Drugs. New York, Four Winds/Scholastic Book, 1971

Hunt M: The Young Person's Guide to Love. New York, Farrar Strauss Giroux, 1975

Hyde MO: Mind Drugs (rev ed). New York, McGraw-Hill, 1974 (also paperback)

Johnson EW: How to Live Through Junior High School. Philadelphia, Lippincott, 1975

Johnson EW: V.D. New York, Bantam, 1974 (paperback)

LeShan E: You and Your Feelings. New York, Macmillan, 1975

Levinson F: What Teenagers Want to Know. Chicago, Budlong, 1971 (paperback)

Lieberman EJ, Peck E: Sex and Birth Control: A Guide for the Young. New York, Crowell, 1973

Rosenthal MS, Mothner I: Drugs, Parents and Children. Boston, Houghton Mifflin, 1972 (also paperback)

PAMPHLETS

Approaching Adulthood (rev ed). AMA, 1972. $1.00

Finding Yourself (rev ed). AMA. $1.00

Understanding Sexuality (rev ed) (Kirkendall LA, Heltsley M). SRA, 1972. $1.20

You and Your Alcoholic Parent (Hornick EL). PAP (#506), 1974. 50¢

Books about Exceptional, Handicapped, and Emotionally Ill Children

Blodgett HE: Mentally Retarded Children: What Parents and Others Should Know. Minneapolis, University of Minnesota Press, 1971

Burt C: The Gifted Child. New York, Halsted, 1975

Clinebell H, Clinebell C: Crisis and Growth: Helping Your Troubled Child. Philadelphia, Fortress Press, 1971 (paperback)

Court JM: Helping Your Diabetic Child: A Guide to Parents and Their Children Who Have Diabetes. New York, Taplinger, 1974

Fleming JW: Care and Management of Exceptional Children. New York, Appleton, 1973

Gardner RA: MBD: The Family Book About Minimal Brain Dysfunction. New York, Aronson, 1973

Gordon S: Living Fully: A Guide for Young People with a Handicap, Their Parents, Their Teachers and Professionals. New York, Day, 1975

Heisler V: A Handicapped Child in the Family: A Guide for Parents. New York, Grune & Stratton, 1972

Lowenfeld B: Our Blind Children: Growing and Learning with Them (3d ed). Springfield, Ill, Thomas, 1971

Mayer G, Hoover M: When Children Need Special Help with Emotional Problems (rev ed). New York, Children Study Press, 1974 (paperback)

Myklebust HR: Your Deaf Child. Springfield, Ill, Thomas, 1974 (paperback)

Park CC: The Siege: The First Eight Years of an Autistic Child. Boston, Little, Brown, 1972 (paperback)

Spock B, Lerrigo MO: Caring for Your Disabled Child. New York, Macmillan, 1965 (also paperback)

Stewart MA, Olds SW: Raising a Hyperactive Child. New York, Harper & Row, 1973

Weiner F: Help for the Handicapped Child. New York, McGraw-Hill, 1973

PAMPHLETS

El Asma—Como Sobrellevarla (Carson R). PAP (#437), 1970 (Spanish). 50¢

The Autistic Child . . . A Guide for Parents (Havelkova M). CMHA, 1970

Behavior Modification. NESSCCA, 1975. 50¢

The Child with Minimal Brain Dysfunction. AOTA, 1974

Facts About Autism. NIMH. USGPO (#1724–0259), 1972. 25¢

A Handicapped Child in Your Home. CB. Single copy: free from CB. Multiple copies: USGPO (#1791–000189), 35¢ per copy

Un Niño Desventajado en Su Casa. CB. Single copy: free from CB. Multiple copies: USGPO (#1791–000195), 35¢ per copy

Help for Your Troubled Child (Barman A, Cohen L). PAP (#454), 1970. 50¢

Helping the Child Who Cannot Hear (Moffat S). PAP (#479), 1972. 50¢

Helping Children Read Better (Witty P). SRA. $1.50

Helping the Gifted Child (Witty P, Grotberg E). SRA. $1.50

Helping the Handicapped Teenager Mature (Ayrault EW). PAP (#504), 1974. 50¢

Helping the Slow Learner (Bienvenu M). PAP (#405), 1967. 50¢

Independent Living: New Goal for Disabled Persons (Dickman I). PAP (#522), 1975. 50¢

The Retarded Child Gets Ready for School (Hill M). PAP (#349), 1963. 50¢

Securing the Legal Rights of Retarded Persons (Ogg E). PAP (#492), 1973. 50¢

When Children Need Special Help with Emotional Problems (Mayer G, Hoover M). CSAA, 1974. $1.25

Books on Self-understanding and Self-help Books

Benson H: The Relaxation Response. New York, Morrow, 1975

Fensterheim H, Baer J: Don't Say Yes When You Want to Say No. New York, Dell, 1975 (paperback)

Fromm E: The Art of Loving. New York, Harper & Row, 1956 (also paperback—New York, Bantam)

Levin, A: Talk Back to Your Doctor: How to Demand and Recognize High Quality Health Care. Garden City, NY, Doubleday, 1975

Liebman JL: Peace of Mind. New York, Simon & Schuster, 1965 (also paperback—New York, Bantam)

Madow L: Anger. New York, Scribner, 1974 (paperback)

Murphy G, Leeds M: Outgrowing Self-Deception. New York, Basic Books, 1975

Newman M, Berkowitz B: How to Be Your Own Best Friend. New York, Random House, 1971

Overstreet HA: The Mature Mind (10th ed). New York, Norton, 1959

Sheehy G: Passages: Predictable Crises of Adult Life. New York, Dutton, 1976

Weiss RS (ed): Loneliness: The Experience of Emotional and Social Isolation. Cambridge, Mass, M.I.T. Press, 1973

Wheelis A: How People Change. New York, Harper & Row, 1973 (also paperback)

PAMPHLETS

How Weather and Climate Affect You (Irwin T). PAP (#533), 1976. 50¢

A Positive Approach to Mental Health (Menninger H). EP. 27¢

Seven Keys to a Happy Life (Menninger WC). NRB, 1973. 25¢

Stress—and Your Health (rev ed). MLIC

Tensions—and How to Master Them (Stephenson GS, Milt H). PAP (#305), 1968. 50¢

Understanding Stress (Freese AS). PAP (#538), 1976. 50¢

Books for Patients with a Mentally Ill Relative

Benziger BF: The Prison of My Mind. New York, Walker, 1969

Benziger BF: Speaking Out: Therapists and Patients—How They Cure and Cope with Mental Illness Today. New York, Walker, 1976

Burch C: Stranger in the Family: A Guide to Living with Emotionally Disturbed. Indianapolis, Bobbs-Merrill, 1972

Milt H: Basic Handbook on Mental Illness (rev ed). New York, Scribner, 1974

Stern EM: Mental Illness: A Guide for the Family (5th ed). New York, Harper & Row, 1968

PAMPHLETS

Depression: Causes and Treatment (Irwin T). PAP (#488), 1973. 50¢

Learning About Depressive Illnesses. NIMH. USGPO (1972)

Mental Illness: A Guide for the Family (5th ed) (Stern E). NAMH, 1968. 80¢

Schizophrenia: Current Approaches to a Baffling Problem (Henley A). PAP (#460), 1971. 50¢

Schizophrenia—Is There an Answer? Center for Studies of Schizophrenia, NIMH. USGPO (#1724–0224). 35¢

When a Mental Patient Comes Home. AMA (OP–329), 1975. 15¢

When a Parent Is Mentally Ill: What to Say to Your Child (rev ed) (Arnstein HS). CSAA, 1974. $1.25

Books on Problems of Retirement and Old Age

Askwith H: Your Retirement. How to Plan for It—How To Enjoy It to the Fullest. New York, Hart, 1974 (paperback)

Huyck MH: Growing Older: What You Need to Know About Aging. Englewood Cliffs, NJ, Prentice-Hall, 1974 (paperback)

May EE et al: Independent Living for the Handicapped and the Elderly. Boston, Houghton, Mifflin, 1974

PAMPHLETS

After 65: Resources for Self-Reliance (Irwin T). PAP (#501), 1973. 50¢

Better Health in Later Years (Irwin T). PAP (#446), 1970. 50¢

A Full Life After 65 (rev ed) (Stern EM). PAP (#347A), 1976. 50¢

Getting Ready to Retire (Close K). PAP (#182A), 1972. 50¢

Health and Physical Fitness in Retirement. AGC—USC. 50¢

Is My Mind Slipping? AGC—USC. 50¢

Nutrition for Health and Enjoyment in Retirement. AGC—USC. 50¢

Pierre the Pelican Retirement Series. Series for Men (1966); Series for Women (1970). FPC

Books for the Advanced Reader

Brown JA: Freud and the Post-Freudians. New York, Penguin, 1961 (paperback)

Encyclopedia of Mental Health, 6 vols (Deutsch A, ed). Metuchen, ND, Scarecrow, 1963

Erikson E: Insight and Responsibility. New York, Norton, 1964

Frank JD: Persuasion and Healing: A Comparative Study of Psychotherapy (2d ed). Baltimore, Johns Hopkins Press, 1973

Freud A: The Ego and the Mechanisms of Defense. New York, International Universities Press, 1946

Freud S: Collected Papers, 5 vols. New York, Basic Books, 1959

Ginsburg SW: A Psychiatrist's Views on Social Issues. New York, Columbia University Press, 1963

Jahoda M: Current Concepts of Positive Mental Health. New York, Basic Books, 1958 (Monograph No. 1, Joint Commission On Mental Illness And Health)

Joint Commission on Mental Illness and Health: Final Report. Action for Mental Health. New York, Basic Books, 1961

Leighton AH: My Name Is Legion. New York, Basic Books, 1959

Lidz T: The Person: His Development

Throughout the Life Cycle (rev ed). New York, Basic Books, 1976

Ruitenbeek HM (ed): Varieties of Personality Theory. New York, Dutton, 1964 (paperback)

Pamphlet Sources

ACEI: Association for Childhood Education International, 3615 Wisconsin Avenue, NW Washington, DC 20016

AGC—USC: Andrus Gerontology Center, University of Southern California, University Park, Los Angeles, California 90007

Al–Anon: Al–Anon Family Group Headquarters, PO Box 182, Madison Square Station, New York, New York 10010

AMA: American Medical Association, 535 North Dearborn Street, Chicago, Illinois 60610

AOTA: American Occupational Therapy Association, 6000 Executive Boulevard, Rockville, Maryland 20852

CB: Children's Bureau, Office of Child Development, Department of Health, Education, and Welfare, Washington, DC 20402. Single copies free on request. For purchase, write to Superintendent of Documents, U.S. Government Printing Office, Washington, DC 20402

CMHA: Canadian Mental Health Association, 52 St. Clair Avenue East, Toronto 7, Ontario, Canada

CSAA: Child Study Association of America, 50 Madison Avenue, New York, New York 10003

CSP: Child Study Press, 50 Madison Avenue, New York, New York, 10003

EP: Economics Press, 12 Daniel Road, Fairfield, New Jersey 07006

FPC: Family Publications Center, PO Box 15690, New Orleans, Louisiana 70115

HES: Health Education Service, PO Box 7283, Albany, New York 12224

HLD: Hazeldon Literature Department, Box 176, Center City, Minnesota 55012

MHMC: Mental Health Materials Center, 419 Park Avenue South, New York, New York, 10016

MLIC: Metropolitan Life Insurance Company, Health and Welfare Division, 1 Madison Avenue, New York, New York, 10016

NAEYC: National Association for the Education of Young Children, 1834 Connecticut Avenue, NW, Washington, DC. 20009

NAMH: National Association for Mental Health, 1800 North Kent Street, Rosslyn Station, Arlington, Virginia 22209

NEA: National Education Association, 1201 Sixteenth Street, NW, Washington, DC 20036

NESSCCA: National Easter Seal Society for Crippled Children and Adults, 2023 West Ogden Avenue, Chicago, Illinois 60612

NIAAA: National Institute on Alcohol Abuse and Alcoholism, 5600 Fishers Lane, Rockville, Maryland 20852

NIMH: National Institute of Mental Health, 5600 Fishers Lane, Rockville, Maryland 20852. Single copies free on request. For purchase, write to Superintendent of Documents, U.S. Government Printing Office, Washington, DC 20402

NRB: National Research Bureau, 424 North Third Street, Burlington, Iowa 56202

OCD: Office of Child Development, Department of Health, Education, and Welfare, Washington, DC 20402. Single copies free on request. For purchase, write to Superintendent of Documents, U.S. Government Printing Office, Washington, DC 20402

PAP: Public Affairs Pamphlets, 381 Park Avenue South, New York, New York 10016

PPFA: Planned Parenthood Federation of America, 810 Seventh Avenue, New York, New York 10019

SIECUS: Sex Information and Education Council of the United States. Publications distributed by Human Sciences Press, 72 Fifth Avenue, New York, New York 10001

Despite efforts to provide current figures, the author reminds the readers that pamphlet prices may change at any time

SRA: Science Research Associates, 259 East Erie Street, Chicago, Illinois 60611

TU: Tufts University, Alumnae Office, Eliot-Pearson Department of Child Study, 105 College Avenue, Medford, Massachusetts 02115

USGPO: Superintendent of Documents, U.S. Government Printing Office, Washington, DC 20402

EDUCATIONAL FILMS

The following is a list of recommended films that the therapist may want to show to patients. The titles have been selected for their value in stimulating group discussions on various aspects of mental health. Films present yet another medium as an adjunct to help change attitudes, provide insight, and increase self-understanding.

Personality Problems

Hassles & Hang-ups. 16 mm, color, 20 min. Distributor: Motivational Media, 8271 Melrose Avenue, Los Angeles, Cal. 90046. Purchase: $380. Rental: $35

Hassles and hang-ups are presented in brief scenes indicating whether professional help is necessary.

How Psychiatry and Psychotherapy Help

Therapy—"What Do You Want Me to Say?" (Part of Conflict and Awareness Series.) 16 mm, color, 15 min. Distributor: CRM Educational Films, Del Mar, California 92104. Purchase: $195. Rental: $15

An acted interview between a young woman (student) and therapist (psychologist) reveals that therapy means dealing with feelings. Misconceptions that young people may have about psychotherapy are dispelled.

Journey. 16 mm, color, 28 min, 1974. Written and directed by Robert M. Anderson; produced by Imagination, Inc., for the National Association for Mental Health. Distributor: NAMH Film Service, 324 North Fairfax, Alexandria, Virginia 22314. Purchase: $300. Rental: $35

A brief explanation of what mental illness and treatment are all about. Pantomime is used to clarify the concepts of mental illness and mental health.

Marriage

How Was Your Day? 16 mm, black and white, 4 min, 1974. Made by Roberta London and Robert Polin. Distributor: Nassau Film Productions, 515 Oxford Street, Westbury, New York 11590. Purchase: $55. Rental: None

The film is a mildly ironic look at middle-class suburban marriage. It is useful for leading into discussion on values, family life, male–female roles.

Human Sexuality

About Sex. 16 mm, color, sound, 23 min, 1972. Produced by Texture Films, 1600 Broadway, New York, New York 10019. Purchase: $290. Rental: $35

The film is intended to facilitate interaction regarding attitudes and values about sexuality. Topics—sexual fantasies, body growth, masturbation, pregnancy, contraception, abortion and sex roles.

Pregnancy and Childbirth

Childbirth, 16 mm, color, 17 min, 1972. Distributor: Polymorph Films, 331 Newberry Street, Boston, Massachusetts 02115. Purchase: $225. Rental: $20

A husband and wife lovingly share the birth of their first child.

The Woman's Role

Sylvia, Fran and Joy. 16 mm, black and white, 25 min, 1973. Distributor: Churchill Films, 662 North Robertson Boulevard, Los Angeles, California 90069. Purchase: $185. Rental: $25

Three young middle-class women—housewife, working mother, and separated woman—discuss their experiences as women.

Primary audience: Young people

Family Problems and Crises

With Just a Little Trust. 16 mm, color, 15 min. Distributor: Teleketics, 1229 S. Santee St., Los Angeles, California 90015. Purchase: $190. Rental: $17

The film depicts how a black welfare family copes with adversity.

Family Living and Adjustment

David and Hazel. 16 mm, black and white, 28 min, 1965. Produced by the National Film Board of Canada. Distributor: McGraw-Hill Films, 1221 Avenue of the Americas, New York, New York 10020. Purchase: $330. Rental: $14

Two middle-class families are contrasted in their ways of coping with changes in the husbands' respective businesses: one couple communicates feelings effectively and one couple quarrels.

Chris and Bernie. 16 mm, color, 25 min, 1975. Made by Bonnie Friedman and Deborah Shaffer of Pandora Films. Distributor: New Day Films, PO Box 315, Franklin Lakes, New Jersey 07417. Purchase: $350. Rental: $35

The film depicts the daily life of two working single mothers and their children, living cooperatively.

Primary audience: General public (high school students, adults)

General Child Care and Guidance

The Development of Feelings in Children. 16 mm, color, 35 min, 1975. Produced by Parents' Magazine Films, Inc. Distributor: Parents' Magazine Films, Inc., 52 Vanderbilt Avenue, New York, New York 10017. Purchase: $295. No rental, but free 30-day preview with no obligation for agencies and organizations

The film depicts parent–infant interaction, play interaction, and parent–child interaction in young children

Primary audience: Adults (parents and teachers of young children)

Infants and Young Children

Adapting To Parenthood. 16 mm, color, 20 min. Produced by Polymorph Films. Distributor: Polymorph Films, 331 Newbury Street, Boston, Massachusetts 02115. Purchase: $285. Rental: $30

New parents, particularly the father, are depicted in their adjustment to baby. Some discussion as well as narration by Dr. Kathryn Kris.

Primary audience: Prospective and new parents

The Child's Middle Years

Self-Incorporated. A series of 15 films. 16 mm, color, 15 min each, 1975. Produced by Agency for Instructional Television. Purchase: $180. Available from Agency for Instructional Television, Box A, Bloomington, Indiana 47401

Available from NET, c/o Audiovisual Service, Indiana University, Bloomington, Indiana 47401. Rental: $15.

These are brief documentaries of topical problems in early adolescence; experiences of social, emotional and physiological change.

Primary audience: Preadolescents; appropriate for adult discussion groups

How to Understand and Relate to the Adolescent

I Just Don't Dig Him. 16 mm, color, 11½ min, 1969. Written and directed by Irving Jacoby for the Mental Health Film Board, Inc. Distributor: International Film Bureau, 332 South Michigan Avenue, Chicago, Illinois 60604. Purchase: $150. Rental: $10

Insights are presented into the communication gap between father and adolescent son.

For Adolescents

Pupae. 16 mm, black and white, 30 min, 1974. Made by Seth Pinsker, age 17. Distributor: Youth Film Distribution Center, 43 West 16th Street, New York, New York 10011. Purchase: $300. Rental: $45

Two adolescent boys explore newly felt sexuality in discussions and action.

Primary Audience: Teenagers and adults in middle-class setting

Exceptional, Handicapped, and Emotionally III Children

Early Recognition of Learning Disabilities. 16 mm, color, 30 min, 1972. Produced by Charles M. Wurtz for the National Institute of Neurological Diseases and Stroke, NIH. Purchase: $99.50 from National Audiovisual Center, National Archives and Records Services, Washington, DC 20409. Available on free loan (allow 3-week delivery): National Medical Audiovisual Center (Annex), Station K, Atlanta, Georgia 30324.

Unusual patterns of behavior clearly depicted as ''warning signs'' in a classroom of children.

STRESS: Parents with a Handicapped Child. 16 mm, black and white, 30 min, 1967. Produced by Derrick Knight & Partners, Ltd. Distributor: McGraw-Hill Films, 1221 Avenue of the Americas, New York, New York 10020. Purchase: $225. Rental: $15

This documentary illustrates how parents cope with the special problems of living with children who are disabled by mental retardation, cerebral palsy, muscular dystrophy, schizophrenia, and epilepsy.

Self-understanding

Everybody Rides the Carousel. 16 mm, animated, color, 3 parts (24 min, each), 1976. Produced by Faith and John Hubley. Distributor: Pyramid Films, Box 1048, Santa Monica, California 90406. Purchase: $900—3 parts; $350 each part. Rental: $60—3 parts, $25 each part.

Carousel is the metaphor for Erik Erikson's eight stages of life: newborn, toddler, childhood, school, adolescence, young adulthood, grown-up, and old age.

Primary audience: High school and college students

For Patients with a Mentally III Relative

Full Circle. 16 mm, black and white, 29 min, 1964. Produced by Affiliated Film Producers for the Mental Health Film Board. Purchase: $175. Available from International Film Bureau, Inc., 332 South Michigan Avenue, Chicago, Illinois. Rental: $11. Available from NYU Film Library, 26 Washington Place (Press Annex Bldg.), New York, New York 10003

This film effectively illustrates the comprehensive mental health treatment services provided a patient in a local general hospital: from intensive care, outpatient service, and work adjustment to vocational rehabilitation.

Problems of Retirement and Old Age

Aging. 16 mm, 22 min, color. Distributor: CRM Educational Films, Del Mar, California 92014. Purchase: $295. Rental: $35

This multifaceted film essay on aging mocks stereotypes. It is good for discussion with various age groups.

Mental Health Film Sources

Agency for Instructional Television
Box A
1111 West 17th Street
Bloomington, Indiana 47401

Indiana University Audiovisual Center
Bloomington, Indiana 47401

Mental Health Training Film Program
58 Fenwood Road
Boston, Massachusetts 02215

NAMH Film Service (National Association for Mental Health)
c/o A-V Media Inc
324 North Fairfax
Alexandria, Virginia 22314

National Audiovisual Center (GSA)
  Washington, DC, 20409

New Day Films
  PO Box 315
  Franklin Lakes, New Jersey 07417

New York University Film Library
  26 Washington Place (Press Annex Bldg)
  New York, New York 10003

Perennial Education
  1825 Willow Road
  Northfield, Illinois 60093

Psychological Cinema Register
  Pennsylvania State University
  University Park, Pennsylvania 16802

University of California
  Extension Media Center
  2223 Fulton Street
  Berkeley, California 94720

54
Short-Term Psychotherapy

The advantages of short-term over long-term therapy may be debated on various grounds. Financial savings, more efficient employment of psychotherapeutic resources, opportunity to reduce waiting lists—these and other expediencies are often presented as justification for short-term programs. Admitting that there may be pragmatic reasons for abbreviating treatment, we may ask a crucial question, "How truly effective are short-term approaches in modifying disturbed neurotic patterns?"

One of the first patients I treated, a few weeks after I started my private practice, many years ago, was a whimsical example of the expediency of short-term therapy. One afternoon I received a desperate telephone call from a man who importuned me to see him immediately because of a problem too delicate to discuss over the telephone. It was impossible, I assured him, to arrange for an appointment that day, but if he talked to me for a while on the telephone, we might be able to handle the emergency, and then we could settle on a time in a day or two for an initial interview.

There was little question, from the sighs, coughs, and hesitancy in his speech that the man was experiencing strong anxiety, and I interpreted his hesitation to reveal to me, a total stranger, over a public communication system, a problem that was understandably of such great personal concern to him. "Doctor," he blurted, "nothing like this ever happened to me before and it is perfectly terrible." But, with all the prompting and support I could give him over the telephone, I could not wrest from him the secret of his concern. Only after assuring him that I probably had come across and handled many problems similar to his did he finally blurt out the source of his suffering. The emergency, it turned out, was that he had just that morning become impotent. This catastrophe had developed without any warning or apparent provocation from his sexual partner. In its wake there followed an awesome feeling of threat greater than anything he had ever before experienced. He started trembling and sweating, and his helplessness struck in him such stark terror that his very survival seemed at stake.

In a quiet, matter-of-fact tone I expressed sympathy at his plight, but I advised him that the incident of his impotence was of little importance, since in the lives of all men temporary ebbs in the stream of desire were common. These sponsored deficiencies in performance spontaneously resolved themselves if one stopped worrying himself to a frenzy. The aspect of real interest was, I continued, why he had responded to so natural and evanescent an event with so violent an explosion. He should, I insisted, push the episode of impotency out of his mind and focus instead on what other problems were undermining his security and interfering with an adequate image of himself. If he did this, in a short time the sexual matter would probably take care of itself. We then settled on an appointment time three days following.

At the initial interview, a dapper young man appeared, with smiling manner and a self-confident tone, scarcely that which had issued out of the telephone receiver a few days ago. He was, he said, this same man; but now he had become transformed—solely on the basis of the few words I had spoken to him. "When I hung up," he said, "the tension oozed out of my shoes onto the floor. I knew I was going to be all right." Later that afternoon he tested his sexual prowess, not caring whether he succeeded or failed, and he was completely potent. "I didn't need to come today," he explained, "except that I wanted to see what kind of fellow you were who could do this for me over the telephone." When it became apparent that he was reconciled to his present state of well-being, and had no desire to do anything more about himself, we terminated our contact at this initial interview.

While the results of my first short-term effort undoubtedly left much to be desired, the point is illustrated that adaptive collapse can rapidly be resolved in some cases once we have induced the sufferer to apply to the symptoms a different meaning. The experiences of patients who, in a few sessions, have been brought to an emotional equilibrium, and who thereafter have remained symptom-free, force us to take a new look at our goals in therapy (Rosenbaum, 1964). In view of the large numbers of patients who seek treatment for whom there is no available time in the busy schedules of our psychotherapists, is it not reasonable to reposition our sights on the extensiveness of our therapeutic efforts? Admitting that short-term therapy cannot possibly approach long-term treatment in the extent and depth of change, can we honestly say that our abbreviated efforts are worth the investment?

A number of studies have appeared that bear out that short-term therapy is a most efficient means of bringing about symptomatic improvement or cure. Notable is the experiment of Group Health Insurance, Inc., in which 1200 participating psychiatrists treated a large sample of patients suffering from a wide spectrum of emotional problems (Avnet, 1962). At the end of the limited treatment period a 76 percent cure or improvement rate was scored. Follow-up investigation 2½ years later recorded 81 percent of patients as having achieved recovery or improvement (Avnet, 1965). On the basis of these studies, it may be grossly predicted that four out of five patients receiving brief forms of treatment will report or feel some kind of improvement, even with current treatment methods executed by long-term oriented therapists. That depth changes are also possible has been reported by psychoanalytically trained psychotherapists who present evidence that far-reaching and lasting changes may occur even with a limited number of sessions (Malan, 1963; Wolberg, LR, 1965).

This contention will understandably be subject to challenge. Personality distortions have a long history. They involve habit patterns and conditionings dating to childhood that have become so entrenched that they resist dislodging in a brief period. Repetitively they force the individual into difficulties with himself and others, and they may persist even after years of therapy with an experienced psychoanalyst have revealed their source, traced their nefarious workings through developmental epochs, and painstakingly explored their present-day consequences. We can hardly expect that the relatively few sessions available for short-term therapy can effectuate the alchemy of extensive reorganization not possible with prolonged treatment. Reconditioning any established habit requires time; and time is of the essence in molding personality change if change is at all possible. *But experience persuades that this time need not be spend in all cases in continuous psychotherapy.* Removing some misconceptions about one's illness and one's background may dislodge the cornerstone, crumble the foundations, and eventually collapse some of the neurotic superstructure. This development may not be apparent until years have passed following a short-term treatment effort. Obviously, this bounty cannot always be realized. We may hypothesize that the more experienced, highly trained, and flexible the therapist, the more likely it is to occur. Yet the environment in which the individual functions will undoubtedly have a determining effect on any reconstructive changes that will evolve, since the milieu may sponsor and encourage or vitiate and crush healthy personality growth. But without having had the benefit of therapy, however brief it may have been, even the most propitious environment will have registered little improvement, save for exceptional cases.

There are patients who by themselves have already worked through a considerable bulk of their problems and who need the mere stimulation of a few sessions with a proficient therapist to enable them to proceed to astonishing development. I may cite in this reference the case of a woman and her husband who brought to my office a 17-year-old boy who was a senior in high school.

The presenting complaint was that he was doing poorly at school. The mother, distraught at the boy's lack of motivation to go to college, believed that I could hypnotize the reluctant scholar to force him to apply himself to his school work and to stimulate him to make formal application to the few schools that might be willing to accept a student with so mediocre a record. The boy, upon interview, seemed not too disturbed about the possibility of terminating his education. He was, he confided, more interested in girls, automobiles, and sports than in getting a college degree. Under the circumstances, I confided to him, I would not undertake to subject him to hypnosis; but I would be willing to help him in any other manner if he wanted this. The only way I could really be useful, he insisted, was to get his mother "off his back."

His concerned parents were, needless to say, quite disappointed at my inability to conjure away their son's indolence. Nevertheless, the mother agreed that it might be best to permit him to work for a year in order to experience the grim realities of earning a living as an unskilled

worker. With this the husband concurred. It turned out that the latter was really the boy's stepparent, the mother having divorced the boy's father, whom she described as a brutal and detached individual, uninterested in his son, as contrasted with her present mate who was a warm and sympathetic husband and stepfather.

Several days later I received a telephone call from the mother who inquired if she could consult with me regarding a problem of her own. During the interview it became apparent that the woman, while astute and intelligent, possessed very little understanding of any psychological factors that might be associated with her migraine attacks and muscle and joint pains for which she sought relief. What she desired, she confessed, was to have me hypnotize away her discomforting symptoms. Because she was completely unmotivated for exploratory psychotherapy, I agreed to teach her how to relax her muscles and to control her pain. During the hypnotic induction I suggested that there might be some reason for her symptoms. While going through the self-relaxation exercises, therefore, she could, if she desired, ask herself whether she was not more upset inside, or resentful, than she imagined herself to be. If so, it might be helpful to explore these areas of trouble. After the session the patient gratefully thanked me for my concern, but she completely denied the possibility that any problems other than her boy's educational failure plagued her. Since she had extricated herself from her first marriage, she had never been so happy. Her second husband was everything a woman could want in a man. They got along ideally with no harsh words or strife to mar the blessedness of their union.

Eight days later, at her second visit, my enthusiastic patient proudly announced that her aches and pains were practically gone. She had faithfully performed her "wonderful relaxing exercises" twice daily. With this revelation, she pulled up her skirt, pulled down her panties, and, to my astonishment, presented me with a view of her buttocks which displayed on the right side a bruise the size of a baseball. "Doctor," she said, "you never would believe that I could bump into a table and get bruised this way without going into shock?" Prior to her first visit with me she could not tolerate the slightest pressure on her skin. Now she was able to withstand even severe pain. For the first time in several years, she had been able to move about freely without distress or agonizing headaches.

This, however, was not the best news she had to offer me. She had followed my advice and had informed her son that she no longer would press him to go to college. The boy's relief was great. It was therefore somewhat of a shock to her when he casually announced, the next day, that he had spontaneously sent off an application for admission to two colleges and was planning a trip to visit one of the schools with a classmate that weekend. When he returned on Sunday, he was extremely buoyed up about his visit and eager to enter college so that he could eventually become an athletic coach.

"The topping of the cake," she continued, "came when I was practicing your exercises and I remembered your wanting me to examine how I felt inside and whether I was angry at anything. I knew I was, but I didn't know why. Then it all came to me. There is something my husband has done from the first day we got married that bothers me. It's so silly I feel foolish to mention it to you. It's so minor compared to the wonderful things he does, that I never wanted to anger him by telling him about it. You see, my first husband could never take criticism and went into rages for practically no reason. I never wanted to give my present husband any cause to be unhappy with me and my boy whom he treats like a son. But, while I was relaxing, I said to myself, 'If this is what is making you sick, you must tell him.' You see, what he does is this: every morning at breakfast, he butters his toast with the toast directly over the butter so that it becomes peppered with crumbs. It upsets me, but I never said anything for years. But, when he came home that evening, I told him that you wanted me to get any resentments off my chest, and I told him about the toast and butter. You know, all he did was laugh and say, 'Dear, if it bothered you, why didn't you mention it. Of course, I'll stop.' 'Another thing,' I said, 'that upsets me about you is that, when you come home from work, you throw your coat and hat on the stairs. Why can't you hang them up!' Again, he was very understanding. He was really surprised that it bothered me so. I was so relieved by all this that I felt twenty pounds lighter. Twenty pounds of grief. I know I'll never carry around so much misery again."

There was only one more visit, with a follow-up a year later that revealed excellent progress reflected not only in the patient's continued loss of symptoms, but in a true strengthening of her personality. For instance, the patient had become aware of a persistent pattern of compliance and repression of resentment that had dominated her life from childhood on. She was, she felt, now able to cope with this constricting trait and to express greater assertiveness.

Such extensive dividends may not come about—nor should they be expected—with many patients in short-term treatment, even where the therapist is sufficiently endowed by personality, training and experience to do reconstructive therapy. However, if treatment is managed well, patients will be given an opportunity to move beyond restoring their customary emotional balances. Should they possess sufficient motivation to propel them toward further development, should neurotic secondary gain elements be minimal, and should their environment be sufficiently accommodating to sponsor their continued movement, they may accept this reconstructive gift as a welcome blessing if it comes, but, should it not, we must be satisfied that the patients have derived something worthwhile, even though goal-limited, out of their sparse sessions. If therapy is interrupted at the peak of the improvement curve, before the idealized relationship projections dissolve in the substratum of transference and resistance, and before dependency has had an opportunity to establish a permanent beachhead in the relationship, the rate of improvement can be substantial.

METHODOLOGY

A variety of short-term therapeutic methods have been proposed by different therapists (Barten, 1969, 1971; Bellak, 1968; Bellak & Small, 1965; Castelnuovo-Tedesco, 1971; Gottschalk et al, 1967; Harris, MR, et al, 1971; Levene et al, 1972; Mann, J, 1973; Patterson, V, et al, 1971; Sifenos, 1967; 1972; Wolberg, LR, 1965). The treatment plan to be pursued will depend on the patient's level of intelligence, the patient's capacities for understanding abstract concepts, and the policy of the agency under whose auspices therapy is being done. If we are dealing with an individual with meager education in an outpatient clinic that sets a firm limit on the number of sessions offered, we may have to confine our therapeutic effort exclusively to supportive efforts, offering the patient whatever psychotropic drugs are needed and spending our therapeutic time reassuring and counseling in relation to the current crisis situation. After the allotted number of sessions have expired, we may invite the patient to return for 15- or 20-minute visits periodically to check on drug status and to permit verbalizing of feelings. Holding out this thread of help may suffice to keep the patient in homeostasis. Even inexperienced therapists may function well in such a supportive role. Of value to some patients, particularly those with phobic reactions, is behavior therapy focused on countercondi-tioning and desensitization.

Employing dynamic therapy presupposes that the patient is motivated toward conceptualizing and digesting complex ideas. To a large extent this is contingent on the therapist's capacity to express what is happening in words that are meaningful to the patient. Individuals with even restricted education have a surprising capacity to understand dynamic concepts if these are coached in simple terms. This requires that the therapist have sufficient training and experience to recognize the operative mechanisms, the skill to arouse the patient's curiosity about them, the sensitivity to perceive the best way of helping the patient to organize and integrate this information, and the personality to provide the patient with an experience that does not reduplicate that which the patient has undergone previously with punitive authority.

But, even though we may accomplish nothing more for many of our patients then to enable them to function at their habitually optimal levels, the treatment of patients with a relatively small number of sessions, or over a short span of time, can offer great advantages. In clinic setups where large numbers of patients must be seen by staffs with uneven training and experience, short-term therapy is the only reasonable approach. Unless limits on time are set, all of the available therapeutic hours will soon be filled by patients who become locked into long-term treatment, which will virtually eliminate the clinic as a community resource.

The experience at the Montreal General Hospital is typical (Straker, 1968). A tenfold increase in the caseload forced a shift in emphasis from long-term to psychodynamic short-term therapy. As a result the previously high dropout rate declined, clinic congestion was eliminated and waiting lists reduced. A 2-year follow-up revealed a remission rate of 84 percent in the briefly treated population. The majority of patients exposed even to an unskilled therapist who is neither too hostile nor detached will, within a few sessions, become the beneficiaries of nonspecific healing agencies, such as derive from forces of placebo, emotional catharsis, suggestion, and projected idealized relationship. There is some evidence that the specific maneuvers practiced by the therapist in short-term therapy are of only secondary value as compared to the nonspecific effects. In a double-blind study by Brill et al. (1964), patients were exposed to the following methods: (1) three different drugs—prochlorperazine, meprobamate, and phenobarbital, (2) placebos, and (3) psychotherapy. A long-term evaluation indicated an absence of any marked difference in the improvement rates of the five groups. On the other hand, patients in all five groups showed a tendency to improve as contrasted with the absence of improvement in a no-treatment control group. One should not be compelled from these statistics to discard the discipline of a structured therapeutic plan, since we are interested in bringing about not only an immediate cessation of symptoms but also a continuing betterment in adjustment. An experienced therapist should be able to influence patients beyond the placebo effect.

What constitutes an ideal short-term treatment span is a matter about which there is considerable difference. Some clinics limit therapy to 6 sessions; others to 15. In private practice some therapists believe 10 to 15 sessions to be adequate; others decide on 25 sessions as a maximum, preferably condensed into a period of less than 4 months; still others regard therapy as "brief" even if it has gone on for a year, provided that the total number of sessions does not exceed 50.

Problems considered to be most suitable for short-term therapy are those in which the treatment goal is an abbreviated one. Crisis intervention lends itself admirably to short-term methods (Kalis et al, 1961; Harris, MR, et al, 1963; Kalis, 1970; Patterson, V, & O'Sullivan, 1974). It is my observation, after treating a sizable number of patients with different syndromes, that the average patient can benefit from a short-term approach. Indeed, it can be the treatment of choice.

Certain aspects of a total problem may often be rectified in a few therapeutic sessions. Here a brief period of treatment suffices to restore the patient to emotional equilibrium, leaving him symptom-free and capable of eluding certain pitfalls previously unavoidable. Additionally, he may learn how to utilize his assets to best advantage, how to minimize his liabilities, how to avoid crises in relationships with people, how to organize his activities around his characterologic weaknesses, and how to discover and release some positive qualities within himself. These therapeutic aims, as will be noted, are not too extensive. Basically, the objective is to stabilize the individual by restoring defenses that had, prior to his upset, enabled him to function satisfactorily, or to provide him with a somewhat better means of interpersonal relatedness.

Persons who respond best to short-term approaches are those who have, prior to coming to therapy, already worked out many of their difficulties on a nonverbal or partially verbal level. Such individuals merely need a helping hand in the form of clarification, a little more support, or a slight challenge in order to think through their problems toward a satisfactory solution. Other susceptible patients are those with flexibility of character structure who are capable of relating easily to others without undue dependency, hostility, or detachment. Where the motivation for treatment is strong, where ego strength is good, and where concurrent environmental distortions are easily remediable, success is more readily insured. A fairly keen intelligence and the ability to work on one's problems between sessions are also of positive value.

The shortening of therapy depends to a considerable degree on the therapist. Unfortunately, there is a tendency to think about brief psychotherapy in terms of utilizing one or another special technique or frill. Actually, the most important factor in shortening psychotherapy is not the method that is used, nor the specific syndrome treated, but *the therapist* and the therapist's understanding of dynamics and of how to use oneself most constructively in the therapeutic interpersonal relationship. What this means is that an incompetent therapist's techniques are not particularly enhanced through the utilization of short-term approaches. Indeed, such a therapist may discover that his or her psychotherapy actually becomes briefer in the wrong sense, in that patients become dissatisfied earlier and terminate therapy much more quickly than if the practitioner had utilized traditional long-term methods.

The therapist must, in short-term therapy, be capable of establishing a rapid rapport with the patient. One must be sensitive, perceptive, and capable of focusing on important problem areas without undue delay. It goes without saying that the therapist must understand how to utilize with skill the specialized techniques that are part of the therapeutic process. A knowledge of hypnotherapy, behavior therapy and drug therapy are also of great advantage.

Problems that do not yield to short-term measures are those that have persisted a long time and perhaps date back to early childhood. An example of the latter are serious personality disturbances caused by destructive conditionings in the formative years of life. Obdurate attitudinal and behavioral patterns usually cannot be resolved except by a prolonged therapeutic experience. Here, time itself is important since extensive reconditioning is required. Time is an essential part of treatment in instances where emotional growth has been thwarted by unfortunate traumas in early life, and where the therapeutic goal is a maturation of the personality structure.

This does not mean that brief psychotherapy precludes extensive personality change; it does mean that the change to take place will require an extensive time interval following treatment in the medium of life experience itself. What is accomplished in therapy here is that seeds of change are planted which slowly germinate in the course of living long after therapy has ceased. Resistances are gradually resolved, sometimes with surprising alterations in the character structure. Well done short-term therapy may offer the reward of continuing reconstructive change.

AN OUTLINE OF SHORT-TERM THERAPY

The following outline may constitute a therapeutic plan:

1. Delineate in rank order the complaints and symptoms that the patient considers most upsetting and that he or she would like to resolve. Verbalize empathically how the patient must feel about these to communicate concern and understanding. Make a contract with the patient during the first session designating the total number of sessions, the target goals, the fee and manner of payment, and possibly the type of therapy to be employed.

2. Identify any important immediate situational problems that were associated with and perhaps continue to be related to the patient's present complaint factor.

3. Explore the patient's ideas and feelings regarding the relationship of symptoms and associated disturbing events that both preceded and followed the development of the complaints.

4. Explore what the patient has done about the symptoms and disturbing environmental situation. Why has the patient been unable to solve the present difficulty without help?

5. Inquire into previous upsets that were similar to the present one, and see if a relationship between symptoms and precipitating events can be established. Is there a similarity to the present crisis?

6. Inquire into other complaints and symptoms, including what measures have been taken to alleviate these. Were any tranquilizing or energizing drugs used? Ask about sleeping habits; does the patient dream much or little? Can the patient relate a remembered dream vividly?

7. Inquire briefly into the patient's early life. Ask, "What was your mother like when you were a child? How did she act toward you? What about your father? Any problems with your sisters and/or brothers? How did you get along as a child? Any nervous difficulties?" Estimate on personality distortions arising from these early conditionings.

8. Try to make a connection between the patient's present complaints, previous episodes of decompensation, and residual personality difficulties.

9. In language the patient can understand, try to give a reasonable and uncomplicated explanation for the difficulties.

10. Try to get the patient to make connections between the immediate situation and past conditionings.

11. Explore the patient's ideas of how he can handle the problem. Implement supportive maneuvers where needed (environmental manipulation, guidance, drug therapy, hypnosis, conditioning techniques, family therapy).

12. Clarify the patient's fears and resistances, and attempt to get the patient to think matters through and to do things for himself.

13. Avoid too involved probings into the past.

14. If any transference manifestations arise that act as resistance, and if these can be detected, resolve them through discussion, reassurance, and clarification.

15. Terminate, refer for further help, or continue with individual or group therapy if absolutely necessary.

It goes without saying that the general principles of interviewing and psychotherapy detailed in previous chapters apply to short-term as well as longer treatment.

THE SUPPORTIVE PHASE OF TREATMENT

Turning to another human being for help is an inevitable consequence of feelings of helplessness, bewilderment, and anxiety. It represents a final acknowledgment by the individual that one is unable to cope with one's difficulty through one's own resources. More or less, every emotionally ill patient overtly or covertly regards the helping authority as a source of inspiration from whom infusions of wisdom must flow that will heal the wounds and lead one to health and self-fulfillment. Such credences are powered by the helplessness that inevitably accompanies a shattering of the sense of mastery. Because habitual coping mechanisms have failed, the patient believes himself incapable of independent judgments and delivers body and soul to the powerful therapeutic agent whose education and experience promises to take over the direction of his life.

This design is obviously unwholesome if it is permitted to continue, for elements will be released that undermine the patient's independence, inspire infantility, and mobilize anachronistic hopes and demands that superimpose themselves on the patient's other troubles, further complicating his existence. If our therapy is to be short-term, we cannot afford to inspire dependency in our patients.

Knowing that the patient covets a scheme to enmesh himself indefinitely in a passive role with an omniscient deity, beneficent protector, and idealized parent, the therapist may plan the strategy of treatment.

First, it is essential to establish as rapidly as possible a working relationship with the patient. This can often be done by a skilled therapist in the initial interview. It is difficult, however, to designate any unalterable rules for the establishing of immediate contact with a patient. Variable factors apply in one case that are not applicable in a second. However, there are certain general principles that are useful to observe within the bounds of which one may operate flexibly. For instance, on meeting the patient the expression of a sympathetic and friendly attitude is remarkably helpful in relaxing him sufficiently to tell his story. As obvious as this may seem, many therapists greet a new patient with a detached and passive attitude in the effort to be objective and nondirective. This can freeze the patient in a resistive bind from which he may not recover during the short span of his contact with the therapist.

Second, it is important to treat the patient, no matter how upset he seems, as a worthwhile individual who has somehow blundered into a neurotic impasse from which he will be able to extricate himself. Neurotic difficulties influence feelings in the direction of being unloved and unlovable. The patient may harbor doubts that he can be accepted or understood. Irrespective of denial mechanisms, he will crave extraordinary reassurance that the therapist is interested in him and cares about what happens to him. This obviously cannot be communicated verbally, but it may be expressed through a manner of respect, considerateness, tact, solicitude, and compassion.

Third, the patient must be inspired to verbalize as much as possible, while the therapist attends to what he is saying, encouraging him by facial expressions, gestures, utterances, and comments that reflect an interest in the patient and an understanding of what he is trying to say. The patient is constantly drawn out to express his problems, pointed questions being phrased to facilitate the flow of ideas and feelings. Whereas in long-term therapy prolonged silences may be sometimes tolerated, in brief therapy they should be interrupted actively.

Fourth, it is vital to avoid arguing or quarreling with the patient, no matter how provocative he may be. The available time for therapy is so limited that one cannot indulge in the challenges and confrontations possible in long-term therapy. One may not agree with what the patient says, but one should convey a respect for the patient's right to express his irritations and misconceptions.

Fifth, empathy is the keynote in establishing contact. Understandably one may not be able, in the limited span available for their exploration, to sympathize with some of the attitudes, feelings, and behavior of the patient. It may also be difficult to put oneself in his place. Yet the therapist may be able to detect an essential dignity in the patient, considering that his problems, destructive to him and to other people, have deviated him away from creative and humanistic aims. While it is inexpedient therapeutically to reassure too readily or to praise, it is essential not to underestimate the patient's constructive qualities. In concentrating his attention on his bad points, the patient will tend to minimize his worthwhile characteristics, which may lend themselves to a recounting by the therapist after he has gathered sufficient data.

Sixth, the therapist may, by verbal and nonverbal behavior, signal confidence in his or her ability to help the patient without promising him a cure. This presupposes that one has faith in what one is doing and a conviction that all people, given even a minimal chance, have the capacity to get well and develop.

Seventh, even in the first interview, the patient may be told that the rapidity of recovery will depend on his willingness to cooperate in working on his problems. The therapist will show him how he can do this and will help him to help himself.

Eight, appropriate drugs, environmental manipulation, hypnosis, desensitization, counterconditioning, and other adjunctive agencies may be introduced in order to bring the individual to homeostasis as rapidly as possible. These instrumentalities may constitute for the patient the chief ingredients of his treatment; yet we know that the profits derived from the interpersonal relationship with the therapist are of cardinal importance.

Restoration to habitual functioning may be all that can reasonably be done for many patients, and the therapeutic effort may be halted at this point.

THE APPERCEPTIVE PHASE

If we are to proceed beyond the supportive phase, toward an attempt at reeducation or reconstruction of personality, we must strive to bring the individual to some recognition of what is behind his disorder. The power of "insight" has, of course, been greatly exaggerated; but irrespective of how valid or invalid an "insight" may be, it constitutes, when it is accepted, a significant means of alleviating tension and of restoring to the individual his habitual sense of mastery. The fact that we couch our "insights" in scientific terminology, being assured that they validate our theoretical preconceptions, does not make them accurate, even though the patient responds to them with relief, hope, and abatement of his complaints.

Yet the principle is a correct one. Some explanation for his trouble is essential, and we must give our patient one that is as close to our current scientific understanding of human nature as possible, always mindful of the fact that as behavioral scientists we are balanced precariously on the pinnacle of profound ambiguities. What seems like the truth of today may be the exploded myth of tomorrow.

But myth thought it be, we have no other more tenable explanation; so we make it, hopeful that it will find its mark. The most effective vehicle that we have for this is the unique relationship that is set up between the patient and therapist. This acts as a corrective experience for the patient. The patient may project into the relationship the same kinds of irrational demands, hopes, and fears such as have shadowed his attitudes toward early authorities and other significant people in his past. But instead of meeting indignation, rejection, ridicule, or hostility—the usual and expected rebuttals—the therapist interprets the patient's reactions with sympathy and understanding. Bringing these, if they are apparent, to his attention in a noncondemning manner helps the patient to arrive at an understanding of the meaning and possible origin of his drives while actually reexperiencing them in the protective relationship with the therapist. Under these circumstances the patient may come to realize that his responses toward the therapist are the product, not of any realistic situation that exists, but rather of what he anticipates or imagines must be as a result of past relationships. He may then appreciate that what is happening with the therapist also happens under some circumstances with other people. Thus, varied defensive reactions become apparent to the patient, not as theories, but as real experiences.

In short-term therapy time prevents the employment of other than focused interviewing techniques, while eschewing extensive dream interpretation and the building up of a transference neurosis. However, an experienced therapist will be able, perhaps even in the first session, to gain knowledge of the operative dynamics from the history given by the patient, particularly the quality of his relationship with his parents and siblings, from one or two dreams, from the nature of the symptomatology, and from the patient's behavior with the therapist during the interview. The therapist may then present at a propitious moment a cautious but firm explanation to the patient of the impact on him and his personality of some of the experiences and deprivations in his childhood—the defenses that he has developed, how environmental precipitating factors have operated to bring his conflicts to a head, and how these are registered in his immediate symptoms and sufferings. Only a fragment of the existing conflicts may lend itself to such exploration and interpretation in short-term therapy, but this can be like a biopsy of the total psychodynamic picture. If the patient grasps the significance of an interpretation and sees the continuity between problems in his development, their crystallization in his general personality structure, and their relation to the current complaint factor, a deep penetration will have been achieved. By concerted self-examination the patient may thereafter progressively widen his own insights. In any equation the shifting of one factor will bring other elements into realignment.

Obviously, interpretations will have to be made that coordinate with the patient's capacities for understanding. The therapist will need to employ language comprehensible to the patient, encouraging the patient to restate what has been expressed to test his comprehension. It is surprising how patients, even those without an extensive education, can grasp the meaning of relatively complex psychological concepts if these are illustrated by examples from the patient's own experience. When a good relationship exists between the therapist and patient, even unconscious repudiated aspects may be explored without provoking too severe reactions of resistance. If skilled at dream analysis, the therapist may advantageously work with dreams (Merrill & Cary, 1975). If the patient is unable to acknowledge the ac-

curacy of an interpretation, the therapist may ask him to consider it, nevertheless, before discarding it entirely. The patient may also be encouraged to alert himself to factors that stir up his tensions, to work on connections between these provocative factors and what is being mobilized inside himself. Are reactions habitual ones; if so, how far back do they go? Are they related to important experiences in childhood? Some patients may be able to get considerable understanding through the discipline of searching within themselves. Some may even learn to interpret their dreams in line with such percipience.

Sometimes the patient will, due to resistance or the lack of time, fail to arrive at any basic realizations in the course of short-term therapy. This need not deter the therapist from encouraging the patient to work on himself toward self-understanding after the treatment period is over. It is quite rewarding to observe how many patients, some months and even years later, arrive at insights that strike them with a dramatic force and that they can utilize constructively. Examining these, one may recognize them as patterned after some of the therapist's original interpretations, which could not be accepted during the short-treatment phase but which were subjected to spontaneous working through following treatment.

THE ACTION PHASE

Insight is not enough. The acid test of therapy lies in the patient's capacity to put his acquired new comprehensions into definitive action. This means that he must challenge conceptions that have up to this time ruled his life. A symptom may rapidly be overcome in the supportive phase of therapy; but a personality pattern, one that disorganizes relationships with other human beings, will scarcely be altered except after a period of working through.

In short-term therapy even the tiniest action opposing neurotic misconceptions can be scored as a gain. The therapist may actively invite the patient to challenge his fears and engage in actions that hold promise of rewards. Discussion of the consequences of his movements may then prove fruitful. Several tactics may be of importance here. First, actively outlined, are specific courses of action, hoping that the patient, prompted to act on suggestion, will achieve a small success that will reinforce his determination to try again. Even after a signal success, patients will need further urging. Having escaped hurt by the skin of their teeth, they may feel that their luck will collapse the next time they engage in an experience that threatens to set off anxiety. Techniques of behavior modification may be advantageously employed (Sloane, RB, et al, 1975), and where the relationship is a good one an anxiety-provoking technique may be cautiously applied (Sifneos, 1972). Any of the adjunctive aids described in Chapter 53 may be employed. Second, a tranquilizer or a barbiturate taken prior to a challenge may reduce anxiety sufficiently so that the patient may allow himself to enter into a fearsome situation and see it through. As soon as possible, a repetition of this action with reduced and finally no drug will be indicated. In borderline patients a phenothiazine derivative such as Stelazine appears to work better than the minor tranquilizing drugs. Third, some patients may be taught self-hypnosis or meditation for purposes of desensitization. In the trance the patient is trained to visualize himself successfully mastering situations that upset him. The patient may fantasy overcoming progressively challenging difficulties, gradually working himself up to more fearsome ones. Suggestions made to himself, during the period of self-relaxation, that he will have the desire to tackle his problems may enable him to handle these with greater and greater ease. Fourth, role playing with the patient in which he imagines himself in challenging or hazardous spots may crystalize his determination to expose himself to the responsibilities that he must face.

THE INTEGRATIVE PHASE

Consolidating therapeutic gains will require practice the remainder of the individual's life. The chinks in the patient's defen-sive armor must be widened by constant challenges and repetitive profitable actions. Complacency, riding on the notion that one feels better and hence can remain at a standstill, invites a recrudescence of symptoms once stress exceeds existent coping capacities. Constant alertness to what is happening within oneself and a resisting of subversive neurotic temptations are mandatory.

In short-term therapy one must depend on the posttherapeutic period to harden what has been molded during the active treatment phases and to restructure into new patterns aspects that were only casually perceived before. Encouraging is the fact that, once the old way of life has been unbalanced in one dimension, new zones of activity and more wholesome modes of being and feeling may present themselves.

Before therapy is terminated, the patient may realize that it is possible to control tension and anxiety once it starts by making connections between symptomatic upsets, precipitating factors in his environment, and his operative personality forces and by recognizing that he is capable of developing a different philosophy that can lend to his life a salutary meaning.

In some cases the patient may be encouraged after he leaves therapy to employ the technique of self-hypnosis or self-relaxation periodically when he is upset, both to resolve his tensions and to explore reasons for the revival of his symptoms. Patients can easily learn to apply this twofold tactic by giving themselves the assignment to figure out the aspects within their environment and within themselves that have precipitated their anxiety. This may result in direct understanding, or stimulated fantasies and dreams may yield some leads. A helpful course of action may then spontaneously be evolved. No more than a few sessions by himself are usually required to restore equilibrium. Sometimes it is advantageous to make a cassette recording for the patient, as described in the section on hypnosis, that the patient may utilize to reinforce his gains.

The patient may also be counseled temporarily to employ a mild tranquilizing drug if tensions do not resolve after a while.

The patient must be cautioned, however, that drugs, while provisionally useful, cannot constitute a way of life. The basic therapeutic factor at all times is self-understanding that leads to constructive action. Drugs cannot and must not replace such self-directed efforts.

Finally, the patient is exhorted to adopt a few basic philosophical principles. Superficial as they sound, they sometimes make a profound impact on him. In long-term therapy the patient is expected to develop new values through his own spontaneous efforts. In short-term therapy a different way of looking at things may be presented in an active educational effort. For example, the following principle may be proferred: "It is useful to remember at all times that while you are not responsible for what happened to you in your childhood and the faulty ideas and fears that you learned in your past, you are responsible for carrying them over into your adult life." This principle, if accepted, may block the patient from making a career out of blaming his parents and crediting to past unfortunate episodes all of his current problems, justifying his neurotic carryings-on by the terrible things done to him as a child over which he had no control. Another principle is, "No matter what troubles or terrible scrapes you have gotten yourself into in the past, you can rise above these in the future with the knowl-edge you now have. You need not indulge in patterns which you know you should be able to control, and really want to control" This precept, if incorporated, may help some patients control certain neurotic patterns realizing that they have powers to inhibit them. The putting together of certain persuasive formulations in this way can be useful to patients who are unable to structure a philosophic formula by themselves. This may help consolidate the gains they have made in therapy.

Within this broad framework, then, the therapist may apply himself or herself to patients' problems, utilizing procedures from various fields blended into a comprehensive approach. The specific techniques in short-term therapy are contingent, first, on the acceptance of electicism, adopting procedures from every field of psychiatry, psychology, sociology, education, and even philosophy that may be of help in the total treatment effort; second, on the existence of flexibility that enables the therapist to adjust stratagems to the immediate needs of the patient and therapeutic situation; and third, on the studied employment of activity in the relationship. All modalities are employed in those combinations that may be of value.

A complete recording of a short-term treatment process of nine sessions may be found immediately following Chapter 62.

55

Handling Emergencies in Psychotherapy

Emergencies sometimes develop during psychotherapy that require prompt and cautious handling. Among such emergencies are suicidal attempts; psychotic attacks; excitement, overactivity, and antisocial behavior; panic states; acute alcoholic intoxication; acute barbiturate poisoning; hallucinogenic and other intoxications; severe psychosomatic symptoms; and intercurrent incurable somatic illness.

SUICIDAL ATTEMPTS

In well-conducted psychotherapy suicidal attempts are rare. Vague suicidal threats may be expressed at the start of treatment, the patient making such comments as that he might be better off dead but that he is "too much of a coward" to try suicide. Where such statements lack the tone of conviction, it is best for the therapist not to subject the patient to concentrated interrogation around the matter of suicide. The therapist's expressed concern may frighten the patient badly and rob him of faith in himself. It is generally found that he is trying to prove something or to hurt someone with his suicidal threat. Actually, he is responsible for his own actions, and

neither the therapist nor anybody else can stop him from destroying himself if this is really what he wants to do. The family of the patient may also be helped to resist being blackmailed by suicidal threats.

The following signs, symptoms and situations, however, do point to a potential suicidal risk:

1. Depressions of a psychoneurotic or psychotic nature.
2. Irrespective of diagnosis, any patient who has made a suicidal attempt in the past or who has a history of a severe depression.
3. A patient who, during therapy, insistently threatens suicide.
4. Loss of appetite, severe weight loss, insomnia, listlessness, apathy, persistent expressions of discouragement and hopelessness, loss of sexual desire, extreme constipation, hypochondriac ideas, continuous weeping, and general motor retardation which are present at the start or appear in the course of therapy.
5. Dreams of death, mutilation, and funerals.

Where during treatment, the patient talks *openly and seriously* about a desire to "end it all," it is important not to change the topic or to reassure the patient unduly. Rather, a frank talk about the reasons why he feels that suicide is the best recourse for him may permit the patient to investigate his feelings. This will enable the therapist to determine whether the threat is real, whether it is casually made as a dramatic gesture, whether it is a hostile stab at the therapist, or whether it constitutes an appeal for reassurance. Under no circumstances should the therapist minimize the importance of the threat, cajole the patient, or subject him to verbal attack. Arguing with the patient is generally useless. Where the threat seems ominous, the therapist might make helpful statements to the effect that suicide *seems* to be a way out of difficulty, but it actually accomplishes nothing; that there may be other solutions than suicide that are not now apparent; and that suicide is a final act that cannot be undone and that it could always be resorted to later on if the patient so wishes. The attitudes conveyed to the patient in such statements are respect for his right to self-determination and a reminder that he is not giving himself an opportunity to explore more constructive actions. Talking frankly about suicide often serves to rob it of its awesome or appealing quality. Where suicide seems imminent in spite of anything the therapist can do or where an abortive attempt is actually made, there is no alternative than to advise responsible relatives to get the patient hospitalized immediately in a closed ward of a psychiatric hospital.

Suicide prevention centers do exist in the larger cities, and they have been used by depressed individuals and their families in crises. How effective these centers are in preventing suicide has not been evaluated adequately. Their impact may be minimal because individuals intent on suicide do not generally call in. Suicide centers do, however, serve a purpose if no more than to act as a referral source.

Hysterical Personalities

Suicidal attempts in hysterical personalities are common and consist of histrionic gestures calculated to impress, frighten, or force persons with whom the patient is in contact to yield attention and favors. Such attempts are incited by motives for display rather than by genuine desires to take one's life. Dramatic performances of an ingenious nature are indulged, during which there is a superficial slashing of the wrists, or feigned unconsciousness with stertorous breathing while placing an empty bottle of sleeping pills alongside the bed, or the gulping of tincture of iodine, or the impetuous opening of gas jets. Feverish demonstrations of suffering and martyrdom continue after the patient is restrained or "revived," until he is convinced that he has emphasized his protests sufficiently. The danger of these pseudosuicidal maneuvers is that the patient's judgment may not be too good during dramatic overacting and he may accidentally go too far and commit suicide even though this was not his original intent.

In treating hysterical cases with suicidal threatenings, we must demonstrate to the patient that we are neither intimidated by nor angry at the actions of the patient. Interpretation of the purpose of the patient's frenzied behavior should be made in terms of the broader neurotic patterns.

Psychopathic Personality

Of a related but more serious nature are the suicidal attempts of the psychopathic personality. During episodes of excitement, violence, deep remorse, excessive drinking, or temporary psychotic outbreaks, the psychopath may slash his wrists or take an overdose of sleeping pills. The desire for self-punishment and death are genuine, though temporary. When their attempt has been aborted and they have been hospitalized, such patients recover rapidly, evidence no further suicidal impulses, and express great remorse at their folly. Yet, a short time later, under propitious circumstances, the attempt will be repeated, with further contrition and promises of abstention. Interpretation of the episode is essential, but it usually fails to act as a deterrent to the patient's actions. When the suicidal episodes are motivated by disturbed interpersonal relationships, as, for instance, a broken love affair or rejection by a love object, the continued exploration of the patient's feelings and patterns is indicated. In addition, the therapist may have to increase the frequency of visits and insist on being telephoned when the patient is tempted to indulge in suicide. Where the patient persists in his impulsive suicidal behavior, after seeming to have acquired insight into his patterns, the therapist may have no other alternative than to tell the patient that treatments will have to be discontinued. It may be suggested that the patient may perhaps want to start treatment with another therapist. This may give the patient enough of a jolt so that he will insist on the therapist's continuing to treat him, on the condition that he will abandon all further suicidal attempts. Whether or not the therapist concedes to the patient's wishes to continue treating him will depend on how the therapist feels about the patient. Unfortunately, with some psychopaths the threat of discontinuance of therapy may be the only force that can control their explosive conduct. Even here the effect may be temporary.

Schizophrenia

In some types of schizophrenia suicide is a grave possibility. It is most common in acute, excited catatonic states, particularly those associated with panic. Hallucinations may drive certain patients to mutilate or kill themselves. Fear of homosexual attack or of being persecuted may also force some paranoidal individuals to suicide. The methods of self-destruction employed in schizophrenia may be bizarre, including such mutilations as disembowelment and genital amputation.

The handling of the suicidally inclined schizophrenic patient is organized around administering ample sedation, communicating with the family so that they may assume some responsibility, and arranging for transportation and admission to a mental hospital. Electric convulsive therapy is often indicated. Chlorpromazine (Thorazine), thioridazine (Mellaril), perphenazine (Trilafon), or haloperidol (Haldol) in ample dosage (see the section on

somatic therapy in Chapter 53) are indicated.

Pathologic Depressions

Depressed episodes may occur in people due to loss of security, status, or a love object; however, the depression is rarely of such depth as to inspire a desire to take one's life. Where the depressed state is extreme, suicide is always a possibility. Among the pathologic depressive conditions are psychoneurotic depression, manic-depressive depressed psychosis, involutional depression, senile depression, and depressions in organic brain disease. Isolated elderly people and middle-aged persons separated from their mates are definite risks.

To manage a patient with a pathologic depression, certain palliative measures are helpful. The watching of diet with the inclusion of stimulating and appetizing foods and the prescription of tonics and vitamins may be indicated in anorexia. In mild depressions Benzedrine or Dexedrine may be useful temporarily to stimulate the patient during the day, while sedation may be required at night for insomnia. In more severe depressions the patient's family or a reliable friend should be interviewed and acquainted with the potential dangers. Where the patient remains at home while in a deep depression, a trustworthy adult person should be in constant attendance. The patient should not be permitted to lock himself into a room, including the bathroom. Sleeping pills, tranquilizers, poisonous drugs, razor blades, rope, and sharp knives and instruments should be removed. Window guards are necessary if there is a chance that the patient may hurt himself by leaping through a window. Hospitalization on a closed ward with constant supervision by efficient nurses or attendants may be essential. The treatment of choice is electroconvulsive therapy, which may prove to be a lifesaving measure. Psychotherapy during severe depression is generally confined to supportive measures, as insight approaches tend to stir up too much anxiety.

Fear and guilt feelings are common in

the therapist who will usually be in a dilemma about hospitalization. It is urgent that a nonmedical therapist secure a consultation with a psychiatrist to share responsibility, to prescribe antidepressive medications, or to arrange for hospitalization should the patient need it and is willing to consider it. Although a patient can end his life in spite of any safeguards if he desperately insists on suicide, there is a lesser chance in a hospital setting, particularly when ECT is immediately started. Usually there is little problem in decision making when the patient has made an unsuccessful attempt. Here relatives and neighbors rush the patient to an emergency hospital service, or the police are brought into the picture and arrange for admission and perhaps transport the patient.

Difficulties in decision are greater in the event a patient has mildly threatened to take his life, but makes no active gesture to do so, and has no history of past suicidal attempts. Under these circumstances the therapist may have to utilize the greatest interviewing skills (Murray, 1972). The patient may be told that the ultimate responsibility for his life is his own. "You probably won't believe this, but you *will* get over this depression and will feel better. Right now it is natural for you to imagine your suffering will continue indefinitely. It will not." Here it is assumed that the patient is started on a regime of antidepressant drugs (Tofranil, Elavil, or Sinequan) in adequate dosage (see the section on somatic therapy in Chapter 53). In the great majority of patients a frank empathic talk will tide them over the crisis.

Suicide is especially possible during the spontaneous resolution of a depression, when the patient begins to recover from a depressive attack after a few electroconvulsive treatments or when, after having started to recover, he suffers a relapse. The patient must consequently be watched carefully during these periods since he is apt to put into practice a suicidal desire that he was previously unable to execute due to retardation.

It is often important to see the patient frequently and to telephone him between sessions to maintain as close a tie as possible.

Miscellaneous Suicidal Conditions

Sometimes a therapist is consulted by the parents or friends of a child who has made a suicidal attempt. Examination may fail to reveal hysteria, depression, or schizophrenia, especially when the child is noncommunicative to the point of mutism. It is possible here that the child is internalizing destructive feelings. Young drug abusers are particularly vulnerable. Because the youth is nonmotivated for therapy and resents having been taken to a psychiatrist, it may be difficult to treat the patient. By following the rules outlined in Chapter 31, Dealing with Inadequate Motivation, and by indicating to the patient that he seems to be angry at someone, it may be possible to establish rapport.

A 14-year-old girl who had made a suicidal attempt by swallowing 50 aspirin tablets was brought in for a consultation. Refusing to talk except in monosyllables, it was difficult to carry on an interview. The therapist finally remarked, "You must have been awfully angry at someone to have done this to yourself." The patient blanched, then brought her hands to her face and started compulsive sobbing, which went on for 15 minutes. Intermittent were outbursts in the form of protestations of how "bad" she was for feeling the way she did about her mother. Ventilation of her resentment produced immediate emotional relief and established sufficient contact with the therapist to start psychotherapy.

Should a suicidal attempt have been made, the immediate injuries will have to be treated and artificial respiration instituted if necessary. If concentrated oxygen is available, it should be given. In asphyxiation with gas or from fumes of an automobile 50 cc of 50 percent glucose, injected intravenously, may help prevent cerebral edema. Intramuscular adrenalin (epinephrine), 0.5 to 1.0 cc of 1 : 1000 concentration, may also be administered.

If suicide was attempted with poisons or drugs, identification of these will permit selection of the proper antidote. Patients who are not unconscious and who have not taken corrosives or petroleum products may be induced to vomit by tickling the pharynx with a finger or spoon, and by giving them a glass of water containing 1 tablespoonful of salt or 1 teaspoonful of powdered mustard or soap suds. This should be repeated several times if necessary and followed by a gastric lavage with 1 quart of water containing 1 tablespoonful of (a) "universal antidote," or (b) 2 parts burnt toast to 1 part strong tea and 1 part milk of magnesia, or (c) table salt. Next, a neutralization of the specific poison with the antidote is attempted and demulcents (flour, starch, gelatin in a paste, or 12 beaten eggs mixed with milk) are given. Finally, the poisons remaining in the intestinal tract are removed by administering magnesium sulfate (Epsom salts: 30 gm in a glass of water). Suicidal attempts with barbiturates are handled by inducing emesis, administering "universal antidote," and preventing shock with measures to be described in a later part of this chapter, under Acute Barbiturate poisoning.

PSYCHOTIC ATTACKS

In the course of psychotherapy anxiety may be released that is beyond the endurance of certain patients. A psychotic episode occurring during treatment may be the product of too early or too avid an attack on resistances and defenses. Often, it is the consequence of a transference neurosis that gets out of control. A good psychotherapist is capable of gauging the ego strength of the patient and of introducing supportive measures should signs of the shattering occur. Nevertheless, even good psychotherapists may be unable to control the outbreak of psychosis in patients with vulnerable ego structures. The quality of the working relationship is a crucial factor. Some therapists are capable of working sensitively and emphatically toward reconstructive goals with potentially psychotic and even overtly psychotic patients. Other therapists, particularly those who are unable to manage their countertransference, may be unable to treat patients whose ego organizations are unstable. Such therapists may refuse to work with infantile dependent personality disorders or with borderline and psychotic patients unless the approach is to be exclusively supportive in nature. They may also have to transfer patients who show tendencies toward psychotic outbursts once the treatment process is under way.

Symptoms that lead one to suspect beginning ego disintegration during psychotherapy are feelings of unreality, depersonalization, excessive daydreaming, ideas of reference, paranoidal ideas, bizarre somatic sensations, motor excitement, uncontrollable sexual and hostile impulses, propensity for perversions, heightened interest in toilet activities, compulsive talking, fears of castration, and fleeting hallucinations and delusions. These symptoms may appear individually or in combination. For a while the patient may maintain a good grasp on reality, recognizing the unusual or irrational nature of his ideas, impulses, and acts. Later on, distortions of reality may occur in the form of fixed delusions and hallucinations, perhaps accompanied by panic reactions, suicidal tendencies, and violent aggression.

Psychotic attacks may be handled within the therapeutic situation by a therapist who has a warm feeling for the patient, who is not disturbed by the existing symptoms, and who is capable of modifying his approach so as to bring about the restoration of repressive barriers. The fact that a psychosis has precipitated is usually indicative of something having gone amiss in the therapeutic relationship. If one can admit to oneself the possibility of errors in handling and if one is able to restore the patient's feelings of trust and confidence, such a therapist may be capable of bringing the retreat from reality to a halt. In line with this objective it is best to discontinue probing for deep conflictual areas and to keep the content of the interview focused on current reality problems. The relationship with the therapist should be kept on as positive a level as possible, the therapist assuming a helpful active role. Under no circumstances should the therapist express alarm at, and condemnation toward, any of the patient's misconceptions. Listening attentively to the patient's productions, the therapist counters with reality, suggesting that perhaps things seem to be as they are because the patient has been so upset. If disturbing transference is at the basis of the patient's turmoil, measures to lessen transference, described in Chapters 40 and 44, may be invoked. Should the patient require more support, the frequency of interviews may be increased.

Where these practices fail to bring relief to the patient, it is likely that the therapeutic relationship has deteriorated and that the patient will have to be referred to another therapist. The referral may be upsetting to the patient, and he is apt to consider it a further manifestation of rejection or an indication of his failure. The therapist may explain that the patient's specific problem will probably be helped more by another therapist with a slightly different approach. If the patient is incapable of thinking rationally and if his difficulties are potentially dangerous to himself and others, a reliable family member should be asked to assume some responsibility in the matter of referral. Should the patient object to the therapist's making contact with his family, the therapist may, if the situation is sufficiently dangerous, have to communicate with the family irrespective of the patient's wishes.

Where self-injury, suicide, homicide, violent aggression, ruinous spending, criminality, or other disasters are possible, hospitalization may be mandatory. If the therapist is a nonmedical person, a consulting psychiatrist should be called in. Discussion with the patient may convince him that he should enter an institution voluntarily. Hospitalization will, however, have to be accomplished against the wishes of the patient where he sees no need for confinement. In the event that he is actively resistent and must be absolutely hospitalized, intravenous Sodium Amytal to the point of deep sleep will permit his transport to an institution without the need for physical restraint. A physician should be in attendance in the ambulance that transports the patient in order to handle such emergencies as respiratory paralysis.

The therapist may have to arrange the details of hospital admission in cooperation with the patient's family and, in addition, may have to explain the reasons for hospitalization to them in a reassuring way. In doing this, the therapist may experience some guilt and anxiety, as if accountable for the patient's collapse. It is important, however, not to castigate oneself for what has happened nor to confess to failure; rather, the family may be informed that the patient's personality structure has been unable to stand his inner tensions and that he has temporarily broken down. A period of hospitalization is necessary to restore his equilibrium.

The specific treatment rendered in the hospital will depend on the severity and type of psychosis. In acute excitement or depression with exhaustion it will be necessary to sedate the patient adequately, to correct dehydration by injecting fluids and salts parenterally, and to administer electroconvulsive therapy or intensive drug therapy, whichever is indicated. In milder excitements or depressions sedatives and hospitalization alone may suffice to restore the patient's stability. It is important that the person assigned to look after the patient avoid arguing with or "psychoanalyzing" the patient, no matter what the provocation, since this will upset the patient even more.

EXCITEMENT, OVERACTIVITY, AND ANTISOCIAL BEHAVIOR

States of excitement and overactivity developing during psychotherapy are signs of acting-out or manifestations of ego shattering.

During acting-out the patient may engage in destructive, antisocial, or perverse sexual behavior. In attempting to understand acting-out, one's first suspicion is that the patient is protecting himself from awareness of transference by projecting it away from the therapist. Hostile or aggressive outbursts, delinquency, criminality, marked promiscuity, and perverse sexuality are often products of hostile and sexual impulses toward the therapist that the patient is unable to acknowledge.

The best way to resolve such acting-out is to explore the patient's feelings and attitudes toward the therapist, to determine which of these are rooted in realities and which are irrational carryovers of the past. As long as he is unaware of and cannot verbalize his proclivities toward the therapist, the patient will continue to "blow off steam" outside of therapy. Skillful use of the interviewing process that brings out verbalizations related to the transference may put a halt to the patient's destructive patterns.

Sometimes it is difficult or impossible to get the patient to analyze transference and in this way to terminate acting-out. The therapist here may attempt to deal with this obstruction (1) by stimulating transference, though devices already described, in order to make its manifestations so obvious that the patient cannot help but talk about his feelings or (2) by controlling acting-out by increasing visits to as many as daily sessions and by the assumption of a prohibitive, authoritative role. If these measures fail to help the situation, therapy will have to be terminated with transfer to another therapist.

Excitement and antisocial behavior that occur as a result of ego shattering may be dealt with after identifying the cause of the present difficulties. Supportive techniques are generally indicated, and the patient may have to be put on a regime of Haldol (2–5 mg), Thorazine (25–100 mg), or Valium (10 mg), repeated at intervals until adequate sedation occurs. If the decline continues, the therapist had best transfer the patient to another therapist, since he himself is probably unable to control the situation. Where a dangerous psychotic condition develops, the patient's family will have to be apprised of it, for hospitalization will in all likelihood be necessary.

INTENSE ANXIETY ATTACKS

Severe anxiety sometimes breaks out in the course of psychotherapy. It may become so overwhelming that the patient feels helpless in its grip. His coping resources have seemingly come to an end, and he can no longer crush the fear of imminent disintegration. His demands on the therapist then may become insistent, and he will bid for protection and comfort.

The handling of intense anxiety reactions will require much fortitude on the part of the therapist. By assuming a calm, reassuring manner, the therapist provides the patient with the best medium in which to achieve stability. Accordingly, the therapist must be able to tolerate the emotions of the patient. One must be able to convey to the patient a constant feeling of warmth, understanding, and protectiveness while respecting the patient's latent strengths that have been smothered by his turmoil. Upbraiding the patient for exhibiting foolish fears and attempting to argue away anxiety serve to stimulate rather than to reduce tension.

The best means of handling acute anxiety is to permit the patient to verbalize freely in an empathic atmosphere. Helping the patient to arrive at an understanding of the source of his anxiety, whether it be rooted in unconscious conflict, transference, resistance, or the too abrupt removal of existing defenses, promises the quickest possibility of relief. The triad of emotional catharsis, insight, and reassurance operates together to permit of a reconstitution of defenses against anxiety.

Where anxiety is intense, it is usually impossible to work with the patient on an insight level. Here, supportive measures will be necessary to restore the habitual defenses. If the paient is living under intolerable environmental circumstances, a change of environment may be indicated to lessen pressures on him. In the event that anxiety has followed intensive mental probing, a holiday from exploration may be necessary, with a focusing on casual or seemingly inconsequential topics. A patient who has spent many sleepless nights tossing about restlessly or, once asleep, has awakened periodically with frightening dreams may benefit from a dose of 3 gr of Sodium Amytal, which may alleviate his tension remarkably and restore his stability. The use of sedatives during the day is to be minimized, if possible, to forestall the sedative habit. If anxiety continues, the frequency of sessions may be increased and the patient may be assured that he can reach the therapist at any time in the event of a real emergency. Referral to an experienced psychiatrist skilled in the somatic therapies may be necessary.

Excessive anxiety in psychoneurotic patients is best handled psychotherapeutically, increasing the frequency of sessions if necessary. Where this fails to bring relief, several sessions devoted to "narcosuggestion," that is, reassurance and suggestion under intravenous Pentothal or Amytal (see Narcotherapy, page 801), may be tried. Librium (25 mg. 3 to 4 times daily) or Valium (10 mg. 3 to 4 times a day) may restore the individual's composure, following which the drugs are diminished, then discontinued. Where anxiety is out of control and constitutes an emergency, 50 to 100 mg of intravenous Librium, repeated in 4 to 6 hours if necessary and followed by oral Librium, may be helpful. Some patients respond better to barbiturates than to tranquilizers. In acute anxiety pentobarbital (Nembutal) ¾ to 1½ gr, or secobarbital (Seconal) ¾ to 1½ gr may dissipate symptoms in about 30 minutes. Some patients prefer to take ¼ to ½ gr of phenobarbital sodium (Luminal) every 3 or 4 hours. Barbiturate administration is to be halted as soon as possible because of the danger of habituation.

In borderline or psychotic patients it is wise to institute drug treatments immediately. Haldol, Thorazine, or Mellaril in adequate dosage (see Table 53–3) may bring anxiety to a halt.

These measures will rarely fail to control severe anxiety in borderline or psychoneurotic patients. In the rare case where they fail, and especially where a transference neurosis is present and cannot be resolved, the patient may have to be referred to another therapist or a short period of hospitalization may be required.

PANIC STATES

The treatment of panic states is more difficult than the management of anxiety. Here the patient is victimized by a wild, unreasoning fear that plunges him into disorganized thinking and behavior or drives him to the point of immobilization. Suicide is always a grave possibility. Admission to an emergency unit in a hospital may be essential, the therapist giving the admission doctor pertinent information about the patient. Where a patient in panic is seen for the first time, the therapist will be somewhat in a dilemma. The initial step in the management of a panic state with a strange patient is attempting to calm down the patient by quiet, empathic listening in a quiet atmosphere. Reassuring the belligerent individual that he is belligerent because he is frightened often has a dramatic effect. Often little more will be needed than to display interested attention and to express sympathy at appropriate times. Sorting out the problem in this way will give the therapist clues about appropriate therapeutic steps to take, including whether psychotropic drugs are necessary (emergency units unfortunately do not usually have a secluded place where quiet interviewing can take place). Where the patient is out of contact with reality, is suicidal, or is aggressively excited, however, he will require rapid sedation or tranquilization and probably hospitalization.

Diagnosis is important. The patient may be psychotic as a result of a functional ailment like schizophrenia. Or he may be manifesting a toxic psychosis as a result of taking too many drugs or because of a physical ailment. Giving the patient more medication in the latter instances will merely compound the injury. Information about the patient from relatives or friends is highly deisrable, even indispensable, in ruling out drug intoxication or physical ailments, such as cardiovascular illness, diabetes, etc., that may be responsible for delirium.

If drug intoxication is ruled out, drug therapy is the treatment of choice for schizophrenic or manic excitements. Rapid tranquilization is indicated to reduce social consequences of morbidity. Not everybody agrees with this, however, In young schizophrenics who are having a first attack there are some who believe that they should be allowed spontaneously in a protected environment to reach a baseline. Thus, Mosher and Feinsilver (1973) state, "We believe that the inner voyage of the schizophrenic person, which is induced by environmental crisis, has great potential for natural healing and growth, and we therefore do not attempt to abort, rechannel, or quell it before it has run a natural course." Whether one heeds this advice or not will depend on the existing social support systems on which the patient will depend. A congenial hospital regime with empathic nurses and attendants is helpful. On the other hand, and particularly in older patients or those who have had a previous minimum absence from work and their families, it may be vital to avoid prolonged disability and unemployment which can operate as stress factors.

Restoration to a nonpsychotic state is possible within a few hours employing powerful neuroleptic drugs that act on the limbic system and influence the psychotic thinking process. The drug often chosen is haloperidol (Haldol) given intramuscularly. The first dose is 5 mg, then 2–5 mg every 30 minutes until the patient is sedated; the blood pressure should be monitored to avoid hypotension. The objective is to get the maximum therapeutic impact with a minimum of side effects (dystonia, akithesia, and other Parkinsonian symptoms). If the patient falls asleep after the first 5 mg injection, he is probably suffering from a toxic psychosis like drug intoxication (e.g., alcoholism), and Haldol is stopped.

Some therapists still prefer chlorpromazine (Thorazine), which is given intramuscularly in 25 to 75 mg dosage according to the size of the patient and degree of disturbance. If the systolic blood pressure standing is below 95, the Thorazine is discontinued; the patient's head is lowered and the feet elevated. If the pressure is maintained satisfactorily, the drug is given every hour until control of the excitement is achieved. The dosage is either increased or decreased depending on how the patient responded to the previous dose. The intramuscular medication is discontinued should the patient fall asleep or quiet down sufficiently. The choice of being subsequently seen on an outpatient basis or immediately hospitalized will depend upon whether the patient is dangerous to himself or others, the attitude of the family, hospital resources in the community, and the patient's cooperativeness.

What dosage of drug orally for ensuing 24-hour periods will be required can be estimated by multiplying the intramuscular dosage of Thorazine that it has taken to tranquilize the patient by 2⅔ (Ketal, 1975).

With Haldol one may give the same dose orally as was given intramuscularly. If the patient is too sedated, this can be cut back. Patients should be seen daily or every other day to make sure that they do not slip back.

Drowsiness and hypotension with Haldol are less than with Thorazine. Extrapyramidal side effects are more common, however. Where such side effects occur with Haldol or other antipsychotic drugs, 1 to 2 mg of Cogentin by mouth (or intravenously if emmergent) or 50 mg of Benadryl by mouth or intravenously may be given. Continuance of the drug for several days is indicated. Reassurance of the patient and his family are important. To avert the pyramidal symptoms, some therapists give Cogentin prophylactically.

Where intramuscular injection is not possible or urgent, oral medications are used. Here 10 to 20 mg of Haldol may be given in liquid concentrate form for the first day; if no response, this is raised to 40 mg the second day and 60 mg the third day until an effect is achieved. Or Thorazine in liquid concentrate form of 50 to 150 mg dose may be given and regulated according to response.

Intravenous Sodium Amytal (up to 15 gr) will put the patient into narcosis. If panic continues following this, the patient may require hospitalization on a closed ward. Electroconvulsive treatments will also often interrupt the excitement. As many as 2 ECTs daily may be needed for a few days, followed by one treatment daily, until equilibrium is established. Where delirium and confusion appear in elderly patients or those with respiratory and cardiovascular disorders, Thorazine may be given for restlessness and paraldehyde or chloral hydrate for insomnia. Should epileptic seizures develop and continue (status epilepticus), intravenous Sodium Amytal, phenobarbital sodium (Luminal), or diphenyl hydantoin (Dilantin) may be administered.

In hospital settings "sleep therapy" is occasionally instituted, especially in psychotic patients, where panic cannot be arrested through other means (Azima, 1958). Here sleep, which lasts 20 to 24 hours a day, is induced by giving the patient a combination of 100 mg (1.5 gr) Seconal,

100 mg Nembutal, 100 mg Sodium Amytal, and 50 mg of Thorazine. The patient is aroused 3 times daily, and the dosage of medication is regulated according to the degree of wakefulness. Good nursing care is urgent; indeed, without it sleep therapy is hazardous. During the waking period the pulse rate, blood pressure, temperature, and respiration are recorded; the patient is gotten out of bed, washed, and fed. Daily 2000 cc of fluid and at least 1500 calories in food are supplied, while vitamins are administered parenterally. A half-hour prior to meals 5 units of insulin are injected to stimulate the appetite. Milk of magnesia is supplied every other day if necessary, and a colonic irrigation is given should a bowel movement not occur in 2 days. Catherization is performed if the patient does not urinate for 12 hours. The bed position of the patient must be changed every 2 hours, and should the patient's breathing become shallow, oxygen and carbon dioxide are administered. Sometimes ECT is instituted with sleep therapy, either daily during the first waking period or three times weekly. In this way a deep regression is induced. The average treatment duration is 15 to 20 days. Rehabilitative therapy must follow the sleep-treatment episode.

In manic reactions, once the acute psychotic process is brought under control, lithium therapy may be started.

TOXIC DRUG PSYCHOSES

Mixed drug intoxications are common and may constitute important emergencies. It is difficult, if not impossible, to determine what substances the patient has imbibed since even he may not know their true nature, purchased as they have been from dubious sources. Knowledge of the local drug scene may be of some help, at least in screening out certain possibilities. The kinds of drugs utilized vary in different parts of the country. They include amphetamine, barbiturates, alcohol, phencyclidine, THC, nonbarbiturate hypnotics (like Doriden, Quaalude), marijuana, morning glory seeds, nutmeg, LSD, mescaline, DMT, STP, MDA, psylocybin, and a variety of mescaline and amphetamine combination compounds.

In many cases adequate therapy can be administered only in a hospital, which unfortunately may not provide the quiet, relaxed atmosphere that excited patients need. Gastric lavage is limited to instances where the drug was recently taken. After a number of hours it is relatively useless. Hemodialysis is valuable for certain drugs and not for others. In all cases maintenance of an airway, of respiration, and of the cardiovascular apparatus is fundamental.

If the nature of the drug that has been taken is known, for example, from the blood or urine analysis, it may be possible to prescribe certain antagonistic medicinal agents. Thus, if amphetamine is the culprit, Thorazine or other neuroleptic or antipsychotic drugs can be given. If the patient has taken STP or LSD, antidotes may block some sympathemimetic effects without influencing the hallucinogenic aspects. As yet there is no totally effective antagonist for these common hallucinogens. Indeed, Thorazine is contraindicated in STP toxicity because of the hypotensive and convulsive potentiating effect, which can be dangerous. Mildly excited patients may respond to a mild tranquilizer like Valium given parenterally.

Global mystagmus is a frequent symptom in drug psychosis and may serve as a valuable diagnostic indicator. Disorientation, confusion, and hallucinations are common, of course. Because, in the average toxic patient, the kinds of drugs that the patient has been taking are difficult to diagnose, it is best to err on the side of caution in administering antipsychotic drugs. Some of the effects of the substances the individual has been taking, like THC (the pure extract of marijuana), may be reinforced by antipsychotics. After reassuring the patient that he will get over his reactions, he may be given 10 to 20 mg of Valium intramuscularly. If there is no improvement in the patient after a few hours and no anticholinergic symptoms, a major psychotic, such as 5 mg of Haldol or 4 mg of Navane or Trilafon, may be given. These drugs have a marked antipsychotic effect without too great sedation.

Handling the "Bad Trip"

Individuals experimenting with hallucinogenic drugs, including marijuana and amphetamines, may occasionally experience a frightening journey away from reality and need emergency intervention. In the street vernacular such an experience is referred to as a "bad trip." Hallucinations may be vivid, and there may be an inability to communicate. Such reactions may be inspired by an overdose of drug or may be the consequence of something frightening that the patient perceives or imagines in his environment or even may occur with small dosage in schizophrenic patients. The atmosphere in which the "bad tripper" is treated is important. It should be as quiet as possible. Sending the person to an emergency hospital unit may induce more panic. The therapist or person managing the patient should be reassuring and gentle and never question the patient about his experience, for this may tend to stir him up. He should be asked to concentrate his attention on something in reality, like an object in the room, in order to shift his focus from his inner life. Rarely are physical restraints or drugs necessary, except when the patient becomes violent. Valium (10 mg intramuscularly, repeated if necessary) is helpful in the latter instance.

The treatment of severe amphetamine psychosis is similar to that of schizophrenic psychosis, namely, prescribing Thorazine or Haldol intramuscularly. In the case of LSD, psylocybin, or marijuana intake with a psychoticlike response, the therapist should stay with the patient while reassuring him that his reactions are temporary and will pass in a few hours. Valium (5–10 mg) or Librium (25–50 mg) may be helpful. Where not successful and panic increases, Thorazine intramuscularly may be utilized with all of the precautions outlined under the section on Panic States. In the event of overdose of sleeping medications containing scopalamine, Thorazine should be avoided. Valium may be utilized as may Physostigmine (2–4 mg).

The most frightening consequence of a toxic drug absorption is a status epilepticus, a constant series of seizures without the patient regaining consciousness in between. Here one must establish an adequate airway, particularly being sure that the patient's tongue does not block respiration. Up to 10 cc of paraldehyde may be given intramuscularly (5 cc in each buttock) or 1 to 3 cc intravenously very slowly over 3 to 4 minutes. Phenobarbital (100–200 mg intramuscularly) is also commonly utilized after a single seizure to prevent status epilepticus. It may be given intravenously (200–400 mg) very slowly. A respirator should be available in the event respiration stops. Phenobarbital may thereafter be given intramuscularly (100–200 mg) every 2 to 6 hours up to 1 gm of the drug in 24 hours. The next day the patient may be started on Dilantin (200 mg intramuscularly). Valium (10 mg) intravenously is also a good anticonvulsant, but it is short-acting, lasting only 3 to 6 hours.

Acute Alcoholic Intoxication

Pathological intoxication sometimes presents itself as a psychiatric emergency. The reactions range from stupor or coma to excited, destructive, combative, homicidal, or suicidal behavior. Comatose states are best treated in a hospital where a neurological study may be made to rule out other causes of unconsciousness, such as apoplexy, brain concussion, status epilepticus, cerebral embolism or tumor, subdural hematoma, toxic delirium, uremic or diabetic coma, and carbon-monoxide or morphine poisoning. Where alcoholic intoxication exists, a hospital with a 24-hour laboratory service permits of the testing of blood sugar and carbon-dioxide levels required for the administration of insulin and dextrose. Nursing care is important. The patient must be turned from side to side regularly and his head lowered to prevent aspiration pneumonia. The pulse, respiration, and blood pressure are recorded every half hour. Oxygen is given by tent or nasal catheter where respiration is depressed. Intravenous sodium chloride should be injected in amounts of 250 cc every 3 or 4 hours.

Where the patient is conscious and gag

reflexes are present, a gastric lavage may be provided, external heat applied, and strong coffee administered by mouth or rectum. Intramuscular caffeine and sodium benzoate (0.5–1.0 gm) may be dispensed every hour until the patient is alert. Intravenous dextrose solution (100 cc of 50 percent dextrose) may be introduced and repeated, if necessary, every hour, and 10 to 20 units of insulin may be provided, repeated in 12 hours. Thiamine hydrochloride (100 mg) intravenously is also a useful medicament.

Excited reactions, including acute alcoholic intoxication, alcoholic hallucinosis, and delirium tremens are treated by intramuscular injection of Haldol (5 mg), or Navane or Trilafon (4 mg), or Thorazine (25–50 mg) repeated if necessary. Some psychiatrists use Librium intramuscularly or intravenously (50–100 mg) or Valium (10–20 mg) repeated, if necessary, in 2 to 4 hours, for alcoholic agitation and impending or active delirium tremens or hallucinosis. Dextrose (100 cc of a 25 percent solution), thiamine hydrochloride (100 mg), and 20 units of insulin are given routinely. If tranquilizers are not used, paraldehyde (10 cc by mouth, rectally, or intramuscular injection) repeated every 2 to 4 hours and chloral hydrate (0.5–1.0 gm) every 4 to 6 hours may help to sedate the patient. Morphine and depressing hypnotics are contraindicated; however, Sodium Amytal (0.5–1.0 gm) is sometimes administered intravenously (1 cc per minute) to quiet a violently disturbed patient. Ample fluids should be given intravenously to combat acidosis and dehydration (approximately 3000 cc daily, containing magnesium and potassium minerals). Other drugs include thiamine hydrochloride (20–50 mg), intramuscularly, and nicotinamide (niacinamide, 100 mg.), intravenously, substituted in several days by oral thiamine hydrochloride; vitamin C (100 mg), caffeine and sodium benzoate (0.5 gm every 4 to 6 hours for 4 to 6 doses) for stimulation, saline laxatives to promote proper elimination, and Compazine (10 mg intramuscularly) for uncontrollable nausea and vomiting. Milk and eggnog may be offered the patient; if not tolerated, 10 percent dextrose and sodium chloride solution intravenously may be required.

Acute Barbiturate Poisoning

The popularity of barbiturates as sedatives has resulted in a relatively large incidence of barbiturate poisoning. Patients who have developed a sedative habit may accidentally take an overdose of barbiturates, or the drugs may be purposefully incorporated with suicidal intent. Sometimes the patient, having swallowed a lethal dose, will telephone the therapist informing him of his act. At other times relatives or friends will chance on the patient before respiratory paralysis has set in.

The usual therapy consists of immediate hospitalization, if possible, and the institution of the following measures:

1. Establishing an airway, such as with an endotracheal tube with suction of secretions.
2. Administration of oxygen, or artificial respiration if necessary, using a mechanical resuscitator.
3. Early gastric lavage carefully administered.
4. Fluids given parenterally (5 percent glucose); in extreme hypotension, plasma injected intravenously.
5. Stimulants—vasopressors like Neosynephrine (2–3 mg) if blood pressure is low or L-norepinephrine (4 mg/L of 5 percent glucose solution).
6. Turning the patient hourly with head slightly lower than feet.
7. Catherization of the bladder if necessary.
8. Prophylactic antibiotics.
9. Hemodialysis with an artificial kidney, if available, or peritoneal dialysis.
10. Digitalis for heart failure.
11. Avoidance of analeptics.

Clemmesen (1963) has described the treatment of poisoning from barbiturates in Denmark, where the incidence of attempted suicide has always been relatively high. A special intoxication center helps control the clinical condition day and night. The pulse, respiration, temperature, blood pressure, and hemoglobin are monitored every 2 or 4 hours, each day the barbiturate acid content of the blood is determined, as is plasma chloride and bicarbonate, blood urea, and serum protein. The gastric contents are *not* aspirated unless the drug was taken within the past 4 or 5 hours, and the pharyngeal and laryngeal reflexes are present. Gastric lavage is avoided. The Trendelenburg position is maintained during the first few days to prevent aspiration of gastric contents. Patients are moved to a different position in bed every 2 hours. There is intensive slapping of the chest and suction of secretion from the air passages. Procaine penicillin (2 million units × 2) are injected each day as a prophylactic against infections. Fluids of 2 to 3 liters are given parenterally. Shock, if present, is managed by blood transfusion and perhaps by drugs such as norepinephrine. Complications, such as pulmonary edema, pneumonia, and atalectasis are treated. Stimulation with analeptics is avoided. In the absence of pronounced hypotension, pulmonary edema, and reduced renal function, after the clinical condition is under control, osmotic diuresis and alkalinization by infusions of urea and electrolyte solutions reduce the duration of coma two to four times. Of 92 patients with severe barbiturate poisoning, 85 recovered with this treatment approach.

Poisoning from overdose of nonbarbiturates or tranquilizers may be managed in essentially the same way, although these drugs are somewhat safer than barbiturates. Amphetamine and pressor amines are contraindicated, although norepinephrine may be given. Should inordinate restlessness or tonic and clonic convulsions follow excessive phenothiazine intake, careful administration of Sodium Amytal may be helpful, recognizing the potentiation possibility. Cogentin or Artane may also be valuable.

SEVERE PSYCHOSOMATIC SYMPTOMS

There are a number of psychosomatic symptoms for which the patient initially seeks treatment, or that develop suddenly in therapy, that may be regarded as emergencies. Most of these are hysterical conversion or dissociative reactions, such as blindness, seizures, fugues, vomiting, aphonia, amnesia, paralysis, astasia-abasia,

violent contractures, and anorexia nervosa. The patient may be so disabled by his symptom that he will be unable to cooperate with any attempted psychotherapeutic endeavor. Immediate removal of the symptom may thus be indicated. Such removal need not block the later use of more ambitious therapeutic measures. In the course of symptom removal, efforts may be made to show the patient that his symptoms are rooted in deeper personality problems, the correction of which will necessitate exploration of conflictual sources.

Hypnosis is an ideal adjunctive technique to expedite the emergency relief of hysterical symptoms. Once symptom removal has been decided upon, it is necessary to determine whether to attempt the removal at one session or whether to extend therapy over a period of several weeks. The severity of the symptom, its duration, the nature of the patient's personality, and the aptitude for hypnosis have to be considered. The approach is an individual one, and suggestions must be so framed that they will conform with the patient's personality, the type of symptom, and its symbolic significance. It is essential to adapt one's language to the patient's intelligence and education. Many failures in symptom removal are due to the fact that what the hypnotist is trying to convey is not clearly understood by the patient.

If hypnotic removal of the symptom at one session is decided upon, sufficient time must be set aside to devote oneself exclusively to the problem. As many as 2 to 3 hours may be necessary. A new patient may be encouraged to discuss past history and symptoms in order for the therapist to determine the patient's reaction to the illness as well as to gain clues to the patient's attitudes, motivations, and personality structure. Accenting of the patient's protestations of how uncomfortable he is, the therapist may emphasize that there is no reason why, if the patient has the motivation, he cannot overcome his symptom.

An optimistic attitude is important because many patients are terrified by their illness and have convinced themselves of the impossibility of cure. However, a cure should not be promised. The patient may be told that hypnosis has helped other people recover and that it can help him, too, if he will allow himself to be helped.

The patient may then be informed that it is necessary to determine how he will respond to suggestions. He is instructed that he need not try to concentrate too hard on what is said because, even though his attention wanders, suggestions will get to his subconscious mind and he will find himself reacting to them. If he has the desire to rid himself of suffering, he will have the desire to relax and to follow suggestions. No indication is given the patient at this time that his symptom will be removed in its entirety since the symptom may have values for him and he may show resistance if he suspects that he will be deprived of it immediately.

Hypnosis is then induced, and confidence in the ability to follow suggestions is built up by conducting the patient through light, medium, and, finally, deep trance states. Where the patient has a symptom that consists of loss of a physical function, it may be expedient to suggest that he is unable to use the part. This is done in order to associate malfunction with the hypnotist's command instead of with a personal inadequacy.

The next step in treatment is to get the patient, if he so desires, to discuss under hypnosis his immediate life situation and his reaction to his illness. A persuasive talk may be given to the patient, avoiding, for the time being, reference to his symptom.

In some patients active participation is encouraged. A reasonable explanation is given for the suggestions that will be made. In some instances the patient may even be encouraged to veto suggestions, if he does not wish to follow them or if he believes them to be against his best interests. Active participation is encouraged in patients with relatively good ego strength who shy away from too authoritarian an approach.

Symptom removal by suggestion is far more effective where it is demonstrated to the patient that he has not lost control over his functions, and hence is not the helpless victim of symptoms that cannot be altered or removed. This is achieved by showing the patient, while he is in a trance, that it is possible to create on command such symptoms as paralysis, spasticity, and anesthesia. Once the patient responds to these suggestions, he is informed about the important influence that the mind has over the body. Then a symptom identical with the patient's chief complaint is produced in some other part of the body. Should the patient respond successfully, a partial removal of his own symptom is attempted. For instance, if he has a paralyzed arm, he is told that his fingers will move ever so little. Then paralysis of the other arm, which has been artifically produced, is increased in intensity, while a strong suggestion is made that the patient will find that function is restored to his ailing part. In the case of a paralyzed arm it is suggested that his hand will move, then his arm, and, finally, that the paralysis will disappear altogether.

The fact that symptoms can be produced and removed so readily on suggestion may influence the patient to accept the fact that he is not powerless and that he can exercise control over his body.

In order to protect the patient, should his symptom have a defensive function, he may be left with some residual symptom that is less disabling than the original complaint but that, it is hoped, will absorb its dynamic significance. For instance, in the case of a paralyzed arm paralysis of the little finger may be induced, and a suggestion may be given the patient that the finger paralysis will have the same meaning for him as the arm paralysis and that the finger paralysis will remain until he understands fully the reasons for the original paralysis and no longer needs the paralysis. In the event of an extensive anesthesia numbness of a limited area may be suggested as a substitute.

Posthypnotic suggestions are next given the patient to the effect that his restored functions will continue in the waking state, except for the induced residual symptom. An activity may then be suggested that brings into use the ailing part; the patient may then be awakened in the midst of this action.

These suggestions are repeated at subsequent visits, and, if desired, the patient is taught the technique of self-hypnosis so that suggestive influences may continue through his own efforts.

Although removal of the patient's

symptom at one sitting may be possible and desirable in certain acute disabling hysterial conditions, it is usually best to extend therapy over a longer period. Suggestions are carried out very much better where the patient is convinced that he has been hypnotized and that hypnosis can have a potent influence on his functions. It may, therefore, be advisable to delay giving therapeutic suggestions until the patient achieves as deep a trance as possible and gains confidence in his ability to experience the phenomena suggested to him. The employment of therapeutic suggestions at a time when the patient is skeptical about his ability to comply, and before he has achieved sufficient faith in himself and in the therapist, may end in failure and add discouragement and anxiety to the patient's other troubles.

A deep trance seems to increase therapeutic effectiveness in most patients. Where only a light trance is possible, the patient may not be able to get to a point where he becomes assured of his capacity to control his symptom.

All suggestions must be as specific as possible and should be repeated several times. The therapist should build, as completely as possible, a picture of what he wants the patient to feel or to do.

The lighter the trance, the less emphatic should the suggestions be. In extremely superficial hypnotic states the patient may be instructed that he need not concentrate too closely on the suggestions of the therapist, but rather he should fixate his attention on a restful train of thought. This technique is based on the idea that the patient's resistances can be circumvented. A logical explanation may be presented of why suggestions will work, along such lines as that the mind is capable of absorbing and utilizing suggestions even though some resistance is present.

If the patient is in a medium or deep trance, suggestions should be framed as simply as possible. The patient, especially when in deep hypnosis, should repeat what is expected of him. Otherwise he may be so lethargic that he may not understand clearly the nature of the commands. If he is a somnambule, he may be instructed to carry out instructions even though he does not remember that they were formulated by the therapist. It is also a good idea in somnambulistic patients to give them a posthypnotic suggestion to the effect that they will be unresponsive to hypnotic induction by any person except the therapist. This will prevent the patient from being victimized by an amateur hypnotist who may very well undo therapeutic benefits.

If facts important in the understanding of the patient's condition are uncovered in hypnosis, these may or may not be brought to the patient's attention, depending upon their significance and upon the ability of the patient to tolerate their implications. It is best to make interpretations as superficial as possible, utilizing knowledge one has gained in working with the patient to guide him into activities of a creative nature that do not stir up too much conflict.

Termination of hypnosis by having the patient sleep for a few minutes before interruption is advantageous. The patient is instructed that he will continue to sleep for a designated number of minutes, following which he will be awakened. The period of sleep may range from 2 to 15 minutes. Where the patient is able to dream on suggestion, this period may profitably be utilized to induce dreams either of a spontaneous sort or of a nature relevant to the particular trends elicited during the trance.

There is no set rule as to how much time to devote to hypnosis during each session. Except for the initial induction period, the trance need not exceed one-half hour. Ample time should be allowed to take up with the patient his problems both before and after hypnosis. His reaction to the trance may also be discussed. Prejudice against symptom removal continues in force. On the whole, it is unjustified. Needless to say, more extensive psychotherapeutic measures will be necessary to insure lasting relief.

INTERCURRENT INCURABLE SOMATIC ILLNESS

The incidence of an intercurrent incurable physical illness constitutes an emergency in some patients. Development of certain conditions, such as multiple sclerosis, brain tumor, Hodgkins disease, cancer, cerebral hemorrhage or thrombosis, or a coronary attack, will make it necessary for the therapist to take stock of the reality situation and perhaps to revise therapeutic goals. Essential also is a dealing with the emotional impact of the intercurrent illness on the individual. Insight therapy may have to be halted, and supportive approaches implemented.

Where the person is suffering from a nonfatal illness and where there is a possibility of a residual disability, as in coronary disease, apoplexy, tuberculosis, and various neurologic disorders, an effort must be made to get the patient to accept the illness. A desensitization technique may be utilized, encouraging the patient to discuss the illness and to ventilate fears concerning it. The need to recognize that this illness does not make one different from others, that all people have problems, some of which are more serious than one's own, that it is not disgraceful to be sick, may be repeatedly emphasized.

Persuasive talks may be given the patient to the effect that the most important thing in the achievement of health is to admit and to accept the limitations imposed on one by one's illness. This need not cause the patient to retire in defeat. He will still be able to gain sufficient recognition and success if he operates within the framework of his handicap. It is most important for his self-respect that he continue to utilize his remaining capacities and aptitudes, expanding them in a realistic and reasonable way. Many people suffering from a physical handicap have been able to compensate for a disability in one area by becoming proficient in another.

In patients who tend to regard their disability as justifying a completely passive attitude toward life, an effort must be made to stimulate activity and productiveness. The dangers of passivity and dependency, in terms of what these do to self-respect, are stressed. The person is encouraged to become as self-assertive and independent as the handicap will allow.

Where it is important for the patient to relax and to give up competitive efforts,

persuasive therapy may be combined with a reassuring, guidance approach aimed at externalizing interests along lines that will be engaging, but not too stimulating. The cultivation of a different philosophy toward life, directed at enjoying leisure and looking with disdain on fierce ambitious striving, will often help the patient to accept this new role.

Tension may be alleviated by barbiturates, Librium, and Valium; nausea, by Compazine; agitation and anxiety, by Thorazine or Haldol; severe pain in dying patients, by regular administration of narcotics such as heroin. Intractable and unbearable pain that does not respond to the usual analgesics and to hypnosis may require psychosurgery (lobotomy). The practice of permitting a terminal patient to die with dignity (passive euthenasia) without burdening him with useless and desperate artificial means and heroic measures is being more and more accepted (Fletcher, MI, 1974; Jaretzki, 1976). Interesting also is the publication called *A Living Will* (Euthenasia Education Council, 1974).

In progressive, incurable, and fatal ailments there may be a temptation to stop therapy on the basis that nothing more can be done for the patient. Actually, the patient may need the therapist more than before the ailment had developed. Where the patient has no knowledge of the seriousness of his condition, as, for instance, inoperable cancer, the decision of whether or not to inform him of his calamity is a grave one that will influence the degree of his suffering in the remaining days of his life. In many cases it is unwise to burden him with the full seriousness of his condition. Statements may be made to the effect that he has a condition that his physician has classified as one that will get worse before it gets better. There is an obligation, of course, not to withhold facts from the patient, but honesty can be tempered with optimistic uncertainty. Many persons cling to a straw extended to them by an authority and maintain a positive attitude to the end.

In other patients it is sometimes practical to inform them, particularly if they already more than suspect it, that they have a progressive ailment. They may be assured that everything will be done to reduce pain and suffering and to keep up their good health as much as possible. Persuasive suggestions to face the remaining months with calmness and courage may be very reassuring. The patient may be told that while his life span is limited, he may extend and enjoy it by the proper mental attitude. A guidance approach helps reduce the disturbing effect of environmental factors and permits the patient to divert interests toward outlets of a distracting nature. Where the patient is so disposed, he may be encouraged to cultivate religious interests in which he may find much solace.

The patient's time may be so arranged that he will not be allowed desolately to sit around waiting for death. He may also be taught the technique of self-hypnosis to induce relaxation, diminish tension, reduce pain, and promote a better mental outlook. Mendell (1965) states that patients respond to his statement: "You are not alone. The struggle is not over. You don't have to worry that what can be done is not being done. I am with you and aware of what you are undergoing. I am with the forces that are to help you, and if anything develops, I will bring it to you immediately." An attitude should be inculcated in the patient that he has fulfilled his task well and that it is now time to let himself relax. Such an attitude may permit of the peaceful, even happy, acceptance of the end of life. Actually, few dying patients do not appreciate the imminence of death, even though their psychological defenses tend to deny it. The therapist may keep emphasizing that the patient, by his courage, is doing a great deal for his family. What the patient needs is someone to understand him, to help him mobilize his resources, to listen to him with respect and not pity, to display a compassionate matter-of-factness, and above all to help him overcome his fear of isolation. The greatest problem in working with the dying patient is the therapist's own feeling of helplessness, guilt, and fear of death.

The work of Cicely Saunders, Director of St. Christopher's Hospice (Liegner, 1975) is evidence that for dying patients a great deal can be done toward making their last days comfortable, painless, and free

from anxiety. Administration of medications ("polypharmacy") to render the patient symptom-free is routine at St. Christopher's. Diamorphine (heroin) every 4 hours orally, thorazine and its derivatives, and other medications that are indicated for special conditions, such as dexamethasone for brain metastases and increased intracranial pressure, are given during the day and night. The physical atmosphere is clean, cheerful, and comfortable. The members of the staff are all supportive and participate in working through the stress of separation anxiety. Discussion about incurability and dying are not avoided, and the fact is accented "that death is a continuum of life and is not to be feared." Under these conditions the patients respond to the passing of another patient with little dread or fear.

If the patient who knows that he is dying can be shown that the acceptance of death is a positive achievement rather than resignation to nothingness, much will have been accomplished in making his remaining days more tolerable. Understanding the patient's anxiety, guilt feelings, and depression through empathic listening may be extremely reassuring. Helping members of the patient's family to deal with their hostility and despair may also be an essential part of the therapist's task. Cautioning them on the futile search for expensive and nonexistent cures may, incidentally, be in order. At all times the focus is on relieving the patient's physical pain and distress, on making him comfortable in his home, and on assuaging his mental turmoil. If this is done, peace will usually follow. A good relationship with the patient's family during the last days will help them to an acceptance of the reality of death.

Where death has occurred, the therapist may be called on to render help to the bereaved. Different members of the family will respond with their distinctive reactions to the incident. The detached and presumably adjusted member may actually need more support than the one who is ostensibly upset and manifestly grief stricken. Since members are bound to respond to the emotional tone of those around them, the manner and mode of communication of the therapist will influence the healing process. Cooperativeness, understanding, sympathetic listening, and an expressed desire to help can inspire friendship and trust in the therapist. As Beachy (1967) has pointed out, it is unwise to whitewash the facts of suffering and death or to try to evade the evolving emotional reactions, however unreasonable they may seem. A completely open, factual manner that is not falsely oversolicitous is best, and where needed, the continued care and attention of a clergyman or other supportive person may be advisable. The value of therapy with groups of terminally ill patients makes this modality one that should be considered in selected cases (Yalom & Greaves, 1977).

Readings on this subject may be found in Aldrich (1963), Cassem (1974), Chodoff (1960), Christ (1961), G. W. Davidson (1975), Eissler (1955), Feifel (1959), J. Fletcher (1972), GAP Symposium (1965), Jeffers et al. (1961), Kennedy (1960), Krupp and Kligfeld (1961), Kubler-Ross (1969), Langer (1957), Morgenthau (1961), Pack (1961), Reeves (1973), P. S. Rhoads (1965), Saul (1959), A. Schwartz (1961), Standard and Nathan (1955), Tagge et al. (1974), Wahl (1960), A. F. C Wallace (1956), Worcester (1935), and Zilboorg (1943).

56
Psychotherapy in Special Conditions

The principles of psychotherapy that have been outlined, and the technical procedures that have been delineated, apply to all emotional problems and conditions irrespective of clinical diagnosis. It is possible, with the proper kind of working relationship and the adroit use of appropriate techniques, to approach goals of personality reconstruction in any syndrome. Experience, however, has shown that certain kinds of conditions make extensive therapeutic objectives difficult to achieve. Experience also indicates that they seem to respond favorably to specific techniques or combinations of methods. In this chapter we shall consider the problems and modifications often encountered in the treatment of the different neurotic, psychophysiologic, personality, and psychotic disorders.

PSYCHONEUROTIC DISORDERS

Anxiety Neuroses (Anxiety States, Anxiety Reactions)

Some anxiety is a universal human experience considered by existentialists as basic to the nature of existence. It is common to all physical and emotional problems where these are conceived of as a threat. Anxiety usually generates a host of defenses marshalled to neutralize its effects. Some defenses, however, contribute to greater maladaptation than the anxiety experience itself, for example, recourse to inhibitions of function or overindulgence in drugs and alcohol. Where anxiety becomes excessive and free-floating, it is regarded as a pathological syndrome to which several labels are appended, like anxiety states, anxiety neurosis, and anxiety reactions.

Anxiety reactions are characterized by panic, terror, and somatic symptoms that occur with little or no relationship to specific situations or objects. In this way they are distinguished from fear reactions, which are stimulated by realistic threatening circumstances. Inner conflicts (fear of death, disease, hostility, sexuality, etc.) are often at the basis of undifferentiated excessive anxiety, which readily may be activated by unfortunate or threatening outside events, for instance, a death in the family, the discovery on physical examination of an organic ailment, a catastrophic environmental happening, and so forth. The rapid heartbeat, rise in blood pressure, chest pains, and distress in breathing may convince the victim that he is suffering from a cardiac illness, initiating persistent visits to practitioners and specialists, who may diagnose the condition as ''neurocirculatory asthenia,'' the functional nature of which the patient usually fails to believe.

The average patient with an anxiety reaction is so upset by his symptoms that relief from suffering constitutes his prime motivation. Because he feels helpless and frightened, he is apt to demand an authoritative, directive relationship in which he is protected and through which he obtains immediate symptomatic relief. To abide by these demands will mean that the therapist will have to employ supportive measures that may or may not be successful in abating anxiety. There are many supportive maneuvers that help to bring the individual to a point where his anxiety is reduced and spontaneous reparative forces come into play (see Supportive Therapy, Chapter 48). Supportive treatment may be all that is needed to eliminate anxiety. This is particularly the case where the basic ego structure is reasonably sound, having broken down under the impact of severe external stress. However, palliative measures may temporarily alleviate anxiety even where the problems are internally inspired. Should supportive tactics prove to be successful, some patients lose their incentive for further help and are contented with their symptom-free state, even though this may be impermanent. Where unsuccessful, they may lose confidence in the therapist and then go off elsewhere in search of relief.

It is important, therefore, to work on the motivation of the patient in order to get him to accept more than supportive therapy. This may prove to be a more formidable task than the therapist had calculated. Because repression is a chief defense against sources of anxiety, the patient may be unable to challenge coping mechanisms that he has elaborated, though they be inadequate in dealing with his difficulty. Where anxiety is inspired by unconscious conflicts, resistances against insight are manifold and sometimes so powerful that only a transference neurosis in psychoanalysis is capable of breaking them down and of revealing their underlying nature.

The treatment of pathological anxiety reactions must be adapted to their intensity, the needs and motivations of the patient, and the readiness to accept psychotherapy. Dynamic psychotherapy is the treatment of choice, and this can be supplemented where anxiety is too disruptive by adjuncts such as relaxation exercises, hypnosis, meditation, biofeedback, behavior therapy, and medications (see Chapter 53). Valium (5–10 mg) or Librium (10–25 mg) are often prescribed at whatever intervals are necessary. Some patients react well to small doses of barbiturates like phenobarbital (0.25 gr). Propranolol (Inderal) is a beta-adrenergic blocking agent that may be helpful especially to quiet sympathetic overactivity. The dose must be adapted to the sensitivities of the patient. Some patients do well on 10 mg two or three times daily. Some require doses up to 160 mg daily or higher. Side effects are not too severe, but signs of cardiac failure may occur in patients with heart ailments and so such patients will require a reduction of dosage or cessation of medication.

Where anxiety interferes with treatment, temporary mild sedation or tranquilization is especially helpful (see Pharmacotherapy in Chapter 53). Under the calming influence of drugs, it may be possible to set up a working relationship and to begin active therapy. One must recognize, however, that sedatives and tranquilizers are props the patient may be reluctant to relinquish. Under circumstances of especially intense anxiety, narcotherapy (q.v.) may be useful; and, where anxiety mounts to panic, the measures advocated in Chapter 55 on ''Panic States'' may prove of value.

Hysterical Neurosis (Conversion and Dissociative Types: Conversion Hysteria)

The basic defense employed in conversion and dissociative reactions is repression. Therapeutic techniques are best organized to resolve repression and to deal with inner conflicts. Transference analysis, especially with the working through of a transference neurosis, is ideally suited to therapy of this disorder. Where transference analysis cannot be used, a less intensive psychoanalytically oriented psychotherapy may be employed. From the viewpoint of mere handling and removal of symptoms, hypnosis is classically of value. However, while hysterical symptoms can often be eliminated in relatively few hypnotic sessions, the dramatic, infantile, and self-dramatizing personality constellation associated with this reaction will require prolonged psychotherapy, preferably along reconstructive lines. Unfortunately, even though insight therapy is accepted by the patient, a great many impediments will become manifest during the course of treatment in the form of intellectual inhibitions and other devices to reinforce repression.

Whereas insight therapy is the best treatment for this condition, circumstances of obstinate resistance, of faulty motivation, and of profound secondary gain may prevent any other than a supportive approach.

Symptom removal by authoritative suggestion, with or without hypnosis, is occasionally indicated, particularly where the symptom produces great physical discomfort and interferes with the individual's social and economic adjustment. There are some symptoms that serve a minimal defensive purpose in binding anxiety. The inconvenience to the patient of such symptoms is an important incentive toward their abandonment. Where the symptom constitutes a plea for help, love, and reassurance on the basis of helplessness, the therapist, by ordering cessation of symptoms, virtually assures the patient of support and love without his needing to utilize symptoms for this purpose.

Such symptoms as paralysis, aphonia, visual disorders, anesthesia, astasia-abasia, and hysterical contractures may often be removed in relatively few sessions with a strong authoritarian suggestive approach. One must not overestimate the permanency of the cure, however, since the original motivations that sponsored the symptom are not altered in the least and a relapse is always possible. Consequently, wherever the therapist can do so, the patient should be prepared for further therapy by explaining the purposeful nature of the symptom and its source in unconscious conflict.

Since hysteria often represents a reaction to unpleasant circumstances that stimulate inner conflicts, a guidance approach is sometimes utilized in appropriate cases to adjust the patient to environmental demands from which he cannot escape and to help him to modify existing remediable situational difficulties. It may be possible to get an hysterical individual to make compromises with his environment so that he will not be inclined to overreact to current stresses. Here, too, an attempt must be made to acquaint the person with the fact that his symptoms, though inspired by external difficulties, are actually internally sponsored. Once the patient accepts this fact, therapy along insight lines may be possible.

The treatment of hysteria through hypnotic symptom removal and by guidance therapy are least successful where the symptom serves the purpose of providing intense substitutive gratification for sexual and hostile impulses.

Difficulty will also be encountered where the symptom tends to reinforce the repression of a traumatic memory or conflict, as in amnesia. The extent of amnesia varies. It may involve a single painful experience in the past, or it may include a fairly wide segment of life. It may actually spread to a point where the person loses his identity and forgets his past completely. Amnesia serves the defensive purpose of shielding the individual from anxiety. The intractibility of an amnesia, consequently, is related to the amount of anxiety bound down and to the ego resources that are available for coping with the liberated anxiety. The fear of being overcome by anxiety may be so great that an impenetrable block to recall will exist despite all efforts to reintegrate the person to past memories. Indeed, the fear of uncovering a memory may be so strong that the person will resist trance induction.

Where resistance to hypnosis is encountered, a light barbiturate narcosis, either oral or intravenous (see the section on Narcotherapy), may remove the block. A trance, once induced, is deepened, and a posthypnotic suggestion is given the patient that he will henceforth be responsive to hypnosis without narcosis.

There are authorities who recommend that dangerous or debilitating hysterical symptoms that do not yield to psychotherapy or hypnosis be treated without further delay with electroconvulsive therapy. For example, hysterical dissociations may yield to 4 to 12 ECTs. Anorexia nervosa, if it has persisted for no more than 3 months, is considered curable with 8 to 10 ECTs (Paterson, AS, 1963). After this time, subcoma insulin and Thorazine may be tried. Where there is no response to these measures, leucotomy may, in the opinion of Paterson, be a lifesaving measure. Hysterical torticollis may, he asserts, also be approached by up to 12 sessions of electronarcosis supported by Librium. These heroic measures are, however, rarely necessary, if at all.

It must again be emphasized that, while certain hysterical symptoms may be treated rapidly through short-term supportive treatment, the basic personality problems associated with the hysterical disorder will require a considerable period of reconstructive therapy.

Phobic Reactions
(Anxiety Hysteria)

As a defense designed to control anxiety, the phobic reaction constitutes one of the most common syndromes that the psychotherapist must handle in everyday practice. When we consider the structure of a phobia, we must recognize that a maze of primary and auxiliary phenomena embrace this defense. First, the phobia, apart from the simple conditioned fear reaction, is generally a facade that conceals an underlying, earlier causative factor. Second, it is a manifestation that protects the individual against the experiencing of constant and intense anxiety. Third, a phobia gradually changes in its dimensions by generalizing to stimuli that are more and more remote from the initiating phobic excitant. Fourth, as the phobia spreads and circumscribes the individual's activities, the person feels increasingly undermined, self-confidence is progressively shattered, self-image is more and more devalued, and the individual may become depressed and even phobophobic. Loss of mastery revives regressive defenses

and needs, including childish dependency promptings, which, if gratified, further contribute to feelings of helplessness.

Anxiety is often relieved by displacement of inner dangers onto external objects or situations. Due to its apparent protective quality, the phobia usually becomes fixed, the patient manifesting the greatest obstinacy in facing it. The treatment of phobic reactions may consequently be difficult. Because the individual feels helpless in dealing with his anxiety, he is apt to seek out a childlike kind of relationship with some person, usually a parent or mate, who becomes a parental substitute, toward whom he displays a hostile, dependent attitude. Complications in this relationship may consume a great deal of the therapist's time, since the patient is so involved with his hostile dependency that he will have little energy left to approach the original conflictual sources.

Phobias may be approached in various ways. Reassurance, support, persuasion, desensitization, reconditioning, and drug therapy may at least partially alleviate the symptom.

Through persuasive tactics an attempt is made to boost the individual's self-confidence and self-esteem, encouraging him to engage in activities that will overcome his symptom. Unfortunately, though the patient is apt to make a better adjustment, and may learn to control his fears on the basis of positive benefits he derives from their conquest, he will usually have to force himself over and over again to face fear-provoking situations.

Associated with persuasive techniques, techniques of self-mastery through autosuggestion are advocated by some therapists as a supportive device. The person fortifies himself to face a phobic situation by minimizing its fearful aspects and by concentrating on the pleasure values incidental to the presenting ordeal. Persistent suggestions to gather courage and to master his fears may inspire sufficient fortitude to pull the person successfully through a situation that he ordinarily would be unable to face. Needless to say, such techniques are palliative, and results are temporary at best.

Another means of supportively treating phobias is by desensitization. The aim in desensitization is to get the patient to master fears by actually facing them. It is essential for the individual to expose himself repeatedly to the phobic situation in order that he may finally learn to conquer it. For example, if a person fears open spaces, or going outdoors, on the first day he can walk several steps from his house and then return. On the second day he may increase the distance between himself and his house, and similarly on each day thereafter until he is able to walk a considerable distance from his home. The hope is that triumph over deliberately stimulated fear will desensitize him to its influence, although this is the exception rather than the rule.

The most expedient way of resolving a phobia is through proficient behavioral therapy; in many cases it may achieve a symptomatic cure. According to conditioning theory, phobias are "habits of anxiety responses" that may be correlated with definite stimulus antecedents. An identification of these antecedents makes it possible to decondition the "anxiety habits" in relatively few sessions. One technique of deconditioning "reciprocal inhibition" relies on the exposure of the individual to gradually increasing increments of anxiety ("stimuli hierarchy") in an anxiety-inhibiting climate, such as deep muscle relaxation. As the patient accepts and endures in fantasy the disturbing excitants in the "stimuli hierarchy," a generalization of response occurs in real life. Implosive therapy and "paradoxical intension," one aspect of logotherapy, attempt to extinguish the phobic response by flooding methods. Other approaches include modeling and relaxation techniques (see Chapter 49).

Some therapists prescribe the minor tranquilizers like Valium and Librium prior to facing a phobic situation. Phobias have also been approached by giving the patient 4 to 8 mg of perphenazine (Trilafon) 3 times daily, along with 15 mg of Nardil or 25 mg of Elavil three times daily. The phenothiazine drug tends to dissociate the phobic experience, while the energizer makes available to the individual greater sources of energy (Kline, NS, 1966).

Whatever the method, it should, if possible, be supplemented with psychoanalytic psychotherapy. An eclectic approach to phobias is increasingly gaining favor (MacKenzie, 1973). Some therapists find hypnoanalysis adjunctively helpful in tracing the origin of a phobia. In cases where a fear has been produced by an incident so terror inspiring that it has been repressed, it may be possible to get the person to recall the original emotional experience under hypnosis and then to reevaluate the situation in terms of his present-day understanding. A helpful technique is to regress the person to a period prior to the development of the phobia and then gradually to reorient him in his age level to later and later periods of life until the original situation associated with the development of the phobia has been uncovered. Where the phobia is complicated by a character disturbance that originated early in life, it will be necessary to produce a more or less drastic reorganization of the personality through further therapy after the phobia has been analyzed and its sources determined.

There are those who believe that classical psychoanalysis, rather than psychoanalytic psychotherapy, offers the individual the greatest opportunity for relief from some phobias by working out the infantile neurosis in the transference neurosis. Phobias are looked upon as repressive defenses shaped by mechanisms of condensation, displacement, and symbolization, which preserve the relationship of the individual to important persons in his life through a transferring and a discharging of dangerous feelings toward apparently unrelated tokens. Among the basic conflicts that are said to set off the phobic coping mechanism are repudiated needs and drives that the individual is unable to accept as aspects of himself and that, therefore, become attached to outside situations and individuals.

Three determinants that are parcels of successive developmental stages condition the most important conflicts:

1. The urge to preserve the symbiosis with a protective parental agency (here the danger is of abandonment, i.e., "separation anxiety").
2. The demand to convince oneself of one's physical intactness (the danger is

conceived of at this level as mutilation, i.e., "castration anxiety").

3. The impulsion to conform to the dictates of one's own conscience (the danger is regarded as of being culpable, guilty, and reprehensible, i.e., "superego anxiety).

The more exigent the need, the more active the conflict and the more intense the phobia that will be required to bind and delimit anxiety. The ego reacts to the external danger as a mask that conceals its internal derivations.

All therapists, it is claimed, should be complemented and eventually replaced by psychotherapy along dynamic lines, particularly where inner conflicts nurture the phobia. In essence, one investigates the imbalance in the structural elements of the personality. As anxiety lessens, learning processes resume and reality functioning is strengthened. The ego restores its ability to tolerate anxiety and to control impulses, the sense of reality is widened, identity is bolstered, and there is an enhanced capacity to manage one's conflicts.

Obsessive-Compulsive Reactions (Obsessive Neurosis, Compulsion Neurosis)

The treatment of obsessive-compulsive reactions is notoriously difficult. Not only is it necessary to deal with nascent anxiety, which becomes particularly pronounced when obsessional ideas break loose, but more significantly one must also manage the hostile, distrusting, dependent character structure that is a component part of the disorder.

Attitudes toward the therapist are so ambivalent that a working relationship may never develop. On the one hand, the patient desires to be dependent on the therapist and toward this end will employ varied techniques like making himself obsequious, ingratiating, and submissive. On the other hand, in spite of the fact that he desires to be dependent, he will resent dependency. He will express hostility toward the therapist, either openly or covertly. While

on the surface he may exhibit a great deal of deference, inwardly he is rebellious and he is fired with much resentment. The dreams that he displays, related to the transference, demonstrate the intense hostility that he feels toward the therapist. The patient looks upon his impulses for dependency and compliance as threats to his independence and to his capacity to function by himself.

The battle with the therapist can go on for a long time without the patient's being aware of how he seeks to make himself dependent and at the same time to detach himself. While he asks the therapist for help, he will stubbornly oppose accepting the therapist's interpretations or suggestions. He may become tremendously demanding and insist on being relieved of his symptoms; yet, when attempts are made to help him in a positive way, he will resist these and then act hostile toward the therapist for not helping him more. The rigidity that he displays during therapy is manifested in intellectualizing what is going on. This serves as a defense against his feelings. Many compulsive persons are capable of learning the mechanisms of their illness, but this seems to have not the slightest effect upon the intensity and severity of their symptoms. Their tendencies to doubt make interpretations difficult. When they do accept interpretations, evincing interest in what goes on in their psyche, it is quite apparent that they do not feel what they intellectually accept. The "isolation" of the intellectual processes from the emotional content makes therapy extremely difficult.

The compulsive individual may attempt to disarm the therapist by obeying punctiliously every suggestion or command expressed or implied. While he may be responsive on the surface, inwardly he maintains a tremendous amount of skepticism about what goes on. One may attempt to change the patient's way of life by pointing out prevailing contradictions. Though the patient seems to have accepted and understood thoroughly the implications of his difficulties and though he voices a desire for change, the way that he acts outside the therapeutic situation indicates that he has not really absorbed the insight he had verbalized. Sometimes the behavior of the patient is in a direction opposite to his intellectual understanding. Partly responsible is the fact that the patient seeks to ridicule the therapist by contradicting the therapist's suggestions.

Compulsion neurosis does not respond to insight therapy as well as do other neurotic syndromes. It can be treated, of course but the therapist must be extremely skilled in the handling of the transference and must have much fortitude to tolerate the vicissitudes that will come up in the course of treatment.

Frequently, the most that can be done is to fortify the patient's failing defenses and to get him to function with the personality makeup that he had prior to the development of disabling symptoms. The complicating element is that detachment, which is one of his primary defenses, may be the symptom the patient desires most to abandon. He seeks to live a better life, and he is thoroughly disgusted with his detachment. He understands that he is missing many of life's pleasures. But he cannot stop being detached. When the patient realizes that yielding his detachment creates in him anxiety and turmoil and when he appreciates that he cannot help being isolated from people, he may become depressed. In some instances desperation can even drive him to suicide.

Salzman (1966) points out rightfully that the obsessive-compulsive defense of persistent doubting, negativism, unwillingness to commit oneself, and strivings for perfection, omnipotence, and omniscience are attempts to control the universe, to guarantee one's safety, security, and survival. This defense acts as an obstruction to constructive learning. Free association and concern with past memories are utilized by the obsessional person as screens behind which to conceal his coping maneuvers. Years of futile probing into the unconscious, and careful unravelment of the sources and meanings of rituals usually accomplish little. The obsessional is an expert in "one-upmanship." He engages in a verbal tug-of-war; he must get in the last word; he undermines psychotherapy as a process; and he derogates the ability of the therapist to

help him. Yet he bitterly complains that he is not being helped. What is important in therapy is dealing with the immediate transactions between therapist and patient and not permitting the patient to enter into gambits through which he conspires to wrest control from the therapist.

Whenever possible, therefore, the therapist must attempt not only to control the patient's symptoms, but to promote sufficient alteration in the character structure to permit of a reasonable functioning with people in a close relationship situation. Where the patient has a motivation to gain normal satisfactions in life and where he realizes that his detachment, obsequiousness, perfectionism, meticulousness, obstinacy, and other character traits create difficulties with people and prevent enjoyment in living, he may then have the incentive to tolerate and to work through the anxieties incumbent upon giving up these traits.

The therapy of compulsion neurosis or compulsive-obsessive personality disorders must, therefore, take into account the patient's dependency, profoundly hostile impulses toward people, need for detachment, tendency to "isolate" intellect from feeling, and magical frame of reference in which the patient's ideas operate. Some leads may be obtained from the articles by Barnett (1972, E. K. Schwartz (1972), and Suess (1972).

Among the most important tasks to be achieved in therapy by the therapist are the following:

1. Demonstrating to the patient that symptoms have a definite cause and that they stem from no magical sources.
2. Demonstrating that aggression is a common impulse originating in hostile attitudes.
3. Demonstrating that one can express a certain amount of hostility without destroying other people or injuring oneself.
4. Demonstrating that one can relate to a person without needing to make oneself dependent or compliant.

Some therapists find a combination of insight and supportive therapy the best treatment for obsessive-compulsive reactions. A transference neurosis is avoided, and techniques like guidance, persuasion, and reassurance are used whenever necessary.

At the start of therapy the patient is often bewildered, tense, and torn by ambivalent strivings. He pleads for relief and often assumes that the therapist is delinquent in responsibility by failing to annihilate his symptoms. He may furiously insist that he feels no better, that he has uncontrollable impulses to do damage to himself and others, that he is impelled to engage in sexual activities that repel him, that he is helpless in coping with his tension and panicky feelings. It is essential to explain to him that his symptoms and feelings have a meaning and that it is necessary to understand some of the factors creating his difficulties before they can be corrected. As a general rule, the patient will be skeptical about this explanation, since inwardly he believes that his trouble is caused by some sort of evil magic. Only when he establishes a feeling of confidence in the therapist is it possible to influence his superstitious nature.

Where the patient is very upset, he may be given reassuring and persuasive suggestions to the effect that he can get well, that others sicker than himself have been able to experience relief from their symptoms, and that if he has the desire to recover, he will want to do what is essential in overcoming his difficulties.

One of the most important things that he must realize is that his symptoms are not the product of supernatural forces but rather follow scientific laws of cause and effect. Victimized by fear, tension, and panicky feelings that seemingly come from unknown sources, the patient understandably has been unable hitherto to ascertain the meaning of his symptoms. The reasons that he suffers will become known to him, however, as he begins to connect events in his environment with how he feels. Nothing in the universe happens by chance. If he hears a sound, he knows very well something has created the sound. Science has definitely shown that a causal relationship exists in the world.

The patient is usually reassured by such a talk, since he does not want to be at the mercy of wicked, inscrutable forces over which he has no control. These forces are nightmarish in quality and give him the feeling of being manipulated by demons. It must be remembered that the compulsion neurotic often thinks in terms akin to witchcraft. To be advised by a person whom he respects that a matter-of-fact cause is responsible for his agony gives him at least temporary solace. Accepting this explanation on faith, however, is not enough. It is essential to point out to him how, when he gets involved in specific environmental difficulties, his symptoms become exacerbated.

A persuasive technique is sometimes expedient. The patient is first reassured about his obsessive fears and impulses. He is told that, were he actually going to execute them into action, he would not now be tormenting himself so. The chances are that he will not perpetrate any of the wicked deeds of which he is so frightened.

For instance, if Mary Jones fears that she may become violently dangerous and kill people, she may be shown that actually she expresses aggression far less freely than the average person. As a matter of fact, she probably fails to exhibit even ordinary amounts of assertive aggressiveness. She is encouraged to observe herself in her daily reactions with people, to see whether she is not restricting a show of aggressive feeling.

One of the tendencies of the compulsive neurotic is to keep tormenting himself with his fears and anxieties. A masochistic element undoubtedly exists here. It is sometimes helpful to point out to the patient that occupying one's mind with frightening ideas stirs up tension and physical symptoms. The patient may be reminded that the mind is closely linked to all of the body organs. Upsetting ideas can thus upset all of the body organs. More perniciously, irritating the mind with frightening and uncomfortable thoughts may delay mental healing.

The patient may be asked to practice changing the type of thinking that preoccupies him. This may not be successful at first, but it will begin to work after a while. What is necessary is that he begin to direct thoughts away from concern with his obsessions to some other group of ideas. This could be some activity, or hobby, or some period in life when his happiness was greatest. The patient is warned about the difficulty of controlling his thinking at first. He will be tempted to tease and torture himself with his fears, just like picking at an irritating sore. Surely the sore may be provoking. It itches, and the person wants to scratch it; but as long as he does, healing will be delayed. It is the same with irritating ideas. Even though these are provoking, it is necessary purposefully to divert thoughts into some other channel. This persuasive approach, though superficial; often helps the patient to exercise some control over his obsessions, which otherwise would tend to preoccupy him to distraction.

In some cases, patients experience relief from their obsessions if they themselves practice bringing them on (paradoxical intention) and even exaggerating them in fantasy. The patient is enjoined not to resist obsessions but to deliberately indulge them in order to gain control over their influence.

A word is necessary concerning dependency in the compulsion neurotic. Because of the patient's desires for dependency and because of the difficulty in controlling a neurotic transference, it may be best not to permit the patient to come too frequently for treatments. Should treatment sessions be too concentrated, the patient may become inordinate in demands on the therapist on the basis that he cannot function by himself. Therapy once or twice weekly is ample in most instances.

In all cases the therapist should be alert to whether any elements of schizophrenia are present. Some compulsion neurotics are very close to schizophrenia, and in such individuals the therapist will have to be careful in offering authoritative interpretations. Rather, one should be reassuring, manipulating the individual's environment so that he can function as effectively as possible with his existing personality equipment. The prognosis for extensive goals here may not be too favorable; nevertheless, a great deal can be done for the patient when therapy is oriented along lines such as are used in schizophrenia. Small doses of phenothiazines, like Stelazine, are some-

times useful. Should a reconstructive approach be attempted, the chances are that the therapist will be rewarded with a therapeutic failure. The ego is usually too weak to handle the anxiety that will be released. Compulsion neurotics with this type of weak ego structure may develop psychoticlike excited episodes, irrespective of the kind of therapy employed. Convulsive therapy may be expedient here. In the event the obsessional pattern alternates with a depressive reaction antidepressant drugs may be needed.

Where the anxiety is violent and uncontrollable with psychotherapy alone, 12 to 18 ECTs, which may have to be concentrated at first, are followed by prolonged drug therapy, for instance 16 mg of Trilafon each day, along with, if anxiety needs further control, 0.75 gr of Sodium Amytal three times daily. Anxiety mingled or alternating with depression may be treated with Trilafon and Elavil (Triavil or Etrafon). (See Table 53–3.)

In certain compulsion neurotics aversive conditioning (see page 694) may prove to be highly effective. Other forms of behavior therapy may also be useful. For example, patients obsessed with fears of contracting disease through contamination may be helped by modeling techniques where the therapist demonstrates that he or she is not harmed by touching the floor and other objects that the patient avoids. The patient is firmly enjoined to follow the therapist's example and to sit out the entire session without scrubbing (Wilson, TG, 1976). Where all attempts at therapy fail, a short period of hospitalization may be helpful. This is particularly important where family problems or attitudes reinforce the patient's symptoms. In the hospital, the patient should be exposed to situations to which the patient customarily acts obsessionally, and his compulsive rituals should be blocked in the hope of extinguishing them (Marks et al, 1975). Coordinate psychotherapy is important as is family therapy after the patient returns home.

The prognosis in compulsion neurosis will depend upon the severity of the condition and the residual ego strength. It will also depend upon the length of time the patient has been ill. In some cases compulsive-obsessive patterns appear to be of relatively recent duration, the compulsive difficulty having developed as a result of external pressures and problems to which the patient could not adjust. The prognosis here is much more favorable than where the compulsive illness has been with the individual ever since puberty. some psychiatrists recommend that patients who do not respond to psychotherapy, and whose anxiety and suffering become unendurable, ultimately submit to transorbital lobotomy, or other forms of brain surgery, which, in some cases, will control symptoms where everything else fails.

Depressive Reactions (Reactive Depression, Psychoneurotic Depression)

Reactive depression is often a consequence of a catastrophic happening affecting the individual's security, self-esteem, or relationship with a cherished love object. It is differentiated qualitatively and quantitatively from the momentary bursts of grief and sadness that afflict the average human being, on the one hand, and from the prolonged despair of endogenous depression, on the other. An examination of the dynamics indicates, however, that the reactive type is closely affiliated with the other members of the family of depressions. In contrast with endogenous depression, neurotic depression constitutes a special way of dealing with anxiety. The depressive symptom picture often alternates with anxiety and with psychophysiological manifestations of anxiety that may mask the underlying hostility, despair, guilt, and grief.

There are three types of treatment—psychotherapeutic, pharmacologic, and electroconvulsive. For certain neurotic depressive reactions formal psychotherapy appears to be the only successful method of treatment (Kline, NS, 1964). Such treatment calls for greater than usual activity on the part of the therapist with "constant, emphatic and authoritative assurances of eventual recovery" (Lemere, 1957). The very presence of the therapist serves to con-

ciliate the patient. This is especially the case in severely morose patients who, lacking the capacity to handle their anxiety, seek comfort in the shadow of an idealized parental figure. Coming to therapy, therefore, in itself constitutes for the patient an inspiration that he is not hopeless. But what is essential in addition to reassurance is helping the patient recognize the active role that he plays in bringing about his own pain as well as the positive personal resources he has available to him toward altering his self-defeating practices (Bonime, 1965).

The use of drugs (see Somatic Therapy in Chapter 53) is purely symptomatic and is best reserved for patients who cannot be helped materially through psychotherapy. Stimulants such as dextroamphetamine (Dexedrine, Dexamyl), methamphetamine (Desoxyn, Methedrine), pipradol (Meratran), and methylphenidate (Ritalin) may be helpful in supplying energy on a temporary basis for fatigued and exhausted patients. Insomnia may be dealt with by various measures, including barbiturate and nonbarbiturate hypnotics. As a tranquilizer with slightly energizing qualities, Librium is the drug of choice. In severe neurotic depressions the MAO inhibitors and imipramine (Tofranil) or desipramine (Norpramine, Pertofrane) may prove helpful. A positive attitude on the part of the therapist toward drug therapy will definitely influence the patient's response to antidepressant medications, neutralizing the negative placebo element. Where suicide is a possibility, no hesitation need be felt in prescribing electroconvulsive therapy.

PSYCHOPHYSIOLOGIC AUTONOMIC AND VISCERAL DISORDERS

Psychophysiologic (psychosomatic) disorders are often rooted in deep disturbances in the personality organization; some are engendered by defects in the earliest contacts of the infant with the mother. The personality structure of the patient, consequently, contains dependent, hostile, and masochistic elements that tend to obstruct a good working relationship. Because the ego is more or less fragile, anxiety, mobilized by the transference and by interpretation, may be intolerable. Insight therapy may, therefore, have to be delayed in favor of discreet supportive techniques, during which the patient is permitted to relate himself dependently to the therapist.

The negative elements of the relationship with the therapist must constantly be resolved, the therapist being on the alert to hostile manifestations, which the patient will perhaps try to conceal. Once a good working relationship is established, exploration of inner strivings, needs, and conflicts with cautious interpretations may be attempted. However, most patients with psychosomatic difficulties find it difficult or impossible to think abstractly, and revelations of conflict seem to do little good. They cannot seem to describe their affects and to relate their fantasies, and they fail to respond to free association and interpretation (Nemiah, 1971). Exaggeration of the patient's physical symptoms is a common sign of resistance. When symptoms increase in intensity, the patient may be tempted to leave therapy. Treatment is generally a long-term proposition, since the deep personality problem associated with the symptoms resolves itself slowly. Essentially, therapy may follow the design for the management of personality disorders (q.v.).

A constant danger during insight therapy is the unleashing of excessive quantities of anxiety, usually the result of too speedy symptom removal or too rapid dissipation of defenses. Often the somatic disturbance represents the most acceptable avenue available to the patient for the discharge of anxiety and hostility. Because the ego has been unable to handle these emotions on a conscious level, the mechanism of repression is invoked. Where coping devices are threatened without a coordinate strengthening of the ego, where the person becomes prematurely aware of unacceptable conflicts and strivings, there is definite danger of precipitating a crisis. The patient may release such intense anxiety that he will employ symptomatic contingencies to bind this emotion. He may, for instance,

develop hysterial or compulsive symptoms, or he may display detachment and other characterologic defenses. Anxiety may, nevertheless, get out of hand and shatter the ego, precipitating a psychosis.

It may be impossible to do more for the patient than to give supportive therapy. For instance, persuasion and guidance may enable the patient to organize his life around his defects and liabilities, to avoid situations that arouse conflict and hostility, and to attain, at least in part, a sublimation of his basic needs. The object here is to bolster the ego to a point where it can handle damaging emotions more rationally as well as to improve interpersonal relationships so that hostility and other disturbing emotions are not constantly being generated. In some instances such therapies help to liberate the individual from the vicious cycle of his neurosis, facilitating externalization of interests, increasing self-confidence, and indicating ways of discharging emotions. Minor tranquilizers, such as Librium and Valium may be administered periodically where symptoms are especially harsh. Considerable relief from symptoms may be obtained through relaxation exercises, meditation, hypnosis, and biofeedback (see pages 761–791). Behavior therapy works better than dynamic psychotherapy.

The therapeutic relationship is kept on as positive a level as possible, an attempt being made to show the patient that the symptoms are not fortuitous, a causal relation existing between symptoms and difficulties in dealing with life. The circumstances under which symptoms become exaggerated are investigated with the object of determining areas of failure in interpersonal functioning. Once a pattern is discerned, its significance and origin are explored. Finally, the patient is encouraged to put into action the retrained attitudes toward life and people. In some cases sufficient ego strength may be developed to make psychoanalytically oriented psychotherapy possible.

Where the patient is coordinately under the care of an internist, cooperation between the therapist and internist will insure the best results.

PERSONALITY DISORDERS

The therapy of severe personality (character) disorders is difficult because of what has been called the "negative therapeutic reaction." The patient almost always utilizes the relationship with the therapist as a focus for various character drives. He may subject the therapist to attitudes of contempt and ridicule. He may seek to vanquish, provoke, and to hurt in subtle ways. He may slavishly subject himself to ingratiating or masochistic tactics to win the tribute, affection, and support he believes that he deserves. Feelings of self-devaluation and hopelessness often permeate his outlook and lead him to anticipate failure in therapy. In spite of the fact that the individual may be talented and outwardly successful, the inner self-image is depleted and contemptible. Self-devaluation acts as a potent block to treatment. The patient seems to utilize the facade of helplessness to avoid making any effort to get well.

Because of the vulnerability of the relationship with the therapist, interpretations are apt to be regarded by the patient as a blow to his self-esteem, initiating depression, rage or anxiety. They are evidences that the therapist does not approve of him. The patient is apt to intellectualize the entire therapeutic process, using his knowledge either as resistance or as a means of fortifying himself against change. Despite all logic, the patient strives to wedge therapy into the framework of his distorted attitudes toward life. He exhibits feelings of rejection and of distrust, and at the slightest challenge from the therapist his defenses crumble, leaving him in a state of collapse and despair. He may then show a psychic rigidity that refuses to yield to reason or entreaty.

The initial aim in therapy in personality disorders must be toward a solidification of the working relationship. This process is expedited where the patient does not feel forced to comply with demands that he believes are against his interests. Analytic probing and exploration of unconscious material should be in the most tentative terms.

Until the patient is capable of understanding that many of his attitudes toward the therapist have no basis in reality, but are rather an outgrowth of personal difficulties, interpretations must be delayed. Attempts are first made to establish a positive relationship without analyzing its source. Hostile feelings toward the therapist and other irrational impulses that interfere with a good relationship must be dealt with actively. It may be necessary to confine the entire treatment hour to current problems, shying away from historical material. Only when the patient's relationship with the therapist becomes more congenial will it be possible for him to benefit from attempts to connect historical data with his present difficulties.

During the course of treatment the patient will seemingly modify attitudes toward the therapist, but in this alteration the therapist must search for areas of resistance. For instance, a submissive, ingratiating attitude, which is a cover for a fear of abandonment, may, upon interpretation, be replaced by an apparently sincere attempt to search for and to analyze inner problems. The therapist may, if the patient is observed closely, detect in this attitude a fradulent attempt to gain security by complying with what the patient feels is expected of him. While the patient appears to be analyzing his problem, his real motive is to gain security by adjusting himself to what he considers are the demands of the therapist. In this way the process of therapy itself becomes a means of indulging his neurosis.

In analyzing resistances, their sources in infantile attitudes and conditionings usually become apparent. Eventually it is essential to bring the patient to a realization of how the machinery with which he reacts to the world now is rooted in early conceptions and misconceptions about life. The interpretation of character strivings does not suffice to change their nature, for they are the only way the patient knows of adjusting; they are to him "ego-syntonic."

A breakdown of character strivings often brings out in sharp focus the repressed needs and impulses from which the strivings issue. When the patient becomes cognizant of the conflicts that produce his destructive interpersonal attitudes, he has the best chance of taking active steps toward their modification.

In certain cases, particularly where there are time limitations, the only thing that can be accomplished is to adjust the person to his neurosis in as expedient a manner as possible. Environmental manipulation may be necessary to take pressures off the patient. He may be shown how to adjust himself to the reality situation. For instance, if a patient has a strong striving for perfectionism that drives her incessantly into positions that she cannot handle with her intellectual and physical equipment, she may be shown how she can confine herself to a project that she can master proficiently. Whereas the scope of her operations may be limited, she can indulge her perfectionistic strivings in a circumscribed way, gaining some measure of gratification in this. If she is inordinately dependent, it may be pointed out that she can maintain a certain freedom of action in spite of the fact that she has to lean on authority. If she has a power impulse, avenues for its exercise through competition may be suggested. This approach, of course, merely panders to the patient's neurosis, but it may be the only practical thing that can be done for the time being; in many cases it will make the patient's life immeasurably more tolerable.

Whenever possible, the patient should be brought to an awareness of the nature, genesis, and dynamic significance of his character trends. He should be encouraged to observe how his strivings and defenses operate in everyday life, and to scrutinize ways in which he can change his attitudes toward people. Desirable as this may be, a shift in therapeutic orientation toward insight may stir up a hornet's nest in the relationship with the therapist.

While character trends can be classified in such categories as dependency, passivity, aggressiveness, power strivings, and detachment, they are usually interrelated and the fusion makes for a picture that is unique for each individual. Behavior is not the static product of a group of isolated trends; rather it is a complex integrate of a number of drives. The product of this intermingling differs from any of the compo-

nent strivings. That is, if the person is compulsively modest, is fired by perfectionism, is unconsciously arrogant and aggressive, some of these traits will tend to neutralize and some to reinforce each other. Nevertheless, for treatment purposes, character disorders may be regarded in terms of the most dominant trend.

"Inadequate," Infantile, Passive-Aggressive, and Dependency Patterns

The treatment of extreme "inadequacy" and dependency reactions poses special problems. Dependent persons are often brought to the therapist for treatment not because they feel a need for change, but rather because parents, marital partners, or friends insist that something be done for them. Visits to the therapist in such cases are kept merely as a formality. The patient expects that no change will occur, and he will be resistant to any effort to get him to participate in the treatment process. The limit of his cooperativeness is to expose himself to the therapist during the allotted hour.

With a defective motivation such as this, little progress can be expected. The patient will particularly resent interpretations that he may regard as unfair criticisms. He will be antagonistic to any implication that there is something wrong with him. He may respond with bewilderment, aggression, or pseudoconformity. Months and even years of therapy may effect little alteration in the inner dynamics of the personality.

As long as the patient has no real incentive for therapy, no change will be possible. The sole hope lies in convincing the patient that in the therapist he has a friend who will not influence him against his will and who understands and sympathizes with the way he feels. The struggle with the therapist will stop only when the patient senses that the therapist is a person who does not challenge his scheme of life but rather seeks to participate in it.

The only real way of aiding the patient is to help him to establish a contact with the therapist that will assume a more mature form than his previous interpersonal relationships. Unfortunately, this is easier said than done, for the dependent individual, if he is not fighting the therapist, will utilize the therapist in the same way that he uses all authorities—as a prop to security.

The patient seeks to establish himself with the therapist in ways that resemble the infant's imposition on the parents. He does not seem to be interested in developing resources within himself. Rather, he desires to maneuver the therapist into a position where constant favors will be forthcoming. He will abide by any rules of therapy in order to obtain this objective, even to the apparent absorption of insight. It is most disconcerting, however, to learn that assimilated insights are extremely superficial, and that the patient is less interested in knowing what is wrong with him than he is in perpetuating the child–parent relationship. He actually seems incapable of reasoning logically, and there is an almost psychotic quality to the persistence of his demands for support and direction. Sometimes the residual hostility is expressed in aggressiveness, which is usually masked by passive maneuvers like procrastination, obstinacy, recalcitrance, and stubbornness, hence the term "passive-aggressive character disorder."

Interpretations of the patient's dependency are usually regarded by him as chastisement. He will assume that any attempt to put responsibility on his shoulders is a form of ill will expressed toward him by the therapist. He will demonstrate reactions of disappointment, rage, anxiety, and depression, and he will repeat these reactions in spite of lip service to the effect that he wants to get well.

In treating a dependency reaction, it is essential to recognize that hostility is inevitable in the course of therapy. The demands of dependent people are so insatiable that it is impossible to live up to their expectations. Only when the patient begins to experience himself as a person with aggressiveness, assertiveness, and independence, will he be able to function with any degree of well-being. This goal, unfortunately, may in some instances never be achieved.

Supportive therapy that propitiates the patient's dependency needs is of extremely temporary effect. It is advisable, where possible, to promote a therapeutic approach in which the individual learns to accept responsibility for his own development in the hope that he will utilize this opportunity to grow.

There are some individuals, however, whose self-structure has been so crushed that they will resist any attempt to make the therapeutic situation a participating one. Here the treatment program may have to be directed at a limited therapeutic goal. The therapist will then have to become resigned to educating the patient to function with his dependency strivings with as little detriment to himself as possible.

As much pressure as the patient can bear must be imposed upon him so that he will make his own choices and decisions. It is to be expected that he will resent this vigorously, accusing the therapist of refusing to accept responsibility. The therapist may then explain to the patient that were he or she to pander to the patient's demands for support and make decisions for him, this would only tend to infantilize the patient. It would make him more dependent and more unable to develop to a point where he could fulfill himself productively and creatively. The therapist does not wish to shirk responsibility but withholds directiveness out of respect for the patient's right to develop. Although the patient may still resent the therapist's intent, he may finally understand that unless he begins to make his own decisions, he will never get to a point where he is strong within himself.

Some patients who seemingly are fixated on a dependent level may, with repeated interpretations and injunctions, finally begin to accept themselves as having the right to make their own choices and to develop their own values. Persistence, however, is the keynote. In therapy the patient will exploit every opportunity to force the therapist to assume a directive role. Nevertheless, when the patient sees that the therapist has his welfare at heart, he may be able to develop more independence and assertiveness. The shift in therapy from a directive to a nondirective role calls for considerable skill, and it must be tempered to the patient's incentives and ego strength.

Unless such a shift is made at some time, psychotherapy will probably be interminable, and the patient will continue on a dependent level requiring the ever presence of the therapist or some other giving person as a condition to his security.

Should it become apparent that one cannot work along participating lines, and that the patient's only objective is to make himself dependent on the therapist, visits may be cut down to 15- to 20-minute sessions once weekly or bimonthly, and/or the patient may be referred to a supportive social or reeducative group. Periodic full-time sessions may be required and tranquilization, sedation, or energizing with the appropriate medications (see the section on somatic therapy in Chapter 53) may temporarily be prescribed.

"Schizoid" and Detached Patterns

The treatment of a patient with a personality problem of detachment also presents many difficulties. Such a patient is usually motivated to seek therapy because detachment interferes with his livelihood or capacity to achieve social or sexual gratification. Often anxiety, which has developed from the individual's effort to emerge from his detachment, is the complaint for which the patient wants help.

The type of therapy employed will depend upon the function of detachment in the life adjustment of the individual. It will also depend on the ego strength of the patient and his capacity to tolerate the anxieties incumbent upon relating himself intimately to other persons.

Detachment may be means elaborated by the individual to protect himself from intense dependency strivings. A close relationship poses dangers of being overwhelmed, for in it the patient may envisage a complete giving up of his independence. Detachment may also be a technique of avoiding injury or destruction that the patient believes will occur when he comes close to a person. Finally, it may be a method by which the patient protects himself from fears of attacking and destroying others. In treating the patient, therefore, the

dynamic significance of detachment must be kept in mind and interventions cautiously applied.

Some therapists believe that they can assess the potentialities of the patient to tolerate interpersonal relationships through the Rorschach test, especially noting his reaction to the color cards. The best way of estimating ego strength is, of course, the patient's actual response to the therapeutic situation and a study of his dreams, fantasies, and feelings mobilized by the transference.

Where the patient's ego is so weak that it must fortify itself against shattering and where there is little practical possibility of modifying its strength, therapy along supportive lines may help the patient to reinforce his character defenses and to modify his detachment to some extent in line with a more comfortable adaptation. Where the ego strength will permit close interpersonal relationships, insight therapy may result in some alteration in the character structure.

In treating a detached patient, one must anticipate that there will be difficulty for a long time in establishing a close relationship, since this tends to mobilize his fears of injury and inspires detachment. Much active work will be required in detecting and dissolving resistances to change. The detached patient often has a tendency to intellectualize the entire therapeutic process. He will particularly shy away from expressing his feelings because he will conceive of them as dangerous.

Great hostility is bound to arise, which may be disconcerting principally because it is usually unexpressed or liberated in explosive outbursts. The therapist must realize that hostility is a defense against interpersonal closeness. It is extremely important that the therapist be as tolerant toward the patient's provocations as possible. The patient will probably attempt to goad the therapist into expressions of counteraggression to justify attitudes toward people as untrustworthy and his withdrawal from the world as potentially menacing.

Sometimes the patient may be encouraged to participate in social activities, competitive games, and sports. Commanding, restrictive directions should, however, be avoided. With encouragement, detached people may begin to relate themselves with others. In groups they drift cautiously from the periphery to the center as they realize that they will not be injured in a close interpersonal relationship. Group therapy may sometimes be most rewarding in certain detached, schizoid individuals, where no pressure is put on them to participate. Social groups with a wide range of activities are particularly suitable.

A common reaction in the therapy of detached persons is anxiety, which is manifested by disturbing nightmarish dreams or by actual anxiety attacks. The reaction will usually be found when the patient experiences for the first time real closeness or love toward the therapist. The emotions terrorize him and cause him to fear injury of an indefinable nature. It is essential to deal with this reaction when it occurs by giving him as much reassurance and interpretation as is necessary. Detached patients whose defenses have crumbled may go into a clinging dependent attitude when they realize the full weight of their helplessness. Supportive therapy may have to be given here, in an effort to provide the patient with an experience in which he receives help without being domineered or smothered with cloying affection. At certain stages in therapy, as when anxiety becomes too disturbing, a phenothiazine drug (Stelazine or Trilafon) may be helpful.

Paranoid Patterns

A type of personality disorder often found in our culture, characterized by a self-entrenched attitude, is one commonly called "paranoid" personality. The core of this personality is one of distrust. This motivates the fear of being overwhelmed and produces great suspiciousness and a desire to preserve oneself by warding off all intrusions through the building up of an impenetrable wall between oneself and others. The individual seems to want to take things in but to give up little. Associated are impulses of stinginess, orderliness, cleanliness, obstinacy, and sadism.

The function of most of these traits is to preserve the wall that protects the person

from others. Cleanliness becomes a means of warding off contacts with the outside world. Orderliness is a technique that keeps things in place so that the individual may not be caught unaware. Obstinacy is a technique of fighting off overwhelming power by negativism. Sadism stems from a feeling of weakness within oneself and from the necessity to deal with others in kind through domination and force. One of the motivants of homosexuality, which often appears in this type of personality, is a fear of people of the opposite sex, who are not to be trusted because they are different from onself and hence potentially evil. Intimacy with persons who are more familiar because they have the same sexual organs is less threatening. Homosexuality here represents a means of destroying others, of making oneself passive and dependent, and of gaining power. Love is conceived of as dangerous; indeed, any outgoing feelings are dangerous.

There is much to indicte in this personality disorder, that difficulties in relationships to parents occurred at the stage of social and toilet training, at which time intolerable frustrations were imposed on the child. During this period of development the ego expands, and the child experiences a desire for mastery and dominance. He is exposed, however, to parental disciplines that challenge his claims for mastery. The child may strive to cling to his sense of power by conforming as little as possible to demands made on him. Toilet training usually becomes the arena in which he proves he can gain mastery over his parents. An ambivalent attitude exists in that he also realizes that by conforming to the demands of his parents in establishing habits of cleanliness, he will obtain their love and support. Nevertheless, his deisres for power and mastery conflict with this aim and create impulses to retain fecal material or to soil. It is probably for this reason that excretory activities become so overvalued and constitute symbols of danger and destructiveness in dream and fantasy life. Punishment inflicted by others and self-punishment may actually be symbolized by anal punishment. The intense hostility that is generated in this condition may be projected outward in a paranoid reaction. An obsessive-compulsive neurosis is also common when the character facade fails. Understandably, the patient, for a long while, will regard therapy as a personal encroachment.

Patients with this type of problem tend to intellectualize the therapeutic process. This serves as a defense against feeling. Sometimes all that can be done for such patients is to give them as much insight as they can tolerate, in this way cooperating with their need to intellectualize therapy. Interpretations should deal with the more superficial character defenses rather than with the deep hostile and sexual content. They must be made in a reassuring manner. A persuasive approach as outlined for compulsion neurosis is usually best, although in some cases insight therapy is possible.

Power Patterns

Another type of personality disorder is one in which power impulses predominate. In this condition all that seems to matter in life is forcefulness and strength. The feelings and rights of other people are disregarded. There is a blind admiration for everything invincible. The person is contemptuous of softness and tenderness, and selfesteem is seemingly dependent on the ability to be dominant. As in dependency, the dynamic force behind the power impulse is a profound sense of helplessness and an inability to cope with life with the individual's available resources. A motive behind the power drive is to coerce people to yield to one's will, which provides bounties of various sorts.

The treatment of the power-driven individual is oriented around a building up of frustration tolerance, an increasing of the capacity to withstand tension, and a gaining of security through one's own resources. A reeducative approach may be effective in permitting the individual to develop inner restraints capable of exercising control of impulses. It is essential to be firmer in this type of disorder than in either dependency or detached reactions. The patient must be shown that there are limits beyond which one cannot go and that one must face responsibility. Whenever possible, the patient should be acquainted with the dynamic significance of his power drive, and he should be encouraged to make efforts toward the expansion of his inner resources.

Where dependency and power drives are fused, the individual functions in a dual manner, seeking security from stronger people by clinging to them helplessly or wresting security from them by force and aggression. An effort may be directed toward correcting the core of selflessness that makes for trends of compulsive submissiveness and dominancy.

Narcissistic Reactions

In treating the character disorder of excessive narcissism, therapists experience much difficulty. Persons with this problem seem to have such a need for personal admiration that they conceive of therapy as a means of making themselves more worthy of praise.

Unlike the mature person who gains security from cooperative endeavors in attitudes of altruism and sympathy, narcissistic individuals concentrate most of their interest on themselves. Self-love may actually become structured into grandiose strivings, omnipotent impulses, and megalomania. Although the image of the individual appears to be bloated, analysis readily reveals how helpless and impoverished he actually feels. There is danger here of precipitating depression or excitement in presenting insights prematurely. The shock-absorbing capacity of the ego must always be weighed, and interpretations must be given in proportion to the available ego strength. In markedly immature individuals little development may be expected other than a somewhat better environmental adaptation through guidance techniques.

Many of these patients often band together in Bohemian groups, posturing and posing, displaying a haughty defiance of convention, garbing themselves in outlandish dress, arranging their hair out of keeping with the accepted style as a way of expressing their exaggerated exhibitionistic, omnipotent, sadistic, and masochistic impulses. Language for them serves to release tension and not as genuine means of communication. As long as they impulsively discharge their tension and anxiety in acting-out, they will not be too uncomfortable. "They are hunting eternally for satisfactory and secure models through which they may save themselves by a narcissistic identification. On the surface it appears later as a scattered, superficial pseudo competitiveness" (Greenacre, 1952). There is little motivation for therapy, which is usually sought, not by the person, but by a concerned parent or friend who is shocked or frightened by the patient's behavior. Under these circumstances psychotherapy proceeds under a great handicap, the patient generally breaking appointments or manifesting such resistance that the therapist's tolerance is put under the severest test. The only incentive that the patient has for treatment is to please the parent or referral agency, usually to avoid the catastrophe of having his allowance cut off. Where the person is unable to release tension due to the absence of or removal from environmental resources, anxiety may then come to the surface. Symptomatic discomfort will then act as a motive for help.

In recent years an interest into the dynamics and therapy of narcissistic subjects has been revived. Scrutiny of the earliest phases of ego development have led to a number of hypotheses on how the disorder evolves and its influence on treatment (Kohut, 1971). Attempts have been made, with variable results, to differentiate narcissistic reactions from borderline cases and schizophrenia, which are distinctive ailments even though a strong bond exists among these entities. Problems in all three have occurred in the primary stages of separation and individuation. Object relationships as a result become distorted and shallow, being oriented around what they can do to enhance the individual's status and interests. Fusion and dependency are basic themes; love objects are imbued with both terrifying and grandiose qualities. In therapy the transference reaction, which is essentially narcissistic, encourages regressive episodes with fear of the loss of the love object, paranoidal symptoms, and a fear of castra-

tion. The regression is never as deep as that in borderline or schizophrenic disorders.

Classical psychoanalysis is contraindicated, but where a semblance of a relationship can be maintained, psychoanalytically oriented psychotherapy, blended with supportive approaches, may be helpful.

Antisocial (Psychopathic) Personality

Allied to narcissistic character disorders is an antisocial personality manifested by poor frustration tolerance, egocentricity, impulsivity, aggressiveness, antisocial acting-out, an inability to profit by experience, undeveloped capacities for cooperative interpersonal relationships, poorly integrated sexual responses, and urgent pleasure pursuits with an inability to postpone gratifications. Because of the severe warping in ego formation, goals in therapy, as in the narcissistic character, are geared toward behavioral rather than character change. Modification of destructive and antisocial behavior is, of course, mandatory. Recognition of the patient's acting-out, the circumstances and needs that initiate it, and the way that the patient draws other people into his maneuvers are not too difficult.

Most authorities agree that the management of antisocial personality is most difficult. All approaches have yielded meager results. In many cases the only thing that can be accomplished is manipulation of the environment to eliminate as many temptations as possible that stimulate the psychopath into expressing his vicarious impulses.

If a psychopathic individual can establish a relationship to a person, the latter may be able, as a kind but firm authority, to supervise the patient's actions. Hypnosis can reinforce this authoritative relationship. The therapist may, by adroit suggestions, act as a repressive moral force and as a pillar of support. The patient may get to the point where he will turn to the therapist for guidance when temptation threatens him. Suggestions may be couched in such terms as to convince the patient that he is actually wiser and happier for resisting certain activities that, as he knows from past experience, are bound to result disastrously. On the basis of a guidance relationship, the patient may be instructed in the wisdom of postponing immediate gratifications for those that in the long run will prove more lasting and wholesome. He is taught the prudence of tolerating frustration and the need to feel a sense of responsibility and consideration for the rights of others. Not that these lessons will be immediately accepted or acted on, but constant repetition sometimes helps the patient to realize that it is to his best interest, ultimately, to observe social amenities and to exercise more self-control.

Experience demonstrates that it is possible to modify to some extent the immature explosive reactions of the psychopath by an extensive training program, particularly in cooperative group work where the individual participates as a member toward a common objective. Adequate group identifications are lacking in the psychopath, and the realization that ego satisfactions can accrue from group experiences, may create a chink in the defensive armor. In cases where the psychopath comes into conflict with the law and where incarceration is necessary, a program organized around building up whatever assets the individual possesses, particularly in a therapeutic community, may, in some instances, bring success. In young psychopaths vocational schools that teach a trade may contribute to self-esteem and provide a means of diverting energies into a profitable channel. Should group therapy be deemed necessary, the constituent members ideally are psychopathic personalities with problems similar to those of the patient. Even where therapy seems successful, intervals of acting-out are to be expected.

ALCOHOLISM

Alcoholism ranks with cancer, heart disease, and mental illness as one of the four major health problems in the nation. It is the most commonly abused and the most dangerous drug habit of today. In most cases alcoholism is incurable; the best that

can be done is to help the individual become a "nondrinking alcoholic."

When the average alcoholic applies for therapy, the therapist is usually confronted with the expressed or secret hope that the patient will learn to drink normally and to "hold his liquor like anyone else." While this may be possible in the anxiety drinker following abatement of his neurosis, it is not true in the case of the real alcoholic.

Although there are some persons who believe that the alcoholic can be cured by weaning him gradually from the bottle, and who are of the opinion he may learn to engage in social drinking without exceeding his capacity, experience has shown that success is possible only where alcohol is completely and absolutely eliminated from the individual's regime. The object in therapy is complete elimination of all alcoholic beverages, including wine and beer.

The treatment of alcoholism not only embraces the removal of the desire for alcohol; it also involves restoration of the patient to some kind of adaptational equilibrium. Without such restoration the person will become pathologically depressed, and his tension will drive him to drink no matter what pressures are put on him.

In the anxiety drinker any attempt to force or to shame the person into sobriety will interfere with the therapeutic relationship. The patient should be made to feel that he need not apologize for his drinking desires. He should be shown that alcohol provides him with an escape and that he may require liquor as long as his fundamental problems remain. The danger of continued drinking may be pointed out. However, while the therapist does not approve of the patient's drinking, the patient will not be ordered to stop. When the patient believes that he is ready to give up alcohol, the therapist will help him to do so. The therapeutic program should be organized around the treatment of the underlying neurotic or character problem. A sympathetic attitude toward the patient's need for alcohol is always appreciated by the patient. Nevertheless, the therapist must insist that the patient come in sober for his sessions.

While a reconstructive approach is sometimes useful in the anxiety drinker, it is usually futile in the real alcoholic. The ego of the alcoholic is immature, and his capacity to integrate and to utilize insight in a constructive manner is impaired. The alcoholic patient will dig out fascinating dynamic structures during psychotherapy, but this effort will have little influence on his drinking. In many cases the therapist must be satisfied with the partial therapeutic objective of weaning the patient from alcohol, thus permitting him to adjust to life with his immature character organization in as adaptive and nondestructive a manner as possible.

The greatest difficulty will be experienced in the handling of those alcoholics who do not wish to stop drinking and who apply for treatment under coercion of parents, mate, or friends. Exposure to therapy is merely a device to retain the good will of the people close to the patient. Treatment here will usually be unsuccessful, the patient utilizing the therapist as a referee who is expected to arbitrate between himself and his family. Sessions are spent lamenting his plight or presenting himself as a misunderstood and abused person who is completely justified in his drinking.

Such alcoholics are best treated in an institution where they cannot obtain drink. The usual reaction to hospitalization is indignation and promises to refrain from alcohol if released. When such release is not forthcoming, the patient will make an exemplary adjustment, creating such an appearance of normality that one may be tempted to discharge him prematurely. One difficulty is the attitude of relatives who will be goaded by the patient to secure his release. In the hospital psychotherapy may be started, and an attempt may be made to get the patient interested in hobbies, crafts, or an occupation that will engage his energies. Supportive therapy of a guidance and persuasive type is useful to help the patient discover and exploit his assets and talents. Reconstructive therapy, if feasible, may be tried. A period of 1 to 2 years of hospitalization is often required, and before the patient is discharged, his environment should be manipulated to assure a minimum of stress.

Where hospitalization is impossible, certain forceful measures may be required, particularly in the alcoholic who has no motivation whatsoever to abandon liquor. The best time to start therapy is when the patient is in an acute alcoholic episode. At this time he is given the usual detoxification therapy (see Acute Alcoholic Intoxication, p. 856). The contact with the patient here will serve a psychotherapeutic purpose in promoting a close relationship. The therapist, utilizing the remorse and self-condemnation of the patient during the "hangover" period, may enjoin him to seek psychotherapy.

The next phase of therapy is a coercive one in which an attempt is made to bring the patient to a point where he refuses to drink or is unable to drink. Cajolery and appeals to reason are usually futile. Sometimes a belittling and challenging manner mobilize in the patient a need to prove that he has the "guts" to master the craving for alcohol. This, however, cannot be depended on. Once the patient verbalizes a desire to stop drinking, conditioned-reflex therapy or antabuse therapy may be started. The patient should be under close supervision during this period.

An attempt must always be made to establish a rapid relationship with the patient. Should the patient become dependent on the therapist, the latter may utilize the dependency situation to reinforce the patient's desire to abstain from drink and to motivate him toward utilizing his assets to best advantage. Interest in hobbies and recreations should be stimulated. The patient should also be urged to join a group like Alcoholics Anonymous.

The approach utilized by the Alcoholics Anonymous organization is a most effective one. Here the person is forced to admit that he is an alcoholic, that he needs help, and that he wishes to do something about his condition. He is enjoined to realize that because of his own powerlessness in managing his drinking, his life has gotten out of control. He is encouraged to feel that a Power greater than himself can restore him to health, and he is advised to turn himself over to this Power in his quest for security. He is furthermore encouraged to make a searching moral inventory of himself, admitting his faults to others in the group as well as to God. He must be willing to make amends to those persons whom he has in any way harmed. At the same time he is shown that he may have overemphasized his bad points.

The alcoholic is never actually urged to say he will stop drinking entirely. Rather, he is informed that each day he will tell himself that he will remain dry, with God's help, for 24 hours. At the end of the day he may take an inventory of himself to see if he did anything that was not constructive or if he had acted intolerant, resentful, jealous, spiteful, or unkind.

The group meetings are extremely useful, since the patient finds companionship with others who share similar emotional problems. Furthermore, when the patient feels tempted to drink, he is able to telephone one of his friends and make an appointment to talk things over. An important part of the program is the patient's participation in helping other alcoholics who are in the grip of their drinking habit. The fact that the workers in the movement are ex-alcoholics enables them to display an enormous amount of tolerance and to convince the patient that he, too, can do what others have done. It goes without saying that only an alcoholic really understands the drinker. An identification is thus expedited.

Many alcoholics stop drinking when they feel that their dependency is appeased by an alliance with God. The religious cure of alcoholism is often dynamically based on the drinker's conviction that if he lives up to God's expectations and stays sober, he will be given bounties, if not now, then in the hereafter. God becomes the ideal parent who is all-wise, all-supporting, and all-forgiving. The alcoholic is unable to challenge this new parental figure or to test his omnipotence or weakness, as he can a flesh-and-blood person. His hostility is consequently held in check. When a drinker "gets religion," he may overcome his alcoholic habit. On the other hand, there are some alcoholics who are "turned off" by any references to God. Such agnostics will need Alcoholics Anonymous or a similar group that has eliminated the God concept from its format.

The treatment of the alcoholic who spontaneously applies to the therapist for help, while difficult, does not present as many problems as that of the person who is maneuvered into therapy through the agency of another concerned individual. In treating such a patient, the following steps may be kept in mind. First, a relationship is started with the patient with the object of developing positive rapport. Second, an effort is made to build up the patient's self-esteem. Third, his interests are externalized, and outlets are provided for his aggression. Fourth, he is taught to handle frustration and deprivation. Fifth, he is encouraged to stop drinking. Sixth, he is urged to make social contacts with individuals and groups.

The first aim is to get the patient to substitute a dependency relationship on the therapist for his alcoholic habit. The alcoholic seeks and needs this type of relationship. When he accepts the therapist and has confidence in the therapist, the latter will then be able to utilize this to help break the drinking habit. It is essential, therefore, to make the alcoholic feel that he is accepted on his own level, drunk or sober. The patient may be told that the therapist wants to help him but is not going to act as a policeman and force him to give up drink, however destructive this may be for him, if he believes it is so vital for his adjustment. He is informed that the therapist realizes that alcohol plays a major role in his life. Drinking does not make him a bad person. If he has the desire for alcohol, it is because of a sequence of conditionings and experiences that have happened to him that he can now overcome.

It may be difficult to convince the patient that the therapist is interested in him, and he will often test the therapist's good faith by indulging in repeated heavy bouts of drinking. Should one fall into this trap and become embittered with the patient, the relationship will terminate. One must remember that the patient habitually tries to wring out of the environment a good parental figure who will supply him with unqualified love and support. It is essential at first, then, to get the patient to accept the therapist in this role.

Any existing remediable elements in

the patient's environment that may be creating conflict for the patient should be straightened out, with the aid of a social worker if necessary. In spite of his expressed optimism, the patient is unable to handle frustration, and any objective source of difficulty may suffice to promote tension that will produce a craving for drink. An inquiry into the patient's daily routine and habits may be expedient. Often one finds a gross defect in the person's diet. Alcoholic overindulgence is coincident with a depletion in dietary intake and with vitamin deficiency. The prescription of a well-balanced diet with sufficient calories and with supplementary vitamin B is of great help. The patient should also be encouraged to appease his hunger whenever he feels a need for food. Hitherto he has propitiated hunger pains by drinking alcohol. He may be surprised to observe that eating three square meals a day can remove much of his craving for liquor.

The numerous difficulties a patient has experienced through his inability to control drinking, the general condemnation of society, and the disdain of his family, all contribute toward a depreciation of his self-esteem. It is difficult to rebuilt self-esteem by reassurance, but an effort must be made to demonstrate to the patient that he has many residual assets that he can expand. Because alcoholics become negligent about their appearnce, it is essential to rebuild interest in their personal care. Appearing neat and well groomed usually has a bolstering effect upon the person. Alcoholic women may be directed toward taking care of their complexions and hair by going to a beauty parlor. Whatever interest the patient shows in hobbies or external recreations should be encouraged. He must be reminded that he is not a hopeless case and that he has many good qualities that he has neglected. His guilt may be appeased by showing him that he is not solely responsible for his alcoholic craving. It will be possible to substitute for it something much more constructive. The therapist will help him make a proper substitution. In discussing his work situation, a battery of vocational tests may disclose that the patient's interests and aptitudes are in a direction other than his existing work. He may be helped to develop along the lines indicated by his tests. The ultimate aim of these efforts is to get the patient to accept himself as a person with value and dignity.

Because the alcoholic often is inwardly hostile, an outlet should be provided for his aggressive tendencies. Joining a YMCA or athletic club, engaging in competitive games and sports, in swimming, archery, or boxing may be of value. As release is provided for the patient's aggression, he will become much less tense.

Teaching the alcoholic to handle frustration will require considerable effort. The patient must be brought around to a realization that everyone has frustrated feelings and that an important job in life is to exercise control. Because of what has happened to him, he is apt to misinterpret any disappointment as a sign of his own personal failure. It is mandatory that he build up a tolerance of frustration, even though he has to extend willful effort in this direction.

Since frustration is usually accompanied by gastric distress, it may stimulate a desire for drink. The patient, therefore, may be advised to carry with him, at all times, a piece of chocolate or candy. Whenever he feels frustrated or under any circumstances where a craving for drink develops, he can partake of this nourishment. Hot coffee, cocoa, and milkshakes are also good for the same purpose and can act as substitutes for alcohol. As the patient gains more respect for himself, it will be possible for him to tolerate greater and greater amounts of frustration.

At some stage in therapy the patient must be encouraged to stop drinking. He may be told that while the therapist does not condemn him for alcoholic indulgence, because liquor has a destructive effect, he must try to control its intake. The close relationship with the therapist, the increased self-esteem that comes from positive achievements, the correction of difficulties in his life situation, and the heightened ability to handle frustration, all help to reduce his thirst for alcohol.

When the propitious time arrives, an explanation may be given the patient of how alcohol is poisonous to him because he has built up an allergy to it. It must be stressed that physiologically he is different from other persons, and for this reason he is unable to tolerate alcohol. Many alcoholics regard their inability to "hold liquor" as a sign of weakness. An organic reason for their intolerance usually has a soothing influence on them. The patient may be told that because of his allergic condition alcohol is as much a poison to him in the long run as cyanide. While he has needed alcohol to appease his tension, he will find that he can utilize other methods now, and he can, therefore, reduce the amount of his alcoholic intake. Gradually, he will want to give up alcohol entirely.

The patient must abandon the prevailing idea, so current among alcoholics, that eventually he will get to a point where he can drink like anyone else. He must be assured that one drink is equivalent to a thousand, and that because of his inability to drink due to allergy, he must make up his mind to forsake alcohol completely. One way to do this is to live his life and make resolutions for only 24 hours in advance.

An important phase of therapy is encouraging the patient to make social contacts and to affiliate himself with groups. If a branch of Alcoholics Anonymous exists in the community, the patient will find that he can make many friends there and that he can involve himself in numerous constructive activities that will engage his energies and consolidate the gains that he has made in therapy. In some communities two offshoot organizations of AA exist for families of alcoholics. Al-Anon is for adults and Alateen is for teenage children of alcoholics. Since families contribute to the reactions of the alcoholic, a resource for them is most helpful. Family therapy and marital therapy may be essential components of an ongoing treatment plan.

In recent years the use of the drug Antabuse has come into prominence. The administration of Antabuse creates an intense sensitivity to alcohol, with such violent reactions upon any consumption of liquor that the pleasure values of drinking are no longer possible. This serves to protect the patient against the uncontrollable urge to imbibe alcohol and gives a sense of secu-

rity. In order to employ Antabuse therapy, the patient's cooperation is necessary. Should the patient refuse to take Antabuse, it will be impossible to force him to do so. With proper medical supervision Antabuse therapy is not dangerous, although disagreeable side effects are possible. Accidents, however, sometimes do happen, as where a patient unintentionally or defiantly swallows an alcoholic beverage. This may result in death if a large amount of drink has been consumed.

Once the patient is reasonably alcohol free, Antabuse therapy may be started by a competent physician. There are several ways of doing this. One method (Fox, R, 1952) consists of prescribing, after the patient has gone at least 12 hours without alcohol, 1 tablet (0.5 gm) of Antabuse each morning for 2 weeks. Following this a test reaction may be made, preferably in a hospital, with 1 to 2 ounces of whiskey or the patient's favorite beverage. The latter is repeated if no response occurs in 20 or 30 minutes. This test may be executed again at weekly intervals. More recently tests have been abandoned, patients merely being warned of the reactions to drinking. Where the patient is taking Antabuse, it is suggested (Fox, R, 1958) that he carry a card on him with identification data, stating that he is on Antabuse and describing the symptoms of the Antabuse-alcohol reaction (Ayerst Laboratories, 685 Third Avenue, New York, N.Y. 10017, will apply such cards on request). All alcohol is to be avoided including wine sauces and wine vinegar. The average maintenance dose is ½ tablet daily (this may range from ¼ to 1 tablet daily), which may be continued indefinitely. It must be remembered that appropriate blood levels of Antabuse are not attained until at least 4 days of continued administration. Minor side effects occur with Antabuse that usually disappear spontaneously with continued medication or with dosage reduction. The drug is contraindicated in severe myocardial disease or coronary occlusion, in psychoses, and in hepatic cirrhosis. Should the patient resume drinking while under Antabuse, he will develop severe symptoms that may be treated by oxygen inhalation, intravenous vitamin C (1 gm), and ephedrine sulfate or antihistamines intravenously. After 6 to 8 hours following the last drink, the patient may return to his Antabuse, taking ¼ of a tablet every 2 or 3 hours for four doses and 25 to 50 mg of Thorazine or Promazine by mouth with each dose if he is emotionally upset.

Each alcoholic must be treated on an individual basis to meet his particular needs (Block, 1964). A general hospital may be required for acute alcoholic intoxication, and this may constitute the first step in the rehabilitation program. Where alcoholism represents a camouflage of a psychosis, a mental hospital may be the best facility. After the acute episode has passed, an outpatient clinic or private treatments may be in order. Employable patients who require supervision when not at work will need a halfway house, which serves as a temporary retreat for those alcoholics whose environment stimulates their drinking. Rehabilitation centers are suited for patients requiring long periods of therapy during which they receive vocational training. The object here is to get the patient to a point where he may be transferred to a halfway house. Further rehabilitation can be carried out in a good foster home that is adequately supervised. On the other hand, a completely sheltered and custodial environment, with recreational and occupational opportunities, may be the best resource for the patient.

Alcoholism demands a multifaced approach "using all disciplines available—medicine, psychotherapy, social and family pressure, in short, a coordinated approach. . . . But treating an alcoholic is a long and complicated process of re-education and rehabilitation" (Fox, R, 1961). Among the therapies employed are physical and occupational rehabilitation, Alcoholics Anonymous, group therapy, psychodrama, counseling, social therapy, recreational therapy, family therapy, and, occasionally, psychoanalysis. Behavior therapy, relaxation exercises, meditation, and hypnosis (for relaxation, improvement of the self-image, and developing of an aversion for alcohol) are other instrumentalities. Finally, assistance with spiritual problems may be necessary. In patients with good motiva-

tion, this total program, according to R. Fox (1966) will bring a 50 to 60 percent recovery rate.

Therapists who have experimented with LSD find that it introduces in some alcoholics the motivation to stop drinking (Abramson, 1966). Employing approximately three LSD exposures during a 6-month period, Kurland et al. (1966), in a controlled study, reported extensive and desirable attitudinal and behavioral changes following psychedelic psychotherapy. In the hands of experienced treatment personnel, the authors believe that alcoholic patients with a wide variety of personality disorders may be treated without complications. However, they warn that relapses and the reestablishment of old patterns are possible unless there is systematic reinforcement, aftercare, and continuing treatment. More recent studies cast some doubt on LSD effectiveness.

Conditioned-reflex therapy may also be employed with the alcoholic. Here the patient is given a short-acting emetic drug, such as apomorphine (0.1 gr) and after 5 to 10 minutes he is allowed to drink his favorite alcoholic beverage. This will readily be disgorged as a wave of nausea descends on the patient. After several treatments on successive or alternate days, the patient is so conditioned that he is nauseated at the sight of alcohol. He vomits if he swallows even a few gulps. To avoid "deconditioning," regular follow-up sessions are required, which most alcoholics resist. A variant of this method is through hypnotherapy. Here the hypnotized subject is exposed to the odor of his favorite alcoholic beverage and given some to drink. Simultaneously it is suggested that the patient will lose his desire for alcohol and that even the odor and taste of it will bring about nausea, dizziness, and severe headache. These sessions are repeated every 2 to 3 days. Once the conditioning is established, the patient may continue with self-hypnosis, returning for reinforcements every three to four months.

During and after an alcoholic episode Librium may be useful. In states of acute agitation parenteral Librium (50–100 mg intramuscularly or intravenously, repeated in

4 to 6 hours if necessary) or chlorpromazine (25–50 mg intramuscularly, repeated if necessary) for a few days may be helpful. Dilantin (150–250 mg intravenously) may be required where the patient has convulsive seizures. In chronic alcoholics 10 mg of Librium three to four times daily, orally, may control tension and anxiety and may reduce the drinker's need for intoxicating beverage. Meprobamate (400 mg one to four times daily) has also been used. Amphetamines and barbiturates should be avoided in the alcoholic because of their habituating potential. Lithium has been utilized experimentally on the basis that a mood disturbance is present in alcoholics. Results have been encouraging.

DRUG DEPENDENCE

Opium Addiction

An occupational hazard for physicians, and pharmacists because of their easy accessibility, a component of pleasure seeking among psychopaths and sociopaths, a means of proving their masculinity among adolescents belonging to gangs, an unfortunate consequence of their prolonged use in pain or anxiety, opiates (particularly heroin) constitute a growing menace to the population. Harsh penalties for the possession and sale of these drugs makes their cost so high that the average addict must engage in stealing and other criminal activities to secure a constant supply. He consequently becomes a social menace. Because he neglects his physical health, the addict suffers from disease and premature aging. Suicide is common as an escape from pain when drugs are not available.

Generally, drug addiction is not a simple matter of physical dependence. It is a manifestation of a long-standing personality problem that has many forms, addiction being one of the symptoms. Drug addiction is also a consequence of social and economic deprivation, many users of drugs coming from areas of poverty and destitution. Juvenile drug users are seriously disturbed youngsters with a delinquent orientation to life who, because of lack of co-

hesiveness, supervision, and discipline in their home, drift toward renegade gangs to supply them with a sense of belonging and, through antisocial actions, to bolster up a stunted sense of identity. Drugs, particularly heroin, provide for them an answer to the tensions and anxieties of growing up. The pleasure rewards of drug intake and the violent discomfort of abstinence make drugs the central interest in the life of the addict. It requires a good deal of money to satisfy the opiate need. This sum is generally obtained through crimes against property and by "pushing" drugs, selling them at profit to other addicts.

The treatment of the drug addict with any of our present methods is frustratingly unsuccessful, principally because of lack of motivation of the addict for cure; the presence in him of narcissistic, immature, schizoidlike personality patterns that stir up incessant inner conflict and interfere with an adaptation to reality; and the existence of a home environment that imposes burdens for which he can find no solution. The following guidelines, nonetheless, may be found useful:

1. The treatment of addiction to narcotic drugs, such as opium, morphine, heroin, dilaudid, demerol, methadone, and cocaine, is best achieved in a specialized institution where withdrawal symptoms can be handled and where there is close supervision to prevent the addict from obtaining drugs. Where the financial condition forbids hospitalization in a private institution, it is advisable to ask the patient to apply for voluntary admission or commitment to the U.S. Public Health Service Hospitals at Lexington, Kentucky, or Fort Worth, Texas (Council on Pharmacy & Chemistry, 1952).

2. Withdrawal or detoxification, which takes 4 to 12 days, is best accomplished with methadone, which may be administered orally. According to Fraser and Grider (1953) and H. A. Raskin (1964), 1 mg of methadone is equivalent to 2 mg heroin, 4 mg morphine, 1 mg Dilaudid, 20 to 30 mg Demerol and 25 mg codeine. The dosage of methadone

must be titrated to the tolerance of the patient. Too concentrated a dosage may produce respiratory depression, circulatory depression, shock, and cardiac arrest. Generally, detoxification treatment is administered daily under close supervision, does not exceed 21 days, and may not be repeated earlier than 4 weeks following the preceding course. A single oral dose of 15 to 20 mg of methadone will usually control withdrawal symptoms. This may have to be repeated if symptoms are not suppressed. A usual stabilizing dose is 40 mg per day in single or divided doses. After 2 or 3 days the dosage is decreased at a daily or 2-day interval. Hospitalized patients generally are reduced by 20 percent each day; ambulatory patients require a slower reduction. In cases of great physical debilitation a high caloric diet, vitamins, hydrotherapy, massage, and glucose infusions are helpful. It is important to prevent all visitors and other persons not concerned with treatment from seeing the patient who is hospitalized since drugs may be smuggled in to him as a result of pitiful pleas to relieve his suffering. Electroconvulsive therapy administered daily has mitigated pain (Paterson, AS, 1963). Librium, Thorazine, Trilafon, or Sodium Amytal may also be given. Hypnotherapy has served to make the patient more comfortable. A prolonged period of hospitalization is best. Follow-up studies have shown that a high percentage of addicts released before 4 months become readdicted within 6 months. The use of Thorazine (25–100 mg four times daily) or Trilafon (4–8 mg four times daily) helps control anxiety.

3. While drug addicts do well in a sheltered, drug-free environment, a return to the pressures and conflicts of their everyday world rekindles tensions, escape from which will be sought in drugs. An aftercare program is mandatory. Some authorities advocate legislation to force the addict to obtain aftercare services.

4. Aftercare is best administered in a day–night hospital or halfway house where the addict may spend a good part of his time, where he may be exposed to the forces of group dynamics and obtain a full range of social, rehabilitative, vocational, recreational, and psychotherapeutic services geared to his needs. The aftercare of drug-free addicts poses many hazards and disappointments principally because of their immature, hypersensitive personalities, their low level of frustration, and their inability to find adequate ways of dealing with their needs and tensions. A return to drugs is easily initiated by one disturbing experience.

5. An aftercare rehabilitative and guidance center is not enough. Rather *constant care and supervision* are required, with daily interactions with some person (social worker, minister, rehabilitation worker, or psychotherapist).

Psychotherapy of the drug addict is usually unsuccessful unless all of the measures outlined supplement the treatment program. In a 12-year follow-up study of addicts who had achieved abstinence, it was found that recovery is possible among delinquent addicts provided there is compulsory supervision and a discovery by the addict of gratifying alternatives to drugs (Vaillant, 1966). Since a considerable number of the patients are borderline or schizophrenic, they must be handled with methods attuned to sicker patients.

Addicts sometimes consult psychiatrists asking that they be given an opiate for renal or gall bladder colic or some other emergent condition that requires temporary narcotic administration. Signs of the addiction include the presence of needle marks on the arms, legs, hands, abdomen, and thighs or physical signs of withdrawal. Withdrawal symptoms may rapidly be brought on in an addict by injecting naloxone (Narcan), which is an antidote to morphine, heroin, and similar narcotics. The presence of an opiate may also be detected from chemical analysis of the urine.

Since it is impractical to treat addiction unless the drug intake is brought under control, the therapist should insist on hospitalization as a preliminary step in the treatment program. During aftercare a small number of addicts will have sufficient ego strength to respond to reeducative or modified reconstructive psychotherapy. But, it must be emphasized, psychotherapy unreinforced by a prolonged, perhaps perpetual program of rehabilitation is unsuccessful as a rule. An important problem in treating a drug addict by psychological means is a countertransference resentment toward and identification with the addict, which interferes with the therapist's capacity to show tolerance and empathy. The addict's acting-out tendencies and his low level of frustration will upset the equilibrium of the most stable therapist.

Some authorities, disappointed with the results of all treatment methods, advocate supplying addicts legally with drugs to keep them in balance, in this way eliminating the illegal supply outlets. Other authorities argue against dispensing drugs, saying that the factor of increasing tolerance enjoins the addict to expand the dose required to secure the desired effect. Having obtained the limit prescribed from the physician or clinic, the addict will return to the illegal market and continue to be exploited by drug peddlers, resorting to crime for funds as usual.

These arguments have been mitigated by the introduction of the narcotic substance methadone (Dole & Nyswander, 1965), which has the potentiality of stabilizing addicts. When administered by medical authorities, it serves to reduce and prevent crime (Cushman, 1972) and to promote a better social adjustment (Sharoff, 1966). Resorting to addicting drugs like methadone, however, is regarded by some authorities as merely a temporary expedient that does not help or control the overall situation (Maddun & Bowden, 1972).

Where maintenance therapy is decided on, doses of methadone must be adjusted on an individual basis. A past heavy user of heroin may be given 20 mg repeated in 4 to 8 hours or 40 mg as a single dose. If the individual has been detoxified or has been a light user, half this dose should suffice. Titration of dosage to control abstinence symptoms may go up to 120 mg daily. Daily administration (or 6 days a week) under supervision is given for 3 months. Following this the patient may come in three times weekly and receive no more than a 2-day home supply. After 2 years the visits can be reduced to twice weekly with a 3-day home supply. Reduction of dosage should be considered on an individual basis as symptoms come under control.

Among the newer treatments for heroin control in addition to methadone is methadyl acetate, a synthetic congener of methadone. Methadyl acetate appears to be equal to methadone in its rehabilitative efficacy, but its duration of action is from 48 to 72 hours, so it can be dispensed three times weekly instead of daily. It may be useful for a certain subgroup of the addict population (Senay et al., 1977).

There are some incurable addicts who are "well-adjusted and leading useful, productive and otherwise exemplary lives which would probably be upset by removing their drugs. They are contented with their present states, do not desire treatment and would resist change. The wisdom of disturbing them is to be questioned, for the result socially and economically might be destructive and bad" (NY Academy of Medicine, 1963). This applies also to elderly addicts with healed lesions of various sorts.

Some addicts seem highly motivated to rehabilitate themselves but require a drug support to sustain them in resisting narcotics. Phenothiazines are helpful in certain situations, particularly where anxiety is an intensely disturbing symptom. Roskin (1966) believes that the schizophrenic addict, who makes up 10 percent of the adult and 30 percent of the adolescent addict group, utilizes narcotics as a tranquilizer when in the throes of severe schizophrenic decompensation. The schizophrenic addict, in his opinion, has a better prognosis than the pure acting-out addict. "If a drug addict seeks help on his own volition, it may be suspected that he is a schizophrenic." Phenothiazine drugs and the supportive relationship with the therapist are helpful replacements for narcotics in the adjustment of the schizophrenic addict.

To remedy overdosage of narcotics or methadone, Cyclazocine, a long-acting narcotic antagonist, has been utilized (Martin, WR, et al, 1965; Jaffe, JH, & Brill, 1966). Recently naloxone (Narcan) has been employed as the drug of choice. It also is used to block the action of narcotics, thus helping the potential user to neutralize dependence on them. In the absence of narcotics or agonistic effects of other narcotic antagonists it has no pharmacologic activity. Where there is a physical dependence on narcotics, it will produce withdrawal symptoms. It is given intravenously, intramuscularly, or subcutaneously (0.4 mg), repeated if necessary intravenously at 2 to 3 minute intervals. It can also exert a 24-hour action given orally in a single 3 mg dose (Zaks et al., 1971). A longer acting antagonist is naltrexone. It is more powerful than naloxone, a dose of 160 to 180 mg inducing opium blockage for 72 hours (Resnick et al., 1974).

Motivated addicts also have been helped in groups by relating themselves to other addicts who have broken the habit. The most successful experiment is that of Synanon under whose care the addict deliberately places himself (Casriel, 1963; Gould, 1965; Walder, 1965). Part of the Synanon idea includes an intensive leaderless form of group therapy—usually three times weekly—during which each member is expected to reveal his feelings truthfully, and to lay bare his fears and hates. "At Synanon we snatch off all the covers of our dirty little secrets. Then we stand there naked for everybody to see" (*Life Magazine,* 1962). Groups with a leader also exist, ideally consisting of three male and three female addicts and one ex-addict ("Synanist"). The Synanist acts as moderator who utilizes his own insight into himself for interpretations. He also employs such tactics as ridicule, cross-examination, and hostile attack to stir up involvement and activity. Another device, used with a new addict is the "haircut," in which four or five significant members of the Synanon family structure "take him apart," criticizing his actions and performances to date. While the "haircut" may be a verbally brutal experience, it is usually quite effective. "When the word gets around that 'haircuts' are being given, people seem to get

in line . . . . Many of the people who have experienced these 'haircuts' reported a change in attitude or a shift in direction almost immediately." Lectures are given daily by one of the more experienced members. The members support each other and come to each other's aid when temptation threatens to disrupt drug abstinence. Each member is also expected to perform household tasks according to his ability, which gives him a sense of participation. Additionally, "a concerted effort is made by the significant figures of the family structure to implant spiritual concepts and values which will result in self-reliance. Members are urged to read from the classics and from the great teachers of mankind—Jesus, Lao Tse, Buddha, etc. These efforts have been successful to a rather surprising degree. The concept of an open mind is part of a program to help the addict find himself, without the use of drugs" (Dederich, 1958). As soon as the addict is adjusted to his new environment, he is encouraged to get a job on the outside, to contribute part of his salary to the group, and to continue living at the Synanon house.

The Synanon idea, which essentially depends for its force on group dynamics, is being adopted in some correctional institutions. The lack of communication between the inmates of an institution and the authorities who run it has always posed a problem. To circumvent this the people chosen to work with offenders are themselves ex-offenders who have modified their own deviant behavior. Offenders, alcoholics, and drug addicts seem to respond to a leader who, like themselves, has gone through criminal, alcoholic, or drug addiction experiences, who talks their language, and who, in having achieved resocialization, becomes a model with whom new identifications may be made. Such a leader usually approaches his work with an evangelical-like zeal to point out new directions in life from which he cannot be outmaneuvered by specious arguments. Another technique that has come into recent use with drug addicts is the "marathon group" of continuous group interaction for 2 or more days with short periods of rest.

Residential treatment centers like

Synanon have been developing in different parts of the country. An example is Daytop. Therapeutic communities like Odyssey House and Phoenix House (DeLeon et al, 1972; Densen-Gerber, 1973) have provided a refuge for some addicts, beneficial effects usually being maintained as long as a patient is an active member.

Recommended readings in narcotic addiction are the following: Brotman et al. (1965), Chein et al. (1964), I. A. Clark (1965), *Comprehensive Psychiatry* (1963), Dobbs (1971), Fawcett (1961), A. M. Freedman (1966), A. M. Freedman et al. (1963), A. M. Freedman and Sharoff (1965), Kaldegg (1966), Lennard et al. (1971), Mueller (1964), New York Academy of Medicine (1963), Nyswander (1956), O'Donnell (1964), Osnos (1963), Ray (1961), Sabath (1964), Savitt (1963), and U.S. Department of Health, Education, and Welfare (nd).

Other Drugs

An addiction problem as serious as that of narcotics is dependence on barbiturates and minor tranquilizers (Miltown, Librium, Valium). In 1962 a survey by the Food and Drug Administration revealed that over 1 million pounds of barbituric acid derivatives were available in the United States (Committee on Alcoholism & Addiction, 1965). This 1-year inventory is enough to supply two dozen 1.5 gr doses to every man, woman, and child in the country. The survey led to the conclusion that "any patient whose psychological dependence on a barbiturate drug has reached a degree sufficient to constitute drug abuse has some form of underlying psychopathology." He is "directly comparable to the opiate-dependent person." There are no specific syndromes involved, practically all diagnostic categories being represented. Sedative, hypnotic, and tranquilizing drugs are incorporated for the purpose of mastering conflict and of maintaining the intrapsychic balance.

Short-acting barbiturates (Pentothal, Seconal, Amytal) are particularly addicting . . . . "they are as truly addicting as heroin or morphine and give the individual

and his physician an even greater problem." (U.S. Department Health, Education, & Welfare, nd). Like alcohol, they are intoxicating, produce confusion, uncoordination, and emotional instability. Sudden or complete withdrawal of barbiturates from an addicted person usually results in convulsions and sometimes in a temporary psychosis such as delirium tremens. Death may follow. Nonbarbiturate hypnotic addiction is also possible, the chief offenders being glutethimide (Doriden), ethinamate (Valmid), ethchlorvynol (Placidyl), and methyprylon (Noludar).

Withdrawal of barbiturates or other hypnotics often becomes a necessity. Treatment should be carried out in a hospital and will require barbiturate substitution, followed by its gradual withdrawal at a rate not to exceed 0.1 gm daily (Ewig, 1966). The daily intake is reduced over a 1- to 3-week period. Phenothiazines, Librium, or Valium may be given temporarily to control agitation, tremor, and insomnia. Supportive restoration of electrolyte balance, vitamins, and intravenous fluids may be in order. Proper nursing care is mandatory. Physical dependence on minor tranquilizers (Miltown, Librium, Valium) will be followed, if withdrawal is abrupt, by abstinence symptoms, convulsions, and even death. Continuing aftercare, as with narcotic addiction, will be necessary. Caution in prescribing sedative drugs with physical dependence-producing properties is essential in "dependence-prone" persons (Bakewell & Wikler, 1966).

Amphetamine addiction has been growing in this country with the continued use of this stimulant by students to prod them into greater alertness, by pleasure seekers in search of "kicks," and by those who habitually try to suppress their appetites to control overweight. Such addiction results in serious disorganization of the personality, even in precipitation of outright paranoid psychoses (Lemere, 1966). Other symptoms are impaired judgment, aggressive behavior, and uncoordination. Amphetamines are being implicated in increasing numbers of automobile accidents and crimes of violence (Med, Soc County of NY, 1966). Treatment of the individual who takes only

2 or 3 tablets a day requires quick withdrawal and administration of ammonium chloride to bring the pH to the acid side. While withdrawal is not as urgent in these cases as in persons who take large amounts, there is always danger that the intake may be increased. Withdrawal that is mandatory for persons who consume large quantities of amphetamines should be carried out in a hospital. The drug is removed abruptly, and the withdrawal effects are treated with intramuscular Thorazine and, if necessary, barbiturates at night, which are especially indicated where amphetamine-barbiturate mixtures, like Dexamyl, have been used (Connell, 1966). Aftercare is as important as with narcotic addiction, and psychotherapy may be an essential part of the rehabilitative program.

Marijuana has become a popular substance, especially among students on college campuses and young people in middle- and upper-income groups. Generally "joints," "dope," or "pot" are smoked experimentally on only one or two occasions. The hallucinogenic ingredient is in too low dosage to create any real difficulties. Harmful physical effects of prolonged marijuana usage have not been consistently demonstrated and probably are minimal compared with the ravages of alcohol intake. Emotionally disturbed persons will, however, continue to indulge in concentrated efforts to experience euphoria, employing the most potent substances like hashish, sometimes to a point where a temporary disturbance in behavior occurs. There is no evidence that the use of marijuana is associated with crimes in the United States (Med, Soc County of NY, 1966). There is no evidence also that the drug is a narcotic or that it is truly addicting. Yet in its usual form it is a mild hallucinogen and may, in some susceptible persons, produce aggressive and psychotic behavior. Moreover, the impaired judgment under drug influence interferes with skilled activities such as driving. Some people with severely disturbed personality problems may proceed from marijuana intake to the heroin habit, although the exact correlation between marijuana and subsequent heroin addiction has not been established. Pressure

to legalize marijuana understandably has brought forth heated debate and controversy.

Indulgence of other hallucinogens has been increasingly reported. In New York the use of dimethyltryptamine, psilocybin, bufotenine, peyote, mescaline, Indian hashish, charas, morning glory seeds, and nutmeg sometimes produces minor problems and glue sniffing among youngsters of school age has become disturbing (Jacobziner, 1963). The chief offender has been LSD, which is obtained from amateur chemists or from organized criminal groups. Usually 100 to 600 micrograms are ingested by individuals on a sugar cube for the purpose of "taking a trip," which is embarked on once or twice a week. Large doses (over 700 micrograms) are also ingested to produce more intense psychotic experiences. Psychotic episodes may persist for days or weeks and, in schizoid personalities, for months or even years, requiring hospitalization. Control of the drug supply is mandatory "until incontrovertible data are available documenting LSD's efficacy and safety" (Med Soc County of NY, 1966).

Cocaine produces many of the effects of amphetamines. While it produces no tolerance or physical dependence, its users commit crimes against property to obtain it.

Summary

In undertaking the treatment of drug addiction, the therapist should be aware of five essential factors: (1) The patient's motivation for therapy, however sincere, may be short-lived, giving way sooner or later to what seems to be self-destructive impulses. Extreme physical and psychological dependence are inescapable with habitual use of opiates, barbiturates, and alcohol. There is some physical dependence and considerable psychological dependence with the long-term use of amphetamines. Psychological dependence is present with cocaine, marijuana, tobacco, and hallucinogens, but there is little or no physical dependence. Great tolerance is soon established with opiates, amphetamines, and hallucinogens; somewhat lesser tolerance with the barbiturates, alcohol, and tobacco. (2)

An individual may derive gratifications from drug indulgence that enable him better than anything else he knows to overcome despair, dissatisfaction, and anxiety. (3) Drug abstinence achieved outside of an addict's habitual environment may not last long when the addict returns to customary surroundings. (4) Single addictions are rare; accordingly removal of one substance does not lessen the craving for others. Indeed, it may provoke the addict to try new experiments with other potentially exciting or calming materials. (5) Detoxification and "cure" of the desire for drugs has little effect on the underlying pathological personality problems, only one manifestation of which was the thrust toward drug intake. Other manifestations will display themselves that justify psychotherapeutic interventions. These may yield meager results and prolonged care in a therapeutic community (Synanon, Phoenix House) may be the only way to achieve a social adjustment.

SEXUAL DISORDERS AND DEVIATIONS

A complex aggregate of physiological, psychological, and environmental factors enter into the sexual reaction. The capacity or incapacity of responsiveness to sexual needs and the distorted or perverted forms of their expression are largely products of past conditionings. Interfering emotions may relate to defects in early training and education (e.g., prohibition of masturbation), to transferential projections (e.g., incestuous feelings toward parental figures), to carryovers of later childhood experiences (e.g., fearsome and humiliating seductions), and to adult unsatisfactory human relationships (e.g., a hostile or nonresponsive partner). Resulting anger and fear are anathema to proper sexual functioning. These affects are not always clearly perceived by the individual suffering from sexual difficulties. Indeed, their existence may be completely denied, and even if the early initiating circumstances are remembered, the emotions

See also the section on sexual therapy in Chapter 53.

relating to them may be shielded under a coat of nonfeelingness. This anesthesia influences sexual behavior, distorting the perception of sexual stimuli or altering the manifestations of the sexual drive. Joining this conspiracy are defects in the self-image prompted by disturbances in personality development and by prolonged exposure to humiliating happenings.

Most common phenomena influencing sexual behavior are premature ejaculation and impotence in the male, and nonorgasmic response, frigidity, dyspareunia, vaginismus, and even infertility in the female, (Practitioners Conference, 1957; Kleegman, 1959; Geijerstam, 1960; Hastings, DW, 1960; Mann, EC, 1960; Nichols, 1961). The degree of failure of response may range from total disinterest in sex and inability to derive any sensation from autoerotic stimulation, to breaking through periodically under special circumstances (e.g., singular dreams, fantasies, and fetishes), to orgasmic response to certain acts (e.g., rape, "bondage," humiliation, pain, or sadistic acting-out), to selective reaction to the embraces of a specific love object, to excited behavior with a variety of sexual objects, to constant preoccupation with sexuality (e.g., nymphomania and satyriasis). People are "turned on" by a host of stimuli that are unique to their personalities and early conditioning experiences. Objects and circumstances accompanying the first sexual arousal may be indelibly imprinted and may motivate actual or symbolic revival for sexual feeling thereafter. Later sexual expression may host consequences dependent on the significance of guilt-ridden experiences (e.g., relaxation and exhilaration or self-punitive mechanisms, like anxiety, migraine, and gastrointestinal symptoms). It is understandable that with the complex array of operative contingencies, a vast assortment of patterns will be displayed by different people and at different times prior to, during, and after the sexual act. The degree of orgasmic reaction will also vary individually, from mild release to violent, ecstatic excitement and even unconsciousness.

Unfortunately, there has been a tendency on the part of some professionals to project their own experiences into their opinions of what constitutes "normal" sexuality instead of dealing with it as a broad spectrum of behavioral repertoires that cannot rigidly be circumscribed in terms of "healthy" and "pathological." Thus, there are writers who insist that oral contacts are abnormal, that manual genital stimulation is immature, that orgasm derived in any other way than through penetration of the penis into the vagina is aberrant if not perverse. These injunctions reinforce any prevailing misconceptions that a patient may be harboring and add to one's misery.

Brief sex therapy (see pages 809–817) may be eminently successful in modifying or curing some of the milder sexual disturbances. In an inspired setting, away from everyday problems and pressures, a couple has the best opportunity for loosening up their inhibitions, relaxing their defenses, and under the prompting of new permissive authorities acquiring better habits of sexual response. Interpersonal hostilities are quietly subdued under these circumstances, and new and more constructive communicative patterns are set up. After therapy is terminated, the real test occurs. Can the improved functioning be sustained in the couple's habitual setting? There is always a possibility that reinstitution of customary pressures and responsibilities may restore tensions and break down the new communication patterns. It would, therefore, seem vital to continue to see the couple after the instruction period is over to help them resolve developing accumulating problems.

The key to successful sexual therapy is the therapist. One's personality, one's casualness, one's flexibility, one's empathy, one's understanding, one's sense of humor, one's capacity to communicate, all of these enter into influencing the techniques. In many couples the strong defenses and resistances to the directives of the therapeutic authority are apt to create frustration and anger in the therapist. The therapist has to know how to deal with this resistance in an easygoing way without taking offense. The therapist actually needs the skills of a good salesperson. It is not possible to adopt a passive analytic stance with this type of treatment.

The short period of therapy can provide a biopsy of the prevailing pathology between the two people. If the pathology is not too severe, if healthy defenses are present, if reasonable flexibility of adaptation prevails, new sexual habits may be maintained. On the other hand, where the sexual difficulty is a reflection of a personality problem, there may still be some improvement sexually, but the personality difficulties will have to be dealt with by more intensive methods.

For example, an impotent single man comes to therapy harboring deep hostile feelings toward women, stemming from a high level of dependency that one may historically trace to his being overprotected by a dominant mother figure—by no means an uncommon condition in problems of impotency. The immediate precipitating factor for the impotency in our present patient, let us imagine, was sexual association with a dominant, demanding woman who somehow undermined his confidence in himself. Let us also hypothesize that, through behavior therapy and in relationship with a cooperative and nondominant woman, the patient is restored to potency. Lacking recognition of his inner drives and needs, however, he may soon lose interest in what he would consider "uninteresting weak females" and seek out domineering women with whom he could act out his dependency and hostility. Without speculating too much, we would probably witness in a new relationship with a controlling woman a revival of his symptom. A thorough understanding of the problem, however, would enable him not only to desensitize himself to domineering women, but also to manage more assertively their specific domineering traits. By seeing that he was projecting attitudes toward his mother into his contemporary relationships, he might better be able to deal with "strong" women. The evolvement of firmer controls may enable him to relate to even manipulating women without fear. Or, realizing his choice of women as a weakness he must overcome, he may decide to restrict his sexual contacts to more passive types, while handling his impulse to goad them into domineering roles.

A complicating factor in many patients

is that the sexual function in the human being is often employed as a vehicle for the expression of varied strivings, interpersonal attitudes and needs. Thus, sexual behavior may embrace, among other things, impulses to hurt or to be hurt, to humiliate or to be humiliated, and to display or to mutilate oneself.

The common kinds of sexual perversion encountered by the therapist are sexual masochism, sexual sadism, exhibitionism, and voyeurism. These conditions are among the most difficult of all syndromes to treat. Because of the intense pleasure values inherent in the exercise of the perversions and the fact that they serve as avenues of discharge of deep needs other than sexual, the patient is usually reluctant to give them up. Although there may be a desire to correct certain disagreeable symptoms, like anxiety or tension, the motivation to abandon the specific kind of sexual expression may be lacking. Due to this lack of incentive, resistance often becomes so intense as to interfere with the therapeutic process.

There is, nevertheless, a growing conviction that sexual deviations are pathological conditions that are susceptible to psychotherapy. The specific approach to perversions will vary with the theoretical orientation of the therapist (Bieber, I, 1962; Bychowski, 1961; Deutsch, H, 1965; Fried, 1962; Lorand, 1956; Marmor, 1965b; Nunberg, 1955; Ovesey, 1954, 1955 a & b; Ovesey et al, 1963; Saul & Beck, 1961; Stark, 1963).

It has been mentioned that unfortunate conditionings in childhood make certain preliminary fantasies or acts mandatory for sexual feeling and performance in adult life. The origin of many of these conditionings are forgotten, repudiated, and repressed, although the individual is mercilessly bound to special stimuli (fetishistic, masochistic, sadistic, etc.) to release his sexuality. In many instances the sexual disturbance reflects improper identity. Where normal masculine identification is lacking (an overly possessive controlling mother, intimidation by an overwhelming father, passive indulgence by a weak father) tendencies toward effeminacy may develop. Lack of a feminine and motherly mother who can

act as a feminine model may divert a girl toward masculinity. Under these circumstances the sexual identification may be altered with eventuating homosexual trends.

Whether all forms of homosexuality should be classified as abnormal is a moot point about which there are differences in opinion among professionals. Under pressure of some groups, the Trustees of the American Psychiatric Association (amidst considerable controversy) officially ruled that the term "homosexuality" be replaced in the Statistical Manual of Mental Disorders by the phrase "sexual orientation disturbance," the latter being applied only to those homosexuals who were in conflict with their sexuality. In justification of this move, we do find many homosexuals who are happy and adjusted, and some studies reveal that symptoms and behavioral disorders among this group are no more frequent than among heterosexuals.

Under these circumstances, it is argued, homosexuality might for some individuals be regarded as a manifestation of a preferred normal life style rather than as a distortion of sexuality. On the other hand, there are those who continue to accent the point that analysis of even so-called well-adjusted homosexuals indicates without question that they have a developmental block in the evolution of the sexual drive. In appraising the pathological nature of homosexuality, we do have to consider the fact that many homosexuals suffer from the abuse and discrimination heaped on them by society, without which they would probably be able to make a better adjustment.

Homosexuals who apply for therapy are in a special category because they are ostensibly disturbed and upset. They seek help for their symptoms, and they may not be motivated to change their sexual orientation. A therapist's forceful attempts to induce change under these circumstances will usually fail. Where there are strong conflicts about homosexuality and desire for heterosexuality, dynamic psychotherapy or psychoanalysis may succeed in a considerable number of cases (Bieber, I, 1962). Adolescents disturbed about homosexuality may well benefit from some brief counseling along the lines suggested by Gadpaille

(1973), which may help resolve their identity problems.

Sometimes homosexual preoccupations in a conflicted individual become so uncontrollably compulsive as to cause the person to act out impulses in a destructive and dangerous manner. Masochistic and sadistic drives are usually operative here. The problem is that the person can easily jeopardize his safety by becoming involved with psychopathic individuals or by getting into trouble with the law. Such individuals may seek from psychotherapy not so much a stoppage of homosexual activity as directing their behavior into less dangerous channels.

Traditional psychotherapy, unfortunately, has had little to offer such applicants, neither insight nor appeals to common sense influencing the driving determination to involve themselves in exciting trouble. A form of therapy still in the experimental state is aversive behavioral treatment. Some behavior therapists recommend that if the patient is insistent on being forced to stop his behavior, and if he is sufficiently motivated, he may be willing to endure exposure to a series of slides that are sexually stimulating to him but are rewarded with a painful electric shock through electrodes attached to the fingertips (Feldman & MacCulloch, 1965). In a technique evolved by McConaghy (1972) the male patient selects 10 slides each of a nude adolescent and of young men and women to which he feels some sexual response. At each session three male slides are shown for 10 seconds, a 2-second shock being delivered during the last second of exposure, the level of shock being as unpleasant as the patient can stand. Following this a slide of a woman is turned on for 20 seconds without accompanying shock. Variable intervals between 3 to 5 minutes are left between showing the three sets of male and female slides. Sessions are given three or more times the first week, gradually reducing these in frequency over the following few months. In female patients the shocks would be delivered with the slides of women, and no shocks would be delivered with the male slides.

The treatment of sexual perversions, like sadism, masochism, voyeurism, exhibitionism, etc., must be organized around removing blocks to personality development in order to correct the immature strivings that are being expressed through the sexual perversion. Fears of adult genitality and of relating intimately and lovingly to persons of the opposite sex must be resolved before adequate sexual functioning is possible. The only rational approach is, therefore, reconstructive in nature. Unfortunately, lack of motivation may inhibit the patient from entering into reconstructive treatment. Additionally, ego weakness and disintegrative tendencies are often present in sexual perversions and act as further blocks to deep therapy. For these reasons the therapeutic objective may have to be confined to the mere control of the perversion and to its possible sublimation. The therapist here may have to function as a supportive, guiding authority who helps the patient to lead a more restrained life.

In treating perversions the therapist must be prepared for a long struggle. Resistances are, as has been mentioned, usually intense, and the patient will repeatedly relapse into the sexual deviation. The patient should not be blamed, reproved, or made to feel guilty for this. Rather, he must be helped to see the purposes served by his perversion and to appreciate why the need to express it becomes more overwhelming at some times than at others. While the ultimate outlook is not as favorable as in some other problems, there is no reason why patients who become motivated for, and who can tolerate reconstructive therapy, cannot achieve a good result.

SPEECH DISORDERS

Functional speech problems, which are sometimes arbitrarily called "stuttering" or "stammering," are the consequence of lack of coordination of various parts of speech wherein the speech rhythm becomes inhibited or interrupted. Associated are vasomotor disturbances, spasm, and incoordination of muscle groups involving other parts of the body. The speech difficulty is initiated and exaggerated by certain social situations, the individual being capable of articulating better under some circumstances than under others. This is confirmed by the fact that the person is usually able to sing and to talk without difficulty to himself and to animals. Some authorities insist that since there is no actual pathology of the speech apparatus, it may be a grave misnomer to label stuttering a speech disorder. Rather it might be conceived of as a manifestation of total adaptive dysfunction.

Martin F. Schwartz (1974) of Temple University has presented evidence that stuttering is produced by an inappropriate vigorous tightening of the larynx (contraction of the posterior cricoarytenoid) triggered off by subglottal air pressures required for speech. Psychological stress reduces the action of the usual supramedullary inhibiting controls of the involved muscle. To correct this, the patient must place the larynx in an open and relaxed position, which helps keep the air pressure in the voice box low. One-way mirrors and videotape equipment are used to couch the patient. The therapy is still in the experimental state but a "reasonable expectation of perhaps a 90 percent success rate with stutterers given the proper therapeutic implementation" may be expected within 2 or 3 months (Pellegrino, 1974). Should the therapy prove itself to be this successful, it will undoubtedly replace the traditional treatment methods.

The counseling of parents of a stuttering child is important in the total treatment plan. Generally, parents react with dismay, frustration, and guilt feelings in relation to their child, many assuming that they are responsible for the problem. At the onset of counseling the parents should be told that we are still unsure of what produces a stuttering child and that worry about complicity in it is not as important as doing something about it. However, there are things that they can do that may help the problem. Constant emphasis of mistakes and subjecting the child to drilling helps aggravate the nonfluency by making the child more self-conscious and aware of his failings. The stuttering child requires a great deal of demonstrated love and affection, and the parents must be enjoined to go out of their way to give these. It is essential also that they encourage the child to express feelings

openly no matter how badly the child enunciates these and that they control themselves if the child bumbles along in front of friends and relatives. This does not mean that proper discipline should not be imposed, even punitive measures when the child merits it, since discipline is an important learning tool for healthy growth. There is in some families a tendency to infantalize and to overprotect a stuttering child. This must be avoided, and the child should be expected to manage whatever responsibilities one of his age must assume. The role of the father is important in providing proper guidance and companionship. Since tension in the home contributes to the child's disturbance, it may be necessary to institute marital therapy or family therapy before appreciable improvement can be expected.

Therapy with a child therapist, particularly one experienced in speech difficulties, may have to be prescribed for the manifestly disturbed child or one who has been undermined by his speech problem.

The usual treatment of adult stuttering proceeds on two different levels: correction of the improper speech habit and the handling of the deeper emotional problem that originally initiated and now sustains the difficulty. A guidance approach is of help in achieving the first objective. The second goal is obtained through a persuasive, reeducative and, where possible, a reconstructive approach. Therapy involves correction of patent difficulties in the environment that stir up the person's insecurity, and a dealing with disturbing inner conflicts. Since the character disturbance in stutterers is usually extensive, therapy is bound to be difficult, prolonged, and, in many cases, unsuccessful insofar as alteration of the underlying personality disorder is concerned. The most that can be done for many stutterers is symptomatic relief in the form of speech correction.

Speech training may do as much harm as it does good. It is valuable only as a means of building up confidence in the individual's powers to articulate. Unfortunately, it may psychologically have the opposite effect since it overemphasizes will power and control and concentrates the stutterer's attention on the mechanics of his speech rather than upon what he says. Instead of becoming less conscious about his speech difficulty, he becomes more involved with it, thus intensifying his problem. This is not to say that proper exercises in diaphragmatic breathing, phonetics, and articulation are of no value in certain patients. Sometimes, with these methods, a symptomatic recovery may take place in mild cases. However, in severe cases, they are relatively ineffectual, and, especially where the person makes a voluntary effort to put his stuttering to a halt, the severity of his speech problem may increase. Rhythmics and eukinetics are sometimes helpful. Training methods, when utilized, should be employed by a therapist experienced in speech techniques.

In supportive approaches with stuttering adults certain evasions and defenses are sometimes taught the stutterer to tide him over situations where he must talk. Drawling, speaking in a rhythmic manner or in a sing-song tone, utilizing distracting sounds like "ah" or a sigh prior to articulation, employing a gesture or engaging in some motor act like pacing or rubbing a watch chain, purposeful pauses, and a variety of other tricks are used. These are entirely palliative and must be considered escapes rather than therapeutic devices.

A persuasive approach is sometimes helpful. The first step in therapy consists of convincing the patient that because of his experience and disappointments, he has come to overemphasize the speech function. To him it constitutes an insignia of aggrandizement and defamation. His self-esteem has become linked with how he performs in his speech. Because of this, he concentrates his attention on the way he talks more than on what he says. It is essential to remember that while his speech problem is important in his mind, it is probably not regarded with the same emphasis by others. He must understand also that he will overcome his stuttering more easily when he stops running away from acknowledging it. He must face the situation and even admit his speech problem to others. When he does this, he will be more at ease and his speech will improve.

A talk such as the following may be indicated:

Th. There is nothing disgraceful about stuttering. Avoiding social situations because of fear of ridicule merely serves to exaggerate the sense of defeat. It is necessary to regard stuttering in the same light as any other physical problem. If you stop being ashamed of it, and do not concern yourself with embarrassing others, people will notice your speech less and less. As you become more unconcerned about *how* you talk, you will concentrate on *what* you say. Keep concentrating on what you say, and pay no attention to how it sounds. Fear and embarrassment exaggerate your speech difficulty, so make yourself act calm and you will feel calm, and your speech will improve.

The next stage of therapy draws on some reeducative techniques and consists of demonstrating to the patient how he becomes upset and loses his sense of calmness in some situations. There will be no lack of material since the patient will bring to the therapist's attention many instances in which his stuttering becomes exaggerated. Examining his emotional reactions to these situations as well as his dreams will give the therapist clues as to the dynamic elements involved in the patient's speech disorder. These may be pointed out to the patient in terms that conform with his existing capacities for understanding. The aim is to show the patient that his speech difficulty appears when he loses his capacity to remain relaxed and when, for any reason whatsoever, emotional instability develops.

In some cases it will be advisable to refer the patient to a good speech therapist. The therapeutic approach that appears most successful comes from the work of Bryngelson, Van Riper, and Wendell Johnson. This aims at the elimination of anxieties about stuttering, which is considered a learned reaction to conscious fears of speech or fluency failure. The patient is enjoined to adopt an "objective attitude" by facing the fact squarely and, instead of avoiding displaying his stuttering, talking about his speech handicap to others, deliberately forcing himself to meet all fearful and difficult speaking situations, and articulating in the best way he can, utilizing, if necessary, the evasions, defenses, and tricks that are so often employed by stutter-ers. The patient is also exposed to various speaking challenges where he is urged to maintain an objective attitude in difficult speaking situations.

Specifically, the patient is taught to open up, in as casual and objective, and even humorous a way as possible, the topic of his speech problem with others, even if the listeners do not know that he has a speech problem. Clearing the atmosphere in this way will put both his listeners and him-self at ease. He is asked to observe how others falter and make mistakes in speaking and by this to realize that normal fluency is imperfect and quite variable. He is re-quested to observe how certain listeners react to what he says and to check his ob-servations with those of others present. In this way he will discover that he projects his own fears and prejudices onto other people. Most important, he is requested to give up running away from fearsome words that cause him to stutter, to utter them deliber-ately, particularly in situations in which he has stumbled over them, while remaining emotionally detached and not caring how the listener reacts. Role playing may be used here to prepare the patient for his stint outside. He is requested to discuss his ex-perience with the therapist at the next ses-sion. The patient is reminded to try to culti-vate a calm, unemotional tone of voice. He may practice this with a friend or with members of his family. One-half hour each day devoted to reading aloud from a book, jotting down those words that are difficult to pronounce, is helpful. He may then practice enunciating words several times during the day. Some persons find it helpful to talk for a short time daily in front of a mirror, watching their facial movements as they utter sounds. Along with these recondition-ing techniques environmental therapy may be used, geared toward an expansion of the assets of the individual and a remedying of liabilities in himself and his situation.

Where these techniques do not yield desired results, the patient may be taught ways of postponing word attempts, of start-ing difficult words or of releasing himself from blockages. He may also be taught a substitutive stuttering pattern, deliberately

prolonging or repeating himself in an unhur-ried, tenseless way. For instance, Van Riper's cancellation technique enjoins the stutterer to pause immediately after he ex-periences a stuttering block and to ask him-self what he did (pressed his lips together? pushed his tongue against the roof of his mouth? felt panic? diverted his gaze from the listener?). He is then to cancel his failure by "stuttering" on the same word deliber-ately in a new way with prolonged relaxa-tion, maintaining eye contact with the lis-tener. This starts a reconditioning process so that he may begin to change his behavior during the first attempt and then to manipu-late his preparatory sets prior to the attempt "to facilitate the production of a 'fluent' pattern of stuttering" (Bloodstein, 1966; Van Riper, 1971).

Three important adjuncts in speech therapy are behavior therapy, self-hypnosis, and group therapy. Certain behavioral ap-proaches may be quite valuable (Brady, 1968) particularly utilizing a metronome. In metronome-conditioned speech retraining (MCSR) a minaturized electronic met-ronome* is worn behind the ear like a met-ronome (Brady, 1971, 1972). This may be especially helpful when the patient is con-fronted with a speaking engagement, the metronome allowing him to pace his speech. Prior to the use of the ear met-ronome, the therapist may expose the pa-tient to an ordinary desk metronome, such as used in piano practice. At first as few as 40 beats per minute may have to be used, the patient pronouncing one syllable for each beat. As soon as the patient is fluent in pronouncing several syllables at this speed, the rate is gradually increased to 90 to 100 per minute. The patient is to procure a met-ronome for practice at home, at first alone; then when he feels confident, with a friend or parent in the room; then with more than one person present. He introduces pauses to some beats and then more than one word to each beat. He also practices while fan-tasizing progressively more anxiety-provoking scenes. When he reaches a satis-

* A metronome known as a "Pacemaker" is made by Associated Auditory Instruments, Inc., 6796 Market Street, Upper Darby, Pennsylvania 19082.

factory fluency, he practices with the minature metronome and then utilizes the fluency outside the home at first in low-stress situations and then after this in high-stress situations. Should difficulty be experienced under some conditions, he may reduce the speed of the metronome and speak more slowly. Gradually as he gains confidence, he may practice speaking without turning on the metronome, first in low then higher stress situations.

Another method is listening to a transistor radio, utilizing earphones while talking to a cassette tape recorder. The radio is played so loudly that one's voice is not heard. At first this is done after practicing relaxation. Then situations of increasing anxiety are imagined, the patient articulating his feelings and thoughts at the same time and particularly pronouncing his name and the words over with which he usually experiences difficulty. As he gains confidence in speaking, he may turn the radio off while speaking, turning it back on should nonfluency return.

Persuasive autosuggestions in a self-induced trance reinforce the patient's desires for self-confidence and assertiveness. Group therapy in which the patient comes into contact with other persons suffering from speech problems removes his sense of isolation. The fact that his companions experience the same trepidations as he does helps him to reevaluate his reaction. An opportunity is provided him to speak and to recite in a permissive setting. The identification with the group, along with the growing confidence in his ability to express himself, may have a most positive effect on his speech performance.

As the patient begins to experience improvement in his interpersonal relationships, his speech problem will plague him less and less. Utilizing the speech group as a bridge, he may be able to integrate himself with other groups and to consider himself on an equal plane with its constituent members. In some cases reconstructive therapy may be possible to deal correctively with the personality disorder (Barbara, 1954, 1957, 1958, 1963). This, however, is associated with many vicissitudes as Glauber (1952) has pointed out.

BORDERLINE CASES (LATENT SCHIZOPHRENIA, PSEUDONEUROTIC SCHIZOPHRENIA)

Patients who diagnostically hover between neuroses and psychoses are very commonly encountered in practice. These patients possess a personality disorder characterized by dependency, immaturity, detachment, tendencies toward autistic thinking, disintegrative ego proclivities, faulty reality testing, transient psychotic episodes, and shifts in defenses from neurotic to psychoticlike processes.

Sometimes borderline patients are classified as schizophrenics. Gunderson et al. (1975) have shown that there is little justification for this, borderline patients exhibiting an absence of distinguishing schizophrenic symptoms as well as a difference in the quality of thought disorder. Kernberg (1974) has described the personality organization of the borderline as one in which there is ego weakness with primitive mechanisms of defense, such as splitting, denial, omnipotence, devaluation, and early projective tendencies; a shift toward primary process thinking that may come through only in projective testing; and pathological internalized object relations. Kohut (1971) has expounded on the early traumatic disturbances in the relationship with the archaic idealized self-object and the damage to the maturing personality that continues because of this trauma. Fixation to aspects of archaic objects fashions the regression that occurs during analytic therapy.

Unlike the mature personality whose coping mechanisms are reality-oriented, the borderline patient retains and employs the archaic defenses which were evolved during infancy and childhood in relationship to parental agencies. Prominent among these, according to A. Wolberg (1952, 1959, 1960), are projection, displacement, withdrawal, autism, dissociative processes (splitting of the ego), denial, and other hysterical and obsessive-compulsive maneuvers. These sponsor a delusional system that is repressed, then utilized as a coping device whenever the patient is under extraordinary stress. The existence of this system may be exposed during narcosynthesis or with the administration of small quantities of the psychotomimetic drugs.

The specific conditionings to which children who become borderline patients are exposed will vary in their manifest forms. Usually the parents utilize the child as a transferential object, i.e., an object of displacement from their own parents. Thus parental associations with children are predicated on the acting-out by the parent of his personal fantasies. The standard relationship with the child is a sadomasochistic one. The impact on the patient is such that he has no alternative but to play a neurotic role with the parents that suits their purpose. He will accordingly organize fantasies of a sadomasochistic nature as defenses against the anxiety that he feels. Although these are repressed, they motivate acting-out tendencies. He develops deep distrust in his interpersonal relationships and detachment emerges as a defense against his ambivalent feelings. Exploitation and aggression are to him elements in all of his interactions with his parents, and he fears and withdraws from these at the same time that he is forced to participate. His later dispositions are patterned after his relationships with his parents. Some perverse neurotic and psychotic reactions are responses to contacts with parents who communicate their wishes and deny them at the same time. In early childhood one may detect perverse rituals concealed within the rearing techniques.

The parent regulates the child's behavior so that it fits the role that will most relieve the parent's pressing anxiety. In performing the neurotic role designed for him, the child has to give up certain developmental needs and to identify with the demands of the parents, acting "as if" this is what he wished. Thus healthy needs are inhibited through the means of defensive stratagems, being replaced by substitutive fantasies, characterologic distortions, and neurotic symptoms. Indeed, normal developmental needs are conceived of in fantasy as expressions of aggression against the parents or others who are substituted and displaced parental figures. In sexual development a confusion of sexual role may be expected. Male and female are intermixed since the mothers and fathers of these patients usually repudiate to a degree their sexual identities.

In the "use" of the child the parent expresses some of his perverse feelings. Latent homosexual trends may thus be set up in the patient. Because the parents feel guilty about their neurotic sexual needs and their aggressions, the child is taught to deny that he is engaging in the transactions arranged for him. This forces him to repress to a considerable degree knowledge of what is going on. Substituted for the existing sadomasochistic relationship with his parents are fantasies (which are defensive reactions) of sadomasochistic situations that involve not his parents but "others." This is a form of projection and displacement that must be taken into consideration during therapy. The neurotic roles that the child is trained to perform by the parents contain "permitted" aggressions of a type that the parents would have wanted to express toward their own parents, but that are now directed toward other persons than the parents, i.e., siblings or people outside the family. A certain amount of hostility, however, is permitted to appease the parents' guilt and their masochistic needs. The "unpermitted" aggressions are those that are directed against the parent as a result of the child's seeing through their facades and thus exposing their dangerous aims. Threatening to the parent and consequently also "unpermitted" are counteraggressions in the child as a consequence of his being "used" in the relationship. The child is made to feel guilt about his perceptions of reality and is thus forced to deny and to act "as if" he could not understand.

The reconstructive treatment of the borderline patient, according to A. Wolberg, must be slowly and carefully organized because of the ever present projective frame of reference and the danger of throwing the patient into anxiety that will force him to use his delusional system as a defense, thus pushing him over the border into an active psychosis. Freud's account of his management of the patient described in his paper "An Infantile Neurosis" contains tactics that may be used with borderline patients: "The patient . . . remained . . . unassailably entrenched behind an attitude of obliging apathy. He listened, understood, and remained unapproachable. His shrinking from an independent existence was so great as to outweigh all the vexations of his illness. Only one way was to be found of overcoming it. I was obliged to wait until his attachment to myself had become strong enough to counterbalance this shrinking, and then played off this one factor against the other" (*Collected Papers*, Vol. III, pp. 477–478). In view of the degree of sadomasochism in the borderline patient, the treatment process must take into account the severe anxiety to which such patients are constantly subjected, the peculiar composition of the ego, which tends to be organized around oppositional tendencies (sadism), stubborn negativism, the need of the patient to fail in certain situations, the passivity, the projective framework, the psychoticlike transference, and the characteristic failure of the various defensive structures. Special techniques are needed.

The first phase of treatment must involve what A. Wolberg (1960, 1973) has called "projective techniques." These are methods of coping with the sadomasochism of the patient, his acting-out tendencies, his denial and dissociative mechanisms, his autism (fantasy life), and his negativism so that the therapist does not become embroiled with him in a sadomasochistic relationship. Three projective techniques are recommended: (1) "the use of the other," (2) "attitude therapy," and (3) "ego construction," i.e., reinforcement of the patient's constructive ego trends.

In the "use of the other" the therapist takes advantage of the patient's tendency to deny his own feelings and ideas and to project them onto others. When he speaks of "others," therefore, he is actually talking about himself in a masked way to avoid anxiety. Should the therapist do what is ordinarily done with a neurotic patient, i.e., interpret the projection and confront the patient with his defense, the borderline patient will be unable to organize himself and to utilize the interpretation constructively. Instead he will become more resistive and deny the validity of the interpretation, incorporating the interpretation into his sadomasochistic operations by beating himself with it and advancing it as another reason why he should hate himself or, on the other hand, by becoming paranoid against the therapist and using the interpretations as a rationalization for his distrust. The relationship with the therapist is bound to disintegrate under these circumstances; a transference neurosis may precipitate out abruptly; psychotic manifestations may emerge. For these reasons the therapist must preserve the projective defenses of the patient and always (at least during the early stages of treatment) talk about the motives and maneuvers of the "others," allowing the patient himself to make personal connections or to deny them as he wishes. Such a method will help cement a positive relationship with the patient. Dreams are handled in the same way, never pointing an accusing finger at the patient. Fantasies that have motivated the acting-out are analyzed in a manner similar to dreams: the therapist does not challenge or confront the patient. One merely explores. One does not justify or reassure the patient, even though one acts empathic with him.

The "others" in the interpersonal encounters are analyzed by conjecturing as to why they feel and act as they do and what their motives could possibly be. The therapist does not charge the patient with the fact that he is like the "others." Eventually when the working relationship consolidates, the patient will acknowledge this himself. When the first statements are made by the patient that "this is like me," the therapist simply agrees and does not pursue it further. Each time that the patient says "this is like me," the therapist agrees that it *might* be true. Should the patient repeatedly bring up the consociation with himself, the therapist may suggest that this is a pattern worth exploring. The therapist may query, "How does the pattern operate? It is not too obvious in the sessions. This could be worth exploring."

"Attitude therapy" is a projective device utilized to point up the patient's patterns of operation within any given interpersonal relationship. Inevitably he will bring up details of a personal encounter that are highly prejudiced and contain a paranoidal flavor. Accurate accounts will be resisted since this will reveal his acting-out proclivities which mobilize his guilt. The therapist must not be put off by the patient's maneuvers; the therapist keeps asking for details, but not to the point where the patient becomes overly defensive. In such a case the therapist discontinues questioning, indicating that it is causing too much anxiety in the patient. However, when other incidents are reported, questioning is begun again.

Eventually the patient's true attitudes and feelings, which contain fragments of the fantasies motivating the acting-out, will be revealed. The therapist may then say, "Incidents like this can be very upsetting." As the patient brings up accounts of further encounters, definite patterns will emerge. Eventually the therapist will be able to help the patient consolidate his thoughts, attitudes, feelings, and behavior in these situations. The interpretations are in the form of broad statements that in a roundabout way, through focusing, indicate a connection between thoughts, feelings, fantasies, anxieties, and patterns of acting-out behavior. Questions are posed in such a manner that the patient himself makes the associations. If the therapist offers the patient an interpretation before he is ready for it, i.e., before he himself has mentioned the possibility several times, then the therapist may become involved in the patient's obsessive mechanisms. He will weave the therapist into the warp and woof of his fantasy life and chew on the information instead of using it to work out his problem.

In the technique of "positive ego construction" the therapist is the projective object, taking positive trends in the patient's ego and reflecting them back to the patient as if they were the therapist's own. This is because the patient cannot accept good things about himself or utilize his own constructive thinking without excessive anxiety. The patient is guilty about his positive trends since he has been taught by his parents to despise them; he has been encouraged to fail in certain ways in order to play the roles consigned to him. Success constitutes a greater threat than failure in specific areas. To reduce his guilt but not to analyze

it is one of the purposes of this technique. For instance, if the patient brings in the tale of his having applied for a job and having bungled the interview by purposefully saying that he could not qualify because of lack of skills, and, if he then reflects back on what happened with the remark, "I should have told him that I know enough about this work to be able to learn the special details rapidly, which is the truth," the therapist may respond in a qualified positive way: "It is definitely *my* opinion that you know enough about this work to be able to learn the special details rapidly." Thus the phrases the patient has uttered are repeated as the therapist's own ideas. The phrases may also be reorganized and the same thing said in different words. For example, the patient states: "Probably I feel I don't deserve the job." The therapist does not reply to this with the conventional, "Why not?" Instead the comment may be, "I've thought of this too. Many people I've worked with feel guilt when a good opportunity presents itself. They shouldn't have to feel this way, but they do."

Role playing may also be employed to rehearse with the therapist what the patient *might* have said, the patient and therapist interchanging roles of patient and employer. After a certain number of incidents have been "role played," the patient may wonder why he acts the way he does. The therapist then replies, "This is an important thing for us to figure out." The therapist does not give the patient the answers when he asks, "Why?" Rather the therapist indicates that the two must seek answers together; this is a cooperative effort between two people who have come to an agreement on certain points.

After the patient is able to accept responsibility for his own actions without developing intense anxiety or manifesting his usual defenses, the treatment may take on a form similar to that of working with a neurotic patient. Should the patient become excessively anxious, projective techniques, as outlined above, should be used. As a rule, some drug therapy will be necessary at certain phases of treatment—Stelazine or Trilafon for anxiety and Tofranil or Elavil for depression—and then stopped when the target symptoms come under control. Where ego shattering is threatened and drug therapy appears unable to restore the equilibrium, a few electroconvulsive treatments may prove effective. In exceptional circumstances "maintenance" ECT may be required.

Therapy is best conducted on a once- or twice-a-week basis. The modifications in method that are necessary include several points:

1. Establishing a warm supportive relationship is of paramount importance, the therapist doing the giving, being careful not to offend the patient.
2. Time restrictions in the session must be elastic.
3. A long testing period is to be expected. It may often be very difficult for the patient to make a relationship with the therapist.
4. Environmental manipulation may be necessary.
5. Working with the patient's family to reduce pressure on the patient is frequently indicated.
6. The interview focus is on reality, the patient's relapse into daydreaming or delusion being interpreted as a reaction to fear or guilt.
7. Avoiding the probing of psychoticlike material is advisable.
8. Active reassurance and advice giving may be necessary.
9. Directive encouragement is given to the patient to participate in occupational therapy, hobbies, and recreations.
10. Neurotic defenses are supported and strengthened.
11. Challenging or disagreeing with the patient's distorted ideas is delayed until a good relationship exists.
12. Therapy may last a long time, perhaps the rest of the patient's life.

The importance of keeping the relationship with the therapist a nondistorted, productive one with a minimum of acting out has been stressed by H. J. Friedman (1975). Utilization of the positive transference to support the therapeutic relationship is also emphasized by Kernberg (1968), along with exposure of defenses and of manifest and latent transference manifestations with (1) elaboration of how they influence the patient's relations with others, (2) confrontation and interpretation of defenses that sponsor the negative transference, (3) the setting of limits in the therapeutic situation, and (4) the employment of modalities like hospitals, foster homes, etc. when needed. Combined individual and group psychotherapy for the borderline patient has special advantages and a specific function. It is at present used widely for extramural cases in private offices and clinics. It is also employed intramurally in institutions where insight into the necessity for treatment and an ability to relate in a therapeutic situation remain at least partially intact.

While the one-to-one relationship of individual therapy satisfies dependency needs, the borderline patient also feels threatened by it. Many of these patients profit in a group therapeutic setting where they feel less dependent and the therapist appears less powerful. In the security of the group the members relate to each other and to the "democratic" authority figure of the therapist with more freedom and less anxiety than in any other situation. The group atmosphere facilitates expression of one's feelings. It makes interaction and with it socialization desirable and rewarding. The all-or-none conflict that leads to emotional inhibition and withdrawal out of fear of one's own destructive impulses is worked through under the protective leadership of the therapist and by testing the reality of anticipated dire consequences following expression of one's emotions. In the social situation of the therapy group, with its graded anxiety-releasing potential and the opportunity for reality testing, the borderline patient may find his first constructive experience in human relationships and may grasp a glimpse of understanding into the positive sides of socialization.

Excellent accounts of the therapy of borderline cases may be found in the writings of Federn (1947), V. W. Eisenstein (1951), Bychowski (1950), Kernberg (1968), A. Wolberg (1973), H. J. Friedman (1975), and Masterson (1976).

Some of the techniques for the treatment of schizophrenia described in the following section of this chapter may also be valuable in treating the borderline patient.

PSYCHOTIC DISORDERS

In most cases the immediate aim in the treatment of a psychosis is to bring the ego back to a realistic level of integration, even though one has to restore habitual character traits and neurotic symptoms that had previously maintained the person in a functional equilibrium. For instance, the individual, responding to a feeling of inner paralysis and helplessness, may have mastered his anxiety on the basis of a strong dependency drive. However, the death of the person on whom he has depended may suddenly confront him with feelings of isolation and despair so profound that his integrative capacities shatter, with a resulting psychosis. In therapy an attempt may be made to restore the balance by providing the patient with a compensatory dependency relationship. Active guidance, manipulation of the environment, drug administration, and other supportive therapies may be useful in achieving this goal. Where the hold on reality is minimal, hospitalization, heavy tranquilization or sedation, and electroconvulsive therapy may be required to bring the ego back to a more realistic stature. A most important element in the treatment program is establishing a relationship with the patient of a nature that will allow for the institution of reeducative and reconstructive measures should the patient require and be able to utilize them.

Involutional Psychotic Reactions

Stresses of a physiological and psychological nature during the period of middle age may produce emotional decompensation with the emergence of disturbed patterns that, up to this time, have been repressed. Features characteristic of manic-depressive psychosis (usually an agitated depressive type) and schizophrenia (generally of a paranoidal quality) are most common, manifesting themselves in the matrix of the individual's unique personality structure.

Mild cases of involutional psychosis are managed by the institution of drug therapy (see Pharmacotherapy, p. 770) directed at target symptoms. Thus, inhibited depressions will require Tofranil; agitated depressions may do well with Elavil (perhaps combined with Trilafon); while aggressive and disturbed paranoid reactions frequently respond to Thorazine or Haldol. Both good and poor results have been reported following the use of estrogenic hormones in females and testosterone in males. As a general rule, endocrine therapy is indicated where there are such evidences of endocrine insufficiency as vasomotor instability, flushes, sweats, headaches, and tension. In certain cases an estrogenic deficiency, as determined by accurate tests, seems to be coincident with the psychosis. Here, substitution therapy produces dramatic results. In other cases tests may show an estrogenic deficiency in which injection of estrogen has little effect. In most patients, however, the psychosis is a product of more complicated factors than endocrine substances.

Milder cases of involutional psychosis may be cared for at home or, better still, in a nursing home under the constant supervision of a nurse or attendant. At all times it is essential to keep in mind the great risk of suicide and to make plans to forestall any suicidal attempt. In some cases treatment is best started by complete bed rest for a few weeks. Attention must be paid to the patient's diet and insomnia. Many patients refuse to eat, and tonics prove of little avail. Forced feedings may have to be utilized to avoid emaciation. Insulin and barbiturates in small doses are often helpful.

In disturbed, agitated, acutely paranoid, and suicidally inclined patients hospitalization is mandatory. Some type of sedative therapy is advisable, at least at first, and in occasional cases prolonged narcosis therapy appears to have a real value. Occupational therapy may be of some help in diverting the interest of the patient from himself. Twenty units of insulin before meals stimulate the appetite.

By far the most effective therapy in involutional melancholia is convulsive treatment. Electroconvulsive therapy (the average ECTs required will be from 12 to 20) is commonly used (see Electroconvulsive Therapy in Chapter 53). The results of convulsive therapy are often dramatic, and experience has shown that physical contraindications to treatment need not be too stringent.

Involutional psychotics are largely inaccessible to psychotherapy. All psychic probing in an analytic sense is to be avoided, and efforts must be directed at increasing repression rather than stimulating and interpreting the material that emerges from the unconscious. Persuasion and reassurance sometimes have the effect of tiding a patient over a crisis. Many patients confide that they have been immeasurably cheered by the physician who reassured them during their acute disorder, even though they were unable at the time to acknowledge the beneficial effect.

In mild cases of involutional melancholia hypnosis may have a calming influence. The trance state is used to induce relaxation and to reinforce reassuring and persuasive suggestions. These aim at helping the individual adjust to his life situation and to limited capacities fostered by advancing years. Psychotherapeutic talks may also be conducted on a waking level. If possible the patient should be diverted from concentrating on his various symptoms, and his attention should be directed to his daily activities, hobbies and recreations.

Psychotherapy along persuasive lines should continue after the acute symptoms have subsided. The interviews are organized around the immediate concerns of the patient, such as discussions of how advancing years bring with them convictions that one's views are considered old-fashioned and intolerable, along with feelings that one may be unable to gain praiseworthy recognition. Various blows to self-esteem, sustained at this time of life, should be clarified and neutralized if possible. Some persons, it may be pointed out, attempt to compensate by becoming markedly egotistic or bigoted in their opinions or by clinging to their convictions stubbornly against logic, hoping thereby to regain their self-respect. Others react by depression, hopelessness, inferiority feelings, hostility, and rage directed at the world at large. One must always recognize the limitations inherent in the process of aging. One should also realize that many creative capacities are unimpaired and that some are actually increased.

It is important for the patient to appreciate and to accept the fact that, as a person grows older, one must modify one's physical and working activities. If the patient is so constituted that he considers an inability to compete physically with younger and stronger persons a blow to his self-esteem, he is bound to respond disastrously. He may become sullen, irritable, and defiant, or else he may evolve expansive notions regarding his own capacities, projecting his inability to function perfectly on the basis that he is misunderstood by others. He will then become more and more unable to withstand frustration, and he will be victimized by his own emotions of rage. He may even withdraw from social contacts and encrust himself in a bitter vituperative shell, isolating himself from relations with other people.

If indicated, discussion may be in order of how some persons attempt to adjust to the problem of their advancing years by a vicarious display of aggressiveness and energy, resenting any curtailment of activities. There is in this a frenzied attempt to regain lost youth by proving to the world that one is still physically virile. Yet it is most essential that the patient be able to tolerate certain frailties within himself. Should one refuse to recognize self-limitations, he may continue to operate under exorbitant expectations that inevitably lead to failure and frustration. It is necessary to appraise oneself honestly in relation to realistic and unrealistic goals. It may be difficult at first to admit weaknesses in oneself; but the gradual understanding that later years bring mellowness and measures of contentment that cannot be approached in the impetuosities of the early decades, can lead to self-tolerance and acceptance. It is essential to remember that in self-acceptance there need be no element of ''giving-up,'' that reasonable physical activity is still essential to health, and that mental and sexual activity can continue in good force. It is urgent also to increase one's social contacts and interests so as not to be upset with the spectre of "aloneness."

Manic-Depressive Reactions

While expansive moods bordering on mania, and depressive symptomatology related to melancholia may occur in various emotional disorders, they are most pronounced in the syndrome of manic-depressive psychosis (Bellak, 1951). Appearing in both cyclic and sporadic form, manic-depressive psychosis manifests itself most commonly during the middle years of life. It is of unknown etiology, although genetic factors have been implicated (Kallmann, 1953). Some authorities credit the mood swings to specific neurohormonal disturbances, perhaps associated with defective indolamine and catecholamine metabolism. Psychogenic factors have also been posited as basic (Freud, 1955; Abraham, K, 1953; Bibring, 1953; Klein, M, 1957a) but, as with the so-called organic determinants, there is no real evidence that they are the true causative forces. Confusion regarding diagnosis stems from imperceptible shadings of manic-depressive psychosis with neurotic depressions and excitements on the one hand, and with schizophrenia on the other. A fusion of syndromes may occur in what Cobb (1943) has called schizoaffective states.

MANIC REACTIONS

The immediate objective in manic reactions is to quiet the patient. This is best achieved with chlorpromazine (Thorazine), which must be administered in ample dosage (up to 1600 mg daily or more). In wild excitements intramuscular injections (25–50 mg repeated in an hour if necessary) are indicated, followed by oral administration. (See also Chapter 55 on Emergencies). Dangerous overactivity may call for electroconvulsive therapy. This may be given twice daily for 3 or 4 days, followed by a treatment every other day. Following this, Thorazine may be substituted. Lithium carbonate (see Chapter 53 on Somatic Therapy) has been employed with considerable suc-cess for recurrent manic states (White et al, 1966). It is essential to keep the serum lithium concentration (this is measured by a flame photometer) below levels of 1.2 or at the most 1.5 mEq/1 and to reduce the dose. as symptoms quiet down.

Psychotherapy is usually ineffective in most manic conditions. The patient's attention is too easily diverted; acting-out is too unrestrained; emotions are too explosive. Because of this, hypomanic and manic patients are extremely difficult to manage in the office. They will seek to involve the therapist in all of their fantastic plans. They will make demands of him which, when unfulfilled, will release great hostility or aggression. They will try to overwhelm and dominate those around them, and they may become uncontrollable when their wishes are not gratified.

One of the chief reasons for hospitalizing the manic patient is to prevent him from involving himself and other people in projects which issue out of his overconfidence. Because he is inclined to be erotic, he must be protected from sexual indiscretions and from a hasty marriage that he may contract on the crest of an ecstatic wave. Another reason for early hospitalization is that some manic cases will go into a state of delirium when they are not treated intensively at the start. These delirious attacks may be fatal due to exhaustion, dehydration and hypochloremia. Sedation, tranquilization, and electroconvulsive therapy are most easily administered in a hospital setup.

DEPRESSIVE REACTIONS

Depression is often ushered in by feelings of loss of self-confidence, absent initiative, and fatiguability. The depressive mood itself may not be apparent; it is often covered by an overlay of hollow humor in what has been called the "smiling depressions." As the depression deepens, loss of appetite, insomnia, diminution of the sexual drive, and a general anhedonia (lack of gratification in the pursuit of pleasure strivings) follow. There are difficulties in attention and concentration and variations in mood, the intense depression during the morning lifting as the evening approaches. Interference with work and interpersonal relationships follow. Extreme suffering and regression to early dependency with masochistic behavior then develops in the course of which suicidal thoughts, impulses, and acts may erupt.

Principal goals in therapy consist of the following:

1. Removal of symptoms and a relief of suffering.
2. Revival of the level of adaptive functioning that the patient possessed prior to the outbreak of the illness.
3. Promotion, if possible, of an understanding of the most obvious patterns that sabotage functioning and interfere with a more complete enjoyment of life.
4. In motivated patients, recognition of conflictual patterns and exploration of their meaning, origins and consequences.
5. Provision of some way of dealing with such patterns and their effects in line with a more productive integration.

Unfortunately, depressions are singularly resistive to treatment in that the mood change imposes a barrier to three of the most important elements in therapy: faith, hope, and trust. Lost is the expectancy of getting well that so often powers the machinery of cure. Gone is the feeling that someone cares, so essential in establishing a therapeutic relationship. Yet beneath his isolation and hopelessness the depressed individual seeks a restoration of his ties with humanity. He resists relationships, and then credits his isolation to the fact that he is unloved.

Among the therapeutic measures that are most effective are the following:

1. Establish as rapidly as possible a relationship with the patient. This is precarious as has been mentioned before. Yet winning the patient over in spite of inertia, gloom, sluggishness, despair, hostility, and self-recriminations is urgent. Depressed patients are insatiable in their demands for help and love. No matter how painstaking are the therapist's attempts to supply their demands, they will respond with rage and aggression, often accusing the therapist of

incompetence or ill will. The patients should, nevertheless, be approached with the attitude that the therapist understands and sympathizes with their suffering. Such measures as active guidance and externalization of interests may be attempted. As in schizophrenic patients, the basis of treatment is a warm relationship between the patient and the therapist. The relationship that the patient establishes with the therapist will, however, be extremely vulnerable. Much lenity and tolerance are needed, and an attempt must be made to show that the therapist realizes the depth of the patient's fears and misgivings. This, however, is more easily said than done, since the depressed patient has a distrustful nature.

Distrust springs from the fusion of hate with love. Hostile feelings generate guilt that may be so disabling that the person will want to discontinue treatment. The slightest frustration during therapy, such as the unavoidable changing or canceling of an appointment, may be equivalent to rejection and will mobilize a tremendous amount of anxiety. Under the surface there is always fear of abandonment, and there is a tendency to misinterpret casual actions. The patient seeks reassurance but resents its being called psychotherapy.

The aim in treatment is to develop and to reinforce all positive elements in the relationship. This will involve much work, since the attitudes of the patient are so ambivalent that he will feel rejected no matter what the therapist does. It is best to let the positive relationship take root in any way it can without attempting to analyze its sources.

One of the means of maintaining the relationship on a positive level is by communicating empathy and by avoiding differences in opinion. It is essential to convey to the patient nonverbally the idea that he is liked and that the therapist is his friend in spite of anything that happens. An attitude of belittling, harshness, ridicule, or irritation must be avoided. The therapist must maintain an optimistic outlook and express the sentiment that although the patient may not believe it now, he *will* get over his depression in a while.

Hypnosis may be of help in some of the milder depressions. The trance state is used primarily as an avenue toward inducing relaxation and toward giving persuasive suggestions to stabilize the person. A number of depressed patients appear to thrive under hypnotic therapy, probably because it appeals to their dependency need.

2. Utilize drug therapy when necessary. In mild depressions Dexedrine, and Dexamyl may be of help in elevating the mood and supplying energy. Librium also has an effect on mild depressions that are associated with anxiety. More severe inhibited depressions may be approached with Tofranil (100–200 mg daily), while agitated depressions appear to respond better to Elavil (100–250 mg daily) combined, if anxiety is present, with Librium (30–40 mg). The effects of the latter drugs may not be felt for several weeks. The MAO inhibitors (Nardil, Parnate) are also of some value in certain depressions. Mellaril has been employed in depressions of the schizoaffective type. Where a schizoid element is present, a phenothiazine drug (Trilafon, Stelazine) may be combined with Tofranil and Elavil. Some doubts as to the real value of antidepressant drugs above the placebo effect has been expressed (Greenblatt et al, 1964; Medical News, 1964), although N. S. Kline (1964) insists that drugs can lessen regression and relieve depression dramatically in most patients. Experience with antidepressant medications confirms this opinion.

Where drugs are employed, the side effects should be explained to the patient to encourage the continuation of the medications in spite of them. The need for sleep may be reduced without harmful effect, and the patient may, if not forewarned, take excessive hypnotics. Constipation and weight gain may occur and require remedial measures. Mouth dryness may be counteracted partly by chewing gum or glycerin-based cough drops. Postural hypotension of a severe nature may be handled by advising the patient not to arise suddenly, to avoid standing unmoving in one place, and, if a woman, to wear elastic stockings and a girdle. Neuralgias or jactitation of the muscles may require 50 mg vitamin B_6 and 100 micrograms of vitamin B_{12} twice daily. Ener-

gizer drugs potentiate barbiturates and alcohol; so these substances should be taken in lower dosage. Coffee intake should also be reduced. The troublesome insomnia in depression is best handled by small doses of barbiturate or nonbarbiturate hypnotics, particularly chloral hydrate. The patient may be given a mimeographed form about drug side effects (see Appendix T). More data on drug therapy will be found in the section on Pharmacotherapy in Chapter 53.

3. Administer electroconvulsive treatments immediately in severe depressions, or where there is any danger of suicide. Electroconvulsive treatments are superior to any of the present-day drugs. (See section on Electroconvulsive Therapy in Chapter 53.) The effect is rapid, 8 ECTs generally eliminating the depression; however, more treatments may be required. In agitated depression, 2 ECTs daily for 2 or 3 days may be followed by 1 ECT daily, and then by treatments twice or three times weekly. Following ECT, energizing drug therapy may be instituted (Tofranil, Elavil) and, if agitation continues, Thorazine or Trilafon can be prescribed. Indokolon may be substituted for ECT, particularly where the patient is not responding to ECT. Unilateral ECT may be employed where even temporary memory loss cannot be countenanced.

4. Hospitalize severe depressions. Mild depressions may be treated at home, preferably under supervision of a psychiatrically trained attendant or nurse, or, better still, the patient should be admitted to a rest home. Isolation from parents and friends, bed rest, and constant care by a motherly attendant may prove very beneficial. Because of anorexia, efforts should be made to bolster the diet with high caloric and high vitamin intake in the form of small but frequent feedings. In severe cases of malnutrition a few units of insulin before meals may be helpful. Where the depression is more than mild, hospitalization is advisable. Suicidal attempts in depression are made in almost one-third of the cases, and deaths resulting from these attempts occur with great frequency. The patient's complete loss of interest in himself makes mandatory the establishment of definite daily routines, such as a hospital can best supply. Electroconvulsive therapy, the treatment of choice, can best be instituted in a hospital setting, and, if the patient requires tube feeding, nursing care is available.

5. Institute psychotherapy as soon as feasible. Psychotherapy is usually ineffective during extremely depressed phases. The only thing that can be done is to keep up the patient's morale. He should not be forced to engage in activities that he resists because this may merely convince him of his helplessness and of his inability to do anything constructive. Where there is little suicidal risk, he should be encouraged to continue his work, if he feels at all capable of managing it, since inactivity merely directs his thinking on his own misery. In many cases contact should be maintained with the patient's family and environment. This is necessary since the family of the patient often chides him for "not snapping out of it" and constantly reminds him that he must make up his mind to get well. The family members may be told that recovery is more than a matter of will power, and they must be urged to avoid a nagging and critical attitude.

The material elicited during the periods of active psychosis, both as to mental content and as to the character of the relationship with the therapist, may yield important clues to the inner conflicts of the patient. Notes may be made for later reference, but all interpretations during the active period must be suspended. Only during a remission can interpretive work be helpful. Many patients spontaneously express a desire to know more about their illness. Here, a modified insight approach may be used. The majority of patients, however, show an unwillingness to go into their difficulties and resist insight therapy. Having recovered, they are convinced they are well, and they desire no further contact with the therapist. Without the "wish" to get well, little can be accomplished in the way of reconstructive psychotherapy. Cognitive therapy *(q.v.)* in the hands of a skilled therapist may prove to be extremely effective.

Once the patient has emerged from his depression, either spontaneously, as a result of convulsive therapy, or through psychotherapy, an attempt may be made to work with character strivings, analyzing the relationship to the therapist actively in an effort to help the patient become more assertive and self-sufficient. It is doubtful that psychotherapy can prevent the onset of a true endogenous manic-depressive reaction. However, it should enable the patient to make a better adjustment between attacks.

Guidelines to psychotherapy in depression are the following:

1. *Permit the patient to express guilt feelings and to verbalize hostilities freely* without challenge. Inviting or provoking motor release of aggression, without the expected recriminations, is valuable in depression.
2. *Avoid analytic probing.* Deal, during the period of depression, with topical manifest material, only tentatively giving interpretations other than reassuring ones.
3. *Employ environmental manipulation wherever the environment imposes burdens on the patient.*
4. *Utilize group therapy where problems in relationship and isolation exist.*
5. *Gradually evolve with the patient a hypothesis about the nature of the presenting problem.* Relate this to underlying conflicts, and, if possible, to early developmental experiences in order to help strengthen the patient's modes of coping with the immediate situation and to provide the patient with a different way of looking at future traumatic happenings.
6. *Help the patient evolve a philosophy of life that enables him to relate himself productively to others and to fulfill himself creatively within the limitations of his capacities and environmental opportunities, without perfectionistic and unrealistic expectations of himself.*

An excellent discussion on therapies helpful in severely depressed suicidal patients may be found in the paper by Lesse (1975).

Schizophrenic Reactions

Schizophrenia, in spite of the massive amount of accumulated data, remains psychiatry's greatest challenge (Bleuler, 1950; Hill, LB, 1955; Arieti, 1959, 1974; Redlich & Freedman, 1966). The very question as to whether it is a special disease entity or a unique way of experiencing has not yet been answered. As one of our most common ailments, it can corrupt all functions—physiological, intrapsychic, interpersonal, and spiritual. Efforts to understand it along neurophysiological, biochemical, genetic, psychosocial, epidemiological, psychoanalytic, existential, anthropological, cultural, and communicative lines have been heroic. But whether the illness is biologically, psychologically, or sociologically determined is still unclear. Neither biochemical nor analytic-psychological investigations have brought us closer to its real essence.

A common theory is that a constitutional, perhaps genetic defect underlies the disorder, disorganizing the biochemical-neurophysiological mechanisms that deal with stress. An abnormal dopaminergic system may be implicated. The psychosocial experiences that make for inadequate defensive systems are superimposed on this faulty substrate and render the individual incapable of mediating certain kinds of stressful pressures. Tension and anxiety beyond a point are potentially disintegrating to the unified thinking, feeling, and behaving functions of the schizophrenic, his defective physiological and psychological machinery indisposing him to dealing with these emotions. The consequences of this are alterations in identity, distortions in communication, diffuseness in ego boundaries, regression, autism, dereism, and disintegration in thinking and feeling. Various levels of defense may be activated to restore homeostatis, with manipulations of the environment, of interpersonal relations, of the intrapsychic structure, and even of the soma and viscera. The resulting coping devices lend to the symptom picture an individual uniqueness; yet the basic schizophrenic constellation is distinguishable within the screen of cultural and personal defensive camouflages. The prognosis depends on the basic adequacy of the prepsychotic personality structure and the degree of its ability to regulate stress.

The treatment of schizophrenia may be schematized in the following way:

1. Restoration of the individual to an adaptive level of integration by (a) removing or reducing the stress source, (b) neutralizing by-products of stress and modulating subcortical neural circuits through drugs, insulin coma or electric convulsive therapy.
2. Strengthening the individual's personality resources so that he can handle more severe environmental pressures.
3. Helping him to develop different attitudes toward inescapable responsibilities so that they may lose their stressful meaning.

The specific treatment will depend upon the stage of the disease, the depth of regression, the grasp on reality that remains, the desire of the patient for therapy, and his ability to establish a relationship with the therapist.

REMOVING THE STRESS SOURCE; HOSPITALIZATION

Where the patient's psychosis has been precipitated by an overwhelming external traumatic situation, simple environmental manipulation may suffice to bring the patient back to his prepsychotic level of adaptation. For example, a man inducted into the armed forces may develop an acute schizophrenic reaction as a result of an inability to adjust himself to the demands and disciplines of army life. The personality resources of the individual, while adequate for satisfactory functioning in civilian life, are not now sufficient to cope with the added burdens imposed on them. In such a case the discharge of the man from the army, and his return to his previous civilian capacity, may achieve a complete cure of the psychosis.

Most schizophrenic reactions, however, are associated with such great weakness of the ego that the person is unable to withstand even average stresses. Ordinary responsibilities of living and relating to people cannot be mediated. Environmental manipulation does not suffice to restore the patient to reality here because he senses menace everywhere, even in the most obviously congenial atmosphere.

Fears rooted in past inimical conditionings and damaging conflicts generate anxiety continuously and prevent the ego from emerging from its regressed level. The patient erects a wall of detachment and isolation to protect himself from further hurt; it is this wall that interferes so drastically with any attempted therapy.

Where the patient feels threatened in his present environment and its regulation does not resolve his tension, where his responses constitute a potential source of danger to himself and others, and where he cannot be treated satisfactorily in the existing milieu, temporary hospitalization may be inevitable. The employment of psychotropic drugs and consultation with the patient's family, helping them to ease their demands on the patient, may enable him to adapt himself outside of an institutional setting. However, there will still be acute emergencies for which no other alternative is available than hospitalization, either on the psychiatric ward of a general hospital, or in a mental institution.

On the other hand, there are certain disadvantages to hospitalization. The most insidious feature of "institutionalization" is that the patient's tendencies to regress will be reinforced enormously by any lack of stimulation in the hospital. As one of a large group of patients, the individual may lose his identity. He becomes dilapidated in his appearance and oblivious to customary habit routines. There may be little in his environment to encourage his latent desires for growth and development. This unfortunate feature is due, to a large extent, to the overcrowding of institutions and to the lack of enlightenment and education of the personnel. The motives governing an employee's choice in working in an institution may not be those helpful to the patient in restoring him as an active unit of society.

That hospitalization can prove itself to be a stimulating rather than a retarding influence is illustrated in institutions with a progressive administration and well-trained personnel. Selected occupational therapy and craftsmanship, carefully applied to the patient's interests and aptitudes, can help prevent the abandonment of reality. Exercises, games, entertainment, dancing, music, social affairs, and group discussions can also be of estimable benefit. Correction of remediable physical defects, or the use of glandular therapy where necessary, and the employment of drugs, insulin coma, and ECT, where indicated, may be helpful. Many of the benefits from such therapies are psychologic. They help convince the patient that he is not considered hopeless, in this way building up a feeling of confidence in the therapist and in himself. It is probable that the so-called Aschner treatment for schizophrenia with its stress on detoxification, stimulation, exercise, baths, sweats, venesection, catharsis, emesis, and hormone therapy was really psychotherapeutic in effect. At any rate, hospitalization should be regarded as a temporary measure; the patient being moved back into the community as soon as possible.

SOMATIC THERAPY

The introduction of neuroleptics has introduced a new and more hopeful outlook in the therapy of many schizophrenics. Phenothiazines (e.g., Thorazine, Mellaril, Prolixin), butyrophenones (e.g., Haldol), thioxanthenes (e.g., Navane), and dihydroindolones (e.g., Moban) in proper dosage may, where indicated, rapidly resolve psychotic states and render the individual more accessible to social demands. (The choice and dosage of neuroleptics have been outlined extensively in the section on Pharmacotherapy in Chapter 53.)

Useful as they have proven to be, neuroleptics unfortunately have their drawbacks since, apart from the side effects and serious sequelae (e.g., tardive dyskinesia) with prolonged employment, they tend to reduce the application of psychologically based therapies. Too frequently young people suffering an initial psychotic break are saturated with massive amounts of drugs which, while restoring homeostasis, prevent them from integrating the significance of the psychotic experience which may, with the help of an empathic therapist, have a great and often beneficial impact on their future development. This in no way minimizes the value of the neuroleptics, but it does necessitate some restraint in their use. Where neuroleptics are resorted to, interruptions of intake with drug holidays are in order.

While the utilization of insulin shock is on the decrease, there are some authorities who believe that it still has a utility in patients whose illness is of a duration of less than six months. Electroconvulsive therapy is also considered to be helpful under certain conditions (see Somatic Therapy, Chapter 53).

HOSPITALIZATION

Hospitalization for severe psychotic disorganization may be mandatory. This not only provides an atmosphere for the protection of the patient and the dispensation of therapeutic measures, but it gets him away from the family and other environmental stresses that may have initiated the breakdown and tend to sustain it.

More and more patients are being admitted for treatment of acute attacks to selected wards of a general hospital rather than to mental institutions. To an extent this is due to the regulations governing compensation by insurance companies and other third-party payment resources. It is due also to the growing deemphasis on institutionalization in mental hospitals. One disadvantage is that payments for hospitalization may be restricted to a limited number of days. This encourages massive tranquilization to bring the patient speedily out of the psychotic state, and it results in discharge before the patient has had an opportunity to establish a relationship with a therapist who may carry on treatment in the posthospital period. What is sorely needed is a unit where the patient may reside for five or six weeks that will provide sufficient time to work through his experience, in part at least, and to consolidate a good therapeutic plan.

To prevent a relapse as much as possible, the home to which the patient returns must be relatively free from stress sources. Where members of his family are hostile, unconcerned, or disturbed, the chances of relapse are great, and the patient, if possible, should be housed elsewhere. If this is not feasible, provision should be made to get the patient out of the house a good part of the day, as in a day hospital or rehabilitation unit. Prescription of maintenance drug therapy will be more essential in the latter case than where the family is loving and understanding. In either instance, continuing psychotherapeutic care is important.

MILIEU THERAPY

Regulation of the environment (see Supportive Therapy, Chapter 48) so that it is therapeutically constructive, both in terms of minimal stress and in providing gratifying experiences, is important in schizophrenia. Occupational, recreational and social therapy may be easily instituted in a hospital or outpatient setting. The atmosphere of a day-and-night hospital, halfway house, or community recreational center also lends itself to environmental control. A total "therapeutic community" program, e.g., with a suitable group may prove rewarding. Settlement in the community and encouragement to engage in some productive work is much better for the patient than assignment to the barren hinterlands of a mental hospital ward.

In many cases family therapy, and individual psychotherapy with other members of the family, may put a halt to destructive stimuli within the household. Schizophrenia, more and more, is being regarded as a manifestation of family pathology. Relationship distortions are not only with the mother, but also with the father and other significant persons in the family constellation (Wynne et al 1958; Bowen, 1960; Lidz & Fleck, 1960). The importance of the "double bind" as a basis for schizophrenia has been underscored by Bateson, Jackson, Haley, and Weakland (1956). These authors, describing the family interactions in schizophrenia, contend that the "victim" who succumbs to schizophrenia is exposed to (1) a repetition of prescriptive themes or experiences, (2) conflicting injunctions in relation to these "themes" with threats of punishment for disobedience, and (3) further restricting "commands" that prevent the "victim" from escaping the field of communication.

The "victim" arrives at a perception of his life as based on a number of key double-bind interactions with family members. For example, a mother's reaction of hostility to her child may be concealed by overprotecting him. The child may be aware of this deception, but to retain her love he cannot communicate this knowledge to her. "The child is punished for discriminating accurately what she is expressing, and he is punished for discriminating inaccurately—he is caught in a double-bind." Incongruence between what is said and what is intended is the essence of the faulty communicative process: ". . . the more a person tries to avoid being governed or governing others, the more helpless he becomes and so governs others by forcing them to take care of him" (Haley, 1959a & b, 1961). Family relationships alternate between overcloseness and overdistance; the members become intrapsychically "fused" so that differentiation of one from the other is often impossible. A psychosis may constitute a mirror image of the patient's unconscious. These factors have focused attention on family therapy as a preferred approach in schizophrenia (Midelfort, 1957; Boszormenyi-Nagy & Framo, 1965). Family psychotherapy increases the chances of breaking the schizophrenic's communication "code" (Jackson, J, 1962).

PSYCHOTHERAPY

Psychotherapy with schizophrenics is an art that graces few therapists. In the face of the patient's stubborn resistance, suspiciousness, withdrawal tendencies, and inability to communicate appropriately most therapists are apt to throw their hands up in surrender. Yet there are few experiences as gratifying to a therapist as providing an empathic bridge to reality for a withdrawn patient. It is difficult to define the qualities a therapist must possess for such a successful eventuality. I once asked Frieda Fromm-Reichmann what she would consider the most desirable characteristic for work with schizophrenics. She replied, "Humility, persistence, sensitivity, compassion, and [*she added drolly*] a good deal of masochism."

It is only human to respond with frustration at repeated therapeutic efforts that slide off the patient with little or no apparent effect. But I am convinced that where such efforts are sustained, with warmth and sincerity, they ultimately will be rewarded.

In my training as a psychiatrist I spent 13 years of my early career working in a state hospital principally with schizophrenics. Those were the days before psychotropic drugs, and the only tools available to the therapist (other than wet packs and hydrotherapy) were his or her skills in establishing a meaningful relationship with patients. No matter how severely withdrawn the patients were from external stimuli (and sometimes our catatonic citizens retained their frozen, statuelike behavior for years), it seemed obvious to me that they craved and needed consistent and kindly communication, even though this seemed to register no impact on them. When some of the patients "spontaneously" emerged from their deathlike repose, it astonished me to hear them recount in minutest detail some of the things that they had observed going on around them, with virtual playbacks of my oneway conversations with them. They particularly recalled the little kindnesses bestowed upon them by the nursing staff and myself, which I am now convinced had a more penetrating effect on them than the most mighty of miracle drugs.

Even wild paranoidal individuals seemed to respond to quiet sympathy and lack of retaliation for their abuses. I remember one of the most disturbed patients I had ever encountered, a middle-aged, distraught, and disheveled, hallucinating woman, who accosted me the first day I was put in charge of the disturbed ward on which she had been sequestered for more than 10 years. Blood-curdling shrieks and cries for the police came from her at the first sight of me as I walked through the ward protected by a bodyguard of nurses and attendants. She identified me positively as her tormentor—the man who had for years been making indecent proposals to her and who had been sending electrical impulses up her rectum and genitals. It was all my bodyguard could do to keep her from assaulting me.

Despite the daily indignities that she heaped on me, I took pains each day briefly to talk quietly to her, expressing my concern at her upset and assuring her that if there were anything that I could do to help her, I would be happy to do it. Her response was stereotyped—anger, vilification, and occasionally expectoration. On one occasion as I left her, she managed to find a flower pot, and she hurled it at me, barely missing my head. Slowly, after many months her response to my consistent reassurances became more attenuated, although she daily repeated her resentment that I had the temerity to persist in talking to her when I was the last person on earth she wanted to see.

And then something dramatic happened. On one occasion I was in a hurry to get ward rounds over with to attend a special meeting, and I breezed through the ward without talking to her. Her reaction was electric. She became more highly disturbed than before, upbraiding the nurses for their neglect in directing me away from her, and accusing me of having no respect for her and her feelings. The next morning, for the first time, I was able to talk to her without fear of bodily harm. We spoke quietly about matter-of-fact subjects, and although she was still psychotic and hallucinating, she spoke calmly and with good sense about many matters, apparently enjoying her exchanges with me. Shortly thereafter, the patient became ill with lobar pneumonia, and she was transferred to the acute medical unit. Sick as she was she refused to allow anyone except myself to treat her. With persuasion I convinced her that she could trust the regular staff members of the unit. Upon her recovery from pneumonia, she returned to her old building and was transferred to a quiet, open ward.

My final victory occurred when the patient requested that I cut her toe nails! Since her admission she had not trusted anyone to get near her feet. Her nails had become thickened like horns, and I had to borrow metal shears from the tool shop to do a half decent job. To my delight and surprise, the patient recovered from her psychosis and was able to leave the hospital. I am not certain what other forces were responsible for the patient's improvement, but I am convinced that the relationship I developed with the patient was a prime vehicle in bringing her back to a reasonable contact with the world.

The ability to enter into the patient's life and to share with him his anguish and despair, to refrain from making demands on him that would ordinarily seem justified, to persist in showing him friendship and respect in the face of his outrageous and irresponsible behavior may ultimately win out. To carry out this formidable task, a therapist needs to possess a good deal of stamina and an undaunted optimism that the healthy elements in a sick human being will eventually bubble through. Obviously, the average custodial unit and the average therapist are not equipped to render ideal psychotherapeutic care for these vulnerable human beings.

While there may be some advantage in working exclusively with psychotherapy in the few instances where there is an especially skilled and dedicated psychotherapist who is specialized in working with schizophrenics (Laing, 1960, 1967; Arieti, 1974), the vast majority of therapists find antipsychotic drugs most helpful, if not indispensable, supplementing such drug therapy with psychotherapy. Certainly drugs are capable of keeping chronic schizophrenics operating on reasonable terms with their responsibilities, preventing them from regressing to a state of work disability and restoring their capacity to communicate. The disadvantages that drugs impose by masking defenses are more than offset by their ability to make hospitalization unnecessary in many cases and in fostering better cooperation with the therapist.

The immediate objective of psychotherapy in schizophrenia is to enhance the adaptive reserves of the patient so that he will be able to come to a rapid equilibrium, to discern his chief sources of stress, and either to help him resolve or to remove himself from them as expeditiously as possible. While the schizophrenic tendency may not be entirely eradicated, however, the patient may be strengthened so that he does not shatter so readily upon exposure to stressful stimuli. In extremely uncooperative and withdrawn patients, behavior therapy, employing operant conditioning, has been used with some success (see Chapter 49, Behavior Therapy). When the patient becomes accessible, formal psychotherapy may begin. Sometimes supportive and reeducative group therapy is utilized adjunctively with individual therapy; at times it constitutes the sole psychotherapeutic modality.

The key to the treatment of schizophrenia lies in the ability to establish some sort of contact with the patient. Most schizophrenics fear relationships with people desperately, and they erect various obstacles to any interpersonal threat. The withdrawal from reality and the archaic type of thinking and symbolism enhance the individual's isolation from people, since there is no common means of communication. Yet beneath the surface the patient yearns for a friendly and loving relationship. He wards it off, however, because he has been injured by past interpersonal contacts. He does not wish to encounter further rebuffs. His apathy, his detachment, and his expressed hostility and aggression are means of protecting him from his desire for a closer union with people. Establishing rapport with the patient is in line with two objectives: first, to reintegrate the patient in his relationships with people to where he can obtain at least partial gratification of personal needs without fear of abandonment or injury and, second, to bring him back to the realistic world by proving to him that reality can be a source of pleasure rather than of pain.

The technique of developing rapport varies with the patient. A great deal of activity is essential. In very sick patients whose productions are seemingly irrelevant and incoherent, a careful analysis of the productions will disclose a language that is very meaningful to the patient. The ability to show the patient that his words and gestures are understood may be the first constructive step. Sullivan (1931) has stressed the need to communicate understanding of the patient's language and gestures as a means of solidifying the interpersonal relationship. In order to do this, it may be necessary to talk to the patient on his own regressed level. J. M. Rosen (1947, 1962) interprets the utter-

ances of the patient in terms of their symbolic meaning, and he has been able to develop a relationship with some of his patients through this method. Entering into the psychotic world of the patient, Rosen and his followers attempt to make contact by intensive daylong sessions, overwhelming the patient with direct interpretations of his unconscious. How valid these interpretations are may be challenged, but the fact that the patient is showered with attention, and is shocked with statements coached in harshly frank and sometimes sexually explicit terms, may in a relatively short time bring the patient out of his regressed state. This approach has been practiced in foster homes where the patient is provided with a therapeutic environment throughout the day and night. It is, consequently, an expensive form of therapy and one that can be indulged by a limited clientele.

Employing symbolic objects, Sechehaye (1951) evolved a nonverbal method of communicating with a regressed schizophrenic girl. This was necessary, Sechehaye believed, because the primary trauma occurred before the stage of verbal language. For example, only by realizing that apples symbolized mother's milk was it possible to offer the patient love through drinking "the good milk from Mummy's apples." In ways similar to this, the therapist may gather clues to essential needs and conflicts from the bizarre symbolic thought content, translating it the same way as if it were a dream. Cryptic as these utterances may be, they contain important messages that may well be heeded by the sensitive therapist who will answer them in ways that indicate to the patient that his plaints are recognized and acknowledged.

Using an existential approach as well as family therapy, Laing (1960) and Laing and Esterson (1965) have explored the despair of patients, siding with them against their families and the environment, in this way establishing intimate contact. The relationship is utilized as a vehicle for recasting a patient's concepts of himself. The approaches of Harry Stack Sullivan (Mullahy, 1967, 1968), Frieda Fromm-Reichmann (Ballard, 1959), Otto Will (1967, 1970), and

Harold Searles (1960, 1965) also make worthwhile reading.

In mute patients therapy may consist of nothing more than sitting with the patient without prodding him to express himself. The very fact that the therapist refrains from probing his trends, and avoids discussing the causes of his breakdown, but accepts him as he is may help the patient to regard the therapist as a less threatening force than he regards other people. In many cases therapy may consist of working with the patient at occupational projects and playing games with him, such as, cards, checkers or chess. Sometimes a more positive approach is made to the patient by giving him food, such as milk, candy, and cake. For a long time it may seem that these gratuities are the only reason that the patient desires to see the therapist. In querying the patient after his recovery, however, one becomes convinced that the patient actually had a desire for closeness and was testing the therapist constantly.

Any relationship that the patient is able to establish with the therapist is at first bound to be extremely unstable. The schizophrenic individual feels very vulnerable and helpless within himself. His level of frustration tolerance is inordinately low. He is distrustful, suspicious, and inclined to misinterpret the motives of the therapist in accordance with his inner fears and prejudices. He feels incapable of coping with life, and he resents the intentions of the therapist to return him to reality, which holds for him unbounded terrors. He fears injury and frustration from people, and it may be months, sometimes years, before he is willing to accept the therapist as a friend. Even then he will sense rejection and neglect in the most casual attitude. Anxiety with a temporary return to regression will interrupt therapy repeatedly, and it must be handled by a consistently reassuring and friendly manner. Violent reactions may punctuate treatment from time to time, especially when the patient senses that his liking for the therapist is forcing him to leave the relative security of his reality retreat.

Fromm-Reichmann (1939) has commented on the unpredictable nature of the schizophrenic's relationship to the therapist. A sympathetic, understanding, and skillful handling by the therapist of the relationship is far more important than an intellectual comprehension of the operative dynamics. She ascribes difficulties in therapy to the fact that the therapist is unable to understand the primitive logic and magical reasoning that governs schizophrenic thinking.

Unless we analyze our own reactions repeatedly, our sense of frustration may arouse strong aggression that will interfere with treatment. It is manifestly impossible to treat any psychotic person where there is no genuine liking for him. If we are able to regard the actions of the patient as essentially childlike, we shall best be able to understand the patient's outbursts. Cold logic fails miserably in explaining the reactions of the schizophrenic. Despite his age the patient seeks an infantile relationship to the therapist, and he desires unlimited warmth, understanding, protection, and help. He seeks a mothering affiliation rather than a give-and-take encounter between two equals.

The therapist should try to be as sympathetic and reassuring as possible, approaching the patient casually and informally and conveying an interest in him and his immediate concerns. Sometimes it is desirable to encourage the patient by touching his shoulder or arm as a gesture of friendship. I have found that I have been able to establish a relationship in a remarkably short time by offering to show the patient how to relax his tensions, utilizing a simple hypnotic relaxing technique (q.v. page 794). Even frightened patients can be helped, but, obviously, they must be willing to cooperate. The therapist may say, "It's been rather tough on you, and you can't avoid being upset by all that has happened. If you'd like, I can show you how to relax yourself, which should make you feel a lot better." If the patient responds positively, he is asked to make himself comfortable in his chair and to shut his eyes while relaxing suggestions are made.

It is important not to cross-examine the patient or subject him to questioning. An attitude of accepting him as he is without reserve is best while conveying sincere interest in his needs and problems. The sicker patients will usually flood the therapist with their irrational ideas and delusions. One way of handling this situation is to focus as much as possible on matter-of-fact reality items. This is not as difficult as it sounds, although the therapist must avoid giving the impression of being bored with or disbelieving of the patient's irrational concerns.

Probing for conflicts is taboo, as is the lying-down couch position. Only when the patient himself brings up topics for discussion is it desirable to discuss these, but this should be done in as a matter-of-fact way as possible. This does not mean that depth interpretations are always to be avoided; they may be made once the therapist–patient relationship is solidified. It may be reassuring to the patient to have a dynamic explanation for some of his problems. This may relieve him of the mystery of what is happening to him.

Therapy in schizophrenia must, in summary, be oriented around the immature ego of the patient. Like an infant, the patient's emotional reactions to people are unstable and ambivalent. He is easily frustrated, and he feels rejection without ostensible cause. He is unreasonable and demanding. His concept of reality is unreliable; he often confuses inner mental processes with outside reality. He may assume that the person on whom he depends is omniscient and will supply his every demand, expressed or unexpressed. He will react with hostility if he is not granted what he believes to be his due. Alone, his ego is so weak that he is unable to tolerate complete responsibility. He needs help and support, and yet he fears and resists assistance.

Federn (1943) has advised enlisting the aid of a relative or friend, preferably a motherly person who can look after the patient. He stressed that no schizophrenic person should be allowed to depend on his own resources. He should at all times be surrounded by an atmosphere of love and warmth. His stability and his strength grow as a result of positive identifications with loved ones. If he is at all able to develop to

self-sufficiency, his independence will grow best in the soil of this positive identification. The hope is to bring him to a point where his own ego can function satisfactorily without the aid of a parental figure. In many cases the latter stage of self-sufficiency is never attained, and all one can do is adapt the individual to reasonable social functioning while attached to some kindly person.

The need to surround the patient with a favorable atmosphere necessitates work with his family or with people with whom he lives. This is essential to relieve the burden on the patient induced by demands and responsibilities that he is incapable of fulfilling. Often the inertia and apathy of the patient stir up resentment in his family, and when the patient is aware of their hostility, he may retreat further from reality. Considerable work with the patient's relatives may be required before they are sufficiently aware of the dynamics of the patient's reactions and before they are willing to aid the therapist in the treatment plan.

The chief emphasis in treatment must be on the creation of a human relationship with the patient that has pleasure values for him. Only by this means will he relinquish the safety and gratification of regression and, utilizing the relationship with the therapist as a bridge, return to reality. The handling of treatment, however, requires considerable tact. No matter how detached the patient is, he is extremely sensitive to everything that the therapist says or does. An avoidance of situations that evoke anxiety in the patient is essential. This is often a very difficult task because the most casual remark may stir up powerful emotions in him.

The patient may choose to remain silent throughout the treatment hour, and he will appreciate the therapist's refraining from forcing him to talk. It is expedient with such a mute patient to point out occasionally that he perhaps abstains from talking because he believes that the therapist is interfering with him or because he is afraid of what he might say. The patient may feel more at ease due to such remarks, and he may finally break through his silence.

In most cases the patient at first will

feel alone, helpless, and misunderstood. He resents the intrusion of the therapist into his private life, and he believes that the therapist, like everyone else, is unable to understand him. The initial task is to show the patient that his impulses and wishes are respected and that he is not required to comply with demands that are unreasonable. Usually in all of his previous interviews he has been bombarded with questions about his breakdown, and, even when he has responded to these questions in a more or less frank manner, he has sensed disapproval. The fact that the therapist accepts him as he is may eventually build up his own self-respect and strengthen his desire to return to reality.

Constantly, during treatment, the patient may react by detachment or withdrawal, or he may subject the therapist to a testing period during which he is recalcitrant and hostile. His purpose may be finding out whether the therapist is the kind of person who can be trusted, or whether the therapist is like all other people in his experience, who make unfair stipulations or react to his hostility with counterhostility. The patient may believe that what the therapist demands of him is to be ''good.'' This ''goodness'' means to the patient that he must comply with standards that all other people impose on him. At first he will act as if the therapist actually expects him to abide by these standards, threatening him with rejection or aggression if he resists. The testing period may be a trying one for the therapist, since it may continue for many months during which the patient constantly rejects the therapist's friendship. When the patient realizes that the therapist does not expect him to do certain things, that the therapist sides with him against the unreasonable demands of his family, he will begin to regard the therapist in a new light.

The beginning of a feeling of closeness may precipitate panic; the patient may try to run away from therapy, or he will exhibit aggression toward the therapist. The ability to see the patient through this stage may finally succeed in breaking down his reserve and in establishing for the first time an identification with a person based upon love. There exists within every schizophrene a psychic tug of war between the spontaneous forces of mental health that drive him to seek gratifying relationships with people and the security of his regressed state that harbors him from the imagined dangers of a hostile world. The therapist's attitudes will determine which of these impulses will triumph.

The method of handling the treatment hour is of signal importance. It is best not to cross-examine the patient because he may interpret this as censure. He must be convinced that the therapist does not want to invade and to remove him from his private world, but rather seeks to participate in it with him. This does not mean assuming a cloying sweetness during sessions, because the patient will be able to see through this. It must be expected that the patient's attitudes will be ambivalent. He may profess little interest in the interview, yet resent its termination at the designated time. He may attempt to defy or to provoke the therapist, or he may refuse to cooperate. If the therapist becomes ill and cannot keep an appointment, the patient may react with rage and refuse to continue treatments. If the therapist is unavoidably late for an appointment, the same thing can occur. The patient may resent the therapist's taking any vacation or assigning another person to care for him. Where customary routines have to be interrupted, it is best to prepare the patient far in advance and, if necessary, to enlist the help of those members of his family with whom he has an attachment. If the patient becomes hostile toward the therapist, every attempt must be made to explore why he believes the therapist has failed him. Should he persist with his hostility and insist on seeing another therapist, his wishes should be respected, for it is futile to do any work with a patient while he is governed by feelings of resentment.

Once a positive relationship has been established, it is necessary to cherish it carefully. Nothing must jeopardize the relationship. For example, the patient must never be led to feel that his delusions are ridiculous. His feelings and attitudes must be respected at all times. It is unnecessary to reinforce these attitudes by agreeing with them; but they should be accepted as something that the patient believes in sincerely. However, it may be impressed on the patient that there might possibly be another explanation for his experiences than the one that he supports. All probing for dynamic material must assiduously be avoided at this point. This is one of the most frequent errors in the handling of psychotic patients. It is also an error to interrogate the patient regarding previous mental upsets.

Because the aim in the psychotic patient at first, at least, is to increase repression, since the ego is already too weak and permits the filtering through of disturbing unconscious material, such techniques as free association are to be discouraged. Rather, the patient should be enjoined to talk about everyday reality happenings. In general, the past had best be avoided, and the patient may be aided in any expressed desire to regard it as a "bad dream" or something that should be forgotten. Under no circumstances should a positive relationship with the therapist be analyzed. Where the patient exhibits inhibitions or phobias, these too should be respected, since they probably have protective values. All resistances he uses to repress psychotic material must be reinforced, although the symbolisms he employs may sometimes be interpreted to him. Unlike neurosis, analysis of resistances should be avoided to prevent the release of the unconscious content that will upset the patient more. When the patient himself brings up delusional material or symptoms and spontaneously talks about the connection with traumatizing circumstances in his past, an effort may then be made to explain in uncomplicated terms how these manifestations originated. The rule never to dissolve resistance does not apply to resistances to getting well or to integrating himself more closely with the therapist and with reality. These impediments should be analyzed and removed if possible. Guilt feelings may be met by reassurance, and hostilities dealt with in a manner that does not put responsibility or blame on the patient.

One of the ways in which a positive relationship with the therapist may be used is to try to show the patient that his thoughts and ideas often appear to be realis-tic but that it is necessary always to differentiate between what seems to be real and what actually is real. In the patient's case, too, he may confuse both, even though there is no question of doubt in his mind that the two states are identical. An excellent sign of restoration of ego strength is the ability of the patient to recognize the irrational nature of his ideas while he was in an upset condition.

While some patients achieve a fairly good grasp of reality and tend to return to their customary occupations, and even to tolerate relationships with other people along the lines of the close attachment they establish with the therapist, it may be necessary to do further work with the patient to prevent a relapse. Some of the patient's problems may be rooted in the fact that he harbors bloated ambitions of what he should accomplish in life. His grandiose expectations may have resulted in constant frustration. Under such circumstances it is essential to modify the patient's goals through the careful use of the therapeutic relationship. It may be possible, for instance, to convince him that it is better to devote his life to the attainment of happiness in the immediate present than to strive for things in the unknown future. Character disturbances may exist that make relationships with people fraught with anxiety. An active manipulation of the patient's environment through consultation with his family may enable him to function more comfortably. Attempts should also be made to introduce him gradually into social contacts with other people.

In spite of such corrective measures, hostility, tension, and anxiety may constantly be created by unconscious inner conflict. The intensity of these emotions may again tend to shatter the patient's ego. The danger of another schizophrenic collapse may, therefore, be imminent. *As a preventive measure, the cautious use of an insight approach may be indicated. It is best here,* as mentioned before, *not to attempt probing for conflicts until the patient evinces an interest in understanding his own problems.* Schizophrenic persons are remarkably intuitive and can grasp the dynamics of their disorder better than most neurotics.

This is probably because they live closer to their unconscious, and because ego barriers to deep impulses and fears are not so strong. It is for this reason that one must proceed very carefully in analyzing the patient's deepest impulses (Bychowski, 1952; Eisenstein, VW, 1952; Fromm-Reichmann, 1952; Bruch, 1964). Haley (1961) has outlined some excellent suggestions for the analytic handling of schizophrenics. Other suggestions, namely the use of projective techniques, may be found in the section on the treatment of the borderline patient (p. 901).

Although the therapist assumes a directive role, it is the patient who is expected to uncover the meaning of his communications (Bruch, 1964). This fact has been stressed by many therapists working with schizophrenics, particularly Sullivan (1962), Fromm-Reichmann (1954), and Lidz and Lidz (1952). In this way the therapist avoids bombarding the patient with useless interpretations or confronting him with a road map of his unconscious that will lead the patient nowhere. Inevitably, the relationship between therapist and patient will begin to stir up feelings in the patient that he will have to clarify with the help of the therapist. For example, if the patient identifies the therapist with his mother, interpreting this may mean little. Exploring in what way the therapist is *acting* like a mother may, on the other hand, become meaningful.

The realization of unconscious guilt, hostility, and erotism has a dual effect on the psychic apparatus. On the one hand, it floods the ego with destructive emotion; on the other, by forcing a more realistic adaptation, it serves to liberate the psyche from incessant conflict. In this way the dynamic probing is like a two-edged sword; the ego has to be traumatized by the liberated emotions before it is able to mobilize defenses less destructive to the person than regression. The ego, however, may still be so weak that it collapses under the impact of emotion before it can adapt itself in a more adequate manner. This is always a danger in psychotic and prepsychotic conditions. All interpretations must, therefore, be very cautiously applied. Reconstructive techniques should be abandoned temporarily if excitement or great hostility develop, for only when the patient is positively attached to the therapist is he able to bear the suffering brought out by a realization of his unconscious trends.

AFTERCARE

The aftercare of hospitalized schizophrenic patients constitutes a serious problem due to the large numbers of such persons in the community and the high rate of psychotic relapse. That aftercare may be arranged economically is brought out in a study by Mendel (1964) in which both professional therapists and nonprofessional "psychiatric aides" were used. All patients were seen individually once a month for a 20- to 30-minute interview. Fifty-seven percent of the patients were given psychotropic drugs in addition to the interviews. The interview focus was on the immediate activities of the patient—what he did since his last visit—rather than on what fantasies or hallucinations he had experienced or was experiencing. No interpretations were given. "The therapist questions perceptions which appear distorted and disorganized, and reinforces a more accurate and conventional view of the world." This may create doubts in the patient as to the construction of the world as he sees it (Mendel, 1963; Mendel & Rapport, 1963) and opens up alternative world perceptions and constructions. Specific instructions are given to the treatment team to stress the reality of the helping situation and the assurance of continuing with the patient in treatment as needed. "Built into the transaction between the doctor and the patient is hope and the possibility of change." The next appointment time is always clearly specified so that the patient has something to look forward to. With this limited therapy, 70 percent of the patients remained functional outside the hospital.

The prescription of maintenance antipsychotic drugs may be required in the chronic schizophrenic. Some patients spontaneously take medications or increase the dosage when their tension grows stronger or when they feel reality slipping away. Cooperation of the family may be necessary in other cases to make sure that the patient takes the medications. Periodic visits to outpatient clinics may help maintain the proper drug balances and help arrangements for drug holidays.

In most cases the patient will feel better if employed in some gainful work. Preliminary referral to a rehabilitation unit or sheltered workshop may be helpful.

LOBOTOMY

Prefrontal lobotomy has been prescribed with variable results for seriously ill patients who have failed to show improvement after 2 or 3 years of psychotropic drugs and psychotherapy. This form of treatment is said to yield best results where the prepsychotic personality was fairly well integrated, where there is no emotional deterioration, and where the patient's current symptoms include tension, restlessness, motor activity, combativeness, and destructiveness. Catatonic and paranoid reactions respond best; hebephrenic reactions poorly. After schizophrenia has existed for 10 years or more, lobotomy is rarely of value. (See the section on lobotomy in Somatic Therapy, Chapter 53).

STRESS REACTIONS

Except for transportation and industrial accidents—and the rare catastrophes of hurricane, flood, and famine—stress reactions (traumatic neuroses) are mainly consequent to the disasters of war. Especially prominent is combat fatigue among the soldiers of the participating armies. The most common reaction is an anxiety state characterized by tension, emotional instability, somatic symptoms, insomnia, and nightmarish battle dreams. Less common are conversion and depressive and psychophysiological reactions. Acute temporary psychoticlike episodes may also occur.

Knowledge of the dynamics of war neurosis made certain preventive measures possible in World War II. Where the soldier had had effective training that made him feel he could defend himself under all circumstances, where he was shown that he

had adequate weapons of attack, where he had confidence in his leaders, and where he had obtained sufficient indoctrination and morale building, he was best prepared to resist a breakdown. An important element in prevention was group identification. Cooperation with others was essential, and the individual had to be made to feel that he was part of a team, with enough of an idea of the battle situation and the planned strategy so that he would not be caught by surprise.

The incidence of war neuroses is proportionate to shattered morale and to feelings of isolation from fellow soldiers. An organized body of men fighting for a cause that they consider just can best overcome war stress and hardship.

The treatment of the soldier with acute battle exhaustion depends upon whether he is or is not to be returned to duty. The sequel of all battles are reactions of fear and great fatigue. Only later are these reactions organized into actual neuroses. Experience in previous wars has shown that evacuation and a too reassuring attitude encourage collapse. Unless the individual anticipates going back to the front in spite of his reactions, he may develop neurotic illness to avoid duty.

Combat exhaustion, if treated early, does not necessarily result in neurosis. Therapy consists of rest, good food and continued assignment to one's combat group, with reassurance and exhortation from company officers. If medical treatment is necessary, the patient is sent to the battalion aid station. A moderate anxiety state may be cleared up in 24 hours with rest, reassurance and 7.5 to 10 gr of oral Sodium Amytal. It is assumed that the soldier will go back to the front. Where there is reluctance to return to battle duty, appeals to patriotism, courage, and "not letting one's buddies down" often build up the person's morale and determination. Encouragment to verbalize fear and disgust is vital, since the soldier in this way releases tension and discovers that others share in his anxieties. The value of respecting the soldier's "gripes" in building morale has long been recognized. The role of the leader is important, too, and an intrepid commanding officer has always been of great service. It is amazing how often a change in attitude in a soldier can prevent neurotic collapse.

Individuals with more severe emotional reactions may be transferred to the division clearing station and put under the care of psychiatrists. Proper sedation is instituted and supportive, reassuring talks continue to emphasize return to full combat duty, while building motivation and morale. The psychiatrist particularly avoids mention of "illness" or "neurosis" or the possibility of the patient's needing long-term treatment in order to avoid sponsoring secondary gain elements. The patient is assured, after a physical examination, that he is physically well and that his "exhaustion" will soon be over. In occasional cases narcosynthesis and hypnosis may be helpful to overcome serious conversion or phobic symptoms. These measures help prevent a structuralization of the neurosis, the effects of which may persist long after discharge from the army has taken place.

Treatment of stress reactions in civilian life (hurricanes, floods, explosions, mass bombings, etc.) should be started as soon as possible, since delay permits the neurosis to become more highly organized and allows the secondary gain element to take hold (American Psychological Association, 1964). First aid rapidly helps victims of disasters to return to proper functioning in a short time. Preventive measures are of incalculable value if a disaster is anticipated and potential victims are apprised of dangers as well as suitable protective and ameliorative actions that may be taken. Practice drills under simulated disaster conditions, faithfully repeated, help to establish appropriate patterns if and when emergencies occur.

Responses of people to both unexpected and to expected dangers will vary with the specific meaning to them of the danger situation and their residual stabilities and habitual coping mechanisms in the face of stress. They will also respond uniquely to any warning signals. Among the gravest dangers to the group are the wildly uncontrolled panic reactions of a few unstable individuals, which can have a contagious influence on the rest of the group. If the leader

knows in advance which members are apt to manifest unrestrained fear, he may select them in advance and assign definite tasks to them so as to divert their energies.

In spite of drills, exercises, and warning signals, the impact of a disaster is bound to provoke immediate reactions of anxiety and confusion. These, however, should soon be replaced by adaptive responses encouraged during the practice sessions. As soon as the violent impact of the disaster has subsided, organized activities will take place. Working together and helping the more physically and emotionally disabled has a profoundly reassuring effect. Where a person is unable to compose himself, he may need special treatment. For example, if a person shows blind panic, he may require firm restraining by two or three people to avoid spreading panic throughout the group. Drug therapy may be necessary as described in dealing with panic reactions in the section on emergencies (see pp. 846–863).

In treating disaster victims whose neurotic or psychotic responses do not subside with the termination of the emergency, the first principle is to permit them to verbalize feelings; the second, to accept their reactions, no matter how unreasonable these may seem. Supportive therapy coupled with sedation or tranquilization will usually suffice to restore the person to his previous state.

Where a patient has a continuing stress reaction that threatens to become chronic, narcotherapy and hypnotherapy are often effective for purposes of symptom removal. In instances where anxiety is extreme, one may utilize an "uncovering" type of technique. Here hypnosis and narcotherapy are also of help. The recovery of amnesias, and the reliving of the traumatic scene in action or verbalization, may have an ameliorative or curative effect.

While hypnotherapy and narcotherapy accomplish approximately the same results, the emotions accompanying hypnotherapy are often much more vivid, and the carthartic effect consequently greater, than with narcotherapy. There are other advantages to hypnosis. The induction of a trancelike state, once the patient has been hypnotized, is brought about easily without the complication of injections and without post-therapeutic somnolence. Additionally, hypnotic suggestions are capable of demonstrating to the patient more readily his ability to gain mastery of his functions. On the other hand, narcotherapy is easier to employ and does not call for any special skills.

Where it is essential to remove an amnesia, the patient is encouraged under hypnosis or narcosis to talk about the events immediately preceding the traumatic episode and to lead into the episode slowly, reliving the scene as if it were happening again. Frequently the patient will approach the scene and then block, or he may actually awaken. Repeated trance inductions often break through this resistance. Also, it will be noted that the abreactive effect will increase as the patient describes the episode repeatedly. Apparently the powerful emotions which are bound down are subject to greater repression that the actual memories of the event.

In the treating of postwar neuroses of traumatic origin, Hadfield's (1920) original technique is still useful. The patient is hypnotized and instructed that when the therapist's fingers are placed on the patient's forehead, the patient will picture before him the experiences that caused his breakdown. This usually produces a vivid recollection of the traumatic event with emotions of fear, rage, despair, and helplessness. The patient often spontaneously relives the traumatic scene with a tremendous cathartic effect. If he hesitates, he must be encouraged to describe the scenes before him in detail. This is the first step in therapy and must be repeated for a number of sessions until the restored memory is complete. The second step is the utilization of hypnosis to readjust the patient to the traumatic experience. The experience must be worked through, over and over again, until the patient accepts it during hypnosis and remembers it upon awakening. Persuasive suggestions are furthermore given him, directed at increasing assurance and self-confidence. After this the emotional relationship to the therapist is analyzed at a conscious level to prevent continuance of the dependency tie.

Horsley (1943) mentions that where the ordinary injunctions to recall a traumatic scene fail, several reinforcing methods can be tried. The first has to do with commanding the patient to remember, insisting that he will not leave the room until his memory is complete. The second method is that of soothing, coaxing, and encouraging the patient, telling him he is about to remember traumatic scenes that will remind him of his experiences. The patient may, if this is unsuccessful, be told that although he does not remember the experience during hypnosis, he will remember it upon awakening. He may also be instructed to recall it in a dream the next night.

Various hypnoanalytic procedures, such as dramatization, regression and revivification, play therapy, automatic writing, and mirror gazing, may be utilized to recover an obstinate amnesia. The reaction of patients to the recall of repressed experiences varies. Some patients act out the traumatic scene, getting out of bed, charging about the room, ducking to avoid the attacking objects and people. Other patients live through the traumatic episode without getting out of bed. Some individuals collapse with anxiety; they should be reassured and encouraged to go on. Where the patient voices hostility, he should be given an opportunity to express his grievances and dislikes. Clarification of his feelings of injustice may afford him considerable relief.

It must be remembered that the object in therapy is to dissipate feelings of helplessness and of being menaced by a world that the patient no longer trusts. The sense of mastery and the ability to readjust oneself to life must be restored. It is necessary to proceed with therapy as rapidly as possible to prevent organization of the condition into a chronic psychoneurosis. Follow-up therapy is essential with integration on a waking level of the material brought up during the trance. Where the anxieties relating to the disaster have precipitated hysterial, phobic, compulsive, and other reactions characteristic of the ways that the patient has dealt with anxiety in everyday life, long-term insight therapy will usually be required.

In chronic stress reactions treatment is

difficult because of the high degree of organization that has taken place and because of the strong secondary gain element involving monetary compensation and dependency. The recovery of amnesias should always be attempted, but even where successful, this may not at all influence the outcome. An incentive must be created in the patient to function free of symptoms, even at the expense of forfeiting disability compensations, which in comparison to emotional health may be shown to be diminutive indeed.

HABIT DISORDERS

A number of symptomatic complaints are commonly encountered among patients that serve either as a prime reason for seeking therapy or become so distracting that they obstruct the therapeutic effort. Their resolution consequently will concern the psychotherapist, who, having satisfactorily managed to overcome them, may proceed with the underlying personality problems of which the symptoms are a surface manifestation. Many of the techniques for habit modification come from the behavioral field. The effectiveness of reinforcement therapy has been validated even with chronic psychotic patients (Gottfried & Verdicchio, 1974).

Insomnia

The complaint of insomnia is a common one in emotionally disturbed people, particularly those suffering from anxiety and depression. The emotional reactions to sleeplessness are usually more serious than any physiological damage that is being promoted. Patterns of insomnia are individual: (1) there are those persons who find it difficult to fall asleep, but once slumber occurs, they do not awake until morning; (2) there are those who fall asleep easily, but awake in a few hours, fall asleep again, and go through the sleep-awakening cycle several times during the night; (3) there are persons who doze off readily, but who awaken at 4 to 6 A.M. and then cannot return to sleep; (4) there are others who sleep throughout the night lightly, fitfully, rest-

lessly, and get up in the morning as exhausted and tired as when they went to bed.

Causes of insomnia are multiple, but by far the most common source is fear, agitation, resentment, or mental overstimulation that prevents the person from assuming the repose essential to a good night's rest. A complicating problem in chronic insomnia is that the patient may be convinced that he is harming himself physically and mentally by not getting his full quota of sleep. He may, as a consequence, become so preoccupied with the challenge of whether he will doze off or not in the evening that he will whip himself into a state of self-defeating alertness.

The treatment of insomnia will depend upon whether or not it is acute, the provocative factors that keep the patient awake, and the degree of addiction to hypnotic drugs.

Acute temporary periods of insomnia are usually readily handled by reassuring the patient that he will not damage himself by sleeping less than his usual quota, by permitting him to verbalize his fears and resentments, and perhaps by prescribing a hypnotic substance if necessary. Commonly employed are the barbiturates (Nembutal, 1.5 gr; Seconal, 1.5 gr; Luminal, 1.5 gr; Tuinal, 1.5 gr; Carbrital, full strength) or the nonbarbiturates (Noludar, 300 mg.; Dalmane, 15 to 30 mg.); Doriden, 500 mg; Placidyl, 500 mg). If anxiety appears to be a primary factor, Valium (5 mg) may be tried. Hypnotics and minor tranquilizers must be taken only temporarily since prolonged use may prove to be habituating.

The treatment of chronic insomnia is a more difficult matter, largely because the patient has established faulty habit patterns, and has probably incorporated his insomnia into his neurotic superstructure. The primary treatment is psychotherapeutic, and hypnotics should be avoided if possible. The patient's preoccupations and vexations during the nighttime may yield clues to basic conflicts that undermine him. Generally, as the patient experiences relief for his neurotic suffering, his insomnia will yield. Where no progress is being made toward better sleep, the following tactics may be tried:

1. Rearranging sleeping habits.
2. Reassuring the patient about sleep needs.
4. Getting the patient to accept insomnia.
3. Teaching the patient relaxing exercises.
5. Treating hypnotic drug dependence.
6. Prescribing medication.

REARRANGING SLEEPING HABITS

(1) The patient should attempt to establish a regular bed time, avoiding naps during the day. (2) Excessive smoking and drinking should be eliminated. (3) In some patients a change of mattresses should be made from hard to soft and vice versa, attention being paid to the bedcovers so that the patient is neither over- nor under-heated, to the wearing of more comfortable night apparel, and to the regulation of the room temperature. Simple as this may sound, it may be all that is required. (4) A change in position during sleep may be indicated if the patient is in an uncomfortable repose. Superstitions such as that one must not sleep on the left side because the heart may be damaged, should, if this position is a preferred one, be corrected. Patients with asthma or orthopnea are more comfortable propped up in bed rather than lying prone. An elevation of the head and upper trunk is sometimes a preferred position. In married persons a change from a double to twin beds, or the reverse, may be considered. (5) A bedtime snack (warm milk, sandwich, cocoa) is reassuring to some people, as is a glass of beer or ale or a small tumbler of sherry, port, or an aperitif. (6) Tea or coffee should be excluded from the evening meal and not taken before going to bed. (7) Reading in bed concentrates the attention away from inner concerns. Television programs selected before bedtime should not be too stimulating. (8) a brisk walk in the evening followed by a hot bath are recommended by some. (9) Should the patient desire to experiment with it, there is on the market, in "sleep shops" or department stores, an oscillating mattress that rhythmically rocks some people to sleep.

(10) Ear plugs, antisnore masks, and eye shades may be utilized to control situations disturbing to sleep. If necessary, one may sleep in a separate room away from a snoring partner.

REASSURING THE PATIENT ABOUT SLEEP NEEDS

The individual's estimate of how much sleep he must have for health reasons is usually far above his true physiological requirements. As people get older, sleep needs get less. A reduction of deep sleep stages (III and IV) is normal. Because lighter stages (I and II) are indulged, older people get the feeling they do not sleep a wink. They also awaken three or four times during the night and fall asleep again, which is normal. If the patient can be convinced that he will not damage himself by merely reposing in bed and not forcing himself to sleep, and if he can develop the philosophy "If I sleep, so much the better; if not, it doesn't matter," he may be able to stop worrying himself into wakefulness. The patient may be told that merely lying in bed and relaxing are usually sufficient to take care of the physiological needs. If one does not sleep as much as he believes is necessary, no real harm will befall him. Of course, he may drive himself to distraction by worrying about not sleeping. Worry will actually cause him more difficulty than not sleeping.

RELAXING EXERCISES

Progressive muscle relaxation with deep breathing exercises and self-hypnosis are valuable adjuncts in insomnia. The techniques of relaxation and self-hypnosis have been outlined previously in this volume (q.v.). They may advantageously be taught to the patient. Repeated suggestions are made to himself that he will be able to "turn his mind off," to focus on a pleasant scene, and to feel himself getting more and more drowsy and relaxed. This may reestablish the sleep rhythm more effectively than any other measure. A useful pamphlet on ways to approach sleep may be prescribed for the patient (Better Sleep, 1963). An interesting article called "The science of sleep," by Joan Arehart-Treichel (1977) in *Science News,* may be recommended.

ACCEPTANCE OF INSOMNIA

Where these tactics are unsuccessful, an effort should be made to get the patient to accept his insomnia as something with which he can learn to live. Indeed he may, as Modell (1955) has pointed out, successfully exploit his symptom. Once the patient is convinced that he needs less sleep physiologically than his habits dictate, he may be encouraged to accomplish something useful during his waking hours at night. Instead of tossing about fitfully in bed, and brooding about problems, he may read or write in bed. Or he may get up, take a shower, and, for an hour or two, apply himself to useful work, particularly work that worries him. He may then return to bed. A cat nap during the day, if absolutely necessary, may supplement his sleeping needs.

TREATING HYPNOTIC DRUG DEPENDENCE

When hypnotic drugs have been utilized over a long period, they usually become less effective and REM sleep markedly is reduced. Therapy is much more difficult since the patient will resist going off hypnotics. Should drugs be abruptly withdrawn, disturbing insomnia will eventuate. The brief snatches of sleep that do occur are interrupted by a rebound in REM sleep, upsetting dreams, and nightmares. Consequently, slow withdrawal is necessary (a good rule is reducing by one nightly dose every 5 or 6 days). The patient should be warned about the possibility of a temporary increase in insomnia, vivid dreams, and nightmares. Relaxation exercises or self-hypnosis are prescribed or biofeedback employed if the therapist has the apparatus. The principles outlined above should also be followed.

DRUG TREATMENT

Where these suggestions fail to give desired results, it may be necessary to prescribe medications, hopefully temporarily. The kind of drugs to use will depend on the type of insomnia. Persons who have difficulty in falling asleep may be started with 2.5 mg of Valium, increased to 5 mg and then 10 mg if smaller doses do not work. This is helpful also in the patient with insomnia due to a situational anxiety. Where the patient falls asleep, but awakens during early hours, a useful drug is Sinequan (25–50 mg). Where both conditions prevail, the drug of choice is Dalmane (15–30 mg). It is best to start with the 15-mg dose and to tell the patient that Dalmane is more effective on the second, third, or fourth night of consecutive use than on the first night. In the event that the dose of 15 mg. fails to work after 1 week, 30 mg is prescribed. In very severe, chronic insomnia one may start initially with the 30-mg dosage.

Should these medications fail and it is judged that the patient is already hopelessly addicted to pills, other drugs may be tried and the dose individually regulated. The choice of drug will depend upon whether short action is desired, i.e., 3 to 4 hours, in which case pentobarbital (Nembutal) 1.5 gr is prescribed; intermediate action, i.e., 4 to 6 hours, will require butabarbital (Butisol) 1.5 gr; or long action, i.e., 6 to 8 hours, for which phenobarbital (Luminal) 1.5 gr will be necessary. Sometimes combination drugs like Tuinal (1.5 gr), which contains Seconal and Amytal for short and intermediate action, or Carbrital, which "full-strength" contains 1.5 gr of pentobarbitol and 4 gr of Carbromal, are well tolerated. Should a "hangover" result the next morning, the doses should be halved. Under no circumstances should a stimulant like benzedrine, dexedrine, or methedrine be prescribed to alert the patient, since a vicious sedating-stimulating habit may be established. The nonbarbiturates are also popular. Among these chloral hydrate is to be preferred (7.5–15 gr). This is available in capsule form (Noctec), which consists of 7.5 gr of chloral hydrate and is taken in doses of one to two capsules nightly; or in syrup form which contains 7.5 gr of chloral per teaspoonful. Placidyl (500 mg), Doriden (500 mg), and Noludar (300 mg) are also commonly prescribed. As psychotherapy proceeds, the patient may be able to reduce the dosage of hypnotics or to eliminate them completely.

Overweight and Obesity

Losing poundage in the chronically overweight person is not a matter of diet or drugs. This is why going on crash diets, relying on dietary foods, and taking appetite suppressants (anorexiants) are so rarely successful. The basic causative factor is a faulty life style, often sustained by psychological factors, which yields best through the application of behavior modification methods (Stunkard, 1972) reinforced when necessary by dynamic psychotherapy.

Lifelong obesity of an intractible nature is usually a symptom of a severe personality problem that dates back to childhood (Bruch, 1957, 1961). More rarely it is a manifestation of an endocrine disturbance that fosters a decreased energy output or of hypothalamic lesions that disturb the perception of satiety. Individuals who have been pampered or rejected in childhood, and who have suffered great insecurity or harsh illness in the first years of life, are most apt to overvalue oral activities. Stuffing the stomach with food materials becomes associated with a feeling of peace and contentment. Analysis of fantasies and dreams often indicates that in eating the person strives to achieve a regressive security equivalent to being breast fed by a bountiful mother. Overeating thus becomes a tension-relieving mechanism as well as a most important source of pleasure fulfillment. The personality structure that provokes the overeating tendency may also motivate the individual toward dependency on a stronger person who acts as a mother substitute (Caldwell, 1965). Moreover the fact that persons in his environment are so overly concerned with the individual's appearance provides him with a weapon to punish and to defy others, to assert his individuality and the right to do as he pleases, or to present himself to the world as a casualty who should not be expected to engage in adult responsibilities. The body image becomes distorted, the person's large size becoming equated with health, strength, and power. To yield his size threatens him with a loss of intactness. Obesity in such conditions does not resolve with behavioral methods, but it may respond to long-term

psychoanalytic psychotherapy sufficiently modified to meet the individual's personality needs (Bruch, 1973). It would seem urgent to treat the basic personality difficulty before any permanent improvement in the craving for oral gratification could be expected. Unfortunately, an alteration in the character organization of individuals with this type of problem is an extremely ambitious undertaking. Even when the patient is motivated toward change, therapy is bound to be prolonged. Unless one is willing to endure hunger and a certain amount of tension, the individual will be unable to follow a diet no matter how scientifically and skillfully it is constructed. Because of these psychological factors, the individual's efforts at dieting are usually unsustained. Tricked, shamed, cajoled, or bribed into restricting food intake, he may manage to relinquish a few pounds, which are ravenously replaced in a week or so of overstuffing. Even though the person has been drilled into knowing what foods are taboo, he displays a peculiar intellectual inhibition about remembering a proper dietary. Rather than expose himself to disciplined food regulation, he will exploit dramatic measures, such as quack "diet specialists," and appetite suppressants, such as the amphetamines. Addiction to the latter drugs may occur with no relief whatsoever of the obesity.

In treating the average adult whose overweight is not caused by such serious psychological problems, some clarification will usually be necessary. Though the patient has been exposed to years of dietary information and may profess to know all about dieting, there are usually large gaps in his knowledge that have been filled with old wives' tales about food and feeding as well as faddist whimseys extracted from magazines and newspapers. Information of what constitutes a good food regime (7 calories per pound of ideal weight with proper protein, mineral, and vitamin content) may have to be supplied that can act as the basis of a living diet to be followed faithfully. In some patients alcohol, taken to appease tension, constitutes a block to dieting. One ounce of drink of any spirit contains about 135 calories. An average martini has as many calories as three slices of bread! Considering that several highballs or cocktails supply 500 to 750 calories, and that the appetite is in addition stimulated by alcohol, food control for the drinker becomes a nonexistent entity. The matter of exercise will also require explanation. A 250-pound man climbing 20 flights of stairs will lose the equivalent of one slice of bread. Exercise firms up muscles, but it cannot take off sufficient poundage without strict dieting. When suggesting a proper diet the therapist should give the patient a basic nutritional list of essential daily foods. This consists of a helping of fresh fruit twice daily; a small helping of cooked vegetables; a salad; lean broiled meat, fish, or fowl twice daily; a glass of milk or cheese twice daily; 2 to 3 eggs weekly; and little or no alcoholic beverages (Tullis, 1973). Fats, nuts, candy, cake, and all desserts are to be avoided. Low-calorie salad dressings, saccharine, and sugar-free drinks may be permitted. Meals should be taken at regular hours with no snacking allowed.

The basic therapy, however, is behavior modification that takes into consideration the prevailing eating patterns of the patient. Detailed questioning is essential regarding not only the kinds and preparation of foods the patient prefers to eat, but also the time of day when overeating occurs, the availability of the food, the exact circumstances under which the appetite is stimulated, propensity for sweets, late evening snacking, social pressures, etc. What is essential is control of environmental eating cues that excite temptation. Once these factors are identified, the patient is instructed in how to rearrange eating routines and given homework assignments to practice the new orientation. For example, snacking while watching television is a common practice. The patient may be told that should the desire be overpowering, he may only eat outside of the TV room. If candy is left around for "guests who may call," this must be replaced by radishes, carrots, and celery kept fresh in the refrigerator. If compulsive eating occurs when the patient gets angry, he is to pound a pillow instead. Some therapists explore with the patient the most unpleasant thoughts he can conjure up as well as the most pleasant. These are used as reinforcers, the unpleasant thoughts being indulged when an old eating temptation occurs; the pleasant thoughts when a constructive pattern is substituted. Other therapists impose a "fine" on the patient whenever he relapses. A point system may be set up, the patient giving himself points when he thinks a punishing thought to control a desire for high-calorie food, or for counting his calories, or for pausing after every mouthful. Points are also deducted for failures. A mate or friend then gives the patient a small amount of money at the end of a week (or day), say a penny for each point gained, and acquires the same amount for each point lost. Finding appropriate reinforcers helps the acquisition of new habits. Should the patient need further instruction or ask for greater details, he may be told to acquire the popular book: *Slim Chance in a Fat World: Behavioral Control of Obesity,* by R. B. Stuart and B. Davis (Champaign, Ill., Research Press), which spells out a system. The book by Earl Ubell, *How to Save Your Life,* (New York, Harcourt Brace Javanovich) also has some helpful ideas. The patient is also instructed to chew his food slowly over a longer period, to avoid all desserts except a small helping of fresh fruit, to leave half the food on his plate when he dines out, etc. The aim is slow weight loss (about 1 pound weekly). Keeping a daily diary of all foods eaten and a semiweekly record of his weight often helps. It takes a long time to retrain one's palate to prefer and enjoy the less fattening foods. Most important is the principle that one cannot change a person by altering his diet; rather one alters his diet by changing his attitude and his behavior.

Most overweight patients are generally interested in shortcuts, particularly weight-losing drugs. Unless there is a low basal metabolism, no purpose is served in supplying medications like thyroid tablets. Amphetamines (Dexedrine, Dexamyl) are virtually of little more than temporary value, although in patients who require a "lift" they may serve to strengthen the resolve to limit the food intake. They should never be used for more than 6 weeks or so. Safer drugs to use are clortermine hydrochloride

(Voranil) 50 mg daily, fenfluramine hydro-chloride (Pondimin) 20 mg three times daily, an hour before meals, which may be increased to 40 mg three times daily, and mazindol (Sanorex) (Dykes, 1974). They are also employed on a short-term basis. An often used aid are supportive groups like Weight Watchers, Overeaters Anonymous, and TOPS (take off pounds sensibly). The effectiveness of these self-help groups is increased by behavior modification techniques (Levitz & Stunkard, 1974). If skilled in hypnosis, the therapist may try hypnosis as an adjunct. Direct suggestions are given as to diet, ego-enhancing suggestions are made, mental imagery is used to accelerate a desired goal, self-hypnosis is encouraged, and a casette tape made for the patient (Stanton, 1975).

Pathological obesity dangerous to life may have to be treated by hospitalizing the patient and putting him on a starvation diet. The patient should be told that he is being hospitalized to ''get something,'' i.e., a thorough checkup. He should not be threatened by the statement that he will be starved or ''put on a diet,'' which he will interpret as having something ''taken'' from him. Psychotherapy following hospitalization is usually necessary. As a last resort when all measures have failed, intestinal bypass surgery has been employed (Solow et al, 1974).

Smoking

Patients, for health reasons, often request that they be helped to give up smoking. This is a difficult task where smoking serves the purpose of alleviating tension. Educational campaigns, psychotherapy, and pharmacological aids have all yielded limited success (Ford & Ederer, 1965). Mark Twain's comment, ''It's easy to quit smoking; I've done it hundreds of times,'' is tragically the experience of most inveterate smokers who force themselves to give up tobacco. Warnings about health hazards of nicotine and coal tar, group therapy with smokers, anesthetic lozenges, astringent mouth washes, anticholinergic drugs, tranquilizers, and lobeline as a nicotine substitute may produce temporary withdrawal

from tobacco with high relapse rates. The entire process of smoking becomes for the inveterate user of tobacco an adjustment mechanism serving to satisfy specific needs: appeasing and reducing tension, providing a facade of nonchalance and poise, controlling anger, overcoming embarrassment in upsetting interpersonal situations, providing mouth and oral gratifications, acting as a substitute for overeating, etc. Giving up smoking leaves a hollow in the life of the tobacco addict, mobilizes tension, and deprives the addict of a powerful adaptational tool.

In treating the individual who seeks to abandon the habit, it is important to keep these points in mind. One may then proceed with behavioral modification methods fashioned after the techniques used in overcoming overweight and obesity. An investigation is launched into the history of the smoking habit, how many cigarettes are consumed daily, under what circumstances, when the frequency increases, what puffing on a cigarette does for the individual, what efforts have been made to stop in the past, why the individual wants to give up smoking now. In many cases the smoker will openly or indirectly reveal that he is convinced that he will be unable to stop. In one case I was consulted by a professional man with Berger's disease, an illness in which smoking is dangerous. When he was admitted to a hospital for the beginning of gangrene of a toe, he had strapped cigarettes across his back to conceal them from the nurses and attendants knowing that they would remove any cigarettes on his doctor's orders!

The ''I can't'' resistance (''I don't have what it takes,'' ''My life is too unsettled now,'' ''I'm not strong enough,'' etc.) is a means of reducing anxiety stemming from the conflicting desires of wanting to smoke and wanting to maintain one's defensive gratifying prop (Clark, R, 1974). The defeatist belief is a way of denying this conflict. In applying for help there is a forlorn hope that someone other than the patient can control his smoking. The resistance if unresolved will defeat any applied therapeutic efforts. The fact that smoking continues in spite of treatment convinces the individual that he is hopeless and provides him with an excuse for continued smoking. The idea that he has exposed himself to therapy appeases his guilt. "I know it's bad for me, but I don't care, it doesn't matter, I'm not going to think about it." In working with any smoker, therefore, this resistance, even if it is not apparent at first, should be tackled at first. The therapist should verbalize the nature of the resistance and explain its purpose. The smoker is encouraged to stop pretending that he is doing all he can to overcome the habit. At the same time the therapist should express confidence that he *can* quit smoking if he wants to and work toward kindling the patient's faith in himself.

Behavior modification techniques described in the section on overweight are useful in providing a routine for the patient. A therapist acquainted with the hypnotic technique, will find it a useful adjunct. Many ways of employing hypnosis have been described with claims of long-term success ranging from 25 to 94 per cent (Crasilneck & Hall, 1968; von Dedenroth, 1968; Spiegel, H, 1970).

In my own experience I have found that hypnosis helps eliminate sources of tension, especially after the smoking habit has been broken. The initial visits should, if possible, be frequent. Suggestions are made in the trance to the effect that the patient will develop a desire to stop smoking, that he will grow so strong that neither temptation nor tension, no matter how intense, will deviate him from his resolve to give up tobacco. This achievement will be rewarded by a feeling of well-being and strength that will be greater with each day of continued abstinence. The patient will, in relinquishing smoking, be able to control his appetite so that he does not overeat. Should the patient inquire about other oral gratifications, such as gum chewing or allowing a hard piece of candy to dissolve in his mouth, "permission" for this may be given him if this is not overindulged. Some patients, who have a need to defy authority, will then, rather than to return to smoking, engage in these harmless oral activities beyond what they believe is permitted. In this way the tobacco habit may become more readily ex-

tinguished, the gum-chewing and candy indulgence gradually being given up on their own. Dictated tape recordings, made by the therapist, which the patient plays on his own machine twice daily (see section on Induction of Hypnosis, p. 793) often help to reinforce suggestions and are useful where the patient cannot come for frequent reinforcing sessions. Self-hypnosis, facilitated by the recording, may prove to be of value also. It is best to encourage the patient to give up cigarettes completely rather than to taper off. Excessive tension may be handled psychotherapeutically, and, if required, minor tranquilizers, such as Librium or Valium, may be prescribed. A Dexamyl spansule in the morning should mild depression develop may be indicated in some patients. Such medications will be needed only temporarily. The patient's feelings of well-being at ridding himself of the tobacco habit, his enhanced physical condition in eliminating nicotine from his body, and the approval he senses from the therapist and his friends for his "courage" will serve to sustain him.

Successful as this program may prove to be, the patient may need psychotherapy to deal with underlying tension-producing problems and conflicts that can engineer a relapse in smoking unless they are resolved or brought under satisfactory control.

Enuresis

Once urologic or general causes for enuresis (a good physical examination is a necessity) are eliminated (for instance, local irritation around the meatal or urethral areas, phimosis, adherent clitoris, balanitis, cystitis, urinary tract infections, pinworms, diabetes, cerebral dysrhythmia, and systemic diseases), its sources in psychological conflict may be explored. If the patient is not mentally defective or of borderline intelligence, the presence of enuresis probably indicates improper habit training, emotional immaturity, or conflicts related to sexuality or aggression (Bakwin, 1961). Frequently enuresis has positive values for the individual as a masturbatory equivalent. In some instances it represents a form of aggression against the parents or against the world in general. Often it signifies an appeal for dependence on the basis of being a childish, passive, helpless person. In this context, enuresis symbolizes for the boy castration and the achieving of feminity. In girls it may connote aggressive masculinity and symbolic functioning with a penis.

For children a record is kept of dry and wet nights, the former being rewarded by praise and the record marked with a star. Rewards like ice cream may also be used. The child when he wets should change his bed clothes himself and see that they are washed. One-third of the children presenting with enuresis may be cured by this regimen alone (McGregor, HG, 1937).

Strong emotional stress sometimes produces enuresis in persons who are ordinarily continent. This was brought out during World War II when certain soldiers subjected to the rigors of induction or warfare displayed the regressive symptom of bed-wetting. Most soldiers who showed this symptom had a history of early bed-wetting or of periodic attacks of the disorder prior to induction.

In treating an enuretic child, he may first be requested to empty his bladder at bedtime; then awakened 2 hours later and induced to urinate again. This interval may gradually be prolonged, and, if enuresis stops, the evening awakening may be discontinued after 6 months. Positive praise and encouragement are given the child when he controls his bladder; however, there should be no scolding or punishment for wetting. Exciting play or activity prior to bedtime is best curtailed, and fluids restricted after four o-clock. Coffee, tea, cocoa, sweets, salts, and spices should be avoided. Sedatives, amphetamine, methyl testosterone, anticonvulsants, belladonna, and other substances have been administered with varying results. Imipramine (Tofranil) has been used (Poussaint & Ditman, 1964; Stewart, MA, 1975) one-half hour before bedtime. The dose is 25 mg for children of 4 to 7 years, 35 mg for children of 8 to 11 years, and 50 mg for children older than 11 years. Partial improvement has been reported with some side effects in certain cases. Friedell (1927) obtained an 80 percent cure rate with intramuscular injections of sterile water. W. A. Stewart (1963) de-

scribed the cure of a young man of 19 with lifelong enuresis in one session by Zulliger, who convinced the patient that he, the therapist, sided with the patient against his father. The fact that so many treatments have yielded positive results indicates the presence of a strong suggestive and placebo element in the management of enuresis (English, OS, & Pearson, 1937; *Hospital Focus,* 1964).

Enuresis developing in an adult is usually a regressive phenomenon connoting a desire to return to a childish adaptation and a defiance of the adult world.

The treatment of enuresis will depend upon whether one wishes to deal with the symptom as an entity, disregarding the emotional undercurrents, or to work with the intrapsychic structure in hopes that the symptom will eventually resolve itself (Pierce, 1975). A focusing on the symptom as preliminary to working with more fundamental dynamic factors is preferred by many since the symptom is an undermining element that robs the individual of self-confidence and vitiates his interest in searching for conflictual sources. Nevertheless, concomitant counseling and carefully conducted psychotherapy should, if necessary, be employed.

A rapid effective conditioning technique which, according to the British Journal, *Lancet* (1964), brings a relief yield of 75 percent, involves a buzzer or bell which sounds off when there is wetting of the bed (Mowrer & Mowrer, 1938). There are advocates and critics of this. However, side-tracking the issue of whether symptom removal is rational or irrational (Winnicott, 1953; Eysenck, 1959) or whether the buzzer treatment is a form of classical or operant conditioning (Lovibond, 1963), this approach to enuresis in controlled studies has been shown to be superior to other therapies (Werry, 1966). While the relapse rate is about 30 percent, relapses respond rapidly to a second course of treatment. There is little evidence that symptom substitution or precipitation of a neurosis develops with the removal of enuresis; on the contrary the emotional well-being seems benefitted (Baller & Schalock, 1956; Behrle et al, 1956; Bostock & Schackleton, 1957; Gillison &

Skinner, 1958; Lovibond, 1963; Werry, 1966). The apparatus consists of two foil electrodes separated by thin gauze placed under the child. The covering over the electrodes should be as thin as possible. Parents and child are reassured there will be no shock, and the child himself is to prepare the bed and set the alarm. Should the alarm go off, he must get up and go to the bathroom. On return he is to remake his bed and reset the alarm. Eventually the child will awaken before the alarm goes off. Should the child fail to awaken when the alarm sounds, the parents should awaken the child and see to it that he goes to the bathroom. A 90 percent cure is reported in six months (Dische, 1971). An improved form of apparatus is the Mozes Detector invented and used in Canada and tested at the Toronto Hospital for Sick Children with impressive results (Medical World News, 1972).

Hypnotherapy is sometimes a useful adjunct. Elsewhere (Wolberg, LR, 1948, vol 2, pp 40–133) a full recording of the hypnotic treatment of enuresis is described. Actually, there is no single hypnotic method suitable for all patients; the specific suggestions and strategems will depend upon the problems and personality characteristics of the patient. One method is to train the patient to enter as deep a trance state as possible. In the trance, an attempt is made to show him that he himself is able to produce various phenomena, such as paralysis, muscle spasm, etc. and that he can shift or remove these by self-suggestions. Fantasies related to the best thing that can happen to a person are obtained for the purpose of reinforcing the conditioning process later on. The patient is then requested to experience a sensation of slight bladder pressure such as occurs immediately prior to urination. As soon as he feels this sensation, it will inspire a dream or will make his hand rise to his face, which action will cause him to open his eyes. Even though no dream or hand levitation occurs, it is suggested that his eyes will open, nevertheless. At that moment he will experience an urgency to get out of bed. Going to the bathroom will be associated with a feeling similar to that accompanying the fantasy of the best thing

that can happen to a person. These suggestions are repeated a number of times.

The next stage in therapy is teaching the patient to control sensations that arise in his bladder, retaining his urine without needing to awaken until morning. Suggestions to this effect are given the patient as soon as he establishes a habit of getting out of bed and going to the bathroom. The positive relationship with the therapist may be utilized as a reinforcing agent in reconditioning, praise and reassurance being offered when suggestions are followed.

In patients who have expressed a willingness to undergo dynamic psychotherapy, conditioning procedures may be delayed until they are deemed absolutely necessary. This is because the symptom can disappear as the origins of bed-wetting are explored, and the unconscious fantasies associated with it clarified. However, there is no reason why psychotherapy cannot be combined with a conditioning approach.

Nail Biting and Hair Plucking

Nail biting and finger sucking are common outlets for tension in preadolescence and adolescence and may persist as a neurotic symptom into adult life. Among other things, nail biting serves as a substitutive release for masochistic, sadistic, and repressed masturbatory needs. Where no other serious emotional problems coexist, the treatment may be symptomatic (Pierce, 1975), or therapy may be focused on inner emotional factors that generate tension, particularly environmental family problems. Unfortunately, most nail biters have little motivation for real psychotherapy, seeking mere measures of control because of embarrassment about their habit. They are usually unaware that the nail-biting symptom has a meaning, and they are often puzzled by the persistence of the urge to chew their finger tips.

Where psychotherapy is resisted, the therapist may have no alternative but to treat the symptom. Hypnosis may be useful here. In hypnosis strong authoritarian suggestions are made to the effect that the patient will have a desire that grows stronger and stronger to give up the childish habit of biting his nails. Should he put his fingers into his mouth, he will discover that his fingernails taste disgustingly bitter. He may even develop nausea with the mere desire to nail bite. Daily hypnotic sessions are best, but since this is usually impractical, a tape recording may be made that the patient may turn on twice daily (see Induction of Hypnosis, p. 793). If the patient is a child, his parents may activate the machine while he is asleep to reinforce suggestions through sleep conditioning. Self-hypnosis may be employed in an adult. Where these tactics fail, aversive conditioning (q.v.) using a small shocking apparatus may be tried (Bucher, 1968). A strong desire to control the symptom must be expressed by the patient and his cooperation secured.

An assessment of the patient's problems will determine whether further reeducative or reconstructive therapy is indicated after nail biting is brought under control.

Hair plucking (head, eyelashes, eyebrows) is generally a manifestation of a severe personality problem often of an obsessive-compulsive or schizoid nature. It may serve as an outlet for revenge and self-punishment, and it is often accompanied by frustration, guilt feelings, and remorse. Psychotherapy is notoriously ineffective in dealing with this symptom. Hypnosis and particularly aversive conditioning (q.v.) with a self-operated shocking apparatus may score some successes.

Anorexia Nervosa

Anorexia nervosa usually invites desperate expediencies. In their anger, anguish, and dismay patients and therapist may take recourse in such measures as cajolery, bribes, tube feedings, and even electroconvulsive therapy. These may have an immediate ameliorative effect, but since they circumvent the core problems they ultimately aggravate self-starvation. Anorexia nervosa mainly affects young adolescent girls of well-to-do families who defend their avoidance of food with a captious

logic that does not yield to common-sense arguments. Where some motivation exists, behavior therapy by itself sometimes brings temporary benefits (White, 1964). Follow-up studies, however, have been discouraging, with relapse and alarming substitutive symptoms being the rule rather than the exception (Bruch, 1973). The malady appears to be on the increase throughout the world with pursuit of thinness a chief obsessive concern.

Psychological studies often reveal an erstwhile "perfect" child struggling to maintain her stature and virtuosity with abstemious relentlessness. Basic is the search for identity and a struggle for independence and control. Paradoxically, short-lived bouts of uncontrollable eating binges further undermine the anorexic's self-esteem and incite an exaggerated refusal to eat.

Therapy is thus understandably difficult. It hinges on two objectives: (1) improving nutrition (the use of the high-calorie diet is sometimes helpful but must not be forced (Maxmen et al, 1974); and (2) rectifying the instrumental psychological causes. In mild cases, where the family warfare is not too extreme, treatment may be achieved at home. In most instances, separation from the home environment (usually with hospitalization) is mandatory in order to remove the patient from the highly charged family situation and from the aversive entourage surrounding the prevailing eating atmosphere. The relationship with the therapist is primary, with a minimum of pressure employed. Focus on food stuffs and calories is avoided. Psychoanalytic psychotherapy reinforced by family treatment (Liebman et al, 1974) and supportive measures has yielded the most encouraging results and helped to rectify identity problems, temper cognitive distortions, and expand autonomy and self-control in relation to eating habits. Continuing psychotherapy with the patient, and perhaps family therapy, will be required after hospitalization (Bruch, 1973, 1975).

57

Supervision of the Psychotherapeutic Process

Supervision of the work of the beginning therapist is an essential requirement in the learning process. Without supervision it will be difficult or impossible for the therapist to translate theoretic knowledge into effective practice, to work through blocks in understanding, and to develop skills to a point where the therapist can help patients achieve the most extensive goals. Supervision, then, in psychotherapy is essentially a teaching procedure in which an experienced psychotherapist helps a less experienced individual acquire a body of knowledge aimed at a more dexterous handling of the therapeutic situation.

Adequate learning necessitates, first, an appropriate presentation of data in terms meaningful to the student, second, the incorporation of this data by the student, and third, the ability of the latter to organize his experiences cognitively and to generalize from them to related aspects of his or her work.

The first requirement presupposes an ability on the part of the teacher to develop an empathic understanding with the student and to discern what aspects of the available material are pertinent to the immediate needs of the student and to the teaching task. The second essential assumes the exis-

tence of motivation, an adequate intellectual capacity to integrate the information, and the relative absence of anxiety. The third requisite entails the presence of a synthesizing function of the ego that enables a student to examine oneself critically, to give up old modes of conceptualizing, and to apply oneself to new creative tasks. Helpful is alertness and ability of the teacher to keep the relationship on a level where transference resistances do not interfere with this process. Helpful also is a detection of the student's specific learning problems and the evolvement of techniques designed especially to deal with them.

Unfortunately, there are many interferences with the expeditious learning of psychotherapy, not the least of which is the ambiguity of the concepts that constitute the marrow and lifeblood of the psychotherapeutic process. It is difficult to authenticate techniques that are universally applicable. A method that works in one case may not be effective in another; it may product good results for one therapist and a string of failures for another with a different kind of personality; it may be highly productive at a certain phase of treatment and backfire in the same patient at another phase. What appears to be necessary is more research into the actual procedures of teaching psychotherapy. Christine McGuire (1964) has pointed out that much of the ongoing clinical teaching is conducted in a manner that runs counter to basic principles about learning long known to educators and psychologists. A professional coach who sends his players out to complete a number of practice games with instructions on what to do and who asks them to provide him at intervals with a verbal description of how they had played and what they intend to do next would probably last no more than one season. Yet this is the way much of the teaching in psychotherapy is done. What is lacking is a systematic critique of actual performances as observed by peers or supervisors. This is not to say that an account, highly screened as it may be, of what a therapist says he or she has done with a patient may not lend itself to a dynamic learning relationship (Ekstein & Wallerstein, 1958); however, it is most valuable when it is compared to what the supervisor has actually observed in a live session between the student and patient through a oneway mirror or in viewing a videotape of the session.

A sensitive question relates to the validity of utilizing data in teaching psychotherapy drawn from the teaching of related disciplines. Can we, for example, apply to psychotherapy the information derived from such areas as social work supervision, the psychology of learning, communication theory, and programmed instruction? On the surface the reply would be "yes." Yet there are special problems in the teaching of psychotherapy that force us to qualify this answer.

An individual who masters a complex skill proceeds through a number of learning phases, namely (1) the acquisition and retention of certain factual information, (2) the development of ways of utilizing this information in a practical way, and (3) the evolvement of a capacity of altering this information when new situations arise that call for different approaches. In psychotherapy modern methods of acquiring information embrace exposure to didactic materials through fact-finding learning (lectures, reading, and observation of therapy performed by expert therapists through a oneway mirror, videotapes, and sound movies) and problem-solving learning (programmed instruction and role playing with immediate feedback). Practical applications of what has been learned are inherent in observing the consequences of treatment techniques by actually *doing* psychotherapy under supervision, by listening to audiotapes and watching videotapes of one's own performances, by observing others performing in psychotherapy through a oneway mirror, by viewing videotapes and sound movies, and by clinical conferences and case seminars. The creative employment of psychotherapy with the development of methods designed for the special problems of each patient are consequences of continued supervision and prolonged experience. Through such a program of scholarship, searching inquiry, observation, and experiment, a body of organized knowledge is eventually developed in the matrix of sophisticated theory.

Research into teaching method indicates that the effectiveness of teaching is increased "when the teacher accepts a teacher's responsibility for directing learning, providing every opportunity and inducement for the student to accept a larger responsibility for his own education, and holding out always his and their goal the maximum achievement of which they are both capable" (Hatch & Bennet, 1960). Fundamental is a spirit of inquiry that provides the motivational fuel for the powering of proper learning (Matarazzo, 1971). This is most trenchantly sustained where the content of teaching is related to the needs and educational level of the students.

Once we have explicated teaching goals in operational terms, and have designed the most effective methods to help the student achieve these goals, we must test the effectiveness of learning experiences by requiring that the student demonstrate how much he has truly mastered. Reliable methods of recording and measuring performance are needed here. This should be more than a matter of clinical impressions, for, as McGuire (1964) has pointed out, these "are no more acceptable in a scientific study of the educational efficacy of a training program than they are in a scientific appraisal of the therapeutic efficacy of a new drug." The crucial obstruction is, of course, our relatively undeveloped methods of evaluation. In psychotherapy, where the clinical data may be interpreted in endless ways and where criteria of competence are so vague, evaluation techniques are still more pedantic than they are precise. Yet we must agree that, however tenuous they may seem, measures of competence must be constructed to require students to demonstrate that they can perform in a desired way. Both the continuous case conference and supervision offer a means of approaching the thorny problem of evaluation. Important leads may perhaps be taken from the study of the evaluation of the teaching of psychiatry at the undergraduate level in the film test series developed at the University of Rochester, the University of Nebraska, and the University of Pittsburgh. At the postgraduate level a number of interview films have been developed—for instance, those at Temple University Medical School, which may be utilized to test clinical judgment and problem-solving skills and which can be adapted to the evaluation of different training programs.

In the field of psychotherapy several notable efforts have been made to identify the factors essential for the teaching and learning of psychotherapy and particularly psychoanalysis. One outstanding investigation is recorded in the publication by Ekstein and Wallerstein (1958). An interesting pilot study on supervision of the analytic therapeutic process was also reported by Fleming (1963) and Fleming and Benedek (1964) utilizing electrically recorded sessions of students with patients and with their supervisors. With such data it was possible for other supervisors to listen to records or to read the transcripts. Evolving from this, a project was organized by Fleming and Benedek (1966) to investigate "the processes of interaction between communicating systems in the teaching-learning relationship" that involved the triadic dimensions of supervisor, student-analyst, and patient. The similarity of the analytic and supervisory situations were found to be

striking. "When we tried to follow the communications between analyst and patient and between student and teacher, what stood out in great clarity were the phenomena of process—that is, the sequential series of actions linked in a continuing pattern of shifting balances of tensions moving toward a goal-directed change."

A model of supervisory activity was constructed around the overall *aims* (to promote the student's psychoanalysis of the patient and to objectify the learning), the *pedagogical diagnosis* (the student's rapport with the patient, the understanding of the material, the technique of communication with the patient, and the rapport with the supervisor), and the *teaching targets* (the dynamics of the patient, the dynamics of transference, general and special techniques, and general and special theory). The supervisory function was conceived of as dealing with all of these factors—i.e., (1) assisting the student in his or her aims while helping the student to develop as an "analytic instrument"; (2) making a pedagogical diagnosis of the learning problem, and particularly noting the student's capacities for (a) maintaining a therapeutic alliance, (b) employing empathic understanding, (c) self-observation, (d) communication with his or her own preconscious motivations, (e) cogent understanding regarding the intrapsychic obstacles to working as an analyst, and (f) awareness of responses to the supervisor that promote or retard learning; and, finally, (3) orienting the student to the teaching targets by pointing out the effect of one's behavior on the patient, one's motivations for a given behavior and one's relationship with the supervisor.

Assessment of the student brought into play a complicated network of motivations in the supervisor, for instance, the preconceived expectations of a student, the supervisor's own investment in teaching, and the defensive reactions to a student's resistances. "Our experience demonstrated again and again the necessity for a supervisor to listen to and evaluate himself in interaction with his student; and it is our opinion that the more aware a supervisor is of the various aspects of his educational role, the more effective he will be as an object for identificatory learning and as a developer of students in general.''

In making an ''educational diagnosis,'' what must be considered, according to Fleming and Benedek (1966), are the aptitude for analytic work and the amount of experience the student 'has had which should be weighed against the level of theoretical learning the student has achieved. This will help select the appropriate teaching target as well as the best educational techniques.

Supervisory teaching tactics include the following:

1. Calling the student's attention to a gap in his or her understanding of the patient.
2. Confronting the student with his or her countertransference or mistakes in technique.
3. Demonstrating the student's analytic work habits.
4. Prescribing the appropriate remedies.

These tactics are based on a fundamental strategy of teaching that embraces the following assumptions:

1. Teaching-learning is similar to psychoanalytic process, requiring diagnosis, interpretation, and the working through of resistance by both student and teacher.
2. The supervisory process moves through many short-term tasks in orderly progression toward the long-range goal of making the student an accomplished analytic instrument.
3. The self-analytic faculties of the student in relation to patients are developed without attempting to analyze the student's personal conflicts.

As the treatment process progresses through various phases, including the transference neurosis and working through to termination, new problems confront the student, and novel teaching paradoxes impose themselves. In the main, three phases—the initial, middle, and terminal—occur in teaching and learning and introduce three coresponding groups of objectives. During the initial phase the basic ob-

jectives are (1) the ability ''to learn to listen with free-floating attention'' to the patient's verbal, paralinguistic and nonverbal communications; (2) to learn and to perceive the meaning of the patient's behavior (diagnostic interpretations) through introspection, which will not yet be communicated to the patient; (3) to learn to estimate the patient's level of anxiety and resistance, which are, of course, reflective of the student's capacity for empathy with the affective and regressive state of the patient; and (4) to learn to respond with proper and timed interpretations. During the middle phase of analysis, when regression and transference come about with their contingent primitive affects and resistances, the ability to detect and to interpret such phenomena constitutes a primary learning task. It is during this phase that the student's cognitive understanding and emotional stability are put to the firmest test. Awareness of transference and countertransference, identification of their genetic sources, the existence and nature of conflict and defense, and the capacity to interpret these accurately to the patient and to oneself concern the student. Coordinate with the supervisor's efforts, self-analytic functions in the student are encouraged in order to free interpretation from its binds in character resistances or neurosis.

In psychoanalysis the dealing with transference and regression will constitute a bulk of the analytic work. Learning problems referable to these areas include the following:

1. The student's inability to recognize transference and its many manifestations, such as defenses that take a form in opposition to a principal affect and serve as a means of neutralizing it.
2. Regression to an earlier defensive conflict-free position.
3. Regression to a shift in conflict from the chief transference figure to another person to minimize anxiety.
4. Arousal of screen memories.
5. Erotizations of transference.
6. The employment of transference as resistance.

Complicating these cognitive blind spots are countertransference reactions of the student toward the patient induced by such factors as (1) identification of the patient with a transference object in the student's past, (2) overidentification with the patient's transference expectations, (3) repetition of defensive character attitudes, and (4) defenses against the patient's affect, regression, transference expectations, and identification. Superimposed on these phenomena are the student's transference reactions to the supervisor.

As the student learns to deal with the changing resistances and the protean forms of the transference neurosis, a working through of the neurosis toward the termination of analysis comes into focus. New learning problems will be encountered here conditioned by the evolvement of many subtle resistances. The confidence of the student may be taxed by retrogressions in treatment progress, stubborn refusal by the patient to implement insight toward change, and the requirement of reworking the material in what seems like an endless chore. The supervisor helps the student manage the patient's and his or her own resistances to termination, by enabling the student to recognize signs of progress in patients and the obstructions erected to leaving the protective wing of the supervisor.

The data from studies of supervision of the psychoanalytic process require a reconciliation with treatment situations of greater activity and more limited goals, as in the supportive and reeducational therapies.

FUNCTIONS OF SUPERVISION

The traditional type of supervision, unfortunately, has become so contaminated with overseeing, directorial, and inspective functions that it has frequently been diverted from its teaching objective. This has particularly been the case in agency work, where the supervisor, as part of the administrative body, is responsible for the quality of service rendered to clients. Many difficulties arise here because the supervisor serves in a dual role—as an overseer and a teacher (Eisenstein, S. 1972).

As overseer, the supervisor may be so concerned with maintaining the standards of the agency that he or she may not be able to exercise the kind of tolerance and patience required in a teacher. For instance, under press of responsibility, the supervisor is likely to "jump in" and interfere with the treatment plan set up by the supervisee, the execution of which, while perhaps less expert than a plan devised by the supervisor, would prove of greatest learning value to the supervisee. Because the student's status is dependent on evaluations by the supervisor, the process of supervision in agencies is apt to become extremely trying. This is less frequently the case in psychotherapeutic supervision, although a parallel situation does develop where the supervisee is in training at a psychotherapeutic or psychoanalytic school and one's career is dependent on the evaluation by one's supervisor. Similarly, where the supervisee is a staff member of a clinic, the supervisor as part of the administration may subordinate the teaching role to a meticulous concern with the total case load. This shift in emphasis cannot help but influence adversely the quality of training received; this is inevitable whenever the training is oriented around circumscribed goals set up in relation to specific kinds of service for which the clinic is responsible. Much less complicated is the supervision of the psychotherapist in private practice, who chooses a supervisor principally to expand technical skills, not being dependent on the supervisor of an evaluation that may destroy his or her career or eliminate the means of livelihood.

In instances where attached to a school or clinic, the supervisor will usually operate as a teacher, an evaluator, an administrator, and a policymaker.

Teaching

The first responsibility of the supervisor is observation of the total functioning of the therapist in order to help in the supervisee's educational growth. Toward this end, it may be essential to bring the supervisee to an awareness of how he or she fails to live up to therapeutic potentialities, either because of insufficient knowledge or because of neurotic character problems that inject themselves into the psychotherapeutic relationship. It is incumbent on the supervisor, among other things, to help the supervisee (1) to gain knowledge that is lacking, (2) to achieve an awareness of the student's own character problems that may interfere with the establishment and maintenance of a therapeutic relationship, and (3) to overcome resistances to learning.

Evaluating

A second responsibility of the supervisor is an evaluation of the capacities and progress of the supervisee for the purposes of determining professional development and current skills as a therapist. Evaluation involves a number of areas including theoretic understanding, therapeutic aptitudes, and the kinds of relationships that are established with patients and the supervisor.

Administration and Policy Making

The third responsibility of the supervisor lies in the administration and policy of the school or clinic under whose aegis the program is being conducted. The supervisor here recommends modifications of the therapeutic and teaching programs in order to accomplish a better cooperation between the therapist and the agency. The supervisor helps also in an analysis of administrative, intake, and pedagogic policies that may influence adversely the training and the work of the therapist as well as the patient's responses to treatment.

To summarize, supervision in psychotherapy is fundamentally a teaching process in which a more experienced participant, the supervisor, observes the work of the less experienced participant, the supervisee, with the aim of helping the supervisee acquire certain essential therapeutic skills through better understanding of the dynamics involved in mental illness and through resolution of personality factors that block performance of effective psychotherapy. Supervision embraces a sharing of experiences: not only those gathered in the relations between therapist and patient, but also those occurring in the relationship between the supervisor and supervisee.

Qualifications of a good supervisor are the following:

1. Ability to function expertly as a psychotherapist.
2. Ability to function effectively as a teacher.
3. Ability to accept the supervisee unconditionally, without contempt, hostility, possessiveness, and other unwarranted attitudes and feelings.

Supervisory problems may roughly be divided into five categories: problems in orientation, problems in recording, problems in technical performance, problems in learning, and problems in termination of supervision.

PROBLEMS IN ORIENTATION

Differences in Theoretic Orientation

Important and often irreconcilable differences occur in the theoretic background and orientation of the supervisor and the therapist who is being supervised, a product usually of varying kinds of preclinical training. Illustrative of such differences are the following:

1. The relative weight to be placed on constitutional as compared with experiential factors in the genesis of neurosis.
2. The importance of biologic as contrasted with sociologic factors.
3. The respective emphasis on past childhood experiences and on current environmental hardships.
4. The degree of stress placed on unconscious conflict as the focus of neurotic difficulties.
5. The extent of acceptance of the Oedipus complex, castration fears, and penis envy as universal phenomena.
6. The primacy of sexual over other drives.

7. The significance of character structure in creating and sustaining neurotic disturbance.

8. The relative emphasis of conditioning theory in accounting for anxiety.

The most effective supervisor is one who respects the right of therapists to their own ideas and opinions, yet who has a broad dynamic orientation, discussed in earlier sections of this book, along the following lines:

1. Emotional difficulties are sponsored by a variety of conflicts operating on different levels of awareness.

2. The most intense conflicts originate in early childhood, issuing from unfavorable experiences with and conditionings by important authoritative personages, particularly the parents.

3. Resultant are blocks in psychosocial development and distortions in the character structure with impairment of the individual's capacity for adaptation.

4. Disturbances in interpersonal relationships and in the expression of basic biologic and social needs inspire threats to mastery and expectations of injury that, in turn, alter the individual's emotional homeostasis and provoke anxiety.

5. Some symptoms of neurosis consist of manifestations of anxiety, as well as defenses against anxiety and its causative conflicts. Other symptoms are learned responses bearing only an indirect relationship to inner conflict.

A dynamic formulation of the treatment of neurosis, agreed on by supervisor and therapist, would conceive of therapy as taking place in a unique relationship that is established between the therapist and the patient. This relationship serves as a corrective experience for the patient, restoring his shattered sense of mastery to a point where he can deal effectively with his inner tensions, as well as with the demands of the outside world. The relationship supports the patient in the vicissitudes that he undergoes while gaining an understanding of the conflictual sources of his difficulty and reconditioning his responses to the demands of

present-day reality. It helps him to reevaluate himself and to discard some of his archaic fears, attitudes, and patterns of behavior, substituting for them strivings that enable him to relate congenially to life and people. Finally, through the resolution of developmental blocks, it enables him to achieve an optimal level of emotional growth and personality maturity.

Formulations such as these will provide considerable latitude for the merging of the views of both supervisor and supervisee.

Differences in Communication

Since communication is the basis of the supervisory relationship, it is important that verbalizations and concepts be understood by both supervisor and supervisee. Assuming that there are no important language differences, problems in communication are usually related to differences in terminology.

One of the most poignant objections to psychiatry voiced by scientists in other fields is that it is so partial to neologisms. The worst offenders in this direction are followers of the Freudian and Meyerian schools and, to a lesser extent, those of the Rank, Horney, and Sullivan schools. Tendencies to utilize neologisms and complex language forms have acted as one of the strongest barriers toward a rapprochement of the varying orientations.

Both supervisor and supervisee may be vitimized by an esoteric terminology. Translation of complex language forms into concepts with which both participants are conversant is vital to a mutual understanding and to the establishment of a common frame of reference.

Differences in Method

Another problem in supervision relates to differences in method; that practiced by the supervisor and that accepted or practiced by the supervisee. Such differences may involve various matters, such as the most desirable number of treatment sessions per week, whether or not to employ routine history taking and psychologic workups, the use of free association, the emphasis on dream material and the manner of its employment, the use of the couch, the degree of activity in the interview, the extent to which a transference neurosis is permitted to develop, and the adjuncts to be utilized during therapy. Resolution of serious differences in method is to be expected in the course of good supervision.

Considerable flexibility will be required in methodologic approaches, particularly where the therapist is expected to handle, in the practice for which he or she is being trained, a wide assortment of clinical problems. Supportive of the principle of technical eclecticism is the fact that no single approach is applicable to all types of emotional difficulties. Some problems seem to respond better to certain kinds of therapeutic intervention than to others.

Differences in Goals

Problems may arise between supervisee and supervisor on the basis of varying concepts of what makes for success in psychotherapy. Is success in therapy the achievement of complete resolution of all blocks in personality maturation with effective functioning in all areas of living? Or is success to be graded in terms of optimal development within the practical limitations imposed on the individual by his existing motivations, his ego strength, and environmental pressures from which he cannot reasonably escape?

While the therapist has a responsibility to the patient in bringing him to the most extensive personality reconstruction possible, the therapist must realize that many circumstances may interfere with extensive goal achievement. A modified treatment objective may be the only possible alternative, at least temporarily. However, a therapist, having been trained in the tradition that any therapeutic change falling short of complete reconstruction is spurious, may look askance at the supervisor who considers goals in terms of optimal functioning within the limitations of the reality situation. Or the supervisor may be unwilling to accept goal

modification and may regard with contempt changes that fall short of absolute psychosocial maturity with complete performance in all areas of living.

PROBLEMS IN RECORDING AND REPORTING

Data on functioning are supplied by the therapist's reporting of activities with patients. Careful listening to the content of the report, to the manner of reporting, to the evasions and points of emphasis, to slips of speech, and to casual off-the-record references to feelings about patients help the supervisor to evaluate the therapeutic work of the therapist.

In making this appraisal, it is important to remember that the role the therapist plays with the supervisor and his or her attitudes toward the supervisor are no reliable index of what the therapist does with patients. For with patients one is operating in an entirely different setting than with the supervisor, with whom one is in a more subordinate status—more vulnerable, and more capable of being challenged or criticized. One may respond to the supervisor with fear, detachment, resentment, and other character patterns related to one's feelings about authority. Therefore, it will not be possible to communicate to the supervisor the capacity to be spontaneous, empathic, and responsive, which may be shown in the relatively secure atmosphere in which one operates with patients. The supervisee's activity in the supervisory session may be contaminated by defenses against the supervisor, and the struggle with the supervisor may reflect itself in the content of the report.

For instance, one therapist presented material to her supervisor in a cocky, superior manner, containing a somewhat contemptuous attitude toward the patient about whom she talked. It soon became obvious to the supervisor, however, in listening to tape recordings of actual treatment sessions, that hostile feelings were not manifest in the therapist's responses nor in her manner of their presentation. A further inquiry revealed that hostility, marshalled by transference feelings toward the supervisor, was seeping into the supervisory session and was influencing the nature of the reporting.

Neurotic feelings toward the supervisor may thus distort the therapist's presentation of material. Pertinent data may be deleted, irrelevant items may be introduced, and secondary elaboration may destroy totally, or in part, the value of the presentation. Fear of exposing deficiencies, of appearing ridiculous, of incurring the displeasure and contempt of the supervisor are among the more common causes of poor reporting.

Some of the difficulties in reporting may be obviated by insisting on process recording in which there is a verbatim account of both the patient's and the therapist's verbalizations. Process recording has the advantage of presenting a reasonably cogent picture of what is going on, since the tendency toward distortion or deletion will be minimized. However, there are certain objections to this method, in that the therapist may be unable to record simultaneously while doing good therapy or because the patient protests that he is unable to make good contact with someone immersed in writing. Furthermore, no matter how careful is the attempt to record, the student will be unable to include everything that is said. There will then be a tendency to curtail the material, consciously or unconsciously eliminating elements that cause him to feel that he is revealing himself unfavorably. In intensive supervision, in which one case is being presented over a long period of time, the supervisor may, nevertheless, have to insist on process recording until convinced of the therapist's ability to report correctly in a more abbreviated way. (See Appendix K for a case outline.)

Perhaps the most effective type of recording is done with a video machine. As such machines are improved and become less expensive, we may predict that they will be indispensable items of equipment, not only for supervision, but also for playback to the patient who observes and listens to himself communicating (Geocaris, 1960). Video recording will also be helpful for playback to the therapist who may learn as much by self-observation as from the supervisor (Moore et al, 1965; Beiser, 1966). Moreover, the supervisor may profit from observing himself in supervisory operation. Audio recordings on tape are cheaper, but less effective. However, for purposes of record keeping and for later transcription audiotapes are sufficient. Few patients object to the use of machine recorders, and once the fears about revealing oneself have been overcome, the therapist can function freely.

The value of video recording cannot be overestimated. One has a most factual picture of what has actually gone on in the session, not only in content, but also in revealing bodily movements of which the therapist is unaware and intonations and subvocal utterances that cannot be communicated in written types of recording. The method enables the supervisor to observe aspects of the interviewing process that are handled well or poorly. It helps to understand how the different kinds of content are dealt with, whether the therapist exaggerates, minimizes, or negates the importance of certain types of material. It permits of observation of how the therapist responds to unreasonable demands of the patient, to hostilities and other transference attitudes that are developing in the relationship. It enables the supervisor to study techniques in interviewing, the handling of dream material, and skill in interpretation in terms of timing and presentation. The difference between the written or verbal account and what actually went on, which is revealed in observing and listening to a playback, is often so astonishing as to leave little question about the value of this kind of recording.

For instance, one therapist's verbal account made no mention of hostile feelings in the patient, to which the therapist was responding by shifting the topic of discussion and by complacent, reassuring utterances whenever the patient introduced a slightly antagonistic remark. The therapist was totally unaware of his responses, but in the playback he could not escape what had happened. Another therapist reported a progressively deepening depression in a borderline patient. The process recording related that the patient talked incessantly about how she had been neglected, particularly by a mother preoccupied with outside activities and a detached father. The therapist, in her recorded responses, appeared to be saying the right things. A session of the therapist working with the patient, which was recorded on videotape, however, demonstrated that the therapist had placed her chair so that she was not facing the patient; was in effect detaching herself from her and repeating a childish trauma. Correction of this position, with the closer interaction that the face-to-face placement encouraged, rapidly brought the patient out of her depression and accelerated her progress.

The advantage of watching the student performing with patients behind a oneway mirror and of recording the session on videotape so that it may be played back for the student is incalculable since immediate feedback is possible. Parenthetically, a session in which the supervisor treats a patient, observed by the student through a oneway mirror or by watching a video recording is helpful in pointing out techniques that are difficult to describe verbally. Understandably, it will be impossible to utilize recordings at every supervisory session due to lack of time. Several recorded sessions presented during each 6 months of supervision will usually suffice to measure the therapist's progress, and in themselves will justify the use of the video machine. A unique device described by Boylston and Tuma (1972) is "bug in the ear," a receiver placed in the therapist's ear through which a supervisor gives instructions via a transmitter from behind a oneway-mirror.

From the standpoint of research, recordings, videotapes, or sound film recordings of interviews permit the researcher to approach the problems of both process and outcome evaluation with greater objectivity (Kubie, 1950b; Strupp, 1960; Davidman, 1964).

While the student's written notes and observations about therapeutic work are valuable (Beckett, 1969; Bush, 1969; Moulton, 1969), they are rendered more significant by studying the inclusions, omissions, and exaggerations in video recordings of the same sessions. As Schlessinger (1966) points out, we are dealing with different kinds of data in both types of recording, each of which has a different potential for teaching but which are by no means mutually exclusive.

Recently computer programs have been made available that have been found useful by some therapists, for example, Harless's Computer-assisted Simulation of the Clinical Encounter (Harless, 1971, 1972), which deals with diagnostic problem solving. Elaborations of this computer-assisted instruction involving typical psychotherapeutic situations will probably have a significant impact on some students since, as Hubbard and Templeton (1973) have pointed out, they can expose the student to a wide variety of clinical problems, provide modes of practice and diagnostic skills in a nontraumatic setting, and permit early feedback by a consensus of experts in the field. The authors predict, because of such technology instruction, a different role for teachers is possible, namely "the management of educational resources: planning educational programs, organizing and implementing the curriculum, staying abreast of national activities, participating in the national development of and sharing of instructional materials, and designing and implementing the intramural evaluation program." Helfer and Hess (1970) and Lomax (1972) have published interesting material on related new trends in teaching.

PROBLEMS IN TECHNICAL PERFORMANCE

The supervisee will experience trouble in various areas in the process of doing psychotherapy. These difficulties are the consequence either of lack of understanding, experience and skill, or of countertransference. They will have to be handled by the supervisor in relation to their origin and function. Most common are the following problems:

1. Difficulties in the conduct of the initial interview.
2. Inability to deal with inadequate motivation.

3. Inability to clarify for the patient misconceptions about psychotherapy.
4. Inability to extend warmth and support to the patient or to establish an initial contact with him.
5. Inability to define for the patient goals in therapy.
6. Inability to structure the therapeutic situation adequately for the patient.
7. Inability to recognize and to handle manifestations of transference in the therapeutic relationship; specifically, dependence, sexual feelings, detachment, hostility, and aggression.
8. Lack of knowledge of how to explore and to bring to awareness conflicts that mobilize anxiety in the patient (in insight therapy).
9. Lack of sensitivity and perceptiveness to what is going on in therapy.
10. Lack of technical skill in the implementation of free association, dream interpretation, and analysis of the transference (in insight therapy).
11. Inability to deal with resistances in the patient toward verbal exploration of his problems.
12. Tendencies to avoid problems of the patient that inspire anxiety in the therapist.
13. Tendency to probe too deeply and too rapidly at the start.
14. Impatience with resistances toward the acquisition of insight (in insight therapy).
15. Faulty techniques of presenting interpretations.
16. Frustration and discouragement at the patient's refusal to utilize insight in the direction of change.
17. Tendency to push the patient too hard or too rapidly toward normal objectives.
18. Fear of being too directive with resultant excessive passivity.
19. Lack of understanding of how to create incentives for change.
20. Lack of understanding in dealing with forces that block action.
21. Lack of understanding of how to help the patient master anxieties surrounding normal life goals.
22. Inability to scale down therapeutic goals when modification of objectives is mandatory.
23. Lack of understanding of how to implement the translation of insight and understanding into action.
24. Inability to deal with resistance toward abandoning primary and secondary neurotic aims.
25. Inability to deal with resistance toward normality.
26. Inability to deal with resistance in the patient toward activity through his own resources.
27. Tendencies to overprotect or to domineer the patient.
28. Inability to assume a nondirective therapeutic role.
29. Lack of understanding of how to deal with the refusal on the part of the patient to yield his dependency.
30. Lack of understanding of how to handle the patient's fear of assertiveness.
31. Lack of understanding of how to analyze dependency elements in the therapist–patient relationship.
32. Lack of understanding of how to terminate therapy.

In observing functioning, the supervisor must exercise great tolerance for the specific style of activity of the therapist. He must remember that irrespective of training and exposure to specific schools of psychiatric thinking, basic personality patterns of the therapist will infiltrate into the treatment situation and cannot help but influence the techniques that are learned. Some modification of techniques will always occur, particularly of those that do not coordinate with the therapist's personality structure. The therapist will probably never be able to duplicate the exact style of the supervisor, nor vice versa, since they are two different people and relate to patients in their own unique ways. Yet certain basic principles in psychotherapy must not be violated, no matter what kinds of relationships one establishes and what types of techniques one employs. By defining the broad bounds of psychotherapy, and by elucidating on the fundamental principles to which every therapist must adhere, the supervisor may help the supervisee perfect skills, yet maintain spontaneity, which is a most cherished characteristic in the psychotherapist.

PROBLEMS IN LEARNING

A number of propositions are involved in the learning of psychotherapy that may be expressed as follows:

1. All learning necessitates a ˙substitution of new patterns for old. This requires a working through of blocks that constantly invest the acquisition of new patterns. Sometimes the struggle is a minimal one; sometimes it is intense.

2. The manner in which learning proceeds is unique for the individual both in relationship to the rate of learning, and the methods by which material is absorbed and integrated. Some persons learn by leaps and bounds, others by cautious precarious crawling. Many variants expedite or interfere with learning in different people. What is taught an individual has to be accepted by him in his own terms.

3. Learning involves both an understanding of theory as well as its integration and translation into effective action. The responsibility for understanding theory is vested in the instructors and teachers with whom the therapist has had preclinical training. The responsibility for execution of theory into practice is vested in the therapist.

4. Little learning is possible without a motivation to learn. This motivation must be sufficiently intense to overcome the difficulties that inevitably envelop all learning. It is assumed that the therapist has sufficient motivation—in terms of a desire to be a psychotherapist—to expose himself or herself to the ordeals of the learning process.

5. Anxiety is present in all learning. Its sources are related to fear of change and the desire to cling to familiar patterns as well as to resistance in altering basic accepted attitudes and behavior tendencies.

6. Resistances to learning are present in all people in response to anxiety. The kind and the degree of resistance will vary with the individual. Most common are lack of attention, lack of retention, amnesia, and simulated stupidity. In addition, resistance may take the form of patterns of dependence, submissiveness, self-depreciation, ingratiation, arrogance, grandiosity, resentment, aggression, and detachment. These are products of specific neurotic character problems; but there may be a universality of expression of such trends in certain cultures, reflecting accepted attitudes toward education and toward the authorities that are responsible for education.

7. Resistances to learning must be overcome before learning can proceed. The attitudes of the supervisor are crucial here. His tolerance, flexibility, and capacity to extend warmth, support and acceptance toward the therapist, irrespective of the errors that the latter makes, promotes the most effective medium for the handling of resistance.

8. Learning is thus facilitated by a warm working relationship between supervisor and therapist. It is impeded by hostility that develops in this relationship. A primary focus, then, in the supervisory process is the existing relationship between student and teacher, with thorough ventilation of negative feelings before these exert a corrosive influence on the learning process. The therapist must be encouraged to express disagreements, criticisms, or feelings in relation to the supervisor. In turn, the therapist must be able also to accept criticism, and this will be possible where there is good rapport with the supervisor.

9. As a general rule, learning blocks are resolved during the first few months of supervision. An inability to master such blocks after several months indicates a severe problem that necessitates incisive investigation.

10. In learning, the therapist has a backlog of past experiences on which to build. One cannot be expected to progress any faster than would be warranted by the degree of this experience, no matter how hard the supervisor may push. As a matter of fact, too severe demands will be of greater hindrance than of help.

11. As a rule, in the early stages of learning the therapist will feel resentful, unsure, and certain of failure. He or she will want to be told how to function; indeed, will

demand that the supervisor demonstrate exactly what to do. The supervisor must accept the dependency and yet treat the therapist as an equal. The setting of supervision is best permissive, the therapist being given the feeling that one is free to act, experiment, and make mistakes. Emphasis is on the sharing of experiences and responsibilities.

12. Learning is a tedious process enhanced by the active participation of one in one's own growth. It is facilitated also by selected cases that serve a specific purpose in filling in gaps in the therapist's experience, as well as by assigned reading and by recommended courses. At all times, critical thinking is to be encouraged, even at the expense of inflicting narcissistic slights on the supervisor.

13. Learning is more an educational than a therapeutic process, and the focus in psychotherapy is on a therapist's work rather than problems. It is essential that the therapist be treated as an adult, and not as a problem child.

14. Learning is expedited by successes, and it is impaired by failures. Provision should be made for some successes that will reinforce learning. Where the therapist encounters repeated failures, damage will be done to the learning process.

PROBLEMS IN TERMINATION OF SUPERVISION

The relationship that a therapist establishes with the supervisor will, in general, proceed through various phases, including the establishing of rapport with the supervisor, the understanding of problems that occur in relationship to the supervisor, the translation of this understanding into corrective action, and, finally, the ending phase in which a therapist develops the capacity to carry on, on his or her own, the working through of the dependence on the supervisor.

Where the supervisor has an authoritarian personality structure, it may be difficult to operate on equal terms with the therapist. The supervisor will want to continue to make decisions, to utter judgments, and to

offer interpretations, consciously or unconsciously resenting the therapist's right to self-determination. Under these circumstances the ending of supervision may impose great hardships on both supervisor and therapist.

On the other hand, the greater the dependency needs in the therapist, the more difficult it will be to countenance termination. An inability to resolve dependence on the supervisor indicates a severe characterologic problem for which the therapist may require further therapeutic help.

During the terminal phases of supervision the supervisor, in anticipation of the trauma of separation, may assume a nondirective role, insisting that the therapist be active and figure things out entirely alone. One may expect that the therapist will respond to such nondirectiveness with anxiety and hostility and that there will be an attempt to force the supervisor to abandon this role. If the supervisor is persistent, however, justifying the passivity displayed on the basis of a respect for the therapist's growth process, the therapist will eventually be convinced of the rationale of the supervisor's behavior.

TECHNICAL DETAILS OF SUPERVISION

Preclinical Training of the Therapist

Before supervision begins, the supervisor will desire information about the preclinical training of the prospective supervisee. Questions that may arise include these: Is the theoretic background of the supervisee adequate for functioning in psychotherapeutic practice? Have the required courses been taken and the essential reading done? Has this theoretic material been integrated satisfactorily? Does the supervisee have the personality qualities that will make for a good therapist? How profound an understanding does the supervisee have of his or her own emotional and interpersonal processes? Will the supervisee be able to resolve or to control the expression of hostility, detachment, sexual interest, overprotection, rejection, and other strivings that will be inimical to the psychotherapeutic relationship? Can we reasonably assume that the supervisee is sufficiently adjusted to life now, so that he or she will not use the therapeutic situation and the experiences of the patient to live through vicariously certain frustrated ambitions, dependencies and hostilities? Does the supervisee have a capacity to empathize with people, to feel and to communicate warmth to them? Is there the capacity to be resolute and firm on occasion, capable of insisting on certain essential actions during the therapeutic process? How much experience has the supervisee had in doing psychotherapy? What kinds of cases have been treated and with what results? Has there been previous supervision, and if so, with whom and for how long? Does the supervisee believe such supervision has been beneficial?

There is general agreement that the prospective psychotherapist requires an extensive amount of preclinical training. A review of training that is being given in most of the recognized schools reveals a close similarity in prescribed courses and requirements. These include the following:

1. Courses in basic neuropsychiatry, normal psychosocial development, psychopathology, psychodynamics, techniques of interviewing, techniques of psychotherapy, dream interpretation, child psychiatry, group psychotherapy, and behavior modifications.
2. Clinical conferences and continuous case seminars that have been attended regularly.
3. Readings in psychiatric literature of sufficient scope to provide the student with a good background in history, theory, and practice.
4. Ideally, enough personal psychotherapy or psychoanalysis to provide the student, first, with an opportunity to study psychodynamics, through self-observation by observing his or her own emotional conflicts, their genesis and their projection into present-day functioning; and, second, to liberate the student from personal problems and character

disturbances that interfere with the establishment and maintenance of a therapeutic interpersonal relationship.

Should the supervisee be lacking in any of these basic requirements, the supervisor must help find ways of making up these deficiencies. (See Appendix L, for a form that supplies the supervisor with essential information.)

The Beginning Stages of Supervision

The first contact of the supervisor with the therapist is in the nature of an exploratory talk. At this time there may be a discussion of the therapist's preclinical training, and arrangements may be made as to the hours, frequency of visits, and the method of recording and presentation. The therapist may be given preliminary orientation as to what will be involved in supervision and how supervisory sessions may best be utilized. Arrangements may furthermore be made for the handling with the supervisor of any emergency situations that may occur during the course of supervision.

In the early months of supervision a period of disillusionment is to be anticipated. The therapist will be brought face to face with practical problems in implementing therapy which may be at variance with what has been learned from books. Student-therapists often are upset by the fact that the specific kinds of problems that provoke their patients may be precisely those that are disturbing to themselves. They may be exposed to certain situations that develop in treatment with a violent impact, that tax their own capacities for adjustment. It is incumbent on the supervisor to extend to the therapist, during this period, a good deal of warmth and understanding. The primary focus in early supervision is the relationship between supervisor and supervisee, since little progress will be possible until good rapport exists.

Later Phases of Supervision

In supervision the supervisor seeks to ascertain whether or not the therapist is living up to his or her potentialities. If not, the sources of this lack must be diagnosed. For instance, the problem may relate to deficiencies in the kind of preclinical training received, or in the assimilation of educational materials presented in training. It may be due to an absence of perceptiveness or to insensitivity about what is going on in the therapeutic situation. It may be the product of personality problems that prevent the therapist from establishing a meaningful contact with the patient.

The areas in which the therapist needs help most will soon become apparent. In the main technical problems break down into difficulties in diagnosis, the conduct of the initial interview, the use of interviewing techniques, the understanding of the operative dynamics, the use of dreams, the detection and handling of transference, the awareness and mastery of countertransference, the dealing with resistance, the use of interpretations, and the termination of therapy.

The task of the supervisor here is not to tell the therapist what to do, but rather to teach him how to think through solutions for himself. Toward this end, it will be essential to ask questions and to structure problems so that the therapist can come to his own conclusions. Learning problems are to be diagnosed and handled along lines indicated previously. Modes of improving sensitivity are described by Fielding and Mogul (1970).

In the course of supervision, the therapist is bound to show transference manifestations. The supervisor will also have emotional attitudes toward the therapist. Both positive and negative feelings will have to be subjected to close scrutiny in order to permit of the development of the proper kind of empathic yet objective attitudes. Furthermore, the supervisor will have to maintain a certain amount of tension in the supervisory sessions to expedite activity.

The beginning supervisor, particularly, may respond to supervision with untoward feelings. There may be a tendency to be pompous and overbearing and to overwhelm supervisees with material. One is apt to feel irritable when a supervisee does not learn rapidly, when the student defies suggestions and criticisms, even though

these are offered in a constructive way. One may be provoked when there is persistence in errors that are so obvious that they scarcely need identification. Such attitudes on the part of the supervisor will, of course, interfere with learning. An honest search for feelings within oneself will often reveal tendencies that stifle the development of the supervisee. It must be emphasized again that countertransference is always present and that it need not be destructive to the teaching objective, provided that the supervisor is capable of understanding his feelings and of modifying and correcting them before they get out of control.

Disagreements between supervisor and therapist are inevitable, even desirable. All learning inspires resistance. The therapist will voice protests in changing habitual patterns. He is bound to be critical. Actually, he cannot change unless he is given an opportunity to voice and to work through his criticisms. The supervisor may be offended by the reactions of the therapist who presumably challenges his judgment with little provocation. The supervisor will best be able to respect the therapist's right to his own opinions when he realizes the unavoidable learning struggle that is involved.

Essential for learning is an open mind to new ideas. Some students have already settled their opinions about psychological theory and process and seal themselves off from fresh points of view. What they seek from the supervisor is a confirmation of their frozen ideologies. Similarly, there are supervisors so rigidly wedded to their credos that they insist on their students becoming a mirror image of themselves. Vital for learning in the supervisory process then is a therapist and supervisor who are both willing to collaborate, to share experiences, and, if necessary, to change. The student must be able to countenance exposure of deficiencies in psychotherapeutic performance. The supervisor must be able constructively to bring the student to an awareness of these deficiencies and to provide the student with an appropriate means of rectifying them.

Illustrative of some of the problems are the following comments of a supervisor:

I have a supervisee who is a chatterbox and who is highly defensive about any comment I make—even a casual comment on the dynamics is interpreted as a criticism of her. Her defense is to interrupt, challenge me, justify herself, etc., without permitting me to finish what I have to say. Often, by the end of the session, I find that I have been able to tell her very little. I have been debating with myself whether to take up the problem with her directly, which might merely provoke additional defensiveness, to pull back and tell her virtually nothing until she complains about it to me, or to go on as I have but being very supportive until she feels less threatened.

These are the remarks of a student:

The trouble with my supervisor is that he is constantly trying to force his point of view on me. I would think that he would know I can't do things exactly how he does them. I would like to have him help me work better with my good points and to help me eliminate by bad points. When I show him what I believe is a gain in my patient, he usually criticizes it as merely defensive, a new resistance.

In both of these illustrations effective learning is being blocked by problems that are influencing the relationship between student and supervisor. The supervisory encounter is far more complex than that of a simple teaching contingency. It embraces unconscious processes that may require mutual exploration. In any of the social sciences where the individual utilizes himself as an investigative or therapeutic tool, there are bound to be differences in theoretical assumptions and methodological approaches. These differences may interfere with the manner in which the individual communicates himself to other professional persons. Even within the same school, problems in communication may be vast. They are particularly annoying in the psychotherapeutic learning and teaching situation.

The supervisor is constantly involved in a process of self-analysis as he relates himself to the supervisee's productions and personality and as he examines his own reactions, transferential and reality determined. He must realize that his student will be doing therapy with his own personality and not with that of the supervisor. The student may not be able to perform exactly as the supervisor performs, nor will the student be able to deduce from interactions with patients all of the nuances that are apparent to the supervisor. A tremendous amount of tolerance and acceptance will be required from the supervisor that may tax the latter's coping capacities and bring countertransference into play. While the supervisor serves as a model for the student, he must be a flexible model who does not insist upon an exact reduplication of himself in his student. These conditions should readily be acceptable to the individual who possesses the sophistication that qualifies him or her as a supervisor, since he or she will realize from experience that there is no single accurate way of doing therapy. There are many ways. What can be taught is a broad framework of psychotherapy with a buttressing up of those elements of the student's functioning that permit of good therapeutic process, while expurgating elements that interfere with treatment.

"Intensive" versus "Technical" Supervision

In practice, two general types of psychotherapeutic supervision may be defined. The first type, "intensive" supervision, consists of the "continuous-case" type of reporting with a single patient, preferably from the initial interview to termination, utilizing video recordings if possible. This enables the supervisor to help the therapist in all phases of treatment, by observing operations with one patient over a long-term period. "Intensive" supervision is the most effective kind of teaching for beginning therapists.

The second type of supervision, arbitrarily called "technical" supervision, may be further divided into two subtypes. The first, or "case-load" supervision, which is usually prescribed especially for the beginning therapist in a clinic, covers the general progress and specific difficulties being encountered in the entire case load of the therapist. One might consider this a kind of administrative supervision. The second subtype, which we may, for want of a better name, call "special-problem" supervision, is handled in a manner similar to a clinical conference. Any pressing problem in diagnosis, psychodynamics, or technical management may be presented, and the discussion centers around the specific difficulty encountered by the therapist.

The latter kind of supervision is more highly advanced than other types and presupposes more experience on the part of the therapist. It may also be effectively practiced in a group of no more than three or four therapists, who participate in the discussion with the supervisor. Each therapist may be given the privilege of presenting material on successive sessions. In practice, this proves to be a highly provocative teaching device, provided all the supervisees are on approximately the same level.

The Evaluation of the Supervisee

Evaluation is a means of helping the therapist develop skills through a continuous assay of strengths and weaknesses. As such, it becomes part of the teaching method, pointing to areas in which more development is needed and helping in a positive way to promote such development. Criteria of evaluation may be along the following lines:

1. Method of presentation, and recording ability.
2. Theoretic understanding.
3. Diagnostic ability.
4. Integration of theory into practice.
5. General therapeutic aptitudes, sensitivity, empathy, and capacity for critical thinking.
6. Kinds of relationships that the therapist establishes with patients and the skill in handling these relationships.
7. Type of relationship that the therapist has with supervisor and the use the therapist makes of the sessions.
8. Types of relationships that the therapist establishes with colleagues and personnel of the clinic, if any, to which he is attached.
9. Therapist's good points and special skills.
10. Therapist's lacks and deficiencies.

11. General learning ability and the progress that has been made in learning.
12. Positive recommendations for increasing learning, including recommended readings, prescribed courses, and preferred kinds of cases to be assigned to the therapist.

Yardsticks of expected progress have never been set. Arbitrarily, a rough gauge such as the following may be useful to indicate minimal levels of achievement:

End of first six months of supervision: Ability to make diagnoses, ability to keep patients in therapy.
End of first year: Ability to understand dynamics; capacity to establish good rapport with patients.
End of one and one-half years: Recognition of personal problems in therapeutic functioning.
End of second year: Ability to overcome most personal problems in therapeutic functioning.
End of two and one-half years: Ability to function without serious mistakes.
End of three years: Ability to do good psychotherapy.

Evaluation imposes burdens on both supervisor and therapist. The supervisor may not want to criticize out of fear of hurting or offending the therapist. The therapist, in turn, may feel humiliated at having weak points exposed. The manner in which evaluation is presented, and the purpose for which it is used, will largely determine the reactions of the therapist. If the understanding is clear that there will be periodic evaluations, let us say every six months, to point out the areas in which the greatest or least development has been made, the experience can prove to be in the interests of learning.

The evaluation conference may be set up in advance and both therapist and supervisor may prepare their observations for mutual discussion and consideration. At the conference a common understanding must be reached, and if a written evaluation must be sent to the head of a clinic or school, agreement on as many points as possible is best achieved in advance of sending the report. The supervisor may assign certain tasks to the therapist (as a questionnaire) to build self-awareness (Purvis, 1972) or to search for personal life experiences in the past or present that parallel those of his or her patient in order to enhance empathic responsiveness (Kaplowitz, 1967).

The point at which the supervisor certifies the student therapist as competent to do psychotherapy will vary with the kind of therapy for which the student is being prepared. Table 57–1 shows the outline for evaluation for certification at the Postgraduate Center for Mental Health.

Administrative Responsibilities

Where the supervisor and therapist are both associated with a clinic, the supervisor will have further responsibilities. For instance, the supervisor may participate in an analysis of administrative or intake policies, making recommendations of alteration of old or the devising of new policies. The object here is that of eliminating influences that are destructive to the patient's therapy or to the therapist's functioning. If supervision is part of a school training program, the supervisor will also probably be engaged in an analysis of administrative and pedagogic procedures in the program. This will include methods of choice of students, modification of curricula, introduction of new courses, and proposed changes in instructors or instructional methods. Routine meetings among the supervisors, or between supervisors and the supervisory head, will cover discussion of such problems in detail, with the introduction of whatever current difficulties the supervisor is having with supervision and routine evaluations of the progress shown by the different therapists.

SUPERVISION AS AN INTERPERSONAL RELATIONSHIP

The supervisory relationship is one to which the supervisee reacts with mingled attitudes of admiration, jealousy, fear, and hostility. Admiration and jealousy are usu-ally inspired by the supervisor's superior knowledge, training, and status. Fear of the supervisor is often the product of the therapist's helplessness in the face of an authority, who, he feels, may judge him unfairly and destroy his career and livelihood in the event he fails to live up to expectations. Hostility issues from many sources. On the one hand, it is the product of dependency on the supervisor, which is especially inevitable at the beginning of supervision. Dependency yearnings that are mobilized are usually accompanied by convictions that these yearnings will be frustrated. Feelings of being victimized by one's own dependency needs, and the threats imposed by these needs on independence and assertiveness, inspire further resentment. The very acceptance of supervision implies to some therapists a kind of subordination that imposes burdens on adjustment, particularly where independence has become the keynote in the person's life struggle. The therapist, in addition, resents demands that he believes the supervisor makes on him. The restrictions imposed on the therapist, the criticisms directed at his functioning, deliver vital blows to his narcissism and contribute to further fears of loss of self.

Supervision will thus produce feelings in the therapist that are related to neurotic attitudes toward authority. Difficulties in relationships to authority may come out toward the supervisor in the nascent state, in the form of verbalizations or behavioral acting-out. They may also be concealed behind a barrage of defenses which reflect the therapist's habitual patterns in his dealings with authority.

The supervisor, in turn, will respond in supervision with feelings toward the therapist, many of which are the product of neurotic attitudes toward subordinates. He may, in a flush of omnipotence, assume a patronizing attitude toward the therapist, presenting his ideas as if they were irrevocable pronouncements. He may feel contempt for the relatively inferior knowledge, skill or status of the therapist. He may develop hostility toward the therapist when the latter challenges his opinions or theories. He may resent the growth or advance of the therapist, seeking to keep him

Table 57–1
Outline of Evaluation for Certification

Technical Skill	Personality of the Therapist	Direction of Growth and Promise	Supervisor-Supervisee Relationship
1. Diagnostic skill. a. Ability to establish diagnosis and tentative psychodynamics after one or two sessions with the patient. b. After six weeks, the ability to describe the patient's character manifestations and how they will most likely work out in relation to the therapist. c. After six weeks, ability to write an organized case report including diagnosis, psychodynamics and estimate of rate of progress. 2. Treatment planning. a. Formulation of a plan of treatment consistent with some theoretical orientation. b. Estimation of areas of difficulty. c. Estimation of what stage of therapy a patient is in and formulation of what to do accordingly. d. Estimation of when the patient is ready to discuss transference. e. Judgment and timing of interpretations and communications. 3. Session-to-session handling of the patient. a. Perception and understanding of continuity and discontinuity of communications of the patient within a session and from session to session. b. Recognition of manifestations of resistance. c. Judgment as to when to give ego support and ability to do so.	1. Ways of relating to the patient. a. Genuine interest in and empathy for the patient. b. Readiness and capacity to relate emotionally with the patient in a healthy way, that is, (1) Disengage oneself from neurotic involvements. (2) Be aware when it is productive; ability to express feelings, positive and negative. (3) Ability to estimate the attitudes and role that one assumes in the therapeutic sessions (awareness of roles that may hurt the patient, such as putting up a front, managerial, being rigid, detached, overconcerned, not showing respect, etc.). c. Appraising factors in the previous experience of the patient. (1) Sorting out real hardships from neurotic ones in the life of the patient. (2) Appraising what might have gone on in a previous therapy. (3) Alertness to grievance collecting. d. Speaking in terms natural to the patient; using technical language only when necessary. e. Ability to use values judiciously, espe-	1. Continuing ability to learn from patients as student develops therapeutic skills. a. Continuing improvement in recognition of similarities and dissimilarities in various patients. b. Awareness that one does not know everything about the psychodynamics of one's patients (accepts the fact that one does not know all the answers). 2. Recognition of areas in which one is competent and in which one needs to learn more in order to become more competent. 3. Ability to develop own individual style without needlessly imitating an idealized supervisor. 4. Progressive diminution of unrecognized countertransference reactions. 5. Continuing interest in scientific problems of personality (diagnosis, prognosis, and psychodynamics) and psychotherapeutic techniques. 6. Estimate by supervisor(s) as to how the therapist will function when on his or her own and in a new status. a. Will the therapist continue in supervision or consult when there is a need? b. Will the therapist feel free to exchange problems with colleagues? 7. After certification will the therapist work in the community, such as to teach, to do research, to work in some organization or clinical setting, or to participate in professional activities?	1. Ease with which supervisor feels he can work with supervisee. Add any statement you wish to make about your evaluation.

4. Skill in handling the middle phases of therapy.
   a. Judgment in the use of dreams in the best interests of the patient's therapy.
   b. Judgment in the use of transference in the patient's best interest (positive and negative transference).
   c. Awareness and use of countertransference.
   d. Ability to recognize acting-out and to help the patient recognize this either in what he does in the session or between sessions, including the patient's desire to terminate prematurely.
5. Skill in handling emergencies, including the recognition of the severity of a crisis.
6. Skill in handling problems of termination.
   a. Recognition of when termination should be planned for.
   b. Preparation of the patient for this.

cially when therapist's value judgments differ from those of the patient.
   f. Ability to learn by mistakes.
2. Ways of relating to supervisor.
   a. Ability to communicate therapy sessions and problems meaningfully to the supervisor.
   b. Relative freedom from defensiveness in relation to what is going on in therapy with a patient.
   c. Respect for and honesty toward the supervisor.
   d. Utilization of supervisory session in order to learn.
   e. Tolerance for new point of view other than one's own.
   f. Ability to discuss one's own evaluation in a mature way.
3. Ways of relating to the administration.
   a. Reliable in relation to requirements (paper work, etc.).
   b. Reliable in relation to class attendance.
   c. Reliable in making arrangements for supervision.
   d. Reliable in relation to patient load.
   e. Honesty in relation to administration.
   f. Reasonable consideration for clerical personnel.
4. Ways of relating to colleagues.
   a. Respect for colleagues in different disciplines.
   b. Ability to cooperate with colleagues on related cases (husband and wife, child and parent).
   c. Mature attitudes, in classroom and professional meetings, toward presenting of case material by colleagues.

on a subordinate level, in an effort to preserve his own superiority. Accordingly, he may minimize successes the therapist achieves, being chary of any praise or admiration he accords him. He may express his feelings directly toward the therapist, or, more likely, he may respond with defenses against his feelings which are intended to conceal them. For instance, he may cloak aggression in a solicitous, ingratiating attitude, with overkindliness and overattentiveness. Or he may show disinterest in the productions of the therapist, offering him little help or reassurance. Searles (1955) and Benedek (1972) have written on the use of the supervisor's feelings and "intuition" as a way of gaining understanding into the problems of the therapist.

The supervisory process will thus arouse feelings and attitudes in both supervisor and therapist. The readiness of dissolution of these attitudes will depend upon their severity, the level of insight possessed, the strength of existing provocative factors, and their functional utility or destructiveness.

Sufficient resolution of transference and countertransference feelings must occur before real learning is possible, since the emotions that contaminate the relationship are apt to divert it from the goals for which it is intended. Neurotic feelings, along the lines indicated above, will always exist to some degree, although the intensity should not ordinarily be so great as to interfere with learning, nor so obdurate so as not to be resolved in the ordinary process of supervision. As a general rule, assuming that both participants are integrated people, capable of facing inimical attitudes and feelings, the initial resistances, fears and distrustful attitudes will be dissipated by the development of positive identification and rapport.

Transference and countertransference, however, may persist, blocking the therapist in development and progress. Certain attitudes that the supervisor displays, for instance, may militate against learning. Among these are tentativeness, indecisiveness, minimization of himself, his knowledge and skill, irritability with the therapist, overprotectiveness, and a benign patronizing attitude that puts a damper on the therapist's need to express criticism and to verbalize doubts and indecisions. Lack of interest in the therapist and in the therapist's growth and absence of praise when an important gain is made, also act as dampers to learning.

The therapist, undergoing a more violent struggle than the supervisor, is bound to show many resistances, some of which will persist with an amazing tenacity. Among these are attitudes of conformity, and a seeming absorption of every utterance of the supervisor. This spurious kind of complacency is accompanied by a constant repetition of mistakes, as if the therapist sheds knowledge immediately after leaving the supervisor's office. A pattern of this kind is often the product of a continuing fear of losing one's independence by yielding to the supervisor's dictates and demands. Clinging to old attitudes then becomes for the therapist a means of retaining identity.

Another kind of resistance is the need to dominate and to take control by outsupervising the supervisor. Here the therapist overwhelms the supervisor with material, editing reports, even falsifying material, in order to impress the supervisor. Belittling and derisive attitudes and feelings may exist toward the supervisor that are only indirectly expressed and that serve to protect the therapist from fancied exploitation and injury.

On the other hand, the therapist may become so terrified about what is happening in the relationship with the supervisor as to seek reassurance, affection, and support in sundry ways. One way is to become helpless and hopeless, assume a defenseless attitude, and seek from the supervisor various panaceas for difficulties, insisting that something positive be done that will help in conducting therapy. In making such demands, the student-therapist may express refusal to work out problems, attempting to force the supervisor to shoulder all obligations for decisions. Self-devaluation may follow in the wake of this attitude, much of which is an effort to avoid criticism and to forestall any responsibilities being put on the therapist. Where there is a strong masochistic bent, there may be attempts to flay oneself, to undermine one's intelligence and adjustment, and then to protest being victimized or unfairly treated.

Resistance to learning may also be expressed in the form of hostility. The patterns that hostility takes are legion, depending upon the individual's habitual modes of dealing with this emotion. Where one finds it difficult to express rage, the response may be depression and discouragement. One individual may seek to terminate supervision on the basis that he is completely incapable of learning. Another may mask her hostility with dependence, with feigned amiability and with strong gestures to force the relationship with the supervisor into social channels. In instances where the therapist is capable of expressing her hostility openly, she may become defiant, challenging, and overcritical. She may develop feelings of being exploited, misunderstood, and humiliated, and she may attempt to find evidence for these feelings by misinterpreting what goes on between herself and the supervisor. She may become suspicious about the supervisor's abilities, training, and personal adjustment. She may enter into active competition with the supervisor, bringing in materials, quotations, and references from authoritative works in order to challenge the supervisor or to nullify suggestions the latter has made. In some instances, the therapist may actually become uncooperative, negativistic, and even mute. In other instances, hostility is masked by apathy and detachment. Here one will get the impression that the therapist, while presenting material and listening to the comments of the supervisor, is mentally "off in the clouds."

The therapist may try to ward off the supervisor by discursive talk about superficial topics or by self-interpretations that are expressed with great vehemence. This attempt to disarm the supervisor by spurts of productivity has little corrective value for the therapist, since it is motivated by an effort to hurt the supervisor rather than to learn.

Other resistances take the form of an inability to think clearly and an incapacity to express one's ideas. There may be an insistence that the therapist has achieved great development which is not supported by facts, and while self-confidence and assertiveness may be expressed, these will be found to be without substance. Another defense against the supervisor is an attempt to seduce him with gifts, lavish praise, and compliments. The overvaluation of the abilities of the supervisor may know few bounds, and unless the supervisor watches himself carefully, he is apt to respond to these devices with omnipotent feelings.

Assuming that the supervisor is capable of controlling or of resolving countertransference, can he help the therapist to overcome such varied resistances to the supervisory relationship?

One must remember that supervision is a student–teacher relationship rather than a patient–therapist relationship. Emotional problems stirred up in the therapist in work with patients cannot entirely be handled by the supervisor in the setting of supervision. While often the outcome of supervision is definitely therapeutic for the supervisee, the goal is toward more adequate functioning in psychotherapy rather than the helping of the therapist with his or her own neurotic difficulties. Naturally, the supervisor does point out neurotic problems of the therapist that express themselves in the latter's countertransference, in order to bring the therapist to an awareness of blocks in functioning. Since some of the problems that the therapist experiences with the supervisor are similar to those being experienced with his or her patients, working them out with the supervisor is bound to have some salubrius effect on overall therapeutic functioning. It is assumed that the therapist has had sufficient personal psychotherapy, or is sufficiently integrated emotionally, to be able to work through blocks with his or her own resources in the supervisory setting. In the event this is not possible by virtue of the depth of disturbance, it may be necessary to refer the therapist for more personal psychotherapy or to enjoin the therapist, if the latter is in the process of receiving psychotherapy, to report to the psychotherapist the problems that have developed in supervision.

However, the supervisor will have to handle those aspects of feeling and attitude that impede the therapist in the acquisition of therapeutic skills. This experience, as has been mentioned, may prove itself to be therapeutic for the supervisee, but, if this occurs, it is a by-product of the chief objective—the learning of psychotherapy. Should the supervisor's effort to help the therapist to resolve difficulties in supervision fail, referral for more personal psychotherapy may be necessary, a contingency the supervisor himself may want to seek where he realizes that he cannot work through his own problems in the existing relationship with his supervisee. In the event mutual trust and respect do not develop between supervisor and therapist after these devices have been exploited, transfer to another supervisor may be necessary.

Among the recommended readings on supervision are Arlow (1963), Balint (1948), Benedek (1954, 1972), Blitzstein and Fleming (1953), Bruner (1957), Collins (1962), De Bell (1963), Dewald (1969), Ekstein (1953, 1960, 1969), Ekstein and Wallerstein (1958), Fleming (1961, 1963, 1967), Fleming and Benedek (1966), Gitelson (1948), Grotjahn (1955), Grinberg (1970), M. Kramer (1959), Kris (1956), Kubie (1958), Langer et al. (1964), P. Sloane (1957), Towle (1954), Solnit (1970), Szasz (1958), and Windholz (1970).

58

Questions Therapists Ask about Psychotherapy

Sundry questions plague the individual doing psychotherapy. Answers to these questions are not easily provided, since there are many ways of accomplishing the same task in psychotherapy, some of which are suitable for one therapist and wholly inappropriate for another. In this chapter a number of common questions, posed by therapists participating in case seminars conducted by the writer, and not answered completely in the text of this book, are considered. The answers given to these questions are, of course, not absolute and will require modification in terms of the individual's unique experience and specific style of working.

Q. If a patient attacks you verbally at the initial interview, how would you handle the situation?

A. An aggressive outburst in the first interview is clearly an indication of great insecurity or fear in the patient. The patient will generally rationalize his hostility on one basis or another. A way of handling the situation is to accept the patient's hostility and to inform him that under the circumstances you do not blame him for being angry. As a matter of fact, it would be difficult for him to feel any other way. If possible, an effort should be made to bring the meaning of the aggressive outburst to the awareness of the patient. If this can be done, it may al-

leviate his tension and initiate more positive feelings toward the therapist.

Q. How do you handle a patient who comes to see you while he is being treated by another therapist?

A. This situation occasionally happens and will have to be managed diplomatically. There are a number of reasons why a patient finds it necessary to consult a second therapist. He may be in a state of resistance, and his visit constitutes an attempt at escape from, or a gesture of hostility toward, his therapist. Or the patient may sense that he is unable to relate to his therapist, or that his therapist is unable to relate to him, and he is reaching out for a new, better therapeutic relationship. In either instance, one must respectfully listen to the patient and focus particularly on the specific meaning of his consultation with you. Under no circumstances should one participate in criticism of the other therapist, no matter what outlandish activities are ascribed to him by the patient. On the contrary, one should alert himself to transference manifestations and attempt to clarify any misconceptions or irrational attitudes about the patient's therapist that present themselves. The ultimate result of the interview may be emotionally cathartic for the patient, and he may return to his therapist with insight into his resistance. Should there be reason for your considering treating the patient, and if he has not informed his therapist about his prospective consultation with you, it will be important to emphasize the need to discuss the situation with his therapist. The patient may be told that for ethical reasons it will be impossible to start treatments with him unless both he and his therapist agree that a transfer is indicated. In the event the patient has, when he consults you, discontinued treatment with his therapist, the visit may, of course, be conducted as an initial interview.

Q. Is it permissible to treat one's friends or relatives?

A. It is extremely difficult to be therapeutically objective with friends or relatives. Nor will they be able to establish the proper kind of relationship with you. For these reasons if they need treatment they are best referred to another therapist.

Q. How far can the therapist go in making interpretations at the beginning of therapy?

A. An experienced therapist may discern important dynamics in the first interview or shortly thereafter. To interpret these to the patient may be fatal. One must bide his time and wait for a strategic moment—which may come many months later—before revealing to the patient what the therapist already knows. New therapists, in their enthusiasm, frequently violate this rule, as do experienced therapists with strong narcissistic leanings who attempt to demonstrate to the patient how much they know about him.

Q. What causes violent feelings that are stirred up in the patient after the first interview?

A. These may be caused by transference or by something the therapist has done in error.

Q. Are mistakes that a therapist makes in doing psychotherapy irretrievably destructive?

A. Even the most experienced psychotherapist makes mistakes in the conduct of therapy. There are many reasons for this, including the fact that the therapeutic relationship is so complex that the therapist cannot see all of its facets. Such mistakes are not too important if the working relationship with the patient is a good one.

Q. Are the various psychotherapeutic approaches ever used together?

A. Practically all forms of psychotherapy purposefully or inadvertently employ a combination of approaches. Even in formal psychoanalysis one may, at times, be unable to avoid suggestion and reassurance. Persuasive and other supportive influences may by design enter into insight therapy from time to time, and disturbing environmental factors may deliberately have to be handled in order to promote maximal progress. Wittingly or unwittingly then, no approach exists in a pristine form. Rather, it is blended with other approaches, made necessary on occa-

sion by the exigencies of the therapeutic situation.

Q. Does one ever start off using one approach and then, in the course of treatment, switch over to another approach?

A. This is very frequently the case. One may start off with an approach aimed at a supportive or palliative goal. In the course of treatment it may become apparent that no real improvement will be possible unless one deals with underlying causative factors. One will consequently have to motivate the patient toward accepting therapy aimed at more extensive goals. On the other hand, one may begin reconstructive treatment and, in the course of administering this, discover that circumstances make less extensive goals desirable. A supportive approach may therefore become advisable.

Q. Should the patient be required to pay for his own treatment?

A. Some patients will get more out of therapy if they feel in some way responsible for its payment. This does not mean that they will not benefit from treatment financed for them if they cannot afford it. With the increasing incidence of third-party payments (insurance, medicare, medicaid, etc.) a considerable body of experience shows that good psychotherapy is possible even though patients do not pay for it themselves. In child and adolescent therapy parents or guardians assume responsibility for fees, and this fact does not denigrate the therapeutic effort. Where therapy is given free, and no payment is made for it by any party, some patients are handicapped in expressing any feelings toward the therapist that they believe will offend him. A perceptive therapist can detect this reluctance and deal with it so as to promote freedom of expression.

Q. How is the matter of fees best handled?

A. The matter of setting a fee satisfactory to both therapist and patient, and of agreeing on the manner in which payments are to be made, is part of the reality situation that therapy imposes on the patient. Most therapists gauge their fees according to the patient's ability to pay. In setting a fee, it is important that the therapist consider the patient's capacity to carry the financial responsibility over the estimated treatment period. Unless this is done, both therapist and patient will find themselves in a difficult situation later on. Though grading the patient's fee according to his ability to pay over the estimated time period of his treatment, the therapist must be assured that he is setting a fee acceptable to himself. Should he enter into an agreement whereby he accepts a fee so low that he is hampered in meeting his own obligations, he will feel insecure. Resentment or anxiety may occur that will impose a destructive influence on the therapeutic relationship. Once a fee is set, it is difficult and unfair to raise it unless the financial situation of the patient has changed for the better. Often a neurotic problem interferes with the work capacity and productiveness of the patient. At the start of therapy, the earning ability of the patient will therefore be minimal. Once therapy gets under way, the patient may be able to earn a great deal more money. Under such circumstances, discussing with the patient the raising of a fee is justifiable, and an adjustment of fees upward usually will be acceptable to the patient. On the other hand, financial reverses may occur during the course of therapy. In such instances a reduction of fee may be required.

Q. What do you do when a patient neglects payments of fees?

A. Lack of punctuality in the payment of fees may be a manifestation of temporary financial shortage, a problem in the patient related to money or to giving, or an indication of resentment toward the therapist and of a desire to frustrate him. Should the patient disregard the payment of the bill for a considerable period, the matter may merit inquiry and therapeutic handling. Where the therapist himself has neurotic problems in relation to money, he may evidence marked anxiety when payments are not being made on time. He may consequently tend to overemphasize the importance of punctuality in payments, and he may introduce the matter of finances completely out of context with the material that concerns the patient. On the other hand, the therapist may be negligent as to the matter of payments, and he may fail to bring to the patient's awareness possible avoidance of a responsibility that is part of the reality situation. Unless justified by financial reverses, the accumulation of a debt creates hardships for the patient which may be harmful to his relationship with the therapist.

Q. If you discover that the patient's finances are greater than those he reported at the beginning of therapy, would you boost the fee?

A. Financial arrangements with a patient may have been made on the basis of a reported low income. If the patient has purposefully concealed his finances from the therapist, this deception will, in all probability, later create guilt and tension. The therapist may assure the patient that there must have been reasons why he felt he had to falsify his income. Understandably, careful handling is necessary to avoid mobilizing further guilt. In the event the set fees require adjustment because of the patient's larger income, this matter must be discussed thoroughly with the patient, no change of fees being made except on mutual agreement. If the patient's fees are arbitrarily raised without his complete cooperation, grave difficulties may be anticipated in the therapeutic relationship.

Q. Should the therapist ever visit a patient in his home?

A. Only in the event of a serious incapacitating illness or accident where it is impossible for the patient to come to the therapist's office and where it is urgent to administer psychotherapy.

Q. What do you do when a patient talks too much and doesn't allow the therapist to speak?

A. If the patient is focused on an important area and is doing good therapeutic work, one does not interrupt. If he is talking about irrelevant things or his rambling seems to be resistance, one interrupts and focuses on pertinent topics. If this does not help, one may question the reason for rambling, or perhaps attempt its interpretation.

Q. Is there not a similarity between friendship and a working relationship?

A. Only peripherally. The therapeutic relationship is a professional one. Implicit in it is the absolute promise of confidentiality, the recognition that the time span is a limited one, and that termination of the relationship will eventually come about.

Q. What do you do if the patient has been in negative transference for a long time and this continues no matter what the therapist does?

A. First the therapist might examine his own feelings and behavior to see if he is provoking these feelings. If he is sure there is nothing in the therapeutic situation that is stirring up the patient, he may attempt to analyze possible projections by the patient into the present relationship of negative attitudes toward important past personages. If this does not help, he may go back to the first phase of therapy and actively try again to establish a working relationship with the patient.

Q. What is the relative merit of focusing on past as compared with present life difficulties in reconstructive therapy?

A. In reconstructive psychotherapy, some controversy exists as to the relative importance of material that deals with the past and material relating to the present. Extremists of both points of view argue the merits of their particular emphasis. On the one hand, there are those who regard the present problems of the individual as a superficial product of personality disturbances arising out of insecurities in childhood. These insecurities have undermined the self-esteem and blanketed sexual and aggressive drives with a mantle of anxiety. Environmental difficulties and current situational distortions stir up hardships for the individual by agitating past problems. Dealing with provocative current situations may restore the equilibrium of the individual. This stability is, however, precarious due to the continued operation of immature strivings. While harmony may be reconstituted, the recurrence of environmental stress will promote a new breakdown in adaptation. It is fruitless, therefore, to concentrate on the present since the roots of the difficulty, imbedded in the past history, will remain firmly entrenched. On the other hand, there are therapists who are opposed to an emphasis on the past. It is claimed that the individual repeats in present-day patterns his important childhood disturbances. A concern with the present must of necessity involve a consideration of the past. To discuss the past in detail results in a mere raking over of dead historical ashes; while interesting material may be exposed, it may bear little relationship to current happenings. A dichotomy may then be set up between the past and the present, with lacking unity of the two. As irreconcilable as these two viewpoints appear, they are not so disparate as the proposed arguments would seem to indicate. In psychotherapeutic practice one constantly utilizes current life experiences as vehicles for discussion, for it is in the present that the individual lives and feels. Yet, a consideration of the past is mandatory in understanding what is happening in the present. Current life experiences may be regarded as reflecting a patterning from the past through the use of present-day symbols. It is therefore necessary to blend the past and the present and to focus on whichever element is of immediate importance.

Q. Is it ever permissible to assign "homework" to the patient?

A. This can be very rewarding particularly where the patient is not too productive and does not work industriously at therapy. Asking him to keep a kind of diary, writing out his reactions, observations, and dreams between sessions, may get him to approach treatment more seriously. Each interview may be organized around discerning and exploring basic patterns which are revealed in the patient's notes or observations. The patient should leave every session with a general problem to focus on up to the time of the next session. He may then work on this problem, observing himself and his reactions, noting which environmental or interpersonal situations tend to aggravate or moderate it. This "homework" may catalyze the patient's thinking and get him to assume more responsibility for his treatment.

Q. If a patient wants information about a subject like sex, do you give it to him?

A. Yes, but only after ascertaining why the patient asked for this data.

Q. Isn't a routine physical examination for all patients a wasteful practice?

A. Every patient about to get psychotherapy should have a good physical examination and preferably a thorough neurologic examination performed by a competent neurologist. The findings will be negative in the vast majority of patients, but the occasional case of early cancer, brain tumor, or other operable maladies that may be detected will justify the precaution of routine physicals.

Q. How would you handle a patient who appears to have read just about everything on the subject of psychiatry and keeps citing the opinions of different authorities which may or may not agree with your point of view?

A. The patient may have read more on psychiatry than you, but this does not mean that he has integrated what he has read. As a matter of fact, he will probably tend to utilize the knowledge he has gained as resistance, by intellectualizing what goes on, or by criticizing the technique or formulations of the therapist. At some point in therapy it may be necessary to mention to the patient that, while his reading has given him a good deal of information, this information may be a hindrance to his therapy rather than a help. No two problems of an emotional nature are alike, and things he has read applying to other people surely do not exactly apply to himself. He can be fair to himself only by observing his feelings and his attitudes, without speculating what they must be like on the basis of his readings. Sometimes it may be necessary to be very blunt and to tell a patient that it is important for him to forget what he has read since this seems to interfere with his spontaneity.

Q. What do you do when the patient asks a question the therapist is unable to answer?

A. The therapist may say that he cannot answer the question at this time but will do so later when the answer becomes more clear.

Q. Is it ever justifiable to lie to a patient?

A. Lies eventually reveal themselves and shatter the patient's trust and confidence in the therapist. Truthfulness is, consequently, the keynote in therapy. In an effort to be truthful, however, one should not reveal things to the patient that may be harmful to him. It may be essential, therefore, where his security and health are menaced, to avoid answering certain questions directly. If, for instance, the patient shows symptoms of an impending psychosis, and is dangerously tottering between sanity and mental illness, and if he is frightened by the upsurge of archaic unconscious material to a point where he believes himself to be insane, it may be harmful to tell him that he is approaching a psychosis. Rather, he may, if he questions the therapist, be told that his preoccupation with becoming insane is more important than the symptoms he manifests. These are evidences of great insecurity. Whenever the patient asks a direct question, an honest answer to which may be upsetting to the patient in view of existing ego weaknesses, he may be asked why he asks this question, and his concern may be handled without upsetting him with a straight reply. It is important to remember that truthfulness must not be confused with necessary caution in divulging information and interpreting prematurely. Where a patient is insistent on a complete answer to his question, it may be helpful to point out to him that therapy involves a mutual inquiry into a problem and an avoidance of premature judgments. One must patiently wait until enough evidence is available before being certain of one's observations. The answer to questions will soon become evident, both to the patient and to the therapist. If for any reason the patient cannot perceive the truth, the therapist will point out to him why it is difficult for him to understand what is happening. The patient will eventually develop confidence in the fact that the truth will not be kept from him but that ideas must be checked and doublechecked for their validity before they can be communicated.

Q. Sometimes it is necessary to break an appointment with a patient. How can this best be done?

A. Appointments should, if possible, never be broken without adequate notice being given to the patient. Unless this is done, the relationship may be injured and a great deal of work may be necessary to undo the damage. Where circumstances make it necessary to break an appointment, the therapist or his secretary should telephone the patient, explain that an emergency has developed that necessitates a revision of the therapist's schedule, and that, consequently, it will be necessary to make a new appointment for the patient or to skip the present appointment. In instances where the therapist is ill, or expects to be away from his practice for an indefinite period, the patient may be informed that the therapist will get in touch with him shortly to give him a new appointment. If a reasonable explanation is given to the patient to account for a broken appointment, there will be no interference with the working relationship.

Q. How would you handle a patient's resentment because you do not keep appointments on time?

A. The patient's resentment may be jus-

tified. Because of ambivalent feelings, the patient usually has difficulties trusting any human being completely. The therapist must, therefore, give the patient as little reality basis for his distrust as possible, always explaining to the patient the reasons for unavoidable irregularities in appointment times, so the patient will not assume that the therapist is irresponsible. Giving the patient an allotted amount of time is part of the reality situation to which both the patient and therapist must adjust. Where appointments are forgotten by the therapist or where the patient has to sit around and wait for the therapist because the therapist has not finished with a preceding patient, resentments will develop which may interfere with therapy. Of course, there will be occasions when the therapist cannot help being late for a session. Emergencies with a preceding patient may develop, and the therapist may have to run over in time into the next session. Under such circumstances an explanation must be given the patient to the effect that an emergency occurred that could not be avoided and that necessitated a delay in starting his session. In order to impress on the patient the fact that he is not being exploited, he may be told also that time taken from his session will be made up. In the event a mistake has been made in the patient's appointment, and the patient appears for his session at a time allotted to another patient, he must be taken aside and given an explanation to the effect that an unfortunate error in scheduling has occurred that resulted in the patient's being given the wrong appointment time. Another appointment should then be given the patient during which any resentment resulting from the error may be handled.

Q. If you are unable to understand what is going on dynamically in a case you are treating, what do you do?

A. Occasions will arise when the therapist may be unable to discern exactly what is going on in treatment. Should this continue for too long a span, it may be indicative of such blocks as unyielding resistance in the patient or of countertransference. In either instance, where the therapist is disturbed by what is happening or where progress is blocked, several supervisory sessions with an experienced psychotherapeutic supervisor may be helpful in resolving the difficulty.

Q. When do you increase the frequency of sessions?

A. During the course of therapy it may be necessary to increase the number of sessions weekly for the following reasons: (1) an upsurge of intense anxiety, depression, or hostility that the patient cannot himself control; (2) violent intensification of symptoms; (3) severe resistance that interferes with progress; (4) negative transference; (5) unrestrained acting-out that requires checking; (6) threats of shattering of the ego unless constant support is given the patient; and (7) where one wishes to stimulate transference to the point of creating a transference neurosis.

Q. When would you decrease the number of sessions weekly?

A. A decrease in the number of weekly sessions is indicated (1) where a patient is becoming too dependent on the therapist, (2) where alarming transference reactions are developing which one wishes to subdue, (3) where the patient has a tendency to substitute transference reactions for real life experiences, and (4) where the patient has progressed sufficiently in therapy so that he can carry on with a diminished number of visits.

Q. How important is adhering to the exact time of a session?

A. From the standpoint of scheduling, adhering to a set time may be necessary. The usual time is between 45 to 60 minutes. But shorter spans, as low as 15 minutes, can be effective in some patients, and certain situations can arise that require extending the scheduled time.

Q. Is advice-giving taboo in reconstructive therapy?

A. Generally. One must keep working on the patient's resistances to the solving of his own problems. The ultimate aim is self-assertiveness rather than reliance on the therapist. On rare occasions, however, advice giving may be unavoidable.

Q. Should the therapist ever insist on the patient's engaging in a specific course of action?

A. Only when it is absolutely necessary that the patient execute it and its rationale is fully explained to and accepted by the patient.

Q. Should the therapist ever try to forbid the patient from making crucial decisions during therapy?

A. While important changes in his life status, like divorce or marriage, may best be delayed until the patient has achieved stability and greater personality maturity, it is obviously difficult for the therapist to "forbid" the patient to make any decisions. The patient may be reminded that it is important not to take any drastic steps in altering his life situation without discussing these thoroughly with the therapist. If the therapist believes the decisions to be neurotic, he may question them, presenting interpretations if necessary. In the event the patient decides, nevertheless, to go through with a move that is obviously impetuous, it means that he is still at the mercy of neurotic forces he cannot control, that his insight is not yet sufficiently developed,

or that he has to defy or challenge the therapist. The therapist may have no other alternative than to let the patient make a mistake, provided the patient realizes that he has acted on his own impulse. It is important not to reject the patient or to communicate resentment toward him for having made a move against advice. Only when the patient is about to take a really destructive or dangerous step is the therapist justified in actively opposing it.

Q. What do you do if the patient brings in written material for you to discuss?

A. Occasional written material may be important, but if large quantities are brought in, this practice should be discouraged.

Q. What would you do if the patient refuses to talk session after session but offers to write out his ideas?

A. If this is the only way the patient will communicate, it should be accepted. However, an attempt must be made to handle the patient's resistance to talk at the same time that he is encouraged to bring in written comments.

Q. What do you do if a patient says he fears he will kill someone?

A. One should not reassure the patient nor minimize what he says. Rather, he may be told that there are reasons why he feels so upset that he believes that he will kill someone. He may then be encouraged to explore his impulses and fears. If the patient is psychotic or destructively dangerous, hospitalization may be required.

Q. Should the therapist permit the patient to express hostility or aggression openly in the therapeutic situation?

A. Any overt behavioral expressions of hostility or aggression are forbidden, although verbalization of these emotions or impulses is permissible, even indispensable.

Q. Do you ever reassure the patient during insight therapy?

A. Reassurance should be kept at a minimum. However, gross misconceptions will require reassuring correction, or the patient may be in an emotional crisis which needs mitigation. Reassurance should never be given the patient when he is in a negativistic state, since this may produce an effect opposite to what is intended.

Q. Are fleeting suicidal thoughts arising in the patient during treatment important?

A. Suicidal thoughts are not uncommon during therapy. They often serve a defensive purpose, acting as a kind of safety valve. Vague ideas of suicide may be entertained as a way of ultimate escape from suffering in the event life should become too intolerable. In most instances such ideas are fleeting and are never put into practice no matter how bad conditions become.

They are handled therapeutically in the same way that any fantasy or idea might be managed. It is important not to convey undue alarm when the patient talks about escape fantasies in taking his life. To do so will frighten the patient or cause him to use suicidal threats against the therapist as a form of resistance. Rather, the therapist may listen respectfully to the patient and then state simply that there may be other ways out of his situation than suicide. Suicide is an irrevocable act. More suitable ways of coping with the situation will present themselves as he explores his difficulty. Where, however, the patient has, in the past, made an attempt at suicide, fleeting suicidal thoughts must be taken very seriously. A careful watch is indicated since the attempt may be repeated. Any evidence of hopelessness or resentment that cannot be expressed as such must be explored and resolved if it is possible to do so. Should resolution be impossible and should the danger of suicide continue to lurk, hospitalization may be required. Suicidal thoughts in patients who are deeply depressed must be considered as dangerous, and the patient must be handled accordingly.

Q. What do you do if a patient you are treating telephones and insists on seeing you that very day?

A. If possible, this request should be respected, provided the situation upsetting the patient is an emergency. Should the therapist be unable to arrange for an appointment, or for a partial appointment, he may promise to telephone the patient at a specified time that day to discuss the situation with him. As early an appointment as possible should be made for the patient.

Q. What would you say to a patient who asks whether he may telephone or write to you whenever he desires?

A. Lack of time will obviously make it difficult for the therapist to answer telephone calls or to read all the material that the patient wishes to communicate in writing. The therapist may handle a request on the part of the patient to telephone by saying simply that it is much better to take up matters during a session, since the limited time available during telephone conversations may create more problems than are solved. In response to excessive written communications, the therapist may remark that verbalization is to be preferred to writing. The patient may be informed that where emergencies occur, he may feel free to telephone the therapist. Where a crisis has developed, the patient may be given specific times at which he may call, or he may be told that the therapist will telephone him at a certain hour. It is usually best to keep such telephone calls at a minimum and to increase the sessions of the patient should a more intensive contact be required.

Q. How would you handle a patient who is insistent that you inform him of your whereabouts at all times so that he can get in touch with you?

A. One would deal with this the way any other symptom in a neurosis would be handled. The patient may be told that it is important to find out why he needs to know the therapist's whereabouts. It may be that he feels so helpless and insecure within himself that he must be convinced that the therapist will not desert him or deny him help in the event of a catastrophe. The patient may be assured that the therapist will, in the instance of an emergency, always be happy to talk with him but that it is important to understand what is behind the patient's insecurity in order that he be able to overcome his feelings of helplessness.

Q. In the event a patient who has been using the couch position manifests anxiety and asks to sit up, would you encourage this?

A. Anxiety may be the product of penetration of unconscious material into preconsciousness, or it may indicate a feeling of isolation from or a fear of the therapist. Encouraging the patient to continue his verbal associations on the couch may enable him to gain awareness of important feelings or conflicts. However, if anxiety becomes too great, his request to assume the sitting-up, face-to-face position should be granted. This will generally permit of a restoration of stability, especially if supportive measures are coordinately employed.

Q. Should a patient be encouraged to use the couch in psychotherapy?

A. In most cases this is not indicated or advisable. The possible exception is in formal psychoanalysis in which free association is employed.

Q. What do you do when a patient has reached a stalemate in therapy? He is completely unproductive, and any attempts of the therapist to mobilize transference and to resolve resistance fail.

A. Group therapy with alternate individual sessions often stimulates activity, as may several sessions of hypnosis or narcotherapy. Continued resistance may justify a vacation from therapy, or, as a last resort, transfer to another therapist.

Q. When is psychotherapy likely to become interminable?

A. A patient whose personality has been so damaged in early childhood that it has never allowed for a satisfactory gratification of needs or for an adequate defense against stress may feel he requires a continuing dependent relationship in order to function. Transference here is organized around maneuvering the therapist into a parental role. There is strong resistance to a more mature relationship. Where the therapist enters into the patient's design, due to his own needs to play parent, therapy is apt to become interminable.

Q. What does dreaming indicate when it becomes so excessive that it takes up the entire session?

A. Where the patient deluges the therapist with dreams, the therapist should suspect that they are being used as resistance, perhaps to divert the therapist from other important material.

Q. Which dreams that the patient presents should one consider of great importance?

A. Repetitive dreams and those with an anxiety content may be of great importance.

Q. What do you do when a patient constantly brings up important material several minutes before the end of a session, leaving no time to discuss it?

A. This is usually a manifestation of anxiety. It may be handled by mentioning to the patient the fact that the material he has brought up sounds important and should be discussed at the next session. If the patient does not spontaneously bring it up, the therapist may do so, handling whatever resistances arise.

Q. How would you handle a parent who brings a child to you for therapy, and you are impressed by the fact that the parent needs treatment more than does the child?

A. It may be important to determine how much motivation the parent has for therapy and his level of understanding. Should the parent be unaware of how he participates in the child's neurosis, it may be necessary to inform him that the treatment of his child will require seeing the parent also, both to determine what is going on at home and to help the parent understand how to handle developing problems. In this way the parent himself may be brought into a treatment situation.

Q. Are interviews with the patient's family or with other persons important to the adult patient of any value?

A. The therapist may frequently get information from persons close to the patient that the patient himself has been unable to convey. Often a conference reveals distortions in the patient's attitudes and behavior that are not based on reality. One or more interviews with important family members may thus serve as a constructive experience. Furthermore, where the patient is unable to correct a disturbed environmental situation by himself, the cooperation of a related person as an accessory may be helpful. Where

the patient is reacting destructively to a relative who then responds in a counterdestructive manner, where demands on the patient by a relative are stirring up problems in the patient, where a related person is opposing the patient's therapy—and his help, financial and other, is needed—an interview with the relative, aimed at the clarification of these issues, may yield many dividends. The relative may require reassurance to neutralize his guilt about the patient. Sometimes relatives can be prepared for contingencies that may arise in therapy, such as rebelliousness and hostility directed at them by the patient. An explanation that such occurrences are inevitable in treatment, and that they are part of the process of getting well, may forestall retaliatory gestures. The patient's need for independence and assertiveness may be explained for the benefit of relatives who unwittingly overprotect the patient. Statements to the effect that the patient will get worse before he gets better and that it will require time before results are apparent often prevent discouragement and feelings of hopelessness among concerned relatives. Because a therapeutically induced change in the patient's attitudes brought about by therapy may impose new and unaccustomed burdens on persons with whom the patient associates, preparing these persons for the change may avoid a crisis. An interpretation of the patient's actions in dynamic terms will often relieve a related person's guilt and lessen his resentment. For instance, if an adolescent is beginning to act cantankerous and resistive, an explanation to the parent that this behavior is to be expected at the patient's time of life, that all adolescents are often difficult to live with, and that parents are bound to feel resentful at the behavior of their offspring, may foster greater tolerance. Or a wife distraught at her husband's inattentiveness may be helped to realize that her spouse is responding not specifically to her as a person, but rather to her as a symbol of some actual past or fantasied personage against whom the patient had to build a wall of detachment. This insight may help avoid the creation of the very situations that would drive her husband deeper into isolation.

Q. How would you approach a patient should you decide a conference with a relative is necessary?

A. The patient may be told that in psychotherapy the therapist may want to have an occasional conference with a relative or other person close to the patient. The purpose is to get to know the relatives and their attitudes. Following this, the therapist may say, "I wonder how you would feel if I thought it necessary to talk with _____ [*mentioning name of person*]?"

The patient may acquiesce; he may question the need for such a conference; or he may refuse indignantly to permit it. If the patient is insistent that no contact be made, his desire should be respected. Important material concerning the relative will undoubtedly be forthcoming and may constitute the material of later interviews.

Q. If an interview with a family member or other significant person is decided on, are there any rules one should follow?

A. Experience has shown that a number of precautions are necessary when it is decided to contact the family. First, the patient's consent should always be obtained, the only exception being where he is dangerously psychotic. Second, confidential material revealed by the patient must never be divulged, since the breach of confidence will usually be flaunted at the patient even where the relative promises to keep the revelations to himself. Third, in talking to the related person, the therapist will often have a temptation to blame, to scold, or to enjoin the person to change his ways or attitudes toward the patient. Distraught, confused, frustrated, and filled with guilt and indignation, the related person will expect the therapist to accuse him of delinquencies toward the patient. Permitting the person to talk freely, sympathizing with his feelings, and encouraging him to express his ideas about the situation will tend to alleviate his tension. It is important to try to establish a rapid working relationship with the person, if this is at all possible. Once the person realizes that the therapist is sympathetic with him, he will be more amenable toward accepting interpretations of the patient's reactions, and he will be more cooperative in the treatment plan. Indeed he may, if he has been hostile to the patient's therapy or to the therapist, become a helpful accessory. Fourth, should the person telephone the therapist, he must be told that it is best that the patient be informed about the call, although the specific details need not be revealed. Fifth, if the patient is insistent on knowing what went on in the conference or conversation with the therapist, he may be told that the conversation was general and dealt with many of the person's own problems, as well as his relationship with the patient. Sixth, it may be necessary to see the person more than once, perhaps even periodically. Seventh, the therapist should not participate with the patient in "tearing down" a family member, nor should the member be defended when the patient launches an attack. A sympathetic, impartial attitude is best.

Q. Under what conditions would you advise a relative of a patient to get psychotherapy?

A. Where the patient is in close contact with a neurotic relative and he is being traumatized by the relative, psychotherapy may be advised, provided the therapist has a sufficiently good relationship with the relative to make this recommendation. Therapy may also be advised when a change in the patient's condition makes a new adjustment by the relative necessary. For instance, a frigid wife, living with an impotent husband, may, as a result of psychotherapy, on the basis of experiencing sexual feelings, make sexual demands on her husband that the latter will be unable to fulfill. In order for the husband to make an adjustment, he may require psychotherapy.

Q. Is it permissible to treat several members of the same family?

A. The situation often becomes complicated, but it can be done. Whether or not simultaneous treatment is possible, will depend on the therapist and his ability to handle the inevitable complications. Reconstructive individual therapy with several members of the same family is not easily managed. Treating all or a number of family members together in a group (family therapy) may effectuate a better family adjustment. Marital problems are often advantageously handled in conjoint marital therapy.

Q. How should one act when one meets a patient on the street or at a social affair?

A. A professional therapeutic relationship requires reducing social contacts to a minimum. Occasions will, however, arise where the therapist will run into the patient on the street, in public places, or at private social affairs. This may prove embarrassing to both therapist and patient. One cannot handle such situations by running away from them. Once the therapist is recognized by the patient, the former may greet him cordially and then proceed with his activities as usual. Understandably, at private gatherings, one's spontaneity will have to be curtailed to some extent. The patient's reactions to seeing the therapist in a different role may have to be handled with him during the ensuing sessions.

Q. Should you expect all your patients to like you?

A. Except for very sick patients, a satisfactory resolution of prejudices, suspicions, and resentments will occur relatively early in therapy, leading to a good working relationship. Periodically, however, the patient's feeling about the therapist will be punctuated by hostility, issuing either out of transference or out of an inadvertent error in the therapist's handling of the patient. Analysis and resolution of hostilities as they develop should bring the relationship back to a working level.

Q. If a patient continues to dislike you no

matter what you do, should you discontinue therapy?

A. A continued dislike is usually indicative of either errors in therapeutic management or of transference that the patient cannot resolve. As long as the dislike persists, little progress can be expected in treatment. Should the therapist be unable to correct the patient's feeling, he may have to suggest the possibility of transfer to a different therapist. This must be done in such a way that the patient realizes that the transfer is being recommended out of consideration for his welfare and not because the therapist rejects him. As a general rule, very few patients will need to be transferred because of persistent negative feelings. Where a therapist encounters this problem frequently, the chances are that he is doing something in the therapeutic situation that is inspiring the dislike of his patients. He should, therefore, seek supervision with an experienced psychotherapist who may be able to help him to understand what is happening.

Q. How should you act to displays of crying or rage on the part of the patient?

A. One generally permits these to go on without reassurance until the meaning of the reaction is explored and determined. If the reaction is dangerous to the patient or to others, it should be controlled by supportive measures.

Q. Should the therapist engage in a confessional, confiding his past or present life to the patient in an effort to show the patient that he too has frailties?

A. This can be very destructive to the relationship, especially at the beginning of therapy. The patient may use any revelations made as a confession of the therapist's weakness and ineptness, and he may then decide to discontinue treatment. The patient will usually discover enough frailties in the therapist spontaneously without being alerted to them.

Q. Should you ever admit to the patient that you may be wrong about certain things?

A. It is important to admit of an error when this is obvious to the patient and he questions the therapist about it.

Q. If a patient asks you if you are ill or tired, would you admit it?

A. If it is true, it may be important to confirm the patient's observation, adding that you do not believe this will interfere with your ability to work with the patient.

Q. What happens in insight therapy if the therapist's personality is authoritarian?

A. If the authoritarianism of the therapist interferes with the patient's ability to express hostility, and with his assertiveness, it will probably limit therapeutic goals.

Q. Is it possible that a therapist may develop a deep hate for a patient?

A. If a circumstance like this develops in therapy, there is something seriously wrong with the therapist or with his technique. It is not possible for the therapist to like all patients to the same degree, nor is it possible to avoid disliking some of his patients temporarily in certain phases of treatment. When this happens, the therapist must resolve the untoward feeling before it interferes with therapeutic progress. If he cannot do this, he should transfer the patient to another therapist, and perhaps seek psychotherapy for himself.

Q. Does a therapist ever fall in love with a patient?

A. If such a situation develops, it is a manifestation of countertransference that will seriously interfere with the therapist's essential objectivity. Failure to analyze his feeling and to resolve it will make it necessary to transfer the patient to another therapist.

Q. Does a therapist ever develop sexual feelings for a patient?

A. It is possible that certain patients may arouse sexual feelings in the therapist. If this happens, such feelings must be subjected to self-analysis and resolved.

Q. Should not the conduct and attitudes of the psychotherapist be as passive and noncommittal as possible?

A. The idea that the therapist should remain detached and completely passive stems from the notion that this attitude will best demonstrate to the patient how he automatically projects onto the therapist attitudes and feelings that are rooted in past relationships. Not having done anything to incite his attitudes, the therapist is in a better position to interpret transference. The passive, detached attitude also is believed to avoid dependency and to throw the patient on his own resources. Experience shows, however, that the projections of the patient, which are sparked by past distortions in interpersonal relationships, will emerge whether the therapist is passive or active. A patient with hostile problems will thus develop hostility toward the therapist who acts detached as well as toward one who acts accepting. If the patient has a problem of dependency, he will get dependent on the most passive therapist. Rather than cripple the spontaneity of the therapist in the dubious quest of interpreting transference phenomena, or of mobilizing assertiveness, it is best for the therapist to act himself and not to assume artificial passivity if he is not normally a passive person. Such an assumption may signify rejection to the patient and, in mobilizing hostility, may interfere with the working relationship.

Q. Are not warmth and emotional support necessary for some patients?

A. Yes, especially when the patient's adaptive resources are at a minimum. Unfortunately, some therapists have been reared in the tradition of passivity and nondirectiveness to a point where they provide for the patient a sterile, refrigerated atmosphere that, in seriously sick patients, is anathema to a working relationship.

Q. Is the assumption of a studied role by the therapist of any help in insight therapy?

A. It has been recommended by some authorities that the therapist play a deliberate role in insight psychotherapy that is at variance with his usual neutral, though empathic, position. Such role playing, however, may inspire intense transference that the therapist may be unable to control. As a general rule, the therapist should not transgress his defined role of a professional person who seeks to enable the patient to help himself through understanding. An exception to this rule is an extremely experienced and skilled therapist who is thoroughly acquainted with the existing dynamics operative in a patient and who, by dramatizing a part and injecting himself actively into the patient's life, strives to expedite change. Such activity is not without risks, but it may, in some cases, produce brilliant results. On the whole, role playing is not to be recommended. Most patients quickly perceive the artificiality in the assumed part played by the therapist.

Q. If the therapist acts consistently permissive and accepting, will this not in itself eventually reduce the patient's irrational responses to authority?

A. The behavior of the therapist, no matter how well controlled will, to some degree, always be subject to distortion in terms of the patient's conceptual framework, which, in turn, is based on his previous experiences with authority. This is not to say that gross deviations of behavior on the part of the therapist will not bring about appropriate reality-determined responses. A brusque, disinterested, detached, or hostile manner will produce untoward reactions in most patients. However, one must not delude himself into thinking that absolutely correct activity and behavior will always bring about good responses, since the patient may interpret the therapist's actions as a hypocritically conceived lure.

Q. Should deprivations ever be imposed on the patient?

A. Occasionally it is necessary to enjoin the patient to deprive himself of certain sources of gratification to help the exploratory process. Thus, a patient with destructive acting-out ten-dencies may be urged to control his sexual impulse so that tensions may accumulate that will facilitate an analysis of his problem. Where the patient is shown the reason for his need to give up certain pleasure promptings, he will be less inclined to resent the therapist.

Q. How would you handle the overanxious and completely unreasonable patient who acts more like a child than an adult?

A. It is essential to remember that while the patient may be chronologically an adult, emotionally he may not have progressed beyond a childhood level. One may expect, therefore, childish tantrums, ambivalent feelings, unrestrained enthusiasms and other reactions. If one can respect the patient despite his unreasonableness, one will best be able to help him.

Q. What do you do when your relationship with the patient starts getting bad?

A. All other tasks cease, and one must concentrate on bringing the relationship back to a satisfactory level. It is useless to explore patterns, to interpret and to engage in any other interviewing tasks so long as good rapport is absent. Essentially one must go back to the first phase of therapy and focus on reestablishing a working relationship.

Q. Why is the handling of transference important in reconstructive therapy?

A. Since much of the suffering of the patient is produced by destructive transference involvements with people, part of the therapeutic task in reconstructive therapy is to put a halt to such reactions and to replace them with those that have a foothold in reality. If, for instance, the patient responds automatically to authority with violent hate, as a result of an unresolved hatred toward a parent or sibling, his reaction may have a disorganizing effect on his total adjustment. The patient usually does not appreciate that this response to all authority is undifferentiated. He may not even be aware of his hate, which, considered to be dangerous in expression, becomes internalized with psychosomatic or depressive consequences. Liberation from such reactions is essential before the patient can get well. This can best be insured in therapy by bringing him to an awareness of his projections. Several means are available to the therapist in executing this goal. First, on the basis of functioning in the role of an objective and impartial observer, one may help the patient realize how many of his reactions outside of therapy have no reality base. Second, by watching for instances of transference toward the therapist, one may demonstrate to the patient, often quite dramatically, the nature of those projections that constitute basic patterns.

Q. What is the difference between "transfer-

ence," "transference neurosis," "parataxic distortions," and "positive relationship?"

A. Stereotyped early patterns, projected into the relationship with the therapist, were called by Freud "transference reactions." When these became so intense that the patient acted out important past situations, this was known as a "transference neurosis." No satisfactory name was given to repetitive early patterns occurring with persons outside of the therapeutic situation until Sullivan invented the term "parataxic distortions," which included all stereotyped patterns that developed inside or outside of therapy. A "positive relationship" usually refers to a good working relationship with minimal transference contamination.

Q. Isn't the accepted idea of transference as a manifestation of purely infantile or childish attitudes or feelings a restricted one?

A. Probably. A broader concept of transference would consider it to be a blend of projections onto the therapist of attitudes and feelings that date back to infancy and childhood, as well as more current attitudes that have had a formative influence on, and have been incorporated into, the character structure.

Q. Does every patient have to go through a transference neurosis in order to achieve very deep, structural personality changes?

A. There is much controversy on this point, but experience shows that some patients can achieve extensive personality growth without needing to live through a transference neurosis.

Q. What activities on the part of the therapist encourage neurotic transference responses?

A. Dependency may be stimulated in the patient by such therapist activities as overprotecting the patient, making decisions for him, and exhibiting directiveness in the relationship. Sexual feelings in the patient may be provoked by seductive behavior displayed toward the patient, by socializing with the patient, and by physical contact of any kind. Fearful attitudes and hostile impulses may be mobilized where the therapist acts excessively passive, detached, authoritarian, overprotective, hostile, pompous, or belligerent. It must, however, be remembered that transference may arise without any provocation whatsoever on the part of the therapist. This is the case where needs are intense and can be voiced and expressed in transference due to the permissiveness of the therapeutic relationship.

Q. What is the best way of handling transference?

A. There is no best way; methods depend on the kind of therapy done and the therapeutic goals. Transference may not be explored or handled in supportive therapy. In reeducative

therapy it may be immediately interpreted in an effort at resolution whenever it becomes apparent as resistance. In some types of reconstructive therapy it may be allowed to develop until it becomes so disturbing that the patient himself achieves awareness of its irrational nature. In Freudian analysis it may be encouraged to the point of evolution of a transference neurosis.

Q. Are so-called "transference cures" ever permanently effective?

A. Structural personality changes rarely occur. However, a "transference cure" may permit a patient to relate better to his life situation. This facilitates the development of more adaptive patterns that can become permanent.

Q. How does countertransference lead to an improper assessment of neurotic traits in the patient?

A. Countertransference may cause the therapist to make incorrect interpretations of the patterns exhibited by the patient. Thus, he may, if he welcomes hostile outbursts, regard these as manifestations of assertiveness rather than as destructive responses. If he relishes a submissive, passive attitude on the part of the patient, he may credit this to cooperation and to the abatement of neurotic aggression rather than to a neurotic need for compliance.

Q. Should you ever emphasize positive aspects of the patient's adjustment?

A. Therapists too often tend to regard the patient as a respository of pathologic strivings, emphasizing these to a neglect of constructive traits, mention of which is very important in the reality assessment.

Q. Is acting-out always a bad sign?

A. No. It may be a transitional phase in therapy indicative of a shift in the psychic equilibrium. Thus a repressed, timid individual, realizing that he has been intimidated by an archaic fear of physical hurt for assertiveness, may become overly aggressive and act out his defiance of authority as a way of combating his terror. Proving himself to be capable of this expression without experiencing the dreaded punishment may enable him to temper his outbursts. In the same way a sexually inhibited person may become temporarily promiscuous, almost as if liberation from fear is tantamount with indulgence in sexual excesses. Incorporated also in the acting-out process are unresolved impulses and conflicts, in relation to early authorities, that have been mobilized by the transference. When the therapist becomes aware of acting-out, it is important for him to discourage it in favor of verbalization. As verbalizations replace impetuous acts and as understanding progresses, a more rational solution is found for neurotic drives and impulses.

Q. *How do the value prejudices of the therapist interfere with treatment?*

A. Whether he wants to or not, the therapist will accent in the interview attitudes and feelings that are in line with his value system, and he will minimize those that are opposed to it. Where, for instance, the therapist has a problem in his own relationships with authority, manifesting submission and ingratiation, he may overvalue these traits. He may then tend to discourage assertiveness or aggressiveness when the patient seeks to take a stand with authority. He may credit his philosophy to "good common sense" and to justify it in terms of the benefits that accrue to ingratiation. This may seriously inhibit the patient from working through neurotic feelings toward authority. On the other hand, where the therapist himself reacts to authority with aggression and hostility, he may inspire defiance or promote aggressive attitudes toward authoritative persons which may seriously endanger the patient's security.

Q. *What value standards should the therapist have?*

A. The values of the therapist should reflect the constructive values of the culture. However, the therapist should be able to tolerate those biologic needs that do not entirely conform exactly with the existing mores, recognizing that cultural values and folkways may inhibit the spontaneous expression of some biologic and social needs. The therapist should also be sensitive to neurotic distortions that are culturally nurtured and help bring the patient to an awareness of these distortions in order that the patient be able to take a more rational stand with life. Respect for the patient's right to autonomy and self-determination must be blended with a realistic appraisal of social disciplines to which the patient will have to make an adjustment.

Q. *Shouldn't the therapist be trained in all therapeutic approaches?*

A. The most effective therapist is one who can implement whatever therapies are indicated, whether these are of a supportive, reeducative, or reconstructive nature. If the therapist has a broad understanding of various therapeutic procedures, if he knows how to execute them, and if he is sufficiently flexible in personality so as not to be tied to a single treatment process, he will score the greatest therapeutic successes. This, however, is an idealistic situation. Most therapists learn only one kind of technique, which enables them to handle only a certain number of problems—those which are amenable to their technique. They may also be limited by

their character structure so as to be unable to utilize certain techniques. For instance, a therapist may be an essentially passive person and, on this account be unable to employ the directiveness and authoritarianism of approach essential for symptom removal, reassurance, guidance, persuasion, environmental manipulation, and other supportive therapies. On the other hand, the therapist may be so extremely authoritarian and dogmatic that he may not be able to allow his patient to make mistakes, to work out his own problems, and to establish his own sense of values, so essential in reconstructive therapy.

Q. *When is supportive therapy justified?*

A. Supportive psychotherapy is aimed at a rapid relieving of the symptoms of the patient, enabling him to function as effectively as possible within the limitations of his neurotic difficulties which cannot or should not, for one reason or another, be dealt with in the present therapeutic effort. In some cases as a result of the relationship with the helping agency, patients with latent resources will proceed beyond sheer symptom relief to greater maturity and characterologic growth. This is especially the case where the environment condones and rewards such changes.

Q. *Is not insight a basic factor in all therapies?*

A. Insight on some level is helpful in all therapies. Even in supportive therapy, an understanding of the existing environmental encumbrances may eventually lead to a correction of remediable difficulties or to an adjustment to irremediable conditions. In reeducative therapy knowledge of the troublesome consequences of existing behavioral patterns may ultimately sponsor a substitution with more wholesome interpersonal relationships. In reconstructive therapy insight into unconscious conflicts and their projected manifestations into his everyday life, encourages the patient toward actions motivated more by the demands of reality than by the archaic needs and fears of his childhood. Obviously, insight alone is not equivalent to cure.

Q. *What is the difference between the level of insight effectuated in reeducative therapy and the kind in reconstructive therapy?*

A. In reeducative therapy an inquiry is conducted into conscious and preconscious drives, impulses, feelings, and conflicts with the object of suppressing or changing those that disorganize adjustment and of encouraging others that expedite adjustment. In reconstructive therapy the exploratory process deals with the more unconscious drives and conflicts. Due to the intensity of repression, one must implement the inquiry through examination of, and the inculcation of insight into, derivatives from the unconscious as revealed in verbal associations, dreams, fantasies, slips of speech, and the transference. The object in reconstructive therapy is to liberate the individual as completely as possible from anachronistic values, attitudes, strivings, and defenses and to remove blocks to personality growth.

Q. What is the best kind of therapy to use when the sole object is symptom relief or mere control of certain obnoxious personality traits?

A. The objective in the treatment effort may practically be limited to the restoration of habitual controls to the individual, to the mediation of any continuing environmental stress, and to the modification of strivings and goals that are inimical to the person's well-being or that are beyond his existing potentialities. Through the use of supportive and conditioning techniques, and by fostering an awareness of some of his character distortions and strivings, we may accomplish these objectives in a satisfactory way. There are, however, some conditions where the character structure is so disturbed, and where elaborated crippling mechanisms of defense are so tenacious, that even the objective of mere symptom relief presupposes an extensive exploration of aspects of the personality that have been repressed. This will necessitate reconstructive approaches.

Q. Is it possible to do reconstructive therapy on the basis of once-a-week sessions?

A. The effectiveness of therapy is dependent upon factors more important than the number of times each week the patient is seen. Reconstructive therapy is possible in some patients on the basis of sessions once weekly; it is not possible in others. Great skill is required to bring about reconstructive changes where there are long intervals between visits. Where a transference neurosis is to be created, four to five sessions weekly will be needed.

Q. What is the difference between an apparent and a permanent recovery as related to reconstructive therapy?

A. An apparent recovery is mere restoration to the premorbid level with the strengthening of the defensive techniques that have served, prior to illness, to maintain the ego free from anxiety. A permanent cure involves a real alteration of the ego to a point where those compromising defensive attitudes and mechanisms are no longer necessary to keep it free from anxiety. Under these circumstances the individual is capable of gratifying his basic needs and strivings without undue conflict. Recovery in psychotherapy is permanent only insofar as it produces a real change in the character structure of the individ-

ual and a reorientation of his relationships with others and with himself. Due to the operation of resistances which blanket offending impulses, and because of repressions which keep from awareness the most important problems of the individual, reconstructive psychotherapy offers the person the greatest chance of overcoming a severe emotional difficulty.

Q. What would you consider an acceptable minimal goal in reeducative therapy?

A. The least we can do for a patient is to bring him to as great an awareness of his problems as is reasonably possible, to enable him to lead as useful, happy and constructive a life as he can with his personality and environmental handicaps, to help him to overcome remediable life difficulties and to adapt to irremediable ones, and to adjust his ambitions to his existing capacities.

Q. What is the difference between a "normal" and "neurotic" person?

A. "Normality" is a social designation that embraces characteristics not entirely consonant with a definition of mental health. The average "normal" person in a culture possesses many neurotic drives that are sanctioned and perhaps encouraged by society. While these drives nurture some anxieties, the "normal" individual is still capable of functioning and of making a satisfactory social adjustment. Where the person is no longer able to adjust himself and he begins to manifest excessive anxiety and maladaptive mechanisms of defense, we may classify him as "neurotic." In therapy our objective may be to restore the person's social adjustment and his "normal" neurotic tendencies. However, a more extensive objective would be a correction of all neurotic traits, even those condoned as "normal."

Q. If ideal goals of complete reconstruction are impossible, what would be reasonably good goals in reconstructive therapy?

A. It is manifestly impossible for any one individual to reach the acme of emotional maturity in every psychic and interpersonal area. One may decide that a satisfactory result has been achieved when the patient loses his symptoms, abandons his disturbing neurotic patterns, deals with his difficulties spontaneously without needing help from the therapist, manifests productivity and self-confidence, shows absence of fear following expression of assertiveness, and exhibits an improvement in his interpersonal relationships with increased friendliness and respect and lessened suspiciousness, detachment, aggression, and dependency.

Q. What is the chief use of short-term or brief psychotherapy?

A. In "brief" psychotherapy the whole object is to achieve as rapid change as possible in a limited period of time. This entails a circumscription of goals. We may achieve symptomatic relief or the facing of one's problems more constructively, but we will usually not effectuate character change within the short treatment span. This will require a long period in or out of treatment. Nevertheless, with all of its limitations, brief therapy has an important and practical utility.

Q. How does the therapist's personality influence his techniques?

A. Each therapist eventually evolves his own therapeutic method, which is a composite of the methods he has learned, the experiences he has had, and his specific personality traits. For instance, an analytically trained therapist, inclined by personality to be authoritarian, may be unable to maintain the traditional silence and passivity demanded by psychoanalysis. To do so robs him of spontaneity; it provokes tension and prevents him from exhibiting the kind of relaxed objectivity that is most helpful in treatment. He may find it necessary to abandon passivity and to permit himself to participate more actively in the treatment process. His patients will perhaps respond to this change in a gratifying way and react more positively than when he was behaving in a stultified manner. This success may encourage the therapist to be himself, and he will probably find that his results continue to justify his alteration of technique. For him, then, the shift is justified since it liberates him from acting in an artificial, inhibited way. Yet another therapist may not be able to do the same thing; for instance, one who by personality is more retiring, quiet, and unobtrusive. For him the passive technique will probably work well; to attempt to force activity would be as artificial as to expect the former therapist to assume a feigned passivity.

Q. How do you explain the misunderstanding that exists among the different schools of psychiatry and psychology?

A. In so virgin a territory as the uncharted psyche, a diversity of theories, interpretations, and methods may be expected. A great deal of animosity has, however, unfortunately come to the surface among groups with divergent points of view. Splinter societies have erupted, justifying their break with the parent body on the basis of discrimination and lack of academic freedom in the older organization. Sparked at first by the impulse to create groups possessed of scientific liberalism, a number of the splinter organizations have, upon achieving stability, fallen victim to the same intolerant forces that initiated their secession, developing their own dogmas and rejecting original thinking among the members. Such entrenched and reactionary attitudes are to be condemned in any scientific group.

Q. Should a good therapist be able to cure or help all patients?

A. No matter how highly trained the therapist may be, he will be able to help some patients more than others. There will be certain patients he will not be able to treat—patients who other therapists may successfully manage. On the other hand, he will probably be able to cure some patients with whom other therapists have failed. He will make some mistakes during the course of therapy with all of his patients, but these mistakes need not interfere with ultimate beneficial results. Finally, he will be rewarded by a large number of successes, but he will also have his quota of failures.

Q. Does it follow that a psychoanalytically trained therapist will do better therapy than one who has not been analytically trained?

A. It is fallacious to assume that a nonanalytically trained therapist is incapable of doing many kinds of psychotherapy as well as one who has been analytically trained. However, where the therapist plans to do reconstructive psychotherapy, utilizing dream interpretation, transference, and resistance, he will require sound training in reconstructive therapy including a personal analysis.

Q. Must the therapist be completely free from neurosis?

A. It is doubtful that any person in our culture is entirely free from neurosis, no matter how much personal psychotherapy he has had. In order to do psychotherapy, however, the therapist must be sufficiently free from neurosis so that his own personal problems do not divert the relationship from therapeutic goals.

Q. Will personal psychotherapy or psychoanalysis guarantee good functioning on the part of an adequately trained therapist?

A. In most instances it will. However, serious personality difficulties may not be resolved to a point where the individual will be able to function as a therapist, although he might work satisfactorily in some other field. In other words, where his ego has been so damaged through a combination of constitutional predisposition and traumatic life experiences, he may not, even with extensive psychotherapeutic help, be able to achieve that kind of personality flexibility, objectivity, sensitivity, and empathy that are prerequisite for functioning as a psychotherapist.

Q. Why should not psychotherapy or psychoanalysis be able to resolve the neurotic problems of the psychotherapist, since he actually is not as *sick as most patients and should benefit greatly from psychotherapeutic help?*

A. The motivation to do psychotherapy, which is what inspires many therapists to seek personal therapy, may not be sufficient to enable the therapist to endure and to work through the anxieties underlying his character distortions. For instance, the individual may, prior to his determination to become a therapist, have been functioning in a more or less detached manner, removing himself from disturbing interpersonal situations periodically when these had become too difficult for him to handle. Under ordinary circumstances, and in average relationships, he would be able to function quite effectively with this kind of a defensive attitude. However, his detachment may seriously affect his capacity to operate in a therapeutic interpersonal relationship, in which he will constantly be brought into contact with critically disturbed people who will seek to extract from him responses he may be unable to give. A tremendous amount of personal psychotherapeutic work may be required before the therapist will be able to give up his detachment as an interpersonal defense. However, where he does not have sufficient anxiety to incite him to seek new modes of adjustment, he may not have the incentive to tolerate the great amount of work and suffering that will be involved in effecting a reconstructive change in his own personality. Consequently, in his personal therapy, he will keep warding off the deepest character change, and he may go through his total treatment without significant modification of his detachment. The fact that many therapists have exposed themselves to extensive personal therapy or psychoanalysis, and have emerged from it without any basic character changes, is no indictment of psychotherapy. Rather, it is an indication of how difficult it is to treat certain kinds of emotional disturbance without adequate motivation. In other words, the desire to become a psychotherapist is not in itself sufficient motivation to promote deep character change.

Q. What can the therapist do whose personality problems interfere with his executing good psychotherapy even after he has gotten extensive personal therapy and supervision?

A. If a qualified supervisor finds that the therapist's problems are interfering with his therapeutic effectiveness, the therapist may be advised to seek further personal psychotherapy. Should no change occur, it may be necessary for the therapist completely to give up psychotherapy as a career. He should not regard this as a personal defeat or as a sign of devaluated status, since he will probably be able to function very effectively in another role. For example, a psychiatrist may decide to do diagnostic, institutional, or other kinds of work that do not bring him into an intimate therapeutic relationship with patients. A caseworker can confine activities to an agency organized around other areas than therapeutic services. A psychologist can restrict functions to diagnostic testing, research, vocational guidance, and counseling.

Q. Don't you believe that every therapist should know the principles of preventive mental health in addition to knowing how to do psychotherapy?

A. Mental health needs are only partially served by an exclusive program of psychotherapy. This is because the impact of emotional problems on the lives of people so often reflect themselves in disturbances in work, family, marital, interpersonal, and social relations without causing collapse in adaptation characteristic of neuroses. The providing of help for these preclinical problems requires an ability to consult with, and to supervise community workers and professionals like social workers, teachers, nurses, physicians, psychologists, correctional workers and ministers, who are unable to handle such problems alone. It is advisable that every therapist be acquainted with the principles of preventive mental health and know how to communicate well with community agencies and the ancillary professions.

Q. What do you do if you make an outlandish error like forgetting a patient's age or marital status?

A. Being human, the therapist will, from time to time, unintentionally commit some blunders. He may forget the patient's age, the details about his family, or items in the history that the patient has already recounted. Distracted, he may even forget the patient's first name. Sometimes a more flagrant blunder may occur, such as calling a patient by the wrong name, or asking him if he has dreamed recently, when he already has in the first part of the interview recounted a dream. Should such slip-ups happen, there is no need to conceal them or to be too apologetic. The therapist may merely say: "Of course, you told me this" (or "I know this"). "It just temporarily slipped my mind." Patients will not make too much of such errors if a good relationship exists. At any rate, it may, if it seems indicated, be important to explore the patient's feelings immediately upon commission of a mistake.

Q. Should the psychiatrist do a physical examination if necessary?

A. A psychiatrist will probably not be as skilled in diagnosis as the internist to whom he can refer a patient needing medical treatment. However, a physical examination, in any other therapy than psychoanalysis, theoretically need not interfere with the therapeutic process, if the patient's reactions to it are examined and explored. It may bring many interesting and important feelings to the surface. This kind of activity will call for a therapist with great experience who can handle complicated reactions should they occur.

Q. Should two therapists, each working on separate members of the same family, confer?

A. A conference may be helpful to clarify the patient's interactions with the other member and to check on data significant to both. Usually, however, this is not routine. If it is done, the therapist should be mindful of his competitiveness with and need to impress the other therapist and of his defensiveness regarding his patient's behavior.

Q. What is multiple therapy, and does it have a utility?

A. Multiple therapy is the treatment of a single patient or a group by two or more therapists. It is preferred by some therapists in the management of difficult patients, such as psychotics and psychopaths. Differences in opinion and transference reactions between the therapists will require careful handling, sometimes within and sometimes outside of the therapeutic session. There may be advantages in employing multiple therapy in cases that do not respond to conventional treatment.

Q. Does not behavior therapy circumvent transference and other resistances?

A. Behavior therapy possesses ingredients that are common to all psychotherapies. Inaugurated almost immediately is a relationship situation, the patient responding to the therapist as an idealized authority who holds the key to his well-being. The trinity of faith, hope, and trust, while not openly expressed, are aspects that cannot be avoided. The placebo element is as much a component of behavior therapy as it is of any other kind of treatment. Factors of motivation and dyadic group dynamics undoubtedly come into play and act as accelerants or deterrants to progress. Where readiness for change is lacking, one might expect a negative result in behavior therapy. Subtley, transference will be set into motion, no matter how assiduously the behavior therapist attempts to avoid it, and resistances of various kinds will rear their obstructive heads at almost every phase of the therapeutic operation. Some behavior therapists refuse to acknowledge the presence of these intercurrent elements, though this obviously will not negate their influence.

Q. If psychological tests indicate that a person is very sick, shouldn't you approach him carefully in therapy, and isn't this a sign that your goals have to be superficial ones?

A. One may be forewarned about the strength of the individual's ego from psychological tests, but this should not prejudice the treatment process. One of the disadvantages of testing is that it puts a label on the patient the therapist may be reluctant to remove, even though his clinical judgment disagrees with the test findings. The therapeutic relationship is a better index of how deep one may go in therapy and the extensiveness of goals to be approached than any psychological test or battery of tests.

Q. Isn't it difficult at present to develop a real science of mind because of the many divergent ideas about psychodynamics?

A. The subject of psychodynamics opens up many founts of controversy because authorities with different orientations have different ways of looking at psychopathological phenomena. Irrespective of orientation, one can always find data that seems to substantiate one's particular point of view. The same interview material may thus be variously interpreted by several observers. Some regard it as confirming their theory that neurosis is essentially a clash between instinctual strivings and the environment. Others as enthusiastically demonstrate cultural forces as the primary provocative agent. Still others may find in the material evidence that neurosis is fostered by disturbances in the integrative functioning of the ego. Such divergent ideas are not too serious; they are to be regarded as the inevitable forerunners of a real science of mind. In the study of the uncharted psyche theories in abundance were bound to emerge, supporting many rifts and controversies. Fortunately, we are witnessing the beginnings of amalgamation, an honest effort to blend the findings of the various schools into a body of knowledge shorn of prejudice and bias.

Q. Is it possible for a therapist to be supervised by several different supervisors who espouse different theoretical viewpoints?

A. Unavoidable, particularly in an eclectic atmosphere, is the fact that the student therapist will be supervised by several supervisors whose approaches reflect wide theoretical differences. It is to be expected that these divergencies will mobilize insecurity in students who are seeking a definite structure in theory and process. The function of the good supervisor is to help the student see that different views of a phenomenon merely expose contrasting aspects of the same thing. These multiform facets may seemingly conflict with each other, though they are actually constituent parts of a unified whole. One must handle the student's desire to make everything harmonize and fit together into a master plan. Should his anxiety prove too great, the student may need special, even psychotherapeutic help. This is to be preferred to subverting the supervision to inept, clandestine treatment. Appreciating that other points of view exist is one of the most important contributions of the supervisor. However, only a supervisor who is sufficiently secure so as not to regard differences in approach as interferences, but rather who can look on them as a challenge toward further scientific inquiry, will be able to bring the kind of help that the student needs and that the student has a right to expect.

Q. Can a dependent patient progress in therapy beyond the goal of achieving freedom from symptoms?

A. It is sometimes contended that where the patient seeks a guidance, authoritarian relationship in therapy that his mental set will prohibit his entering into the participating activity essential for the exploratory process. His desire for paternalism, it is said, will block essential collaboration. This is not always correct. The majority of patients, even those who have read tomes on psychoanalysis, seek a relationship with a strong, idealized parental-like agency, who can lift them out of their distress. The stronger the anxiety, the greater the dependency. The task of the therapist is to promote a shift in motivation toward expanding the patient's inner resources and working cooperatively with the therapist. A fundamental task in all therapy is to promote the conviction in the patient that he has the resources within himself to resolve his feelings of helplessness. Good technique in psychotherapy takes this factor into account. Understandably, there are some characterologically dependent souls and borderline patients so inwardly damaged that they will need a dependency prop in order to function. No amount of therapeutic work will deviate them from this aim. But even here the therapist owes it to the patient to make an effort to promote greater self-sufficiency. Patients may diagnostically be written off as candidates for reconstructive psychotherapy in view of the depth of their disturbance, their habitual infantile relationships with people, wretched past conditionings with emotionally ill parents, uncontrollable acting-out propensities, paranoidal-like ideas, etc. On this basis, a supportive relationship is provided the patient, only to find that he presses for deeper self-understanding. Yielding to this pressure, the therapist may institute reconstructive treatments, helping the patient to rise out of his de-

pendent morass and to utilize his understanding toward great self-actualization.

Q. Are there any diagnostic signs that will indicate how a patient will actually respond to psychotherapy?

A. Very few diagnostic or other rules can be laid down to anticipate a patient's responses to therapy. The only true test is the way he takes hold of the opportunity offered him in psychotherapy to approach his life from a different perspective. Trial interpretations may be instituted to determine how the patient will respond in the relationship. Will he deny, resist, fight against, or accept the interpretation; and will he or will he not act on it?

Q. What is the effect on the patient of passivity in the therapist?

A. Passivity on the part of the therapist may produce frustration and anxiety, which, if not too intense, may mobilize the patient to think things through for himself and to act on his own responsibility. However, should excessive hostility and anxiety be engendered or should the patient interpret the therapist's passivity as rejection or incompetence, it may have a paralyzing effect on his progress. This is particularly the case where the patient, in his upbringing, has been victimized by a neglectful or uninterested parent who put too much responsibility on his immature shoulders. The therapeutic situation then will merely tend to recapitulate the early traumatizing experience and reinforce the sense of rage and helplessness.

Q. Should a trial period be instituted in psychotherapy to see how the patient will react?

A. Freud [1913] originally recommended that a trial period of a week or two be instituted to see if the patient is suitable for psychoanalysis. More or less, a trial period is inherent in all psychotherapeutic endeavors. The patient and therapist mutually survey each other to see whether they feel comfortable and confident about working together. The patient tests the therapist. Does he like him? Does he have confidence in him? Does he trust him? The therapist subjects the patient to an empirical scrutiny. Can he interact with the patient? Is the patient properly motivated and if not how can incentives be developed? Is the patient operating under misconceptions about treatment? How far will he be able to go in therapy—toward symptom relief? toward reconstructive personality change? He may, during this trial phase, make a few interpretations to test the patient's receptivity, flexibility, and capacities for change; at the same time ground rules are established, a working hypothesis laid down, and the beginnings of treatment instituted. Reformulations of this early hypothesis will have to be made periodically in accord with the patient's reactions, resistances and rate of movement.

Q. Shouldn't a therapist always remain neutral?

A. The therapist as a human being has feelings, values, prejudices, and needs. He will reveal these to the patient sooner or later, if not verbally then nonverbally, both directly in his interpretations and indirectly in his silences, pauses, content of questions, and emphasis. While ideally the therapist should avoid prejudicial pronouncements, he should not deceive himself into thinking that he can always maintain such a neutral stand. Nor is this desirable. It may be quite suitable to apply value pressure where it is needed and sometimes, as in acting-out proclivities, it is the only tactic that makes sense. Though maintaining the philosophy that the patient has an inalienable right to his point of view, decisions, and behavioral twistings and turnings, the therapist does not need to accept the validity of such ideas and actions. There is no such thing as true "neutrality" in the therapist. Otherwise he would not care whether the patient remained sick or got well. The therapist has opinions, and he has prejudices. He will display these in one way or another, if not one day then the next.

Q. Are there differences among psychoanalysts regarding the use of activity as opposed to passivity in psychoanalysis?

A. Polemics have been organized around the matter of activity versus passivity. On the one hand there are purists like Glover who defend the sanctity of the passive classical procedure. There are nonpurists, like Franz Alexander, who insist that the rejection of activity can only lead to therapeutic stagnation. Activity is generally eschewed in the classical technique on the basis that it tends to produce a refractory and insoluble as opposed to an ameliorative transference neurosis [Mitchell, 1927]. Since the time of Ferenczi [1926, 1928] who instituted "active" approaches, many analysts have introduced manipulations that to Glover [1964] exceed the limits of pure analytic practice on the basis that "deliberately adopting special attitudes and time restrictions for special cases changes the character of therapy in these cases, converting it into a form of rapport therapy." While such methodological innovations may produce excellent results and even be the best therapy for cases inaccessible to the customary technique, they should not be confused with "psychoanalysis" in which one analyzes and does not manipulate the transference. Supporting rigidity in approach, Glover avows that "flexibility in both psychoanalytic theory and practice has in the past been a frequent preamble to abandonment of basic principles." Passivity and the adoption of a "blank screen" are advocated as the best of deliberately nurtured attitudes to reduce complications. On the other hand, there are analysts who disagree with Glover, recommending modifications in method from the manipulation of the transference to the open exhibition of interest in and modulated demonstrations of affection toward the patient [Nacht, 1957, 1958; Bouvet, 1958; Eissler, 1958]. Commenting on the fact that few cases of simple transference neurosis are seen in practice, Lorand [1963] points out that psychoanalytic technique today "is quite different from that of earlier periods of analysis." Unless active interference is used in certain cases, for example in character disorders and infantile patterns of behavior, the analysis may stagnate or break down. Obviously, it is impossible at all times to adhere to the basic rules of psychoanalysis. Directiveness and active interference are sometimes essential, especially during stages of resistance "where the standard technical methods are of little help." Such variations in technique within the framework of classical psychoanalysis may be used to further therapeutic progress. The "dosing" of interpretations may also be necessary to activate the unconscious, to eliminate defenses as well as to prevent their too ready emergence. In a past contribution, Glover [1955] himself considered *complete* neutrality a myth and wondered whether adhering to the rule of not making important decisions was really desirable. When deviations from classical technique are in order, however, they must, he insisted, be dictated by the needs of the situation and not by countertransference. In practice, modification of analytic rules is frequently necessary. But whether we should label such deviations as "psychoanalysis" is another matter. There would seem to be some justification in restricting the term "psychoanalysis" to the classical technique and to entitle procedures incorporating modifications and active interventions as "modified psychoanalysis" or "psychoanalytically oriented psychotherapy."

Q. What is the theory behind cognitive therapy, and does it have a utility?

A. The theory underlying cognitive therapy is that people are dragooned into maladaptive actions by distortions in thought that they can both understand and control; within themselves they possess capacities for awareness of such understanding and solution of their difficulties. Therapeutic techniques organized around this hypothesis are directed toward correcting deformities in thinking and developing alternative and more realistic modes of looking at life experiences. It is said that this is a much more direct approach to problems than other approaches since it draws on patients' previous learning encounters. Interventions are aimed at rectifying misconceptions and conceptual blemishes that are at the basis of individual difficulties. This technique involves explorations of the stream of consciousness with the object of modifying the ideational content associated with the symptoms. Among the basic assumptions here are that the quality of one's thinking will inevitably influence the prevailing mood and that the *meaning* of a stimulus to the individual is more important than the nature of the stimulus itself.

There is a good deal of overlap of cognitive therapy with behavior therapy. Albert Ellis [1962, 1971] in his rational–emotive therapy has pioneered in cognitive approaches in a behavioral setting. Meichenbaum [1977] attempts to blend cognitive–semantic modification with behavioral modification. Aaron T. Beck [1976] has written extensively on cognitive therapy and has claimed advantages for it in treating depression over all other therapeutic methods, including drug therapy. A new magazine, *Cognitive Therapy and Research* (Plenum), is devoted to explicating the role of cognitive processes in human adaptation and adjustment. Whether cognitive therapy is useful for a therapist depends on the skill and conviction of the therapist and on the special learning capacities of the patient.

59
Recording in Psychotherapy

Satisfactory recording is conducive to good psychotherapy. It acts as a kind of discipline to the beginning therapist. It is helpful even to experienced therapists, facilitating the following of the progress of a case and helping in the rendering of a report. It is indispensible for purposes of research (Wolberg, LR, 1964b).

Except in those clinics where an ample budget provides dictating facilities and secretarial services, records of patients receiving psychotherapy are apt to be pitifully sparse. To some extent this is due to the absence of an organized routine recording system. Additionally, note taking during the treatment session is distracting to the therapist and annoying to some patients. Of utmost value, therefore, would be a recording system that is both simple to follow and not too disturbing to the patient.

Most patients expect that some kind of record will be kept. They usually accept note taking during the initial interview and do not object to occasional notes being written during later sessions. Where objections are voiced, these may be dealt with by an explanation to the effect that the keeping of a record is helpful in following the progress of the patient. Should the patient continue to object to notes being taken during sessions because this distracts him, or should

the practice distract the therapist, a note may be entered into the record following each session. If fear is expressed that confidential material may be read by another person, the patient may be informed that under no circumstances will the record be released, nor any information divulged, even to the patient's family physician, unless the patient gives written permission for this. Excellent outlines and suggestions for recording may be found in the books by Menninger (1952) and Beller (1962).

CASE RECORD

The case record should minimally contain the following data: (1) statistical data sheet, (2) initial interview, (3) daily progress notes, (4) monthly progress notes, (5) termination note, (6) summary, and (7) follow-up note.

Statistical Data

Basic statistical data include the following:

1. Patient's name
2. Address, home and business telephone

3. Age
4. Sex
5. Marital status, how long married, previous marriages, ages and sex of children
6. Age and occupation of mate
7. Education
8. Occupation, salary, sources of income if unemployed
9. Military record
10. Referral source

This data may be entered on a separate sheet or on a form (see Appendix A), or the first sheet of the initial form interview (see Appendix C). A more complete statistical form, which is useful in clinics, is illustrated in Appendix B.

Sometimes the patient may be asked to fill out certain questionnaires to help get statistical data without taking up too much of the therapist's time. Short forms are included under Appendix D, which is a Personal Data Sheet, and Appendix E, which is a Family Data Sheet. In using these forms, the Personal Data Sheet is given to the patient to fill out immediately prior to the initial interview. The Family Data Sheet is filled out after the therapist has accepted the patient for treatment.

Initial Interview

The data to be included in the recording of the initial interview are the following:

1. Chief complaint
2. History and development of complaint
3. Other symptoms and clinical findings
4. Patient's attitudes toward his family
5. Previous emotional upsets
6. Previous treatment
7. Estimate of existing insight and motivation
8. Tentative diagnosis
9. Tentative dynamics
10. Disposition of the case

A convenient initial interview form is included under Appendix C, the first sheet of which is for statistical data.

Daily Progress Notes

At the end of each session, the date and a brief note, which may consist of no more than one sentence, should be entered on a progress note sheet. This should contain the dominant theme of the session. Other entries may be:

1. Present state of symptoms or complaints (absent, improved, the same, worse)
2. How the patient feels (anxious, placid, depressed, happy)
3. Important life situations and developments since last visit and how they were handled
4. Content of the session
5. Significant transference and resistance reactions
6. Dreams

Since the wording of the patient's dreams is important, it is best to write dreams down during the session while they are related by the patient.

Appendix F is a convenient form for progress notes.

Monthly Progress Notes

A summarizing monthly progress note is of value in pulling together the events of the month. This may be a succinct recapitulation of what has been going on in treatment. In clinic setups where supervision of the total caseload is essential, a monthly progress summary, such as illustrated under Appendix G, which is routinely reviewed by the supervisor, may make for a more efficient kind of reporting.

Termination Note

A termination note is important containing the follow:

1. Date of initial interview
2. Date of termination interview
3. Reason for termination
4. Condition at discharge (recovered, markedly improved, moderately improved, slightly improved, unimproved, worse)
5. Areas of improvement (symptoms,

adjustment to environment, physical functions, relations with people)

6. Patient's attitude toward therapist at discharge
7. Recommendations to patient
8. Diagnosis

A termination form will be found under Appendix H.

Summary

The summary should contain the following information:

1. Chief complaint (in patient's own words)
2. History and development of complaint (date of onset, circumstances under which complaint developed, progression from the onset to the time of the initial interview)
3. Other complaints and symptoms (physical, emotional, psychic, and behavior symptoms other than those of the complaint factor)
4. Medical, surgical, and, in women, gynecologic history
5. Environmental disturbances at onset of therapy (economic, work, housing, neighborhood, and family difficulties)
6. Relationship difficulties at onset of therapy (disturbances in relationships with people, attitudes toward the world, toward authority, and toward the self)
7. Hereditary, constitutional and early developmental influences (significant physical and psychiatric disorders in patient's family, socioeconomic status of family, important early traumatic experiences and relationships, neurotic traits in childhood and adolescence)
8. Family data (mother, father, siblings, spouse, children—ages, state of health, personality adjustment, and patient's attitude toward each)
9. Previous attacks of emotional illness (as a child and later). When did patient feel himself to be completely free from emotional illness?
10. Initial interview (brief description of condition of patient at initial interview, including clinical findings)
11. Level of insight and motivation at onset of therapy (How long ago did the patient feel that he needed treatment? For what? Awareness of emotional nature of problem. Willingness to accept psychotherapy.)
12. Previous treatments (When did the patient first seek treatment? What treatment did he get? Any hospitalization?)
13. Clinical examination (significant findings in physical, neurologic, psychiatric, and psychologic examinations)
14. Differential diagnosis (at time of initial interview)
15. Estimate of prognosis (at time of initial interview)
16. Psychodynamics and psychopathology
17. Course of treatment:
    (a) Type of therapy employed, frequency, total number of sessions, response to therapist
    (b) Significant events during therapy, dynamics that were revealed, verbatim report of important dreams, nature of transference and resistance
    (c) Progress in therapy, insight acquired, translation of insight into action, change in symptoms, attitudes, and relationships with people
18. Condition on discharge (areas of improvement, remaining problems)
19. Recommendations to patient
20. Statistical classification

A summary form with spaces for the above items will be found under Appendix I.

Follow-up Note

A note on follow-up visits, or the inclusion of follow-up letters from patients, helps the therapist to evaluate the effectiveness of treatment. A follow-up letter may be mailed out 1, 2, and 5 years after therapy. A form letter such as the following may be used:

Dear ____:

In the past year I have wondered how things were progressing with you. Would you drop me a note telling me how you feel, and indicating any new developments. You may perhaps want to comment on your experience in treatment and how this was of help to you.

Sincerely yours,

———

Case Folder

A manila folder is advisable to hold the case record of the patient. The name of the patient is written on the flap, and, if the patient is being treated in a clinic, the case number is also entered. Some therapists prefer a folder which has several pockets that may be used for correspondence in relationship to the patient, as well as for detailed notes. Under Appendix J, there is a folder the writer has found useful in private practice as well as in clinic practice. Printed on the front of an ordinary folder are spaces for entry of the date of each visit, payments made, and certain items that are pertinent to the treatment of the patient. It is a simple matter of only a few seconds to check on the total number of visits, the number of broken or cancelled appointments, the payments that have been made and the dates of completion of the statistical data sheet, initial interview, monthly progress notes, consultations (psychiatric, medical, psychologic and casework) if these were obtained, tests administered by the therapist, termination note, summary and follow-up notes. There is space also for entry of supervisory sessions if these were obtained in relation to the patient. Printed on the back of the folder are lines for entry of dates for more visits if the space on the front of the folder is not sufficient.

Miscellaneous Enclosures

Included in the case record, in addition to the above data, are other notations and forms used by the therapist, such as psychologic test results, notes on medical and other consultations, detailed notes made by the therapist, written comments and notes of the patient (see Appendix S), and correspondence in relation to the patient.

ELECTRICAL RECORDING IN PSYCHOTHERAPY

Recording is being revolutionized by advances in computer technology and by the development of machines that electronically record auditory, visual, and physiological data. Machines can never replace the heuristic propensities of man. But machines can supplement his decision-making, contemplative facilities by sorting, storing, categorizing, and retrieving vast amounts of information with astonishing rapidity, efficiency, and accuracy. As new developments in switching, information theory, and automatic coding techniques become incorporated into computers, their potentialities will undoubtedly be expanded so that they can prepare their own programs from instructions fed into them. Computers, even at the present time, have become indispensible instruments in medicine, aiding in diagnosis by categorizing and analyzing symptoms and physical findings (Brodman et al, 1959, 1960; Weinrauch & Hetherington, 1959; van Woerhom & Brodman, 1961; Brodman & Van Woerhom, 1966).

New means of cataloging, storing, and dealing with complex variables have made it possible to employ the modern digital computer in psychiatric hospital systems (Laska et al, 1967; Glueck & Stroebel, 1975b) and even statewide systems (Sletten et al, 1970). In clinical practice attempts have been made to computerize data regarding the history of the patient, his mental status, and symptom clusters in an attempt to aid in diagnosis, prognosis, progress evaluation, and treatment outcome (Colby et al, 1969; Spitzer & Endicott, 1969). The making of computer diagnosis has been especially challenging and has attracted an increasing number of experimenters (Glueck & Stroebel, 1969; Maxwell, 1971). Glueck and Stroebel (1975b) have estimated that classification-assignment techniques are now available to permit an accuracy in diagnostic labeling comparable to that of expert clinicians with an accuracy nearing 100 percent, but they point out that there is a lack of ability of any classification system to achieve "more than 70 to 75 percent interrater reliability in the prediction of psychopathological criteria.'' Some attempts have also been made to refine computerized analysis of the electroencephalographic and neurologic findings, and innovative tactics have been evolved for various other types of data recording. The development of automated files will in the future undoubtedly help expedite the tabulation and retrieval of diagnostic, treatment, progress and disposition information. Simple and effective methods for computer programming immeasurably help administrators, auditors, researchers, and ultimately clinicians by simplifying the massive amount of memoranda included in the traditional case record, enabling the scanning of essential elements of a case without needing to spend endless hours looking for pertinent facts.

The programming of computers to process the data of psychotherapy requires that we reduce the complex interpersonal transactions that take place to mathematical symbols that can be coded. Because the full encoding of human pursuits is not now, and probably never will be, complete, only limited parameters can be assigned to the circuitry of electronic computers. A number of interesting experiments have been reported. For instance, Colby (1963) has described the simulation of a neurotic process by a computer, and Bellman (1957, 1961) has, through dynamic programming, attempted to contribute insights into the interviewing process. A computer-assisted simulation of the clinical encounter is described by Harless and his associates (1971, 1972) and Hubbard and Templeton (1973).

It is posited that eventually improved computer methods will revolutionize education with replacement of our present-day teaching technologies by computer systems that permit active personalized conversational dialogue between student and instrument, thereby eliminating the highly inefficient lecture techniques that reduce the student to an immobilized, passive, and resistive receiving station. An actual attempt in this direction, the teaching of interviewing by employing a suitably programmed digital computer to simulate an initial psychiatric interview, has met with some suc-

cess (Bellman et al, 1963, 1966). Here a trainee assumes the role of the therapist, and the digital computer, properly programmed, replies as a patient would respond. The computer may be programmed to represent a range of problems and patients. Jaffe (1964) has described specific techniques for interview analysis with the aid of digital computers with special methods of coding interpersonal phenomena that have potential research applications.

The flexibility of digital computers in selection, orderly storage, and rapid recovery of data, beyond the capacities of human performance, puts them in the forefront as instruments for research in the mental health field, not only for the calculating of results in experiments designed around specific hypotheses, but also in delineating trends and significances and in generating new hypotheses (Cappon, 1966). Computer programs capable of carrying out principle components factor analysis with varimax rotation may measure clinical change with greater objectivity and probable reliability than other methods (Cole, 1964). By proper programming it may be possible to ask computers to make decisions between alternate futures, thus expediting the predictability of human behavior.

More mundane operations that are being performed by computers include work with psychiatric records and other data related to the patient's history, symptomatology, and responses to therapy that may speedily and systematically be "memorized," synthesized, and retrieved. Feeding into the machine the recorded history, the psychological test results, and the symptoms of the patient, computers will quickly process these facts against the statistics of relative possibilities of diagnosis, prognosis, and treatment approaches (Rome et al., 1962; Swenson et al, 1963).

The employment of videotape recorders (see also Videotape Recording, p. 804) has also introduced a new dimension into psychotherapeutic recording, with vast potentials for teaching and the expediting of treatment (Stoller, 1967, 1969; Torkelson & Romano, 1967; Czajkoski, 1968; Danet, 1969; Alger & Hogan, 1969; Berger MM, 1970; Melnick & Tims, 1974). Therapists, viewing themselves interacting with their patients may learn as much as they do in a good supervisory session (Geocaris, 1960; Moore, FJ, et al, 1965; Beiser, 1966). However, the initial shock value of seeing oneself performing inadequately usually induces one to change for a limited time only. One will soon adapt oneself to one's television image unless there is a reworking of the material by a supervisor to reinforce one's learning. Observance by the supervisor of the therapist in actual operation with patients is feasible by videotape, the contrast between what the therapist's report of what he or she believes has been going on and the recorded events lending itself to emotional learning in the student. Supervisors also may be able to sharpen their own techniques in supervision by videotaping some of their supervisory sessions. Finally, beginning therapists may learn the process of interviewing and the management of various stages in treatment by watching videotapes (or sound movies) of expert therapists working with patients.

While useful, written records and sound tape recordings alone are limited in bringing about an awareness on the part of patients of incongruous or paradoxical communication patterns. Sound films (Scheflen, 1963) and videotapes are more useful. Alger and Hogan (1966), employing videotape recordings in conjoint marital therapy, have pointed out that many levels of communication, as well as discrepancies between levels, become readily apparent to patients watching themselves immediately after interacting during a session. Differences between the televised actions and remembered feeling responses are beneficially registered on the patient. In individual therapy the videotaped interview may help the patient see himself as others see him. This is an excellent way of demonstrating to the patient how he communicates. Use of the playback technique has proven valuable for many syndromes, including speech problems and alcoholism. A view of himself in a drunken state often helps motivate an alcoholic to stop drinking. Videotaping may be of value in group and family therapy.

Obviously, it is impossible to record all of the treatment sessions of any single patient even if the therapist possesses the proper equipment. Apart from the expense of recording materials, and the problem of storage of the recordings, transcription of even a single recorded session is an item of considerable, and in many instances prohibitive, cost. Occasional recordings that are saved until they have served their purpose will, however, be found valuable. Exceptional videotapes may be transferred over to 16-mm sound film at a reasonable cost. From a practical viewpoint, *audio casette tape recordings* may serve the purpose of preserving the verbal interactions of patient and therapist. While not nearly as valuable as videotapes, they are less expensive and they are easily transcribed.

Where the therapist is not resistive to recording sessions, generally there will be relatively little difficulty in gaining the patient's permission and cooperation. The apparatus is placed unobtrusively (it must not be concealed) in the room. When the patient enters the room (usually when recordings are to be made, it is best to introduce this possibility to the patient at the initial interview), he may be approached in a way somewhat similar to this:

Th. Hello, I'm Dr. ____.
Pt. Hello.
Th. Won't you sit down in this chair so we can talk things over?
Pt. Yes, thank you.
Th. (pointing to the tape recorder) Don't mind this machine. Sometimes I record an important session during therapy. It saves me the need to write everything down, so I can pay attention better to what is said.
Pt. I see.
Th. (smiling) Does this scare you?
Pt. Oh, no, if it's useful, I've never been recorded.
Th. Of course, what is recorded is completely confidential between us, but if you object for any reason, we don't really have to record.
Pt. No, I don't mind.
Th. If, for any reason, it interferes in any way or bothers you, tell me and I'll turn it off.
Pt. All right, I really don't mind.
Th. All right then, would you like to tell me about your problem so we can decide the best thing to do for you?

The recorder may be turned on at this point, or, if it has been on, no further attention should be paid to it. During later sessions it may be started prior to the patient's entering the room, so that the first comments may be recorded. If the recording is to be used for teaching purposes or transcribed for publication, a signed release is usually necessary. If, for any reason, the patient objects to the machine, it should immediately be turned off and not used again unless the patient's permission has been obtained.

60

Psychotherapy during Childhood, Adolescence, and Old Age

There are critical stages in the development of personality at which times crucial incidents and experiences have a destructive impact that are not registered at another period. The stages of weaning, habit training, bodily exploratory activities, entry into school, puberty and adolescence, marriage, pregnancy, child rearing, and retirement and old age pose special problems that influence psychotherapeutic interventions when these are needed.

CHILD AND ADOLESCENT THERAPY

Psychopathology in children must at all times be viewed against the backdrop of developmental norms. Moreover, it must be considered in relation to existing family and social distortions that deprive children of needs essential to their growth or subject them to rejection, violence, or overstimulation with which they cannot cope. Among common noxious influences are parental absence, rejection, seduction, overprotection, or cruelty. Contemporary disruptions in family life, such as a detached and disinterested father, subjection to television bombardments of violence and sexuality,

poverty, lack of intimate family ties, racial conflicts at school, etc., exaggerate the normal problems inherent in growing up, for instance, fears of separation, resistance to socialization, defiance of discipline, sibling rivalry, and Oedipal crises, interfering with their resolution. Emotional difficulties in childhood usually express themselves in symptoms of excessive irritability, hyperkinesis, fearfulness, daydreaming, obsessions, compulsions, bed-wetting, and excessive masturbation. Sleep, speech, eating, and learning disturbances are common, as are psychophysiological manifestations such as tics, spasms, vomiting, diarrhea, and asthma.

During the first three years of life excessive and continuous crying unrelieved by attention from the mother signals a state of unresolved tension (Cramer, 1959). Inordinate rocking, thumb sucking, head rolling, sleeplessness, food refusal, vomiting, fecal retention, soiling, temper tantrums, ritualistic behavior, defiance, stammering, and aggression often indicate disturbances in the child's environment, particularly in the relationship with the mother. In a small number of instances these are manifestations of organic physical or neurological ailments.

During the fourth and fifth years extravagant fears, nightmares, excessive masturbation, and enuresis reflect sexual-identity difficulties. Overactivity, tantrums, negativism, and destructiveness constitute another type of patterning for conflicts developed during this period. Such difficulties are often nurtured by sexual and hostile acting-out in parents and by their seductive use of the child to satisfy their own neurotic needs.

Neurosis during the sixth to ninth years of life frequently manifests itself in failing adjustment at school, the outcroppings taking the form of school phobias, truancy, aggression toward fellow pupils and teachers, and learning disabilities. Outright neurotic symptoms may appear in other types of phobias, tics (blinking, grimacing, jerking of the head and extremities), stammering, compulsions, and conversion phenomena. Excessive withdrawal and daydreaming or aggressiveness and antisocial activities (stealing, exhibitionism, fetishism, peeping, etc.) interfere with social adjustment. Frank, unbound anxiety may erupt. Eventuating psychophysiological disturbances may derange various organ systems.

In the preadolescent (latency) stage, between nine and twelve, there is enhanced aggressiveness, fighting with siblings and friends, and occassional depressive states stimulated by disappointments and failures.

During adolescence potential problems incorporate the full spectrum of psychopathology from behavior disorders to psychoneuroses to psychoses. The emotional disorders that are most common in adolescence, however, are adjustment difficulties, personality pattern and trait disturbances, scholastic failure, school phobia, enuresis, psychosomatic complaints, and delinquency.

In the tumultuous growth period of adolescence, with the extensive alterations in the physical, biochemical, and emotional make-up characteristic of this epoch, we must, in judging the degree of disturbance, take into consideration the normal anxieties and concerns that plague the individual.

Adolescents have a need for both uniqueness and difference, a desire to conform as well as a fear of being different from others of their age and sex. Strong and strange impulses dominate the body as the sexual glands mature and the adolescent comes under the influence of erotic thoughts and feelings. New demands are made by family and community; no longer is the youth considered a child. Swings into independence and aggressiveness are followed by refuge in childish dependency and passivity. The need for recognition vies with the impulse to defy. Drives for success and prestige are paramount, while conflict rages over issues of religion and death. A fluctuating sense of values and confusion in identity add to the adolescent's turmoil.

Constructive solutions will be needed. The adolescent must first dissipate dependency ties sufficiently to enter into a more aggressive and independent attitude toward the world. This is especially necessary in a society where the burden of one's own support and ultimately that of one's family will fall on the individual's shoulders. Second, the adolescent must learn to control sexual function so that there will be a proper balance between restraint and expression. Evolvement of adequate sexual role identification is mandatory. Third, one must change from the subordinate manner of a child to the dominant habitude of a grown-up, in order to feel equal with other adults. Fourth, one must develop a cooperative attitude toward authority, without feeling victimized or excessively hostile. Fifth, one must learn to be assertive and creative and to assume leadership on occasion, without ulterior motives of control or power. A proper educational and career choice must be made.

In primitive cultures the adolescent struggle is less intense than in civilized societies because there is much more continuity in the behavior patterns of child and adult. Primitive economies are less complex and consequently afford an easier and earlier emancipation from parental support. Child marriage and premarital intercourse are more or less condoned. This sanction affords the growing child an outlet for energies. Civilized societies impose barriers against which the adolescent will struggle. While relatively mature biologically, the adolescent cannot become economically self-sufficient until well along in adult life. A large proportion of today's young people are forced by the requirements of their chosen careers to enter upon a long and expensive period of study that must be financed by their parents.

Hostility and resentment are frequently the outcome of the conflict between the impulse to break dependency ties and the need for material help and support. Although adolescents feel an urge to lash out at their parents, most realize that such action will result in retaliatory measures that threaten one's security. In addition, the hostile urge clashes with some of the adolescent's ideals. Thus a youth is at the mercy of many ambivalent and conflicting values and goals. For example, one may desire a career in line with the projected ambitions and wishes of one's parents. On the other hand, an impulse to become self-directing may intrude, even though this involves interrupting one's education and taking a menial job. The youth is torn between devotion to parents and anger at them for hampering freedom of action. The adolescent is hindered by adult moral judgments and taboos against unrestrained expression of sexual curiosities, yet is driven in the direction of gratifying outlets that, in an ambivalently permissive society with many sources of stimulation (movies, television, pornographic materials), spur acting-out. Sometimes the child is driven by contradictory impulses reflecting both the secret sexual and delinquent wishes of one or more parents that they have projectively and covertly conveyed to their offspring, as well as guilt feelings of the parents that have prevented them from personally expressing these impulses. The child here acts as a messenger for the parents, who stealthily relish the exploits of their offspring and then heap blame on him or her.

Under the best of circumstances the adolescent period is a chaotic one and is characterized by a recrudescence of problems that had their origin in childhood and were never adequately resolved. Often parents have not been aware of these problems, and they are dismayed and frightened by the eruption of severe behavioral disturbances in a previously exemplary child. The early adolescent (12 to 15 years) is plagued by regressive thrusts that conflict with the

new growth demands of this stage. The child ambivalently veers between submitting and rebelling, sociability and isolation, friendships and enmities, overactivity and retreat, depression and overexcitement. Delinquency and acting-out are common. The struggle in this period is a process of resolution of sexual identity, object ambivalence, and needs for separation and individuation. In middle adolescence (14 to 17 years) there is some resolution of sexual conflicts with greater ability to relate. Narcissistic defenses alternate with more mature coping mechanisms. Homosexual episodes, depersonalization, anxiety, and runaway tendencies may occur. In late adolescence (17 to 21 years) separation-individuation accelerates, object choice solidifies, identifications strengthen. Identity crises, depression, and adjustment difficulties continue, however, often encouraged by available peer groups involved in sexual and delinquent exploits.

The average child at all stages undergoes a great upheaval in the clash between inner strivings and personal and parental standards. A resolution of these discordancies results in greater ability both to function independently and to engage in cooperative relationships with people.

In many cases the adolescent conflict does not resolve easily. It is influenced adversely by unfortunate conditionings and experiences in earlier relationships. Overprotected children, particularly those who have been dominated and overstimulated by neurotic, adulating mothers, are tremendously disturbed by thoughts of independence. A striving toward self-sufficiency conflicts with the need to cling to the protecting parent. The child here is plunged into catastrophic helplessness when his dependency drive is threatened. In the quest for uniqueness, a defiance of convention may be indulged with eccentric hair style, dress, speech, and conduct that are at odds with custom and traditional proprieties. The youth may indulge in drugs and engage in reckless and even dangerous pursuits, often in cooperation with a peer group that gives support and a spurious security.

Resultant behavior patterns depend upon the facility with which the individual externalizes aggression. Verbal or physical assaults on the parents, runaway tendencies, and behavior problems result when overt aggression does not precipitate too much anxiety. In cases where the child has been intimidated and cannot express rage openly or where he senses that his resentment will result in abandonment and punishment, he may be unable to give vent to his anger. Resentment creates such anxiety that it may not gain conscious recognition. It may instead be shunted off into autonomic channels, with resultant depression and psychosomatic symptoms. Coincidentally, elaborated defenses, in the form of phobias, compulsions, and conversion symptoms help reinforce the repression of aggression. Guilt feelings may be appeased by ascetic acts or religious preoccupations. In pathologically weak ego structures the intensity of conflict may produce ego shattering, with the precipitation of psychoses, usually of a schizophrenic nature.

In summary, *adjustment reactions* to growing up are a normal by-product of socialization. They occur in all children. The reactions become exaggerated in those who are subjected to extraordinary stress, or whose developmental needs are not being met by parents, or who are being grossly mismanaged, improperly disciplined, or subjected to cruel and abusive treatment. The constitutional makeup of the child will influence the severity of reactions and the ability to cope with the stress being experienced. The responses of the parents to the child's reactions will also influence the outcome. If they are kindly and caring adults, capable of maintaining control of the situation and their own emotions, the child may be helped through the critical adjustment years. Where they are not so equipped, minor maladjustment reactions may explode into severe behavior disorders that can persist and influence adversely later stages of development. The ultimate outcome may be a pathological neurotic or psychotic reaction for which treatment will be needed.

General Principles of Child and Adolescent Therapy

The basic rule in treating disorders in childhood is providing an adequate climate in which developmental needs are met,

opportunities for impulse gratification supplied, and proper disciplines and restraints imposed. Alterations of the milieu are usually required and the cooperation of the parents and family may be essential even to the point of exposing them to independent counseling, psychotherapy and family therapy. Unless this is done, work with the child alone may prove to be fruitless, the parents and other family members sabotaging the child's efforts at adjustment.

Therapeutic interventions will accord with the accepted theoretical model. Thus, if we regard deviant behavior as originating through reinforcement of unhealthy patterns by the family, we will organize treatment tactics around modifying the consequences of such patterns through behavior therapy (Ross, A, 1972). Should we adopt a psychoanalytic family interaction model, we will embark on a search for pathogenic conflicts and their resolution through insight and working through in the patient–family–therapist relationships. If we consider constitutional organic neurological factors as most significant, we will look for developmental and language lags that interfere with the timetable in the evolution of essential functions, the prescription of proper medications, and the institution of adequate training routines.

Treatment techniques among good child therapists of divergent schools are not too dissimilar in spite of theoretical differences. The existence in childhood of relatively undeveloped personality functions, the strivings for independence and mastery that inevitably conflict with dependency yearnings, the heightened motor activity and fantasy life, the lowered frustration tolerance, the greater needs for discipline, and the extraordinary plasticity of the developing ego will require innovations in technique. Environmental manipulation, crisis intervention *(q.v.)*, family therapy *(q.v.)*, drawings *(q.v.* art therapy), the use of play materials *(q.v.* play therapy), and the employment of greater activity and supportiveness with efforts at symptom control are more or less standard. The key to management is a proper diagnosis with assessment of the potential of the child as well as the role the mother and family will play in organizing a therapeutic milieu.

The majority of child therapy clinics utilize eclectic methods that stress the interpersonal relationship, focus on the present, and encourage therapist activities of a friendly, active, and supporting nature in order to provide a corrective experience for the child. Psychotherapy is considered a new and unique growth experience that is family-centered with the focus of concern on the child (Allen, FH, 1962, 1963).

Thus at the beginning of therapy parents require help in expressing their feelings about the plans being made for therapy. Prior to bringing the child into a treatment situation, the mother and father are aided in ventilating their hopes, doubts, and fears. Discussions consider the part they can play in preparing their offspring for treatment. In these early interviews the role distortions of the parents with each other and their children usually become apparent. It is essential to involve both parents in the planning to avoid distorting the family drama further. The beginning phase of treatment with the child is diagnostic for the therapist. The therapist witnesses how the child reacts to a unique experience of acceptance and empathy, his degree of accessibility, the content and manner of his communications, and the ways that he expresses or conceals feeling. At the start the child will probably perceive the therapist as he does other adults—hostile, dogmatic, overprotective, omnipotent, etc. "He will project on the therapist both what he expects, what he wishes, and what he fears him to be. The child will invest him with the magic to cure without having to do anything himself. The therapist will both allow and help the child to test out these preconceptions, but will maintain his own integrity and not become the projection. While the child tries to make him be the good or bad parent, the therapist remains himself and thus provides a new, differentiating experience for the child." But even in the first interview a therapeutic process may begin. Winnicott (1969), utilizing the child's drawings, has brought out that we can score a significant imprint on motivation in this one interview.

Emerging from this "diagnostic" phase is a therapeutic plan determined by the child's physical condition, the evaluative studies of the psychologist, the ability of the child to form a relationship with the therapist, and the cooperation of the parents. A definite schedule is set up, usually once weekly, the child and parents having separate and sometimes concurrent appointments. In a team plan different team members may see the parents and the child.

Changing paradigms of therapy have placed an accent on *child behavior therapy*. Its briefness, ease of administration, and effectiveness in behavior and habit disorders have enabled therapists to help many children, especially young ones, who because of their lack of motivation, cooperation, intelligence, and verbal skills have not been able to utilize traditional interview and play techniques. The focus is on altering the environmental circumstances that initiate and support deviant patterns. No effort is made to probe for conflicts or to promote insight. There is little emphasis on the importance of the child–therapist relationship except to establish sufficient rapport to enhance the acceptance of social reinforcement. The traditional diagnostic categories are not considered of great importance.

Initially, a behavioral assessment is made of the problem, consisting of an exact description of its nature, its history, its frequency, the circumstances under which symptoms occur, the reactions of the parents or teachers, and the consequences to the child. Many pertinent techniques are delineated in Chapter 49 on Behavior Therapy. The selective method used with a particular child will depend on the specific behavior to be altered. Bijou and Redd (1975) have outlined some useful methods. Monitoring procedures are set up to provide data about progress, and parents are trained in proper responses, and at home they act as accessory behavior therapists.

Thus, where a child has behavior tendencies that are upsetting to others (such as pushing, fighting, hitting, etc.), a program may be organized that grants rewards (candy, a token or points exchangeable for something the child likes to receive or do, praise, etc.) for each instance of desirable social behavior. Coordinately, an aversive contingency may be employed whenever the obnoxious behavior occurs, for example, removal of the child from the room for a period and placement in a room without toys. Or the child may be penalized for conduct by taking away some tokens or points.

Where a child is withdrawn or shows shy or phobic behavior, he is rewarded with praise and attention when he manifests sociable and nonphobic behavior. He is ignored when he does not. Reinforcements are gradually spaced and delayed, and requirements for reinforcement gradually are made more stringent to shape behavior. Modeling appropriate behavior may be utilized both for the child and the parents, the latter observing how the therapist responds through a one-way mirror if one is available. Systematic desensitization may also be employed. Thus, a school phobia is treated by gradual introduction to the school environment for slowly increasing periods, each success being rewarded.

The acquisition of new and desirable behavior repertoires will call for contingent positive reinforcement for first approximations then increasing intensities of the new behavior. Inappropriate normal responses (of speech, conduct, etc.) may gradually be extinguished and displaced to suitable situations by adequate reinforcements.

These operant techniques are also applicable to hospitalized adolescent patients. Their effectiveness is illustrated by the experience in the Adolescent Service of the Boston State Hospital (Lehrer et al, 1971). A token economy is tailored to individual needs or problems. Patients are given points that can be redeemed for money, school attendance, and participation in various activities. Points buy food (hot dogs, pizza, hamburgers), soda, and ice cream. Then they permit playing a jukebox, games (pinball, table tennis, and board games) as well as purchasing various things and goods in a special teenage lounge that has a soda fountain and grill. Points are also exchangeable for parties, dances, camping expeditions, etc. Points are taken away for infraction of the rules. Serious violations, like assaultiveness and abuse of property, lead to restriction of all activities until the patient has worked out with a psychologist strategies for controlling his behavior and proper

point payment for any damages that he has done to property.

Some therapists utilize the findings of dynamic psychology to conceptualize the development and problems of children. The therapeutic focus of *child psychoanalysis* following this model is on bringing to the child's awareness the anxieties, unconscious wishes, and defenses that produce his difficulties. Since children do not respond to therapy like adults, the classical technique accordingly must be modified taking into account the child's tendencies to project problems onto the environment and the lack of motivation for therapy. The parents and other important members of the family also have to be brought into the therapeutic situation on some level (counseling, family therapy, individual therapy) in accordance with what is required in each individual case. Because children express themselves most readily in play, play therapy may be an important tool for probing conflicts and for interaction with the therapist.

Child psychoanalysis was originally explicated by Sigmund Freud in his "Analysis of a Phobia in a Five-Year-Old Boy." The two main orientations that emerged were those of Anna Freud (1928, 1945, 1946) and Melanie Klein (1932, 1961). According to Anna Freud, children as young as 3 years of age may be analyzed. Free association and the couch position, however, cannot be employed. Instead the child's activities in movement, play, and random talk are used for interpretation, as are stories, dreams, and the child's reactions to the therapist. Caution in making interpretations is essential since the ego of the child is not as firmly developed as the adult. Generally the child does not evolve a transference neurosis, reflecting more of the immediate situation than the past. The cooperation of the parents should be enlisted, but no attempt is made to offer advice or to manipulate the environment on the theory that to change the milieu is to remove what will help the gaining of insight into the child's conflicts and responses. In Melanie Klein's technique children as young as 2 may be treated. Unlike Anna Freud's method, the deepest interpretations to fantasies revealed by the child in play are given, starting with the first interview. These are concerned with Oedipal wishes, awareness of parental intercourse, the desire to destroy the mother's body, and the desire to incorporate the father's penis. Since the reality situation is not considered significant, the cooperation of the parents is not sought; indeed, it is considered an unnecessary inconvenience. Interesting descriptions of the psychoanalytic process in children may be found in the writings of Aichorn (1936), Winnicott (1958), Erikson (1963), Isaacs (1930), Bornstein (1949), Gyomroi (1963), and Blos (1962, 1970).

There is some disagreement among analysts regarding how thoroughly one should probe the unconscious. Generally with adolescents between 12 and 15 years of age and even up to 17 or 18, there is a tendency to keep therapy on a reality level. Work with these adolescents has dimensions that vary from those with younger children because of the different problems the adolescent faces in adaptation. Required are great activity, flexibility in approach, consistent strengthening and supporting of ego functions, focusing on current and immediate problems with avoidance of probing into the psychodynamics of the past, and involvement where necessary of the parents in therapy on an individual and family basis. While it's necessary to become acquainted as thoroughly as possible with the unconscious problems of the adolescent, the therapist does not deliberately explore them, except when they are obviously and openly linked to present problems. Countertransference must be rigidly controlled since unresolved problems with one's own parents may subtly get one to encourage acting-out in the patient. For instance, the therapist's innuendoes, interest, and manner may catalyze defiant and sexual behavior. A psychoanalyst will need to modify techniques radically, the analyst providing "a collaborative setting where closeness and intimacy are possible without being imposed. Adolescents need to test reality, to validate their perceptions, and to assess their value systems. The analyst must be ready to state his position on important issues and, when appropriate, let the patient

know some of his personal reactions to him" (Bryt, 1965). The sex of the therapist is also important. With girls it is urgent to have a female analyst. With boys a male therapist is a preferred but not essential choice. Blos and Finch (1975) state that visits twice a week are more than doubly effective as those on a once weekly basis.

Attempts to utilize more formal psychoanalytic therapy in late adolescence are more successful. A search is made for fixations and problems in the infantile period and in early childhood that reappear in direct or disguised forms as well as the defenses against regression, castration anxieties, and superego guilt. From these we may better understand how a hitherto adjusted child becomes converted into a disorganized, willful, and violent adolescent. The youthful patient is, however, usually a resisting participant in probing noxious early experiences and reactions, not seeing the connection with what is happening in the present.

Gladstone (1964) describes three major groupings of adolescents for whom different treatment approaches are applicable. The first group consists of acting-out character problems and offenders who will require extreme therapist activity to promote a relationship, a firm setting of limits, and a constant emphasis on human values and their communication in the relationship. In another study, he points out how this may be done (Gladstone, 1962). The second group includes neurotic disorders and dependency problems. Here observant and interested objectivity is offered the patient, emotional catharsis is encouraged, there is a probing of underlying conflicts toward insight, and there is a minimum of interference from the therapist in working out the conflicts. Illustrations of such tactics are provided by Josselyn (1952, 1957). The third group is composed of withdrawn schizoid reactions. With such patients one best employs supportive techniques, experience sharing, continuous correction of distorted perceptions with efforts at reality testing, and educational correction and filling in of learning deficits. Silber (1962) gives examples of these procedures.

Group therapy (q. v.) with children was

described by Slavson (1949, 1952) and has become an accepted way of dealing with problems in childhood, both as a principal therapy and as an adjunct to individual therapy. Of note, too, are Moreno's methods of utilizing psychodramatic play with groups of children (Moreno, 1965).

The size of children's groups must be kept below that of adult groups (Geller, 1962). For instance, in the age group up to 6 years, two or three children constitute the total. Both boys and girls can be included. Single-sex groups are those (1) from 6 to 8 years, which optimally consist of three to five members; (2) from 8 to 12 years, which may have four to six members; and (3) from 12 to 14 years, which have the same number. Mixed-sex groups at the oldest age level are sometimes possible. Play therapy is the communicative device up to 12 years, the focus being on feelings and conflicts. It is obvious that the ability to communicate is a prerequisite here. Beyond 12, discussions rather than play constitute the best activity medium. Techniques include confrontation, analysis of behavior in the group, and dream and transference interpretation. Both activity (during which acting-out may be observed) and discussions are encouraged at various intervals. Interventions of the therapist should be such so as not to hamper spontaneity. Discussion is stimulated by the therapist, and silences are always interrupted. Ideally, individual therapy is carried on conjointly with group therapy, particularly at the beginning.

Group therapy is particularly ideal for adolescents even though resistance may be prominent. Identity crises and confusion may respond better to group treatment than to any other approach (Rachman, AW, 1972a & b). The therapist must function in roles in addition to that of psychotherapist, for example, as guide, counselor, and teacher (Slavson, 1965). Exposure to an intensive, dynamic, analytically oriented focus is often intolerable to the adolescent; hence a flexible, active format is best. A behavioral group approach is often helpful, for example, with disturbed adolescents in a hospital, such as was previously described, as well as in a residential setting (Carlin & Armstrong, 1968). The introduction of several young adults of ages 21 to 24 helps foster healthier transference reactions and provides identification models. The therapist amidst the impulsive active behavior in the group (which is spontaneous among adolescents) cautiously introduces interpretations.

Some therapists find a cotherapist (preferably of the opposite sex) useful (Evans, 1965; Godenne, 1965). Countertransference phenomena that often occur in cotherapy include excessive attraction to young patients of the opposite sex, fear of "liking too much" certain patients of the same sex (due to homosexual fears), projection of feelings toward the therapist's own mate onto the cotherapist or a patient of the opposite sex, competition with the patients of the opposite sex for the cotherapist, competition with the cotherapist for the group's admiration and support, and transfer of emotions originally felt for a child of the therapist onto a member of the group.

The *drug therapy* of children with behavior disorders, schizophrenia, and chronic brain syndromes has included the use of a number of substances (Fish, 1963, 1965, 1966). The most important drug influence has been registered on psychomotor excitement, a control of which reduces other symptoms, such as perceptual and thought disorders. As a result of being calmed down, the child may become amenable to group activities, educational offerings, and psychotherapy (Fish, 1960 a & b).

Generally no drug is given until it is proven that environmental manipulation and psychotherapy have had no effect on the prevailing symptoms. Diphenhydramine (Benadryl 2 mg per pound of body weight daily; average dose 100–200 mg daily, maximum dose 300 mg) is valuable in behavior disorders with hyperactivity in children over 20 pounds of weight and in anxiety reactions in children under 10 years of age. Since it produces drowsiness, it may be employed as a bedtime sedative. Meprobamate (Equanil, Miltown—200–600 mg daily) is useful in some neurotic and behavior disorders, including mild organic brain disease (Freedman, AM, 1958). Other drugs that can be utilized are chlordiazepoxide (Librium) for children over 6 years of age, 5 mg two to four times daily, increased if necessary to as much as 10 mg two or three times daily; and diazepam (Valium), 1 to 2.5 mg three or four times daily, increased gradually as needed and tolerated for anxiety. Promethazine (Phenergan) for severely disturbed children (Bender & Nichtern, 1956) acts as a sedative when 25 mg are given at bedtime or 6.25 mg to 12.5 mg are given three times daily. Phenothiazines may be tried for primary behavior disorders, as well as schizophrenia and organic brain disease where milder therapies are ineffective. Chlorpromazine (Thorazine, 1 mg per pound of body weight daily, or 50–400 mg daily) is used in excited states; should an emergency necessitate intramuscular injection, 0.25 mg per pound of body weight every 6 to 8 hours as needed are given. Trifluoperazine (Stelazine, 0.15 mg per pound of body weight daily, or 1–20 mg daily) is used sometimes in apathetic withdrawn children. Taractan (in children over 6 years of age) in dosage of 10 to 200 mg daily, Navane (in adolescents) in dosage of one to 40 mg daily, Haldol (in adolescents) 0.5 to 16 mg daily, and Moban (in adolescents) in dosage of 1 to 2.5 mg daily may be tried, in this order, where phenothiazines are ineffective. The employment of Ritalin, Dexedrine, and Benzedrine will be described later in drug therapy for hyperactive minimal brain dysfunctional children. Barbiturates should not be given to children. Should hypnotics become necessary, Miltown or chloral hydrate may be used. The latter is prescribed as Noctec Syrup (each teaspoon equals 500 mg) in a single dose of 25 mg/kg of body weight up to 1 g. The use and dosage of imipramine (Tofranil) in enuresis is described in the section on Habit Disorders.

The Treatment of Aggression

The management of aggression constitutes an important aspect of working with children. Methods of handling aggression range from extreme permissiveness—even to the undesirable extent of allowing physical attacks on the therapist—to rigid disciplinary measures and physical restraint.

Aggression is representative of many diverse conditions. It may be a reaction to frustration of a fundamental need or impulse. It may be a means of coping with overwhelming inner fears stirred up by terror of a menacing world. In the detached child it may signify an averting of close relationships with people; in the child with power strivings, a way of gaining control; and in the masochistic youngster, a technique of provoking others to a point where they retaliate in kind. In some children it is the only form of relationship to another human being that they know, being a frenzied appeal for companionship or help. Aggression may be a camouflage for a deep feeling of inner helplessness, and as such it is motivated by the conviction that the only way to escape hurt is to overwhelm others. It may be a manifestation in the compulsively dependent child of disappointment in the adult to whom he clings, on the basis that his whims are not being satisfactorily gratified or because more favors are being shown to others than to himself. Before adequate therapy can be instituted, it is essential to know the symbolic significance of aggression to the child and the situations under which it is most likely to appear.

A number of children who exhibit behavior problems in the form of direct or subversive aggression never seem to have developed an inner system of moral restraint or the ability to tolerate an average amount of frustration. Neglected children—those reared in slum areas without proper guidance or discipline or those brought up by parents who themselves fear aggression and are consequently unable to take a stand with the child—frequently develop a defective repressive mechanism that is incapable of inhibiting rage or of directing it into socially approved channels. The child here usually has no fear of, or respect for, authority. He is narcissistically oriented and uses aggression as a coercive tool to force others to yield to his will. There is little contrition or guilt associated with his destructive acts, and the child usually takes the attitude that persons or objects on which he vents his rage are worthy of its consequences. Retaliatory measures have little deterrent influence and actually may incite the child to further bouts of aggression.

In treating a child showing this form of aggression, a permissive environment is worse than useless. This is because a sympathetic tolerance of the child's rage plays into the child's contemptuous attitudes toward authority as deserving little or no consideration. Actually, the child himself sees no necessity for change, and a permissive atmosphere merely perpetuates aggressive strivings.

The treatment objective in this type of child is to build up a superego capable of exercising control of his inner impulses. Much as the growing infant develops a conscience from external restraints and prohibitions, so the child with a diminutive superego needs discipline to nourish this impoverished portion of his personality. A kindly but firm expression of disapproval, and even irritation in response to destructive behavior, are much more rational approaches than its sanction or tolerance. The child must be taught that there are limits to his conduct beyond which he cannot go, that he has responsibilities for his daily acts that he must face, that definite things are expected of him, and that he has to live up to these expectations. When, in the therapeutic setting, limits to the child's conduct are first established, the child is apt to react violently; but as firm discipline continues, he will himself discover that he is much more comfortable knowing that there are boundaries beyond which he cannot go. This is not to say that he yields himself readily to such a circumscription of his freedom. The usual reaction is to engage in a prolonged struggle with the therapist to break down the limits imposed on behavior.

The therapeutic situation differs from any previous atmosphere because the child soon begins to feel in it a warmth and expectation such as he has never before experienced. Indeed, while in the realistic world his impulses have brought him a measure of security, they have also isolated him from people. He gradually begins to understand that the therapist is one adult who is not threatened by his aggression and does not yield to it or withdraw his love even in the face of the most provoking tantrum.

As the child continues therapy, affection for the therapist gradually increases. Eventually, he seems to go through a stage in development similar to that of the normal evolution of the conscience, namely, he feels it essential to win the therapist's approval and love. Whereas punishment and threats of abandonment have had little influence on the child's aggression, the fear of losing the approval of the one adult who has become significant to him has an extremely potent effect on the ability to inhibit rage. Needless to say, the process during which the child reintegrates himself with authority, in which he identifies himself with a loving adult and seeks to win his love and approval, is a long and tedious one. But the conscience, even in the normal child, never develops precipitiously; rather it extends over a period of years. One must not get too discouraged if the youthful patient has temporary setbacks in relationships with authority, including the therapist.

There is another type of aggression in the form of a power striving that resembles the aggression in the child with an undeveloped superego, but it has an entirely different dynamic significance and calls for a radically different kind of treatment. The superego, instead of being diminutive, is hypertrophied and takes on a terrifying and punitive aspect. The image of authority is that of a fearful and destructive force that can overpower and mutilate the child if he yields to its control. The way that the child copes with his helplessness is by overwhelming others with his power drive and aggression.

The object in therapy here is not so much to reinforce and solidify the superego, but rather to undermine it and replace it with one that does not threaten the child for the exercise of his impulses or functions. It is consequently necessary to tolerate aggression as much as is possible within reasonable limits of safety and decorum. Unlike the case of the first type of aggression, a permissive environment is essential. The permissive atmosphere at first often incites power-driven children to exaggerated acts of aggression. These seem to be defensive techniques by such children to avoid yielding their vigilance against authority.

Power-driven children often have difficulty in expressing softness, love, or tenderness. These emotions conflict with their self-ideals, and this is especially the case in children reared in environments where toughness and strength are the only admirable qualities in life. During therapy in a permissive situation such children gradually begin to let down their guards. One sees them working cautiously with creative materials, and there often emerges from their depths a great deal of esthetic feeling that has been buried previously under a crust of hardness. The amount of anxiety that accompanies the expression of tender emotions is amazing. As the attitude toward authority gradually undergoes a change, the child usually finds it more permissible to enjoy softer impulses. In a hospital ward, for example, many children who have been egocentric and destructive may be seen, after a while, making active attempts to help the crippled and defenseless children in dressing, in their habit training, and in other routines.

Another form of aggression frequently encountered is that in the dependent child who clings to the therapist or to other children in a submissive and ingratiating way. The aggression is stimulated by a feeling in the child that he has not received a sufficient amount of attention or love. The demands of dependent children are often so inordinate that it is impossible to live up to their expectations. There is involved an element of magical wish fulfillment, and rage occurs when wishes are not automatically granted. There is another important reason for aggression in the dependent child, and this emerges from a conviction in the child that independence is being crushed by the person upon whom he leans. As long as dependency remains the keynote of living, assertiveness, activity, and creative self-fulfillment are constantly subdued. Great hostility may be underneath the outer core of submissiveness and ingratiation, and the child may regard the adults who care for him as overpowering beings who prevent him from attaining to self-sufficiency. This is one reason why aggression is precipitated without any apparent cause in the child who receives unlimited privileges and favors. It is essential for personnel who deal with children to understand this, for the eagerness of the adult to overprotect the dependent child may actually rob the child of the necessity of participating actively in his own growth.

The dependent child may burn up his energy cajoling or forcing others to carry him, for he feels too helpless to accomplish things through his own efforts. Therefore, a program must be instituted in which the child learns to accept responsibility for daily routines of living. Self-growth is attained primarily through achievement. It is understandable that the child will exhibit episodes of aggression when he senses that others insist that he stand on his own feet. It is important not to yield to the child's aggression when it is obvious that he is trying to force the therapist to carry him.

Finally, it is necessary to consider the aggression exhibited by shy and detached children. Such children constitute a most serious problem and are usually referred to a clinic or to a hospital because of neurotic difficulties, psychosomatic complaints, or psychoses. Aggression, here, is at first not expressed, and the outward behavior of the child is usually of a compliant and innocuous nature. The detached child is threatened constantly by life and by people. He maintains his safety either by submitting to others or by building a defensive chasm that separates him from the world. In individual play therapy he will sit quietly awaiting instructions with little show of spontaneity. In a group of other children he will isolate himself and play alone. He possesses an enlarged and punishing superego as well as a great undermining of self-esteem. Beneath the shell of compliance are great quantities of hostility that he fears expressing openly. The object in treatment is to get him to mingle intimately with other children, to engage in competitive activities freely, and to express his aggression without counteraggression on the part of surrounding adults. This necessitates an extremely permissive environment.

Detached children are driven by a spontaneous force to assert themselves with other children and with adults, but their efforts in a normal environment are usually frustrated. In the permissive environment of the clinic or hospital the child gradually experiments with self-expressiveness. In play therapy he may reach a point where he breaks through his reserve and begins working with pliable materials that he can manipulate or destroy. Later on, he may begin to penetrate from the periphery of the group to its center, participating in activities that bring him into contact with others.

As the child realizes that he will not be hurt in closer relationships with others, he may engage gradually in mild competitive activities. Later, he may actually take a stand in life, defending his own rights and demands. At this point a tremendous amount of aggression is released, and he may become very destructive or assaultive. The aggression frequently is in the nature of a test to provoke adults around him into acts of retaliation in order to prove to himself that his previous concepts of the world as menacing were justified. Furthermore, as the permissive environment begins eating away at his repressive image of authority, he may begin experiencing feelings of love toward the therapist. He may become so overwhelmed with terror out of fear of getting close to a person that he may direct his aggression at the therapist with little external provocation. Therefore, a tolerance of the child's aggression is, as much as possible, therapeutically indicated.

Aggressive acting-out children have been helped significantly with a total behavioral reinforcement program. Rewarding of desired behavior with complete ignoring of unacceptable behavior has resulted in significant improvement. Working with parents and teachers to educate them regarding the meaning of the disturbed behavior is indispensable as a way of helping the children retain their gains. Where behavior therapy does not help the problem, a program of psychotherapy (which may be a long-term one) with the child and parents will be required.

The Hyperkinetic Child (Minimal Brain Dysfunction)

Whenever one encounters an aggressively hyperkinetic child, it is important to rule out organic syndromes that may manifest themselves purely as a behavior disor-

der (Wender, P, 1971). Symptoms of aggression, frustration intolerance, hyperactivity, and disturbed behavior occurring prior to 6 years and even 10 years of age may be a consequence of damage to the brain brought about by such etiological factors as a high forceps delivery, severe infantile infectious illness (whooping cough, measles, etc.), and frequent spells of high fever without apparent cause (Levy, S, 1966). Before making a diagnosis, however, it will be necessary to rule out ordinary physiologic hyperactivity, reactive and neurotic behavior disorders, childhood schizophrenia, and mental retardation. A rule of thumb has been applied to the effect that if a child does not have enough control over himself to sit still while watching his favorite television program, an organic brain problem should be suspected. In true hyperactivity there is a limited attention and concentration span, emotional lability along with impulsiveness, an inability to delay gratification, and poor frustration tolerance. Minor neurological signs and an abnormal electroencephalogram may be present. Often a learning disability is the reason why a child is referred for treatment. Because of sadistic uncontrollable behavior, the child may be ostracized by other children and may be excluded from school. This undermines self-esteem and sponsors paranoidal ideas and more violent behavior.

Therapy is difficult and prolonged and must be administered by a child therapist, preferably one who has had experience with hyperactive children. Involved is work with both child and parents. The latter must be counseled and educated regarding the nature of the problem and the need to refrain from applying the labels of "good" and "bad" to the child. It is often difficult for parents to accept the diagnosis of organicity and to control their desperate fears and guilt feelings. The cooperation of a neurologist may be helpful. Tutoring for special learning difficulties may be essential as may exercise programs to improve motor skills. A comprehensive treatment approach is thus best. Feighner and Feighner (1974) describe one such program consisting of a complete evaluation of the child, pharmacotherapy, behavior modification, curriculum counseling, training for parents and teachers, parent–child interaction videotaping, and feedback sessions while coordinating the treatment of the child, family, and school.

Drug therapy is usually symptomatically effective, the object being to stimulate the braking mechanisms of the brain in order to inhibit the motor overactivity. The drug that is most popular is methylphenidate (Ritalin), which is used in children over 6 years of age. Before breakfast and before lunch 5 mg are given, gradually increasing by increments of 5 to 10 mg weekly up to a total of 60 mg if necessary. Usually 20 to 40 mg will be effective. If there is no improvement in one month, the drug should be discontinued. Other drugs are the amphetamines. Dextroamphetamine (Dexedrine) may be given to children over 3 years of age as tablets or elixir. In children of 3 to 5 years 2.5 mg are given daily, increased at weekly intervals by 2.5 mg until an optimal response occurs. In children over 6 years of age 5 mg are given once or twice daily, raised weekly in increments of 5 mg until the best response is obtained, which is usually below 40 mg. Amphetamine (Benzedrine) for children of 3 to 5 years of age is given in 2.5 mg single dosage at first, raised at weekly intervals by 2.5 mg to an optimal response. After 6 years of age 5 mg once or twice daily (on awakening and the additional dose 4 to 6 hours later), the dosage being raised at weekly intervals by 5 mg to the optimal response. The usual dose is below 40 mg. A spansule capsule of Benzedrine may be used once daily as soon as the dosage is regulated. All of these medications may be reduced or discontinued over weekends or during school vacations. After puberty they may not be needed at all.

Coordinately, other adjunctive modalities previously mentioned should be employed. Parent groups of six weekly sessions have proven beneficial. Reading materials should be assigned to parents, such as the article by M. A. Stewart (1970). Teacher groups also have their use. Reinforcements (behavior medication) for the child to produce acceptable behaviors, play therapy, contact with teachers, videotape sessions with the parents to play back interactions, remedial tutoring, and special exercises are other useful techniques.

In the medium of his relationship with the therapist, the child is encouraged to explore his feelings and attitudes. The poor impulse control and the motor incoordination of the child during treatment may stir up countertransference reactions in the therapist, at home in the parents, and at school in the teachers. A passive neutral attitude will create insecurity in the child. On the other hand, counteraggression will add fuel to the fire. A firm kindly attitude is best. Should the child become violent, he should physically be removed from the disturbing situation so as not to perpetuate his behavior. Slowly, with proper management, mastery of behavior may be established, and there will be an ability to cope with increasingly challenging situations.

Juvenile Delinquency

A famous writer presented the problem of juvenile delinquency in these words: "Our youth now love luxury. They have bad manners, contempt for authority, disrespect for older people. Children nowadays are tyrants. They no longer rise when their elders enter the room. They contradict their parents, chatter before company, gobble their food, and tyrannize their teachers." These are the words of Socrates, written in the fifth century B.C. In the thousands of years that have passed since Socrates, we are not only still grappling with how to control youth's defiance of convention, but also with serious infractions of law that are represented by offenses of violence, stealing, fire setting, vandalism, dangerous drug indulgence, rape, and other crimes.

Delinquency among children who belong to asocial gangs is common in economically depressed areas. Here a cultural-transmission theory has been posited by such authorities as Tannenbaum (1938) and Topping (1943). Other authorities insist that the quality of family life is what is of greater etiological significance. Susceptible children are those from families in which there is no cohesiveness, no clear-cut authoritative model with which to identify, and little or no constructive supervision and discipline (Glueck & Glueck, 1950). Delinquent groups are powered by forces in opposition to the social world. (Cohen, AK, 1955). Collective solutions are evolved that though antisocial gain mutual support and identification. Work with the sociologic delinquent, therefore, must take into account both the disruptive family organization and the deprived environment from which he comes. Therapeutic directions are milieu-oriented. These focus on a broad community approach, enlisting the aid of religious leaders, social agencies, and police groups. Economic help, counseling, and casework for the delinquent's family and rehabilitative group work with the delinquent himself are essential. Individual psychotherapy generally fails miserably unless coordinate environmental approaches are employed.

Delinquency does not restrict itself to children from deprived and lower socioeconomic families. It affects upper- and middle-class groups as well. A. M. Johnson and Szurek (1952) have shown that the inability of parents to set limits due to poorly integrated impulses and "superego lacunae" (Johnson, AM, 1949) and the goading of a child to act out unconscious perverse and hostile parental strivings that were unresolved in the parent's own relationships with parental figures, produced delinquent behavior. "It is possible, in every case adequately studied, to trace the specific conscience defect in the child to a mirror image of similar type and emotional charge in the parent" (Johnson, AM, 1959). A specific superego defect may thus be created in the child that reflects the parental flaw. Szurek (1942) insists that many cases of psychopathic personality are products of unconsciously determined promptings from both mothers and fathers that encourage amoral and antisocial behavior. The child "victim" chosen has communicated to him subtle insinuations and suggestions that may often, even though the parents are not aware of their presence or implications, be detected by a good clinician during an interview. Indeed, psychotherapy with delinquents may have to be focused on the parents rather than the child since they will tend to undermine the child's treatment should he stop responding to their messages.

Modifications of analytic technique are obviously very much in order in working with a dynamic family neurosis, and this was years ago pointed out by Aichhorn (1936). Aichhorn's methods, employed during the residential treatment of delinquent adolescents, inspired the founding of special residential units organized around providing emotionally corrective experiences (Redl, 1959; Brady, S, 1963). Bettelheim (1950), Szurek (1949), Szurek, Johnson, and Falstein (1942), E. Glover (1956), and Noshpitz (1957), among others, have introduced methods that have proven of value in dealing with the problems of the delinquent child and his family. However, the treatment of delinquency is eminently unsuccessful no matter what stratagems are utilized. This is in large part due to the effect on the people handling the child of his unreliable promises and violent behavior. The child's expectation of rejection and punishment promote rampancy and rowdyism, to which the human targets of this turbulence respond with retreat, outrage, and often brutality. The self-fulfilling prophecy of the child that he will be hurt creates a feeling of hopelessness and distrust. He moves from one situation to another with the same result. Ultimately, the child may be placed in a *residential treatment unit* organized around the philosophy of a structured therapeutic community (Noshpitz, 1975; Alt, 1960; Balbernie, 1966; Noshpitz, 1975). Various orientations exist among different centers. Thus, a center may be a school, casework, or hospital, principally operated as such with teachers, caseworkers, nurses, and physicians. Some psychotherapy of a psychoanalytic group and behavioral nature is usually available, depending on the philosophies and skills of the therapists in the unit.

Residential centers have increased in numbers—but unfortunately not in quality. An exception is the unit in England known as Finchen Manor (Langdell, 1967), which is organized for selected multiproblem families. An optionally effective unit requires a special design (Roche Report, 1966). Most present day units are not too well designed or operated for the best management of delinquent children. Moreover, placement is too short-term (at least 2 years of residency are usually required for any change to register itself). In addition, there is a lack of coordinated services (provision for educational and vocational opportunities, outlets for aggression, need for privacy, etc.), and an absence of a well-trained staff and other personnel who are both caring and capable of maintaining adequate control. Too often the aggression of the children leads to remedies of isolation, punishment, and drug treatment, which, while temporarily effective, do not alter the existing difficulty. A pertinent problem in some settings is the insistence in retaining the medical model in the institution, which is an inappropriate one for children (Linton, 1973). Here the responsible psychiatrists, clinical psychologists, and psychiatric caseworkers are not in as intimate contact with the children as would be child-care workers, teachers, and other persons who can intimately be related to the daily life and behavior of the children. A reeducational model that involves total millieu planning is more appropriate than a medical model. It has been recommended that a different type of professional is needed for residential units, one who has received comprehensive training designed for the tasks that he or she will pursue. In France, Denmark, and the Netherlands, for example, a new discipline is evolving concerned with mediating child problems ("education, orthopedagogue").

A great deal of the failure in treatment is also due to the paucity of aftercare services once the child leaves the residential unit. Little continuity usually exists between the residential center and the environment to which the child is returned, which continues to impose on him the original traumas and deprivations. *Intensive home therapy* by medical and nonmedical personnel have been employed with some success. Therapist activities will vary from guidance and support to formal marital or family therapy depending on the needs of the family. The home therapist usually works under the supervision of the child therapist who is in charge of the program. Among the conditions for which home therapy is especially indicated are the presence of a psychotic parent at home, refusal of children or parents to accept office treatment, the dealing with double and multiple binds, adverse reactions of a mother to a baby or her pregnancy, and projective mechanisms in parents which activate a child's disturbed behavior.

A *day care center* constitutes a useful modality for some children, particularly those who manifest such problems as severe withdrawal, lack of object relationships, impulse control, and lack of use of language. Reinforcements are provided for constructive conduct (North, 1967). Day care treatment often avoids prolonged hospitalization, providing the child with a therapeutic environment for many hours a week while remaining a part of the family. A disadvantage is the low therapist-to-child ratio, which is ideally one to one. One way of meeting this dilemma is to train ancillary workers, some of whom can be recruited as part of a corps of volunteers.

Learning and Reading Disabilities

Learning and reading disabilities are the commonest single immediate causes for the referral of children to guidance clinics (Rabinovitch, 1959). In prescribing appropriate treatment psychological tests are in order to ascertain the general intelligence and to assess the potentials, the achievement level, the developmental readiness, and the degree of emotional disturbance; neurological examinations are recommended to rule out brain injury and aphasic disorders. Generally there is a close relationship between learning disabilities and emotional disturbance, but the presence of emotional illness itself does not presuppose that there will be failure in school work. A psychological inability to learn or to read is usually a symptom that serves a specific purpose, such as to punish the parents, to defy authority, to refuse to grow up, to avoid competition, or to punish oneself. Anxiety that emerges from the child's school failures adds to his inability to attend and to concentrate on work. Even where the problem is organically determined, as where there is damage to the associational patterns controlling visual-motor functioning, such anxiety may act as a prime disorganizing factor. The treatment of learning and reading difficulties will depend upon their cause. Problems rooted in organic brain disorders will require retraining, utilizing visual, auditory, and kinesthetic approaches (Strauss, AA, & Lehtinen, 1947; Strauss, AA, & Kephart, 1955; Vernon, 1957). Disabilities provoked by emotional factors will call for psychotherapy, aided, if necessary, by special tutoring and remedial reading.

Schizophrenic Children

Residential treatment of children and adolescents is sometimes essential in youngsters who are out of control and who constitute a danger to themselves or others (Wolberg, LR, 1959). Psychotic children particularly will need hospitalization (Gralnick, 1966) as may severe cases of anaclitic depression (Spitz, RA, 1946), certain delinquencies (Aichhorn, 1936), and severe psychosomatic and organic conditions (Rapaport, HG, 1957).

Childhood schizophrenia (Bender, 1947; Despert, 1948), early infantile autism (Kanner, 1959), and the "symbiotic psychosis syndrome" (Mahler, 1952) are characterized by profound disturbances of behavior on every level of functioning—physiological, psychological, and interpersonal. Withdrawal tendencies and problems in communication make treatment extremely difficult. Therapy aims at establishing a better integrity of body image, a sense of entity and identity, a consolidation of object relationships, and a restoration of defective developmental ego functions (Mahler et al, 1959). The therapist provides for the patient an auxiliary ego and encourages a living through of those developmental phases that were thwarted in his actual growth experience. An interesting account of a working-through of problems with a schizophrenic in an intensive relationship is described by Sechehaye (1956). Due to the primary process nature of the child's behavior and communication, it may be difficult to comprehend the meaning of his verbalizations and actions. Here the therapist may have to serve an educational function. With autistic children, operant conditioning techniques may serve to bring

them to some measure of social conformity and relationship with reality.

Emergencies

Sometimes emergencies arise in children that the psychotherapist may be called on to resolve. Usually they are the climax of a long preceding period of maladjustment to which the parents may have been oblivious or indifferent. They are differentiated from the normal developmental crises that call for minimal interventions since they may be the means to conflict resolution. Acute disturbances in adolescents may occur as a result of an identity crises. Here a quiet youngster may suddenly become aggressive and destructive to furniture. Often we find this among adolescents who have been forced to be "good." As they enter into the turmoil of adolescence they break through their passivity by outbursts of aggressiveness. On the other hand, aggressive and violent behavior, as toward people, may be the result of a psychosis, which will call for entirely different management. To put a youngster with an identity crisis into a psychiatric institution as a result of the crisis will only contribute to the identity confusion.

True emergencies will call for accurate assessment of underlying causes. A detailed history of the child's development and interviews with the parents and perhaps teachers and other significant adults is in order. The therapeutic plan will then be discussed with these people. The plan may follow a crisis interventional model.

One of the most common emergencies is *running away* from home (Jenkins, RL, 1973). It is estimated that there are 600,000 to 1 million runaway children yearly in the United States. Often the elopement is to communes of peers who encourage drug and promiscuous sexual indulgence. Some runaways are normal children escaping from a situation of intolerable stress or complete rejection. Some seek constructively to effectuate separation-individuation, which is impossible in a home that continues to infantilize them. Some schizophrenic children resort to disorganized runaway tendencies and may be accepted in a group that seeks to protect them though they offer little in return. Commonly, running away is a delinquent response all the more dangerous since the child may be attracted to delinquent gangs that wreak havoc in the community. Diagnosis is important since *why* the child runs away will determine the kind of treatment that must be instituted. In all runaway problems work with the family as well as the child is mandatory.

Another emergency is a *suicidal attempt,* which most frequently occurs at age 10 and between 15 to 19 years of age. These are often impulsive in nature, precipitated by disproportionately minor provocative incidents that, for the child, are interpreted as of major importance. What is behind the attempt (conflict over sexual impulses, self-punishment for forbidden impulses or thoughts, projected aggression against a parent or sibling, frustrated dependency, persecutory delusions, toxic drug reaction, hopelessness, depression, etc.) will require persistent probing. Whether or not hospitalization will be needed must be assessed. At any rate, environmental rearrangements may be required along with therapy for the child and at least counseling for the parents.

The easy accessibility of *drugs* during periods of school attendance or during leisure hours has, particularly in adolescents, produced emergencies brought on both by the discovery of the indulgence by parents and by an overdose of the intoxicating substance. While casual temporary experimentation with such drugs as marijuana may not be too significant, substances like the amphetamines, barbiturates, codeine, and heroin can lead to addiction. Alcohol has recently been increasingly utilized by children. The use of mind-expanding drugs, such as LSD, substances in glue (glue sniffing), and gasoline is fraught with dangerous consequences. Usually combinations of drugs have been taken, and their exact identification is difficult when the child is admitted to a detoxification center, since he himself usually will not know what he has been taking. Behind the taking of such destructive drugs may be efforts to escape from depression, boredom, stresses of separation-individuation, and impulses of

aggression. Often the only signs that these youngsters exhibit are anxiety, excitement, and overactivity. The temptation is immediately to use sedatives. Without knowing whether or not drugs have been taken, and their nature, it is dangerous to contribute to the drug toxicity by adding other substances to an already overloaded nervous system. In recent years there has been a shift from hallucinogenic and tranquilizing drugs to alcohol, and it may be anticipated that cases of acute alcoholic toxicity will be increasing among adolescents. After successful detoxification, a psychotherapeutic program, often prolonged, will be required.

In *car crash cases* where one youngster is killed and another survives with minor injuries, it is often helpful in the emergency room for the doctor or nurse to communicate to the survivor that it is common in such cases to feel guilty and, if this happens, to recognize that one will eventually get over it. Allowing the youth to verbalize his feelings while listening sympathetically may be important. Sedatives should not be offered since refuge may henceforth be found in drugs. The parents should also be informed regarding the turmoil the child is likely to experience and to anticipate it.

In the event of *death of a parent* the surviving parent should be encouraged to talk about the departed member openly with the children and not to cover the matter up by denying the validity of the pain that the children are bound to suffer. A great area of prevention can be instituted in the emergency room where an adult with a coronary attack is brought dead on arrival. The surviving parent may have no opportunity to see any other professional people than the personnel in the emergency room. A few minutes spent with the parent explaining the need not to cover matters over with a pall of silence may prevent a great deal of misery in the family, particularly among adolescents.

Other emergencies include school phobias, anorexia nervosa, parental beating of the child ("the battered child"), sexual and other violent assaults, and deaths in the family. These will call for special handling and perhaps extended treatment.

PSYCHOTHERAPY IN OLD AGE

Aging is an inexorable sculptress. The "golden years" are characterized by declining hearing, thinning hair, dimming eyesight, loss of 100,000 brain cells daily, the heart pumping less blood, the lungs absorbing less oxygen, bladder control and capacity lessening, the drying and wrinkling of skin, the weakening of muscles, the lowering of hormone output, and swelling of joints. As medical advances add years to peoples' lives, diseases of aging (arthritis, cardiac ailments, kidney diseases, arteriosclerosis, cataracts, cancer, etc.) and the infirmities that they bring complicate the existence of the elderly person. But even more devastating are the ravages of fear and insecurity.

Unfortunately, our culture fails to provide adequate roles for the many old people who retire or who, due to their age, are pushed aside by younger and more energetic citizens. Loss of family and the companionship of children, reduced income, and lowered status combine with diminishing strength and increasing physical disability to encourage conflict and to accelerate mental deterioration.

In making efforts at facilitating adjustment, counseling and casework methods may help resolve problems of housing, finances, health, occupation, socialization, and recreation. Proper information and guidance may be all that an older person requires to continue to maintain self-respect and to shore up feelings of self-sufficiency.

A shift in living arrangements alone may eliminate a host of difficulties. Any changes must obviously take into account both the person's desire to live in familiar surroundings and the practical needs of one's situation. Dwelling units especially designed for older persons have become increasingly popular, and retirement villages containing medical, recreational, and rehabilitative services are available. In some cases private-home placement may be a more suitable solution, supplemented with the facilities of community centers that have programs for the aged. On the other hand, where the individual is unable to care for himself, a hospital or old-age nursing or convalescent home may be what is required.

Finding suitable work for an active older person may restore vitality, interest, and self-esteem. It is totally unrealistic to assume that leisure alone can bring contentment to one who has been occupied productively all of his or her life. Nor is it sensible for the community to turn people out to pasture who have acquired skills and knowledge that cannot easily be duplicated.

The problems of retirement make pre-retirement counseling an important preventive measure. New adaptations will be required. Wives should be prepared for resentment at having their husbands at home full time, particularly since they can become more grouchy and irritable. Role playing is helpful in preparing the retiree for what is inevitable—time on one's hands, a feeling that one is out of the mainstream of life and a "has been." A search for new meanings to existence will be needed.

Education in an aging society is an important aspect of a comprehensive program. Properly implemented, it supplies information to the older person regarding the physical changes in the body and new emotional requirements that take place with ongoing years. It clarifies confusion about sexuality. It furnishes guidelines for continued creativity and vocational usefulness. It encourages enjoyment of positive assets and minimization of liabilities. Programs of adult education to prepare the individual for aging and to help develop new leisure-time interests must include instruction for persons working with older people about various phases of geriatrics. The booklet, *Planning for the Later Years,* issued by the U.S. Department of Health, Education and Welfare (Washington, D. C., U. S. Government Printing Office) contains some excellent suggestions for health maintenance, nutrition, emotional adjustment, housing and living arrangements, retirement income, work, and legal problems. It may be profitably read by the aging person. Other reading materials for the aged or their relatives are given elsewhere in this volume (see the section on Old Age, in the Addenda, Recommended Texts). For professional persons the writings of Weinberg (1975), Butler and

Lewis (1973), Rossman (1971), and Simon and Epstein (1968) and the publications *Medical World News, Geriatrics,* (1973) and *Psychiatric Annals,* (vol. 2, no. 10 and 11, 1972) are recommended.

Among the most useful measures are the development of appropriate recreational facilities in churches, schools, community centers, and the various old-age institutions to encourage hobbies, handicrafts, dancing, lectures, and discussions. Social participation increases morale and counteracts withdrawal and deterioration.

The above measures designed to meet the diversified needs of older people may avert or delay the development of untoward senile reactions. The most common of these are confusional syndromes that come on suddenly, particularly when the individual is moved to unfamiliar surroundings or subjected to situations to which he cannot adjust. Old people have a tendency to prowl around at night and during the day to wander away from home. Providing them with activities to occupy their minds tends to keep them more focused on reality.

Perhaps the most difficult problem in providing a solution to the aging person in a family setting is the inability of children to accept the inevitable change in role that will be demanded of them as their parents become more helpless and dependent. The psychotherapist consulted by the family will usually have to involve the entire family in the treatment plan, helping them to face the physical and emotional changes in their parents, and educating them into the need for becoming substitute parents for their own parents in response to the latter's developing dependency needs. What the aged person often requires is "a surrogate-protector in much the same way that he approached a parent as a child. . . . It is possible for the therapist to use this delegated authority to foster and maintain an illusion that the patient has found a protector and one who will satisfy many psychological needs" (Goldfarb, AI, 1964).

Mental disorders in elderly people are characterized by a superimposition of psychological reactions (usually depression and paranoidal projections) on an organic substrate. Assessment of the degree of organic involvement is essential in outlining an appropriate program of therapy. This will require clinical observation, laboratory tests, and an electroencephalogram. Once the degree of affective and organic components implicated are estimated, a comprehensive treatment plan includes physical care, rehabilitation, drugs, and psychotherapy. With good supervision the vast majority of older people may be treated outside of a hospital. Transfer to a mental institution causes great anxiety and agitation and may shorten life. Where home conditions are unsuitable or upsetting, institutionalization may be inevitable, and, if proper facilities can be found, the last years of life may be made tolerable if not enjoyable.

The treatment of depression in old age differs in some respects from that in younger years (Charatan, 1975). Modest treatment goals are indicated with limited symptom relief employing a directive, supportive approach with brief sessions. Where drugs are needed, imipramine (Tofranil), amitriptyline (Elavil), and doxepin (Sinequan) are utilized starting with 10 mg three times daily, gradually building up the dose. Glaucoma, pyloric stenosis, and urinary retention are contraindications to the use of these tricyclics. The patient should be reassured about side effects and about the need to wait for 10 days to 2 weeks before the full effect of the drug registers. Should mental confusion occur, intramuscular neostigmine methylsulfate (Prostigmin) in 1 to 2 mg dosage may be given. Severe depressions may require electroshock after a thorough physical examination, blood count, urinalysis, electrocardiogram, and x-ray of the chest and spine show no contravening abnormalities. A total of eight to ten biweekly treatments are best.

Other drugs are prescribed in the treatment of the aged, but they must be used with care since overreactions to ordinary doses are possible. For anxiety Librium (5 mg twice daily, gradually increased to four times daily if needed) or Valum (1 to 2.5 mg three or four times daily, increased gradually as needed or tolerated) may be used. Agitated and paranoidal reactions require antipsychotic drugs (Haldol, Navane, Mellaril, Trilafon, Thorazine). Frequent blood counts are indicated to detect oncoming agranulocytosis, which, though rare, is in old people often fatal. Cogentin or Artane will neutralize complications of Parkinsonism. A combination of a phenothiazine and antidepressant (Triavil, Etrafon) is sometimes prescribed in agitated depression. It is generally wise to try different antipsychotic drugs should the patient not respond to a selected one. Insomnia may require chloral hydrate (Noctec), paraldehyde, or Dalmane. Barbiturates should be given sparingly, if at all, and central analeptics should never be utilized in confusional states. Oxazepam (Serax) in 10 mg doses, three times daily is recommended by some for anxious agitated reactions. There are many other substances in use whose virtues are contradictory (Hollister, 1975). These include the cerebral dilators Pavabid, Cyclospasmol, Vasodilan, and Riniacol, the ergot alkaloids (Hydergine), and procain (Gerovital), although the latter can produce a mild antidepressant effect. Small doses of stimulants like Ritalin sometimes help fatigue and mild depression. Vitamin supplements are often used, but a good balanced diet is extremely vital and makes excessive vitamin intake unnecessary.

The conditions requiring psychotherapy in geriatric patients include all of those in younger groups as well as syndromes arising with the deteriorative, metabolic, and systemic disturbances of old age. Relationship and interpretative therapies are employed in combination as needed (Goldfarb, AI, 1955, 1959; Meerloo, 1955). The question arises as to whether we can approach reconstructive changes in the older person with alteration of the basic character structure and the development of new potentialities. Or must we be content with a holding operation, with symptom relief and better adaptation in areas of living in which the patient is failing, with at best a reorganization of attitudes and values? An elderly person with a basically good ego structure, in whom organic brain damage is minimal, if sufficiently motivated may be brought to some reconstructive change. Generally, however, extensive alterations in character structure are not to be anticipated.

Psychotherapy serves to alleviate the anxieties of aging individuals, to provide a means for emotional catharsis; to reassure them about their physical condition; to help them deal with depression and grief and the death of members of their family and friends, frustrated sexual longings and impairment, problems of retirement, difficulties in living alone and paranoidal projections; and to convince them that somebody cares and that their basic needs will be satisfied. The chronically ill patient who lives in fear of death appreciates a friend and counselor. In psychotic states psychotherapy may be coordinated with drug therapy even in the brain-damaged (Hader, 1964). Short sessions (10 to 15 minutes once weekly or bimonthly) may be all that is required. This usually suffices to support dependency needs and to give the patient a feeling of being protected. Group therapy and group discussions are ideally suited to the needs of elderly people, fostering group belongingness, reducing the sense of isolation, and enabling them to deal with feelings of separation and fears of death. The goals to be achieved in group methods are to support the existing personality strengths, to inculcate knowledge of human behavior, to expand tolerance and flexibility toward individual differences, to accept a changing role in life, to deal with personal prejudices, to facilitate group membership, and to promote better interpersonal relationships (Klein, WH, et al 1966; Goldfarb, AI, & Wolk, 1966; Burnside, 1970).

One of the problems, however, is getting older persons to break through their isolation and join a group. Often the individual will come to an outpatient clinic in search of help for somatic complaints and will resent being referred to a psychiatrist. A skillful referral, however, will often be accepted, such as that physical problems and suffering always give rise to tensions that make it difficult or impossible for a physical problem to heal and that group therapy often will help resolve tensions and aid the healing process. Most patients experience great relief as a result of the group process. This may ameliorate somatic complaints as well as help problems of living.

61

Failures in Psychotherapy

Psychotherapy was never designed to cure everybody. With our present techniques we are able to effectuate symptomatic improvement in almost all emotional problems, behavioral changes in the majority, and complete cure in some. The fact that extensive reconstructive alterations are possible in approximately one-third of cases is an encouraging sign, however, since it contradicts the commonly accepted adage that human nature cannot be changed. With continued empirical research our understanding of personality will undoubtedly be advanced, and with more clinical experience our therapeutic methods should become enriched. In the meantime, we may follow an old Chinese proverb that says, "It is better to light one candle than to curse the darkness."

Failures in psychotherapy are generally the product of mismanagement of the therapeutic relationship. Most commonly the patient is pushed toward reconstructive goals that are beyond his competence. The patient may himself seek extensive personality change even though he is incapable of achieving more than symptom relief.

No matter how ambitiously we as therapists may pursue treatment, we are confronted with limitations in all patients in their potentials for growth. Three kinds of patterns may be clinically observed. First, there are promptings so deeply imbedded in the personality matrix that they seem to pursue an autonomous course. No amount of insight or authoritative pressure seems capable of modifying their expression or lessening their force. These tendencies are rooted in conditionings sustained during early childhood, perhaps in the preverbal period before the individual was able to conceptualize experiences. They may, if sufficiently intense, disorganize adult adjustment. For instance, separation from a mother for extended periods during infancy may sponsor profound feelings of distrust. Apathy, depression, pressing drives for oral gratification, suspicion regarding the motives of people, and a view of the world as menacing may survive in traits that distort the most bountiful reality situation in later years. The ego, structured on an infirm basis, sustains disintegrative proclivities. In most persons, however, symptomatic residues of early conditionings, though present, are not so pronounced. Minor as they are, they still defy change and energize maladjustment.

A second group of patternings develops somewhat later, which are remembered, at least in part, and can be verbalized. Serving spurious neurotic functions, they may in execution promote conflict. This group is subject to some control through willful inhibition once the individual appreciates the nature and consequences of his inclinations. While they may continue to press for expression, their mastery becomes an important goal. Many of these strivings are rooted in needs and drives that, in promoting anxiety, are repressed. Their recognition, if the individual is sufficiently motivated, may enable him to bring them under control and, in fortunate instances, to eliminate them completely.

For example, a child whose assertiveness during second and third years of life was inhibited by parents wedded to the doctrine that children are to be seen and not heard, may discover that when she mobilizes sufficient aggression and rage she can get her own way. "Hell-raising" then becomes a pattern essential to the expression of assertiveness. Recognition that her aggression is resented by her colleagues, and insight into the sources of her affiliation of assertiveness with aggression, may enable her to experiment with modes of assertive display dissociated from violence. A child fondled seductively by a parent may become too stimulated sexually and detach from his sexual feelings. Intimate relationships in adult life may precipitate an incestuous association that inhibits sexual expression. Awareness of the roots of his difficulty may enable the individual to experiment sexually with the objective of establishing new habit patterns. A host of pathological conditionings may, as Freud pointed out, invest the sexual and aggressive drives, and the person may develop inhibitions of function or distorted and perverse modes of expression. Burdened by essentially childish needs, he may be fixated in activities that survive as outlets for sex or aggression. To gratify these drives, he must pay a toll in insecurity and damaged self-esteem. This group of neurotic promptings with proper therapy, should the individual strongly desire it, may undergo modification. The patient thus either learns to live with his handicaps, once he understands them more thoroughly, or he is better able

to control them. With reconstructive therapy an individual may be able to develop more mature ways of sexual and aggressive feeling and behaving.

A third group of patterns present in all people are relatively flexible. They are not subject to severe repression, and do not press for release against all reason. Developing both during early and late childhood and in adult life, they constitute a bulk of the individual's coping maneuvers. These, the most malleable of tendencies, may be influenced most significantly in therapy.

Disappointment in psychotherapy is often registered when, after an ambitious, carefully designed and prolonged program of treatment, the patient continues to resist giving up the first set of patterns and must exercise his will power constantly to keep the second group in check. All human beings are so constituted that no amount of therapy, as we practice it today, can alter some personality components, since they have become so firmly entrenched that they function like organic fixtures. Yet, properly designed psychotherapy offers the individual a substantial opportunity to rectify many destructive personality traits and to achieve a measure of happiness that, prior to treatment, was outside his grasp.

UNTOWARD REACTIONS DURING PSYCHOTHERAPY

The bulk of patients in psychotherapy move along well. Obstructions in progress and inimical emotional outbursts are readily handled. There are conditions, however, that pose hazards even for the experienced psychotherapist. Personality structures in whom emotional instability is ingrained, having existed since early childhood, will in all probability erupt with greater bursts of violence, responding with insurgency and defying control. Impartial as one may try to be, the therapist will be drawn into the patient's onslaught and may be unable to maintain an even tenor, either yielding to unreasonable demands or counterattacking in retaliation. The greatest incidence of untoward reactions in psychotherapy occurs where the relationship between therapist and patient is faulty. Inexperience and improper conduct of treatment, as well as countertransference, account for a large percentage of unfortunate results although we are not certain how these take place. The work of Bergin (1963, 1971) and Strupp et al. (1976) accents the need for further research into deterioration effects and reasons for failures in psychotherapy.

It may not be amiss to mention the virtue of a therapist's seeking consultation or supervision for a case that is not going well. This will necessitate courage and an honest confrontation with oneself in facing the fact that one may be acting nontherapeutically with a patient or that one may be employing interventions that do not satisfy the patient's needs. Talking things out with a colleague will often somehow break through the current obstruction and promote satisfactory movement.

Without justification, one may classify as treatment failures the emergence during therapy of certain disturbed reactions. These are most apt to erupt when the customary defenses of the individual are challenged or blocked, as in reeducative and reconstructive therapy; however, they may break loose in certain patients as a consequence of mere contact with the therapist, however supportive one may try to be. Thus, borderline patients who are perched precariously on the razor edge of reality are particularly vulnerable to any kind of interpersonal relationship. Even ordinary human encounters stimulate undue tension and conflict. Underlying morbid traits, kept under control by tenuous defenses, may emerge, often with explosive violence. Depressive manifestations may deepen into suicidal attempts; psychopathic aberrations may be acted out in total disregard of consequences; feelings of unreality and depersonalization may spread into an outright psychosis. During any kind of psychotherapy with borderline patients the course of treatment is customarily stormy, punctuated by fluctuations in the sense of reality. The patient may interpret the relationship as an assault on his integrity, particularly where the therapist is excessively authoritarian or has unresolved hostile or sexual difficulties that filter through in his or her manner and speech. Borderline patients sensitively divine these from the tiniest cues (Schmideberg, 1959). Emotional crises more or less constitute the usual climate in which therapy is conducted.

Problems are also commonly encountered in the treatment of psychosomatic problems in the form of recrudescence of symptoms in an intensified form. Where the erupting symptoms are minor, there is no great danger; however, severe outbreaks of somatic disturbance may occur, such as a "thyroid crisis," violent asthmatic attack, or fulminating ulcerous colitis that may lead to death. Suicide is also a possibility. The most disturbing reactions occur in patients who have habitually had a tenuous relationship with other persons and a precarious evaluation of themselves since childhood. "In these individuals there is a serious feeling of helplessness, considerable expectation of rejection, frustration and injury from other individuals, and considerable feelings of guilt about their impulses. . . . These individuals easily react . . . with a violent frenzied emotional flood, or with destructive violence at times turned in on themselves, or with a more complete withdrawal and inaccessibility. Any of these reactions may be fused with various disturbances of organ function (oral, excretory, circulatory, and also genital) and may reach the point of abandoning adequate contact with reality" (Mittelman, 1948).

Patients suffering from brain injuries are apt, during psychotherapy, to manifest outbreaks of euphoric, paranoidal, sexually aggressive, or suicidal behavior (Weinstein & Kahn, 1959). Probing procedures employed in manic-depressive psychosis and involutional psychosis may release great anxiety and resentment and activate latent suicidal drives (Arieti, 1959). A treatment relationship in dependent individuals who mask their hopelessness by a thin overlay of indifference may precipitate a deep depression when the patient realizes the limitations in the degree of closeness possible with the therapist imposed by the reality situation. Exploratory activities in reactive depressions notoriously excite intense anxiety (Muncie, 1959).

Paranoid reactions respond adversely to almost any kind of human contact. Thus an individual who is burdened merely with self-doubt and suspicion may in a relationship of even moderate intensity find himself responding with strong mechanisms of denial and projection. Ego defenses may then shatter with oversensitivity, estrangement, preoccupation, distrust, suspicion, fears of physical and sexual attack, litigious tendencies, homosexual impulses, delusional jealousies, and grandiose delusions (Cameron, N, 1959). Schizophrenics who interpret psychotherapy as an intrusion on their privacy often will be provoked into fearful or aggressive reactions (Arieti, 1959). Personality disorders manifest diverse reactions to therapeutic contacts. Urgent dependency needs may be projected onto the therapist with excessive clinging, release of intense erotic feelings, and liberation of resentment at the inevitable frustration. Detachment with needs for control may be threatened by the patient's belief that yielding to another person implies a trap from which there is no escape. Masochistic promptings may enjoin the individual to torture himself with luxurious symptoms. Homosexual strivings kept in check prior to treatment may suddenly appear promoting panic. Impulsive characters may exhibit acting-out proclivities without warning, engaging in outlandish and dangerous activities (Michaels, 1959).

Psychopathic personalities may when challenged respond with excited and even psychotic behavior. Alcoholics and drug addicts are notoriously treacherous, indulging in defiant and occasionally destructive practices. Some conversion reactions display alarming conduct when an attempt is made to alleviate or reduce their symptoms. A psychotic disorder of a depressive or paranoidal type may supervene (Abse, 1959). In obsessive reactions frightening extremes of anxiety and rage may from time to time be released, along with guilt feelings and expiatory self-punishment, the therapist being accused of promoting the appearance of these symptoms (Rado, 1959).

RISKS OF PSYCHOTHERAPY

Difficulties will also develop as a consequence of the new adaptations forced on the individual as a result of removal of the problem for which he originally sought help. Sometimes a neurotic disorder constitutes the best compromise the individual can make with life and with himself. While he may complain bitterly about the disabling effects of his condition, when he is relieved of it, he may be exposed to new circumstances that will or will not terminate happily. This, of course, is something for which the practitioner cannot be held responsible. There is no crystal ball with which to predict the ultimate outcome of any problem. A therapist's responsibility is to help the patient overcome an illness and to enable him as best he can to make a constructive future adjustment.

The end issues, however, may leave much to be desired, under which circumstances therapy may be scored as a failure. Thus a patient with migraine gets insight into the fact that she is complying, with strong internalized rage, to the authoritative demands of a widowed mother who seeks to infantilize her only child as an outlet for her controlling needs. Therapy helps the patient to liberate herself from her mother. The latter, unable to accept her daughter's freedom, commits suicide. The ensuing guilt, recriminations, and depression in the patient make her regret having started psychotherapy. An obese girl, helped to diet by psychological treatments, finds herself attractive to men. Unable to cope with the sexual demands made on her by her admirers, she responds with panic. A patient with frigidity dramatically overcomes her sexual indifference. Responding passionately to a seductive male, her episode terminates in pregnancy and the birth of an illegitimate child, which complicates her life to her detriment.

It is often impossible to foresee and to forestall future calamities that follow even traditional medical and surgical treatments. Thus the relieving of anginal pain, through prescription by an internist of a monoamine oxidase derivative, may encourage a cardiac patient to overtax his heart through physical efforts beyond his endurance, initiating a massive coronary attack. Plastic surgery often exposes the patient to responsibilities that his devalued self-image is unable to countenance, initiating many adverse reactions.

To refuse to treat a travel phobia by psychotherapy in order to protect a patient from the possibility of an airplane crash would consititute a foolish if not irresponsible shirking of one's duty. The best course to follow is to attempt to anticipate possible consequences of therapy and to work with a patient until a reasonable stabilization is reached in his life situation.

FAILURES IN
RECONSTRUCTIVE THERAPY

There are certain patients in whom long-term reconstructive treatment is not only useless but constitutes a definite hazard. Such patients, in good faith, enter into treatment with well-trained psychotherapists, and after years of futile probing they reach a desperate dead end. In many instances the hope of cure enjoins the patient to engage a succession of psychotherapists, each espousing a well-documented theoretical system that promises success but ultimately results in failure.

If we take a hard look at what has been happening, we often find that the therapist has become incorporated by the patient into his neurotic system. It becomes obvious that what the patient is seeking from treatment is not cure, but satisfaction of his dependent needs, a relief from suffering that his conflicts foster, but which he refuses to relinquish, and a replacement of amputated aspects of his self that, at our present state of knowledge, are far beyond the power of science to supply. Freud, astute clinician that he was, recognized that not all people were ready for the long-term pull of psychoanalysis when he advised that only individuals able to develop a transference neurosis be treated with his method. While the diagnostic boundaries are diffuse, empirically it is possible to designate the kinds of conditions in which failures are common with reconstructive therapy.

The most unacceptable of candidates are a body of patients who seem to be unable to get along on their own. These persons are possessed of such great fragility in their defenses that they tend to fall apart in the face of even reasonable stress. Often they protect themselves from hurt by restricting their needs and circumscribing the zones of their interpersonal operations. Yet their helplessness enjoins them to fasten themselves to some host who, they insist, must supply them with love, support, and other intangible bounties. Such unfortunate individuals have been so damaged in their upbringing that no amount of help, affection, discipline, entreaty, supplication, or castigation can seem to repair their hurt. They tend to find and fasten themselves to individuals, movements, and institutions from whom and from which they hope to gain sustenance and strength. They act like an exsanguinated people in need of perpetual transfusions.

Diagnostically these persons spread themselves over a wide nosologic spectrum. They include schizophrenics, borderline patients, alcoholics, drug addicts, and psychopathic personalities. We find them among obsessive-compulsive, depressive, phobic, and psychosomatic reactions. Essentially they are characterologically immature, never having achieved inner freedom and independence. It is as if they have become marooned on an island of infantile affect. Outwardly they may present a facade of assurance, but inwardly they are anchored to pitifully dependent moorings.

When such persons enter into psychotherapy, they soon sweep the therapist into the orbit of their dependent designs. The grim objective of making the therapist an idealized parental agency is not diverted in the least by the therapist's technical skills, astute observations, lucid interpretations, management of countertransference, encouragement of emotional catharsis, transference revelations, and expert unraveling of dream symbolisms nor by the uncovering of forgotten memories, free association, structured interviews, firm directiveness, punishment, kindness, support and reassurance, suggestion, hypnosis, or drugs nor by any other method the therapist may exploit or devise. A therapist who is deceived by the earnestness with which the patient applied himself to the therapeutic task will credit the patient's lack of progress to the obstinacy of his resistances, which, the therapist imagines, will eventually be resolved. And the patient, coasting along on the premise that time itself brings the cherished gift of unconscious motive or memory, will become increasingly helpless and will then supplicate for greater professions of dedication from the therapist. The liberated hostility serves no purpose other than that to make the mutual lives of patient and therapist miserable in a futile tug of war.

With expanded public education and the exciting promises of fulfillment through psychotherapy, more and more individuals, unable to gratify their pathological dependency promptings in their habitual relationships, or through religion, or by affiliation with special movements, have flocked to the offices of therapists seeking the elusive pot of gold that never quite materializes. And because hope springs eternal, the therapeutic diggings go on for years in the vain quest of bringing up treasure that somehow, according to legend, must eventually be exposed. Both patient and therapist enter into this undeliberate deception only marginally aware that the quest is a useless one and that what the patient really seeks from therapy is supportive aliment for his emptiness.

The great danger in long-term reconstructive psychotherapy is not only its becoming a never-ending placebo to such characterologically dependent persons who would otherwise find an object of faith outside of therapy, but, more insidiously, the activation of latent dependency needs in persons who have managed their lives, prior to treatment, with a modicum of independence and assertiveness. As treatment continues, the defenses, organized around avoiding dependency, break down and are swept away. This contingency is useful, of course, in patients who have a solid enough core to reconstitute themselves. Indeed, unless one removes the shaky superstructure, the defective underpinnings cannot be strengthened to support more adequate defenses. But what happens in individuals who do not have the materials, let alone the tools, to rebuild their lives? That which once served to carry the individual through daily chores, albeit not as mature as it might be, no longer can be used. The patient has

thrown away his crutches, and his legs are now too weak to propel him in any direction. The specter of patients being damaged by prolonged therapy is one that unfortunately haunts every psychotherapist.

Can we, by proper diagnosis, select patients for reconstructive therapy more appropriately, eliminating those who will present us with the dependency hazard? Are there ways that we can spot poor therapeutic risks in advance? As psychotherapists, we find ourselves in a quandary because morally and ethically we are committed to helping people develop and grow no matter how sick they are. We may, therefore, append a corollary to our questions: When we do detect poor therapeutic risks, are there ways of treating them effectively?

Before we attempt to answer these questions, let us try to designate the qualities of a good therapeutic risk for protracted reconstructive treatment. In order for a person to benefit from such therapy, the following conditions should prevail.

1. The presence of a personality disorder serious enough to justify the sacrifices inherent in an extended period of treatment.
2. The presence of symptoms or behavioral difficulties that are intensely annoying to the patient.
3. An ability to accept the conditions related to time, finances, and cooperation with techniques that probe the unconscious.
4. The presence of rigid resistances that cannot be resolved by less ambitious approaches.
5. A level of dependency that is not too high.
6. The ability to tolerate anxiety without severe disintegrative reactions.
7. The presence of some flexible defenses, ample enough to support the patient when anxiety is mobilized.

In advance of starting an actual therapeutic program, there are a few prognostic indicators that may be of value. If the patient has been seriously maladjusted since childhood—has failed to achieve goals ordinary for his age level; has been in psychotherapy for a number of years, particularly with a series of therapists without achieving benefits; has been institutionalized in a mental hospital; and manifests symptoms of schizophrenia, manic-depressive psychosis, organic brain disease, severe compulsion neurosis, psychopathic personality, alcoholism, drug addiction, severe psychosomatic illness, or obstinate sexual perversion—one should be alerted for trouble. Projective psychological testing is helpful diagnostically, but it may not reveal much in relation to the outcome.

The best clues will be supplied by the psychotherapeutic experience itself. If the patient shows favorable responses to interpretations, evidenced by constructive reactions inside and outside of therapy, and particularly an ability to implement insight in the direction of change, the therapist may be encouraged. Material from free associations, dreams, and transference reactions will reveal much that is not apparent on the surface. These are usually good indicators of therapeutic movement. If the patient responds catastrophically to interpretations, or if he does not respond at all; if he manifests few or no transference reactions, or if his transferences are too violent; if acting-out persists in spite of interpretation; if his associations and dreams consistently reveal no constructive developments—these are warnings that danger may shadow continued intensive explorations.

TREATMENT OF THE POOR THERAPEUTIC RISK

Where signs signal the patient as a poor therapeutic risk, the objective will be to bring him to homeostatis as rapidly as possible with short-term supportive and reeducative approaches. It may be useful to confront the patient frankly with the realities of his situation. Remarks may be couched in terms such as these:

Th. You have problems that date way back in your life. It will require some time to reverse these completely. There may be some things we may not be able to alter entirely because they go so far back and are so firmly welded into your personality that they may not budge. But you can still live a comfortable and happy life. Now

one of the problems in a situation like yours is that you feel helpless to do things by yourself. You will then get very dependent upon me, and it will set you back. For this reason we will keep our treatment short. Please don't feel that I am neglecting you if I encourage you to do things on your own.

These directives obviously will pass over the patient's head. Even though he may acknowledge them intellectually, emotionally he will continue to press for a long-term dependent relationship. In some cases he will really need to be dependent on someone or something the rest of his life since he cannot get along by himself. If this is a possibility, one may still acquaint the patient with the dynamics of his problem in the hope of enlisting his reasonable ego as an ally. By showing the patient the relationship of his dependency to other elements of his personality, of how and why he gets angry, of what he does with his anger, of how he undermines his self-esteem, of why he detaches, he is given a reality explanation for manifestations that he has hitherto considered to be mysteriously ordained.

If the patient persists in retaining the therapist as his dependency agent—and there are many patients who are able to afford this luxury and some therapists who are willing to play such an exhausting role—the therapist may graciously accept the post and inform the patient that he or she is willing to treat the patient and work with him on his daily problems. However, the therapist may add, the situation will be very much like in diabetes where insulin must be taken constantly. There are some emotional problems that are like diabetes and that will require help on a regular basis. He need not be ashamed if this is the situation in his case.

There is hardship in working on any depth level under these circumstances. The patient will merely regurgitate his insights and recite his dynamics like a catechism. The best practice is to settle back with the patient and handle his immediate reactions with logical, persuasive arguments, attempting to inculcate in him a philosophy of living that will help him to accept his limitations and difficulties with grace. At the same time depth material is interpreted whenever it is propitious to do so. Should the patient rail at the therapist and objurgate him for failing to transform him, the therapist must try to control his or her feelings. A simple reply is best here: ''Maybe it is impossible for you to change.'' This may have a startling effect on the patient for the good, often shaking him out of his therapeutic lethargy.

Recognizing that there are patients who will require aid the rest of their lives and cognizant of the ever-expanding waiting lists, one may attempt to provide these sicker patients with a dependency prop that does not require a tie-up of services. For instance a 15-, 20-, or 30-minute interview may be all that is needed. Drugs are prescribed if necessary, and the patient may be encouraged to join a therapeutic group. Group approaches offer advantages to the patient since they help him to diffuse his dependency. The patient generally will select one or two persons as his dependency target, but he knows he can draw on the group at large when necessary. It is helpful, therefore, to encourage patients to join various activity groups, such as social and discussion groups. These may eventually replace the therapist and the therapeutic group.

62

The Psychotherapist in Community Mental Health

There is a story about a unique way of diagnosing mental illness developed in a small community in Scotland. The suspected person is placed in a basement room that has a water tap. The faucet is turned on, the person handed a mop and asked to dry the floor. If he continues to do his job without turning off the faucet, the diagnosis of "madness" is confirmed. This droll story is sometimes utilized to illustrate the situation of mental disturbances in the community. By concentrating our efforts on managing the pressing disorders of the mentally and emotionally ill, we often lose sight of the fact that we coordinately fail to turn off the faucet in our polluted social system that is pouring out more patients than we can treat.

Such a statement assumes that we know enough about what causes emotional illness, and that we have the means of remedying the causes, to turn off the faucet. Such assumptions are only partially true, but we certainly have sufficient knowledge at the present time, if not to dry the floor, to keep the basement from being flooded. The point is that we are not utilizing such knowledge, nor does our society yet support with adequate economic and other means its implementation.

On the debit side we must admit that community mental health is still a relatively uncharted field that embodies a variety of theoretical systems and methodological approaches (Caplan, 1964, 1970, 1974; Glasscote et al, 1964, 1969). Designs for essential services vary with the characteristics and problems of the community being accommodated, with the needs of the individuals and agencies who constitute the consumers or the client systems, and with the philosophies and training of the personnel staffing the center or clinic that is executing the program. The problem areas for attack potentially are limitless, and, obviously, a rigid selection of zones of involvement will be in order. These range from clinical services for severe emotional problems, to counseling or casework for circumscribed personal and environmental difficulties, to educational projects for the public geared to preventive objectives, to training programs for allied professionals and paraprofessionals, to hospitalization and day care facilities for the mentally ill, to rehabilitative and work adjustment programs for the handicapped, to consultation aids to organizations or groups in the community.

There are many existing models in community mental health that deal with how these services may be integrated, and many more will undoubtedly be developed with changing politico-socio-economic conditions. Caplan (1974) in explicating some of these models states that "since we are grappling with a highly complex multifactorial field, no single model can be expected to do more than focus our attention and pattern our expectations about one aspect of the field." What would be applicable in one community does not necessarily conform with the special problems and conditions of another community. The mental health worker must consequently maintain flexibility and utilize whatever models seem pertinent, always altering these as new accomodations become necessary. At the Post-graduate Center for Mental Health in New York City we have worked in different communities and with almost 350 different agencies, institutions, and community groups in cities and counties in New York, New Jersey, and Connecticut. We have found that rigid adherence to any one model of operation can cripple a program and that a great deal more innovative flexibility is required than in working with individual and group psychotherapy.

There are times in the career of most psychotherapists when they are called on to apply their mental health skills to the social system. For example, a local school is experiencing an extraordinary increase in dropouts. A community is being plagued with an epidemic of misdemeanors and crimes perpetrated by juvenile delinquents. A center is being organized to provide recreational and rehabilitative services for older people, and the founders insist that it be oriented around sound mental health principles. A social agency wants to know how to start a mental health clinic. A group of ministers need help in doing more effective pastoral counseling. Vocational rehabilitative workers request a course in the psychiatric and psychological aspects of work readjustment. A parent-teacher's association desires a lecture on child development illustrated by a good film. A fraternal society is setting up a series of discussion groups dealing with family life education and need a discussion leader. The roles which the psychotherapist will be ex-

pected to play in servicing any of these requests go beyond those he conventionally assumes in the clinic or his office. He must take on among other responsibilities those of educator, public health expert and mental health consultant. If he has had the traditional residency and post-residency training, he will not be equipped to do this, the focus of his education being more on clinical than on community functions.

It is beyond the scope of this book to explicate the details of community mental health or the full operations of the mental health specialist. Ample literature exists on these subjects. Mannino, MacLennan, and Shore (1975) have compiled an excellent reference guide to the consultation literature as well as a serviceable list of films and tapes. A full bibliography may be found in *Community Mental Health and Social Psychiatry,* prepared by Harvard Medical School and Psychiatric Service of the Massachusetts General Hospital (Cambridge, Harvard University Press, 1962), and *Community Mental Health, Selected Reading List 1961–1965* (Canada's Mental Health Supplement No. 50; November-December, 1965), as well as Bindman (1966), Hume (1966), NIMH (1967–1970), Bellak et al., (1969, 1972, 1975), and Braceland et al. (1975). Nevertheless, some guidelines will be indicated in this chapter that the therapist may find of practical value.

Let us assume that the therapist receives a letter requesting a consultation from the director of a boy's club that has been organized around activities, such as carpentry and other handicrafts, for adolescents from deprived economic areas. The presenting problem is poor staff morale, which the director credits to the fact that the staff members feel themselves to be ineffectual in dealing with psychiatric problems. Delinquency and drug addiction among many of the boys, for example, continue uninterrupted. The director believes that a course on psychopathology would be good for his staff and may help them to function more efficiently. The therapist replies affirmatively to the letter and sets up an appointment with the director. Prior to the conference, he may make several assumptions:

1. The director's diagnosis of what is needed, namely, a course on psychopathology, may or may not be what is required to resolve the problem.

2. In entering into the picture, the consultant (therapist) most likely will find among different levels of the administration, supervisory group, and staff workers, as well as among the recipients of the service, i.e., the adolescents, a hotbed of interlocking psychopathological constellations. The consultant will, with full justification, be tempted to prescribe psychotherapy for the most disturbed individuals. To do this would probably prove fatal. Limited finances, absent motivation, and the dearth of treatment facilities render psychotherapy impractical. Solutions other than therapy will be required.

3. A series of conferences will be needed with the director, the supervisors, and the staff individually and collectively to determine what they believe is wrong and to observe the way that they interact with each other in the work situation.

4. A series of conferences with the adolescents, particularly the leaders, may be desirable at some time once the picture has crystallized.

5. The entry of the consultant into the organization will probably stir up initial anxiety and resistance on all levels of the organization that will require handling.

6. Being involved in the dynamics of a social system, the consultant will have to keep communication channels open between the administrative, supervisory, and staff levels of the organization. The boundaries of his operations will require explicit definition; i.e., the director may need to be informed about what is going on, but may not have to be involved in the project itself; written communications will have to be sent by the consultant to the director outlining what decisions are reached and what the consultant proposes to do; written agreement to proposals must be received by the consultant; a liaison person must be appointed by the director to represent the administration; and a decision must be made in joint conference as to the persons with whom the consultant will work in the project.

With these assumptions in mind, the consultant sets up an appointment with the director, who visits the consultant in his office. The director appears to be an intelligent, interested, and knowledgeable person, a social worker who has had considerable experience in the field of group work. He is very active in community affairs and has affiliations with many community organizations. He is sociable and relates well. The consultant, inquiring about the program, discovers that 1000 boys are being serviced who live in the area of the club. During the summer the club runs a camp outside of the city. The activity program is managed by a staff of expert craftsmen who have had no mental health orientation. The initial impression of the consultant is that if the staff had some mental health information, they may be able to utilize this in their work with the adolescents. For instance, many of the boys are expressing the usual defiant gestures of adolescents, and some of the staff, he believes, are responding with feelings of not being appreciated. Moreover, a good number of the adolescents have severe character disturbances and are engaging in antisocial activities that may be upsetting the staff. Clarification about the dynamics would, therefore, seem indicated.

The consultant makes an appointment to visit the club and arranges to meet with the staff and supervisory groups individually. Several meetings are also held jointly with the staff supervisors and director. It soon becomes obvious to the consultant that the relationship of the staff and supervisors with the director leaves much to be desired. They consider the director an autocrat who overrides their decisions and who does not allow them freedom in their work. They respond to this by sullen withdrawal and disinterest in their duties. Most of the staff believe that they might learn something constructive from a course in mental health principles and practices. However, the consultant is convinced that little will be accomplished until better relationships are established among the personnel. The director is not at all aware of the role that he is playing with his staff or of their hostile reactions to him. From the way he had communicated in the initial conference, the consultant could not diagnose what was wrong until the work situation and the ongoing interactions had been observed.

In discussion with the staff the following plan is elaborated: (1) a group process to enable the staff to verbalize feelings and to become aware of sabotaging reactions that paralyze their functions and interfere with their relationships with the adolescents, (2) conferences with the director to give him an opportunity to express himself and to test his flexibility, (3) group meetings with the staff, supervisors, and director, during which they are encouraged to discuss how they feel about each other in their work roles. Such sessions help the director play a more cooperative role with his staff and encourage them to talk to him about their "gripes."

The consultant does not consider the group participants as "patients" for very good reasons. First, they do not regard themselves as patients; second, he is principally concerned with their work problems and not their neuroses; and third, group process, employing principles of group dynamics, is the instrumentality that he will use, not probing techniques into defenses and unconscious conflicts. The upshot may be therapeutic for all participants, but this is a by-product. The focus is on conscious feelings in relation to their ongoing interactions.

Another example of how a therapist-consultant may respond to a community need is contained in the request of a suburban psychiatric clinic for staff training in psychotherapy. Upon visiting the clinic, the consultant finds that the problem confronting the clinic is that all of the available time of the staff members is occupied in treating a stationary caseload that does not seem to be going anywhere. The waiting lists are long; intake has more or less been frozen for months due to the absence of available therapeutic hours.

Examining the records of the kinds of patients being treated, the consultant finds that most of them are schizophrenic, borderline, or dependent personality problems who have fastened themselves onto their therapists and have settled into what is turning out to be a permanent niche. The director of the clinic believes that what is required is more sophisticated training of the staff in depth approaches so that the basic inner problems of their patients may be influenced, in this way resolving the stalemate. An interview with the staff reveals frustration and demoralization contingent on disappointment that they are unable to effectuate cures and because of pressures on them to open up more time for new patients.

The consultant sets up conferences with the staff members, and what is finally decided is the following: (1) establishment of a special clinic for sicker patients organized around drug therapy and no more than 15-minute supportive interview sessions once weekly or bimonthly, (2) transfer of the bulk of patients to this clinic, (3) development of a social rehabilitative unit in a neighboring church recreational center to which the patients may be referred for adjunctive social programs, (4) organization of a group therapy clinic and training of the staff in group therapeutic techniques, (5) concentration on short-term therapy as standard for the clinic and staff training in brief psychotherapy, (6) since this plan is long-term, requiring a period of years for its full development, a training program in group therapy and short-term therapy, for which the consultant will help recruit appropriately qualified trainers, (7) work by the consultant, if possible, with this group over the 3 or 4 years of transition, since there will be much staff anxiety that will require handling.

Let us give a third example of how the psychotherapist engages in community life. A therapist-consultant is called into a school as a consultant to determine why so large a percentage of the students are failing their college entrance examinations. Upon studying the school program, and after conferences with the principal, the teachers, and some of the students, she comes to the conclusion that what is needed in the school is a school psychologist to service only the high school who can help student with problems in school and personal adjustment. An expanded budget is presented by the principal to the school board, some of whose members accuse the principal of being delinquent in his duties and oppose his recommendations. A group of irate taxpayers organize themselves into a political-action body and argue that a psychologist in the school will "make the students crazy" or give them "new-fangled foolish ideas." The principal of the school is greatly disturbed and realizes that the community will not accept a psychologist to serve the high school. The consultant and the principal discuss the problem with the teachers, and it is decided that an educational program is needed for the community. The help of the PTA is enlisted, and an educational program is planned. A series of community lectures is organized employing mental health films, with discussion groups following the lectures around problems of child development and family life. There results a change in attitude, and the psychologist is accepted into the school system.

It will be seen from these illustrations that the operations of a community mental health specialist go beyond those of mere psychotherapist. If he or she is to live up to community responsibility, the psychotherapist will need skills not now developed in the traditional residency and postresidency programs. It so happens that by the nature of education and background the psychotherapist may not know as much about the community and his or her proper role in it as do certain professionals, such as community organizers, public health officers, and other social scientists. Yet the knowledge of human dynamics and of the irrational forces that prompt people and groups qualifies the psychotherapist to understand the disorganizing emotional cross-currents that operate in society. What the specialist needs, as has been mentioned before, is the acquisition of a completely new set of professional talents in addition to psychotherapy, since psychotherapy as such may not be suited to the client group or will require reinforcement with other techniques.

The lines along which this supplementation may be organized is perhaps best conceptualized in an ecological model of community mental health that draws its theories and techniques from clinical psychiatry, social science, and public health. Since one objective is the control en masse of emotional disturbance, it is essential to bring into the orbit of techniques methods that not only influence the individual but also the family and other groups. A network of coordinated services are consequently employed that act independent of psychotherapy. By the very nature of one's functioning, the psychotherapist who works in the community must collaborate with other professionals in the fields of education, medicine, nursing, welfare, correction, law, religion, and other disciplines. This does not mean a watering down of psychotherapy where it is indicated in individual cases; however, one must acknowledge the limitations of psychotherapy in dealing with community problems. Essential is a broadening of the base of operations to include every measure—psychological and sociotherapeutic—that can help people relate better and function better.

Actually our understanding of dynamics and psychopathology have widened the horizons of illness to include deviant behavior in addition to the traditional neurotic and psychotic syndromes. With this insight has come the need to provide services for disorders up to recently not considered within the province of psychotherapeutic concern. As a consequence, it has been necessary to blend our therapeutic methodologies with educational, social, and rehabilitative approaches and to modify our ideas and methods within the context of the communities medical and social organizations.

Alterations in line with community need inevitably must include psychotherapy. In extending the benefits of psychotherapy to the masses, however, it becomes necessary to adapt our tactics to abbreviated objectives. Short-term psychotherapy devoid of ambiguous abstractions and amorphous theoretical concepts that applies itself to the immediate problems of the patient becomes essential. The effect of these modified treatment techniques can be both reparative and reconstructive, although goal compromise may be necessary to meet the practical needs of the millions who require aid.

In addition to psychotherapy, the total involvement of the community and its resources in a comprehensive program is unavoidable. One form particularly suited for sicker patients is the "therapeutic community" (Edelson, 1964; Kraft, AM, 1966). The therapeutic community is actually an old concept, dating far back in history. But the ways in which therapeutic communities have operated have varied with the level of our understanding of group and interpersonal processes. The mental health specialist will need to know how to help each member of the community achieve as maximal a development as is within the individual's potential.

Because emergencies in the lives of people most commonly motivate them to seek help, some mental health centers have largely devoted their efforts to working with crises. According to Caplan and Grunebaum (1972), the following points are essential in crisis intervention:

1. Timing: Intensive and frequent visits during the first 4 to 6 weeks are mandatory, rather than spacing interviews at weekly intervals over a long-term period.
2. Family orientation: The integrity of the family should be preserved to help support the member in crisis. Interviews with the family at their home may be required.
3. Avoiding dependency: Undue dependency is avoided by dealing with the current situation rather than focusing on past problems.
4. Fostering mastery: All efforts are made to encourage understanding of a problem and modes of coping with it effectively. This may require intensive short-term education.
5. Outside support: Enlisting the help of available outside support (friends, clergy, and other agencies) facilitates treatment.
6. Goals: The objective is to improve adjustment and the immediate coping with the current situation rather than "cure." Trained nonprofessionals may be helpful in carrying out the therapeutic plan.

Helping people to deal constructively with crises necessitates less a focus on etiology than on encouraging existing health-promoting forces of an interpersonal and social nature that are present or latent. Caplan (1974) points out appropriately that capacities for adaptation of individuals are bolstered by help from the social network "which provide them with consistent communications of what is expected of them, supports and assistance with tasks, evaluations of their performance, and appropriate rewards." While the intensity of stress and the existing ego strength of the individual are important, the quality of the support that the person gets from his group is even more important in adjusting to the noxious effects of an environment or in coping with crises. Supportive groups are many, the individual involving himself consistently with some of these such as in his work area, his church, and his political and recreational associations, or they may be selected and utilized only in times of need like self-help groups, physicians, social workers, ministers, lawyers, or other nonprofessionals, and concerned friends who have had and perhaps conquered problems akin to those of the individual. These helping aids may be exploited spontaneously by the individual or, where a community is lacking in them, organized and stimulated by a knowledgeable professional person. Where they exist and the individual isolates himself from them, the task of the community mental health worker may be to motivate the clients to utilize them or to deal with the resistances against their exploitation. Adequate support programs are vital in any comprehensive program of community mental health (Caplan & Killilea, 1976).

COMMUNITY PSYCHIATRY

The reduction of psychiatric morbidity through preventive, rehabilitative, and therapeutic measures is the objective of "community" or "social psychiatry." Elaboration of community-based treatment and aftercare services draws upon principles of public health and incorporates epidemiological and biostatistical precepts even though psychiatric techniques are ultimately employed. An ample body of literature has accumulated on community psychiatry: Bellak (1964, 1974); Bernard (1954; 1960); Blain and Gayle (1954); Caplan (1959); Carstairs (1962); Clausen and Kohn (1954); J. V. Coleman (1953); Columbia University School of Public Health (1961); Dax (1961); Dohrenwend et al. (1962); Duhl (1963); Dunham and Weinberg (1960); Faris and Dunham (1939); Felix (1957, 1961); Forstenzer (1961); L. K. Frank (1957); H. Freeman and Farndale (1963); GAP (Reports 1949, 1956b; Symposium, 1965); Goldsten (1965); Greenblatt et al. (1957); Gruenberg (1957); Hanlon (1957); Harvard Medical School (1962); Hume (1964, 1965, 1966); M. Jones (1952); I. Kaufman (1956); Kotinsky and Witmer (1955); Lebensohn (1964); Leighton (1960); Leighton et al. (1957, 1963); Lemkau (1955); Lin and Standley (1962); Milbank Memorial Fund (1956, 1957, 1959); Mintz and Schwartz (1964); NIMH (1961); Pepper et al. (1965); Plunkett and Gordon (1960); Redlich and Pepper (1963, 1964); Rennie and Woodward (1948); Ruesch (1965); Stainbrook (1955); G. S. Stevenson (1956); Weston (1975); and WHO (1960).

Preventive Psychiatry

Originally community psychiatrists considered their mission the caring for sicker mental patients. However, the emphasis on prevention has shifted attention to the less severe emotional ailments, i.e., the psychoneuroses, the character disorders, the addictions, and even the milder adjustment problems. As Caplan (1965) has pointed out, "The community psychiatrist accepts responsibiltiy for helping those of all ages and classes, who are suffering from disorders of all types, wherever they occur in the community."

A public health model of prevention divides the program into primary, secondary, and tertiary categories (Caplan, 1964; Zus-

man, 1975) In *primary prevention* attempts are made both to modify the environment and to reinforce constructive elements within the individual to aid in his coping capacities and to reduce the incidence of mental disorder. In *secondary prevention* the aim is to diagnose and to treat patients who had already developed mental disorders in order to lower the severity and duration of morbidity. In *tertiary prevention* the object is to rehabilitate persons with emotional difficulties so that they may make some kind of adaptation to their environment.

Efforts at prevention require a knowledge of community organization and planning as well as cooperation with other productive community programs that are operative within the community. There are relatively few psychiatrists and psychologists who have gone beyond their clinical training to acquire required skills to work at prevention. But even where the mental health worker has had adequate knowledge and training, there are regressive forces within the community that will resist change and will even attempt to restore the prior pathogenic elements once change is effectuated. Indeed, there are professionals who insist that the present-day community mental health movement is geared predominantly toward social control and toward preserving the politicoeconomic system and that change will be possible only by the assumption of a radical position with centers becoming politically involved while utilizing methods that reach large masses of people (Kunnes, 1972). Advocated is turning over the control of policies and priorities of services to the citizenry of the community, the "consumers." On the other hand, it is pointed out by oppositionists that where such a radical position has been taken, the results have been sadly wanting and that, therefore, a more conservative stance is to be preferred. One can only do for a community what it is willing to accept. This should not dampen enthusiasm about what can be accomplished nor discourage efforts at public education that can reduce the resistance threshold.

Primary prevention, while "the most desirable and potentially most effective approach to a solution of the problem of mental disorder in our communities, is clearly more a hope than a reality'' (Caplan & Grunebaum, 1972). The provision of adequate health, housing, police, sanitation, educational, welfare, social, and recreational facilities require outlays of public funds so vast that any effective provision would threaten other priorities, such as space exploration, which are deemed more essential by political authorities than dealing with the problems of the citizenry. Increasing taxation and the issuing of bonds to bolster flagging budgets have acted like a time bomb that threaten fiscal solvency. For the most part, community mental health operations have served, in some cases at least, quite successfully to supply services for secondary and tertiary prevention.

The Community Mental Health Center

Broadening the base of services to the mentally ill and emotionally disturbed and focusing on early treatment and ambulatory services result in a minimal disruption of personal, family, work, and social life. Essentially the psychiatrist functions as a consultant both for the treatment of individual cases and for the development and implementation of programs. The therapist's major area of competence is in diagnosis and treatment.

Two patterns of community psychiatry appear to be emerging. The first is organized around the community mental health center, which aims at decentralization, regionalization and local service and is not too intimately related to other health services. The second is the integrated blending together of psychiatric services orbited around the general hospital, which has consultative, outpatient, inpatient, day-and-night care facilities, but which is relatively isolated from community welfare and educational services.

The assembly under one umbrella of all services for the mentally ill was one of the recommendations of the National Congress on Mental Illness and Health held by the American Medical Association Council on Mental Health in 1962 (NIMH: *The Comprehensive Community Mental Health Center,*

Public Health Service Pamphlet No. 1137, 1964; see also *Community Mental Health Advances,* Public Health Services Publication No. 1141). The Joint Commission on Mental Illness and Health, in its report to Congress in 1961, also emphasized the need for community services as a way of prevention and treatment to avert the debilitating effects of long hospitalization. The Joint Commission recommended expanded services in the community, a shift of focus from mental hospital institutionalization to smaller inpatient units as well as increased community care, a concentration on prevention and rehabilitation, greater cooperation among the different professions toward improving mental health research and treatment, and a more intimate coordination of hospital and community resources (*Action for Mental Health: Joint Commission on Mental Illness and Health.* New York, Basic Books, 1961). These recommendations have sponsored the organization of community mental health centers that offer the following:

1. Inpatient services, including a 24-hour emergency service
2. A day hospital
3. Outpatient clinic services for adults, children, and families without a waiting period
4. Partial hospitalization for day care and night care
5. Consultation services
6. Diagnostic services
7. Rehabilitative services of an educational, vocational, and social nature
8. Precare and aftercare services, such as placement in foster homes and halfway houses
9. Training of all types of mental health personnel
10. Research and evaluation

These instrumentalities may not be under one roof or one sponsorship but are administered so that a continuity of care is achieved (NAMH, 1963a & b; Downing et al, 1966; McKinley et al, 1966; Dorsett & Jones, 1967).

The concentration of services around a general hospital is recommended by some authorities, and a selected annotated bibliography has been prepared by the National Institute for Mental Health detailing how it may function as a psychiatric resource (*The Community General Hospital as a Psychiatric Resource,* Public Health Service Publication No. 1484, Public Health Bibliography Series No. 66).

The experience of implementing the community mental health center program in the first few years of its development was not entirely a happy one. Glasscote et al. (1969) believed the flaw to have been in the timetable: "Lack of experience, lack of staff, and lack of definition have all played a role, but they have been less of a problem than bad timing." The urgency to spend allocated funds for construction of community mental health centers over a 2-year period encouraged the building of centers prior to planning how the centers would be utilized in comprehensive statewide designs. Problems also developed in providing for adequate staffing, a prime key to the adequate operation of a center. Much of the fault in fulfilling the original purpose of Congress in creating the program lay in the fact that providing for the mental health needs of all people in all parts of the state with adequate preventive, screening, diagnostic, therapeutic, rehabilitative, consultative, educational, research, and training services was a too ambitious, and perhaps unrealistic, goal that awaited a good deal of experiment over many years before it could be even minimally fulfilled. This is perhaps why unfavorable publicity and reports of failure of the community mental health programs have appeared in the literature. For instance, Ralph Nader (Medical Tribune, 1972) has claimed that the programs in action have perpetuated a two-class system of care that is sterile in ideas and operations. An overcommitment to broad social problems at the expense of the immediate needs of clients "wastes professional staff and is both expensive and unfruitful, thus causing public disillusionment and endangering the whole community psychiatry program" (Wachpress, 1972). Under the circumstances it is remarkable that many community mental health centers have functioned as well as they have (New York Times,

1972). It is hoped that profitting from what has happened in the past, with adequate governmental funding and more sophisticated staffing, the centers may ultimately bring to fruition some of Congress's original goals. It is hoped, too, that aftercare programs for the patients discharged from mental hospitals will become richer and better organized so that readmissions to hospitals are less necessary. Some of the statistics are impressive. The number of hospital beds for mental patients has been halved, and the average stay has been reduced from 8 years to 17 months. Without adequate support systems in the community, however, the benefits are questionable.

Expanded Functions of the Psychiatrist

Since diagnostic and treatment resources are deployed in relationship to large groups of patients, the community psychiatrist will usually make no personal contact with them. Because preventive methods entail the detection and remedying of social forces and environmental pressures that have a potentially pathogenic effect on people, "the psychiatrist begins to include in his treatment plan the active manipulation of the organizational aspect of his patient's life" (Caplan, 1965). This often requires the offering of individual or group consultation to administrators and others in an organization. Advice may be given affecting any phase of organizational functioning, including policy-making. In expanding operations, the psychiatrist will, as has been mentioned before, have to go beyond habitual clinical theoretical models.

It is obvious that community work foists on the psychiatrist responsibilities that differ from those of clinician in line with the new tools being used (i.e., consultation, in-service training, and general public education) and the people in the organization (executives, foremen, staff workers) with whom one is working. The theory and practice of community psychiatry, the practical implementation of community research methodology, the planning of services in line with the most efficient use of resources, and the development and administration of community programs are functions that will require specialized training beyond that of the psychiatric residency. Such training will undoubtedly be organized in the future as part of a career program and may be as eagerly sought after as psychoanalytic training has been for the past generations of psychiatrists. One design of training has been that offered at the Columbia Presbyterian Medical Center, which has been carried out jointly by the Department of Psychiatry and the School of Public Health and Administrative Medicine through an interdepartmental Division of Community Psychiatry (Columbia University, 1961; Bernard, 1960, 1965). Others have been at the Johns Hopkins School of Hygiene and Public Health (Lemkau, 1955), at Harvard (Caplan, 1959), and at Berkeley (Bellak, 1964). There are some who believe that it is possible to teach community psychiatry in a traditional residency training program (Daniels & Margolis, 1965). Some favor the Community Mental Health Center (Sabshin, 1965). Others have developed programs in relationship to state and local health departments and university, state, and private training centers (Kern, 1965).

Comprehensive Training in Community Mental Health

There is a wide disparity in the level of professional development required for courses in community psychiatry and community mental health. Some schools train psychiatrists on a residency level exclusively; others believe that psychiatric nurses, clinical psychologists, and psychiatric social workers are fully capable, with training, of learning skills in community psychiatry (Hume, 1966). Community mental health is, according to Lemkau (1965), of medical concern, but it is not identical or coincident with psychiatry. It is much broader; it is a communitywide responsibility that sponsors the concept that "the program is to be under professional and lay auspices, and that mental health is promoted and fostered not solely through medical treatment, but also through a variety of institutions and agencies with numerous disciplines joining in the effort."

The multidisciplinary accent on community mental health will probably incubate rivalries and hostilities between the disciplines engaged as soon as adequate financing for services becomes available. Arguments of who can practice, and under what auspices and supervision, will perhaps be as vehement as in the practice of psychotherapy. With added information about epidemiology and biostatistics, and with a somewhat greater public health orientation, the average psychiatrist can very well adapt to a community-based design for the mentally ill and, if creative and experienced, can evolve, implement, and supervise treatment programs. The therapist may also be able to develop and carry out public education projects. Properly trained nonmedical people, particularly psychiatric nurses, clinical psychologists, and psychiatric social workers, may assist in programs for the severely mentally ill. They may also quite capably be able to organize, direct, and execute projects of public education and consultation in mental health. However, to do consultation, in-service staff training, and the training of allied professionals, such as ministers, nurses, social workers, physicians, rehabilitation workers, speech therapists, and teachers, in techniques in mental health (counseling, group process, etc.), even experienced psychiatrists, clinical psychologists, psychiatric nurses, and psychiatric social workers will need to fulfill certain requirements. They will preferably have to be skilled psychotherapists, which means that following their residencies they will have completed postgraduate work in a psychoanalytic or psychotherapeutic training center. They must ideally also have completed a structured course in community mental health that draws its substance from the public health and behavioral sciences fields. Work in community projects under supervision will have taught them the fundamentals of mental health consultation and how to gear teaching methods to the needs of the different professionals who handle people with problems. It is hardly conceivable that a mental health consultant and professional trainer can be on a level below that of supervising psychotherapist.

One of the chief difficulties for most psychotherapists launching into the field of mental health is that, with the possible exception of the social worker, their training, experience, and hence conceptual framework is largely clinical. While this framework may operate effectively in psychotherapy, it does not apply to many, perhaps most, of the problems encountered in the community. An ideal community mental health worker should in part be a sociologist, anthropologist, psychologist, educator, political scientist, community organizer and planner, psychoanalyst, psychiatrist, physiologist, social worker, historian, public health specialist, biologist, social philosopher, researcher, and administrator. Since no therapist has or will ever have a complete combination of skills relating to the above professions, one will have to accommodate existing talents to a complex, difficult, and constantly changing community atmosphere, utilizing oneself as constructively as one can while preserving the open mind of a student and scholar who is in constant search for new information and knowledge. Training is helpful within a community mental health center to equip a therapist with the specialized abilities required to work in the community. Where one has the motivation and is fortunate enough to live in an area where there is a training course in community mental health, the experience may be very profitable.

The kind of training that is most suited for a community mental health specialist is, in addition to psychotherapy, experience with group processes and group dynamics, research design and methods, community organization and planning, communication techniques, teaching, various rehabilitation procedures, administration, and legal and legislative processes. A knowledge of public health objectives and measures is also helpful. It is rare that an individual can be interested in all of these fields. Generally one concentrates on a special area, such as mental health education, but comprehensive knowledge will enhance functioning even though greatest weight is given one kind of activity. Work in rehabilitation, law enforcement, industry, recreation, religion, etc., requires an extensive repertoire of techniques. The broader the education of the therapist, the greater use the therapist will be to consultee groups.

Since substantial impact may be made on people during periods of crisis, nonpsychiatric professionals who are in contact with persons in trouble may be of incalculable help if they have fundamental information about how to recognize an emotional problem, how to interview, how to utilize themselves constructively in a relationship situation, and how to refer. Educating such persons is a fundamental task of the mental health consultant, and for this he or she will require an understanding of teaching method.

TECHNIQUES IN COMMUNITY MENTAL HEALTH

Mental Health Consultation

Consultation is a basic tool of the mental health specialist. It consists of an interaction between a specialist or consultant and one or more consultees (usually agency professionals) aimed at the mental health components of their work, including program and practices of the consultee organization. In the course of such consultation the consultee is also, according to Gerald Caplan, "being educated in order that he will be able in the future to handle similar problems in the same or other clients in a more effective manner than in the past" (U.S. Public Health Service, 1962).

Mental health consultation must be differentiated from psychotherapy, supervision, professional education, in-service training, and collaboration (Haylett & Rapaport, 1964). In psychotherapy the interaction is with a patient toward resolving symptoms and strengthening personality assets; in consultation the relationship is with a professional consultee and is geared toward enhancing his knowledge and broadening his skills. In supervision the supervisor assumes an administrative in addition to an educative role; in consultation, the consultant does not play an administrative authority role. In professional education a student is schooled in a skill that equips one to enter a certain profession; in consultation the consultee has already fulfilled the minimum requirements for his profession. In in-service training the focus is on improving competence in the tasks for which one has been hired; in consultation new tasks are envisioned to expand the consultee's functions in mental health areas.

Consultation is usually offered to individuals in key administrative and supervisory positions in order to maximize the effect and to reach the greatest numbers of people, i.e., the working staffs. It is generally done at the consultee's place of work unless the consultant possesses or arranges for special facilities.

Stages of consultation may be divided into a beginning or "entry" phase, a problem-solving phase, and a termination phase. It is assumed that the consultee is acquainted with the consultant or the consultant's work and is oriented regarding the nature of consultation services. If not, a preparatory interpretive meeting or group of meetings may have to be arranged. A contract is drawn up either verbally or, preferably, in the form of an exchange of letters. The consultant and consultee agree on details as to participating personnel, the extent of time of the project, and physical arrangements. It may be necessary to clarify the consultant's role, for instance, that services are not given directly to the consultee's clients. The next phase is that of problem solving, which is the core of the consultation process. Here the consultee's motivations and readiness for change mingle with the consultant's skill, experience, and capacity to handle emotional aspects of the relationship. This interaction will determine the rapidity with which movement and change are registered. The final phase is that of a mutually agreed upon termination.

The methods employed by the mental health consultant will have to be adapted to the special needs and problems of the agency, group, or individual who is seeking help. Generally, methods derived from the clinical model, i.e., therapeutic work with individuals, are not too applicable to consultation. As an example, let us suppose that the specialist is engaged by a social agency as a consultant to help in making their functions more effective. The first step is the "entry process" into the agency— "consultee system," or "client-system" as R. Lippitt et al. (1958) call it. This entails a proper diagnosis of the problem determined by setting up a series of meetings with key personnel. The objective is to help the consultee arrive at an understanding of what is needed and which aspects of the problem to approach immediately and which later on. A problem-solving plan is evolved, and the consultant then focuses on facilitating and enhancing the problem-solving skills of the individuals who will execute the plan. Communication channels are opened up between the various levels of the agency (executive, supervisor, and staff) to handle the effects of feedback, and resistances to change and to learning. The consultant then continues to work with the agency until the plan is proceeding satisfactorily. Where the agency is large, the consultant may restrict efforts just to training the supervisory staff, expanding their information and skills so that they may by themselves manage and continue the program that has been instituted. The consultant may have to use some research techniques and engage in nine or ten group conference services, getting details of work habits, studying records, and becoming familiar with the functions of the organization. Then attention may be directed to training. If the consultant cannot personally enter into the problem-solving process, help may be obtained from the proper outside resources for this task. Finally, the consultant withdraws from the agency or "consultee system" (Wolberg, A, & Padilla-Lawson, 1965).

Considerable numbers of writings have accumulated detailing theory and method in mental health consultation. Recommended reading are the following: Argyris (1961); Berlin (1956, 1960, 1964); Bindman (1959, 1960, 1966); Boehme (1956); Brashear et al. (1954); Caplan (1961b, 1963, 1964, 1970); L. D. Cohen (1966); J. V. Coleman (1947); Covner (1947); Croley (1961); Davies (1960); W. E. Davis (1957); Family Service

Association (1956); GAP (1956a); Garrett (1956); Gibb (1959); Gibb and Lippitt (1959); Gilbert (1960); Gilbertson (1952); Glidewell (1959); Gordon (1953); Greenblatt (1975); Halleck and Miller (1963); Kazanjian et al. (1962); Leader (1957); Lifschutz et al. (1958); G. Lippitt (1959); R. Lippitt et al. (1958); Maddux (1950, 1953); Malamud (1959); Mannino et al. (1975); Mental Hygiene Committee (1950); Nunnally (1957); K. B. Oettinger (1950); Parker (1958, 1962); L. Rapaport (1963); M. J. Rosenthal and Sullivan (1959); San Mateo County (1961); G. S. Stevenson (1956); Valenstein (1955); A. Wolberg and Padilla-Lawson (1965); Zander (1957).

More specifically, the entry phase is characterized by an exploration during conferences of the manifest problems and needs of the consultee. During this phase relationships will be established. If possible, a personal interview should be made by the consultee for the consultant with the head of the agency to affirm his support for the project. Answers are needed:

1. What is the structure of the agency, including the history, budget, and financing?
2. What is the organizational structure involving the personnel in the agency? What are the authority lines and policy-making bodies?
3. What are the supervisory policies?
4. Are there any apparent personality problems of, and conflicts in relation to, the leadership?
5. Are there any apparent conflicts in policies and aims?
6. What are the existing functions of the agency and are these being fulfilled?
7. What are the proposed future functions, if any, and are these realistic?
8. What is the community setting in which the agency operates? Are there conflicts between policies and functions of the agency and the community? What are the areas of community support and the areas of opposition? (For example, a school may wish to focus its resources and energies on the most gifted children who are showing learning blocks. The parents' association may be pressing for better tutoring to prepare the students for college boards. Some community organizations, courts, social agencies, etc., may be insistent that juvenile delinquents and retarded children receive special attention, which will conflict with a program for brighter students.)
9. What is the community organization; is there now or will there be a duplication of services? Is there cooperation with other agencies?
10. What are the existing and anticipated conflicts regarding programming and policy changes?
11. What were the previous experiences of the agency with consultants?

During the next (problem-solving) phase of the consultation there is an ordered gathering of information about the consultee system, including needs and difficulties. A true working relationship begins to develop. Diagnostic assessments are made and a plan of action is agreed upon. It will be essential in dealing with the consultee (or consultees) to educate him (or them), as one goes along, to handle anxieties and resistances. A periodic review of services and problems may be required and role limitations defined. It is to be expected that some untoward reactions will crop up among the staff, supervisors, and administration when changes in program are proposed or implemented. Great tact must be exercised in dealing with these. It may be that the staff's proposals for change may not be consonant with the personal philosophies of the administrator, in which case exploratory conferences will be necessary.

In the course of problem solving, transference and countertransference will come into evidence. One's own analysis and experience as a psychotherapist will help the consultant to deal with these contingencies. Obviously, psychotherapy will not be done; however, inimical reactions may tactfully be interpreted on the "here-and-now" level. Temptation to fall back on clinical methods must be resisted. If the consultee recognizes an emotional problem in himself and requests help for this, the consultant may offer advice as to resources. Plunging in blindly and trying to get a consultee to accept personal therapy without his desire for this may destroy the working relationship.

What is discouraging to most consultants is the slowness with which attitude change can be brought about. Personality difficulties among the professionals in an agency are the greatest deterrents to change and constructive action, and the consultant will have to work with these obstructions painstakingly. Honest, frank communication in the matrix of a working relationship is the best way of dealing with emerging resistances and problems. The consultant must expect that some of the intrusions proffered will be challenged and that discrimination may be exercised that will not always be in the consultant's favor. Questions one asks about the organization and its functions may arouse suspicions of "trespassing" and may mobilize guilt feelings in those who consider that their negligence in duty will be discovered. Some may resent being told how to do their jobs. The consultant during conferences should convey no implication of blame or criticism, no "eyebrow lifting." A casual reassuring manner is best punctuated by occasional approving remarks for praiseworthy things the consultee is doing. Attempts should be made to build up confidence and trust, realizing that no matter how meritorious or urgently needed are changes, they are bound to be resisted. Even a poorly functioning organization has achieved a shaky equilibrium, which will be defended.

Among the rules to follow are these:

1. Do not be hasty with advice. Community problems are complex and a thorough exploration will be essential before conclusions are valid.
2. Consider carefully the ideas and opinions of the people with whom you are working.
3. Expect power groups to try to involve you; avoid taking sides.
4. Try to see both sides of a question if there is conflict. Verbalize how the opponents must feel. Let them offer suggestions regarding proposed courses of action.
5. Try to exhibit tact and to retain a sense of humor.

The withdrawal phase of consultation will take place after the problem for which the consultant was retained has been solved, or prior to its solution by mutual consent. An evaluation of the service and plans for future cooperation (reports, personal contact, etc.) are made.

It is apparent that the consulting specialist, will need to know something about community organization and planning for mental health, social planning, organizational management, administration, public relations, public health, individual and group dynamics, research, legal and legislative aspects, teaching, supervision, social psychology, cultural anthropology, sociology, and political action.

At the Postgraduate Center for Mental Health in New York City, an interdisciplinary specialty program trains psychiatrists, psychiatric social workers, and clinical psychologists to function as community mental health consultants only after they have completed a postgraduate psychoanalytic training program (which requires an average of 4 years of didactic courses, personal psychoanalysis and intensive supervision) and who thereafter spend an additional 2 years, part time, in active consultative work in the community under supervision (Wolberg, A, & Padilla-Lawson, 1962; Hamburger, 1976). In practically all cases students have become so interested in community work that they have participated substantially as community workers after completing their course in addition to operating as a therapist in private practice. The model for the consultation process taught has been developed and organized in part around the paradigms of G. Lippitt (1959) and Gibb and R. Lippitt (1959), which emphasize systems theory and group dynamics, and in part around concepts of a mental health "multilevel-planning-activity group (MPAG)" developed by A. Wolberg and Padilla-Lawson (1959), an outline of which is given in Table 61–1.

To utilize oneself most effectively in

Table 62–1

A Multilevel, Multisystem, Method for the Study of Problems of Organizations and the Individual Functioning in these Organizations as They Attempt the Solution of Problems: A Mental Health Consultation Technique—Directives to the Consultant

Part I. Definition of Problem

Succinctly formulate the chief problem for which the study is undertaken based on the subjective estimation of the problem by members from three levels of the organization. The statement must include what the problem means to the organization and to the individuals functioning in the setting. Important administrative, supervisory, and line staff members should be interviewed.

Part II. Detection, Identification, and Descriptions of the Problem

A. Study of the individuals in the organization who have the particular problem or who are affected by it.
  1. Study formal records.
  2. Study anecdotal records.
  3. Study questionnaires which have been answered by the individual for the study.
  4. Direct interviews with three or four individuals affected by this problem.
  5. Study the work records of individuals affected by this problem in relation to skill, absenteeism, illness.
B. Study peer groups in three levels of the organization, members of which are affected by the problem (administrative, supervisory, and line staff personnel).
  1. Hold a series of four group discussions with peers from each organizational level and answer these questions:
     (a) How does each individual react in the group?
     (b) Can the members communicate?
     (c) Do subgroups form as the discussion proceeds?
     (d) Are some members disruptive?
     (e) Are any of these group members emotionally disturbed?
     (f) Does this disturbance cause trouble in the group?
     (g) Does the emotional difficulty affect work roles?
C. Study of the organization in relation to this particular problem.
  1. What is the function of this organization?
  2. Study the institutional records for the purpose of determining how the problem affects the operation of the organization.
  3. What disposition has been made of the problem up to the present?
  4. How seriously does the problem affect the organization?
  5. Has the problem affected individuals in a destructive way?
  6. What institutions or organizations or agencies in the community is this organization responsible to with respect to this problem?
  7. Is this trend or problem a unique one which exists only in this organization? Or does it exist in all organizations? Or only in some? Specify.
  8. What efforts have been made to reverse this trend? And what techniques have been used? By whom? Where?
  9. Typical day in the organization with respect to this problem.
  10. Group discussion with at least four or more individuals on the supervisory level with respect to the information collected to date.
  11. Is there any discrepancy between the ideas of the supervisors and those of the staff with respect to the problem?
  12. Are there subgroups within the organization that are competing or are antagonistic to one another?
  13. Is the consultative process threatening to individuals within the organization, and do they build up resistance to it? Illustrate.

Part III. Analysis of Data

A. What are the motivations of the individuals who requested the consultation?
B. Where are the main pressures in the organization?
C. What groups of individuals need more skills?
D. Can the supervisory staff give the members of the group the appropriate training for the skills, or do they themselves need further education?
E. Can you determine the point at which information is acceptable and at which it can be integrated by the supervisors and by the staff?
F. Are other resources than skills of the consultant needed to assist in the retraining of the staff?
G. Is there conflict between workers and supervisors? Between supervisors and administrators?
H. Are there intra-agency clashes between departments? Between persons due to lack of role boundary? Due to personality problems?
I. What are the main problems as you see them according to the analysis of the data? List.
J. Will the changes in role by training or retraining cause dislocation of a temporary nature in the organization?

Part IV. Planning and Decision Making

A. What plan do you suggest?
B. How will you explain this plan to the administration? To the supervisors? To others who may have to be informed?
    1. Illustrate the types of communication that you will use with the above categories in the social organization.
C. Where do you anticipate that resistance will occur and for what reasons?
    1. Can anything be done to counteract this?
D. What is the nature of your relationship with the members of the organization with whom you will have to work? Explain.
E. Steps in working out the plan.
    1. List the steps you will take to carry out the plan.
    2. How will this reverse the trend or help the problems which you have found?
        (a) Document this plan and the rationale for the steps you are taking with theoretical concepts from the literature.
    3. What are the specific techniques you will employ?
    4. What do you anticipate as a result of the carrying out of this plan?

Table 62–2

Mental Health Consultation Guide for Multisystem Consultation Method

Within an Organization Tensions are Expressed on the:	Expressions of Problems Found on Entry into an Organization:	Psychological, Social and Health Factors Contributing to Organizational Difficulties:
Individual Level:	Lack of clarity in goals	Characterologic, neurotic and psychotic difficulties
by	Inability to achieve objectives	Frequent illnesses
Executives	Lack of skills (inadequate training)	Alcoholism
Supervisors	Rigidity; confused "ordering"	Delinquency and crime
Staff	Inability to change practices	Drug addiction
	Apathy, boredom and lack of interest in work	Chronic disease
	Procrastination, lack of initiative	Absenteeism
	Sense of hopelessness	Other
	Inability to undertake responsibility	
	Self-excuse	
Internal Relationships Level:	Inadequate administration	Projection of difficulties on others
by individuals who belong to sub-groups involved with agency philosophy, policy making and establishing rules and regulations.	Cluttered and inoperative channels of communication; divisive techniques; unclear administrative channels; lack of coordination of activities	Hostility, agression or compulsive competitiveness
	Confusion in giving and taking orders	Acting out of sadomasochistic fantasies
Management in relation to owners, stockholders and Boards of Trustees	Interdisciplinary and departmental conflicts (prestige, control, status and authority problems)	Withdrawal
Intra-management relationships	Unqualified staff	Obsessive doubting, indecisiveness
Administrative actions	Conflicts between policy makers and those who carry out policy	Resistance to change
Staff-management relationships		Recurrent frustrations in work effort
Staff interaction	Lack of participation in group process	Conflicting interpersonal relations
	Fear of democratic process and need for authoritarian system	Unconscious sabotaging
Staff-client relationships	Inadequate system of rewards and recognition for personal achievement	Paranoid feelings (griping, complaining, undermining)
	Inadequate personnel practices, training programs and counseling	Laissez-faire attitudes
	Vague and conflicting aims	
	Inadequate programming for goal achievement	
	Inadequate Board of Trustees, owners or corporate personnel	
External Relationships Level:	Difficulties in obtaining cooperation of community leaders	Failure of staff and/or organization to satisfy standards acceptable to the community
by individuals who are working with	Inadequate interagency cooperation on programs	Failure of staff to meet standards of professionals in the community
Organized Professional Groups	Failure in communication with groups	Inadequate service
Labor	Failure in obtaining acceptance from professional groups	Failure to meet community needs
Religious organizations	Difficulty in obtaining acceptance of community groups	
Civic organizations	Inability to reduce conflicts with groups in the community	
Political groups	Poor image of performance and role of organization	
Business groups	Inadequate techniques to deal with community criticism and pressures	
Press		
Government		

Consequences to Organization:	Consultation Activity Aimed at Problem Resolution; Consultant Assists Staff Toward:	Recommendations and Plans
Inadequate service	Presenting of problems through case method	Programming for individual counseling, psychotherapy and/or referral sources
Loss of work due to high rate of lateness and absenteeism	Discussing staff studies and staff understanding of problems presented by individuals	
		Clarification of roles
	Collecting of information on staff attitudes based on opinions expressed	Clarification of duties
		Clarification of supervisory practices
	Observing of interaction of staff members (in framework of group dynamics)	
	Making inferences as to problems presented and their analysis and evaluation	
Organization goals not achieved due to inappropriate planning and programming	Discussing of organizational chart to obtain clarification of lines of authority and channels through which decisions are made and implemented	Changes in staff orientation and role
Inadequate supervision and controls; unclear responses and practices	Identifying needs and problems of staff and making inferences as to the kinds of and intensity of problems in the organization; establishing the expertness of staff and agency resources to cope with the problems	Education for new roles through training
Inability of staff to meet requirements of job		Adaptation of mental health information and techniques to the needs of the organization and its goals and practices
High turnover of qualified persons	Exchange of ideas	
Duplication, errors, minimization of benefit from skills of expert staff	Handling feed-back from communication	
Difficulty in rendering service		
Failure on collaboration efforts		
Low morale		
Low prestige	Interpreting goals and purposes to community	Joint programs with agencies
Confused public image	Organizing services useful to the district in which the organization exists	Community Education
Lack of community acceptance		Consultation Services
	Public relations	
Difficulty in raising funds or obtaining credit	Fund-raising (for non-profit organizations)	Work in professional societies
Difficulty in obtaining adequate staff	Changes in Board membership	Explicit public relations programs which are educational as well as informative
	Programming in relation to other organizations	
		Reporting of work done

the community, a therapist-consultant will have to fulfill a number of roles. Ideally, one should be able to plan, develop, and implement programs for prevention of mental illness, for reduction of psychiatric morbidity, for training of mental health manpower, for agency evaluation and reorganization, for education of professionals (physicians, teachers, ministers, lawyers, correctional workers, etc.) who deal with people blocked in learning, work, and interpersonal and social relationships, for upgrading of skills of institutional staffs (schools, industry, social agencies, etc.), and for public education in mental health. Obviously, neither one's background nor available time will enable a therapist to be equally effective as "community psychiatrist," mental health consultant, professional trainer, and public health educator. Consequently, it will be necessary to restrict efforts to areas within one's competence while acquiring further training that will equip one to play an expanded mental health role. Thus if zones of interest and ability are in the field of treatment, administration, research, or teaching, a therapist will most likely seek out and be sought for selective projects in line with one's focus.

In some of these projects the consultant will become involved in organizing, administrating, and supervising a variety of other services some of which he or she can do better than others. These include preventive care, home treatment, walk-in clinics, admission procedures, partial hospitalization, work programs, social rehabilitation, planning and developing the locus of care, rural program development, metropolitan mental health center development, legal issues in establishment and operation, record keeping and research, etc. (Grunebaum, H, 1970).

The Training of Mental Health Manpower

Mental disorders constitute a major public health problem resulting not only in syndromes that totally incapacitate a large section of the population, but also, in their early stages and incipient forms, directly or indirectly influence the happiness and efficiency of every individual alive. Because of the ubiquity of the problem, psychotherapists are being increasingly drawn into programs of training on federal, state, and local levels. The broadening of vistas of mental health to penetrate into every nook and cranny of the community and the diffusion of psychiatric knowledge into programs of education, correction, health, and welfare have resulted in an enlistment of the psychotherapist toward planning programs and participating in their development in accordance with the needs, readiness, and practical limitations existing in a specific area of the country. The psychotherapist is also playing a vital role in the recruitment of mental health manpower.

In view of the great shortage of manpower, training programs are being sponsored with federal and state support, which include not only professional groups such as general practitioners, nurses, social scientists, health officers, health educators, ministers, teachers, social workers, occupational therapists, recreational therapists, speech therapists, and vocational counselors, but also subprofessional and technical personnel such as psychiatric aids. While it is difficult to estimate the precise manpower requirements, it is safe to assume that at least twice the number of mental health professionals will be needed to cope even minimally with the existing demand for services. In recognition of these needs, the Surgeon General's Ad Hoc Committee on Mental Health Activities (NIMH, 1962) encouraged the in-service training in mental health of professional personnel in organizations that deal with problems confronting human beings on every level of functioning, the introduction of mental health courses in schools of public health, more intensive exposure of psychiatric residents to social science and public health methods, and support for the training of greater numbers of high-level professional mental health personnel, particularly for work in community mental health programs.

In designing a training program for an agency or organization, the therapist-consultant will need to utilize some of the processes of consultation. This may be illustrated by a problem presented to the Postgraduate Center by the casework staff of the case study unit of one of the bureaus of a school system (Wolberg, A, 1964). The staff was concerned with the need to learn new techniques in order to approach the hard-to-reach children expressing their emotional problems in poor school attendance or persistent absenteeism. Home visits, referrals to community agencies, supervision of the children, consultation with community agencies, and appearances in court constituted the work done by the social work staff. After a series of conferences of the consultees with the casework staff, it was agreed that some of the children might benefit from group approaches. It was decided to organize a training program to teach the social workers the group-counseling method within casework process.

Four broad phases in this program were planned: (1) Six to eight exploratory sessions with the case study supervisors of the bureau and the consulting supervisory staff of the Postgraduate Center to discuss typical cases handled by the bureau, with the hope (a) of developing a set of criteria for the choice of clients who would participate in the groups and (b) of evolving group techniques appropriate to this situation. (2) A regular 15-session seminar in group process for the case study supervisory staff of the bureau and for the three caseworkers who were to handle the first three trial groups. (3) Three consultants assigned to the first trial groups were to teach the caseworkers how to utilize group dynamic methods in handling their groups of children, and to teach the supervisors how to supervise this group process. Other supervisors and social workers were to observe the supervision of the worker. This phase was to continue for 2 or 3 years in a progressively diminishing manner as the bureau staff acquired greater skills. (4) In 4 or 5 years the project was to be expanded to train social workers in the bureau to assume responsibility for a citywide group program in the schools. After this the Center was to withdraw, and the consultation program terminated. According to the plan, each caseworker (attendance teacher) carried two groups of eight children each, weekly, over a period of one semester (15 weeks), in addition to the caseworker's regular work. The objective was not to make group therapists out of the social workers, but to adapt group methods to casework procedure to enhance the mental health of the children.

The value of this program was scored by the marked improvement by the participant children in actual school attendance (complete cessation of absenteeism in 53 percent, marked reduction in 20 percent), in scholastic achievement, in attitudes toward the school, and in general attitudes toward their classmates and adults. The school personnel expressed enthusiasm regarding the results of the program. A total of 25 attendance teachers were trained to carry groups, most of whom became supervisors and in turn began to train others.

Training programs must be tailor-made, designed for the specific needs of the professionals who are seeking further tutelage, taking into consideration their present education and the functions that they intend to fulfill. Generally, a consultation process will be required to assess what the training requirements are and the best means of executing the proposed goals. It is essential that the training equip the individual to work more effectively within one's particular profession and not be geared to making the "trainee" a psychotherapist. Didactic lectures are secondary to case discussions and supervised work with clients. A group process is often helpful for the professionals themselves, enabling them to become aware of some of their personal problems and resistances.

Public Education in Mental Health

The great need for public education in mental health was pointed out by Frances Braceland (1955) in view of the fact that "public information on what constitutes illness and health is a hodgepodge of folklore, information, and misinformation." However, he appropriately warns that the techniques and particularly the use of mass propaganda methods may present a distorted picture of any public health problem. Data about mental and emotional disease may easily arouse fears and anxieties. The ineffectiveness of intensive educational programs utilizing a wide variety of materials is, unfortunately, not too uncommon an experience, established attitudes rarely being changed. Braceland affirms the need to avoid calling attention to the ravages of mental illness; rather it is essential to stress hope and the promise of recovery with early diagnosis and treatment, "to reassure rather than to threaten or frighten . . . the presentation should clarify rather than confuse . . . the audience . . . spared technical language and abstruse, complex material that they are not prepared to handle." What requires emphasis is normal behavior, the fluctuations in emotional well-being, the universality of anxiety and some of its common manifestations, the determining (but not necessarily irreversible) influences of past experiences, the impact of social and cultural factors on personality development and functioning, the psychological needs at various developmental phases, the stress situations that create emotional insecurity at different age periods, and a description of how emotion influences man toward unrealistic goals and immature behavior.

Mass approaches to public education in mental health must await the development of television and radio programs as well as the kinds of press reporting and magazine writing that does not emphasize the destructive, dramatic, and violent aspects of mental illness and emotional disturbance. If the sponsors of programs and the controlling forces in the publication field were to apply the organizational and creative skills they use to sell advertised products, they undoubtedly would be able to adapt mental health materials that would change attitudes. This would necessitate a shift in the content of mass media away from preoccupations with violence and disturbed relationships among people.

In the meantime, mental health workers may have to confine themselves to the influencing of small, motivated groups who need and ask for special kinds of information. Materials pertinent to the topics of interest may be procured, and leads regarding appropriate films, pamphlets, plays, and other audiovisual and graphic aids may be obtained, from such educational organizations as the Mental Health Materials Center, 419 Park Avenue South, New York, New York 10016. There is a Public Health Service Publication (No. 218, Washington, D. C., 1960) entitled *Mental Health Motion Pictures: A selective Guide.* The *Index to 16 mm Educational Films* is published by NICEM, University of Southern California, National Information Center for Educational Media, University Park, Los Angeles, California 90024. The Library of Congress publishes a catalogue of motion pictures and filmstrips on many educational topics. Films may also be obtained from Psychological Cinema Register, Audiovisual Service, Pennsylvania State University, University Park, Pennsylvania 16802; and New York University Film Library, Washington Square North, New York, New York 10003. Where audio materials alone would be ample a catalogue with a full listing may be obtained from The Center for Casette Studios, 8110 Webb Avenue, North Hollywood, California 91605; and from Xerox University Microfilms, 300 North Zeeb Road, Ann Arbor, Michigan 48106.

In the section on Bibliotherapy (p. 817), books, pamphlets, and films on different subjects written for the general public will give the educator ideas of content and methods of presentation.

A brief outline of suggested methods of working with films and conducting discussion groups follows.

SUGGESTIONS ON METHODS
OF INTRODUCING AND
DISCUSSING MENTAL
HEALTH FILMS

1. *General.* Mental health films presented to lay groups are mainly informational in objective. This means that the discussion leader functions as an "expert." He or she must make the largest contribution elaborating on the theme of the film and clarifying the questions brought up by the audience. Nevertheless, audience participation must be encouraged. This can be done by stimulating discussion on several points illustrated by the film.

Many members in the audience will

identify with characters in the film. Consequently, the tone of the discussion must always be sympathetic and reassuring. *Never* belittle or ridicule any character; *never* say a condition is hopeless or incurable.

2. *Previewing the film.* If possible, preview the film, at least an hour before the actual showing. Make a notation in writing of the following: (a) What is the theme of the film? (b) What three or four points does it illustrate? The discussion that follows the film may be organized around these points.

If a preview of the film is not possible, study the *leader's guide* issued with the film, if there is such a guide, at least an hour before the showing. Make notations in writing of the film theme and of several psychiatric points that are illustrated.

If a preview of the film is not possible and if there is no leader's guide, make a mental note of the theme and points raised while watching the film at the actual showing.

3. *Starting the class or meeting.* The class or meeting must be started sharply on time. Latecomers will probably come on time at the next meeting if this is done.

4. *Introducing the film.* There are two methods of introducing the film: Method 1—Give a brief lecture (10 to 15 minutes) on the general topic illustrated by the film, indicating which points the audience are to observe. Method 2—Describe the film briefly (1 to 5 minutes) indicating the general theme and the points the audience are to watch for especially.

5. *Film showing.* Arrangements will probably have been made with a projector operator so that the film is ready for showing on a signal from the discussion leader. Since breakdowns in equipment are common, the leader should determine in advance if the projector is in good working order.

6. *Discussing the film.* The discussion leader reviews the film and then proceeds along several lines:

a. *Lecture.* If there is to be a lecture, this should last no more than 15 minutes. The points in the film are introduced in the content as illustrative material. Following this,

the meeting is opened to discussion.

b. *Presentation of the salient points of the film.* The chief points illustrated by the film are mentioned, following which there is discussion.

c. *Asking pertinent questions about the film.* The points illustrated by the film are presented as questions. This is a very good way to get audience participation.

7. *Handling group situations.*

a. *Group failing to participate.* When the group fails to enter into the discussion, ask one or two provocative questions. If no one responds, call on one member of the group.

b. *A member arguing too much.* Simply say, "I understand your reaction; perhaps other people here would like to comment on it." The group usually has a way of subduing the disturbed member. If this does not work, invite the person to discuss matters with you after the meeting.

c. *One member talking too much.* At a pause in his talk, cut him off with a summarizing statement and direct a question at someone else.

d. *A member persisting on talking off the subject.* Cut him off with the statement, "That is interesting, and we may come back to that later." Direct a question at someone else.

8. *Terminating meeting.* The meeting should be terminated after about one hour of discussion, or lecture and discussion. A brief summary is sometimes helpful, as is assignment of reading material.

SUGGESTIONS ON
CONDUCTING A
DISCUSSION GROUP

1. *General.* A discussion group provides the participants with perhaps the best opportunity for learning. Sharing ideas and experiences promotes an exchange of information. Verbalizing attitudes and doubts helps to resolve resistances and learning

blocks. Furthermore, the discussion group may serve a therapeutic function, enabling the individual to gain a measure of assuredness in expressing his ideas and opinions and in working through fears, hostilities, and other disabling attitudes in relation to a group.

2. *Physical arrangements.*

a. *Size of group.* The ideal size of the group ranges from six to ten people. This number makes it possible for all members to contribute actively. In exceptional or unavoidable instances, a larger group may be handled although this will involve some sacrifice in individual activity.

b. *Position of chairs.* Seating arrangement is important to avoid the leader being placed in too prominent a position, which is apt to stifle discussion. Members and leader may be seated facing each other around a table, or, if this is impractical, in chairs placed in a circle or semicircle. It goes without saying that proper ventilation, comfortable lighting and sufficient ash trays add to the relaxed atmosphere that is most conducive to good discussion.

c. *Length of discussion session.* This will vary depending on the circumstances, but a good average is 1½ hours.

d. *Starting the session on time.* The session should begin sharply on time. Latecomers will probably come on time at the next session if this is done.

3. *The first session.*

a. Once members are seated, a good way to start is to ask each member to introduce himself to the group by stating his name, his discipline, if he has one, and the organization, if any, with which he is associated. This serves to "break the ice" and to introduce an air of informality into the atmosphere.

b. Next introduce the general subject to be discussed and relate it to the interests of the group members. A distributed outline, prepared in advance, designating material to be considered is a very helpful adjunct.

c. Where essential information needs to be conveyed to the members before discussion begins, a short talk is in order. If desired, introduce an auxilliary lecturer, or a movie, filmstrip, or other audiovisual aid. Make this preliminary presentation as brief as possible.

d. Following this begin the discussion. If there is any doubt in the minds of the members about procedure, inform them that no one will be called on formally, that any person may speak up when he desires, and that a person should limit his comments to 2 or 3 minutes at most.

e. Encourage the group to participate by any of the following methods:
(1) Ask a provocative question relating to the outline or to the material under discussion.
(2) If there are two points of view on a topic germaine to the discussion, call for a show of hands of those who share the different viewpoints. Then ask a question as to why one or the other point of view is taken.
(3) Selecting a topic related to the general subject, ask if there is any one in the group who has had experience with this topic.
(4) Using a blackboard, list the different opinions or ideas of the members about a topic, or possible approaches to the topic. Group these into specific categories, and then ask questions about the various listings.

4. *Subsequent sessions.* At the start of each subsequent session the leader may summarize the salient points about the pre-

vious session and then bring up the topic for the present session. Where new information is to be introduced, this may be done by assigned readings, written reports from the members, an informative talk by an expert, films, etc.

5. *Activity of the leader.* The function of the leader in a discussion group is to help the members verbalize their ideas and integrate their thinking about a specific subject. The leader participates in the discussion only when the members stop talking, when they deviate from the topic under consideration, or when they are not able to think things through for themselves. Such participation does not mean that one delivers a lecture, gives advice, or shows off one's own knowledge.

In order to fulfill this function, the leader must have respect for all of the members in the group, and for their opinions, resistances and resentments. One must accept the fact that the learning process requires time and that people must resolve their doubts and suspicions before they can accept ideas, no matter how logical these may seem. This will necessitate great tolerance and the ability to handle aggression that is projected by some members toward the group and toward the leader. Required is an informal manner and a sense of humor. Essential also is an ability to talk the same "down-to-earth" language as the group, eschewing complicated formulations and avoiding impressing the members with abstruse talk.

From time to time, clarify the material presented, particularly conflicting issues, and summarize the contributions that have been made by the members. If certain points are not covered, ask questions about these. Never argue, belittle, or disagree with a person. If you have a contribution to make yourself, make it briefly, saying, "This is what I have come to believe," or "This is what is generally believed."

6. *Handling special situations.* This is, on the whole, handled as done in this category under the section on discussing films.

a. *Group fails to participate.* When the group fails to enter into discussion, ask one or two provocative ques-

tions. If no one responds, call on one member of the group. If, after this person comments, nobody else volunteers, say, "Perhaps someone has a different slant on this."

b. *A member arguing too much.* Simply say, "I can understand your reaction; perhaps other people here would like to comment on it." The group usually has a way of subduing the disturbed member. If this does not work, invite the person to discuss matters with you after the meeting.

c. *One member talking too much.* At a pause in this talk, cut him off with a summarizing statement and direct a question at the group.

d. *A member persisting on talking off the subject.* Cut him off with the statement, "That is interesting, and we may come back to that later." Direct a question at the group.

e. *A side argument developing between two or more members.* Rap on the table or chair and say, "May I interrupt please. Perhaps others here would like to comment on this question that is causing controversy." If this does not stop the argument, or if the argument spreads, say, "Obviously there are several points of view; perhaps I can help integrate them." Attempt then to explain why the differences exist and how they can be resolved. If no resolution is possible, say, "Let us think about this matter further, and we may have a chance to come back to it later." Following this, ask another question directing the discussion into another channel.

f. *One member constantly interrupting the comments of others.* Firmly say to the person at each interruption, "Mr. X [the person interrupted] has not finished talking, let us permit him to continue." If this does not stop the person from interrupting, say to him, "There is something that is bothering you, and it may be helpful for you to see me after the session." Arrange then to have a talk or talks with the person, and if his disruptive activity does not halt, suggest that he drop out from the group.

g. *Side conversations.* Rap on the table or chair and say, "Please let us all concentrate on what is being said."

h. *The discussion straying too far afield from the subject.* Say, "This is interesting, but how does it apply to the subject we are discussing?"

i. *A member refusing to budge from an opinionated and obviously erroneous point of view.* Do not take sides against him. Merely say, "Perhaps Mrs. Y would like to bring in source material next time to back up his point of view." Then pass on to another person.

j. *A member refusing to participate.* Respect his silence. After a number of sessions, if he raises his hand, call on him immediately. Rarely you may say, "Perhaps Mr. Z may want to comment on this subject." If he shakes his head or remains silent, gloss this over with, "Not at this time; well, perhaps later."

k. *Lags in the discussion.* Point out the differences in ideas or opinions that have been presented, and ask how these differences may be reconciled.

l. *Unnecessary repetition.* Summarize what has been said, point out important aspects and highlights; then introduce a different question.

7. *The recorder and observer.* In some discussion groups it is helpful to appoint a volunteer who will record the salient features of the discussion for purposes of transcription or for summarization at the end of the present or at the beginning of the next session. Another volunteer, an observer, may be appointed to record the activity or passivity of the various members and leaders, the interpersonal reactions, and the dynamics of the group process, which may also be prepared at the end of the session or at the beginning of the next session.

8. *Summarizing the discussion.* Before the session ends, it may be helpful to summarize the discussion, mentioning the salient points that have been covered, relating the material to what has gone on in previous sessions, restating differences of opinion, tying together topics that have not been coordinated, and adding suggestions as to procedure and areas of future exploration. It is essential that the summary contain the conclusions of the group rather than your own conclusions. If the group conclusions are in your opinion inadequate or erroneous, a statement may be made to the effect that further discussion on the subject will open up areas that may yield important data.

9. *Reading assignments and reports.* Assigned readings, and verbal or written presentations by the members are helpful as teaching aids. They serve also to introduce new material for group consideration. Suggestions regarding readings may be obtained in the section on Bibliotherapy in Chapter 53.

VI

Addenda

Case History

The case history presented here illustrates many of the techniques described in previous chapters. The case was chosen, not for its dramatic interest—since there was nothing spectacular about the involved dynamics—but because it delineates within the nine sessions that comprised the total treatment period, important processes observed in the opening, middle, and terminal phases of therapy. A 5-year follow-up was obtained to see how many of the gains in therapy continued. The material in these interviews has been utilized by Strupp (1957) to compare the processes of psychoanalytically oriented brief therapy with those of client-centered therapy and to test his system for the abstracting and measuring of relevant aspects of therapeutic communications (Strupp, 1960, pp. 263–286); by Auerbach (1963) to compare with the therapeutic activity of other psychotherapists; and by Jaffe (1964) for purposes of interview analysis with the aid of digital computers.

The treatment sessions, which had been recorded on tape, where then typed and minor changes were made to conceal the identity of the patient. The original transcription was read at a seminar of psychiatrists in training, and interpolations were made by me during the reading. The seminar sessions were additionally recorded on plastic discs, and the recordings, which contained the treatment sessions as well as my comments, were transcribed and then minimally edited for purposes of inclusion in this chapter. The complete transcription follows:

In preparing this course I was somewhat in a dilemma as to the best kind of case material to present. The goals I had in mind were, first, to demonstrate the actual process of therapy from the first contact with the patient to the terminal interview; second, to illustrate the procedure of interviewing; and third, to try to give you an idea of the thinking that went into the total handling of the case. I felt I might do this by reading to you a full transcription of the tape recordings of a patient whom I had treated, interpolating comments as to what I believed was going on in the patient's mind, what conscious thoughts were in my mind, and the reasons I employed the methods I used.

To do this it was necessary to select a case that illustrated typical situations encountered in psychotherapy. Because I wanted to cover beginning, middle, and terminal phases of treatment, it was essential to describe a patient who had been handled on a short-term basis. One should not interpret from this that all patients will respond to short-term measures as well as did the patient chosen. Even in this patient, while some personality changes occurred, many more would undoubtedly have eventuated had the patient remained longer in treatment. Nevertheless, for the purposes outlined, the case presented will suffice.

The type of treatment employed was insight therapy with reeducative goals. The problem for which therapy was sought was a "run-of-the-mill" type of situation often encountered in practice. I was happy that the psychopathologic material elicited in this case was not so startling as to excite concentration on psychodynamics. In teaching therapy there is so often a temptation to focus on the spectacular, to wallow so in symbolic representations of conflict and in the manifold defenses that the human mind employs in seeking surcease from turmoil, that one may fail to emphasize what is really important in treatment: the study of the relationship that develops between the patient and the therapist. I felt that the case I chose would permit us to explore such aspects as the conduct of an initial interview, the establishment of a working relationship with the patient, the techniques for arriving at the dynamics of a neurosis, the promotion of activity toward therapeutic change, and the termination of therapy.

In the course of my presentation I expect that you will, from time to time, be puzzled and perhaps even critical of some of the things I said and did. Psychotherapy, after all, is essentially a blend of the personality of the therapist and the method he has learned. Since no two personalities are exactly alike, the blend must always be different no matter how similar the training may have been. Your personalities will make you see things differently from the way I see them, and perhaps to emphasize and to focus on different areas. Your specific character traits will enable you to employ varying degrees of directiveness and nondirectiveness in therapy and, even, to some extent, to strive for divergent objectives. This need not disturb you because your results will be good, provided you do not violate certain basic principles in therapy. As I present the material, I shall try to show you how I personally function within the bounds of these basic principles. But I do not expect that you will be able to accept or to follow my techniques precisely as I present them to you. These techniques are germane to my own personality structure; all may not be germane to yours. Indeed, it would be remarkable if you saw things exactly the same way as I see them. Yet you should be able to derive out of the material presented a method through which you can fulfill the basic principles of a good psychotherapeutic program. Appreciating your own personality assets and limitations, you may then be able to work out means by which you can reach satisfactory goals in therapy in ways that coordinate with your unique personality traits.

It may be proper at this time to say something about the interview process utilized in this case. The fact that I made certain responses and focused on special problems does not mean that they were the only responses that could have been offered the patient. Other comments and different areas of focus may have been chosen, and the therapeutic result would probably have turned out equally satisfactorily. But there were special reasons why I selected the responses I did; and I shall point out the reasons to you. Again, you may have seen things in another light, and, if you conducted yourself within the bounds of good therapeutic procedure, your personal selection of responses would probably have ensured success in treatment.

In going over the transcription, I can see certain things that I did, and that I failed to do, that I shall point out to you as mistakes. Mistakes are commonly made in the conduct of therapy; understandably they are more frequently perpetrated by inexperienced than by experienced therapists. You are bound to make many mistakes in the course of learning psychotherapy. These will probably wound your ego, but without mistakes you will probably be unable to develop into good therapists. Even experienced psychotherapists sometimes make mistakes. The process of treatment is so complex that one cannot always be right. As a matter of fact, mistakes need not hurt the patient nor interfere with the relationship, provided the therapist has a good feeling for the patient and does not violate the general principles of a good psychotherapeutic structure.

Now a word of warning—while case presentations such as this, and other didactic teaching aids, are important in learning psychotherapy, supervised clinical experience is indispensable. Without supervision, the person seeking to do psychotherapy is truly handicapped because he will be unable to develop himself to his full potential. The psychotherapist is, after all, merely a human being, and he may react to his patients with an array of prejudices, likes and dislikes of which he may be partially or completely unaware. Even though he has been psychoanalyzed, he may be unable to control feelings that will interfere with the execution of sound therapeutic procedures. In supervision, the supervisor may be able to detect and to help the therapist to overcome blocks that strangle the therapist's effectiveness.

With this brief introduction I should like to

tell you something about the patient in the case. I received a telephone call from a former patient who asked if I could see a friend of hers in consultation. Her friend, a retired business woman, had, during the past 2 years, become progressively more depressed, and in the past 6 months she had retreated from her customary social contacts. An attractive widow, and comfortably situated financially, there was no objective reason why she should act in this manner. The caller had tried to convince her friend to seek therapy 6 months previously, but the reaction to this suggestion was a bad one. However, her friend had telephoned her this morning and had asked to be referred. My comment was that I would want to see her friend in consultation before I could decide whether I was the best person to treat her particular problem. If she would ask her friend to call me, I would be pleased to give her an appointment. That afternoon the patient telephoned me, and I set up an appointment for an initial interview.

FIRST SESSION

The goals of this interview are (1) to establish rapport with the patient, (2) to make a tentative diagnosis, (3) to get an idea of some of the involved psychodynamics, (4) to determine the extent of motivation for therapy and to help motivate the patient, if this is necessary, (5) to elicit and correct misconceptions about therapy, (6) to test the existing level of insight, (7) to determine if the therapist is capable, with his skills, of treating the patient, (8) to make the essential time and financial arrangements for therapy, (9) to refer the patient to another therapist if necessary, (10) to prepare the patient for psychologic testing if testing is required, and (11) to make any other disposition of the case that is necessary.

Because so much data must be collected, the therapist is inclined to be very much more active during the first interview than during later interviews.

(The patient enters the office with a depressed worried expression on her face. She is an attractive, well-groomed, middle-aged woman.)

Th. Hello. I'm Dr. Wolberg. [*Most patients are frightened at the first session, anticipating censure or rejection. The mysteries of psychiatry both intrigue and terrify them. They expect to have their minds dissected by a cold, detached,*

scientific wizard. A friendly greeting may help put them at their ease.]

Pt. How do you do. [*This conventional remark may conceal various feelings. In some patients there is deep despair and hopelessness. In others there is tension or panic related to expectations of injury. Some patients are quite resentful that they have been finally forced to seek help. By listening closely, the therapist may detect the feeling behind the content of the patient's verbalizations.*]

Th. Won't you sit here in this chair opposite me so we can talk things over? [*Sitting in a chair opposite the patient sets the stage for a more cooperative relationship. Interviewing from behind a desk in the traditional doctor–patient position helps maintain the authoritative station of the therapist, which is best minimized in insight therapy.*]

Pt. Thank you. *(pause)* [*There are many reasons why the patient may pause here. She may be waiting for the therapist to ask her questions. She may be fearful, hostile, or frustrated. These emotions may block her speech or ideation.*]

Th. Would you like to tell me something about your problem? [*This question is necessary only because the patient hesitates. Most patients are only too eager to talk about their problems.*]

Pt. Well, doctor. I don't know what's wrong, but there is something seriously the matter with me. I am upset, and depressed, and I have pains around my heart. I'm frightened that I have a heart condition. *(pause)* [*These symptoms indicate that the patient is experiencing adaptational collapse. Her defenses apparently are no longer capable of protecting her or of mediating a satisfactory adjustment. She is concerned with her symptoms, and she realizes that something is wrong.*]

Th. I see. *(pause)* Have you had your heart checked by your physician? [*Whether her heart complaint is organic, psychosomatic, or hypochondriac is not known, and this question attempts to probe further into this.*]

Pt. Yes, I have. He gave me an electrocardiograph.

Th. Uh huh. *(nodding)* [*nonverbal encouraging responses to signal the patient to keep on talking*]

Pt. He said that I had a heart condition. *(pause)* [*It seems probable to me that this patient will need much activity in interviewing to keep her talking. Most patients are only too willing to tell their story, and therefore few responses from the therapist will be required. Some patients, like this one, do not communicate well, and need constant responses by the therapist to keep them verbalizing.*]

Th. What was your reaction to this? [*This question was asked to determine the patient's reactions to a potentially serious condition.*]

Pt. I was upset, but he reassured me it wasn't serious. *(pause)*

Th. Do *you* feel that your heart condition is a serious one? [*Even though reassured by her physician, the patient may still worry about the seriousness of her heart condition. This question is to test her own evaluation of the condition.*]

Pt. No, I don't. I don't think about it as being serious. You know doctor, I don't feel very good. I don't feel strong. I don't . . . *(pause)* well, maybe it's nerves. [*She returns to her provocative symptoms and acknowledges at least a possibility of their being emotional in origin.*]

Th. Nerves? [*focusing on the word "nerves" to explore the depth of her insight*]

Pt. That's right. I have a good doctor, and I trust him as far as my physical condition is concerned. *(pause)*

Th. But?

Pt. Well, doctor, I know that there's something wrong. And I don't know what it is. There is something wrong with me. I can't seem to get interested in anything.

Th. I see. *(nodding)*

Pt. I don't have any interests . . . of course, I have the theater, but I haven't been going. I've had no desire to go. I just don't feel like it. I've been going to bed every night about 9 o'clock cause I guess I think I'm sick and I should go to bed and rest. I mean, I mean I don't do anything that would be pleasant. I just sit home and read, and I can do those things, but that isn't the way to live. [*It would seem from this that her insight is not too extensive. A profound dissatisfaction with her symptoms is, however, apparent, which is good in the sense that it can provide strong motivation to get well.*]

Th. It must be very frustrating. [*communicating sympathy*]

Pt. I have a feeling that life makes no sense. I suppose I worry too much about things like my heart. [*This sounds as if she recognizes her worry about her heart as emotionally determined.*]

Th. And you get little real pleasure out of life. [*I feel that it would be of little avail to talk any more about her heart condition.*]

Pt. That's right. And I tell myself it's because of the heart, but I know it isn't a heart condition.

Th. I see. *(pause)* You're sure it's not a heart condition? [*testing her conviction*]

Pt. I haven't had a pain in 2 months. I used to get a pain across here, in my back. But that really doesn't bother me.

Th. I see. *(nodding)*

Pt. Yes. And I was talking to an old friend of mine. She's the one that recommended you. She said you helped her a lot and she was sure you could help me.

Th. You would really like to get rid of this trouble?

Pt. Doctor, there is nothing I wouldn't do to get rid of it. Life doesn't mean anything, you know, the way things are going. *(pause)*

Th. How did you come to the conclusion that it was your nerves that were at fault? [*again probing the extent of her insight*]

Pt. Well doctor, you know Mrs. Henshaw, and I'm very fond of her, and I've seen how she's come along so nicely that I thought that maybe I could get something out of it too [*Mrs. Henshaw is the friend who referred her to me.*]

Th. Mm hmm. *(nodding)* [*encouraging her verbalizations along this line*]

Pt. I said to her, "You know, really I should do something for myself. This is awful what's happening to me, now." This was only last week, because, really, I said I don't do anything, but just sit at home. I don't want to see anyone, and I get into bed and can't wait to get into bed. I just look at my bed, and it looks so good that . . . but I guess, I don't know whether it's health or what it is, doctor, whether it's mental or . . . I don't know. *(pause)*

Th. Well, let's see. You do seem to have a problem, and perhaps I can help you with it. First, however, I should like to get a little more information, and then we'll talk things over and see what can be done. [*We seem to have reached a deadend in her talking about her difficulties. Direct questioning seems necessary to gather essential information.*]

Pt. Anything that I can tell you, doctor, that will be of help, I wouldn't hesitate.

Th. Do you have any ideas about what is causing this trouble? [*more probings for insight*]

Pt. I really do not, except that I find that nothing really matters. It's so discouraging, you know. I don't feel as if I'm living. You know that . . . you know about that song "Old Man River?" Scared of living and afraid of dying? Well, that's it.

Th. Mm hmm. *(nodding)*

Pt. It goes back further than I think, because while I was in business my mind was occupied and I didn't think about myself so much. You know, we had a book business, my husband and I. We built it up into something very substantial. And then when he died I was left with the business. That was 6 years ago. *(pause)*

Th. I see. *(pause)* Perhaps if I ask you a few pointed questions, it may make it unnecessary to come back to preliminary things later on. [*To permit the patient to ramble on in this interview would result in a failure to obtain essential data.]

Pt. All right, anything you say, doctor.

Th. How old are you? [*questioning for essential statistical data*]

Pt. Fifty.

Th. Your husband died 6 years ago you say?

Pt. Yes.

Th. How long were you married?

Pt. About 23 years.

Th. Any children?

Pt. No.

Th. And you were in the book business. When did you give that up?

Pt. About a year ago.

Th. Have you been doing any work since?

Pt. No, doctor, I've been retired and haven't wanted to do anything. I gave up my business because I felt I couldn't stand working any more.

Th. Now briefly, what other symptoms do you have besides those you told me about? [*The patient is questioned as to symptoms other than the complaint factor.*]

Pt. I don't know what you mean.

Th. Do you feel depressed?

Pt. Very much so—most of the time.

Th. Any panicky feelings that scare you?

Pt. (*pause*) No, not anything like that.

Th. Any fears?

Pt. No.

Th. Any thoughts that crowd into your mind that you can't get out of your mind?

Pt. I don't think so.

Th. How about compulsions? Do you feel compelled to do anything over and over?

Pt. No.

Th. What about headaches and dizziness?

Pt. I do get dizzy feelings from time to time.

Th. Any stomach trouble?

Pt. No.

Th. Any sexual problems?

Pt. Well . . . there just is no sex, and I don't seem to miss it.

Th. Upset by that?

Pt. I don't think so.

Th. Any tension?

Pt. I am tense most of the time.

Th. How do you sleep?

Pt. Very poorly. I average 4 to 5 hours of sleep a night.

Th. Any nightmares?

Pt. No.

Th. Do you dream a lot or a little? [*This question is better phrased this way rather than asking the patient if she ever dreams. Many patients will answer the latter in the negative who*

might respond positively to the former phrasing.]

Pt. I rarely remember any dreams.

Th. Can you recall a dream that seems vivid in your mind? [*A therapist trained in dream interpretation can sometimes get the essential dynamics of the patient's problem from a vivid dream.*]

Pt. (*pause*) No, not a single one.

Th. How about drinking? I mean alcohol.

Pt. Just an occasional drink.

Th. How about sedatives?

Pt. I take none.

Th. Do you feel fatigued or exhausted?

Pt. A good deal of the time.

Th. In other words, the chief problems are this lack of energy, the exhaustion, and depressed feelings. [*summarizing*]

Pt. Yes. If I could get rid of those, I would be happy.

Th. You have no financial worries? [*Information as to the financial status is important in planning a psychotherapeutic program that the patient can afford.*]

Pt. I don't have to worry. I mean, of course, I can't go crazy, do a lot of stupid things with money, but I can get along nicely with what I got for the business. And there's another thing, I like to do things. If I can get things for someone else, I break my neck to go out and get it. For myself I just haven't any interest. I'd walk miles to find the right thing for a friend or any one that I'd want to do something for, but I haven't . . . I don't even want to go out and get anything for myself. I need a hat, and one night I should go out and buy a hat. This hat is about 5 years old. I should go out and buy a couple of hats. You see what I mean? [*Why the patient does not buy things for herself is of interest. Does she value herself minimally, does her guilt prevent her from getting nice things she can enjoy, or is she masochistically punishing herself?*]

Th. I believe I do. You find this very annoying? [*reflecting feeling*]

Pt. I do very much. It's about time I did do something for this trouble.

Th. To get back to the origin of this trouble, was there ever a period when you felt happy? [*This question is asked to determine whether the patient ever experienced a period of good adjustment, and whether the present complaint is an outgrowth of earlier maladjustment.*]

Pt. That's hard to say. I suppose there were times.

Th. How about your childhood? [*questioning to elicit family data*]

Pt. Well, that was bad. We had a tough time. My father died when I was 5 years of age.

Th. Do you remember him?

Pt. No, but I do remember going to live with my mother's cousin. I saw my mother though, occasionally. [*This remark is significant. A child wrested from the mother is one whose security mechanism is damaged and whose self-esteem is apt to be undermined.*]

Th. What sort of a person was she?

Pt. She was a sweet person. I was very close to her, a wonderful mother, and understanding. She lived with my sister and I before I was married, and with my husband and I after my marriage. She passed away 5 years ago. [*One wonders how she could both have been separated from and have been close to her mother. This should be explored later.*]

Th. I see.

Pt. My husband liked my mother too.

Th. What about your husband?

Pt. Well doctor, that's where a lot of my trouble was. He was a playboy type, and didn't pay enough attention to me. Well, it hurt; my pride was hurt, but then I thought he's probably seen so much of me, he's tired of me, you know. You work with someone all day long, and you have all the troubles together. You know, doctor, we've been through so much, through the depression and through so many problems we had to work out. And I thought maybe he was just tired of the whole thing. I don't know whether I resented it or not. I don't know. [*This area is undoubtedly a painful one that should also be explored later.*]

Th. You were attached to him?

Pt. Well, I was crazy about him. And, of course, he was very good, he was very good to my mother, see, and I appreciated that. And after all, I got along with him.

Th. And then he passed away, and after that your mother died. Were you alone then?

Pt. Well, I had my sister, and I, we, have a great deal in common; and besides being a sister, she's a good friend. I can talk to her.

Th. Do you see her?

Pt. Every week. She comes in to see me once a week, and we have lunch at my home together and we visit. She stays a few hours and that's about all. I haven't anyone else. I mean not anyone else to confide in or go over anything else that I might feel.

Th. How old is your sister?

Pt. A few years older than I am.

Th. Any other children in the family?

Pt. Yes, an older brother who I don't see often.

Th. How do you get along with him?

Pt. Very well, but we don't see each other often.

Th. I see.

Pt. You see, doctor, while I was working I wasn't thinking about how bad things were, but I haven't regretted getting out of my business, doctor, not for one minute—that I haven't because it was too much for me. *(pause)*

Th. It was too much? [*helping to maintain the flow of verbalizations*]

Pt. And I wasn't too happy in there because I was forcing myself, see. It was evening work too, and I'd find myself, oh so depressed going in there every night from my home, and then going home alone from there, and tired and everything, don't you know? And I have not regretted that for one minute in spite of the fact that I am very lonely. But I haven't regretted selling it, not once. But, I don't know, maybe I should get a little something to do. Get out into something different again. I don't know.

Th. You've been very lonesome. [*accenting her expressed feelings of lonesomeness*]

Pt. Yes, as far back as I can remember. You see, my husband was a playboy type, as I said, and he didn't pay enough attention to me. Up until he had his kidney condition, he was a very strong fellow, but he got a condition, and he had that for 8 years, and, of course, I worried about that, and I never knew but that when I'd come home that I'd, well, that he wouldn't be there. You know what I mean. His doctor told me he might pass away any time.

Th. You worried a great deal about him? [*accenting her expressed feeling of worry*]

Pt. Well, he was a wonderful man, but he was a playboy—a lot of fun for himself, and toward the end I really was neglected, in a sexual sense, and, and that went on a long time. [*Her emphasis of unhappiness in her relations with her husband points to one of her past conflictual concerns.*]

Th. How come you stuck to him for so long? Did you feel a loyalty to him?

Pt. Well, I did, and I felt that he needed me, doctor, that he was ill; and I felt that being with him I would probably see that he would take better care of himself than if I wasn't there. You know how it is, and I was married to him for a good many years by that time. [*One may ask himself if the patient is describing a character trait of abnegating herself for the benefit of others.*]

Th. You were in love with him? [*Since the patient is focusing on her husband, I decide to explore this relationship more completely.*]

Pt. Oh, yes, definitely.

Th. How did his not paying attention to you affect you?

Pt. Well, I felt very hurt about it, naturally,

because we had been together so long, and we had worked so long together.

Th. And did you bring to his attention the fact that he paid no attention to you?

Pt. Oh, yes, of course I did.

Th. How did he react?

Pt. Well, he said that he felt that we were together too much, and that had something to do with it, because we worked together in the business, you see. *(pause)*

Th. And he tried to explain the fact that he was detaching himself from you because you had been together so much?

Pt. Well, that's the way he explained it, yes, and we took vacations separately, which isn't bad. That isn't anything, a lot of people do that.

Th. What about your own personal life? Had you become interested in anybody else?

Pt. No.

Th. During the period when you were sexually active with your husband, were there any sexual problems?

Pt. Perfectly normal. I enjoyed it.

Th. After he stopped having relations with you, didn't you feel that you wanted to continue?

Pt. Well, yes, I did doctor, but you see, it was just about that time, it was about in 1938 that I had had this operation, and that also did something to me.

Th. What operation was that?

Pt. A hysterectomy, removal of the womb because of fibroids.

Th. I see.

Pt. Ater that I felt I was out of things because it made me feel there was something lacking. I was ashamed of it, or something. [*another possible conflictual focus*]

Th. You were ashamed of this operation?

Pt. Yes, and then it took me a long time to recover from it. It's quite a shock, it's quite an operation. And, of course, that started during that time. From that time on, doctor, that we weren't . . . ah . . . that I, that we, ah weren't . . .

Th. Together?

Pt. It's just that I had been ill, you see. I was in the French Hospital for about 5 weeks with this thing. And then when I came home, things seemed changed for me because my husband started withdrawing from me more than ever.

Th. There were no other people you could be close to as friends?

Pt. Yes, I'll tell you, doctor. In that business you meet a lot of people. It's all a part of the whole work. You know what I mean. And my having, well my working with my husband there,

and all the help that had been with us for so many years, I mean, that I felt that there was a certain amount of dignity along with my position there. And I didn't at any time give anyone any encouragement, and even after I was a widow, I just did what I should, and I don't know why I just thought it should be that way.

Th. You mean for 6 years you have been leading a solitary life?

Pt. Yes, isn't that awful?

Th. You feel that's pretty bad. [*To agree with the patient might substantiate her feelings that she is "awful" rather than she feels what she has done is "awful."*]

Pt. Well, I guess it's myself doctor. [*indulging in self-recriminations*]

Th. Do you think that you could be very attractive to men? [*This question is related to one aspect of her feelings about herself.*]

Pt. I don't know . . . *(pause)* I suppose if I had a child things would be different. [*Could this possibly be another source of conflict?*]

Th. Did you want children?

Pt. Yes, but I suppose I couldn't have them. I never used contraceptives, but just couldn't have them, and then, of course, after the operation it was impossible.

Th. And now there doesn't seem to be any person with whom you are close?

Pt. No.

Th. Is it possible that a block exists in you that prevents a relationship from starting? Is it possible that such a block made you more and more discouraged toward your getting intimate with any person? [*attempting to bring the patient to an awareness of a problem more fundamental than her isolation*]

Pt. Well, you see, now even in this present time, when I've so much time on my hands, time to think, which I didn't have before, that is to think about myself—I didn't have any time before to think about myself—now I can't imagine myself being married again, which would be the logical thing to think about now when I haven't any other responsibilities or problems that I had had in the past. I can't imagine it, that I would meet someone now, someone that I could care for, which would be a wonderful thing, but I just can't conceive it. I can't imagine how I could do it, doctor.

Th. You can't find within yourself any possibility of this?

Pt. I've met many men, but can't get interested.

Th. You've met a lot of men—probably many of them that would want to take you out?

Pt. Yes, yes.

Th. But could you warm up to them?

Pt. No, no. I didn't believe it, and I don't know what it was.

Th. What is it about a man that would appeal to you, what type of man particularly?

Pt. Someone that would be understanding and sympathetic, a nice person.

Th. A nice person. And haven't you met any such people?

Pt. No. Well, I don't know, it seems to me that . . . well, I know some married men—and I resent that sort of thing, and, I mean, that someone would think as little of you as to think that, you know, that you'd go out with them, and they were married.

Th. Primarily your desire is not to have a pure sexual affair.

Pt. No.

Th. Companionship and understanding.

Pt. Someone you know that you could be with. I'm absolutely alone, because my sister is married, my brother is married, and he has his daughters, and they all have their lives, and I understand that, and I don't expect them to give me their time, because they have their interests. But I should have mine too.

Th. You would like to be able to have your interests too.

Pt. Yes, yes.

Th. So it seems that you have been frustrated a good deal. You were a loving wife and were rejected. You wanted love and companionship and these were not forthcoming. You had your business on your mind to divert your attention; but after you gave that up, all your frustrations piled up on you. And now nothing seems worth while. [*An attempt is made here to summarize as succinctly as possible the various points brought out by the patient.*]

Pt. That's it exactly, doctor; that's exactly how it is.

Th. The important thing is doing something about it.

Pt. If there is anything you can do to help me, doctor, I do need help. You can see that. [*The patient is obviously well motivated, and it will not be necessary to spend any time creating an incentive for therapy.*]

Th. Do you have any ideas about psychiatry or psychotherapy? [*This is to determine any misconceptions she may have about therapy.*]

Pt. No, nothing other than I've read in the papers and what Mrs. Henshaw told me. I think it's a wonderful thing to be able to help these problems.

Th. Well, then we can get started. We will meet once weekly. How would Tuesdays at 4:30 P.M. suit you? [*Apparently the patient is quite naive about psychotherapy but has no misconceptions about therapy. For a number of reasons I was unable to see her more frequently during the next few weeks. I somehow felt she would do well on a twice-a-week, or three-times-a-week basis; but I decided to observe her progress with one session weekly and then to increase the visits if necessary. This was no arbitrary decision; it was conditioned by practical necessity.*]

Pt. That's fine, doctor.

Th. You say there is no financial problem?

Pt. No, not really.

Th. I should like to obtain a psychologic examination. Often this can be of help in expediting treatments. If you agree, my secretary will give you the name and address of a good psychologist.

Pt. Anything that you say will help, doctor. Do you think I can really be helped? [*The patient is so well motivated that it is unnecessary to go into a detailed explanation of why a psychologic test would be helpful.*]

Th. All people can be helped. The extent to which they can be helped, however, varies. The most important item is the desire for help, which enables a person to do what is necessary in the treatment process to get well. [*No false promises are given the patient with this explanation.*]

Pt. I know—I do want to do all I can because things are no good the way they are.

Th. All right, then, we will meet next week. One thing more, in the event you have any dreams, try to remember them and mention them to me next week. [*A better way to have approached the patient would have been to tell her that sometimes dreams reveal a story about one's fears and wishes that could be helpful and that it might be important for her to try to remember any dreams she may have so that she can discuss them with me.*]

Pt. All right, doctor, I'll try.

Th. Good. So I'll see you next week. Goodbye.

Pt. Goodbye, doctor.

If, at the end of the first session, we attempt to see how many of the goals enumerated for the initial interview have been fulfilled, we would list the following: (1) rapport seemed to be satisfactorily established; (2) the tentative diagnosis is psychoneurotic depression engrafted on a personality disorder; (3) the involved psychodynamics were unclear, but a number of elements were suggested, namely, the possibility of having experienced shattered security and self-esteem due to maternal neglect, the need to submit herself to exploitation as evidenced in her relationship with her husband, the low estimation of herself along with self-neglect, and the blocking of her ability to relate to people; (4) she seemed well motivated for therapy; (5) ideas about psychotherapy were few, but no misconceptions were apparent; (6) the existing level of insight was minor; (7) I felt I could adequately treat the patient with my skills; (8) we were able to make agreeable time and financial arrangements; (9) no outside referral was necessary; and (10) I prepared the patient for psychological testing and my secretary gave her the address of the psychologist.

SECOND SESSION

Most patients, except perhaps those who have had psychiatric treatments in the past, are somewhat bewildered at the techniques employed in psychotherapy. Reassured by the first interview, they question more openly the value of "mere talking." Since they expect some mysterious remedy or device, they are disappointed at the relative passivity of the therapist. It is, therefore, usually essential to clarify the therapeutic situation for the patient in order to give him an idea of why "talking things out" helps and why his active participation is necessary. This we may have to do as soon as the patient begins to display any doubts about treatment.

A word about psychological testing may be helpful at this point. Projective testing is useful as an aid to diagnosis, and as a means of providing brief glimpses into dynamics. It is no substitute for a clinical appraisal. Its value, for the inexperienced psychotherapist, is to give the therapist a feeling of confidence by providing a rough blueprint of the involved dynamics. This blueprint is usually revised, and perhaps even discarded, as the therapist gets deeper into the clinical material. As one grows more experienced, one relies less and less on projective testing and more and more on one's clinical judgment. But even a seasoned therapist can get something of value out of psychological testing, provided one does not go "overboard" on its virtues and ascribe to it properties it does not possess. Some clinical psychologists attempt to give the therapist too much data about the patient. It is difficult or impossible to determine such things as the prognosis or the best kind of therapy to employ from psychological tests alone, since the most crucial determining factor here is the therapist and how skillful he or she is in the conduct of therapy. Psychological tests cannot give one too accurate predictions about such factors. On the whole, if the tests are regarded as tentative, not absolute, and one's therapeutic spontaneity is not crippled by advance information, some of which may be inaccurate, psychological testing has a place in psychotherapy.

During the last session with our patient we arranged for psychological testing. The patient was referred to a clinical psychologist who did a Rorschach and Thematic Apperception Test, which are appended at the end of this session. Of the two tests, the Thematic Apperception Test was the most useful. Some of the interpretations of the tester were not valid in terms of what happened in therapy; others were remarkably accurate.

Pt. Doctor, I saw the psychologist, and she showed me some ink blots. [*The fact that the patient brings this matter up in her first sentence indicates some concern about the test or its meaning.*]

Th. Yes.

Pt. What does this show? [*Apparently she is concerned with its meaning. It would be fatal to read the test results to the patient. Whenever a patient insists on getting test results, a brief watered-down version indicating the good points revealed and merely stating that there are certain problems that have to be substantiated by clinical findings are all that should be told to the patient.*]

Th. The interpretation is a rather technical one, and it would mean little to you at this point. As you know, these tests are merely signposts of problems and must be correlated with clinical observation.

Pt. Did it show anything? [*She is pressing for some answer.*]

Th. Yes, of course. It shows that you have many potentials that are being hindered by an emotional problem. That's what we're going to work at so that you can be unblocked.

Pt. I have not been feeling too well, doctor. I feel like staying in all the time. I am wondering if there is any medicine I can take. [*The fact that the patient wants medicine brings out her feeling that I should do something immediate and dramatic. She may be puzzled about how psychologic measures can be of help to her.*]

Th. It's natural that you want medicines. However, problems of this kind cannot be treated by medicines or injections. They require understanding through conversations together, such as we are having now. [*If the patient has already been taking medicines to no avail, this fact can be brought out. Yet the patient may believe a new, more powerful, medicine to be indicated.*]

Pt. But how can just talking help? [*My prediction seems to be borne out in this question.*]

Th. This question puzzles everybody when they are about to start psychotherapy. Certainly it sounds unusual that talk can remedy as power- ful feelings of despair, hopelessness, and fatigue as you have. But you know there are reasons why these symptoms exist in you. [*Some pa- tients already have gone through the experience of talking at length with people about their prob- lem to no avail. It is important to bring the patient to an understanding that talking about oneself to the therapist is different from the usual kind of conversations.*]

Pt. I know there must be, doctor, you know. It's been there so long.

Th. Do you have any idea what causes these feelings, what is actually behind these symptoms? [*focusing her attention on the fact that there are causes that underlie her symptoms*]

Pt. I have thought about it all week, doctor, and I see what you mean. I know my life was unsatisfactory, you know what I mean, doctor, with the business worries and the worrying about my husband and all. But that's all over now, and I can't seem to be myself. [*Obviously the patient has no idea about the sources of her problem. Because she sees no reason for her symptoms, she is puzzled that they persist.*]

Th. This is where psychotherapy comes in—to help you understand the connection be- tween your symptoms and basic causes for the symptoms. This is why talk is important. [*again attempting to bring out that there are causes and that discovering these through psychotherapy will help her*]

Pt. I see what you mean, doctor. [*This is a cliché. One would justifiably doubt that she really can see what I mean at this point*]

Th. And once we really know what is behind your suffering, you can do something construc- tive about yourself aimed at correcting the sources of your trouble. [*Some patients through reading get the idea that all that is required in psychotherapy is to find out what causes their trouble. Cure then will follow automatically. The statement I made tends to put responsibility on the patient to do something constructive about herself after the causes have been explored.*]

Pt. I would like to do this because I am so miserable. It's been so long since I last felt good at all. [*Her suffering will undoubtedly provide a good incentive to get well, if she can overcome her other resistances.*]

Th. Then it will be important for you to talk to me about your thoughts and your feelings and I will help you clarify what is going on. This will really help you a lot more than medicines. In fact, it's the only way. [*attempting to show her that she can do something positive about her problem in cooperating with me*]

Pt. I don't know what to talk about. Is there anything you want me to talk about? [*Apparently the patient believes she has told me all about her- self and that there is nothing more she need tell me. Perhaps she is irritated that I haven't helped her with all the information she has already given me.*]

Th. Any problem that is immediately on your mind is what you might explore, particu- larly any feelings that are of concern to you. I will help you as you go along. [*I am provided here with an opportunity to structure the therapeutic situation for the patient, to show her how therapy might help her and how she can cooperate with me.*]

Pt. For instance, doctor, what?

Th. Well . . . for instance, you were just bothered about how talk might be of any help to you in mastering your symptoms, so you men- tioned your feelings to me. Any other important thoughts or feelings would be topics of conversation.

Pt. Yes, I see what you mean, doctor. So if I can understand why I feel the way I do, every- thing will be all right? I would like you to tell me what is wrong, doctor, and I'll do anything you say. [*Obviously the patient has not integrated what I said about activity on her own part; she continues to request that I tell her what is wrong, which is what the traditional physician should do in her opinion.*]

Th. Now I'd like to tell you how I feel about this situation. First, I very much want to help you work this problem out. It seems a shame that a person as manifestly gifted as yourself should feel the way you do, where you retreat from practically everybody and everything. And I would like to work with you so that you can get well as soon as possible. [*expressing sympathy in the attempt to consolidate the relationship— actually, this is really how I feel.*]

Pt. I am very thankful to you for this.

Th. So that I would like to acquaint you with how we can best make progress in getting you well. [*again preparing her for a recital of how she can cooperate*]

Pt. Yes, I will do anything I can to help.

Th. First, as we begin to talk about your problems, things will become more obvious to me than to you. This is because I can be more objective than you. You live too close to your problems to be objective about them. Second, I'm trained to do psychotherapy and can see the connections better. Now the funny thing we have found is that a therapist's telling a person about what he observes about him does not really help him much in getting well. What really helps is for the person to figure things out for himself, with the therapist's help. This really helps. [*explaining why her role must be an active one*]

Pt. You can help me figure out why I don't feel well, and then things will get better? [*This is an encouraging comment and may indicate the beginnings of an intellectual grasp of her responsibilities.*]

Th. Yes. Because you live so close to your problems, it's difficult to see them for what they are. I might be able to tell you what the problems are very fast, but this wouldn't help you as much as my showing *you* why *you* aren't able to see what is going on in you, so that *you* then can really figure things out. It's like learning French. If I were your French teacher and did all the talking, you'd never learn *how* to talk French.

Pt. Well, that sounds reasonable.

Th. I know all this is a little difficult to understand, but we will clarify matters as we go along.

Pt. You know, doctor, I want to do everything I can, but I don't know how to go about it. You asked me to remember my dreams, but I don't dream much. Sorry to disappoint you. [*Perhaps the patient felt I expected her to dream, and if she didn't dream, it meant she was a bad girl who didn't cooperate.*]

Th. You felt that you ought to have dreamt?

Pt. Well, I thought you mentioned that dreams would help.

Th. I see. . . . Yes, I did mention that.

Pt. I didn't have them. Does it really have something to do with all of this? [*Not having read anything on the subject, the patient must have been puzzled to have me mention the fact that dreams were important.*]

Th. Well, let's look upon it this way. A person's mind is never absolutely inactive. One often has thoughts in sleep that are very significant, that one won't allow oneself to think about when one's awake. The content of these thoughts will sometimes reveal what a person is worried about and what paralyzes one in daily activity. Thoughts in sleep often take the form of dreams. Now one of the things that is bothering you a great deal is that you used to be very active and mingled with people, and now you do not. You have no idea what caused this change? [*The reason for the shift from dreams to a personal reference is that I later want to tell her that dreams may help tell us why she has retreated from people.*]

Pt. No, not really.

Th. Then it is possible that we might learn something from your exploring your feelings about this. And maybe if you do remember a dream or two, we may get a clue to what is behind this problem.

Pt. It's like a shock, the things that happened. I am not myself at all. I don't like to have people around. *(pause)*

Th. You don't like to have people around. [*repeating what the patient has said in an attempt to stimulate more verbalizations about this point*]

Pt. It's just the opposite to the way it's been. It's a mystery to me. *(pause)* [*Apparently the patient feels blocked in knowing how she can pursue this trend.*]

Th. There's a mystery to it for you that we will try to work out together.

Pt. But I don't know what I'm supposed to do. [*She again expresses her helplessness here. I will have to explain more fully, by giving her an example, of how one works in psychotherapy.*]

Th. Let me give you an example. A young woman I treated came to see me because of unhappiness in marriage. She was on the verge of divorce. It turned out that this was her third marriage, the first two terminating in divorce because she was so unhappy with her husbands. After her second divorce, she got into three or four affairs, and each affair ended with her dismissing the man. She finally married the third time, and the marriage was about to break up when she came to see me, at the insistence of her lawyer. "Well," she said, "this is awfully silly, I know that there's nothing wrong with me. I don't have anything wrong with my mind. I don't see why I should see a psychiatrist." I replied that psychiatric practice these days didn't confine itself to treating very severe mental problems, but also helped people with normal problems. She was quite certain, she answered, that there was nothing wrong with her; there was no reason in the world why anyone should feel that she had any real problems. She could not see that there was anything wrong in any of her relationships with men, except that they turned out to be the wrong kind of people for her. At the second session she reported a dream. She was about to be married. At the altar she was confronted with choosing one of two men. One of them was a small, wiry person, and the other was a tall, rather austere fellow. And she chose the tall austere man. When she got home, he turned out to be a Jack-the-Ripper character who went after her with an ax. She ran away in terror, but he caught her and started hacking her up. She awoke from her sleep in a cold sweat. She thought that was a rather silly dream, but I urged her to talk about the dream and particularly about her associations to the incidents and people in the dream. In her talk she revealed that the only type of man she really respected was one who had great qualities that she could admire and respect. She went on to associate that her father was an unusually wonderful person, even though her mother had a great deal of difficulty with him. Her father treated her mother badly, and on several occasions he had slapped her around. As she talked, she remembered that she had been quite terrified of her father as a child. This seemed to clear up certain doubts in her mind as to why she chose men who bore no resemblance to her father. She liked very passive, suave men who were no threat or challenge to her. But when she began to relate herself to a man like this, she realized that he didn't have the qualities she admired in a man. Then she developed a lot of contempt for his passivity and broke up the relationship. This is what happened in each marriage. Now the dream was the first clue as to what was going on.

Pt. But she didn't know, she didn't recognize it.

Th. She became aware of it by talking. Now, when she was aware of what she was doing to herself, when she became conscious that even her third marriage was to a man she felt no respect for, she was able then to reevaluate the whole situation. [*Examples such as this one are invaluable in helping to structure the therapeutic situation.*]

Pt. And she's happy?

Th. And she's happy.

Pt. Well, that's wonderful that you could help her just like that.

Th. That's what we want to do with you. Now in your particular case, there are reasons why *you* suddenly got to a point in your life where you don't want to see people.

Pt. Well, I've probably had some disappointments. There's no question about that. I think my husband, John, was a disappointment to me. I mean the way I helped him and went along with him and gave up everything practically. And, of course, that's all right. I think I've benefitted by it. I mean, it's experience. Sometime maybe I'll . . . but it took a lot out of me. It was an awful hurt, you see. I didn't have any children. I took an interest in helping crippled children, and, of course, I don't feel too badly about that because again I feel that I've done something good. I mean, aside from the fact that I could have had a child that was normal and it would have been a nice thing for me, a companion and all, to enjoy—but it didn't happen. So, well, I'm taking that as it was given to me. There must be a reason, I guess. I don't know, I was happy helping crippled children, especially in institutions. They are happy in that little atmosphere over there. They live in their own little world, doctor, you know. They have no worries and, being protected that way, they aren't hurt.

Normal children hurt little children, you know, that aren't up, and being able to be as alert as they are. And these little children are protected. So, I mean, that really doesn't hurt me too much. I feel badly about it, but I don't think that has anything to do with it, with what's happened to me, you know. [*The patient is unblocked to some extent. The meaning of her interest in crippled children is not clear.*]

Th. There are other things? [*attempting to get her to explore things more thoroughly*]

Pt. It goes further. *(pause)*

Th. It goes further? It involves your own feelings about yourself? [*I am not sure why I introduced the last statement. Perhaps I had a hunch at the time that this area was important.*]

Pt. Yes, and people. *(pause)*

Th. And people? [*repetition of the last word in the form of a question to maintain the flow of verbalizations*]

Pt. Now, I have some friends, and, of course, they're nice, but they aren't too interesting. They're people I met in business, and John liked them. They're along more on the sporting type, like he was, you see. And I could take a drink or two, but, I mean, it didn't interest me. It isn't everything with me to go out for an evening, and just see how much I can drink, or how drunk I can get. That doesn't mean anything to me. You see, I like to be with people, but I like to be with interesting people. Someone I . . . as you say . . . someone that you can respect. It goes back to the same thing too. Now, these friends of mine now are all carryovers. They are friends of his that we both used to go out with. And those are the people that I see, and those are the only people that I know. Now the result of that is that when I go away for a winter vacation, I always go where they are, because I don't want to be alone. Now I feel that I want to go somewhere and be alone. Before I was afraid to go without anyone. Now this year I'm thinking differently. I'd like to get away from all that and be alone, you see. I don't know which is the worse of the two, doctor. [*One may ask whether she is bored with these persons specifically, or whether they are being used as an expression of general boredom with people. Is there something that happens in her relationships with people that upsets her, and if so, is it with certain kinds of persons or with all people?*]

Th. What type of people are they specifically?

Pt. Well, they are business people.

Th. They don't have similar interests to yours?

Pt. Well, I've been going a long time with these people, 15 or 20 years. You know how it is, doctor. And I feel as if I'm neglecting them if I don't call them and say, "How are you?" You know how it is. Isn't it awful?

Th. It must be kind of tough for you. [*The patient may want to be blamed. I try to avoid expanding her guilt by sympathizing with her suffering.*]

Pt. It is. It really is. You see what I mean. And that's about all there is to it.

Th. Do you think you need a few new interests?

Pt. Well, there's no question about this.

Th. Have you ever done anything—hobbies, art, anything?

Pt. No, all I've ever done, as I've told you, is work at our book business. You see what I mean? And see that the books were in order and then get everything going. People start coming in at all times. You'd have to see that the girls were on the job and everything. And then readying for new customers again. Well, you know, doctor, you do that for 22 years, and then I finally got out of it because this thing began working on me that I have now. And I couldn't stand it any more. *(pause)*

Th. Apparently, it was more than you could stand.

Pt. That's why I got out of it. *(cries)*

Th. You suffered a great deal. *(conveying sympathy)*

Pt. You see, that's really why I got out. Because this was coming, and I was forcing myself. Every step that I took to go in there, doctor, was an effort. It was agony, just like a person who didn't know how to say a word, but was always forced to say something. It was the same thing. I was dragging myself, and I did that about 2 years. That's what I went through, and I was foolish to do it. Well, finally I got out of it, and I think it was the best thing that ever happened. I think I might have cracked up very badly. *(pause)*

Th. There wasn't anything in it that was of real value to you, that you enjoyed?

Pt. Suddenly, it all . . . everything took the opposite. When people talked to me, I just could hardly stand it, you see. And everything, the whole picture was just the reverse of what it had been before. Before I loved it, and then it took that sudden turn. It all seems impossible. *(cries)*

Th. Look, we've got to work so you can get out of this thing. It may take a short time, or it may take a long time. Your vitality and creativeness seem to have been snowed under by this hopelessness. [*The patient seems to be in need of some reassurance and support and this was the intention behind these comments.*]

Pt. Whatever it is, the worst part is that I'm being forced to see these old friends who are bores and whom I don't want to see. What can I do? [*The thing that comes to my mind here is why she feels she is forced to see these old friends who are bores.*]

Th. It may be that you have to take a stand with some of your friends. [*I make the assumption here that she feels forced to see them.*]

Pt. Yes, I see, I could tell them that I'm busy. They are things in my past, like the business.

Th. You may feel toward them the same thing that you finally felt toward your business.

Pt. Yes, doctor, that's how I feel. I think a person needs to have something or do something with meaning. Regardless of what it is, you must have something with meaning. Money isn't everything, you know. If it was, I'd have stayed in business. *(pause)*

Th. Your business was a profitable one?

Pt. You see, if I had thought that that was everything to me, I would have stayed in there because I had a wonderful thing. But I got so, that I knew that that wasn't the thing that I was interested in any more. That had no more interest for me. I knew that I was getting nothing out of life, and I realized that all I was doing was working and sleeping and eating. And there wasn't anything else. You see, so I mean that, doctor, money is not everything. I'd have traded everything for a nice life.

Th. And your life was not too satisfactory. [*focusing on what she seems to consider the basic problem of her life.*]

Pt. No, for several years before my husband died, he had no intercourse with me at all. You know how that is, doctor . . . leave you there, just leave you there, and, I mean, just completely ignore me, that way.

Th. How did you take that?

Pt. How did I take that? Well, as I say, he had a kidney condition, and he blamed it on that. And then, of course, I finally found out that he was running around, you see. And I knew that it really wasn't true that he was so sick that we couldn't do anything that way. So then, of course, I knew that it wasn't true, that he was lying to me about that. And, of course, that went on and on. You know, doctor, there's so many things. And then my sister was on my mind. I had to take care of her. You know, there was that responsibility, which was quite an expense. And it wasn't always all right. We had gone through that last depression in '29, you know, and it took a long time for us to get back again, you know. You have ups and downs. You know how that is, doctor. And it was all, you know, one of those things. And then, you know, that my mother lived with us. So there were some things that I had to think about. The same old thing again. You know, you can't always do what you want to do. And so that was that. And, of course, at that time I had a lot of opportunity to go out with others, but I didn't. Naturally, I wouldn't. [*The patient presents a picture here of having been exploited by others. The question is whether she was really exploited, whether she is complaining without adequate basis, or whether she insisted on being exploited out of some personal need.*]

Th. You felt you didn't want to be unfaithful?

Pt. Well, I wouldn't. Not only for him, but for myself, you see. You see what I mean?

Th. I believe I do.

Pt. I wasn't thinking of whether I was being honest about it for his sake, but just for my own sake, I wouldn't do that, you see. But it took an awful lot out of me, seeing that I was hurt, and I suffered surely. But then he passed away, and I had to take care of the business. *(pause)*

Th. Then you were left with the business. [*repetition of the last phrase to maintain the flow of verbalization*]

Pt. Then I was left with the whole thing, which I knew how to take care of, fortunately. Because he, being ill so many years, I was really preparing for that, and didn't know it. I mean gradually taking more and more over, you see. *(pause)*

Th. So you absorbed yourself in business. [*summarizing*]

Pt. What I needed was affection, and understanding and love from people. [*This may be a focal conflict. The lack of affection and understanding may be something she brings on herself in some way.*]

Th. Which you didn't get. You couldn't find another man?

Pt. Well, you see, I suppose I should tell you that I did have an affair with someone for 3 years. It's just over now, and maybe it was my fault.

Th. How did it terminate? [*It may be important to explore this affair as a reflection of a general pattern.*]

Pt. Well, he's had another sweetheart for about 20 years. I always played second fiddle to her. He didn't tell me about it, and then I found out. It upset me, and I stopped seeing him. Things like that keep happening to me. [*Is her playing "second fiddle" a pattern in which she participates as part of her neurotic problem?*]

Th. That same pattern as with your husband?

Pt. Isn't it awful? And, of course, when we first started going around together, he said that

he would absolutely get rid of this other woman, but he didn't. I mean it still exists. This girl works for him, you see. And in the capacity of a buyer. She's been with him; he's had her in business. It's one of those jumbled things. And then I just got fed up with it, see, doctor? *(pause)*

Th. It must have been very difficult.

Pt. Well, you see, he said that this affair with the girl didn't exist any more, you see.

Th. He was just telling you this?

Pt. I suppose so, because she's still around.

Th. And he had very little time for you?

Pt. I'll tell you why I never did see him over weekends, and it sounds like the same old story. Saturday and Sunday he was always busy. He has three children. They're married, three daughters. And, well, I just got a little tired of the whole thing. I mean, it just didn't seem right, and I guess it wasn't. And I just sort of cooled off, you know, and when he called, I just didn't encourage him. He called again, he called a couple of times. And that was that. That's how it is. I haven't heard from him in 3 months. [*Is it possible that her difficulties with and her breaking off of her affair with this man precipitated her present serious depression?*]

Th. Do you miss him?

Pt. Well, there is a little . . . well, an interest.

Th. He hasn't pursued you?

Pt. No, he hasn't at all since, but I haven't given him any encouragement to call again.

Th. He hasn't shown any sort of an interest?

Pt. No, and if he was interested, he would call. [*Apparently the patient is still interested.*]

Th. How old a man is he?

Pt. About 62, too old for me.

Th. What else was there about him?

Pt. He was always in a lot of trouble. He always had troubles and always brought them to me. He's involved a lot, and there's an ex-wife. He's divorced, and, oh, I get myself into the worst kinds of things. Just one of those things, just being lonesome, you see. You see, to get someone to pay a little attention to you, have an interest, go to the theater or dinner or something. But there wasn't anything to it. That isn't for me, doctor. You have too many troubles then. He's too involved. He has this girl, which is probably still going on. *(pause)*

Th. If he were a special person, perhaps you wouldn't give him up so easily. [*I test her desire here to continue seeing him.*]

Pt. Well, I feel this way, as you say, if he was interested, he would have tried to see me again, I think.

Th. And he only called you that once, you say.

Pt. Twice.

Th. Twice, and what did he say specifically?

Pt. Well, he was going to Europe, you see, and he said, "I'll call you before I leave," and that was supposed to be the next day, and he didn't call. *(pause)*

Th. And he didn't call.

Pt. And he hasn't called since he came back. So that's that. I'm not, I just . . . I wouldn't, just . . . *(pause)*

Th. He may come back . . .

Pt. Forget it. And even if he doesn't, it's probably the best thing.

Th. It may be hard to give him up. [*testing how much she wants him to pursue her*]

Pt. I can get somebody better than that. *(pause)*

Th. You feel perhaps that it is important for you to be discriminating with people you get mixed up with from now on? [*reflecting an attitude that may be behind her previous statements*]

Pt. Because they do something to me . . . You see, doctor, people do something to me. And I seem to go along in that pattern. Now, I know another girl that's with a doctor, and she isn't married to him. Isn't it funny, and I get involved in those kinds of pictures, and that isn't good and I know it isn't. You know what I mean, you can't respect yourself. *(pause)*

Th. Because it makes for complications that are destructive to you as a person? [*reflecting her feeling of being devalued in being involved with certain men*]

Pt. Yes. *(pause)*

Th. You just get to a point where you don't respect yourself any more, after a while. [*continuing to reflect her feeling devalued*]

Pt. You see what I mean. And I don't need that because, after all, I . . . ah . . . people respect me, and I should really get something, something for myself. Which I haven't been smart enough to, apparently. I don't know. I've missed a lot of opportunities on the way, you see. [*She expresses her feeling here of having been exploited by people.*]

Th. There must have been some reason for this. [*focusing on the motives behind what has been happening to her*]

Pt. You know, maybe I don't put enough of a value on myself, doctor. That's very possible, you see. I always bring myself down to the other person's level instead of trying to bring myself up to a better level, that is, something I could look up to. You know what I mean? Like I feel sorry for other people, you know, and I go along with them. And I find myself with them instead of others that would do me some good. Some-

how I avoid the others. [*The patient here is verbalizing what may be insight, that is, a feeling that she is underestimating her value and that she is yielding to the impulse of feeling sorry for other people.*]

Th. What happens when you meet the other kind of people, those that you could look up to?

Pt. I am not interested. *(pause)*

Th. Not interested?

Pt. Why? Because I suppose they haven't all these troubles and complications. I seem to go for that for some reason. [*Does the patient have an awareness of a need to take care of helpless or disturbed people?*]

Th. In other words, you find that your interests are for getting involved with people who are in a lot of trouble, who need your help. And you get involved with them, and then you find that after a while that . . . [*attempting to consolidate insight if it exists*]

Pt. That it isn't any good, it's a nuisance, and then I'm where I started, only worse off, because I have my head filled with that other thing.

Th. So that the type of person who might be able to help you . . .

Pt. I'm not interested in them. [*Again this has the sound of some insight.*]

Th. Perhaps you feel that . . .

Pt. They're above me and . . . *(pause)*

Th. They're above you and that they might not accept you? [*This is merely a guess, and it is presented as a possible interpretation.*]

Pt. I really do, I really do. It's exactly like that. *(pause)* [*The patient apparently accepts the interpretation.*]

Th. Now let's investigate that. How far back does that go? [*If we are on the track of an important trend, it would be helpful to explore how far back it goes in her estimation.*]

Pt. Oh, I didn't have any childhood days, at all. I told you that I was 5 years old when my father died. My mother was left without anything at all. And she had a furnished-room house. That was the only way she knew how to make a living, in order to take care of us. And then there was, I don't know, some talk about . . . oh . . . I don't know, that the place wasn't right. She wasn't running it right. And we children were taken away from her for a short period. [*This must have been a painful period in her childhood.*]

Th. Oh, is that so, where were you taken?

Pt. Put into an asylum for a little while. Then my mother's cousin took me. I lived with her, and she was married to a very nice man. He was in the avocado business. He had a ranch in California. And then my oldest brother was about 12, and he was all right. And I lived with mother's cousin, oh, until I was about 14. [*Her account of her childhood is that of great insecurity. One wonders if she harbors resentment about it. We must ask if her insecure childhood could be linked with her feelings of self-devaluation. Our time is up at this point, which will be indicated in the next remark.*]

Th. All right. We meet again at the same time next week.

Pt. Thank you, doctor, I'll be here.

During this session a structuring of the therapeutic situation has enabled her to open up and to explore several painful areas of her life including that of her childhood. She brings out the inkling of a trend in which she feels exploited by people whom she feels forced to help.

PSYCHOLOGIC TEST INTERPRETATIONS

Rorschach Test

The record is that of an intelligent woman whose cognitive and conative processes at this stage are being distorted by her tremendous fear and apprehension. The intensity of her apprehension seems to be related to her inability to adequately suppress her hostility. She is constantly at war with herself and the external reality so that at certain points reality is misperceived and distorted on the basis of her struggle.

This is a woman who cannot conceive of relationships except in terms of aggression. The whole outer environment is a place of hostility—people are aggressive toward one another and, to her mind, this is the source of interaction. She is sufficiently integrated to be able to doubt her own perception and interpretations, but cannot work out a more positive and constructive approach to living. When she does attempt this, she is most likely to end up with masochistic activity. There is some indication that her self-destructiveness is restraining impulsive, aggressive acting-out, upon and in the environment.

This patient seems to function, generally, on the basis of fear, ensuring retreat and withdrawal, rather than on the basis of permitting any overt anxiety.

The record reveals much oral emphasis

and suggests strivings to be nurtured, dependent, and protected. At the same time (in consideration of what has been mentioned) she is likely to be highly resentful of such a position, since it would inevitably expose her marked aggressiveness, and she would very easily become panicked by the upsurge of hostile attitudes.

She cannot tolerate much external pressure or excitation and has to detach herself. When this occurs, her masochistic fantasies take over and she actually has no "place."

This is a woman who can experience shallow emotionality in her interpersonal relationships, more in the order of sentimentality than warmth and affection (except for explosive, highly immature and intense outbursts).

It is felt that she could not accept deep insight analysis of a probing nature and will attempt to structure therapy herself on a guidance basis. The possibility of her dealing with aggressive impulses (on herself and toward others), by some indirect means, could be considered (art, needle work, etc.).

At the present time she is sufficiently integrated to be able to detach herself, but the possibility of released anxiety leading to a paranoid process should be considered.

Thematic Apperception Test

The record suggests a woman struggling with a deep feeling of inadequacy, isolation and dissatisfaction. She feels herself to be misunderstood and lacking in an understanding of others. Her confusion regarding the nature of relationships has led to an interpretation of the total environment as hostile and unsympathetic to her. Her expectation is to be hurt, deprived, and maligned. This results in hostile and aggressive attitudes toward others—a constant struggle with environment and her inner impulses.

This woman appears to conceive of relationships in terms of aggression. That is, that the basis of interaction of people is hurting one another. She is sufficiently integrated to be able to doubt her perception; she has a close enough contact with reality for this doubt to occur; and when things do happen that impinge on her illusions and distortion, she can experience much anxiety. At such times she is likely to end up with highly masochistic activity. One gets the impression that self-destructive attitudes restrain acting-out aggressive impulses.

The record suggests a striving for nurture and dependence, as though she lives under a sense of loss and, burdened by life's vicissitudes, she seeks protection. However, she is the kind of person who would be highly resentful of a position of dependence; also, it would inevitably expose her aggressiveness and she would be panicked in such a situation. Her difficulties in relationships are marred, too, by her inability to integrate effective stimuli into an emotionally meaningful and rich experience. She tries not to become involved with situations that carry pressure or excitation. When she does, she struggles to detach herself, to remain on the periphery and to become evasive. She is likely to reveal emotional shallowness, to demonstrate much feeling in terms of sentimentality rather than any depth toward or about people.

It appears as though one of her needs to be detached is in order to avert any open anxiety.

Some of the difficulties she is experiencing at this time seem to be around questions of age, with resentment and bitterness in regard to her present status. This appears to express itself in questions of sexuality and some doubt and confusion regarding femininity.

It is rather doubtful whether this patient can accept deep insight therapy or analysis of a probing critical nature. She is more likely to structure therapy by herself on a supportive-guidance basis. The possibility of released anxiety leading to a paranoid process should be considered. On the whole, however, the record suggests a neurotic process with an hysteria syndrome.

THIRD SESSION

The structuring of the therapeutic situation during the last session might be expected to provoke certain reactions in the patient. She may respond by greater activity, or she may manifest further hopelessness or discouragement which will have to be worked through.

Pt. I had a dream, doctor.

Th. Good.

Pt. I had a dream. I am in a store buying presents, pocketbooks and purses, and I have them wrap them into nice little bundles. It is like I get them for . . . I mean . . . like I have to get them home; important like . . . almost as if my life depended on it. Then I am home and my husband and sister are there—waiting. They open up the presents, and everything is gone—just empty boxes. I feel awful, and my husband laughs at me. You know, doctor, I felt so awful in my sleep that I woke up crying. *(pause)* [*My own associations to this dream–tentative, of course–are that something valuable that she has to offer people close to her is found to be without content. She feels ridiculed for her gesture and becomes upset. The fact that she awoke crying indicates the intense emotional feeling associated.*]

Th. Does the dream bring any thoughts to your mind?

Pt. Why no, doctor, should it? [*Either the patient is extremely naive or shows resistance to the dream's latent content.*]

Th. You may have certain ideas or associations to the different events or objects in the dream. For instance, what does buying presents in a store bring to your mind?

Pt. We . . . I like to buy presents and really do enjoy giving things.

Th. I see. *(pause)* What about this business of having to get the presents home, as if your life depended on it?

Pt. I don't know about that—that's funny, isn't it? *(pause)*

Th. Any associations to your husband and sister waiting?

Pt. Well . . . they are just waiting for me. *(pause)*

Th. Any feelings about this?

Pt. No. *(pause)*

Th. What about the rest of the dream?

Pt. Well, the last part makes me feel foolish, and as if I failed them. It's like I had been fooled, you see. Buying the presents and then having been given a raw deal.

Th. How do you feel about being given a raw deal?

Pt. Very upsetting. It makes you feel like you are a perfect fool.

Th. Did anything like this ever happen?

Pt. You mean like in the dream?

Th. Yes.

Pt. Why no, that is, I never bought anything and came home with an empty box.

Th. How about feeling like a perfect fool?

Pt. Why, yes, I felt that way a good part of my life. *(pause)*

Th. What other feelings do you have?

Pt. *(pause)* I am tired today, I suppose I get up too early. *(yawning)* [*There seems to be little point in pursuing the dream due to the resistance that is present. It is possible that her feeling tired may be a manifestation of resistance, and I decide to explore it.*]

Th. What time do you get up?

Pt. I get up about 8:30, and I fix my own breakfast. I used to have my girl come in—my maid—come in the morning at 8:30 to fix my breakfast, but I've changed that because I wanted to be alone in the mornings. And I have her come in now at 11. I fix my own breakfast for myself now, so I'll have a little time alone again in the mornings instead of her being there. This girl that's been with me for 22 years, and a lovely girl, I can't even stand her. *(pause)*

Th. She irritates you? [*I decide to explore her feelings about her maid to see if any patterns are apparent.*]

Pt. I even resent her doctor. *(pause)* And she is a wonderful girl. *(pause)*

Th. She gets on your nerves?

Pt. Yes. *(pause)*

Th. What does she do that gets on your nerves?

Pt. Everything. *(pause)*

Th. Just irritating?

Pt. Yes, and I just hate myself for it, because she is a nice girl. *(pause)*

Th. Perhaps you're blaming yourself too much for this, because, after all, you have a problem that disturbs you very much. [*One of the worst blocks the patient can get into is to flagellate herself with her shortcomings. I attempt to point out that her difficulty is a problem, not a personal defect.*]

Pt. *(crying)* It's ridiculous for me to feel this way about people that have been good to me. I miss the nice girl when I don't even want to be around her. [*The patient does not pick up my statement, and she continues to blame herself.*]

Th. You blame yourself for your feelings. *(pause)* It upsets you to feel irritated by the girl who actually has been nice to you.

Pt. Yes, I do.

Th. Well, there may be things she does that are very disturbing to you. [*In this comment there is an intent to get the patient to test reality; the opportunity is offered to her to project her difficulties if she wishes to do so.*]

Pt. I don't think so, doctor.

Th. Is there anything that she does that is unusual?

Pt. Oh no, I don't think so. It must be me. [*The patient continues to blame herself, although her recognition of her role may indicate some insight.*]

Th. All right then, we have to determine why your resentment piles up. [*stressing the sources of her feeling*]

Pt. Well, doctor, I don't know. I know that I have nice friends, and I just haven't any patience with them. *(pause)*

Th. I see.

Pt. I don't get mad at them, but I lose my interest in them after I've been with them a little while, and . . . oh, I don't know . . . start criticizing them to myself, and there's no reason for it. They're the same as they've ever been. *(pause)*

Th. Is there any person with whom you now feel comfortable? [*This is asked to see what exceptions there may be to the patient's feelings about being critical of people.*]

Pt. No. *(long pause)*

Th. There isn't a single person with whom you feel comfortable?

Pt. No.

Th. You may, in coming to see me, perhaps, not feel comfortable with me either. [*probing for possible transference reactions*]

Pt. No, I think you're wonderful, doctor, I do. I like you very much. [*This may or may not be transference, or it may be a way of expressing her awareness that we have a good working relationship.*]

Th. Why do you like me, why do you think I'm wonderful? [*inquiring into what "wonderful" means to her to test the extent of transference*]

Pt. Why I think you're wonderful to be in the profession you're in, helping people.

Th. Look, I'm going to try to help you, but you may happen to get critical of me too sometime. After all, if you feel this toward other people, you're likely to feel it toward me. If you do, it would be helpful to mention this to me so we can see what it means. [*giving her "permission" to express any irrational feelings she may have toward me as part of the therapeutic process*]

Pt. No, I mean I think anyone who would do this work is very . . . must be very good and kind, to listen to all these things all day. And I imagine it must take a lot out of you. [*Her concern with what listening to patients does to me may be a projection of her own resentment and fatigue at helping people.*]

Th. Actually, this is my work and I enjoy doing it. And I am going to do what I can to help you solve *your* problem. This thing has got you by the throat, and it's sort of shaking you all over. Now, what I'd like to work out with you is the best approach to the handling of your problem.

Pt. Yes, so that I can enjoy being with people, which is the natural thing. *(pause)*

Th. Now what *we* have to understand is why these feelings of irritation with people occur.

Pt. Doctor, I just don't know why. All I know is that they come. Why should they come? [*The patient's curiosity is understandable, but she still may be trying to force me to give her the answers.*]

Th. Now, that's a good question. You realize that they are not natural feelings and that they interfere with your happiness. They are, nevertheless, significant in that there is a reason for their existence. The reason may not be known to you now. You don't know why these feelings develop; they just creep up and overwhelm you, and you feel guilty about them. Now, what we're going to try to do is understand what these feelings mean and why they develop. [*I am trying to create motivation here to explore her feelings.*]

Pt. Well tell me, doctor, why is it that I don't do the things that I want to do? There's so many things even in my own home that I know that I should do, that I would be very much happier for doing. [*The patient is beginning to question certain things about herself, which is a good sign, but I get the feeling she still wants me to give her the reasons for her behavior.*]

Th. For instance?

Pt. Well there's, for instance, order in my home. I know that there are some things that I should take care of myself. No one can do that for me. I can't get myself to do these things. *(long pause)*

Th. You can't do them. [*restating*]

Pt. Well, why is that? [*apparently trying to force an answer out of me*]

Th. All right now, that's a very good question. [*throwing the question back at her*]

Pt. Well, what is it? [*She is still trying to make me act directive.*]

Th. I wish I could give you the answer right now, but it wouldn't do you any good if I presented you with an answer. We'll have to find out about what it is together. Let's find out what it is that makes you feel that there's nothing you can . . .

Pt. Do.

Th. Yes.

Pt. There isn't anything that I can do. I read a little article the other day about a person who did a great deal with just a little organized knowledge. It is worth so much more than some-

one that has a fund of knowledge but with no organization behind it. You see what I mean?

Th. You mean that's how you feel?

Pt. Well, I have a lot of ideas, but I can't put one of them across. I can't do a thing. I can't do anything or be well. Why is that? [*Again she tries to put me on the spot.*]

Th. If you really have a desire to get well, you will have the best chance of understanding what causes you to feel the way you do. [*What I am saying here is that if she really wants to overcome her suffering, she will have to figure out the answers for herself with my help.*]

Pt. I do want to get well. I do.

Th. There's no question in your mind about that?

Pt. I certainly do, because this isn't living. I'm willing to do anything to get well. [*If her incentive is strong enough, she will break through her block and start working actively on her problem.*]

Th. So you are willing to do what is absolutely necessary to bring yourself to a point where you can experience yourself as a different person, where you can really start living. [*implying that if the patient works at understanding herself she can achieve the objective of getting well*]

Pt. Yes, of course, of course. This isn't living—I mean it's nothing. You're here and you are not here. *(cries)*

Th. It must have been terribly difficult for you. [*expressing sympathy*]

Pt. Well, I want to be helped, be normal like other people, be able to enjoy life.

Th. This runs through your mind a good deal?

Pt. Yes.

Th. You've suffered terribly haven't you?

Pt. Oh terribly, for an awful long time. Always fighting with myself. There isn't anything that I want to do that I do. *(cries)*

Th. You feel almost as though you're completely defeated. [*reflecting possible feeling*]

Pt. Yes. It's all so futile. I mean, there isn't a thing that I make up my mind to do that I can fulfill. It's just as if I didn't have the, well, the mind or even anything else to do it with, doctor. It's a terrible thing, awful, awful. It's an awful thing. I get up in the morning and I think I'm going to have so much ambition today, and I'm going to take care of these things, one after the other. I have them laid out, and I say I'll do it this way. And I don't do it. Not a thing, not one of them. Isn't that awful, doctor?

Th. Why awful? You mean it's awful in the sense that you have the capacity?

Pt. And I can't do it. *(pause)* But the fact that I think of it doctor, and I have hands and I have legs and I'm breathing and living, and why can't I do it, if I think that I want to do it? [*Again she tries to force me to do something positive for her, or tell her something positive.*]

Th. If you have the desire to do it, I will help you figure out what is wrong. You act and feel almost as if you gave up life years ago, as if your whole life is over. You act almost as if you are as old as Methuselah, and at the end of your rope. *(long pause, using silence to stir up tension)* [*We seem to be having a contest here. She is trying to force me to do something active for her; I sidestep this attempt by putting her on the spot to think things through for herself.*]

Pt. Well, I don't know what to do. *(pause)*

Th. There isn't anything?

Pt. Well, yes. You see there's a couple of things that I want to do, and I feel, well, now I'm going to do that, and then I don't care if I die. You know what I mean?

Th. Like what, for instance?

Pt. Well, there's a little girl that I've taken care of, and I want to put a little trust fund aside for her. She's a little paralytic. And I want to adopt her so that there won't be any trouble when I pass on, that she'll get this to help her to grow up. [*This may possibly be an opening wedge into a more unconscious focus of conflict.*]

Th. Who is the little girl?

Pt. A little orphan.

Th. A little orphan—and is she with you?

Pt. No, she's in a boarding school.

Th. In school?

Pt. Yes, for backward children who require special care.

Th. Where is this?

Pt. In Michigan.

Th. How long have you known her?

Pt. About 27 years.

Th. Oh, she's a big girl.

Pt. About 28 or so. You know how it is, they're like babies, I mean.

Th. I see.

Pt. It's partial paralysis, doctor, and she needs special care. *(pause)*

Th. Special care?

Pt. She's utterly dependent. *(pause)*

Th. What sort of a place is she in?

Pt. It's a private school. They have about, they take care of a small number of children. *(pause)*

Th. And you're paying for her.

Pt. Surely.

Th. How'd you get interested in that?

Pt. Well this is a long story doctor. You see I took an interest in the baby when she was an infant. I felt it was what I needed. It was after my divorce. I had been married to this man at 16,

then 2 or 3 years later we separated. I was living in Detroit. Then I got divorced. Afterward I met someone who got very much interested in me. It was his idea that I get this little girl from an orphanage. You see, he was married and he knew that he could never be to me . . . I mean, well, he thought I ought to have a child that I adopt, and be in the community, established like. [*Now we have opened up a pocket of material that must be very difficult for her to verbalize. One would speculate that the incidents to which she refers casually must create intense conflict and guilt.*]

Th. I see.

Pt. Give me a home environment. When I got the infant, she was about, she was only about 4 months old. Of course, I didn't know that she had this paralysis, you see.

Th. It wasn't apparent at first, it wasn't noticeable?

Pt. No, no doctor, not at 4 months.

Th. I see.

Pt. And I only found that out after I had had her about 2 years, you see, when the time came for her to talk and walk.

Th. You took care of her yourself when she was a baby?

Pt. Of course, myself. And then about 2 years later, I found out that she had this handicap, see, and along about that time I met John. And we were married. So, about when she was about 5 years old, we put her in this school. But we had never put a trust away for her, you see. That's one of the things that I want to do. And I can't seem to get around to it. And you know why?

Th. Why?

Pt. Because I'm afraid there might be a lot of embarrassing questions.

Th. What would be embarrassing?

Pt. But I should do it though doctor. [*She avoids my question.*]

Th. Well, maybe you can work out something so that you won't be embarrassed. [*I decide not to press her for an answer at this time.*]

Pt. That would be good. *(pause)*

Th. It means a good deal to you?

Pt. Yes, it does. Because I don't want her to be a public charge. I want her to be looked after, you know, and taken care of.

Th. Were you devoted to this child? [*Unlike most patients who are only too eager to talk, this patient must practically be forced to verbalize by much activity on the part of the interviewer. In this respect she is not typical, but from a teaching standpoint, presenting a case of a passive patient, showing how she is approached in interviewing, its probably advantageous.*]

Pt. Yes, she's a lovely girl. Her mentality is low though.

Th. Does she recognize you?

Pt. Oh yes, surely. *(pause)*

Th. She looks forward to seeing you?

Pt. Sure. *(pause)*

Th. She thinks that you're her mother?

Pt. Oh, yes, certainly, surely. *(pause)*

Th. You'd like to make security provision for her then?

Pt. Yes, I would. That would give me pleasure—I mean it's what I think I should do. *(pause)*

Th. I see. *(pause)* But the big problem is what is behind how you feel about yourself and your inability to do what you'd like. [*This is about as far as the patient seems to want to go in talking about her adopted child. I decide to focus again on the larger problem of how she feels about herself.*]

Pt. Yes, yes. I keep wondering about what has happened to me. It all seems funny, I mean. Because, when I was working—hard like—I could go on and on, could do a thousand things, and now I can hardly drag myself around. I want to do nothing and see nobody. *(pause)* Why is that? [*The patient resumes her effort to force me to give her the answers.*]

Th. There are reasons for it. [*Again I dodge this intent and throw the responsibility back to her.*]

Pt. I surely do not know why. I do feel ashamed of what has happened to me. I mean, doctor, that man I told you about, his having . . . I mean . . . not being frank with me. You see, I can't understand why I let this go on so. [*A great deal of guilt and resentment seem to lurk behind these remarks.*]

Th. Do you possibly resent what has happened? [*reflecting possible feeling*]

Pt. I . . . I . . . I feel that maybe nothing else . . . that is . . . I think maybe I expect him not to want to see me any more. *(pause)* I always felt like I wasn't wanted—just do, do, do for others. *(pause)* With John, I think I felt that I was being used and all that, you see. I never had . . . I mean things as they were, I never felt I was happy except with this middle man. [*The patient expresses again an idea that she is not wanted for herself, that she must do things for other people. It is possible that the patient, feeling little value in herself, believes she must do material things for people to be liked.*]

Th. With him you did feel a sense of happiness. [*I might better have focused on the matter of her feeling she had to do things constantly for other people.*]

Pt. Yes, yes, it was the only thing that I ever had, that meant something. Except, of course, I was in love with John, and he meant everything, until this thing happened, where he didn't . . . well, I mean where he paid no attention to me. *(pause)*

Th. I see. *(pause)*

Pt. So maybe what I feel now, hopeless like, doctor, is no mystery considering what I've been . . . what's happened to me, and my not feeling I am, I amount to anything, you see. [*Her verbalized comment that she feels hopeless because she amounts to nothing may be significant, in that it may be used in later interpretations. Of course, we will want to find out why she feels she amounts to nothing.*]

Th. You mean, except with the man you knew before you married John?

Pt. Yes, he was the one that suggested the little girl, so I could feel settled, and as if I had a place in the community.

Th. Uh huh.

Pt. So I got this little girl, and then it turned out the way it did. Things like that are always happening, I suppose, and I shouldn't regret it because, after all, how do you know?

Th. Nevertheless, it must have been a blow to you.

Pt. It was, it was. And it made me feel guilty too, because when I married John, he just assumed it was my little girl. [*another guilt pocket opened*]

Th. You didn't tell him?

Pt. Why, no . . . well, I felt that it all would be very hard to explain, so I let him go on thinking that, you see what I mean? After all, there was no sense . . . Oh, it all seems terrible.

Th. You must have felt guilty about that. *(reflecting her guilt)*

Pt. I did, oh, I did. But the poor child. It was not her fault. She is so much better off in boarding school, away from, away from others, where she might be hurt.

Th. Perhaps you feel embarrassed and guilty about this whole situation? *(reemphasizing her guilt feeling)*

Pt. Oh . . . I . . . I . . . I never told anybody about that before, doctor. And it hurts me when I think how things went. [*Suppression of past experiences and partial repression of her guilt probably have contributed to her emotional illness.*]

Th. Do you blame yourself? [*continuing to encourage her to explore this area*]

Pt. No, I did everything, everything. I didn't stop at expense or anything. She has the best, the poor thing *(long pause)* The thing that bothers me is that I've always been so unhappy. There seems no way out.

Th. No way out?

Pt. With John, it was all right at first, but then he lost his interest, and I felt sorry for him and did everything I could, doctor, you see. It couldn't be helped. And I tried, but I felt it was all of no use. *(pause)* I kept thinking that with my first husband, you know, the one I married to get away from it all, it was nothing—there was nothing there. I tried and I gave, but there was nothing, nothing. *(pause)* [*again the theme that she gives, gives, gives, and there is no return*]

Th. Hmm. *(shaking head)* [*expressing sympathy*]

Pt. Yes, you see how it went, doctor, I never would have married him had it not been for what happened to me when I was little, you see. No home and being put away, I mean, and all that.

Th. I see.

Pt. And that was only part of it. *(pause)*

Th. You mean there was more?

Pt. Well, I've always been disappointed. Like that man I told you about who I went with after John died, who just . . . just . . . well, who didn't seem to think that my feelings shouldn't be hurt. *(cries)*

Th. So, as a child you were unhappy, and you married to get away from it; but you were still unhappy. Then you met the middle man, and you put everything into that relationship, but it ended. You took care of an orphan and that ended tragically for you, too. You married John and felt exploited and used. And with the last man, too, things ended by your feeling you got little out of it. That's quite a series of depriving incidents. [*summarizing the events the patient discussed to point out that they all add up to the same thing–her feeling deprived*]

Pt. Oh, that's the way it's been. *(cries)*

Th. No matter what you did and give, it ended as if you has nothing to give. [*The tentative interpretation here is made largely from the cue in the dream that the packages she had to offer were empty. From her verbalizations, too, it would seem that she feels she has little to offer people within herself.*]

Pt. Yes, yes, it all seems so hopeless. [*Should the assumption be true that she has nothing to give, she would be justified in feeling hopeless.*]

Th. Particularly when you give, give, give, and nothing happens. [*implying indirectly that she gives materially to make up for a lack of substance within herself*]

Pt. I always enjoy doing things for people.

Th. I guess you do. *(pause)* [*This is said a little ironically.*]

Pt. Why, is that wrong, doctor? [*The patient picks up the irony from my tone.*]

Th. Why should it be wrong?

Pt. I don't know.

Th. Let me ask you this, do *you* enjoy having people do things for *you?*

Pt. Why, why, when it happens, doctor, it makes me want to cry. When it happens. [*The implication here seems to be that people do little or nothing for her.*]

Th. You mean it happens so rarely? [*reflecting how she may feel*]

Pt. Yes, rarely. *(pause)* It's more the other way. But, don't mistake me, doctor, I don't expect people to return favors. They seldom do anyway, I find. But I do enjoy giving, you know. I like to help people arrange things. Before I felt so terrible I helped a friend fix up her entire apartment. Went shopping for things, seeing that the draperies and things were all done. That's easy for me, you see, because we . . . I . . . being in business, you see, had to do these things all the time. I know about these things, like decorating. [*The positive virtues she finds in doing things for people may be linked to a need for self-exploitation and to a desire to win the favors of others.*]

Th. I see.

Pt. I noticed, for instance, in your waiting room, doctor, and the landing, why, I can do many things there to help. I would be delighted if you wanted me to, doctor. [*This is the first real projection. She apparently would like to act out her problem with me. To allow her to do this would foster her feeling exploited by me and her becoming resentful toward me. I will later use this episode to point out the active workings of her problem.*]

Th. Thank you very much. I do appreciate your offer to help, but maybe it's more important that we understand this need to help and to give. [*To allow her to decorate my waiting room would have been a fatal therapeutic mistake, probably involving her immediately in a transference neurosis.*]

Pt. I don't know what you mean, doctor.

Th. Do you think you have an impulse to do things that serves a purpose of some kind? *(pause)* [*posing a basic question which is probably still far beyond her comprehension–yet, it should set her thinking.*]

Pt. I don't know. It's all been that way, you see. *(pause)* With everyone . . . why do you think this is so, doctor? [*again trying to force me to give her the answers*]

Th. Why do you think it's so? [*throwing the question back at her*]

Pt. Can't you tell me? [*She persists.*]

Th. I'd really like to do this for you, but *my* doing it really wouldn't help *you.* If you think this thing through for yourself, it will make a tremendous difference. [*I also persist.*]

Pt. Yes, doctor, I see what you mean. *(laughing)* Well, I'd like to have *you* do it for me, but if you can't, you can't.

Th. It isn't that I don't want to help, you know, it's that . . .

Pt. (laughing) It will do me good if *I* do it. [*I finally seem to have made my point.*]

Th. (laughing) That's right.

Pt. All right, doctor.

During this session we engage in a struggle of her wanting me to be active and to give her the answers to her problems. I bring out the need for her own activity and participation in terms of her finding the answers for herself with my help. As tension accumulates in the interview, she comes out with suppressed and partially repressed material, with some catharsis. She attempts to act-out an impulse to be exploited in the transference, which I circumvent. She continues to try to force me into a directive role, and finally she becomes aware of her intent. At the end she seems to accept my structuring of the therapeutic situation. We seem to be entering into the middle phase of treatment.

FOURTH SESSION

During the following session the patient explores the dynamics of her problem with beginning insight. She may be considered in the middle phase of treatment.

Th. Hello.

Pt. (laughing) Well I'm feeling pretty good. I feel very quiet and the same.

Th. (smiling) What do you mean very quiet and the same?

Pt. (still laughing) Well, I haven't done anything.

Th. How about your own feeling?

Pt. Better, much better—lighter.

Th. Lighter?

Pt. I've been doing a little more around the house. I seem to be able to accomplish a little more anyway. I mean, I have a little more ambition for things that I didn't before, so I'm quite pleased about that.

Th. I see. *(nodding)*

Pt. I do think that you're helping me, so far.

Th. In what way?

Pt. In the first place, I've felt better. My mind has been a little more at ease. And I've been able to pass my time a little in the house, by doing things that I wasn't able to do before.

Th. Why do you think you are feeling better?

Pt. Well, I think talking to you and getting rid of these things that I've held in all these years, without ever having told them to anyone.

Th. Particularly what?

Pt. Well, I think my relationship with John. And I think my first marriage which, I mean, wasn't good. And the little bit of my childhood that I told you the other day. *(pause)*

Th. Mm hmm. *(nodding)* *(pause)* Perhaps there is more about your early childhood you'd like to talk about?

Pt. Well, I think I've really told you about all of it, doctor. I had very little schooling. I went through the lower grades, as I recall, and I went to work just as soon as I was able to. I mean there was a child law at that time. I think I went when I was about 15 years old. And I had taken up a little business course that my cousin paid for, something like 3 months or something like that. I'd taken up typewriting and a little shorthand. Then I went to work doing that, and I think I worked for about 2 years. And, as I've said, then I was married. I was married when I was about 16 or 17, something like that.

Th. I see.

Pt. I was able to support myself. Yes, and I mean I always found time to help the family too, you see.

Th. Uh huh. *(nodding)*

Pt. Well, I mean, well, for instance, my sister wasn't able to; she didn't seem to work. I did. And she wore my things that I was able to buy, and when I was working, she wore my clothes, and that sort of thing. I mean, I helped her along that way. *(pause)*

Th. What was the difference in the ages between the two of you?

Pt. Well, she was 4 years older.

Th. Older? [*It seems unusual for her to have had to care for an older sister.*]

Pt. That's right. I'm the youngest.

Th. She seems to have been more passive than you. [*This comment is to stimulate her to discuss why she believes she had to take care of the sister.*]

Pt. Well, I don't know; well, probably because she had a few more advantages; she went to school longer than I did, and, I don't know, my mother seemed to favor her. Oh, I don't know. Maybe I just thought so. *(pause)* [*This may be a significant remark perhaps pointing to a feeling her mother did not value her sufficiently.*]

Th. Did your mother insist that you go out and work?

Pt. Well, doctor, my mother couldn't do anything for me. You see, as I told you, we were taken away from her. And then my cousin was taking care of me, you see. After she took me out of the asylum. And then I went to work. Naturally I felt that I should.

Th. Mm hmm.

Pt. I felt I had to do it. All my life.

Th. Mm hmm.

Pt. That's right. I felt I had to do things for people.

Th. Why?

Pt. I don't know. That's me, I guess.

Th. If you didn't do things for people, what then?

Pt. I . . . I . . . felt they wouldn't like me. *(long pause)*

Th. You always did things for people then?

Pt. Always, yes.

Th. Why?

Pt. I don't know. I always did things. I don't know why.

Th. Perhaps you felt that if you did things, people would like you. [*Interpretation reemphasizes statement patient has made.*]

Pt. Yes . . . yes . . . that's so [*Apparently she accepts this interpretation.*]

Th. Now it would seem then that the way you got approval and understanding and love and recognition was through the ability to demonstrate that you could take care of yourself and do things for others? [*elaborating on the interpretation*]

Pt. Of course.

Th. Did the same thing hold true after your marriage? Who did most of the giving? [*At this point I feel it might be fruitful to explore the theme of her being exploited.*]

Pt. Well, I think I was so happy to be married, you see, and I really was in love with John. I did do most of the giving. You see, John was sick and I felt I had to.

Th. What about your first marriage?

Pt. The first one, well, that was something to get away from, to get away from all that I had been through, and sort of to be free.

Th. Did your husband do anything for you?

Pt. No, no.

Th. You did most of the giving?

Pt. Yes.

Th. Now what about the boy friend you had after you divorced your first husband?

Pt. This man was very wonderful.

Th. Was he warm to you?

Pt. Yes, yes, and very kind, and a very wonderful person in every way.

Th. And what did he do for you?

Pt. Well, he really helped me. He was married; that I knew. He helped me. He suggested that I get established in the community. That's

why I thought I would adopt a child, to give me a feeling I was established. *(pause)* [*The fact that the pattern of exploitation has one exception, at least, sounds like a hopeful sign. We must remember, however, that she was being exploited even here, since she was living with a married man who was using her for his own gratification.*]

Th. I see. *(pause)*

Pt. To feel a nicer life, surroundings, in every way, doctor. Do you see what I mean? I got into a nice little community, and people respected me, and then I was able to take my mother with me and get her away from the others, you see. [*The question that crosses my mind is whether she also allowed herself to be exploited by her mother.*]

Th. You felt you had to do something for your mother?

Pt. Well, I do that all the time.

Th. Why do you think you do that all the time?

Pt. Why *(pause)* that's the way I am.

Th. Are other people like this? [*challenging "the way she is"*]

Pt. Why, no. They expect *me* to do things. [*Undoubtedly the patient feels herself to be unique.*]

Th. Do you think *you* are made up differently than others in that *you* have to do things and they do not? [*again challenging her concept of uniqueness*]

Pt. Why, it's always been this way. I feel it's expected. *(pause)*

Th. If you don't do things that are expected, how do you feel? [*I am trying to get the patient to explore a painful area. I attempt to deal with her resistances to verbalizing by challenging her with questions.*]

Pt. Awful and guilty.

Th. So this is why you feel forced to do things?

Pt. (pause) I . . . I . . . *(pause)*

Th. Does this needing to do things for others go on all the time?

Pt. Why, of course.

Th. How about with me?

Pt. What do you mean?

Th. Remember last time when you asked me about my waiting room? You wanted to help me fix it all up, to do things for me. [*Nothing has as much impact on a patient as to point out a pattern happening in the relationship with the therapist.*]

Pt. Yes, yes, I remember. I would, too.

Th. Isn't this the same kind of pattern: your putting yourself out to do what you can for me?

Pt. Yes, I understand. *(pause)*

Th. So, whatever the reasons for it, you feel

obliged to do things and put yourself out for other people.

Pt. But I've always done this, doctor. *(pause)* [*The patient seems to be resisting even acknowledging the abnormality of her pattern.*]

Th. You've always done this. With John, too?

Pt. Of course.

Th. All right then, the repetitive pattern of this thing seems to have worked out with John too. You were the understanding and giving wife. You had to make allowances for him.

Pt. I did.

Th. You had to make the adjustments. All right. Now, what do you think a pattern of this kind does, first, to your security, and, second, to your feelings about yourself?

Pt. Well, I did find out, doctor, that it didn't help me. With John, he didn't respect me for it.

Th. Uh huh.

Pt. Truly. I mean, you see, at that time I was so happy to be married, you see, and get a position, you know what I mean, to have a husband after all the rest of what happened to me, you see. And I kept living with him all the time because I kept thinking, had to think, he did so much for me. See what I mean?

Th. And did he do much for you?

Pt. Well . . . *(pause)* Yes and no.

Th. I see.

Pt. I kept giving, giving, giving. Like working in the place long hours because I wanted to help him. And then he felt as long as I could do it, he wouldn't. I mean, he was only having fun and I was always working. *(long pause)*

Th. You must have resented this. [*reflecting feeling*]

Pt. I never learn. I keep taking on things on myself all the time. Still get myself in the same messes over and over, no matter who I meet.

Th. No matter where you are and whom you meet the pattern repeats itself. [*restating*]

Pt. Well, I like to do it you see. [*This is an important statement. To acknowledge the values of a neurotic pattern is a sign of insight.*]

Th. You must then get some value out of what you are doing.

Pt. But I'm getting nothing for myself. [*She is not sure about the real value of her pattern.*]

Th. You're getting absolutely nothing for yourself?

Pt. No pleasure, no happiness, not even . . . I like to do things for people, don't misunderstand me, but this isn't compensating me enough within myself doctor, you see.

Th. No?

Pt. And I'm a very unhappy person.

Th. Then why do you have to put yourself out when you get little or nothing in return? *(pause)*

Pt. I guess I do it to be liked. What else do I need to do it for? I was just thinking why do I do it, why do I get into these messes with people. *(pause)*

Th. That's a very good question. Why?

Pt. I *must* have to do it—why, why? *(cries)*

Th. Why do you think?

Pt. I don't know. *(pause)*

Th. Maybe you feel people wouldn't like you unless you did. [*restating what she already has said*]

Pt. Unless I would do something.

Th. If this is so, how do you think this would make you feel?

Pt. Terrible, feeling always they won't like me. *(pause)*

Th. That they'd reject you. And, if this is so, isn't it possible that if you have to keep doing things to keep people liking you, you would either want to run away from the relationship or else continue to have to do things for the person over and over? [*interpreting more deeply*]

Pt. That's the whole thing. Now you see, in this last affair, this man I told you about, you see . . . well the last time we were out to dinner, I don't know, I don't know how he found out these things, but he said to me, "You were married twice." When he said that to me, I never wanted to see him again. He did call me a couple of times, but I just ran away from the whole thing, because the fact that he told me that, I figured that he must know an awful lot more, and I was afraid that he'd tell me more and hurt me, you see. Do you understand? Isn't it the truth?

Th. What do you think he'd know about you or say about you that is so bad?

Pt. Why, he's worse than I am, really. He has someone, and he was absolutely deceitful about the whole thing. *(pause)*

Th. But? *(pause)*

Pt. I feel *I'm* the bad one. Oh, yes, everything, everything bad. *(pause)*

Th. As if you've done something that is terrible?

Pt. I'm afraid to see him again for fear he has found out more about me that's bad, and hurt me by telling me. But that's silly because I haven't done anything. Yet I feel bad. *(pause)*

Th. You seem to be carrying around the feeling that you are no good, the feeling that there's something damaged about yourself.

Pt. Well, there was. I mean, really. *(pause)* Well, what I mean, according to the . . . well, that isn't the normal thing. I've been through so much and everything that . . . that . . . *(pause)*

Th. Like what?

Pt. All in all, I've had to struggle through the whole thing. *(pause)*

Th. You've had to struggle through the whole thing?

Pt. You know, I have absolutely no one to do anything for me, nobody. My mother was sweet, but she didn't know.

Th. So what does this have to do with *you* as a person?

Pt. But look at all that I've had to go through.

Th. You feel that because you had to go through a lot, and had no one to do anything for you, that you are a bad, damaged person?

Pt. It's something like that—like I went through what I went through because I'm bad. [*The thought crosses my mind that the patient may have felt her mother separated from her because she was a bad girl.*]

Th. What you are saying then is this: "Because I am a bad person, and always was bad, I had to go through all this. Because, if I were a good person, then I wouldn't have to go through all this."

Pt. It's terrible how I've had to do this and act as if it didn't matter. Now here I am 50 years old, and I feel as if I am a child, bad, bad—not as good as other people. *(cries)*

Th. Now what material evidences do you have that you are not as good as other people?

Pt. Well, when I was little and mother was away so much, I felt terrible. *(pause)* [*This remark may indicate a source of her feeling "bad."*]

Th. Perhaps you felt she was away because you were bad? Perhaps you felt that if you were good, your mother would have spent more time with you?

Pt. I felt as if I were different, almost as if she didn't really like me. *(pause)*

Th. That must have been frightening to you.

Pt. It was. *(cries)* I felt that when anybody was good to me, I could cry, like I didn't deserve it. *(cries)*

Th. What other evidence do you have that you were not as good as other people?

Pt. Well, I didn't have the education.

Th. How does that jibe with the fact that you were able to build up and handle such a good business?

Pt. I know I am intelligent; that's what's so funny about it.

Th. So that what you know and what you feel are two different things. What else is there different about you now, that makes you feel as if you are bad?

Pt. Well, when I had this operation I felt this was because I was different. *(pause)* I know it's silly. *(pause)*

Th. Again the difference between how you think and how you feel. [*reemphasizing the disparity between thinking and feeling*]

Pt. I know my life isn't any worse than a lot of other people. They do worse than I have done.

Th. It is possible for you to find many things in your life that you don't like. All people do things about which they may have shame. You can catalogue all the bad things you have done and make testimony that sounds overwhelming, but when you compare your life to any other person's life, your sins will probably compare to theirs. So far, you haven't told me a thing that would justify your feeling the way you do. [*This reassurance is given the patient to try to counteract the extreme tension evoked by the material discussed up to this time.*]

Pt. I've told you all the important things in my life that I thought were important. [*The patient apparently grasps at this reassurance.*]

Th. There isn't any more?

Pt. I haven't done anything, doctor. I've never hurt anyone. I mean, an injury of any kind, you know; but it's myself that I injure, I guess. Like I crossed myself up with this man. *(pause)* Three and one-half years I went with him, imagine! And he hasn't called me up in 3 months. But he did call me twice and he . . . *(pause)*

Th. He did call you twice?

Pt. Yes, but after he asked me these questions, I felt things were changed.

Th. You resented the fact that he was prying into your life?

Pt. He was, apparently, wherever he found it out. Maybe someone that he met or some talk maybe around the business. I don't know. You never can tell.

Th. What do you think would be so bad if he knew the truth?

Pt. Then he would be disappointed in me.

Th. Why? What have you done that's so terrible?

Pt. Nothing, except that I didn't tell him everything about myself. I guess I kept a lot of things to myself. I never let anybody into my life . . . except you. [*This may be interpreted as evidence of a good working relationship.*]

Th. Uh huh. *(nodding)*

Pt. I didn't really think it was necessary. You understand, he didn't ask me to marry him or anything like that. You see.

Th. This secretiveness that you kept about yourself, never letting anybody in on your life, could that be a cover for a fear that you will be considered a terrible person?

Pt. Yes, that's it.

Th. But how terrible are you really?

Pt. It's only those things that I told you.

Th. You believe that they make you a terrible person?

Pt. I . . . I don't know.

Th. If you feel you are a terrible person, then you would have to act in a certain way with people, wouldn't you?

Pt. About the way I do now. I have to show them that I'm all right. *(pause)*

Th. In other words, by doing what you do—being secretive, buying presents, giving people things, being nice to them—you cover up the fear that you will show yourself as being a terrible person. [*interpreting her defense mechanism*]

Pt. (pause) Well, I . . . . *(pause)* Well, I find that I do start doing all kinds of things, and I am always fearful that they'll leave me. Like with this man, I kept it up for a long time, but I felt mad about how things were going. *(pause)*

Th. Mad?

Pt. Well, I sort of resented that with him; see, we'd only go out maybe once a week, you see.

Th. Uh huh.

Pt. Yes, and well, that's really the only affair I had, since John died. And so only once a week, and, as I say, I never used to see him over the weekends, and, of course, that did something to me too. That gave me an inferiority complex, to think he didn't think enough of me to give me more of his time. You see what I mean?

Th. Mm hmm.

Pt. Well, I felt that at least I had someone interested in me, and that's something. You see what I mean? Someone to go to the theater with, even if it was someone that saw me only once a week, instead of nobody at all. Well, and it was something to look forward to, and that was that. But still I knew that it wasn't right. I knew that he wasn't treating me right. That it wasn't the right thing to do. Do you understand?

Th. You must have suffered a great deal because of this conflict.

Pt. Just going along and suffering, and not realizing it until I came to see you, never realizing how I *should* be, and am not. I mean, other people get some happiness out of life. I didn't get any, and I'm not getting any.

Th. Why do you think you aren't getting any happiness from life?

Pt. Because there is no one I can feel close to.

Th. Why do you think that is?

Pt. I'm afraid of being hurt.

Th. You're afraid of being hurt. Rejected?

Pt. That's right, and it takes a lot out of me, you see. When I've been with people, I never say anything or contribute anything to the conversation, as far as myself is concerned, because I'm very much more interested in what *they're* doing—do you know what I mean?—than to tell them anything about what I've been doing. What I do doesn't matter—I mean it's all the other people. With me it's everybody else, and I just don't count.

Th. All right, now, there must have been a reason why you minimized yourself so much. Could it be that you just accepted the fact that you were a terrible person?

Pt. Well, certainly, well, I've told you things that I've never told, and never would have told, anyone else, honestly, because I would be ashamed.

Th. Because telling them such things would make them feel about you what you felt about yourself. [*interpreting her tendency toward secretiveness*]

Pt. Maybe that's why I did those things.

Th. Mm hmm.

Pt. Like put on a front, and act dumb and try to please.

Th. Mm hmm.

Pt. Exactly, you see, it's the same way if someone would ask me to go out. For instance, if a man would ask me to go out. It's my own fault that I don't go because I think that I have to give something to him. Now I'm being very honest with you. Do you see what I mean?

Th. You mean you'd do anything *they* wanted to please them, and you'd feel that was not what *you* wanted to do?

Pt. Do you understand? I mean to sleep with them. If they take me out, I feel, well, why would they otherwise want to take me out? Do you understand? Doctor, that's a terrible thing, so I don't go out.

Th. Isn't that the same thing we've been talking about, that you feel the only reason they want you is so that you can do something for *them,* to give *them* something? [*relating what she has said to a general pattern*]

Pt. Well, that's the thing that hurt me with this other man. To see me just to go out once every week; I felt that that was all that he was interested in. And you know I'm not like that.

Th. If you're not like that, what else could you have done?

Pt. Well, all right, what could I do about it?

Th. We could at first find out what this is all about. We're doing that now, and we see a pattern in your life that goes back as far as you can remember.

Pt. It's terrible. That's right.

Th. The same thing, that you feel that you can't be wanted for yourself.

Pt. Unless I could give something or just

please people. *(pause)* [*The patient seems to have achieved some insight.*]

Th. Unless you give something—money, time, your services—or unless you sleep with a man.

Pt. Isn't that terrible, doctor? Truly, I mean I'm not common; I haven't any of those things really in me.

Th. It's just that you feel forced to comply.

Pt. I shouldn't ever see any man unless he is worthy.

Th. Mm hmm.

Pt. Sure, then it would be worthwhile, you would get something out of it. *(pause)* I want to be respected for myself.

Th. Yes.

Pt. Well, I didn't give anything to this other man. He's very nicely situated, and I wouldn't do that because I . . . *(pause)*

Th. Because you . . .

Pt. Because I felt that he didn't respect me. I felt that he only went out with me once a week just for that, do you understand?

Th. Well, it's going to take a little time for you to think this thing through and see how you've got yourself in a kind of vicious cycle. You may be afraid to break out of that cycle. The next time you get into a situation with a person, you will be tempted to repeat the same pattern, to feel that you aren't liked for yourself, that you aren't going to be respected, that you will be found out for your past. It's going to be hard. [*emphasizing the compulsiveness of the neurotic pattern*]

Pt. I am ashamed of my past.

Th. What really is wrong with your past?

Pt. Well, I just felt it was bad.

Th. What particularly?

Pt. Just that people would think I was common and . . . to do that sort of thing. *(pause)*

Th. What sort of thing?

Pt. What I did. *(pause)*

Th. Which is what?

Pt. Well, having that other married man in between my marriages. [*This is a pocket of guilt that must torture the patient.*]

Th. I see.

Pt. And then the way John treated me, too, that hurt me terribly. And then this last thing that didn't turn out right.

Th. Let's take the thing about John. [*focusing on the situation with John to see how the repetitive pattern operates here*]

Pt. He ignored me.

Th. I see.

Pt. Well, doctor, it's not a nice thing to have it known your husband ignores you.

Th. Were you sure other people knew this?

Pt. Well . . . I thought they must. *(pause)* But I see what you mean, that I go about blaming myself for everything. *(pause)* [*Insight seems to be dawning on her.*]

Th. All right, what about this love affair between your marriages? [*again focusing to explore for a pattern*]

Pt. I felt very guilty about it because he was married.

Th. You had a need for affection and love and understanding. [*This reassuring interpretation is given to help counteract her guilt.*]

Pt. Yes, doctor, and he gave that to me.

Th. Do you have to be ashamed of such needs? Do you think such needs are abnormal?

Pt. You mean all people need this. I see what you mean, doctor, I see that.

Th. Now what about this last man, are you ashamed of what happened there? [*I continue to explore the pattern by focusing on her last affair.*]

Pt. I really couldn't go on with it because it took too much out of me.

Th. Couldn't you have been reaching for the same affection and understanding, and not really have got it with him?

Pt. He couldn't give it; he was too involved. I did everything I could.

Th. But the interesting thing is that you see that you haven't done anything unusual or really bad; yet you turn all of these incidents against yourself.

Pt. Then how can I, doctor, how can I rise above this thing, and get it out of my system, so to speak? How can I get this over?

Th. Well that's what our job is in therapy here. Our job is to get you out of this morass and for you to see if you are as terrible a person as you imagine or whether you might be mistaken in some ways. [*It will be noted that whenever the patient asks for an answer, she is told that we will have to work the problem out between us.*]

Pt. I see.

Th. What do *you* think the answer is?

Pt. For me to convince myself that I just don't have to please everybody all the time.

Th. In other words, not have to give presents and practically stand on your head to convince people you amount to something.

Pt. *(laughing)* Really, isn't that awful, doctor? And, I mean, I did feel bad about it myself, I mean I did that. This is something I'm going to stop. All this nonsense. You see what I mean? [*Naturally it is too early for the patient to have integrated any insight; yet her verbalization of determination to change is encouraging.*]

Th. You mean you feel it's unnecessary to give, give, give, all the time?

Pt. I felt that the only thing I have to give

them is something material. [*more indications of insight*]

Th. Material. How could you ever have a real friendship on this basis?

Pt. Oh, I don't know; it's my own fault. [*Self-recriminations emerge.*]

Th. It's your fault only because you felt there was nothing else for you to give. [*The session time is up, but since my next session is open, due to a cancellation, and because we are dealing with important material, I decide to go on.*]

Pt. I shouldn't do this any more. [*This determination is easier said than done, due to the habit patterns that must have been established.*]

Th. It's going to be very hard to give up the old patterns. You'll automatically find yourself reacting the same way. [*To warn the patient that her old patterns will persist even though she realizes their futility is a wise move and helps prevent discouragement.*]

Pt. I may lose all my friends, but that's all right. They're no friends of mine, if they're that kind, where they expect me to give all the time and where they just don't take me for myself. [*The warning also serves to bolster the patient's determination to experiment with new ways of life.*]

Th. Uh huh.

Pt. (laughing) Isn't that awful doctor? People are funny, you know. Don't you think I'm terrible to be this way? [*more masochism*]

Th. Now you're tearing yourself down in front of me by saying what a terrible person you are. [*interpreting what she is doing*]

Pt. Of course not, doctor; I don't really mean that.

Th. Do you think you have the right to expect people to accept you for yourself, instead of for what you do for them? [*challenging her verbal determination to change her compulsive pattern*]

Pt. I do, sure, I lose all my own self-respect along with it, you see, when it's the other way. I only see that now, not before. Before, I thought it was the thing to do, not because I felt I had nothing else to give, but because I thought I wanted to help everyone, be nice to them in that way, you see. That goes all the way down the line with my family. (pause)

Th. Uh huh.

Pt. All the way down the line, you see. Gosh, I've given, I mean, I've given more to my family than, well, than I've ever had for myself really. And for myself, I hate to spend anything on me really, you know.

Th. Really?

Pt. Yes, really.

Th. Why?

Pt. Oh, I don't know. I'd rather do it for somebody else. That's one of those things.

Th. Do you think you should start spending money on yourself?

Pt. I should.

Th. And not for anybody else?

Pt. I should.

Th. Nobody else?

Pt. Well, you see, this man that I was going around with for 3 years, he used to send me things. He really was very nice that way to me. He was really the nicest that I've met so far. At least . . .

Th. At least he gave you *things*. That's something.

Pt. At least he did. That's something. But that isn't for me doctor, though.

Th. That isn't for you?

Pt. That man isn't for me.

Th. No?

Pt. He was too involved, and he isn't for me. There's not the warmth. (pause) If he were the sort of a person that really loved me, he'd be a little bit more warm; he'd come around. (pause) [*Her protest is a little too vigorous and points to a wish to resume the relationship. Apparently her break-up with this man was the precipitating factor in her present upset.*]

Th. But he didn't call you?

Pt. Well, he called me twice, I told you.

Th. Mm hmm.

Pt. And I didn't encourage him; that's it, you see.

Th. I see.

Pt. I mean, there's another thing again. That 3½ years where I should have had really a wonderful time—all in all, I didn't. I suffered through it.

Th. You sat around waiting?

Pt. For him to call. You see what I mean?

Th. And you wonder why you got yourself in this mess?

Pt. Oh, now I see it, little by little as the dawn is coming.

Th. You stood in the dark for many years.

Pt. Yes, but it isn't good. That isn't good, doctor. I mean showing myself how much will power I have; that isn't good for me, doctor. You don't want to live that way, challenging your own happiness. That's what I've been doing, you see. You understand? Never ever doing what I want to do, always doing what the other person wants to do, you see. And never giving in to a feeling, you understand, and that's a terrible thing. That isn't being strong. You're really killing yourself. You're killing everything that's in you. I only know that now that you've just . . . talking to you about these things. I never thought of it that way before. But I realize now just what it has done to me. It's almost inhuman really. And I don't want to be that way.

Th. You have a right not to.

Pt. I'm really a very unhappy person and have never been happy as far back as I can remember. *(pause)*

Th. If you begin to think into your whole life, things will begin taking shape. As you yourself say, this did not start just yesterday; your difficulty goes back much farther.

Pt. Well, you see, I really didn't have any love in the first place. All I can remember when I was 5 years old was all commotion. And then my mother was dispossessed from where she lived and all, and didn't have anything, I mean. That's the thing that stood out in my mind. Even the gas stove was taken out, you see, the little house and all. And then I remember going into this other place, and then we were all taken away, see, and that had a, oh, that made a tremendous hurt in me, you see. And I didn't have any childhood really. Like kids have friends and they come in and have a lot of fun and play after school, and all that. I didn't have any of that, see. So then my cousin was very kind. But there wasn't anything there, you see. She was married to this very old man, and it was a very funny relationship there too, you know. And I felt that I was just a relative, you know, and it wasn't my mother, it was my cousin and it was more or less pity that she did it for me. You see what I mean? So as soon as I was able to go out and work, I did. I didn't have any fun at all like other children, anything like other children have. You know how children are brought up in a home and have a lot of little parties and things, you know, doctor. It does something to you. So when that first man came along, I married him to get out of all this. But it didn't work. The one kindness, I mean warmth, that I felt was the man in between. [*The patient is exploring the genetic determinants of her devaluated self-esteem.*]

Th. Perhaps that's why he's so important to you.

Pt. It was the nicest experience, the nicest in my whole life. *(pause)*

Th. How did it terminate?

Pt. He died. Yes, and we were friends to the end. Before he died, I married John, and I didn't have anything more to do with him. He was happy that I was married, of course; he felt that that had been the thing he wanted to happen. He wanted for me to be established in the community. That's really what he had in mind.

Th. It was a good experience. [*attempting to alleviate her guilt*]

Pt. The best thing that's ever happened to me, you see.

Th. Why should you be ashamed of it, then?

Pt. Well, because I'd hidden it so long I feel doubts about it now that it's way in the past.

Th. Perhaps you've been ashamed too much for what has happened?

Pt. You're right; I have nothing to hide. I haven't killed anyone. I haven't hurt anyone.

Th. It was a good experience for you.

Pt. You know, that's true. Oh, it's really terrible, doctor, but that's the situation I'm in. I'm in a very bad way. [*The patient is beginning to realize that she has been ashamed of a relationship that had much meaning for her.*]

Th. Maybe you can begin breaking out of that situation—in little ways with different people.

Pt. Oh, how I'd like to do that.

Th. It may take a lot of courage. [*warning her of the hardships involved*]

Pt. But this, what I've been going through, is so bad. [*This indicates a realization that her patterns cause her much suffering.*]

Th. It might frighten you. [*more warnings*]

Pt. I couldn't be worse off. [*She again responds well.*]

Th. It's going to take time. [*additional cautions*]

Pt. Sure it will. You know what? Tonight I was invited to a big dinner, and these people invited me and I thought I would *(laughs)* send them a present, some nice bottles of Scotch. [*This may be a turning point in that the insight she has gained may be translated into action, at least in her mind.*]

Th. I see.

Pt. The idea occurred to me. *(laughs)*

Th. The idea occurred to you?

Pt. I won't send it. [*If she can follow through on this, and if she discovers that she is not rejected for her failure to give presents, it may begin to undermine her neurotic pattern.*]

Th. Think you can go through with it? [*challenging her determination*]

Pt. But I was going to, though, this afternoon. I mean, I was going to send it before I came here.

Th. Do you think you can go there without sending or bringing anything?

Pt. I think I can all right. Thanks for helping me, and do you think I'm going to be all right?

Th. Having the desire to get well is nine-tenths of the battle. But you mustn't be impatient. You're going to find that you will want to act the way you always have, even though you understand how destructive it is to you. [*again warning her of the possibility of a relapse*]

Pt. Yes, I know. But you do think I will be all right?

Th. You seem to have a doubt about it. [*To tell her that she will get well, which is what she wants to hear, would put me in an omniscient position. Actually, I do not know that she will get well; all I know is that she has the best chance of getting well if she is active in therapy. I do not wish to discourage her, so I focus on the doubts that lurk behind her question.*]

Pt. Well, I've had this so long, It's a long time, isn't it doctor? However, I hope that I'm going to be able to get something out of living.

Th. You really want to, don't you?

Pt. Because this is, I mean, I've suffered, and it's been so hard for me.

Th. The important thing is to understand your patterns of living thoroughly, see how they cross you up, why they occurred and are still occurring, and then challenge them.

Pt. Well, I hope I can do this, doctor. Then I'll see you Monday at 11:40.

Th. That's right.

Pt. All right, thank you, 'bye, 'bye.

In this session the patient has arrived at several insights. She sees a pattern weaving through her life and connects it with what happened to her in her childhood. She realizes the values of her neurotic patterns, but also appreciates their destructive effects. At the end of the session she challenges her need to pursue the pattern of her giving presents to be loved.

FIFTH SESSION

The patient here shows signs of utilizing her insight in the direction of change.

Pt. Doctor, I bought you a nice pencil. I noticed that you were looking for one the other day.

Th. Thank you. *(not accepting pencil)* But why did you get it? [*Could this be her "giving" pattern coming through again in our relationship?*]

Pt. I felt it would be nice to get it.

Th. All right now, why did you feel that way? Mind you, I appreciate the gesture, but, as you know, we have to inquire into everything that happens here.

Pt. 'Cause I wanted to help you. [*This would seem to corroborate my suspicion.*]

Th. *(laughing)* Isn't that the same thing you've always been doing, helping people, being nice and considerate?

Pt. *(laughing)* I suppose it is, and I suppose I

tell myself that's because *he* needs it. Well anyway, I've been quite well the past few days. *(puts pencil into bag)*

Th. Uh huh. *(smiling)*

Pt. How have *you* been, doctor?

Th. Quite well, thank you, and you?

Pt. Well, doctor, things have been a lot better for me. I find myself a lot more active. The other day I joined an art class. I had a card on me given me by a friend a long while ago. I put it away and then remembered it. I began to think I should get active. So, well, you know, I took that art class lesson on Friday afternoon, and I enjoyed it. [*Her getting out of her house into outside activities is an encouraging sign.*]

Th. You did.

Pt. It was fun. Yes, and Friday evening, what did I do? Oh, I went up and read to the blind for an hour and a half. And then I went to a movie, saw "Foreign Affair." Have you seen it?

Th. No, I haven't.

Pt. With Marlene Dietrich; it was excellent. And Saturday I didn't do very much. I stayed home, and took a little walk in the afternoon. Yesterday, I went to church in the morning, came back home and read the Sunday papers. In the evening I listened to the radio. I did some things around the apartment, hung some curtains. That's about all. [*This sounds like a break in her neurotic pattern with a lifting of depression.*]

Th. I see. *(pause)*

Pt. I feel better. The depression isn't as depressed as it was.

Th. And you find yourself being a bit more active.

Pt. Yes, and sort of releasing some things. I mean, this is only an instance. I was coming from the movies on Friday evening and I'd been looking for some large serving platters, you know. Well, before I saw you, I wouldn't even cross the street. I saw one in the window across the street, so I crossed over and at least looked at it before I would leave, and had the ambition to do it. Little things like that encourage me.

Th. I see.

Pt. And I had another dream.

Th. Mm hmm.

Pt. I dreamed I was jumping over a creek of water. And had my pocketbook in one arm, and I dropped it in the water because I had to use my two hands to save myself from falling in the water. And then after that I don't know how these people came around, but there were a couple of . . . like nurses or something, and one girl was a tall girl with red hair, and apparently she was queer because she was making advances to me. Said how wonderful it would be if she and I got together, and that's all I remember about it. [*The patient used the symbol of the pocketbook also in her first dream. What the significance of this may be will be explored. In this dream she drops her pocketbook to save herself from falling in water. Following this, a woman makes homosexual advances toward her. The latter, an eruption of deep unconscious wishes and fears, is on a different level from the characterologic conflicts we have been working on so far.*]

Th. Any associations to the dream? [*To give her my associations would have been disastrous.*]

Pt. There were a couple of nurses like, yes, just in white.

Th. I see.

Pt. That's all I can remember, doctor. [*This inability to associate may be the product of repression. If, as I suspect, she is dealing in the dream with deep unconscious fears, she may be expected to show resistance.*]

Th. What about the stream?

Pt. I don't know. I don't recall ever having jumped over a stream.

Th. What does an episode like that suggest? Here you're walking and you're crossing a creek.

Pt. That had some water in between and I had to jump over it, you see, and I thought it would be an easy jump. Instead of that I almost fell in, and then I had the pocketbook in my arm and I had to grab hold of something that was something like a log or some arrangement there. But I didn't fall in and I got up over this trespass, or whatever it was. And then this, this girl, these two girls were there, and I don't know how it happened, but kind of a homely looking girl with red hair approached me. That I remember.

Th. Red hair?

Pt. Yes, I don't know what that is. It reminds me of nothing. *(pause)*

Th. I see.

Pt. She was ugly. *(pause)*

Th. Ugly? [*I hope to stimulate associations by these questions.*]

Pt. Well, she wasn't nice.

Th. But she was making a pass at you.

Pt. Oh, oh yes. Oh, I wouldn't think of it . . . nothing like that.

Th. What about your ideas about homosexuality?

Pt. Well, I . . . it disgusts me. I think it's an awful thing.

Th. Awful?

Pt. Well, I mean, with women particularly, I mean. *(pause)*

Th. Mm hmm.

Pt. Yes, I think it's awful, two women or two men. Because, I mean, anything isn't normal like that.

Th. Do you know anything about homosexuality?

Pt. Well, after all, I've lived a little while, doctor, and I've heard things and that sort of thing, but I've never entered into anything like that.

Th. But you haven't any idea as to what the reasons for it are?

Pt. No. . . . Is it ever normal, doctor?

Th. Well, in puberty and adolescence children of the same sex often experiment sexually with each other.

Pt. Until they don't . . . until they know better, is that it, doctor?

Th. Well, until they go to a relationship with a person of the opposite sex. Now, very often when a child is brought up so that she is afraid of the opposite sex, the only type of sexual activity that she can stand, because she is afraid of the other, is this early type of activity. A lot of homosexual people have never quite developed normally. They've sort of been arrested at a certain stage of their development. [*The purpose of this explanation is to attempt to allay a sense of guilt and to encourage associations to homosexuality, if this is a problem.*]

Pt. In other words, timid or bashful or something.

Th. Timid or bashful or frightened. Or very frequently what happens is that a person may have a bad experience with a person of the opposite sex, like being rejected. Then they may continue to be afraid of rejection, and they may prefer a person of the same sex.

Pt. Well, I've never had anything like that, so that as far as I can see there is nothing like that. [*The patient seems to repudiate the exploration of the area of homosexuality.*]

Th. To get back to the dream, do you have any other associations?

Pt. I don't know, doctor.

Th. What about the pocketbook?

Pt. Well, I had this pocketbook and I dropped it to save myself from falling into the water. *(pause)*

Th. What does the pocketbook remind you of?

Pt. Should it remind me of something?

Th. No, not necessarily. But what ideas come to your mind when you think of pocketbook? *(pause)*

Pt. Well . . . this is funny, you know, doctor, because . . . well, you know how people talk . . . they talk about a woman's private parts . . . some people do . . . as a pocketbook. Isn't that awful?

Th. A pocketbook is often a sexual organ in dreams.

Pt. Is that so? *(pause)*

Th. And in the process of jumping over and crossing a creek, the implication would be that you lost your femininity, and you're left like a sexless person. [*interpreting an aspect of the dream to encourage further associations*]

Pt. Well, that's something like it, isn't it? I mean with this last experience that I had, isn't it, doctor?

Th. So that your fear is that the only thing that is left is you as a sexless person.

Pt. You mean the pocketbook that I dropped?

Th. You dropped your pocketbook.

Pt. Yes, it's true, I dropped my pocketbook, and I was really quite disturbed about it, that I dropped it, because there was some money in it. But that's all that happened. And then that ugly looking red head on the top of it. She had to come along, and say that to me, that she and I would be wonderful together.

Th. Well, in the dream, if you are left with no femininity, your relations with men would be gone. The idea then might be that the next best thing is a relationship with a woman. [*Interpreting more deeply. It is possible that the patient feels that she has lost her sexual attractiveness and her femininity. This may symbolize a loss of self and account for some of her depression.*]

Pt. Well, I wouldn't do that in spite of it. I'd rather go in alone, 'cause that would be awful.

Th. Do you really feel that you've lost your capacity to establish a relationship with a man?

Pt. Well, it seems so, you know.

Th. Admittedly, you've gone through something pretty terrible, with the experiences as you've reported them to me.

Pt. Well, I have, all the way down the line. And I think that's why I've been afraid to take a chance in many instances where I did have opportunities, don't you see? And I saw this friend of mine yesterday getting in a car. He lives just a block or two from me, and I saw him getting in his car, with one of these women that he's involved with.

Th. With *one* of them?

Pt. Well, there's two of them. I thought I told you there were two. I was walking, and I just happened to see it, so I stopped. I was on the other side of the street and I didn't want to pass. *(pause)*

Th. How did you feel about this?

Pt. I'm better off without him.

Th. Mm hmm.

Pt. Oh, I know I am, because it would only be worse.

Th. You'd get yourself into a bigger mess?

Pt. Possibly.

Th. Do you feel that you just don't want to get involved with *any* men?

Pt. No, I don't feel that way.

Th. You don't feel that way?

Pt. No, I do not. I mean, I'm game. I'll take a chance if there's a good prospect in view. Why not? It's the only way you can succeed. Isn't it? [*This verbalized determination is hopeful.*]

Th. It would seem so.

Pt. I hope I never . . . I don't keep on making mistakes, that's all. That's the thing I'd like to avoid, if it can be helped.

Th. Mm hmm.

Pt. Well, that would be fine if it happens. Of course, the way I'm going along now, I'm not going out with anybody. I don't really have a chance to meet anyone. But that's all right. That's all right. That'll take care of itself. *(pause)*

Th. Within a few months things may be different. [*said tentatively*]

Pt. Well, who knows; you never know anyway. *(pause)* At any rate I'm feeling better. . . . Yes, I'm feeling better, and I'm happier, and I'd like to have a little more activity though. You see, I could do it; I feel well enough. I feel better since I've been coming to see you.

Th. Mm hmm.

Pt. One should be busy. *(pause)* [*Her desire to be busy is commendable and evidence of her having overcome some derpession. I get a feeling at this point that the patient may not be motivated for deep therapy, involving exploration of the more repressed unconscious conflicts. She may be satisfied with a break up of her neurotic character patterns, which will lead to a more effective kind of life devoid of her former unhappiness. In view of her age, this may constitute an optimal goal.*]

Th. You should be busy?

Pt. Well, because I'm an active person. *(pause)*

Th. Can you, would you object to getting a job? [*At this point I decide to work on her finding some useful occupation or recreation to give her a purpose in living, greater than she has had.*]

Pt. Oh no, not one bit. You mean be ashamed?

Th. Do you feel that you just wouldn't want to work?

Pt. Oh, no, no. That doesn't matter to me, doctor. I like to.

Th. Is there any specific thing you're most interested in?

Pt. Well, you know I thought of taking up a course in antique furniture. I like antiques a great deal. And then my friends talked me out of that. I was going to enlist on the fourth of October, and they said, "Oh, you'll get up there with a lot of old women and you won't get any fun out of it." Well, I wanted to do that, but they talked me out of that. Now that's all over. There's several good schools in New York. But they're all closed now, and I can't get in. But I wanted to do that. I felt that it would be nice.

Th. Well, are you interested in antiques?

Pt. Yes, I would like to do that work. And I mean I could develop what taste I have. And I thought maybe I would go further with it, you know.

Th. How did you let them talk you out of it?

Pt. Well, because I just listen to everybody. I go around asking advice, you know. Well, that's how I get in trouble.

Th. I see.

Pt. Well, they felt that I wouldn't meet anybody that I'd be interested in or something like that. And I wasn't thinking about that. They said, "You'll meet a lot of old women up there."

Th. Well, the school is one thing. Your contacts with people outside are another thing.

Pt. Exactly, I mean, that's it.

Th. The study of antiques can be a very exciting thing.

Pt. Wonderful.

Th. You have to use your brain; you have to know what's in the field.

Pt. And every home presents a different problem. *(pause)*

Th. Every home has a different problem.

Pt. Don't you see. So I thought it would be nice. 'Cause I'm accustomed to all that, because every day in my business there were always different problems cropping up.

Th. When does the next term begin in this school?

Pt. I think in the spring, you see, I missed that.

Th. Perhaps you can take specific courses without matriculating. [*This is a direct suggestion presented to her as a possibility for action.*]

Pt. Well, I'll find out. But, you see, I did want to go to a good school, naturally.

Th. Naturally.

Pt. 'Cause I felt if I'm going to learn something, I'll learn something from the people who have the best knowledge.

Th. But even though you can't get into a good school to matriculate, perhaps you can get your application in, and you can take scattered courses here and there, and also get some good books on the subject. Perhaps you can start getting into the field so that when you start taking the courses you'll have a pretty good background. [*I am pushing her a bit here to get in-*

volved in something that may turn out to be of value to her.]

Pt. I think there is a school that has a few classes, you know. Let me find out what's going on around.

Th. Are you able to do it? [*challenging her as to her ability to follow through*]

Pt. Well, I'll tell you what I'll do. *Vogue* has about five or six pages of different schools, you know, on adult education. Supposing I look around. *(pause)* The trouble with me is that I haven't enough confidence in myself. I'll tell you why. My friends ask me to go shopping with them 'cause they like the things I select, you see. And I see very often people follow through on things that I've just talked about. I notice it, but they would never say to me that you gave us this idea or something, you know.

Th. Well, maybe you can make a different start. [*What I do here is get her off the track of beating herself with how badly she is treated by others, focusing on a positive course of action.*]

Pt. Well, that would be nice. You see, when I get in contact with people I'm accustomed to, I know how to talk with them, and I think I can sell somebody a bill of goods if it's necessary. I mean, if they would have enough confidence in me, doctor, that if I make suggestions they would feel that I could follow through on it. But everybody talks me out of everything I want to do, doctor. Really it's . . . but why do I let them?

Th. Why do you let them?

Pt. Because, well, I haven't enough confidence in myself.

Th. Precisely in what way?

Pt. Don't you see what I mean?

Th. You feel you make mistakes?

Pt. Well, everyone does.

Th. Everyone does, but your ability to feel that even though you made a mistake, you're all right, would be the liberating thing for you.

Pt. Why do I feel as if I amount to nothing?

Th. That's a good question.

Pt. As far back as I remember, as a child, because of the way I had been going from one place to another, I didn't feel loved. I just didn't feel that I had anything. I felt that I just sort, just had to push myself and give in order to be liked and approved of.

Th. Now that wound seems to be carrying over to your present-day life, and it's necessary for you to evaluate yourself and see what you really are.

Pt. Yes, I think I have very excellent taste and can use my own judgment. *(pause)* Except, doctor, as you say, I haven't any confidence. You see, I feel that lack of education very, very much. It gives me, in the sense of the word, an inferiority complex.

Th. Can you explain that?

Pt. I really do, well, I'll tell you about it. I've worked hard for everything, for everything that I have. That is really working hard, you see. And very often I'm around people, and there are lots of things that I'd like to say, but I'm afraid to say them for fear that I will make a grammatical error, in the way that I express myself. Therefore, I just sit and listen, and never become, hardly ever become, a part of the conversation. It's true. And I thought when I'd sell the business, I was going to go and take up some language, and so forth, and I didn't do it, because I didn't have the ambition. Now that you've been talking to me, I feel entirely different. I felt lost.

Th. You felt lost, absolutely lost, and didn't know where to start.

Pt. Don't you see?

Th. If you take up antiques, you could also take up language and things to improve your vocabulary, if that's what you want. Antiques could give you valuable topics for discussion and develop you. [*I do not feel that it would be too fruitful to continue talking about her devaluated self-esteem and I focus on her doing something about herself.*]

Pt. Certainly, and I may have an office, and open a nice little office like you have here. And get some clients and give the work out to be done, and all of that.

Th. You've got enough contacts?

Pt. Oh, wonderful. I know some of the nicest people in New York, really, and they all like me.

Th. I see.

Pt. You see. *(pause)*

Th. And it's necessary to start right in then, if that's what you decide.

Pt. All right, no matter what.

Th. No matter what.

Pt. Just start in—all right.

Th. Start right in and get the ground laid. It might take you a little while to get into the field.

Pt. But, of course. It's what I want to do.

Th. After all, you've got to have something to do. Every person has to be involved in something he feels is important.

Pt. I see, to get some pleasure out of it. Doctor, then later I could go to Europe and study some of the furniture over there. I would really have a wonderful time.

Th. Mm hmm.

Pt. It's a tremendous outlook. I mean it could grow and grow to no end of things. [*Her*

enthusiasm means little unless she does something about her plans in reality. This we will have to wait for.]

Th. The educational value of it alone, without even considering the practical value is important—the different periods and things.

Pt. That alone, too, is wonderful for the mind.

Th. Yes.

Pt. Well, those are the things I need, you see. I've never had any of it. The only thing I've ever known was to just work and work and worry, and that's all. But that's all over now. It's all over and I feel that that's a wonderful thing. *(pause)*

Th. Have you traveled through the museums and seen the period pieces?

Pt. No.

Th. You never have?

Pt. Never.

Th. Perhaps that's one thing you can put on your agenda before I see you again next week. Perhaps you could go to the Metropolitan Museum. [*again a positive suggestion to encourage action*]

Pt. All right. Is that up here on Fifth Avenue, doctor, on eighty . . .

Th. Yes, on 83rd Street.

Pt. I could just casually go around and see the old American, the various periods. It'll show all the different things . . .

Th. All right, now that's the first step. And also before I see you next time, perhaps you may want to start taking other steps in regard to getting the best training in antique furniture. [*I am being as positive in my suggestions as I can be without being too directive.*]

Pt. That's what I want, you see.

Th. Perhaps you can get matriculated, even if it's in the spring.

Pt. Then I can look onward. *(pause)* Materials, designs, fabrics—all interesting.

Th. You may get a kick out of this.

Pt. Oh, I think it will be a wonderful thing for me. See, I could have been in it already if I went before.

Th. Of course, you were down in the dumps then.

Pt. Oh, but so low, you see, but so low.

Th. You were down in the dumps.

Pt. Yes, well it's all going to work out all right, isn't it, doctor?

Th. It has to if you really set your heart on it. [*implying her responsibility in making things turn out right*]

Pt. I must. I just must, that's all. It's ridiculous to just absolutely have no confidence in what you think, and what people who haven't nearly as much sense as I have say . . . I mean, I follow their advice. Do you understand?

Th. Why do you follow their advice?

Pt. Same old thing.

Th. Same old thing?

Pt. Well, now about my friends. Tell me doctor, something about that. I mustn't let them all go and neglect them. Well, now how do I go about it? *(pause)* [*The patient wants me to give her the answers here, which I must try to avoid.*]

Th. Well, now let's see if we can identify the problem. What is the problem?

Pt. Well, now, it's that I have nobody close.

Th. Do people call you?

Pt. Well, now they haven't called me. I have to call them, don't you see, call and say "hello." I can do that.

Th. What people, what friends do you have?

Pt. Well I have quite a few. Now a girl called me this morning. She's the girl that I always take out, you know, well, to lunch occasionally, and pay her checks and everything. She calls herself the perennial guest. Well, I mean, she never attempts to pay the check, so this morning she called me up and said, "Look, I'd love to go to the Horse Show tonight." She didn't say, "Would you like to go?" She said that she would like to go. So then I felt, well, now, Dr. Wolberg showed me that I shouldn't be taking everybody out, and all that and paying. [*The patient apparently has integrated the material we discussed in the last session.*]

Th. So what did you say?

Pt. So I said, "Well, I have an engagement this evening." Well, before I would have had to take her to dinner and the Horse Show.

Th. Did you want to go to the Horse Show?

Pt. Well, I don't want to keep taking her out.

Th. All right, but if you wanted to go to the Horse Show, mightn't you have said to her, "Fine, why don't *you* buy the tickets and take *me* out to dinner then."

Pt. I see.

Th. Well, that's what you *might* have said to her.

Pt. Well, she didn't ask me to go. She said that *she* would like to go. Why didn't she say would *I* like to go to the Horse Show tonight?

Th. Why do you think?

Pt. To pay her way somewhere, I know.

Th. To sponge on you?

Pt. Then I don't need her for this. I should ask her to take me out sometime.

Th. Put her on the spot this way. But it would be hard. [*challenging her determination*]

Pt. I know, but you have to do it.

Th. You have to do it to get these sponges off your neck.

Pt. She'll have more respect for me.

Th. She'll have more respect for you, and for herself, too.

Pt. And then I'll handle it that way. Yes.

Th. Now with your other friends?

Pt. Well, of course, there are a lot of married couples, the carryovers from the time we all went out together. So I see them, and, of course, they entertain me in their homes, and then I entertain them. Now that's all right, isn't it?

Th. Who were the people who objected to your going ahead with your antique course? [*I dodge the question here by posing another.*]

Pt. This one girl that I know in Pennsylvania that's married. She's a very aggressive person.

Th. How often do you see her?

Pt. I don't see her very often.

Th. Do you have a desire to talk to her at all?

Pt. Not necessarily. Now that's another thing. I don't tell people what I do. That's another thing that's wrong with me. I keep all these things to myself.

Th. You're entitled to do what *you* want. [*encouraging her to think of herself*]

Pt. Yes, yes, and I'll do that. And that's true of a lot of other things too. But I'll cross my bridges when I come to them.

Th. You've got to repair your bridges now, but you've got to do it slowly and surely.

Pt. Surely. I'm glad I mentioned it to you, you see. I'm very glad I mentioned it to you, about the antiques.

Th. And it should open up many, many avenues to you.

Pt. Oh, it'll be wonderful. I'll meet people again. There's the contacts, you see, which will be nice for me. And it's creative too. It's nice to take a room and fix it and see that it looks so nice after you've worked on it, worked on it, you know.

Th. Mm hmm.

Pt. I think I'll enjoy it. Oh, I had thought of it, but they had talked me out of it, you see. That's probably why I don't tell about a lot of these things that I feel. I shouldn't listen.

Th. You apparently get yourself into a situation with people in which you're kind of—well, they feel that they've got to boss you around and tell you what to do.

Pt. Well, a lot of people call me and ask my opinion of things, too.

Th. (*It is time for the session to end.*) I see. All right, then I'll see you again next week.

Pt. Goodbye, doctor.

In this session the patient begins to make positive plans for the future. An attempt to deal with deeper unconscious material is revealed in a dream; however, the patient resists this effort and seeks to keep the interview on her immediate environmental situation. I act more directive in suggesting a positive course of action.

SIXTH SESSION

This session is illustrative of sessions in which not much seems to be happening. The working-through process may be going on, nevertheless.

Pt. Hello, how are you. I'm sorry to be late. I couldn't get a taxi. The rain is awful. How are you?

Th. Fine, and you? [*One might suspect resistance when a patient comes late, but the weather is bad and her explanation is a reasonable one.*]

Pt. Very good. *(pause)* I've been really very quiet, thinking over the situation, giving it a great deal of thought.

Th. Mm hmm.

Pt. Agreeing with you all along the line, that you have got it absolutely figured out. And I feel very much better for it.

Th. You do?

Pt. Positively.

Th. The depression has left you?

Pt. Yes, I'm much happier. Things seem to be much easier for me to do, I mean, that is, any little things ghat before, that I couldn't take care of, now I can get around to it. And I enjoy doing some little things around the house, even, and writing letters that I haven't been able to get around to in some time. These little things like that. *(pause)*

Th. Did you do anything about the school? [*I am perhaps a little overanxious to hear whether or not she did anything positive about the plans she made last week.*]

Pt. Well I tell you, doctor, I was going to go yesterday, but it was a miserable day. It rained all day and my sister came in and I had her with me most of the day. But I thought I'd go up there between this time now, when I leave you and when I go to the art class. I did inquire about a school which may be adequate. I'll tell you, I'll look into this one. It sounds interesting. I'll take care of that this afternoon. [*For some reason she has not followed through. There seems to be resistance of some kind.*]

Th. Mm hmm.

Pt. Very nice.

Th. What else has been happening? *(pause)*

Have you felt a little bit depressed? [*testing her professed improvement*]

Pt. No. No. I've been good. *(pause)*

Th. Anything happening on other levels, like at home?

Pt. Well, the maid, I've been giving her orders and she just doesn't know what's happened to me. Poor girl, she seems to wonder what's happened to me. She looks at me, you know. "What goes on here," I guess she thinks. Because I've been having her do a lot of things that I've been doing, which had been perfectly ridiculous. I mean, for instance, I like to have my things done nicely, and so sometimes I do them myself because she doesn't do them well. So I said to her the other day, "I want you to do these things. I've been doing them and that's foolish for me to do them when you're here." And I said, "I did them because I didn't like the way you were doing them, but I want you to be more careful." She said, "Thank you." I said, "No. You were just a little careless, you can do them nicely, I'm sure." So she looked puzzled; she was wondering what's happened. [*This looks like a sign of returning assertiveness.*]

Th. Perhaps she'll have more respect for you.

Pt. Of course. *(pause)*

Th. And you may have more respect for yourself. *(pause)* Anything else?

Pt. I guess not. *(pause)*

Th. Any dreams since I saw you last? [*Since the patient seems to be blocking, an inkling of more unconscious happenings, such as revealed by dreams, may be helpful.*]

Pt. No, I haven't, I haven't, not since that last one. I guess that last one cured me. After me telling you what happened, and you asking what it meant, I guess I'll never dream again. That'll be the end of the dreams. I'm afraid now. *(laughs)* [*The levity displayed probably masks her fear of revealing unconscious conflicts. Even though great care was displayed in not interpreting, she seems to have been frightened by the implications of her last dream. Resistance is apt to become more intense.*]

Th. So the last dream really upset you?

Pt. Cured me. *(laughs)* [*What she means, perhaps, is "cured" her of going too deeply into herself.*]

Th. Cured you?

Pt. *(laughing)* That was quick.

Th. What was there in the last dream that upset you.

Pt. You mean the dream? Oh, I don't want to be that way, that's why.

Th. Be that way?

Pt. Well, I mean I don't want to be sexless.

You said it might mean that I had no femininity, and I don't want that. [*This is a misinterpretation of what I said, but I decide to let it pass.*]

Th. That's a very healthy attitude on your part, not to want that.

Pt. Certainly.

Th. Because you don't want to cast sex out to the winds. It's important for you to envisage a life eventually with a man who's worthy and deserving. You don't want to live a solitary life.

Pt. No, certainly I want to live a normal life. And I'm not living a normal life now. *(pause)*

Th. What do you think the first step is to get yourself out of this groove you've been in, so that your estimate of yourself will gradually rise? You and I know how valueless and little you felt inside all these years.

Pt. Well, I think the reason for that was, doctor, that, you see, while I was capable of doing so many things, I wasn't recognized because John always kept me in the background. And that's really worthy of. He always, well, he was *it*, you see. With a capital "I," and I was out. And I thought, well, I just thought I'm not doing very well after all, and he's doing it, and these things are unimportant. And then by the time I did take over, well, that thing was so deep in me that I couldn't get over it, that I, you know, didn't have the ability. I mean, for so many years, he impressed me that I didn't have any brains, you see. [*This may be the dominant theme of the present session, that is, an exploration of feelings of having been, and of being undermined.*]

Th. Really?

Pt. Oh, yes, yes, yes.

Th. In what way did he do that?

Pt. Well, just that, oh, I could make suggestions, and he would say "Oh, what do you know?" and all this, and then I just wouldn't say anything. Then I would see that it would be done, but I just thought, well, all right then. And, I mean, it went on for so long that I thought, well, I guess maybe I don't know anything. And then, you see, when I was alone, I still didn't think that I had the capabilities. And that is really, I mean, that is the truth. I'm being absolutely honest about it. And that's what it is. That's what was done to me. That's a fact. And that goes all the way down the line, Dr. Wolberg.

Th. I see.

Pt. In business and in my own personality. Well, it's too bad, but it is, it happened.

Th. It happened. And he kept undermining you?

Pt. Yes, undermining me, instead of building me up, you see, which would have been a wonderful thing for me, because I had never had any

opportunities, until I married him, that is, to get out into this public work, and so forth, you see. And, well, he always . . . *(pause)*

Th. He always minimized . . .

Pt. Minimized my ability, my thinking capabilities.

Th. When you started in this career, when you started working with him, what aspect of the work did you handle?

Pt. Well, I'll tell you how it happened. You see this work, in this work, you're very confined, and you put in a good many hours a day. And when I married him, I was very much in love with him, and I felt, well, now if I don't become interested in this, I will hardly never see my husband, you see. So I said, well maybe I can be of some use; I could shop for supplies and things and supervise the details in the store, and see that it's kept immaculate—that sort of thing. Because I didn't have any experience along any other line, but I did know that I could buy these things that were needed. And then gradually I got into it more and more. If a saleslady was out ill for a day or two days, then I got in and took over her place, and, little by little, I began to learn everything about the business, you see, everything.

Th. Over how long a period was this?

Pt. Twenty years.

Th. Over a period of 20 years. When did he begin undermining you?

Pt. Oh, after I began to learn more of it, and, you see, then I took a course, then I used to express my ideas about certain things.

Th. And what did he do?

Pt. Oh, he pooh-poohed me out, you know. "What do *you* know?" and then walk away and light a cigarette. I'd be just left there and I'd say, "Well, maybe I don't know." So that's all right, I'll go along with it, and see what happens. *(pause)*

Th. That must have made you feel that you weren't respected.

Pt. Well, I'd feel that, I did, you know.

Th. That you weren't . . .

Pt. That I wasn't clever, capable of thinking of things, and so forth. But it did, over a period of time, it does something to you. Dr. Wolberg, you know that. Like somebody keeping on beating you down, and beating you down, and you . . . and that's why even today when I'm with people, I mean, I'm afraid to express myself or say what I think about things. You see what I mean?

Th. And you never felt that you contributed much?

Pt. No, after he died, then I still thought, well all of this is still what he built up, and it isn't mine. Do you understand, doctor, at no time did I ever get any credit for ever doing anything on my own.

Th. I see.

Pt. Exactly, you see. Oh, I've heard a lot of the customers say, "Oh, if it wasn't for you, the place wouldn't be the way it is, and we all know that you were the brains behind everything," and all that sort of thing. But I never took any stock in it because he never built me up, you see. And he was the one that I looked up to, to do that for me, and he never did, you see.

Th. And you needed that.

Pt. And I needed that so badly, because, I mean, that's all that there really was to it, you see. And gradually toward the end, that was very important when a lot of the other things were over. So I didn't get it, and it really, you know, Dr. Wolberg, it does, it sort of becomes a part of you, and you just don't have any confidence in yourself. It's a terrible thing, in spite of all the things that I know that I can do. But, however, I'm very glad I got out of the business. That was one thing that I never regretted, not for one instant, not an instant. I'm so glad I'm out of it. It was a tremendous responsibility, and it was getting worse and worse. *(pause)*

Th. You felt you were getting nothing out of working.

Pt. As if I couldn't do anything. He gave me that idea.

Th. He didn't really build you up.

Pt. A new estimate—I must get that.

Th. Perhaps you have a feeling that you are inferior because you didn't get a great deal of formal education? [*exploring material reasons she may give to explain her devaluated self-esteem*]

Pt. I haven't any of the, I mean, I never, I don't like to brag about things. And I know that some of my friends they brag, but to me it's sort of ridiculous because I see through the whole thing and it's so shallow. But, I mean, I haven't any of that, Dr. Wolberg, because to me it isn't important. I mean I don't brag about having done well financially in the business.

Th. Mm hmm.

Pt. You know, and I've . . . well, I mean, I don't brag about anything at all, and maybe that's another thing too. I don't know, maybe this is another inferiority I have. I don't know.

Th. You may feel that what you have isn't worth very much.

Pt. I do, I do. I don't place any importance on it at all.

Th. Well, there must be things that are important to you.

Pt. Well, I . . . a friendship to me is of great value and, of course, it starts me to thinking again of the good that I could ever do, and that to me means a great deal. And I like to live a nice clean life. But I don't want to do all the giving. *(pause)*

Th. You really feel you haven't been on the receiving end? You've been on the giving end.

Pt. All the way through.

Th. To be on the receiving end, you'll have to think enough of yourself so that you feel you deserve receiving. [*focusing on the need for better self-esteem before she can get a modicum of what she wants out of life*]

Pt. I feel I am lacking in personality. How can I build up my feeling about myself? *(pause)*

Th. The best way is through good relations with people. *(pause)* Perhaps you minimize a lot of things that you have about yourself.

Pt. Oh, I never think of it, you see.

Th. You feel it's all bad things you've got, no good things?

Pt. I never think of it, you see, I haven't any of those thoughts which I should really develop. It would be good to get some of these because it would help me. *(pause)* Ever since I've been coming to see you, I've been giving more thought to myself than I've ever done in my whole life. Believe me, believe me. Because all through these years I just never think of myself, never, never, doctor. Nothing that *I* do ever amounts to anything; believe me, it was what everybody else did. That was the big thing with me. [*The patient doesn't yet see her own masochistic participation in and need for tearing herself down.*]

Th. Other people were important to you then?

Pt. Oh, but definitely, definitely. No matter how small, no matter who they were, you see. And I never, never think of myself. Lately is the first time. Because I've been going along, I've always thought about my mother, thought about John, and thought about the little girl, my brother and my sister. I've always helped. It's always all of those things that I had to think about, and do, you see. Before, I never had time to think about myself.

Th. Well, it isn't too late to change, if you're really fed up with that sort of thing.

Pt. It isn't too late.

Th. If you really thought it was too late, you'd just resign yourself and say there's no hope.

Pt. Well, I never will do that no matter how things are going to go. I'm never ever going to feel that way again because I want to live a normal life. If I'm lucky enough to, you know, really meet somebody nice, and that I'd be interested in, I think it would be wonderful.

Th. Maybe they'd be lucky to meet you. [*emphasizing how she undervalues herself*]

Pt. Well, that's the idea I should hold. It's really me. I know I should. Oh, I know I should. Yesterday, twice I had a call, and I said I wasn't home, and this chap is very, very wealthy, very wealthy. But he drinks, and I don't want that, that isn't for me, and I don't need his money.

Th. It's important for you to be discriminating, even if you wait. [*trying to put into words what the patient may feel, but has not yet verbalized*]

Pt. I don't care, doctor, I will not get in with somebody that's going to pull me down. I don't think that's good at all.

Th. No. *(shaking head)* [*reinforcing her conviction*]

Pt. I've struggled too hard.

Th. Another experience that tears you down will be very hard to bear. [*emphasizing the need to avoid another masochistic experience*]

Pt. Just one more will be too much.

Th. You've already gone through enough, except for that one interlude of your life.

Pt. With this man that did some good for me. That really pulled me out of all the other things; the only real relationship I had.

Th. Maybe you need another interlude.

Pt. Yes, like that, with someone nice. Well, of course, I was so much younger then, you see. I had more opportunities then. But it'll be a different thing, something different, if it comes again.

Th. If it comes again you have to be ready for it. You can't expect to be ready if you have a bad opinion of yourself. If you correct the bad opinion of yourself, when someone worthy comes along, you'll be able to accept the situation. [*linking her desire for a better life with the task to rectify her bad feelings about herself*]

Pt. Sure, no matter how good *they* were, if *I* felt good, it wouldn't matter.

Th. There is one thing you may have to watch for when you meet a worthwhile person. In the face of this man's apparent good qualities, you may say to yourself, "Well, gosh, he'll never see anything in *me*. Why should I get myself messed up over him? If he sees something in me, it's because he just wants sex, or because he wants to take advantage of me, or something like that; it isn't likely that he respects me for myself." And after that, you won't give him a chance; you'll just run like a deer. Now you've got to build up this estimate of yourself, if things are to be different. We have a fairly good idea of the origin of this bad estimate of yourself in your

early upbringing. But this has produced in you an extremely insidious situation, in which you keep on despising yourself, in which you feel you have no inherent qualities, in which you feel that you can only be loved for what you can do for people, and not for yourself. Now these patterns keep messing you all up. [*This summation attempts to link up all the random bits of information we have. It also warns her that her problems still are with her even though she feels better. Anticipating her neurotic reactions when she relates to people will give her the best opportunity to learn about her drives and to modify them. Another thing that an anticipatory comment does for the patient is to prevent her from becoming depressed and hopeless when her neurotic reactions reappear after she knows about them and feels that therapy has annihilated them. Most patients want to rid themselves of symptoms so earnestly that they cannot accept the truism that time itself is necessary for the complete eradication of a neurotic pattern, even after insight into the pattern has been achieved.*]

Pt. Well, all right, now what will I do about this other thing?

Th. Which other thing?

Pt. Getting on with people.

Th. All right, now the first step is getting started on a program of building up your value in yourself. What do you think the first step might be?

Pt. Like going to school or meeting a new group of friends or a new group of people . . . like building an entirely new personality.

Th. A new personality and a new life for yourself. Does this mean you have to discharge all of your present friends?

Pt. No, but, I don't . . . not too much of them. Because that'll be all in that old type of thinking again, and surroundings and all the old ideas.

Th. Not that the old type of thinking isn't going to pop up again from time to time, even if your attitudes do change. [*again anticipating the old reactions*]

Pt. I know. I know what you mean.

Th. But it's starting with a new base, starting off with the idea that you're going to be frank with people that you meet, and, by George, if they like you, fine, they like you for yourself.

Pt. It'll give me an entirely different outlook, and then I'll be surrounded with an entirely different environment.

Th. And the people . . .

Pt. Will like me as I am. [*How much she is voicing what she says to please me and how much is real insight and determination to react in a different way, the future will tell.*]

Th. Like you as you are, the way you are, not because you do things for people.

Pt. Well, that doesn't mean anything; they haven't anything to offer. They come to me to try to have me to give something of myself to them. Because most of these people are so, oh, just don't have any real interest to offer, you know.

Th. Yes.

Pt. They're a lot of negative people with a lot of money to spend and go around drinking every day, and live that way. Well, that's not of interest to me. I mean, I don't want anything like that. To me that's a waste of time. Now this last man . . . I decided to give him up. It was too much [*The fact that the patient keeps bringing this man up shows that she has not resolved her problem with him, and probably wants to resume a relationship.*]

Th. Mm hmm.

Pt. One of my friends, she said, "You're foolish if you don't go with him." I said, "No, I'm not, I know what I'm doing." No, doctor, I couldn't go on with that.

Th. Why did she think you were foolish.

Pt. Well, because she thought he was good to me, see?

Th. Good?

Pt. I said he took too much out of me, he hurt me.

Th. You felt it wasn't worth what it did to your ego.

Pt. Oh, am I glad now that I'm rid of it. It's wonderful. At least now if I'm alone over weekends, it's my choice, at least.

Th. Yes.

Pt. Yes, and I don't feel like a dog for it. Don't you know what I mean?

Th. Mm hmm.

Pt. The other way you think, well, gosh, here I am by myself. You see other people along the avenue with company, you know, men, and all of them together Saturdays and Sundays, and I'm alone. Well, what's the matter with me, I think. That's where all this trouble came, you see, when I saw this man. [*It is more apparent now that the rupture of her relationships with this man was a prime precipitating factor in her emotional illness.*]

Th. Torturing yourself with thoughts that you're not worthy.

Pt. That's right. And what is it worth?

Th. Mm hmm.

Pt. It's my fault.

Th. Your fault?

Pt. I'll get over it. (pause) I'll get over it.

(pause) I'll get over this thing; I'll straighten myself out with your help, doctor.

Th. Mm hmm.

Pt. I need new surroundings. It'll be a nice type of people I'll be meeting.

Th. It'll be a nice type of people with whom you can establish the best kind of relationships. [*The question comes to my mind at this point as to whether the patient is "whistling in the dark," so to speak. Her capacity to put her insight into action will tell the story.*]

Pt. You see what I mean. It'll be nice. And then you see, doctor, before I was in a business where the people I met, they were forced on me 'cause I had to cater to them. And then I wasn't given any credit for it before because John would never give me any credit for it, and then, you see, I was always in the background. He used to put me—make me do the most simple things, like assist in the cleaning.

Th. Why?

Pt. Well, when things were so bad during the depression, and I had to watch everything and work out where I was needed most.

Th. And you had to just keep this up all the time?

Pt. And it ran me down physically. (pause) Oh, I, well, I really got a bad break all the way through on this thing. Now I will come through it all right though, now I will.

Th. Well, are you worried about this all now?

Pt. Well, I'm not worried about it since I came to see you, 'cause I see it doesn't really matter. It's how I feel about myself that counts.

Th. How do you feel about yourself now?

Pt. You mean now? I thought I was different, you know, when I had that operation on my womb.

Th. Well, virtually there is a difference, but . . .

Pt. Of course there is.

Th. But it isn't so extensive a difference that would make it significant. I shouldn't think you have anything to worry about on that score.

Pt. Well, I haven't thought of it since I came to you. But I'm going to straighten myself out and I see that I have the right idea on it, and I'm thinking along the right lines with your help, and I'm going to get along fine. There's no question about it. I know that. [*This sounds good, but the future will tell whether she will or will not sustain her symptomatic improvement. There is also a possibility that she fears getting too deeply involved analyzing herself, and is showing a "flight into health" to get out of therapy. In the latter instance, a relapse in her symptoms will occur after leaving treatment.*]

Th. Good.

Pt. I know that Dr. Wolberg.

Th. You're making plans for yourself?

Pt. Oh, sure, there's no doubt about it.

Th. Well, let's make sure about next week's appointment.

Pt. O.K.

Th. (*checking my schedule*) So I'll see you the same time as last week.

This session was spent in listening to the patient express a more hopeful outlook on life. She has stopped beating herself with her inadequacies and with the wastefulness of her life. I get a feeling that she has broken up a neurotic pattern of allowing herself to be exploited in order to be loved. Feeling little value within herself, she has had to "give" to make up her imagined deficiencies. Genetically, this is related to a shattered security and devaluated self-esteem originating in depriving childhood experiences. Her fear of rejection and the hostility mobilized by a feeling she is exploited by people may drive people from her, or may cause her to withdraw from relationships. She has started to assert herself with others, and she is talking about leading a more active and independent life. That she has deeper unconscious conflicts that have not yet been explored, there is no doubt. Whether she will have the motivation to explore them, we do not know. A hunch I have at this point is that she will go into resistance and run from therapy if I push her into deeper anxiety material. We must remember that our goal may have to be a more abbreviated one than complete personality reconstruction, because of her age.

SEVENTH SESSION

In this session the patient seems to be moving out of her neurotic pattern into more constructive relationships with people. The old patterns, have, of course, not been completely resolved and we continue exploring them.

Pt. Hello.

Th. Hello.

Pt. Well . . . (*pause*)

Th. Well, what's happened since I saw you?

Pt. Oh, everything is all right.

Th. Everything?

Pt. Yes, fine. I went to two parties since I saw you—Friday evening and Saturday evening. Been stepping out, had a good time. (*laughs*)

Th. Did you?

Pt. Yes.

Th. You didn't have to force yourself?

Pt. No, no, I didn't think about it. Just got there and entered into the thing, didn't think about the people or anything, just had a good time, relaxed. (*smiles and pauses to light a cigarette*)

Th. You didn't think about having to do things for others? [*I say this almost as if I take it for granted.*]

Pt. Not having to do anything for anyone, no, no.

Th. Mm hmm. (*nodding*)

Pt. Certainly it makes all the difference in the world. (*pause*)

Th. How did the other people respond to this?

Pt. Better, better. I think they paid more attention to me, than they did before, I mean it. [*This, if true, is a real achievement, since she has not been allowing herself to give presents and to "knock herself out" to please others.*]

Th. Well, that's something we can talk about. [*The implication here is that she has accomplished a notable thing.*]

Pt. It was Friday night; this was a very lovely party. There were two married couples there and a professor from a university. This one couple are very old friends of mine, about 10 years. I had introduced this girl to her husband, and, oh, we really had a wonderful time. All in all, it was very, very pleasant.

Th. What about the professor? [*I say this hopefully. Perhaps this man may be eligible and enable her to experiment with new attitudes.*]

Pt. The professor was all right. I would have liked to have had a talk with him, but another girl buttonholed him as soon as she got in the place, as soon as she got in the apartment. She got hold of him, and she had him all evening. He was a very pleasant fellow; he was a bachelor. As a matter of fact, I think they probably invited him there to have an extra man for me, but I didn't even get a chance to talk to him. (*pause*)

Th. Who was the girl?

Pt. Well, her husband was away. He had to go to Washington for that evening.

Th. Mm hmm.

Pt. He was very, very nice, but I didn't have very much chance to talk with him, or find out about him.

Th. Perhaps they might be able to arrange another meeting. [*My disappointment reflects itself in this statement.*]

Pt. Well that's just it; I wish they would.

Th. Do you know these people well enough to say, "How about arranging a party where I will be able to buttonhole him before anyone else does?"

Pt. Because that's really what happened, and he, let's see, I think I left . . . there's this couple that live at Park Avenue, and they took me home. They were going downtown, so naturally they said, "Come on and we'll give you a lift. And we'll all go down together." So he stayed on at the apartment.

Th. Did you feel that you should have stayed on?

Pt. Well not necessarily, I didn't. Same old thing.

Th. I wonder if you felt that you just couldn't get him interested. [*reflecting possible feelings*]

Pt. Same old thing.

Th. What same old thing?

Pt. Well, that I wasn't really interested enough.

Th. You weren't interested enough in him?

Pt. There was not enough there to appeal to me.

Th. Maybe you felt there was no sense in your even wasting your time. Unless you wanted to run away on the basis that he might reject you. [*opening up the possibility of a neurotic reaction*]

Pt. Well, you see, I didn't have a chance to find out whether he likes me or not.

Th. Yes.

Pt. That's very true. To enjoy each other's company you need a small group. You know when there's a big party—there were eight people altogether, you know that's quite a few people in an apartment—you never really get a chance to see very much of your hostess and host, for that matter. But it was pleasant and I enjoyed it; it was very nice. And Saturday night was a great big party too, twenty-four people. It was a birthday party. So we had a lot of fun, singing songs and dancing, and they had a lady there playing the piano. She was a school teacher and she came and played. We had a nice party.

Th. Did you go because you felt forced to go?

Pt. No, I wanted to; I enjoyed it. As a matter of fact, they wanted me to come back yesterday, and I did. I went back for dinner. That's something I never would have done before, but never. I mean, because I wouldn't even be interested enough. You know what I mean doctor? I want to do all those things that were hard for me to do before, you know. [*more encouraging signs*]

Th. You can sense that in your running away from people, there was something very neurotic in it? [*attempting to get her to talk about the meaning of her neurotic behavior*]

Pt. It was wrong. Isn't that right?

Th. What do you think?

Pt. Sure it was wrong, what it did to me.

Th. With all the resentment you must have carried around with you on the basis of being forced to do something that you didn't want to do, the feeling that you couldn't be accepted for yourself, but only for what you did for people, it's understandable that you'd want to drift away more and more from people. [*interpreting*]

Pt. Well, that's just exactly why I came to see you. Because I knew something bad was happening to me, you see. It was getting worse and worse, you see. I would be only happy when I was alone, and without anyone at all to disturb me. I mean just to sit there and think, you see. And really, I mean, I just . . . when anyone disturbed me I just hated it. It was just . . . to me it was a wonderful thing to be alone and just go over and over and over in my mind all these things. But it wasn't any good; it was just a waste of time. *(pause)*

Th. Mm hmm.

Pt. I had a dream last night. I dreamed that I was walking around in some strange place, and I came into an auction room, and there were some glass platters there, and I stole one and ran and cut all around corners and everything to get away. Now isn't that a peculiar thing. A cheap glass platter, it wasn't anything; it was just an ordinary glass platter.

Th. What are your associations to the dream?

Pt. Why, I really don't know what it is.

Th. All right now, what do you associate with auction rooms?

Pt. Well, auction rooms—this one girl that was at the party Friday night said, "I was down in your neighborhood, I always like to go down there about once or twice a week and run into the auction rooms there. See what they have." They've got a lot of them all around, down there in that neighborhood. Well, that's the only thing I can think of.

Th. Which girl was this?

Pt. The one I had introduced to her husband.

Th. Oh, I see. And what about lifting a plate, a cheap platter?

Pt. Yes, it was nothing, doctor. It might be worth a quarter maybe. It was just a very inexpensive ordinary glass platter like a little glass . . .

Th. What are your associations to stealing the glass?

Pt. Terrible, why I think that's an awful thing to do, to steal anything. But imagine me doing that! And if I remember, I think I threw it away. I think I got frightened and I think I threw it away, or something like that—and ran.

Th. Have you ever stolen anything?

Pt. No!

Th. Never?

Pt. I might have when I was a kid, stolen a piece of cake from the ice box or something like that, if they didn't want me to have any more.

Th. But you never stole anything else?

Pt. Oh, no.

Th. And here you dream of being kind of a thief, and doing this thing and just running off. And in the other dream you dreamed about . . . [*I am trying to make a connection.*]

Pt. Jumping over a stream and dropping my pocketbook in the water.

Th. Dropping your pocketbook in the water. And this woman . . .

Pt. Making a pass at me, yes.

Th. Making a pass at you, and you feeling it was a terrible thing. All right, now in both the dreams the common denominator is being kind of a terrible person, isn't it? [*The connection that I make is that there is a deep feeling of being a terrible person in both dreams.*]

Pt. Well, yes.

Th. Now what does that suggest to you? Here in two dreams you dream about your doing something that's wrong or bad.

Pt. Yes.

Th. What does that suggest to you?

Pt. Well, it suggests to me that it's the same old thing, that I don't think I'm all right.

Th. Here you dream that you're a sneaky selfish person. Does this show the feeling that you have about yourself? That, if true, is in line with what we've been talking about, isn't it—a disparity about what you feel about yourself and what is actually so? Now again, what does this mean? Why do you have to keep teasing yourself with thoughts that you're a terrible person? [*She is aware of some reasons for her self-devaluation. What I am trying to do is get her to bring out more guilt feelings, inner fears, and repulsive experiences, if there are any.*]

Pt. Well, I certainly don't get any pleasure out of it because I'm not happy about it. And I don't know why I should even feel that way. I mean, I want to get over this feeling, but it isn't so easy, doctor. When you've been thinking a thing so long, you can't do it in just a few weeks, just throw it out the window. It isn't like taking a piece of furniture and saying I don't want that any more. I mean, that's a part of me. I've been thinking that way so long. It takes time. I can't do that so quickly. I'm doing it gradually. [*This is factual thinking; but is it also subtle resistance?*]

Th. These patterns and habits are so rigid—they go back so far into a person's life that it takes time. You know, for instance, if you were going to break a cigarette habit . . .

Pt. Yes, I know. I did.

Th. You know how long it took you. You know that you craved smoking. Now, this is just a very simple little cigarette habit. Some people can't even break a cigarette habit. And that's a simple habit. Now, just imagine how complex the habits of a personality are.

Pt. For years, for an accumulation of years and years and years.

Th. Yes, for years and years, your whole life seems to have been the same.

Pt. The same pattern.

Th. The same pattern, and it's a monumental thing to change now. But you can change, and the only way one can change is to find out why one has been just beating one's head against a stone wall. The only way you can change is to find out how the patterns you've been accepting as normal are abnormal.

Pt. Oh, the whole thing is that, I know it. Well, I have to work it out. I'm doing it now to the best of my ability, I mean the best I can. [*I get a feeling she is being defensive.*]

Th. You seem to feel that I'm impatient with you.

Pt. No I don't, no I don't.

Th. Well, I hope you don't because I'm not.

Pt. No, I don't, I really don't feel that.

Th. I certainly understand how difficult it is for you, and how deep these trends are, and that it's going to take time—time, time, time.

Pt. Of course, and a lot of practice, doing things that are entirely different from what I've been doing, and thinking along an entirely different trend of thought. See, I'm alone so much you see. That's bad. And still I don't know of anybody that I could get any good from that I know, and that would be a good influence. You see, the people I know, they look to *me* to help *them* with their problems. Now you can imagine, I mean . . . they couldn't help *me*, could they? [*This may reflect her determination not to let people influence her toward exploiting herself.*]

Th. You feel you need a new set of companions.

Pt. Positively, you see—people that I would respect for their way of living, and their ideas of themselves, and so forth, you see.

Th. Mm hmm.

Pt. People who would give me stimulation in the right direction.

Th. Would any of your present friends be able to do that for you?

Pt. No, and not have a good influence.

Th. Mm hmm.

Pt. This man I went out with, well, I saw him yesterday. I was standing out in front of my house waiting for a taxi. He only lives three blocks from me, and he was over in front of his house.

Th. Did he see you?

Pt. I suppose he did. I didn't pretend that I saw him, because I don't want to pick that up, I don't want any part of that. *(pause)* [*Because she constantly brings the man up in her conversation, I get the feeling she dropped him because of a "sour-grapes" attitude, that in not being able to command more of his attention, she concluded, he was no good in the first place. I decide to focus on him again to see if she has more ideas about the relationship.*]

Th. How'd you happen to meet him in the first place?

Pt. In my business.

Th. He came in and met you this way?

Pt. Oh, he'd been coming in for years, you know. No, I don't want any part of that any more. That is the best thing that happened to me in a long time, that getting rid of that situation. I'm very happy about it. [*The thought occurs that "the lady doth protest too much."*]

Th. You seem to miss him, however.

Pt. No, to the contrary, I mean I feel worse about him than I ever did. I almost hate him to a point, now.

Th. But even after all that time, it wasn't worth a row of pins?

Pt. No, no.

Th. Not worth emotionally what you went through?

Pt. It didn't help for 3 years to go through *that*. That certainly isn't living.

Th. Mm hmm.

Pt. There wasn't much to it, you see, as I got nothing. He used to expect everything from me, tell me all his troubles. *(pause)*

Th. He was the type of person that would make you the confessor, tell you about how he felt about things?

Pt. Oh, yes, yes, completely, everything—his daughters, his sons-in-law—and I was listening to all the troubles about everything.

Th. You were listening and acting understanding.

Pt. Oh yes, wonderful. *(said sarcastically)* He used to come out with all these things and get it off his chest and put it in my lap, you see. Yes . . . well, that's all over. I don't want any part of it. I don't want to even . . . if he would call me, I would tell him I don't want to have anything more to do with him. Just don't call me, I'd say. I don't like it. I wouldn't even go out and have dinner with him. I don't want to hear from him any more. I'm finished with it; that's the end of that. I'll go out to parties and things and have fun, like the last party. [*The explorative attempt I*

made was not too fruitful; so I decide to focus back onto the party she talked about.*]

Th. Well now, let's go back to this party. This woman that you introduced her husband to, what sort of a couple do they make?

Pt. They're very nice. She has entirely different ideas about things than I have. I mean, she's the sort of a person that likes to have an easy life, and definitely all for herself, you see. The fact that I would want to do anything again, you see, like when I said that I'm going to take up a course in antiques—oh, she thinks that's ridiculous. "You just got out of business, so you could play and have fun," she says. "Why don't you go down to Florida and stay there for 3 or 4 months and have a good time." But I'm not in the mood for that. I wouldn't have a good time, I said, if I went to Florida. See, so that's her idea, just to have fun and play.

Th. What kind of a man did she marry?

Pt. Oh, a very nice fellow, very nice fellow. He's very good to her, and I think they're very compatible. They seem to be.

Th. Does he appeal to you at all? [*I am thinking of the dream in which she steals a platter. Her associations suggest a competitive attitude toward the woman. I am trying to bring this out, if present, through questioning.*]

Pt. To be married to? No.

Th. Not at all?

Pt. Well, he's nice, I like him, I respect him, but for marriage, no.

Th. There's no jealousy at all?

Pt. No, not at all.

Th. No envy of this woman?

Pt. No, no. Why, did you feel that there might have been?

Th. Well, I don't know, I'm just thinking about that dream . . . the association of the auction, you see, and this woman. You going in and stealing something, might give us an inkling, but there is nothing definite.

Pt. Well, I . . . she went to Florida with me on this trip that one winter I was driving down, and I said for her to come on down. She was a widow. I said, "You've never been down, and I'd love to have the company. Come on down with me. It won't cost you anything in the car—come on down. We'll have a nice drive down together." I wanted to do something for her.

Th. Which is?

Pt. That same old thing. [*She does have good insight into her neurotic pattern in that she picks it out when simple cues are presented to her.*]

Th. Mm hmm.

Pt. And so she came down there with me,

and I knew this fellow, and I introduced them, and they were married 6 months later. So that was one of those things, and it seems to be working out, so that's fine and I'm very glad of it. That was 10 years ago. But I don't see an awful lot of her, and, as a matter of fact, she never mentions the fact that she's happy or ever says that that's the best thing that ever happened to her. She never mentions that I introduced her or anything like that. Never, never once has she ever said it. However, I'm not going to ask her if she's happy. She seems to be happy. I mean, I should think she'd say it to me because I introduced her to him, and he certainly is good to her.

Th. And she never shows any gratitude at all to you.

Pt. She has never shown any appreciation, I mean, by way of doing anything for me. I don't want it, but I mean that's the way the picture is.

Th. I see.

Pt. And I wonder if she really is happy. She appears to be happy. He's been very, very good to her, like I said, and they live beautifully.

Th. Aren't you sort of . . . well, disgusted? [*The meaning of the dream may be that while this woman can go into auction rooms and pick out beautiful things, the patient must be contented with cheap things, and she has to steal them at that. This may refer to what she gets from life, or to her own feelings of self-worth. Resentment toward the woman may have sparked off the dream.*]

Pt. Yes, I mean, I'm sorry for her, because I'm sorry that she hasn't a little more . . . I don't know whether you should call it gratitude or a little more graciousness maybe, to sometime just express it to me, that she had a nice life with him, and it was so wonderful that I introduced her to him, something like that. But never ever, ever once, never. It's one of those things; but that isn't anything. Why are people like that, doctor? They have no part of feelings for others.

Th. Some people are like that, others not. [*attempting to introduce reality into her thinking*]

Pt. Not everyone does that I suppose, but I get stuck with them that have no feeling.

Th. I know, but why should *you* get tangled up with those people?

Pt. Well, I won't I don't have to now.

Th. You know there are some people who are sponges; their whole life is integrated around sponging on others.

Pt. Either in one way or another. Now, you see, this girl I told you I used to see a lot of, the one that lives with this doctor. He hasn't married her . . . why he hasn't married her, I don't know. He's free to do so; he's been divorced and she's divorced, and why should they live in sin

when they don't have to, that's something I can't understand. It seems silly to me, because why not be married and have a perfectly normal life together; then if you disagree, all right, then get a divorce after 10 years, but why do that? Well, any rate that's the picture. So I, so Saturday night they were at the party also, this doctor and the girl, and there's about a 23-year age difference there, and I just looked at her and I thought, "Oh, my, I should get into anything like that." This old man . . . old, I mean, real old—65, 66—that's old, doctor, when you're 50 or something like that, don't you think so? [*Is the patient expressing a "sour-grapes" attitude here too?*].

Th. Mm hmm.

Pt. That's a terrific difference.

Th. Of course, but it depends on the person too. There are individual differences. Some people at 65 can be still young; some people at 45 can be awfully old. [*This statement of fact is intended again to introduce reality into her thinking.*]

Pt. Yes, but this man is—well, the fact that he doesn't marry her, he doesn't even think enough of her to marry her in spite of their age difference. He should be so happy to have her.

Th. Maybe *she* doesn't want to get married? [*placing possible responsibility on the woman, in case the patient is trying to prove that all men are nefarious*]

Pt. Well, she says so, but I wonder what woman wouldn't want to be married, instead of living that way.

Th. There are some.

Pt. Really?

Th. I believe so.

Pt. She says *this* way she can walk out whenever she feels like it. Well, that I can't understand.

Th. Could she just be holding on to him for security?

Pt. Well, then—this is what I really started to tell you—then this girl I introduced to this man who married her, said to me, when this girl and the doctor were quarreling one time, she said, "Can't you introduce *her* to someone?" "Why," I said, "Why, I wouldn't think of it." I said, "What about the doctor?" I said, "I don't do—I wouldn't do things like that."

Th. Mm hmm.

Pt. "Well, but," she said, "can't you introduce her to someone else?" [*The implication is that the patient has a responsibility to introduce other women to nice men. People expect her to "give."*]

Th. Just like that. [*sympathizing with the patient's feeling*]

Pt. Just like that. So you see, that's the type of person this other one is.

Th. Apparently you size her up as a selfish person.

Pt. Well, that's the picture then; now you've got it, see?

Th. I certainly have the picture you've been used to following.

Pt. I guess you have.

Th. The defender of the rights of others, but not so much of your own.

Pt. (indignantly) Yes, almost to the extent that I would be a procurer if it comes to that. "Can't you introduce her to someone?" I said, "I don't do that." I said, "What about the doctor? She's with him, isn't she?" Now how do you like that? Well, now there it is. I get into awful—some awful kind of pictures.

Th. Apparently you've given people the impression that you are there to serve.

Pt. It's my fault.

Th. It's not a matter of fault or blame. You've given them that impression because you needed to have that kind of relationship with people. And you got yourself into spots where others . . . [*bringing up the matter of her "need" to do things for people, the satisfaction she gets from doing things for others*]

Pt. Take things for granted.

Th. And that must burn you up inside.

Pt. Well it does, it hurts.

Th. Of course, it hurts.

Pt. Every time I see this girl that married this fellow, it hurts. You say there may be a jealousy. No, there isn't any jealousy because there isn't anything that she has that I haven't. I mean as far as that goes. While he is an awfully nice fellow, I wouldn't want to be married to him. And I mean he has no appeal for me. I like him as a person, and he's a very regular little fellow, you know; he's very nice, but . . . *(pause)*

Th. He's not the sort of a fellow that would really suit you.

Pt. No, no, that's right. He was a very good friend of my husband's, you see.

Th. I see.

Pt. And, so that's the picture, but I still don't think she has taken the right attitude toward me.

Th. Very obviously you don't think that.

Pt. That is a fact.

Th. Mm hmm.

Pt. Not once, as I say, has she ever given me a single thank you for that. Well, I just think it's a little abnormal, that's all. It's just something wrong about it. Because I know what I would do. I mean, I would mention it once in a while, just to

make someone feel good about it. [*The patient is obviously fired with the indignation and resentment at how she has been exploited by others. Prior to therapy this suppressed resentment may have produced depression.*]

Th. That would be the . . .

Pt. The natural thing. But I would take up with people like that. As you say, I must have needed them, doctor, but they are hard on you, I mean they expect everything.

Th. It's natural for you to feel angry at people who like you only if you continue doing things for them. You know there's a story which explains that personality very well. It's about a man who had the same kind of problem that you have, always kept doing things for people. Now, on one occasion he was told by a friend that a person he had helped considerably in the recent past was hostile to him, spreading vicious and unfounded tales about his character. So he went over to see the man and said, "Look, why do you treat me this way? Why do you talk about me the way you do? Haven't I given you a car, found a job for you that pays you well, and even introduced you to several young women you've been dating." And the fellow replied, "Yes, that's true, but what have you done for me lately?" [*I passed up an opportunity to talk about her "need" to take up with the kind of people she detests. I was probably anxious to tell her a good story before it slipped my mind.*]

Pt. (laughter) That's good, he wanted him to keep on with the giving, and when he let down, well, then everything stopped, he didn't even act in any way grateful.

Th. The minute he let down on the giving, then he was his enemy.

Pt. That's right, doctor, that describes me all over. *(laughs)* [*The story apparently clicked.*]

Th. Could these attitudes on your part really be the things that are at fault, causing you to feel that people expect things from you, while you yourself secretly hope *they* will be the ones who will do things for *you?*

Pt. You know I take it too seriously. I should be a little more impersonal about these things. True, everyone's troubles are my troubles, and I get involved in these things. I should just mind my own business, in other words. How about it, doctor? [*The patient is unwilling to explore the provocative question I asked her.*]

Th. You find yourself drifting into things, not even wanting to?

Pt. Yes, and that's what I'll have to watch.

Th. You mean, you feel you'll have to watch yourself from wanting to take people over, do things for them, act the hostess, so to speak.

[*again emphasizing her own responsibility in perpetuating the pattern*]

Pt. Yes, I can see, I can see how what you've told me is so true.

Th. Maybe you participate in this, encouraging them to depend on you more than you think.

Pt. I don't want to get involved, I don't, I don't.

Th. But you *do* get involved somehow.

Pt. Well, I tell you, you talk about those things—why, even my bookkeeper, when I was in business, don't you know, that he said, "Well, now I'd like to put a little money into this business." Now imagine, he wants to get in on an income from my business. Oh, that shows you, you're so right about it. Everybody has the impression that—well, I was theirs. [*The patient evades my implication.*]

Th. What I was saying was that by your manners and actions you may have encouraged their thinking you were theirs. [*This is a "perhaps" interpretation, but it is given emphatically.*]

Pt. Well, whatever the reason was, it was all one-sided.

Th. One-sided, and then you stopped the supplies, they got mad at you.

Pt. Well now, I'm just going to . . . I've been doing that . . . and now I'm not going to do anything for anybody. [*This would, of course, be unhealthy, but I doubt that she means it. In resentment, a statement like this is apt to come out.*]

Th. You might feel if you didn't do anything for anybody, that they might not like you.

Pt. I'm through with it, honest and truly.

Th. Completely?

Pt. It's just something that will help me to build up a different impression of myself. I've got to do that, doctor, because things are no good the way they have been. That's why I thought I'd go ahead with studying, to build myself up to feel different.

Th. Have you thought any more about the course in antiques?

Pt. Yes, I'm going to go through with it. I am. I'm going to do it.

Th. Mm hmm. (*nodding*)

Pt. Now you see, doctor, if I wanted to really go ahead, I might go into the extended course, which is 8 months a year for 2 years, and that would give me time for vacations, you see. I might as well do it.

Th. Mm hmm. (*nodding*)

Pt. And do it right, and get a great deal of satisfaction out of it, the whole thing, you know. And then if I ever want to use it, I'll have it.

Th. You haven't had an opportunity to yet investigate yet when to register in the school?

Pt. Yes, I've done something about it. I have a catalogue there, and they have some of the dates there written. I'm sure I can get started on that. And I am going to. And then later, if I want to go in for myself, in business I mean, I can if I want to.

Th. Mm hmm.

Pt. You know what I mean?

Th. Not only for purposes of business, but better still, an education.

Pt. Everything, you see. The business angle is only part.

Th. Yes.

Pt. There are wonderful possibilities in this thing, too.

Th. And it's not only from the standpoint of having an interesting thing to do, but you can meet a lot of people in this way.

Th. Yes.

Pt. It's wonderful, it's certainly wonderful that I have the energy to do it. Go back to school, it'll be all so new.

Th. New and exciting.

Pt. Yes.

Th. All right, see you next week.

Pt. Yes, doctor, goodbye.

This session is characterized by greater hopefulness, and accounts of positive achievement. There is, however, reluctance to get into deeper, more unconscious, aspects of herself. In the seventh interview this could scarcely be expected, even if we desired to get into them. She seems to be moving along extremely well.

EIGHTH SESSION

This session is illustrative of some of the activity that occurs in the middle phase of treatment.

Pt. Hello, doctor.

Th. Hello.

Pt. Well, this man comes into it again. [*This is apparently the dominant theme today. It may give us an opportunity to explore her deepest feelings about the man.*]

Th. Well!

Pt. His sister passed away last week. I happened to hear of it very . . . it was quite an accident the way I heard of it. But at any rate I was tempted to write a letter and I was tempted to send a card, but I said, "Oh, no, don't start, don't let yourself in for that all over again." It would have been nice to write a letter to him, of sympathy or something, but I said it isn't the thing to do, so I just won't do it. Now I'm so glad I didn't, today I'm so glad I didn't. *(pause)*

Th. You were almost tempted to write. [*focusing on latent desires to see the man in question*]

Pt. Yes, and then I felt, well, Dr. Wolberg says no, that sort of thing is just poison for me, and why do I want anything that isn't good. [*The patient puts me in an authoritative position, as if I think it's wrong for her to make contact with the man.*]

Th. If I weren't around, what would *you* say?

Pt. The same.

Th. But after all, he's the last man in your life, and it is understandable that you would want to see him. [*This comment is intended to be both reassuring and provocative, stimulating her to associate more about her desire to renew the relationship.*]

Pt. You understand, it was no good for me.

Th. Is this because *I* implied he was no good for you? [*attempting to bring patient to the realization that she is defining her values, not I*]

Pt. You are right that he was no good for me. [*continues to put me in the authoritative role*]

Th. But there are still some memories about him.

Pt. Yes, but it wasn't the thing for me to, and this morning I was so glad I didn't do it, see? Because, I said, well now here I'll be right back where I started. If he should get the card or letter of sympathy, you know, he'll call me, and then it'll just be that hanging and dangling on, and what good will it do? [*This is the first time she has openly admitted a yearning to go back into the relationship. Her admitting the desire and her making a choice not to on the basis of intelligent judgment rather than resentment, will help her resolve her conflict. I might earlier have caused a verbalization of the desire by saying something like, "Most women would want to see their boy friend, and miss him, even if he was mean. You probably miss him too in some ways." Nevertheless, the patient did well with the tactics I employed.*]

Th. You may be tempted some more.

Pt. But I'm glad I didn't.

Th. Did you avoid doing it to please me? [*testing her use of me as an authority*]

Pt. (laughs) No, no, doctor, it would be bad for *me*.

Th. Do you think *I'd* disapprove if you did see him again?

Pt. No, but that is not what I want. Why, I feel so good today about that, that was such a

lift, you know, that I thought, well, I did have enough common sense, and I wasn't swayed by my emotions or sympathy again, you know, to do something to help or be very obliging. [*This is a forthright, honest attempt to handle her feelings.*]

Th. Mm hmm. *(nodding)*

Pt. Oh, I'm so glad I did it, doctor, I just feel so good about it. That in itself is wonderful. Because I know just what would happen. See, he'd get the card, and he'd wait a few days to call. And, say I saw him, and then I'd be waiting again, you know, I don't want it. I'm so much better off without him. [*She seems finally to have made a choice.*]

Th. Mm hmm. *(nodding)*

Pt. Much better off.

Th. At least you feel independent, even though you may not have the pleasure of having him around once in a while.

Pt. Yes, but it wasn't worth it when I did have him.

Th. It actually undermined you in a lot of ways?

Pt. Breaking me down. So that's number one. And then I had a lovely Thanksgiving, it was a hen party, but it was fun. [*The patient shifts the topic, apparently having dealt with it to her satisfaction.*]

Th. That's good.

Pt. Well, it was at the house of this old friend of John's and me. We were about six girls and the old boy, he's about 81.

Th. Well!

Pt. Well, he was just so happy; we really had a lovely evening. So I had a nice day. And then there's been a death in my brother's wife's family since I saw you, so I went over there, and helped my sister-in-law a little bit while she took care of some of the things for her father. That's really about all. And let's see now, and then last night I was to go to a cocktail party. I just went up for one drink to see this couple, and said "hello" to them and then left. About a half hour . . . I went up there. But I was glad I did that, because I want to take care of everything, don't you know, that I was afraid to do before. [*The patient diverts from the theme of her former boy friend, and her frustrations with him, to the constructive efforts she is making with life.*]

Th. It wasn't too hard?

Pt. No, no, it was all right. I'm glad I did go.—I want to do all the things that are hard for me to do, that I didn't do before. Isn't that right?

Th. Well?

Pt. Isn't it?

Th. Instead of just withdrawing, you do things, but more importantly, if you can get a little pleasure out of doing them, this would make it really worth while. [*Instead of answering "yes" to her question, I give her a possible reason for continuing in the path she is going.*]

Pt. Yes, well I am. I'm seeing things in a different way. I seem to, I seem to understand more about doing the things now than I did before. I mean, in a different way. I mean, before I thought, well, I *have* to do it, you see. Now I look forward to it with a little pleasure, you know?

Th. You were depressed before.

Pt. Terribly.

Th. And you didn't want to get out of the house. You wanted to stay within yourself. Anything you did outside the home was an effort.

Pt. Yes, that wasn't good. Now I want to talk to you about the going up to the Institution for the Blind and reading. I've been going there recently to read to this one man there, and he isn't completely blind. The way for him to read something, he has to look at it this way. *(brings hand approximately 2 inches from eyes)* I see that when he looks at his watch for the time, this way you see. So I've been reading to him for about 3 weeks. This isn't the young boy I read to before. I only substituted for a reader for this young boy. This chap is a different thing again. I've been reading to him about three weeks. So he's interested in psychiatry; so he had a book there. *Between Us and the Dark* is the name of it. I don't know if you know it. Well, it was about a woman that during the change of life, went all through all this emotional period, and was put away in a hospital, and so forth, and so on, and stayed there 4 years. Well, at any rate, I finished that book, reading it to him. It was very interesting. So now last week, last Tuesday, he has a book written by a Dr. Flanders Dunbar, *Mind and Body.*

Th. Yes.

Pt. Well, at any rate, he has a certain amount of it that isn't read, and then I come to the part almost immediately where it's marked off here. This is the chapter that I'm to read, and it's all about this girl that's having intercourse, that's being whipped, flogged, and all that. Oh, it's the worst, I mean, I never heard anything like it. First time I ever read anything like that. Well . . .

Th. Did he know that that was the material he wanted you to read?

Pt. Well, now wait. So then he said, in referring to that, he said, "Turn back to page 202, about the third chapter, and then there's more of this filthy stuff." He knew the book.

Th. Yes.

Pt. He must, he must have known the book,

and he knew the page, you see. So now, how do you like that?

Th. And he wanted you to read that?

Pt. Oh, yes. So I don't think I'm going to go back there any more.

Th. It shocked you.

Pt. Yes, but isn't that awful. I mean, you go up to read and you want to do some good, and then here this thing is thrown at you. What is the idea with those people? [*The possibility crosses my mind that the patient may be employing this example to illustrate the uselessness of her making constructive efforts for herself.*]

Th. Well, again, doesn't it resolve itself to the fact that sometimes you feel taken in, taken advantage of?

Pt. But, doctor, isn't that a shame?

Th. You want to do the best for people, and they use you for their own selfish personal interests?

Pt. Yes, but well, isn't that a shame, doctor, now, really, I mean it. You go up there and you want to help somebody. And that's the reason I went up there. I felt that I would be doing some good, and I might get some, you know, pleasure out of it. And imagine to find this filth. I mean, I don't understand this.

Th. Well, if his interest is in something pornographic, he's not interested in the scientific attitude.

Pt. You don't think so? Why shouldn't he be?

Th. Should he be?

Pt. He's not a doctor.

Th. He's not a doctor.

Pt. Well, it's just that . . . *(pause)*

Th. Maybe all he wants is to be stimulated.

Pt. It's just filth.

Th. It disgusts you.

Pt. Reading these things, you see.

Th. These things are what sick people do, not healthy people. [*By emphasizing that constructive efforts may fail on sick people, but not necessarily on healthy people, I am hopeful that she will conclude that she need not seek out sick people to do things for.*]

Pt. Yes, I know it. And it's certainly for no one's pleasure to read to them. So then he said, "Well, you turn back to this page and there's a little of it on that 202 page." And he said, "Well, I'll have to return this book." He gets these books from the library, you see. He can't keep this book, but he wanted me to get all that old, all that filthy stuff out of it, you see, and read it to him. So I don't think I'm going to go back anymore. I don't, I don't like the fellow now, after that.

Th. Not all blind people are like that. [*in-*

troducing reality into the situation to forestall, if possible, retirement from further activity]

Pt. Well, you know. So I'm going to forget that. I'll call it off.

Th. If that's what you want to do.

Pt. I will, I'll do that. Now that's that. Now isn't that something. I guess I just run in hard luck, because it looks like the other people go up there, and it seems to be all right.

Th. You do the best you can. The fact that people don't turn out to be the kind of people you imagine them to be is just unfortunate.

Pt. It is.

Th. But . . . this person, he's probably a very sick person emotionally. *(pause)*

Pt. Well, I don't know whether he's sick or not, doctor, but at any rate, he shouldn't be taking advantage of people who are coming up there, and with all good faith.

Th. Did you tell him you didn't want to read the material?

Pt. No I didn't. Do you think I should?

Th. You had a right to.

Pt. I can go there and ask if I can get someone else to read to. *[I was wrong in my thought that the patient seeks to run out of the situation. She does seem to be evaluating reality better.]*

Th. Mm hmm. Do you enjoy reading?

Pt. I would enjoy reading to the right type of person, and the right sort of thing, yes. I enjoy it very much.

Th. Well then, why don't you go up there and tell the people in charge what happened, and give them the reasons why you don't want to return. *[a suggestion for constructive action]*

Pt. All right. That's all right.

Th. Wouldn't that be better than not showing up at all, if you get any kind of pleasure out of reading?

Pt. Well I do, I do. I'd like it very much to be able to go there once or twice a week and read.

Th. There's no reason why you shouldn't.

Pt. I was enjoying it until this thing came along.

Th. You certainly owe it to the person in charge there to tell him what happened. Maybe some people don't object to reading things of that sort, but you object very much. And you enjoy reading. Maybe they could get somebody else for you to read to.

Pt. Sure, I'll do it then. I certainly am not going back there to him. He's probably, as you say, a sick fellow, and he's sort of getting something out of this thing here, you know, probably something to have him believe, maybe, that he's all right, and he isn't.

Th. Mm hmm.

Pt. The book was all right you see, the book was interesting.

Th. Mm hmm.

Pt. It's good, but in its place, don't you know what I mean? I'm not interested about reading about some poor unfortunate that has to have those things. But the other book was an interesting novel. You know, it was a story that, well the woman that had written about the Snake Pit, it was her own experience. But this other thing, I don't want any part of it. And then he did say something very funny. He said, "I," he said, "I sell novocaine." He said, "Do you know anyone that has any use for it?" I said, "No, I don't."

Th. The man sounds like a dope peddler?

Pt. I said, "No, I don't know anyone at all."

Th. The man sounds as if he is a very sick man.

Pt. Well, I thought novocaine is only for dentist work, when they pull your teeth. It isn't like that other drug, heroin, or whatever you call it. Well, you see, he said, "Do you know anyone." And I said, "No, I don't know anybody."

Th. That sounds very suspicious.

Pt. I haven't any idea of going back there to read to him. As a matter of fact, I was going to forget the whole thing, but I think your suggestion is good. Let them know there, what kind of a man he is.

Th. They have a right to know, don't they?

Pt. Yes, only I wouldn't want to get involved in it. I wouldn't want to have anybody hurt you know.

Th. No.

Pt. You know what I mean?

Th. You don't want to get involved.

Pt. Exactly.

Th. But, they do have a right to know.

Pt. I'll do it.

Th. Do you think you can?

Pt. I'll do it.

Th. Good.

Pt. I enjoy reading, and I'd like to have them assign someone else to me, you understand. *(pause)* I think that it's the best thing. So that's been . . . that. *(laughs)* I certainly do get into things, don't I?

Th. Well?

Pt. I surely do. *(laughing still)*

Th. It involves you anyway. *(laughs)*

Pt. I certainly do. *(laughs)* The time will come, I suppose, when I won't have any of that stuff; it'll all disappear. I'll always have some, but I'll know how to take care of myself too, I mean.

Th. Now you sound more optimistic.

Pt. I am. I wouldn't be surprised if I met someone nice soon.

Th. Now if you did, you'd be tempted to act how? [*testing her insight*]

Pt. And that's another thing again. *(laughs)* Do things for him, I suppose, and then get mad at him for not liking me for myself.

Th. You can get yourself adjusted without that eventually, if the right sort of person comes along. [*presenting the possibility of a different way of reacting*]

Pt. I'll be attracted to them, and they'll be attracted to me, and it'll be so much better. Because what's the use, the way it is now. I suppose I'm not really ready completely, only partly. Really, I wouldn't know what I wanted, so what's the use of starting anything. [*This shows that she is not really "whistling in the dark." She seems to be assessing reality quite well.*]

Th. You feel there isn't any use?

Pt. Unless I was sure of the person. I'd only get in trouble, and that would just be another disappointment, then . . . oh, I'll just go along and I'll work it out. I know I will.

Th. On the other hand, you still just don't want to lose your faith in people, because there are still some very nice and decent people alive.

Pt. I know.

Th. And it's a matter of knowing where and how to find them. The people you've been most attracted to are the people who have needed help. They've been exploiting, they've used you. That type of relationship is a one-way affair. And it's bound to explode because you can't be adjusted in a situation of that type. [*repeating the same interpretation*]

Pt. Be giving all the time, you can't.

Th. You'll despise yourself too much, you'll feel as if you resent the time you put into it. And then such people become demanding and make you feel guilty because you don't do enough for them.

Pt. And then in the end, unless you keep on, and then when you do stop . . . well, then you find out that they don't really care anything about you. When you don't continue to keep giving of yourself, you know what I mean? That's really the way it works out. Because, I suppose people don't want you to be that way after all, do they?

Th. But if you have a *need* to be needed, you'll act that way in spite of everything—in spite of the kind of person you meet. [*again emphasizing her own need for participating in the pattern*]

Pt. But most of the people I met wanted mothering.

Th. Certainly there are some people who want to have a mother around that supplies things all the time. And they won't start any relationship except with a person of that type. You'll find them everywhere you go. There are always people wanting to sponge on you. They're always willing to give you their time, that is, unless they're busy doing something else that is more profitable for them.

Pt. That's right, then they don't even give you the time of day.

Th. Any time you spend with them, you'll have to be doing something for them, but the minute you stop doing something for them, they . . .

Pt. They don't want you anymore.

Th. I told you that story, "What have you done for me lately?"

Pt. Oh, yes, I love that story. It's cute.

Th. That's the type of person who saw in you a supplying mother. But on the other hand . . .

Pt. *(interrupting)* You don't have to be around them.

Th. They're sick people, immature, undeveloped. They're like children.

Pt. But don't you see, doctor, you learn all that, I mean just . . . well, I'll be on my guard, and I don't want to lose faith because that would be terrible to go through life like that, and I won't. But the way I feel now, it's been a letdown, the whole thing has been a letdown for me, and you don't get over it overnight.

Th. You still have the need for people, and still have the need for a nice relationship, but you're afraid to get involved again.

Pt. Well, not for long, I hope.

Th. Because you've been hurt so much. And before you'll let yourself get involved with anybody, you may want to make sure he's the right person.

Pt. That's what I intend—and don't you think I'm thinking along the right lines?

Th. What do you mean?

Pt. 'Cause I could find any number of people that I could pick out that I could do things for.

Th. You probably could. Do you think you still have a need to get involved with sick people to whom you can give things? [*confronting her with responsibility for her pattern, which she had previously blamed on others.*]

Pt. Oh, listen, I told you I could, but I don't want to. Why should I just do things to make those other people—make other people happy? *I* want to be happy, I really do.

Th. You have a right to be happy.

Pt. Yes, I want a man to be attracted just to me, for myself.

Th. A reliable and a responsive person who's not a baby and who doesn't want a mother?

Pt. Fine.

Th. Fine, but until that time comes you've got to supplement your activities with some outside interests.

Pt. No matter what they may be, I must do that. *(pause)*

Th. To feel you are doing something constructive.

Pt. Yes, yes.

Th. But it may be very hard to do. [*challenging her determination*]

Pt. I know, I know, but I've got to do things, doctor, I know I can't just hang around the house. Yes, and I will. *(long pause)*

Th. What are you thinking about?

Pt. About a dream I had. It's not clear.

Th. Do you remember anything about it?

Pt. It was a dream with a fellow.

Th. Tell me about it.

Pt. Oh, that was it.

Th. Well, what?

Pt. Well we were . . . yes, that . . . yes . . . *(pause)*

Th. Well . . .

Pt. Intimate, having relations with him.

Th. Yes. What was your feeling about it?

Pt. Pleasant. *(pause)* There was another part. I gave him my pocketbook with valuables. He protected it, picked me up and carried me over a stream, and kissed me. Then we walked hand in hand. Yes. Well that was all, that's that. [*My own associations to the dream are that it indicates a trust in a man and a feeling that she has something valuable to offer. It sounds like a good dream, reflecting constructive tentative changes. It may also refer to the transference situation.*]

Th. Well, that dream is different from the other.

Pt. I should say it is. *(laughs)* It was a good dream.

Th. What do you think of it?

Pt. Nice, if it was true.

Th. Well?

Pt. Maybe it will come true.

Th. Do you think you would want it?

Pt. I think so.

Th. But it may not be for some time.

Pt. No, but as long as I know I am ready for it.

Th. It may not be forthcoming though, for some time—I mean in terms of you meeting someone worthwhile.

Pt. Will I be ready to accept it the right way when it comes?

Th. Do you really want to accept it? [*dodging the question and throwing it back to her*]

Pt. Surely, surely.

Th. You'd miss relations with a man.

Pt. Yes, yes. Well then, I can wait for the right one.

Th. Is it intense, I mean, do you miss it intensely?

Pt. Yes, well, ah, it just, it was one of those things, and I don't know, I suppose. It's been quite some time, you know, so I just had that dream, and that's all. I didn't have any others.

Th. Are you impatient for things to happen?

Pt. Well, I don't, I don't . . . no, and I'm not . . . I'm glad I'm not. I wouldn't think of starting anything over again, doctor. I haven't any idea of it, simply none, until I'm sure of the person and of myself. I don't want to get in with another one like the last man.

Th. He's too much involved.

Pt. Too involved, too much. He's too involved.

Th. If he could be free?

Pt. No, there's too much intrigue there. He's all tied up.

Th. He's all tied up.

Pt. Sure, what's the use?

Th. You may still want him. [*testing her*]

Pt. I doubt it very much. So that's over and that's that.

Th. If he were different.

Pt. Maybe that would be different.

Th. Mm hmm.

Pt. But he's too damn selfish.

Th. Mm hmm.

Pt. He doesn't want to give up anything.

Th. He wants everybody to come to him?

Pt. That's right. That's it.

Th. But you still sound as if you miss him. [*testing her again*]

Pt. No, I feel that he probably did me a great favor. *(pause)* Because eventually I know that I will meet someone worthwhile, and I wouldn't if I hung around with him. Waste my time! So it's all right then. That's a closed chapter, I'm just through with it, and I'm perfectly happy about it.

Th. You might meet a person who's worth twenty times more. [*I attempt here to reinforce her hopefulness.*]

Pt. Oh, sure, doctor. He wasn't for me. He was just a very conceited guy that just thought that money was everything and money could pay for anything he wanted. And you know, there's a lot of people that believe that. They think they can get what they want if they have money. And if they're that type of people, then it probably doesn't make any difference to them how they get it. Do you understand?

Th. It's no compliment to you to have a person like that around.

Pt. Well, it certainly is not. It certainly is not.

Th. It makes you feel cheap.

Pt. Sure, I don't need him.

Th. You don't need him?

Pt. I should say not. He didn't help me. I helped him. I mean, I was so far above him in every way, and I knew it and he knew it too.

Th. You were doing most of the giving?

Pt. And it didn't amount . . . and then always on the run, that wasn't anything, you know.

Th. He just popped in and out.

Pt. Yes, sure. I told you, one night a week.

Th. Mm hmm.

Pt. Silly. Well, it was my fault. However, I'm learning. I'll bet he expected a card or a letter from me this morning.

Th. Mm hmm.

Pt. Oh sure, and then he thought I'd be waiting again. No, no, oh I wouldn't go through that again, not for anything in the world. Now when I look back, I don't know how I did it. That's what happened to me.

Th. And then, when he didn't respond, when you got fed up finally and threw him out . . .

Pt. I did.

Th. You sort of hoped that he'd come back again. [*trying to get her to accept the fact that she secretly did want to get involved with the man until relatively recently*]

Pt. (*laughs*) I suppose I did. (*laughs*) But that's silly. I'd really be in a fix if he did. And now I'm so glad. And now, even if he did, I won't . . . I don't even, I wouldn't even see him. I wouldn't even go out with him for dinner. Because I know how aggressive he is, you know, he'd . . .

Th. Persist?

Pt. Oh, sure.

Th. And then you'd be right in it again.

Pt. Oh, certainly. What is it the fellow said? I need that like I need a something in the head?

Th. A hole in the head?

Pt. A hole in the head. (*laughs and then suddenly becomes very serious*) No, I'll just go along a little way, and then I'll get there just the same. (*long pause*)

Th. What are you thinking of?

Pt. I was wondering if I should find out about getting a job or something?

Th. Yes.

Pt. I was wondering if I should.

Th. Well, what were you thinking of?

Pt. Well, you remember I talked with you about it. I said that maybe I could get something part time.

Th. Mm hmm. And then you began to feel what?

Pt. Well, and then I was just wondering if I should. I don't know.

Th. You feel that maybe you're not up to it?

Pt. Well, you can't get over it overnight, so quickly, I mean, get well entirely, I mean.

Th. You won't get over it until you really start getting out of your shell, and begin to integrate and feel like a part of the world again. Perhaps a man will come along too—a good man.

Pt. I know, it's very important. I know it. But I will not get mixed up with any more of those married men, doctor. I mean I'm through with that. I mean it now, I mean it. No more. I don't want any part of it. Not any more. That's nothing. Waste all your time and you get nowhere, and it's a letdown for your pride.

Th. Your ego gets deflated.

Pt. Surely, you're playing second fiddle, or third, or whatever it is. Why should you? Find someone for yourself. Why not? And then you're somebody, and no matter who I mean, if he's a nice man, no matter if he doesn't have an awful lot. But as long as he is a really nice person, at least he's your husband or he's your sweetheart. There isn't all that other intrigue, and all that lying and conniving, and all that, that sort of thing.

Th. Mm hmm.

Pt. I do feel so much better, doctor. Really better than I've felt, as far back as I can remember. The cobwebs lifted. I'm sure I'm never going to fall back into that again, I mean. I'm very grateful to you, doctor, because I couldn't see what I was doing to myself, bringing this on myself, I mean, and blaming it on hard luck and things. Now I'm going to have people take me as I am, and not go doing, doing. No, no, that is no good, no good.

Th. No good at all.

Pt. Doctor, I may be leaving town. I got a letter from a friend in California. It will be a nice rest and a vacation. I'd like to go in a couple of weeks. It will be fun to go and see things.

Th. Mm hmm. We'll talk about that next week.

Pt. Goodbye, doctor.

This session is a good one and indicates that the patient is utilizing her insight in the direction of change. Life is opening up to her and she seeks to partake more of its joys. She does not yet trust herself, and recognizes that she may act out her neurotic patterns in her relations with people. But she understands these patterns and she has a determination to rectify them. Her desire for a vacation is both a sign of her development and an indication that she may feel satisfied that she has achieved all she wants from therapy. If the latter is the case, I will have to decide on whether to deal with this as resistance or to satisfy myself with the results of therapy; namely, a more reeducative than reconstructive effect, or, at most, a partial reconstructive result.

NINTH SESSION

This is the terminal session and illustrates some of the techniques employed in the terminal phase of treatment. The patient seems to have decided that she has achieved all she desires from therapy. I respect her conclusions and terminate treatment.

Pt. Hello, doctor.

Th. Hello.

Pt. Things have been so well, wonderful. I'm really feeling fine. *(laughs)* Like I can do things again. I am being just matter-of-fact and not worrying that I hurt people by doing that, like I used to worry about before.

Th. Mm hmm.

Pt. Not worrying about that at all. *(pause)*

Th. Yes.

Pt. I told you how I would call people, you know, and wondered how they were, and think I was neglecting them if I wouldn't call them. But you know, I don't do that any more, and it's perfectly all right. Nobody seems to think anything of it. As a matter of fact, I might have been annoying them. It's very possible. *(laughing)*

Th. At any rate, you feel that it isn't necessary for you to make the rounds. You're not a postman to have to keep calling on them all the time. [*said facetiously*]

Pt. Exactly, I don't. *(laughs)*

Th. Do you find that they do come to *you,* if you don't come to them?

Pt. Oh, sure.

Th. Mm hmm.

Pt. Now, don't you see, going away for a vacation, like I mentioned last time, I made a few calls to my close friends and said I'm going away, and I want to wish you a Merry Christmas, and so forth. So a couple of them wanted to come to see me before I left, but I really haven't the time, I've got a lot of things to do. Why add

all that confusion to it? [*The patient seems to have decided to go away. Also she is acting, perhaps for the first time, normally assertive.*]

Th. And you told them that?

Pt. I did, I said, "I'm sorry, but time is short, and I have so many things to do, so that I'll see you when I get back home."

Th. Mm hmm.

Pt. It all helps. You use so much up of yourself the other way, doctor, you do. You don't realize it. That's what I've been doing, you know.

Th. And it's been draining you.

Pt. Giving, giving, giving of myself.

Th. Mm hmm.

Pt. Giving, giving . . . things like that. The sponge is just being wrung out. No wonder I didn't want to mix with people. No wonder I didn't want to see anybody, because every new contact meant so much more . . . and the burden was just mighty miserable. Just terrible what I did to myself, just horrible.

Th. Yes.

Pt. I see it all now. *(pause)* And it's just a matter of being . . . getting a little horse sense in you to realize it that you've been going on wrong, the idea that people aren't going to like you, that people are going to reject . . . and that I'm a terrible person by not acting in this way they want. [*The patient says these things as if she really knows them and means them.*]

Th. I see.

Pt. And bend over backwards to try to get people to like you. *(pause)*

Th. Mm hmm. *(pause)* Have you had any dreams since I saw you last? [*I am trying to look under the surface for deep anxieties as a reaction to her present assertiveness.*]

Pt. Only about furniture. What does that mean?

Th. Well, let's see what the dream was.

Pt. Well, I was looking at all these books about furniture, and that's all. So what does that mean? Am I turning into a piece of wood or something like that? *(laughs)*

Th. What do you think it means?

Pt. Well, the feeling was good, I mean it was pleasant.

Th. What does looking at books of the furniture bring to your mind?

Pt. Well, it must have something to do with how I've been feeling lately.

Th. Mm hmm.

Pt. More action, more doing.

Th. Yes.

Pt. Yes . . . furniture, that's all; I mean, something new I want.

Th. You feel it indicates a new orientation?

[*The dream sounds like a constructive one. At least no anxieties seem apparent.*]

Pt. Good.

Th. A new life?

Pt. Good, good, that's it, that's it.

Th. And?

Pt. I had two wonderful volumes sent to me from this lawyer, this old, old friend of the family's. It's all the pictures, of all the originals of individual owners, doctor.

Th. Of furniture?

Pt. Yes.

Th. Mm hmm.

Pt. Oh, beautiful—two volumes. Macmillan publishes it. It really is something.

Th. Real authentic antiques?

Pt. Yes, and the original owners, their names are down, people who possess these things. Even in their homes, 'cause they're so rare. They have the pictures in these two volumes. Wonderful, doctor . . . everything imaginable, even old clocks and beautiful old tables, and chests and . . . *(pause)*

Th. Mm hmm.

Pt. Of course its wonderful.

Th. This book made you feel well.

Pt. Sure, because they're real possessions, you know. They have beautiful things.

Th. All right, what does this have to do with *you*, now?

Pt. Well . . . *(pause)*

Th. Yes.

Pt. (laughing) Well, you see I'm planning for the future . . . a foundation that . . . *(pause)*

Th. A foundation that . . .

Pt. (still laughing) I don't know. I'll be careful though, I don't want to be too hasty.

Th. You have to be careful?

Pt. I've made arrangements to go to this school to study antiques. It starts after I get back from California. After that I'll go to school, and I was thinking I could go into business after that. But I will be careful.

Th. You've decided on going to California?

Pt. I'd like to, doctor. I believe I am ready, and I've been invited. Do you think I can do it?

Th. Do you feel you'd like to do it?

Pt. I would, doctor, I would. I feel so thankful to you . . . I don't know what to say. . . . It's so hard to know how what happened, happened. It's hard to realize that a little while—a while ago, I mean, things were so hard, so hard for me. I gave up, things were no good for me. I felt that I never would be able to feel well again. I can see it . . . how it was, how it came, I mean . . . I mean, doctor, that is how I was before . . . feeling, feeling I was nothing and had nothing to give of me . . . so I gave, gave of every-

thing I could do for the person, doctor. And then hated myself and the person because you never know, this way, where you stand. *(pause)* [*This sounds like good insight.*]

Th. And how do you feel about that now?

Pt. Oh different, so different, doctor. I'm beginning to see that I placed no value on me . . . like I was no good. And that's silly, doctor, so silly, doctor, for me to feel that. The only way things will work out is for me to stop doing things, and be accepted for what I am. I have nothing to be ashamed of . . . I haven't done anything bad, you know. I'm as good as anybody. I really feel that, doctor.

Th. Good. And what about your going away? [*I decide here to explore what may be behind her going on vacation.*]

Pt. If you feel I shouldn't go, doctor, I'll stay.

Th. I'd rather have *you* decide that.

Pt. I'd like to go, doctor. It's an opportunity I'd like. It will be so much fun, you know.

Th. There is no reason why you shouldn't go, if you wish.

Pt. When I get back, doctor, can I see you if I need to come to do some more about me? I feel confident though now, as if the future had something for me.

Th. Of course, you can see me any time you want when you get back. You are likely to have ups and downs. People always do. In fact, you may still get yourself into the same position with people you were before, and then get infuriated and depressed. [*I am warning her here that a relapse of her neurotic reaction is quite possible. This is not too significant if she realizes her neurotic reaction for what it is and is capable of mastering it.*]

Pt. I don't think so, doctor. [*The patient hopefully believes she will have no relapses. Unless I warn her in advance of the possibility, she may react badly should a relapse occur.*]

Th. Well, after all, these old patterns are very deep, practically part of yourself, and the new patterns are of recent origin.

Pt. You mean the old way may come back if I don't watch myself?

Th. And even if you watch yourself. It takes time to overcome a problem that's been part of you all your life. If the old patterns return, you will better be able to correct them before they get you down.

Pt. Well, I won't let myself get into that same thing again, doctor.

Th. Maybe it won't happen, but if it does, at least you'll know better what's going on.

Pt. Yes, yes, I will, I won't be a fool if I can help it.

Th. Another thing, you may have some problems that still need further treatment, and you may later decide to get more treatment for them. [*It may be that the patient wishes to terminate therapy. Giving her a reason for returning is important.*]

Pt. I know that, I know that there are many things I can straighten out. I mean, I see what I did all my life, the damage of that early thing with my . . . that home situation. And it hurts.

Th. Yes, you may want to go further into yourself later on. As far as your present situation goes, do you feel you've got out of your treatment what you want?

Pt. Oh yes, yes. I have gotten more than I thought it was possible.

Th. Perhaps you may be able to avoid the patterns that get you into troubles with yourself; but the chances are they may try to repeat. [*I am reemphasizing a point I believe to be important.*]

Pt. You mean I might do that again, and get upset all over?

Th. Yes, the chances are you will. But the difference is that you will know what you are doing better, or catch yourself doing it. What will happen then is that you will learn again how automatic the pattern is, and not allow yourself to sink into it.

Pt. Catch yourself before it's too late.

Th. Yes.

Pt. Well, I can see that . . . you know it takes a long time to overcome this . . . but I know now I can . . . I will, I mean, because the other is just, just no good for me. And if they don't want me for myself, they can just go to blazes.

Th. Mm hmm.

Pt. Yes, they can. I mean that, doctor. Either they like me or they don't.

Th. Well, what about that? Do you believe you are likeable and that there are people who can like you for yourself?

Pt. I know it now, with what's been happening in the past few weeks. People are very nice to me, and I don't do anything for them. It's funny I never thought of that before.

Th. Disappointments are apt to occur, however; you will still meet people who will want you for what they can get out of you. [*forewarning the patient again so she will alert herself to acting-out*]

Pt. Certainly, take it in slow easy doses, isn't that right, doctor?

Th. What do *you* think?

Pt. Absolutely, absolutely, and the person must accept me with my cards on the table.

Th. You have nothing to hide, nothing to conceal.

Pt. After a little while, after I feel that I'm interested, there is no reason why I can't tell them everything.

Th. Absolutely none. [*reinforcing her determination*]

Pt. You know that's so.

Th. Mm hmm.

Pt. Yes, after I know them real well, and I know what they're interested enough in me to really know what's what.

Th. But you're apt to have one old enemy—and that is you're likely to start saying, "Oh, I don't want to lose this person, I better not say anything about myself."

Pt. Well, that's the way I've always been, you see.

Th. Yes, that's the way it's been all along.

Pt. And like this other fellow, you know, that I went around with for 3 years, you know, I was always afraid that if I would ask him to be with me over the weekend, I'd never see him again. And well, now I don't see him anyways, even if I didn't ask him. I haven't heard a word from him, and I'm not sending him a Christmas card. I want to get rid of the whole thing.

Th. Mm hmm.

Pt. I want to get him out of my hair completely.

Th. You feel the sooner you get that thing out of your hair, the sooner you'll be able to concentrate on something else.

Pt. He just isn't . . . he isn't any good. That's all.

Th. There may be a lot of temptations still, to see him, because, after all, it's the last affair you had and he's around all the time. There's a lot of temptation to crawl back into that thing again. [*testing her resolution not to see the man*]

Pt. I won't do it.

Th. You may really want to.

Pt. It would be a waste of time.

Th. Maybe you feel you couldn't find another man?

Pt. No, doctor, it would take away all the good that I've gained so far, if I went back.

Th. And you'd be right back.

Pt. And I'd be right back where I started.

Th. But maybe you feel you couldn't find another man?

Pt. No, I don't think I will have trouble there.

Th. Suppose he happens to call you up or something, or insists you see him. [*continuing to test her*]

Pt. I wouldn't.

Th. If he did come back into your life, and crossed you up again?

Pt. I'd throw him right out.

Th. You'd throw him out.

Pt. But I 'wouldn't even want to do that. Why do it?

Th. Well, you may not have thrown him out of your thoughts.

Pt. Why do I need it for? He isn't any good for me. He's just a . . . he's really an awful person.

Th. Mm hmm.

Pt. Period. I could say a lot of other things. *(pause)*

Th. Well?

Pt. But what's the use? But he is, and I'm through with it. And I'm not going to bother with his daughter because he'll think that if I send her a card, all of that, he will want to try to get back in with me again, you know. Not a chance!

Th. You've given him plenty of opportunity.

Pt. Oh, to call me.

Th. And to come back again. And . . . *(pause)*

Pt. It's 5 months that I haven't even heard a word. Imagine! [*There seems to be an inkling of a desire to resume the relationship; however, she is resolute in her stand not to let her desires get the best of her better judgment.*]

Th. It must be terribly irritating.

Pt. Well, it shows me what a fool I was. It's irritating in that angle of the picture—that I was just a fool. *(pause)*

Th. Well?

Pt. He's too aggressive for me, doctor.

Th. He was very aggressive, he used you?

Pt. That's right. Just a fool.

Th. And you let yourself be carried away.

Pt. Well, of course.

Th. Maybe because you were afraid to lose him. Maybe you said to yourself, "Here's a nice man, maybe he'll be kinder to me, maybe he'll come to me eventually and I'll be the only one. I better not say anything to upset him."

Pt. Well, I thought in time, see, it would change. I thought he would get rid of this other girl, but . . . *(pause)*

Th. But?

Pt. He hasn't enough character to clean . . . to make a clean sheet of the whole thing, throw out the rest and start with something he really wants.

Th. Mm hmm.

Pt. Do you see? He will keep on dabbling with the women he has, and finish it that way. That's a lot of . . . that goes on in New York all the time. But do you know, another thing: I say, "Yes, all right, I'll be here; all right, I'll see you." And as soon as I say it, I *know* I shouldn't have said it. I know I'm wrong. I know I'm being too soft, too easy about things.

Th. Mm hmm.

Pt. Now, I . . . I don't know· why I should do these things. I should think about it before I give an answer to something.

Th. There are reasons why you feel you have to do this.

Pt. Do you understand? *(pause)* You see? I say, "Yes," or "All right, I'll do it," and if I say I will, I'll do it, no matter what. But I shouldn't, I should be very careful of what I answer and say. I have to be . . . *(pause)*

Th. Yes. *(pause)*

Pt. See, I should think a little more. I should use my noodle.

Th. You have to be very careful about the situations that you can get yourself into?

Pt. Exactly.

Th. In other words, there'll be a lot of opportunities.

Pt. Exactly.

Th. So?

Pt. There'll be a lot of opportunities, but I must watch out not to start anything with someone—well, a man who isn't deserving; and I'm not going to get too involved, no matter what demands are made.

Th. Mm hmm.

Pt. No matter what people want from me. Because, if I do, there'll be some people who will just really wring. My big problem you showed me is what I do to myself because I feel I'm no good.

Th. It's not exactly what you want to do, because you really want to be liked for yourself. *(pause)*

Pt. Now you see, one of my people turned up that worked for me for about 12 years, a boy that I had a lot of trouble with. I knew he was stealing, but he was a good worker and I did the best I could to control it as much as I could, but I knew he was stealing from me every day. But at any rate, he took ill about 3 weeks ago, and he went to the hospital. So I had a Christmas card last week from his wife, and she said—on the card—Joe is very, very ill in the St. Francis Hospital, you see. Well, I know what that means, you know. Well, I called up—day before yesterday—to find out how he got through his operation. He was operated on 2 or 3 days ago, and they said he was doing nicely. So this morning I sent a little Christmas plant to him, and it said, "With all good wishes for a speedy recovery," but I'm not going to give him any money. I mean, I just did that, just with a little good feeling toward the fellow, because I knew he was wrong all the time he worked for me, too, see?

Th. Good.

Pt. See? You know?

Th. The moment you got that card you realized that it was just a touch?

Pt. I knew, sure. Sure she would have liked me to have gotten in touch with her and said, "Is there anything he needs?" Well, you know, she wouldn't say no, and I'd be right in for it, let myself in for the whole thing.

Th. You resisted it.

Pt. I mustn't do it.

Th. If you did, you would have resented it.

Pt. I know. Now you see, going back into the book shop now for the holidays, I'm not going to go in there. All those old help, they think I should give them something.

Th. Yes?

Pt. I'm just going to keep away from it. I really have nothing in common with these people. The only reason I saw them was because I felt I had to.

Th. Mm hmm.

Pt. I'm not going in at all. I'm not going to go in there.

Th. What do they think you are, Santa Claus?

Pt. Well, it's possible, you know. I have been to all of them. Around Christmas, I gave all of them a bonus, you know, Christmas money. *(long pause)* . . . *(laughs)* But that's all in the past. I won't do anything like that any more because I know it's wrong. And then it annoys me after, you see. See? It annoys me after I do it. I know it's the wrong thing for me to do. These people are using me, and I know it's not right.

Th. Mm hmm. And you are tired of being used.

Pt. Right.

Th. It's also the thing that it does to them. The most insidious thing is that this type of giving and this type of patronizing are bad for the people who accept it. And it's bad for them, and deep down they hate to have anybody just be in a position where they can give them presents. It makes them feel dependent and helpless.

Pt. I understand. Everyone likes independence. Everyone likes to do things for themselves. That's what they appreciate . . . *(pause)* the things that they can do for themselves.

Th. You can see the pattern, and the way it's working in you. All your lifetime you have had to give. All your lifetime you've had to give in order to feel accepted. You believed that this was the only thing left for you, that you couldn't possibly be accepted on your own terms, that you couldn't have things done for you, and still be loved and respected. Now this is one of the ways this thing started. But the more insidious

thing was that it kept up. It kept up. When you see this clearly, you'll say, "Hey, stop this business." *[summarizing]*

Pt. Just cut it all out, that's all. And I'm doing it too. But I'm just going to keep away from the book shop—I'm not going to go in there at all. I don't have to go in. I'm not going.

Th. Your own guilt feelings inside may keep telling you, well, wouldn't it be nice to just go in there? People will think more of you, and they will like you better if you go in, and so on. *[challenging her]*

Pt. Well, I don't have to go in. I can just simply send them a Christmas card.

Th. Mm hmm.

Pt. One nice card.

Th. Mm hmm.

Pt. "Merry Christmas," it will say.

Th. Merry Christmas.

Pt. "And a Happy New Year," period.

Th. Mm hmm.

Pt. Good. I'll do that this afternoon, and I'll send it tomorrow, and that'll take care of the whole thing.

Th. Mm hmm.

Pt. That is good. *(pause)*

Th. And?

Pt. That takes care of that.

Th. That takes care of that.

Pt. Yes, and they'll have more respect for me.

Th. Mm hmm. *(long pause)* Well, what would you like to talk about now?

Pt. The thing that's on my mind now is about what I'll do when I get back from California.

Th. Mm hmm. *[Since she is leaving on a long trip, I decide not to stir up tension in this interview by provocative focusing on possible conflictual areas.]*

Pt. I don't like this being retired. I'm naturally very active.

Th. There are some people who are able to retire gracefully, and there are some people who are not.

Pt. Well, people that are very phlegmatic maybe.

Th. And you are not phlegmatic.

Pt. No, no.

Th. Well?

Pt. People who haven't any interest, and you just . . . it's a slow death. It really is.

Th. It's a slow death. That is not for you, is it? You're too active a person.

Pt. Yes, but still I always force that other part, you see. See, I have that drive, you know. I have, I mean I never give up, and I could just, well . . . the antiques thing interests me.

Th. The antiques interest could keep you occupied.

Pt. It'll be wonderful.

Th. If you really make a career out of it, then you'd feel accepted on a different level, not merely as John's wife.

Pt. Exactly.

Th. You'd be accepted for yourself.

Pt. Exactly. Yes, and if I do go in business, I can, I can just use my own name. It would be good.

Th. Mm hmm.

Pt. Yes, I have a different feeling about all that now.

Th. Mm hmm.

Pt. Not being afraid to face things.

Th. Fine.

Pt. Feeling real good.

Th. Mm hmm.

Pt. It makes me feel good that I could ever think of going ahead.

Th. Mm hmm.

Pt. You know.

Th. It may give you a better feeling of value, a feeling of worth.

Pt. Well, you know, doctor, one thing always leads to another. You know, when you do one thing, there's always so many other things that come out of it. You know what I mean? That through this thing, there are other happenings. It always works that way—in things you never realize.

Th. Yes.

Pt. You know, that you never think of. You can imagine what I mean.

Th. What?

Pt. Oh, everything—a lot of things.

Th. For instance.

Pt. Oh, *(laughs)* I did get involved so with the customers. *(laughs)* They had me run ragged.

Th. Doing things for them?

Pt. Oh, loved it. *(laughs)* When they let me do it, I would love to do it. There was politics in it too.

Th. Politics?

Pt. Oh yes, they used to bring me tickets. *(pause)*

Th. Tickets?

Pt. Yes, yes . . . Oh sure, there was one judge out in Connecticut. *(laughs)* He really was wonderful. I just took advantage of it because he was just so good about these tickets, you know, that he'd get. Put it in an envelope and send it to me. I made some good contacts.

Th. You've still got some good connections that you can utilize?

Pt. Oh, it'll be wonderful. I can use them too, later.

Th. You mean if you go into business?

Pt. Oh, it's a good contact with the good people—I really did know some wonderful people, I mean, and they all liked me, you know, and I can really, I can pick up some of those nice contacts when I get started, you see.

Th. When you get back from . . .

Pt. California, yes.

Th. I see.

Pt. Yes, when I get back from California I'll get in touch with a few people, the very nice ones.

Th. Mm hmm.

Pt. Yes, that would be good, sure. All you need really is a few good contacts, you know, a few good ones. And then they have guests that come in to see their homes, and they say, well, where did you get these antiques, you know. Here I go again, planning. *(laughs)*

Th. At least the planning is something constructive.

Pt. I've been thinking about that a lot, dreaming of a place I can set up, getting some people to work for me—real crackerjack people. *(pause)*

Th. Real crackerjack people.

Pt. Yes, workmen. *(pause)*

Th. Workmen.

Pt. That's the stuff, and that should be a big secret. No one should know who they are, either. Dig up someone that's very, very, very good.

Th. Your assistants.

Pt. That's right.

Th. Mm hmm.

Pt. They have to be very good, do excellent workmanship. You see, that's the secret of it all, because if you buy beautiful fabrics, and if it isn't done well, then the whole thing is lost. You know there's a big difference between good work and . . . shoemaker work, they call it, you know.

Th. This whole new field that you're exploring, it'll probably take quite a while.

Pt. Oh, of course, it will, of course it will.

Th. Yes.

Pt. In the meantime I will meet a lot of people, and I need to get out of myself.

Th. You do need people.

Pt. Here's another thing, doctor, you're going to like.

Th. Mm hmm.

Pt. I got new clothes, and a couple of new hats. Imagine? *(laughs)* [*This may be a reflection of better self-esteem.*]

Th. *(laughs)* That sounds like a revolution.

Pt. *(laughs)* For me it is. Imagine, new hats that I thought I deserved for myself. And I used to feel I could only, only get things for another person.

Th. Is that one of the new hats you have on?

Pt. (laughs) Yes, it is.

Th. It's very attractive, becomes you well. [*This is a response which I believe I should express openly to her.*]

Pt. (laughs) Thank you, doctor.

Th. Do you think it's attractive? *(pause)*

Pt. Well . . . *(laughs)*

Th. Well?

Pt. Well, yes, I do. There I go boasting.

Th. Boasting?

Pt. (laughs) Yes, I do like it.

Th. Do you like the way *you* look in it?

Pt. You want me to say I like myself.

Th. Well?

Pt. I was looking in the mirror and I said I'm not bad looking at all, not hard on the eyes. *(laughs)*

Th. I should say not. Do you think men would find you attractive?

Pt. Wouldn't be surprised if they did. *(laughs)*

Th. If you gave them a chance.

Pt. Oh, I think everything will be all right there too.

Th. You'd give them a chance then?

Pt. Well, I wouldn't run if they came around, because, after all, I'm not so bad.

Th. Good. *(pause)* So I won't see you until you get back from the trip.

Pt. I'll drop you a line and call you when I get back. Doctor, I want to thank you ever so much for all you've done for me. It's wonderful, this work.

Th. (laughs) Thank yourself, too. After all, *you* did most of the work.

Pt. (laughs) Goodbye, doctor.

This was the last session I had with the patient. After a 2-month stay in California she returned to New York. She telephoned me and cheerfully announced that she felt completely well and did not believe she needed further therapy. Periodically she communicated with me by letter, and 2 years after therapy, she paid me a personal call. Her entire manner indicated a satisfactory adjustment. Five years after therapy, this adjustment was being maintained.

CONCLUSION

In evaluating what happened in the treatment of this patient, it must be remembered that rarely is treatment this short. In most instances, many more sessions are required to achieve a comparable result. The case was presented not to demonstrate short-term therapy, but merely to illustrate some of the essential processes that are involved in treatment.

One thing that will be apparent is that the patient did not get bogged down in too much resistance. Her motivation to get well was probably a great help here. Also, I did not let her get too dependent on me by giving her the answers to her questions; I let her, or I should say, forced her, to think things out for herself. We established a good working relationship, rapidly, and in relatively few sessions we were well into the middle phase of treatment. If the patient had developed resistances to the working relationship, especially transference resistances, we would probably have been involved in therapy for many, many months before we could have begun working constructively on her problems. Were there a strong secondary gain element to perpetuate her neurotic patterns, we would also have had to work through this resistance, which may have required many additional months. Had she established a transference neurosis with me, we also probably would have become involved in difficulties for a long time. Finally, had she become dependent on me, we would have had to resolve the trauma of separation, and this also would have required a considerable treatment period. While I was able to avoid these snags in this patient, I might not have been able to circumvent them in others.

Now I should like to say a few things about the quality of change achieved in this patient. We worked practically entirely on a characterologic level. She was able to recognize a prevailing pattern in her relations with people; she could see its repetitive and compulsive nature; and she realized how it was engendered by early feelings of insecurity and devaluated self-esteem. She did not reach levels of the deepest unconscious conflicts, namely, oral, anal and homosexual strivings, incestuous impulses, and penis envy. She might have done so had therapy been more intensive and prolonged and had we established a transference neurosis. Whether she would have responded with more reconstructive changes in her personality than she achieved in her present therapeutic effort, we cannot say.

Actually, in view of the fact that she was 50 years of age, and chiefly because she moved rapidly in treatment to a point of losing her symptoms and of relating herself better to people, the goals she achieved were probably optimal ones. Nevertheless, she might have progressed even further with more therapy.

The classification of the kind of therapy I

used would fall into that of insight therapy with reeducative goals, even though I dealt with resistance, and, at least in several instances, with transference. Also, I employed dream analysis. I did not use free association, relying entirely on the focused interview. The effect was mostly of a reeducative nature.

A follow-up study of 5 years has shown that the gains the patient achieved from therapy were sustained and that she has continued to grow in self-stature and in the kinds of relationships she establishes with people. There has not been any relapse of symptoms throughout the 5-year period. The patient could see how compulsive her patterns were, and she was, on a number of occasions, tempted to revert to her previous role with people. After a brief interlude of acting-out, however, she would interrupt her pattern, and enter into a different kind of relationship. She has developed outside interests along the lines planned in our talks, and she has, according to her own expression "never been so happy" in her life. These results are, under any standards, estimable ones.

Recommended Texts

The literature in the field of psychotherapy flourishes with ever increasing contributions from all divisions of the behavioral sciences. Accordingly, the selection of recommended reading becomes progressively more difficult as new books and periodicals accumulate. The present section contains a representative sampling of the most popular texts among students and reviewers. A more complete bibliography explicating specific topics will be found in the various chapters of this book. Obviously it will be difficult or impossible for any therapist to read or even to acquire all the recommended texts, which will undoubtedly be found on the shelves of any good psychiatric library. Readers, nevertheless, will be able discriminately to cull from the suggested lists items that suit their interests and needs. New books, as well as revisions, will undoubtedly appear as time goes by. Nevertheless, many of the present texts will in all probability continue to survive as classics.

A Weekly Psychiatry Update Series is published by Biomedia Inc., Princeton, New Jersey 08540. While not in the textbook category, it offers a review of timely topics on a weekly basis written by authorities in different fields and is organized as part of a continuing education program.

The list of books that follows has been divided into 82 main categories. To make it easier for readers to find the particular section or sections that are of interest to them, Addenda Table 1 gives the subject organization of the texts recommended.

Addenda Table 1
Contents of Recommended Texts

1. Reference Works	26. Psychoanalytic Psychotherapy
a. Dictionaries and Glossaries	27. Group Process
b. Psychiatry	28. Group Psychotherapy
c. Psychology	29. Family Therapy and Marital Therapy
d. Psychotherapy	30. Hypnosis
e. Psychoanalysis	31. Somatic Therapies
f. Behavior Therapy	32. Miscellaneous Adjuncts
g. Social Work	a. Occupational Therapy
h. Anthropology	b. Recreational Therapy
2. History	c. Music Therapy
3. Personality Development	d. Dance Therapy
4. Culture and Personality	e. Poetry Therapy
5. Human Behavior and Adaptation	f. Art Therapy
6. Mental Functions	g. Bibliotherapy
a. Perception	h. Videotape
b. Cognitive Processes	i. Biofeedback
c. Conditioning and Learning	j. Relaxation Methods and Meditation
d. Thinking	33. Short-term Psychotherapy
e. Problem Solving	34. Hospital Psychiatry
f. Intelligence	35. Emergencies in Psychotherapy and Crisis Intervention [Suicide]
g. Creativity	36. Rehabilitation and Recreation
h. Motivation	37. Consultation-Liaison Psychiatry
i. Opinions, Beliefs, and Values	38. Psychosomatic Disorders
7. Basic Neuropsychiatry	39. Sexual Problems
8. Diagnosis	40. Depressive Disorders
9. Psychopathology	41. Schizophrenic Reactions
10. Psychodynamics	42. Borderline Cases
11. Conditioning Theory	43. Delinquency and Criminality
12. General Systems Theory	44. Speech and Voice Disorders
13. Psychoanalytic Theory	45. Alcoholism
14. Schools of Psychotherapy	46. Drug Addiction
a. General	47. Organic Brain Disease
b. Individual Schools	48. Mental Deficiency
15. Introduction to Psychotherapy	49. Case Material
16. Values in Psychotherapy	50. Child Psychiatry and Child Therapy
17. Tactics of Psychotherapy	51. Adolescence: Problems and Therapy
18. Interviewing	52. Old Age: Problems and Approaches
19. Counseling and Casework	53. Behavioral Sciences
20. Behavior Therapy	54. Neurophysiology
21. Freudian Psychoanalysis	55. Neurology, Neuroanatomy, and Neuropathology
22. Ego Analysis	56. Sleep and Dreams
23. Kleinian Psychoanalysis	57. Biochemistry
24. Non-Freudian Psychoanalysis [Adler, Ferenczi, Horney, Jung, Rank, Reich, Stekel, Sullivan]	58. Genetics
25. Existential Analysis	59. Ethology

60. Sociology
      a. General
      b. Social Theory
      c. Social and Family Problems
      d. Social Behavior
      e. Family Interaction
      f. Bureaucracy
      g. Social Stratification
      h. Social Class and Mental Illness
      i. Ethnic Relations
      j. Discrimination
      k. Crime
      l. Suicide and Homicide
      m. Military
      n. Adoption
61. Anthropology
62. Psychology
      a. Testing
      b. Experimental Psychology
      c. Educational Psychology
      d. Physiological Psychology
      e. Clinical Psychology
      f. Abnormal Psychology
      g. Social Psychology
63. Communication
      a. General
      b. Mass Communication
      c. Propaganda
      d. Language
      e. Interactional Process

64. Group Dynamics
65. Economics
66. Politics
67. Religion
68. Education
69. Schools
70. Community Organization and Planning
71. Community Mental Health
72. Community Mental Health Centers and
     Clinics
73. Administration
74. Legal Aspects
75. Public Health
76. Epidemiology
77. Mental Health Manpower
      a. General
      b. Psychiatrists
      c. Psychologists
      d. Social Workers
      e. Nurses
      f. Nonpsychiatric Physicians
      g. Teachers
      h. Clergy
      i. Nonprofessionals (Paraprofessionals)
      j. Volunteers
78. Industrial Mental Health
79. Research in Psychotherapy
80. Continuing Education
81. Teaching and Supervision
82. Death and Dying

REFERENCE WORKS

Dictionaries and Glossaries

American Psychiatric Association: A psychiatric Glossary (4th ed). New York, Basic Books, 1975
American Psychoanalytic Association: A Glossary of Psychoanalytic Terms and Concepts (2d ed). New York, the Association, 1968
English HB, English AC: A Comprehensive Dictionary of Psychological and Psychoanalytical Terms (4th ed). New York, McKay, 1958
Freud S: Freud: Dictionary of Psychoanalysis. Fodor N, Gaynor F (eds). New York, Philosophical Library, 1950
Hinsie LE, Campbell RJ: Psychiatric Dictionary (4th ed). New York, Oxford University Press, 1970

Psychiatry

Arieti S: American Handbook of Psychiatry (2d ed), 6 vols. New York, Basic Books, 1974–1975
Freedman AM, Kaplan HI, & Sadock BJ (eds): Comprehensive Textbook of Psychiatry–II (2d ed), 2 vols. Baltimore, Williams & Wilkins, 1975
Wolman BB: Encyclopedia of Psychiatry, Psychology, Psychoanalysis, and Neurology, 12 vols. New York, Van Nostrand Reinhold for Aesculapius Publishers (in press)

Psychology

Eysenck HJ (ed): Encyclopedia of Psychology, 3 vols. New York, Seabury, 1972
Koch S (ed): Psychology: A Study of Science, 6 vols. New York, McGraw-Hill, 1959–1963

Psychotherapy

Masserman JH (ed): Current Psychiatric Therapies. New York, Grune & Stratton, annually from 1961*

Psychoanalysis

Eidelberg L (ed): Encyclopedia of Psychoanalysis. New York, Free Press, 1968
Freud S: Standard Edition of the Complete Psychological Works of Sigmund Freud, 24 vols. Strachey J (trans). London, Hogarth, 1964

Behavior Therapy

Franks CM, Wilson GT (eds): Annual Review of Behavior Therapy and Practice. New York, Brunner/Mazel, annually from 1973

---

* Works marked with an asterisk appear in the list for medical practitioners by West KM, Wender RW, May RS: Books in clinical practice 1971–75: A selected and annotated list for medical practitioners. Postgrad Med 56(7)60–61, 1974.

** Works marked with a double asterisk appear in Brandon AN: Selected list of books and journals for the small medical library. Bull Med Libr Assoc 63(2)149–172, 1975.

† Works marked with a dagger appear in Allyn R: A library for internists. Recommended by the American College of Physicians. Ann Intern Med 84:346–373, 1976.

†† Works marked with a double dagger are the most recommended books of the basic psychiatry literature from recommended reading lists of residency training programs that appear in Woods JB, Pieper S, Jr, Frazier SH: Basic psychiatric literature. I. Books. Bull Med Libr Assoc 56(3)295–309, 1968.

Social Work

Lindzey, G, & Aronson E (eds): Handbook of Social Psychology, (2d ed), 5 vols. Reading, Mass, Addison-Wesley, 1954–1969

Morris R (ed): Encyclopedia of Social Work, 2 vols. New York, National Association of Social Workers, 1971

Anthropology

Kroeber AL (ed): Anthropology Today: An Encyclopedic Inventory. Chicago, University of Chicago Press, 1953

HISTORY

Ackerknecht EH: A Short History of Psychiatry (2d ed). New York, Hafner, 1969

Altschule MD: Roots of Modern Psychiatry (2d ed). New York, Grune & Stratton, 1965

Deutsch A: The Mentally Ill in America (2d ed). New York, Columbia University Press, 1949   ††

Ehrenwald J (ed): History of Psychotherapy: From Healing Magic to Encounter. New York, Aronson, 1974

Ellenberger H: The Discovery of the Unconscious: The History and Evolution of Dynamic Psychiatry. New York, Basic Books, 1970

Havens LL: Approaches to the Mind: Movement of the Psychiatric Schools from Sects Toward Science. Boston, Little, Brown, 1973

Howells JG (ed): World History of Psychiatry. New York, Brunner/Mazel, 1975

Jones E: The Life and Work of Sigmund Freud, 3 vols. New York, Basic Books, 1953–57 (1961 abridged—Trilling L, ed)   ††

Misiak H, Sexton VS: History of Psychology: An Overview. New York, Grune & Stratton, 1966

Zilboorg G, Henry GW: A History of Medical Psychology. New York, Norton, 1967

PERSONALITY DEVELOPMENT

Bowlby J: Maternal Care and Mental Health, (2d ed). Monograph Series No. 2. Geneva, World Health Organization, 1952

Bowlby J: Attachment and Loss. New York, Basic Books. Vol. 1: Attachment, 1969. Vol. 2: Separation, 1973

Conger JJ: Adolescence and Youth: Psychological Development in a Changing World. New York, Harper & Row, 1973

Erikson EH: Identity and the Life Cycle: Selected Papers. Psychological Issues, Monogr 1: Vol. 1, No. 1 New York, International Universities Press, 1967

Escalona SK: Roots of Individuality: Normal Patterns of Development in Infancy. Chicago, Aldine, 1968

Foss BM: New Perspectives in Child Development. New York, Penguin, 1975 (paperback)

Fraiberg SH: The Magic Years. New York, Scribner, 1968

Josselyn I: Psychosocial Development of Children. New York, Family Service Association of America, 1948

Knobloch H, Pasamanick B (eds): Gesell and Amatruda's Developmental Diagnosis (3d ed). New York, Harper & Row, 1974

Lidz T: The Person: His and Her Development Throughout the Life Cycle (rev ed). New York, Basic Books, 1976

Mahler M, et al.: Psychological Birth of the Human Infant. New York, Basic Books, 1975

Mussen P (ed): Carmichael's Manuel of Child Psychology (3d ed), 2 vols. New York, Wiley, 1970

Piaget J, Inhelder B: Psychology of the Child. New York, Basic Books, 1969

Spitz R: The First Year of Life: A Psychoanalytic Study of Normal and Deviant Development of Object Relations. New York, International Universities Press, 1965

Wiedeman GH (ed): Personality Development and Deviation: A Textbook for Social Work. New York, International Universities Press, 1975

CULTURE AND PERSONALITY

Abel TM, Metraux R: Culture and Psychotherapy. New Haven, Conn, College and University Press, 1974

Bergen BJ, Thomas CS (eds): Issues and Problems in Social Psychiatry: A Book of Readings. Springfield, Ill, Thomas, 1966

Ginsburg SW: Psychiatrist's Views on Social Issues. New York, Columbia University Press, 1963

Hollingshead AB, Redlich FC: Social Class and Mental Illness. New York, Wiley, 1958 (paperback) ††

Kardiner A, et al: The Psychological Frontiers of Society. New York, Columbia University Press, 1945

Kardiner A: The Individual and His Society (rev ed). Westport, Conn, Greenwood, 1974

LeVine RA (ed): Culture and Personality: Contemporary Readings. Chicago, Aldine, 1974

Masserman J, Schwab JJ (eds): Social Psychiatry, vol. 1. New York, Grune & Stratton, 1974

Mead M: Male and Female: A Study of Sexes in a Changing World. New York, Morrow, 1975 (paperback)   ††

Moos RH: The Human Context: Environmental Determinants of Behavior. New York, Wiley, 1976

Myers JK, Bean LL: A Decade Later: A Follow-up of Social Class and Mental Illness. New York, Wiley, 1968

Opler ME: Culture, Psychiatry and Human Values. Springfield, Ill, Thomas, 1965

Voth HM, Orth MH: Psychotherapy and the Role of the Environment. New York, Behavioral Publications, 1973

HUMAN BEHAVIOR AND ADAPTATION

Berelson B, Steiner G: Human Behavior: An Inventory of Scientific Findings. New York, Harcourt, 1964 (paperback, 1967)

Dollard J: Frustration and Aggression. New Haven, Yale University Press, 1939

Erikson EH: Childhood and Society (2d ed). New York, Norton, 1963

Freedman AM, Kaplan HI (eds): Human Behavior: Biological, Psychological and Sociological. New York, Aronson, 1973

Grinker RR (ed): Toward a Unified Theory of Human Behavior. New York, Basic Books, 1956

Harvey OJ (ed): Experience, Structure and Adaptability. New York, Springer, 1966

Jahoda M: Current Concepts of Positive Mental Health. New York, Basic Books, 1958

Levi L (ed): Emotions: Their Parameters and Measurement. New York, Raven, 1975

Sadock BJ, Kaplan HJ, Freedman AM (eds): The Sexual Experience. Baltimore, Williams & Wilkins, 1976

Selye H: Stress in Health and Disease. Reading, Mass, Butterworths, 1976

MENTAL FUNCTIONS

Perception

Allport FH: Theories of Perception and the Concept of Structure. New York, Wiley, 1955

Geldard F: The Human Senses (2d ed). New York, Wiley, 1972

Cognitive Processes

Inhelder B, Piaget J: The Growth of Logical Thinking from Childhood to Adolescence. New York, Basic Books, 1958

Conditioning and Learning

Hilgard ER, Bower GH: Theories of Learning (4th ed). Englewood Cliffs, NJ, Prentice-Hall, 1974

Skinner BF: The Behavior of Organisms. New York, Appleton-Century-Crofts, 1938

Thinking

Bruner JS, et al: A Study of Thinking. New York, Wiley, 1956 (paperback)

Problem Solving

Davis GA: Psychology of Problem Solving: Theory and Practice. New York, Basic Books, 1973
Wertheimer M: Productive Thinking (rev ed). New York, Harper & Row, 1959

Intelligence

Block NJ, Dworkin G (eds): The IQ Controversy. New York, Pantheon, 1976
Butcher HJ: Human Intelligence: Its Nature and Assessment. London, Methuen, 1968

Creativity

Stein M: Stimulating Creativity: Vol. 1, Individual Procedures. New York, Academic Press, 1974

Motivation

Maslow AH: Motivation and Personality (2d ed). New York, Harper & Row, 1970 (paperback)
Weiner B: Theories of Motivation: From Mechanism to Cognition. Chicago, Rand McNally, 1972

Opinions, Beliefs, and Values

Maslow AH (ed): New Knowledge in Human Values. New York, Harper & Row, 1959 (paperback, 1970)
Morris C: Varieties of Human Value. Chicago, University of Chicago Press, 1956 (paperback, 1973)
Robinson JP, Shaver PR (eds): Measures of Social-Psychological Attitudes (rev ed). Ann Arbor, Institute for Social Research, University of Michigan, 1973

BASIC NEUROPSYCHIATRY

Alexander F, Ross H (eds): Dynamic Psychiatry. Chicago, University of Chicago Press, 1952   ††
Detre T, Jarecki HG: Modern Psychiatric Treatment. Philadelphia, Lippincott, 1971   * **
Freedman AM, Kaplan HI, Sadock BJ: Modern Synopsis of Comprehensive Textbook of Psychiatry, II, (2d ed). Baltimore, Williams & Wilkins, 1976   * ** †
Kolb LC: Modern Clinical Psychiatry (8th ed). Philadelphia, Saunders, 1973   * ** †
Masserman JH: Theory and Therapy of Dynamic Psychiatry. New York, Aronson, 1973
Redlich FC, Freedman DX: The Theory and Practice of Psychiatry. New York, Basic Books, 1966

DIAGNOSIS

American Psychiatric Association, Committee on Nomenclature and Statistics: Diagnostic and Statistical Manual of Mental Disorders (2d ed). Washington, DC, the Association, 1968
Freedman AM, Kaplan HL: Diagnosing Mental Illness: Evaluation in Psychiatry and Psychology. New York, Atheneum, 1972 ("One of a series of volumes based on the first edition of the Comprehensive Textbook of Psychiatry")
Hoch P: Differential Diagnosis in Clinical Psychiatry. New York, Aronson, 1972
Katz MM (ed): The Role and Methodology of Classification in Psychiatry and Psychopathology. Chevy Chase, Md, NIMH, 1968
Woodruff RA: Psychiatric Diagnosis. New York, Oxford University Press, 1974   *

PSYCHOPATHOLOGY

Angyal A: Neurosis and Treatment: A Holistic Theory (Hanfman E, Jones R, eds). New York, Viking, 1973 (paperback)

Davis DR: Introduction to Psychopathology (3d ed). New York, Oxford University Press 1973 (paperback)

Freeman T: Psychopathology of the Psychoses. New York, International Universities Press, 1969

Millon T: Theories of Psychopathology. Philadelphia, Saunders, 1967

Nemiah J: Foundations of Psychopathology. New York, Aronson, 1973

Sahakian WS (ed): Psychopathology Today: Experimentation, Theory and Research. Itasca, Ill, Peacock, 1970

White RB: Elements of Psychopathology: The Mechanisms of Defense. New York, Grune & Stratton, 1976

Zax M, Stricker G: Patterns of Psychopathology. New York, Macmillan, 1963

PSYCHODYNAMICS

Cheshire NM: The Nature of Psychodynamic Interpretation. New York, Wiley, 1975

Weiss E: Structure and Dynamics of the Human Mind. New York, Grune & Stratton, 1960

CONDITIONING THEORY

Bandura A, Walters RH: Social Learning and Personality Development. New York, Holt, 1963

Lieberman D: Learning and Control of Behavior: Some Principles, Theories, and Applications of Classical and Operant Conditioning. New York, Holt, 1974

Mowrer OH: Learning Theory and Personality Dynamics. New York, Ronald, 1950

Skinner, BF: Science and Human Behavior. New York, Macmillan, 1953

GENERAL SYSTEMS THEORY

Bertalanffy L von: Robots, Men and Minds. New York, Braziller, 1967

Buckley W: Modern Systems Research for the Behavioral Scientist. Chicago, Aldine, 1968

Gray W, Duhl FJ, Rizzo ND (eds): General Systems Theory and Psychiatry. Boston, Little, Brown, 1969

Grinker RR, Sr: Toward a Unified Theory of Human Behavior. New York, Basic Books, 1967

Jones M: Maturation of the Therapeutic Community: An Organic Approach to Health and Mental Health. New York, Human Sciences Press, 1976

Ruesch J: Knowledge in Action. New York, Aronson, 1975

PSYCHOANALYTIC THEORY

Brenner C: An Elementary Textbook of Psychoanalysis (enl & rev ed). New York, International Universities Press, 1973

Fenichel, O: The Psychoanalytic Theory of Neurosis. New York, Norton, 1945   ††

Freud S: New Introductory Lectures on Psychoanalysis. Strachey J (ed & trans). New York, Norton, 1933

Freud S: Outline of Psychoanalysis (rev ed). Strachey J (ed & trans). New York, Norton, 1970 (paperback)

Menninger KA, Holzman PS: The Theory of Psychoanalytic Technique (2d ed). New York, Basic Books, 1973

Rickman J: Selected Contributions to Psychoanalysis. New York, Basic Books, 1957

SCHOOLS OF PSYCHOTHERAPY

General

Alexander F, Eisenstein S, Grotjahn M (eds): Psychoanalytic Pioneers. New York, Basic Books, 1966
Brown JAC: Freud and the Post-Freudians. New York, Penguin, 1961
Corsini RJ (ed): Current Psychotherapies. Itasca, Ill, Peacock, 1973
Harper RA: Psychoanalysis and Psychotherapy: 36 Systems. New York, Aronson, 1974   *
Munroe R: Schools of Psychoanalytic Thought. Hinsdale, Ill, Dryden, 1955   ††
Usdin G (ed): Overview of the Psychotherapies. New York, The American College of Psychiatrists and Brunner/Mazel, 1975

Individual Schools

CLIENT-CENTERED THERAPY

Rogers C: Client-Centered Therapy: Its Current Practice, Implications, and Theory. Boston, Houghton Mifflin, 1951

COGNITIVE THERAPY

Beck AT: Cognitive Therapy and Emotional Disorders. New York, International Universities Press, 1976

CONFRONTATION THERAPY

Adler G, Myerson PG (eds): Confrontation in Psychotherapy. New York, Aronson, 1973

GESTALT THERAPY

Perls F: Gestalt Therapy Verbatim. Moab, Utah, Real People Press, 1969
Smith WWL (ed): Growing Edge of Gestalt Therapy. New York, Brunner/Mazel, 1976

ORIENTAL THERAPY

Reynolds DK: Morita Psychotherapy. Berkeley, University of California Press, 1976
Suzuki DT: Zen Buddhism and Psychoanalysis. New York, Grove, 1963

RATIONAL EMOTIVE THERAPY

Ellis A: Humanistic Psychotherapy: The Rational-Emotive Approach. New York, McGraw-Hill, 1974 (paperback)

REALITY THERAPY

Glasser W: Reality Therapy: A New Approach to Psychiatry. New York, Harper & Row, 1965

TRANSACTIONAL ANALYSIS

Berne E: Transactional Analysis in Psychotherapy: A Systematic Individual and Social Psychiatry. New York, Ballantine, 1975 (paperback)

INTRODUCTION TO PSYCHOTHERAPY

Balsam RM, Balsam A: Becoming a Psychotherapist: A Clinical Primer. Boston, Little, Brown, 1974
Bruch H: Learning Psychotherapy: Rationale and Ground Rules. Cambridge, Harvard University Press, 1974
Cameron DE: Psychotherapy in Action. New York, Grune & Stratton, 1968
Colby K: Primer for Psychotherapists. New York, Ronald, 1951   ††
Dewald P: Psychotherapy (2d ed). New York, Basic Books, 1971
Diethelm O: Treatment in Psychiatry (3d ed). Springfield, Ill, Thomas, 1955
Dollard J, Miller ND: Personality and Psychotherapy. New York, McGraw-Hill, 1950 (paperback)

Martin DG: Introduction to Psychotherapy. Monterey, Calif, Brooks-Cole, 1971
Rogers CR: On Becoming a Person: A Therapist's View of Psychotherapy. Boston, Houghton,
    Mifflin, 1961
Tarachow S: An Introduction to Psychotherapy. New York, International Universities Press, 1970
    (paperback also)

VALUES IN PSYCHOTHERAPY

Buhler C: Values in Psychotherapy. New York, Free Press, 1962
Hartmann H: Psychoanalysis and Moral Values. New York International Universities Press, 1960
Levine M: Psychiatry and Ethics. New York, Braziller, 1972

TACTICS OF PSYCHOTHERAPY

Masserman JH (ed): Current Psychiatric Therapies. New York, Grune & Stratton, annually from
    1961   *
Murphy W: The Tactics of Psychotherapy: The Application of Psychoanalytic Theory to
    Psychotherapy. New York, International Universities Press, 1965
Wolberg LR: The Technique of Psychotherapy (3d ed). New York, Grune & Stratton, 1977
Wolman BB (ed): The Therapist's Handbook: Treatment Methods of Mental Disorders. New York,
    Van Nostrand Reinhold, 1976

INTERVIEWING

Argelander H: The Initial Interview in Psychotherapy. Bernays HF (trans). New York, Human Sci-
    ences Press, 1976
Deutsch F, Murphy WF: The Clinical Interview, 2 vols. Vol. 1: Diagnosis. Vol. 2: Therapy. New York,
    International Universities Press, 1955   ††
Garrett AM: Interviewing: Its Principles and Methods. New York, Family Service Association of
    America, 1972
Gill MM, Newman R, Redlich F: The Initial Interview in Psychiatric Practice. New York,
    International Universities Press, 1954
Kahn RL, Cannell CF: The Dynamics of Interviewing. New York, Wiley, 1957
MacKinnon RA, Michels R: The Psychiatric Interview in Clinical Practice. Philadelphia, Saunders,
    1971   *
Masserman JH, Schwab JJ: The Psychiatric Examination. New York, Stratton Intercontinental, 1974 *
Sullivan HS: The Psychiatric Interview. New York, Norton, 1954 (paperback)   ††

COUNSELING AND CASEWORK

Ard B: Counseling and Psychotherapy. Palo Alto, Calif, Science & Behavior Books, 1975
Bordin ES: Psychological Counseling (2d ed). Englewood Cliffs, NJ, Prentice-Hall, 1968
Edinburg GM: Clinical Interviewing and Counseling: Principles and Techniques. Englewood Cliffs,
    NJ, Prentice-Hall, 1975
Hart JT, Tomlinson TM (eds): New Directions in Client-Centered Therapy. Boston, Houghton Mifflin,
    1970
Hollis F: Casework: A Psychosocial Therapy (2d ed). New York, Random House, 1972
Perez JF: Counseling; Theory and Practice. Reading, Mass, Addison-Wesley, 1965
Perlman HH: Social Casework, a Problem-solving Process. Chicago, University of Chicago Press,
    1957
Rogers CR: Counseling and Psychotherapy: Newer Concepts in Practice. Boston, Houghton Mifflin,
    1942

Traxler AE: Techniques of Guidance (3d ed). New York, Harper & Row, 1966
Turner FJ (ed): Differential Diagnosis and Treatment in Social Work (2d ed). New York, Free Press, 1976

BEHAVIOR THERAPY

APA Task Force on Behavior Therapy: Behavior Therapy in Psychiatry: A Report. New York, Aronson, 1974 (repr of APA Task Force Report 5)
Eysenck HJ (ed): Case Studies in Behavior Therapy. Boston, Routledge & Kegan, 1976
Franks CM, Wilson T (eds): Annual Review of Behavior Therapy: Theory and Practice, vol. 1. New York, Brunner/Mazel, 1973
Kanfer FH, Phillips S: Learning Foundations of Behavior Therapy. New York, Wiley, 1970
Lazarus AA (ed): Multimodal Behavior Therapy. New York, Springer, 1976
Sloane RB, et al: Psychotherapy Versus Behavior Therapy. Cambridge, Harvard University Press, 1975
Wolpe J: The Practice of Behavior Therapy (2d ed). Elmsford, NY, Pergamon, 1974

FREUDIAN PSYCHOANALYSIS

Freud S: Therapy and Technique. New York, Macmillan, 1963 (paperback)
Glover E: The Technique of Psychoanalysis (rev ed). New York, International Universities Press, 1968
Greenson R: The Technique and Practice of Psychoanalysis. New York, International Universities Press, 1967
Kubie L: Practical and Theoretical Aspects of Psychoanalysis (rev ed). New York, International Universities Press, 1975
Meltzer D: The Psychoanalytic Process. Perth, Scotland, Clunie, 1973
Nunberg H: Practice and Theory of Psychoanalysis, 2 vols. New York, International Universities Press, 1961

EGO ANALYSIS

Blanck G, Blanck R: Ego Psychology. New York, Columbia University Press, 1974
Freud A: The Ego and the Mechanisms of Defense (rev ed). Writings of Anna Freud, vol. 2. New York, International Universities Press, 1967   ††
Hartmann H: Essays on Ego Psychology: Selected Problems in Psychoanalytic Theory. New York, International Universities Press, 1965
Loevinger J: Ego Development: Conceptions and Theories. San Francisco, Jossey-Bass, 1976
Parad HJ (ed): Ego Psychology and Dynamic Casework. New York, Family Service Association of America, 1958 (Papers from the Smith College School for Social Work)

KLEINIAN PSYCHOANALYSIS

Klein M: Contributions to Psychoanalysis. London, Hogarth, 1950
Klein M: Envy and Gratitude. London, Tavistock, 1957
Rosenfield H: Psychotic States: A Psycho-analytical Approach. New York, International Universities Press, 1965
Segal H: Introduction to the Work of Melanie Klein. New York, Basic Books, 1964

NON-FREUDIAN PSYCHOANALYSIS

Adler A: The Practice and Theory of Individual Psychology. Atlantic Highlands, NJ, Humanities Press, 1971 (repr of 1929 ed)
Ferenczi S: Further Contributions to the Theory and Techniques of Psychoanalysis. London, Hogarth, 1960

Hall CS, Nordby VJ: A Primer of Jungian Psychology. New York, Taplinger, 1973
Horney K: The Neurotic Personality of Our Time. New York, Norton, 1937   ††
Horney K: New Ways in Psychoanalysis. New York, Norton, 1939
Jung CG: Psychology of the Unconscious. New York, Dodd, Mead, 1931 (orig 1916)
Kelman H: Helping People: Karen Horney's Psychoanalytic Approach. New York, Science House, 1971
Rank O: Will Therapy and Truth and Reality. New York, Knopf, 1945
Reich W: Character Analysis. New York, Farrar, Strauss & Giroux, 1972   ††
Stekel W: Techniques of Analytic Psychotherapy. New York, Liveright, 1950
Sullivan HS: Conceptions of Modern Psychiatry. New York, Norton, 1953

EXISTENTIAL ANALYSIS

Boss M: Psychoanalysis and Daseinalysis. New York, Basic Books, 1963
May R (ed.): Existential Psychology. New York, Random House, 1964
May R, Angel E, Ellenberger H (eds): Existence: A New Dimension in Psychiatry and Psychology. New York, Basic Books, 1958
Misiak H, Sexton VS: Phenomenological, Existential and Humanistic Psychologies. New York, Grune & Stratton, 1973
Ruitenbeek HM (ed): Psychoanalysis and Existential Philosophy. New York, Dutton, 1962
Sonneman U: Existence and Therapy. New York, Grune & Stratton, 1954
Van den Berg JJ: A Different Existence. Atlantic Highlands, NJ, Duquesne University Press, distributed by Humanities Press, 1972

PSYCHOANALYTIC PSYCHOTHERAPY

Alexander F: Fundamentals of Psychoanalysis. New York, Norton, 1963 (paperback)
Chessick RD: Technique and Practice of Intensive Psychotherapy. New York, Aronson, 1974
Fromm-Reichmann F: Principles of Intensive Psychotherapy. Chicago, University of Chicago Press, 1950
Giovacchini P (ed): Tactics and Techniques in Psychoanalytic Therapy, 2 vols. Vol. 1: Tactics and Techniques, 1972. Vol. 2: Countertransference, 1975. New York, Aronson
Giovacchini P: Psychoanalysis of Character Disorders. New York, Aronson, 1975
Greenacre P (ed): Affective Disorders. New York, International Universities Press, 1953   ††
Langs R: The Technique of Psychoanalytic Psychotherapy, 2 vols. New York, Aronson, 1973–1974
Lorand S: Technique of Psychoanalytic Psychotherapy. New York, International Universities Press, 1961
Shainberg D: The Transforming Self: New Dimensions in Psychoanalytic Process. New York, Stratton Intercontinental, 1973

GROUP PROCESS

Bales RF: Interaction Process Analysis: A Method for the Study of Small Groups. Reading, Mass, Addison-Wesley, 1950
Kawin E: Parenthood in a Free Nation: Manual for Group Leaders and Participants, vol. 4. Bloomington, Ind, Purdue Research Foundation, 1970
Lippitt R, Watson J, Westley R: The Dynamics of Planned Change: A Comparative Study of Principles and Technique. New York, Harcourt, 1958

GROUP PSYCHOTHERAPY

Bion WR: Experiences in Groups. New York, Basic Books, 1961
Durkin H: The Group in Depth. New York, International Universities Press, 1964
Foulkes SH: Introduction to Group Analytic Psychotherapy. London, Heinemann, 1948

Kadis A: Practicum of Group Psychotherapy (2d ed). New York, Harper & Row, 1974

Liff ZA (ed): The Leader in the Group. New York, Aronson, 1975

Rosenbaum M, Berger MM (eds): Group Psychotherapy and Group Function (rev ed). New York, Basic Books, 1975

Shaffer JB, Galinsky MD: Models of Group Therapy and Sensitivity Training. Englewood Cliffs, NJ, Prentice-Hall, 1974

Slavson SR: An Introduction to Group Therapy. New York, International Universities Press, 1943 (paperback, 1970)   ††

Wolberg LR, Aronson ML (eds): Group Therapy: An Overview. New York, Stratton Intercontinental, 1973, annual

Wolf A, Schwartz EK: Psychoanalysis in Groups. New York, Grune & Stratton, 1962

Yalom ID: The Theory and Practice of Group Psychotherapy (2d ed). New York, Basic Books, 1975

FAMILY THERAPY AND MARITAL THERAPY

Ackerman NW: The Psychodynamics of Family Life. New York, Basic Books, 1958   ††

Ackerman NW: Treating the Troubled Family. New York, Basic Books, 1966

Boszormenyi-Nagy I, Framo JL: Intensive Family Therapy. New York, Harper & Row, 1965

Glick ID, Kessler DR: Marital and Family Therapy. New York, Grune & Stratton, 1974

Grunebaum H: Contemporary Marriage: Structure, Dynamics and Therapy. Boston, Little, Brown, 1976

Haley J, Hoffman L: Techniques of Family Therapy. New York, Basic Books, 1967

Howells JG: Theory and Practice of Family Psychiatry. New York, Brunner/Mazel, 1971

Martin P: A Marital Therapy Manual. New York, Brunner/Mazel, 1976

Minuchin S: Families and Family Therapy. Cambridge, Harvard University Press, 1974

Sager C: Marriage Contracts and Couple Therapy. New York, Brunner/Mazel, 1976

Satir VM: Conjoint Family Therapy. Palo Alto, Calif, Science & Behavior Books, 1964

Satir VM: Helping Families to Change. New York, Aronson, 1975

Skynner ACR: Systems of Family and Marital Psychotherapy. New York, Brunner/Mazel, 1976

Zuk GH, Boszormenyi-Nagy I (eds): Family Therapy and Disturbed Families. Palo Alto, Calif, Science & Behavior Books, 1967

HYPNOSIS

Dorcus RM (ed): Hypnosis and Its Therapeutic Applications. New York, McGraw-Hill, 1956

Gill MM, Brenman M: Hypnosis and Related States. New York, International Universities Press, 1959

Sheehan PW, Perry CW: Methodologies of Hypnosis: A Critical Appraisal of Contemporary Paradigms of Hypnosis. New York, Wiley, 1976

Wolberg LR: Medical Hypnosis, 2 vols. New York, Grune & Stratton, 1948

Wolberg LR: Hypnoanalysis (2d ed). New York, Grune & Stratton, 1964

SOMATIC THERAPIES

American Medical Association, Department of Drugs: AMA Drug Evaluations (3rd ed). Action, Mass, Publishing Sciences Group, 1977   ** †

Ban T: Psychopharmacology. Baltimore, Williams & Wilkins, 1969

Cole JO, et al (eds): Psychopathology and Psychopharmacology. Baltimore, Johns Hopkins Press, 1973   *

Goodman LS, Gilman A: The Pharmacological Basis of Therapeutics (5th ed). New York, Macmillan, 1975.   * ** †

Hollister LE: Clinical Use of Psychotherapeutic Drugs. Springfield, Ill, Thomas, 1973

Kalinowsky LB, Hippius H: Pharmacological, Convulsive and Other Somatic Treatments in Psychiatry (2d ed). New York, Grune & Stratton, 1969

Klein DF, Gittelman-Klein R (eds): Progress in Psychiatric Drug Treatment, vol. 2. New York, Brunner/Mazel, 1976
Sargant WW, Slater ET (eds): Introduction to Physical Methods of Treatment in Psychiatry (4th ed). New York, Aronson, 1973
Schildkraut JJ: Neuropsychopharmacology and the Affective Disorders. Boston, Little, Brown, 1970
Simpson LL (ed): Drug Treatment of Mental Disorders. New York, Raven, 1976
Williams RL, Webb WB: Sleep Therapy. Springfield, Ill, Thomas, 1966

MISCELLANEOUS ADJUNCTS

Occupational Therapy

MacDonald EM: Occupational Therapy in Rehabilitation (3d ed). Baltimore, Williams & Wilkins, 1970
Willard HS, Spackman CS: Occupational Therapy (4th ed). Philadelphia, Lippincott, 1970

Recreational Therapy

Frye V, Peters M: Therapeutic Recreation: Its Theory, Philosophy and Practice. Harrisburg, Pa, Stackpole, 1972
Mosey AC: Activities Therapy. New York, Raven, 1973

Music Therapy

Alvin J: Music Therapy. New York, Basic Books, 1975

Dance Therapy

American Dance Therapy Association. Monographs. Monogr 1: 1971; Monogr 2: 1972. Columbia, Md, the Association, issued irregularly
Rosen E: Dance in Psychotherapy. New York, Teachers College Press, Columbia University, 1957

Poetry Therapy

Leedy J (ed): Poetry Therapy. Philadelphia, Lippincott, 1969

Art Therapy

Naumberg M: Dynamically Oriented Art Therapy: Its Principles and Practice. New York, Grune & Stratton, 1966
Ullman E, Dachinger P (eds): Art Therapy: Art in Education, Rehabilitation and Psychotherapy. New York, Schocken, 1975

Bibliotherapy

Brown EF: Bibliotherapy and Its Widening Applications. Metuchen, NJ, Scarecrow Press, 1975

Videotape

Berger MM (ed): Videotape Techniques in Psychiatric Training and Treatment. New York, Brunner/Mazel, 1970

Biofeedback

Biofeedback and Self-Control: An Aldine Annual on the Regulation of Bodily Processes and Consciousness, vols. 1–4. Chicago, Aldine, 1971–1974

Schwartz GE, Shapiro D (eds): Consciousness and Self-Regulation: Advances in Research, vol. 1. New York, Plenum Press, 1976

Relaxation Methods and Meditation

Benson H: The Relaxation Response. New York, Morrow, 1975

Carrington P: Freedom in Meditation. New York, Doubleday, 1977

Jacobson E: Progressive Relaxation: A Psychological and Clinical Investigation of Muscular States and Their Significance in Psychology and Medical Practice (3d rev ed). Chicago, University of Chicago Press, 1974

Naranjo C, Ornstein R: On the Psychology of Meditation. New York, Viking, 1971

SHORT-TERM PSYCHOTHERAPY

Barten HH: Brief Therapies. New York, Behavioral Publications, 1971

Malan DH: The Frontier of Brief Psychotherapy. New York, Plenum Press, 1976

Mann J: Time-Limited Psychotherapy. Cambridge, Harvard University Press, 1973

Sifneos P: Short-Term Psychotherapy and Emotional Crisis. Cambridge, Harvard University Press, 1972

Small L: Briefer Psychotherapies. New York, Brunner/Mazel, 1971

Wolberg LR (ed): Short-Term Psychotherapy. New York, Grune & Stratton, 1965

HOSPITAL PSYCHIATRY

Gralnick A (ed): The Psychiatric Hospital as a Therapeutic Instrument: Collected Papers of High Point Hospital, New York, Brunner/Mazel, 1969

Greenblatt M, Levinson DJ, Williams RH (eds): The Patient and the Mental Hospital. New York, Free Press, 1957

Group for the Advancement of Psychiatry: Crisis in Psychiatric Hospitalization, vol. 7. New York, the Group, 1969

Linn LA: A Handbook of Hospital Psychiatry: A Practical Guide to Therapy. New York, International Universities Press, 1955   ††

Smith CG, King JA: Mental Hospitals. Lexington, Mass, Lexington Books, 1975

Stanton AH, Schwartz MS: The Mental Hospital: A Study of Institutional Participation in Psychiatric Illness and Treatment. New York, Basic Books, 1954   ††

EMERGENCIES IN PSYCHOTHERAPY AND CRISIS INTERVENTION

Aguilera DC, Messick JM: Crisis Intervention: Theory and Methodology (2d ed). St. Louis, Mosby, 1974

Glick RA, et al (eds): Psychiatric Emergencies. New York, Grune & Stratton, 1976

Lieb J: The Crisis Team: A Handbook for the Mental Health Professional. New York, Harper & Row, 1973

Parad HJ: Crisis Intervention. Selected Readings. New York, Family Service Association, 1965

Resnik HLP (ed): Suicidal Behaviors: Diagnosis and Management. Boston, Little, Brown, 1968

Resnik HLP, Ruben HL (eds): Emergency Psychiatric Care: The Management of Mental Health Crises. Bowie, Md, Charles, 1975

REHABILITATION AND RECREATION

Csikszentmihalyi M: Beyond Boredom and Anxiety. San Francisco, Jossey-Bass, 1976
Edelson M: The Practice of Sociotherapy. New Haven, Yale University Press, 1970
Glasscote R: Rehabilitating the Mentally Ill in the Community. Washington, DC, Joint Information
    Service of the American Psychiatric Association, and the National Association for Mental Health,
    1971
Haun P: Recreation: A Medical Viewpoint. New York, Teachers College Press, Columbia University,
    1965 (paperback)
Lamb R: Rehabilitation in Community Mental Health. San Francisco, Jossey-Bass, 1976
Michaux WW: First Year Out: Mental Patients After Hospitalization. Baltimore, Johns Hopkins Press,
    1969
Patterson CH: Rehabilitation Counseling: Collected Papers. Champaign, Ill, Stipes, 1969 (paperback)
Rusk HA: Rehabilitation Medicine (3d rev). St. Louis, Mosby, 1971   * ** †
Silverstein M: Psychiatric Aftercare. Philadelphia, University of Pennsylvania Press, 1968

CONSULTATION-LIAISON PSYCHIATRY

Castelnuovo-Tedesco P (ed): Psychiatric Aspects of Organ Transplantation. New York, Grune &
    Stratton, 1971
Cullen JW, et al (eds): Cancer: The Behavioral Dimensions. New York, Raven, 1976 (National Cancer
    Institute Monogr)
Gentry WD, Williams RB: Psychological Aspects of Myocardial Infarction and Coronary Care. St.
    Louis, Mosby, 1974   †
Lief HI, et al (eds): The Psychological Basis of Medical Practice. New York, Harper & Row, 1963
Lipowski Z (ed): Psychological Aspects of Physical Illness. Advances in Psychosomatic Medicine Ser,
    vol. 8. Basle, Karger, 1972
Shader RI (ed): Psychiatric Complications of Medical Drugs. New York, Raven, 1972

PSYCHOSOMATIC DISORDERS

Alexander F: Psychosomatic Medicine. New York, Norton, 1965
Black P (ed): Physiological Correlates of Emotion. New York, Academic Press, 1970
Dunbar HF: Emotions and Bodily Changes: A Survey of Literature on Psychosomatic Interrelation-
    ships, 1910–1953 (4th ed). Columbia University Press, 1954, 1975 repr
Grinker RR: Psychosomatic Concepts (rev ed). New York, Aronson, 1973
Hill OW (ed): Modern Trends in Psychosomatic Medicine, vol. 2. New York, Appleton-Century-
    Crofts, 1970
Merskey H, Spear FG: Pain: Psychological and Psychiatric Aspects. London, Baillière, Tindall &
    Cassell, 1967
Wolstenholme GEW, Knight J (eds): Physiology, Emotions and Psychosomatic Illness. Amsterdam,
    Elsevier, 1972 (CIBA Foundation Symposium)

SEXUAL PROBLEMS

Abse DW: Marital and Sexual Counseling in Medical Practice (2d ed). New York, Harper & Row, 1974
Bullough VL: Sexual Variance in Society and History. New York, Wiley, 1976
Hartman WE, Fithian MA: Treatment of Sexual Dysfunction: A Bio-Psycho-Social Approach. Long
    Beach, Calif, Center for Marital and Sexual Studies, 1972
Kaplan HS: The Illustrated Manual of Sex Therapy. New York, Quadrangle, 1975
    Mazel, 1974
Kaplan HS: The Illustrated Manuel of Sex Therapy. New York, Quadrangle, 1975
Masters WH, Johnson VE: Human Sexual Inadequacy. Boston, Little, Brown, 1970

Money J: Sex Errors of the Body: Dilemmas, Education, Counseling. Baltimore, Johns Hopkins Press, 1968

Ostow M (ed): Sexual Deviation: Psychoanalytic Insights. New York, Quadrangle, 1974

Saghir MT, Robbins E: Male and Female Homosexuality: A Comprehensive Investigation. Baltimore, Williams & Wilkins, 1973

DEPRESSIVE DISORDERS

Anthony EJ, Benedek T (eds): Depression and Human Existence. Boston, Little, Brown, 1975

Beck AT: Diagnosis and Management of Depression. Philadelphia, University of Pennsylvania Press, 1973

Gaylin W (ed): The Meaning of Despair: Psychoanalytic Contributions to the Understanding of Depression. New York, Science House, 1968

Jacobson E: Depression: Comparative Studies of Normal, Neurotic, and Psychotic Conditions. New York, International Universities Press, 1971

Mendels J (ed): Psychobiology of Depression. New York, Halsted, 1975

Mendelson M: Psychoanalytic Concepts of Depression (2d ed). New York, Halsted, 1974

Schuyler D: The Depressive Spectrum. New York, Aronson, 1974

SCHIZOPHRENIC REACTIONS

American College of Psychiatrists: Schizophrenia: Biological and Psychological Perspectives (Usdin G, ed). New York, Brunner/Mazel, 1975

Arieti S: Interpretation of Schizophrenia (2d ed). New York, Basic Books, 1974

Bellak L: Ego Functions in Schizophrenics, Neurotics and Normals: A Systematic Study of Concepts, Diagnosis and Therapeutic Aspects. New York, Wiley, 1973

Bleuler E: Dementia Praecox or the Group of Schizophrenias. New York, International Universities Press, 1966

Cancro R, et al (eds): Strategic Intervention in Schizophrenia: Current Developments in Treatment. New York, Behavioral Publications, 1974

Greenblatt M (ed): Drug and Social Therapy in Chronic Schizophrenia. Springfield, Ill, Thomas, 1965

Gunderson JG, Mosher LR (eds): Psychotherapy of Schizophrenia. New York, Aronson, 1975

Hill LB: Psychotherapeutic Intervention in Schizophrenia. Chicago, University of Chicago Press, 1955   ††

Jackson DD: The Etiology of Schizophrenia. New York, Basic Books, 1960   ††

Lidz T: The Origin and Treatment of Schizophrenic Disorders. New York, Basic Books, 1973

Searles HF: Collected Papers on Schizophrenia and Related Subjects. New York, International Universities Press, 1966

Weiner IB: Psychodiagnosis in Schizophrenia. New York, Wiley, 1966

World Health Organization: Schizophrenia: A Multinational Study: A Summary of the Initial Evaluation Phase of the International Pilot Study of Schizophrenia. Public Health Papers Publication No. 63. Geneva, WHO, 1975

BORDERLINE CASES

Grinker R, et al: The Borderline Syndrome: A Behavioral Study of Ego-Functions. New York, Basic Books, 1968

Kernberg O: Borderline Conditions and Pathological Narcissism. New York, Aronson, 1975

Mack J (ed): Borderline States in Psychiatry. Seminars in Psychiatry. New York, Grune & Stratton, 1975

Masterson JF: Psychotherapy of the Borderline Adult: A Developmental Approach. New York, Brunner/Mazel, 1976

Wolberg AR: The Borderline Patient. New York, Stratton Intercontinental, 1973

DELINQUENCY AND CRIMINALITY

Aichhorn A: Wayward Youth. New York, Viking Press, 1965 (paperback)   ††
Cortes JB, Gatti FM: Delinquency and Crime, A Biopsychosocial Approach: Empirical, Theoretical, and Practical Aspects of Criminal Behavior. New York, Academic Press, 1972
Eissler KR (ed): Searchlights on Delinquency: New Psychoanalytic Studies. New York, International Universities Press, 1967   ††
Glueck S, Glueck E: Of Delinquency and Crime: A Panorama of Years of Search and Research. Springfield, Ill, Thomas, 1974
Halleck SL: Psychiatry and the Dilemmas of Crime. New York, Harper & Row, 1967
Khanna JL: New Treatment Approaches to Juvenile Delinquency. Springfield, Ill, Thomas, 1975
MacIver RM: The Prevention and Control of Delinquency. New York, Atherton, 1966
Redl F, Wineman D: The Aggressive Child. New York, Free Press, 1957
Zilboorg G: Psychology of the Criminal Act and Punishment. Westport, Conn, Greenwood, 1968 (repr 1954 ed)

SPEECH AND VOICE DISORDERS

Abse DW: Speech and Reason: Language Disorder in Mental Disease and a Translation of Philipp Wegener's *The Life of Speech*. Charlottesville, University Press of Virginia, 1971
Damste PH, Lerman JW: An Introduction to Voice Pathology: Functional and Organic. Springfield, Ill, Thomas, 1975
Mysak ED: Pathologies of Speech Systems. Baltimore, Williams & Wilkins, 1975
Vetter HJ: Language Behavior and Psycho-Pathology. Chicago, Rand McNally, 1969

ALCOHOLISM

Blum EM, Blum RH: Alcoholism: Modern Approaches to Treatment. San Francisco, Jossey-Bass, 1967
Bourne P, Fox R (eds): Alcoholism: Progress in Treatment. New York, Academic Press, 1973
Catanzaro RJ (ed): Alcoholism, the Total Treatment Approach. Springfield, Ill, Thomas, 1968
Kissin B, Begleiter H (eds): The Biology of Alcoholism, 5 vols. Vol. 1: Biochemistry. Vol. 2: Physiology and Behavior. Vol. 3: Clinical Pathology. Vol. 4: Social Aspects. Vol. 5: Rehabilitation. New York, Plenum Press, 1971–1976

DRUG ADDICTION

Ausubel D: Drug Addiction: Physiological, Psychological, and Sociological Aspects. New York, Random House, 1958
Bourne PG (ed): Addiction. New York, Academic Press, 1974
Brill L, Lieberman L (eds): Major Modalities in the Treatment of Drug Abuse. New York, Behavioral Publications, 1972
Fisher S, Freedman AM (eds): Opiate Addiction: Origins and Treatment. Washington, DC, Winston, 1973
Glasscote RM: The Treatment of Drug Abuse: Programs, Problems, Prospects. Washington, DC, Joint Information Service of the American Psychiatric Association and NIMH, 1972
Johnson RB, Lukash WM (eds): Summary of Proceedings of the Washington Conference on Medical Complications of Drug Abuse. Washington, DC, AMA Committee on Alcoholism and Drug Dependence, 1972
National Commission on Marijuana and Drug Abuse: Drug Use in America: Problem in Perspective. Washington, DC, Government Printing Office, 1973
Rosenbaum M (ed): Drug Abuse and Drug Addiction. New York, Gordon & Breach, 1974

ORGANIC BRAIN DISEASE

Elizur A: Psycho-Organic Syndrome: Its Assessment and Treatment. Los Angeles, Western Psychological Services, 1969 (paperback)
Goldstein K: The Organism: A Holistic Approach to Biology Derived from Pathological Data in Man. New York, American Book, 1939
Ho BT, McIsaac WW (eds): Brain Chemistry and Mental Disease. Advances in Biology, vol. 1. (Proceedings of the Symposium on Brain Chemistry and Mental Disease held at the Texas Research Institute, Houston, 1970.) New York, Plenum Press, 1971
Luria AR: Higher Cortical Functions in Man. New York, Basic Books, 1966
Luria AR: The Man with a Shattered World: The History of a Brain Wound. New York, Basic Books, 1972
Small L: Neuropsychodiagnosis in Psychotherapy. New York, Brunner/Mazel, 1973
Walker AE, Caveness WF (eds): The Late Effect of Head Injury. Springfield, Ill, Thomas, 1969

MENTAL DEFICIENCY

Khanna JL: Brain Damage and Mental Retardation: A Psychological Evaluation (2d ed). Springfield, Ill, Thomas, 1973
Koch R, Dobson JC: The Mentally Retarded Child and His Family: A Multidisciplinary Handbook. New York, Brunner/Mazel, 1971
Menolascino FJ (ed): Psychiatric Approaches to Mental Retardation. New York, Basic Books, 1970
Tredgold RF, Soddy K: Tredgold's Mental Retardation (11th ed). Baltimore, Williams & Wilkins, 1970
Wolfensberger W, Kurtz RA (eds): Management of the Family of the Mentally Retarded. Chicago, Follett, 1969

CASE MATERIAL

Adler A: The Case of Mrs. A. (2d ed). Chicago, Alfred Adler Institute, 1969
Baruch DW: One Little Boy. New York, Dell, 1952 (paperback)
Bettelheim B: Truants From Life: The Rehabilitation of Emotionally Disturbed Children. New York, Free Press, 1955 (paperback)
Davitz LJ: The Psychiatric Patients: Case Histories. New York, Springer, 1971
Deutsch F, Murphy WF: The Clinical Interview, 2 vols. New York, International Universities Press, 1967
Freud S: Fragment of an analysis of a case of hysteria, pp 13–146; Analysis of a phobia in a five-year-old boy, pp 149–289; Notes upon a case of obsessional neurosis, pp 293–383; Psycho-analytic notes upon an autobiographical account of a case of paranoia (dementia paranoides), pp 387–470. In Collected Papers, Vol. 2. London, Hogarth, 1952
Grinker, RR, Robbins FP (eds): Psychosomatic Case Book. New York, Blakiston, 1954
Klein M: Narrative of a Child Analysis: The Conduct of Psycho-Analysis of Children as Seen in the Treatment of a Ten-Year-Old Boy. New York, Basic Books, 1961 (rev ed—New York, Delacorte, 1975)
Masserman JH: The Practice of Dynamic Psychiatry. Part III, Case Studies and Communications. Philadelphia, Saunders, 1955
Niederland WG: The Schreber Case: Psychoanalytic Profile of a Paranoid Personality. New York, Quadrangle, 1974
Sechehaye MA: Symbolic Realization: A New Method of Psychotherapy Applied to a Case of Schizophrenia. New York, International Universities Press, 1960   ††
Stekel W: Compulsion and Doubt (rev ed), 2 vols. (Case material.) New York, Liveright, 1949
Ullman LP, Krasner L (eds): Case Studies in Behavior Modification. New York, Holt, 1965
Wolberg LR: Hypoanalysis (2d ed). (The Case of Johann, R.) New York, Grune & Stratton, 1964
Wolberg LR: The Technique of Psychotherapy. (Case histories.) New York, Grune & Stratton, 1977
The Wolf-Man by the Wolf-Man, (Gardiner M, ed). With the Case of the Wolf-Man by Sigmund Freud, and a Supplement by Ruth Mack Brunswick. New York, Basic Books, 1971

CHILD PSYCHIATRY AND CHILD THERAPY

Allen F: Psychotherapy with Children. New York, Norton, 1942   ††
Anthony EJ: The Child in His Family, vols. 1, 2, 3. International Yearbook for Child Psychiatry and Allied Disciplines. New York, Wiley, 1970
Axline VM: Play Therapy (rev ed). New York, Ballantine, 1969 (paperback)
Chess S, Thomas A (eds): Annual Progress in Child Psychiatry, vol. 1. New York, Brunner/Mazel, annually from 1968
Eissler RS, Freud A et al: Psychoanalytic Study of the Child. New Haven, Yale University Press, annually from 1945
Freud A: Writings, 7 vols. New York, International Universities Press, 1966–1974
Gardner RA: Psychotherapeutic Approaches to the Resistant Child. New York, Aronson, 1975
Graziano AM (ed): Behavior Therapy with Children, vol. 1. Chicago, Aldine, 1971
Haworth MR (ed): Child Psychotherapy: Practice and Theory. New York, Basic Books, 1964
Kanner L: Child Psychiatry (4th ed). Springfield, Ill, Thomas, 1972   **
Klein M: The Psychoanalysis of Children. New York, Norton, 1975 (orig, 1932)
Moustakas CE: Children in Play Therapy (rev ed). New York, Aronson, 1973
Pearson GH (ed): Handbook of Child Psychoanalysis. New York, Basic Books, 1968
Sapir SG, Nitzburg AC (eds): Children with Learning Problems: Readings in a Developmental-Interaction Approach. New York, Brunner/Mazel, 1973
Shaw CR, Lucas AR: The Psychiatric Disorders of Childhood (2d ed). Englewood Cliffs, NJ, Appleton, 1970   **
Sperling M: The Major Neuroses and Behavior Disorders in Children. New York, Aronson, 1974
Stedman JM: Clinical Studies in Behavior Therapy with Children, Adolescents, and Their Families. Springfield, Ill, Thomas, 1973
Szurek, SA, Berlin IN (eds): Clinical Studies in Childhood Psychoses. New York, Brunner/Mazel, 1973
Winnicott DW: Therapeutic Consultations in Child Psychiatry. New York, Basic Books, 1971
Wolman BB (ed): Handbook of Child Psychoanalysis: Research, Theory, and Practice. New York, Van Nostrand Reinhold, 1972

ADOLESCENCE: PROBLEMS AND THERAPY

Blos P: On Adolescence: A Psychoanalytic Interpretation. New York, Free Press, 1962
Esman AH (ed): The Psychology of Adolescence. New York, International Universities Press, 1975
Howells JG (ed): Modern Perspectives in Adolescent Psychiatry. New York, Brunner/Mazel, 1971
Josselyn IM (ed): Adolescence. A Report. Published under the auspices of the Joint Commission on Mental Health of Children. New York, Harper & Row, 1971
Masterson JF: Treatment of the Borderline Adolescent: A Developmental Approach. New York, Wiley, 1972
Rachman AW: Identity Group Psychotherapy with Adolescents. Springfield, Ill, Thomas, 1975
Weiner IB: Psychological Disturbance in Adolescence. New York, Wiley, 1970

OLD AGE: PROBLEMS AND APPROACHES

Bellak L, Karasu TB (eds): Geriatric Psychiatry: A Handbook for Psychiatrists and Primary Care Physicians. New York, Grune & Stratton, 1976
Butler RN, Lewis MI: Aging and Mental Health, Positive Psychosocial Approaches. St. Louis, Mosby, 1973 (paperback)
Eisdorfer C, Lawton MP (eds): The Psychology of Adult Development and Aging. Washington, DC, American Psychological Association, 1973
Howells, JG (ed): Modern Perspectives in the Psychiatry of Old Age. New York, Brunner/Mazel, 1975

BEHAVIORAL SCIENCES

Behavioral and Social Sciences Survey Committee: The Behavioral and Social Sciences: Outlook and
    Needs: A Report. Washington, DC, National Academy of Sciences, 1969
Berelson B (ed): The Behavioral Sciences Today. New York, Basic Books, 1963
Hine FR: Behavioral Science: A Selective View. Boston, Little, Brown, 1972
Regan PF, Pattishall EG (eds): Behavioral Science Contributions to Psychiatry. Boston, Little,
    Brown, 1965
Wolberg LR: Psychotherapy and the Behavioral Sciences. New York, Grune & Stratton, 1966

NEUROPHYSIOLOGY

American Physiological Society: Handbook of Physiology, Section 1: Neurophysiology, 3 vols. Ma-
    goun HW (ed). Baltimore, Williams & Wilkins, 1959–1960
Kursunoglu B (ed): Progress in the Neurosciences and Related Fields. Studies in Natural Sciences
    Series, vol. 6. New York, Plenum, 1974
Magoun, HW: The Waking Brain (2d ed). Springfield, Ill, Thomas, 1969

NEUROLOGY, NEUROANATOMY, AND NEUROPATHOLOGY

Brain L: Diseases of the Nervous System (7th ed). Rev by Walton JN. New York, Oxford University
    Press, 1969
Chusid JG: Correlative Neuroanatomy and Functional Neurology (15th ed). Los Altos, Calif, Lange,
    1973   **
Malamud N: Atlas of Neuropathology. Berkeley, University of California Press, 1957
Merritt, HH (ed): A Textbook of Neurology (5th ed). Philadelphia, Lea & Febiger, 1973   * ** †
Truex RC, Carpenter MB: Human Neuroanatomy. Baltimore, Williams & Wilkins, 1969

SLEEP AND DREAMS

Altman LL: The Dream in Psychoanalysis (rev ed). New York, International Universities Press, 1975
Bonime W: The Clinical Use of Dreams. New York, Basic Books, 1962
Foulkes D: Psychology of Sleep. New York, Scribner, 1966 (paperback)
French TM, Fromm E: Dream Interpretation: A New Approach. New York, Basic Books, 1964
Freud S: The Interpretation of Dreams. Strachey J (ed). New York, Basic Books, 1955   ††
Gutheil EA: The Handbook of Dream Analysis. New York, Liveright, 1951
Kales A (ed): Sleep Physiology and Pathology. A Symposium. Philadelphia, Lippincott, 1969
Usdin G (ed): Sleep Research and Clinical Practice. New York, Brunner/Mazel, 1973

BIOCHEMISTRY

Grenell RG, Gabay S (eds): Biological Foundations of Psychiatry. New York, Raven, 1976
Harlow HF, Woolsey CN: Biological and Biochemical Bases of Behavior. Madison University of
    Wisconsin Press, 1958
Jevons FR: The Biochemical Approach to Life. New York, Basic Books, 1964
Michael R (ed): Endocrinology and Human Behavior. New York, Oxford University Press, 1968
Sachar EJ (ed): Hormones, Behavior and Psychopathology. New York, Raven, 1976
Weil-Malherbe H, Szara S: The Biochemistry of Functional and Experimental Psychoses. Springfield,
    Ill, Thomas, 1971

GENETICS

Bergsma D (ed): Birth Defects: Atlas and Compendium. Baltimore, Williams & Wilkins, 1973
Fuller JL, Thompson WR: Behavior Genetics. New York, Wiley, 1960
Slater E, Cowie V: The Genetics of Mental Disorders. New York, Oxford University Press, 1971

ETHOLOGY

Eibl-Eibesfeldt I: Ethology: The Biology of Behavior (2d ed). New York, Holt, 1975
Lorenz K: On Aggression. New York, Harcourt, 1966
Serban G, King A (eds): Animal Models in Human Psychobiology. Proceedings of the Second International Symposium of the Kittay Scientific Foundation. New York, Plenum Press, 1976
Tinbergen N: The Study of Instinct. New York, Oxford University Press, 1969
Tobach E, et al: Biopsychology of Development. New York, Academic Press, 1971
Wilson EO: Sociobiology: The New Synthesis. Cambridge, Harvard University Press, 1975

SOCIOLOGY

General

Becker HS: Social Problems: A Modern Approach. New York, Wiley, 1966
Society Today (2d ed). CRM Books Editorial Staff. Del Mar, Calif, Communications Research Machines, 1973

Social Theory

Coser LA, Rosenberg B (eds): Sociological Theory: A Book of Readings (4th ed). New York, Macmillan, 1976
Merton RK: Social Theory and Social Structure. New York, Free Press, 1968

Social and Family Problems

Kantor D, Lehr, W: Inside the Family. San Francisco, Jossey-Bass, 1976
Merton RK, Nisbet RA (eds): Contemporary Social Problems (3d ed). New York, Harcourt, 1971
Rainwater L (ed): Social Problems and Public Policy: Inequality and Justice. Chicago, Aldine, 1974

Social Behavior

Homans GC: Social Behavior: Its Elementary Forms (rev ed). New York, Harcourt, 1974
Weinstein F, Platt GM: Psychoanalytic Sociology: An Essay on the Interpretation of Historical Data and the Phenomena of Collective Behavior. Baltimore, Johns Hopkins University Press, 1973

Family Interaction

Parsons T, Bales RF: Family Socialization and Interaction Process. New York, Free Press, 1955

Bureaucracy

Bennis WG (ed): American Bureaucracy (2d ed). New Brunswick, NJ, Transaction Books, Rutgers-The State University, 1972
Blau P: The Dynamics of Bureaucracy (rev ed). Chicago, University of Chicago Press, 1973 (paperback)

Social Stratification

Lejeune, R (ed): Class and Conflict in American Society. New York, Random House, 1972

Social Class and Mental Illness

Finney JG (ed): Culture Change, Mental Health and Poverty. Lexington, University Press of Kentucky, 1969

Hollingshead AG, Redlich FC: Social Class and Mental Illness: A Community Study. New York, Wiley, 1958

Myers JK: A Decade Later: A Follow-up of Social Class and Mental Illness. New York, Wiley, 1968

Ethnic Relations

Gelfand, DE, Lee RD (eds): Ethnic Conflicts and Power: A Cross-National Perspective. New York, Wiley, 1973

Discrimination

Becker G: The Economics of Discrimination (rev 2d ed). Chicago, University of Chicago Press, 1971 (paperback)

Crime

Cohen AK: Delinquent Boys. New York, Free Press, 1971 (paperback)

Cressey DR, Ward DA (eds): Delinquency, Crime and Social Process. New York, Harper & Row, 1969

Suicide and Homicide

Douglas JD: Social Meanings of Suicide. Princeton, NJ, Princeton University Press, 1967

Palmer S: The Violent Society. New Haven, Conn, College and University Press, 1972

Military

Janowitz M: Sociology and the Military Establishment, vol. 5. New York, Russell Sage Foundation, 1974

Adoption

Ansfield J: The Adopted Child. Springfield, Ill, Thomas, 1971

ANTHROPOLOGY

Mead M: An Anthropologist at Work: Writings of Ruth Benedict. New York, Avon, 1973 (paperback)

Mering O von, Kasdan L: Anthropology and the Behavioral and Health Sciences. Pittsburgh, Pa, University of Pittsburgh Press, 1970

Muensterberger M (ed): Man and His Culture: Psychoanalytic Anthropology After "Totem and Taboo." New York, Taplinger, 1970

Williams TR (ed): Psychological Anthropology. The Hague, Mouton, 1975 (distributed by Aldine)

PSYCHOLOGY

Testing

Cronbach LJ: Essentials of Psychological Testing (3d ed). New York, Harper & Row, 1970
Harrower M: Appraising Personality. New York, Simon & Schuster, 1968 (paperback)
Matarazzo JD: Wechsler's Measurement and Appraisal of Adult Intelligence (5th ed). Baltimore, Williams & Wilkins, 1972
Murstein BI (ed): Handbook of Projective Techniques. New York, Basic Books, 1965
Rapaport D, Gill MM, Schafer R: Diagnostic Psychological Testing (rev ed). Robert R. Holt (ed). New York, International Universities Press, 1968
Rickers-Ovsiankina MA: Rorschach Psychology (rev ed). Huntington, NY, Krieger, 1977

Experimental Psychology

Kling JW, Riggs LA (eds): Woodworth-Schlossberg's Experimental Psychology, 3d ed. New York, Holt, 1971
Nuttin J, et al (eds): Experimental Psychology. Vol. 5: Motivation, Emotion and Personality. New York, Basic Books, 1968
Plutchik R: Foundations of Experimental Research (2d ed). New York, Harper & Row, 1974
Stevens SS (ed): Handbook of Experimental Psychology. New York, Wiley, 1951

Educational Psychology

Cronbach LJ: Educational Psychology (2d ed). New York, Harcourt, 1963

Physiological Psychology

Brown H: Physiological Psychology: An Integrative Approach. New York, Oxford University Press, 1975
Morgan CT: Physiological Psychology (3d ed). New York, McGraw-Hill, 1965

Clinical Psychology

Bachrach AJ: Experimental Foundations of Clinical Psychology. New York, Basic Books, 1962
Korchin SJ: Modern Clinical Psychology: Principles of Intervention in the Clinic and Community. New York, Basic Books, 1976
Rubinstein EA, Lorr M (eds): Survey of Clinical Practice in Psychology. New York, International Universities Press, 1954
Weiner IB (ed): Clinical Methods in Psychology. New York, Wiley, 1976
Wolman BB (ed): Handbook of Clinical Psychology. New York, McGraw-Hill, 1965

Abnormal Psychology

Coleman J: Abnormal Psychology and Modern Life (5th ed), Glenview, Ill, Scott, Foresman, 1976
Eysenck, HJ (ed): Handbook of Abnormal Psychology (2d ed). San Diego, Calif, Knapp, 1973
White RW, Watt NF: Abnormal Personality (4th ed). New York, Ronald, 1973

Social Psychology

Brehm SS: The Application of Social Psychology to Clinical Practice. New York, Halsted/Wiley, 1976
Wechsler H, Solomon L, Kramer BM (eds): Social Psychology and Mental Health. New York, Holt, 1970

COMMUNICATION

General

Steinberg DD, Jakobovits LA: Semantics: An Interdisciplinary Reader in Philosophy, Linguistics and Psychology. London, Cambridge University Press, 1971

Mass Communication

McLuhan M: Understanding Media: The Extensions of Man. New York, McGraw-Hill, 1964 (paperback)

Schramm W, Roberts DF (eds): Process and Effects of Mass Communications (rev ed). Urbana, University of Illinois Press, 1971

Propaganda

Berelson B, Janowitz M (eds): Reader in Public Opinion and Communication (2d ed). New York, Free Press, 1966

Language

Brown R: Psycholinguistics. New York, Free Press, 1970

Fishman J: Sociolinguistics: Brief Introduction. Rawley, Mass, Newbury House, 1970

Interactional Process

Birdwhistell RL: Kinesics and Context: Essays on Body Communication. Philadelphia, University of Pennsylvania Press, 1970

Ruesch J, Bateson, G: Communication: The Social Matrix of Psychiatry. New York, Norton, 1968 (paperback)

Scheflen AE: Communicational Structure: Analysis of a Psychotherapy Transaction. Bloomington, Indiana University Press, 1973

Watzlawick P, Beavin JH, Jackson DD: Pragmatics of Human Communication: A Study of Interactional Patterns, Pathologies, and Paradoxes. New York, Norton, 1967

Weitz S (ed): Nonverbal Communication: Readings with Commentary. New York, Oxford University Press, 1974

GROUP DYNAMICS

Cartwright D, Zander A (eds): Group Dynamics: Research and Theory (3d ed). New York, Harper Row, 1968

Homans GC: The Human Group. New York, Harcourt, 1950

Kissen M (ed): From Group Dynamics to Group Psychoanalysis: Therapeutic Applications of Group Dynamic Understanding. Series in Clinical and Community Psychology. New York, Halsted, 1976

Zander A: Motives and Goals in Groups. New York, Academic Press, 1971

ECONOMICS

Brenner MH: Mental Illness and the Economy. Cambridge, Harvard University Press, 1973

Piven F, Cloward RA: Regulating the Poor: The Functions of Public Welfare. New York, Random House, 1972

POLITICS

Knutson JN (ed): Handbook of Political Psychology. San Francisco, Jossey-Bass, 1973
Lasswell HD, Kaplan A: Power and Society: A Framework for Political Inquiry. New Haven, Yale
    University Press, 1950
Money-Kyrle RE: Psychoanalysis and Politics: A Contribution to the Psychology of Politics and
    Morals. Westport, Conn, Greenwood, 1951 (repr, 1973)
Riesman D, Glazer N: Faces in the Crowd: Individual Studies in Character and Politics (rev ed). New
    Haven, Yale University Press, 1964

RELIGION

Argyle M, Beit-Hallahmi B: Social Psychology of Religion. Boston, Routledge & Kegan, 1975
Cox RH: Religious Systems and Psychotherapy. Springfield, Ill, Thomas, 1973
Doniger S (ed): The Nature of Man in Theological and Psychological Perspective. Plainview, NY,
    Books for Libraries, 1973 (1963 ed repr)
Farnsworth DL: Psychiatry, the Clergy and Pastoral Counseling. Collegeville, Minn, St. John's Uni-
    versity Press, 1969
Linn L, Schwartz L: Psychiatry and Religious Experience. New York, Random House, 1958

EDUCATION

Dewey J: Democracy and Education. New York, Free Press, 1966
Farnsworth DL: Psychiatry, Education, and the Young Adult. Salmon Lecture Series. Springfield, Ill,
    Thomas, 1969
Halsey AH, et al (eds): Education, Economy, and Society. New York, Free Press, 1965 (paperback)

SCHOOLS

Bower EM (ed): Orthopsychiatry and Education. Detroit, Wayne State University Press, 1971
Clark DH, Kadis AL: Humanistic Teaching. Columbus, Ohio, Merrill, 1971
Kaplan L: Education and Mental Health (rev ed). New York, Harper & Row, 1971
Perry WG: Forms of Intellectual and Ethical Development in the College Years. New York, Holt, 1970

COMMUNITY ORGANIZATION AND PLANNING

Bonjean CM, et al: Community Politics: A Behavioral Approach. New York, Free Press, 1971
Cox FM, et al (eds): Strategies of Community Organization: A Book of Readings (2d ed). Itasca, Ill,
    Peacock, 1974
Marris P, Rein M: Dilemmas of Social Reform: Poverty and Community Action in the United States
    (2d ed). Chicago, Aldine, 1973
Mechanic D: Politics, Medicine and Social Science. New York, Wiley, 1974
Sharaf MR, Greenblatt M (eds): Dynamics of Program Development. New York, Grune & Stratton,
    1971

COMMUNITY MENTAL HEALTH

Bellak L (ed): A Concise Handbook of Community Psychiatry and Community Mental Health. New
    York, Grune & Stratton, 1974
Caplan G: Principles of Preventive Psychiatry. New York, Basic Books, 1964
Caplan G: The Theory and Practice of Mental Health Consultation. New York, Basic Books, 1970

Caplan G: Support Systems and Community Mental Health: Lectures on Concept Development. New York, Behavioral Publications, 1974

Duhl L, Leopold RL (eds): Mental Health and Urban Social Policy: A Casebook of Community Action. San Francisco, Jossey-Bass, 1968

Evans D, Claiborn, W (eds): Mental Health Issues and the Urban Poor. Elmsford, NY, Pergamon, 1974

Golann SE (ed): Current and Future Trends in Community Psychology. New York, Behavioral Publications, 1975

Grunebaum H (ed): The Practice of Community Mental Health. Boston, Little Brown, 1970

Joint Commission on Mental Illness and Health: Action for Mental Health Final Report. New York, Basic Books, 1961   ††

Kaplan BH: Further Explorations in Social Psychiatry. New York, Basic Books, 1976

Lamb HR, Heath D, Downing JJ (eds): Handbook of Community Mental Health Practice: The San Mateo Experience. San Francisco, Jossey-Bass, 1969

Miller DH: Community Mental Health: A Study of Services and Clients. Lexington, Mass, Lexington Books, 1974

Murrell SA: Community Psychology and Social Systems: A Conceptual Framework and Intervention Guide. New York, Behavioral Publications, 1973

Shore MF, Mannino FV (eds): Mental Health and the Community: Problems, Programs and Strategies. New York, Behavioral Publications, 1969

COMMUNITY MENTAL HEALTH CENTERS AND CLINICS

Barhash AZ, et al: The Organization and Function of the Community Psychiatric Clinic. New York, National Association of Mental Health, 1952

Beigel A, Levenson AI (eds): Community Mental Health Center: Strategies and Programs. New York, Basic Books, 1972

Beisser AR: Mental Health Consultation and Education. Palo Alto, Calif, National Press Books, 1972

Bellak L, Barten HH (eds): Progress in Community Mental Health, 3 vols. New York, Grune & Stratton, vol. 1, 1969: vol. 2, 1972: vol. 3, 1975

Butterfield A: Sixteen Indices: An Aid in Reviewing State and Local Mental Health and Hospital Programs. Washington, DC, Joint Information Service of the American Psychiatric Association and the National Association for Mental Health.

Fairweather GW, et al: Creating Change in Mental Health Organizations. Elmsford, NY, Pergamon, 1974

Glasscote RM: Halfway Houses for the Mentally Ill: A Study of Programs and Problems. Washington, DC, Joint Information Service of the American Psychiatric Association and the National Association for Mental Health, 1971

Glasscote RM: Rehabilitating the Mentally Ill in the Community: A Study of Psychosocial Rehabilitation Centers. Washington, DC, Joint Information Service of the American Psychiatric Association and the National Association for Mental Health, 1971

Glasscote RM: Children and Mental Health Centers: Programs, Problems, Prospects. Washington, DC, Joint Information Service of the American Psychiatric Association and the National Association for Mental Health, 1972

Glasscote RM, et al: The Community Mental Health Center: An Analysis of Existing Models. Washington, DC, Joint Information Service of the American Psychiatric Association and the National Association for Mental Health, 1964 (paperback)

Glasscote RM, et al: The Community Mental Health Center: An Interim Appraisal. Washington, DC, Joint Information Service of the American Psychiatric Association and the National Association for Mental Health, 1969

Kaplan SR, Roman M: The Organization and Delivery of Mental Health Services in the Ghetto: The Lincoln Hospital Experience. New York, Praeger, 1973

Kolb LC (ed): Urban Challenges to Psychiatry: The Case History of a Response. (Columbia–Washington Heights Community Mental Health Project, New York.) Boston, Little, Brown, 1969

Mannino FV (ed): The Practice of Mental Health Consultation. New York, Halsted, 1975

New York State Department of Mental Hygiene: Guide to Communities in the Establishment and
    Operation of Psychiatric Clinics. Albany, the Department, 1954
Sharaf MR, Greenblatt M (eds): Dynamics of Program Development. New York, Grune & Stratton,
    1971
Singh RKJ: Community Mental Health Consultation and Crisis Intervention. Berkeley, Calif, Book
    People, 1971
Whittington HG: Development of an Urban Mental Health Center. Springfield, Ill, Thomas, 1971

ADMINISTRATION

Barrett JH: Individual Goals and Organizational Objectives: A Study of Integration Mechanism. Ann
    Arbor, Institute for Social Research/University of Michigan, 1970
Feldman S: The Administration of Mental Health Services. Springfield, Ill, Thomas, 1973
Leavitt HJ: Organizations of the Future. New York, Praeger, 1974
Levinson H: Organizational Diagnosis. Cambridge, Harvard University Press, 1972

LEGAL ASPECTS

Allen RC, Ferster EZ, Rubin JG: Readings in Law and Psychiatry (2d ed). Baltimore, Johns Hopkins
    University Press, 1975
American Bar Foundation: The Mentally Disabled and the Law (rev ed). Chicago, University of
    Chicago Press, 1971
Ayd FJ: Medical, Moral and Legal Issues in Mental Health Care. Baltimore, Williams & Wilkins, 1974
Brooks A: Law, Psychiatry and the Mental Health System. Boston, Little, Brown, 1974
Davidoff DG: Malpractice of Psychiatrists. Springfield, Ill, Thomas, 1973
Group for the Advancement of Psychiatry: Confidentiality and Privileged Communication in the
    Practice of Psychiatry. No. 45. New York, Group for the Advancement of Psychiatry, 1960
Katz J, Goldstein J, Dershowitz AM: Psychoanalysis, Psychiatry and Law. New York, Free Press,
    1967
Mental Health Law Project: Basic Rights of the Mentally Handicapped. Washington, DC, Mental
    Health Law Project, 1973
Slovenko R: Psychiatry and Law. Boston, Little, Brown, 1973
Stone AA: National Institute of Mental Health, Center for Studies of Crime and Delinquency:
    Mental Health and Law: A System in Transition. Crime and Delinquency Issues Monogr
    Series. Washington, DC, U.S. Government Printing Office, 1975

PUBLIC HEALTH

American Public Health Association: Mental Health, the Public Health Challenge. Washington, DC,
    the Association, 1975
Andreano R, Weisbrod BA: American Health Policy: Perspective and Choices. Institute for Research
    on Poverty Monogr Series. Chicago, Rand McNally, 1974
Hargreaves GR: Psychiatry and the Public Health. New York, Oxford University Press, 1958
Wilner DM, et al: An Introduction to Public Health (6th ed). New York, Macmillan, 1973   *

EPIDEMIOLOGY

Dohrenwend BP, Dohrenwend BS: Social Status and Psychological Disorder: A Causal Inquiry. New
    York, Wiley, 1969
Hughes CC, et al: The Stirling County Study of Psychiatric Disorder and Sociocultural Environment.
    Vol. 2: The People of Cove and Woodlot. New York, Basic Books, 1960
Kaplan BH, Cassel JC (eds): Family and Health: An Epidemiological Approach. Chapel Hill, NC,
    Institute for Research in Social Science, 1975

Langner TS, Michael ST: The Midtown Manhattan Study. Vol. 2: Life, Stress and Mental Health. New York, McGraw-Hill, 1963

Leighton AH: The Stirling County Study of Psychiatric Disorder and Sociocultural Environment. Vol. 1: My Name Is Legion: Foundations for a Theory of Man in Relation to Culture. Vol. 3: The Character of Danger. New York, Basic Books, vol. 1, 1959; vol. 3, 1963

Srole L, et al: The Midtown Manhattan Study. Vol. 1: Mental Health in the Metropolis. New York, McGraw-Hill, 1962

MENTAL HEALTH MANPOWER

General

Goldston SE, Padilla-Lawson E: Mental Health Training and Public Health Manpower. Rockville, Md, National Institute of Mental Health, 1971

Henry WE, Sims JH, Spray SL: The Fifth Profession: Becoming a Psychotherapist. San Francisco, Jossey-Bass, 1971

Holt RR (ed): New Horizons for Psychotherapy: Autonomy as a Profession. New York, International Universities Press, 1971

Simon R (ed): Explorations in Mental Health Training: Project Summaries. Rockville, Md, National Institute of Mental Health, 1975

Psychiatrists

Rosenfeld AH (ed): Psychiatric Education: Prologue to the 1980's. Report of the Conference on the Education of Psychiatrists, Lake of the Ozarks, Mo, June 9–15, 1975. Washington, DC, American Psychiatric Association, 1976

Psychologists

Dorken H: The Professional Psychiatrist Today. San Francisco, Jossey-Bass, 1976

Social Workers

Strean HS: The Social Worker as Psychotherapist. Metuchen, NJ, Scarecrow Press, 1974

Nurses

Leininger MM (ed): Contemporary Issues in Mental Health Nursing. Boston, Little, Brown, 1973

Nonpsychiatric Physicians

Balint M: Treatment or Diagnosis: A Study of Repeat Prescriptions in General Practice. London, Tavistock, 1970

Teachers

ATE Yearbook: Mental Health and Teacher Education. Washington, DC, Association of Teacher Educators, 1967

Clergy

Clinebell HJ, Jr: Basic Types of Pastoral Counseling. Nashville, Tenn, Abingdon, 1966

Nonprofessionals (Paraprofessionals)

Guerney BG, Jr (ed): Psychotherapeutic Agents: New Roles for Nonprofessionals, Parents and Teachers. New York, Holt, 1969
Sobey F: The Nonprofessional Revolution in Mental Health. New York, Columbia University Press, 1970

Volunteers

Ewalt PL (ed): Mental Health Volunteers: The Expanding Role of the Volunteer in Hospital and Community Mental Health Services. Springfield, Ill, Thomas, 1967

INDUSTRIAL MENTAL HEALTH

Argyris C: Integrating the Individual and the Organization. New York, Wiley, 1964
Bass BM, Barrett GV: Man, Work, and Organization: An Introduction to Industrial and Organizational Psychology. Boston, Allyn & Bacon, 1972
Levinson H: Men, Management, and Mental Health. Cambridge, Harvard University Press, 1962
Marrow AI: Management by Participation. New York, Harper & Row, 1967
Tredgold RF: Human Relations in Modern Industry, (2d rev ed). New York, International Universities Press, 1963

RESEARCH IN PSYCHOTHERAPY

Bergin AE, Strupp HH: Changing Frontiers in the Science of Psychotherapy. Chicago, Aldine, 1972
Chassan JB: Research Design in Clinical Psychology and Psychiatry. New York, Appleton-Century-Crofts, 1967
Gottshalk LA, Auerbach AH: Methods of Research in Psychotherapy. New York, Appleton-Century-Crofts, 1966
Meltzoff J, Kornreich M: Research in Psychotherapy. Chicago, Aldine, 1970
National Institute of Mental Health: Division of Biometry and Epidemiology: Mental Health Statistical Notes. Rockville, Md. National Institute of Mental Health: Division of Biometry and Epidemiology: Report Series on Mental Health Statistics. Rockville, Md, National Institute of Mental Health
    Series A: Mental Health Facility Reports
    Series B: Analytical and Special Study Reports
    Series C: Methodology Reports
    Series D: Conference or Committee Reports and Analytical Reviews of Literature
National Institute of Mental Health: Psychotherapy Change Measures: Report of the Clinical Research Branch Outcome Measures Project. Waskow I, Parloff M (eds). Washington, DC, U.S. Government Printing Office, 1975
Orlinsky DE, Howard KI: Varieties of Psychotherapeutic Experience: Multivariate Analysis of Patients' and Therapists' Reports. New York, Teachers College Press, Columbia University, 1975
Psychotherapy and Psychoanalysis: Final Report of the Menninger Foundation's Psychotherapy Research Project. Kernberg OJ (ed). Bull Menninger Clin 36(1/2), 1972
Research Task Force, NIMH: Research in the Service of Mental Health. Summary Report. Segal J (ed). National Institute of Mental Health, Washington, DC, U.S. Government Printing Office, 1975
Spitzer RL, Klein DF (eds): Evaluation of Psychological Therapies: Psychotherapies, Behavior Therapies, Drug Therapies, and Their Interactions. Baltimore, Johns Hopkins University Press, 1976

CONTINUING EDUCATION

Carmichael HT: Prospects and Proposals: Lifetime Learning for Psychiatrists. Washington, DC, American Psychiatric Association, 1972
Carmichael HT: Continuing Education and Psychiatrists. Sixth annual Seymour Vestermark Memorial Award Paper. Rockville, Md, National Institute of Mental Health, 1975

Group for the Advancement of Psychiatry, Recertification: A Look at the Issues. Task Force on Recertification: Report No. 96. New York, the Group, 1976
Weiner IB (ed): Postdoctoral Education in Clinical Psychology. Proceedings of the Menninger Conference on Postdoctoral Education in Clinical Psychology, Topeka, May 18–21, 1972. Topeka, Menninger Foundation, 1973

TEACHING AND SUPERVISION

Bruch H: Learning Psychotherapy: Rationale and Ground Rules. Cambridge, Harvard University Press, 1974
Doehrman MJ: Parallel Processes in Supervision and Psychotherapy. Bull Menninger Clin 40 (1), 1976
Ekstein R, Wallerstein RS: The Teaching and Learning of Psychotherapy (rev ed). New York, Basic Books, 1972
Fleming J, Benedek T: Psychoanalytic Supervision. New York, Grune & Stratton, 1966
Scheflen AE: Communicational Structure: Analysis of a Psychotherapy Transaction. Bloomington, Indiana University Press, 1973
Schuster DB, Sandt JJ: Clinical Supervision of the Psychiatric Resident. New York, Brunner/Mazel, 1972

DEATH AND DYING

Becker E: The Denial of Death, New York, Free Press, 1973
Easson WM: Dying Child: The Management of the Child or Adolescent Who Is Dying. Springfield, Ill, Thomas, 1972
Eissler KR: The Psychiatrist and the Dying Patient. New York, International Universities Press, 1970 (paperback)
Furman E: A Child's Parent Dies: Studies in Childhood Bereavement. New Haven, Yale University Press, 1974
Kastenbaum R: Psychology of Death. New York, Springer, 1972
Kübler-Ross E: Death: The Final Stage of Growth. Englewood Cliffs, NJ, Prentice-Hall, 1975
Schoenberg B, Gerber I (eds): Bereavement: Its Psychological Aspects. New York, Columbia University Press, 1975
Weisman A: On Dying and Denying: A Psychiatric Study of Terminality. New York, Behavioral Publications, 1972

Recommended Films, Audiotapes, and Videotapes

Films, audiotapes, and videotapes are excellent teaching vehicles that are useful for functional purposes for both lay audiences and for professional education. A good discussion leader, of course, will enhance their value. In this section 408 films, audiotapes, and videotapes that relate to the topics discussed in these volumes are listed, along with pertinent details concerning their themes and where to obtain them. They are valuable adjuncts to an educational program. The same film or tape may be utilized to stress different points with a variety of audiences, serving as an introductory conveyance for lectures or discussions. The prices given for rentals or sales, obviously, will not necessarily remain the same in the future. Addenda Table 2 summarizes all those listed as to subject area.* All order sources and distributors have been abbreviated in the particular lists. At the end of each list there is a complete listing of sources for that section with their addresses and other pertinent information. Methods of using mental health films have been suggested on page 1034.

* Media are also listed alphabetically by subjects in the general index.

Addenda Table 2
Guide to Films, Audiotapes, and Videotapes

Subject Areas	Film No.	Audio No.	Video No.
History	1–4	173, 174	
Personality Development	5–19	175–181	
Culture and Personality	20, 21	182	
Human Behavior and Adaptation	22, 23	183–185	338
Mental Functions	(24–26)		
Conditioning and Learning	24		
Cognitive Processes	25	186	
Basic Neuropsychiatry	27	187	
Diagnosis	28, 29		339, 340
Psychopathology	30–35	188–192	341–343
Psychodynamics	36	193	344
Conditioning Theory	37		
General Systems Theory	38	194	
Schools of Psychotherapy	(39–49)	(195–206)	
General	39	195	
Client-centered Therapy	40, 41	197, 198	
Confrontation Therapy	42	199	
Gestalt Therapy	43	196, 200	345
Rational Emotive Therapy	44	201	
Reality Therapy		202	
Transactional Analysis	45–47	196, 203	
Primal Therapy	48	204	
Humanistic	49	205, 206	
Introduction to Psychotherapy	50	207, 208	
Values in Psychotherapy		209	
Tactics of Psychotherapy		210–216	
Interviewing	51, 52		346, 347
Counseling and Casework	53–55		
Behavior Therapy	56–59	217–223	
Freudian Psychoanalysis	60		
Ego Analysis		224	
Non-Freudian Psychoanalysis	61, 62	225–227	
Existential Analysis	63	228	
Psychoanalytic Psychotherapy		213, 214	
Group Process	64	229	
Group Psychotherapy	65–68	230–239	348–351
Family Therapy and Marital Therapy	69–75	240–247	352, 353
Hypnosis	76–77a	248–252	354–357
Somatic Therapies		253–260	
Miscellaneous Adjuncts	(78–83)	(261–264)	(358–362)
Dance Therapy	78, 79	261	358
Music Therapy	80		
Art Therapy	81		359, 360
Video Therapy	82		361
Biofeedback	83	262, 263	362
Relaxation Methods and Meditation		264	
Hospital Psychiatry	84, 85		
Emergencies in Psychotherapy and			
Crisis Intervention (Suicide)	86, 87	265, 266	363–367

FILMS

History

1. Freud: The Hidden Nature of Man. Western Civilization: Majesty and Madness Series, 16 mm, color, 29 min, 1970. Order Source: UIAC (also GFL). Rental: $12.50. Freud's revolutionary theories of the power of the unconscious.
2. Geel: A Changing Tradition. 16 mm, color, 41 min, 1973. Order source: UCEMC. Purchase: $490. Rental: $28. A documentary about Geel, the Belgian town where foster care of mental patients originated in the Middle Ages.
3. Karl Menninger Looks at Psychiatric History. 16 mm, color, 21 min, 1966. Made by Karl Menninger, MD. Order Source: AMAFL. Order #05722. Rental: free. Service Charge: $10.
4. Sigmund Freud: His Offices and Home, Vienna, 1938. 16 mm, color, 17 min, 1975. Order Source: UCEMC. Rental: $20.

Personality Development

5. Emotional Ties in Infancy. (Vassar Films for Head Start Training.) 16 mm, 12 min, nd. Order Source: NYUFL. Rental: $9. Compares four 8- to 10-month olds brought up under different conditions of mothering.
6. Erik Erikson. 16 mm, b & w, 110 min, 1966. Produced by RI Evans for the National Science Foundation. Order Source: GFL. Rental: $20 base service charge for 2 days
7. Genesis of Emotions. (Film Studies of the Psychoanalytic Research Project on Problems in Infancy Series.) 16 mm, b & w, 30 min, silent, nd. Produced by Rene A Spitz, MD. Order Source: GFL. Rental: $20 base service charge for 2 days. Earliest evidence of interpersonal interests.
8. Grief. (Film Studies of the Psychoanalytic Research Project on Problems in Infancy Series.) 16 mm, b & w, 30 min, silent, nd. Produced by Rene A Spitz, MD. Order Source: GFL (also NYUFL). Rental: $20 base service charge for 2 days. Effect upon infants of prolonged absence of the mother.
9. Growth and Intelligence in the Preschool Years. 16 mm, color, 31 min, nd. Produced by Drs Bettye M Caldwell, & Julius B Richmond. Order Source: GFL. Rental: $20 base service charge for 2 days. Developmental advances made by infants during the first year of life.
10. Konrad Lorenz. Film 2: Motivation. 16 mm, b & w, 30 min, nd. Order Source: GFL. Rental: $20 base service charge for 2 days. Instinctive basis of social motives and intelligence.
11. Konrad Lorenz. Film 3: Aggression. 16 mm, b & w, 30 min, nd. Order Source: GFL. Rental: $20 base service charge for 2 days. Effects of sex and violence as depicted in the mass media.
12. Learning to Learn in Infancy. (Vassar Films for Head Start Training.) 16 mm, b & w, 30 min, nd. Order Source: NYUFL. Rental: $13. How adults can help infants differentiate between objects and develop earliest communication skills.
13. Mother–Infant Interaction. Film 6: Resemblances in Expressive Behavior. 16 mm, b & w, 40 min, nd. Order Source: GFL. Rental: $20 base service charge for 2 days. Mother–infant interaction with different forms of maternal behavior.
14. Mother Love. (Film Studies of the Psychoanalytic Research Project on Problems in Infancy Series.) 16 mm, b & w, 20 min, silent, nd. Produced by Rene A Spitz, MD. Order Source: GFL. Rental: $20 base service charge for 2 days. Impact of mother love on the social relations of a child.
15. Normal Child. 16 mm, b & w, 25 min, 1967. Made by Margaret D Griffel, MD, Robert C Prall, MD, Jacques Van Vlack. Order Source: PCR. Purchase: $125. Rental: $5.90. Shows a 6-year-old boy interacting normally and positively with his environment.

† Titles marked with a dagger apply to recommended media cited in AVLINE (Audio Visuals On-Line), the data base maintained by the National Library of Medicine. These materials have been professionally reviewed for technical quality, currency, accuracy of subject content, and educational design.

16. Nursery School Child–Mother Interaction. 16 mm, b & w, 60 min, nd. Produced by Marianne Marschak. Order Source: GFL. Rental: $20 base service charge for 2 days. Common forms of interaction encountered by professionals; demonstrated by three Head Start children with their mothers.
17. Overdependency. (Mental Mechanisms Series.) 16 mm, b & w, 32 min, nd. Produced by NFB. Order Source: NYUFL. Rental: $11. A young man crippled by overdependency seeks psychiatric help.
18. Prevention–Early Intervention, Mother–Child Groups. 16 mm, b & w, 20 min, 1975. Made by Henry Parens, MD, Leafy Pollack, MSW, Robert C Prall, MD. Order Source: EPPI. *Restricted Use.* Rental: $8. Helping mothers to understand their behavior in relation to the needs of their children.
19. A Study in Maternal Attitudes. 16 mm, b & w, 30 min, nd. Produced by NY Fund for Children (NYU). Order Source: NYUFL. Purchase: $165. Rental: $15.

Culture and Personality

20. Karba's First Years. (Character Formation in Different Cultures Series.) 16 mm, b & w, 19 min, nd. Produced by Gregory Bateson, Margaret Mead (NYU). Order Source: NYUFL. Purchase: $135. Rental: $9.50. A series of scenes in the life of a Balinese child.
21. Trance and Dance in Bali. (Character Formation in Different Cultures Series.) 16 mm, b & w, 20 min, nd. Produced by Gregory Bateson, Margaret Mead (NYU). Order Source: NYUFL. Pruchase: $135. Rental: $9.50. The Balinese ceremonial dance drama.

Human Behavior and Adaptation

22. Anna N. Life History from Birth to Fifteen Years. The Development of Emotional Problems in a Child Reared in a Neurotic Environment. (Film Studies on Integrated Development Series.) 16 mm, b & w, 60 min, silent, nd. Produced by Margaret Fries, MD. Order Source: GFL. Rental: $20 base service charge for 2 days
23. Growing Up Without Sight. 16 mm, color, 20 min, nd. Order Source: GFL (also NYUFL). Rental: $20 base service charge for 2 days. Compensations in functioning by blind children.

Mental Functions

24. Ernest R. Hilgard. 16 mm, b & w, 30 min, nd. Order Source: GFL. Rental: $20 base service charge for 2 days. Hilgard's views on contemporary learning theory.
25. Evan's Dialogues with Piaget and Inhelder. 16 mm, color. Parts I & II, 40 min each. Order Source: ASF. Purchase: $425 each part. Rental: $25 each part. Part I: Piaget's stages of cognitive development. Part II: His contact with Freud.
26. Perception. (Psychology Series.) 16 mm, b & w, 17 min, nd. Produced by McGraw-Hill. Order Source: NYUFL. Rental: $10.50. Basic principles of perception as an organizing process.

Neuropsychiatry (World-Wide)

27. Mental Health Year. 16 mm, b & w, 59 min, nd. Produced by the Mental Health Film Board. Order Source: NYUFL. Rental: $22. Psychiatric treatment and facilities in 22 countries.

Diagnosis

28. Diagnosis of Childhood Schizophrenia. 16 mm, b & w, 35 min, nd. Produced by Brooklyn Juvenile Guidance Center, Inc. Narrator: Abraham A Fabian. Order Source: NYUFL. Purchase: $195. Rental: $15.
29. An Exercise in the Differential Diagnosis of Psychiatric Syndromes of Childhood. 16 mm, b & w, 25 min, 1970. Produced by MD Griffel, JD Van Vlack. Order Source: PCR *Showing Restricted.* Purchase: $175. Rental: $8.70.

Psychopathology

30. Folie A Deux. (Mental Symptoms Series.) 16 mm, b & w, 15 min, nd. Order Source: GFL. Rental: $20 base service charge for 2 days. A psychosis developed first in the daughter and was then communicated to the mother.
31. Manic State. (Mental Symptoms Series.) 16 mm, b & w, 15 min, nd. Order Source: GFL. Rental: $20 base service charge for 2 days. Hypomania.
32. No In-Between: The Manic Depressive. 16 mm, b & w, 23 min, 1970. Made by T Rusk, B Addis. Order Source: BSML. Rental: $15. Manic and depressive symptomatology.
33. Obsessive-Compulsive Neurosis. (The Disordered Mind Series.) 16 mm, b & w, 28 min, nd. Produced by Robert Anderson. Order Source: NYUFL. Rental: $12.50
34. A Pathological Anxiety (The Disordered Mind Series.) 16 mm, b & w, 28 min, nd. Produced by Robert Anderson. Order Source: NYUFL. Rental: $12.50
35. A Psychopath (Disordered Mind Series.) 16 mm, b & w, 28 min, nd. Produced by Robert Anderson. Order Source: NYUFL. Rental: $12.50

Psychodynamics

36. Neurotic Behavior: A Psychodynamic View. 16 mm, color, 19 min, nd. Order Source: PCR. Rental: $14

Conditioning Theory

37. BF Skinner. 16 mm, b & w, 50 min, nd. Order Source: GFL. Rental: $20 base service charge for 2 days. Operant conditioning and shaping behavior.

General Systems Theory

38. Whither or Wither Mental Health. 16 mm, color, 30 min, 1971. Order Source: AHSS. Purchase: $210. Rental: $50. The application of systems technology to community mental health.

Schools of Psychotherapy

39. Three Approaches to Psychotherapy. 16 mm, b & w. Part 1, Carl Rogers, 48 min; Part 2, Frederick Perls, 32 min; Part 3, Albert Ellis, 37 min, 1964. Order Source: NYUFL. Rental: Part 1, $20; Part 2, $20; Part 3, $20. Three-part series depicting one patient undergoing therapy with therapists of different orientations.
40. Behavioral Therapy or Client Centered Therapy: A Debate (John D Krumboltz and CH Patterson). 16 mm, color, 35 min, 1970. Order Source: APGA. Purchase: $250. Rental: $25
41. Client-Centered Counseling (CH Patterson). 16 mm, color, 35 min, 1970. Order Source: APGA. Purchase: $250. Rental: $25
42. Come Out, Come Out, Whoever You Are. 16 mm, b & w, 50 min, 1971. Order Source: UCEMC. Rental: $20. Confrontation therapy with long-term mental patients.
43. What is Gestalt? 16 mm, color, 24 min, 1971. Order Source: UCEMC. Rental: $21. Basic principles of Gestalt therapy explained by Frederick Perls.
44. Albert Ellis: A Demonstration with a Young Divorced Woman. 16 mm, color, 30 min, 1972. Order Source: APGA. Purchase: $250. Rental: $25
45. Games People Play: The Theory. 16 mm, b & w, 30 min, nd. Produced by NET. Order Source: NYUFL. Rental: $11. Transactional analysis explained by Eric Berne.
46. Games People Play: The Practice. 16 mm, b & w, 30 min, nd. Produced by NET. Order Source: NYUFL. Rental: $11. A patient analyzed by Eric Berne during a group session at Berne's home.
47. I'm OK—You're OK: Can TA [Transactional Analysis] Free the Child in Us? 16 mm, color, 22 min, 1974. Order Source: UCEMC. Rental: $28. Introduction to the principles and techniques of transactional analysis; commentary by Thomas A Harris.
48. The Inner Revolution. 16 mm, b & w, 80 min, 1971. Order Source: ETC. Rental: Contact ETC. The highlights of a 3-week session in primal therapy.
49. Maslow and Self-Actualization. Two film series. 16 mm, color, 30 min each, nd. Order Source: PFI. Purchase: $450 for the series. Rental: $35 for the series.

Introduction to Psychotherapy

50. An Introduction to Psychotherapy. 16 mm, b & w, 20 min, 1974. Order Source: VG. Purchase: $140. Rental: $35. Some general issues discussed by two patients.

Interviewing

51. General Practitioner as a Psychiatric Interviewer. 16 mm, b & w, 50 min, 1973. Made by Paul Jay Fink, MD, Jacques Van Vlack. Order Source: EPPI. Rental: $15. Good and bad examples of interviewing shown.
52. Psychiatric Interview Series. 16 mm, b & w, 1967. Authors: Robert L Stoller, MD, Robert H Geertsma, PhD. Order Source: UCEMC. *Restricted to medical education or medical research;* signed agreement required.
     Psychiatric Interview 1, 2: Evaluation for Diagnosis. 30 min each. Purchase: $240 each. Rental: $19 each
     Psychiatric Interview 3: The Thinking Disorder. 30 min. Purchase: $240. Rental: $19
     Psychiatric Interview 5: Problems in Gender Identity. 10 min. Purchase: $80. Rental: $11
     Psychiatric Interview 6: Evaluation for Treatment. 30 min. Purchase: $240. Rental: $19
     Psychiatric Interview 8: Forensic Medicine. 30 min. Purchase: $360. Rental: $25
     Psychiatric Interview 9: Follow-up Treatment. 30 min. Purchase: $360. Rental: $25
     Psychiatric Interviews 10–13, 15–17: Problems in Gender Identity. 10 min each. Purchase: $130 each. Rental: $14 each
     Psychiatric Interviews 18, 21: Evaluation for Diagnosis. 10 min each. Purchase: $130 each. Rental: $14 each

Counseling and Casework

53. Behind Client Behavior. 16 mm, b & w, 30 min, 1969. Order Source: UIAC. Purchase: $150. Rental: $7.25. Investigates the cause of social service client behavior.
54. Casework With Groups. 16 mm, b & w, 30 min, 1969. Order Source: UIAC. Purchase: $150. Rental: $7.25. How the elements of social casework with individuals are also applicable to a group.
55. Leona Tyler on Counseling. 16 mm, color, 50 min, 1973. Order Source: APGA. Purchase: $250. Rental: $25. Presentation of a series of significant issues in counseling.

Behavior Therapy

56. Behavioral Therapy Demonstration. 16 mm, color, 32 min, 1969. Produced by the Eastern Pennsylvania Psychiatric Institute. Order Source: PCR. *Showing Restricted.* Purchase: $311.50. Rental: $11.60
57. Behavior Therapy in a Case of Overdependency. 16 mm, kinescope, b & w, 130 min, 1970. Made by Joseph Wolpe, MD. Order Source: TUSM. Rental: Contact TUSM. The behavioral analysis and essentials of treatment.
58. Broad Spectrum Behavior Therapy in a Group. 16 mm, b & w, 29 min, 1969. Produced by A Lazarus, MD, J Van Vlack. Order Source: PCR. *Showing Restricted.* Purchase: $145. Rental: $6.40. Similarities and differences between conventional group psychotherapy and Lazarus' brand of group behavior therapy.
59. Reinforcement Therapy. 16 mm, b & w, 45 min, 1966. Prepared by OI Loaas, PhD, University of California (Los Angeles). Order Source: AMAFL. Order #05611. Rental: Free. Service Charge: $10. Shows how reinforcement therapy can be used to create an environment that will help direct patients toward normal, socially desirable behavior.

Freudian Psychoanalysis

60. Ernest Jones. 16 mm, b & w, 30 min, nd. Order Source: GFL. Rental: $20 base service charge for 2 days. Interesting sidelights on Freud and psychoanalysis.

Non-Freudian Psychoanalysis

61. Carl G Jung. 16 mm, b & w, 32 min, nd. Order Source: GFL. Rental: $20 base service charge for 2 days. Jungian ideas and theories.
62. Interview with Dr. Erich Fromm. (Two parts.) 16 mm, b & w, 50 min each part, nd. Order Source: ASF. Purchase: $275 each. Rental: $17.50 each, $30 both. Part I: Productive and nonproductive orientations. Part II: Fromm's approach to psychotherapy: His theories and techniques.

Existential Analysis

63. Logotherapy: Viktor Frankl. 16 mm, b & w, 27 min, 1965. Made by OA Parsons, GH Deckert, B Addis. Order Source: BSML. Rental: $10

Group Process

64. Group Leadership: The History of the Group Process Movement. 16 mm, b & w, 28 min, 1976. Order Source: UCEMC. Purchase: $225. Rental: $18.

Group Psychotherapy

65. Group Psychotherapy: The Dynamics of Change. 16 mm, color, 30 min, nd. Order Source: AMAFL. Order #05721. Rental: Free. Service Charge: $10. A psychoanalytically oriented group therapy session portraying some of the dynamics operative in the group process.
66. Group Therapy. 16 mm, b & w, 60 min, 1972. Order Source: GPF. Purchase: $295. Rental: $50. Social, psychological, and interpersonal aspects of a group session illuminating its dynamics.
67. Psychodrama in Group Processes. 16 mm, b & w, 110 min, 1970. Order Source: NYUFL. Purchase: $275. Rental: $20
68. Three Approaches to Group Therapy. (Three parts.) 16 mm, color, Part I—38 min, Part II—40 min, Part III—38 min, nd. Part I: Actualizing Therapy, Everett Shostrom; Part II: Reason and Emotion in Therapy, Albert Ellis; Part III: Decision Therapy, Harold Greenwald. Order Source: PFI. Purchase : $400 each. Rental: $35 each

Family Therapy and Marital Therapy

69. A Context Analysis of Family Interviews: Part I. 16 mm, color, 28 min, 1974. Produced by J Van Vlack, C Beels, J Ferber. Order Source: PCR. *Restricted Use.* Purchase: $336. Rental: $15. Natural history method of context analysis developed by Birdwhistell and Scheflen.
70. The Enemy in Myself. 16 mm, b & w, 50 min, nd. Made by Nathan Ackerman. Order Source: NAI. Rental: $40. Composite of four interviews with a family group over a period of 1½ years.
71. Family Therapy with Follow-up. 16 mm, kinescope, b & w, 62 min, 1972. Made by Gerald H Zuk, PhD, Jacques Van Vlack. Order Source: EPPI. *Restricted Use.* Rental: $15. Demonstration of problems of family interaction and discussion of methods of treatment.
72. Hillcrest Family: Assessment Series. (Series of two films.) 16 mm, color, 1968. Order Source: PCR.
    Assessment Interview 1: Dr Nathan W Ackerman. 32 min. Purchase: $355. Rental: $11.60
    Assessment Consultation 1: Drs Ackerman and Peachey. 12 min. Purchase: $130. Rental: $5.40
    Assessment Interview 2: Dr Carl A Whitaker. 31 min. Purchase: $355. Rental: $11.60
    Assessment Consultation 2: Drs Whitaker and Peachey, 14 min. Purchase: $150. Rental $5.40
    Assessment Interview 3: Dr Don Jackson. 32 min. Purchase: $340. Rental: $11.60
    Assessment Consultation 3: Drs Jackson and Peachey. 11 min. Purchase: $115. Rental: $4.40
    Assessment Interview 4: Dr Murray Bowen. 28 min. Purchase: $300. Rental: $10.60
    Assessment Consultation 4: Drs Bowen and Peachy. 16 min. Purchase: $175. Rental: $6.40
    A series of four separate interviews with the Hillcrest family, which has sought psychiatric help because of problems with the children. Discussion by each psychiatrist of his views on the dynamics of the family situation with a therapist who has been working with the family.

73. In and Out of Psychosis. 16 mm, b & w, 2 hr, nd. Made by Nathan Ackerman. Order Source: NAI. Rental: $40. Treatment of a family with a 16-year-old daughter, an only child, who is mentally ill.

74. Runaway Wife. 16 mm, b & w, 60 min, 1975. Produced by Gerald H Zuk, PhD. Order Source: GHZ. Rental: Contact GHZ. Viewing is restricted to mental health personnel and students.

75. A Social Learning Approach to Family Therapy. 16 mm, color, 30 min, nd. Order Source: RP. Purchase: $425. Rental: $50. Demonstration (for counseling professionals and students) of an intervention technique to control outbursts of destructive behavior in families.

Hypnosis

76. Hypnotic Behavior. 16 mm, b & w, 20 min, nd. Produced by Association Films. Order Source: NYUFL. Rental: $9.50. A psychological film on common phenomena of hypnosis demonstrating, among others, induction of trance, abnormal illusions, awakening, posthypnotic amnesia, and execution of posthypnotic suggestion.

77. Unconscious Motivation. 16 mm, b & w, 39 min, 1949. Made by LF Beck. Order Source: PCR. Rental: $11. Effects of unconscious motives; projective techniques and dream analysis used to discover and release repressed ideas implanted under hypnosis.

77a. The Use of Hypnosis in Psychotherapy. 16 mm, b & w, 30 min, 1976. Produced by James R Hodge, MD, University of Akron. Order Source: JRH. *Restricted Use.* Rental: $35 plus mailing. Gives the physician or therapist an idea of what to expect in different levels of trance and also shows what he can do to help the patient.

Miscellaneous Adjuncts

78. Moving True. 16 mm, b & w, 19 min, 1973. Produced by Betty Shapiro. Order Source: MTC. Purchase: $200. Rental: $25. The rationale and technique of dance therapy.

79. Looking for Me. 16 mm, b & w, 29 mins, 1969. Order Source: GFL (also UCEMC). Rental: $20 basic service charge for 2 days. Therapeutic benefits of patterned movement in working with three types of pupils—normal preschool children, emotionally disturbed children, autistic children—and a group of adult teachers.

80. A Song for Michael. 16 mm, b & w, 22 min, 1966. Produced by the Music Therapy Center; Creative Arts Rehabilitation Center, Inc. Order Source: PCR. Rental: $5.40. How music is used as a functional tool to promote emotional and social growth as an adjunct to psychotherapy.

81. Art Therapy Session with an Emotionally Disturbed 16-Year-Old Boy. 16 mm, kinescope, b & w, 44 min, 1971. Made by Leah Freedman, Robert C. Prall, MD, Jacques Van Vlack. Order Source: EPPI. Rental: $15.

82. Perspectives on Mental Health (10-part Series). 16 mm, b & w, nd. Produced by Ari Kiev. Order Source: BHES. Rental: Contact BHES. ''Videotherapy'' utilizing videotapes.

83. Dialogue on Biofeedback. 16 mm, color, 50 min, nd. Order Source: VAFL. (also USDA). Rental: See information on VAFL in Source List. A trip through a variety of laboratories and clinical facilities where biofeedback experimentation is being conducted.

Hospital Psychiatry

84. Developing a Therapeutic Community: A Staff Training Series. A series of four filmstrips, color, 1972. Order Source: UMAVEC. Purchase: $85. A series on the materials necessary for a 5-day workshop for teaching hospital staff about the process of implementing an intensive treatment program in milieu therapy.

85. Psychiatric Services in General Hospitals. 16 mm, color, 25 min, 1965. Presented by the American Hospital Association, American Psychiatric Association, ER Squibb and Sons. Order Source: AMAFL. Order #05598. Rental: Free. Service Charge: $10. How a general hospital established a psychiatric service.

Emergencies in Psychotherapy and Crisis Intervention (Suicide)

86. The Suicidal Patient. 16 mm, b & w, 60 min, 1968. Produced by Richard Scott for Medical Television Network (UCLA, USC). Order Source: NAC. Rental: Free. Case histories providing descriptions of suicidal types and guidelines for management.
87. Suicide Prevention and Crisis Intervention. Multimedia package of 12 films (16 mm), 6 audiotapes. Order Source: CPP. Rental: Contact CPP. The films illustrate various kinds of potential suicides, teach interviewing skills, and test students.

Rehabilitation and Recreation

88. Bitter Welcome. 16 mm, b & w, 26 min, 1959. Order Source: NYUFL (also PCR). Rental: $11. Describes the struggle of a discharged mental hospital patient to overcome the fears and prejudices of his fellow workers and to regain his place in the community.
89. The Day Hospital. 16 mm, b & w, 22 min, nd. Produced by NYU. Order Source: NYUFL. Purchase: $160. Rental: $11. Portrays Marlborough Day Hospital, London, England, where nonresident patients come for such therapies as individual counseling, activity therapy, electroshock, chemotherapy, and group therapy.
90. Full Circle. 16 mm, b & w, 27 min, nd. Produced by the Mental Health Film Board. Order Source: NYUFL. Rental: $11. Describes the importance of the job situation to the well-being of the discharged mental patient; shows the role of the psychiatric ward of the hospital in preparing the patient to find and keep a job.
91. They're Your People. (To Save Tomorrow Series.) 16 mm, b & w, 29 min, 1969. Order Source: UIAC. Rental: $7.75. A description of the rehabilitation process used by the Singer Zone Center in Rockford, Illinois, showing how the center aids short-term psychiatric patients and helps local communities develop their own mental health facilities.   †
92. Wellmet House. (To Save Tomorrow Series.) 16 mm, b & w, 30 min, 1969. Order Source: UIAC. Rental: $7.75. Depicts the program at Wellmet House, whose program aim is to rehabilitate the mentally ill not by gaining conforming behavior but by helping them relate to other people in natural and unstructured ways.   †

Consultation-Liaison Psychiatry

93. Emotional Factors in General Practice: Their Recognition and Management. 16 mm, b & w, 43 min, 1961. Produced by Robert Anderson Associates. Order Source: GP. Rental: Contact GP. Includes case history and treatment of a patient whose severe physical symptoms during 2 years begin to improve over a 2-month period when the emotional elements of her condition are recognized, accepted, and dealt with by a general practitioner.

Psychosomatic Disorders

94. A Coronary (The Disordered Mind Series.) 16 mm, b & w, 28 min, nd. Produced by Robert Anderson. Order Source: NYUFL. Rental: $12.50. Illustrates the relationship of the patient's personality to his attack.
95. Psychosomatic Conditions—Obesity. (Disordered Mind Series.) 16 mm, b & w, 28 min, nd. Produced by Robert Anderson. Order Source: NYUFL. Rental: $10. Case study in which a 13-year-old girl and her parents are made aware, through treatment, of the relationship between her unmet emotional needs and her overeating.

Depressive Disorders

96. Depressive States: I. (Mental Symptoms Series.) 16 mm, b & w, 12 min, nd. Produced by the National Film Board of Canada. Order Source: NYUFL. Rental: $8.50. A demonstration of some manifestations of the agitated form of severe depression.
97. Depressive States: II. (Mental Symptoms Series.) 16 mm, b & w, 11 min, nd. Produced by the National Film Board of Canada. Order Source: NYUFL. Rental: $8.50. The retarded form of depression and severe depression that has reached the point of attempted suicide.

98. Feelings of Depression. (Mental Mechanisms Series.) 16 mm, b & w, 30 min, nd. Produced by the National Film Board of Canada. Order Source: NYUFL. Rental: $11. Case study that traces the genetic development of a neurotic depression by examining the emotional significance of a series of experiences in one man's life.

99. Uncovering Depression in the Anxious Patient. 16 mm, color, 24 min, nd. Order Source: MSD. Rental: Free loan to professional groups. The use of interviewing techniques for diagnosing and treating depression in anxious patients. For the physician in general practice.

Schizophrenic Reactions

100. Asylum. 16 mm, color, 95 min, 1974. Order Source: VQ. Purchase: $950. Rental: Contact VQ. A record of the life style inside RD Laing's radical therapeutic community in London. Presents an alternative to traditionalized institutional mental health treatment.

101. Breakdown. 16 mm, b & w, 40 min, 1951. Produced by National Film Board of Canada. Order Source: NYUFL. Rental: $12. A vivid and authentic case study of a young woman who develops a schizoid personality. The course of her treatment in a mental health clinic and a state hospital and finally her rehabilitation as a member of her family.

102. The Magic Mirror of Aloyse. 16 mm, color, 27 min, 1965, Produced by Center for Mass Communication Columbia University. Order Source: NYUFL. Rental: $22. Presents a 77-year old schizophrenic, Aloyse, who cannot communicate except through pictures. Shows how her pictures explain some of the mechanisms of the psychosis.

103. Paranoid Conditions. (Mental Symptoms Series.) 16 mm, b & w, 13 min, nd. Order Source: GFL. Rental: $20 base service charge for 2 days.

104. Schizophrenia: Catatonic Type. (Mental Symptoms Series.) 16 mm, 12 min, nd. Produced by the National Film Board of Canada. Order Source: NYUFL. Rental: $8.50

105. Schizophrenia: Hebephrenic Type. (Mental Symptoms Series.) 16 mm, b & w, 13 min, nd. Produced by the National Film Board of Canada. Order Source: NYUFL. Rental: $8.50

106. Schizophrenia: Simple-Type Deteriorated. (Mental Symptoms Series.) 16 mm, b & w, 11 min, nd. Produced by National Film Board of Canada. Order Source: NYUFL. Rental: $8.50

107. The Treatment of Acute Schizophrenia. 16 mm, color, 29 min, 1972. Order Source: P. Rental: Free. Treatment of four women with acute schizophrenia with a neuroleptic agent for 14 to 24 days. Patients shown before and after treatment.

108. Victorian Flower Paintings: Pictorial Record of a Schizophrenic Episode. 16 mm, color, 7 min, 1968. Made by Institute of Psychiatry, London. Order Source: NYUFL. Rental: $12. Rare and unusual clinical history of schizophrenia as manifested in a folio of watercolors painted by an unknown person between 1863 and 1868. The first serene paintings give way to grotesqueries; at the climax of the illness the paintings are chaotic, wild; then the mood gradually subsides, violence disappears, and the last few paintings are as tranquil as the first. Modern commentary points out distortions and explains them.

Delinquency and Criminality

109. Four Gray Walls. 16 mm, color, 29 min, 1973. Order Source: BYU. Purchase: $265. Rental: $15.90. A film about a program that has been called one of the most significant advancements to be made in prison reform in the last 200 years with a recidivism rate of less than 2 percent compared to 80 percent nationally.

110. Release. 16 mm, color, 28 min, 1975. Produced by Church Women in the U.S.A. with a grant from Lilly Endowment, Inc. Order Source: OF. Purchase: $350. Rental: $30 (plus $3 shipping charge). The true story of a Hispanic-American woman who after four years in prison (for drug-related theft and prostitution) is released to a halfway house where she begins the long process of rehabilitation.

111. Young Convicts: Prison in the Streets. 16 mm, color, 36 min, 1972. Order Source: ABCMC. Purchase: $350. Rental: $35. Some alternatives to prison in operation in California and Massachusetts, two states that are attempting to implement such alternatives, with arguments for and against this philosophy by articulate officials. Examples of homes where group therapy sessions are an integral part of house activity, halfway houses, foster homes, intensive probation programs, and parole programs using volunteers. Shows counselors, psychiatrists, social workers, and volunteers working to help the offender while keeping him in his own or a near normal environment.

Speech and Voice Disorders

112. Identifying Speech Disorders: Language. 16 mm, b & w, 20 min, nd. Produced by Harper & Row. Order Source: NYUFL. Rental: $12. A variety of language disorders illustrated by individuals of different ages.
113. Identifying Speech Disorders: Stuttering. 16 mm, b & w, 20 min, nd. Produced by Harper & Row. Order Source: NYUFL. Rental: $12

Alcoholism

114. Alcoholism: Disease in Disguise. 16 mm, color, 27 min, nd. Order Source: ASF. Rental: Free. Addressed to physicians. Emphasis on alcohol's role in society's tendency toward "sedativism." Statements by authorities on alcohol, drugs, addiction, treatment, chemistry, etc., and an interesting feature on a detox center in a St. Louis general hospital.
115. Trigger Films on Alcoholism. 16 mm, color, 15 min, nd. Order Source: ASF. Purchase: $185. Rental: $25 per week. Five short vignettes about drinking designed to spark discussion among professionals who work with alcoholics.

Drug Addiction

116. Hooked. 16 mm, b & w, 20 min, nd. Produced by Churchill Films. Order Source: NYUFL. Rental: $11. A vivid description of the experience of drug addiction provided by statements from young (ages 18–25) former addicts.
117. Methadone: An American Way of Dealing. 16 mm, color, 60 min, nd. Order Source: NDF. Rental: Contact NDF. An antimethadone documentary that takes an in-depth look at a midwest clinic with 400 patients—mostly young blacks and poor white ghetto dwellers—who speak candidly about lack of supportive therapies. Also a comprehensive historical review of opiate use in the United States and a look at a drug-free alternative to a methadone program.
118. Professional Drug Films. (A series of nine films.) 16 mm, color, 118 min, 1971. (1) Drug Dialogue—Orientation; (2) Bunny; (3) Guy; (4) Tom; (5) Rick—File X-258375; (6) Treatment—New Teams; (7) Drug Dialogue—Involvement; (8) Confrontation—A Nurse and a Drug Addict; (9) Counseling—A Critical Incident. Produced by NIMH. Order Source: NAC. Purchase: $358.25. Rental: $80. For health and social service professionals concerned with drug-abuse prevention and treatment.
119. The Treatment of Acute Drug Abuse. 16 mm, color, 25 min, nd. Order Source: EL. Rental: Free. Some specific treatment modalities for overdoses of heroin, barbiturates, LSD, and other drugs of abuse. Intended for the physician in general practice.

Mental Deficiency

120. Clinical Types of Mental Deficiency. 16 mm, b & w, 29 min, 1957. Produced by Audio-Visual Education Service, University of Minnesota in cooperation with Faribault State School and Hospital, Cambridge State School and Hospital. Order Source: PCR. *Showing Restricted.* Purchase: $175. Rental: $7.90. Magnitude of problems and social implications suggested.
121. The Evaluation of the Retarded Client. (Counseling the Mentally Retarded, Part II.) 16 mm, color, 18 min, 1969. Produced by the Audiovisual Department, Parsons State Hospital. Order Source: NAC. Rental: Free. Shows how vocational counseling develops rehabilitation potential in retarded clients. Demonstrates the use of evaluative procedures. †
122. The Nature of Mental Retardation. (Counseling the Mentally Retarded, Part I.) 16 mm, color, 21 min, 1968. Produced by the Audiovisual Department, Parsons State Hospital. Order Source: NAC. Rental: Free. Presents examples of the eight etiological categories and five adaptive behavior levels of retardation. Contrasts severe with mild cases and defines rehabilitation potential for each. †
123. Post Placement Counseling. (Counseling the Mentally Retarded, Part V.) 16 mm, color, 22 min, 1968. Produced by the Audiovisual Department, Parsons State Hospital. Order Source: NAC. Rental: Free. Shows the counselor's contribution to rehabilitation after the client is employed and living in the community. †
124. Training Resources and Techniques. (Counseling the Mentally Retarded, Part III.) 16 mm, color, 28 min, 1968. Produced by the Audiovisual Department. Parsons State Hospital. Order Source: NAC. Rental: Free. Explores the counselor's role in helping the retarded client adapt to new situations and new jobs. †

Case Material

125. Case Study of Multiple Personality. 16 mm, b & w, 30 min, 1957. Order Source: PCR. *Restricted Use.* Rental: $14

126. Character Neurosis with Depressive and Compulsive Trends in the Making: A Life History of Mary from Birth to Fifteen Years. (Film Studies on Integrated Development Series.) 16 mm, b & w, 40 min, silent, nd. Produced by Margaret E Fries, MD, Paul J Woolf, MS. Order Source: GFL. Rental: $20 base service charge for 2 days. Shows how a child with superior biological capacity and an active congenital-activity type develops a neurosis through interactions with those in her environment.

127. The Feeling of Rejection. (Mental Mechanisms Series.) 16 mm, b & w, 23 min, nd. Produced by the National Film Board of Canada. Order Source: NYUFL. Rental: $10. Case history of a young woman who learned in childhood not to risk social disapproval by independent action.

128. Harold—A Character Disorder in the Making from Preconception to 32 Years. (Studies on Integrated Development: Interaction Between Child and Environment.) 16 mm, b & w, silent, 36 min, 1973. Produced by Margaret E Fries, MD, Paul J Woolf, MS. Order Source: NYUFL. (also GFL). Rental: $11. Unique in that predictions at 7 weeks were revalidated at 32 years re physically healthy, active mode of adaptation, character disorder. Predictions based on his active healthy constitution interacting with a disturbed family.

129. The Rat Man (Notes on a Case of Obsessional Neurosis.) 16 mm, b & w, 50 min, nd. Order Source: GFL. Rental: $20 base service charge for 2 days. A movie of Freud's case, The Rat Man. (This has been presented before the British and American Psychoanalytic Associations.)

Child Psychiatry and Child Therapy

130. Autistic Syndrome Series. (Series in four parts.) 16 mm, b & w, sound, English narration, nd, Part I, 43 min; Part II, 42 min; Part III, 36 min; Part IV, 43 min. Produced by Stichting Film en Wetenschap-Universiaire Film, Utrecht, the Netherlands; Scientific Hospital for Child Psychiatry, Utrecht, the Netherlands. Order Source: NYUFL. Purchase: Parts I, II, IV, $200; Part III, $170. Rental: Parts I, II, IV, $15; Part III, $12   †

131. A Boy Named Terry Egan. 16 mm, b & w, 53 min, nd. Order Source: GFL. (also NYUFL). Rental: $20 base service charge for 2 days. Shows a 9-year-old boy making measurable gains against autism. Comments by Bruno Bettelheim on behalf of the 80,000 autistic children in this country.

132. Clinical Aspects of Childhood Psychosis. 16 mm, b & w, silent, 55 min, nd. Produced by the Institute of Psychiatry, London. Order Source: NYUFL (also GFL, PCR). Purchase: $165. Rental: $11

133. He Comes from Another Room. (Part of NIMH's series, One to Grow On.) 16 mm, color, 28 min, nd. Made by Ed Mason, MD. Order Source: NAC. Purchase: $113.50. Rental: $12.50. A sensitive documentary about integrating two emotionally disturbed children into a regular classroom.

134. Jane: Aged 17 months in Fostercare for 10 Days. 16 mm, b & w, 37 min, nd. Produced by James and Joyce Robertson, Tavistock Child Development Research Unit, London. Order Source: GFL. Rental: $20 base service charge for 2 days. Emotional sequelae in an infant after a 10-day separation from her mother.

135. John: 17 months—Nine Days in a Residential Nursery. 16 mm, b & w, 45 min, 1969. Produced by James and Joyce Robertson. Order Source: PCR. Rental: $15. Follows the daily increasing distress and deterioration as John is defeated in efforts to secure a "mother" while residing in a residential nursery during his mother's hospitalization.

136. Natural History of Psychotic Illness in Children. 16 mm, b & w, 19 min, nd. Produced by Institute of Psychiatry, London (NYU). Order Source: NYUFL (also GFL). Purchase: $160. Rental: $10.50. Describes the evolution of a psychotic child from infancy to adolescence, showing the change from normal to abnormal. The "behavior day" of a psychotic child fully documented.

137. The Neurotic Child. 16 mm, b & w, 28 min, 1968. Produced by MD Griffel, RC Prall, Eastern Psychiatric Institute. Order Source: PCR. *Showing Restricted.* Purchase: $145. Rental: $6.40. Depicts a 7-year-old boy diagnosed as a psychoneurotic in clinical interview situation.   †

138. Personality Disorganization in a 12-Year-Old Negro Boy. 16 mm, b & w, 23 min, 1969. Produced by P Toussieng, L Wright, OA Parsons, B Addis. Discussion by P Toussieng, LJ West. Order

Source: BSML. Rental: $15. Povl Toussieng's interview with a 12-year-old black boy who is undergoing an acute psychotic break.

139. Two-Year-Old Goes to Hospital. 16 mm, b & w, 50 min, 1952. Produced by James Robertson. Order Source: GFL. Rental: $20 base service charge for 2 days. Research described sponsored by the World Health Organization in a project directed by John Bowlby, MD.

140. We Won't Leave You. 16 mm, color, 17 min, 1975. Made by Edward A Mason, MD. Order Source: MHTFP. Purchase: $195. Rental: $20. A film record about meeting the emotional needs of hospitalized young children.

Adolescence: Problems and Therapy

141. The Adolescent Iliad. 16 mm, color, 25 min, 1970. Order Source: LP. Purchase: $250. Rental: $20. Unusual methods of treating emotionally disturbed teenagers; demonstrated at Mendocino State Hospital in Talmage, California.

142. Psychological Adjustment to College. 16 mm, 43 min, 1971. Order Source: UCEMC. Rental: $19

Old Age: Problems and Approaches

143. Aging. 16 mm, color, 22 min, nd. Order Source: CRM. Purchase: $295. Rental: $35. A diversified, up-beat film essay that effectively flouts stereotypes—including those held by workers with the elderly.

143a. Home for Supper. 16 mm, color, 14 min, nd. Order Source: NAC. Rental: Free. The day hospital as an alternative to institutionalization for the elderly and infirm.

144. The Rights of Age. 16 mm, b & w, 28 min, nd. Produced by the Mental Health Film Board. Order Source: NYUFL. Rental: $12.50. Examination of a number of older people in need of physical, psychological, or legal assistance.

145. To Live With Dignity. 16 mm, color, 29 min, 1972. Produced by Institute of Gerontology, University of Michigan, Wayne State University. Order Source: UCEMC. Purchase: $200. Rental: $15 per day ($5 each additional day over contracted period). Documentary of a 3-month project involving milieu therapy with 20 institutionalized elderly patients.

146. Trigger Films on Aging. 16 mm, color, 15 min, nd. Order Source: UMTVC. Purchase: $180. Rental: $25. Five very brief dramatized vignettes on various aspects of growing old.

Neurophysiology

147. Brain and Behavior. 16 mm, b & w, 22 min, nd. Produced by McGraw-Hill. Order Source: NYUFL. Rental: $10.50. Demonstrates two ways of studying different brain areas: (1) the artificial stimulation of the brain by electrodes and (2) measuring by tests behavioral changes following brain injuries.

Sleep and Dreams

148. The Secrets of Sleep. 16 mm, color, 60 min, nd. Order Source: GFL. Rental: $20 base service charge for 2 days. A comprehensive documentary that reviews research into the world of sleep and dreams.

Ethology

149. Behavior and Ecology of Vervet Monkeys. 16 mm, color, 40 min, nd. Produced by Thomas T Struhsaker, New York Zoological Society, Rockefeller University. Order Source: GFL. Rental: $20 base service charge for 2 days

150. Konrad Lorenz. Film 1: Ethology and Imprinting. 16 mm, b & w, 30 min, nd. Order Source: GFL. Rental: $20 base service charge for 2 days

151. Mother Love. 16 mm, b & w, 26 min, nd. Produced by CBS. Order Source: NYUFL. Rental: $11. Testing by Harry F Harlow of reactions of newborn rhesus monkeys to unusual mother substitutes. Shows that the single most important factor is body contact and that deprivation causes deep emotional disturbances.

Sociology

152. Social Class in America. (Sociology Series.) 16 mm, b & w, 16 min, nd. Produced by McGraw-Hill. Order Source: NYUFL. Rental: $10. Shows significant contrasts in the lives of three boys who come from three different social classes—lower, middle, and upper.
153. Uptown. 16 mm, b & w, 27 min, nd. Produced by Lincoln Hospital, New York City. Order Source: NYUFL. Rental: $12. Graphic portrait of a disadvantaged community in South Bronx, New York City, showing way of life of its people through the external reality revealing their desperation and hopes.

Communication

154. A Communication Primer. 16 mm, color, 20 min, 1953. Order Source: MOMA. Rental: $12.50. Some basic messages on aspects of communications that affect our lives in this classic by Charles Eames.
155. This Is Marshall McLuhan: The Medium Is the Message. 16 mm, color, 53 min, nd. Produced by NBC-TV. Order Source: NYUFL. Rental: $44. Presents McLuhan's basic ideas through pictorial techniques and his own comments as well as the reactions of others to his views. Examines the way in which all media of communication shape and alter society.

Group Dynamics

156. Anatomy of a Group. 16 mm, b & w, 30 min, 1961. Produced by NET. Order Source: PCR. Rental: $8.50. Structure of a group, goals to be achieved during meetings, participation patterns, group standards and procedures.

Schools

157. What Is Teaching—What Is Learning. 16 mm, color, 30 min, 1971. Produced by NIMH. Order Source: NAC. Purchase: $66. Rental: $12.50. Discussion by teachers of their first year's experiences in the "open classroom" as flashbacks illustrate their conversation.
158. A Nice Kid Like You. 16 mm, b & w, 40 min, nd. Produced by the University of California. Order Source: NYUFL. Purchase: $250. Rental: $18. Articulate college students speaking candidly about some of their most important concerns: drugs, sex, political action, faculty and curriculum, their relationships with their peers, and the generation gap.

Community Mental Health

159. Chain of Care. 16 mm, b & w, 38 min, 1962. Produced by MHFB. Order Source: NYUFL. Rental: $12.50. Shows patients in the various institutions that make up a coordinated statewide program of prevention, treatment, aftercare, and rehabilitation of mental illness.
160. Community Treatment of the Psychotic Patient. 16 mm, color, 30 min, nd. Order Source: Sq. Rental: Free to professionals. "Highlights" of a seminar consisting of presentations by several psychiatrists on the advantages and drawbacks, as well as the appropriate implementation of a community treatment approach. Moderated by Jonathan O Cole, MD.
161. One Day a Week. 16 mm, b & w, 33 min, nd. Produced by CMC. Order Source: NYUFL. Rental: $12. The experiences of a community psychiatrist on his visit to the Rodman Job Corps Center in Massachusetts, where he offers mental health consultation.
162. Storefront. 16 mm, b & w, 49 min, nd. Produced by Lincoln Hospital, New York City. Order Source: NYUFL. Rental: $22. Describes how a neighborhood service center can be a vital part of a community mental health program. Shows the selection, training, and development of nonprofessional staff members.

Community Mental Health Centers and Clinics

163. Community Mental Health. 16 mm, b & w, 32 min, nd. Produced by MHFB. Order Source: NYUFL. Rental: $11. Dramatizes the public health approach of the mental health center that is concerned with prevention and mental health promotion as well as treatment of disease.

Legal Aspects

164. Psychiatry and Law—How Are They Related? Part I, Part II: Concepts and Controversies in Modern Medicine. 16 mm, b & w, 29 min, 1970. Produced by National Medical Audiovisual Center. Order Source: NAC. Rental: Free

Public Health

165. Broken Appointment. 16 mm, b & w, 30 min, nd. Produced by MHFB. Order Source: NYUFL. Rental: $11. Describes the experience of a young public health nurse who discovers it is as important to understand a patient's feelings as well as to interpret physical symptoms.

Mental Health Personnel

166. On Becoming a Nurse-Psychotherapist. 16 mm, color, 42 min, 1970. Order Source: UCEMC. Purchase: $490. Rental: $28
167. Man to Man. 16 mm, b & w, 30 min, nd. Produced by the Mental Health Film Board. Order Source: NYUFL. Rental: $11. Story of Joe Fuller who takes a temporary job in a state hospital and through a deep and moving relationship with one of his patients decides to stay permanently.
168. Workshop for Another Dimension. 16 mm, b & w, 39 min, 1969. Order Source: MHALA. Rental: Contact MHALA. Sale: $125. New techniques for training volunteers.

Teaching and Supervision

169. Interstaff Communications. (Psychodrama in Group Process Series.) 16 mm, b & w, 42 min, nd. Produced by Ira Pauly (NYU). Order Source: NYUFL. Purchase: $335. Rental: $24. The use of psychodrama techniques to facilitate interstaff communications.

Death and Dying

170. Counseling the Terminally Ill. 16 mm (in preparation). Produced by Charles Garfield and the Cancer Research Institute, University of California Medical Center. Rental: Contact NIMH. A training film designed for the medical and mental health communities regarding the social and psychological needs of the dying.
171. Passing Quietly Through. 16 mm, b & w, 26 min, 1971. Order Source: GPF. Purchase: $300. Rental: $30. An encounter between a nurse and an aging man.
172. Until I Die. 16 mm, color, 30 min, nd. Order Source: UCEMC. Rental: Contact UCEMC. Concise presentation of the work of Elisabeth Kübler-Ross, noted researcher and writer in the field of psychological reaction and adjustment to the process of dying.

Film Sources

ABCMC: ABC Media Concepts, 1330 Avenue of the Americas, New York, NY 10019. (212) 581–7777

AHSS: Applied Human Service Systems, Heller Graduate School, Brandeis University, Waltham, Mass 02154. (617) 647–2944

AMAFL: American Medical Association Film Library, c/o Association Films Inc. At the following addresses:
600 Grand Avenue, Ridgefield, NJ 07657
512 Burlington Avenue, La Grange, Ill 60525
6644 Sierra Lane, Dublin, Calif 94566
5797 New Peachtree Road Atlanta, Ga 30340
8615 Directors Row, Dallas, Texas 75247
(Films are available on loan to individual physicians, medical societies, medical schools, hospitals, and professional medical groups. No entrance fee may be charged to audiences.)

APGA: American Personnel and Guidance Association, 1607 New Hampshire Avenue, NW, Washington, DC 20009. (202) 483–4633

ASF: Association-Sterling Films, 866 Third Avenue, New York, NY 10022. (212) 736–9693

BHES: Blue Hill Educational System, PO Box 113, Monsey, NY 10952. (914) 425–4466

BSML: Behavioral Sciences Media Laboratory, The Neuropsychiatric Institute, University of California at Los Angeles, 760 Westwood Plaza, Los Angeles, Calif 90024

BYU: Department of Motion Picuture Productions, MPS, Brigham Young University, Provo, Utah 84602

CPP: Charles Press Publishers, Inc, PO Box 830, Bowie, MD 20715

CRM: CRM Educational Films, Del Mar, Calif 92014

EL: Eli Lilly & Company, Indianapolis, Ind 46206

EPPI: Audio-Visual Media, Eastern Pennsylvania Psychiatric Institute, Henry Avenue & Abbottsford Road, Philadelphia, Pa 19129. (215) 842–4075

(Restricted Use: Films marked with this notation are intended to be shown only on advanced classes in psychology; classes of medical students; classes of nurses in training; hospital or clinic staff meetings of psychological, medical, or psychiatric societies. Identification of the group leader and composition of the group is required before the film can be supplied.)

ETC: Education Through Communication, Inc, 15354 Weddington Street, Van Nuys, Calif 91401

GFL: Maxwell Gitelson Film Library, 180 North Michigan Avenue, Chicago, Ill 60601. (312) 726–6300

GHZ: Gerald H. Zuk, PhD, Family Psychiatry Department, Eastern Pennsylvania Psychiatric Institute, Henry Avenue & Abbottsford Road, Philadelphia, Pa 19129

GP: Geigy Pharmaceuticals, Saw Mill River Road, Ardsley, NY 10502

GPF: Grove Press Films, 196 West Houston Street, New York, NY 10014. (212) 242–4900

JRH: James R Hodge, MD, 2975 West Market Street, Akron, Ohio 44313. *(Restricted use: Members of The American Society of Clinical Hypnosis or The Society for Clinical and Experimental Hypnosis only.)*

LP: Lawren Productions, Inc, PO Box 1542, Burlingame, Calif 94010. (415) 697–2558

MHALA: Mental Health Association of Los Angeles County, 247 North Western Avenue, Los Angeles, Calif 90004. (213) 466–3491

MHTFP: Mental Health Training Film Program, 58 Fenwood Road, Boston, Mass 02215

MOMA: Museum of Modern Art, Film Rentals, 21 West 53rd Street, New York, NY 10019

MSD: Merck, Sharp, & Dohm, Teterboro, NJ 07608

MTC: Music Therapy Center, 251 West 51st Street, New York, NY 10019

NAC: National Audiovisual Center (GSA), Order Section, Washington, DC 20409. (301) 763–7420

NAI: Nathan W. Ackerman Institute, Inc, 149 East 78th Street, New York, NY 10021

NDF: New Day Films, PO Box 315, Franklin Lakes, NJ 07417

NIMH: National Clearinghouse for Mental Health Information, 5600 Fishers Lane (Rm 15c-26), Rockville, Md 20852

NYUFL: New York University Film Library, 26 Washington Place (Press Annex Bldg), New York, NY 10003

OF: Odeon Films, Inc, 1619 Broadway, New York, NY 10019

P: Pfizer & Company, 235 East 42nd Street, New York, NY 10017. (212) 573–2536

PCR: Psychological Cinema Register, Pennsylvania State University, University Park, Pa 16802

PFI: Psychological Films, Inc, 110 North Wheeler Street, Orange, Calif 92666. (714) 639–4646

RP: Research Press, PO Box 31774, Champaign, Ill 61820

Sq: ER Squibb & Sons, PO Box 4000, Princeton, NJ 08540

TUSM: Behavior Therapy Productions, Department of Psychiatry, Temple University School of Medicine, % EPPI, Henry Avenue & Abbottsford Road, Philadelphia, Pa 19129

UCEMC: University of California Extension Media Center, 2223 Fulton Street, Berkeley, Calif 94720. (415) 642–0460

UIAC: University of Indiana, Audiovisual Center, Bloomington, Ind 47401. (812) 337–8087

UMAVEC: University of Michigan Audio-Visual Education Center, 416 4th Street, Ann Arbor, Mich 48103. (313) 764–5361

UMTVC: University of Michigan TV Center, 400 South 4th Street, Ann Arbor, Mich 48103

USDA: U. S. Department of Agriculture, Office of Communications, Motion Picture Service, Room 1081-S, 14th & Independence Avenue, SW, Washington, DC 20250

VAFL: Central Film Library, 037B1, Audiovisual Service, Veterans Administration Central Office, Washington, DC 20420. (202) 389–2793 *(free loan to hospitals, university departments, and appropriate professional organizations)*

VG: Videographics, Inc, Prospect Center, 26 Trumbull Street, New Haven, Conn 06511. (203) 562–9872

VQ: Vision Quest, Inc, Box 206, Lawrenceville, NJ 08648. (609) 896–1359

AUDIOTAPES

Most of the available audiotapes are in the convenient form of cassettes. These are distributed by a number of companies designated in the descriptions of the audiotapes in this section. Several companies issue cassettes regularly to subscribers. For example, Audio-Digest Foundation Psychiatry, 1250 South Glendale, Avenue, Glendale, California, has issued a cassette every 2 weeks on a timely psychiatric topic since July 1972. Practical Reviews in Psychiatry, Educational Reviews, Leeds, Alabama, sends out a monthly cassette reviewing important articles in the current psychiatric literature.

History

173. The Development of Psychoanalytic Thought. Speaker: Reuben Fine, PhD. Distributor: JA. 12 cassettes (1 hr each). $72
174. Why Freud? An Intellectual and Cultural Study. (Series.) Speaker: Robert Albert, PhD. Distributor: BSTL. 2 cassettes (1 hr each). $14

Personality Development

175. Development of Body Concept and Psychological Differentiation. Speaker: Herman Witkin, PhD. Distributor: JA. One side of 1 cassette (30 min). $10 for cassette. (Other side: Loneliness in Childhood and Adolescence—Rudolf Ekstein, PhD.)
176. Lectures in Child Development, 1974. Distributor: UCP. $25. Lectures from the 1973 convention of the Society for Research in Child Development: LS Kubie, Loss of the Freedom to Change Through Acquisition of the Symbolic Process; MJ Senn, History of the Child Development Movement; J Loevinger, Ego Development and Its Measurement.
177. Loneliness in Childhood and Adolescence. Speaker: Rudolf Ekstein, PhD. Distributor: JA. One side of 1 cassette (30 min). $10 for cassette. (Other side: Development of Body Concept and Psychological Differentiation—Herman Witkin, PhD.)
178. The Meaning of Sleep Disturbances in Early Childhood. Speaker: Humberto Nagera, MD. Distributor: JA. 1 cassette (90 min). $15. Contents: The First Year of Life; The Second Year of Life: Developmental Disturbances; The 3- to 5-Year-Old: Latency.
179. On Aggression. Speaker: Anna Freud. Distributor: JA. 1 cassette (22 min). $10. How aggression works in the service of the merging ego to shape personality and character.
180. Separation and Loss. A symposium by the San Francisco Psychoanalytic Institute Extension Division. Major Speaker: John Bowlby, MD. Distributor: JA. 5 cassettes (1 hr each). $50
181. Women and Achievement. (Series.) Speaker: Susan Darley, PhD. Distributor: BSTL. 3 cassettes (1 hr each). $21. Topics: (1) The way it is and an explanation from the Freudian perspective; (2) An introduction to the situational approach: Role differences between men and women; (3) Differences between ascribed and achieved roles: How the combination works against women.

Culture and Personality

182. Understanding Behavior and Psychiatric Theory Through Ethnic Culture. (Series.) Proceedings of the International Man, Culture, and Humanities Film Festival. Speaker: Harry Wilmer, MD, PhD. Distributor: BSTL. 3 cassettes (1 hr each). $21. A series of lectures that relate the development of psychiatric theory to specific cultural factors.

Human Behavior and Adaptation

183. Role of Stress in the Psychogenesis of Disease. Speaker: Kenneth Pelletier, PhD. Distributor: EMCA. 1 cassette or 1 open-reel (88 min). Available for purchase only: $15. The actual and potential uses of meditation and biofeedback in clinical settings.
184. Spatial Behavior in Human Beings. (Series.) Speaker: Gary Evans, PhD. Distributor: BSTL. 3 cassettes (1 hr each). $21
185. Stress Response Syndromes and Character Types. Speaker: Mardi J. Horowitz, MD. Distributor: JA. 2 cassettes (1 hr each). $20

Mental Functions

186. Cognitive Developments in Children. Speaker: Jules Bemporad, MD. Distributor: JA. 2 cassettes (1 hr each). $20. Cassette 1: Rene Spitz, John Money, Heinz Werner, Jean Piaget; Cassette 2: Piaget, ego development and Hartmann's work, Arieti's work.

Basic Neuropsychiatry

187. Topics in Clinical Psychiatry. (Series.) Distributor: BSTL. 12 cassettes (1 hr each). $6.95 each. Topics: (1) Introduction and General Systems and Diagnostic Concepts; (2) The Therapeutic Community and the Therapeutic Community—Subsystems and Supersystems; (3) Cerebral Dysfunction; (4) Cerebral Dysfunction—Seizure Disorders; (5) Cerebral Dysfunction—14 and 6 Cycles Positive EEG Spiking; (6) Acute Schizophrenia (in two parts); (7) Violence in Clinical States—Syndromes; (8) Violence in Clinical States—Treatment; (9) Depression—Clinical Pictures and Treatment; (10) Depression—Differential Diagnosis and Recent Biochemistry and Paranoia; (11) Geriatric Psychiatry.

Psychopathology

188. Clinical Psychopathology. (Series.) Distributor: BSTL. 12 cassettes (1 hr each). $6.95 each. Viewpoints on 12 salient issues in clinical psychopathology. Topics: (1) The Use of Somatic Treatments in Schizophrenia; (2) Sleep and Psychopathology; (3) Depression—Reaction or Disease; (4) The Definition of Alcoholism; (5) The Diagnosis and Treatment of Pseudoneurotic Schizophrenia; (6) Emergency Psychiatric Treatment; (7) Regrief Work for the Pathological Mourner; (8) The Inpatient Management of Borderline Patients; (9) Regression and Semantic Speech in Hysteria and Schizophrenia; (10) Obsessions and Phobias; (11) Recent Contributions Toward a Theory of Pain Behavior; (12) Who Can Be Hypnotized, Experimental and Clinical Studies in the Control of Pain, etc.

189. The Disorganized Personality Recorded Case Interviews (2d ed). Speaker: GW Kisker. 8 cassette tapes, 1972. Distributor: McH. $100. Topics: (1) Behavior Problems of Childhood and Adolescence; (2) Sexual Deviations; (3) Folie A Deux? (4) Childhood Psychosis; (5) Undifferentiated Schizophrenia; (6) Paranoid Schizophrenia; (7) Affective Psychosis; (8) Brain Disorders.

190. Managing the Potentially Dangerous Patient. Speakers: Miller, Goldzband, Distributor: ADF. 1 cassette. $5.40

191. Paranoid States: Theory and Therapy. Speaker: Leon Salzman, MD. Distributor: JA. 1 cassette (1 hr). $10

192. Therapy of the Obsessional States. Speaker: Leon Salzman, MD. Distributor: JA. 3 cassettes (1 hr each). $30. Topics: (1) Clinical Description of the Obsessive Personality; (2) General Strategies and Maneuvers; (3) The Doubting.

Psychodynamics

193. The Nature of Anxiety. Speaker: Kurt Goldstein, MD. Distributor: JA. One side of 1 cassette (30 min). $10 for cassette. (Other side: Loneliness in Mature Age—Charlotte Buhler, PhD.)

General Systems Theory

194. General Systems Science and Psychoanalysis. Speaker: Joseph C. Solomon, MD. Distributor: BSTL. 6 tapes (1 hr each). #80200. $42

Schools of Psychotherapy

195. AAP Research. Tape: 6 Therapists. Cassette only. Distributor: AAPTL. $10 including script. Extra scripts $1.50 each. Short samples of the work of Albert Ellis, Richard Felder, Abraham Levitsky, Ira Progoff, Carl Rogers, and John Rosen chosen by Nat Raskin as the basis for the American Academy of Psychotherapists (AAP) Psychotherapy Research Project, which compared different approaches to psychotherapy, including ratings by 83 judges on 12 different variables.

196. Transactional Analysis and Gestalt: A Teachable System for Psychoanalytically Oriented Psychotherapy. (Series.) Speaker: Robert Drye, MD. Distributor: BSTL. 3 cassettes (1 hr each). $21

197. Carl Rogers at 70. Cassette only. Distributor: AAPTL. $12 including script. Extra scripts $1.50 each. A joint release of AAP and the Division of Psychotherapy of the American Psychological Association. Client-centered counseling.

198. Mrs. P.S. Reel only. 43 min. Distributor: AAPTL. $10 including script. Extra scripts $1 each. An initial interview by Carl Rogers with a young woman of low socioeconomic status. As a first interview, unusually revealing and illustrative of many aspects of the therapeutic process.

199. Provocative Theory and Therapy. Reel only. 55, 63 min. Distributor: AAPTL. $15 including script. Extra scripts $2 each. Theoretical concepts and examples involved in provocative therapy.

200. Gestalt Therapy and How It Works. Speaker: Fritz Perls, MD. Distributor: JA. 1 cassette (1 hr). $10. The basic principles of Gestalt therapy and how it differs from psychoanalysis explained by Fritz Perls.

201. Interview With Dr. Albert Ellis. Cassette only. 22 min. Distributor: AAPTL. $10 including script. Extra scripts $1 each. A joint release of AAP and the Division of Psychotherapy of the American Psychological Association.

202. Reality Therapy in Child and Marital Counseling. Speaker: W Glasser. Distributor: ADF. 1 cassette. $5.40

203. Transactional Analysis. (American Psychiatric Association Postgraduate Course/Continuing Medical Education Program.) Distributor: ADF. 1 cassette (4 hr). $39.95. Qualifies for AMA Continuing Medical Education credits, Category I.

204. Critique of Primal Therapy. Cassette only. 25, 25 min. Speaker: Hans Strupp. Distributor: AAPTL. $10 including script. Extra scripts $1 each. A critical discussion of Arthur Janov's primal therapy.

205. Basic Concepts of Humanistic Psychology. Speaker: Charlotte Buhler. Distributor: JA. 1 cassette (1 hr). $10

206. Self-Actualization. Speaker: Abraham Maslow, PhD. Distributor: JA. 1 cassette (1 hr). $10 The core concept of Maslow's approach, self-actualization.

Introduction to Psychotherapy

207. Contemporary Psycho-social Issues. (Series.) Distributor: BSTL. 12 cassettes (1 hr each). $6.95 each. Psychiatric psychoanalysis and sociological investigations in contemporary psychosocial issues such as racism, marijuana and encounter groups reviewed. Topics: (1) Psychodynamics of Racial Conflicts; (2) Character Types and Political Action; (3) Radical Interpretation of Psychoanalysis; (4) Role of Psychiatrist on the College Campus; (5) Psychoanalysis and Unconscious Racism; (6) Sexual Behavior and the Law; (7) Therapeutic, Educational, and Recreational-Expressive Uses of Groups: The Behavioral Scientist's Perspective; (8) The Dying Patient; (9) The Behavioral Revolution in Psychiatry and Psychology; (10) Marijuana: A Review of the Research; (11) Legal and Behavioral Perspectives on Privacy; (12) A Model of Psychohistorical Change.

208. Psychotherapy: What, Why, and How. Speakers: Enelow, Engelert, Kolb. Distributor: ADF. 1 cassette. $15.40

Values in Psychotherapy

209. Patient Values and the Clinical Enterprise. (Series.) Speaker: Larry Beutler, PhD. Distributor: BSTL. 3 cassettes (1 hr each). $21. Topics: (1) Influencing Patient Values Through Psychotherapy; (2) Diagnostic Assessment for Maximizing Value Change; (3) Value Change, Personality Theory, and Inducing Therapeutic Dissonance.

Tactics of Psychotherapy

210. The Process of Intensive Psychotherapy. Speaker: Richard Chessick, MD. Distributor: JA. 12 cassettes (1 hr each). $72. A guide to understanding the psychotherapeutic process. Topics: (1) Psychotherapy in the Context of Civilization; (2) Mental Health and Psychological Healing; (3)

The Psychotherapist; (4) On Beginning the Treatment; (5) The Opening Phase; (6) Transference and Countertransference; (7) Resistance and Intervention; (8) The Art of Interpretation; (9) Analysis of a Psychotherapy; (10) Therapeutic Interaction; (11) Ending the Treatment; (12) Progress in Psychotherapy.

211.   Psychotherapy and Behavior Change. Cassette only. Speaker: Hans Strupp. 30, 23 min. Distributor: AAPTL. $12 including script. Extra scripts $1.50 each. Discussion of differences in inputs and outcomes among various philosophies of psychotherapy, the equivalence of therapeutic techniques, etc.

212.   Psychotherapy and Psychoanalysis. (Series.) Distributor: BSTL. 12 cassettes (1 hr each). $6.95 each. Review of current development in the practice and theory of psychotherapy and psychoanalysis. Topics: (1) Common Errors in the Psychotherapeutic Management of Schizophrenic Patients; (2) Power and Paranoia; (3) The Use of Video Tapes in Psychotherapy; (4) The Aims and Outcomes of Psychotherapy; (5) Confusion of Goals in Psychotherapy—Mental Health, the Good Life, and Happiness; (6) Psychotherapeutic Features of Psychotherapy; (7) Creativity and Character; (8) The Development and Relevance of "Existential" Themes in the Practice of Psychotherapy; (9) Brief Psychotherapy: Technique, Indications, and Limitations; (10) Psychoanalytic Treatment of Male Homosexuality; (11) Recent Advances in Behavior Therapy; (12) Image Techniques in Psychotherapy.

213.   The Technique of Psychoanalytic Psychotherapy. Speaker: Robert Langs, MD. Distributor: JA. 12 cassettes (1 hr each). $72. A series of teaching tapes in an ongoing conference for second- and third-year residents in psychiatry. Topics: (1) Case 1: Interpretations and Confrontations; (2) Case 2: The Patient's Attempt to Cure the Therapist; (3) Missed Interpretations and Maladaptive Responses; (4) Adaptive Context and the Interpsychic Conflict; (5) Forced Terminations, Acting-out, Free Associations, and Unconscious Derivatives; (6) Case 3: Transference Fantasies: The Use of Silence and Misalliance; (7) Premature and Intellectualized Interventions; (8) Patient's Unconscious Perception of the Therapist; Dreams, the Process by which the Therapist Picks up His Own Errors; (9) Close Derivatives of Unconscious Fantasies: Confirmation by Recall; (10) Case 4: Patient–Therapist Relationship; Unconscious Fantasies and the Therapeutic Context; (11) Termination; (12) Consultations, Confidentiality, Deviations in Technique.

214.   A Comprehensive Course in Psychoanalytic Psychotherapy. (A continuing series, to be produced on a bimonthly schedule, 2 at a time.) Speaker: Robert Langs, MD. Distributor: JA. $20 for each 2-hr unit. A record of ongoing supervision in a seminar setting. Topics: (1) Interpretation of Early Resistances; (2) The Boundaries of the Therapeutic Relationship; (3) Patient–Therapist Relationship. Further topics in process.

215.   The Process of Intensive Psychotherapy. (Series.) Distributor: BSTL. 12 cassettes (1 hr each). $6.95 each. The process of intensive psychotherapy described in 12 parts, from the initial interview to the complex problems involved in termination. Topics: (1) Psychotherapy in the Context of Civilization; (2) Mental Health and Psychological Healing; (3) The Psychotherapist; (4) On Beginning the Treatment; (5) The Opening Phase; (6) Transference and Countertransference; (7) Resistance and Intervention; (8) The Art of Interpretation; (9) Analysis of a Psychotherapy; (10) Therapeutic Interaction; (11) Ending the Treatment; (12) Progress in Psychotherapy.

216.   The Theory and Practice of Individual Psychotherapy. Speaker: Paul A Dewald, MD. Distributor: JA. 12 cassettes (1 hr each). $72. Focuses on insight-directed and supportive therapy and the goals, strategies, and processes appropriate to each. Topics: (1) Psychopathology and the Treatment Process; (2) General Clinical Theory of the Therapeutic Process; (3) The Therapist as Catalyst; (4) Insight-Directed vs. Supportive Therapy; (5) Various Treatment Modalities: When Indicated; (6) Diagnosis and Evaluation; (7) Establishing Treatment Goals; (8) The Beginning Phase of Therapy; (9) Middle Phase; (10) Termination; (11) Brief Therapy; (12) Special Therapeutic Problems.

Behavior Therapy

217.   Behavior Therapy. (American Psychiatric Association Postgraduate Course/Continuing Medical Education Program.) Distributor: ADF. 1 cassette (3 hr). $29.95. Qualifies for AMA Continuing Medical Education credits, Category I.

218.   Behavior Therapy. Reel only. 65 min. Distributor: AAPTL. $12 including script. Extra scripts $1 each. A demonstration by Joseph Wolpe of behavior therapy including the use of relaxation and reciprocal inhibition with a phobic girl.

219. Behavior Therapy Technique of Assertive Training. (Series.) Speaker: John Galassi, PhD. Distributor: BSTL. 4 cassettes (1 hr each). $28
220. Behavior Therapy: Techniques, Principles and Patient Aids. (Series.) Edited by Cyril Franks, PhD. Distributor: BMA. 12 cassettes in 2-vol series. Vol I, $55 for 6-cassette folio; Vol II, $59.70 for 6 cassettes in 12-cassette folio. Each cassette available individually for $9.95. Vol I: (1) Relaxation Training in Clinical Practice—Ian Evans, PhD; (2) Therapist Guidelines in Weight Control—Michael Mahoney, PhD; (3) Regulation of Body Weight—Michael Mahoney, PhD; (4) Behavioral Treatment of Depression: A Guide for Clinicians—Peter Lewinsohn, PhD; (5) Combating Depression: Practical Techniques—Peter Lewinsohn, PhD; (6) Cognitive Behavior Modification Techniques: Stress Innoculation—Donald Meichenbaum, PhD. Vol II: (1) Behavioral Treatment of Obsessive-Compulsive Disorders—G. Terence Wilson, PhD; (2) Behavioral Treatment of Sexual Dysfunction—Joseph LoPiccolo, PhD; (3) Behavioral Treatment of Smoking: Clinical Alternatives—Edward Lichenstein, PhD, Brian Danaher, MS (2 cassettes); (4) Rational Emotive Therapy: Clinician's Guide—Albert Ellis, PhD. (2 cassettes).
221. Implosive Therapy. Reel only. 52, 46 min. Distributor: AAPTL. $15 including script and material. Extra scripts $2 each. Dramatic demonstration by Robert Hogan of implosive deconditioning by extinction using as examples snake and rat phobias. (The snake tape has been used experimentally in the treatment of frigidity.)
222. Multimodal Behavior Therapy. (Series.) Distributor: BSTL. 6 cassettes (1 hr each). $6.95 each. Concepts pertinent to multimodal behavior therapy. Topics: (1) Some Free Associations upon Broad-Spectrum Behavior Therapy; (2) Aspects of Broad-Spectrum Behavior Therapy in Groups; (3) Modality Therapy: An Introduction; (4) The Relation of Theory to Practice—with Special Reference to "Technical Eclecticsm"; (5) Two Important Issues in Behavior Therapy: Symptom Substitution, Transference and Relationship Factors; (6) Training Broad-Spectrum Behavior Therapists—Trainees' Comments on Training.
223. Unlearning Fears: The Behavioral Extinction Technique of Implosive Therapy. (Series.) Speaker: Donald Levis, PhD. Distributor: BSTL. 3 cassettes (1 hr each). $21. Topics: (1) A Learning Model on How Psychopathology Is Acquired, Maintained, and Extinguished; (2) The Implosive Therapy Procedure and Cue Classification Schemes; (3) Theory and Application of the Implosive Technique to Various Nosologies.

Ego Analysis

224. Ego Psychology. Speaker: Gertrude Blanck, PhD, Rubin Blanck, MS. Distributor: JA, 6 cassettes (1 hr each). $60

Non-Freudian Psychoanalysis

225. Adlerian Therapy: Two Interviews. Reel only. 34, 35 min. Distributor: AAPTL. $10 including script. Extra scripts $1 each. Two interviews with hospitalized women conducted by Bernard Shulman.
226. Gregg. Reel only. 61 min. Distributor: AAPTL. $12 including script. Extra scripts $1.50 each. An example of Jungian analysis with a focus on exploring dreams—the therapist, Ira Progoff; the subject, a young man.
227. Interview with Dr. John N. Rosen. Cassette only. 17, 16 min. Distributor: AAPTL. $10 including script. Extra scripts $1 each. A joint release of AAP and the Division of Psychotherapy of the American Psychological Association. Changes in the theory and practice of direct analysis, treatment aims, long-term results with patients, etc.

Existential Analysis

228. Existentialism and Psychiatry. (Series.) Speaker: Irwin Savodnik, MD, PhD. Distributor: BSTL. 6 cassettes (1 hr each). $42. Provides the background of how existential concepts came to psychiatry and the impact of existentialism upon psychiatric thinking. Clear presentation of the clinical aspects of existential psychiatry. Topics: (1) Philosophy and Psychiatry; (2) Cultural and Historical Foundations of Existentialism; (3) Kierkegaard, Heidegger, and Psychiatry; (4) Heidegger's Impact on Existential Psychiatry; (5) Clinical Aspects of Existential Psychiatry; (6) The Concept of the World in Existential Psychiatry.

Group Process

229.   Group Process and Group Therapy. Speakers: Hawkins, Colman, Ziferstein. Distributor: ADF.
       1 cassette. $5.40

Group Psychotherapy

230.   The Art and Technique of Analytic Group Therapy. Speaker: Martin Grotjahn, MD. Distributor: JA. 1 cassette (2 hr). $20
231.   Current Developments in Group Psychotherapy. Speaker: Max Rosenbaum, PhD. Distributor: BSTL. 1 cassette (1 hr). $6.95. Current developments in group psychotherapy.
232.   Group-analytic Psychotherapy. (Series.) Distributor: BSTL. 3 cassettes (1 hr each). $6.95 each. Topics: (1) Group-analytic Psychotherapy: Principles and Orientation; (2) Group-analytic Situation and Therapeutic Process; (3) The Group Analyst and His Training: Method and Technique.
233.   How to Use Encounter Groups. (A program in series.) Speaker: Carl Rogers, PhD. Distributor: ID. Series I: $64.95; Series II, $64.95; Series III: $38.95. Three-series program: $164.95
234.   The Intensive Group. Speaker: Carl Rogers, PhD. Distributor: JA. 1 cassette (1 hr). $10
235.   Interview with JL Moreno. Cassette only. 27, 27 min. Distributor: AAPTL. $10 including script. Extra scripts $1.50 each
236.   An Introduction to Group Psychotherapy. Speaker: Benjamin Sadock, MD. Distributor: BSTL. 1 cassette (1 hr). $6.95
237.   Introduction to Psychodrama. Cassette only. 30 min. Distributor: AAPTL. $10 including script. Extra scripts $1 each. Demonstration by James Sacks with a group the basic techniques of psychodrama including the empty chair, use of the double.
238.   My Experiences with Psychoanalytic Group Psychotherapy. Speaker: Martin Grotjahn, MD. Distributor: BSTL. 1 cassette (1 hr). $6.95
239.   Rules of Thumb for Open Encounter. Speaker: William Schutz, PhD. Distributor: JA. 1 cassette (1 hr). $10

Family Therapy and Marital Therapy

240.   Divorce Counseling. Speaker: Esther Oshiver Fisher, JD, EdD. Distributor: JA. $40 1 cassette (4 hr).
241.   Families and Family Therapy. (Series.) Distributor: BSTL. 5 cassettes (1 hr each). $6.95 each. Topics: (1) Introduction to Family Therapy; (2) Family Homeostatic Mechanisms (in two parts); (3) Family Role Relationships; (4) Family Therapy; (5) Family Therapy and Individual Therapy and Social Homeostasis: Individual, Family and Social Interactions.
242.   Family Communication and Growth. Speaker: Virginia Satir. Distributor: JA. 1 cassette (1 hr). $10. Satir working with three married couples to help find a way of satisfactorily quarreling without permanently damaging their marriages.
243.   Family Therapy and Diagnosis. Speaker: Gerald H Zuk, PhD. Distributor: JA. 6 cassettes (1 hr each). $50. Topics: (1) The Engagement Phases/The Termination Phase; (2) Runaway Wife; (3) Description of Pathogenic Relating; (4) Truants from School; (5) The Therapist as Celebrant; (6) A Family with a Drug-using Teenager.
244.   Family Therapy with Follow-up. Speaker: Gerald H Zuk, PhD. Distributor: BSTL. 1 cassette (1 hr). $6.95
245.   Indications and Contraindications for Family Therapy. Speaker: Ira D Glick, MD. Distributor: BSTL. 1 cassette (1 hr). $6.95
246.   Marital Disharmony. (American Psychiatric Association. Postgraduate Course/Continuing Medical Education Program.) Distributor: ADF. 1 cassette (2 hr). $19.95. Qualifies for AMA Continuing Medical Education credits, Category I.
247.   Training Family Therapists. (Series.) Speaker: Bruce Peck, PhD. Distributor: BSTL. 6 cassettes (1 hr each). $42. A comprehensive view of the implications and ramifications of the training of family therapists. Topics: (1) Introduction; (2) Cotherapy and the Consultant; (3) Training for Style; (4) Failure Experiences and Growth; (5) The Therapist's Family; (6) After Training.

Hypnosis

248. Hypnosis for Students. 2 reels only. 146, 103 min. Distributor: AAPTL. $40 including script. Extra scripts $5 each. A joint release of AAP and the Society for Clinical and Experimental Hypnosis. Eight excerpts on two tapes from an introductory course in hypnotism given by Irwin Rothman and associates.
249. Hypnosymbolic Psychotherapy (Part I, Part II). Speaker: C Scott Moss. Distributor: BSTL. 2 cassettes (1 hr each). $6.95 each
250. Hypnotic Age Regression. Reel only. 82, 41 min. Distributor: AAPTL. $15 including script plus explanatory material. Extra scripts $2.50 each. A joint release of AAP and the Society for Clinical and Experimental Hypnosis. A detailed induction by Erika Fromm.
251. Hypnotic Relief of Pain. Cassette only. 44, 22 min. Distributor: AAPTL. $12 including script. Extra scripts $1.50 each. A joint release of the AAP and the Society for Clinical and Experimental Hypnosis.
252. Uses and Abuses of Hypnosis. Speaker: Lewis R Wolberg, MD. Distributor: JA. 1 cassette (1 hr). $10

Somatic Therapies

253. Clinical Psychopharmacology. (American Psychiatric Association Postgraduate Course/ Continuing Medical Education Program.) Distributor: ADF. 1 cassette (3 hr). $29.95. Qualifies for AMA Continuing Medical Education credits, Category I.
254. Clinical Use of Psychotropic Drugs. Speaker: David J Greenblatt, MD. Distributor: MSTL. 3 tapes (1 hr each). $24. Discussion of recent findings regarding the rational use of psychotropic agents.
255. Drugs in Treatment of Aggression. Speakers: Monroe, Blumer, Bosma. Distributor: ADF. $5.40
256. Hope and Scope of Psychopharmacotherapy. Audio Digest 4(2). Distributor: ADF, 1 cassette (1 hr). $5.40
257. Impact of Pharmacology on Psychiatry. Speakers: Lehman, Hollister, Mandell. Distributor: ADF. 1 cassette. $5.40
258. Psychoactive Drugs. Speakers: Dernberg, Glassman, Smith. Distributor: ADF. 1 cassette. $5.40
259. Psychopharmacologic Treatment of Affective Disorders. Speaker: Baron Shopsin, MD. Distributor: MSTL. 4 tapes (1 hr each). $32. Topics: (1) Psychopharmacology of Depression; (2) Psychopharmacology of Mania; (3) Use of Lithium in Psychiatry; (4) Use of Lithium in Psychiatry (cont'd).
260. Psychopharmacology. Speaker: Scott L Carder, MD. Distributor: MSTL. 6 tapes (1 hr each). $48. Provides a clear and concise outline of what the physician must know in order to use psychochemotherapeutic agents safely and effectively. Topics: (1) Major Tranquilizers Used in Medicine; (2) Antianxiety Drugs; (3) Lithium Treatment of Mood Disorders; (4) The Practical Use of Long-acting Phenothiazines; (5) Specific Psychoactive Drug Uses in Children; (6) The Treatment of Depression.

Miscellaneous Adjuncts

261. The New Body Therapies. Cassette only. 33, 31 min. Distributor: AAPTL. $10 including script. Extra scripts $1.50 each. A review by Harold Streitfeld of the important shift from mind to body in current therapy. Discussion at length of sensory awareness, Gestalt therapy, Rolfing, the Reichian therapies, and dance or movement therapy.
262. Biofeedback Techniques in Clinical Practice. (Series.) Edited by John Basmajian, MD, Johann Stoyva, PhD. Distributor: BMA. 26 cassettes in 3 vol. Vol I, $90 for 10-cassette folio; Vol II, $90 for 10-cassette folio; Vol III, $110 for 12-cassette folio. $9.95 for individual cassettes. Vol I: (1) Biofeedback: Clinical Applications and Research—Sidney Rosenberg, PhD; (2) Relaxation Procedures—Alan Rappaport, PhD; (3) Voluntary Stress Release and Behavior Therapy in the Treatment of Clenching and Bruxism—Andrew Cannistraci, DDS; (4) EMG Biofeedback: Therapeutic Applications—William Love, Jr, PhD; (5) EEG Biofeedback: Clinical Applications and Research Frontiers—Barbara Brown, PhD; (6) Biofeedback in Psychotherapy—Charles Adler, MD, Sheila Morrissey Adler, PhD; (7) The Proper Selection of Headache Patients for

Biofeedback—Seymour Diamond, MD (2 cassettes); (8) The Application of Biofeedback to Headache Patients—Seymour Diamond, MD; (9) Biofeedback in Pain Management—Arnold Gessel, MD. Vol II: (1) Stress Disorders: Why Use Biofeedback—Johann Stoyva, PhD; (2) Diagnosis and Treatment of Insomnia and Other Sleep Disorders—Peter J Hauri, PhD; (3) Systems Approach to Biofeedback Training—Thomas H Budzynski, PhD; (4) Thermal Biofeedback: Clinical Applications—Clarence E Carnahan, MD, Barbara A Pearse; (5) Clinical Biofeedback and Vasoconstrictive Syndromes—Charles F Stroebel, PhD, MD; (6) Biofeedback in Physical Rehabilitation: An Overview—John V Basmajian, MD; (7) Biofeedback in Control of Cardiac Function—Bernard T Engel, PhD; (8) GSR Biofeedback in Clinical Practice—Keith Sedlacek, MD; (9) Biofeedback in Cognitive Behavior Modification—Donald Meichenbaum, PhD; (10) Evaluating and Selecting Biofeedback Instrumentation—John Rugh, PhD. Vol III: (1) Biofeedback, Patterning, and the Treatment of Essential Hypertension—Gary Schwartz, PhD (2 cassettes); (2) How to Use Biofeedback in Physical Therapy: Audio-Visual Neuro-Muscular Reeducation Techniques—C Kumarlal Fernando, RPT; (3) Mixed Scanning Relaxation Training Program: Introductory and Advanced Instructions—CH Hartman, PhD; (4) Biofeedback in Systematic Desensitization—Thomas Budzynski, PhD (2 cassettes); (5) Fundamentals of Clinical Biofeedback for Self-control Skills Learning—T Mulholland (2 cassettes); (6) Thermal Biofeedback in Migraine Headache Treatment—The Menninger Foundation Studies; (7) Biofeedback in Treatment of Gastro-Intestinal Disorders—KA Hubell, JD Sargeant; (8) Biofeedback Applications in Pregnancy and Labor—RH Gregg; (9) Selecting Patients for Biofeedback Therapy—KR Gaarder.

263. Fact and Fancy About Biofeedback and Its Clinical Implications. Speaker: Neal Miller. Distributor: APA. $10

264. Relaxation Techniques: Clinical and Training Procedures. (Series.) Edited by Ian Evans, PhD. Distributor: BMA. 6 cassettes. $55 for series; $9.95 for individual cassettes. Topics: (1) Relaxation Procedures—Alan Rappaport, PhD; (2) Yoga as a Relaxation Technique: Instructions—Judith Proctor; (3) Auto-Induction Procedures for Relaxation—Andrew Cannistraci, DDS; (4) Breathing and Meditative Techniques—Judith Procter; (5) Relaxation Training in Clinical Practice—Ian Evans, PhD; (6) Mixed Scanning Relaxation Training Program: Introductory and Advanced Instructions—CH Hartman, PhD.

Emergencies in Psychotherapy and Crisis Intervention (Suicide)

265. Crisis Intervention. (Series.) Speaker: Harvey Ruben, MD, MPH. Distributor: BSTL. 3 cassettes (1 hr each). $21. Topics: (1) Introduction; (2) Techniques; (3) Treatment of Alcoholism.

266. Suicide Prevention and Crisis Intervention. 6 audiotapes and 12 16 mm films in a multimedia package. Distributor: CPP. Simulated telephone interviews designed to train crisis center workers.

Consultation-Liaison Psychiatry

267. Organic Ills in Psychiatric Clothing. Caveat, Doctor! Speakers: Waggoner, Escamilla, Moser. Distributor: ADF. 1 cassette. $5.40

268. Pediatric Psychology for Pediatricians. (Series.) Speaker: Kenneth Berry, PhD. Distributor: BSTL. 3 cassettes (1 hr each). $21. A comprehensive guide to understanding and achieving effective interaction with children. For the psychotherapist working with children hospitalized for the treatment of physical disorders.

269. The Psychiatrist in the General Hospital. 60 min, 1973. Distributor: BSTL. $6.95. The role of the psychiatrist in the general hospital examined in three parts, emphasizing problems in dealing with the psychiatric concomitants of physical illness. Topics: (1) Consultation Psychiatry and the General Hospital; (2) Psychological Aspects of Chronic Hemodialysis; (3) The Psychological Reactions to Cardiac Surgery.

270. Psychiatry's Role in Therapeutic Abortion. Speakers: Pasnau, Marmer, Cushner, Kirkpatrick, Straker. Distributor: ADF $5.40

Psychosomatic Disorders

271. Current Perspectives in Psychosomatic Medicine. Edited by Robert Martin, MD. Distributor: BMA. 6 cassettes in folio. $55

272. Psychiatric Overlays in Somatic Illness. Speakers: Chaffin, Zeifert. Distributor: ADF. 1 cassette. $5.40

273. Psychosomatic and Psychological Factors in Medicine. Speaker: Kenneth Pelletier, PhD. Distributor: EMCA. 1 cassette or 1 open-reel (103 min). $20. Rapid overview of the psychogenesis of disease. Outlines some things the individual can do by means of biofeedback, patterning, meditation, and autogenic exercises. Exercises demonstrated with the audience; can be duplicated by listener.

274. Psychosomatic Medicine. (Series.) Speaker: Hoyle Leigh, MD. Distributor: BSTL. 3 cassettes (1 hr each). $21.

275. Psychosomatic Medicine. (Series.) Speaker: Alistair Munro, MD. Distributor: BSTL. 6 cassettes (1 hr each). $42

Sexual Problems

276. Dealing with Sexual Material. Cassette only. 30, 30 min. Distributor: AAPTL. $10 including script. Extra scripts $1 each. A joint release of AAP and the Division of Psychotherapy of the American Psychological Association. A symposium on the inner feelings of the therapist when dealing with sexual material.

277. Homosexuality. Should It Be in the APA Nomenclature? Speakers: Gold, Bieber, Marmor, Socarides. Distributor: ADF. 1 cassette. $5.40

278. Human Sexuality. (American Psychiatric Association. Postgraduate Course/Continuing Education Program.) Distributor: ADF. 1 cassette (4 hr). $39.95. Qualifies for AMA Continuing Medical Education credits, Category I.

279. Phenomenon of Transsexualism. Speakers: Hastings, Newman. Distributor: ADF. 1 cassette. $5.40

280. Sexual Dysfunctions in Married Couples: Psychodynamics and Treatment. (Series.) Speaker: Leo Jacobs, MD. Distributor: BSTL. 3 cassettes (1 hr each). $21. Topics: (1) Sexual Dysfunctions in Married Couples; (2) Psychodynamics in Married Couples; (3) Treatment of Sexual Dysfunctions in Married Couples.

Depressive Disorders

281. Depression. Speaker: Leon Salzman, MD. Distributor: JA. 1 cassette (1 hr). $10. Clarifies normal, neurotic, and psychotic depressions; covers both the psychopharmacologic and psychotherapeutic approaches to treatment.

282. Depression and Insomnia: Current Treatment Approaches. Speakers: Ayd, Wahl. Distributor: ADF. 1 cassette. $5.40

283. The Diagnosis and Treatment of Depression. Speaker: Martin G Blinder, MD. Distributor: JA, 1 cassette (1 hr). $10

Schizophrenic Reactions

284. Biochemical Substrates of Schizophrenia. Speaker: Larry Stein. Distributor: APA. $10

285. Common Errors in the Psychopharmacologic Treatment of Schizophrenia. Speaker: Ivan K Goldberg, MD. Distributor: BSTL. 1 tape (1 hr). $7.95

286. Common Errors in the Psychotherapeutic Management of Schizophrenic Patients. Speaker: Harold F Searles, MD. Distributor: BSTL. 1 cassette (60 min). Behavioral Sciences Tape Library (Psychotherapy and Psychoanalysis No. 1). $7.95

287. Family Dynamics and Schizophrenia. Speakers: Jerry Higgins, PhD, Irving B Weiner, PhD. Distributor: JA. $10. Psychopathology of schizophrenia.

288. Psychotherapy of Schizophrenia. Speakers: Friedman, Schulz, Will. Distributor: ADF. 1 cassette. $5.40

289. Schizophrenia. Speakers: Lidz, Sarwer-Foner, Dyrud. Distributor: ADF. 1 cassette. $5.40

290. Schizophrenia: Causes, Characteristics, and Cures. Speaker: Bernard Shulman, MD. Dis-

tributor: MSTL. 6 tapes (1 hr each). $43. Discussion of the origins and treatments of schizophrenia.

Borderline Cases

291. The Borderline Patient. Speaker: Richard Chessick, MD. Distributor: JA. 12 cassettes in a permanent album (1 hr each). $72
292. The Borderline Patient. Speaker: Arlene Wolberg, MSS. Distributor: JA. 3 cassettes (1 hr each). $30. Topics: (1) The Walking Borderline; (2) Early Life of Borderline Patient; (3) Techniques of the Therapeutic Process.
293. Special Considerations in the Treatment of Borderline Patients. (Series.) Speaker: Melvin Singer, MD. Distributor: BSTL. 2 cassettes (1 hr each). $14

Delinquency and Criminality

294. Criminal Behavior and Reform. (Series.) Speaker: George Solomon, MD. Distributor: BSTL. 3 cassettes (1 hr each). $21. Topics: (1) Psychodynamics of Criminal Behavior; (2) Prisons and the Psychopath; (3) Criminal Behavior and Reform—"Joe," An Inmate Speaks.

Speech and Voice Disorders

295. Behavioral Treatment of Stuttering. Reel only. 60, 9 min. Distributor: AAPTL. $12 including script and material. Extra scripts $2. Demonstration by John Paul Brady of the deconditioning of stuttering using the Pacemaster, a miniaturized electronic metronome.

Alcoholism

296. Alcoholism and Drug Abuse. (American Psychiatric Association Postgraduate Course/ Continuing Medical Education Program.) Distributor: ADF. 1 cassette (4 hr). $39.95. Qualifies for AMA Continuing Medical Education credits, Category I.
297. Counseling the Children of Alcoholics. Speaker: Kathleen Michael. Distributor: ARF. 1 cassette (26 min). $9. Illustrates the problems confronting children of alcoholics and offers counseling suggestions for the therapist.
298. Treatment of Alcoholism. Speakers: Beard, Moore, Goodwin. Distributor: ADF. 1 cassette. $5.40

Drug Addiction

299. Drug Abuse Education. Speaker: Russell N. Cassel, PhD. Distributor: MSTL. 6 tapes (1 hr each). $42. The causes, identification, prevention and treatment of drug abuse. A long, hard look at current drug treatment programs. Topics: (1) Introduction to PLUDRUG. History of Dangerous Drugs; (2) Classes of Dangerous Drugs. Nature of Dangerous Drugs; (3) Drug Addiction and Dependence. Evidence of Dangerous Drug Abuse; (4) Cause of Drug Abuse. Drug Treatment Programs; (5) Dialogue with Drug Abusers. Drug Control Laws and Procedures; (6) Drug Abuse Education. Drug Abuse Prevention.
300. National Commission on Marijuana and Drug Abuse. Speakers: Grinspoon, Bozzetti, Ungerleider, Fort. Distributor: ADF. 1 cassette. $5.40
301. Professional Drug Tapes. (Series.) Distributor: NAC. 8 talks on 4 cassette audiotapes. $10. For health and social service professionals concerned with drug-abuse prevention and treatment. Topics: (1) Abuse of Stimulants, Depressants, and Anesthetics; (2) The Bad Trip; (3) Hallucinogens; (4) History of Drug Abuse and Legal Control; (5) Marijuana; (6) Methadone Maintenance. (7) Narcotics; (8) Principles of Counseling.
302. The Psychiatrist and the (Horse, Coke, Grass, Acid, and Speed) Drug Scene. Speakers: Yolles, Louria, Primm, Abruzzi. Distributor: ADF. 1 cassette. $5.40

Organic Brain Disease

303.   Stroke: Recovery with Aphasia. Cassette only. 30, 25 min. Distributor: AAPTL. $12 including script. Extra scripts $1.50 each. The subjective reports of a therapist, Scott Moss, and his wife, Betty, about his stroke, consequent aphasia, and long recovery from both internal and external language loss, the accompanying physical and psychological trauma, factors in his recovery, and suggestions for the treatment of aphasic patients and their families.

Case Material

304.   Problems Case Seminar with Bruno Bettelheim. Speakers: Bruno Bettelheim, MD, Oliver JB Kerner, PhD. Distributor: JA. 3 hr. $30

Child Psychiatry and Child Therapy

305.   Behavior Disorders of Children. (Series.) Distributor: BSTL. 12 cassettes (1 hr each). $6.95 each. Emphasizes innovative therapeutic approaches to the disturbances of childhood. Treatment of children with disordered psychosexual development, school phobias, work in preschool learning, preventive mental change in children's behavior.
306.   A Child Goes to the Hospital. 2 cassettes only. 40, 29, 27 minutes. Distributor: AAPTL. $15 including script. Extra scripts $3 each. Extra Cassette B only, for parents, no script, $5. On Cassette A discussion by Harold Geist of the dynamics and impact of pediatric illness on parents and children.
307.   Child Therapy, Child Analysis, and Prevention. Speaker: Judith Kestenberg, MD. Distributor: JA. 1 cassette (1 hr). $10
308.   Dealing with Common Practical Problems in Child and Adolescent Therapy. Speaker: Richard Gardner, MD. Distributor: JA. 3 hr. $30
309.   Hysteria in Children. Speakers: Malmquist, Laybourne. Distributor: ADF. 1 cassette. $5.40
310.   The Mutual Storytelling Technique. Speaker: Richard Gardner, MD. Distributor: JA. 12 cassettes (1 hr each). $72. Describes a particular form of child therapy in which the child tells a story that the therapist reiterates, adding alternative corrective behaviors.
311.   Psychotherapeutic Approaches to the Resistant Child. Speaker: Richard Gardner, MD. Distributor: JA. 2 cassettes (1 hr each). $20
312.   Some Views on Child Psychiatry. Speakers: Brunstetter, Fish, Anderson, Jacobs, Distributor: ADF. 1 cassette. $5.40
313.   Spotlight on Child Psychiatry. Speakers: Enzer, Peters, Laybourne. Distributor: ADF. 1 cassette. $5.40
314.   Techniques of Child Psychotherapy. Speaker: Richard Gardner, MD. Distributor: JA. 12 cassettes (1 hr each). $72. Critical explanation of the techniques most widely employed by child therapists today. Topics: (1) Introduction and Pretreatment Evaluations; (2) Play Therapy; (3) Relationship Therapy; (4) Nondirective and Structured Play Therapy; (5) The Mutual Storytelling Technique; (6) Work with Parents; (7) Analytically Oriented Child Psychotherapy; (8–10) Child Psychoanalysis; (11–12) Common Therapeutic Problems.

Adolescence: Problems and Therapy

315.   Adolescence. Speaker: Derek Miller, MD. Distributor: JA. 5 cassettes (1 hr each). $50. Details the dependency-autonomy struggles of early, middle and late adolescence.
316.   Adolescent Schizophrenia. Speakers: Masterson, Miller, Einspruch, Gadpaille. Distributor: ADF. 1 cassette.
317.   Psychotherapy of Adolescents. (Series.) Distributor: BSTL. 12 cassettes (1 hr each). $6.95. Technical problems unique in the psychoanalytic treatment of adolescents. Emphasizes transference difficulties, rebellion, the problem of confidentiality versus responsibility, and conflicting loyalties within the therapist. Topics: (1) The Initial Evaluation; (2) The Diagnostic Process and the Planning of Treatment; (3) The Therapeutic Alliance and the Early Stages of Treatment; (4) Transference Manifestations and Their Management; (5) Transference and Countertransference; (6) Regression and Its Prevention; (7) Management of the Dependent Adolescent; (8) The Adolescent and His Parents; (9) Depression and Suicide; (10) Learning Disabilities—

Psychotherapy and Adolescent Subcultures; (11) Delinquent and Promiscuous Homosexual Behavior; (12) Termination of the Treatment of Adolescents.

Old Age: Problems and Approaches

318. Geriatric Psychiatry. (American Psychiatric Association Postgraduate Course/Continuing Medical Education Program.) Distributor: ADF. 5 cassettes (1 hr each). $49.95. Qualifies for AMA. Continuing Medical Education credits, Category I.

319. Loneliness in Mature Age. Speaker: Charlotte Buhler, PhD. Distributor: JA. 1 side of 1 cassette (30 min). $10 for cassette. (Other side: The Nature of Anxiety—Kurt Goldstein, MD.)

320. Retirement Counseling. Cassette only. 30, 30 minutes. Distributor: AAPTL. $10 including script. Extra scripts $1.50 each

Behavioral Sciences

321. Social Science Research and Social Policy. (Series.) Speaker: Eli Rubinstein, PhD. Distributor: BSTL. 3 cassettes (1 hr each). $21. A look at the integrity of social research and the practical and moral implications of its influence on policymaking social situations. Topics: (1) Characteristics of Research for Policy. TV Violence Study as Case Illustration; (2) Joint Commission on Mental Illness as Case Illustration. Translating Joint Commission Report into Action; (3) Should Research Lead to Policy. The Need for Continuity.

Neurophysiology

322. Psychiatric Aspects of Acupuncture. Cassette only. 30, 30 min. Distributor: AAPTL. $10 including script. Extra scripts $1 each. Principles of acupuncture—its applications in psychotherapy as well as its psychophysiological ramifications.

Neurology

323. Neurology of behavior. (Series.) Speaker: D Frank Benson, MD. Distributor: BSTL. 8 cassettes (1 hr each). $56. Topics: (1) Mental Status Evaluation; (2) Memory and Amnesic Syndromes; (3) Dementia-Pseudodementia; (4) Disorders of Verbal Expression; (5) Aphasia: Testing, Classification, and Localization; (6) Hysteria and Psychogenic Pain Syndromes; (7) Clouding of Consciousness, Confusion, and Delirium Denial of Illness; (8) Psychiatric Aspects of Frontal Lobe Pathology. Psychiatric Aspects of Temporal Lobe Pathology.

Sleep and Dreams

324. Current Sleep Research: Methods and Findings. Speaker: Wilse B Webb. Distributor: APA. 1 cassette. $10

Genetics

325. Behavior Genetics: Current Status and Perspective. Speaker: Kurt Schlesinger. Distributor: APA. 1 cassette. $10

326. The Genetics of Mental Disorders. Speaker: Julien Mendlewicz, MD. Distributor: MSTL. 3 tapes (1 hr each). $24. Topics: (1) Review of Classical Genetics: Types and Structures of Genetic Studies; the Genetics of Schizophrenia; (2) The Genetics of Manic-Depressive Illness; Experimental Studies and Their Interpretations; (3) Continuation of the Genetics of Manic-Depressive Illness.

Sociology

327. Violence: Child Abuse. Speakers: Menninger, Saldinger, Jack. Distributor: ADF. 1 cassette. $5.40

Community Mental Health

328. Mental Health Consultation to Schools. (Series.) Speaker: L Eugene Arnold, MEd, MD. Distributor: BSTL. 6 cassettes (1 hr each). $42. Topics: (1) School Consultation: Definition, Basic Concepts, and Conceptual Options; (2) The School as a Social Institution. The American Educational System. Roles and Skills of School Personnel. Confidentiality in the School Setting; (3) Consultant Attitudes, Skills, Knowledge Training, and Role Conflicts; (4) Planning Strategy, Project Development Assessment, and Accountability. (5) Consultation to Specific Categories of School Personnel; (6) Special Problems of Children: Children at Risk and Their Management in the School Setting.
329. Revolutionary Trends in Mental Health Care. Cassette. 60 min, 1973. Distributor: BSTL. $6.95

Legal Aspects

330. Dialogue. Cassette. 1972. Distributor: ORS. $7.50. A dialogue of mental health experts and practicing psychiatrists with Thomas Szasz about psychiatry and law and the myth of mental illness.
331. Forensic Psychiatry. Speakers: Suarez, Randolph, Sheldon. Distributor: ADF. 1 cassette. $5.40
332. Psychiatry and Law. (Series.) Ralph Slovenko, LLB, PhD. Distributor: BSTL. 6 cassettes (1 hr each). $42. Lucid explanation of the various aspects of legal involvement in psychiatric settings and clear definition of the significance of these involvements for the psychiatrist. Topics: (1) Introduction to Psychiatry and Law; (2) Hospitalization and the Rights of the Mentally Ill; (3) Privileged Communication and Confidentiality; (4) Criminal Responsibility and Competency to Stand Trial; (5) Psychiatric Malpractice and Regulation; (6) Panel Discussion: Medical Malpractice—the Social Issues.

Epidemiology

333. Urban Personality. (Series.) Speaker: James Hill Parker, PhD. Distributor: BSTL. 5 cassettes (1 hr each). $35. Topics: (1) Urbanization and Mental Illness. Urbanization and Alienation; (2) Myth of Urban Decline. The Sixties and Urban Personality; (3) Models of Urban Personality. Conceptions and Misconceptions of City Life and Personality; (4) Human Needs and the Urban Crisis; (5) Identity: The Case of the French-Americans.

Teaching and Supervision

334. Group Relations and Psychotherapy. (Series.) Distributor: BSTL. 3 cassettes (1 hr each). $6.95 each. Topics: (1) The Tavistock—AK Rice Group Relations Conferences and Concepts of Organization Derived from AK Rice; (2) The Experience of a Conference and Some Issues Concerning Professionals and Nonprofessionals in the Mental Health Field; (3) Teaching and Training Graduate Students in Psychotherapy and Supervision.

Death and Dying

335. Belief Systems and Cancer. Speakers: O Carl Simonton, MD, DABR; Stephanie Simonton. Distributor: EMCA. 1 cassette or 1 open-reel (118 min). Purchase: $20. On relevant research literature that cites accumulating evidence that certain psychological factors predispose individuals to cancer, also other psychological factors that are shared by patients who appear to be combating cancer successfully. A moving definition of the orientation that therapists themselves must achieve to work effectively with terminal cancer patients.
336. Death and Dying. (Series.) Speaker: Thomas Garrity, PhD. Distributor: BSTL. 3 cassettes (1 hr each). $21. Topics: (1) The Sociocultural Context of Death and Dying in the United States; (2) The Experiences of Dying and Grieving; (3) Terminal Care in the Institutional Context.
337. Helping Children Deal with Parental Death. (Series.) Speaker: Richard Gardner, MD. Distributor: BSTL. 3 cassettes (1 hr each). $21. A child-oriented approach to dealing with parental death. Topics: (1) The Child's Early Life Preparation for Dealing with Death; (2) The Normal Mourning Process; (3) Factors That Can Impede or Prevent a Healthy Mourning Experience.

Audio Cassette and Reel Sources

AAPTL: American Association for Psychotherapists (AAP) Tape Library, 1040 Woodcock Road, Orlando, Fla 32803. (305) 894–0921

ADF: Audio-Digest Foundation, 1250 South Glendale Avenue, Glendale, Calif 91205

APA: American Psychological Association Publications Sales Department, 1200 17th Street, NW, Washington, DC 20036

ARF: Addiction Research Foundation, 33 Russell Street, Toronto, Ontario, Canada M552S1

BMA: Biomonitoring Applications, Inc, 270 Madison Avenue, New York, NY 10016. (212) 258–2724

BSTL: Behavioral Sciences Tape Library, % Sigma Information, Inc, 485 Main Street, Ft Lee, NJ 07024. (201) 947–4154

CPP: Charles Press Publishers, Inc, PO Box 830, Bowie, Md 20715

EMCA: Extension Media Center Audiotapes, University of California Extension Media Center, 2223 Fulton Street, Berkeley, Calif 94720

ID: Instructional Dynamics, Inc, 166 East Superior Street, Chicago, Ill 60611. (313) 943–1200

JA: Psychotherapy Tape Library, 59 4th Avenue, New York, NY 10003. (212) 677–1280

McH: McGraw-Hill, Inc, 1221 Avenue of the Americas, New York, NY 10036. (212) 997–1221

MSTL: Medical Sciences Tape Library, 240 Grand Avenue, Leonia, NJ 07605

NAC: National Audiovisual Center (GSA), Order Section, Washington, DC 20409. (202) 763–7420

ORS: Orosonic Recording Services, PO Box 1517, Silver Spring, MD 20902. (301) 949–5650

UCP: University of Chicago Press, 5801 Ellis Avenue, Chicago, Ill 60637. (312) 753–3344

VIDEOTAPES

It has already been pointed out in the opening remarks of this section that videotapes make excellent teaching supplements, particularly when directed by a good discussion leader. Both lay and professional audiences can benefit greatly from their use. An effort has been made to include as much information as possible about the tapes. Data for reel or tape width is indicated where it appears in producers' catalogues. Owing to lack of standardization in the industry, readers are advised to determine the compatability of desired videotape programs with existing videotape recorders in their institutions.

Human Behavior and Adaptation

338.   Selye on Stress, with Hans Selye, MD, PhD, DSc. 17 min, color. Distributor: NCME. Apply to NCME for subscription information.

Diagnosis

339.   Body Language in Diagnosis, with Gordon H. Deckert, MD. 17 min, color. Distributor: NCME. Apply to NCME for subscription information.

340.   Mental Health Assessment Form. 26 min, ¾-in videotape. Produced by James H Ryan, MD. Distributor: ER. Apply to ER for purchase information. The Electronic Textbook of Psychiatry accompanying script. *Restricted Audience*

Psychopathology

341.   Anxiety and Symptom Formation. 51:46 min, ¾-in videotape. Produced by James H Ryan, MD. Distributor: ER. Apply to ER for purchase information. The Electronic Textbook of Psychiatry accompanying script. *Restricted Audience*   †

342.   Inferiority and Compensation. 35 min, ¾-in videotape. James H Ryan, MD. Distributor: ER. Apply to ER for purchase information. The Electronic Textbook of Psychiatry accompanying script. *Restricted Audience*   †

343.   Passive-Aggressive Personality. 25 min, ¾-in videotape. Produced by James H Ryan, MD. Distributor: ER. Apply to ER for purchase information. The Electronic Textbook of Psychiatry accompanying script. *Restricted Audience*

Psychodynamics

344. Mechanisms of Defense, with LC Hanes, MD. 17 min. Distributor: NCME. Apply to NCME for subscription information.

Schools of Psychotherapy

345. Gestalt Therapy. 56 min, b & w, 1970. Distributor: TCL. Purchase: $85. Rental: $25

Interviewing

346. Psychiatric Interview Technique: The Brief Interview. 23 min, ¾-in videotape. Produced by James H Ryan, MD. Distributor: ER. Apply to ER for purchase information. The Electronic Textbook of Psychiatry accompanying script. *Restricted Audience*   †
347. Psychiatric Interview Technique: Demonstration and Critique. 54 min, ¾-in videotape. Produced by James H Ryan, MD. Distributor: ER. Apply to ER for purchase information. The Electronic Textbook of Psychiatry accompanying script. *Restricted Audience*   †

Group Psychotherapy

348. The Experience of Psychodrama. 30 min, ¾-in videocassette, 1975. Distributor: FF. Purchase: $235. Rental: $40
349. Psychodrama—The Prologue: Part I. 26 min. Presented by James Enneis, MD, Director of Psychodrama, St. Elizabeths Hospital, Washington, DC, and U.S. Department of Health, Education, and Welfare. Distributor: NCME. Apply to NCME for subscription information.
350. Psychodrama—The Play: Part II. 29 min. Distributor: NCME. Apply to NCME for subscription information. An actual psychodrama, conducted by James Enneis.
351. Psychodrama—The Critique: Part III. 14 min. Distributor: NCME. Apply to NCME for subscription information.

Family Therapy and Marital Therapy

352. Contracting—A Therapist's Aid to Family Counseling. 47 min, color, videocassette, 1975. Distributor: ARF. Purchase: $95. In this initial interview with a young married couple, obtaining a commitment from the spouses to work on their marital problems is therapist's central goal.
353. Making the Invisible Visible. Peggy Papp and the Nathan W Ackerman Family Institute. Distributor: NWAFI. Rental: $50. A demonstration of the use of sculpting as a therapeutic technique in an initial family interview. The basic dysfunctional triangle spatially staged and subsequently corrected.

Hypnosis

354. Hypnosis: Techniques of Induction and Clinical Applications. 60 min, ¾-in videotape. Produced by James H Ryan, MD. Distributor: ER. Apply to ER for purchase information. The Electronic Textbook of Psychiatry accompanying script. *Restricted Audience*
355. Hypnotic Dreaming: Some Physiological Correlates and Psychological Mechanisms: Part I, with Milton V Kline, EdD. 26 min. Distributor: NCME. Apply to NCME for subscription information.
356. Hypnotic Induction Techniques—Part I, 13 min. Distributor: NCME. Apply to NCME for subscription information. Demonstration of an induction method by Milton Jabush, MD.
357. Hypnotic Induction Techniques—Part II, Positive Hallucinations. 21 min. Distributor: NCME. Apply to NCME for subscription information.

Miscellaneous Adjuncts

358. Looking In Reaching Out: Learning to Become a Dance Therapist. 18 min, b & w, ½-in videotape, 1973. Distributor: ETC. Purchase: $50. Rental: $15
359. Art Therapy with an Emotionally Disturbed 16-Year-Old Boy. 44 min, 1971. Produced by Leah Freedman, Robert C Prall, MD, Jacques Van Vlack. Distributor: EPPI. Rental: $15
360. Group Projective Art Therapy. 60 min, 1-in videotape, 1969. Distributor: TCL. Purchase $85. Rental: $25
361. Perspectives on Mental Health. b & w, 10-part series. Produced by Ari Kiev, MD. Distributor: BHES. Rental: Contact BHES. Demonstration by Ari Kiev, pioneer in "videotherapy," of his techniques with a variety of patients. Indicated for training programs in psychotherapy.
362. Sensory Feedback Therapy, with Joseph Brudny, MD. 18 min, color. Distributor: NCME. Apply to NCME for subscription information.

Emergencies in Psychotherapy and Crisis Intervention (Suicide)

363. Counseling the Post-Abortion Patient. Ronald J Pion, MD, Nathaniel N Wagner, PhD. 18 min, color. Distributor: NCME. Apply to NCME for subscription information.
364. Crisis Intervention Theory. 41 min, b & w, 1-in videotape, 1971. Distributor: TCL. Purchase: $85. Rental: $25
365. Crisis Intervention Therapy. Distributor: TCL. Purchase: $85. Rental: $25. Three scenes acted out to illustrate the use of crisis intervention as therapy.
366. Suicide—Practical Diagnostic Clues. Matthew Ross, MD. 13 min. Distributor: NCME. Apply to NCME for subscription information.
367. Suicide Prevention: The Physician's Role. Includes a summary by Karl Menninger, MD. Distributor: NCME. Apply to NCME for subscription information.

Psychosomatic Disorders

368. Does Type A Personality Affect Your Heart? with Ray H Rosenman, MD, William B Kannel, MD, Campbell Moses, MD. 18 min, color. Distributor: NCME. Apply to NCME for subscription information.
369. Influence of the Emotions on the Outcome of Cardiac Surgery: Diagnosis and Decision, with Janet A Kennedy, MD, Hyman Bakst, MD. 20 min. Distributor: NCME. Apply to NCME for subscription information.
370. Influence of the Emotions on the Outcome of Cardiac Surgery: Psychological Categories, with Janet A Kennedy, MD, Hyman Bakst, MD. 24 min. Distributor: NCME. Apply to NCME for subscription information.
371. Problems and Pitfalls in Psychosomatic Medicine: Hypertension, with Roy R Grinker, MD, F Theodore Reid, MD. 15 min, color. Distributor: NCME. Apply to NCME for subscription information.   †
372. Problems and Pitfalls in Psychosomatic Medicine: Peptic Ulcer, with Roy R Grinker, MD, F Theodore Reid, MD. 16 min, color. Distributor: NCME. Apply to NCME for subscription information.   †

Sexual Problems

373. Impotence, with Philip A Sarrel, MD, Lorna Sarrel. 18 min, color. Distributor: NCME. Apply to NCME for subscription information.   †
374. Male Homosexuality. 50 min, ¾-in videotape. Produced by James H Ryan, MD. Distributor ER. Apply to ER for purchase information. The Electronic Textbook of Psychiatry accompanying script. *Restricted Audience*
375. Sexuality: Getting It Together. Harold Lear, MD, Helen Kaplan, MD. 20 min, color. Distributor: NCME. Apply to NCME for subscription information.

Depressive Disorders

376. Depression: Coping with Loss. 36 min, ¾-in videotape. Produced by James H Ryan, MD. Distributor: ER. Apply to ER for purchase information. The Electronic Textbook of Psychiatry accompanying script. *Restricted Audience* †

377. Depression: Retarded and Agitated Forms. 30 min, ¾-in videotape. Produced by James H Ryan, MD. Distributor: ER. Apply to ER for purchase information. The Electronic Textbook of Psychiatry accompanying script. *Restricted Audience* †

378. The Diagnosis and Treatment of Depression. (Three programs produced with the cooperation of the Council on Scientific Assembly of the American Medical Association.) (1) Masked Depression: The Interview and the Recognition and Delineation of Depression (30 min); (2) Biogenic Amine Theories of Depression (14 min); (3) Managing the Depressed Patient (34 min). Distributor: NCME. Apply to NCME for subscription information.

379. Differential Diagnosis of Depression, with F Theodore Reid, Jr, MD. 23 min, color. Distributor: NCME. Apply to NCME for subscription information. †

380. Manic-Depressive Illness. 31 min, ¾-in videotape. Produced by James H Ryan, MD. Distributor: ER. Apply to ER for purchase information. The Electronic Textbook of Psychiatry accompanying script. *Restricted Audience*

381. Treating the Depressed Patient, with F Theodore Reid, Jr, MD. 19 min, color. Distributor: NCME. Apply to NCME for subscription information. †

Schizophrenic Reactions

382. Paranoid Schizophrenia. 28 min, ¾-in videotape. Produced by James H Ryan, MD. Distributor: ER. Apply to ER for purchase information. The Electronic Textbook of Psychiatry accompanying script. *Restricted Audience* †

383. Schizophrenia: Hebephrenic and Schizo-Affective Forms. 42:30 min, ¾-in videotape. Produced by James H Ryan, MD. Distributor: ER. Apply to ER for purchase information. The Electronic Textbook of Psychiatry accompanying script. *Restricted Audience*

384. Schizophrenia: Thought Disorder and Social Isolation. Videotape. 23 min, ¾-in videotape. Produced by James H Ryan, MD. Distributor: ER. Apply to ER for purchase information. The Electronic Textbook of Psychiatry accompanying script. *Restricted Audience*

385. Schizophrenic Language. 40 min, ¾-in videotape. Produced by James H Ryan, MD. Distributor: ER. Apply to ER for purchase information. The Electronic Textbook of Psychiatry accompanying script. *Restricted Audience*

Alcoholism

386. Drinkers in Crisis, with Henry D Abraham, MD. 16 min, color. Distributor: NCME. Apply to NCME for subscription information.

387. The Multiphasic Treatment of Alcoholism, with Albert N Brown-Mayers, MD. 29 min, color. Distributor: NCME. Apply to NCME for subscription information.

Drug Addiction

388. Current Trends in Therapy for Narcotic Addiction. (Series: Concepts and Controversies in Modern Medicine.) 29 min, b & w. Distributor: NAC. Apply to NAC for subscription information. Contrasts intensive psychotherapy with methadone treatment.

389. Drug Abuse: Recognizing and Treating Acute Reaction to Amphetamines and Sedative Hypnotics, with David E Smith, MD. 19 min. Distributor: NCME. Apply to NCME for subscription information.

390. Drug Abuse: Recognizing and Treating Acute Reactions to Hallucinogens, with David E Smith, MD. 19 minutes. Distributor: NCME. Apply to NCME for subscription information.

391. Medical Problems of Adolescent Heroin Abuse, with Michael I Cohen, MD. 14 min, color. Distributor: NCME. Apply to NCME for subscription information. An in-depth interview conducted with a 14-year-old heroin addict under treatment.

Child Psychiatry and Child Therapy

392. Child Development: The Early Years. 30 min, ¾-in videotape. Produced by James H Ryan, MD. Distributor: ER. Apply to ER for purchase information. The Electronic Textbook of Psychiatry. Accompanying script. *Restricted Audience*
393. Child Development: The Middle Years. 28 min, ¾-in videotape. Produced by James H Ryan, MD. Distributor: ER. Apply to ER for purchase information. The Electronic Textbook of Psychiatry accompanying script. *Restricted Audience*
394. Diagnosis of Learning Disabilities, with Dorothy L DeBoer, PhD, Lowell M Zollar, MD. 16 min, color. Distributor: NCME. Apply to NCME for subscription information.
395. Modern Little Hans. Color, ½-in videocassette, 1974. Distributor: PCGC. Rental: $70. A series of excerpts and an analysis of an entire treatment sequence where the presenting problem is a patient with a fear of dogs.

Adolescence: Problems and Approaches

396. Child Development: The Adolescent Boy. 22 min, ¾-in videotape. Produced by James H Ryan, MD. Distributor: ER. Apply to ER for purchase information. The Electronic Textbook of Psychiatry accompanying script. *Restricted Audience*
397. Child Development: The Adolescent Girl. 25 min, ¾-in videotape. Produced by James H Ryan, MD. Distributor: ER. Apply to ER for purchase information. The Electronic Textbook of Psychiatry accompanying script. *Restricted Audience*

Neurology, Neuroanatomy, and Neuropathology

398. Essentials of the Neurological Examination, with Houston Merritt, MD. 50 min, ¾-in videotape. Produced by James H Ryan, MD. Distributor: ER. Apply to ER for purchase information. The Electronic Textbook of Psychiatry accompanying script. *Restricted Audience*

Sleep and Dreams

399. "Doctor, I Can't Sleep Nights," with Julius Segal, PhD. 15 min, color. Distributor: NCME. Apply to NCME for subscription information.
400. Dream Therapy. 60 min, b & w, 1-in videotape, 1969. Distributor: TCL. Purchase: $85. Rental: $25. The use of therapeutic guided daydreams in a group setting.

Sociology

401. Management of the Battered Child Syndrome, with C Henry Kempe, MD, Brandt F Steel, MD, Helen Alexander. 18 min, color. Distributor: NCME. Apply to NCME for subscription information.

Teaching and Supervision

402. Use of Video Tape in Counseling Skills in Training. 40 min, color, videocassette, 1975. Distributor: ARF. Purchase: $70. Demonstrates how videotape tools and techniques can be introduced into specialized counseling skills training.

Death and Dying

403. Terminal Illness: Reactions of a Patient, His Family, Friends, and Physicians. Part I: Interviews with the Patient. 25 min, b & w, videocassettes, 1974. Produced by the Health Sciences Learning Resources Center and CCTV Services of the University of Washington, through the cooperation of Dr. Gary E. Leinbach, his family, friends, and physician. Source: UWP. Purchase: $125. Rental: $25
404. Terminal Illness: Reactions of a Patient, His Family, Friends, and Physicians. Parts 5, 6: The

Grieving Process. Part 5, 25 min; Part 6, 45 min; b & w, ¾-in videocassettes, 1974. Produced by the Health Sciences Learning Resources Center and CCTV Services of the University of Washington, through the cooperation of Dr. Gary E Leinbach, his family, friends and physician. Distributor: UWP. Purchase: $125. Rental: $25 each part

405. Learning to Live with Dying. 39 min, color. Distributor: NCME. Apply to NCME for subscription information.

406. Management of the Terminally Ill: The Family, with Elizabeth Kübler-Ross, MD. 16 min. Distributor: NCME. Apply to NCME for subscription information.

Videotape Sources

ARF: Addiction Research Foundation, 33 Russell Street, Toronto, Ontario, Canada M552S1

BHES: Blue Hill Educational System, PO Box 113, Monsey, NY 10952. (914) 425–4466

EPPI: Eastern Pennsylvania Psychiatric Institute, Henry Avenue & Abbottsford Road, Philadelphia, Pa 12129

ER: Educational Research, New York State Psychiatric Institute, 722 West 168th Street, New York, NY 10032. (212) 508–4000
(Videotapes in "The Electronic Textbook of Psychiatry" series are restricted to audiences of professionals-in-training in the mental health sciences. The videotape cassettes are only available in groups of 10 titles to accredited medical institutions. For further information contact James H Ryan, MD, director.)

ETC: Educational Technology Center, Hunter College-CUNY, 695 Park Avenue, New York, NY 10021. (212) 360–5182

FF: Forum III Films, 230 Park Avenue, New York, NY 10017. (212) 889–7915

NAC: National Audiovisual Center, Order Section, Washington, DC 20409

NCME: Network for Continuing Medical Education, 15 Columbus Circle, New York 10023. (212) 541–8088 *(The programs produced by the Network are limited to use by physicians affiliated with institutional subscribers to NCME's biweekly videocassette service. For information on how to become a subscriber, contact the organization.)*

NWAFI: Nathan W Ackerman Family Institute, 149 East 78th Street, New York, NY (212) 879–4900

PCGC: Philadelphia Child Guidance Clinic, 1700 Bainbridge Street, Philadelphia, Pa 19146

TCL: Telecommunications Center Library, Department of Health, Camarillo State Hospital, Box A, Camarillo, Calif 93010

UWP: University of Washington Press, Audiovisual Division, Seattle, Wash 98105

VII

Appendices and References

The following forms include all the information that appears on the forms used in actual practice; in order to make these reproductions conform to the page size of the book, however, the layout has had to vary from the original in some instances, and occasionally spacing between items has been considerably reduced. For example, some forms, which in reproduction here appear on one page, appear in practice on two pages, or two sides of one page. The actual forms are on standard 8½ × 11 inch sheets, with sufficient space between items to allow for complete entry of data.

APPENDIX A

Statistical Data*

PATIENT'S NAME: Date:

ADDRESS: Interviewer:

TELEPHONE: BUSINESS PHONE: Referred by:

Informant *(if any):* Name and address:

With whom is patient now living? *(list people)*

Age of patient: Sex: Religion:

Education: Occupation: Salary:

If unemployed, sources of income:

Marital status: How long married?   Any previous marriages?

When?   Age of mate: Occupation of mate:

                                        Salary of mate:

Military record:

Miscellaneous:

---

* Short form: To be filled out by therapist, initial interviewer, or intake worker in a clinic set-up.

APPENDIX B

Statistical Data[*]

Patient's Name _____   Case No._____

1. GENERAL DATA:

　　a. Age:　　Date of birth:　　　　　b. Sex (M, F)

　　c. Race (W, B, Y, R):　　　　　　　d. Religion:

　　e. Birthplace:

　　f. If foreign-born, date of arrival in U.S.A.:

　　g. Naturalization dates:　　1st Papers:　　　　2nd Papers:

　　h. Education:

　　i. Occupation:

　　j. Employed (yes, no):

　　k. Salary:

　　l. Yearly income, all sources:

　　m. If unemployed, on what sources of income, or on what person is patient dependent, giving occupation and relationship to patient of this person:

　　n. Military Service (yes, no); dates:

　　o. Name and address of nearest relative or friend:

　　p. With whom is patient living at present?

2. RESIDENTIAL DATA:

　　a. Address:

　　b. Character of residence: ( )house ( )apartment ( )room; ( )self-owned ( )rented, rental cost:

　　c. Place of legal settlement:

　　d. Length of residence in this town or city:

　　e. Length of residence in state:

f. Home telephone no.:   Business telephone no.:

g. Previous addresses *(giving dates):*

3. MARITAL STATUS:

a. M, S, W, Div, Sep:

b. Date of marriage:

c. Date termination of marriage:

d. Name of mate, if any:

e. Dates of previous marriages, if any:

f. Dates of termination of previous marriages and reasons:

g. Names and ages of children:

4. FAMILY IDENTIFICATION DATA:

a. Father's name: Living or dead?

Age at present, or, if dead, age at death and year of death:

Birthplace:

If foreign-born, date arrival U.S.A.:   Citizenship:

b. Mother's maiden name: Living or dead?

Age at present, or, if dead, age at death and year of death?

Birthplace:

If foreign-born, date arrival U.S.A.:   Citizenship:

c. Siblings (list names, ages, and sex):

5. SOCIAL SERVICE EXCHANGE *(for clinic patients):*

---

* Long form: Complete statistical data outline to be filled out by therapist or social worker.

APPENDIX C

Initial Interview

PATIENT'S NAME: Date:

ADDRESS: Interviewer:

HOME TELEPHONE: BUSINESS PHONE: Referred by:

Informant *(if any):* Name and address:

With whom is patient now living? *(list people)*

Age of patient: Sex: Religion:

Education: Occupation: Salary:

In unemployed, sources of income:

Marital status: How long married?   Any previous marriages?

When?   Age of mate: Occupation of mate:

                                           Salary of mate:

Military record:

Miscellaneous:

* To be filled out by initial interviewer.

(Use additional blank sheets if necessary indicating item number.)

1. CHIEF COMPLAINT *(patient's own words):*

2. HISTORY AND DEVELOPMENT OF COMPLAINT *(from onset to present):*

3. OTHER SYMPTOMS AND CLINICAL FINDINGS AT PRESENT:

☐ Tension	☐ Physical symptoms	☐ Phobias
☐ Depressed	☐ Fatigue	☐ Obsessions
☐ Severe depression	☐ Exhaustion	☐ Compulsions
☐ Suicidal	☐ Headaches	☐ Excessive sedatives
☐ Severe anxiety	☐ Dizziness	☐ Excess alcohol
☐ Hallucinations	☐ GI Symptoms	☐ Insomnia
☐ Delusions	☐ Sexual problem	☐ Nightmares
☐ Dangerous	☐ Impotency	☐ Other symptoms *(specify)*
☐ Excited	☐ Homosexuality	☐ Present medications *(dosage and how long taken)*

Description of above:

4. DREAMS *(patient's own words):*

5. FAMILY DATA *(health and personality of mother, father, siblings, spouse, children; and patient's attitudes toward them):*

6. PREVIOUS EMOTIONAL UPSETS *(from childhood to present illness):*

7. PREVIOUS TREATMENT *(including hospitalization):*

8. PSYCHOLOGIC TESTS:

9. TENTATIVE DIAGNOSIS:

10. TENTATIVE DYNAMICS:

11. TENTATIVE PROGNOSIS:

12. PATIENT'S RESPONSE TO INTERVIEWER: ( ) cooperative ( ) fearful ( ) suspicious ( ) hostile
13. INTERVIEWER'S RESPONSE TO PATIENT: ( ) positive ( ) ill-defined ( ) negative
14. PHYSICAL APPEARANCE: ( ) meticulous ( ) presentable ( ) untidy ( ) disheveled
15. PATIENT'S ESTIMATE OF PRESENT PHYSICAL HEALTH: ( ) satisfactory ( ) poor
16. COMMUNICATIVENESS: ( ) garrulous ( ) satisfactory ( ) underproductive ( ) answers questions only
17. Insight and motivation:

( ) aware of a problem   ( ) desires to correct problem
( ) aware of emotional nature of problem ( ) willing to accept psychotherapy
( ) accepts present therapist   ( ) accepts conditions of therapy
( ) can arrange time for therapy   ( ) can afford treatment

18. DISPOSITION:

	FEE:
	Initial interview

( ) Case accepted	Hours Patient Can Come for Treatment:
( ) Case referred	
( ) Case closed	

	Testing
	Therapy

( ) Emergency	( ) Appointment given patient	( ) Paid
( ) ℞ Urgent	( ) Notify patient of appointment	( ) Charge
( ) ℞ Not urgent	( ) Patient will call for appointment	( ) Send Bill

TYPE OF THERAPY:

CORRESPONDENCE REQUIRED:

RECOMMENDATIONS AND REMARKS:

APPENDIX D

Personal Data Sheet*

Please fill out the following blank as completely as possible. This will save time and make it unnecessary to ask you routine questions. All material is confidential and will not be released except on your written request.

Name _____

Address _____

    (Will it be all right to write to you at the above address for billing, changes of appointment, etc? _____)

Home phone _____   Business phone _____

    (Can we call you at either of these? _____)

    In the event of a change in appointment, at what time can we reach you at either of these phones? _____
_____

Age _____ Birthday _____ Sex (M,F) _____

Birthplace _____

If foreign-born, date of arrival in U.S.A. _____

If foreign-born, are you a citizen? _____

Approximately how long have you lived in this city? _____

Marital status (Single, Married, Separated, Divorced) _____

If married, how long ago? _____ If separated or divorced, when? _____

If married more than once, list dates of marriage, length of time married, whether

marriage terminated by divorce, annulment, death: _____

Number and ages of children, if any _____

Occupation _____ Approximate gross yearly salary _____

How long have you been doing your present kind of work? _____

If unemployed, source of income at present: _____

How far through school did you go? _____

Name and address of nearest relative or friend: _____

_____

Any army service? _____

Whom are you living with at present? _____

Who referred you here? _____

How strongly do you want treatment for your problem? *(check)*

   ( ) very much   ( ) much   ( ) moderately   ( ) could do without it, if necessary

   ( ) do not want treatment

What days and times can you come here for treatments?*_____

If your answer to above is after 5 p.m., can you, if necessary, get away for an hour once

   weekly during the day? _____

If psychologic or other tests are necessary to help your condition, would you object to

   them for any reasons? _____

Do you know what psychotherapy is?

_____

   * To be filled out by patient.

APPENDIX E

Family Data Sheet*

NAME:

Please fill out the following blank as completely as possible. This will save time and make it unnecessary to ask you routine questions. All material is confidential and will not be released except on your written request.

1. List the first names of your father, mother, brothers, and sisters, in chronologic order, and supply the following information about each:

List first names.	Age.	Live in what city?	If dead, what year and cause?	Marital status— M, Div, Sep, Wid	Do you see them often or write often to them? (yes, no)	Personality adjustment (good, fair, poor)	How do (or did) you get along with them (good, fair, poor)?
Father:							
Mother:							
Sisters:							
Brothers:							

2. If married, age of mate: _____ Are you living with spouse now? _____
   Occupation of spouse: _____
   Personality adjustment of spouse (good, fair, poor): _____
   How are you getting along with spouse (good, fair, poor)? _____

3. List all of your children of both present and previous marriages, by first names in chronologic order, giving the following information on each:

Name	Living or dead	Ages	Living with whom at present?	Check if by previous marriage	Personality adjustment (good, fair, poor)	How do you get along with child (good, fair, poor)?

* To be filled out by patient.

APPENDIX F

Examiner:	**Daily Progress Note***	Date:

PATIENT'S NAME:

At each visit enter (1) present state of symptoms or complaints (absent, improved, the same, worse), (2) how patient feels (anxious, placid, depressed, happy), (3) important life situations and developments since last visit and how they were handled, (4) general content of session, (5) significant transference and resistance reactions, (6) dreams.

* On the standard form, this Daily Progress Note is given two full sides of an 8½ by 11 inch sheet, to allow for as complete a report as is required.

APPENDIX G

Monthly Progress Summary***

Month covered in this report:

(Fill out this side and on back of sheet elaborate on any checked items as well as other items of importance, using additional sheets if necessary.)†

NAME OF PATIENT: NAME OF THERAPIST:

NUMBER OF SESSIONS THIS   TOTAL NUMBER OF SESSIONS TO
  MONTH: DATE:

NUMBER OF MISSED SESSIONS   *Reason for this:*
  THIS MONTH:

PATIENT'S RESPONSE TO THERAPY:

1. *General progress to date:*   ( ) excellent   ( ) satisfactory   ( ) poor
     Symptoms are: ( ) better   ( ) the same   ( ) worse

2. *Appointments:*   ( ) comes on time   ( ) comes early   ( ) comes late

3. *Communicativeness:*   ( ) satisfactory   ( ) overproductive   ( ) incoherent
     ( ) underproductive   ( ) responds only to questions
     ( ) long periods of silence   ( ) other, describe:

4. *Relationship with therapist:*   Working relationship: ( ) good   ( ) fair
     ( ) poor   ( ) intense dependency   ( ) sexual feelings   ( ) fear
     ( ) detachment   ( ) negativism   ( ) hostility   ( ) other, describe:

5. *Resistance:*   ( ) low   ( ) moderate   ( ) strong   ( ) interferes with progress
     ( ) "acting-out" tendencies

6. *Insight:*   ( ) achieving insight   ( ) curiosity about dynamics
     ( ) intellectual, but no emotional, insight   ( ) resists insight

7. *Translation of insight into action:*   ( ) excellent   ( ) satisfactory   ( ) poor

8. *Present symptoms:*   (Describe any checked items on back.)

    ( ) new physical   ( ) sexual disturbance   ( ) intense anxiety
      symptoms or   ( ) intense depression   ( ) hallucinations
      complaints   ( ) suicidal threats   ( ) delusions
    ( ) exaggerated old   ( ) suicidal attempts   ( ) excess alcohol
      physical symp-   ( ) overactivity   ( ) excess sedatives or
      toms   ( ) destructive tend-   drugs
    ( ) work disability   encies   ( ) other, describe:
    ( ) marked insomnia

9. *Severe environmental problems:*   ( ) finances   ( ) work   ( ) family   ( ) other

---

** This form will be found helpful in clinics where there is routine supervision of the entire case load. It is turned over monthly to supervisor.

† The original Monthly Progress Summary is on one side of a sheet only.

REMARKS:

1. (   ) Supervisory Conference Needed: (   ) emergency foreseen
      (   ) dynamics not clear   (   ) treatment going poorly
      (   ) patient wants to discontinue   (   ) may need medication
      (   ) therapist considering closing   (   ) other, describe:

2. (   ) Consultation Needed: (   ) with caseworker   (   ) with psychologist
      (   ) with medical consultant   (   ) with psychiatric consultant
      (   ) other, describe:

3. *Other* (describe briefly on back of sheet what has been going on in treatment during the last month):

APPENDIX H

Termination Note

1. NAME OF PATIENT: _____

2. DATE OF INITIAL INTERVIEW: _____

3. DATE OF TERMINAL INTERVIEW: _____

4. TOTAL NUMBER OF SESSIONS: _____

5. REASON FOR TERMINATION: ( ) planned termination
   ( ) withdrawal by patient (explain)

6. CONDITION AT DISCHARGE:
   ( ) a. *Recovered:* Asymptomatic with good insight
   ( ) b. *Markedly improved:*
         ( ) Asymptomatic with some insight
         ( ) Asymptomatic with no insight
   ( ) c. *Moderately improved:*
         ( ) Partial reduction of symptoms with good insight
         ( ) Partial reduction of symptoms with some insight
   ( ) d. *Slightly improved:* Partial reduction of symptoms with little or no insight
   ( ) e. *Unimproved*
   ( ) f. *Worse* (Describe)

7. AREAS OF IMPROVEMENT *(use back of sheet, if necessary):*
      a. Symptoms:

      b. Adjustment to environment: (work, community, etc.)

      c. Physical functions: (appetite, sleep, sex, etc.)

      d. Relations with people:

8. PATIENT'S ATTITUDE TOWARD THERAPIST AT DISCHARGE *(use back of sheet, if necessary):*
   ( ) friendly ( ) indifferent ( ) unfriendly
9. Would patient object to a follow-up letter inquiring about progress?
   ( ) Yes   ( ) No
10. RECOMMENDATIONS TO PATIENT AT DISCHARGE *(if any. Use back of sheet, if necessary):*

11. DIAGNOSIS AT DISCHARGE:

12. ADDITIONAL COMMENTS (use back of sheet).

APPENDIX I

Summary*

PATIENT'S NAME:

Date of Summary:		Therapist:
Prepared by:	Total Treatment Sessions:	Initial Interview Date:

    I. CHIEF COMPLAINT:

    II. HISTORY AND DEVELOPMENT OF COMPLAINT:

    III. OTHER COMPLAINTS AND SYMPTOMS:

    IV. MEDICAL, SURGICAL, AND GYNECOLOGIC HISTORY:

    V. ENVIRONMENTAL DISTURBANCES (at onset of therapy):

    VI. RELATIONSHIP DIFFICULTIES (at onset of therapy):

    VII. HEREDITARY, CONSTITUTIONAL, and EARLY DEVELOPMENTAL INFLUENCES:

    VIII. FAMILY DATA:

    IX. PREVIOUS ATTACKS OF EMOTIONAL ILLNESS:

* Type this form, if possible. Use and attach additional blank sheets in the event space for any item is not sufficient, carrying over the same item number. *Note:* This form has been condensed to two pages here; it is ordinarily in four pages, with considerable space between items.

X. INITIAL INTERVIEW (brief summary of condition of patient):

XI. LEVEL OF INSIGHT AND MOTIVATION (at onset of therapy):

XII. CLINICAL EXAMINATION (significant physical, neurologic, psychiatric, and psychologic findings):

XIII. DIFFERENTIAL DIAGNOSIS:

XIV. ESTIMATE OF PROGNOSIS:

XV. PSYCHODYNAMICS AND PSYCHOPATHOLOGY:

XVI. COURSE OF TREATMENT (type of therapy employed, frequency, total sessions, significant events during therapy, nature of transference and resistance, progress in therapy, insight, change in symptoms, attitudes, and relationships with people):

XVII. CONDITION ON DISCHARGE:

XVIII. RECOMMENDATIONS TO PATIENT:

XIX. STATISTICAL CLASSIFICATION:

APPENDIX J*

NAME OF PATIENT: NAME OF THERAPIST:
(L–Late; B–Broken;
C–Cancelled)

	DATE	L,B or C	BILLING
1			
2			
3			
4			
5			
6			
7			
8			
9			
10			
11			
12			
13			
14			
15			
16			
17			
18			
19			
20			
21			
22			
23			
24			
25			
26			
27			
28			
29			
30			
31			
32			
33			
34			
35			
36			
37			
38			
39			
40			
41			
42			
43			
44			
45			
46			
47			
48			
49			
50			
51			
52			
53			
54			

DATE	FORM
	Personal Data Sheet
	Family Data Sheet
	INITIAL INTERVIEW
	Personality Inventory
	Rorschach Responses
	Man–Woman Drawing
	Consultations:
	Psychiatric
	Medical
	Neurological
	Psychological
	Casework
	TERMINAL NOTE
	SUMMARY
	Transfer
	Follow-up 1 yr.
	Follow-up 2 yrs.
	Follow-up 5 yrs.
	Case Re-opened

MONTHLY NOTES

1		13		25	
2		14		26	
3		15		27	
4		16		28	
5		17		29	
6		18		30	
7		19		31	
8		20		32	
9		21		33	
10		22		34	
11		23		35	
12		24		36	

SUPERVISION

Date	Supervisor	Date	Supervisor
1		13	
2		14	
3		15	
4		16	
5		17	
6		18	
7		19	
8		20	
9		21	
10		22	
11		23	
12		24	

* Case folder. This form is printed on the front of a heavy manila correspondence folder, and the numbered record of appointments (left-hand column) is continued in two columns on the back of the folder, provision being made for 165 appointments. (The above reproduction has been reduced in size from an original 9 × 11¾ inch folder.)

APPENDIX K

Outline for Case Presentation

1. Age of patient.
2. Sex.
3. Marital status.
4. How long married?
5. Number and ages of children.
6. Age and occupation of mate.
7. Any previous marriages? When?
8. Religion.
9. Education.
10. Occupation.
11. Employed? Salary.
12. If unemployed, source of income.
13. CHIEF COMPLAINT (in patient's own words).
14. HISTORY AND DEVELOPMENT OF COMPLAINT (date of onset, circumstances under which complaint developed, progression from the onset to the time of the initial interview).
15. OTHER COMPLAINTS AND SYMPTOMS (physical, emotional, psychic, and behavioral symptoms other than those of the complaint factor).
16. MEDICAL, SURGICAL, AND, IN WOMEN, GYNECOLOGIC HISTORY.
17. ENVIRONMENTAL DISTURBANCES AT ONSET OF THERAPY (economic, work, housing, neighborhood, and family difficulties).
18. RELATIONSHIP DIFFICULTIES AT ONSET OF THERAPY (disturbances in relationships with people, attitudes toward the world, toward authority, and toward the self).
19. HEREDITARY, CONSTITUTIONAL, AND EARLY DEVELOPMENTAL INFLUENCES (significant physical and psychiatric disorders in patient's family, socioeconomic status of family, important early traumatic experiences and relationships, neurotic traits in childhood and adolescence).
20. FAMILY DATA (mother, father, siblings, spouse, children—ages, state of health, personality adjustment, and patient's attitudes toward each).
21. PREVIOUS ATTACKS OF EMOTIONAL ILLNESS (as a child and later. When did patient feel himself to be completely free from emotional illness?).
22. INITIAL INTERVIEW (brief description of condition of patient at initial interview, including clinical findings).
23. LEVEL OF INSIGHT AND MOTIVATION AT ONSET OF THERAPY (How long ago did the patient feel that he needed treatment? For what? Awareness of emotional nature of problem, willingness to accept psychotherapy).
24. PREVIOUS TREATMENTS (When did the patient first seek treatment? What treatment did he get? Any hospitalization?).
25. CLINICAL EXAMINATION (significant findings in physical, neurologic, psychiatric, and psychologic examinations).
26. DIFFERENTIAL DIAGNOSIS (at time of initial interview).
27. ESTIMATE OF PROGNOSIS (at time of initial interview).
28. PSYCHODYNAMICS AND PSYCHOPATHOLOGY.
29. COURSE OF TREATMENT (up to time of presentation).
    (1) Type of therapy employed, frequency, total number of sessions, response to therapist.

   (2) Significant events during therapy, dynamics that were revealed, verbatim report of
       important dreams, nature of transference and resistance.
   (3) Progress in therapy, insight acquired, translation of insight into action, change in
       symptoms, attitudes, and relationships with people.
   (4) Verbatim account of all or part of a typical session, if desired.
30. STATISTICAL CLASSIFICATION.

Application Blank for New Staff Members*

NAME: ADDRESS:

AGE: MARITAL STATUS: TELEPHONE:

1. DEGREES (where obtained and dates—undergraduate and postgraduate):

2. DIDACTIC INSTRUCTION:

a. BASIC COURSES	WHERE TAKEN, YEAR, INSTRUCTOR
Psychosocial Development	
Psychopathology	
Psychodynamics	
Techniques of Interviewing	
Basic Neuropsychiatry	
Readings in Psychiatric Literature	
Techniques in Psychotherapy	
Clinical Conferences	
Continuous Case Seminars	
Child Psychiatry	
Group Psychotherapy	

   b. What schools of psychotherapy or psychoanalysis have you attended as a matriculated student?

Dates:

Were you ever certified?
Have you been qualified by any Board?
Date of license, if any, to practice profession:
Membership in which professional societies?

3. PERSONAL PSYCHOANALYSIS OR PSYCHOTHERAPY:

When started:

With whom:

Number of sessions per week:

Total number of sessions:

Additional therapy:

4. CLINICAL EXPERIENCE (*indicate names of therapeutic centers, clinics, institutions, or agencies; date of affiliation; capacity in which you have functioned*):

5. CASE EXPERIENCE:

When did you begin practicing psychotherapy?

Can you estimate the total number of patients treated?

Can you estimate the total number of patient sessions to date?

Underline the kinds of problems you have handled: character disorder

psychopathic personality   anxiety neurosis   anxiety hysteria

conversion hysteria   obsessive compulsive neurosis

psychosomatic problem   alcoholism   drug addiction

borderline case   schizophrenia   psychoneurotic depression

manic-depressive psychosis   involutional melancholia

paranoid condition   marital problem   childhood behavior problem

childhood psychoneurosis   childhood psychosis   convulsive disorder

6. SUPERVISED CLINICAL EXPERIENCE *(give names of supervisors, place of supervision, dates, total number of sessions with each supervisor):*

7. SUPERVISORY EXPERIENCE:

Have you ever supervised therapists in psychotherapy?

If yes, how many therapists?

Total number of supervisory sessions:

Have you ever had a course of instruction in psychotherapeutic supervision?

8. GROUP THERAPY:

Have you ever done group therapy?

If so, underline types: inspirational and supportive groups

educational groups   discussion groups   analytic groups

social and activity groups   psychodrama   other

Total number of group therapy sessions

9. PSYCHOTHERAPEUTIC TEACHING EXPERIENCE *(courses taught, dates, places):*

10. HAVE YOU EVER PUBLISHED ANY MATERIAL ON PSYCHOTHERAPY *(papers, pamphlets)?* If so, list:

---

* This form is useful in determining the didactic and experimental equipment of an applicant for a clinic position.

APPENDIX M

Questions You May Have about Psychotherapy*

1. DO I NEED PSYCHOTHERAPY?

   If you have nervous symptoms such as tension, depression, fears, fatigue, and certain physical complaints for which your doctor finds no physical basis; if you find it difficult to get along in your work or in your relations with people; if you have a school, sex, or marital problem; or if you merely feel irritable, unhappy, and believe you are not getting the most out of life, psychotherapy will be of help to you.

2. HOW DOES PSYCHOTHERAPY WORK?

   Nervous symptoms and unwarranted unhappiness are the product of inner emotional troubles. In psychotherapy you are helped to understand your problems. In this way it is possible for you to do something constructive about solving them.

3. CAN PHYSICAL SYMPTOMS BE CAUSED BY EMOTION?

   Many physical symptoms are psychosomatic in nature, which means that they have an emotional or nervous basis. When you come to think of it, it is not really so strange that emotional strain or worry should produce physical symptoms. After all, every organ in your body is connected with your brain by nerve channels; and so it is logical that when your nervous system is upset by some crisis or conflict, you may feel the effects in various organs of the body.

4. IF I CANNOT SOLVE MY PERSONAL PROBLEMS WITHOUT HELP, DOES THAT MEAN THAT I HAVE A WEAK WILL OR AM ON THE WAY TO A MENTAL BREAKDOWN?

   No. Even if you have no serious symptoms, it is difficult to work out emotional problems by yourself because you are too close to them and cannot see them clearly. More and more people, even those with a great deal of psychologic knowledge, are seeking help these days because they realize this. The fact that you desire aid is a compliment to your judgment and is no indication that you are approaching a mental breakdown. Psychotherapy has helped countless numbers of people to overcome serious emotional symptoms and has enabled many others to increase their working capacities and to better their relationships with people.

5. WHAT KIND OF TREATMENT WILL I NEED?

   The kind of treatment best suited for you can be determined only by a careful evaluation of your problem by a professional therapist.

6. WHAT HAPPENS TO THE INFORMATION ABOUT ME?

   In scientific work records are necessary, since they permit of a more thorough dealing with one's problems. It is understandable that you might be concerned about what happens to the information about you, because much or all of this information is highly personal. Case records are confidential. *No outsider, not even your closest relative or family physician, is permitted to see your case record without your written permission.*

7. HOW CAN I HELP TO COOPERATE WITH THE TREATMENT PLAN?

   The general practitioner has medications; the surgeon works with instruments; the heart specialist has x-rays and delicate recording apparatus. But for the most part, the psychotherapist has only one aid besides knowledge—YOU. Your cooperation and trust in the therapist are essential. You must feel free to take up with your therapist anything about the treatment process that disturbs you or puzzles you in any way. By doing this you have the best chance of shortening your treatment and of insuring its fullest success.

---

* Informational sheet that may be given the patient prior to the initial interview.

APPENDIX N

Personal History Sheet*

Name _____   _____
                    LAST   FIRST   DATE

This material is necessary for the completion of your records. In answering the questions use extra sheets if required, noting the number of the question that is being answered. This, as all other information, will be kept confidential. If you are particularly troubled by any question and do not desire to answer it, merely write in "Do not care to answer."

1. How would you describe your health (excellent, good, fair, poor)?

     a. Physical _____
     b. Emotional _____

2. What physical illnesses have you had? When?

3. When was your last examination by a physician? _____

          For what condition? _____

4. Have you in the last 2 years had

     a. Chext x-ray _____
     b. Urine examination _____
     c. Blood tests _____

5. Have you ever been turned down for life insurance? _____

          If yes, why?

6. Have you ever been in a hospital? _____ If yes:

          Name of hospital _____
          Nature of illness _____
          Date and length of hospitalization _____

7. When was the last time you felt well both physically and emotionally for a sustained period? _____

8. Have you received treatment for "nervous" or emotional difficulties? _____
   If so:

Date _____
Frequency of visits _____
Nature of treatment _____
Whom treated by _____

9. Does your present job satisfy you?

   If not, in what ways are you dissatisfied?

10. Do you think you could handle a job more difficult than those you have held? _____

    If yes, describe.

11. What is your ambition?

12. Do you make friends easily? _____ Do you keep them? _____

13. Are most of your friends of one sex? _____ Which? _____

14. Can you confide in your friends? _____

15. How is most of your free time occupied?

16. What medications are you taking at the present time?
    Dosage?

Check any of the following that apply to you:

( ) headaches	( ) depressed
( ) dizziness	( ) suicidal ideas
( ) fainting spells	( ) always worried about something
( ) palpitations	( ) unable to relax
( ) stomach trouble	( ) unable to have a good time
( ) no appetite	( ) don't like weekends and vacations
( ) bowel disturbances	( ) over-ambitious
( ) fatigue	( ) sexual problems
( ) insomnia	( ) shy with people
( ) nightmares	( ) can't make friends
( ) take sedatives	( ) can't make decisions
( ) alcoholism	( ) can't keep a job
( ) feel tense	( ) inferiority feelings
( ) feel panicky	( ) home conditions bad
( ) tremors	( ) financial problems

* To be filled out by the patient when indicated.

APPENDIX O

Medical Form

RE: _____

DEAR DR. _____ :

The above patient has given me (us) permission to ask you for the results of his recent physical examination. I would appreciate your filling out this form and returning it in the enclosed envelope: (The patient's signed release is attached.)

Head: EENT

Neck:

Cardiovascular:

Pulmonary:

Genito-urinary:

Neurologic:

Additional:

Diagnosis:

From your findings is there any evidence of physical illness which requires treatment as this time?   NO _____   YES _____

If, yes, what medical treatment do you recommend?

Sincerely yours,

_____

Address _____

Telephone No. _____

APPENDIX P

Physical, Neurologic, and Laboratory Examinations

(Check items in which abnormality exists and explain below.)

I. *Physical Examination:*

( ) Stature	( ) Tongue	( ) Abdomen
( ) Nutrition	( ) Gums and teeth	( ) Hernia
( ) Weight	( ) Pharynx	( ) Genitals
( ) Skin	( ) Tonsils	( ) Muscles
( ) Hair	( ) Neck	( ) Bones
( ) Scalp	( ) Thyroid gland	( ) Joints
( ) Eyes	( ) Chest	( ) Spine
( ) Nose	( ) Breasts	( ) Extremities
( ) Sinuses	( ) Lungs	( ) Nails
( ) Ears	( ) Heart	( ) Lymphatic glands
( ) Lips	( ) Blood vessels	( ) Other (explain
( ) Mouth	( ) Blood pressure	below)

II. *Neurologic Examination:*

( ) Station	( ) Oculomotor, trochlear, and
( ) Gait	abducens nerves
( ) Tactile sense	( ) Trigeminal nerve
( ) Pressure sense	( ) Facial nerve
( ) Temperature	( ) Auditory nerve
( ) Pain	( ) Glossopharyngeal nerve
( ) Muscular sense	( ) Vagus nerve

( ) Stereognostic sense   ( ) Spiral accessory nerve

( ) Olfactory nerve   ( ) Hypoglossal nerve

( ) Optic nerve   ( ) Knee jerk

( ) Achilles reflex   ( ) Abdominal and epigastric reflexes

( ) Ankle clonus   ( ) Sphincteric reflexes

( ) Wrist, biceps, triceps   ( ) Motor disturbances

     reflexes   ( ) Paresis

( ) Babinski reflex   ( ) Muscles weakness

( ) Oppenheim's reflex   ( ) Hypotonia

( ) Gordon reflex   ( ) Tremors, tics, spasms

( ) Cremasteric reflex   ( ) Other (explain below)

III. *Miscellaneous Examinations:*

( ) Urinalysis   ( ) X-ray examination

( ) Blood analysis   ( ) Electrocardiogram

( ) Endocrine analysis   ( ) Electroencephalogram

                  ( ) Other (specify)

IV. *Summary of Physical, Neurologic, and Laboratory Examinations:* If examinations are

    essentially negative, check below. Explain items that have been checked above.)

( ) Physical examination negative

( ) Neurologic examination negative

( ) Miscellaneous examinations negative

APPENDIX Q

Mental Examination

NAME OF PATIENT:

(Check the following and elaborate below.)

I. *Attitude and General Behavior:*

    A. Physical appearance: ( ) disheveled ( ) untidy ( ) unkempt

    B. Degree of cooperativeness: ( ) fair ( ) poor

    C. General manner: ( ) mistrustful ( ) suspicious ( ) antagonistic

        ( ) negativistic ( ) defiant ( ) preoccupied

    D. General activity: ( ) motor retardation ( ) hyperactivity ( ) stereotypy

        ( ) mannerisms ( ) tics ( ) echolalia ( ) echopraxia

        ( ) perseveration ( ) compulsion

II. *Stream of Mental Activity:*

    A. Accessibility: ( ) indifferent ( ) self-absorbed ( ) inaccessible

    B. Productivity: ( ) voluble ( ) circumstantial ( ) flight of ideas

        ( ) under-productive ( ) retardated ( ) mute

    C. Progression of thought: ( ) illogical ( ) irrelevant ( ) incoherent

        ( ) verbigeration ( ) blocking

    D. Neologisms:

III. *Emotional Reactions:*

    A. Quality of affect: ( ) elation ( ) exhilaration ( ) exaltation ( ) euphoria

        ( ) mild depression ( ) moderate depression ( ) severe depression

        ( ) apprehension ( ) fear ( ) anxiety ( ) irritability

        ( ) morbid anger ( ) apathy ( ) emotional instability

    B. Appropriateness of affect: ( ) incongruity with thought content ( ) ambivalence

        ( ) emotional deterioration

IV. *Mental Trend—Content of Thought:*

    A. Thinking disorders: ( ) phobias ( ) obsessive ideas ( ) psychosomatic complaints ( ) persecutory trend ( ) ideas of reference ( ) grandiose ideas ( ) depressive delusions ( ) nihilistic delusions ( ) hypochondriac ideas ( ) ideas of unreality ( ) deprivation of thought ( ) delusions of influence ( ) autistic thinking

    B. Perceptive disorders: ( ) auditory hallucinations ( ) visual hallucinations ( ) olfactory hallucinations ( ) tactile hallucinations ( ) reflex, microptic, hypnagogic, or psychomotor hallucinations ( ) illusions

V. *Sensorium, Mental Grasp, and Capacity:*

    A. Disorders of consciousness: ( ) confusion ( ) clouding ( ) dream state ( ) delirium ( ) stupor

    B. Disorders of apperception: ( ) mild ( ) severe

    C. Disorders of orientation: ( ) time ( ) place ( ) person

    D. Disorders of personal identification and memory: ( ) general amnesia ( ) circumscribed amnesia ( ) confabulation ( ) retrospective falsification ( ) hypermnesia

    E. Disorders of retention and immediate recall: ( ) mild ( ) severe

    F. Disorders of counting and calculation: ( ) mild ( ) severe

    G. Disorders of reading: ( ) mild ( ) severe

    H. Disorders of writing: ( ) mild ( ) severe

    I. Disorders in school and general knowledge: ( ) mild ( ) severe

    J. Disorders in attention, concentration and thinking capacity: ( ) mild ( ) severe

    K. Disorders in intelligence: ( ) inconsistent with education ( ) mild ( ) severe

    L. Disorders in judgment: ( ) mild ( ) severe

    M. Disorders in insight: ( ) mild ( ) severe

VI. *Summary of Mental Examination* (check and describe abnormality, if any):

    ( ) Mental examination essentially negative
    ( ) Disturbance in attitude and general behavior
    ( ) Disturbance in stream of mental activity
    ( ) Disturbance in emotional reaction
    ( ) Disturbance in mental trend—content of thought
    ( ) Disturbance in sensorium, mental grasp and capacity

APPENDIX R

Authorization for Release of Medical Records

TO: _____

ADDRESS: _____

I would appreciate your releasing to _____
all records or abstracts pertaining to my case. I herewith grant permission for this
release.

SIGNED: _____

Witness: _____

Date: _____

APPENDIX S

Progress Report*

NAME: DATE:

(At the beginning of each month, it would be helpful if you would write a brief report on how you feel and what you believe has been accomplished in the past month.)

Checking the following:

The symptoms are complaints for which I sought treatment originally are: (   ) the same

(   ) better   (   ) worse

My understanding of my condition is: (   ) excellent   (   ) good   (   ) fair   (   ) poor

I believe my relationship with my therapist to be: (   ) good   (   ) fair   (   ) in need of improvement

I would consider my progress to be: (   ) excellent   (   ) good   (   ) fair   (   ) poor

ADDITIONAL COMMENTS:

---

* This sheet may be given monthly to selected patients for a progress report.

APPENDIX T

Antidepressant Medications: Special Instructions for Patients*

TYPE OF MEDICINE

These medications properly taken can relieve depression *immediately or take up to 4 weeks of continuous medication*. The percentage of success with these medications is very high, and if the patient cooperates by not skipping medication and not under or overdosing, hospitalization is rarely (less than 5%) necessary. The average time for signs of recovery to appear is 1 to 4 weeks.

DOSAGE

It cannot be overstressed that the medication should be taken as prescribed and not skipped. It is common for depressed persons to be their own worst enemies and thus, on one pretext or another, not take the medication as prescribed or most frequently to skip doses or days.

SIDE EFFECTS

Almost all good modern medicines have some mildly undesirable or minor reactions which are usually unimportant. Do not become alarmed. Usually it is best to tell the doctor if you do get them.

1. Dryness of the mouth is probably most frequent. Ignore it, or chew gum, keep hard candy in the mouth, or take liquids often.
2. Blurring of vision—is usually due to a temporary enlargement of the pupil. If it bothers you a great deal or interferes with your work, tell the doctor.
3. Lowered blood pressure—*Do not stand suddenly*. If you should forget and stand suddenly after having been on the medicine for some time, you may get nauseous or dizzy. If you are afraid of fainting, lie flat. Get an elastic bandage to wrap tightly around the abdomen (belly). The wrapping should be at least 8 inches wide. A tight girdle or similar support may be enough. An abdominal support purchased in a surgical supply house or drugstore is best. Put the support on before getting out of bed in the morning and continue to wear it daily until the doctor says you may stop. It is rarely necessary to wear elastic stockings or wrap elastic bandages around the legs to the hip. The belly support tightly and properly applied is usually adequate. If it is not, tell the doctor and have him check your blood pressure *in the standing position*. The doctor can also use additional medicines to raise your pressure.
4. Constipation—Your body can adjust to bowel movements occuring every 2–3 days, and, thus, if medication or depression does this, laxatives are not required. Do not take any laxative but mineral oil or milk of magnesia except on the doctor's advice.
5. Minor and rare inconveniences—never reason for stopping medication.
   a. Sweating—excessive perspiration may occur in some persons. This is usually a sign that an adequate dosage is being used. Excessive sweating may also be caused by nervousness, so do not stop medication under these circumstances; discuss it with your doctor.
   b. Sleepiness—most fatigue and sleepiness is due to emotional problems. Rarely, temporary sleepiness of a week's duration is caused by medication. Under no circumstances stop the medication entirely because of this. Dose may be taken

more toward bedtime, decreased with doctor's consent, or sleepiness will stop after a week on the medication.

  c. Shakiness—most shakiness is due to the emotional problem. Rarely is it due to medication. Discuss this with your doctor.

6. *IMPORTANT!* Most antidepressants will mix well with foods or other medicines. However, if you are treated by another doctor for anything, even a cold, you should remind him that you are taking an antidepressant or have been in the last two weeks.

  a. DO NOT USE ALCOHOL IN ANY FORM.

  b. Do not take any medication without the doctor's knowledge, especially over-the-counter medicines with the exception of aspirin, mineral oil, or milk of magnesia. In particular, avoid cold and cough medicines, antihistamines, and reducing or sleeping medicine. It is also well to avoid coffee and "colas" as they increase nervousness.

7. *MOST IMPORTANT*—For those on MAO antidepressants only. If the doctor tells you that you are on an especially strong antidepressant, such as an MAO (monoamineoxidase inhibitor) for depression, then:

  a. Do not use alcohol in any form, especially chianti wine.

  b. Do not eat cheese, except cottage cheese.

  c. Do not eat prepared herring or similar products, no wax beans, or other foods that the doctor may prohibit.

DEPRESSION AND ITS FUTURE

Almost all people get the "blues" or are depressed for some period of time. You have a longer period of depression than is healthy. You may usually feel that there is no hope for you . . . that you're not worth taking the time and money to cure . . . that you're too tired to make any effort . . . or that you're the one person who can't be cured. Usually your concentration and memory have temporarily declined. You may have little feeling for those you have loved before, even in your own family, and you may have little interest in sex. These and some other things are characteristic of depression. *They respond easily to treatment—do not give up hope.*

---

* Reprinted from mimeographed sheets by permission of the author, Dr. Irwin Rothman.

APPENDIX U

Questions You May Have About Hypnosis

---

1. EXACTLY WHAT IS HYPNOSIS?

Hypnosis is a state of altered consciousness that occurs normally in every person just before one enters into the sleep state. In therapeutic hypnosis we prolong this brief interlude so that we can work within its bounds.

2. CAN EVERYBODY BE HYPNOTIZED?

Yes, because it is a normal state that everybody passes through before going to sleep. However, it is possible to resist hypnosis like it is possible to resist going to sleep. But even if one resists hypnosis, with practice the resistance can be overcome.

3. WHAT IS THE VALUE OF HYPNOSIS?

There is no magic in hypnosis. There are some conditions in which it is useful and others in which no great benefit is derived. It is employed in medicine to reduce tension and pain that accompany various physical problems and to aid certain rehabilitative procedures. In psychiatric practice it is helpful in short-term therapy and also, in some cases, in long-term treatment where obstinate resistances have been encountered.

4. WHO CAN DO HYPNOSIS?

Only a qualified professional person should decide whether one needs hypnosis or could benefit from it. In addition to other experience, the professional person requires further training in the techniques and uses of hypnosis before being considered qualified.

5. WHY DO SOME DOCTORS HAVE DOUBTS ABOUT HYPNOSIS?

Hypnosis is a much misunderstood phenomenon. For centuries it has been affiliated with spiritualism, witchcraft, and various kinds of mumbo jumbo. It is a common tool of quacks who have used it to ''cure'' every imaginable illness, from baldness to cancer. The exaggerated claims made for it by undisciplined persons have turned some doctors against it. Some psychiatrists too doubt the value of hypnosis because Freud gave it up 60 years ago and because they themselves have not had too much experience with its modern uses.

6. IF HYPNOSIS IS VALUABLE, SHOULDN'T IT BE EMPLOYED IN ALL PSYCHOLOGICAL OR PSYCHIATRIC PROBLEMS?

Most psychological and psychiatric problems respond to treatment by skilled therapists without requiring hypnosis. Where blocks in treatment develop, a therapist skilled in hypnosis may be able to utilize it effectively. But only a qualified professional person can decide whether this is necessary or desirable.

7. IS THE USE OF HYPNOSIS ENDORSED BY THE PROPER AUTHORITIES?

Both the American Medical Association and the American Psychiatric Association have qualified hypnosis as a useful form of treatment in the hands of skilled doctors who have had adequate training and who employ it in the context of a balanced treatment program.

3. CAN'T HYPNOSIS BE DANGEROUS?

The hypnotic state is no more dangerous than is the sleep state. But unskilled operators may give subjects foolish suggestions, such as one often witnesses in stage hypnosis, where the trance is exploited for entertainment purposes. A delicately balanced and sensitive person exposed to unwise and humiliating suggestions may respond with anxiety. On the whole, there are no dangers in hypnosis when practiced by ethical and qualified practitioners.

9. I AM AFRAID I CAN'T BE HYPNOTIZED.

All people go through a state akin to hypnosis before falling asleep. There is no reason why you should not be able to enter a hypnotic state.

10. WHAT DOES IT FEEL LIKE TO BE HYPNOTIZED?

The answer to this is extremely important because it may determine whether or not you can benefit from hypnosis. Most people give up hypnosis after a few sessions because they are disappointed in their reactions, believing that they are not suitable subjects. The average person has the idea that he will go through something different, new and spectacular in the hypnotic state. Often he equates being hypnotized with being anaesthetized, or being asleep, or being unconscious. When in hypnosis, he finds that his mind is active; that he can hear every sound in the room; that he can resist suggestions if he so desires; that his attention keeps wandering, his thoughts racing around; that he has not fallen asleep; and that he remembers everything that has happened when he opens his eyes, and thus he believes himself to have failed. He imagines then that he is a poor subject, and he is apt to abandon hypnotic treatments. *The experience of being hypnotized is no different from the experience of relaxing and of starting to go to sleep.* Because this experience is so familiar to you, and because you may expect something startlingly different in hypnosis, you may get discouraged when a trance is induced. Remember, you are not anaesthetized, you are not unconscious, you are not asleep. Your mind is active, your thoughts are under your control, you perceive all stimuli, and you are in complete communication with the operator. The only unique thing you may experience is a feeling of heaviness in your arms and tingliness in your hands and fingers. If you are habitually a deep sleeper, you may doze momentarily; if you are a light sleeper, you may have a feeling you are completely awake.

11. HOW DEEP DO I HAVE TO GO TO GET BENEFITS FROM HYPNOSIS?

If you can conceive of hypnosis as a spectrum of awareness that stretches from waking to sleep, you will realize that some aspects are close to the waking state, and share the phenomena of waking; and some aspects are close to sleep, and participate in the phenomena of light sleep. But over the entire spectrum, suggestibility is increased; and this is what makes hypnosis potentially beneficial, provided we put the suggestibility to a constructive use. The depth of hypnosis does not always correlate with the degree of suggestibility. In other words, even if you go no deeper than the lightest stages of hypnosis and are merely mildly relaxed, you will still be able to benefit from its therapeutic effects. It so happens that with practice you should be able to go in deeper, but this really is not too important in the great majority of cases.

12. HOW DOES HYPNOSIS WORK?

The human mind is extremely suggestible and is being bombarded constantly with suggestive stimuli from the outside, and suggestive thoughts and ideas from the inside. A good deal of suffering is the consequence of "negative" thoughts and impulses invading one's mind from subconscious recesses. Unfortunately, past experiences, guilt feelings, and repudiated impulses and desires are incessantly pushing themselves into awareness, directly or in disguised forms, sabotaging one's happiness, health, and efficiency. By the time one has reached adulthood, he has built up "negative" modes of thinking, feeling, and acting that persist like bad habits. And like any habits they are hard to break. In hypnosis we attempt to replace these "negative" attitudes with "positive" ones. But it takes time to disintegrate old habit patterns; so do not be discouraged if there is no immediate effect. If you continue to practice the principles taught you by your therapist, you will eventually notice change. Even though there may be no apparent alterations on the surface, a restructuring is going on underneath. An analogy may make this clear. If you hold a batch of white blotters above the level of your eyes so that you see the bottom blotter, and if you dribble drops of ink onto the top blotter, you will observe nothing different for a while until sufficient ink has been poured to soak through the entire thickness. Eventually the ink will come down. During this period while nothing seemingly was happening, penetrations were occurring. Had the process been stopped before enough ink had been poured, we would be tempted to consider the process a failure. Suggestions in hypnosis are like ink poured on layers of resistance; one must keep repeating them before they come through to influence old, destructive patterns.

13. HOW CAN I HELP IN THE TREATMENT PROCESS?

It is important to mention to your therapist your reactions to treatment and to him or her, no matter how unfounded, unfair, or ridiculous these reactions may seem. Your dreams may also be important. If for any reason you believe you should interrupt therapy, mention your desire to do so to your doctor. Important clues may be derived from your reactions, dreams, and resistances that will provide an understanding of your inner problems and help in your treatment.

14. WOULDN'T HYPNOTIC DRUGS BE VALUABLE AND FORCE ME TO GO DEEPER?

Experience shows that drugs are usually not necessary. Often they complicate matters. If you should require medications, these will be employed.

15. WHAT ABOUT SELF-HYPNOSIS?

"Relaxing exercises," "self-hypnosis," and "auto-hypnosis" are interchangeable terms for a reinforcing process that may be valuable in helping your therapist help you. If this adjunct is necessary, it will be employed. The technique is simple and safe.

APPENDIX V

Relaxing Exercises

These exercises may be performed the first thing in the morning before getting out of bed. They may be repeated during the day if desired. They should always be done at night prior to retiring; relaxing suggestion will eventually merge into sleep. The total time for each session should be at least 20 minutes.

After shutting your eyes, proceed with the following steps:

1. Deep slow breathing for about 10 breaths.
2. Progressive muscle relaxation from forehead, face, neck to fingertips; from chest to toes, visualizing and purposefully loosening each muscle group.
3. Visualizing a wonderfully relaxed scene or simply a blank white wall.
4. Slow counting to self from 1 to 20 while visualizing the relaxed scene (or white wall).
5. Relaxing or sleeping from 1 to 2 minutes during which visualization of the relaxed scene continues.
6. Make the following suggestions to yourself (using the word ''you'').

   a. *Symptom relief* (disturbing symptoms, like tension, etc., will get less and less upsetting).
   b. *Self-confidence* (self-assuredness will grow).
   c. *Situational control* (visualize impending difficult situations and successful mastery of them).
   d. *Self-understanding* (make connections if possible between flare-ups of symptoms and precipitating events and inner conflicts).
7. Relax or sleep for several more minutes.
8. During daytime arouse yourself by counting from one to five.

At night do not arouse yourself; continue relaxing until sleep supervenes.

If sleep begins developing during the 4th step before the count comes to an end, interrupt counting and proceed immediately to suggestions (6th step above). Then continue with count and go as deeply as you wish. A racing of the mind and a tendency to distraction are normal. When this occurs force your attention back to the exercises.

Remember, you will not really be asleep during these exercises. You will be aware of your thoughts and of stimuli on the outside. If, for any reason, before you finish you want to bring yourself out of the relaxed state, tell yourself that at the count of 5 you will be out of it. Count from 1 to 5 and say to yourself: ''Be wide awake now, open your eyes.'' If negative thoughts crop up, bypass them, and continue with the steps outlined above. *Results are rarely immediate.* It takes a while to neutralize negative suggestions you have been giving yourself all your life. So be patient. Persistence is the keynote to success.

References

Abbot FK, Mack M, Wolf S: The action of banthine on the stomach and duodenum of man with observations of the effects of placebos. Gastroenterology 20:249–261, 1952

Abraham K: Notes on the psychoanalytical investigation and treatment of manic-depressive insanity and allied conditions, in Selected Papers. New York, Basic Books, 1953

Abraham W: Common Sense About Gifted Children. New York, Harper & Row, 1958

Abrahams J: Maternal Dependency and Schizophrenia: Mothers and Daughters in a Therapeutic Group. Abrahams J, Varon E (eds). New York, International Universities Press, 1953

Abrams R: Daily administration of unilateral ECT. Am J Psychiatry 124:384–386, 1967

Abrams R: Recent clinical studies of ECT. Semin Psychiatry 4:3–12, 1972

Abrams R, Fink M: Clinical experiences with multiple electroconvulsive treatments. Compr. Psychiatry 13:115–122, 1972

Abramson HA: LSD-25 as an adjunct to psychotherapy with elimination of fear of homosexuality. J Psychol 39:127–155, 1955

Abramson HA: LSD-25 XIX. As an adjunct to brief psychotherapy with special reference to ego enhancement. J Psychol 41:199, 1956(a)

Abramson HA: LSD-25 XXII. Effect on transference. J Psychol 42:51, 1956(b)

Abramson HA (ed): The Use of LSD in Psychotherapy. New York, Josiah Macy, Jr, Foundation, 1960

Abramson HA: LSD in psychotherapy and alcoholism. Am J Psychother 20:414–438, 1966

Abroms GM: The new eclecticism. Arch Gen Psychiatry 20:514–523, 1969

Abroms GM: Who prescribes drugs? Paper presented at the May 1972 meeting of the American Psychiatric Association. Audio-digest cassette 1(1), 1972

Abse DW: Hysteria, in Arieti S (ed): American Handbook of Psychiatry, vol. 1. New York, Basic Books, 1959, pp 290–291

Abt LE: Acting out in group psychotherapy: A transactional approach, in Abt LE, Weissman SL (eds): Acting Out Theoretical and Clinical Aspects. New York, Grune & Stratton, 1965

Abt LE, Bellak L: Projective Psychology. New York, Grove, 1959, p 357

Ackerman NW: The training of case workers in psychotherapy. Am J Orthopsychiatry 19:14–24, 1949

Ackerman NW: Psychoanalysis and group psychotherapy. Group Psychother 3:204–215, 1950

Ackerman NW: Interpersonal disturbance in the family: Some unsolved problems in psychotherapy. Psychiatry 17:359–368, 1954

Ackerman NW: Five issues in group

psychotherapy. Z Diagnost Psychol 5:167, 1957

Ackerman NW: An orientation to psychiatric research on the family. Marr Fam Living 19:68–74, 1957

Ackerman NW: Behavior trends and disturbances of the contemporary family, in Galdston I (ed): The Family in Contemporary Society. New York, International Universities Press, 1958(a)

Ackerman NW: The Psychodynamics of Family Life. New York, Basic Books, 1958(b)

Ackerman NW: Family-focused therapy of schizophrenics, in Sher SC, David HR (eds): The Out-Patient Treatment of Schizophrenia. New York, Grune & Stratton, 1960

Ackerman NW: The schizophrenic patient and his family relationships, a conceptual basis for family-focused therapy of schizophrenia, in Greenblatt M, Levinson DJ, Klerman GL (eds): Mental Patients in Transition, Steps in Hospital Community Rehabilitation. Springfield, Ill, Thomas, 1961

Ackerman NW: The psychoanalytic approach to the family. Fam Process 1:i, 1962

Ackerman NW: Family therapy in schizophrenia: Theory and practice. Int Psychiatry Clin 1:929–43, 1964

Ackerman NW: Rational of family therapy. Roche Report 2:1–9, 1965

Action for Mental Health: Final Report of the Joint Commission on Mental Illness and Health. New York, Basic Books, 1961

Adamson FK: The psychiatric nurse in the outpatient clinic. Nurs Outlook 5:25–27, 1957; 6:24, 1957

Adler A: Study of Organ Inferiority and its Psychical Compensation. Washington, DC, Nervous & Mental Disease Publishing Co, 1917(a)

Adler A: The Neurotic Constitution. Glueck B, Lind JE (trans). New York, Moffat Yard, 1917(b)

Adler A: The Practice and Theory of Individual Psychology. New York, Harcourt, 1929

Adler A: The Education of Children. New York, Greenberg, 1930

Adler A: Social Interest: A Challenge of Mankind. London, Faber & Faber, 1938

Adler, Alexandra: Guiding Human Misfits, A Practical Application of Individual Psychology. New York, Philosophical Library, 1948

Adler G, Buie DH: The misuses of confrontation with borderline patients, in Masserman JH (ed): Current Psychiatric Therapies, vol. 14. New York, Grune & Stratton, 1974, pp 89–94

Adler G, Myerson PG: Confrontation in Psychotherapy. New York, Aronson, 1973

Adler KA, Deutsch D (eds): Essays in Individual Psychology: Contemporary Application of Alfred Adler's Theories. New York, Grove, 1959

Agrin A: The Georgian Clinic: A therapeutic community for alcoholics. Q J Stud Alcohol 21:113–124, 1960

Ahsen A: Basic Concepts in Eidetic Imagery. New York, Brandon House, 1968

Ahsen A: Eidetic Parents Test and Analysis. New York, Brandon House, 1972

Aichorn A: Wayward Youth. London, Putnam, 1936

Albert RS: Stages of breakdown in the relationship and dynamics between the mental patient and his family. Arch Gen Psychiatry 3:682–690, 1960

Aldrich CK: Psychiatry for the Family Physician. New York, McGraw-Hill, 1955

Aldrich CK: The dying patient's grief. JAMA 184:329–331, 1963

Aldrich CK: An Introduction to Dynamic Psychiatry. New York, McGraw-Hill, 1966

Aldrich CK, Nighswonger C: Pastoral Counseling Casebook. Philadelphia, Westminister, 1968

Alexander ED: In-the-body travel—a growth experience with fantasy. Psychother: Theory Res Prac 4:319–324, 1971

Alexander F: Five-Year Report of the Chicago Institute for Psychoanalysis, 1932–1937. Chicago, the Institute, 1937

Alexander F: Psychoanalysis revised. Psychoanal Q 9:1–36, 1940

Alexander F: Fundamentals of Psychoanalysis. New York, Norton, 1948

Alexander F: Psychosomatic Medicine, Its Principles and Application. New York, Norton, 1950

Alexander F: Psychoanalysis and psychotherapy. Am J Psychoanal 2:722–733, 1954

Alexander F: Psychoanalytic contributions to short-term psychotherapy, in Wolberg LR (ed): Short-Term Psychotherapy. New York, Grune & Stratton, 1965, pp 84–126

Alexander F, French TM, et al: Psychoanalytic Therapy. New York, Ronald, 1946

Alexander L: Effects of psychotropic drugs on conditioned responses in man, in Rothlin E (ed): Neuropsychopharmacology. Amsterdam, Elsevier, 1961

Alexander L: Objective evaluation of antidepressant therapy by conditional reflex technique, in Franks CM (ed): Conditioning Techniques in Clinical Practice and Research. New York, Springer, 1964, pp 71–85

Alger I: The clinical handling of the analyst's responses. Paper presented at the New York Medical College, Department of Psychiatry, Symposium on Transference and Counter-Transference, October 1964

Alger I: Joint sessions: Psychoanalytic variations, applications, and indications, in Rosenbaum S, Alger I (eds): Psychoanalysis and Marriage. New York, Basic Books, 1967(a)

Alger I: Joint psychotherapy of marital problems, in Masserman, JH (ed): Current Psychiatric Therapies, vol. 7. New York, Grune & Stratton, 1967(b)

Alger I: Television image confrontation in group therapy, in Sager CJ, Kaplan HS (eds): Progress in Group and Family Therapy. New York, Brunner/Mazel, 1972, pp 135–150

Alger I, Hogan P: The use of videotape recordings in conjoint marital therapy. Paper presented at the Annual Meeting of the American Psychiatric Association, Atlantic City, NJ, May 13, 1966

Alger I, Hogan P: The use of videotape recordings in conjoint marital therapy. Am J Psychiatry 123:1425–1430, 1967

Alger I, Hogan P: Enduring effects of videotape playback experience on marital and family relationships. Am J Orthopsychiatry 39:86–96, 1969

Allen CM: Day Care Centers for School Children. New York, Child Welfare League of America, 1947

Allen EK, Hart B, Buell, JS, et al: Effects of social reinforcement on isolate behavior of a nursery school child. Child Dev 35:511–518, 1964

Allen FH: Therapeutic work with children: A statement of a point of view. Am J Orthopsychiatry 4:193–202, 1934

Allen FH: Psychotherapy with children. New York, Norton, 1942

Allen FH: Child psychotherapy, in Masserman JH (ed): Current Psychiatric Therapies, vol. 2. New York, Grune & Stratton, 1962, pp 41–47

Allen FH: Positive Aspects of Child Psychiatry. New York, Norton, 1963

Allen WY, Campbell D: The Creative Nursery Center. New York, Family Service Association of America, 1949

Allinsmith W, Goethals GW: The Role of Schools in Mental Health. Joint Commission on Mental Illness and Health, Monogr Ser No 7. New York, Basic Books, 1962

Allport GW: The Individual and His Religion. New York, Macmillan, 1950

Alt H: Residential Treatment for the Disturbed Child. New York, International Universities Press, 1960

Altshuler IM: Four years' experience with music as therapeutic agent at Eloise Hospital. Am J Psychiatry 100:792–794, 1944

Alvarez WC: Psychosomatic medicine that every physician should know. JAMA 135:705, 1947

American Association of Psychiatric Social Workers: Better social services for mentally ill patients, in Knee RI (ed): Proceedings of the Institute for Social Work in Psychiatric Hospitals, 1955

American Association of Schools of Social Work: Preprofessional Education for Social Work. New York, the Association, 1946

American Board of Examiners in Professional Psychology: Annual Report. Am Psychol 12:620–622, 1957

American Nurse: Nurse psychotherapists analyze current issues: Roles. Am Nurse 5:6, 1973

American Nurses' Association: Guidelines for the Establishment of Peer Review Committees. Developed by the Ad Hoc Committee on Implementation of Standards of Nursing Practice. Kansas City, Mo, the Association, 1973(a)

American Nurses' Association: Standards: Psychiatric-Mental Health Nursing Practice. Kansas City, Mo, the Association, 1973(b)

American Occupational Therapy Association: Occupational therapy: Its definition and functions. Am J Occup Ther 26:204, 1972

American Psychiatric Association: Newsletter 3(9), May 15, 1951

American Psychiatric Association: First aid for psychological reactions in disasters. Washington, DC, the Association, 1964

American Psychiatric Association, Committee on Nomenclature and Statistics: Diagnostic and Statistical Manual of Mental Disorders (2d ed). Washington, DC, the Association, 1968

American Psychiatric Association: Task Force Report: Psychiatric Education and the Primary Physician. Washington, DC, the Association, 1970

American Psychiatric Association: Discussion Guide on National Health Insurance. Washington, DC, the Association, 1974

American Psychoanalytic Association: Conference on Psychoanalytic Education and Research—Position Paper. Commission II—The Ideal Institute. New York, the Association, February 1974

American Psychological Association: Ethical

Standards of Psychologies. Washington, DC, the Association, 1953

American Psychological Association: Conference on Level and Patterns of Training in Psychology, Vail, Col, July 1973

American Psychological Association: APA Monitor June, July, November, December 1973

American Psychologist: Professional Standards and Accreditation. Proceedings of the 57th Annual Business Meeting of the American Psychological Association in Denver, Colorado 4:445, 1949

Anderson HH: Domination and integration, in: The social behavior of young children in an experimental play situation. Genet Psychol Monogr 19:341–408, 1937

Anderson HH: Domination and social Integration in the behavior of kindergarten children and teachers. Genet Psychol Monogr 21:287–385, 1939

Anderson HH, Anderson GL: An Introduction to Projective Techniques. Englewood Cliffs, NJ, Prentice Hall, 1951

Anderson HH, Anderson GL: Social development, in Carmichael L (ed): Manual of Child Psychology (2d ed). New York, Wiley, 1954

Anderson HH, Brewer JE: Dominative and socially integrative behavior of kindergarten teachers. Appl Psychol Monogr No. 6, 1945

Anderson HH, Brewer JE: Effects of teachers' dominative and integrative contacts on children's classroom behavior. Appl Psychol Monogr No. 8, 1946(a)

Anderson HH, Brewer JE, Reed, MF: Studies of teachers' classroom personalities: III. Follow-up studies of the effects of dominative and integrative contacts on children's behavior. Appl Psychol Monogr No. 11, 1946(b)

Anderson VV, Kennedy WM: Psychiatry in college—a discussion of a model personnel program. Ment Hyg 16:353–383, 1932

Andrews JS: Directive psychotherapy: Reassurance, in Watson RI (ed): Readings in the Clinical Method in Psychology. New York, Harper & Row, 1949, pp 654–673

Andronico MP, Guerney BG: The potential application of filial therapy to the school situation. J School Psychol 6:2–7, 1967

Angell JR: Mental hygiene in colleges and universities. Ment Hyg 17:543–547, 1933

Ansbacher HL, Rowena R: The Individual Psychology of Alfred Adler. New York, Basic Books, 1956

Ansbach HL, Rownea R: Superiority and Social Interest, Alfred Adler. Evanston, Ill, Northwestern University Press, 1964

Antebi RN: Seven principles to overcome resistances in hypnoanalysis. Br J Med Psychol 36:341–349, 1963

Anthonisen MR: The practice of the college psychiatrist. Dis Nerv Syst 3:175–184, 1942

Appel KE: Drawings by children as aids to personality studies. Am J Orthopsychiatry 1:129–144, 1931

Appel KE: Religion, in Arieti S (ed): American Handbook of Psychiatry, vol. 2. New York, Basic Books, 1959, pp 1777–1782

Appel KE, Lhamon ST, Myers JM, Harvey WA: Long-Term Psychotherapy, in Association for Research in Nervous and Mental Disease: Psychiatric Treatment. Research Pub 31. Baltimore, Williams & Wilkins, 1953, pp 21–24

Appel KE, Ormsby R, Myers JM: Family casework agencies, psychiatric clinics and the Joint Commission Report. Am J Psychiatry 121:839–846, 1965

Arehart-Treichel J: The science of sleep. Science News 111:203–207, 1977

Argyris C: Explorations in consulting-client relationships. Human Organization 21:121–133, 1961

Arieti S: Some basic problems common to anthropology and modern psychiatry. Am Anthrop 58:26–29, 1956

Arieti S: Manic-depressive psychosis, in Arieti S (ed): American Handbook of Psychiatry, vol. 1. New York, Basic Books, 1959(a) p 450

Arieti S: Schizophrenia, in Arieti S (ed): American Handbook of Psychiatry, vol. 1. New York, Basic Books, 1959(b), p 494

Arieti S (ed): American Handbook of Psychiatry, vol. 3. New York, Basic Books, 1966

Arieti S: Interpretation of Schizophrenia (2d ed). New York, Basic Books, 1974

Arje FB: The fine arts as an adjunct to rehabilitation. J Rehab 26:28–29, 1960

Arlow JA: The supervisory situation. J Am Psychoanal Assoc 11:576–594, 1963

Arlow JA, Kadis A: Finger painting in the psychotherapy of children. Am J Orthopsychiatry 16:134–146, 1946

Aron KW, Smith S: The Bristol psychiatric day hospital. J Ment Sci 99:564–571, 1953

Aronson ML: Acting-out in individual and group psychotherapy. J Hillside Hosp 13:43, 1964

Aronson ML: Technical problems in combined therapy. Int J Group Psychother 14:425, 1964

Aronson ML: Resistance in individual and group therapy. Am J Psychother 21:86–95, 1967

Aronson ML: A group program for overcoming the fear of flying, in Wolberg LR, Aronson

ML (eds): Group Therapy 1974: An Overview. New York, Stratton Intercontinental, 1974, pp 142–157

Arsenian J, et al: An analysis of integral functions in small groups. Int J Group Psychother 12:421, 1962

Aserinsky E, Kleitman N: Regularly occurring periods of eye motility and concomitant phenomenon during sleep. Science 118:273–274, 1953

Aserinsky E, Kleitman N: Two types of ocular motility occurring in sleep. J Appl Psychol 8:1–10, 1955

Ash WE, Mahoney JD: The use of conditioned reflex and antabuse in the therapy of alcoholism. J Iowa Med Soc 41:456–458, 1951

Ashbrook J: Judgment and pastoral counseling. J Pastoral Care 20:1–9, 1966

Assagioli R: Psychosynthesis: A Manual of Principles and Technique. New York, Hobbs, Dorman, 1965

Association for Supervision and Curriculum Development: Fostering Mental Health in Our Schools, 1950 Yearbook. Washington, DC, National Education Association, 1950

Astor MH: Hypnosis and behavior modification combined with psychoanalytic psychotherapy. Int J Clin Exp Hypn 21:18–24, 1973

Astrup C: The effects of psychotherapy. Int J Psychiatry 1:152–153, 1965

ATE Yearbook: Mental Health and Teacher Education. Washington, DC, Association of Teacher Educators, 1967

Atkinson RC, et al: Public Employment Service in the United States. Chicago, Public Administration Service, 1938

Auerbach AA: An application of Strupp's method of content analysis to psychotherapy. Psychiatry 26:137–148, 1963

Auerswald EH: "Interdisciplinary" vs "Systems" approach in the field of mental health. Paper presented at the 122d Annual Meeting of the American Psychiatric Association. Atlantic City, NJ, May 1966

Austin LN: Trends in differential treatment in social casework. J Soc Casework 29:203–211, 1948

Austin LN: Qualifications for psychotherapists, social caseworkers. Am J Orthopsychiatry 26:47–57, 1956

Austin LN: Diagnosis and treatment of the client with anxiety hysteria, in Parad HJ (ed): Ego Psychology and Dynamic Casework. New York, Family Service Association of America, 1958

Avnet HH: Psychiatric Insurance: Financing Short-Term Ambulatory Treatment. New York, Group Health Insurance, 1962

Avnet HH: How effective is short-term therapy? in Wolberg LR (ed): Short-term Psychotherapy. New York, Grune & Stratton, 1965, pp 7–22

Axel M: Treatment of schizophrenia in a day hospital. Int J Soc Psychiatry 5:174–181, 1959

Axline VM: Play Therapy. Boston, Houghton Mifflin, 1947 (rev ed—New York, Ballantine, 1969)

Ayd FJ: The current status of major antidepressants. Washington, DC, American Psychiatric Association, February 1960, pp 213–222

Ayd FJ: A critique of antidepressants. Dis Nerv Syst 22:5–32, 1961(a)

Ayd FJ: Toxic somatic and psychopathologic reactions to anti-depressant drugs. J Neuropsychiatry 2(1):119, 1961(b)

Ayd FJ: Chlorpromazine: Ten years' experience. JAMA 184:173–176, 1963

Ayd FJ: The future of pharmacotherapy: New drug delivery systems. Int Drug Ther Newsletter 1973

Ayllon T, Azrin NH: The Token Economy: A Motivational System for Therapy and Rehabilitation. New York, Appleton-Century-Crofts, 1968

Ayllon T, Houghton E: Control of the behavior of schizophrenic patients by food. J Exp Anal Behav 5:343–352, 1962

Ayllon T, Michael J: The psychiatric nurse as a behavioral engineer. J Exp Anal Behav 2:323–334, 1959

Ayllon T, Michael J: The psychiatric nurse as a behavioral engineer, in Franks CM (ed): Conditioning Techniques in Clinical Practice and Research. New York, Springer, 1964, pp 275–289

Azima H: The effects of Vesprin in mental syndromes. Squibb Inst Med Res Monogr Ther 2:203, 1957

Azima H: Sleep treatment in mental disorders. Dis Nerv Syst 19:623–530, 1958

Bach GR: Intensive Group Psychotherapy. New York, Ronald, 1954

Bach GR: Observations on transference and object relations in the light of group dynamics. Int J Group Psychother 7:64–76, 1957

Bach GR: The marathon group: Intensive practice in intimate interaction. Psychol Rep 18:995–1002, 1966

Bach GR: Marathon group dynamics: I. Some

functions of the professional group facilitator. Psychol Rep 20:995–999, 1967(a)

Bach GR: Marathon group dynamics: II. Dimensions of helpfulness: Therapeutic aggression. Psychol Rep 20:1147–1158, 1967(b)

Bach GR: Marathon group dynamics: III. Disjunctive contacts. Psychol Rep 20:1163–1172, 1967(c)

Bach GR: Group and leader phobias in marathon groups. Voices 3:41–46, 1967(d)

Bach GR: Fight with me in group therapy, in Wolberg LR, Aronson ML (eds): Group Therapy 1974: An Overview. New York, Stratton Intercontinental, 1974, pp 186–195

Bachrach AJ: Experimental Foundations of Clinical Psychology. New York, Basic Books, 1962

Back KW: Beyond Words: The Story of Sensitivity Training and the Encounter Movement. New York, Russell Sage Foundation, 1972

Baer DM, Harris FR, Wolf MM: Control of nursery school children's behavior by programming social reinforcement from their teachers. Paper presented at a meeting of the American Psychological Association, Philadelphia, August 1963

Bagchi BK: Mental Hygiene and the Hindu doctrine of relaxation. Ment Hyg 20:424–440, 1936

Bailey P: The great psychiatric revolution. Academic lecture. Am J Psychiatry 113:387, 1956

Baily P: Sigmund the Unserene: A Tragedy in Three Acts. Springfield, Ill, Thomas, 1965

Baker BL: Symptom treatment and symptom substitution in enuresis. J Abnorm Psychol 4:42–49, 1969

Baker EFW: The use of lysergic acid diethylamide (LSD) in psychotherapy. Can Med Assoc J 91:1200–1202, 1964

Bakewell WE, Wikler A: Symposium: Nonnarcotic addiction. Incidence in a university hospital ward. JAMA 196:710–713, 1966

Bakker CB, Bakker-Rabdau MK: No Trespassing, Explorations in Human Territoriality. Corte Madera, Calif, Chandler & Sharp, 1973

Bakwin H: Enuresis in children. J Pediatr 58:806, 1961

Balbernie R: Residential Work with Children. Elsmford, NY, Pergamon, 1966

Baldwin AL, Kalkorn J, Breese FH: Patterns of parent behavior. Psychol Monogr 58, No. 3, 1945

Bales RF: Interaction Process Analysis: A Method for the Study of Small Groups. Reading, Mass, Addison-Wesley, 1950

Bales RF: Small-group theory and research, in Mertin RK, Broom L, Cottrell LS, Jr (eds): Sociology Today: Problems and Prospects. New York, Basic Books, 1958, pp 293–305

Balint M: The final goal of psychoanalytic treatment. Int J Psychoanal 17, 1936

Balint M: On the psychoanalytic training system. Int J Psychoanal 29:163–173, 1948

Balint M: Training general practitioners in psychotherapy. Br Med J 1:115–131, 1954

Balint M: The doctor, his patient and the illness. Lancet 1:683–688, 1955

Balint M: The Doctor, His Patient and the Illness. New York, International Universities Press, 1957 (2d ed—London, Pitman, 1964)

Balint M: The other part of medicine. Lancet 1:40–42, 1961(a)

Balint M: Psychotherapeutic Techniques in Medicine. London, Tavistock, 1961(b)

Balint M: The doctor's therapeutic function. Lancet 1:1177–1180, 1965

Balint M: Psychoanalysis and medical practice. Int J Psychoanal 47:54–62, 1966

Balint M: Medicine and psychosomatic medicine: New possibilities in training and practice. Comp Psychiatry 9:267–274, 1968(a)

Balint M: The Basic Fault: Therapeutic Aspects of Regression. London, Tavistock, 1968(b)

Balint M: Research-seminars: Its implications for medicine. J R Coll Gen Pract 17:201–211, 1969

Balint M: Research in psychotherapy and the importance of the findings for psychoanalysis. Rev Med Psychosom Psychol Medicale 12:225–240, 1970

Balint M, Balint E: On transference and countertransference. Int J Psychoanal 20:223–230, 1939

Balint M, Balint E: Psychotherapeutic Techniques in Medicine. London, Tavistock, 1961

Balint M, Balint E, Gosling R, Heidebrand P: A Study of Doctors. Philadelphia, Lippincott, 1966

Balint M, Hunt J, Joyce D, et al: Treatment of Diagnosis: A Study of Repeat Prescriptions in General Practice. Philadelphia, Lippincott, 1970

Balint M, Ornstein PH, Balint E: Focal Psychotherapy—An Example of Applied Psychoanalysis. Philadelphia, Lippincott, 1972

Ballard J: Long Way Through. Boston, Houghton-Mifflin, 1959

Baller WR, Gianareco JC: Correction of nocturnal enuresis in deaf children. Volta Rev 72:545–547, 1970

Baller WR, Schalock HD: Conditioned response treatment of enuresis. Except Child 22:233–236, 247–248, 1956

Bambrace F: Effects of chlordiazepoxide in severely disturbed outpatients. Am J Psychiatry 118:69, 1961

Ban TA, Levy L: Physiological patterns: A diagnostic test procedure based on the conditioned reflex method, in Franks CM (ed): Conditioning Techniques in Clinical Practice and Research. New York, Springer, 1964, pp 56–60

Bancroft FW, Pilcher C (eds): Surgical Treatment of the Nervous System. Philadelphia, Lippincott, 1946

Bandura A: Social learning through imitation, in Jones MR (ed): Nebraska Symposium on Motivation. Lincoln, University of Nebraska Press, 1962(a), pp 211–269

Bandura A: Punishment revisited. J Consult Psychol 26:298–301, 1962(b)

Bandura A: Behavioral modification through modeling procedures, in Krasner L, Ullmann LP (eds): Research in Behavior Modification. New York, Holt, 1965(a)

Bandura A: Psychotherapy conceptualized as a social learning process. Unpublished paper, 1965(b)

Bandura A: Principles of Behavior Modification. New York, Holt, 1969

Bandura A, Blanchard ED, Ritter J: The relative efficacy of desensitization and modelling therapeutic approaches for attitudinal changes. Unpublished manuscript. Stanford University, 1968

Bandura A, Huston AC: Identification as a process of incidental learning. J Abnorm Soc Psychol 63:311–318, 1961

Bandura A, Lipsher DH, Miller PE: Psychotherapists' approach-avoidance reactions to patients' expression of hostility. J Consult Psychol 24:1–8, 1960

Bandura A, McDonald FJ: The influence of social reinforcement and the behavior of models in shaping children's moral judgments. J Abnorm Soc Psychol 67:274–281, 1963

Bandura A, Rosenthal TL: Vicarious classical conditioning as a function of emotional arousal. J Pers Soc Psychol 1, 1965

Bandura A, Ross D, Ross SA: Transmission of aggression through imitation of aggressive models. J Abnorm Soc Psychol 63:575–582, 1961

Bandura A, Ross D, Ross SA: Imitation of film-mediated aggressive models. J Abnorm Soc Psychol 66:3–11, 1963(a)

Bandura A, Ross D, Ross SA: Vicarious reinforcement and imitative learning. J Abnorm Soc Psychol 67:601–607, 1963(b)

Bandura A, Ross D, Ross SA: A comparative test of the status envy, social power and secondary reinforcement theories of identificatory learning. J Abnorm Soc Psychol 67:527–534, 1963(c)

Bandura A, Walters RH: Adolescent Aggression, New York, Ronald, 1959

Bandura A, Walters RH: Social Learning and Personality Development. New York, Holt, 1963

Banks SA: Psychotherapy: Values in action, in Regan PF, Pattishal EG (eds): Behavioral Science Contributions to Psychiatry. Boston, Little, Brown, 1965

Barahal HS: Resistances to community psychiatry. Psychiatr Q 45:333–343, 1971

Barbara DA: Stuttering. New York, Julian, 1954

Barbara DA: Working with the stuttering problem. J Nerv Ment Dis 125:329, 1957

Barbara DA: Communication in stuttering. Dis Nerv Syst 9(47):1, 1958

Barbara DA: The psychotherapy of stuttering, in Masserman JH (ed): Current Psychiatric Therapies, vol. 3. New York, Grune & Stratton, 1963

Barber TX: Hypnotic phenomena: A critique of experimental methods, in Gordon JE (ed): Handbook of Experimental and Clinical Hypnosis. New York, Macmillan, 1967

Barber TX: Hypnosis: A Scientific Approach. New York, Van Nostrand, 1969

Barber TX: An alternative hypothesis, in Fromm E, Shor RE (eds): Hypnosis: Research Development and Perspectives. Chicago, Aldine, 1972

Bard M, Berkowitz B: Training police as specialists in family crisis intervention. A community psychology action program. Community Ment Health J 3:315–317, 1967

Barendregt JT: A psychological investigation of the effects of psychoanalysis and psychotherapy, in Research in Psychodiagnostics. Paris, Mouton, 1961

Barendregt JT: The effects of psychotherapy. Int J Psychiatry 1:161–163, 1965

Barnett J: Therapeutic intervention in the dysfunctional thought processes of the obsessional. Am J Psychother 26:338–351, 1972

Baron S: Limitations of the teacher in guidance. Am J Psychother 6:104–110, 1952

Barret BH: Reduction in rate of multiple tics by free-operant conditioning methods, in Franks CM (ed): Conditioning Techniques in Clinical Practice and Research. New York, Springer, 1964, pp 303–314

Barrett EB: Strength of Will. New York, PJ Kennedy, 1915

Barrett EB: The New Psychology. New York, PJ Kennedy, 1925

Barrios AA: Posthypnotic suggestion as higher ordered conditioning: A methodological and experimental analysis. Int J Clin Exp Hypn 21:32–50, 1973

Barron F, Learly TF: Changes in psychoneurotic patients with and without psychotherapy. J Consult Psychol 19:239–245, 1955

Bartemeier LH: The attitude of the physician. JAMA 145:1122–1125, 1951

Bartemeier LH: Psychoanalysis and religion. Bull Menninger Clin 29:237–244, 1965

Barten HH: The coming of age of the brief psychotherapies, in Bellak L, Barten HH (eds): Progress in Community Mental Health, vol. 1. New York, Grune & Stratton, 1969

Barten HH: Brief Therapies. New York, Behavior Publications, 1971

Bartlett MR: A six-month follow-up of the effects of personal adjustment counseling of veterans. J Consult Psychol 14:393–394, 1950

Barton WE, Malamud W: Training the Psychiatrist to Meet Changing Needs. Washington, DC, Port City Press, 1964

Baruch DW: Procedures in training teachers to prevent and reduce mental hygiene problems. Pedagog Semin J Genet Psychol 67:143–178, 1948

Basescu S: Existential therapy, in Deutsch A, Fishman H (eds): The Encyclopedia of Mental Health, vol. 2. New York, Franklin Watts, 1963, p 589

Bates ES, Dittemore JV: Mary Baker Eddy. New York, Knopf, 1932

Bateson G: Panel review, in Masserman JH (ed): Individual and Familial Dynamics. New York, Grune & Stratton, 1959

Bateson G: Discussion of Samuel J. Beck's "Families of schizophrenic and of well children; method, concepts and some results." Am J Psychiatry 30:263–266, 1960

Bateson G: The challenge of research in family diagnosis and therapy, summary of panel discussion: I. Formal research in family structure, in Ackerman NW, Beatman FL, Sanford S (eds): Exploring the Base for Family Therapy. New York, Family Service Association, 1961

Bateson G, Jackson DD: A note on the double bind. Fam Process 1962. 2:154–161, 1963

Bateson G, Jackson DD, Haley J, Weakland JH: Toward a theory of schizophrenia. Behav Sci 1:251–264, 1956

Bauman G, Douthit VB: Vocational rehabilitation and community mental health in deprived urban areas. Paper presented at the 122d Annual Meeting of the American Psychiatric Association, Atlantic City, NJ, May 1966

Bavelas A: A mathematical model for group structure. Appl Anthrop 7(3):16–30, 1948

Bavelas A: Communication patterns in task-oriented group, in The Policy Sciences: Recent Development in Scope and Method. Stanford, Calif, Stanford University Press, 1952, pp 193–202

Baynes HG: Mythology of the Soul: A Research into the Unconscious from Schizophrenic Dreams and Drawings. London, Bailliere, Tindall & Cox, 1939

Beachy, WN: Assisting the family in time of grief. JAMA 202:559–560, 1967

Beatman, FL: Family interaction: Its significance for diagnosis and treatment. Soc Casework 38:111–118, 1957

Beck AT: Cognition, affect, and psychopathology. Arch Gen Psychiatry 24:495–500, 1971

Beck AT: Cognitive Therapy and Emotional Disorders. New York, International Universities Press, 1976

Beck AT, Kovacs M: A new fast therapy for depression. Psychol Today 10(8):94, 1977

Beck RL, Delaney W, Kraft IA: Moving through resistance: A multimedia approach to family therapy using dance therapy, video feedback and behavioral observation, in Wolberg LR, Aronson ML (eds): Group Therapy 1975: An Overview. New York, Stratton Intercontinental, 1975, pp 49–62

Beck SJ: Rorschach's Test, 3 vols. Vol. 1, Basic Processes; vol. 2, A Variety of Personality Pictures; vol. 3, Advances in Interpretation. New York, Grune & Stratton, 1944, 1945, 1952

Beck SJ: The Rorschach Test: A multidimensional test of personality, in Anderson HH, Anderson GL (eds): An Introduction to Projective Techniques. Englewood Cliffs, NJ, Prentice-Hall, 1951

Becker A, Goldberg HL: Home treatment services, in Grunebaum H (ed): The Practice of Community Mental Health. Boston, Little, Brown, 1970

Becker WC, Madsen CH, Jr, Arnold CR, Thomas, DR: The contingent use of teacher attention and praise in reducing classroom behavior problems. J Spec Ed 1:287–307, 1967

Beckett T: A candidate's reflections on the supervisory process. Contemp Psychol 5:169–179, 1969

Beecher HK: The powerful placebo. JAMA 159:1602–1606, 1955

Beecher HK: Research and the Individual: Human Studies. Boston, Little, Brown, 1970

Behanan KT: Yoga: A Scientific Evaluation. New York, Dover, 1937

Behnken P, Merrill E: Nursing care following prefrontal lobotomy. Am J Nursing 49:431, 1949

Behrle FC, Elkin MT, Laybourne PC: Evaluation of a conditioning device in treatment of nocturnal enuresis. Pediatrics 17:849–856, 1956

Beier EG: The Silent Language of Psychotherapy. Chicago, Aldine, 1966

Beiser HR: Self-listening during supervision of psychotherapy. Arch Gen Psychiatry 15:135–139, 1966

Belinkoff J: The effect of group psychotherapy on anaclitic transference. Am J Group Psychother 14:474–481, 1964

Belinkoff J, et al: The effect of a change of therapist on the group psychotherapy in an outpatient clinic. Int J Group Psychother 12:456, 1962

Bell F, Moore RR: Let's Create Activities and a Philosophy for Creative Teaching. Bedford, Mass, Creative Classrooms, 1972

Bell JE: Family group therapy. Pub Health Monogr No. 64, 1961

Bell JE: Recent advances in family group therapy. J Child Psychol Child Psychiatry 3:1–15, 1962

Bell NW, Vogel EF: The emotionally disturbed child as the family scapegoat, in Bell NW, Vogel EF (eds): The Family. New York, Free Press, 1960(a)

Bell, NW, Vogel EF (eds): The Family. New York, Free Press, 1960(b)

Bellak L: The use of oral barbiturates in psychotherapy. Am J Psychiatry 105:849–850, 1949

Bellak L: Manic-Depressive Psychosis. New York, Grune & Stratton, 1951

Bellak L: Psychiatry applied to medicine, surgery and the specialties, in Bellak L (ed): Psychology of Physical Illness. New York, Grune & Stratton, 1952

Bellak L: The Thematic Apperception Test and the Children's Apperception Test in Clinical Use. New York, Grune & Stratton, 1954

Bellak L: Handbook of Community Psychiatry and Community Mental Health. New York, Grune & Stratton, 1964

Bellak L: The role and nature of emergency psychotherapy. Am J Pub Health 2:58, 1968

Bellak L (ed): A Concise Handbook of Commu-nity Psychiatry and Community Mental Health. New York, Grune & Stratton, 1974

Bellak L, Barten HH (eds): Progress in Commu-nity Mental Health, 3 vols. New York, Grune & Stratton, vol. 1, 1969: vol. 2, 1972: Brunner/Mazel, vol. 3, 1975

Bellak L, et al: Psychiatric training program for nonpsychiatric physicians. JAMA 184:470–472, 1963

Bellak L, Small L: Emergency Psychotherapy and Brief Psychotherapy. New York, Grune & Stratton, 1965

Beller EK: Clinical Process. New York, Free Press, 1962

Bellman R: Dynamic Programming. Princeton, NJ, Princeton University Press, 1957

Bellman R: Adaptive Control Processes: A Guided Tour. Princeton, NJ, Princeton University Press, 1961

Bellman R, Friend MB, Kurland L: Psychiatric interviewing and multistage decision pro-cesses of adaptive type. The Rand Corp. RM–3732–NIH, June 1963

Bellman R, Friend MB, Kurland L: Simulation of the initial interview. Behav Sci 11:389–399, 1966

Bellville, TP, Raths ON, Bellville CJ: Conjoint marriage therapy with a husband and wife team. Am J Orthopsychiatry 39:473–483, 1969

Ben-Avi A: Zen Buddhism, in Arieti S (ed): American Handbook of Psychiatry, vol. 2. New York, Basic Books, 1959, pp 1816–1820

Bender L: Art and therapy in the mental distur-bances of children. J Nerv Ment Dis 86:249–263, 1937

Bender L: Childhood schizophrenia. Am J Or-thopsychiatry 27:68, 1947

Bender L, Goldschmidt L, Siva-Sankar DV: Treatment of autistic schizophrenic children with LSD-25 and UML-491. Recent Adv Biol Psychiatry 4:170–177, 1962

Bender L, Nichtern S: Chemotherapy in child psychiatry. NY State J Med 56:2791–2796, 1956

Bender L, Woltmann AG: The use of puppet shows as a psychotherapeutic method for behavior problems in children. Am J Or-thopsychiatry 6:341–354, 1936

Bender L, Woltmann AG: The use of plastic ma-terial as a psychiatric approach to emotional problems in children. Am J Orthopsychiatry 7:283–300, 1937

Benedek T: Countertransference in the training analyst. Bull Menninger Clin 18:12–16, 1954

Benedek T: Countertransference in the training analyst. Am J Psychiatry 129:156–160, 1972

Benedict R: Patterns of Culture. New York, Mentor, 1953

Benjamin JD: Psychoanalysis and nonanalytic psychotherapy. Psychoanal Q 16:169–176, 1947

Bennett AE, Eaton JT: The role of the psychiatric nurse in the newer therapies. Am J Psychiat 108:169, 1951

Bennett AE, Hargrove FA, Engle B: The Practice of Psychiatry in General Hospitals. Berkeley, University of California Press, 1956

Bennett IF: Clinical studies with phenothiazine derivatives in psychiatry, in Braceland FJ (ed): The Effect of Pharmacologic Agents on the Nervous System. Baltimore, Williams & Wilkins, 1957

Bennett LR: A therapeutic community. Nurs Outlook. 9:423–425, 1961

Benney C, Black BJ, Niederland WG: Rehabilitation of the mentally ill for the world of work. Proceedings of the Institute for the Rehabilitation of the Mentally Ill. New York, Altro Health and Rehabilitation Services, April 1962, pp 52–63

Benson H, Beary JF, Carol MP: The relaxation response. Psychiatry 37:37–46, 1974

Bentler PM: An infant's phobia treated with reciprocal inhibition therapy. J Child Psychol Psychiatry 3:185–190, 1962

Berelson B (ed): The Behavioral Sciences Today. New York, Basic Books, 1963

Berg C: Psychotherapy—Practice and Theory. New York, Norton, 1948, pp 349–457

Berg IA: Measures before and after therapy. J Clin Psychol 8:46–50, 1952

Berger D: Guidance in the elementary school. Teachers Coll Rec 49:44–50, 1947

Berger MM: Nonverbal communication in group psychotherapy. Int J Group Psychother 8:161, 1958

Berger MM: Videotape Techniques in Psychiatric Training and Treatment. New York, Brunner/Mazel, 1969

Berger MM: Videotape Techniques in Psychiatric Training and Treatment. New York, Bruner/Mazel, 1970

Berger MM: Self-confrontation through video. Am J Psychoanal 31:48–58, 1971

Berger MM, Sherman B, Spalding J, Westlake R: The use of videotape with psychotherapy groups in a community mental health service program. Int J Group Psychother 18:504–515, 1968

Berger SM: Conditioning through vicarious instigation. Psychol Rev 69:450–466, 1962

Bergin AE: The effects of psychotherapy: Negative results revisited. J Counsel Psychol 10:244–250, 1963

Bergin AE: Some implications of psychotherapy research for therapeutic practice. J Abnorm Psychol 71:235–246, 1966

Bergin AE: The deterioration effect: A reply to Braucht. J Abnorm Psychol 75:300–302, 1967

Bergin AE: The evaluation of therapeutic outcomes, in Bergin AE, Garfield, SL (eds): Handbook of Psychotherapy and Behavior Change: An Empirical Analysis. New York, Wiley, 1971, pp 217–270

Bergler E: Homosexuality, Disease or Way of Life. New York, Collier, 1956

Berkowitz L: Aggressive cues in aggressive behavior and hostility catharsis. Psychol Rev 71:104–22, 1964

Berkowitz S: Some specific techniques of psychosocial diagnosis and treatment in family casework. Soc Casework 36:399–496, 1955

Berle B, Nyswander M: Ambulatory withdrawal treatment of heroin addicts. NY State J Med 64:1846–1848, 1964

Berlin IN: Some learning experiences as a psychiatric consultant in the schools. Ment Hyg 40:215–236, 1956

Berlin IN: Mental health consultation in schools as a means of communicating mental health principles. J Am Acad Child Psychiatry 30:827–828, 1960

Berlin IN: Learning mental health consultation. Ment Hyg 48:257–265, 1964

Berlin JI, Wycoff B: Human relations training through didactic programmed instruction. Atlanta, Human Development Institute, 1964 (mimeo)

Berliner B: Short psychoanalytic psychotherapy: Its possibilities and its limitations. Bull Menninger Clin 5:204–213, 1941

Berman EM, Lief HJ: Marital therapy from a psychiatric perspective: An overview. Am J Psychiatry 132:583–593, 1975

Berman L: Countertransference and attitudes of the analyst in the therapeutic process. Psychiatry 12:159–166, 1949

Berman L: Some problems in the evaluation of psychoanalysis as a therapeutic procedure. Psychiatry 18:387–390, 1955

Bernal JD: Science in History. New York, Penguin, 1969

Bernard HW: College mental hygiene—decade of growth. Ment Hyg 24:413–418, 1940

Bernard HW: Psychiatric consultation in the social agency. Child Welfare 33:3–8, 1954

Bernard HW: A training program in community psychiatry. Ment Hosp 11:7–10, 1960

Bernard HW: Some aspects of training for community psychiatry in a university medical center, in Goldston SE (ed): Concepts of Community Psychiatry: A Framework for Training. Pub Health Service Publ No. 1319. Bethesda, Md, National Institute of Mental Health, 1965, pp 57–67

Bernard HW: Mental Health in the Classroom. New York, McGraw-Hill, 1970

Berne E: The Mind in Action. New York, Simon & Schuster, 1947

Berne E: Transactional Analysis in Psychotherapy. New York, Grove, 1961

Berne E: The Structure and Dynamics of Organization and Groups. Philadelphia, Lippincott, 1963

Berne E: Games People Play. New York, Grove, 1964

Berne E: Principles of Group Treatment. New York, Oxford University Press, 1966

Berne E: Staff-patient staff conference. Am J Psychiatry 125:3, 42, 1968

Bernfeld S: Sisyphos, or the Boundaries of Education. Vienna, Int Psa Press, 1925

Bettelheim B: Love Is Not Enough. New York, Free Press, 1950

Better Sleep Inc: Relax and Go to Sleep. Berkeley Heights, NJ, Better Sleep Inc, 1963

Betz BJ: Experiences in research in psychotherapy with schizophrenic patients, in Strupp HH, Luborsky L (eds): Research in Psychotherapy, vol. 2. Washington, DC, American Psychological Association, 1962, pp 41–60

Betz BJ: Studies of the therapist's role in the treatment of the schizophrenic patient. Am J Psychiatry 123:963, 1967

Beukenkamp C: Beyond transference behavior. Am J Psychother 10:467, 1956

Bibring E: The mechanism of depression, in Greenacre P (ed): Affective Disorders. New York, International Universities Press, 1953

Bibring E: Psychoanalysis and the dynamic psychotherapies. J Am Psychoanal Assoc 2:745–770, 1954

Bibring-Lehner G: A contribution to the subject of transference resistance. Int J Psychoanal 17:181–189, 1936

Bieber I: A critique of the libido theory. Am J Psychoanal 18:52–65, 1958

Bieber I: Homosexuality: A Psychoanalytic Study of Male Homosexuals. New York, Basic Books, 1962

Bieber TB: The emphasis on the individual in psychoanalytic group therapy. Int J Soc Psychiatry 2:275–280, 1957

Bieber TB: The individual and the group. Am J Psychother 13:635–650, 1959

Bierer J: A new form of group psychotherapy. Proc Roy Soc Med 37:208–209, 1943

Bierer J: A new form of group psychotherapy. Ment Health (London) 5:23–26, 1944

Bierer J: Therapeutic Social Clubs. London, Lewis, 1948

Bierer J: The Day Hospital. London, Lewis, 1951

Bierer J: Modern social and group therapy, in Harris NC (ed): Modern Trends in Psychological Medicine. London, Butterworth, 1958

Bierer J: Theory and practice of psychiatric day hospitals. Lancet 2:901–902, 1959

Bierer J: Day hospitals, further developments. Int J Soc Psychiatry 7:148–151, 1961

Bierer J: The Marlborough experiments, in Bellak L (ed): Community Psychiatry: The Third Psychiatric Revolution. New York, Grune & Stratton, 1963

Bijou SW, Redd WH: Behavior therapy for children, in Arieti S (ed): American Handbook of Psychiatry (2d ed), vol. 5. New York, Basic Books, 1975, pp 319–344

Billings EG: A Handbook of Elementary Psychobiology and Psychiatry. New York, Macmillan, 1939

Bilmes M, Civin G: Psychiatric Education for the Non-Psychiatrist Physician. Community Project Publication. New York, Postgraduate Center for Mental Health, 1964

Bindman AJ: Mental health consultation: Theory and practice. J Consult Psychol 23:473–482, 1959

Bindman AJ: Bibliography on Consultation. Boston, Department of Mental Health, 1960

Bindman AJ: The clinical psychologist as a mental health consultant, in Abt L, Riess T (eds): Progress in Clinical Psychology. New York, Grune & Stratton, 1966, pp 78–106

Binger C: The Role of Training in Clinical Psychology in the Education of the Psychiatrist. Transactions of the First Conference. New York, Josiah Macy, Jr, Foundation, 1947, pp 57–58

Bingham J: The Inside Story: Psychiatry and Everyday Life. Redlich F (compiler). New York, Knopf, 1953

Binswanger L: Grundformen und Erkenntnis menschlichen Daseins. Zurich, Max Niehaus Verlag, 1942

Binswanger L: Ausgewählte Vorträge und Aufsätze, 2 vols. Bern, Switz, Francke, 1947, 1955

Binswanger L: Existential analysis and psychotherapy, in Fromm-Reichmann F, Moreno J (eds): Proress in Psychotherapy, vol. 1. New York, Grune & Stratton, 1956

Binswanger L: Sigmund Freud: Reminiscences of a Friendship. Gutermann (transl). New York, Grune & Stratton, 1957

Bion WR: Experiences in groups. Hum Relations 1:314–320, 1948; 2:487–496, 1948; 3:13–22, 1949; 4:295–303, 1949; 5:3–14, 1950; 6:395–402, 1950; 7:221–227, 1951

Bion WR: Group Dynamics, in Klein M, et al (eds): A Re-View in Psychoanalysis. New York, Basic Books, 1951, pp 440–447

Bion WR: Experiences in Groups. London, Tavistock, 1959; New York, Basic Books, 1961

Bion WR: Learning from Experience. London, Heinemann, 1962

Bion WR: Elements of Psycho-Analysis. London, Heinemann, 1963

Bion WR: Transformations. London, Heinemann, 1965

Bion WR: Second Thoughts. London, Heinemann, 1967

Bion WR: Attention and Interpretation. London, Tavistock, 1970

Bird HW, Martin PA: Countertransference in the psychotherapy of marriage partners. Psychiatry 19:353–360, 1956

Birdwhistell RL: Introduction to Kinetics. Louisville, Ky, University of Louisville Press, 1952

Birdwhistell RL: Contributions of Linguistic Kinetic Studies to the Understanding of Schizophrenia—An Integrated Approach. Auerbach A (ed). New York, Ronald, 1959

Birk L, et al: Behavior Therapy in Psychiatry. A Report of the APA Task Force on Behavior Therapy. Washington, DC, American Psychological Association, 1973

Bischoff A: Uber eine therapeutische verwendung der sogenannten "Weck-amine," in Der Behandlung Schizophrener Erregungszustande, Monatsschr Psychiat u Nuerol 121:329, 1951

Blachly PH: Recent developments in the therapy of addictions, in Masserman JH (ed): Current Psychiatric Therapies, vol. 12. New York, Grune & Stratton, 1972

Black BJ: The protected workshop in the rehabilitation of the mentally ill. Psychiatr Q Suppl 33:107–118, 1959

Black BJ: Psychiatric rehabilitation in the community, in Bellak L (ed): Community Psychiatry: The Third Psychiatric Revolution. New York, Grune & Stratton, 1963

Blackman N: Ward therapy—a new method of group psychotherapy. Psychiatr Q 16:660–666, 1942

Blackman N: The effects of group psychotherapeutic techniques on community attitudes. J Soc Ther 3:197–205, 1957

Blackwell B: Drug therapy. N Engl J Med 289:249, 252, 1973

Blain D: The world around us. Roche Report 2:1–9, 1965

Blain D, Gayle RF: Distribution, form and extent of psychiatric consultation. JAMA 154:1266–1270, 1954

Blaine GH, et al: Music as a therapeutic agent. Ment Hyg 41:228–245, 1957

Blair BAS: The therapeutic social club. Ment Hyg 39:54–62, 1955

Blair O, et al: The value of individual music therapy as an aid to individual psychotherapy. Int J Soc Psychiatry 7:54–64, 1960

Blake RR: The other person in the situation, in Tagiuri R, Petrulio L (eds): Person Perception and Interpersonal Behavior. Stanford, Calif, Stanford University Press, 1958, pp 229–242

Blakemore CB, Thorpe JG, Barker JC, et al: The application of faradic aversion conditioning in a case of transvestism. Behav Res Therapy 1:29–34, 1963

Blanchard EB, Young LD: Clinical applications of biofeedback training: A review of evidence. Arch Gen Psychiatry 3:573–589, 1974

Blanton S, Peale NV: Faith Is the Answer. New York, Abington-Cokesbury, 1940

Blau A, Slaff B: A brief analysis of the nature of psychotherapy. NY State J Med 56:3319–3322, 1957

Blay Neto B: Group psychotherapy of married couples: Communications observed, in Wolberg LR, Aronson ML (eds): Group Therapy 1975: An Overview. New York, Stratton Intercontinental, 1975, pp 175–186

Bleuler E: Dementia Praecox or the Group of Schizophrenias. New York, International Universities Press, 1950

Blinder MG, Kirschenbaum M: The technique of married couple group therapy. Arch Gen Psychiatry 17:44–52, 1967

Blitzstein NL, Fleming J: What is a supervisory analysis? Bull Menninger Clin 17:117–129, 1953

Block MA: Rehabilitation of the alcoholic. JAMA 188:84–86, 1964

Blofeld J: The Zen Teaching of Huang Po, on the Transmission of Mind. New York, Grove, 1959

Bloodstein O: The speech therapist's need for training in psychodynamic principles. Conference on Speech Therapy, Postgraduate

Center for Mental Health, New York City, March 25, 1966

Bloom JB, Davis N, Wecht CH: Effect on the liver of long-term tranquilizing medication. Am J Psychiatry 121:788–797, 1965

Bloomberg W: Developments in community psychiatry, in Masserman JH (ed): Current Psychiatric Therapies, vol. 7. New York, Grune & Stratton, 1967

Blos P, Jr; Finch SM: Psychotherapy with children and adolescents, in Arieti S (ed): American Handbook of Psychiatry (2d ed), vol. 5. New York, Basic Books, 1975, pp 133–162

Blos P, Sr: On Adolescence: A Psychoanalytic Interpretation. New York, Free Press, 1962

Blos P, Sr: The Young Adolescent: Clinical Studies. New York, Free Press, 1970

Boag TJ: Further developments in the day hospital. Am J Psychiatry 116:801, 1960

Boas C Van Emde: Intensive group psychotherapy with married couples. Int J Group Psychother 12:142–153, 1962

Boehme W: The professional relationship between consultant and consultee. Am J Orthopsychiatry 26:241–248, 1956

Bojar S: The psychotherapeutic function of the general hospital. Nurs Outlook 6:151–153, 1958

Bolte GL: A communications approach to marital counseling. Fam Coordinator 19:32–40, 1970

Bonime W: The liking and disliking of one's patients, in Schizophrenia in Psychoanalytic Office Practice. New York, Grune & Stratton, 1957

Bonime W: Intellectual insight, changing consciousness, and the progression of processes during psychoanalysis. Compr Psychiatry 2:106–112, 1961

Bonime W: The Clinical Use of Dreams. New York, Basic Books, 1962

Bonime W: A psychotherapeutic approach to depression. Contemp Psychoanal 2:48–53, 1965

Bonstein I: Conditioning technique of psychoprophylactic preparation of the pregnant woman, in Psychoprophylactic Preparation for Painless Childbirth. London, Heinemann, 1958, pp 26–44. [Reprinted in Franks CM (ed): Conditioning Techniques in Clinical Practice and Research. New York, Springer, 1964]

Bookhammer RS, Meyers R, Schober C, Piotrowski Z: A five-year clinical follow-up study of schizophrenics treated by "direct analysis" (Rosen's) compared with controls. Paper presented at the 122d Annual Meeting of the American Psychiatric Association, Atlantic City, NJ, May 1966

Bornstein B: The analysis of a phobic child, in Eissler RS, et al (eds). The Psychoanalytic Study of the Child, vol. 3/4. New York, International Universities Press, 1949, pp 181–226

Boss M: Psychoanalyse und Daseinsanalytik. Bern and Stuttgart, Hans Huber, 1957

Boss M: Psychoanalysis und Daseinsanalysis. New York, Basic Books, 1963

Bostock J, Schackleton M: Pitfalls in the treatment of enuresis by an electric awakening machine. Med J Aust 2:152–154, 1957

Boszormenyi-Nagy I: The concept of schizophrenia from the perspective of family treatment. Fam Proc 1:103–113, 1962

Boszormenyi-Nagy I, Framo JL: Intensive Family Therapy. New York, Harper & Row, 1965

Bott E: The Family and Social Network. London, Tavistock, 1957

Bottome P: Alfred Adler: A Biography. New York Putnam, 1939 (Alfred Adler: A Portrait from Life. New York, Vanguard, 1957)

Boulougouris JC, Marks IM: Implosion—a new treatment for phobias. Br Med J 2:721–723, 1969

Bouvet M: Technical variations and the concept of distance. Int J Psychiatry 39, 1958

Bowen M: A family concept of schizophrenia, in Jackson DD (ed): Etiology of Schizophrenia. New York, Basic Books, 1960

Bowen M, Dysinger R, Basmania B: Role of fathers in families with a schizophrenic patient. Am J Psychiatry 115:1017–1020, 1959

Bowen M, et al: Study and treatment of five hospitalized family groups each with a psychotic member. Paper presented at the American Orthopsychiatric Association, Chicago, March 1957

Bower EM: Early Identification of Emotionally Handicapped Children in School. Springfield, Ill, Thomas, 1960; 2d ed, 1970

Bowers KS, Bowers PG: Hypnosis and creativity, in Fromm E, Shor RE (eds): Hypnosis: Research Developments and Perspectives. Chicago, Ill, Aldine, 1972

Bowers MK, et al: Counseling the Dying. New York, Thomas, Nelson, 1964

Bowers S: Social Work Year Book. Hodges MB (ed). New York, American Association of Social Workers, 1951

Bowman KM, Simon A, Hine CH, et al: A clinical evaluation of tetraethylthiuramdisulphide (antabuse) in the treatment of problem drinkers. Am J Psychiatry 107:832–838, 1951

Boylston WH, Tuma JM: Training of mental health professionals through the use of the "bug in the ear." Am J Psychiatry 129:124–127, 1972

Braceland FJ: Present status of preventive psychiatry. JAMA 159:1187–1190, 1955

Braceland FJ: Comprehensive psychiatry and the mental hospitals. Ment Hosp 8:2–7, 1957

Braceland FJ, et al: Yearbook of Psychiatry and Applied Mental Health. Chicago, Year Book Medical Publishers, 1975

Braceland FJ, Stock M: Modern Psychiatry: A Handbook for Believers. New York, Doubleday, 1963

Bradford LP, Gibb JR, Benne KD: T-Group Theory and Laboratory Method: Innovation in Re-Education. New York, Wiley, 1964

Bradley C: Benzedrine and dexedrine in the treatment of children's behavior disorders. Pediatrics 5:24, 1950

Brady JP: Brevital-relaxation treatment of frigidity. Behav Res Ther 4:71–77, 1966

Brady JP: A behavioral approach to the treatment of stuttering. Am J Psychiatry 125:843–848, 1968

Brady JP: Metronome-conditioned speech retraining for stuttering. Behav Ther 2:129–150, 1971

Brady JP: Behavior therapy of stuttering. Folia Phoniat (Basel, Switz) 24:355–359, 1972

Brady JP, Lind DL: Experimental analysis of hysterical blindness, in Franks CM (ed): Conditioning Techniques in Clinical Practice and Research. New York, Springer, 1964, pp 290–302

Branch HCH: Should the medical student be trained to refer or to handle his own psychiatric patients. Am J Psychiatry 121:847–851, 1965

Brashear AD, et al: A community program of mental health education using group discussion methods. Am J Orthopsychiatry 24:554–562, 1954

Brennan EC: College students and mental health programs for children. Am J Public Health 57:1767–1771, 1967

Breuer J, Freud S: Studies in Hysteria. Washington, DC, Nervous & Mental Disease Publishing Co, 1936

Brick M: Mental hygiene value of children's art work. Am J Orthopsychiatry 14:136–146, 1944

Brill NQ: Psychologists' useful role in medicine requires supervision of a physician. Modern Med, June 15, 1957, p 207

Brill NQ, Beebe GW: A follow-up study of war neuroses. VA Med Monogr. Washington, DC, Veterans Administration, 1955

Brill NQ, Glass JF: Hebephrenic schizophrenic reactions. Arch Gen Psychiatry 12:545–550, 1965

Brill NQ, Koegler RR, Epstein LJ: Controlled study of psychiatric outpatient treatment. Arch Gen Psychiatry 10:581–595, 1964

Brim OG: Family structure and sex-role learning of children, in Bell NW, Vogel EF (eds): The Family. New York, Free Press, 1960

Brister CW: Pastoral Care in the Church. New York, Harper & Row, 1964

Britton C: Casework techniques in child care services. Soc Casework 36:3–13, 1955

Brockbank R: Analytic group psychotherapy, in Masserman JH (ed): Current Psychiatric Therapies, vol. 6. New York, Grune & Stratton, 1966, pp 145–156

Brodman K: Diagnostic decisions by machine. IRE Trans Med Electronics. ME-7:216–219, July 1960

Brodman K: Interpretations of symptoms with a data-processing machine. Arch Med 103:776–782, 1959

Brodman K, et al: The Cornell Medical Index: An adjunct to medical interview. JAMA 140:530–534, 1949

Brodman K, van Woerhom AJ: Computer-aided diagnostic screening of 100 common diseases. JAMA 197:901–905, 1966

Brody MW: Observations on Direct Analysis: The Therapeutic Technique of John Rosen. New York, Vantage, 1959

Brody MW: Prognosis and results of psychoanalysis, in Moyer JH, Nodine JH (eds): Psychosomatic Medicine. The first Hahnemann Symposium. Philadelphia, Lea & Febiger, 1962

Brody S: Simultaneous psychotherapy of married couples, in Masserman JH (ed): Current Psychiatric Therapies, vol. 1. New York, Grune & Stratton, 1961, pp 139–144

Brody S: Community therapy of child delinquents, in Masserman JH (ed): Current Psychiatric Therapies, vol. 3. New York, Grune & Stratton, 1963, pp 197–204

Bromberg W: Advances in group therapy, in Masserman JH (ed): Current Psychiatric Therapies, vol. 1. New York, Grune & Stratton, 1961, pp 152–158

Brook A, Bleasdale JK, Dowling SJ, et al: Emotional problems in general practice: A sample of ordinary patients. J Coll Gen Pract 11:184–194, 1966

Brooks GW: Opening a rehabilitation house, in Greenblatt M, Simon B (eds): Rehabilitation of the Mentally Ill. Washington, DC, American Association for the Advancement of Science, 1959, p 127

Brooks GW: Rehabilitation house. NY State J Med 60:2400–2403, 1960

Brotman R, Meyer AS, Freedman AM: An approach to treating narcotic addicts based on a community mental health diagnosis. Compr Psychiatry 6:104–118, 1965

Brown BS, Wienckowski LA, Stoltz SB: Behavior Modification: Perspective on a Current Issue. DHEW Publ No. (ADM) 75–202. Bethesda, Md, National Institute of Mental Health, 1975

Brown GI: Human Teaching for Human Learning. New York, Viking, 1971

Brown JAC: Freud and the Post-Freudians. New York, Penguin, 1964

Brown MM, Fowler GR: Psychodynamic Nursing. Philadelphia, Saunders, 1961

Brown W, Jaques E: Product Analysis Pricing. Carbondale, Southern Illinois University Press, 1964

Brown W, Jaques E: Glacier Project Papers. Carbondale, Southern Illinois University Press, 1965

Browning JS, Houseworth, JH: Development of new symptoms following medical and surgical treatment for duodenal ulcer. Psychosom Med 15:328–336, 1953

Bruch H: The Importance of Overweight. New York, Norton, 1957

Bruch H: Conceptual confusion in eating disorders. J Nerv Ment Dis 133:46–54, 1961

Bruch H: Psychotherapy with schizophrenics, in Kolb LC, Kallmann FJ, Polatin A (eds): International Psychiatric Clinics, vol. 1. Boston, Little, Brown, 1964

Bruch H: Eating Disorders: Obesity, Anorexia Nervosa and the Person Within. New York, Basic Books, 1973

Bruch H: Learning Psychotherapy: Rational and Ground Rules. Cambridge, Harvard University Press, 1974(a)

Bruch H: Perils of behavior modification in treatment of anorexia nervosa. JAMA 230:1419–1422, 1974(b)

Bruch H: How to treat anorexia nervosa. Roche Report 5(8), 1975

Bruder EE: Ministering to Deeply Troubled People. Englewood Cliffs, NJ, Prentice-Hall, 1963

Bruner JS: Going beyond the information given, in Contemporary Approaches to Cognition. Cambridge, Harvard University Press, 1957

Bruner JS: Towards Theory of Instruction. Cambridge, Harvard University Press, 1966

Bruno FJ: Trends in Social Work as Reflected in the Proceedings of the National Conference of Social Work. New York, Columbia University Press, 1948

Bruyn GW, deJong UJ: The Midas-syndrome. An inherent psychological marriage problem. Am Imago 16:251–262, 1959

Bry A (ed): Inside Psychotherapy. New York, Basic Books, 1972, pp 57–60

Bry T: Varieties of resistance in group psychotherapy. Int J Group Psychother 1/2:106–114, 1951

Bry T: Acting-out in group psychotherapy. Int J Group Psychother 3:42–48, 1953

Bryt A: Psychoanalysis and its modifications in the treatment of emotional disturbance in adolescents. Psychiatr Spectator 3:1–2, 1965

Buber M: I and Thou. New York, Scribner, 1937

Buber M: Das Problem des Menschen. Heidelberg, Schneider, 1948

Buber M: Lecture, March 17, 1957, Washington, DC, as reported in Newsletter (William Alanson White Institute) 5(2), April 1957

Bucher BD: A picket portable shocking device with application to nailbiting. Behav Res Ther 6:389, 1968

Buck JN: Administration and Interpretation of the H-T-P Test (House-Tree-Person). Richmond, Va, VA Hospital, August 1950

Budson RD: The psychiatric half-way house. Psychiatr Ann 3:65–83, 1973

Budzynski TH, Stoyra JM, Adler C: Feedback-induced muscle relaxation: Application to tension headache. J Behav Ther Exp Psychiatry 1:205–211, 1970

Buehler RE, Patterson GR, Furniss JM: The reinforcement of behavior in institutional settings. Behav Res Ther 4:157–167, 1966

Bullard DM: Psychoanalysis and Psychotherapy. Selected Papers of Frieda Fromm-Reichmann. Chicago, University of Chicago Press, 1959

Bullis HE, O'Malley EE: Human Relations in the Classroom. Course I. Wilmington, Delaware State Society for Mental Hygiene, 1947

Bullis HE, O'Malley EE: Human Relations in the Classroom. Course II. Wilmington, Delaware State Society for Mental Hygiene, 1948

Burke JL, Lee H: An acting-out patient in a psychotic group. Int J Group Psychother 14:194, 1964

Burnside IM: Group work with the aged: Selected literature. Gerontologist 10:241–246, 1970

Buros OK: The Fourth Mental Measurements Yearbook. Highland Park, NJ, Gryphon, 1953

Burrow T: Social images versus reality. J Abnorm Soc Psychol 19:230–235, 1924

Burrow T: The laboratory method in psychoanalysis. Its inception and development. Am J Psychiatry 5:345–355, 1926(a)

Burrow T: Our mass neurosis. Psychol Bull 23:305–312, 1926(b)

Burrow T: Our social evasion. Med J Rec 123:793–795, 1926(c)

Burrow T: Psychoanalytic improvisations and the personal equation. Psychoanal Rev 13:173–186, 1926(d)

Burrow T: The Social Basis of Consciousness: A Study in Organic Psychology Based upon a Synthetic Societal Concept of the Neurosis. New York, Harcourt, 1927

Burrow T: The physiological basis of neurosis and dream. A societal interpretation of the sensori-motor reactions reflected in insanity and crime. J Soc Psychol 1:48–65, 1930

Burrow T: A phylogenetic study of insanity in its underlying morphology. JAMA 100:648–651, 1933

Burrow T: Kymograph records of neuromuscular (respiratory) patterns in relation to behavior disorders. Psychosom Med 3:174–186, 1941(a)

Burrow T: Neurosis and war. A problem in human behavior. J Psychol 12:235–249, 1941(b)

Burrows WG: Human sexuality: A program for sex education in the public school system. Psychosomatics 11:31–35, 1970

Burtness JH, Kildahl JP (eds): New Community in Christ. Minneapolis, Augsburg, 1963

Burton A: A commentary on the problem of human identity. J Existentialism 5(19), 1965

Burton A: Encounter: The Theory and Practice of Encounter Groups. San Francisco, Jossey-Bass, 1969

Burton A: Operational Theories of Personality. New York, Brunner/Mazel, 1974, p 406

Bush G: Transference, countertransference and identification in supervision. Contemp Psychol 5:158–162, 1969

Butler RN, Lewis MI: Aging and Mental Health: Positive Psychological Approaches. St Louis, Mosby, 1973

Bychowski G: The rebirth of a woman: A psychoanalytic study of artistic expression and sublimation. Psychoanal Rev 34:32–57, 1947

Bychowski G: Therapy of the weak ego. Am J Psychother 4:407, 1950

Bychowski G: Psychotherapy of Psychosis. New York, Grune & Stratton, 1952

Bychowski G: The ego and the object of the homosexual. Int J Psychoanal 13:255–260, 1961

Cade JFJ: Lithium salts in the treatment of psychotic excitement. Med J Aust 2:349–352, 1949

Cairns RB: The influence of dependency inhibition on the effectiveness of social reinforcers. J Personal 29:466–488, 1961

Caldwell J: Lifelong obesity—a contribution to the understanding of recalcitrant obesity. Psychosomatics 6:417–426, 1965

Call AP: Power Through Repose. Boston, Little, Brown, 1891

Calvin AD, Clifford LT, Clifford B, et al: Experimental validation of conditioned inhibition. Psychol Rep 2:51–56, 1956

Cameron DE: The day hospital: An experiment of hospitalization. Mod Hosp 3:64, 1947

Cameron DE: General Psychotherapy. Dynamics and Procedures. New York, Grune & Stratton, 1950, pp 270–288

Cameron DE: The conversion of passivity into normal self-assertion. Am J Psychiatry 108:98–102, 1951

Cameron DE: Psychotherapy in Action. New York, Grune & Stratton, 1968

Cameron DE, MacLean RR, et al: Special areas involving hospital-community relations, the day hospital. Ment Hosp 9:54–56, 1958

Cameron DE, Sved S, Solyom L, Wainrib B: Ribonucleic acid in psychiatric therapy, in Masserman JH (ed): Current Psychiatric Therapies, vol. 4. New York, Grune & Stratton, 1964

Cameron N: Paranoid conditions and paranoia, in Arieti S (ed): American Handbook of Psychiatry. New York, Basic Books, 1959, pp 508–539

Cameron N, Margaret A: Behavior Pathology. Boston, Houghton Mifflin, 1951

Cammer L: Treatment methods and fashions in treatment. Am J Psychiatry 118:447, 1961

Campbell D: Counseling service in the day nursery. Family, March 1943

Campbell JH, Rosenbaum CP: Placebo effect and symptom relief in psychotherapy. Arch Gen Psychiatry 16:364–368, 1967

Campbell RJ: Facilitation of short-term clinic therapy, in Masserman JH (ed): Current Psychiatric Therapies, vol. 7. New York, Grune & Stratton, 1967

Canada's Mental Health: Suppl No. 36. Preventive Psychiatry: If Not Now—When? April 1963

Canada's Mental Health: Suppl No. 44. Prevention of Mental Illness and Social Maladjustment. November–December 1964

Canada's Mental Health: Vol. 13, Community Mental Health. November–December 1965

Cancro R, Fox H, Shapiro L (eds): Strategic Interventions in Schizophrenia. New York, Behavioral Publications, 1974

Cantor MB: Karen Horney on psychoanalytic technique: Mobilizing constructive forces. Am J Psychoanal 17:118–199, 1967

Cantor MB: Personal communication. 1976

Cantor N: The Dynamics of Learning. Buffalo, NY, Foster & Stewart, 1946

Cantor P: The effects of youthful suicide on the family. Psychiatr Op, 12:6–11, 1975

Caplan G: An approach to the education of mental health specialists. Ment Hyg 43:268–280, 1959

Caplan G: Prevention of Mental Disorders in Children. New York, Basic Books, 1961(a)

Caplan G: An Approach to Community Mental Health. New York, Grune & Stratton, 1961(b)

Caplan G: Types of mental health consultation. Am J Orthopsychiatry 33:470–481, 1963

Caplan G: Principles of Preventive Psychiatry. New York, Basic Books, 1964

Caplan G: Community psychiatry, introduction and overview, in Goldston SE (ed): Concepts of Community Psychiatry: A Framework for Training. Pub Health Service Pub No. 1319. Bethesda, Md, National Institute of Mental Health, 1965

Caplan G: The Theory and Practice of Mental Health Consultation. New York, Basic Books, 1970

Caplan G: Support Systems and Community Mental Health: Lectures on Concept Development. New York, Behavioral Publications, 1974

Caplan G, Grunebaum H: Perspectives on primary prevention: A review, in Gottesfeld H (ed): The Critical Issues of Community Mental Health. New York, Behavioral Publications, 1972

Caplan G, Killilea M: Support Systems and Mutual Help. New York, Grune & Stratton, 1976

Cappon D: Results of psychotherapy. Br J Psychiatry 110:35–45, 1964

Cappon D: Computers in psychiatric research. Paper presented at the 122d Annual Meeting of the American Psychiatric Association, Atlantic City, NJ, May 1966

Carlin AS, Armstrong HE: Rewarding social responsibility in disturbed children: A group play technique. Psychother: Theory Res Prac 5:169–174, 1968

Carmichael DM: A psychiatric day hospital for convalescent patients. Ment Hosp 11:7, 1960

Carmichael DM: Community aftercare services, in Masserman JH (ed): Current Psychiatric Therapies, vol. 1. New York, Grune & Stratton, 1961, pp 210–215

Carmichael HT, Masserman JH: Results of treatment in a psychiatric outpatients' department. JAMA 113:292–298, 1939

Carr M: School Phobia. Can Counselor 4:41–45, 1970

Carrera RN: Observable difference between rolfed and unrolfed bodies. Psychother: Theory Res Prac 11:215–218, 1974

Carrington P: Freedom in Meditation. New York, Doubleday, 1977

Carrington P, Ephron HS: Clinical use of meditation, in Masserman JH (ed): Current Psychiatric Therapies, vol. 15. New York, Grune & Stratton, 1975

Carroll EJ: Treatment of the family as a unit. Pa Med J 63:57–62, 1960

Carroll HA: Mental Hygiene: The Dynamics of Adjustment. Englewood Cliffs, NJ, Prentice-Hall, 1963

Carstairs GM, et al: The Burden on the Community. The Epidemiology of Mental Illness: A Symposium. London, Oxford University Press, 1962

Cartwright D: Emotional dimensions of group life, in Raymert ML (ed): Feelings and Emotions. New York, McGraw-Hill, 1950

Cartwright D: Annotated bibliography of research and theory construction in client-centered therapy. J Consult Psychol 4:82, 1957

Cartwright D, Lippitt R: Group dynamics and the individual. Int J Group Psychother 7:86–101, 1951

Cartwright D, Zander A (eds): Group Dynamics: Research and Theory (2d ed). Evanston, Ill, Row, Peterson, 1960 (3d ed–New York, Harper & Row, 1968)

Casey GA: Behavior rehearsal: Principles and procedures. Psychother: Theory Res Prac 10:331–333, 1973

Casey JF, Lindley CJ: Recent advances in Veterans' Administration psychiatry, in Masserman JH (ed): Current Psychiatric Therapies, vol. 2. New York, Grune & Stratton, 1962, pp 233–246

Casriel D: So Fair a House: The Story of Synanon. Englewood Cliffs, NJ, Prentice-Hall, 1962

Casriel D: A Scream Away from Happiness. New York, Grosset & Dunlap, 1972

Casriel D, Deitch D: The Marathon: Time Extended Group Therapy, in Masserman JH (ed): Current Psychiatric Therapies, vol. 8. New York, Grune & Stratton, 1968

Cassem NH: Confronting the decision to let death come. Crit Care Med 2:113, 1974

Castelnuovo-Tedesco P: The twenty-minute hour: An experiment in medical education. N Engl J Med 266:283, 1962

Castelnuovo-Tedesco P: The Twenty-Minute Hour. Boston, Little, Brown, 1965

Castelnuovo-Tedesco P: Decreasing the length of psychotherapy: Theoretical and practical aspects of the problem, in Arieti S (ed): The World Biennial of Psychiatry and Psychotherapy, vol. 1. New York, Basic Books 1971, pp 55–71

Castelnuovo-Tedesco P, Greenblatt M, Sharef M: Paraprofessionals: A discussion. Psychiatr Op 8:13–21, 1971

Catanzaro RJ: Telephone therapy, in Masserman JH (ed): Current Psychiatric Therapies, vol. 11. New York, Grune & Stratton, 1971

Cerletti V, Bini L: Electric shock treatment. Bull Acad Med Rome 64:36, 1938

Chalfen L: Use of dreams in psychoanalytic group psychotherapy. Psychoanal Rev 51:461, 1964

Chambers DW: Storytelling and Creative Drama. Dubuque, Iowa, Brown, 1970

Chance E: A study of transference in group psychotherapy. Int J Group Psychother 2:1–40, 53, 1952

Chance E: Families in Treatment. New York, Basic Books, 1959

Chandler AL, Hartman MA: LSD-25 as a facilitating agent in psychotherapy. Arch Gen Psychiatry 2:286, 1960

Chapman LS, Chapman JD: Genesis of popular but erroneous psychodiagnostic observations. J Abnorm Psychol 72:193–204, 1967

Charatan FB: Depression in old age. NY State Med 75:2505–2509, 1975

Chein I, Gerard DL, Lee RS, Rosenfeld E: The Road to H. New York, Basic Books, 1964

Chessick RD: How Psychotherapy Heals. New York, Science House, 1969

Chessick RD: Why Psychotherapists Fail. New York, Science House, 1971

Chien CP, Cole JO: Depot phenothiazine treatment in acute psychosis: A sequential comparative clinical study. Am J Psychiatry 130:13–18, 1973

Child GP, Osinski W, Bennett RE, Davidoff E: Therapeutic results and clinical manifestations following the use of tetraethylthiuramidisulphide (antabuse). Am J Psychiatry 107:774–780, 1951

Chittenden GE: An experimental study in measuring and modifying assertive behavior in young children. Monogr Soc Res Child Devel No. 1, Ser No. 31, 1942

Chodoff P: A psychiatric approach to the dying patient. CA 10:29, 1960

Chodoff P: Medical insurance and private psychiatric practice. Psychiatr Ann 4:45, 1974

Christ AE: Attitudes toward death among a group of acute psychiatric patients. J Gerontol 16:56–69, 1961

Christensen C: The minister—a psychotherapist. Pastoral Psychol 17:31–39, 1966

Christmas JJ: Group methods in training and practice. Nonprofessional mental health personnel in a deprived community. Am J Orthopsychiatry 34:410–419, 1966

Church RM: The varied effects of punishment on behavior. Psychol Rev 70:369–402, 1963

Chwelos N, Blewett DB, Smith B, Hoffer A: Use of d-lysergic acid diethylamide in the treatment of alcoholism. Q J Study Alcohol 20:577–590, 1959

Ciancilo PJ: Children's literature can affect coping behavior. Personnel Guid J 43:897–903, 1965

Clancy HG, McBride G: Therapy of childhood autism in the family, in Masserman JH (ed): Current Psychiatric Therapies, vol. 12. New York, Grune & Stratton, 1972

Clarizio HF (ed): Mental Health and the Educative Process. Chicago, Rand McNally, 1969

Clark DH: Administrative Therapy: The Role of the Doctor in the Therapeutic Community. New York, Barnes & Noble, 1971

Clark DH, Cooper LW: Psychiatric half-way hostel. Lancet 1:588–590, 1960

Clark DH, Kadis AL: Humanistic Teaching. Columbus, Ohio, Merrill, 1971

Clark IA: Opiate addiction. Proc Roy Soc Med 58:412–414, 1965

Clark R: The "I can't" resistance to quitting smoking. Int Ment Health Res Newsletter 14:9–10, 1974

Clausen JA, Kohn MA: The ecological approach in social psychiatry. Am J Soc 60:140–151, 1954

Clawson G, Peasley E: Nursing care in insulin therapy. Am J Nurs 49:621, 1949

Clebsch W, Jaekle C: Pastoral Care in Historical Perspective. Englewood Cliffs, NJ, Prentice-Hall, 1964

Clements CC: Acting out vs acting through: An interview with Frederick Perls, MD. Voices, 4:66–73, 1968

Clemmesen C: The treatment of narcotic poisoning. Med Sci 14:74–82, 1963

Clinebell HJ, Jr: The challenge of the specialty pastoral counseling. Pastoral Psychol 15:17–28, 1964

Clinebell HJ, Jr: The future of the specialty of pastoral counseling. Pastoral Psychol 16:18–26, 1965

Clinebell HJ, Jr: Basic Types of Pastoral Counseling. Nashville, Tenn, Abingdon, 1966

Clinebell HJ, Jr: The Mental Health Ministry of the Local Church. Nashville, Tenn, Abingdon, 1972(a) (published in 1965 as Mental Health Through Christian Community)

Clinebell HJ, Jr: Is pastoral counseling a credible alternative in the ministry? J Pastoral Care 26:272–275, 1972(b)

Cobb S: Borderland of Psychiatry. Cambridge, Harvard University Press, 1943

Cockerill E, et al: A Conceptual Framework for Social Casework. Pittsburgh, University of Pittsburgh School of Social Work, 1952

Cohen AK: Delinquent Boys: The Culture of the Gang. New York, Free Press, 1955 (paperback, 1971)

Cohen LD: Consultation as a method of mental health intervention, in Abt L, Riess B (eds): Progress in Clinical Psychology. New York, Grune & Stratton, 1966, pp 107–128

Cohen M: Counter-transference and anxiety. Psychiatr J Stud Interpers Proc 15:231, 1952

Cohen M: The therapeutic community. Psychiatry 20:173–175, 1957

Cohen S: Lysergic acid diethylamide: Side effects and complications. J Nerv Ment Dis 130:30–40, 1960

Cohen S, Eisner BG: Use of LSD in a psychotherapeutic setting. Arch Neurol Psychiatry 81:615, 1959

Cohn RC: A group-therapeutic workshop on countertransference. Int J Group Psychother 11:284–296, 1961

Colbert J: On the musical effect. Psychiatr Q 37:429–436, 1963

Colby KM: Energy and Structure in Psychoanalysis. New York, Ronald, 1955

Colby KM: Computer simulation of a neurotic process, in Tomkins SS, Messick S (eds): Computer Simulation of Personality. New York, Wiley, 1963

Colby KM, et al: An on-line computer system for initial psychiatric inventory. Am J Psychiatry 125:8, 1969

Cole JO: Evaluation of drug treatments in psychiatry, in Hoch PH, Zubin J (eds): The Evaluation of Psychiatric Treatment. New York, Grune & Stratton, 1964, p 24

Coleman JS: The Adolescent Society: The Social Life of the Teacher and Its Impact on Education. New York, Free Press, 1961

Coleman JV: Psychiatric consultation in casework agencies. Am J Orthopsychiatry 17:533–539, 1947

Coleman JV: Mental health education and community psychiatry. Am J Orthopsychiatry 23:265–270, 1953

Collins ER: Teaching and learning in medical education. J Med Educ 37:671–686, 1962

Columbia University School of Public Health and Administrative Medicine. Mental Health Teaching in Schools of Public Health. New York, Columbia University Press, 1961

Committee on Alcoholism and Addiction and Council on Mental Health: Dependence on barbiturates and other sedative drugs. JAMA 193:673–723, 1965

Committee on Alcoholism and Addiction and Council on Mental Health: Dependence on amphetamines and other stimulant drugs. JAMA 197:1023–1027, 1966

Commission on Preventive Psychiatry of the Group for the Advancement of Psychiatry: Promotion of Mental Health in the Primary and Secondary Schools: An Evaluation of Four Projects. Rep No. 18. Topeka, Kans, the Group, 1951

Commission on Teacher Education: Helping Teachers Understand Children. Washington, DC, American Council on Education, 1945

Committee on Clinical Psychology of the Group for the Advancement of Psychiatry: The Relation of Clinical Psychology to Psychiatry. Rep No 10. Topeka, Kans, the Group, July 1949

Committee on the Function of Nursing: A Program for the Nursing Profession, Ginzberg E (ed): New York, Macmillan, 1949

Committee on Nomenclature and Statistics of the American Psychiatric Association: Diagnostic and Statistical Manual Mental Disorders. Washington, DC, the Association, 1952

Committee on Private Practice, Division of Clinical Psychology, New York State Psychological Association: The Clinical Psychologist in the Private Practice of Psychotherapy in New York State. New York, the Association, 1963

Committee on Psychiatric Nursing and the Committee on Hospitals of the Group for the Advancement of Psychiatry: The Psychiatric Nurse in the Mental Hospital. Rep No. 22. Topeka, Kans, the Group, May 1952

Committee on Psychiatric Social Work of the Group for the Advancement of Psychiatry: Circular Letter No. 21. Topeka, Kans, the Group, 1946

Committee on Psychiatric Social Work of the Group for the Advancement of Psychiatry:

The Psychiatric Social Worker in the Psychiatric Hospital. Rep No. 2. Topeka, Kans, the Group, January 1948

Committee on Psychiatric Social Work of the Group for the Advancement of Psychiatry: Psychiatric Social Work in the Psychiatric Clinic. Rep No. 16. Topeka, Kans, the Group, September 1950

Committee on Training in Clinical Psychology of the American Psychological Association: Recommended graduate training program in clinical psychology. Am Psychol 2:548, 1947

Comprehensive Psychiatry (special issue on drug addiction) 4:135–235, 1963

Conant MA: Progressive therapy for herpes simplex. Med Op 3:12, 1974

Conference Group on Psychiatric Nursing Practice of the American Nurses' Association: Facing up to Changing Responsibilities. Kansas City, Mo, the Association, 1963

Conference Group on Psychiatric Nursing Practice of the American Nurses' Association: Psychiatric Nursing, Kansas City, Mo, the Association, 1966

Conigliaro V: Counseling and other psychological aspects of religious life. Rev Religion 24:337–362, 1965

Conn JH: A psychiatric study of car sickness. Am J Orthopsychiatry 8:130–141, 1938

Connell PH: Amphetamine Psychosis. Maudsley Mongr No. 5. London, Oxford University Press, 1958

Connell PH: The day hospital approach in child psychiatry. J Ment Sci 107:969–977, 1961

Connell PH: Clinical manifestations and treatment of amphetamine type of dependence. JAMA 196:718–723, 1966

Conte WR: Occupational therapy in the psychoses, in Masserman JH (ed): Current Psychiatric Therapies, vol. 2. New York, Grune & Stratton, 1962, pp 227–232

Conze E: Buddhism, Its Essence and Development. New York, Philosophical Library, 1951

Conze E (ed): Buddhist Texts through the Ages. New York, Philosophical Library, 1954

Conze E: Buddhist Wisdom Books. London, Allen & Unwin, 1958

Cooper AJ: A case of fetishism and impotence treated by behaviour therapy. Br J Psychiatry 109:649–652, 1963

Cooper JE: A study of behavior therapy in thirty psychiatric patients. Lancet 1:411–415, 1963

Cooper LM: Hypnotic amnesia, in Fromm E, Shor RE (eds): Hypnosis: Research Developments and Perspectives. Chicago, Aldine, 1972

Corsini RJ: Methods of Group Psychotherapy. New York, McGraw-Hill, 1957

Corsini RJ: Role playing in Psychotherapy: A Manual. Chicago, Aldine, 1966

Corsini RJ: The behind-the-back encounter, in Wolberg LR, Schwartz EK (eds): Group Therapy 1973: An Overview. New York, Stratton Intercontinental, 1973, pp 55–70

Cosin LZ: The place of the day hospital in the geriatric unit. Int J Soc Psychiatry 1:33–40, 1955

Costello CG: The essentials of behavior therapy. Can Psychiatr Assoc J 8:162–166, 1963

Cottle WC: Beginning Counseling Practicum. New York, Grune & Stratton, 1973

Coué E: La Maitresse de Soi-Même Par L'Autosuggestion Consciente. Paris, Oliven, 1936

Coulter G: Exercise as group therapy. Staff (Am Psychol Assoc) 3:6–7, 1966

Council of the American Psychiatric Association: Principles Underlying Interdisciplinary Relations Between the Professions of Psychiatry and Psychology. Washington, DC, the Association, 1964

Council on Pharmacy and Chemistry: What to do with a drug addict. JAMA 149:1220–1223, 1952

Covner BJ: Principles of psychological consulting with client organizations. J Consult Psychol 11:227–244, 1947

Cowen EL, et al: A preventive mental health program in the school setting: Description and evaluation. J Psychol 56:307–356, 1963

Cox RH: Do pastoral counselors bring a new consciousness to the health professions? J Pastoral Care 26:250, 1972

Craft M: Treatment of depressive illness in a day hospital. Lancet 2:149–151, 1958

Craft M: Psychiatric day hospitals. Am J Psychiatry 116:251, 1959

Cramer JB: Common neuroses of childhood, in Arieti S (ed): Handbook of American Psychiatry, vol. 1. New York, Basic Books, 1959, pp 798–815

Crane GE: Prevention and management of tardive dyskinesia. Am J Psychiatry 129:466–467, 1972

Crank HH: The use of psychoanalytic principles in outpatient psychotherapy. Bull Menninger Clin 4:35, 1940

Cranswick EH, Hall TC: Desoxycortone with ascorbin acid in mental disorder. Lancet 1:540, 1950

Crasilneck HB, Hall JA: The use of hypnosis in controlling cigarette smoking. South Med J 61:999–1002, 1968

Crasilneck HB, Hall JA: Clinical Hypnosis:

Principles and Applications. New York, Grune & Stratton, 1975, pp 167–175

Crawford AL, Buchanan B: Psychiatric Nursing—A Basic Manual. Philadelphia, Davis, 1963

Crisp AH: "Transference," "symptom emergence," and "social repercussion" in behavior therapy: A study of fifty-four treated patients. Br J Med Psychol 39:179–196, 1966

Crocket R, Sandison RA, Walk A (eds): Hallucinogenic Drugs and Their Psychotherapeutic Use. Springfiled, Ill, Thomas, 1963

Croley HT: The Consultive Process. Contin Educ Mongr No. 1. New York, American Public Health Association, 1961

Cronbach LJ: Essentials of Psychological Testing (2d ed). New York, Harper & Row, 1960

Crow HJ, Cooper R, Phillips DG: Progressive leucotomy, in Masserman JH (ed): Current Psychiatric Therapies, vol. 3. New York, Grune & Stratton, 1963

Crowley RM: Harry Stack Sullivan: His Contributions to Current Psychiatric Thought and Practice. Nutley, NJ, Hoffman-LaRoche, 1971

Crutcher HB: Foster home care, in Arieti S (ed): American Handbook of Psychiatry, vol. 2. New York, Basic Books, 1959, pp 1877–1884

Cumming J: A psychiatrist looks at the psychiatric nurse. Psychiatr Op 9:22–25, 1972

Cummings NA, Kahn BI, Sparkman B: Psychotherapy and medical utilization. Paper presented at the conference on Protecting the Emotionally Disabled Worker, University of California Extension Center, San Francisco, June 11, 1963

Curran CA: Counseling in Catholic Life and Education. New York, Macmillan, 1952

Curran D: The problem of assessing psychiatric treatment. Lancet 2:1005–1009, 1937

Curran FJ: Art techniques for use in mental hospitals and correctional institutions. Ment Hyg 23:371–378, 1939

Cushman PJ: Methadone maintenance treatment of narcotic addiction. NY State J Med 72:1752–1755, 1972

Cutner M: Analytic work with LSD-25. Psychiatr Q 33:715–757, 1959

Czajkoski EH: The use of videotape recordings to facilitate the group therapy process. Int J Group Psychother 18:516–524, 1968

Dahlberg CC: LSD as an aid to psychoanalytic treatment, in Masserman JH (ed): Science

and Psychoanalysis. New York, Grune & Stratton, 1963(a)

Dahlberg CC: Pharmacologic facilitation of psychoanalytic therapy, in Masserman JH (ed): Current Psychiatric Therapies, vol. 3. New York, Grune & Stratton, 1963(b)

Danet BN: Videotape playback as a therapeutic device in group psychotherapy. Int J Group Psychother 14:433–444, 1969

Daniels RS, Margolis PM: Community psychiatry training in a traditional psychiatric residence, in Goldston SE (ed): Concepts of Community Psychiatry: A Framework for Training. Pub Health Service Pub No. 1319. Bethesda, Md, National Institute of Mental Health, 1965, pp 69–77

Davidman D: Evaluation of psychoanalysis: A clinician's view, in Hoch PH, Zubin J (eds): Evaluation of Psychiatric Treatment. New York, Grune & Stratton, 1964, pp 32–43

Davidoff E, Best JL, McPheeters HL: The effect of Ritalin (methylphenidylacetate hydrochloride) on mildly depressed ambulatory patient. NY State J Med 57:1753, 1957

Davidson GW: Living with Dying. Minneapolis, Augsburg, 1975

Davidson HA: The effects of psychotherapy. Int J Psychiatry 1:171–173, 1965

Davidson JR, Douglass E: Nocturnal enuresis: A special approach to treatment. Br Med J 1:1345–1347, 1950

Davies SP: Toward Community Mental Health. New York, New York Association for Mental Health, 1960

Davis DR: Introduction to Psychopathology (2d ed). New York, Oxford University Press, 1966

Davis JA: Education for Positive Mental Health. NORC Monogr Soc Res, No. 5. Chicago, Aldine, 1966

Davis JE: Play and Mental Health. New York, Barnes & Noble, 1938

Davis JE: An introduction to the problem of rehabilitation. Ment Hyg 29:217–230, 1945

Davis JE, Dunton WR: Principles and Practice of Recreational Therapy for the Mentally Ill. New York, Barnes & Noble, 1946

Davis JM: Overview: Maintenance therapy in psychiatry: I. Schizophrenia. Am J Psychiatry 132:1237–1245, 1975

Davis WE: Psychiatric consultation—the agency viewpoint. Child Welfare 36:4–9, 1957

Dax EC: Asylum to Community. Melbourne, Aust, Cheshire, 1961

Dean SR: Self-help group psychotherapy: Mental patients rediscover will power. Int J Soc Psychiatry 17:72–78, 1970–1971

DeBell D: A critical digest of the literature on

psychoanalytic supervision. J Am Psychoanal Assoc 11:546–575, 1963

DeCharms R, Levy J, Wertheimer M: A note on attempted evaluation of psychotherapy. J Clin Psychol 10:233–235, 1954

Dederich CE: Synanon Foundation. Paper presented before the Southern California Parole Officers, October 1958

deGroat AF, Thompson GG: A study of the distribution of teacher approach and disapproval among sixth-grade children. J Exp Educ 18:57–75, 1949

Dejérine J, Gaukler E: Psychoneurosis and Psychotherapy. Philadelphia, Lippincott, 1913

Dekker D, Pelser HE, Groen J: Conditioning as a cause of asthmatic attacks: A laboratory study, in Franks CM (ed): Conditioning Techniques in Clinical Practice and Research. New York, Springer, 1964, pp 116–131

Delay J, Deniker P: Apport de la clinique à la connaissance de l'action des neuroleptiques, in Bordeleau JM (ed): Extrapyramidal System and Neuroleptics. Montreal, Editions Psychiatriques, 1960, p 301

Delay J, Deniker P: Méthodeschimiothérapiques en psychiatrique: Les noveaux medicaments psychotropes. Paris, Masson et Cie, 1961

Delay J, Hart JM: Utilisation en thérapeutique psychiatrique d' une phenothiazine d'action centrale élective. Ann Med Psychol (Paris) 110(2):112, 1952

DeLeon G, Holland S, Rosenthal MS: Phoenix House criminal activity of dropouts. JAMA 222:686, 1972

DeLeon G, Mandel W: A comparison of conditioning and psychotherapy in the treatment of functional enuresis. J Clin Psychol 22:326–330, 1966

Demarest EW, Teicher A: Transference in group therapy. Psychiatry 17:187–202, 1954

Dement W: The effect of dream deprivation. Science 31:1705–1717, 1960

Dement W: REM sleep linked to psychophysiological changes. Roche Report 3:1–8, 1966

Dement W, Kleitman N: The relation of eye movements during sleep to dream activity: An objective method for the study of dreaming. J Exper Psychol 53:339–346, 1957

Denber HCB (ed): Research Conference on Therapeutic Community. Springfield, Ill, Thomas, 1960

Denber HCB, Merlis S: Studies on mescaline. I. Action in schizophrenic patients. Psychiatr Q 29:421, 1955

Denker PG: Results of treatment of psychoneurosis by the general practitioner: A follow-up study of 500 cases. NY State J Med 46:2164–2166, 1946

Densen-Gerber J: We Mainline Dreams: The Odyssey House Story. New York, Doubleday, 1973

Deri, S: Introduction to the Szondi Test. New York, Grune & Stratton, 1949

DeRosis L: The existential encounter in group psychoanalysis. J Psychoanal Groups 1:38–46, 1964

Despert JL: Technical approaches used in the study and treatment of emotional problems in children. Psychiatr Q 2:267–95, 1937

Despert JL: Delusional and hallucinatory experiences in children. Am J Psychiatr 104:528, 1948

Deutsch D: Group subgroup and individual therapy combined to treat the family. Roche Report 3:3, 1966

Deutsch D: Personal communication, 1966

Deutsch F: The associative anamnesis. Psychoanal Q 8:354–381, 1939

Deutsch F: Applied Psychoanalysis. New York, Grune & Stratton, 1949(a)

Deutsch F: Applied Psychoanalysis. Selected Objectives of Psychotherapy. New York, Grune & Stratton, 1949(b)

Deutsch F, Murphy WF: The Clinical Interview. Vol. 1, Diagnosis—A Method of Teaching Associate Exploration. Vol. 2, Therapy—A Method of Teaching Sector Psychotherapy. New York, International Universities Press, 1955 (1967)

Deutsch H: Neurosis and Character Type. Clinical Psychoanalytic Studies. New York, International Universities Press, 1965

Deutsch M: A theory of cooperation and competition. Hum Relations 2:129–152, 1949(a)

Deutsch M: The effects of competition on the group process. Hum Relations 2:199–223, 1949(b)

Deutsch M: Mechanism, organism, and society. Phil Sci 18:230–262, 1951

Dewald PA: Psychotherapy—A Dynamic Approach. New York, Basic Books, 1964

Dewald PA: Learning problems in psychoanalytic supervision. Compr Psychiatry 10:107–121, 1969

Dickel HA: The physician and the clinical psychologist. JAMA 195:121–126, 1966

Dicks HV: Experience with marital tensions seen in the psychological clinic. Br J Med Psychol 26:181–197, 1953

Diehl HS, Baker AB, Cowan DW: Cold vaccines, further evaluation. JAMA 115:593–594, 1940

Dies RR, Hess AK: An experimental investigation of cohesiveness in marathon and conventional group psychotherapy. J Abnorm Psychol 77:258–262, 1971

Diethelm O: Treatment in Psychiatry. Springfield, Ill, Thomas, 1950, p 177

DiFuria G, et al: A milieu therapy program in a state hospital. Neuropsychiatry 17:3–10, 1963

Dinkmeyer D: Developing Understanding of Self and Others. Play Kit and Manual, 1. Circle Pines, Minn, American Guidance Service, 1970

Dische S: Management of enuresis. Br Med J 3:33–36, 1971

Dittes JE: Extinction during psychotherapy of GSR accompanying "embarrassing" statements. J Abnorm Soc Psychol 55:187, 1957(a)

Dittes JE: Galvanic skin responses as a measure of patient's reaction to therapist's permissiveness. J Abnorm Soc Psychol 55:295–303, 1957(b)

Dixon HH, Dickel HK, Coen RA, Hangen GO: Clinical observations on tolserol in handling anxiety tension states. Am J Med Sci 220–23, 1950

Dobbs WH: Methadone treatment of heroin addicts. JAMA 218:1536, 1971

Dohrenwend BP, Bernard VW, Kolb LC: The orientation of leaders in an urban area toward problems of mental health. Am J Psychiatry 118:683–691, 1962

Dole VP, Nyswander M: A medical treatment. for diacetyl-morphine (heroin) addiction. JAMA 193:646–650, 1965

Dole VP, Nyswander M: Rehabilitation of heroin addicts after blockade with methadone. NY State J Med 66:2011–2017, 1966

Dollard J, Miller NE: Personality and Psychotherapy. New York, McGraw-Hill, 1950

Domhoff B: Night dreams and hypnotic dreams. Int J Clin Exper Hypnosis 12:159–168, 1964

Doniger S (ed): Religion and Human Behavior. New York, Association Press, 1954

Donner L, Guerney BG, Jr: Automated group desensitization for test anxiety. Behav Res Ther 7:1–13, 1969

Dorfman W: Masked depression. Dis Nerv Sys 22(5):Pt2, 41, 1961

Dorsett CH, Jones C: Architectural Aspects for the Community Mental Health Center. Bethesda, Md, Community Mental Facilities Branch, National Institute of Mental Health, 1967

Downing JJ, et al: Planning Programming and Design for the Community Mental Health Center. Western Institute for Research in Mental Health, 1966

Draper G: The concept of organic unity and psychosomatic medicine. JAMA 124:767–771, 1944

Dreikurs R: Techniques and dynamics of multiple psychotherapy. Psychiatr Q 24:788–799, 1950

Dreikurs R: Psychology in the Classroom. New York, Harper & Row, 1957

Dressel PL: Some approaches to evaluation. Personnel Guid J 31:284–287, 1953

Driscoll GP: Child Guidance in the Classroom. New York, Columbia University Press, 1955

DuBois P: The Psychic Treatment of Mental Disorders. New York, Funk & Wagnalls, 1909

DuBois P: Education of Self. New York, Funk & Wagnalls, 1911

Duhl LJ (ed): The Urban Condition. New York, Basic Books, 1963

Duncan M: Environmental therapy in a hospital for maladjusted children. Br J Delinq 3:248–286, 1953

Dunhan HW, Weinberg SK: The Culture of the State Mental Hospital. Detroit, Wayne University Press, 1960

Dunlap K: Habits: Their Making and Unmaking. New York, Liveright, 1932

Dunton WR: Occupation Therapy. Philadelphia, Saunders, 1915

Dunton WR: Prescribing Occupational Therapy (2d ed). Springfield, Ill., Thomas, 1945

Dupont H (ed): Educating Emotionally Disturbed Children: Readings. New York, Holt, 1969

Durkin H: The analysis of character traits in group therapy. Int J Group Psychother 1:133–143, 1951

Durkin H: Group dynamics and group psychotherapy. Int J Group Psychother 4:56–64, 1954

Durkin H: Acting out in group psychotherapy. Am J Orthopsychiatry 24:644, 1955

Durkin H: Towards a common basis for group dynamics. Group and therapeutic processes in group psychotherapy. Int J Group Psychother 7:115, 1957

Durkin H: The Group in Depth. New York, International Universities Press, 1964

Durkin H: Current problems of group therapy in historical content, in Wolberg LR, Aronson ML (eds): Group Therapy 1974: An Overview. New York, Stratton Intercontinental, 1974, pp 116–141

Durkin H: The development of systems theory and its implications for the theory and practice of group therapy, in Wolberg LR, Aronson ML (eds): Group Therapy 1975: An Overview. New York, Stratton Intercontinental, 1975, pp 8–20

Durkin H, et al: Acting out in group psychotherapy. Am J Psychother 12:87–105, 1948

Durkin H, Glatzer HT: Transference neurosis in group psychotherapy: The concept and the reality, in Wolberg LR, Schwartz EK (eds): Group Therapy 1973: An Overview. New York, Stratton Intercontinental, 1973, pp 129–144

Dykes HM: Evaluation of three anorexiants. JAMA 230:270–272, 1974

Dymond RF: Adjustment changes in the absence of psychotherapy. J Consult Psychol 19:103–107, 1955

Eaton A: Some implications and effects of intra-group acting out of pregenital conflicts. Int J Group Psychother 12:435, 1962

Ebaugh FG: Evaluation of interviewing techniques and principles of psychotherapy for the general practitioner. J Omaha Med-West Clin Soc 9:29–35, 1948

Edelson M: Ego Psychology. Group Dynamics and the Therapeutic Community. New York, Grune & Stratton, 1964

Edmonson BW, Amsel A: The effects of massing and distribution of extinction trials on the persistence of a fear-motivated instrumental response. J Comp Physiol Psychol 47:117–123, 1954

Efron R: The conditioned inhibition of uncinate fits, in Franks CM (ed): Conditioning Techniques in Clinical Practice and Research. New York, Springer, 1964, pp 132–143

Egan MH: Home treatment—an addition to our continuum of therapies, in Masserman JH (ed): Current Psychiatric Therapies, vol. 7. New York, Grune & Stratton, 1967

Ehrenwald J: New Dimensions of Deep Analysis. London, Allen & Unwin, 1954

Ehrenwald J: Neuroses in the Family and Patterns of Psychosocial Defense. New York, Hoeber, 1963

Einstein A: Ideas and Opinions. New York, Crown, 1954

Eisenbud J: Psychology of headache. Psychiatr Q 11:592–619, 1937

Eisenbud J: Psi and Psychoanalysis. New York, Grune & Stratton, 1970

Einstein S: Psychoanalytic education—a critical view from within. Psychiatr Op 9:31–36, 1972

Eisenstein VW: Differential psychotherapy of borderline states. Psychiatr Q 25:379–401, 1951

Eisenstein VW: Differential psychotherapy of borderline states, in Bychowski G, Despert JL (eds): Specialized Techniques in Psychotherapy. New York, Basic Books, 1952

Eisenstein VW: Neurotic Interaction in Marriage. New York, Basic Books, 1956

Eisler RM, Hersen M, Miller PM: Effects of modeling on components of assertive behavior. J Behav Ther Exp Psychiatry 4:1–6, 1973(a)

Eisler PM, Hersen M, Miller PM: Components of assertive behavior. J Clin Psychol 29:295–299, 1973(b)

Eisler PM, Hersen M, Miller PM: Shaping components of assertive behavior with instructions and feedback. Am J Psychiatry 131:12, 1974

Eisner BG: Notes on the use of drugs to facilitate group psychotherapy. Psychiatr Q 38:310–328, 1964

Eisner BG, Cohen S: Psychotherapy with LSD. J Nerv Ment Dis 126:127–528, 1958

Eissler KR: The Psychiatrist and the Dying Patient. New York, International Universities Press, 1955 (paperback, 1970)

Eissler KR: Citation in Lowenstein R: Remarks on some variations in psycho-analytic technique. Int J Psychoanal 39:203, 1958

Eissler KR: Medical Orthodoxy and the Future of Psychoanalysis. New York, International Universities Press, 1965

Ekstein R: On current trends in psychoanalytic training, in Lindner R (ed): Explorations in Psychoanalysis. New York, Julian, 1953, pp 230–265

Ekstein R: Report of the panel on the teaching of psychoanalytic technique. J Am Psychoanal Assoc 8:167–174, 1960

Ekstein R: Concerning the teaching and learning of psychoanalysis. J Am Psychoanal Assoc 17:312–332, 1969

Ekstein R, Motto RL: From Learning for Love to Love of Learning. New York, Brunner/Mazel, 1969

Ekstein R, Wallerstein R: The Teaching and Learning of Psychotherapy. New York, Basic Books, 1958 (rev ed, 1972)

Eliasberg WG: Psychotherapy in cancer patients. JAMA 147:525, 1951

Elkin M: Short-contact counseling in a conciliation court. Soc Casework 43:184–190, 1962

Ellen F: A psychiatric nurse's experience in community nursing. Perspect Psychiatr Care 3(6), 1965

Ellis A: Outcome of employing three techniques

of psychotherapy. J Clin Psychol 13:344–350, 1957

Ellis A: Neurotic interaction between marital partners. J Consult Psychol 5:24–28, 1958(a)

Ellis A: Rational psychotherapy. J Gen Psychol 59:35–49, 1958(b)

Ellis A: Reason and Emotion in Psychotherapy. New York, Lyle Stuart, 1962

Ellis A: An answer to some objections to rational-emotive psychotherapy. Psychotherapy 2:108–111, 1965

Ellis A: A weekend of rational encounter, in Burton A (ed): Encounter. San Francisco, Jossey-Bass, 1970

Ellis A: An experiment in emotional education. Educ Tech 11:61–64, 1971

Ellis A: My philosophy of psychotherapy. J Contemp Psychol 6:13–18, 1973

Ellis NR, Barnett CD, Pryer MW: Operant behavior in mental defectives: Exploratory studies. J Exp Anal Behav 3:63–69, 1960

Endicott NA, Endicott J: Improvement in untreated psychiatric patients. Arch Gen Psychiatry 9:575–585, 1963

Ends EJ, Page CW: A study of three types of group psychotherapy with hospitalized male inebriates. Q J Stud Alcohol 13:263–277, 1957

Enelow AJ, Adler L: Psychiatric skills and knowledge for the general practitioner. JAMA 189:91–96, 1964

English HB: Three cases of the "conditioned" fear response. J Abnorm Soc Psychol 24:221–225, 1924

English HB, English AC: A Comprehensive Dictionary of Psychological and Psychoanalytical Terms. New York, McKay, 1958, p 169

English OS: Who should be trained for psychotherapy? in Hoffman FH (ed): Teaching of Psychotherapy. International Psychiatry Clinics. Boston, Little, Brown, 1964, p 281

English OS, Hamper WW Jr, Bacon CD, Settlage CF: Direct Analysis and Schizophrenia: Clinical Observations and Evaluation. New York, Grune & Stratton, 1961

English OS, Pearson GHJ: Common Neuroses of Children and Adults. New York, Norton, 1937, p 119

Enright JB: An introduction to Gestalt techniques, in Fagan J, Shepherd IL (eds): Gestalt Therapy Now. Palo Alto, Calif, Science & Behavior Books, 1970

Erickson CE: A Basic Test for Guidance Workers. Englewood Cliffs, NJ, Prentice-Hall, 1947

Erickson MH: The investigation of a specific amnesia. Br J Med Psychol 13:143–150, 1933

Erickson MH: A study of experimental neurosis hypnotically induced in a case of ejaculation praecox. Br J Psychol 15:34–50, 1935

Erickson MH: Development of apparent unconsciousness during hypnotic reliving of a traumatic experience. Arch Neurol Psychiatry 38:1282–1288, 1937

Erickson MH: The successful treatment of a case of acute hysterical depression by a return under hypnosis to a critical phase of childhood. Psychoanal Q 10:583–609, 1941

Erickson MH: Hypnotic investigation of psychosomatic phenomena: A controlled experimental use of hypnotic regression in the therapy of an acquired food intolerance. Psychosom Med 5:67–70, 1943

Erickson MH, Hill LB: Unconscious mental activity in hypnosis-psychoanalytic implications. Psychoanal Q 13:60–78, 1944

Erickson MH, Kubie LS: The permanent relief of an obsessional phobia by means of communications with an unsuspected dual personality. Psychoanal Q 8:471–509, 1939

Erikson EH: Dramatics Production Test, in Murray HA, et al (eds): Explorations in Personality. New York, Oxford University Press, 1939, pp 552–582

Erikson EH: Studies in the interpretation of play, in Tomkins SS (ed): Contemporary Psychopathology. Cambridge, Harvard University Press, 1944

Erikson EH: Ego development and historical development, in Eissler RS, et al (eds): Psychoanalytic Study of the Child. New York, International Universities Press, 1946, pp 359–396

Erikson EH: Childhood and Society. New York, Norton, 1950, 1963

Erikson EH: Sex differences in the play configuration of preadolescents. Am J Orthopsychiatry 21:667–692, 1951

Erikson EH: Identity and the Life Cycle. New York, International Universities Press, 1959

Esdaile J: Hypnosis in Medicine and Surgery. New York, Julian, 1957

Esquibel AJ, et al: Hexafluorodiethyl ether (Indokolon): Its use as a convulsant in psychiatric treatment. J Nerv Ment Dis 126:530, 1958

Essig CF: Addiction to nonbarbiturate sedative and tranquilizing drugs. Clin Pharmacol Ther 5:334–343, 1964

Eustace CG: Rehabilitation: An evolving concept. JAMA 195:1129–1132, 1966

Euthanasia Education Council: A Living Will. New York, the Council, 1964

Evans FJ: In-patient analytic group therapy of neurotic and delinquent adolescents. Some specific problems associated with these groups. Psychother Psychosom 13:265–270, 1965

Evans FJ: Hypnosis and sleep, in Fromm E, Shor RE (eds): Hypnosis: Research Developments and Perspectives. Chicago, Aldine, 1972

Evans FJ, Reich LH, Orne MT: Optopinetic nystagmus, eye movements, and hypnotically induced hallucinations. J Nerv Ment Dis 152:419–431, 1972

Ewig CF: Newer sedative drugs that can cause states of intoxication and dependence of barbiturate type. JAMA 196:714–717, 1966

Eysenck HJ: The effects of psychotherapy: An evaluation. J Consult Psychol 16:319–324, 1952

Eysenck HJ: A reply to Luborsky's note. Br J Psychol 45:132–133, 1954

Eysenck HJ: The effects of psychotherapy: A reply. J Abnorm Soc Psychol 50:147–148, 1955

Eysenck HJ: The Dynamics of Anxiety and Hysteria. London, Routledge, 1957

Eysenck HJ: Learning theory and behavior therapy. J Ment Sci 105:61–75, 1959

Eysenck HJ: The effects of psychotherapy, in Eysenck HJ (ed): Handbook of Abnormal Psychology: An Experimental Approach. London, Pitman, 1960(a) pp 697–725

Eysenck HJ: Behaviour Therapy and Neuroses. Elmsford, NY, Pergamon, 1960(b)

Eysenck HJ: Conditioning and personality. Br J Psychol 53:299–305, 1962

Eysenck HJ: The outcome problem in psychotherapy: A reply. Psychother 1:97–100, 1964

Eysenck HJ: The effects of psychotherapy. Int J Psychiatry 1:99–142, 1965

Eysenck HJ: The Effects of Psychotherapy. New York, International Science Press, 1966

Eysenck HJ: The non-professional psychotherapist. Int J Psychiatry 3:150–153, 1967

Eysenck HJ: A mish-mash of theories. Int J Psychiatry 9:140–146, 1970

Eysenck HJ: Psychotherapy and the experimental approach. J Contemp Psychol 6:19–27, 1973

Eymiew A: Le Gouvernement du soi-même. Paris, Perrin, 1922

Ezriel H: A psychoanalytic approach to the treatment of patients in groups. J Ment Sci 96:774–779, 1950

Ezriel H: Notes on psychoanalytic group therapy: II. Interpretation and research. Psychiatry 15:119–126, 1952

Ezriel H: Role of transference in psychoanalytic group psychotherapy and other approaches to group treatment. Acta Psychother 7:101, 1959

Ezriel H: Psychoanalytic group therapy, in Wolberg LR, Schwartz EK (eds): Group Therapy 1973: An Overview. New York, Stratton Intercontinental, 1973, pp 183–210

Fabing HD, Hawkins JR, Moulton JAL: Clinical studies on alpha-(2-piperidyl) benzhydrol hydrochloride, a new antidepressant drug. Am J Psychiatry 111:832, 1955

Fagan J, Shepherd IL: Gestalt Therapy Now. Palo Alto, Calif, Science Behavior Books, 1970

Fairbairn WRD: Prolegomena to a psychology of art. Br J Psychol 28:288–303, 1938(a)

Fairbairn WRD: The ultimate basis of aesthetic experience. Br J Psychol 29:167–181, 1938(b)

Fairbairn WRD: Endopsychic structure considered in terms of object-relationships. Psychoanal Q 5:54, 1946(a)

Fairbairn WRD: Object-relationships and dynamic structure. Int J Psychoanal 17:30, 1946(b)

Fairbairn WRD: An Object-Relations Theory of the Personality. New York, Basic Books, 1954

Family Service Association of America: Psychiatric Consultation in the Family Service Agency. New York, the Association, 1956

Farau A: Fifty years of individual psychology. Compr Psychiatry 3:242–254, 1962

Farber L: Casework treatment of ambulatory schizophrenics. Soc Casework 39:9–17, 1958

Faris R, Dunham HW: Mental Disorders in Urban Areas. Chicago, University of Chicago Press, 1939

Farndale J: The Day Hospital Movement in Great Britain. Elmsford, NY, Pergamon, 1961

Farnsworth DL: Mental Health in College and University. Cambridge, Harvard University Press, 1957

Farnsworth DL, Blaine GB Jr (eds): Counseling and the College Student. Boston, Little, Brown, 1970

Farnsworth DL, Braceland F: Psychiatry, the Clergy and Pastoral Counseling. Collegeville, Minn, St. John's University Press, 1969

Farrell MP: Transference dynamics of group

psychotherapy. Arch Gen Psychiatry 6:66–76, 1962

Faucett EC: Multiple-client interviewing: A means of assessing family processes. Soc Casework 43:114–120, 1962

Fawcett MS: Motivating group therapy in narcotic addicts in a woman's prison. Int J Group Psychother 11:339–346, 1961

Feather BW, Rhoads JM: Psychodynamic Behavior Therapy. Arch Gen Psychiatry 26:496–511, 1972

Federn P: Psychoanalysis of psychosis. Psychiatr Q 17:3–17, 470–487, 1943

Federn P: Principles of psychotherapy in latent schizophrenia. Am J Psychother 1:129–145, 1947

Feifel H (ed): The Meaning of Death. New York, McGraw-Hill, 1959, pp 251–258

Feighner AC, Feighner JP: Multimodel treatment of the hyperkinetic child. Am J Psychiatry 131:459–462, 1974

Fein LG: The Changing School Scene: Challenge to Psychology. New York, Wiley, 1974

Feld M, Goodman JR, Guido JA: Clinical and laboratory observations on LSD-25. J Nerv Ment Dis 126:176, 1958

Feldman MP, MacCulloch MJ: The application of anticipatory-avoidance learning to the treatment of homosexuality. Behav Res Ther 2:165–183, 1965

Feldman PE: Psychotherapy and chemotherapy (amitriptyline) of anergic states. Dis Nerv Syst 22(5): Sect 2, 27, Suppl, 1961

Feldman Y: A casework approach toward understanding parents of emotionally disturbed children. Soc Casework 3:23–29, 1958

Felix RH: The dynamics of community mental health, in Panel Discussion on Creating a Climate Conducive to Mental Health, National Health Forum, Cincinnati, 1957

Felix RH: Second report on the relations between medicine and psychology. NY State District Branch Bull (American Psychiatric Association) December 1960

Felix RH: A comprehensive community mental health program, in Felix RH (ed): Mental Health and Social Welfare. New York, Columbia University Press, 1961

Fellows L, Wolpin M: High school psychology trainees in a mental hospital, in Guerney BG (ed): Psychotherapeutic Agents: New Roles for Nonprofessionals, Parents and Teachers. New York, Holt, 1969

Felsenfield N, et al: The Training of Neighborhood Workers. Washington, DC, Institute for Youth Studies, 1966

Fenichel O: Ten Years of the Berlin Psychoanalysis Institute, 1920–1930.

Fenichel O: Problems of Psychoanalytic Technique. Albany, NY, Psychoanalytic Quarterly, 1941

Fenichel O: The Psychoanalytic Theory of Neurosis. New York, Norton, 1945, p 582

Fensterheim H: Help without Psychoanalysis. New York, Stein & Day, 1971

Fensterheim H: Behavior therapy: Assertive training in groups, in Sager CS, Kaplan HS (eds): Progress in Group and Family Therapy. New York, Brunner/Mazel, 1972, pp 156–169

Ferenczi S: The Further Development of the Active Therapy in Psychoanalysis (1921). Further contributions to Psychoanalysis. London, Hogarth, 1950(a)

Ferenczi S: Contra-Indications to the "Active" Psychoanalytical Technique (1926). Further Contributions to Psychoanalysis. London, Hogarth, 1950(b)

Ferenczi S: The Elasticity of Psycho-Analytical Technique (1928). Further Contributions to Psychoanalysis. London, Hogarth, 1950(c)

Ferenczi S: The Future Development of the Active Therapy in Psychoanalysis (1921). Further Contributions to Psychoanalysis. London, Hogarth, 1950(d)

Ferenczi S: Further Contributions to the Theory and Technique of Psychoanalysis. New York, Basic Books, 1952 (London, Hogarth, 1960)

Ferenczi S: Present-day Problems in Psychoanalysis (1926), in Balint M (ed): The Problems and Methods of Psychoanalysis. New York, Basic Books, 1955

Ferenczi S: The elasticity of psychoanalytic technique (1928), in Balint M (ed): The Problems and Methods of Psychoanalysis. New York, Basic Books, 1955

Ferenczi S, Rank O: The development of psychoanalysis. Washington, DC, Nervous & Mental Disease Publishing Co, 1925

Ferreira AJ: The "double bind" and delinquent behavior. Arch Gen Psychiatry 3:359–367, 1960

Ferster CB: Positive reinforcement and behavioral deficits of autistic children. Child Dev 32:426–456, 1961

Ferster CB: Positive reinforcement and behavioral deficits of autistic children, in Franks CM (ed): Conditioning Techniques in Clinical Practice and Research. New York, Springer, 1964, pp 255–274

Ferster CB: Classification of behavioral pathology, in Ullman LP, Krasner L (eds): Behavior Modification Research. New York, Holt, 1965

Ferster CB, DeMyer MK: The development of performance in autistic children in an automatically controlled environment. J Chronic Dis 13:312–345, 1961

Feshbach S: The stimulating versus cathartic effects of a vicarious aggressive activity. J Abnorm Soc Psychol 63:381–385, 1961

Festinger L: Wish expectation and group performance as factors influencing level of aspiration. J Abnorm Soc Psychol 37:184–200, 1942

Festinger L: The role of group belongingness is a voting situation. Hum Relations 1:154–181, 1947

Fiddler GS: The role of occupational therapy in a multi-discipline approach to psychiatric illness. Am J Occupat Ther 6:1, 1957

Fiedler FE: A comparison of therapeutic relationships in psychoanalytic, non-directive, and Adlerian therapy. J Consult Psychol 14:436–445, 1950(a)

Fiedler FE: The concept of an ideal therapeutic relationship. J Consult Psychol 14:239–245, 1950(b)

Fiedler FE: Factor analyses of psychoanalytic non-directive and Adlerian therapeutic relationships. J Consult Psychol 15:32–38, 1951

Fiedler FE: Quantitative studies on the role of therapist's feelings toward their patients, in Mowrer H (ed): Psychotherapy: Theory and Research. New York, Ronald, 1953, pp 296–315

Fielding B, Mogul D: Sensitivity training of psychotherapists. Int Ment Health Res Newsletter 12:5, 1970

Fierman LB: Myths in the practice of psychotherapy. Arch Gen Psychiatry 12:412, 1965

Filmer BG, Hillson JS: Some child therapy practices. J Clin Psychol 15:105–106, 1959

Finesinger JE: Psychiatric interviewing. I. Some principles and procedures in insight therapy. Am J Psychiatry 105:187–195, 1948

Fink M, Abrams M: Selective drug therapies in clinical psychiatry: Neuroleptic, anxiolytic and antimanic agents, in Freeman AM, Kaplan HI (eds): Treating Mental Illness. New York, Atheneum, 1972

Fink P, Goldman M, Levick M: Art therapy: A new discipline. Pa Med 70:61, 1967

Finney BC: Some techniques for teaching psychotherapy. Psychother: Theory Res Prac 5:115–119, 1968

Fischer J, Gochros HL: Planned Behavior Change: Behavior Modification in Social Work. New York, Free Press, 1975

Fish B: Drug therapy in child psychiatry: Psychological aspects. Compr Psychiatry 1:55–61, 1960(a)

Fish B: Drug therapy in child psychiatry: Pharmacological aspects. Compr Psychiatry 1:212–227, 1960(b)

Fish B: Evaluation of psychiatric therapies in children. Paper presented at the American Psychopathologic Association meeting, February 1962

Fish B: Pharmacotherapy in children's behavior disorders, in Masserman JH (ed): Current Psychiatric Therapies, vol. 3. New York, Grune & Stratton, 1963, pp 82–90

Fish B: A topology of children's psychiatric disorders. I. Its application to a controlled evaluation. J Am Acad Child Psychiatry 4:32–52, 1965

Fish B: Treatment of children, in Kline NS, Lehman HE (eds): Supplement to International Psychiatric Clinics, vol. 2, no. 4. Boston, Little, Brown, 1966

Fisher C: Hypnosis in treatment of neuroses due to war and to other causes. War Med 4:563–576, 1943

Fisher C: REM and NREM nightmares. Int Psychiatry Clin 7:183–187, 1970

Fisher SH: The recovered patient returns to the community. Ment Hyg 42:463–473, 1958

Fisher SH, Beard JH: Fountain House: A psychiatric rehabilitation program, in Masserman JH (ed): Current Psychiatric Therapies, vol. 2. New York, Grune & Stratton, 1962, pp 211–218

Fisher SH, Beard JH, Goertzel V: Rehabilitation of the mental hospital patient: The Fountain House program. Int J Soc Psychiatry 4:295–298, 1960

Fishman HC: A study of efficacy of negative practice as a corrective for stammering. J Speech Dis 2:67–72, 1937

Fitzgerald RO: Conjoint marital psychotherapy: An outcome and follow-up study. Fam Process 8:260–271, 1969

Flach FF, Regan PF: Chlorpromazine and related phenothiazine derivatives, in Flach FF, Regan PF (eds): Chemotherapy in Emotional Disorders. New York, McGraw-Hill, 1960

Flade JK: Milieu therapy for the mentally ill. J Rehab 27:12–13, 1961

Fleck S: Family dynamics and origin of schizophrenia. Psychosom Med 22:333–344, 1960

Fleischl MF: The understanding and utilization of social and adjunctive therapies. Am J Psychother 26:255, 1962

Fleischl MF: Specific problems encountered in

social rehabilitation. Am J Psychother 18:660, 1964

Fleischl MF, Waxenberg SE: The therapeutic social club, a step toward social rehabilitation. Int Ment Health Res Newsletter 6(1), 1964

Fleischl MF, Wolf A: Techniques of social rehabilitation, in Masserman JH (ed): Current Psychiatric Therapies, vol. 7. New York, Grune & Stratton, 1967

Fleming J: Observations on the use of finger painting in the treatment of adult patients with personality disorders. Char Personal 8:301–310, 1940

Fleming J: What analytic work requires of an analyst: A job analysis. J Am Psychoanal Assoc 9:719–729, 1961

Fleming J: Evolution of a research project in psychoanalysis, in Gaskill HS (ed): Counterpoint. New York, International Universities Press, 1963

Fleming J: Teaching the basic skills of psychotherapy. Arch Gen Psychiatry 16:416–426, 1967

Fleming J, Benedek T: Supervision: A method of teaching psychoanalysis. Psychiatr Q 33:71–96, 1964

Fleming J, Benedek T: Psychoanalytic Supervision. New York, Grune & Stratton, 1966

Flescher J: On different types of countertransference. Int J Group Psychother 3/4:357–372, 1953

Flescher J: The economy of aggression and anxiety in group formation. Int J Group Psychother 7:31, 1957

Fletcher J: Indicators of humanhood: Tentative profile of man. Hastings Center Rep 2:1, 1972

Fletcher MI: The Adult and the Nursery School Child. Toronto, University of Toronto Press, 1974

Flumerfelt JM: Referring your patient to a psychiatrist. JAMA 146:1589–1591, 1951

Folsom GS: The music therapist's special contributions. Ment Hosp 14:638–642, 1963

Ford S, Ederer F: Breaking the cigarette habit. JAMA 194:139–142, 1965

Forem J: Transcental Meditation: Maharishi Mahesh Yogi and the Science of Creative Intelligence. New York, Dutton, 1973

Forstenzer HM: Problems in relating community programs to state hospitals. Am J Pub Health and the Nation's Health 51:1152–1157, 1961

Foster LE: Religion and psychiatry. Pastoral Psychol 1:7–13, 1950

Foulkes D: Psychology of Sleep. New York, Scribner, 1966

Foulkes SH: Introduction to Group Analytic Psychotherapy; Studies in the Social Integration of Individuals and Groups. London, Heinemann, 1948, pp 10–18, 28–31; New York, Grune & Stratton, 1949

Foulkes SH: Group-analytic dynamics with specific reference to psychoanalytic concepts. Int J Group Psychother 7:46, 1957

Foulkes SH: Group processes and the individual in the therapeutic group. Br J Med Psychol 34:23, 1961

Foulkes SH: Therapeutic Group Analysis. New York, International Universities Press, 1964

Foulkes SH, Anthony EJ: Group Psychotherapy. New York, Penguin, 1957, pp 31–43, 76–87

Fox R: Psychotherapeutics of alcoholism, in Bychowski G, Despert JL (eds): Specialized techniques in Psychotherapy. New York, Basic Books 1952, pp 239–260

Fox R: Antabuse as an adjunct to psychotherapy in alcoholism. NY State J Med 57:1540–1544, 1958

Fox R: No "sure" therapy for alcoholism. Med News, pp 14–15, July 14, 1961

Fox R: A multi-disciplinary approach to the treatment of alcoholism. Paper presented at the 122d Annual Meeting of the American Psychiatric Association, Atlantic City, NJ, May 1966

Foxx RM, Azrin NH: Restitution: A method of elimination of aggressive-disruptive behavior of retarded and brain-damaged patients. Behav Res Ther 10:15–27, 1972

Fraiberg SH: Psychoanalytic Principles in Casework with Children. New York, Family Service Association of America, 1954

Framo JL: The theory of the technique of family treatment of schizophrenia. Fam Process 1:119–131, 1962

Framo JL: Marriage therapy in a couples group. Semin Psychiatry 5:207–217, 1973

Frank GH: The literature on counter-transference: A survey. Int J Group Psychother 34:441–452, 1953

Frank JD: Problems of controls in psychotherapy as exemplified by the Psychotherapy Research Project of the Phipps Psychiatric Clinic, in Rubenstein EA, Parloff MB (eds): Research in Psychotherapy. Washington, DC, American Psychological Association, 1959

Frank JD: Persuasion and Healing: A Comparative Study of Psychotherapy. Baltimore, Johns Hopkins Press, 1961, pp 65–74 (rev ed, 1973)

Frank JD: The effects of psychotherapy. Int J Psychiatry 1:150–152, 1965

Frank JD: Psychotherapy: The restoration of morale. Am J Psychiatry 131:271–274, 1974

Frank JD, et al: Immediate and long-term symptomatic course of psychiatric outpatients. Am J Psychiatry 120:429–439, 1963

Frank JD, Gliedman LH, Imber SD, et al: Patient's expectancies and relearning as factors determining improvement in psychotherapy. Am J Psychiatry 115:961–968, 1959

Frank LK: Research for what? J Soc Issues, Suppl Ser 10, 1957

Frankel BL, Buchbinder R, Snyder F: Ineffectiveness of electrosleep in chronic primary insomnia. Arch Gen Psychiatry 29:563–568, 1973

Frankl VE: Arztliche Seelsorge. Vienna, Deuticke, 1948

Frankl VE: The Doctor and the Soul: An Introduction to Logotherapy. New York, Knopf, 1955

Frankl VE: The spiritual dimension in existential analysis and logotherapy. J Indiv Psychol 15:157–165, 1959

Frankl VE: Beyond self-actualization and self-expression. J Existen Psychiatry 1(1):5–20, 1960

Frankl VE: Basic concepts of logotherapy. Confin Psychiatr (Basel, Switz) 4:99–109, 1961(a)

Frankl VE: Logotherapy and the challenge of suffering. Rev Existen Psychol Psychiatry 1:3–7, 1961(b)

Frankl VE: From psychotherapy to logotherapy, in Walters A (ed): Psychology. Westminister, Md, Newman, 1963(a)

Frankl VE: Existential dynamics and neurotic escapism. Paper presented at the Conference on Existential Psychiatry, Toronto, Canada, May 6, 1962. J Existen Psychiatry 4:27–42, 1963(b)

Frankl VE: Fragments from the logotherapeutic treatment of four cases, in Burton A (ed): Modern Psychotherapeutic Practice. Palo Alto, Calif, Science & Behavior Books, 1965

Frankl VE: Logotherapy and existential analysis—a review. Am J Psychother 20:252–260, 1966

Frankl VE: Psychotherapy and Existentialism. New York, Washington Square Press, 1967

Franks CM: Conditioning Techniques in Clinical Practice and Research. New York, Springer, 1964

Franks CM: Behavior therapy, psychology and the psychiatrist. Am J Orthopsychiatry 35:145–151, 1965

Franks CM: Behavior Therapy: Appraisal and Status. New York, McGraw-Hill, 1969

Franks CM: Can behavior therapy find peace and happiness in a school of professional psychology? J Clin Psychol 28:11–15, 1974

Franks CM, Wilson GT: Annual Review of Behavioral Therapy, Theory, and Practice, vol. 3. New York, Brunner/Mazel, 1975

Fraser HF, et al: Degree of physical dependence induced by secobarbital or pentobarbital. JAMA 166:126–129, 1958

Fraser HF, Grider JA Jr: Treatment of drug addiction. Am J Med 14:571, 1953

Freedman AM: Drug Therapy in Behavior Disorders. Baltimore, Saunders, 1958

Freedman AM: Beyond "action for mental health." Paper presented at the symposium, Community Mental Health—Implementation of Recommendations of Joint Commission on Mental Illness and Health, at the 40th Annual Meeting of the American Orthopsychiatric Association, Washington, DC, March 8, 1963

Freedman AM: Drug addiction: An eclectic view. JAMA 197:156–160, 1966

Freedman AM: Opiate dependence, in Freedman AM, Kaplan HJ, Sadock BJ (eds): Comprehensive Textbook of Psychiatry II, vol. 2 (2d ed). Baltimore, Williams & Wilkins, 1975, pp 1298–1317

Freedman AM, Sager CJ, Rabiner E, Brotman RE: Response of adult heroin addicts to a total therapeutic program. Am J Orthopsychiatry 33:890–899, 1963

Freedman AM, Sharoff R: Crucial factors in the treatment of narcotics addiction. Am J Psychother 19:397–407, 1965

Freedman DA: Various etiologies of schizophrenia. Dis Nerv Syst 19:1–6, 1958

Freedman DX, Gordon RP: Psychiatry under siege: Attacks from without. Psychiatr Ann 3(11):23, 1973

Freedman MB, Sweet BS: Some specific features of group pschotherapy and their implications for selection of patients. Int J Group Psychother 4:355–368, 1954

Freeman FS: Theroy and Practice of Psychological Testing (3d ed). New York, Holt, 1962

Freeman H, Farndale J (eds): Trends in the Mental Health Services. New York, Macmillan, 1963

Freeman RW, Friedman I: Art therapy in a total treatment plan. J Nerv Ment Dis 124:421–425, 1956

Freeman WJ, Watts JW: Psychosurgery. Springfield, Ill, Thomas, 1942

French JRP Jr: The disruption and cohesion of

groups. J Abnorm Soc Psychol 36:361–377, 1941

French JRP Jr: Organized and unorganized groups under fear and frustration. University of Los Angeles Stud Child Welf 20:299–308, 1944

French LM: Psychiatric Social Work. London, Commonwealth Fund, 1940

French TM: The Integration of Behavior. Vol. 1, Basic Postulates. Chicago, University of Chicago Press, 1952

French TM, Fromm E: Dream Interpretation: A New Approach. New York, Basic Books, 1964

Freud A: Introduction to the Technique of Child Analysis. Washington, DC, Nervous & Mental Disease Publishing Co, 1928

Freud A: Psychoanalysis for Teachers and Parents. Stuttgart, Hippocrates Press, 1930

Freud A: The Ego and the Mechanisms of Defense. London, Hogarth, 1937

Freud A: Indications for child and analysis, in Eissler RS, et al (eds): The Psychoanalytic Study of the Child, vol. 1. New York, International Universities Press, 1945, pp 127–149

Freud A: The Psychoanalytical Treatment of Children: Technical Lectures and Essays. London, Imago, 1946

Freud A, Burlingham DT: Infants Without Families. New York, International Universities Press, 1944

Freud S: Introduction to Pfister's the Psychoanalytic Method, in Standard Edition, vol. 12. London, Hogarth, 1913, pp 329–331

Freud S: A General Introduction to Psychoanalysis. New York, Boni & Liveright, 1920

Freud S: On psychotherapy, in Collected Papers, vol. 1. London, Hogarth, 1924(a), p 249

Freud S: On the history of the psychoanalytic movement, in Collected Papers, vol. 1. London, Hogarth, 1924(b), p 287

Freud S: Papers on technique, in Collected Papers, vol. 2. London, Hogarth, 1924(c)

Freud S: Turnings in the ways of psychoanalytic therapy, in Collected Papers, vol. 2. London, Hogarth, 1924(d), p 392

Freud S: The Future of an Illusion. London, Hogarth, 1928

Freud S: The Ego and the Id. London, Hogarth, 1927

Freud S: Three Contributions to the Theory of Sex. Washington, DC, Nervous & Mental Disease Publishing Co, 1930

Freud S: New Introductory Lectures on Psychoanalysis. New York, Norton, 1933

Freud S: On narcissism, in Collected Papers, vol. 4. London, Hogarth, 1934, pp 30–59

Freud S: The Problem of Anxiety. New York, Norton, 1936 (1926 transl)

Freud S: Analysis terminable and interminable. Int J Psychoanl 18:373–405, 1937

Freud S: Three Contributions to the Theory of Sex, in The Basic Writings of Sigmund Freud. New York, Modern Library, 1938(a)

Freud S: The Interpretation of Dreams, in The Basic Writings of Sigmund Freud. New York, Modern Library, 1938(b)

Freud S: The Ego and Id. London, Hogarth, 1947 (orig publ 1923)

Freud S: An Outline of Psychoanalysis. New York, Norton, 1949, pp 63–64

Freud S: Analysis terminable and interminable, in Collected Papers, vol. 5. London, Hogarth, 1952, pp 316–357

Freud S: Psychoanalysis (1922), in Collected Papers, vol. 5. London, Hogarth, 1952, p 125

Freud S: Postscript to a discussion on lay analysis (1927), in Collected Papers, vol. 5. London, Hogarth, 1952, pp 205–214

Freud S: Mourning and Melancholia (1917), in Standard Edition, vol. 14. London, Hogarth, 1955

Freud S: The Interpretation of Dreams. New York, Basic Books, 1959; Wiley, 1961 (orig publ 1900)

Freud S: Resistances to Psychoanalysis, in Standard Edition, vol. 19. London, Hogarth, 1961

Freund K: Some problems in the treatment of homosexuality, in Eysenck HJ (ed): Behavior Therapy and the Neuroses. Elmsford, NY, Pergamon, 1960, pp 312–325

Freudlich D: Primal experience groups. A flexible structure. Int J Group Psychother 26:29–41, 1976

Freyhan FA: Schizophrenia. Initial separation rates for first admissions: Comparison of selected cohorts, 1908–58, in Rothlin E (ed): Neuro-psychopharmacology, vol. 2. Amsterdam, Elsevier, 1961, p 192

Freynan FA: On the psychopathology of psychiatric education. Compr Psychiatry 6:221–226, 1965

Freytag FF: The Hypnoanalysis of an Anxiety Hysteria. New York, Julian, 1959

Fried E: On Love and Sexuality. New York, Grove, 1962

Fried E: Some aspects of group dynamics and the analysis of transference and defenses. Int J Group Psychother 15:44–56, 1965

Friedell A: A reversal of the normal concentration of urine in children having enuresis. Am J Dis Child 33:717–721, 1927

Friedman AS: Family therapy as conducted in the home. Fam Process 1:132–145, 1962

Friedman DE, Silverstone JT: Treatment of phobic patients by systematic desensitization. Lancet 1:470–472, 1967

Friedman E: Nursing aspects of the treatment of lobotomized patients. Bull Menninger Clin 14:138, 1950

Friedman HJ: Patient-expectancy and symptom reduction. Arch Gen Psychiatry 8:61–76, 1963

Friedman HJ: Psychotherapy of borderline patients: The influence of theory on technique. Am J Psychiatry 132:1048–1052, 1975

Fromm E: Uber Methods and Aufgabe einer analytischen Sozialpsychologie. Ztschr. Soziale I, 1932

Fromm E: Authoritat und Familie, in Horkheimer M (ed): Socialpsychologischen. Paris, Alcan, 1936, pp 77–135, 230–238

Fromm E: Escape from Freedom. New York, Holt, 1941

Fromm E: Man for Himself. New York, Holt, 1947

Fromm E: Psychoanalysis and Religion. New Haven, Yale University Press, 1950

Fromm E: The Sane Society. New York, Holt, 1955

Fromm E: The Forgotten Language. New York, Harper & Row, 1959(a)

Fromm E: Sigmund Freud's Mission. New York, Harper & Row, 1959(b)

Fromm E: Value, psychology and human existence, in Maslow AE (ed): New Knowledge in Human Values. New York, Harper & Row, 1959(c)

Fromm-Reichmann F: Transference problems in schizophrenia. Psychoanal Q 8:412, 1939

Fromm-Reichmann F: Principles of Intensive Psychotherapy. Chicago, University of Chicago Press, 1950

Fromm-Reichmann F: Notes on the development of the treatment of schizophrenics by psychoanalytic psychotherapy, in Bychowski G, Despert JL (eds): Specialized Techniques in Psychotherapy. New York, Basic Books, 1952(a), pp 159–179

Fromm-Reichman F: Psychoanalysis and psychotherapy, in Bullard DM (ed): Selected Papers. Chicago, University of Chicago Press, 1952(b)

Fromm-Reichmann F: Psychoanalytic and general dynamic conceptions of theory and of therapy. J Am Psychoanal Assoc 2:711–721, 1954

Fuerst RW: Problems of short-time psychotherapy. Am J Orthopsychiatry 8:260, 1938 8:260, 1938

Fulkerson SE, Barry SR: Methodology and research on prognostic use of psychological tests. Psychol Bull 58:177–204, 1961

Fultz AF: Music therapy. Psychiatr Op 3:32–35, 1966

Furst W: Homogeneous versus heterogeneous groups. Int J Group Psychother 1:120–123, 1950

Fry WF, Heersema P: Conjoint family therapy: A new dimension in psychotherapy, in Kadis AL, Winick CH (eds): Topical Problems of Psychotherapy, vol. 5. New York, Karger, 1965, pp 147–153

Gadpaille WJ: Observations on the sequence of resistances in groups of adolescent delinquents. Int J Group Psychother 9:275–286, 1959

Gadpaille WJ: Adolescent concerns about homosexuality. Med Asp Hum Sex 17:105–106, 1973

Galdston I: The problem of medical and lay psychotherapy. The medical view. Am J Psychother 4:421, 1950

Galdston I: An existential analysis of the case of Miss L. Paper presented at the Mid-Winter Conference on Existential Psychiatry, New York, December 15, 1963

Gallant DM, Mielke DH, Spirtes MA, et al: Penfluridol: An efficacious long-acting oral antipsychotic compound. Am J Psychiatry 131:699–702, 1974

Gans RW: Group therapists and the therapeutic situation: A clinical evaluation. Int J Group Psychother 12:82–88, 1962

Gantt WH: The conditioned reflex function as an aid in the study of the psychiatric patient, in Franks CM (ed): Conditioning Techniques in Clinical Practice and Research. New York, Springer, 1964, pp 25–43

GAP Report No. 8: An Outline for Evaluation of a Community Program in Mental Hygiene. New York, Group for the Advancement of Psychiatry, 1949

GAP Report No. 34: The Consulting Psychiatrist in a Family Service Agency. New York, Group for the Advancement of Psychiatry, 1956(a)

GAP Report No. 35: The Psychiatrist in Mental Health Education. New York, Group for the Advancement of Psychiatry, 1956(b)

GAP Report No. 73: Psychotherapy and the Dual Research Tradition. New York, Group for the Advancement of Psychiatry, 1969

GAP Report No. 77: Toward Therapeutic Care—A Guide for Those Who Work with the Mentally Ill (2d ed). New York, Group for the Advancement of Psychiatry, 1970

GAP Report No. 93: The Community Worker: A Response to Human Need. New York, Group for the Advancement of Psychiatry, 1974

GAP Symposium No. 10: Urban America and the Planning of Mental Health Services. New York, Group for the Advancement of Psychiatry, 1964

GAP Symposium No. 11: Death and Dying: Attitudes of Patient and Doctor. New York, Group for the Advancement of Psychiatry, 1965

GAP Symposium No. 12: The Right to Die. New York, Group for the Advancement of Psychiatry, 1973

Gardner E: Newsletter. Psychiatric Socieity of Westchester, October 1965

Gardner G: Conflicting Needs and Models in Respect to the Delivery of Mental Health Service for Children. Washington, DC, National Institute of Mental Health, 1974

Gardner GE: Training of clinical psychologists. Round Table, 1951. The development of the clinical attitude. Am J Orthopsychiatry 22:162–169, 1952

Garfield SL: Research on client variables in psychotherapy, in Bergin AE, Garfield SL (eds): Handbook of Psychotherapy and Behavior Change: An Empirical Analysis. New York, Wiley, 1971

Garner HH: Brief psychotherapy. Int J Neuropsychiatry 1:616, 1965

Garner HH: Psychotherapy: Confrontation Problem-Solving Techniques. St Louis, Green, 1970

Garrett A: Counseling Methods for Personnel Workers. New York, Family Welfare Association of America, 1945

Garrett A: Psychiatric consultation. Am J Orthopsychiatry 26:234–240, 1956

Garrett A: Modern casework: The contributions of ego psychology, in Parad HJ (ed): Ego Psychology and Dynamic Casework. New York, Family Service Association of America, 1958, pp 38–52

Garrison EA, Forward in Leninger MM (ed): Contemporary Issues in Mental Health Nursing. Boston, Little, Brown, 1973

Gaston ET (ed): Music in Therapy. New York, Macmillan, 1968

Gayle R, Neale C: Subshock insulin therapy. Dis Nerv Syst 10:231, 1949

Geertsma RH, et al: Auditory and visual dimensions of externally mediated self-observation. J Nerv Ment Dis 148:437–448, 1969

Geertsma RH, Reivich RS: Repetitive self-observation by videotape playback. J Nerv Ment Dis 141:29–41, 1965

Geijerstam G: The psychosomatic approach in gynecological practice. Acta Obst Gynecol Scand 30:346–390, 1960

Geist J, Gerber NM: Joint interviewing: A treatment technique with marital partners. Soc Casework 41:76–83, 1960

Gelb LA: Rehabilitation of mental patients in a comprehensive rehabilitation center. NY State J Med 60:2404–2411, 1960

Gelb LA, Ullman M: "Instant psychotherapy" in an outpatient psychiatric clinic—philosophy and practice. Paper presented at the 122d Annual Meeting of the American Psychiatric Association, Atlantic City, NJ, May 1966

Geller J: Parataxic distortions in the initial stages of group relationships. Int J Group Psychother 12:27–34, 1962

Gellhorn E, et al: Emotions and Emotional Disorders: A Neurophysiological Study. New York, Harper & Row, 1963

Gendzel IB: Marathon group therapy and nonverbal methods. Am J Psychiatry 127:286–290, 1970

Gendzel IB: Marathon group therapy: Rationale and techniques, in Masserman JH (ed): Current Psychiatric Therapies, vol. 12. New York, Grune & Stratton, 1972

Geocaris K: The patient as a listener. Arch Gen Psychiatry 2:81–88, 1960

Geppert TV: Management of nocturnal enuresis by conditioned response, in Franks CM (ed): Conditioning Techniques in Clinical Practice and Research. New York, Springer, 1964, pp 189–195

Gershon S, Shopsin B: Lithium: Its Role in Psychiatric Research and Treatment. New York, Plenum, 1973

Gerty FJ: Roles and responsibilities in mental health planning. Am J Psychiatry 121:835–838, 1965

Gerty FJ, Holloway JW Jr, MacKay EP: Licensure or certification of clinical psychologists. JAMA 148:271–273, 1952

Gerwitz JL: A learning analysis of the effects of normal stimulation, privation, and deprivation on the acquisition of social motivation and attachment, in Foss BM (ed): Determinants of Infant Behavior. New York, Wiley, 1961, pp 213–283

Gibb JR: The role of a consultant. J Soc Issues 15:1–4, 1959(a)

Gibb JR: Lippitt R (eds): Consulting with groups and organizations. J Soc Issues 15(11):2, 1959(b)

Gilbert R: Functions of the consultant. Teachers Coll Rec 61:117–187, 1960

Gilbertson EC, Williamson EM: The consultation process in public health nursing. Pub Health Nurs 44:146–147, 1952

Giles HH, McCutchen SP, Zeckiel AN: Exploring the Curriculum. New York, Harper & Row, 1942, p 5

Gill MM: Ego psychology and psychotherapy. Psychoanal Q 20:62–71, 1951

Gill MM: Psychoanalysis and exploratory psychotherapy. J Am Psychoanal Assoc 2:771–797, 1954

Gill MM, Brenman M: Treatment of a case of anxiety hysteria by a hypnotic technique employing psychoanalytic principles. Bull Menninger Clin 7:163–171, 1943

Gill MM, Brenman M: Hypnosis and Related States. New York, International Universities Press, 1959

Gill MM, Newman R, Redlich FC: The Initial Interview in Psychiatric Practice. New York, International Universities Press, 1954

Gilliland EG: Uses of music therapy. Int J Group Psychother 14:68–72, 1961

Gilliland EG: Progress in music therapy. Rehab Lit 23:298–306, 1962

Gillison TH, Skinner JC: Treatment of nocturnal enuresis by the electric alarm. Br Med J 2:1268–1272, 1958

Ginott HG: Group Psychotherapy with Children. New York, McGraw-Hill, 1961

Ginott HG: Driving children sane. Today's Educ 62:20–25, 1973

Ginsburg EL: The Training and Function of a Psychiatric Social Worker in a Clinical Setting. Transactions of the First Conference. New York, Josiah Macy, Jr, Foundation, 1947, pp 31–40

Gitelson M: Clinical experience with play therapy. Am J Orthopsychiatry 8:466, 1939

Gitelson M: Problems of psychoanalytic training. Psychoanal Q 17:198–211, 1948

Gitelson M: The emotional position of the analyst in the psychoanalytic situation. Int J Psychoanal 33:1–10, 1952

Gitelson M: On the identity crisis in American psychoanalysis. J Am Psychoanal Assoc 12:451–476, 1964

Glad D: Operational Values in Psychotherapy. New York, Oxford University Press, 1959

Gladstone HP: A study of techniques of psychotherapy with youthful offenders. Psychiatry 25:147–159, 1962

Gladstone HP: Psychotherapy with adolescents: Theme and variations. Psychiat Q 2:304–309, 1964

Gladstone RD: Do maladjusted teachers cause maladjustment? A review. J Except Child 15:65–70, 1948

Glasscote RM, Fishman ME: Mental Health on the Campus: A Field Study. Washington, DC, American Psychiatric Association, 1973

Glasscote RM, Sanders D, Forstenzer HM, Foley AR: The Community Mental Health Centers: An Analysis of Existing Models. Washington, DC, Joint Information Service of American Psychiatric Association and the National Association for Mental Health, 1964

Glasscote RM, Sussex JN, Cumming E, Smith LH: The Community Mental Health Centers: An Interim Appraisal. Washington, DC, Joint Information Service of the American Psychiatric Association and the National Association for Mental Health, 1969

Glasser W: Reality Therapy: A New Approach to Psychiatry. New York, Harper & Row, 1965

Glasser W, Zunin LM: Reality therapy, in Masserman JH (ed): Current Psychiatric Therapies, vol. 12. New York, Grune & Stratton, 1972

Glatzer HT: Transference in group psychotherapy. Am J Orthopsychiatry 22:449–509, 1952

Glatzer HT: Handling transference resistance in group psychotherapy. Psychoanal Rev 40:36, 1953

Glatzer HT: The relative effectiveness of clinically homogeneous and heterogeneous psychotherapy groups. Int J Group Psychother 6:258, 1956

Glatzer HT: Notes on the preoedipal fantasy. Am J Orthopsychiatry April 1959(a)

Glatzer HT: Analysis of masochism in group therapy. Int J Group Psychother 9:158–166, 1959(b)

Glatzer HT: Narcissistic problems in group psychotherapy. Int J Group Psychother 12(4), 1962

Glatzer HT: Practice of group psychotherapy based on classical psychoanalytic concepts. Am J Orthopsychiatry 34:395, 1964

Glatzer HT: Aspects of transference in group therapy. Int J Group Psychother 15:167–177, 1965

Glatzer HT, Pederson-Krag G: Relationship group therapy with a mother of a problem child, in Slavson SR (ed): The Practice of Group Therapy. New York, International Universities Press, 1947, p 219

Glauber IP: Dynamic therapy for the stutterer, in Bychowski G, Despert JL (eds): Specialized

Techniques in Psychotherapy. New York, Basic Books, 1952, pp 207–238

Glidewell JC: The entry problem in consultation. J Soc Issues 15:51–59, 1959

Gliedman LH, Nash EH, Imber SD, et al: Reduction of symptoms by pharmacologically inert substances and by short-term psychotherapy. Arch Neurol Psychiatry 79:345–351, 1958

Glover BH: The new nurse-therapist. Paper presented at the 122d Annual Meeting of the American Psychiatric Association, Atlantic City, NJ, May 1966

Glover E: Lectures on technique in psychoanalysis. Int J Psychoanal 8/9, 1927

Glover E: The therapeutic effect of inexact interpretations: A contribution to the theory of suggestion. Int J Psychoanal 12:397–411, 1931

Glover E: An Investigation of the Technique of Psychoanalysis. London, Bailliere, 1940

Glover E: Research methods in psychoanalysis. Int J Psychoanal 33:403, 1952

Glover E: The Technique of Psychoanalysis. New York, International Universities Press, 1955 (rev ed, 1968)

Glover E: Functional Group of Delinquent Disorders: On the Early Development of Mind. New York, International Universities Press, 1956

Glover E: Freudian or neo-Freudian. Psychiatr Q 33:97–109, 1964

Glover E: The effects of psychotherapy. Int J Psychiatry 1:158–161, 1965

Glover E, Fenichel O, Strachey J, et al: On the theory of therapeutic results of psychoanalysis. Symposium. Int J Psychoanal 18:125–189, 1937

Glueck BC, Stroebel CF: The computer and the clinical decision process. Am J Psychiatry 125:2, 1969

Glueck BC, Stroebel CF: Biofeedback and meditation in the treatment of psychiatric illnesses, in Masserman JH (ed): Current Psychiatric Therapies, vol. 15. New York, Grune & Stratton, 1975(a)

Glueck BC, Stroebel CF: Computers and clinical psychiatry, in Freedman AM, Kaplan HI, Sadock BJ (eds): Comprehensive Textbook of Psychiatry II, vol. 1 (2d ed). Baltimore, Williams & Wilkins, 1975(b), pp 413–428

Glueck S, Glueck ET: Unraveling Juvenile Delinquency. Cambridge, Harvard University Press, 1950

Glynn JD, Harper P: Behaviour in transvestism. Lancet 1:619, 1961

Godenne GD: Outpatient adolescent group psychotherapy. Am J Psychiatry 18:584, 1964

Godenne GD: Outpatient adolescent group psychotherapy. I. Review of the literature on use of co-therapists, psychodrama, and parent group therapy. Am J Psychol 19:40–53, 1965

Goertzel V, Beard JH, Pilnick S: Fountain House Foundation: Case study of an expatient club. J Soc Issues 16:54–61, 1960

Golan SE, Eisdorfer C: Handbook of Community Mental Health. New York, Appleton-Century-Crofts, 1972

Goldberg C: Peer influence in contemporary group psychotherapy, in Wolberg LR, Aronson ML (eds): Group Therapy 1975: An Overview. New York, Stratton Intercontinental, 1975, pp 232–241

Goldberg HL: Home treatment. Psychiatr Ann 3:59–61, 1973

Goldberg HL, DiMascio A, Chaudhary B: A clinical evaluation of prolixin enanthate. Psychosomatics 2:173–177, 1970

Goldberg SC: Prediction of response to antipsychotic drugs, in Efron D (ed): Psychopharmacology. A Review of Progress, 1957–1967. Pub Health Service, Publ No. 1836. Washington, DC, U.S. Government Printing Office, 1968, pp 1101–1118

Goldfarb AI: Psychotherapy of aged persons. IV. One aspect of the psychodynamics of the therapeutic situation with aged patients. Psychoanal Rev 42:180–187, 1955

Goldfarb AI: Minor maladjustments in the aged, in Arieti S (ed): American Handbook of Psychiatry, vol. 1. New York, Basic Books, 1959, pp 378–397

Goldfarb AI: Management of aged patients who are mentally ill. Roche Report 1(7), 1964

Goldfarb AI, Wolk RL: The response of group psychotherapy upon recent admissions to a mental hospital. Paper presented at the 122d Annual Meeting of the American Psychiatric Association, Atlantic City, NJ, May 1966

Goldfarb W: Infant rearing and problem behavior. Am J Orthopsychiatry 13:249–265, 1943

Goldiamond I: Fluent and nonfluent speech (stuttering): Analysis and operant techniques for control, in Krasner L, Ullman LP (eds): Research in Behavior Modification. New York, Holt, 1965

Goldman D: Drugs in treatment of psychoses: Clinical studies, in Solomon P (ed): Psychiatric Drugs. New York, Grune & Stratton, 1966

Goldman G: Reparative psychotherapy, in Rado S, Daniels GE (eds): Changing Concepts of

Psychoanalytic Medicine. New York, Grune & Stratton, 1956, pp 101–113

Goldman RK, Mendelsohn GA: Psychotherapeutic change and social adjustment; a report of a national survey of psychotherapists. J Abnorm Psychol 74:164–172, 1969

Goldstein AP: Patient's expectancies and nonspecific therapy as a basis for (un) spontaneous remission. J Clin Psychol 16:399–403, 1960

Goldstein AP: Therapist-Patient Expectancies in Psychotherapy. Elmsford, NY, Pergamon, 1962

Goldstein AP, Heller K, Sechrest LB: Psychotherapy and the Psychology of Behavior Change. New York, Wiley, 1966

Goldstein AP, Wolpe J: Behavior therapy in groups, in Kaplan HI, Sadock BJ (eds): Comprehensive Group Psychotherapy. Baltimore, Williams & Wilkins 1971, pp 292–327

Goldstein SE: Marriage and Family Counseling. New York, McGraw-Hill, 1945.

Goldston SE (ed): Concepts of Community Psychiatry: A Framework for Training. Pub Health Service Pub No. 1319. Bethesda, Md, National Institute of Mental Health, 1965

Golton M: Private practice in social work, in Encyclopedia of Social Work, vol. 2. New York, National Association of Social Workers, 1971

Gomberg RM: Family-oriented treatment of marital problems. Soc Casework 37:3–10, 1956

Gondor EI: Art and Play Therapy. New York, Doubleday, 1954

Good Education for Young Children. Flushing, NY, New York State Council for Early Childhood Education, 1947

Goodman G: An experiment with companionship therapy: College students and troubled boys—assumptions, selection and design, in Guerney BG (ed): Psychotherapeutic Agents: New Roles for Nonprofessionals, Parents and Teachers. New York, Holt, 1969

Goodman JA: Social work services for alcoholics and their families. California's Health, December 1, 1962

Goodman M: Ethical guidelines for encounter group leadership. A committee report for the New Jersey State Psychological Association, 1972

Goodman M, et al: Resistance in group psychotherapy enhanced by the countertransference reactions of the therapists. Int J Group Psychother 14:322, 1964

Goodman M, Marks D: Oral regression as manifested and treated analytically in group psychotherapy. Int J Group Psychother 13:3, 1963

Goodwin HM, Mudd EH: Marriage counseling, in Ellis A, Abarbanel A (eds): Encyclopedia of Sexual Behavior. New York, Hawthorn Books, 1961, pp 685–695

Gordon DE: The function of the consultant. Nurs Outlook 1:575–577, 1953

Gordon T: Group Centered Leadership: A Way of Releasing the Creative Power of Groups. Boston, Houghton Mifflin, 1955

Gordon T, Grummon DL, Rogers CR, Seeman J: Developing a program of research in psychotherapy, in Rogers CR, Dymond RF (eds): Psychotherapy and Personality Changes. Chicago, University of Chicago Press, 1954, pp 12–34

Gorton JV: A Guide for the Evaluation of Psychiatric Nursing Services. New York, National League for Nursing, 1961

Goshen CR: New concepts of psychiatric care with special reference to the day hospital. Am J Psychiatry 115:808, 1959

Gottesfeld H: The Critical Issues of Community Mental Health. New York, Behavioral Publications, 1972

Gottfried AW, Verdicchio FG: Modifications of hygienic behaviors using reinforcement therapy. Am J Psychother 28:122–128, 1974

Gottschalk LA, Mayerson P, Gottlieb AA: Prediction and evaluation of outcome in an emergency brief psychotherapy clinic. J Nerv Ment Dis 144:77, 1967

Gough HG: A sociological theory of psychotherapy. Am J Soc 53:359–366, 1948

Gould I: Specialized group techniques with the narcotics addict. Paper presented at the Gracie Mansion Conference on Drug Addiction, New York City, February 4, 1965

Goulding RL: Four models of transactional analysis. Int J Group Psychother 26:385–392, 1976

Grad B: Some biological effects of the "laying on of hands": A review of experiments with animals and plants. J Am Soc Psychical Res 59:95–127, 1965

Graham SR: The effects of psychoanalytically oriented psychotherapy on levels of frequency and satisfaction in sexual activity. J Clin Psychol 16:94–95, 1960

Gralnick A: Psychoanalysis and the treatment of adolescents in a private hospital, in Masserman JH (ed): Science and Psychoanalysis, vol. 9. New York, Grune & Stratton, 1966, pp 102–108

Gralnick A, D'Elia F: A psychoanalytic hospital becomes a therapeutic community. Hosp Community Psychiatry, May 1969

Grant N Jr: Art and the Delinquent. New York, Exposition Press, 1959

Gray W: Psychiatry and general systems—an introduction. Paper presented at the 122d Annual Meeting of the American Psychiatric Association, Atlantic City, NJ, May 1966

Green DO, Reimer DR: The methohexital-methylphenidate interview. Bull Menninger Clin 38:76–77, 1974

Green RJ: Therapy with hard science professionals. J Cont Psychother 8:52–56, 1976

Green S: Psychoanalytic contributions to casework treatment of marital problems. Soc Casework 35:419–424, 1954

Greenacre P: Trauma, Growth and Personality. New York, Norton, 1952

Greenacre P, et al: Symposium on the evaluation of therapeutic results. Int J Psychoanal 29:7–33, 1948

Greenbaum H: Combined psychoanalytic therapy with negative therapeutic reactions, in Rifkin AH (ed): Schizophrenia in Psychoanalytic Office Practice. New York, Grune & Stratton, 1957, pp 56–65

Greenblatt M: Formal and informal groups in a therapeutic community. Int J Group Psychother 11:398–409, 1961

Greenblatt M: Mental health consultation, in Freedman AM, Kaplan HI, Sadock BJ (eds): Comprehensive Textbook of Psychiatry (2d ed). Baltimore, Williams & Wilkins, 1975, pp 2346–2354

Greenblatt M, Grosser GH, Wechsler H: Differential response of hospitalized depressed patients to somatic therapy. Am J Psychiatry 120:935–943, 1964

Greenblatt M, Levinson DJ, Williams RH (eds). The Patient and the Mental Hospital. New York, Free Press, 1957

Greenblatt M, Simon B: Rehabilitation of the Mentally Ill. Pub No. 58. Washington, DC, American Association for the Advancement of Science, 1959

Greenblatt M, York RH, Brown EL: From Custoidal to Therapeutic Care in Mental Hospitals. New York, Russell Sage Foundation, 1957

Greene BL: Marital disharmony: Concurrent analysis of husband and wife. Dis Nerv Syst 21:1–6, 1960

Greene BL (ed): The Psychotherapies of Marital Disharmony. New York, Free Press, 1965

Greene BL: A Clinical Approach to Marital

Problems: Evaluation and Management. Springfield, Ill, Thomas, 1970

Greene BL: Psychiatric therapy of marital problems: Modern techniques, in Masserman JH (ed): Current Psychiatric Therapies, vol. 12. New York, Grune & Stratton, 1972

Greene BL, et al: Treatment of marital disharmony where the spouse has a primary affective disorder (manic-depressive illness). I. General review—100 couples. J Marr Fam Counsel 1:82–101, 1975

Greene BL, Solomon AP: Marital disharmony: Concurrent psychoanalytic therapy of a husband and wife by the same psychiatrist (the triangular transference transactions). Am J Psychother 17:443–456, 1963

Greenson R: The Technique and Practice of Psychoanalysis. New York, International Universities Press, 1967

Greenspoon J: in Dollard J, Miller NG (eds): Personality and Psychotherapy. New York, McGraw-Hill, 1950

Greenspoon J: The effect of two nonverbal stimuli on the frequency of members of two verbal response classes. Am Psychol 9:384, 1954(a)

Greenspoon J: The reinforcing effect of two spoken sounds on the frequency of two responses. Am J Psychol 68:409–416, 1954(b)

Greenwald H: The integration of behavioral, existential and psychoanalytic therapy into direct decision therapy. J Contemp Psychol 4:37–43, 1971

Greenwald H: Decision therapy. Personal Growth, No. 20, 1974

Greenwald JA: The ground rules in gestalt therapy. J Contemp Psychother 5:3–12, 1972

Gregg DE: The therapeutic roles of the nurse. Perspect Psychiatr Care 1:18–24, 1963

Griffiths R: A Study of Imagination in Early Childhood and Its Function in Mental Development. London, Routledge, 1935

Grinberg L: The problems of supervision in psychoanalytic education. Int J Psychoanal 51:371–304, 1970

Grinker RR: A demonstration of the transactional model, in Stein MI (ed): Contemporary Psychotherapies. New York, Free Press, 1961

Grinker RR: Psychiatry rides madly in all directions. Arch Gen Psychiatry 10:228–237, 1964

Grinker RR: Complementary psychotherapy—treatment of "associated" pairs. Paper presented at the 122d Annual Meeting of the American Psychiatric Association, Atlantic City, NJ, May 1966

Grinker RR, et al: Psychiatric Social Work: A Transactional Casebook. New York, Basic Books, 1961, pp 11–14

Grinker RR, Spiegel JP: Men Under Stress. Philadelphia, Blakiston, 1945

Grinker RR, Werble B, Drye RC: The Borderline Syndrome. New York, Basic Books, 1968

Groom D: Some applications of psychiatry in general medicine. JAMA 135:403, 1947

Gross M, Hitchman IC, Reeves WP, et al: Discontinuation of treatment with ataractic drugs, in Wortis J (ed): Recent Advances in Biological Psychiatry, vol. 3. New York, Grune & Stratton, 1961, p 44

Grosser C: A polemic on advocacy: Past, present, and future, in Kahn AS (ed): Shaping New Social Work. New York, Columbia University Press, 1973

Grotjahn M: Brief psychotherapy on psychoanalytic principles. Illinois Psychiatry 2:1, 1942

Grotjahn M: The role of identification in psychiatric and psychoanalytic training. Psychiatry 12:141–151, 1949

Grotjahn M: The process of maturation in group psychotherapy and in the group therapist. Psychiatry 13:63–67, 1950

Grotjahn M: Special concepts of countertransference in analytic group psychotherapy. Int J Group Psychother 3:4, 407–416, 1953

Grotjahn M: Problems and techniques of supervision. Psychiatry 18:9–15, 1955

Grotjahn M: The efficacy of group therapy in a case of marriage neurosis. Int J Group Psychother 9:420–428, 1959

Grotjahn M: Psychoanalysis and the Family Neurosis. New York, Norton, 1960

Grotjahn M: Selected clinical observations from psychoanalytic group psychotherapy, in Wolberg LR, Aronson ML (eds): Group Therapy 1973: An Overview. New York, Stratton Intercontinental, 1973, pp 43–54

Grotjahn M, Treusch JD: A new technique of psychosomatic consultations. Psychoanal Rev 44:176–92, 1957

Gruenberg EM: Application of control methods to mental illness. Am J Pub Health & Nation's Health 47:944–952, 1957

Grummon DL: Personality changes as a function of time in persons motivated for therapy, in Rogers CR, Dymond RF (eds): Psychotherapy in Personality Changes. Chicago, University of Chicago Press, 1954

Grunebaum H (ed): The Practice of Community Mental Health. Boston, Little, Brown, 1970

Grunebaum MG: A study of learning problems of children: Casework implications. Soc Casework 42:461–468, 1961

Guerney BG, Jr: Filial therapy: Description and rationale. J Consult Psychol 28:304–310, 1964

Guerney BG, Jr (ed): Psychotherapeutic Agents: New Roles for Nonprofessionals, Parents and Teachers. New York, Holt, 1969

Guiora AZ, Hammann A, Mann RD: The continuous case seminar. Psychiatry 30:44–59, 1967

Gunderson JG, Carpenter WT Jr, Strauss JS: Borderline and schizophrenic patients: A comparative study. Am J Psychiatry 132:1257–1264, 1975

Gunderson JG, Singer MT: Defining borderline patients. Am J Psychiatry 132:1–10, 1975

Gurin G, et al: American's View Their Mental Health. New York, Basic Books, 1960

Gustin JC: Supervision in psychotherapy. Psychoanal & Psychoanal Rev 45:63–72, 1958

Gutheil EA: Psychoanalysis and brief psychotherapy. J Clin Psychopath 6:207, 1945

Gutheil EA: Music as an adjunct to psychotherapy. Paper presented at the Association for the Advancement of Psychotherapy, New York, February 27, 1953

Gutheil EA: Music as an adjunct to psychotherapy. Am J Psychother 8:94–109, 1954

Guze SB, Murphy GE: An empirical approach to psychotherapy: The agnostic position. Am J Psychiatry 120:53–57, 1963

Gyomroi EL: The analysis of a young concentration camp victim, in Eissler RS, et al (eds): The Psychoanalytic Study of the Child, vol. 18. New York, International Universities Press, 1963, pp 484–510

Haas LJ: Practical Occupational Therapy. Milwaukee, Bruce, 1946

Hadden SB: Counter-transference in the group psychotherapist. Int J Group Psychother 3:417, 1953

Hader M: Psychotherapy for certain psychotic states in geriatric patients. J Am Geriatr Soc 12:607–617, 1964

Hadfield JA: Functional Nerve Disease. London, Crichton-Miller, 1920

Hagelin A, Lazar P: The Flomp method. Int Ment Health Res Newsletter 15:1–8, 1973

Haggard EA, Hiken JR, Isaacs KS: Some effects of recording and filming on the psychoanalytic process. Psychiatry 28:169–191, 1965

Hain JD, Smith BM, Stevenson I: Effectiveness

and processes of interviewing with drugs. J Psychiatr Res 4:95–106, 1966

Hald J, Jacobson E, Larsen V: Sensitizing effect on tetraethylthiuramdisulphide (antabuse) to ethyl alcohol. Acta Pharmacol Toxicol 4:285, 1948

Haley J: The family of the schizophrenic: A model system. J Nerv Ment Dis 129:357–374, 1959(a)

Haley J: An interactional description of schizophrenia. Psychiatry 22:321–332, 1959(b)

Haley J: Control in psychotherapy with schizophrenics. Arch Gen Psychiatry 5:340–353, 1961

Haley J: Family experiments: A new type of experimentation. Fam Process 1:265–293, 1962(a)

Haley J: Whither family therapy? Fam Process 1:69–103, 1962(b)

Haley J: Marriage therapy. Arch Gen Psychiatry 8:213–234, 1963(a)

Haley J: Strategies of Psychotherapy. New York, Grune & Stratton, 1963(b)

Haley J: An interactional description of schizophrenia, in Jackson D (ed): Communication, Family and Marriage, vol. 1. Palo Alto, Calif, Science & Behavior Books, 1968

Hall BH, Gassert RG: Psychiatry and Religious Faith. New York, Viking, 1964

Hall RV, Lund D, Jackson D: Effects of teacher attention on study behavior. J Appl Behav Anal 1:1–12, 1968

Halleck SL: The Politics of Therapy. New York, Science House, 1971

Halleck SL, Miller MH: The consultation; questionable social precedents of some current practice. Am J Psychiatry 20:164–169, 1963

Halpern H, Lesser L: Empathy in infants, adults, and psychotherapists. Psychoanal Rev 47:32–42, 1960

Hamburger B: Analysis of eleven school projects undertaken by community mental health consultants at the Postgraduate Center for Mental Health. Transnatl Ment Health Res Newsletter 18(2):2, 7–12, 1976

Hamilton DM, Vanney IH, Wall TH: Hospital treatment of patients with psychoneurotic disorders. Am J Psychiatry 99:243–247, 1942

Hamilton DM, Wall TH: Hospital treatment of patients with psychoneurotic disorders. Am J Psychiatry 98:551–557, 1941

Hamilton G: Theory and Practice of Social Casework. New York, Columbia University Press, 1940

Hamilton G: Psychotherapy in Child Guidance. New York, Columbia University Press, 1947

Hamilton G: Psychoanalytically oriented casework and its relation to psychotherapy. Am J Orthopsychiatry 19:209–223, 1949

Hammer LI: Family therapy with multiple therapists, in Masserman JH (ed): Current Psychiatric Therapies, vol. 7. New York, Grune & Stratton, 1967

Hammer LI, Shapiro I: Multiple therapist impact on family therapy. Paper presented at the 23rd Annual Conference of the American Group Therapy Association, 1965

Hammons HG (ed): Hereditary Counseling. New York, Hoeber, 1959

Handlon JH: The effects of psychotherapy. Int J Psychiatry 1:169–171, 1965

Hanlon JG: The role of the mental health service in the local health department. Pub Health Rep 72:1093–1097, 1957

Hare AP: Handbook of Small Group Research. New York, Free Press, 1962

Hargrove EA, Bennett AE, Steele M: An investigational study using carbon dioxide as an adjunct to psychotherapy in neuroses. Paper presented at the 109th Annual Meeting of the American Psychiatric Association, Los Angeles, May 7, 1953

Haring NG, Phillips EL (eds): Educating Emotionally Disturbed Children. New York, McGraw-Hill, 1962

Harless WG, Dennon GG, Marxer JJ: CASE: A computer-assisted stimulation of the clinical encounter. J Med Educ 46:443–448, 1971

Harless WG, Templeton B: The potential for CASE for evaluating undergraduate psychiatric education. Paper presented at the NIMH Congress on Evaluation of Undergraduate Psychiatry, June 22–23, 1972

Harms E: The psychotherapeutical importance of the arts. Occup Ther 18:235–239, 1939

Harms E: Child art as an aid in the diagnosis of juvenile neuroses. Am J Orthopsychiatry 2:191–209, 1941

Harper RA: Psychoanalysis and Psychotherapy—36 Systems. Englewood Cliffs, NJ, Prentice-Hall, 1959 (repr—New York, Aronson, 1974)

Harper RA: Marriage counseling as rational process-oriented psychotherapy. J Individ Psychol 16:197–207, 1960

Harrington JA, Mayer-Gross W: A day hospital for neurotics in an industrial community. J Ment Sci 1:224–234, 1959

Harris A: Day hospitals and night hospitals in psychiatry. Lancet 272:729, 1957

Harris FR, Wolf MM, Baer DM: Effects of adult social reinforcement on child behavior, in Guerney BG (ed): Psychotherapeutic Agents: New Roles for Nonprofessionals,

Parents and Teachers. New York, Holt, 1969

Harris HI: Efficient psychotherapy for the large outpatient clinic. N Engl J Med 221:1–5, 1939

Harris MR, Kalis BL, Freeman EH: Recipitating stress: An approach to brief therapy. Am J Psychother 3:465, 1963

Harris MR, Kalis BL, Freeman EH: An approach to short-term psychotherapy, in Barten HH (ed): Brief Therapies. New York, Behavioral Publications, 1971

Harris T: I'm OK—You're OK. New York, Harper & Row, 1967

Harrower MR: The Evolution of a Clinical Psychologist. Transactions of the First Conference. New York, Josiah Macy, Jr, Foundation, 1947, p 12

Harrower MR: The measurement of psychological factors, in Eisenstein VW (ed): Interaction in Marriage. New York, Basic Books, 1956(a), pp 169–191

Harrower MR: "Projective counseling." A psychotherapeutic technic. Am J Psychother 10:74–86, 1956(b)

Harrower MR: The therapy of poetry, in Masserman JH (ed): Current Psychiatric Therapies, vol. 14. New York, Grune & Stratton, 1974

Hart JT, Tomlinson TM: New Direction in Client-Centered Therapy. Boston, Houghton Mifflin, 1970

Hartert D, Browne-Mayers AN: The use of methylphenidate (Ritalin) hydrochloride in alcoholism. JAMA 106:1982–1984, 1958

Hartland J: Ego building suggestions. Am J Clin Hyp 3:89–93, 1965

Hartley D, Roback HB, Abramowitz SI: Deterioration effects in encounter groups. Am Psychol 31(3):247–255, 1976

Hartley RE, Frank LK, Goldenson RM: Understanding Children's Play. New York, Columbia University Press, 1952(a)

Hartley RE, Frank LK, Goldenson RM: New Play Experiences for Children. New York, Columbia University Press, 1952(b)

Hartley RE, Goldenson RM: The Complete Book of Children's Play. New York, Crowell, 1957, pp xiv, 462

Hartley RE, Gondor EI: The use of art in therapy, in Brower D, Abt LE (eds): Progress in Clinical Psychology, vol. 2. New York, Grune & Stratton, 1956

Hartmann H: Comment on the psychoanalytic theory of the ego, in Eissler RS, et al (eds): The Psychoanalytic Study of the Child, vol. 5. New York, International Universities Press, 1950, pp 74–96

Hartmann H: Technical implications of ego psychology. Psychoanal Q 20:31–43, 1951

Hartmann H: Ego Psychology and the Problem of Adaptation. New York, International Universities Press, 1958

Harvard Medical School and Psychiatric Service, Massachusetts General Hospital: Community Mental Health and Social Psychiatry: A Reference Guide. Cambridge, Harvard University Press, 1962

Hashagen JM: Supervision. J Psychiatr Soc Work 17:94–99, 1947–1948

Haskell D, Pugatch D, McNair DM: Time-limited psychotherapy. Arch Gen Psychiatry 21:546–552, 1969

Hastings DW: The psychiatrist and the clergyman. Northwest Med 47:644–647, 1948

Hastings DW: Psychologic impotence. Postgrad Med 27:429–432, 1960

Hastings PR, Runkle L, Jr: An experimental group of married couples with severe problems. Int J Group Psychother 13:84–92, 1963

Hatch WR, Bennet A: Effectiveness in Teaching New Dimensions in Higher Education, No. 2. Washington, DC, Office of Education, U.S. Department of Health, Education, & Welfare, 1960

Hathaway SR, Meehl PE: An Atlas for the Clinical Use of the MMPI. Minneapolis, University of Minnesota Press, 1952

Haun P: Psychiatry and the ancillary services. Am J Psychiatry 107:102–107, 1950

Haun P: Recreation: A Medical Viewpoint. New York, Teachers College Press, Columbia University, 1965

Haun P: Recreation in medical psychiatric therapy, in Masserman JH (ed): Current Psychiatric Therapies, vol. 7. New York, Grune & Stratton, 1967

Havens LL: The development of existential psychiatry. J Nerv Ment Dis 154:309–331, 1972

Havens LL: The existential use of the self. Am J Psychiatry 131:1–10, 1974

Havens LL, Jaspers K: American psychiatry. Am J Psychiatry 124:66–70, 1967

Hawkins D, Pauling L (eds): Orthomolecular Psychiatry. San Francisco, Freeman, 1973

Hawkins RP, et al: Behavior therapy in the home: Amelioration of problem parent-child relations with the parent in a therapeutic role. J Exp Child Psychol 4:99–107, 1966

Hawkinshire FBW: Training procedures for offenders working in community treatment programs, in Guerney BG, Jr (ed): Psychotherapeutic Agents: New Roles for Nonprofessionals, Parents and Teachers. New York, Holt, 1969

Haylett CH, Rapaport L: Mental health consultation, in Bellak L (ed): A Concise Handbook of Community Psychiatry and Community Mental Health. New York, Grune & Stratton, 1964

Hayman M: A unique day therapy center for psychiatric patients. Ment Hyg 41:245–249, 1957

Heath RG, et al: Brain activity during emotional states. Am J Psychiatry 131:858–862, 1974

Hecht MH: The development of a training program in pastoral counseling at a mental health center. Int Ment Health Res Newsletter 7:12–16, 1965

Heckel R, et al: Conditioning against silences in group therapy. J Clin Psychol 18:216, 1962

Heckel R, et al: The effect of musical tempor in varying operant speech levels in group therapy. J Clin Psychol 19:129, 1963

Heidegger M: Being and Time. New York, Harper & Row, 1962

Heilbrunn G: Results with psychoanalytic therapy. Am J Psychother 17:427–435, 1963

Heiman P: On counter-transference. Int J Psychoanal 31:81–84, 1950

Heimlich EP: Paraverbal techniques in the therapy of childhood communication disorders. Int. J Psychother 1:65–83, 1972

Helfer R, Hess J: An experimental model for making objective measurements of interviewing skills. J Clin Psychol 26:327–331, 1970

Hellenbrand S: Client value orientation: Implications for diagnosis and treatment. Soc Casework 42:163–169, 1961

Henderson RB: In defense of clinical psychology. Can Men Health 14:17–19, 1966

Hendrick I: Facts and Theories of Psychoanalysis (3rd ed). New York, Knopf, 1958

Hendry CE (ed): Decade of Group Work. New York, Association Press, 1948

Henry WE, Sims JH, Spray SL: The Fifth Profession: Becoming a Psychiatrist. San Francisco, Jossey-Bass, 1971

Herbert WL, Jarvis FV: The Art of Marriage Counseling. A Modern Approach. New York, Emerson Books, 1959

Herr VV: Mental health training in catholic seminaries. J Rel Health 1:127–152, 1962

Herr VV: Mental health training in catholic seminaries. J Rel Health 5:27–34, 1966

Herrigel E: Zen in the Art of Archery. New York, Pantheon, 1953

Herschelman P, Freundlich D: Large group therapy with multiple therapists, in Masserman JH (ed): Current Psychiatric Therapies, vol. 12. New York, Grune & Stratton, 1972

Hersen M, Eisler RM, Miller PM: Development of assertive responses: Clinical measurements and research considerations. Behav Res Ther 11:505–522, 1973(a)

Hersen M, Eisler RM, Miller PM, et al: Effects of practice instructions, and modeling on components of assertive behavior. Behav Res Ther 11:443–451, 1973(b)

Herz MI, Endicott J, Spitzer RL, Mesnikoff A: Day versus inpatient hospitalization: A controlled study. Am J Psychiatry 127:1371, 1971

Herzberg A: Short treatment of neurosis by graduated tasks. Br J Med Psychol 19:36–51, 1941

Herzberg A: Active Psychotherapy. New York, Grune & Stratton, 1945, p 49

Herzog E: Some Guide Lines for Evaluative Research. Washington, DC, U.S. Department of Health, Education, & Welfare, 1959

Heyder DW: LSD-25 on conversion reaction. J Am Psychol Assoc 120:396–397, 1963

Hilgard ER: Theories of Learning (2d ed). New York, Appleton-Century-Crofts, 1956 (4th ed, 1974)

Hill G, Armitage SG: An analysis of combined therapy—individual and group—in patients with schizoid, obsessive-compulsive, or aggressive defenses. J Nerv Ment Dis 119:113–134, 1954

Hill JA: Therapist goals, patient aims, and patient satisfaction in psychotherapy. J Clin Psychol 25:455–459, 1969

Hill LB: Psychotherapeutic Intervention in Schizophrenia. Chicago, University of Chicago Press, 1955

Hiltner S: Religion and Health. New York, Macmillan, 1943

Hiltner S: Religion and pastoral counseling. Am J Orthopsychiatry 17:21–26, 1947

Hiltner S: Pastoral Counseling. New York, Abington, 1949

Hiltner S: Hostility in counseling. Pastoral Psychol 1:35–42, 1950

Hiltner S: Pastoral Counseling. New York, Abington, 1952

Hiltner S: The American Association of Pastoral Counselors: A critique. Pastoral Psychol 15:8–16, 1964

Hiltner S: An appraisal of religion and psychiatry since 1964. J Rel Health 4:220, 1965

Hiltner S, et al: Clinical Pastoral Training. New York, Federal Council of Churches of Christ in America, 1945

Hinckley RG: Group treatment in psychotherapy. Minneapolis, University of Minnesota Press, 1951

Hinsie LE, Campbell RJ: Psychiatric Dictionary. New York, Oxford University Press, 1960 (4th ed, 1970)

Hoagland H (ed): Hormones, Brain Function and Behavior. New York, Academic Press, 1957

Hobbs N: Helping disturbed children: Psychological and ecological strategies. Am Psychol 21:1105–1115, 1966

Hobbs N: Mental health's third revolution, in Guerney BG, Jr (ed): Psychotherapeutic Agents: New Roles for Nonprofessionals, Parents and Teachers. New York, Holt, 1969

Hobbs N, Rogers CR (eds): Client-centered Psychotherapy. Boston, Houghton Mifflin, 1951, pp 278–319

Hoch PH: Drugs and psychotherapy. Am J Psychiatry 116:305–308, 1959

Hoch PH, Kalinowsky L: Somatic Treatments in Psychiatry. New York, Grune & Stratton, 1961

Hoch PH, Polatin P: Narcodiagnosis and narcotherapy, in Bychowsky G, Despert JL (eds): Specialized Techniques in Psychotherapy. New York, Basic Books, 1952, pp 1–23

Hoch PH, Zubin J: Relation of Psychological Tests to Psychiatry. New York, Grune & Stratton, 1951

Hoch PH, Zubin J (eds): Comparative Epidemiology of Mental Disorders. New York, Grune & Stratton, 1961

Hodgson RJ, Rachman S: An experimental investigation of the implosion technique. Behav Res Ther 8:21–27, 1970

Hoffer A: An alcoholism treatment program—LSD, Malvaria, and Nicotinic Acid. Preprint of the 2d Conference on the Use of LSD in Psychotherapy, May 1965

Hoffer A: How to Live with Schizophrenia. New York, University Books, 1966

Hoffer A: Megavitamin B-3 therapy for schizophrenia. Can Psychiatr Assoc J 16:499–504, 1971

Hofling CK, Leininger MM: Basic Psychiatric Concepts in Nursing. Philadelphia, Lippincott, 1960

Hofling CK, Meyers RW: Recent discoveries in psychoanalysis. A study of opinion. Arch Gen Psychiatry 26:518–523, 1972

Hofmann H: Religion and mental health. J Rel Health 1:319–336, 1962

Hogan RA, Kirchner JH: Preliminary report of the extinction of learned fears via short-term implosive therapy. J Abnorm Psychol 72:106–109, 1967

Hollander D, Harland J: Antacids vs. placebos in peptic ulcer therapy. A controlled double-blind investigation. JAMA 226:1181–1185, 1973

Hollander FI: The specific nature of the clergy's role in mental health. Pastoral Psychol 10:14, 1959

Hollander FI: Mental health teaching materials for the clergy. J Rel Health 1:273–282, 1962

Hollander M: The Practice of Psychoanalytic Psychotherapy. New York, Grune & Stratton, 1965

Hollis F: The techniques of casework. Soc Casework 30:235–244, 1949

Hollis F: Casework: A Psychosocial Therapy. New York, Random House, 1964; 2d ed, 1974

Hollister LE: Optimum use of antipsychotic drugs, in Masserman JH (ed): Current Psychiatric Therapies, vol. 12. New York, Grune & Stratton, 1972

Hollister LE: Clinical Use of Psychotherapeutic Drugs. Springfield, Ill, Thomas, 1973

Hollister LE: Psychopharmacology. Audio-Digest Foundation Cassette 3(23), December 9, 1974

Hollister LE: Drugs for mental disorders of old age. JAMA 234:195–198, 1975

Holman CT: The Care of Souls: A Socio-Psychological Approach. Chicago, University of Chicago Press, 1932

Holmes M: The Therapeutic Classroom. New York, Aronson, 1974

Holt H: Existential psychoanalysis: A new trend in the field of psychoanalysis. Trans. New York Institute of Existential Analysis 2(2), 1965

Holt H: The problems of interpretation from the point of view of existential psychoanalysis, in Hammer EE (ed): Use of Interpretation in Treatment. New York, Grune & Stratton, 1968

Holt H: Existential group therapy, in Kaplan HI, Sadock BJ (eds): New Models for Group Therapy. New York, Dutton, 1972(a)

Holt H: Existential psychoanalysis, in Freedman AM, Kaplan HI (eds): Treating Mental Illness. New York, Atheneum, 1972(b)

Holt H: Existential psychoanalysis, in Freedman AM, Kaplan HI, Saddock BJ (eds): Comprehensive Textbook of Psychiatry II (2d ed), vol. 1. Baltimore, Williams & Wilkins, 1975, pp 661–668

Holt RR, Luborsky L: Personality Patterns of Psychiatrists, vol. 1. New York, Basic Books, 1958

Homan WG: Child Sense. New York, Bantam, 1969

Homans GC: The Human Group. New York, Harcourt, 1950

Hora T: Beyond countertransference. Am J Psychother 10:18–23, 1956

Hora T: Ontic perspectives in psychoanalysis. Am J Psychother 13:134–141, 1959(a)

Hora T: Existential group psychotherapy. Am J Psychother 13:83–92, 1959(b)

Horney K: The Neurotic Personality of Our Time. New York, Norton, 1937

Horney K: New Ways in Psychoanalysis. New York, Norton, 1939

Horney K: Self-Analysis. New York, Norton, 1942

Horney K: Our Inner Conflicts. New York, Norton, 1945

Horney K: Neurosis and Human Growth. New York, Norton, 1950

Horowitz FD: Social reinforcement effects on child behavior. J Nurs Ed 18:276–284, 1963

Horowitz L: Transference in training groups and therapy groups. Int J Group Psychother 14:202, 1964

Horsley JS: Narcoanalysis. J Ment Sci 82:416, 1936

Horsley JS: Narco-Analysis. London, Oxford University Press, 1943

Horsley JS: A critical discussion of the relationship between hypnosis and narcosis and of the value of these states in psychobiological medicine, in LeCron LM (ed): Experimental Hypnosis. New York, Macmillan, 1952

Hospital Focus: Enuresis-therapies, luck and devices. May 15, November 1, 1964

Howard KI, Orlinsky DE: Psychotherapeutic processes, in Mussen P, Rosenzweig M (eds): Annual Review of Psychology. Palo Alto, Calif, Annual Reviews, 1972, pp 615–668

Howe HS: Progress in neurology and psychiatry. NY State J Med 51:102, 1951

Hubbard JP, Templeton B: The future of medical education and its implications for psychiatry, in Usdin G (ed): Psychiatry: Education and Image. New York, Brunner/Mazel, 1973

Hubbard LR: Dianetics: The Modern Science of Mental Health. New York, Hermitage House, 1950

Hubbs R: The sheltered workshop. Ment Hosp 11:7–9, 1960

Huddleson JH: Psychotherapy in two hundred cases of psychoneurosis. Mil Surg 60:161–170, 1927

Hughes EC: Psychology: Science and/or profession. Am Psychol 7:441–443, 1952

Hulse WC: The therapeutic management of group tension. Am J Orthopsychiatry 20:834, 1950

Hulse WC: Transference catharsis, insight and reality testing during concommitant individual and group psychotherapy. Int J Group Psychother 5:45, 1955

Hulse WC (ed): Controversial issues, Part 2, in Stokvis B (ed): Topical Problems of Psychotherapy, vol. 2. Basel, Switz, Karger, 1960

Hulse WC, Lowinger L: Psychotherapy in general practice. Am Practitioner Digest Treatment 1:141–145; 588–598; 926–932; 1024–1030, 1950

Hulse WC, Lulow WV, Rinesberg B, Epstein NB: Transference reactions in a group of female patients to male and female co-leaders. Int J Group Psychother 6:430, 1956

Hume PB: Community psychiatry, social psychiatry and community mental health work: Some interprofessional relationships in psychiatry and social work. Am J Psychiatry 121:340–343, 1964

Hume PB: Searchlight on community psychiatry. Commun Ment Health J 1:109–112, 1965

Hume PB: General principles of community psychiatry, in Arieti S (ed): American Handbook of Psychiatry, vol. 3. New York, Basic Books, 1966, pp 515–541

Hunt J McV, Kogan LS: Measuring Results in Social Casework: A Manual of Judging Movement. New York, Family Service Association of America, 1950

Hurvitz N: Interaction hypotheses in marriage counseling. Fam Coordinator 19:64–75, 1970

Huseth B: Half-way houses—a new rehabilitation measure. Ment Hosp 9:5–8, 1958

Huseth B: What is a halfway house? Function and type. Ment Hyg 45:116–121, 1961

Hussain A: Behavior therapy using hypnosis, in Wolpe J, et al (eds): The Conditioning Therapies. New York, Holt, 1965, pp 54–61

Hussain MZ: Desensitization and flooding (implosion) in treatment of phobias. Am J Psychiatry 127:1509–1514, 1971

Husserl E: Ideas. New York, Macmillan, 1931, 1962

Huston P: Treatment of depression, in Masserman JH (ed): Current Psychiatric Therapies, vol. 11. New York, Grune & Stratton, 1971

Irvine LF, Deery SJ: An investigation of problem areas relating to the therapeutic community concept. Ment Hyg 45:367–373, 1961

Isaacs S: Social Development in Young Children. London, Routledge, 1930

Ishiyama T: Music as a therapeutic tool in the treatment of a catatonic. Psychiatr Q 37:437–461, 1963

Jackson DD: The question of family homeostasis. Psychiatr Q (Suppl) 31:79–90, 1957

Jackson DD: The family and sexuality, in Whitaker C (ed): The Psychotherapy of Chronic Schizophrenic Patients. Boston, Little, Brown, 1958

Jackson DD: Family interaction, family homeostasis, and some implications for conjoint family psychotherapy, in Masserman JH (ed): Individual and Familial Dynamics. New York, Grune & Stratton, 1959

Jackson DD: Action for mental illness—what kind? Stanford Med Bull 20:77–80, 1962

Jackson DD, Satir VM: Family diagnosis and family therapy, in Ackerman N, Beatman FL, Sherman SN (eds): Exploring the Base for Family Therapy. New York, Family Service Association, 1961

Jackson DD, Weakland JH: Conjoint family therapy, some considerations on theory, technique and results. Psychiatry 24 (2, Suppl):30–45, 1961

Jackson J: A family group therapy technique for a stalemate in individual treatment. Int J Group Psychother 12:164–170, 1962

Jackson J, Grotjahn M: The treatment of oral defenses by combined individual and group patient interview. Int J Group Psychother 8:373, 1958(a)

Jackson J, Grotjahn M: The reenactment of the marriage neurosis in group psychotherapy. J Nerv Ment Dis 127:503–510, 1958(b)

Jackson J, Grotjahn M: The efficacy of group therapy in a case of marriage neurosis. Int J Group Psychother 9:420–428, 1959

Jacobsen C: Preclinical Training of the Clinical Psychologist. Transactions of the First Conference. New York, Josiah Macy, Jr, Foundation, 1947, pp 16–21

Jacobson E: Progressive Relaxation. Chicago, University of Chicago Press, 1938 (3rd rev ed, 1974)

Jacobson E: Psychotic Conflict and Reality. New York, International Universities Press, 1967

Jacobson E, Kehlet H, Larsen V, et al: The autonomic reaction of psychoneurotics to a new sedative: Benactyzine, NFN, Suavitil (benzilic acid diethylaminoethylester hydrochloride). Acta Psychiatr Kbh 30:637, 1955

Jacobson GF, Wilner DM, Morley WE, et al: The scope and practice of an early-access brief treatment psychiatric center. Am J Psychiatry 121:1176–1183, 1965

Jacobziner H: Glue sniffing. NY State J Med 63:2415–2418, 1963

Jaffe J: Verbal behavior analysis in psychiatric interviews with the aid of digital computers. Disorders Commun, vol. 42. Research Publications Association for Research in Nervous and Ment Disorders, 1964

Jaffe JH: Cyclazocine in the treatment of narcotic addiction, in Masserman JH (ed): Current Psychiatric Therapies, vol. 7. New York, Grune & Stratton, 1967

Jaffe JH, Brill L: Cyclazocine—a long-acting narcotic antagonist: Its voluntary acceptance as a treatment modality by narcotic abusers. Int J Addict 1:86–99, 1966

JAMA: Editorial: An evaluation of psychoanalysis. 101:1643–1644, 1933

JAMA: Editorial: Music therapy. 162:1626, 1956

JAMA: Editorial. 183:879, 1963

Jameison GR, McNiel EE: Some unsuccessful results with psychoanalytic therapy. Am J Psychiatry 95:1421–1428, 1939

James W: The Varieties of Religious Experience. New York, Longmanns, Green, 1941

Janov A: The Primal Scream: Primal Therapy. The Cure for Neurosis. New York, Putnam, 1970

Jaques E: Measurement of Responsibility. London, Heinemann, 1956

Jaques E: Equitable Payment (rev ed). Carbondale, Southern Illinois University Press, 1961

Jaques E: Time-Span Handbook. Carbondale, Southern Illinois University Press, 1964

Jaques E: Progression Handbook. Carbondale, Southern Illinois University Press, 1968

Jaques E: Changing Culture of a Factory. London, Routledge & Kegan, 1970(a) (repr 1951 ed)

Jaques E: Work, Creativity and Social Justice. New York, International Universities Press, 1970(b)

Jaques E: Measurement of Responsibility. New York, Halsted, 1972

Jaretzki A: Death with dignity-passive euthenasia. NY State J Med 76:539–543, 1975

Jaspers K: Von der Wahrheit. Munich, Germany, Piper, 1947

Jaspers K: General Psychopathology. Chicago, University of Chicago Press, 1963

Jeffers FC, Nichols CR, Eisdorfer C: Attitudes of older persons toward death: A preliminary study. Gerontology 16:67–70, 1961

Jellinek EM: Clinical tests on comparative effectiveness of analgesic drugs. Biometrics Bull 2:87, 1946

Jenkins RL: Behavior Disorders of Childhood and Adolescents. Springfield, Ill, Thomas, 1973

Jenkins SR: The development and evaluation of a musical thematic apperception test. Proceedings of the National Association of Music Therapy, pp 101–113, 1955

Jens R: Desoxycorticosterone in certain psychotic cases. Northwest Med 48:609, 1949

Jensen SE: A treatment program for alcoholics in a mental hospital. Q J Stud Alcohol 23:243–251, 1962

Jensen-Nelson K: Massage in Nursing Care (2d ed). New York, Macmillan, 1941

Jersild AT: When Teachers Face Themselves. New York, Columbia University Press, 1955

Jersild AT: What teachers say about psychotherapy. Phi Delta Kappan 44:313–317, 1963

Jersild AT: Personal communication. 1966

Jersild AT, Lazar EA, Brodkin AM: The Meaning of Psychotherapy in the Teacher's Life and Work. New York, Teachers College Press, Columbia University, 1962

Jewish Board of Guardians: Conditioned Environment in Case Work Treatment. New York, the Board, 1944

Jewish Board of Guardians: The Case Worker in Psychotherapy. New York, the Board, 1946

Johnson AM: Sanctions for superego lacunae, in Eissler KR (ed): Searchlights on Delinquency: New Psychoanalytic Studies. New York, International Universities Press, 1949, pp 225–245

Johnson AM: Juvenile delinquency, in Arieti S (ed): American Handbook of Psychiatry, vol. 1. New York, Basic Books, 1959, pp 840–856

Johnson AM, Szurek SA: The genesis of antisocial acting out in children and adults. Psychoanal Q 21:323, 1952

Johnson JA: Group Therapy, a Practical Approach. New York, McGraw-Hill, 1963

Johnson PE: The pastor as counselor. NY Acad Sci 63:423, 1955

Johnson PE: Personality and Religion. New York, Abingdon, 1957

Johnson PE: The church's mission to mental health. J Rel Health 12:30–40, 1973

Johnson W: People in Quandaries. New York, Harper & Row, 1946

Johnston R: Some casework aspects of using foster grandparents for emotionally disturbed children. Children 14:46–52, 1967

Joint Commission on Mental Illness and Health: Americans View Their Mental Health. Report 4. New York, Basic Books, 1960

Joint Commission on Mental Illness and Health: Digest of Action for Mental Health. New York, Basic Books, 1961

Jolesch M: Casework treatment of young married couples. Soc Casework 43:245–251, 1962

Jones CH: A day-care program for adolescents in a private hospital. Ment Hosp 12:4–6, 1961

Jones E: The relation of technique to theory. Int J Psychoanal 8:1–4, 1924

Jones E: Decannual Report of the London Clinic of Psychoanalysis, 1926–1936

Jones HG: The application of conditioning and learning techniques to the treatment of a psychiatric patient. J Abnorm Soc Psychol 52:414–419, 1956

Jones M: Social Psychiatry. London, Tavistock, 1952

Jones M: The concept of the therapeutic community. Am J Psychiatry 112:647–651, 1956

Jones M: The treatment of personality disorders in a therapeutic community. Psychiatry 20:211–220, 1957

Jones M: Toward a clarification of the therapeutic community concept. Br J Med Psychol 32:200–205, 1959

Jones M: Therapeutic millieu innovator assails institutional conservatism. Roch Report 3:1–2, 1973

Jones MC: The case of Peter. Pediatr Sem 31:308–318, 1924(a)

Jones MC: The elimination of children's fear. J Exp Psychol 7:382–390, 1924(b)

Jones WHS: Hippocrates, vol. 1. London, Heinemann, 1928, p 318

Joseph H, Heimlich EP: The therapeutic use of music with "treatment resistant" children. Am J Ment Defic 64:41–49, 1959

Josselyn I: The Adolescent and His World. New York, Family Association of America, 1952

Josselyn I: Psychotherapy of adolescents at the level of private practice, in Balser B (ed): Psychotherapy of the Adolescent. New York, International Universities Press, 1957

Jourard SM: I–Thou relationship versus manipulation in counseling and psychotherapy. J Individ Psychol 15:174–179, 1959

Jourard SM: Self-disclosure and other-cathexis. J Abnorm Soc Psychol 59:428–431, 1959

Journal of Pastoral Care: Pastoral Counseling at a Crossroad. 26, 1972 (entire issue)

Journal of School Health: Mental Health in the Classroom. Columbus, Ohio, American School Health Association, 1968

Jung CG: Psychology of the Unconscious. New York, Moffat, Yard, 1916

Jung CG: Studies in Word Association. London, Heinemann, 1919

Jung CG: Psychological Types or the Psychology of Individuation. New York, Harcourt, 1923

Jung CG: Modern Man in Search of a Soul. New York, Harcourt, 1933, 1934

Jung CG: The Structure and Dynamics of the Psyche. Hull RFC (trans). New York, Pantheon, 1960

Jung CG: Memories, Dreams, Reflections. Jaffe A (ed). New York, Pantheon, 1961

Kadis AL: The alternate meeting in group psychotherapy. Am J Psychother 10:275–291, 1956

Kadis AL: Early childhood recollections as aids in group psychotherapy. J Individ Psychol 13:182, 1957

Kadis AL: The role of co-ordinated group meetings in group psychotherapy, in Moreno J (ed): Progress in Psychotherapy. New York, Grune & Stratton, 1958

Kadis AL: Alternate meeting, in Hulse W (ed): Topical Problems of Psychotherapy, vol. 2. Basel, Switz, Karger, 1960

Kadis AL: The exploratory phase in the treatment of married couples: The phase of decision making. Int Ment Health Res Newsletter No. 3/4, p 7, 1963

Kadis AL, Krasner JD, Winick C, Foulkes SH: A Practicum of Group Psychotherapy. New York, Hoeber, 1963

Kadis AL, Markowitz M: The therapeutic impact of co-therapist interaction in a couples group. Paper presented at the 3rd International Congress of Group Psychotherapy, Milano-Stresa, July 16–22, 1963

Kahn RL, Perlin S: Hospital-community integration in psychiatric therapy, in Masserman JH (ed): Current Psychiatric Therapies, vol. 4. New York, Grune & Stratton, 1964, pp 246–252

Kaldegg A: Interaction testing: An engaged couple of drug addicts tested separately and together. J Project Tech Pers Assess 30:77–87, 1966

Kalinowsky LB: The use of somatic treatments in short-term therapy, in Wolberg LR (ed): Short-term Psychotherapy. New York, Grune & Stratton, 1965, pp 201–211

Kalinowsky LB, Hippius H: Pharmacological, Convulsive and Other Somatic Treatments in Psychiatry. New York, Grune & Stratton, 1969

Kalinowsky LB, Hoch PH: Shock Treatments, Psychosurgery and Other Somatic Treatments in Psychiatry (2d ed). New York, Grune & Stratton, 1952

Kalinowsky LB, Hoch PH: Somatic Treatments in Psychiatry. New York, Grune & Stratton, 1961

Kalis BL: Crisis theory: Its relevance for community psychology and directions for developments, in Adelson D, Kalis BL (eds): Community Psychology and Mental Health: Perspectives and Challenges. Scranton, Pa, Chandler, 1970

Kalis BL, Freeman EH, Harris, MR: Influences of previous help-seeking experiences on application for psychotherapy. Ment Hyg 48:267–272, 1964

Kalis BL, Freeman EH, Harris MR, Prestwood AR: Precipitating stress as a focus in psychotherapy. Arch Gen Psychiatry 5:219–226, 1961

Kallmann FJ: Heredity in Health and Mental Disorder. New York, Norton, 1953

Kallmann FJ: Psychiatric aspects of genetic counseling. Am J Hum Genet 8:97–101, 1956

Kallmann FJ: Some aspects of genetic counseling, in Neel JV, Shaw, MW, Schull WJ (eds): Genetics and the Epidemiology of Chronic Diseases. Washington, DC, U.S. Department of Health, Education, & Welfare, 1965

Kallmann FJ, Rainer JD: Psychotherapeutically oriented counseling techniques in the setting of a medical genetics department, in Stokvis B (ed): Topical Problems of Psychotherapy. Basel, Switz, Karger, 1963

Kallmann FJ, Rainer JD: The genetic approach to schizophrenia: Clinical, demographic, and family guidance problems, in Kolb LC, Kallmann FJ, Polatin P (eds): Schizophrenia. Boston, Little, Brown, 1964

Kanfer FH, Phillips S: Behavior therapy. Arch Gen Psychiatry 15:114–127, 1966

Kanfer FH, Phillips S: Learning Foundations of Behavior Therapy. New York, Wiley, 1970

Kanfer FH, Saslow G: Behavioral analysis. Arch Gen Psychiatry 12:529–538, 1965

Kanner L: Early infantile autism. Am J Orthopsychiatry 19:416, 1959

Kant O: Deceptive psychoneurosis. Psychiatr Q 20:129, 1946

Kantorovich NV: An attempt at associative-reflex therapy in alcoholism. Nov Refleflsol Fiziol Nerv Syst 3:436–447, 1929 (Abstract appears in Psychol Abstr 4:493, 1930)

Kaplan HI, Sadock BJ: Comprehensive Group Psychotherapy. Baltimore, Williams & Wilkins, 1971

Kaplan HS: The New Sex Therapy. New York, Brunner/Mazel, 1974

Kaplan HS: The illustrated Manual of Sex Therapy. New York, Quadrangle, 1975

Kaplan L: Mental Health and Human Relations in Education. New York, Harper & Row, 1959

Kaplowitz D: Teaching empathic responsiveness. Am J Psychother 4:774–781, 1967

Kardiner A: The Individual and His Society. New York, Columbia University Press, 1939 (rev ed—Westport, Conn, Greenwood, 1974)

Kardiner A, Linton R, DuBois C, West J: The Psychological Frontiers of Society. New York, Columbia University Press, 1945

Karle W, Corriere R, Hart J: Psychophysiological changes in abreactive therapy. Psychother: Theory Res Prac 10:117–122, 1973

Karliner W: Indokolon therapy, in Masserman JH (ed): Current Psychiatric Therapies, vol. 6. New York, Grune & Stratton, 1966, pp 252–259

Karliner W, Wehrheim HK: Maintenance convulsive treatments. Am J Psychiatry 121:113, 1965

Karnosh LJ, Mereness D: Psychiatry for Nurses: Essentials of Psychiatric Nursing. St Louis, Mosby, 1962

Karon BP, Vandenbos GR: The consequences of psychotherapy for schizophrenic patients. Psychother: Theory Res Prac 9:111–119, 1972

Karpf FB: The Psychology and Psychotherapy of Otto Rank. New York, Philosophical Library, 1953

Karpf FB: Rankian will or dynamic relationship therapy, in Masserman JH, Moreno JL (eds): Progress in Psychotherapy, vol. 2. New York, Grune & Stratton, 1957, pp 132–139

Karpman B: Objective psychotherapy. J Clin Psychol 5:189–342, 1949

Karpman SB: Developments in transactional analysis, in Masserman JH (ed): Current Psychiatric Therapies, vol. 12. New York, Grune & Stratton, 1972

Karush A: Adaptional psychodynamics, in Stein MI (ed): Contemporary Psycho-therapies. New York, Free Press, 1961, pp 305–318

Kasius C (ed): A Comparison of Diagnostic and Functional Casework Concepts. New York, Family Service Association of America, 1950, pp 78–169

Katz M: Agreement on connotative meaning in marriage. Fam Process 4:64–74, 1965

Kaufman I: The role of the psychiatric consul-tant. Am J Orthopsychiatry 26:223–224, 1956

Kaufman MR: Psychiatry: Why "medical" or "social" model? Arch Gen Psychiatry 17:347–358, 1967

Kazanjian V, Stein S, Weinberg WL: An Introduction to Mental Health Consultation. Pub Health Monogr No. 69. Washington, DC, U.S. Government Printing Office, 1962

Kellam SG, et al: Mental Health and Going to School. Chicago, University of Chicago Press, 1974

Kelly G: The Psychology of Personal Constructs. New York, Norton, 1955

Kelman H: Techniques in dream interpretation. Am J Psychoanal 25:3–26, 1965

Kelman H: Helping People: Karen Horney's Psychoanalytic Approach. New York, Science House, 1971

Kempler W: Family therapy of the future. Int Psychiatry Clin 6:135–158, 1969

Kennedy N: Section Three (untitled) on the social worker's role, in Helping the Dying Patient and His Family. New York, National Association for Social Workers, 1960

Kepinski A, et al: Group psychotherapy as an approach to a psychotherapeutic community. Int J Group Psychother 13:182–187, 1960

Kern HM, Jr: Community psychiatric training—a public health approach, in Goldston SE (ed): Concepts of Community Psychiatry: A Framework of Training. Pub Health Service Publ No. 1319. Bethesda, Md, National Institute of Mental Health, 1965, pp 79–87

Kernberg O: The treatment of patients with borderline personality organization. Int J Psychonal 49:600–619, 1968

Kernberg O: Borderline personalities. Bull NY State Distr Branches, Am Psychiatr Assoc Nos. 1 & 6, 1974

Kernberg O: Borderline Conditions and Pathological Narcissism. New York, Aronson, 1975

Kernberg O, et al: Psychotherapy and psychoanalysis: Final report of the Menninger Foundation's Psychotherapy Research Project. Bull Menninger Clin 36 (1, 2), 1972

Kessel K, Hyman HT: The value of psychoanalysis as a therapeutic procedure. JAMA 101:1612–1615, 1933

Ketal RM: Psychotropic drugs in emergency care. Audiodigest Psychiatry. Psychiatric Emergencies, vol. 4, no. 9, May 12, 1975

Kettle J: The EST Experience. New York, Kensington, 1976

Kierkegaard S: A Kierkegaard Anthology. Bretall R (ed). Princeton, NJ, Princeton University Press, 1951

Kiev A: Magic, Faith and Healing. New York, Free Press, 1964

Killins CG, Wells, CL: Group therapy of alcoholics, in Masserman JH (ed): Current Psychiatric Therapies, vol. 7. New York, Grune & Stratton, 1967

Kimble GA: Hilgard and Marquis' Conditioning and Learning (2d ed). New York, Appleton-Century-Crofts, 1961

Kimble GA, Kendall JW, Jr: A comparison of two methods of producing experimental extinction. J Exp Psychol 45:87–90, 1953

King GF, Armitage SG, Tilton JR: A therapeutic approach to schizophrenics of extreme pathology. J Abnorm Soc Psychol 61:276–286, 1960

Kinross-Wright J: Observations upon the therapeutic use of benactyzine (Suavitil). Am J Psychiatry 114:73, 1957

Kinross-Wright J: The current status of phenothiazines. JAMA 200:461–464, 1967

Kirchner JH, Hogan RA: The therapist variable in the implosion of phobias. Psychotherapy 3:102–104, 1966

Klaesi J: Über die therapeutische Anwendung der "Dauernarkose" Mittels Somnifen bei Schizophrenen, Ztschr f d ges Psychiat u Neurol 74:557, 1922

Klapman JW: Group Psychotherapy: Theory and Practice. New York, Grune & Stratton, 1946 (2d rev ed, 1959)

Klapman JW, Lundin JW: Objective appraisal of textbook-mediated group psychotherapy with psychotics. Int J Group Psychother 2:116–126, 1952

Kleegman SJ: Frigidity in women. Q Rev Surg Obstet Gynecol 16:243–248, 1959

Klein G: Two theories or one? Bull Menninger Clinic 37:102–131, 1973

Klein M: The Psychoanalysis of Children. London, Hogarth, 1932; New York, Norton, 1935 (repr, 1975)

Klein M: Notes on some schizoid mechanism. Int J Psychoanal 27:89–110, 1946

Klein M: Contributions to Psychoanalysis, 1921–1948. London, Hogarth, 1948

Klein M: In Richman J (ed): On the Bringing up of Children by Five Psychoanalysts (2d ed). New York, Brunner/Mazel, 1952

Klein M: The psychoanalytic play technique. Am J Orthopsychiatry 112:418–422, 1955(a)

Klein M: The psychoanalytic play technique, its history and significance, in Klein M, Heiman P, Money-Kyrle R (eds): New Directions in Psychoanalysis. The Significance of Infant Conflict in the Pattern of Adult Behavior. New York, Basic Books, 1955(a)

Klein M: New Directions in Psychoanalysis. New York, Basic Books, 1957(a)

Klein M: Envy and Gratitude: A Study of Unconscious Sources. London, Tavistock, 1957(b)

Klein M: On the development of mental functioning. Int J Psychiatry 39:84–90, 1958

Klein M: Über das Seelenleben des Kleinkindes. Psyche (Stuttg) 14:284–314, 1960

Klein M: Narrative of a Child Analysis. New York, Basic Books, 1961 (rev ed—Delacorte, 1975)

Klein M: Our Adult World and Other Essays. New York, Basic Books, 1963

Klein WH, et al: The Training of Youth Counselors. Washington, DC, Institute for Youth Studies, 1966

Klein WH, LeShan ES, Furman SS: Promoting Mental Health of Older People Through Group Methods: A Practical Guide. New York, Mental Health Materials Center, 1966

Klein-Lipshutz E: Comparisons of dreams in individual and group psychotherapy. Int J Group Psychother 3:143–149, 1953

Kleitman N: Patterns of dreaming. Scientific Am 203:82–88, 1960

Klemperer E: Changes of the body image in hypnoanalysis. Paper presented at the Annual Meeting of the Society for Clinical and Experimental Hypnosis, New York Academy of Science, New York, 1953

Kline F: Personal Group Therapy and Psychiatric Training. New York, Stratton Intercontinental, 1975

Kline NS: The practical management of depression. JAMA 190:732–740, 1964

Kline NS: Treatment of phobic disorders. Paper presented at the 122d Annual Meeting of the American Psychiatric Association, Atlantic City, NJ, May 1966(a)

Kline NS: Drugs in the treatment of depression: Clinical studies, in Solomon P (ed): Psychiatric Drugs. New York, Grune & Stratton, 1966(b)

Klopfer B, Kelly DM: The Rorschach Technique. Yonkers, World Book, 1942

Knee RI: Psychiatric social work, in Hurtz RH (ed): Social Work Yearbook. New York, National Association of Social Workers, 1957, p 431

Knight GC: Bi-frontal sterotactic tractotomy: An atraumatic operation of value in the treatment of intractable psychoneurosis. Br J Psychiatry 115:257–266, 1969

Knight RP: Evaluation of the results of

psychoanalytic therapy. Am J Psychiatry 98:434–446, 1941

Knight RP: A critique of the present status of the psychotherapies (1949), in Knight RP, Friedman CR (eds): Psychoanalytic Psychiatry and Psychology. New York, International Universities Press, 1954, pp 52–64

Knobloch F: On the theory of a therapeutic community for neurotics. Int J Group Psychother 10:419–429, 1960

Knobloch F: Czech-type therapeutic unit successfully used in Canada. Psychiatr News 8:32–33, 1973

Koegler R, Brill Q: Treatment of Psychiatric Outpatients. New York, Appleton-Century-Crofts, 1967

Kohl RN: Pathologic reaction of marital partners to improvement of patients. Am J Psychiatry 118:1036–1041, 1962

Kohut H: The Analysis of the Self. New York, International Universities Press, 1971

Kolb LC: Consultation and psychotherapy, in Masserman JH (ed): Current Psychiatric Therapies, vol. 8. New York, Grune & Stratton, 1968

Kolb LC, Montgomery J: An explanation for transference cure: Its occurrence in psychoanalysis and psychotherapy. Am J Psychiatry 115:414–421, 1963

Koltes JA, Jones M: A type of therapeutic community. Ment Hosp 8:16–19, 1957

Konia C: Orgone therapy: A case presentation. Psychother: Theory Res Prac 12:192–197, 1975

Konopka G: Group therapy in overcoming racial and cultural tension. Am J Orthopsychiatry 17:593–699, 1947

Konopka G: Group work and therapy, in Hendry CE (ed): A Decade of Group Work. New York, Association Press, 1948

Konopka G: Eduard C. Lindeman and Social Work Philosophy. Minnesota, University of Minnesota Press, 1958

Konopka G: Group Work: A Heritage and a Challenge. Social Work with Groups. New York, National Association for Social Workers, 1960, pp 7–21

Konopka G: Social Group Work: A Helping Process. Englewood Cliffs, NJ, Prentice-Hall, 1963

Koppitz EM: The Bender Gestalt Test for Young Children. New York, Grune & Stratton, 1963, pp 73–83

Korzybski A: Science and Society. An Introduction to Non-Artistotelian Systems and General Semantics (2d ed). Lancaster, Pa, Science Press, 1941

Kosbab FP: Imagery techniques in psychotherapy, Arch Gen Psychiatry 31:283–290, 1974

Kotinsky E, Witmer HL (eds): Community Program for Mental Health. Cambridge, Harvard University Press, 1955

Kotkov B: Common forms of resistance in group psychotherapy. Psychoanal Rev 44:88, 1957

Kotkov B: Favorable clinical indications for group attendance. Int J Group Psychother 8:419–427, 1958

Kotler SL: Role theory in marriage counseling. Sociol Soc Res 52:50–62, 1967

Kraft AM: The therapeutic community, in Arieti S (ed): American Handbook of Psychiatry, vol. 3. New York, Basic Books, 1966, pp 542–551

Kraft IA, Vick J: Flexibility and variability of group psychotherapy with adolescence girls, in Wolberg LR, Schwartz EK (eds): Group Therapy 1973: An Overview. New York, Stratton Intercontinental, 1973, pp 71–91

Kraines SH: The Therapy of the Neuroses and Psychoses. Philadelphia, Lea & Febiger, 1943

Krakowski AJ: Protriptyline in treatment of severe depressions. A long-range pilot study. Am J Psychiatry 121:807–808, 1965

Kramer BM: The day hospital: A case study. J Soc Issues 16:14–19, 1960

Kramer E: Art Therapy in a Children's Community. Springfield, Ill, Thomas, 1958

Kramer E: Art as Therapy with Children. New York, Schocken, 1972

Kramer M: On the continuation of the analytic process after psychoanalysis (a self-observation). Int J Psychoanal 40:17–25, 1959

Krantz C, Jr, Truitt EB, Jr, Speer L, Ling ASC: New pharmaco-convulsive agent. Science 126:353, 1957

Krasner J: The psychoanalytic treatment of the elder people via group psychotherapy. Acta Psychother (Suppl 7), 205, 1959

Krasner L: Studies of the conditioning of verbal behavior. Psychol Bull 55:148–170, 1958

Krasner L: The psychotherapist as a social reinforcement machine, in Strupp HH, Luborsky L (eds): Research in Psychotherapy, vol. 2. Washington, DC, American Psychological Association, 1962, pp 61–94

Krasner L: The operant approach in behavior therapy, in Bergin A, Garfield S (eds): Handbook of Psychotherapy and Behavior Change. New York, Wiley, 1971

Krause MS: Defensive and non-defensive resistance. Psychoanal Q 30:221–231, 1961

Krause MS: A cognitive theory of motivation for treatment. J Gen Psychol 75:9–19, 1966

Krause MS: Behavioral indices of motivation for treatment. J Couns Psychol 14:426–435, 1967

Kremer MW: A reconsideration of change and insight in therapy. Paper presented at the 122d Annual Meeting of the American Psychiatric Association, Atlantic City, NJ, May 9, 1966

Krich A: A reluctant counselee: A specimen case, in Mudd EH, Krich A (eds): Man and Wife. New York, Norton, 1957, pp 258–275

Kringlen E: Obsessional neurosis: A long-term follow-up. Br J Psychiatry 11:709, 1965

Kringlen E: Schizophrenia in male monozygotic twins. Acta Psychiatr Scand (Suppl 178), Munksgaard, 1965

Krippner S, Kline MV: Passages: A Guide for Pilgrims of the Mind. New York, Harper & Row, 1972

Krippner S, Rubin D (eds): Galaxies of Life: The Human Aura in Acupuncture and Kirlian Photography. New York, Gordon & Beach, 1973

Kris E: On preconscious mental processes, in Rapaport D (ed): Organization and Pathology of Thought. New York, Columbia University Press, 1951, pp 474–493

Kris E: Psychoanalytic Explorations in Art. New York, International Universities Press, 1952

Kris E: On the vicissitudes of insight. Int J Psychoanal 37:445, 1956

Kris EB: Simplifying chlorpromazine maintenance therapy. Am J Psychiatry 114:836, 1958

Kris EB: Intensive short-term therapy in a day care facility for control of recurrent psychotic symptoms. Am J Psychiatry 115:1027, 1959

Kris EB: Effects of pharmacotherapy on work and learning ability—a five-year follow-up study, in Wortis J (ed): Recent Advances in Biological Psychiatry, vol. 3. New York, Grune & Stratton, 1961, p 30

Kris EB: The role of the day hospital in the rehabilitation of mental patients. Proceedings of the Institute for the Rehabilitation of the Mentally Ill. New York, Altro Health and Rehabilitation Service, April 1962, pp 33–36

Kroger WS, Fezler WD: Hypnosis and Behavior Modification: Imagery Conditioning. Philadelphia, Lippincott, 1976

Krug O: The dynamic use of the ego functions in casework practice. Soc Casework 36:443–450, 1955

Krumboltz JD (ed): Revolution in Counseling: Implications of Behavioral Science. Boston, Houghton Mifflin, 1966

Krupp GR, Kligfeld B: The bereavement reaction, a cross-cultural evaluation. Paper presented at the 38th Annual Meeting of the American Orthopsychiatric Association, New York, March 23–25, 1961

Kubie LS: The use of hypnagogic reveries in the recovery of repressed amnesic data. Bull Menninger Clin 7:172–182, 1943

Kubie LS: Elements in the Medical Curriculum Which Are Essential in the Training for Psychotherapy—Training in Clinical Psychology. Transactions of the First Conference. New York, Josiah Macy, Jr, Foundation, 1947, pp 46–51

Kubie LS: Psychoanalysis and healing by faith. Pastoral Psychol 1:13–18, 1950(a)

Kubie LS: Practical and Theoretical Aspects of Psychoanalysis. New York, International Universities Press, 1950(b)

Kubie LS: Research into the process of supervision in psychoanalysis. Psychoanal Q 27:226–236, 1958(a)

Kubie LS: Some theoretical concepts underlying the relationship between individual and group psychotherapies. Int J Group Psychother 8:3, 1958(b)

Kubie LS: Psychoanalysis and scientific method. J Nerv Ment Dis 131:512, 1960

Kubie LS: Neurotic Distortion of the Creative Process. New York, Farrar, Straus, 1961

Kubie LS: The process of evaluation of therapy in psychiatry. Arch Gen Psychiatry 26:880–884, 1973

Kubie LS, Margolin S: The therapeutic role of drugs in the process of regression, dissociation and synthesis. Psychosom Med 17:147, 1945

Kubie LS, Landau G: Group Work with the Aged. New York, International Universities Press, 1953 (rev ed, 1975)

Kubler-Ross E: On Death and Dying. New York, Macmillan, 1969

Kuehn JL, Crinella FM: Sensitivity training: Interpersonal "overkill" and other problems. Am J Psychiatry 126:840–844, 1969

Kuhn R: Problems der praktischen Durchführung der Tofranil-Behandlung. Wien Med Wochenschr 110:245, 1960

Kunnes R: Radicalism and community mental health, in Gottesfeld H (ed): The Critical Issues in Community Mental Health. New York, Behavioral Publications, 1972

Kunstler P: Social Group Work in Great Britain. London, Faber & Faber, 1955

Kurland AA, Savage C, Pahnke WN, et al: LSD in the treatment of alcoholics. Pharmakopsychiatr Neuropsychopharmakolog (Stuttg) 4(2), 1971

Kurland AA, Savage C, Unger S, Shaffer JW: Psychedelic psychotherapy (LSD) in the treatment of alcoholic patients. Paper presented at the 122d Annual Meeting of the American Psychiatric Association, Atlantic City, NJ, May 1966

Kwiatkowska HY: The use of families' art productions for psychiatric evaluation. Bull Art Ther 6(2):52–72, 1967

LaForgue R: Exceptions to the fundamental rule of psychoanalysis. Int J Psychoanal 18:35–41, 1937

Laidlaw RW: The psychiatrist as marriage counselor. Am J Psychiatry 106:732–736, 1960

Laing RD: The Divided Self. London, Tavistock, 1960

Laing RD: The Politics of Experience. New York, Pantheon, 1967

Laing RD, Esterson A: Sanity, Madness and the Family; Families of Schizophrenics (2d ed). New York, Basic Books, 1971

Laitinen LV: Stereotactic lesions in the knee of the corpus callosum. Lancet 1:472–475, 1972

Lancet: Editorial: Treatment of enuresis. 1:1425, 1964

Lander J, Schulman R: The impact of the therapeutic milieu on the disturbed personality. Soc Casework 4:227–234, 1960

Landis C: A statistical evaluation of psychotherapeutic methods, in Hinsie LE (ed): Concepts and Problems of Psychotherapy. New York, Columbia University Press, 1937; London, Heinemann, 1938

Landy D: Rutland corner house: Case study of a halfway house. J Soc Issues 16:27–32, 1960

Landy D, Greenblatt M: Halfway House. Washington, DC, U.S. Department of Health, Education, & Welfare, 1965

Lang PJ: Experimental studies of desensitization therapy, in Wolpe J (ed): The Conditioning Therapies. New York, Holt, 1964

Lang PJ, Lazovik AD: Experimental desensitization of a phobia. J Abnorm Soc Psychol 66:519–525, 1963

Lang PJ, Lazovik AD, Reynolds DJ: Desensitization, suggestibility, and pseudotherapy. J Abnorm Soc Psychol 70:395–402, 1965

Langdell JI: A unique English therapeutic community for adolescents: Finchen Manor, in Masserman JH (ed): Current Psychiatric Therapies, vol. 7. New York, Grune & Stratton, 1967, pp 36–42

Langen D, Volhard R: Zschr Psychotherapie 5:215, 1955

Langer M: Learning to Live as a Widow. New York, Messner, 1957

Langer M, Puget J, Teper E: A methodological approach to the teaching of psychoanalysis. Int J Psychoanal 45:567–574, 1964

Laqueur HP: General systems theory and multiple family therapy, in Masserman JH (ed): Current Psychiatric Therapies, vol. 8. New York, Grune & Stratton, 1968

Laqueur HP: Mechanisms of change in multiple family therapy, in Sager CJ, Kaplan HS (eds): Progress in Group and Family Therapy. New York, Brunner/Mazel, 1972, pp 400–415

Laqueur HP, LaBurt HA: Conjoint family group therapy–a new approach. Paper presented at the 122d Annual Meeting of the American Psychiatric Association, Atlantic City, NJ, May 1966

Lasagna L, Mosteller F, Felsinger JM, Beecher HK: A study of the placebo response. Am J Med 16:770–779, 1954

Laska E, et al: The use of computers at a state psychiatric hospital. Compr Psychiatry 8:476, 1967

LaVietes R, et al: Day treatment center and school: Seven years' experience. Am J Orthopsychiatry 35:160, 1965

Law SG: Therapy Through Interview. New York, McGraw-Hill, 1948

Lawrence MM: The Mental Health Team in the Schools. New York, Behavioral Publications, 1971

Lazarus AA: Group therapy of phobic disorders by systematic desensitization. J Abnorm Soc Psychol 63:504–510, 1961

Lazarus AA: In support of technical eclecticism. Psychol Rep 21:415–416, 1967

Lazarus AA: Behavior therapy in groups, in Gazda G (ed): Basic Approaches to Group Psychotherapy and Group Counseling. Springfield, Ill, Thomas, 1968

Lazarus AA: Behavior Therapy and Beyond. New York, McGraw-Hill, 1971

Lazarus AA (ed): Clinical Behavior Therapy. New York, Brunner/Mazel, 1972

Lazarus AA (ed): Multimodel Behavior Therapy. New York, Springer, 1976

Lazarus AA, Abramovitz A: The use of "emotive imagery" in the treatment of children's phobias. J Ment Sci 108:191–195, 1962

Lazell EW: The group treatment of dementia praecox. Psychoanal Rev 8:168–179, 1921

Lazovik AD, Lang PJ: A laboratory demonstration of systematic desensitization in psychotherapy. J Psychol Stud 11:238–247, 1960

Leader AL: Social work consultation in psychiatry. Soc Casework 38:22–28, 1957

Leake CD: The Amphetamines, Their Actions and Uses. Springfield, Ill, Thomas, 1958

Lebensohn ZM: American psychiatry and the general hospital. Med Ann DC 33:47–52, 1964

Ledney DM: Psychiatric nursing: Breakthrough to independence. Reg Nurse, August 1971, pp 29–35

Lee RS: Religion psychotherapy and Freud. Paper presented at the Postgraduate Center for Mental Health, Carnegie Endowment Center, New York, April 9, 1957

Leedy J: Poetry therapy. Psychiatr Op 3:20–25, 1966

Lehman HE, Ban TA: Pharmacotherapy of tension and anxiety, in Masserman JH (ed): Current Psychiatric Therapies, vol. 12. New York, Grune & Stratton, 1972

Lehner GFJ: Negative practice as a psychotherapeutic technique. J Gen Psychol 51:69–82, 1954

Lehrer P, Schiff L, Kris A: Operant conditioning in a comprehensive treatment program for adolescents. Arch Gen Psychiatry 25:515–521, 1971

Leichter E: Group psychotherapy of married couples' groups: Some characteristic treatment dynamics. Int J Group Psychother 12:154–163, 1962

Leighton AH: An Introduction to Social Psychiatry. Springfield, Ill, Thomas, 1960

Leighton AH, Clausen JA, Wilson RN (eds): Explorations in Social Psychiatry. New York, Basic Books, 1957

Leighton AH, et al: The Stirling County Study. Vol. 1: My Name is Legion. Vol. 2: People of Cover and Woodlot. Vol. 3: The Character of Danger. New York, Basic Books, 1959, 1960, 1963

Lemere F: Treatment of mild depressions in general office practice. JAMA 164:516–518, 1957

Lemere F: The danger of amphetamine dependency. Paper presented at the 122d Annual Meeting of the American Psychiatric Association, Atlantic City, NJ, May 1966

Lemere F, Voegtlin WL: An evaluation of the aversion treatment of alcoholism. Q J Stud Alcohol 11:199–204, 1950

Lemere F, Voegtlin WL, Broz WR, et al: Conditioned reflex treatment of chronic alcoholism: VII. Tech Dis Nerv Syst 3:243–247, 1942

Lemkau PV: Mental hygiene in public health. Pub Health Rep 62:1151–1162, 1947

Lemkau PV: What can the public health nurse do in mental hygiene. Paper presented at the Mental Hygiene Conference for U.S. Public Health Service Nursing Consultants, Washington, DC, February 1948

Lemkau PV: Mental Hygiene in Public Health. New York, McGraw-Hill, 1955

Lemkau PV: Operation of the New York State Community Mental Health Services Act in New York, 1956. Paper presented at the Annual Meeting of the American Psychiatric Association. (Abstract in Goldston SE (ed): Concepts of Community Psychiatry: A Framework for Training. Pub Health Service Publ No. 1319. Bethesda, Md, National Institute of Mental Health, 1965, p 197

Lennard HL, Epstein LJ, Rosenthal MS: The methadone illusion. Science 176:881, 1972

Leopold HS: Selection of patients for group psychotherapy. Am J Psychother 11:634, 1957

Leopold HS: The problem of working through in group psychotherapy. Int J Group Psychother 9:287, 1959

Lerner RC: The therapeutic social club: Social rehabilitation for mental patients. Int J Soc Psychiatry 6:101, 1960

Lesse S: Management of apparent remissions in suicidal patients, in Masserman JH (ed): Current Psychiatric Therapies, vol. 7. New York, Grune & Stratton, 1967

Lesse S: The range of therapies in the treatment of severely depressed suicidal patients. Am J Psychother 29:308–326, 1975

Lester D: The unique qualities of telephone therapy. Psychother: Theory Res Prac 11:219–221, 1974

Lester D, Brockopp GM (eds): Crisis Intervention Counseling by Telephone. Springfield, Ill, Thomas, 1973

Lester MW: Counterpoint in psychoanalytic thinking, in Abt LE, Riess BF (eds): Progress in Clinical Psychology, vol. 5. New York, Grune & Stratton, 1964

Leuner H: Guided affective imagery (GAI): A method of intensive psychotherapy. Am J Psychother 23:4–22, 1969

Levene H, Breger L, Patterson V: A training and research program in brief psychotherapy. Am J Psychother 26:90, 1972

Levick M: Adjunctive Techniques in Psychotherapy: Art Therapy in Psychiatric Patients. Nutley, NJ, Roche Laboratories, 1973

Levine A: The time has come. Bull NY State

Distr Branches Am Psychiatr Assoc 8:1, 1965

Levine A: The present status of relations between psychiatry and psychology. Psychiatric Op 8(3):6–9, 1971

Levine M: Psychotherapy in Medical Practice. New York, Macmillan, 1942

Levitt EE: The results of psychotherapy with children: An evaluation. J Consult Psychol 21:189–196, 1957

Levitt EE: Psychotherapy with children: A further evaluation. Behav Res Ther 1:45–51, 1963

Levitz LS, Stunkard AJ: Therapeutic coalition for obesity: Behavior modification and patient self-help. Am J Psychiatry 131:423–427, 1974

Levy D: Attitude therapy. Am J Orthopsychiatry 7:103–113, 1937(a)

Levy D: Studies in sibling rivalry. Res Monogr 2. New York, American Orthopsychiatric Association, 1937(b)

Levy D: Trends in therapy: III. Release therapy. Am J Orthopsychiatry 9:713–737, 1939

Levy D: Development of psychodynamic aspects of oppositional behavior, in Changing Concepts of Psychoanalytic Medicine. New York, Grune & Stratton, 1956

Levy J: The use of art technique in treatment of children's behavior problems. J Psycho-Asthenics 39:258, 1934

Levy J: Relationship therapy. Am J Orthopsychiatry 8:64–69, 1938

Levy RA: A practical approach to community psychiatry in a remote city—What is sex-session psychotherapy? Paper presented at the 122d Annual Meeting of the American Psychiatric Association, Atlantic City, NJ, May 1966

Levy S: The hyperkinetic child—a forgotten entity: Its diagnosis and treatment. Int J Neuropsychiatr 2:330–336, 1966

Lewin K: Frontiers in group dynamics: Concept, method and reality in social science: Social equilibrium and social change. Hum Relations 1:5–41, 1947

Lewin K: Resolving Social Conflicts: Selected Paper on Group Dynamics. New York, Harper & Row, 1948

Lewin K: Field Theory in Social Science: Selected Theoretical Papers. New York, Harper & Row, 1951

Lewin K, Lippit R, White RK: Patterns of aggressive behavior in experimentally created "social climates." J Soc Psychol 10:271–299, 1939

Lewin W: Observations on selective leucotomy.

J Neurol Neurosurg Psychiatry 24:37–44, 1961

Lewinson TS, Zubin J: Handwriting Analysis. New York, King's Crown, 1942

Lewis DJ, Sloane RB: Therapy with LSD. J Clin Exp Psychopathol 19:19, 1958

Lewis M, Solnot AJ: Residential treatment, in Freedman AM, Kaplan HI, Sadock BJ (eds): Comprehensive Textbook of Psychiatry II (2d ed) Baltimore, Williams & Wilkins, 1975, pp 2246–2249

Lewis NDC: The practical value of graphic art in personality studies. I. An introductory presentation of the possibilities. Psychoanal Rev 12:316–322, 1925

Lewis NDC: Graphic art productions in schizophrenia. A Res Nerv Ment Dis Proc 5:344–368, 1928

Liberman RA: Behavioral approach to group dynamics. I. Reinforcing and prompting of cohesiveness in group therapy. Behav Ther 1:141–175, 1970

Licht S: Music in Medicine. Boston, New England Conservatory of Music, 1946

Lichtenberg B: On the selection and preparation of the big brother volunteer, in Guerney BG (ed): Psychotherapeutic Agents: New Roles for Nonprofessionals, Parents and Teachers, New York, Holt, 1969

Lidz T: Schizophrenia and the family. Psychiatry 21:21–27, 1958

Lidz T: The Person. New York, Basic Books, 1968

Lidz T, Edelson M (eds): Training Tomorrow's Psychiatrist. New Haven, Conn, Yale University Press, 1970

Lidz T, Fleck S: Schizophrenia, human integration and the role of the family, in Jackson DD (ed): Etiology of Schizophrenia. New York, Basic Books, 1960

Lidz T, Lidz RW: Therapeutic consideration arising from the intense symbiotic needs of schizophrenics, in Symposium, Psychotherapy of Schizophrenia. New York, International Universities Press, 1952

Lieberman D: Follow-up studies on previously hospitalized narcotic addicts. Am J Orthopsychiatry 35:601–604, 1965

Liebman JS (ed): Psychiatry and Religion. Boston, Beacon, 1948

Liebman R, Minuchin S, Baker L: An integrated program for anorexia nervosa. Am J Psychiatry 131:432–436, 1974

Liederman PC, Liederman VR: Group therapy: An approach to problems of geriatric outpatients, in Masserman JH (ed): Current Psychiatric Therapies, vol. 7. New York, Grune & Stratton, 1967

Lief HI: Subprofessional training in mental health. Arch Gen Psychiatry 5:660–664, 1966

Liegner LM: St. Christopher's Hospice, 1974. JAMA 234:1047–1048, 1975

Life Magazine: Synanon. March 9, 1962, p 56

Lifschutz JE, et al: Psychiatric consultation in the public assistance agency. Soc Casework 39:3–9, 1958

Lifton W: Working with Groups: Group Process and Individual Growth. Palo Alto, Calif, Science Research Associates, 1961

Lillie FR: General biological introduction, in Allen E (ed): Sex and Internal Secretions. Baltimore, Williams & Wilkins, 1931

Lin T-Y, Standley CC: The Scope of Epidemiology in Psychiatry. Geneva, Switz, World Health Organization, 1962

Lindeman EC: Group Work and Education for Democracy. Proceedings of the National Conference of Social Work. New York, Columbia University Press, 1939, pp. 342–347

Lindner RM: Rebel Without a Cause: The Hypnoanalysis of a Criminal Psychopath. New York, Grune & Stratton, 1944

Lindner RM: Who shall practice psychotherapy? Am J Psychother 4:432–442, 1950

Lindner RM: Hypnoanalysis as a psychotherapeutic technique, in Bychowski G, Despert JL (eds): Specialized Techniques in Psychotherapy. New York, Basic Books, 1952, pp 25–39

Lindsley OR: Characteristics of the behavior of chronic psychotics as revealed by free-operant conditioning methods. Dis Nerv Syst 22:66–78, 1960

Lindsley OR: Characteristics of the behavior of chronic psychotics as revealed by free-operant conditioning methods, in Franks CM (ed): Conditioning Techniques in Clinical Practice and Research. New York, Springer, 1964, pp 231–254

Lindstrom PA, Moench LG, Rovnanek A: Prefrontal sonic treatment, in Masserman JH (ed): Current Psychiatric Therapies, vol. 4. New York, Grune & Stratton, 1964

Linn L: The use of drugs in psychotherapy. Psychiatr Q 38:138–148, 1964

Linn, L: Occupational therapy and other therapeutic activities, in Freedman AM, Kaplan JH, Sadock BJ (eds): Comprehensive Textbook of Psychiatry II (2d ed). Baltimore, Williams & Wilkins, 1975, pp 2003–2009

Linn L, Schwartz LW: Psychiatry and Religious Experiences. New York, Random House, 1958

Linn L, Weinroth LA, Shamah R: Occupational Therapy in Dynamic Psychiatry. Washington, DC, American Psychiatric Association, 1962

Linton TE: Services for "problem" children: Contrasts and solutions. Int J Ment Health 2:3–14, 1973

Lipkin S: Round robin time-limited therapy. Amer Acad Psychotherapists Newsletter 2:37–42, 1966

Lippitt GL: Consulting with a national organization: A case study. J Soc Issues 15:20–27, 1959

Lippitt R, Polansky N, Redl F, Rosen S: The dynamics of power. Hum Relations 5:37–64, 1952

Lippitt R, Watson J, Westley B: The Dynamics of Planned Change. New York, Harcourt, 1958

Lippitt R, White RK: The "social climate" of children's groups, in Barker RG, Kounin JS, Wright HF (eds): Child Behavior and Development. New York, McGraw-Hill, 1943, pp 485–508

Lipschutz DM: Combined group and individual psychotherapy. Am J Psychother 11:336–344, 1957

Lipton MA, Ban TA, Kane FJ, et al: Megavitamin and orthomolecular therapy in psychiatry. American Psychiatric Association Task Force Report No. 7. Washington, DC, the Association, July 1973

Liss E: The graphic arts. Am J Orthopsychiatry 8:95–99, 1938

Liston MF: Educational issues confronting mental health nursing, in Leninger MM (ed): Contemporary Issues in Mental Health Nursing. Boston, Little, Brown, 1973

Little KB, Shneidman ES: Congruencies among interpretations of psychological test and anamnesic data. Psychol Monogr. Gen Appl 73:1–42, 1959

Little M: Counter-transference and the patient's response to it. Int J Psychoanal 32:32–40, 1951

Littner N: The impact of the client's unconscious on the caseworker's reactions, in Parad HJ (ed): Ego Psychology and Dynamic Casework. New York, Family Service Association of America, 1958, pp 73–87

Litton EM: Psychiatric aspects of symptom removal by hypnosis. Paper presented at the Conference on Hypnosis, Center for Continuation Study, University of Minnesota, Minneapolis, June 16, 1966

Liversedge LA, Sylvester JD: Conditioning

techniques in the treatment of writer's cramp. Lancet 2:1147–1149, 1955

Livingston MS: On barriers, contempt, and the "vulnerable moment" in group psychotherapy, in Wolberg LR, Aronson ML (eds): Group Therapy 1975: An Overview. New York, Stratton Intercontinental, 1975, pp 242–254

Locke N: The use of dreams in group psychoanalysis. Am J Psychother 11:98, 1957

Locke N: Group Psychoanalysis: Theory and Practice. New York, New York University Press, 1961

Loeser L, Bry T: The position of the group therapist in transference and countertransference. An experimental study. Int J Group Psychother 3:389–406, 1953

Loewenstein RM: Drives, Affects and Behavior. New York, International Universities Press, 1953

Logsdon A: Why primary nursing? Nurs Clin N Am 8:283–291, 1973

Lomax DE: A review of British research in teacher education. Rev Educ Res 42:289–326, 1972

London P: The Modes and Morals of Psychotherapy. New York, Holt, 1964

Long EL, Jr: Religious Beliefs of American Scientists. Philadelphia, Westminster, 1951

Loomis EA: The Self in Pilgrimage. New York, Harper & Row, 1960

Loomis EA: Religion and psychiatry, in Deutsch A, Fishman H (eds): The Encyclopedia of Mental Health. New York, Encyclopedia of Mental Health, 1963, pp 1748–1759

Lorand S: Technique of Psychoanalytic Therapy. New York, International Universities Press, 1946 (repr, 1961)

Lorand S: Persuasions, Psychodynamics and Theory. New York, Gramercy, 1956

Lorand S: Modifications in classical psychoanalysis. Psychiatr Q 32:192–204, 1963

Lorand S: Present trends in psychoanalytic therapy, in Masserman JH (ed): Current Psychiatric Therapies, vol. 3. New York, Grune & Stratton, 1963

Lovibond SH: The mechanism of conditioning treatment of enuresis. Behav Res Ther 1:17–21, 1963

Lovibond SH: Aversive control of behavior. Behav Ther 1:80–91, 1970

Low AA: Recovery, Inc, a project for rehabilitating postpsychotic and long-term psychoneurotic patients, in Soden WH (ed): Rehabilitation of the Handicapped. New York, Ronald, 1950, pp 213–226

Low AA: Mental Health Through Will-Training. Boston, Christopher, 1952

Low NL, Myers GG: Suvren in brain-injured children. J Pediatr 3:259–263, 1958

Lowen A: Physical Dynamics of Character Structure. New York, Grune & Stratton, 1958

Lowenfeld M: The world pictures of children: A method of recording and studying them. Br J Med Psychol 18:65–101, 1939

Lowinger P, Dobie S, Reid S: What happens to the psychiatric office patient treated with drugs? A follow-up study. Paper presented at the 120th Annual Meeting of the American Psychiatric Association, Los Angeles, May 1964

Lowrey LG: Psychiatry for Social Workers. New York, Columbia University Press, 1946, pp 342–366

Lowry F: A Philosophy of Supervision in Social Case Work. New York, National Council of Social Workers, 1936, pp 108–113

Lowy S, Gutheil EA: Active analytic psychotherapy (Stekel), in Fromm-Reichmann F, Moreno J (eds): Progress in Psychotherapy. New York, Grune & Stratton, 1956, pp 136–143

Luborsky L: A note of Eysenck's article, the effects of psychotherapy: An evaluation. Br J Psychol 45:129–131, 1954

Luborsky L, Singer B, Luborsky L: Comparative studies of psychotherapies. Arch Gen Psychiatry 32:995–1008, 1975

Lucas D, et al: Group psychotherapy with depressed patients incorporating mood music. Am J Psychother 18:126–136, 1964

Luchins AS: Group structures in group psychotherapy. J Clin Psychol 3:269–273, 1947

Ludwig AM: Altered states of consciousness. Arch Gen Psychiatry 15:225–234, 1966

Ludwig AM, Levine J: Hypnodelic therapy, in Masserman JH (ed): Current Psychiatric Therapies, vol. 7. New York, Grune & Stratton, 1967

Luff MC, Garrod M: The after-results of psychotherapy in five hundred adult cases. Br Med J 2:54–59, 1935

Lundin LH, Aranov BM: Use of co-therapists in group psychotherapy. J Consult Psychol 16:76–80, 1952

Lundin RW: Personality—An Experimental Approach. New York, Macmillan, 1961

Luthe W: Autogenic training: Method, research and application in medicine. Am J Psychother 17:174–195, 1963

Luthe W (ed): Autogenic Training. New York, Grune & Stratton, 1965

Luthe W (ed): Autogenic Therapy, vol. 1–6. New York, Grune & Stratton, 1969–1973

Luthe W, Jus A, Geissman P: Autogenic state and autogenic shift: Psychophysiologic and neurophysiologic aspects. Acta Psychother 11:1–13, 1963

Lyle J, Holly SB: The therapeutic value of puppets. Bull Menninger Clin 5:223–226, 1941

Maas H: Social casework, in Friedlander WA (ed): Concepts and Methods of Social Work. Englewood Cliffs, NJ, Prentice-Hall, 1958, pp 48–65

McCabe OL: Psychedelic (LSD) psychotherapy: A case report. Psychother: Theory Res Prac 11:2–10, 1974

McCabe OL, Savage C, Kurland AA, Unger S: Psychedelic (LSD) therapy of neurotic disorders: Short-term effects. J Psychedelic Drugs 5:18–28, 1972

McCann RV: The Churches and Mental Health. New York, Basic Books, 1962

McCarthy BW: A modification of Masters and Johnson sex therapy model in a clinical setting. Psychother: Theory Res Prac 10:290–293, 1973

McConaghy N: Aversion therapy of homosexuality, in Masserman JH (ed): Current Psychiatric Therapies, vol. 12. New York, Grune & Stratton, 1972

McDonald E: The masking function of self-revelation in group therapy. Int J Group Psychother 1:59–63, 1951

MacDonald JM, Daniels M: The psychiatric ward as a therapeutic community. J Nerv Ment Dis 124:148–155, 1956

McGovern WM: An Introduction to Mahayana Buddhism, with Especial References to Chinese and Japanese Phases. London, Routledge & Kegan, 1922

McGovern WM: A Manual of Buddhist Philosophy. London, Routledge & Kegan, 1923

McGraw RB, Oliven JF: Miscellaneous therapies, in Arieti S (ed): American Handbook of Psychiatry. New York, Basic Books, 1959

McGregor HG: Enuresis in children. Br Med J 1:1061–1066, 1937

MacGregor R, Ritchie AM, Serrano AC, Schuster FP, Jr: Multiple Impact Therapy with Families. New York, McGraw-Hill, 1964

McGuire C: Teaching of psychotherapy. Paper presented at the Postgraduate Center for Mental Health, New York, November 1964

McGuire MT: The instruction nature of short-term insight psychotherapy. Am J Psychother 22:218–232, 1968

McGuire RJ, Vallance M: Aversion therapy by electric shock: A simple technique. Br Med J 1:151–153, 1964

Machover K: Personality Projection in the Drawing of the Human Figure. Springfield, Ill, Thomas, 1948

Machover K: In Anderson HH, Anderson GL (eds): An Introduction to Projective Techniques. Englewood Cliffs, NJ, Prentice-Hall, 1951, pp 341–360

McIntosh JR, Pickford RW: Some clinical and artistic aspects of a child's drawings. Br J Med Psychol 19:342–362, 1943

MacKay HA, Laverty SG: G.S.R. changes during therapy of phobic behavior. Unpublished manuscript. Queens University, Ontario, Canada, 1963

Mack-Brunswick R: The preoedipal phase of the libido development. Psychoanal Q 9:293–319, 1940

MacKenzie KR: An eclectic approach to phobias. Am J Psychiatry 130:1103–1106, 1973

Mackie R, Wood J: Observations on two sides of a one-way screen. Int J Group Psychother 18:177–185, 1968

McKinley DA, Jr. et al: Architecture for the Community Mental Health Center. NIMH School of Architecture, Rice University, 1966. Available from the Mental Health Materials Center, New York, NY

McKinney F: Explorations in bibliotherapy. Psychother: Theory, Res Prac 12:110–117, 1975

MacLean JR, MacDonald DC, Bryne UP, Hubbard AM: Use of LSD-25 in the treatment of alcoholism and other psychiatric problems. Q J Stud Alcohol 22:34–45, 1961

McLean P: Psychiatry and philosophy, in Arieti S (ed): American Handbook of Psychiatry. New York, Basic Books, 1959

MacLennan BW, et al: Training for new careers. Commun Ment Health J June 1966

McNeill J: History of the Cure of Souls. New York, Harper & Row, 1951

McNemar A: Psychological Statistics. New York, Wiley, 1949

Maddun JF, Bowden CL: Critique of success with methadone maintenance. Am J Psychiatry 129:440–446, 1972

Maddux JF: Psychiatric consultation in a public welfare agency. Am J Orthopsychiatry 20:754–764, 1950

Maddux JF: Psychiatric consultation in a rural setting. Am J Orthopsychiatry 23:775–784, 1953

Mahler MS: On child psychosis and schizophrenia. Autistic and symbiotic infantile psychoses, in Eissler R, et al (eds): The

Psychoanalytic Study of the Child, vol. 7. New York, International Universities Press, 1952, pp 286–305

Mahler MS: Autism and symbiosis: Two extremes of identity. Int J Psychoanal 39:77, 1958(a)

Mahler MS: On two crucial phases of integration of the sense of identity: Separation-individuation and bisexual identity. Abstracted in Panel on problems of identity, rep Rubinfine DI. J Am Psychoanal Assoc 6:136–139, 1958(b)

Mahler MS: A study of the separation-individuation process and its possible application to borderline phenomena in the psychoanalytic situation, in Eissler R, et al (eds): Psychoanalytic Study of the Child, vol. 26. New Haven, Yale University Press, 1971, pp 403–424

Mahler MS, Furer M, Settlage CF: Severe emotional disturbances in childhood, in Arieti S (ed): American Handbook of Psychiatry, vol. 1. New York, Basic Books, 1959, pp 816–839

Mahoney MJ: Cognition and Behavior Therapy. Cambridge, Mass, Ballinger, 1974

Main TF: The hospital as a therapeutic institution. Bull Menninger Clin 10:66–76, 1946

Majumdar SK: Introduction to Yoga—Principles and Practices. New Hyde Park, NY, University Books, 1964

Malamud DL: Objective measurement of clinical status in psychopathological research. Psychol Bull 43:240–258, 1946

Malamud IT: Volunteers in community mental health work. Ment Hyg 39:300–309, 1959

Malan DH: A Study of Brief Psychotherapy. Springfield, Ill, Thomas, 1963

Malan DH: The outcome problem in psychotherapy research. Arch Gen Psychiatry 29:719–729, 1973

Malan DH, Heath ES, Bacal HA, Balfour FHG: Psychodynamic changes in untreated neurotic patients. Arch Gen Psychiatry 32:110–126, 1975

Malhotra JC: Yoga and psychiatry: A review, J Neuropsychiatry 4:375–385, 1963

Maltz M: Psycho-cybernetics. Englewood Cliffs, NJ, Prentice-Hall, 1960 (paperback—New York, Pocket Books, 1973)

Manaser JC, Werner AM: Instruments for Study of Nurse–Patient Interaction. New York, Macmillan, 1964

Mangus AR: Role theory in marriage counseling. Soc Forces 35:200–209, 1957

Mann EC: Frigidity. Clin Obstet Gynecol 3:739–759, 1960

Mann J: Encounter: A Weekend with Intimate Strangers. New York, Grossman, 1970

Mann J: Time-Limited Psychotherapy. Cambridge, Harvard University Press, 1973

Mann NM, Conway EJ, Gottesfeld BH, Lasser LM: Coordinated approach to antabuse therapy. JAMA 149:40–46, 1952

Mannino FV, MacLennan BW, Shore MF: The Practice of Mental Health Consultation. New York, Gardner, 1975

Marcus EH: Gestalt therapy, in Masserman JH (ed): Current Psychiatric Therapies, vol. 11. New York, Grune & Stratton, 1971

Markowitz M: Analytic group psychotherapy of married couples by a therapist couple, in Rosenbaum S, Alger I (eds): Psychoanalysis and Marriage. New York, Basic Books, 1967

Markowitz M, Kadis A: Parental interaction as a determining factor in social growth of the individual in the family. Int J Soc Psychiatry, Congress Issue, 1964

Marks I, Hodgson R, Rachman S: Treatment of chronic obsessive-compulsive neurosis by in-vivo exposure. Br J Psychiatry 127:349–364, 1975

Marmor J: Some considerations concerning orgasm in the female. Psychosom Med 16:240–245, 1954

Marmor J: Psychoanalytic therapy as an educational process: Common denominators in the therapeutic approaches of different psychoanalytic "schools," in Masserman JH (ed): Science and Psychoanalysis, vol. 5. New York, Grune & Stratton, 1962, pp 286–299

Marmor J: Sexual Inversion: The Multiple Roots of Homosexuality. New York, Basic Books, 1965

Marmor J: Theories of learning and the psychotherapeutic process. Br J Psychiatry 112:363–366, 1966

Marmor J (ed): Modern Psychoanalysis: New Directions and Perspectives. New York, Basic Books, 1968

Marmor J: The future of psychoanalytic therapy. Am J Psychol 130:1197–1202, 1973

Marmor J: Limitations of free association, in Psychiatry in Transition. New York, Brunner/Mazel, 1973, pp 265–275

Marsh LC: Group treatment of the psychoses by the psychological equivalent of the revival. Ment Hyg 15:328–349, 1931

Marsh LC: Group therapy and the psychiatric clinic. J Nerv Ment Dis 82:381–393, 1935

Martin AJ: LSD treatment of chronic psychoneurotic patients under day hospital conditions. Int J Soc Psychiatry 3:188, 1957

Martin AJ: LSD analysis. Int J Soc Psychiatry 10:165–169, 1964

Martin AR: A psychoanalytic contribution to the study of effort. Am J Psychoanal 4:108, 1944

Martin AR: Reassurance in therapy. Am J Psychoanal 9:17, 1949

Martin AR: The fear of relaxation and leisure. Am J Psychoanal 11:52, 1951

Martin HH: American minister. Saturday Evening Post, April 24, 1965, p 21

Martin PA, Bird HW: An approach to the psychotherapy of marriage partners: The stereoscopic technique. Psychiatry 16:123–127, 1963

Martin PA, Lief HI: Resistance to innovation in psychiatric training as exemplified by marital therapy, in Usdin G (ed): Psychiatry: Education and Image. New York, Brunner/Mazel, 1973

Martin WR, Fraser HF, Gorodetzky CW, Rosenberg DE: Studies of the dependence producing potential of the narcotic antagonist 2-cyclopropylmethyl-2'-hydroxy-5, 9-dimethyl-6, 7-benzomorphan (cyclazocine, Win 20, 740, ARCII-C3). J Pharmacol 150:426–436, 1965

Mason AA: Psychotherapeutic treatment of asthma. Trans World Asthma Conference, 1965, pp 89–91

Mason AA: Personal communication. 1966

Mason AS, Tarpy EK: Foster home preparation cottage: A transitional program for the chronic mental patient, in Masserman JH (ed): Current Psychiatric Therapies, vol. 4. New York, Grune & Stratton, 1964, pp 218–221

Masserman JH: Behavior and Neurosis. Chicago, University of Chicago Press, 1943

Masserman JH: Music and the child in society. Am J Psychother 8:63–68, 1954

Masserman JH: Practice of Dynamic Psychiatry. Philadelphia, Saunders, 1955

Masserman JH (ed): Individual and Family Dynamics. New York, Grune & Stratton, 1959

Masserman JH: Principles of Dynamic Psychiatry. Philadelphia, Saunders, 1961

Masserman JH (ed): Current Psychiatric Therapies, vol. 3. New York, Grune & Stratton, 1963

Masserman JH, Carmichael HT: Diagnosis and prognosis in psychiatry. J Ment Sci 84:893–946, 1938

Masters WH, Johnson VE: A team approach to the rapid diagnosis and treatment of sexual incompatibility. Pacif Med Surg 72:371–375, 1964

Masters WH, Johnson VE: Human Sexual Response. Boston, Little, Brown, 1966

Masters WH, Johnson VE: Human Sexual Inadequacy. Boston, Little, Brown, 1970

Masterson JF: Psychotherapy of the Borderline Adult. New York, Brunner/Mazel, 1976

Matarazzo RG: Research on the teaching and learning of psychotherapeutic skills, in Bergin A, Garfield S (eds): Handbook of Psychotherapy and Behavior Change. New York, Wiley, 1971

Matheney R, Topalis M: Psychiatric Nursing. St Louis, Mo, Mosby, 1965

Mathews S: On the Effects of Music in Curing and Palliating Diseases. Philadelphia, Wagner, 1906

Mathewson RH: The role of the counselor. Harvard Educ Rev 17:10–27, 1947

Mathewson RH: Guidance, Policy and Practice. New York, Harper & Row, 1949

Matte-Blanco I: The effects of psychotherapy. Int J Psychiatry 1:163–165, 1965

Matz PB: Outcome of hospital treatment of ex-service patients with nervous and mental disease in the U.S. Veteran's Bureau. U.S. Vet Bur Med Bull 5:829–842, 1929

Maultsby M: Against technical eclecticism. Psychol Rep 22:926–928, 1968

Maultsby M: Routine tape recorder use in REI. J Rational Living 5:823, 1970

Maves PB, Cedarleaf JL: Older People and the Church. Nashville, Tenn, Abingdon, 1949

Max LM: Conditioned reaction technique, a case study. Psychol Bull 32:734, 1935

Maxmen JS, Silberfarb PM, Ferrell, RB: Anorexia nervosa. JAMA 229:801–803, 1974

Maxwell AE: Multivariate statistical methods and classification problems. Br J Psychiatry 119:121, 1971

May PRA: Treatment of Schizophrenia. New York, Science House, 1968

May PRA: For better or worse? Psychotherapy and variance change: A critical review of the literature. J Nerv Ment Dis 152:184–192, 1971

May R: The Meaning of Anxiety. New York, Ronald, 1950

May R: The nature of creativity, in Anderson HH (ed): Creativity and Its Cultivation. New York, Harper & Row 1959

May R: Existential bases of psychotherapy. Am J Orthopsychiatry 30, October 1960

May R, et al (eds): Existence. New York, Basic Books, 1958

May R, Van Kaam A: Existential theory and therapy, in Masserman JH (ed): Current

Psychiatric Therapies, vol. 3. New York, Grune & Stratton, 1963

Mayeroff M: On Caring. New York, Harper & Row, 1971

Meacham ML, Wiesen AE: Changing Classroom Behavior: A Manual for Precision Teaching (2d ed). New York, IEP, 1974

Mead GH: Mind, Self and Society. Chicago, University of Chicago Press, 1934

Mead M: From the South Seas. New York, Morrow, 1939

Mead M: Sex and Temperament. New York, Mentor, 1952

Meador BD: Client-centered group therapy, in Gazda GM (ed): Counseling and Group Psychotherapy (rev ed). Springfield, Ill, Thomas, 1975

Mebane JC: Use of Deanol with disturbed juvenile offenders. Dis Nerv Syst 21:642, 1960

Medical News: Value of antidepressant drugs over other therapy questioned. 190:37, 1964

Medical Society of County of NY: The dangerous drug problem. NY State J Med 66:241–246, 1966

Medical Tribune: 4(19): 10, 1963

Medical Tribune: 130 cases of spontaneous cancer regression surveyed. 4(92), November 18, 1963

Medical Tribune: Ralph Nader organization attacks mental health centers. 13:1, 1972

Medical World News: Shocking device for bedwetters. May 12, 1972

Medical World News: Sex counseling and the primary physician. March 2, 1973

Meduna LJ: Carbon Dioxide Therapy. A Neurophysiological Treatment of Nervous Disorders. Springfield, Ill, Thomas, 1950

Meduna LJ: Physiological background of carbon dioxide treatment of the neuroses. Paper presented at the 109th Annual Meeting of the American Psychiatric Association, Los Angeles, May 7, 1953

Meehl PE: Psychopathology and purpose, in Hoch PH, Zubin J (eds): The Future of Psychiatry. New York, Grune & Stratton, 1962

Meehl PE: The effects of psychotherapy. Int J Psychiatry 1:156–157, 1965

Meerloo AM: Transference and resistance in geriatric psychotherapy. Psychoanal Rev 42:72–82, 1955

Meichenbaum DH: Cognitive Behavior Modification. New York, Plenum, 1977

Meier EG: Social and cultural factors in casework diagnosis. Soc Casework 41:15–26

Meijering WL: The interrelation of individual, group, and hospital community psychotherapy. Int J Group Psychother 10:46–62, 1960

Meissner JH: The relationship between voluntary nonfluency and stuttering. J Speech Dis 11:13–33, 1946

Meissner WW: Annotated Bibliography in Religion and Psychology. New York, Academy of Religion and Mental Health, 1961

Melnick J, Tims AR: Application of videotape equipment to group therapy. Int J Group Psychother 24:199–205, 1974

Meltzer D: The Psychoanalytic Process. Perth, Scot, Clunie, 1973(a)

Meltzer D: Sexual States of Mind. Perth, Scot, Clunie, 1973(b)

Meltzer D: Explorations in Autism. Perth, Scot, Clunie, 1975

Mendel W: Hospital treatment for chronic schizophrenics. J Existen Psychiatry 4:49, 1963

Mendel W: Outpatient therapy of chornic schizophrenia, in Masserman JH (ed): Current Psychiatric Therapies, vol. 4. New York, Grune & Stratton, 1964

Mendel W, Rapport S: Outpatient treatments for chronic schizophrenic patients. Arch Gen Psychiatry 8:100, 1963

Mendell D: Discussion, in Death and Dying: Attitudes of Patient and Doctor. GAP Symposium No. 11, 1965, p 649

Mendelson D: Patient's prior expectation and discrepancies between expectation and actual perception of psychotherapy as factors in session absences. Unpublished doctoral dissertation, Postgraduate Center for Mental Health, New York, 1973

Mennell JB: Physical Treatment by Movement, Manipulation and Massage (5th ed). Philadelphia, Blakiston, 1945

Menninger KA: Religious applications of psychiatry. Pastoral Couns 1:13–22, 1950

Menninger KA: What are the goals of psychiatric education? Bull Menninger Clin 16:156, 1952(a)

Menninger KA: A Manual for Psychiatric Case Study. New York, Grune & Stratton, 1952(b)

Menninger KA: Theory of Psychoanalytic Technique. New York, Basic Books, 1958; 1961

Menninger KA, Holzman PS: Theory of Psychoanalytic Technique (2d ed). New York, Basic Books, 1973

Menninger RW: Observations on absences of member patients in group psychotherapy. Int J Group Psychother 9:195–203, 1949

Menninger WC: Psychiatric social work in the army and its implications for civilian social work. Proceedings of the National Conference of Social Work, 1945

Menninger WC: Psychiatry and religion. Pastoral Psychol 1:14–16, 1950

Mental Hygiene Committee, National Organization of Public Health Nursing: Nurse as a mental health consultant: Functions and qualifications. Pub Health Nurs 42:507–509, 1950

Mereness D: The psychiatric nursing specialist and her professional identity. Perspect Psychiatr Care 1:18–19, 1963(a) 18–19

Mereness D: The potential significant role of the nurse in community mental health services. Perspect Psychiatr Care 1:34–40, 1963(b)

Mereness D: Problems and issues in contemporary psychiatric nursing. Perspect Psychiatr Care 2:14–21, 1964

Merlis S, Beyel V, Fiorentino D, et al: Polypharmacy in psychiatry: Empiricism, efficacy, and rationale, in Masserman JH (ed): Current Psychiatric Therapies, vol. 12. New York, Grune & Stratton, 1972

Merrill S, Cary GL: Dream analysis in brief psychotherapy. Am J Psychother 29:185–193, 1975

Mesnikoff AM: Ward group projects as a focus for dynamic milieu therapy. NY State J Med 60:2395–2399, 1960

Meyer A: Objective psychology and psychobiology. JAMA 65:860–863, 1915

Meyer A: The Commonsense Psychiatry of Dr. Adolf Meyer. New York, McGraw-Hill, 1948

Meyer E, et al: Contractually time-limited psychotherapy in an outpatient psychotherapy clinic. Am J Psychiatry 124(Suppl):57–68, 1967

Meyer HJ, Borgatta EF: An Experiment in Mental Patient Rehabilitation. New York, Russel Sage Foundation, 1959

Meyerson A: Effect of benzedrine sulphate on mood and fatigue in normal and neurotic persons. Arch Neurol Psychiatry 36:816, 1936

Michaels J: Character structure and character disorders, in Arieti S (ed): American Handbook of Psychiatry, vol. 1. New York, Basic Books, 1959, pp 365–366

Midelfort CF: The Family in Psychotherapy. New York, McGraw-Hill, 1957

Migler B, Wolpe J: Automated desensitization: A case report. Behav Res Ther 5:133–135, 1967

Milbank Memorial Fund: The Elements of a Community Mental Health Program. New York, the Fund, 1956

Milbank Memorial Fund: Programs for Community Mental Health. New York, the Fund, 1957

Milbank Memorial Fund: Progress and Problems of Community Mental Health Services. New York, the Fund, 1959

Miles H, Barrabee EL, Finesinger JE: Evaluation of psychotherapy. Psychosom Med 113:83–105, 1951

Miller D: Adolescence: Psychology, Psychopathology and Psychotherapy. New York, Aronson, 1974

Miller EC, Dvorak A, Turner DW: A method of creating aversion to alcohol by reflex conditioning in a group setting. Q J Stud Alcohol 21:424–431, 1960. Also in Franks CM (ed): Conditioning Techniques in Clinical Practice and Research. New York, Springer, 1964, pp 157–164

Miller JG: Elements in the Medical Curriculum Which Should be Incorporated in the Training of the Clinical Psychologist. Transactions of the First Conference. New York, Josiah Macy, Jr, Foundation, 1947, pp 41–46

Miller JG: Criteria and measurement of changes during psychiatric treatment. Bull Menninger Clin 18:130–137, 1954

Miller WB: The telephone in outpatient psychotherapy. Am J Psychother 27:15–26, 1972

Mills Report: Bull Assoc Am Med Coll 6:62, 1971

Minkowski E: Lived Time: Phenomenological and Psychopathological Studies. Nancy Metzel (trans). Evanston, Ill, Northwestern University Press, 1970

Mintz EE: Time-extended marathon groups. Psychother: Theory Res Prac 4:65–70, 1967

Mintz EE: Marathon Groups, Reality and Symbol. New York, Appleton-Century-Crofts, 1971

Mintz EE: On the rationale of touch in psychotherapy, in Sager CJ, Kaplan HS (eds): Progress in Group and Family Therapy. New York, Brunner/Mazel, 1972, pp 151–155

Mintz EE: On the dramatization of psychoanalytic interpretations, in Wolberg LR, Aronson ML (eds): Group Therapy 1974: An Overview. New York, Stratton Intercontinental, 1974, pp 175–185

Mintz NL, Schwartz DT: Urban ecology and psychosis. Int J Soc Psychiatry 10:101–119, 1964

Minuchin S: Conflict-resolution family therapy. Psychiatry 28:278–286, 1965

Minuchin S: Families and Family Therapy. Cambridge, Harvard University Press, 1974(a)

Minuchin S: Structural family therapy, in Arieti

S (ed): American Handbook of Psychiatry, vol. 2 (2d ed). New York, Basic Books, 1974(b), pp 178–192

Minuchin S, Montalvo B: Techniques for working with disorganized low socioeconomic families. Am J Orthopsychiatry 37:880–887, 1967

Mira E: Myokinetic psychodiagnosis: A new technique for exploring the conative trends of personality. Proc Roy Soc Med 33:9–30, 1940

Misiak H, Sexton VS: History of Psychology: An Overview. New York, Grune & Stratton, 1966

Missildine WH: Your Inner Child of the Past. New York, Simon & Schuster, 1963

Mitchell C: Family interviewing in family diagnosis. Soc Casework 40:381–384, 1959

Mitchell HE: Application of the Kaiser method to parital pairs. Fam Process 2:265–279, 1963

Mitchell KB: Do pastoral counselors bring a new consciousness to the health professions? J Pastoral Care 26:245, 1972

Mitchell TW: Problems in Psychopathology. New York, Harcourt, 1927

Mittelman B: Complementary neurotic reactions in intimate relationships. Psychoanal Q 13:491–497, 1944

Mittelman B: The concurrent analysis of married couples. Psychoanal Q 17:182–197, 1948(a)

Mittelman B: Failures in psychosomatic case treatments, in Hoch P (ed): Failures in Psychiatric Treatment. New York, Grune & Stratton, 1948(b) pp 106–117

Mittelman B: Analysis of reciprocal neurotic patterns, in Family Relationships. New York, Basic Books, 1956

Modell W: The Relief of Symptoms. Philadelphia, Saunders, 1955

Moench LG: Office Psychiatry. Chicago, Year Book Publishing, 1952

Money-Kyrle RE: Man's Picture of His World. New York, International Universities Press, 1961

Montgomery GT, Crowder JE: The symptom substitution hypothesis and the evidence. Psychother: Theory Res Prac 9:98–102, 1972

Moore FJ, Chernell E, West MJ: Television as a therapeutic tool. Gen Psychiatry 12:217–220, 1965

Moore GE: Some Main Problems of Philosophy. New York, Macmillan, 1953

Moreno JL: Who Shall Survive? Washington, DC, Nervous & Mental Disease Publishing Co, 1934

Moreno JL: Psychodrama, vol. 1. Beacon, NY, Beacon House, 1946

Moreno JL: The First Book on Group Psychotherapy (3d ed). Beacon, NY, Beacon House, 1957

Moreno JL: Introduction. Psychodrama, vol. 1 (3d ed). Beacon, NY, Beacon House, 1964

Moreno JL: Psychotherapie de Group. Paris, Presse Universitaire de France, 1965, pp 169–180

Moreno JL: Therapeutic aspects of psychodrama. Psychiatr Op 3:36–42, 1966(a)

Moreno JL (ed): The International Handbook of Group Psychotherapy. New York, Philosophical Library, 1966(b)

Morgenthau HJ: Death in the nuclear age. Commentary 32:231–234, 1961

Morris RD: The essential meaning of clinical pastoral training, in Hiltner S (ed): Clinical Pastoral Training. New York, Federal Council of Churches of Christ in America, 1945

Morse PW, et al: The effect of group psychotherapy in reducing resistance to individual psychotherapy. A case study. Int J Group Psychother 5:261–269, 1955

Mosher LR, Feinsilver RD: Current studies on schizophrenia. Int J Psychiatry 11:7–52, 1973

Moss CS: The Hypnotic Investigation of Dreams. New York, Wiley, 1967

Moss CS, Bremer B: Exposure of a "medical modeler" to behavior modification. Int J Clin Exp Hypn 21:1–12, 1973

Mosse EP: Painting-analysis in the treatment of neuroses. Psychoanal Rev 27:65–82, 1940

Moulton R: Multiple dimensions in supervision. Contemp Psychol 5:151–158, 1969

Mowrer OH: Learning Theory and Personality Dynamics. New York, Ronald, 1950

Mowrer OH: Anxiety theory as a basis for distinguishing between counseling and psychotherapy, in Berdie RF (ed): Concepts and Progress of Counseling. Minneapolis, University of Minnesota Press, 1953

Mowrer OH, Mowrer WM: A new method for the study and treatment of enuresis. Psychol Bull 33:611–612, 1936

Mowrer OH, Mowrer WM: Enuresis—a method for its study and treatment. Am J Orthopsychiatry 8:436–457, 1938

Mueller EE: Rebels with a cause. Am J Psychother 18:272–284, 1964

Muench GA: An investigation of the efficiency of time-limited psychotherapy. J Counsel Psychol 12:294–299, 1965

Muench GA, Schumacher R: A clinical experiment with rotational time-limited psychotherapy. Psychother: Theory Res Prac 5:81–84, 1968

Mulac MD: Educational Games for Fun. New York, Harper & Row, 1971

Mullahy P: Harry Stack Sullivan's theory of schizophrenia. Int J Psychiatry 4:492–521, 1967

Mullahy P: Psychoanalysis and Interpersonal Psychiatry. New York, Science House, 1968

Mullan H: Conflict avoidance in group psychotherapy. Int J Group Psychother 3:243, 1953(a)

Mullan H: Countertransference in groups. Am J Psychother 7:680, 1953(b)

Mullan H: Transference and countertransference. New Horizon. Int J Group Psychother 5:169–180, 1955

Mullan H: Group Psychotherapy, Theory and Practice. With Rosenbaum M. New York, Free Press, 1962

Mullan H, Sangiuliano IA: Interpretation as existence in analysis. Psychoanal Rev 45:52–64, 1958

Muller TG: The Nature and Direction of Psychiatric Nursing. Philadelphia, Lippincott, 1950

Muller-Hegemann D: The effects of psychotherapy. Int J Psychiatry 1:157–158, 1965

Muncie W: Psychobiology and Psychiatry 2d (ed). St Louis. Mosby, 1948

Muncie W: The psychobiologic approach, in Arieti S (ed): American Handbook of Psychiatry, vol. 2. New York, Basic Books, 1959, p 1326

Muncie W: Personal communication. 1976

Munster AJ, Stanley AM, Saunders JC: Imipramine (tofranil) in the treatment of enuresis. Am J Psychiatry 118:76, 1961

Munzer J: The effect on analytic therapy groups of the experimental introduction of special "warm-up" procedures during the first five sessions. Int J Group Psychother 14:60, 1964

Muro JJ: Play media in counseling: A brief report on experience and some opinions. Elem School Guide Counsel 3:104–110, 1968

Murphy LB: Personality in Young Children. Vol. 1, Methods for the Study of Personality in Young Children. New York, Basic Books, 1956

Murphy LB: Adaptional tasks in childhood in our culture. Bull Menninger Clin 28:309–322, 1964

Murphy M: The Social Group Work Method in Social Work Education. Vol. 2, A Project Report of the Curriculum Study, Werner W Boehm, Director and Coordinator. New York, Council on Social Work Education, 1959

Murray DC: The suicide threat: Base rates and appropriate therapeutic strategy. Psychother: Theory Res Prac 9:176–179, 1972

Murray EJ: A content-analysis method for studying psychotherapy. Psychol Monogr 70, No. 14 (Whole No. 420), 1956

Murray EJ, Cohen M: Mental Illness, milieu therapy and social organization in ward groups. J Abnorm Soc Psychol 58:48–55, 1959

Murray HA: Explorations in Personality. London, Oxford University Press, 1938, pp 530–545

Murray VF, Burns MM: The use of sodium amytal in the treatment of psychosis. Psychiatr Q 6:273, 1932

Muscatenc LC: Principles of group psychotherapy and psychodrama as applied to music therapy. Int J Group Psychother 14:176–185, 1961

Mussen PH, Conger JJ: Child Development and Personality. New York, Harper & Row, 1956

Muth LT: Aftercare for the mentally ill: A world picture. Philadelphia, Smith, Kline & French Labs, 1957

Muthard JE, et al: Guide to Information Centers in the Social Services. Gainesville, Regional Rehabilitation Research Institute, University of Florida 1971

Myers ES: National health insurance: Prospects and problems. Psychiatr Ann 4:17, 1974

Myerson A: Effect of benzedrine sulphate on mood and fatigue in normal and neurotic persons. Arch Neurol Psychiatry 36:816, 1936

Myrick RD, Moni LS: The counselor's workshop. Elem School Guid Counsel 6:202–295, 1972

Nacht S: Technical remarks on the handling of the transference neuroses. Int J Psychoanal 38:196–203, 1957

Nacht S: Variations in techniques. Int J Psychoanal 39:2352—237, 1958

Napoli PJ: Finger-painting and personality diagnosis. Genet Psychol Monogr 34, No. 2, 1946

Napoli PJ: Interpretive aspects of finger-painting. J Psychol 23:93–132, 1947

Naranjo C: Contributions of gestalt therapy, in Otto H, Mann J (eds): Ways of Growth. New York, Pocket Books, 1971

Nash EM, Jessner L, Abse DW (eds): Marriage Counseling in Medical Practice. Chapel Hill, University of North Carolina Press, 1964

National Association for Mental Health (NAMH): The Mental Health Association in Planning for Comprehensive Community Mental Health Services, Sixth Annual Mental Health Association Staff Council Institute. New York, the Association, 1963(a)

National Association for Mental Health: The Mental Health Services, Seventh Annual Mental Health Association Summer Staff Training Institute. New York, the Association, 1963(b)

National Institute of Mental Health (NIMH): Planning of Facilities for Mental Health Services. Washington, DC, U.S. Government Printing Office, 1961

National Institute of Mental Health, Surgeon General's Ad Hoc Committee on Mental Health Activities: Mental Health Activities and the Development of Comprehensive Health Programs in the Community. Department Pub Health Service Publ No. 995. Bethesda, Md, the Institute, 1962

National Institute of Mental Health: Mental Health and Social Change: An Annotated Bibliography. DHEW Publ No. (HSM) 72–9149, 1967–1970. Washington, DC, U.S. Government Printing Office, 1970

National Institute of Mental Health: Community Mental Health Center Program: Operating Manual. Washington, DC, U.S. Government Printing Office, 1971

National Institute of Mental Health: Mental Health Consultation to Programs for Children. DHEW Publ No. (HSM) 72–9088. Washington, DC, U.S. Government Printing Office, 1972

National Institute of Mental Health: NIMH: Promoting Mental Health in the Classroom. DHEW Publ No. (HSMO) 73–9033. Washington, DC, U.S. Government Printing Office, 1973

Naumburg M: The drawings of an adolescent girl suffering from conversion hysteria with amnesia. Psychiatr Q 18:197–224, 1944

Naumburg M: Studies of the "Free" Art Expression of Behavior Problem Children and Adolescents as a Means of Diagnosis and Therapy. Monogr No. 71. Washington, DC, Nervous & Mental Disease Publishing Co, 1947

Naumburg M: Schizophrenic Art: Its Meaning in Psychotherapy. New York, Grune & Stratton, 1950

Naumburg M: Psychoneurotic Art: Its Use in Psychotherapy. New York, Grune & Stratton, 1953

Naumburg M: Dynamically Oriented Art Therapy: Its Principles and Practice. New York, Grune & Stratton, 1966

Naumburg M: Dynamically oriented art therapy, in Masserman JH (ed): Current Psychiatric Therapies, vol. 7. New York, Grune & Stratton, 1967

Naumburg M, Caldwell J: The use of spontaneous art in dynamically oriented group therapy of obese women. Acta Psychother 7:254–287, 1959

Nelson RC: Pros and cons of using play media in counseling. Elem School Guid Counsel 2:143–147, 1967

Nemiah JC: The psychological management and treatment of patients with peptic ulcer, in Weiner H (ed): Advances in Psychosomatic Medicine, vol. 6. Basel, Switz, Karger, 1971, pp 169–185

Neufeld W: Relaxation methods in United States Navy air schools. Am J Psychiatry 108:132–137, 1951

New York Academy of Medicine: Report on drug addiction, II. NY State J Med 63:1977–2000, 1963

New York State Counselors Association: Practical Handbook for Counselors. Palo Alto, Calif, Science Research Associates, 1945

New York Times: Growth of community mental health in reducing the number of patients in hospitals. July 30, 1972

Nicholls G: Treatment of a disturbed mother–child relationship: A case presentation, in Parad HJ (ed): Ego Psychology and Dynamic Casework. New York, Family Service Association of America, 1958, pp 117–125

Nichols LA: The presentation and diagnosis of impotence in general practice. Coll Gen Practit 4:72–87, 1961

Nickerson ET: Recent trends and innovations in play therapy. Int J Child Psychother 2:53–70, 1973

Nickerson ET: Bibliotherapy: A therapeutic medium for helping children. Psychother: Theory Res Prac 12:258–261, 1975

Nictern S, et al: A community educational program for the emotionally disturbed child. Am J Orthopsychiatry 34:705–713, 1964

Niebuhr HR, William DD, Gustafson AM: The Advancement of Theological Education. New York, Harper & Row, 1957

Niebuhr R: The Self and the Dramas of History. New York, Scribner, 1955

Norris CM: The trend toward community mental

health centers. Perspect Psychiatr Care, January-February, 1963, pp 36–40

North EF: Day care treatment of psychotic children, in Masserman JH (ed): Current Psychiatric Therapies, vol. 7. New York, Grune & Stratton, 1967

North Central Association of Colleges and Secondary Schools: General Education in the American High School. Chicago, Ill, Scott Foresman, 1942, p xii

Noshpitz J: Opening phase in the psychotherapy of adolescents with character disorders. Bull Menninger Clin 21:53, 1957

Noshpitz J: Youth pervades half-way house, at NIMH. Ment Hosp 10:25–30, 1959

Noshpitz J: Residential treatment of emotionally disturbed children, in Arieti S (ed): American Handbook of Psychiatry, vol. New York, Basic Books, 1975, pp 634–651

Noyes AP, Haydon EM, van Sickel M: Textbook of Psychiatric Nursing. New York, Macmillan, 1964

Noyes AP, Kolb LS: Modern Clinical Psychiatry. Philadelphia, Saunders, 1963

Nunberg H: Practice and theory of psychoanalysis. Nerv Ment Dis Monogr No. 74, 1948

Nunberg H: Principles of Psychoanalysis. New York, International Universities Press, 1955

Nunnally J: The communication of mental health information. Behav Sci 2:222–230, 1957

Nyswander M: The Drug Addict as a Patient. New York, Grune & Stratton, 1956

Oates WE: Religious Factors in Mental Illness. New York, Association Press, 1955

Oates WE: Protestant Pastoral Counseling. Philadelphia, Westminster, 1962

Oates WE: Association of pastoral counselors; its values and its dangers. Pastoral Psychol 15:5–7, 1964

Oates WE: Do pastoral counselors bring a new consciousness to the health professions? J Pastoral Care 26:255–257, 1972(a)

Oates WE, Neely K: Where to Go For Help. Revised enlarged edition. Philadelphia, Westminster, 1972(b)

Oberndorf CP: Psychoanalysis of married couples. Psychoanal Rev 25:453–475, 1938

Oberndorf CP: Consideration of results with psychoanalytic therapy. Am J Psychiatry 99:374–381, 1942

Oberndorf CP, Greenacre P, Kubie LS: Symposium on the evaluation of therapeutic results. Int J Psychoanal 29:7–33, 1948

O'Connor JF, Daniels G, Karush A, et al: The effects of psychotherapy on the course of ulcerative colitis: A preliminary report. Am J Psychiatry 120:738–742, 1964

O'Connor JF, Stern LO: Results of treatment in functional sexual disorders. NY State J Med 72:1927–1934, 1972

Odenheimer JF: Day hospital as an alternative to the psychiatric ward. Arch Gen Psychiatry 13:46–53, 1965

O'Donnell JA: A follow-up of narcotic addicts. Am J Orthopsychiatry 34:948–954, 1964

Oettinger KB: Why a nurse mental health consultant in public health? J Psychiatr Soc Work 19:162–168, 1950

Oettinger L: Meratran. Preliminary report of a new drug for the treatment of behavior disorders in children. Dis Nerv Syst 16:299, 1955

Oettinger L: Use of Deanol in treatment of disorders of behavior in children. J Pediatr 53:671–675, 1958

Offenkrantz WCE, Elliot R: Psychiatric management of suicide problems in military science. Am J Psychiatry 114:33, 1957

Olds V: Role theory and casework: A review of the literature. Soc Casework 43:3–8, 1962

O'Leary KD, Becker WC: Behavior modification of an adjustment class: A token reinforcement program. Except Child 33:637–642, 1967

O'Leary KD, Drabman R: Token reinforcement programs in the classroom: A review. Psychol Bull 75:379–398, 1971

O'Leary KD, et al: Modification of a deviant sibling interaction pattern in the home. Behav Res Ther 5:113–120, 1967

O'Leary KD, Wilson GT: Behavior Therapy: Application and Outcome. Englewood Cliffs, NJ, Prentice-Hall, 1975

Olshansky S: The transitional sheltered workshop: A survey. J Soc Issues 16:33–39, 1960

Opler M: Schizophrenia and culture. Sci Am 197:103–112, 1957

Opler M: Discussion: Scientific social psychiatry encounter existentialism. Phil Phenom Res 24:240–243, 1963(a)

Opler M: Need for new diagnostic categories in psychiatry. J Natl Med Assoc 55:133–137, 1963(b)

Orgel SZ: Effect of psychoanalysis on the course of peptic ulcer. Psychosom Med 20:117–125, 1958

Orgler H: Alfred Adler, the Man and His Work. New York, Liveright, 1963

Orlando IJ: The Dynamic Nurse-Patient Relationship. New York, Putnam, 1961, (paperback)

Ormont L: Establishing the analytic contrast in a newly formed therapeutic group. Br J Med Psychol 35:333, 1962

Ormont L: The resolution of resistances by conjoint psychoanalysis. Psychoanal Rev 51:425, 1964

Ornstein P: Selected problems in learning how to analyze. Int J Psa 48:448–461, 1967

Ornstein P: What is and what is not psychotherapy. Dis Nerv Sys 29:118–123, 1968

Ornstein P, Goldberg A: Psychoanalysis and medicine: I. contributions to psychiatry, psychosomatic medicine and medical psychology. Dis Nerv Sys 34:143–147, 1973

Orr DW: Transference and countertransference: A historical survey. J Am Psychoanal Assoc 2:621, 670, 1954

Osipow SH, Walsh WD: Strategies in Counseling for Behavior Change. New York, Appleton-Century-Crofts, 1970

Osnos RJB: The treatment of narcotic addiction. NY State J Med 63:1182–1188, 1963

Ostow M: Religion, in Arieti S (ed): American Handbook of Psychiatry, vol. 2. New York, Basic Books, 1959, pp 1789–1801

Ostow M: The Use of Drugs in Psychoanalysis and Psychotherapy. New York, Basic Books, 1962

Outler A: Psychotherapy and the Christian Message. New York, Harper & Row, 1954

Overall JE, Hollister LE: Computer procedures for psychiatric classification. JAMA 187:583–588, 1964

Overall JE, Hollister LE, Johnson M, Pennington V: Nosology of depression and differential response to drugs. JAMA 195:162, 1966

Overholser W: Physical medicine and psychiatry, some interrelationships. JAMA 138:1221, 1948

Ovesey L: The homosexual conflict: An adaptational analysis. Psychiatry 17(3), August 1954

Ovesey L: The homosexual anxiety. Psychiatry 18(1), February 1955(a)

Ovesey L: Pseudohomosexuality, the paranoid mechanism and paranoia. Psychiatry 18(2), May 1955(b)

Ovesey L: Pseudohomosexuality and homosexuality in men: Psychodynamics as a guide to treatment, in Marmor J (ed): Sexual Inversion. New York, Basic Books, 1965

Ovesey L, Gaylin W, Hendin H: Psychotherapy of male homosexuality. Arch Gen Psychiatry 9(1), July 1963

Oxford Universal Dictionary: Oxford, Eng, Clarendon, 1955, p 584

Pacella BL: A critical appraisal of pastoral counseling. Paper presented at the 122d Annual Meeting of the American Psychiatric Association, Atlantic City, N.J., May 1966

Pack GT: Counseling the cancer patient. Surgeon's counsel. The physician and the total care of the cancer patient. Scientific Session of the American Cancer Society, 1961

Pahnke WN, Kurland AA, Unger S, et al: The experimental use of psychedelic (LSD) psychotherapy. JAMA 212:1856–1863, 1970

Palmer HD, Braceland FJ: Six years with narcosis therapy in psychiatry. Am J Psychiatry 94:35–37, 1937

Palmer MB: Social rehabilitation for mental patients. Ment Hyg 42:24–28, 1958

Palmer RD: Desensitization of the fear of expressing one's own inhibited aggression: Bioenergetic assertive techniques for behavior therapists. Paper presented at the Association for the Advancement of Behavior Therapy, Washington, DC, September 1971

Paneth HG: Some observations on the relation of psychotic states to psychosomatic disorders. Psychosom Med 21:106–109, 1959

Panzetta AF: Toward a scientific psychiatric nosology. Arch Gen Psychiatry 30:154–161, 1974

Papanek E: Das Kinderheim Seine Theorie und Praxis im Lichte der Individual Psychologie. Acta Psychother 4:53, 1956

Papanek E: In-service training of educators for maladjusted youth. Proceedings of the 4th Congress of the International Association of Workers for Maladjusted Children, Laussanne-Paris, 1958

Papanek E: A new approach to institutional care for children, in Adler K, Deutsch, D (eds): Essays in Individual Psychology. New York, Grove, 1959, pp 139–152

Papanek E, Papanek H: Individual psychology today. Am J Psychother 15:4–26, 1961

Papanek H: Combined group and individual therapy in the light of Adlerian psychology. Int J Group Psychother 6:136–146, 1956

Papanek H: Recent developments and implications of the Adlerian theory for clinical psychology, in Abt LE, Riess BF (eds): Progress in Clinical Psychology, vol. 5. New York, Grune & Stratton, 1963

Papanek H: Adler's concepts in community psychiatry. J Individ Psychol 21:117–126, 1965

Papanek H: Personal communication. 1966

Paredes A, Gogerty JH, West LJ: Psychopharmacology, in Masserman JH (ed): Current Psychiatric Therapies, vol. 1. New York, Grune & Stratton, 1961

Paredes A, Ludwig KD, Hassenfeld IN, et al: A

clinical study of alcoholics using audiovisual self-image feedback. J Nerv Ment Dis 148:449–456, 1969

Park LC, Covi L: Nonblind placebo trial. Arch Gen Psychiatry 12:336–345, 1965

Parker B: Psychiatric Consultation for Non-psychiatric Professional Workers. Pub Health Monogr No. 53, Washington, DC, U.S. Government Printing Office, 1958

Parker B: Some observations on psychiatric consultation with nursery school teachers. Ment Hyg 46:559–562, 1962

Parloff MB: The family in psychotherapy. Arch Gen Psychiatry 4:445–451, 1961

Parsons T, Shils EA: Toward a General Theory of Action. Cambridge, Harvard University Press, 1951

Paschalis AP, Kimmel HD, Kimmel E: Further study of diurnal instrumental conditioning in the treatment of enuresis nocturna. J Behav Ther Exp Psychiatry 3:253–256, 1972

Paterson AS: Electrical and Drug Treatments in Psychiatry. London, Elsevier, 1963

Patterson CH: Theories of Counseling and Psychotherapy. New York, Harper & Row, 1966

Patterson GR: A learning theory approach to the treatment of the school phobic child, in Ullmann LP, Krasner L (eds): Case Studies in Behavior Modification. New York, Holt, 1965

Patterson GR: Behavioral intervention procedures in the classroom and the home, in Bergin AE, Garfield SL (eds): Handbook of Psychotherapy and Behavior Change. New York, Wiley, 1970

Patterson GR: Families: Applications of Social Learning to Family Life. Champaign, Ill, Research Press, 1971

Patterson GR, Gullion ME: Living with Children: New Methods for Parents and Teachers. Champaign, Ill, Research Press, 1968

Patterson GR, Reid JB, Jones, RR, et al: A social learning approach to family intervention, in Families of Aggressive Children, vol. I. Eugene, Ore, Castelia, 1975

Patterson V, Levene HI, Breger L: Treatment and training outcomes with two time-limited therapies. Arch Gen Psychiatry 25:161, 1971

Patterson V, O'Sullivan M: Three perspectives on brief psychotherapy. Am J Psychother 28:265–277, 1974

Patton GO: Foster homes and rehabilitation of long-term mental patients. Can Psychiatr Assoc J 6:20–25, 1961

Paul GL: Effects of insight, desensitization, and attention-placebo treatment of anxiety: An approach to outcome research in psychotherapy. Unpublished doctoral dissertation, University of Illinois, 1964

Paul GL: Insight Versus Desensitization in Psychotherapy: An Experiment in Anxiety Reduction. Stanford, Calif, Stanford University Press, 1966

Paul GL: Insight versus desensitization in psychotherapy two years after termination. J Consult Psychol 31:333–348, 1967

Paul GL: Inhibition of physiological response to stressful imagery by relaxation training and hypnotically suggested relaxation. Behav Res Ther 7:249–256, 1969(a)

Paul GL: Physiological effects of relaxation training and hypnotic suggestions. J Abnorm Psychol 74:425–437, 1969(b)

Paul GL, Shannon DT: Treatment of anxiety through systematic desensitization in therapy groups. J Abnorm Psychol 71:124–135, 1966

Paul GL, Tobias LL, Holly BL: Maintenance psychotropic drugs in the presence of active treatment programs. Arch Gen Psychiatry 27:106–115, 1972

Paul NL: Cross-confrontation procedure via tape recordings in conjoint family therapy. Paper presented at the 122d Annual Meeting of the American Psychiatric Association, Atlantic City, NJ, May 1966

Pauling L: Pauling blasts APA report on orthomolecular psychiatry. Psychiatr News 9:4, 1974

Payne J: Omsbudsman roles for social worker. Soc Work January 17, 1972

Payot I: The Education of the Will. New York, Funk & Wagnalls, 1909

Pellegrino V: A new voice: A new life. Todays Health 52:44–49, 1974

Pelletier KR: Theory and applications of clinical biofeedback. J Contemp Psychother 7:29–34, 1975

Pepper M, Redlich FC, Pepper A: Social psychiatry. Am J Psychiatry 121:662–666, 1965

Perelman JS: Problems encountered in group psychotherapy of married couples. Int J Group Psychother 10:136–142, 1960

Perlman H: Social Casework: A Problem-Solving Process. Chicago University of Chicago Press, 1957.

Perlman H: Intake and some role consideration. J Soc Casework 41:171–177, 1960(a)

Perlman H: Social casework, in Kurtz RH (ed): Social Work Year Book—1960. New York, National Association Social Workers, 1960(b), p 535

Perlman H: The role concept and social

casework: Some explorations. I. The "social" in social casework. Soc Serv Rev 35:370–381, 1961. II. What is social diagnosis. Soc Serv Rev 36:17–31, 1962

Perlmutter F, Durham D: Using teen-agers to supplement casework service. Soc Work 10:41–46, 1965

Perls FS: Gestalt therapy and human potentialities, in Otto HA (ed): Explorations in Human Potentialities. Springfield, Ill, Thomas, 1966

Perls FS: Gestalt Therapy Verbatim. Moab, Utah, Real People Press, 1969

Perls FS, Hefferline RF, Goodman P: Gestalt Therapy. New York, Julian, 1951

Peters GA, Phelan JG: Practical group psychotherapy reduces supervisor's anxiety. Personnel J 35:376–378, 1957(a)

Peters GA, Phelan JG: Relieving personality conflicts by a kind of group therapy. Personnel J 36:61–64, 1957(b)

Peterson S: The psychiatric nurse specialist in a general hospital. Nurs Outlook 17:56–58, 1969

Pfister HP: Farbe und Bewengung in der Zeichnung Geisterskranken. Schweiz. Arch Neurol Psychiatry 34:325–365, 1934

Phillips EL: Psychotherapy: A Modern Theory and Practice. London, Staples, 1957

Phillips HU: Essentials of Social Group Work Skill. New York, Association Press, 1957

Phillips JS, Kanfer FH: The viability and vicissitudes of behavior therapy, in Frederick CJ (ed): The Future of Psychotherapy. Boston, Little, Brown, 1969, pp 75–131

Pickford RW: Some interpretations of a painting called "abstraction." Br J Med Psychol 18:219–249, 1938

Pierce CM: Enuresis and encopreses, in Freedman AM, Kaplan HI, Sadock BJ (eds): Comprehensive Textbook of Psychiatry, vol. II (2d ed). Baltimore, Williams & Wilkins, 1975, pp 2116–2125

Pierce CM, et al: Music therapy in a day care center. Dis Nerv Syst 25:29–32, 1964

Piers MA: Play and mastery, in Ekstein R, Motto RL (eds): From Learning for Love to Love of Learning. New York, Brunner/Mazel, 1969

Pietropinto A: Poetry therapy in groups, in Masserman JH (ed): Current Psychiatric Therapies, vol. 15. New York, Grune & Stratton, 1975, pp 221–232

Pinckney ER, Pinckney C: The Fallacy of Freud and Psychoanalysis. Englewood Cliffs, NJ, Prentice-Hall, 1965

Pines M: Group therapy with "difficult" patients, in Wolberg LR, Aronson, ML (eds):

Group Therapy 1975: An Overview. New York, Stratton Intercontinental, 1975, pp 102–119

Pins A: Changes in social work education and their implications for practice. Soc Work 16:5–15, 1971

Piotrowski Z, Schreiber M: Rorschach, perceptanalytic measurement of personality changes during and after intensive psychoanalytically oriented psychotherapy, in Bychowski G, Despert JL (eds): Specialized Techniques in Psychotherapy. New York, Basic Books, 1952, pp 337–361

Pittman FS, DeYoung MS, Flomenhaft K, et al: Crisis family therapy, in Masserman JH (ed): Current Psychiatric Therapies, vol. 6. New York, Grune & Stratton, 1966, pp 185–196

Plunkett RJ, Gordon JE: Epidemiology and Mental Illness. New York, Basic Books, 1960

Plutchik R, Kellerman H: Emotions Profile Index. Los Angeles, Western Psychological Services, 1974

Polak P, Laycob L: Rapid tranquilization. Am J Psychiatry 128:640–643, 1971

Poole N, Blanton S: The Art of Real Happiness. Englewood Cliffs, NJ, Prentice-Hall, 1950

Poussaint AF, Ditman KS: A controlled study of imipramine (tofranil) in the treatment of childhood enuresis. Paper presented at the 120th Annual Meeting of the American Psychiatric Association. Los Angeles, May 1964

Powdermaker FB: Psychoanalytic concepts in group psychotherapy. Int J Group Psychother 1:16, 1951

Powdermaker FB, Frank JD, et al: Group Psychotherapy; Studies in Methodology of Research and Therapy. Cambridge, Harvard University Press, 1953

Powers E: An experiment in prevention of delinquency. Ann Am Acad Pol Soc Sci 77–88, 1949

Powers E, Witmer H: An Experiment in the Prevention of Delinquency. New York, Columbia University Press, 1951

Practitioners Conference, NY Hospital, Cornell Medical Center. Sterility and impotence. NY State Med J 57:120–144, 1957

Pratt JH: The influence of emotions in the causation and cure of psychoneuroses. Int Clinics 4:1, 1934

Pratt JH: The use of Dejerine's methods in the treatment of the common neuroses by group psychotherapy. Bull N Engl Med Ctr 15:1–9, 1953

Pratt JH, et al: Extrasensory Perception After Sixty Years. New York, Holt, 1940

Pray KLM: The place of social casework in the treatment of delinquency. Soc Serv Rev 19:235–248, 1945

Pray KLM: A restatement of the generic principles of social casework practice. J Soc Casework 28:283–390, 1947

Prescott D, et al: Helping teachers understand children. Understanding the Child 14:67–70, 1945

Proceedings of the Brief Psychotherapy Council, under the auspices of the Chicago Institute for Psychoanalysis, October 1942

Proceedings of the Second Brief Psychotherapy Council (1. Psychosomatic medicine. 2. Psychotherapy for children. Group psychotherapy. 3. War psychiatry), under the auspices of the Chicago Institute for Psychoanalysis, January 1944

Proceedings of the Third Brief Psychotherapy Council, under the auspices of the Chicago Institute for Psychoanalysis, October 1946

Prowse M: A night care program. Nurs Outlook 5:518–519, 1957

Pruyser PW: Towards a doctrine of man in psychiatry and theology. Pastoral Psychol 9:9–13, 1958

Pruyser PW: Religion and psychiatry. A polygon of relationships. JAMA 195:197–202, 1966

Psychiatric Bulletin: Houston, Tex, Medical Arts Publishing Foundation, 1950–1951, and issues thereafter

Psychiatric Manpower Bulletin: (American Psychiatric Association) No. 2, May 1963

Psychiatry and Medical Education. Report of the 1951 Conference on Psychiatric Education. Washington, DC, American Psychiatric Association, 1952

Psychotherapy and Casework. Symposium of the Boston Psychoanalytic Society and Institute. J Soc Casework, June 1949, entire issue

Psychotherapy Curriculum Consultation Committee, American Psychological Association: Recommended standards for psychotherapy education in psychology doctoral programs. Professional Psychol Spring, 1971

Pumpian-Mindlin E (ed): On Psychoanalysis as Science. New York, Basic Books, 1956

Pumpian-MindlinE: Considerations in the selection of patients for short-term therapy. Am J Psychother 7:641–652, 1957

Purvis LC: Self-awareness: A proposal for supervision. J Contemp Psychother 4:107–112, 1972

Quarti C, Renaud J: A new treatment of constipation by conditioning: A preliminary report, in Franks CM (ed): Conditioning Techniques in Clinical Practice and Research. New York, Springer, 1964, pp 219–227

Quaytman W: Impressions of the Esalen (Schutz) phenomenon. J Contemp Psychother 2:57–64, 1969

Rabin HM: Any answers to the compelling arguments against encounters and marathons? Psychother Bull 4:16–19, 1971

Rabiner EL, et al: The therapeutic community as an inside catalyst, expanding the transferential field. Am J Psychother 18:244–258, 1964

Rabinovitch RD: Reading and learning disabilities, in Arieti S (ed): American Handbook of Psychiatry, vol. 1. New York, Basic Books, 1959, pp 856–869

Rachman AW: Marathon group psychotherapy: Its origins, significance and direction. J Group Psychoanal Proc 2:57–74, 1969

Rachman AW: Group psychotherapy in treating the adolescent identity crisis. Int J Child Psychother 1:97–117, 1972(a)

Rachman AW: Identity Group Psychotherapy with Adolescents. Springfield, Ill, Thomas, 1972(b)

Rachman AW: The issue of countertransference in encounter and marathon group psychotherapy, in Wolberg LR, Aronson ML (eds): Group Therapy 1975: An Overview. New York, Stratton Intercontinental, 1975, pp 146–163

Rachman S: The Effects of Psychotherapy. International Series of Monographs in Experimental Psychology, vol. 15. Elmsford, NY, Pergamon, 1972

Rachman S, Teasdale J: Aversion Therapy and Behavior Disorders. Coral Gables, Fla, University of Miami Press, 1969

Rachman S, Hodgson R, Marks IM: The treatment of chronic obsessive-compulsive neuroses. Behav Res Theory 9:237–247, 1971

Rado S: Developments in the psychoanalytic conception and treatment of the neuroses. Psychoanal Qt 8:427, 1939

Rado S: Mind, unconscious mind, and brain. Psychosom Med 11:165, 1949

Rado S: Emergency behavior: With an introduction to the dynamics of conscience, in Hoch PH, Zubin J (eds): Anxiety. New York, Grune & Stratton, 1950, pp 150–175

Rado S: Psychoanalysis of Behavior: Collected Papers, vol. 1. New York, Grune & Stratton, 1956

Rado S: Obsessive behavior, in Arieti S (ed): American Handbook of Psychiatry, vol. 1. New York, Basic Books, 1959, p 342

Rado S: Psychoanalysis of Behavior: Collected Papers, vol. 2. New York, Grune & Stratton, 1962

Rado S: Relationship of short-term psychotherapy to development stages of maturation and stages of treatment behavior, in Wolberg LR (ed): Short-term Psychotherapy. New York, Grune & Stratton, 1965, pp 67–83

Rado S, Daniels G: Changing Concepts of Psychoanalytic Medicine. New York, Grune & Stratton, 1956

Rafferty FT: Day treatment of adolescents, in Masserman JH (ed): Current Psychiatric Therapies, vol. 1. New York, Grune & Stratton, 1961, pp 43–47

Raginsky BB: Sensory hypnoplasty with case illustration. Int J Clin Exp Hypn 10:205–219, 1962

Rainer JD: Genetic counseling in a psychiatric setting, in Masserman JH (ed): Current Psychiatric Therapies, vol. 7. New York, Grune & Stratton, 1967

Rangell L: Similarities and differences between psychoanalysis and dynamic psychotherapy. J Am Psychoanal Assoc 2:734–744, 1954

Rank O: The Trauma of Birth. New York, Harcourt, 1929

Rank O: Will Therapy and Truth and Reality. New York, Knopf, 1947

Rapaport D: Emotions and Memory (2d ed). New York, International Universities Press, 1950

Rapaport D: The autonomy of the ego. Bull Menninger Clin 15:113–123, 1951

Rapaport D: The theory of ego autonomy: A generalization. Bull Menninger Clin 22:13–35, 1958

Rapaport D: On the Psychoanalytic Theory of Motivation. Lincoln, University of Nebraska Press, 1960

Rapaport D, Gill M, Schafer R: Diagnostic Psychological Testing, vol. 1. Chicago, Year Book Publishers, 1946 (rev ed—New York, International Universities Press, 1968)

Rapaport HG: Psychosomatic aspects of allergy in childhood. JAMA 165:812–815, 1957

Rapaport L (ed): Consultation in Social Work Practice. New York, National Association of Social Workers, 1963

Rapaport RN: A social scientist looks at the therapeutic community: Suggestions for developing action research, in Proceedings of the World Congress of Psychiatry, Montreal, Canada, 1961

Rapaport RN: Principles for developing a therapeutic community, in Masserman JH (ed): Current Psychiatric Therapies, vol. 3. New York, Grune & Stratton, 1963, pp 244–256

Rapaport RN, et al: Community as Doctor: New Perspectives on a Therapeutic Community. Springfield, Ill, Thomas, 1960

Raskin DE: Problems in the therapeutic community. Am J Psychiatry 128:492, 1971

Raskin HA: Rehabilitation of the narcotic addict. JAMA 189:956–958, 1964

Raush HL, Bordin ES: Warmth in personality development and in psychotherapy. Psychiatry 20:351–364, 1957

Ravenette AT: Maladjustment: Clinical concept or administrative convenience: Psychologists, teachers and children: How many ways to understand? Assoc Educ Psychol J Newsletter 3:41–47, 1972

Ray MB: The cycle of abstinence and relapse among heroin addicts. Soc Prob 9:132–140, 1961

Raymond MJ: Case of fetishism treated by aversion therapy. Br Med J 2:854–856, 1956

Redkey H: Rehabilitation Centers Today. DHEW Rehab Service Ser No. 490. Washington, DC, U.S. Government Printing Office, 1959

Redl F: Resistance in therapy groups. Hum Relations 1:307, 1948

Redl F: The concept of a therapeutic milieu. Am J Orthopsychiatry 29:721–737, 1959

Redl F: When We Deal with Children. New York, Free Press, 1966

Redl F, Wattenberg WW: Mental Hygiene in Teaching. New York, Harcourt, 1959

Redlich FC, Freedman DX: The Theory and Practice of Psychiatry. New York, Basic Books, 1966

Redlich FC, Pepper MP: Social psychiatry. Am J Psychiatry 119:637–642, 1963

Redlich FC, Pepper MP: Social psychiatry. Am J Psychiatry 120:657–660, 1964

Rees TP: Back to moral treatment and community care. J Ment Sci 103:303–313, 1957

Reese HH: In Podolsky E (ed): Music Therapy. New York, Philosophical Library, 1954

Reeve M: The role of the supervisor in helping the student to a professional orientation, in FSSA pamphlet: Some Emotional Elements in Supervision. (Report of a group discussion.) 1937

Reeves RB: When is it time to die? Prolegomenon to voluntary euthanasia. N Engl Law Rev 8:183, 1973

Reich A: Symposium on the termination of psychoanalytic treatment and on the criteria for the termination of an analysis. Int J Psychoanal 31:78–80, 179–205, 1950

Reich W: Zur Technik der Deutung und der Widerstandsanalyse. Int Ztschr Psychoanal 13, 1927

Reich W: Über Charakteranalyse. Int Ztschr Psychoanal 14, 1928

Reich W: The Function of the Orgasm. New York, Orgone Institute Press, 1942

Reich W: Character-Analysis (3d ed). New York, Orgone Institute Press, 1949

Reider N: Remarks on mechanisms of nonanalytic psychotherapy. Dis Nerv Syst 5(1), 1944

Reiff R: Mental health manpower and institutional change. Am Psychol 21:540–548, 1966

Reik T: Dogma and Compulsion: Psychoanalytic Studies of Religion and Myths. New York, International Universities Press, 1951

Rein M: Social work in search of a radical profession. Soc Work 15(2):13–28, 1970

Reinherz H: The therapeutic use of student volunteers. Children 2:137–142, 1964

Reinkes JH: The use of unfamiliar music as a stimulus for a projective test of personality, in Proceedings of the National Association of Music Therapy. Kansas City, Kans, the Association, 1952, pp 224–230

Reisman JM: Toward the Integration of Psychotherapy. New York, Wiley, 1971

Reitman F: Facial expression in schizophrenic drawings. J Ment Sci 85:264–272, 1939

Rennie TAC: What can the practitioner do in treating the neuroses? Bull NY Acad Med, January 1946

Rennie TAC: Trends in medical education (discussion). Commonwealth Fund. New York, NY Acad Med Inst Med Educ, 1949

Rennie TAC, Woodward LE: Mental Health in Modern Society. New York, Commonwealth Fund, 1948

Resnick R, Volavka J, Freedman AM, Thomas M: Studies of EN–1639A (Maltexone): A new narcotic antagonist. Am J Psychiatry 131:646, 1974

Reyna LJ: Conditioning therapies, learning theory, and research, in Wolpe J, et al (eds): The Conditioning Therapies: The Challenge of Psychotherapy. New York, Holt, 1964, pp 169–179

Reynolds DK: Morita Psychotherapy. Berkeley, University of California Press, 1976

Reynolds R, Siegle E: A study of casework with sado-masochistic marriage partners. J Soc Casework 40:545–551, 1959

Rhine SB: Experiments bearing on the precognition hypothesis. J Parapsychol 2:38, 1938

Rhoades W: Group training in thought control for relieving nervous disorders. Ment Hyg 19:373–386, 1935

Rhoads JM, Feather BW: Transference and resistence observed in behavior therapy. Br J Med Psychol 45:99–103, 1972

Rhoads PS: Management of the patient with terminal illness. JAMA 192:661–667, 1965

Rhys-Davids TW: Dialogues of the Buddha, Translated from the Pali of the Digha nikāya, 3 vols. London, Frowde, 1899–1938

Richardson C: The formal rites and ceremonies of the church, in Maves PB (ed): The Church and Mental Health. New York, Scribner, 1953

Richmond ME: Social Diagnosis. New York, Russell Sage Foundation, 1917

Rickels K: Drugs in the treatment of neurotic anxiety and tension: Controlled studies, in Solomon P (ed): Psychiatric Drugs. New York, Grune & Stratton, 1966

Rickels K: Anti-anxiety drugs in neurotic outpatients, in Masserman JH (ed): Current Psychiatric Therapies, vol. 7. New York, Grune & Stratton, 1967

Rickels K, Baumm C, Raab E, Taylor W, Moore E: A psychopharmacological evaluation of chlordiazepoxide, LA-1 and placebo, carried out with anxious medical clinic patients. Med Times 93:238–245, 1965

Rickels K, Clark TW, Ewing JH, Klingensmith WC: Evaluation of tranquilizing drugs in medical out-patients (meprobamate, prochlorperazine, amobarbital sodium and placebo). JAMA 171:1649–1656, 1959

Rickers-Ovsiankina MA: Rorschach Psychology. New York, Wiley, 1960, p 441 (repr—Huntington, NY, Krieger, 1976)

Rieff R, Riesman F: The Indigenous Nonprofessional: A Strategy of Change in Community Action and Community Mental Health. New York, National Institute of Labor Education, 1964

Riess BF: Consensus techniques in diagnosis and group therapy of adolescents, in Wolberg LR, Schwartz EK (eds): Group Therapy 1973: An Overview. New York, Stratton Intercontinental, 1973, pp 92–100

Riessman F: The "helper" therapy principle. Soc Work 10(2):27–31, 1965

Riessman F: New Approaches to Mental Health Treatment for Labor and Low Income Groups. New York, National Institute of Labor Education, 1964

Rimm DC, Masters JC: Behavior Therapy:

Techniques and Empirical Findings. New York, Academic Press, 1974

Ringness TA: Mental Health in the Schools. New York, Random House, 1967

Rioch MJ: The transference phenomenon in psychoanalytic therapy. Psychiatry 6:147–156, 1943

Rioch MJ: Changing concepts in the training of therapists. J Consult Psychol 30:290–292, 1966

Rioch MJ, Elkes C, Flint AA: Pilot Project in Training Mental Health Counselors. Pub Health Service Publ No. 1254. Washington, DC, U.S. Government Printing Office, 1965

Rioch MJ, Elkes C, Flint AA, et al: National Institute of Mental Health pilot study in training mental health counselors. Am J Orthopsychiatry 33:678–679, 1963

Rippon TS, Fletcher P: Reassurance and Relaxation. London, Routledge & Kegan, 1940

Roazen P: Freud, Political and Social Thought. New York, Knopf, 1968

Robbins BS: The theoretical rationale for the day hospital, in Proceedings of the 1958 Day Hospital Conference of the American Psychiatric Association, Washington, DC, 1958, p 5

Robertiello RC: Telephone sessions. Psychoanal Rev 59:633–634, 1972

Robertiello RC, Forbes SF: The treatment of masochistic character disorders. J Contemp Psychol 3:41–44, 1970

Roberts DE: Psychotherapy and a Christian View of Man. New York, Scribner, 1950

Roberts JAF: An Introduction to Medical Genetics. London, Oxford University Press, 1963

Roberts R, Hee R (eds): Theories of Social Casework. Chicago, University of Chicago Press, 1970

Robertson WMF, Pitt B: The role of a day hospital in geriatric psychiatry. Br J Psychiatry 111:635–640, 1965

Robinson AM: The Psychiatric Aide, His Part in Patient Care. Philadelphia, Lippincott, 1964

Robinson DS, Nies A, Ravaria CL, et al: The monoamine oxidase inhibitor, phenelzine, in the treatment of depressive-anxiety states. Arch Gen Psychiatry 29:407–413, 1973

Robinson RL: Criticisms of psychiatry, in Usdin G (ed): Psychiatry: Education and Image. New York, Brunner/Mazel, 1973, pp 1–25

Roche Report: California dialogue: Defining psychotherapy, insight. 2:1–9, 1965

Roche Report: Civic treatment centers recommended for adolescents. 3(18):3, 6, 1966

Roche Report: Distorted video images quickly elicit repressed material. 3(5):1–11, 1973

Roche Report: Video psychiatry comes of age. 4(4):1–8, 1974(a)

Roche Report: Psychiatrists urged to abdicate therapeutic roles. 4(5):3, 1974(b)

Rochkind M, Conn JH: Guided fantasy encounter. Am J Psychotherapy 27:516–528, 1973

Rogers CR: Counseling and Psychotherapy: Newer Concepts in Practice. Boston, Houghton Mifflin, 1942

Rogers CR: Therapy in guidance clinics. J Abnorm Soc Psychol 38:284–289, 1943

Rogers CR: The development of insight in a counseling relationship. J Consult Psychol 8:331–341, 1944

Rogers CR: Significant aspects of client-centered therapy. Am Psychologist 1:415–422, 1946

Rogers CR: Some implications of client-centered counseling for college personnel work. Personal Counselor 3:94–102, 1948

Rogers CR: Client-Centered Therapy. Boston, Houghton Mifflin, 1951

Rogers CR: Client-centered therapy: A current view, in Fromm-Reichmann F, Moreno JL (eds): Progress in Psychotherapy. New York, Grune & Stratton, 1956

Rogers CR: A theory of therapy, personality, and interpersonal relationships, as developed in the client-centered framework, in Koch S (ed): Psychology: A Study of Science. Vol. II, General Systematic Formulations, Learning and Special Processes. New York, McGraw-Hill, 1959

Rogers CR: On Becoming a Person: A Therapist's View of Psychotherapy. Boston, Houghton Mifflin, 1961(a)

Rogers CR: The characteristics of a helping relationship, in Stein MI (ed): Contemporary Psychotherapies. New York, Free Press, 1961(b)

Rogers CR (ed): The Therapeutic Relationship and Its Impact: A Study of Psychotherapy with Schizophrenics. Madison, University of Wisconsin Press, 1967

Rogers CR: Freedom to Learn: A View of What Education Might Become. Columbus, Ohio, Merrill, 1969

Rogers CR: Carl Rogers on Encounter Groups. New York, Harper & Row, 1970

Rogers CR: My philosophy of interpersonal relationships and how it grew. J Hum Psychol 13:3, 1973

Rogers CR: Client-centered psychotherapy, in Freedman AM, Kaplan HI, Sadock BJ (eds): Comprehensive Textbook of Psychiatry, vol. II (2d ed). Baltimore, Williams & Wilkins, 1975, pp 1831–1843

Rogers CR, Becker RJ: A basic orientation for counseling. Pastoral Psychol 1:26–28, 1950

Rogers CR, Truax CB: The therapeutic conditions antecedent to change: A theoretical view, in Rogers CR (ed): The Therapeutic Relationship and Its Impact: A study of Psychotherapy with Schizophrenics. Madison, University of Wisconsin Press, 1976

Rogers D: Mental Hygiene in Elementary Education. Boston, Houghton Mifflin, 1957

Rogers F: Patients respond to music program. Ment Hosp 14:642–643, 1963

Rolf I: Structural Integration. San Francisco, The Guild for Structural Integration, 1958

Romano J: Has psychiatry resigned from medicine? Med Op 2:13–16, 1973

Rome HP: Group psychotherapy. Dis Nerv Syst 6:237–241, 1945

Rome HP: Psychiatry growing up. Editorial. Psychiatr News 1:4, 1966

Rome HP, et al: Symposium on automation. Technics in personality assessment. Proc Mayo Clin 37:61–82, 1962

Ropschitz DH: The role of extra-mural therapeutic social clubs in the mental health services of Derbyshire. Int J Soc Psychiatry 5:165–173, 1959

Rorschach H: Psychodiagnostics: A Diagnostic Test Based on Perception. Berne, Switz, Huber, 1942

Rose AE, Brown CE, Metcalfe EV: Music therapy at Westminister Hospital. Ment Hyg 43:93–104, 1959

Rosen E: Dance in Psychotherapy. New York, Bureau of Publications, Teachers College, Columbia University Press, 1957

Rosen JM: The treatment of schizophrenic psychosis by direct analytic therapy. Psychiatr Q 21:3–37, 117–119, 1947

Rosen JM: Direct Psychoanalytic Psychiatry. New York, Grune & Stratton, 1962

Rosen JM: Direct psychoanalysis, in Masserman JH (ed): Current Psychiatric Therapies, vol. 4. New York, Grune & Stratton, 1964, pp 101–107

Rosen JM, Chasen M: A study of resistance and its manifestations in therapeutic groups of chronic psychotic patients. Psychiatry 12:279, 1949

Rosen V: The initial psychiatric interview and the principles of psychotherapy: Some recent contributions. J Am Psychoanal Assoc 6:157, 1958

Rosenbaum CP: Events of early therapy and brief therapy. Arch Gen Psychiatry 10:506–512, 1964

Rosenbaum M: Group psychotherapy and psychodrama, in Wolman BB (ed): Handbook of Clinical Psychology. New York, McGraw-Hill, 1965

Rosenbaum M: The responsibility of the group psychotherapy practitioner for a therapeutic rationale. J Group Psychoanal Process 2:5–17, 1969

Rosenbaum M, Berger M (eds): Group Psychotherapy and Group Function: Selected Readings. New York, Basic Books, 1963

Rosenberg PP, Fuller M: Human relations seminar: A group work experiment in nursing education. Ment Hyg 39:406–432, 1955

Rosenfeld HA: Psychotic States. London, Hogarth, 1965

Rosenthal D, Frank JD: Psychotherapy and the placebo effect. Psychol Bull 53:294–302, 1956

Rosenthal L: Countertransference in activity group therapy. Int J Group Psychother 3:431–440, 1953

Rosenthal L: A study of resistances in a member of a therapy group. Int J Group Psychother 13:315, 1963

Rosenthal L, Nagelberg L: Limitations of group therapy: A case presentation. Int J Group Psychother 6:166–179, 1956

Rosenthal MJ, Sullivan ME: Psychiatric Consultation in a Public Welfare Agency. Washington, DC, Children's Bureau, 1959

Rosenthal SH: A qualitative description of the electrosleep experience, in Wulfsohn NL, Sances A (eds): The Nervous System and Electric Currents, vol. 2. New York, Plenum, 1971, pp 153–155

Rosenthal SH: Electrosleep: A double-blind clinical study. Biol Psychiatry 4:179–185, 1972

Rosenthal SH, Wulfsohn NL: Studies of electrosleep with active and simulated treatment. Curr Ther Res 12:126–130, 1970(a)

Rosenthal SH, Wulfsohn NL: Electrosleep: A preliminary communication. J Nerv Ment Dis 151:146–151, 1970(b)

Rosenthal SH, Wulfsohn NL: Electrosleep—a clinical trial. Am J Psychiatry 127:175–176, 1970(c)

Rosenzweig A: A transvaluation of psychotherapy: A reply to Hans Eysenck. J Abnorm Soc Psychol 49:298–304, 1954

Rosenzweig S: Some implicit common factors in diverse methods of Psychotherapy. Am J Orthopsychiatry 6:412–415, 1936

Roskin G: Drug addiction and its treatment: An analysis. Roche Report 3:1–8, 1966

Ross A: Behavior therapy, in Wolman BB (ed): Manual of Child Psychopathology. New York, McGraw-Hill, 1972

Ross H, Johnson AM: The growing science of case work. J Soc Casework 27:273–278, 1946

Ross TA: An enquiry into prognosis in the neuroses. London, Cambridge University Press, 1936

Rossi EL: Dreams and the Growth of Personality. Elmsford, NY, Pergamon, 1972

Rossman I: Clinical Geriatrics. Philadelphia, Lippincott, 1971

Roth J: An intervention strategy for children with developmental problems. J School Psychol 8:311–314, 1970

Rothman T, Sward K: Studies in pharmacological psychotherapy. Arch Neurol Psychiatry 75:95–105, 1956

Rubenstein C: The treatment of morphine addiction in tuberculosis by Pavlov's conditioning method, in Franks CM (ed): Conditioning Techniques in Clinical Practice and Research. New York, Springer, 1964, pp 202–205

Rubinstein D: Family therapy, in Hoffman FH (ed): Teaching of Psychotherapy. International Psychiatric Clinics. Boston, Little, Brown, 1964

Rubinstein MA, Chipman A, Nemiroff RA: Simultaneous family and individual therapy of a hospitalized mother and daughter. Paper presented at the 122d Annual Meeting of the American Psychiatric Association, Atlantic City, NJ, May 1966

Ruck F: Alkoholentziehungskur mit Hilfe eines bedingten Reflexes (Apormophinentpziehungskur). (Conditioned reflex treatment of alcoholism.) Psychiatr Neurol Med Psychol (Leipz) 8:88–92, 1958

Ruesch J: Social factors in therapy, in Psychiatric Treatment, vol. 31. Assoc Res Nerv Ment Dis. Baltimore, Williams & Wilkins, 1953

Ruesch J: Disturbed Communication. New York, Norton, 1957

Ruesch J: General theory of communication in psychiatry, in Arieti S (ed): American Handbook of Psychiatry, vol. 1. New York, Basic Books, 1959, pp 895–908

Ruesch J: Social psychiatry. Arch Gen Psychiatry 5:501–509, 1965

Ruesch J, et al: Psychiatric Care. New York, Grune & Stratton, 1964

Rutherford BR: The use of negative practice in speech therapy with children handicapped by cerebral palsy, athetoid type. J Speech Dis 5:259–264, 1940

Rutledge KA: The professional nurse as primary therapist: Background, perspective, and opinion. J Operational Psychiatry 5:76–86, 1974

Ryan WC: Mental Health Through Education. New York, Commonwealth Fund, 1939

Ryle G: Philosophical Arguments. New York, Oxford University Press, 1945

Sabath G: The treatment of hard-core voluntary drug addict patients. Int J Group Psychother 14:307–317, 1964

Sabshin M: Theory and practice of community psychiatry in the medical school setting, in Goldston SE (ed): Concepts of Community Psychiatry: A Framework for Training. Pub Health Service Publ No. 131. Bethesda, Md, National Institute for Mental Health, 1965, pp 49–56

Sager CJ: The effects of group psychotherapy on individual psychoanalysis. Int J Group Psychother 9:403, 1959

Sager CJ: Insight and interaction in combined individual and group therapy. Int J Group Psychother 30:14, 1964

Sager CJ: The treatment of married couples, in Arieti S (ed): American Handbook of Psychiatry, vol. 3. New York, Basic Books, 1966(a), pp 213–224

Sager CJ: The development of marriage therapy: A historical review. Am J Orthopsychiatry 36:458–467, 1966(b)

Sager CJ: Transference in the conjoint treatment of married couples. Newsletter (Society of Medical Psychoanalysts) 7:9–10, 1966(c)

Sager CJ: Marital psychotherapy, in Masserman JH (ed): Current Psychiatric Therapies, vol. 7. New York, Grune & Stratton, 1967

Sager CJ, et al: The married in treatment. Arch Gen Psychiatry 19:205–217, 1968

Sager CJ, Kaplan HS: Progress in Group and Family Therapy. New York, Brunner/Mazel, 1972

Sakel M: The Pharmacological Shock Treatment of Schizophrenia. Wortis J (trans). New York, Nerv & Ment Dis Monogr, 1938

Salk L: What Every Child Would Like His Parents to Know. New York, McKay, 1972

Salter A: Conditioned Reflex Therapy: The Direct Approach to the Reconstruction of Personality. New York, Putnam, 1961

Salter A: The theory and practice of conditioned reflex therapy, in Wolpe J, et al (eds): The Conditioning Therapies. New York, Holt, 1966

Salzinger K: Experimental manipulations of verbal behavior: A review. J Gen Psychol 61:65–94, 1959

Salzman L: Countertransference: A therapeutic tool, in Masserman JH (ed): Current Psychiatric Therapies, vol. 2. New York, Grune & Stratton, 1962

Salzman L: Therapy of obsessional states. Am J Psychiatry 122:1139–1146, 1966

Sanderson RE, et al: An investigation of new aversive conditioning treatment for alcoholism, in Franks CM (ed): Conditioning Techniques in Clinical Practice and Research. New York, Springer, 1964, pp 165–177

Sandison RA, Whitelaw JDA: Further studies in the therapeutic value of lysergic acid diethylamide in mental illness. J Ment Sci 103:332–343, 1957

Sandison RA, Whitelaw JDA, Spencer AM: The therapeutic value of lysergic acid diethylamide in mental illness. J Ment Sci 100:491–507, 1954

San Mateo County Department of Public Health and Welfare: Spectrum of San Mateo County Mental Health Services. San Mateo, Calif, San Mateo Department of Public Health & Welfare, 1961

Santayana G: The Life of Reason (2d ed). New York, Scribner, 1948

Sargant W, Shorvon HJ: Acute war neuroses. Arch Neurol Psychiatry 54:231, 1945

Sargant WW, Slater ETU: Introduction to Physical Methods of Treatment in Psychiatry (4th ed). Baltimore, Williams & Wilkins, 1963 (New York, Aronson, 1973)

Sarlin CN, Berezin MA: Group psychotherapy on a modified analytic basis. J Nerv Ment Dis 104:611–667, 1946

Sarwer-Foner GJ: Patterns of marital relationship. Am J Psychother 17:31–44, 1963

Sasaki RF: Rinzai Zen Study for Foreigners in Japan. Kyoto, The First Zen Institute of America in Japan, 1960

Saslow G, Matarazzo J: A setting for social learning. Ment Hosp 13:217–226, 1962

Saslow G, Peters AD: A follow-up study of "untreated" patients with various behavior disorders. Psychiatr Q 30:283–302, 1956

Satir VM: Schziophrenia and family therapy, in Social Work Practice, 1963. (Published for the National Conference on Social Welfare, Columbus, Ohio. New York, Columbia University Press, 1963

Satir VM: Conjoint Family Therapy. Palo Alto, Calif, Science & Behavior Books, 1964(a)

Satir VM: Symptomatology: A family production. Palo Alto, Calif, Family Project Institute, 1964(b)

Satir VM: Conjoint marital therapy, in Green BL (ed): The Psychotherapies of Marital Disharmony. New York, Free Press, 1965

Saul LJ: On the value of one or two interviews. Psychoanal Q 20:613–615, 1951

Saul LJ: The Technic and Practice of Psychoanalysis. Philadelphia, Lippincott, 1958

Saul LJ: Reactions of a man to natural death. Psychoanal Q 28:383, 1959

Saul LJ, Beck AT: Psychodynamics of male homosexuality. Int J Psychoanal 42:43–48, 1961

Saul LJ, et al: Can one partner be successfully counseled without the other? Marr Fam Living 15:59–64, 1953

Saul LJ, Rome H, Leuser E: Desensitization of combat fatigue patients. Am J Psychiatry 102:476–478, 1946

Savage C: Countertransference in the therapy of schizophrenics. Psychiatry 24:53–60, 1961

Savage C, Harman W, Fadiman J, Savage E: LSD: Therapeutic effects of the psychedelic experience. Psychol Rep 14:111–120, 1964

Savage C, McCabe OL: Residential psychedelic (LSD) therapy for the narcotic addict: A controlled study. Arch Gen Psychiatry 28:808–814, 1973

Savage C, McCabe OL, Olsson JE, et al: Research with psychedelic drugs, in Hicks RE (ed): Psychedelic Drugs. New York, Grune & Stratton, 1969

Savitt RA: Psychoanalytic studies on addiction: Ego structure in narcotic addiction. Psychiatr Q 32:43–57, 1963

Scarborough HE, Denson BW: Treatment of therapeutic blockades with theopental (Pentothal) sodium and methamphetamine (Desoxyn), 1948–1957. Psychosom Med 20:108–116, 1958

Schaefer DL, Smith JJ: A dynamic therapy for schizophrenia. Am J Occup Ther 7:5, 1958

Schaefer R: The Clinical Application of Psychological Tests. New York, International Universities Press, 1948

Scheflen AE: Analysis of thought model which persists in psychiatry. Psychosom Med 20:235–241, 1958

Scheflen AE: A Psychotherapy of Schizophrenia. Springfield, Ill, Thomas, 1961

Scheflen AE: Communication and regulation in psychotherapy. Psychiatry 26:126–136, 1963

Scheflen AE: The significance of posture in communications systems. Psychiatry 27:316, 1964

Schedlinger S: Psychoanalysis and Group Behavior. New York, Norton, 1952

Scheidlinger S: Group process in group psychotherapy. A critical analysis of some current trends in the integration of individual and group psychology. Am J Psychother 14(1,2—entire issues), 1960

Scheidlinger S: Concept of regression in group

psychotherapy. Int J Group Psychother 18:20, 1968

Scherz FH: Multiple-client interviewing: Treatment implications. J Soc Casework 43:120–125, 1962

Schilder P: Results and problems of group psychotherapy in severe neuroses. Ment Hyg 23:87–98, 1939

Schilder P: The cure of criminals and the prevention of crime. J Crim Psychopathol, pp 149–161, 1940

Schindler W: Countertransference in family-pattern group psychotherapy. Int J Group Psychother 3:424–440, 1953

Schlessinger N: Supervision in psychotherapy. Arch Gen Psychiatry 15:129–134, 1966

Schmideberg M: The mode of operation of psychoanalytic therapy. Int J Psychoanal 19, 1938

Schmideberg M: The borderline patient, in Arieti S (ed): American Handbook of Psychiatry, vol. 1. New York, Basic Books, 1959, p 415

Schmideberg M: A major task of therapy: Developing volition and purpose. Am J Psychother 15:251–259, 1961

Schmiege GR: The current status of LSD as a therapeutic tool: A summary of the clinical literature. J Med Soc NJ 60:203–207, 1963

Schneck JM: Hypnoanalysis. Personality 1:317–370, 1951

Schneck JM: Self-hypnotic dreams in hypnoanalysis. J Clin Exp Hypn 1:44–53, 1953

Schneck JM: Hypnosis in Modern Medicine (3rd ed). Springfield, Ill, Thomas, 1963

Schneck JM: The Principles and Practice of Hypnoanalysis. Springfield, Ill., Thomas, 1965

Schofield W: In Welsh GS, Dahlstrom WG (eds): Basic Readings on the MMPI in Psychology and Medicine. Minneapolis, University of Minnesota Press, 1956

Schopbach RR: Art in psychotherapy. Henry Ford Hosp Med Bull 12:301–316, 1964

Schorer CE, Lowinger P, Sullivan T, Hartlaub GH: Improvement without treatment. Paper presented at the 122d Annual Meeting of the American Psychiatric Association, Atlantic City, NJ, May 1966

Schullian D, Schoen M (eds): Music and Medicine. New York, Schuman, 1948

Schultz JA, Luthe W: Autogenic Training—A Psychophysiologic Approach in Psychotherapy. New York, Grune & Stratton, 1959

Schut JW, Himwich HE: The effect of Meratran on twenty-five institutionalized mental patients. Am J Psychiatry 111:837–840, 1955

Schutz W: Interpersonal Underworld. (Original title: Firo: A Three-Dimensional Theory of Interpersonal Behavior.) Palo Alto, Calif, Science & Behavior Books, 1967(a)

Schutz W: Joy: Expanding Human Awareness. New York, Grove, 1967(b)

Schwab JJ, Schwab RB: The epidemiology of mental illness, in Usdin G (ed): Psychiatry: Education and Image. New York, Brunner/Mazel, 1973, p 67

Schwartz A: Parameters in the psychoanalytic treatment of a dying patient. Assoc Psychoanal Med, December, 1961

Schwartz CG: Rehabilitation of Mental Hospital Patients. Pub Health Monogr No. 17. Washington, DC, U.S. Government Printing Office, 1953

Schwartz EK: The development of clinical psychology as an independent profession. Prag Clin Psychol 3:10–21, 1958

Schwartz EK: Non-Freudian analytic methods, in Wolman B (ed): Handbook of Clinical Psychology. New York, McGraw-Hill, 1965

Schwartz EK: The treatment of the obsessive patient in the group therapy setting. Am J Psychother 26:352–361, 1972

Schwartz EK, Abel TA: The professional education of the psychoanalytic psychotherapist. Am J Psychother 9:253–261, 1955

Schwartz EK, Wolf A: Psychoanalysis in groups: Three primary parameters. Am Imago 14:281–297, 1957

Schwartz EK, Wolf A: Psychoanalysis in groups: The role of values. Am J Psychoanal 19:37–52, 1959

Schwartz EK, Wolf A: Psychoanalysis in groups: The mystique of group dynamics, in Hulse W (ed): Topical Problems of Psychotherapy, vol. 2. Basel, Switz, Karger, 1960

Schwartz EK, Wolf A: Psychoanalysis in groups: Some comparisons with individual analysis. J Genet Psychol 64:153–191, 1961

Schwartz EK, Wolf A: Psychoanalysis in groups: As creative process. Am J Psychoanal 24:46–59, 1964(a)

Schwartz EK, Wolf A: On countertransference in group psychotherapy. J Psychol 57:131, 1964(b)

Schwartz MF: The core of the stuttering block. J Speech Hear Disord 39:169–177, 1974

Schwartz MS, Shockley EL: The Nurse and the Mental Patient. New York, Russell Sage Foundation, 1956

Schwartz W: Group work and the social scene, in Kahn A (ed): Issues in American Social Work. New York, Columbia University Press, 1959, pp 110–137

Schwitzgebel R: Reduction of adolescent crime by a research method. J Soc Ther Correct Psychiatry 7:212–215, 1961

Schwitzgebel R, Kolb DA: Inducing behavior change in adolescent delinquents. Behav Res Ther 1:297–304, 1964

Searl MN: Some queries on principles of technique. Int J Psychoanal 17:471–493, 1936

Searles HF: The informational value of the supervisor's emotional experiences. Psychiatry 18:135, 1955

Searles HF: The Nonhuman Environment in Normal Development and in Schizophrenia. New York, International Universities Press, 1960

Searles HF: Collected Papers on Schizophrenia and Related Subjects, New York, International Universities Press, 1966

Sechehaye MA: Symbolic Realization: A New Method of Psychotherapy Applied to a Case of Schizophrenia. Wursten B, Wursten H (trans). New York, International Universities Press, 1951

Sechehaye MA: A New Psychotherapy in Schizophrenia. New York, Grune & Stratton, 1956

Seeman J, Raskin NJ: Research perspectives in client-centered therapy, in Mowrer OH (ed): Psychotherapy: Theory and Research. New York, Ronald, 1953, p 205

Segal H: Introduction to the Work of Melanie Klein. New York, Basic Books, 1964

Segal J: Biofeedback as a medical treatment. JAMA 232:179–180, 1975

Seitz PFD: Experiments in the substitution of symptoms by hypnosis, II. Psychosom Med 15:405–422, 1953

Senay EC, Dorusw, Renault PF: Methadylacetate and methadone. JAMA 237:138–142, 1977

Servadio E: Transference and thought-transference. Int J Psychoanal 37:1, 1956

Shapiro AK: Etiological factors in placebo effect. JAMA 187:712–714, 1964

Shapiro D: Neurotic Styles. New York, Basic Books, 1965

Shapiro D, Schwartz GE: Biofeedback and visceral learning: Clinical applications. Semin Psychiatry 4:171–184, 1972

Sharoff RL: Therapy of drug addiction. Curr Psychiatr Ther 6:247–251, 1966

Sharoff RL: Narcotherapy, in Freedman AM, Kaplan HI (eds): Comprehensive Textbook of Psychiatry. Baltimore, Williams & Wilkins, 1967

Sharpe EF: The technique of psychoanalysis. Int J Psychoanal 11:251–277, 361–386, 1930; 12:24–60, 1931

Shick JFE, Freedman DX: Research in nonnarcotic drug abuse, in Arieti S (ed): American Handbook of Psychiatry, vol. 4. New York, Basic Books, 1975, pp 592–593

Shlien JM: Cross-theoretical criteria in time-limited therapy. Paper presented at the 6th International Congress of Psychotherapy, London, 1964

Shlien JM, Mosak HM, Driekers R: Effects of time limits: A comparison of two psychotherapies. J Counsel Psychol 9:31–34, 1962

Shlien JM, Zinring FM: Research directives and methods in client-centered therapy, in Hart JT, Tomlinson TM (eds): New Directions in Client-Centered Therapy. Boston, Houghton-Mifflin, 1970, p 33

Shobe FO, Gildea MCL: Long-term follow-up of selected lobotomized private patients. JAMA 206:327–332, 1968

Shor RE: The fundamental problem viewed from historic perspective, in Fromm E, Shor RE (eds): Hypnosis: Research Developments and Perspectives. Chicago, Aldine, 1972

Shore MF, Massimo JL: Comprehensive vocationally oriented psychotherapy for adolescent delinquent boys: A follow-up study. Am J Orthopsychiatry 36:609–615, 1966

Shorr JE: Psycho-imagination Therapy. New York, Stratton Intercontinental, 1972

Showalter L: Mental health counselors—new professionals? The NIMH pilot group ten years later. Semin Psychiatry 3:288–291, 1971

Siegel NH: What is a therapeutic community? Nurs Outlook, 12:49–51, 1964

Sifneos PE: Two different kinds of psychotherapy of short duration. Paper presented at the 122d Annual Meeting of the American Psychiatric Association, Atlantic City, NJ, May 1966 (Am J Psychiatry 123:1069, 1967)

Sifneos PE: Short-Term Psychotherapy and Emotional Crisis. Cambridge, Harvard University Press, 1972

Sigerist HE: In Roemer MI (ed): On the Sociology of Medicine. New York, MD Publications, 1960

Silber E: The analyst's perception in the treatment of an adolescent. Psychiatry 25:160–169, 1962

Sills GM: Historical developments and issues in psychiatric mental health nursing, in Leninger MM (ed): Contemporary Issues in Mental Health Nursing. Boston, Little, Brown, 1973

Simmons JQ, Leiken SJ, Lovaas DI, et al: Modifications of autistic behavior with LSD-25. Am J Psychiatry 122:1201–1211, 1966

Simms LM: Use of hydroxyzine in neuropsychiatric states. Dis Nerv Syst 19:225, 1958

Simon A, Epstein LJ (eds): Aging in Modern Society. Washington, DC, American Psychological Association, 1968

Simon B, et al: The recognition and acceptance of mood in music by psychotic patients. J Nerv Ment Dis 114:66–78, 1951

Simon RM: On eclecticism. Am J Psychiatry 131:135–139, 1974

Singer E: Key Concepts in Psychotherapy. New York, Random House, 1965

Skinner BF: Science and Human Behavior. New York, Macmillan, 1953

Sklar AD, Yalom ID, Zim A, et al: Time-extended group therapy: A controlled study. Comp Group Studies 1:373–386, 1970

Slack CW: Experimenter-subject psychotherapy: A new method of introducing intensive office treatment for unreachable cases. Ment Hyg 44:238–256, 1960

Slack CW, Schwitzgebel R: A Handbook: Reducing Adolescent Crime in Your Community. Privately printed, 1960

Slavin S: Education, learning and group work. J Educ Sociology 24:143, 1950

Slavson SR: An Introduction to Group Therapy. New York, Commonwealth Fund, 1943 (paperback—New York, International Universities Press, 1970)

Slavson SR: Current practices in group therapy. Ment Hyg July 1944

Slavson SR: Differential methods of group psychotherapy in relation to age level. Nerv Child, pp 196–210, 1945

Slavson SR: The field and objectives of personality disorders, in Glueck B (ed): Current Therapies of Personality Disorders. New York, Grune & Stratton, 1946, pp 166–193

Slavson SR: Recreation and the Total Personality. New York, Association Press, 1946

Slavson SR: The Practice of Group Therapy. New York, International Universities Press, 1947

Slavson SR: Child-Centered Group Guidance of Parents. New York, International Universities Press, 1949

Slavson SR: Analytic Group Psychotherapy with Adults, Adolescents and Children. New York, Columbia University Press, 1950

Slavson SR: Transference phenomena in group psychotherapy. Psychoanal Rev 37:39, 1950

Slavson SR: Child Psychotherapy. New York, Columbia University Press, 1952

Slavson SR: Sources of countertransference and group-induced anxiety. Int J Group Psychother 3:373–388, 1953

Slavson SR: Criteria for selection and rejection of patients for various types of group psychotherapy. Int J Group Psychother 5:3–22, 1955

Slavson SR: The Fields of Group Psychotherapy. New York, International Universities Press, 1956

Slavson SR: The nature and treatment of acting out in group psychotherapy. Int J Group Psychother 6:3, 1956

Slavson SR: Are there "group dynamics" in the therapy group? Int J Group Psychother 7:131, 1957

Slavson SR: When is a "therapy group" not a therapy group? Int J Group Psychother 10:3–21, 1960

Slavson SR: A Textbook in Analytic Group Psychotherapy. New York, International Universities Press, 1964

Slavson SR: Reclaiming the Delinquent by Para-Analytic Group Psychotherapy and the Inversion Technique. New York, Free Press, 1965, p 766

Sletten I, Ulett G, Altman H, et al: The Missouri standard system for psychiatry. Arch Gen Psychiatry 23:73, 1970

Sloane P: Report of the second panel on the technique of supervised analysis. J Am Psychoanal Assoc 5:539–545, 1957

Sloane RB, Staples FR, Cristol AH, et al: Short-term analytically oriented psychotherapy versus behavior therapy. Am J Psychiatry 132:373–377, 1975

Small IF, Matarazzo R, Small JG: Total ward therapy groups in psychiatric treatment. Am J Psychother 17:254–265, 1963

Smallwood JC: Dance-movement therapy, in Masserman JH (ed): Current Psychiatric Therapies, vol. 14. New York, Grune & Stratton, 1974

Smith AB, Berlin L, Brassin A: Problems in client-centered group therapy with adult offenders. Am J Orthopsychiatry 33:550–553, 1963

Smith BK: No Language But a Cry. Boston, Beacon, 1964

Smith BM, Hain JD, Stevenson I: Controlled interviews using drugs. Arch Gen Psychiatry 22:2–10, 1970

Smith CM: A new adjunct to the treatment of alcoholism: The hallucinogenic drugs. Q J Stud Alcohol 19:406–417, 1958

Smith ER, Tyler R: Appraising and recording student Progress, in Adventures in American Education, vol. 3. New York, Harper & Row, 1942, p 18

Smith G: Psychotherapy in General Medicine. New York, Commonwealth Fund, 1946

Smith ME: Perphenazine and amitriptyline as

adjuncts to psychotherapy. Am J Psychiatry 120:76–77, 1963

Snell JE: The use of music in group psychotherapy, in Masserman JH (ed): Current Psychiatric Therapies, vol. 5. New York, Grune & Stratton, 1965, pp 145–149

Snyder F: Progress in the new biology of dreaming. Am J Psychiatry 122:377–391, 1965

Snyder F: Toward an evolutionary theory of dreaming. Paper presented at the 122d Annual Meeting of the American Psychiatric Association, Atlantic City, NJ, May 1966

Snyder WU: A short-term nondirective treatment with an adult. J Abnorm Soc Psychol Clin Suppl 38:87–137, 1943

Snyder WU: Casebook of Non-Directive Counseling. Boston, Houghton Mifflin, 1947(a)

Snyder WU: The present status of psychotherapeutic counseling. Psychol Bull 44:297–386, 1947(b)

Soal SG, Bateman F: Modern Experiments in Telepathy. New Haven, Yale University Press, 1954

Sobey F: The Nonprofessional Revolution in Mental Health. New York, Columbia University Press, 1970

Soibelman D: Therapeutic and Industrial Uses of Music. New York, Columbia University Press, 1948

Solnit AJ: Learning from psychoanalytic supervision. Int J Psychoanal 51:359–362, 1970

Solomon A, Loeffler FJ, Frank GH: An analysis of co-therapists interaction in group psychotherapy. Int J Group Psychother 3:171–180, 1953

Solomon AP, Greene BL: Marital disharmony: Concurrent therapy of husband and wife by the same psychiatrist. Dis Nerv Syst 24:21–28, 1963

Solomon JC: Active play therapy. Am J Orthopsychiatry 8:479, 1938

Solomon JC: Active play therapy: Further experience. Am J Orthopsychiatry 10:763–781, 1940

Solomon JC: Therapeutic use of play, in Anderson HH, Anderson GL (eds): Introduction to Projective Techniques. Englewood Cliffs, NJ, Prentice-Hall, 1951

Solomon JC, Axelrod PL: Group psychotherapy for withdrawn adolescents. Am J Dis Child 68:86–101, 1944

Solomon P (ed): Psychiatric Drugs. New York, Grune & Stratton, 1966

Solow C, Silverfarb PM, Swift K: Psychosocial effects of intestinal bypass surgery for severe obesity. N Engl J Med 290:300–304, 1974

Sonneman U: Handwriting Analysis. New York, Grune & Stratton, 1951

Soskin RA, Grof S, Richards WA: Low doses of dispropyltryptamine in psychotherapy. Arch Gen Psychiatry 28:817–821, 1973

Spangaard J: Transference neurosis and psychoanalytic group psychotherapy. Int J Group Psychother 9:31–42, 1959

Spector S: Behavior therapy in anorexia nervosa. JAMA 233:317, 1975

Spencer AM: Modifications in the technique of LSD therapy. Compr. Psychiatry 5:232–252, 1964

Sperber E, Feitas, R, Davis D: Bulletins of Structural Integration, vol. I, II, 1969

Spiegel H: Is symptom removal dangerous? Paper presented at the 122d Annual Meeting of the American Psychiatric Association. Atlantic City, NJ, May 1966

Spiegel H: A single-treatment method to stop smoking using ancillary self-hypnosis. Int J Clin Exp Hypn 18:235–250, 1970

Spiegel JP: Homeostatic mechanisms within the family, in Galdston I (ed): The Family in Contemporary Society. New York, International Universities Press, 1958

Spiegel JP: The resolution of role conflict within the family, in Bell NW, Vogel EF (eds): The Family. New York, Free Press, 1960

Spiegel JP: Our colleagues. Psychiatr News 9:2, 1974

Spiegel R: Specific problems of communication in psychiatric conditions, in Arieti S (ed): American Handbook of Psychiatry, vol. 1. New York, Basic Books, 1959, pp 909–949

Spiegelberg H: The Phenomenological Movement, A Historical Introduction. The Hague, Neth, Martinus, Nijhoff, 1960

Spitz HH, Kopp SB: Multiple Psychotherapy. Psychiatr Q Suppl 3:295–311, 1957

Spitz RA: Hospitalism, in Eissler RS, et al (eds): The Psychoanalytic Study of the Child, vol. 1. New York, International Universities Press, 1945

Spitz RA: Anaclitic depression, in Eissler RS, et al (eds): The Psychoanalytic Study of the Child, vol. 2. New York, International Universities Press, 1946, p 313

Spitz RA: Genese des premiéres relations objectales (Development of the first object relationships). Rev Fran Psyche, 1954

Spitzer RL: Clinical criteria for psychiatric diagnosis and DSM-III. Am J Psychiatry 132:1187–1192, 1975

Spitzer RL, Cohen J: Common errors in quantitative psychiatric research. Int J Psychiatry 6:109–131, 1968

Spitzer RL, Endicott J, Diagno II: Further

developments in a computer program for psychiatric diagnosis. Am J Psychiatry 125:12, 1969

Spotnitz H: Group therapy as a specialized psychotherapeutic technique, in Bychowski G, Despert JL (eds): Specialized Techniques in Psychotherapy. New York, Basic Books, 1952(a) pp 85–101

Spotnitz H: A psychoanalytic view of resistance in groups. Int J Group Psychother 2:3, 1952(b)

Spotnitz H: Resistance reinforcement in affect training of analytic group psychotherapists. Int J Group Psychother 8:395, 1958

Spotnitz H: The Couch and the Circle. A Story of Group Psychotherapy. New York, Knopf, 1961

Spotnitz H: Discussion of Stoller's accelerated interaction. Int J Group Psychother 18:236–239, 1968

Spotnitz H: Touch countertransference in group psychotherapy. Int J Group Psychother 22:455–466, 1972

Spotnitz H: Acting out in group psychotherapy, in Wolberg, LR, Schwartz EK (eds): Group Therapy 1973: An Overview. New York, Stratton Intercontinental, 1973, pp 28–42

Spotnitz H, Gabriel B: Resistance in analytic group therapy: A study of the group therapeutic process in children and mothers. Q J Child Behav 2:71, 1950

Staats AW, Staats CK: Complex Human Behavior. New York, Holt, 1963

Stace WT: Religion and the Modern Mind. Philadelphia, Lippincott, 1952

Stainbrook E: The hospital as a therapeutic community. Neuropsychiatry 3:69–87, 1955

Stainbrook E: The hospital as a therapeutic community, in Freedman AM, Kaplan HI (eds): Comprehensive Textbook of Psychiatry. Baltimore, Williams & Wilkins, 1967, pp 1296–1300

Stampfl TG: Implosive therapy in behavior modification techniques in the treatment of emotional disorders. Armitage S (ed). Battle Creek, Mich, Veterans Administration, 1967

Standard S, Nathan H: Should the Patient Know the Truth! New York, Springer, 1955

Stanton A: Milieu therapy and the development of insight. Psychiatry 24(Suppl):19–30, 1961

Stanton HE: Weight loss through hypnosis. Am J Clin Hypn 18:94–97, 1975

Starfield B: Enuresis: Its pathogenesis and management. Clin Pediatr 11:343–349, 1972

Stark P: A psychoanalytic view of male homosexuality. J L Is Consultation Center 3:3–13, 1963

Stein A: Some aspects of resistance in group psychotherapy. J Hillside Hosp 1:79–88, 1952

Stein A: Indications for group psychotherapy and the selection of patients. J Hillside Hosp 12:145, 1963

Stein A: The nature of transference in combined therapy. Int J Group Psychother 14:413, 1964

Stein A: Reconstructive family therapy. Newsletter (Bleuler Psychotherapy Center) February 1966

Stein C: Practical pastoral counseling, in Masserman JH (ed): Current Psychiatric Therapies, vol. 12. New York, Grune & Stratton, 1972

Stein J, Euper JA: Advances in music therapy, in Masserman JH (ed): Current Psychiatric Therapies, vol. 14. New York, Grune & Stratton, 1974

Steinhaus AH: Neuromuscular relaxation and mental health. Psychiatr Spectator 3:1, 1963

Steinman LA, Hunt RC: A day care center in a state hospital. Am J Psychiatry 117:112, 1961

Stekel W: Der Vetischismus. Berlin, and Wein, Urban and Schwarzenberg, 1923

Stekel W: Peculiarities of Behavior. New York, Liveright, 1924

Stekel W: Frigidity in Women. New York, Liveright, 1926

Stekel W: Impotence in the Male. New York, Liveright, 1927

Stekel W: Sadism and Masochism. New York, Liveright, 1929

Stekel W: Sexual Aberrations: The Phenomenon of Fetishism in Relation to Sex, vol. 2. New York, Liveright, 1930

Stekel W: Sexual Aberrations. New York, Liveright, 1949

Stekel W: Technique of Analytical Psychotherapy. New York, Liveright, 1950

Stekel W: Patterns of Psychosexual Infantilism. New York, Liveright, 1952

Sterba R: The dynamics of the dissolution of the transference resistance. Psychiatric Q 9, 1940

Sterba R, Lyndon BH, Katz A: Transference in Casework. New York, Family Service Association of America, 1948

Stern A: On the counter-transference in psychoanalysis. Psychoanal Rev 9:166–174, 1924

Stern K, et al: Observations on a ceramics workshop for psychiatric patients. Can Psychiatr Assoc J 2:114–125, 1957

Stern MM: Free painting as an auxiliary technique in psychoanalysis, in Bychowski G, Despert JL (eds): Specialized Techniques in

Psychotherapy. New York, Basic Books, 1952(a) pp 65–83

Stern MM: Spontaneous art in therapy and diagnosis. Prog Clin Psychol 1:290–311, 1952(b)

Sterne S: The validity of music on effective group psychotherapeutic technique, in Proceedings of the National Association of Music Therapy. Kansas City, Kans, the Association, 1955, pp 130–140

Stevenson GS: Mental Health Planning for Social Action. New York, McGraw-Hill, 1956

Stevenson I: Processes of "spontaneous" recovery from the psychoneuroses. Am J Psychiatry 117:1057–1064, 1961

Stevenson I: The use of rewards and punishments in psychotherapy. Compr Psychiatry 3:20–28, 1962

Stevenson I: Discussion, in Wolpe J, et al (eds): The Conditioning Therapies. New York, Holt, 1966

Stevenson I, Buckman J, Smith BM, Hain JD: The use of drugs in psychiatric interviews: Some interpretations based on controlled experiments. Am J Psychiatry 131:707–710, 1974

Stewart MA: Hyperactive children. Sci Am 222:94–98, 1970

Stewart MA: Treatment of bedwetting. JAMA 232:281–283, 1975

Stewart WA: Psychoanalytic therapy, in Frosch J, Ross N (eds): The Annual Survey of Psychoanalysis. A Comprehensive Survey of Psychoanalytic Theory and Practice, vol. 7. New York, International Universities Press, 1963, pp 354–355

Stieper DR, Wiener DN: Dimensions of Psychotherapy. Chicago, Aldine, 1965

Stock D: Interpersonal concerns during the early sessions of therapy groups. Int J Group Psychother 12:14, 1962

Stock D, Thelen H: Emotional Dynamics and Group Culture. New York, New York University Press, 1958

Stollak GE: An integrated graduate-undergraduate program in the assessment, treatment, and prevention of child psychopathology. Professional Psychol 4:158–169, 1973

Stollak GE: Education for early childhood consultation. J Clin Child Psychol 3:20–24, 1974

Stoller FH: Marathon Group Therapy. Los Angeles, Youth Studies Center, University of Southern California, 1967

Stoller FH: Accelerated interaction: A time-limited approach based on the brief intensive group. Int J Group Psychother 18:220–235, 1968

Stoller FH: Videotape feedback in the group setting. J Nerv Ment Dis 148:457–466, 1969

Stone L: Psychoanalysis and brief psychotherapy. Psychiatr Q 20:215–236, 1951

Stone WN, Tieger ME: Screening for T-groups: The myth of healthy candidates. Am J Psychiatry 127:1485–1490, 1971

Storrow HA: Money as a motivator. Pub Welfare 20:199–204, 1962

Storrow HA: Psychotherapy as interpersonal conditioning, in Masserman JH (ed): Current Psychiatric Therapies, vol. 5. New York, Grune & Stratton, 1965

Strachey J: The nature of the therapeutic action of psychoanalysis. Int J Psychoanal 15:127, 1934

Strachey J: Symposium on the theory of the therapeutic results of psychoanalysis. Int J Psychoanal 18:125–189, 1937

Strachstein H: Bibliography—Group Analysis. New York, Postgraduate Center for Mental Health, 1965

Straker M: Brief psychotherapy in an outpatient clinic: Evolution and evaluation. Am J Psychiatry 124:1219–1226, 1968

Strang R: Educational Guidance: Its Principles and Practice. New York, Macmillan, 1947

Straus E: The Primary World. New York, Free Press, 1963

Strauss AA, Kephart NC: Psychopathology and Education of the Brain-Injured Child, vol. 2. New York, Grune & Stratton, 1955

Strauss AA, Lehtinen LE: Psychopathology and Education of the Brain-Injured Child, vol. 1. New York, Grune & Stratton, 1947

Strauss BV: The role of the physician's personality in medical practice (psychotherapeutic medicine). NY State J Med 51:753, 1951

Strauss JB: Two face the group: A study of the relationship between co-therapists, in Wolberg LR, Aronson ML (eds): Group Therapy 1975: An Overview. New York, Stratton Intercontinental, 1975, pp 201–210

Strauss JS: A comprehensive approach to psychiatric diagnosis. Am J Psychiatry 132:1193–1197, 1975

Strean HS: Non-verbal intervention in psychotherapy. Psychother: Theory Res Prac 6:235–237, 1969

Strean HS: Social change and the proliferation of regressive therapies. Psychoanal Rev 58:581–594, 1971–1972

Stringer LA: Children at risk: II. The teacher as change agent. Elem School J 73:424–434, 1973

Stroebel CF, Glueck BC: Biofeedback treatment

in medicine and psychiatry: An ultimate placebo? Semin Psychiatry 5:379–393, 1973

Stroh G: A therapist's reactions as reflected in his reporting on a psychotherapeutic group. Int J Group Psychother 8:403–409, 1958

Strunk O, Jr: Empathy: A review of theory and research. Psychol Newsletter 9:47–57, 1958

Strupp HH: An objective comparison of Rogerian and psychoanalytic techniques. J. Consult Psychol 19:1–7, 1955

Strupp HH: A multidimensional analysis of therapist activity in analytic and client-centered therapy. J Consult Psychol 21:301–308, 1957

Strupp HH: Psychotherapists in Action. New York, Grune & Stratton, 1960

Strupp HH: The effects of psychotherapy. Int J Psychiatry 1:165–169, 1965

Strupp HH: On the technology of psychotherapy. Arch Gen Psychiatry 26:270–278, 1972(a)

Strupp HH: Needed: A reformulation of the psychotherapeutic influence. Int J Psychiatry 10:119, 1972(b)

Strupp HH: Psychotherapy: Clinical, Research, and Theoretical Issues. New York, Aronson, 1973, pp 377–418

Strupp HH, Hadley SW, Gomes B, Armstrong SH: Negative effects in psychotherapy: A review of clinical and theoretical issues together with recommendations for a program of research. Support provided by NIMH, Contract 278–75–0036(ER). To be published

Stueks AM: Working together collaboratively with other professionals. Community Ment Health J 1:316, 1965(a)

Stueks AM: The community mental health view of mentally ill and mentally restored patients. Perspect Psychiatr Care 3(1), 1965(b)

Stunkard A: New therapies for the eating disorders. Arch Gen Psychiatry 26:391–398, 1972

Subcommittee on Occupational Therapy, American Psychiatric Association: An opinion survey concerning occupational therapy. On file with the Council of the American Psychiatric Association. Washington, DC, the Association

Suess JF: Milieu and activity therapy with chronically disturbed female patients. Psychiatric Q 32:1–12, 1958

Suess JF: Short-term psychotherapy with the compulsive personality and the obsessive-compulsive neurotic. Am J Psychiatry 129:270–275, 1972

Sullivan HS: The modified psychoanalytic treatment of schizophrenia. Am J Psychiatry 11(3), 1931

Sullivan HS: Conceptions in Modern Psychiatry. Washington, DC, William Alanson White Psychiatric Foundation, 1947

Sullivan HS: The Meaning of Anxiety in Psychiatry and in Life. Washington, DC, William Alanson White Foundation, 1948

Sullivan HS: The theory of anxiety and the nature of psychotherapy. Am J Psychiatry 12:3–12, 1949

Sullivan HS: The Interpersonal Theory of Psychiatry. New York, Norton, 1953

Sullivan HS: The Psychiatric Interview. New York, Norton, 1954

Sullivan HS: Clinical Studies in Psychiatry. New York, Norton, 1956

Sullivan HS: Schizophrenia as a Human Process (1930). New York, Norton, 1962

Sundberg ND, Tyler LE: Clinical Psychology. New York, Appleton-Century-Crofts, 1962

Super DE: Guidance and counseling, in Social Work Year Book. New York, American Association for Social Workers, 1951, p 220

Sutherland JD: Notes on psychoanalytic group therapy. I. Therapy and training. Psychiatry 15:111–117, 1952

Suzuki DT: An Introduction to Zen Buddhism. London, Rider, 1947

Suzuki DT: Essays in Zen Buddhism (1st ser, 2d ed). New York, Harper & Row 1949

Suzuki DT: Essays in Zen Buddhism (2d ser, 2d ed). London, Rider, 1952

Suzuki DT: Essays in Zen Buddhism (3rd ser, 2d ed). London, Rider 1953

Suzuki DT: An Introduction to Zen Buddhism (2d ed). London, Rider, 1957(a)

Suzuki DT: A Manual of Zen Buddhism (2d ed). London, Rider, 1957(b)

Suzuki DT: The Training of the Zen Buddhist Monk (1st Am ed). New York, University Books, 1959

Swenson WM, Pearson JS, Rome HP: Automation technics in personality assessment: Fusion of three professions, in Proceedings of Conference on Data Acquisition and Processing in Biology and Medicine. Elmsford, NY, Pergamon, 1963, pp 149–156

Swenson WM, Pearson JS, Rome HP, Brannick TL: A totally automated psychological test. JAMA 191:925–927, 1965

Syz H: The concept of the organism-as-a-whole and its application to clinical situations. Hum Biol 8:489–507, 1936

Syz H: Trigant Burrow's thesis in relation to psychotherapy. Prog Psychother 2:147–155, 1957

Syz H: Reflections on group of phyloanalysis. Acta Psychother Suppl ad 2:37–88, 1963

Szasz TS: Psychiatric aspects of vagotomy II. A

psychiatric study of vagotomized ulcer patients with comments on prognosis. Psychosom Med 11:187–199, 1949

Szasz TS: Psychoanalytic training: A socio-psychological analysis of its history and present status. Int J Psychoanal 39:1–16, 1958

Szasz TS: Myth of mental illness. Am Psychol 15:113–118, 1960

Szasz TS: The Myth of Mental Illness. New York, Hoeber, 1961

Szasz TS: Law, Liberty and Psychiatry. New York, Macmillan, 1963

Szasz TS: Ethics of Psychoanalysis. New York, Basic Books, 1965(a)

Szasz TS: Psychiatric Justice. New York, Macmillan, 1965(b)

Szurek SA: Notes on the genesis of psychopathic personality trends. Psychiatry 5:1, 1942

Szurek SA: Remarks on training for psychotherapy. Am J Orthopsychiatry 19:36–51, 1949(a)

Szurek SA: Some impressions from clinical experience with delinquents, in Eissler KR (ed): Searchlights on Delinquency. New Psychoanalytic Studies. New York, International Universities Press, 1949(b), pp 115–127

Szurek SA, Johnson A, Falstein EI: Collaborative psychiatric treatment of parent-child problems. Am J Orthopsychiatry 12:511, 1942

Taba H: With Perspective on Human Relations. Washington, DC, American Council on Education, 1955

Taffel C: Anxiety and the conditioning of verbal behavior. J Abnorm Soc Psychol 5:496–501, 1955

Taft J: The Dynamics of Therapy in a Controlled Relationship. New York, Macmillan, 1933

Taft J (ed): Family Case Work and Counseling: A Functional Approach. Philadelphia, University of Pennsylvania Press, 1948

Tagge GF, Adler D, Bryan-Brown CW, Shoemaker WC: Relationship of therapy to prognosis in critically ill patients. Crit Care Med 2:61, 1974

Taggert M: The AAPC information project. J Pastoral Care 26:219–244, 1972

Takakusu J: The Essentials of Buddhist Philosophy. Honolulu, University of Hawaii Press, 1947

Talbot E, White RB, Miller SC: Some aspects of self-conceptions and role-demands in a therapeutic community. J Abnorm Soc Psychol 63:338–345, 1961

Talbott DR: Are tranquilizer combinations more effective than a single tranquilizer? Am J Psychiatry 121:597–600, 1964

Talbott JA, et al: The paraprofessional teaches the professional. Am J Psychiatry 130:805–808, 1973

Tallent N: Clinical Psychological Consultation. Englewood Cliffs, NJ, Prentice-Hall, 1963

Tallman FF: Treatment of Emotional Problems in Office Practice. New York, McGraw-Hill, 1961

Tannenbaum F: Crime and the Community. Boston, Ginn, 1938

Tanner BA: Two case reports on the modification of the ejaculatory response with the squeeze technique. Psychother: Theory Res Prac 10:297–300, 1973

Tanner LN, Lindgren HC: Classroom Teaching and Learning. A Mental Health Approach. New York, Holt, 1971

Tarachow S: An Introduction to Psychotherapy. New York, International Universities Press, 1963, p 41

Tart CT: A comparison of suggested dreams occurring in hypnosis and sleep. Int J Clin Exp Hypn 12:263–289, 1964

Tart CT: The hypnotic dream. Psychol Bull 63:87–99, 1965

Tart CT: Types of hypnotic dreams and their relation to hypnotic depth. J Abnorm Psychol 71:377–382, 1966

Tarumianz MD, Bullis HE: The human relations class: A preventive mental hygiene program for schools. Understanding the Child 13:3–10, 1944

Tauber ES: Exploring the therapeutic use of the countertransference data. Psychiatry 17:331–336, 1964

Taylor FK: A history of the group and administrative therapy in Great Britain. Br J Med Psychol 31:153–173, Parts 3, 4, 1958

Teicher A, de Freitas L, Osherson A: Group psychotherapy and the intense group experience: A preliminary rationale for encounter as a therapeutic agent in the mental health field. Int J Group Psychother 24:159–173, 1974

Terman LM, Merrill MA: Stanford-Binet Intelligence Scale; Manual for the Third Revision, Form L-M. Boston, Houghton-Mifflin, 1960

Teuber HL, Powers E: Evaluating therapy in a delinquency preventive program, in Association for Research in Nervous and Mental Disease: Psychiatric Treatment. Res Publ 31. Baltimore, Williams & Wilkins, 1953, pp 138–147

Tharp RG: Psychological patterning with marital partners. Psycho Bull 60:97–117, 1963

Thelen HC: Dynamics of Groups at Work. Chicago, University of Chicago Press, 1954

Thelen HC, et al: Methods of Studying Group Operation. Chicago, Human Dynamics Laboratory, 1954

Thigpen CH, Cleckley H: A case of multiple personality. J Abnorm Soc Psychol 49:135–151, 1954

Thomas A: Simultaneous psychotherapy with marital partners. Am J Psychother 10:716–728, 1956

Thomas DR, Becker WC, Armstrong M: Production and elimination of disruptive classroom behavior by systematically varying teacher's behavior. J Appl Behav Anal 1:35–45, 1968

Thomas EJ: The Life of Buddha as Legend and History. London, Routledge & Kegan, 1931

Thomas EJ: The History of Buddhist Thought. London, Routledge & Kegan, 1933

Thomas EJ: Early Buddhist Scriptures. London, Routledge & Kegan, 1935

Thomas EJ: Selected socio-behavioral techniques and principles: An approach to interpersonal helping. Soc Work 13(1), 1968

Thomas EJ: Behavioral modification and casework, in Roberts R, Nee R (eds): Theories of Social Casework. Chicago, University of Chicago Press, 1970

Thompson C: Psychoanalysis: Evolution and Development. New York, Hermitage, 1950, pp 241–242

Thompson CE: The attitudes of various groups toward behavior problems of children. J Abnorm Soc Psychol 35:120–125, 1940

Thorndike EL: The Psychology of Wants, Interests, and Attitudes. New York, Appleton-Century, 1935

Thorndike RL, Hagen E: Measurement and Evaluation in Psychology and Education (2d ed). New York, Wiley, 1961

Thorne FC: A critique of nondirective methods of psychotherapy. J Abnorm Soc Psychol 39:459–470, 1944

Thorne FC: Directive psychotherapy: IV. The therapeutic implications of the case history. J Clin Psychol 1:318–330, 1945

Thorne FC: Directive psychotherapy: VII. Imparting psychological information. J Clin Psychol 2:179–190, 1946

Thorne FC: Principles of directive counseling and psychotherapy. Am Psychol 3:160–165, 1948

Thorne FC: Principles of Personality Counseling. Brandon Vt, Journal of Clinical Psychology, 1950

Thorne FC: An eclectic evaluation of psychotherapeutic methods, in Jurjevich RM (ed): Direct Psychotherapy, vol. 2. Coral Gables, Fla, University of Miami Press, 1973, pp 847–883

Thorne RB: Bibliography—Group analysis. New York, Postgraduate Center for Mental Health, 1966

Thornton EE: Professional Education for the Ministry: A History of Clinical Pastoral Education. Nashville, Tenn, Abingdon, 1970

Tibbetts RW, Hawkings JR: The placebo response. J Ment Sci 102:60, 1956

Tiemann WH: The Right to Silence. Richmond, Va, Knox, 1964

Tien HC: From couch to coffee shop: A new personality via psychosynthesis. Roche Report 2(18, 19), 1972

Tillich P: The Courage to Be. New Haven, Yale Union Press, 1952

Titmuss RM: Community care of the mentally ill. Can Ment Health Suppl No. 49, November–December 1965

Tobias M: Disturbed child—a concept. Am Pract Dig Treat 10:1759–1766, 1959

Tompkins SS: Thematic Apperception Test. The Theory and Technique of Interpretation. New York, Grune & Stratton, 1947

Topping R: Treatment of the pseudo-social boy. Am J Orthopsychiatry 13:353, 1943

Torkelson LO, Ramano MT: Self-confrontation by video tape: A remedial measure in teaching diagnostic evaluation. JAMA 201:773–775, 1967

Torraine EP, Strom RD (eds): Mental Health and Achievement: Increasing Potential and Reducing School Dropout. New York, Wiley, 1965

Torrance EP: Guiding Creative Talent. Englewood Cliffs, NJ, Prentice-Hall, 1962

Toulmin S: The Philosophy of Science: An Introduction. New York, Longmans, Green, 1953

Tourney G: Therapeutic fashions in psychiatry, 1800–1965. Paper presented at the 122d Annual Meeting of the American Psychiatric Association, Atlantic City, NJ, May 1966

Towle C: Social case work in modern society. Soc Serv Rev 20:165–180, 1946

Towle C: The Training and Function of a Psychiatric Social Worker in a Clinical Setting. Transactions of the First Conference. New York, Josiah Macy, Jr, Foundation, 1947, pp 31–40

Towle C: The Learner in Education for the Professions. Chicago, University of Chicago Press, 1954

Trager H: The Primary Teacher, in Intercultural

Attitudes in the Making. 9th Yearbook of the John Dewey Society, 1949

Trager H, Yarrow MR: They Learn What They Live: Prejudice in Young Children. New York, Harper & Row, 1952

Trail PM: An account of Lowenfeld technique in a child guidance clinic, with a survey of therapeutic play technique in Great Britain and the U.S.A. J Ment Sci 91:43–78, 1945

Traxler AE: Techniques of Guidance. New York, Harper & Row, 1945 (3d ed, 1966)

Trecker HB: Social Group Work, Principles and Practices. New York, New York Women's Press, 1946, pp 16–18; Whiteside, 1955

Trosman H: Dream research and the psycho-analytic theory of dreams. Arch Gen Psychiatry 9:27–36, 1963

Truax CB, Carkhuff RR: For better or for worse: The process of psychotherapeutic personality change, in Recent Advances in the Study of Behavior Change. Montreal, McGill University Press, 1964, pp 118–163

Truax CB, Carkhuff RR: Toward Effective Counseling and Psychotherapy: Training and Practice. Chicago, Aldine, 1967

Truax CB, Mitchell KM: Research on certain therapist interpersonal skills in relation to process and outcome, in Bergin AE, Garfield SL (eds): Handbook of Psychotherapy and Behavioral Change. New York, Wiley, 1972, pp 299–244

Truax CB, Wargo DC: Psychotherapeutic encounters that change behavior: For better or for worse. Am J Psychol 20:499–520, 1966

Tullis F: Rational diet construction for mild and grand obesity. JAMA 226:70–71, 1973

Tuteur W, Stiller R, Glotzer G: Chlorpromazine—five years later (fifth of a series, a five-year study), in Wortis J (ed): Recent Advances in Biological Psychiatry, vol. 3, New York, Grune & Stratton, 1961, p 35

Tyhurst JS: The role of transition states—including disasters—in mental illness. Symposium on Preventive and Social Psychiatry sponsored by the U.S. Walter Reed Army Institute of Research, Walter Reed Army Medical Center, Bethesda, Md, April 1957

Tyler R: The influence of the curriculum and teaching on the development of creativity, in Ekstein R, Motto RL (eds): From Learning for Love to Love of Learning. New York, Brunner/Mazel, 1969

Ulett GA, Akpinar S, Itil TM: Quantitative EEG analysis during hypnosis. Electroencephalogr Clin Neurophysiol 33:361–368, 1972(a)

Ulett GA, Akpinar S, Itil TM: Hypnosis: Physiological, pharmacological, reality. Am J Psychiatry 128:799–805, 1972(b)

Ulett GA, Goodrich DW: A Synopsis of Contemporary Psychiatry. St. Louis, Mosby, 1956

Ullman M: On the occurrence of telepathic dreams. J Am Soc Psychical Res 53:50, 1959

Ullman M, Krippner S: Dream Studies and Telepathy. New York, Parapsychology Foundation, 1970

Ullmann LP, Berkman VC: Efficacy of placement of neuropsychiatric patients in family care. Arch Gen Psychiatry 1:273–274, 1959

Umbarger CC, et al: College Students in a Mental Hospital. New York, Grune & Stratton, 1962

Upham F: Ego Analysis in the Helping Professions. New York, Family Service Association of America, 1973

Urban HB, Ford DH: Some historical and conceptual perspectives on psychotherapy and behavior change, in Bergin AE, Garfield SL (eds): Handbook of Psychotherapy and Behavior Change: An Empirical Analysis. New York, Wiley, 1971

U.S. Children's Bureau: Trends and Developments in Public Child Welfare Services. Child Welfare Reports No. 4. Washington, D.C, U.S. Government Printing Office, 1949

U.S. Department of Health, Education, & Welfare, Public Health Service: Narcotic Drug Addiction, Ment Health Mongr 2. Washington, DC, U.S. Government Printing Office

U.S. Department of Health, Education, & Welfare, Public Health Service: The Protection and Promotion of Mental Health in Schools. Ment Health Mongr 5. Washington, DC, U.S. Government Printing Office

U.S. Department of Health, Education, & Welfare. Secretary's Committee to Study Extended Roles for Nurses: In Extending the Scope of Nursing Practice. Washington, DC, U.S. Government Printing Office, 1971. (See also Am J Nurs 7:12:2346–2351, 1971)

U.S. Department of Health, Education, & Welfare: Report on Licensure and Related Health Personnel Credentialing. Washington, DC, U.S. Government Printing Office, June 1971

U.S. Office of Education, National Institute of Mental Health: Mental Health and Learning. Washington, DC, U.S. Government Printing Office, 1972

U.S. Public Health Service: An Introduction to

Mental Health Consultation. Washington, DC, U.S. Department of Health, Education & Welfare, 1962

U.S. Social Security Administration: Annual Report of the Federal Security Agency, 1949

Vahia NS: Hindu philosophy and psychology. Lecture presented at the Postgraduate Center for Mental Health, New York, 1962

Vaillant GE: A twelve-year follow-up of New York City addicts—characteristics and determinants of abstinence. Paper presented at the 122d Annual Meeting of the American Psychiatric Association. Atlantic City, NJ, May 1966

Valenstein AF: Some principles of psychiatric consultation. Soc Casework 36:253–256, 1955

Van De Wall W: Music in Institutions. New York, Russell Sage Foundation, 1936, pp 48–73

Van Dyke PB: Hypnosis in surgery. J Abdominal Surg 7(1, 2), 1965

Van Ophuijsen JHW: Therapeutic criteria in social agencies. Am J Orthopsychiatry 9:410–420, 1939

Van Putten T: Milieu therapy: Contraindications. Arch Gen Psychiatry 29:640–643, 1973

Van Riper C: The Nature of Suttering. Englewood Cliffs, NJ, Prentice-Hall, 1971

van Woerhom AJ, Brodman K: Statistics for a diagnostic model. Biometrics 17:299–318, 1961

Vasconcellow J, Kurland AA: Use of sustained-release chlorpromazine in the management of hospitalized chronic psychotic patients. Dis Nerv Syst 19:4, 1958

Vass I: The acting-out patient in group therapy. Am J Psychother 19:302–308, 1965

Vassilou G, Vassilou V: Introducing operational goals in group psychotherapy, in Arieti S (ed): Second Biennial of Psychiatry and Psychotherapy. New York, Basic Books, 1973

Vassilou G, Vassilou V: On the synallactic aspects of the grouping process, in Wolberg LR, Aronson ML (eds): Group Therapy 1974: An Overview. New York, Stratton Intercontinental, 1974, pp 158–174

Verhulst J: The couples communication center: Experience with a new therapeutic model. Int J Balint Groups 2–3/4/5–6. Special Edition, Congress Brussels, 1974, pp 129–135

Vernon MD: Backwardness in Reading: The Study of Its Nature and Origin. New York, Cambridge University Press, 1957

Vernonon PE: The significance of the Rorschach Test. Br J Med Psychol 15:199–217, 1935

Verplanck WS: The control of the content of conversation: Reinforcement of statement of opinion. J Abnorm Soc Psychol 51:668–676, 1955

Vigilante J: The future: Dour or rosy. Soc Work 17(4), 1972

Visher JS, O'Sullivan M: Nurse and patient responses to a study of milieu therapy. Am J Psychiatry 127:451, 1971

Vitoz R: Treatment of Neurashenia by Means of Brain Control. Brooks HB (trans). London, Longmans, Green, 1913

Voegtlin W, et al: Conditioned reflex therapy of alcoholic addiction, III. An evaluation of present results in the light of previous experience with this method. Q J Stud Alcohol 1:501–516, 1940(a)

Voegtlin W, et al: The treatment of alcoholism by establishing a conditioned reflex. Am J Med Sci 199:802–809, 1940(b)

Volgyesi FA: "School for Patients," hypnosis-therapy and psychoprophylaxia. Br J Med Hypn 5:8–17, 1954

von Dedenroth TEA: The use of hypnosis in 1000 cases of "tobaccomaniacs." Am J Clin Hypn 10:194–197, 1968

Wachpress M: Goals and functions of the community mental health center. Am J Psychiatry 129:187–190, 1972

Wageneder FM, St Schuy G: Electrotherapeutic sleep and electroanaesthesia. Proceedings of the Second International Symposium, Graz, Austria, September 1970. Amsterdam, Excerpta Medica, 1970

Wagner JA: Children's Literature Through Storytelling. Dubuque, Iowa, Brown, 1970

Wagner PS: Prospects for psychiatry and psychoanalysis. Int Psychiatry Clin 6(3):5–28, 1969

Wahl CW: Section Two (untitled) on the psychiatrist's role, in Helping the Dying Patient and His Family. New York, National Association for Social Workers, 1960

Walder E: Synanon and the learning process: A critique of attack therapy. Correct Psychiatry J Soc Ther 11:299–304, 1965

Walker HM, Mattson RH, Buckley NK: Special class placement as a treatment alternative for deviant behavior in children, in Modifying Deviant Social Behaviors in Various Classroom Settings. Mongr No. 1. Eugene, Department of Special Education, University of Oregon, 1969

Walker RG, Kelley FE: Short-term psychotherapy with hospitalized schizophrenic patients. Act Psychiatr Neurol Scand 35:34–56, 1960

Wallace AFC: Human Behavior in Extreme Situations. National Academy of Sciences, National Research Council, Publ No. 390, Diaster Study No. 1. Washington, DC, the Council, 1956

Wallace RK: Physiological effects of transcendental meditation. Science 167:1751–1754, 1970

Wallerstein RS: The goals of psychoanalysis. A survey of analytic viewpoints. J Am Psychoanal Assoc 13:748–770, 1965

Wallerstein RS: The current state of psychotherapy: Theory, practice, research. J Am Psychoanal Assoc 14:183–225, 1966

Wallin JEW: Education of Mentally Handicapped Children. New York, Harper & Row, 1955

Walsh J: Continuous narcosis: The advantages of oral somnifaine—a comparison. J Ment Sci 93:255, 1947

Walsh JJ: Health through Will Power. Boston, Stratford, 1913

Walsh JJ: Psychotherapy. New York, Appleton-Century, 1913

Walter CJS, Mitchell-Heggs N, Sargant W: Modified narcosis, ECT and antidepressant drugs: A review of technique and immediate outcome. Br J Psychiatry 120:651–662, 1972

Walter WG: Electrophysiologic contributions to psychiatric therapy, in Masserman JH (ed): Current Psychiatric Therapies, vol. 6. New York, Grune & Stratton, 1966, pp 13–25

Walters L: In Podolsky E (ed): Music Therapy. New York, Philosophical Library, 1954

Walters RH, Leat M, Mezei L: Inhibition and disinhibition of responses through empathetic learning. Can J Psychol 17:235–243, 1963

Walters RH, Llewellyn TE: Enhancement of punitive behavior by visual and audiovisual displays. Can J Psychol 17:244–255, 1963

Walton D, Mather MD: The application of learning principles to the treatment of obsessive-compulsive states in the acute and chronic phases of illness. Behav Res Ther 1:163–174, 1963(a)

Walton D, Mather MD: The relevance of generalization techniques to the treatment of stammering and phobic symptoms. Behav Res Ther 1:121–25, 1963(b)

Walton HJ: Outcome in treated alcoholism. Paper presented at the 122d Annual Meeting of the American Psychiatric Association, Atlantic City, NJ, May 1966

Walzer H: Casework treatment of the depressed patient. Soc Casework 42:205–512, 1961

Wasson BG: Mushroom rites in Mexico. Harvard Rev 1:14, 1963

Watkins JG: Hypnotherapy of War Neuroses: A Clinical Psychologist's Casebook. New York, Ronald, 1949

Watson AS: The conjoint psychotherapy of married partners. Am J Orthopsychiatry 33:912–922, 1963

Watson G: The role of the teacher, in Witty PA, Skinner CE (eds): Mental Hygiene in Modern Education. New York, Ferrar & Rinehart, 1939

Watson G: Areas of agreement in psychotherapy. Am J Orthopsychiatry 10:698–709, 1940

Watterson DJ: Problems in the evaluation of psychotherapy. Bull Menninger Clin 18:232–241, 1954

Watts AW: The Way of Zen. New York, Pantheon, 1957

Watts MSM, Wilbur DL: Clinical management of "functional" disorders. JAMA 148:704–708, 1952

Watzlawick P: A review of the double-bind theory. Fam Process 2:132–153, 1963

Watzlawick P, Beavin JH, Jackson DD: Pragmatics of Human Communication: A Study of Interactional Patterns, Pathologies, and Paradoxes. New York, Norton, 1967

Waxenberg SE, Fleischl MF: Referring therapist's impressions of a therapeutic social club. Int J Soc Psychiatry 11:3, 173, 1965

Wayne GJ: The hospital-affiliated halfway house, in Masserman JH (ed): Current Psychiatric Therapies, vol. 4. New York, Grune & Stratton, 1964, pp 213–217

Weakland JH: Family therapy as a research arena. Fam Process 1:63–68, 1962

Webster DR, Azrin NH: Required relaxation: A method of inhibiting agitative-disruptive behavior of retardates. Behav Res Ther 11:67–78, 1973

Wechsler D: WAIS: Manual: Wechsler Adult Intelligence Scale. New York, Psychological Corporation, 1955, p 20

Wechsler H: The ex-patient organization: A survey. J Soc Issues 16:47–53 1960(a)

Wechsler H: Halfway houses for former mental patients: A survey. J Soc Issues 16:20–26, 1960(b)

Wechsler H: Transitional residences for former mental patients: A survey of halfway houses and related rehabilitation facilities. Ment Hyg 45:65–76, 1961

Weinberg J: Geriatric psychiatry, in Freedman

AM, Kaplan HI, Sadock BJ (eds): Comprehensive Textbook of Psychiatry, vol. II (2d ed). Baltimore, Williams & Wilkins, 1975, pp 2405–2420

Weinrauch H, Hetherington AW: Computers in medicine and biology. JAMA 169:238–245, 1959

Weinroth LA: Occupational therapy, in Freedman AM, Kaplan HI (eds): Comprehensive Textbook of Psychiatry. Baltimore, Williams & Wilkins, 1967

Weinstein EA, Kahn RL: Symbolic reorganization in brain injuries, in Arieti S (ed): American Handbook of Psychiatry, vol. 1. New York, Basic Books, 1959, pp 974–976

Weir-Mitchell S: Fat and Blood (4th ed). Philadelphia, Lippincott, 1885

Weiss DM, Margolin RJ: The use of music as an adjunct to group therapy. Am Arch Rehab Ther 3:13–26, 1953

Weiss E, English OS: Psychosomatic Medicine. Philadelphia, Saunders, 1957

Weissman MM, Klerman GL, Paykel ES, et al: Treatment effects on the social adjustment of depressed patients. Arch Gen Psychiatry 30:771–778, 1974

Wender L: Dynamics of group psychotherapy and its applications. JNMD 84:54–60, 1936

Wender L: Group psychotherapy: A study of its application. Psychiatr Q 14:708–718, 1940

Wender L: The psychodynamics of group psychotherapy. J Hillside Hosp 12:134, 1963

Wender P: Minimal Brain Dysfunction in Children. New York, Wiley, 1971

Wenkart A: Existential Psychotherapy: Its Theory and Practice. Nutley, NJ, Roche Laboratories, 1972

Werner H, Kaplan E: The acquisition of word meanings: A developmental study. Child Dev Mongr 15, Ser No. 1, 1950

Werry JS: The conditioning treatment of enuresis. Am J Psychiatry 123:226–229, 1966

Wershub LP: The plague of impotence, J NY Med Coll, Flower Fifth Ave Hosp 1:17–26, 1959

Weston WD: Development of community psychiatric concepts, in Freedman AM, Kaplan HI, Sadock BJ (eds): Comprehensive Textbook of Psychiatry, vol. II (2d ed). Baltimore, Williams & Wilkins, 1975, pp 2310–2326

Wharton RN, Fieve RR: The use of lithium carbonate in the effective psychoses. Paper presented at the 122d Annual Meeting of the American Psychiatric Association, Atlantic City, NJ, May 1966

Wheelwright J: Jung's psychological concepts, in Fromm-Reichmann F, Moreno JL (eds): Progress in Psychotherapy, vol. 1. New York, Grune & Stratton, 1956, pp 127–135

Whiles WH: Treatment of emotional problems in children. J Ment Sci 87:359–369, 1941

Whitaker CA: Psychotherapy with couples. Am J Psychother 12:18–24, 1958

Whitaker CA, Malone TP: The Roots of Psychotherapy. New York, McGraw-Hill, 1963

Whitaker DS, Lieberman MA: Psychotherapy Through the Group Process. New York, Atherton, 1964

White A, et al: Measures for predicting dropping out of psychotherapy. J Consult Psychol 28:326, 1964

White JG: The use of learning theory in the psychological treatment of children, in Franks CM (ed): Conditioning Techniques in Clinical Practice and Research. New York, Springer, 1964, pp 196–201

White RB, Schlagenhauf G, Turpin JP: The treatment of manic depressive states with lithium carbonate, in Masserman JH (ed); Current Psychiatric Therapies, vol. 6. New York, Grune & Stratton, 1966, pp 230–242

White RB, Talbot E, Stuart CM: A psychoanalytic therapeutic community, in Masserman JH (ed): Current Psychiatric Therapies, vol. 4. New York, Grune & Stratton, 1964, pp 199–212

White V: Studying the Individual Pupil. New York, Harper & Row, 1958

Whitehead AN: Science and the Modern World. New York, Macmillan, 1925

Whitehorn JC: Guide to Interviewing and clinical personality study. Arch Neurol Psychiatry 52:197–216, 1944

Whitehorn JC, Betz BJ: Further studies of the doctor as a crucial variable in the outcome of treatment with schizophrenic patients. Am J Psychiatry 117:215, 1960

Whitelaw JDA: A case of fetishism treated with LSD. J Nerv Ment Dis 129:573, 1959

Whittington HG, Zahourek R, Grey L: Pharmacotherapy and community psychiatric practice. Am J Psychiatry 126:551–554, 1969

Wickes IG: Letters to the editor: Treatment of enuresis. Lancet 2:413, 1964

Wickes TA: Examiners' influence in a testing situation. J Consult Psychol 20:23–26, 1956

Wickman EK: Difference in the attitudes of teachers and mental hygienists, in Children's Behavior and Teacher's Attitude. New York, Commonwealth Fund, 1928

Wilcox PH: Psychopenetration. Dis Nerv Syst 12:1, 1951

Wilder J: Facts and figures on psychotherapy. J Clin Psychopathol 7:311–347, 1945

Wilder J: The law of initial values. Psychosom Med 12:392, 1950

Wilder J: Modern psychotherapy and the law of initial values. Am J Psychother 12:199, 1958

Wilder JF, Caulfield S: A "high-expectations" half-way house—a follow-up. Paper presented at the 122d Annual Meeting of the American Psychiatric Association, Atlantic City, NJ, May 1966

Wilkins GD et al: A therapeutic community development in a state psychiatric hospital. Med J Aust 2:220–224, 1963

Wilkins LG, Stein SH: A dynamic approach to symptom amelioration: An integration of psychoanalysis, hypnotherapy and behavior modification. Paper presented at the meeting of the American Psychological Association, Honolulu, Hawaii, September 1972

Will OA: Schizophrenia: Psychological treatments, in Freedman AM, Kaplan H (eds): Comprehensive Textbook of Psychiatry. Baltimore, Williams & Wilkins, 1967

Will OA: The psychotherapeutic center and schizophrenia, in The Schizophrenic Reactions. New York, Brunner/Mazel, 1970

Willard H, Spackman CS (eds): Principles of Occupational Therapy. Philadelphia, Lippincott, 1947

Williams CD: The elimination of tantrum behavior by extinction procedures. J Abnorm Soc Psychol 59:269, 1959

Williams DB: California experiments with half-way house. Ment Hosp 7:24, 1956

Williams DD: Therapy and salvation. Union Seminary Q Rev 15:303–317, 1960

Williams DD: The Minister and the Care of Souls. New York, Harper & Row, 1961

Williams RL, Webb WB: Sleep Therapy. Springfield, Ill, Thomas, 1966

Williams T: Telephone therapy: The faceless therapist. Crisis Intervention 3:39–42, 1971

Williamson EG: How to Counsel Students. New York, McGraw-Hill, 1939

Williamson EG, Darley JG: Student Personnel Work, An Outline of Clinical Procedure. New York, McGraw-Hill, 1937

Williamson FE: Art therapy as creative activity. Ment Hosp 10:18–19, 1959

Willis RW, Edwards JA: A study of the comparative effectiveness of systematic desensitization and implosive therapy. Behav Res Ther 7:387–395, 1969

Wilmer HA: Social Psychiatry in Action: A Therapeutic Community. Springfield, Ill, Thomas, 1958

Wilmer HA: Television as participant recorder. Am J Psychiatry 124:1157–1163, 1968

Wilson G: Group Work and Case Work—Their Relationship and Practice. New York, Family Welfare Association of America, 1941

Wilson G, Ryland G: Social Group Work Practice: The Creative Use of the Social Process. Boston, Houghton Mifflin, 1949

Wilson TG: Behavioral treatment of obsessive-compulsive disorders. Cassette Tape T29. New York, Biomonitoring Applications, 1976

Windholz E: The theory of supervision in psychoanalytic education. Int J Psychoanal 51:393–406, 1970

Winick C: Psychiatric day hospitals: A survey. J Soc Issues 8, 1960(a)

Winick C, Holt H: Uses of music in group psychotherapy. Int J Group Psychother 13:76–86, 1960(b)

Winick C, Holt H: Seating position as non-verbal communication in group analysis. Psychiatry 24:171–182, 1961

Winkelman HW, Jr, Saul SD: The riddle of suggestion. Am J Psychiatry 129:477–481, 1972

Winnicott DW: Hate in the counter-transference. Int J Psychoanal 30:69–74, 1949

Winnicott DW: Symptom tolerance in paediatrics. Proc Roy Soc Med 46:675–684, 1953

Winnicott DW: Collected Papers—Through Pediatrics to Psycho-Analysis. New York, Basic Books, 1958

Winnicott DW: Playing and Reality. Roche Report 6(6), 1969

Winston S: Dance and movement therapy. Psychiatr Op 3:26–31, 1966

Winter G: The pastoral counselor within the community of faith. Pastoral Psychol 10:26–30, 1959

Wisdom JO: Foreword, in Lazerowitz M (ed): The Structure of Metaphysics. New York, Humanities, 1955

Wise CA: Pastoral Counseling: Its Theory and Practice. New York, Harper & Row, 1951

Wise CA: A meeting of American Association of Pastoral Counselors in St. Louis: A Report. Pastoral Psychol 15:47–52, 1964

Witmer H: The later social adjustment of problem children: A report of thirteen follow-up investigations. Smith College Studies in Social Work 5:1–98, 1935

Witmer HL (ed): Teaching Psychotherapeutic Medicine. New York, Commonwealth Fund, 1947

Wittkower ED, La Tendresse TD: Rehabilitation of chronic schizophrenics by a new method of occupational therapy. Br J Med Psychol 28:42, 1955

Wolberg A: The "borderline" patient. Am J Psychother 6:694–710, 1952

Wolberg A: Lectures given in class No. 218 at the Postgraduate Center for Mental Health, New York, 1959

Wolberg A: The psychoanalytic treatment of the borderline patient in the individual and group setting, in Hulse W (ed): Topical Problems of Psychotherapy, vol. 3. Basel, Switz, Karger, 1960, pp 174–197

Wolberg A: The contribution of social casework to short-term psychotherapy, in Wolberg LR (ed): Short-term Psychotherapy. New York, Grune & Stratton, 1965, pp 305–327

Wolberg A: The Borderline Patient. New York, Stratton Intercontinental, 1973

Wolberg A, Padilla-Lawson E: MPAG: A generic concept of mental health consultation. Paper presented at the Postgraduate Center for Mental Health, New York, October 1959

Wolberg A, Padilla-Lawson E: The training of mental health consultants at the Postgraduate Center for Mental Health. Int Ment Health Newsletter 4:3–8, 1962

Wolberg A, Padilla-Lawson E: The psychotherapist as a mental health consultant. Paper presented at the Annual Meeting of the American Orthopsychiatric Association, Chicago, March 1964

Wolberg A, Padilla-Lawson E: The goals of community mental health consultation, in Masserman JH (ed): Science and Psychoanalysis, vol. 8. New York, Grune & Stratton, 1965, pp 243–261

Wolberg LR: The Psychology of Eating. New York, McBride, 1936

Wolberg LR: The spontaneous mental cure. Psychiatr Q 18—105–117, 1944

Wolberg LR: Hypnotic experiments in psychosomatic medicine. Psychosom Med 9:337–342, 1947

Wolberg LR: Medical Hypnosis, vol. 1, 2. New York, Grune & Stratton, 1948

Wolberg LR: Current practices in hypnotherapy, in Fromm-Reichmann F, Moreno JL (eds): Progress in Psychotherapy, vol. 1. New York, Grune & Stratton, 1956

Wolberg LR: Hypnosis in psychoanalytic psychotherapy, in Masserman JH, Moreno JL (eds): Progress in Psychotherapy, vol. 2. New York, Grune & Stratton, 1957

Wolberg LR: Child institutionalization as a psychotherapeutic procedure, in Glueck S (ed): The Problem of Delinquency. Boston, Houghton Mifflin, 1959, pp 755–762

Wolberg LR: Hypnotherapy, in Arieti S (ed): American Handbook of Psychiatry, vol. 2. New York, Basic Books, 1959, pp 1466–1481

Wolberg LR: The efficacy of suggestion in clinical situations, in Estabrooks GH (ed): Hypnosis: Current Problems. New York, Harper & Row 1962, pp 127–136

Wolberg LR: Hypnoanalysis. New York, Grune & Stratton, 1945; 2d ed, 1964(a)

Wolberg LR: The evaluation of psychotherapy, in The Evaluation of Psychiatric Treatment. New York, Grune & Stratton, 1964(b), pp 1–13

Wolberg LR: Short-term Psychotherapy. New York, Grune & Stratton, 1965

Wolberg LR: Psychotherapy and the Behavioral Sciences. New York, Grune & Stratton, 1966

Wolberg LR: The Technique of Psychotherapy (2d ed). New York, Grune & Stratton, 1967, pp 44–51, 293–312

Wolf A: The psychoanalysis of groups. Am J Psychother 3:525–558, 1949; 4:16–50, 1950

Wolf A: Psychiatry and Religion. M.D. International Symposium No. 3, New York, M.D. Publishers, 1955

Wolf A: The arcadian ingredient in group psychotherapy, in Wolberg LR, Schwartz EK (eds): Group Therapy 1973: An Overview. New York, Stratton Intercontinental, 1973, pp 1–11

Wolf A: Remembering Mannie: Emanuel K. Schwartz, PhD, DSSc, June 11, 1912–January 22, 1973, in Wolberg LR, Aronson ML (eds): Group Therapy 1975: An Overview. New York, Stratton Intercontinental, 1975

Wolf A et al: Sexual acting out in the psychoanalysis of group. Int J Group Psychother 4:369–380, 1954

Wolf A, Schwartz EK: Psychoanalysis in groups: Clinical and theoretic implications of the alternate meeting. Acta Psychother Psychosom Orthopsychiatry 7 (Suppl):404, 1959

Wolf A, Schwartz EK: Psychoanalysis in groups: The alternate session. Am Imago 17:101–106, 1960

Wolf A, Schwartz EK: Psychoanalysis in Groups. New York, Grune & Stratton, 1962

Wolf M, Risley T, Mees H: Application of operant conditioning procedures to the behaviour problems of an autistic child. Behav Res Ther 1:305–312, 1964

Wolf S: Effects of suggestion and conditioning on the action of chemical agents in human subjects—the pharmacology of placebos. J Clin Invest 29:100–109, 1950

Wolf S, Pinsky RH: Effects of placebo administration and occurrence of toxic reactions. JAMA 155:339–341, 1954

Wolfe J, et al: Emotional education in the classroom: The living school. Rational Living 4:22–25, 1970

Wolff IS: The psychiatric nurse in community mental health centers. Perspect Psychiatr Care 1:11–18, 1964

Wolman BB: Hostility experiences in group psychotherapy. Int J Soc Psychiatry 10:57, 1964

Wolman BB (ed): Psychoanalytic Techniques. New York, Basic Books, 1967, pp 147–559

Wolpe J: Objective psychotherapy of the neuroses. S Afr Med J 26:825–829, 1952

Wolpe J: Reciprocal inhibition as the main basis of psychotherapeutic effects. AMA Arch Neurol Psychiatry 72:205–226, 1954

Wolpe J: Psychotherapy by Reciprocal Inhibition. Stanford, Calif, Stanford University Press, 1958

Wolpe J: The systematic desensitization treatment of neurosis. NNMD 132:180–203, 1961

Wolpe J: Behavior therapy in complex neurotic states. Br J Psychiatry 110:28–34, 1964(a)

Wolpe J: The comparative clinical status of conditioning therapies and psychoanalysis, in Wolpe J, Salter A, Reyna LJ (eds): The Conditioning Therapies. New York, Holt, 1964(b)

Wolpe J: The effects of psychotherapy. Int J Psychiatry 1:175–178, 1965

Wolpe J: The Practice of Behavior Therapy. Elmsford, NY, Pergamon, 1969

Wolpe J: Orientation to Behavior Therapy. Nutley, NJ, Hoffman-LaRoche, 1971

Wolpe J: Advances in behavior therapy, in Masserman JH (ed): Current Psychiatric Therapies, vol. 12. New York, Grune & Stratton, 1972

Wolpe J, Flood J: The effect of relaxation on the galvanic skin response to repeated phobic stimuli in ascending order. J Behav Ther Exp Psychiatry 1:195–200, 1970

Wolpe J, Lazarus AA: Behavior Therapy Techniques. New York, Pergamon, 1966

Wolpe J, Salter A, Reyna LJ (eds): The Conditioning Therapies. New York, Holt, 1964

Wolpin M: Guided imagining to reduce avoidance behavior. Psychotherapy: Theory Res Prac 6:122, 1969

Wolstein B: Countertransference. New York, Grune & Stratton, 1959

Woltmann AG: The use of puppets in understanding children. Ment Hyg 24:445–458, 1940

Woltmann AG: Mud and Clay. Personality Symposium No. 2. New York, Grune & Stratton, 1950

Woltmann AG: The use of puppetry as a projective method in therapy, in Anderson HH, Anderson GL (eds): Introduction to Projective Techniques. Englewood Cliffs, NJ, Prentice-Hall, 1951

Woltmann AG: Play therapy and related techniques, in Brower d, Abt LE (eds): Progress in Clinical Psychology, vol. 1. New York, Grune & Stratton, 1952

Woltmann AG: Concepts of play therapy techniques. Am J Orthopsychiatry 25:771–783, 1955

Woltmann AG: Play therapy and related techniques, in Brower D, Abt LE (eds): Progress in Clinical Psychology, vol. 2. New York, Grune & Stratton, 1956

Woltmann AG: Play therapy and related techniques, in Brower D, Abt LE (eds): Progress in Clinical Psychology, vol. 3. New York, Grune & Stratton, 1959

Wood E: Yoga. New York, Penguin, 1959

Woodward LE: Family life education, in Social Work Year Book. New York, American Association of Social Workers, 1951, pp 181–182

Woody RH: Behavioral Problem Children in the Schools. Recognition, Diagnosis, and Behavioral Modification. New York, Appleton-Century-Crofts, 1969

Woody RH: Psychobehavioral Counseling and Therapy: Integrating Behavioral and Insight Techniques. New York, Appleton-Century-Crofts, 1971

Worcester A: Care of the Sick, the Dying and the Dead. Springfield, Ill, Thomas, 1935

Worcester A: Care of the Aged, the Dying, and the Dead. Springfield, Ill, Thomas, 1961

Worchel P, Byrne D: Personality Change. New York, Wiley, 1964

World Health Organization (WHO): Occupational Health. WHO Tech Rep Ser No. 66, 1953, p 11

World Health Organization: The Mentally Subnormal Child. WHO Tech Rep Ser No. 75, 1954

World Health Organization: Epidemiology of Mental Disorders. WHO Tech Rep Ser No. 185, 1960

World Health Organization: International Classification of Diseases, vol. 1. Geneva, Switz, WHO, 1965

Wortis RP: Music therapy for the mentally ill. J Gen Psychol 62:311–318, 1960

Wright MW: Clinical psychology—progression or regression. Can Ment Health 14:20–25, 1966

Wright R: Hydrotherapy in Psychiatric Hospitals. Boston, Tudor, 1940

Wynne LC, Ryckoff IM, Day J, Hirsch SI: Pseudo-mutuality in the family relations of schizophrenics. Psychiatry 21:205–220, 1958

Yalom ID: The Theory and Practice of Group Psychotherapy. New York, Basic Books, 1970, p 83; 2d ed, 1975

Yalom ID, Greves C: Group therapy with the terminally ill. Am J Psychiatry 134:396–400, 1977

Yalom ID, Lieberman MA: A study of encounter group casualties. Arch Gen Psychiatry 25:16–30, 1971

Yamakami S: Systems of Buddhist Thought. Calcutta, University of Calcutta, 1912

Yaskin JC: The psychoneuroses and neuroses. A review of a hundred cases with special reference to treatment and results. Am J Psychiatry 93:107–125, 1936

Yates AJ: The application of learning theory to the treatment of tics. J Abnorm Soc Psychol 56:175–182, 1958

Yates AJ: Behavior Therapy. New York, Wiley, 1970

Yates AJ: Theory and Practice in Behavior Therapy. New York, Wiley, 1975

Yates DH: An association set method in psychotherapy. Psychol Bull 36:506, 1939

Yates DH: Relaxation in psychotherapy. J Genet Psychol 34:213–237, 1946

Yeats-Brown F: Yoga Explained. New York, Vista House, 1958

Yeomans NT: Notes on a therapeutic community. I. Preliminary report. Med J Aust 2:382, 1961

Yesudian S, Haich E: Yoga Uniting East and West. New York, Harper & Row, 1956

Young H: A Rational Counseling Primer. New York, Institute for Advanced Study in Rational Psychotherapy, 1974

Young RA: Treatment problems of the psychologist. Round table, 1949. I. The status of the clinical psychologist in therapy. Am J Orthopsychiatry 22:312, 1950

Ytrehus A: Environmental therapy of chronic schizophrenic patients. Acta Psychiatry 34:126–140, 1959

Zabarenko L, Pittenger RA, Zabarenko RN: Primary Medical Practice. A Psychiatric Evaluation. St Louis, Green, 1968

Zabarenko RN, et al: Teaching psychological medicine in the family practice office. JAMA 218:392–396, 1971

Zachry CB: The psychotherapist and the school. Nerv Child 3:249–257, 1944

Zaks A, Jones T, Fink M, Freedman AM: Naloxone treatment of opiate dependencies: A progress report. JAMA 215:408, 1971

Zander A, et al: Role Relations in the Mental Health Professions. Ann Arbor, University of Michigan Press, 1957

Zetzel EA: The effects of psychotherapy. Int J Psychiatry 1:144–150, 1965

Ziferstein I, Grotjahn M: Group dynamics of acting out in analytic group psychotherapy. Int J Group Psychother 7:77–85, 1957

Zigler E, Phillips L: Psychiatric diagnosis: Critique. J Abnorm Soc Psychol 63:607–618, 1961

Zilboorg G: The fundamental conflict with psychoanalysis. Int J Psychoanal 20:480–492, 1939

Zilboorg G: Fear of death. Psychoanal Q 12:465–475, 1943

Zilboorg G: Scientific psychopathology and religious issues. Theolog Studies 14:283–297, 1953

Zilboorg G: Psychoanalytic borderlines. Am J Psychiatry 112:706–710, 1956

Zilboorg G: Psychoanalysis and Religion. New York, Farrar, Strauss, 1962

Zilboorg G: Psychiatry and Medical Practice in a General Hospital. New York, International Universities Press, 1964

Zimmerman EH, Zimmerman J: The alteration of behavior in a special classroom situation. J Exp Anal Behav 5:59–60, 1962

Ziskind E: Training in psychotherapy for all physicians. JAMA 147:1223–1225, 1951

Zrull JP, Patch D, Lehtinen P: Hyperkinetic children who respond to d-amphetamine. Paper presented at the 122d Annual Meeting of the American Psychiatric Association. Atlantic City, NJ, May 1966

Zubin J: Standard control groups for the evaluation of therapy. Proceedings of the 2d Conference of Mental Hospital Administrators and Statisticians. Pub Health Serv Publ No. 226. Bethesda, Md, National Institute of Mental Health, 1953, p 63

Zubin J: The effects of psychotherapy. Int J Psychiatry 1:153–155, 1965

Zucker H: Problems of Psychotherapy. New York, Free Press, 1967

Zucker KB: Teacher or teacher-therapist: Training for special educators? Contemp Educ 42:115–116, 1971

Zucker LJ: Psychoanalytic assessment of ego

weakness. Am J Psychother 17:275–285, 1963

Zuk GH: Family therapy, in Haley J (ed): Changing Families. New York, Grune & Stratton, 1971(a)

Zuk GH: A Triadic-Based Approach. New York, Behavioral Publications, 1971(b)

Zuk GH: Engagement and termination in family therapy, in Wolberg LR, Aronson, ML (eds): Group Therapy 1974: An Overview. New York, Stratton Intercontinental, 1974, pp 34–44

Zuk GH, Boszormenyi-Nagy I (eds): Family Therapy and Disturbed Families. Palo Alto, Calif, Science & Behavior Books, 1967

Zulliger H: Psychoanalytic experiences in public schools practice. Am J Orthopsychiatry 10:37–85; 595–609, 1940; 11:151–171, 356–370, 1941

Zusman J: Primary prevention. Secondary prevention. Tertiary prevention, in Freedman AM, Kaplan HI, Sadock BJ (eds): Comprehensive Textbook of Psychiatry, vol. II (2d ed). Baltimore, Williams & Wilkins, 1975, pp 2326–2346

Zweben JE, Miller RL: The systems games: Teaching, training, psychotherapy. Psychother: Theory Res Prac 5:73–76, 1968

Zwerling I, Wilder JF: An evaluation of the applicability of the day hospital in treatment of acutely disturbed patients. Isr Ann Psychiatry 2:162–185, 1964

Author and Subject Indexes

Author Index[*]

---

[*] See also References, pages 1210–1301, and the section on Bibliotherapy, pages 818–832.

Subject Index